FIFTH EDITION

MANAGEMENT
CONCEPTS & PRACTICES

Tim Hannagan

With contributions from

ROGER BENNETT
RUTH BOADEN
LESLIE CHADWICK
DOMINIC COOPER
HELEN DAVIS
DAVID EDELSHAIN
LINDA GUNNELL
MIKE HARRY
VIRA KRAKHMAL
CLAIRE MOXHAM
KATE PRESCOTT
DAVID ROBOTHAM
MIK WISNIEWSKI

FT Prentice Hall
FINANCIAL TIMES

An imprint of **Pearson Education**
Harlow, England • London • New York • Boston • San Francisco • Toronto
Sydney • Tokyo • Singapore • Hong Kong • Seoul • Taipei • New Delhi
Cape Town • Madrid • Mexico City • Amsterdam • Munich • Paris • Milan

Pearson Education Limited
Edinburgh Gate
Harlow
Essex CM20 2JE
England

and Associated Companies throughout the world

Visit us on the World Wide Web at:
www.pearsoned.co.uk

First published in Great Britain under the Pitman Publishing imprint in 1995
Second edition published 1998
Third edition published 2002
Fourth edition published 2005
Fifth edition published 2008

© Longman Group UK Limited 1995
© Pearson Professional Limited 1998
© Pearson Education Limited 2002, 2005, 2008

ISBN: 978-0-273-71118-6

British Library Cataloguing-in-Publication Data
A catalogue record for this book is available from the British Library

Library of Congress Cataloging-in-Publication Data

Hannagan, Tim.
  Management : concepts & practices / Tim Hannagan ; with contributions from
Roger Bennett ... [et al.]. -- 5th ed.
      p. cm.
  "An Imprint of Pearson Education."
  Includes bibliographical references and index.
  ISBN 978-0-273-71118-6 (alk. paper)
  1. Management. I. Bennett, Roger, 1944- II. Title.
  HD31.H316 2007
  658--dc22
                                    2007039395

10 9 8 7 6 5 4 3 2 1
11 10 09 08 07

Typeset in 9.5/12 pt Stone Serif by 30
Printed and bound by Ashford Colour Press Ltd., Gosport
The publisher's policy is to use paper manufactured from sustainable forests.

CONTENTS AT A GLANCE

CONTENTS

Section A

MANAGING CHANGE

Section E

MANAGEMENT ISSUES

Companion Website resources
Visit the Companion Website at **www.pearsoned.co.uk/hannagan**

For lecturers
- Complete, downloadable Instructor's Manual
- PowerPoint slides that can be downloaded and used as OHTs

LIST OF CONTRIBUTORS

Dr Roger Bennett, Reader, London Metropolitan University (*Chapter 11*)

Professor Ruth Boaden, Professor of Service Operations Management, Manchester Business School University of Manchester (*Chapter 14*)

Leslie Chadwick, Head of Work Experience Placements and Senior Lecturer in Accounting and Finance, Bradford University School of Management (*Chapter 16*)

Dominic Cooper, Chartered Psychologist applying motivational theories in organisations and CEO of BSMS Inc, Franklin, Indiana, USA *(Chapter 12)*

Helen Davis, Principal Lecturer in Human Resource Strategies, London Metropolitan University (*Chapter 11*)

David Edelshain, Senior Lecturer in International Business and Director of the Undergraduate Business Studies Degree programme at Cass Business School, London, and an Adjunct Professor at New York University in London (*Chapter 19*)

Linda Gunnell, Senior Lecturer in Human Resource Strategies, London Metropolitan University; and Private Consultant in Organisation and Senior Management Development (Euphyia l td) (*Chapter 11*)

Dr Mike Harry, MBA/MIBM supervisor for the TiasNimbas Business School (Utrecht). Previously Senior Teaching Fellow in Management and Information Systems, University of Bradford Management Centre (*Chapter 15*)

Dr Vira Krakhmal, Lecturer in Accounting, OU Business School, The Open University (*Chapter 16)*

Dr Claire Moxham, Lecturer in Operations Management, Manchester Business School, University of Manchester *(Chapter 14)*

Kate Prescott, former Lecturer in International Business, University of Bradford Management Centre (*Chapter 19*)

Dr David Robotham, Senior Lecturer in Organisational Behaviour, Department of Human Resource Management, Leicester Business School, De Montfort University (*Chapter 10*)

Mik Wisniewski, Senior Research Fellow, Strathclyde Business School (*Chapter 13*)

PREFACE

This new revised edition has been extensively rewritten and reorganised in order to reflect the latest changes in management thinking and the best practice in the application of management concepts. The management of change remains the great challenge to managers in most organisations and the objective of this book is to provide an understanding of the way organisations are managed, and an appreciation of the most recent developments in management practice and theory. This analysis, while being grounded in past experience, recognises changes that are taking place and looks forward towards developments likely to take place in the future. A number of topics have been developed in this edition including teamwork, innovation, entrepreneurship, green issues, ethical issues, global developments, legal factors, public/private partnerships, branding, emotional intelligence and politics in organisations.

The book is intended for teachers and students on management and business studies programmes such as the Diploma in Management and the MBA, first degree programmes, Higher National Diplomas and Certificates, and professional courses such as marketing, personnel and accounting. This general introduction to management is also important in project management, engineering, building and construction, as well as the public sector, the voluntary sector and other areas of study and work.

In the twenty-first century managers are facing the challenge of a surge in technology, the crisis in environmental issues linked to the highlighting of corporate social responsibility and changes in the social and economic structures of the world. The development of new economic giants, such as India and China, and the enlargement of the European Community have also altered the environment in which managers operate. Rapid developments in the application of information technology are matched by equally rapid changes in the structure of organisations, in the role of managers, their career path and the economies and societies in which they operate. This puts pressure on managers which helps to emphasise the importance of understanding both the practices and concepts of management.

Managers have to face changes in the environment in which they work, in the organisations they work in, in competition, in the demands of their customers and society and in people's expectations as their great challenges whether they work in the private, public or voluntary sectors and irrespective of the size of organisation for which they work. The importance of leadership and a focus on the customer is emphasised in the first section of the book, while the focus on management strategy has been sharpened in order to emphasise the importance of creativity and innovation in the management of organisations and the increasing importance of teamwork in many work situations. While clear strategic objectives are seen as crucial for managers in all areas, marketing and environmental assessment is considered to be an integrating force both in business and in the public sector. Organisational theory and design are increasingly important areas of management as working practices become more fluid and more global and the importance of communicating in organisations is stressed by a rewritten chapter.

Alterations to the way that companies are managed are highlighted in the chapters on decision making, operational management and technology. The chapter on finance and accounting has been updated to include the latest accounting standards, legislation and financial requirements. The increasing emphasis on corporate social responsibility, environmental management and green issues has been recognised in the section on twenty-first century management issues, along with the effects of the globalised economy on the work of many managers. Managers' careers depend increasingly on their own initiative and an understanding of management ideas, as well as the skills now required for their role.

There are two sections after this preface which give help in getting to know your way round the book – a 'guided tour' and a more detailed 'travel guide'. Another potentially helpful section called 'How to pass Management Exams' is included as an appendix just before the Glossary.

This new edition brings the information up to date and includes the very latest ideas on management development. The structure of the book encourages an active approach to learning. All the chapters begin with a list of outcomes and give a summary of the main features covered in the chapter. Each chapter ends with questions for review and discussion, while examples and case studies litter the text and are included at the end of every chapter to provide a basis for further discussion and comment. Expert contributors have written or contributed to specialist chapters.

References to books, articles and websites are provided for each chapter in order to facilitate wider reading and research, and this edition includes an enhanced section on further reading for each chapter to provide guidance and advice for those who want to carry the discussion further. The content of this book and the examples used in it provide both a European and global perspective. It has been designed to be user-friendly and to appeal to undergraduates as well as graduates and post-experience managers on business, management and related professional programmes and courses. A *Lecturer's Guide*, including questions on the case studies, answer points and additional materials, is available free of charge to tutors and lecturers on our website at **www.pearsoned.co.uk/hannagan**

While the whole book takes an integrated approach to management in order to establish the manager's role and a sense of direction for the organisation, specific chapters have been contributed by experts in their fields. In dealing with these issues the book is divided into main sections focusing on the major functions of management, which can be summarised as *organising, controlling* and *planning* – or as *managing change, strategy, people, the organisation* and finally *contemporary issues*. It is concerned with management in a time of change, also looking forward to those issues which will be particularly important in the future.

Organisational restructuring has meant that the career expectations of managers have changed dramatically. Managers now have to take control of their own careers to an extent unknown in the past. This provides a personal challenge as well as a challenge in working with other people. It is argued that this is a dynamic factor in a situation where, more than ever, effective and efficient management can make, and is making, a real difference in all types of organisations. Managers make a difference in private companies, in public sector institutions and in voluntary organisations because of changes in technology, the pressure of competition, the problems of understanding customer needs, along with cultural developments and environmental challenges. The role of the manager has never been more rewarding or challenging and it has never been more important to understand this role.

Tim Hannagan

Note: Where a word is set in **colour** in the main text, this indicates that is is a significant occurrence of a **Glossary term** (please refer to the Glossary on pages 732–43).

GUIDED TOUR

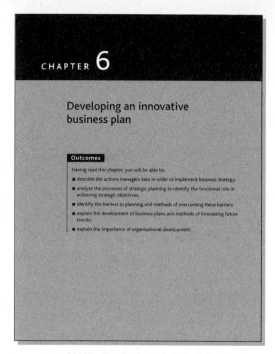

Learning **Outcomes** clearly establish what is covered in each chapter and introduce important topics.

Exhibits illustrate theory with examples and bring the subject to life.

Key terms are highlighted for easy reference. Definitions for each key term can be found in the glossary at the end of the book.

Orientation arrows help you to find your way around the book and develop an understanding of the links between different management functions.

578 SECTION D · MANAGING THE ORGANISATION

Discounted payback

This method simply calculates the payback using the discounted cash flows.

Taxation aspects

Taxation allowances must be included in the cash flows for the period that benefits from those allowances. Tax payments must be included in the cash flows for the period in which they are to be paid over. Thus care needs to be exercised in taking the tax factor into account by considering the various time lags – for example the tax on the income from year 1 could be paid in year 2 and so on.

Non-quantitative aspects

Frequently the cost or benefits arising from a particular investment decision are difficult, if not impossible, to quantify. Yet non-quantitative aspects should not be ignored. There is a real danger of accountants being so preoccupied with the financial aspects of capital investment appraisal that they may tend to ignore other important factors. Such non-quantitative factors include:

- efficiency of servicing
- reliability
- risks associated with buying from overseas
- desire for technical superiority
- flexibility.

SUMMARY

- Major aspects of the legal and regulatory framework of accounting were introduced by covering Companies Act, national accounting standards, international accounting standards and listing rules.
- In financial accounting the profit and loss account and balance sheet were reviewed together with the terminology associated with them – e.g. prepayments, depreciation, assets and liabilities – and the way in which the figures are arrived at. In addition, their limitations were highlighted – for example, the way in which 'creative accounting' can affect the figures.
- Financial analysis was also introduced via a selected number of ratios such as profitability and liquidity ratios, and some possible explanations for movements in them were provided.
- The management accounting area covered decision-making techniques, budgetary control and an introduction to standard costing. In budgeting the key words should act as a reminder of the principles of good budgeting practice. They are:
  - preparation in advance
  - control by responsibility
  - setting targets
  - participation

CHAPTER 13 · DECISION-MAKING PROCESSES IN ORGANISATIONS **451**

- Such models are particularly valuable in decision-making situations where incomplete or inadequate information is available, where a number of alternatives are typically available and where uncertainty exists.
- A number of these models have been introduced in this chapter but it must also be said that the last two or three decades have seen a veritable explosion of such models being developed and used. The subject area known as management science has provided many of these model developments and a number of texts are detailed in the references for further reading which introduce additional models of potential use to the decision maker.

Review and discussion questions

1 From a management perspective what is the difference between decision making and problem solving?

2 Consider an organisation with which you are familiar. What is the organisation's attitude to risk? How does this affect its decision-making process?

3 As a manager facing a decision-making situation which has areas of uncertainty associated with it, is it possible to quantify such areas of uncertainty?

4 What are the key differences between management decision making and personal decision making?

5 Discuss how time affects the various stages of the decision-making process.

6 Consider the various decision-making support models introduced in this chapter. What factors would discourage managers from utilising the information derived from such models in the decision-making process?

7 'Decision making is the most important task for any manager.' Discuss this statement.

8 A manager in an organisation has been offered a considerable promotion. However, the promotion would involve moving to another part of the country.

   a. Using the decision-making process model consider how the manager would try to reach an appropriate decision.

   b. Draw a decision tree representing the decision-making situation.

   c. Assume the manager has decided to take the promotion. Draw a forcefield diagram to assess the critical factors which will affect the success of the move.

The chapter **Summary** recaps the issues covered to check you have achieved the learning outcomes and understood the chapter.

Review and discussion questions can be used for group discussion or on an individual basis to help with understanding and in examination revision.

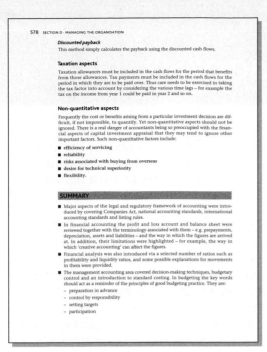

452 SECTION D · MANAGING THE ORGANISATION

CASE STUDY

Jaguar Cars

A Jaguar car, instantly recognisable almost anywhere in the world and a global brand.

However, Jaguar has had a very chequered history over the last few decades and illustrates many of the issues relating to effective decision making discussed in this chapter. In the early 1980s the company came close to disappearing, with reducing market share, decreasing financial viability, outdated technology and working practices, and major product quality problems. With the introduction of new management it was able – painfully – to turn itself around and achieve improvements in efficiency, quality and profitability. Towards the end of the 1980s a worldwide recession emerged and the company again hit problems. In 1989 the company was bought by Ford Motor Company for around US$2.5 billion, with the new owner then having to find a further $700 million to help keep the company going in the short term.

Jaguar starkly illustrates the difficulties involved in decision making in today's environment. On the face of it, the company had tremendous potential. On the other hand it faced a number of major short-term problems. These included:

- the company was operating at a loss – it was estimated that in 1992 it actually lost $18,000 on each car sold;
- in motor industry terms it was very small, even when compared with its competitors in the luxury car market – Mercedes Benz, for example,

The new management of Jaguar faced an array of interlinked problems as well as considerable uncertainty about markets, demand, customer loyalty and competitor strategy. It was also constrained by the desire to keep Jaguar as a unique product and not simply another variety of Ford car. A number of decisions were made so as to try to move the company forward. These included:

- immediate improvements in operating efficiency – assembly man-hours per car, for example, were reduced by almost 40 per cent in a two-year period, with a further 50 per cent reduction planned;
- significant quality improvements – with defects down by over 70 per cent on the XJ6 model alone;
- a major cost-reduction programme leading to a reduction in the workforce of almost 50 per cent;
- the introduction of, and development of, new models, but with decisions related to different timescales. In the short term the company decided to introduce a redesigned version of the XJ6 – which was a relatively quick and low-cost option – and longer term to invest in the design and production of a totally new car aimed at the business executive market.

The decisions faced by the company's management in the 1990s were clearly a mixture of the strategic and the operational. At the operational level, decisions had to be made about how best to improve the company's immediate position. These needed to be made quickly and needed to have an

FURTHER READING

Dive, B (2002) *The Healthy Organization: A Revolutionary Approach to People and Management*, Kogan Page.
This book provides a wealth of information about the situational aspects of motivation, which links strategic attempts to motivate with operational and individual aspects.

Hayes, N (2001) *Managing Teams: A Strategy for Success*, London: Thompson Learning.
Uses much of motivational theory to develop organisational culture and teamworking, and can provide many scenarios for practical application.

Hinds, J M (1995) *Hinds Model of Company Success: How to Overcome Boredom Through Instant Teams and Transform Your Workplace*, Millenium Books.
Provides a useful antidote to the notion that applications of motivational theory are always successful.

Thomas, K (2003) *Intrinsic Motivation at Work: Building Energy and Commitment*, Berrett-Koehler Publishers Inc.
Provides a study of personal motivation at work. It explains why extrinsic rewards (wages, benefits, perks) are no longer enough to motivate people and details four intrinsic rewards that make work compelling – a sense of meaningfulness, a sense of choice, a sense of competence and a sense of progress.

WEBSITES

http://www.accel-team.com/motivation/index.html
Commercial website full of articles on motivation.

http://www.themanager.org/knowledgebase/hr/motivation.htm
A managerial self-help resource site containing interesting material and an original article by Maslow.

http://www.behavioral-safety.com
Contains practical information about OBM techniques to motivate people to comply with safety requirements.

http://www.siop.org/rvtirbin/shtml.dll/search.htm
Society of Industrial/Organizational Psychologists (USA). Type in 'Motivational Theory' as a search term.

http://www.zigonperf.com
Dedicated to human resources/performance management techniques.

Each chapter ends with a **Case study** to show how the theory is applied in practice, and to help you relate your learning to real life management situations.

Further reading and **Websites** at the end of each chapter provide you with the opportunity to explore the subject in more detail.

Lecturers can access a secure website with teaching resources such as an **Instructor's Manual**, including questions and answers to case studies, and downloadable **PowerPoint slides**. Go to **www.pearsoned.co.uk/hannagan**

TRAVEL GUIDE FOR THE BOOK

Travel guides of cities and countries provide information for visitors, suggest itineraries, the main tourist sites to visit and hints on customs, language and other aspects. The travel guide for this book suggests different ways of using it, highlights the main themes to consider, provides hints on its main features and plans of action on reading it.

The major theme of this book is **management at a time of change**. This is to reflect the challenges facing managers with increasingly rapid changes in terms of technology, the culture and environment in which they work and the globalisation of ideas and of business activity. Organisations in the private and public sectors (and the voluntary sector for that matter) have to meet customer needs (however customers may be defined), and as these needs change so too organisations have to change. According to the chief executive of Tesco, the 'secret' of successful retailing is 'never stop listening to customers and giving them what they want – it's that simple' (Chris Blackhurst, 'Sir Terry Leahy', *Management Today*, February 2004). Customers can be considered to be the 'end-users' of a product or service whether they are paying customers in a supermarket or the recipients of a health service or an education service. At the same time, the context in which organisations are operating is altering in one way or another as a result of increased or reduced competition, changes in the availability of resources, changes in regulations or as a result of new technology.

This book is about what managers do now and what they will be expected to do in the future. For this reason the historical perspective is mainly left until the last chapter and is included there to emphasise the fact that ideas about how to manage change over periods of time build on and adapt the ideas of the past. As a result of globalisation and improved communications, management ideas move between countries and regions of the world even more easily than goods and services. This is not meant to suggest that there are no differences between the way people manage in different countries. Local customs vary, and legislation and management styles are not the same in different countries, or for that matter in different organisations.

The book often refers to 'organisations' as a way of suggesting that the same, or at least similar, concepts and practices can be applied in the public and voluntary sectors as in the private sector. There are important differences in the management of public sector corporations and services (such as the BBC, universities and hospital trusts), voluntary organisations (such as charities and societies) and private sector companies. Private sector companies succeed or fail depending on whether they make profits or not; voluntary sector organisations depend on donations of one kind or another; and public sector corporations and trusts depend on government funding. However, many of the concepts and practices of management are the same or similar in these different sectors. They are all involved in **strategic management**, in **managing people**, in **managing operations** and in a range of **management issues**, and all need to face the **management challenge** involved in leadership, meeting the needs of their customers and coping with change. The contrasts between managing in the private and public sectors is analysed in the chapter on managing in the public sector.

The changing face of management is illustrated by the rise of the e-commerce, 'dot-com' companies, which are well illustrated in Chapter 15, and in fact throughout the book. Although these companies are different from more traditional ones in some of the ways in which they operate, they still have to manage operations and people; they still require leadership and a focus on their customers. They need to market their services, they face multinational competition as well as ethical and environmental issues, they have to have a strategy in order to survive, and in the end they have to make a profit. All organisations – from the local football club to the multinational company with a turnover larger than the GDP of some countries – need good management if they are going to succeed in their purpose. This book builds up an understanding of the complexity of this process.

An itinerary or **route** or **road map** through this book could suggest that it should be read from the first page through to the last. Another approach would be to pick out topics of particular interest by referring to the **contents**, the **index** or the **glossary**. For example, if your main interest at the moment is 'financial management', then Chapter 16 is a starting point; if 'motivation in the workplace' is important then Chapter 12 would be a better place to start. The **glossary** provides meanings of many of the terms used in the book and can be used as a starting point in a similar way to the **index**. If you need to investigate a subject in more detail, the list of references at the end of each chapter provide guidance on **further reading**, while detailed references for each chapter are provided at the end of the book. A different approach to the book would be to start each chapter by considering the **review and discussion questions** and then working through the chapter to compare the analysis in it with this consideration. For example, 'What is the function of organisational design?' Or, 'How does the span of management affect the role of a manager?' Such questions could be thought about individually or discussed in a group before reading Chapter 9 and comparing the analysis there with the ideas raised in the general discussion.

Websites are included at the end of every chapter in order to provide further information on the topics described and discussed in that chapter and to provide illustrations of the main issues that are raised. These can be used for initial research into these topics and as a basis for discussion and review of the issues. The websites are examples of the very many that are available in these areas, such as the large number of individual websites opened by companies. There is a range of search engines which can be used to access information on particular topics and subjects, for example *Excite*: **http://www.excite.com/**, *Altavista*: **http://www.altavista.com/** and *Lycos*: **http://www.lycos.co.uk**.

The whole process of management is complex and is full of 'noise' and distraction and each chapter represents a facet of this complexity. Managers work in places where computers sometimes go down, where lifts break down, where transport systems to and from a particular location are unreliable and, above all, where people behave in unpredictable ways. In an ideal world managers arrive at the office after a hassle-free journey, travel up to their floor in the lift to find that their personal assistant has already put the reports required later in the day on the desk or in the laptop with a list of the day's appointments. In practice, the train arrives late or there has been a flood on the main road causing a time-consuming diversion; the lift does not work and the PA has telephoned in sick; the reports necessary for meetings later in the day have not arrived and have to be chased up; the computer is down and the list of appointments for the day has to be deduced from hastily scribbled notes or a few computer references from the previous day. This is the 'noise' – the forms of distraction – which surrounds a manager in reality, and the skill of a manager is working through this to keep in focus the main objectives of the job.

CUSTOM PUBLISHING

Custom publishing allows academics to pick and choose content from one or more texts for their course and combine it into a definitive course text.

Here are some common examples of Custom solutions which have helped over 500 courses across Europe:

- Different chapters from across our publishing imprints combined into one book
- Lecturer's own material combined together with textbook chapters or published in a separate booklet
- Third party cases and articles that you are keen for your students to read as part of the course
- Or any combination of the above

The Pearson Education Custom text published for your course is professionally produced and bound- just as you would expect from a normal Pearson Education text. You can even choose your own cover design and add your university logo. Since many of our titles have online resources accompanying them we can even build a Custom website that matches your course text.

Whatever your choice, our dedicated Editorial and Production teams will work with you throughout the process, right until you receive a copy of your Custom text.

Some lecturers teaching Principles of Management have found that the flexibility of Custom publishing has allowed them to include additional material on certain aspects of their course.

To give you an idea of combinations which have proved popular, here is a list of subject areas in which Pearson Education publish one or more key texts that could provide extra chapters to match the emphasis of your course:

- Business Environment / Business in Context
- Organisational Behaviour / Organisational Theory
- Human Resource Management
- Marketing
- Accounting & Finance
- Operations Management
- Information Systems
- Economics / Business Economics
- Business Law and Ethics
- Study Skills

For more details on any of these books or to browse other material from our entire portfolio, please visit: **www.pearsoned.co.uk**

If, once you have thought about your course, you feel Custom publishing might benefit you, please do get in contact. However minor, or major the change – we can help you out.

You can contact us at: **www.pearsoncustom.co.uk** or via your local representative at: **www.pearsoned.co.uk/replocator**

ACKNOWLEDGEMENTS

EDITOR'S ACKNOWLEDGEMENTS

A number of people have contributed to the production of this book. I would like to thank the contributors from a range of university business schools and management centres, who have used their expertise to provide chapters in their specialist fields – Linda Dhondy and everybody at Pearson Education for their support in producing the book; Yvonne for providing me with the time to work on the book; and the many other people who have supported the project.

PUBLISHER'S ACKNOWLEDGEMENTS

We would like to thank the following reviewers for their valuable comments and feedback on the book:

George Bell
Johan Bosch
Mark Gifford-Gifford
James Gordon-Hall
Paul Griseri
Branka Krivokapic-skoko
Nigel van Zwanenberg

We are grateful to the following for permission to reproduce copyright material:

Figure 2.1 from New Management Grid: The Key to Leadership Excellence in *Harvard Business Review*, 1985, Blake. R.R. & Mouton, J.S., Adapted from Blake. R.R., Mouton. J.S., Barnes, L.B. and Greiner, L.E., Breakthrough in Organizational development, *Harvard Business Review*, Nov-Dec, p.136. Copyright © 1964 by Harvard Business School Publishing Corporation; Figure 2.2 from *Harvard Business Review*, Adapted from Tannenbaum, R., & Schmidt, W.H., How to choose a leadership pattern, *Harvard Business Review*, May–June 1973, Copyright © 1973 by Harvard Business School Publishing Corporation; Figure 2.3 © Copyright 2006 Reprinted with permission of the Center For Leadership Stuides, Inc. Escondido, CA 92025. All Rights Reserved; Figure 2.4 from Fiedler/Chemers, *Leadership and Effective Management*, first edition. © 1974. Reprinted with permission of Pearson Education Inc., Upper Saddle River, NJ.; Figure 2.6 from Self-leadership: Towards an expanded theory of self-influence processes in organizations in *Academy of Management Review*, Vol.II, No. 3, 1986, by Manz. C.C. Reprinted with permission from the author Charles.C. Manz.; Table 5.1, This article was published in *Accounting, Organizations and Society*, Vol. 15, No. 1 / 2, Simons, R. The role of management control systems in creating competitive advantage: New perspectives, pp. 127–43, Copyright © Elsevier, 1990; Table 5.1 from Kald, Magnus, Nilson, Fredrik, Rapp and Birger (Sept 2000), On Strategy and Management Control: The importance of

Classifying the Strategy of the Business, *British Journal of Management*, Vol. 11. Issue 3., Blackwell Publishing.; Figure 10.1 from *The Mathematical Theory of Communication*. Copyright 1949, 1977, 1998 by the Board of Trustees of the University of Ilinois. Used with permission of the University of Illinois Press.; Table 10.1 reproduced by permission of SAGE Publications, London, Los Angeles, New Delhi and Singapore, from Hyman, J. and Mason, B. Managing Employee Involvement and Participation, Copyright (© Hyman, Mason, 1995); Figure 10.3 from Hartley, P., *Interpersonal Communication*, 2nd edition, 1999; Table 10.4 from Luft, J., (1970), *Group Processes: An Introduction to Group Dynamics*, 1970, McGraw-Hill. Reprinted with permission of The McGraw-Hill Companies.; Table 10.5 from Guirdham, M. (2002), *Interactive Behaviour at Work*, Pearson Education Ltd.; Table 10.7 from Guirdham, M. (2002), *Interactive Behaviour at Work*, Pearson Education Ltd.; Figure 12.1 from Badura, Albert, *Social Foundations of Thought and Action: A Social Cognitive Theory*, 1st Edition, © 1986, pp.22–5. Reprinted by permission of Pearson Education, Inc., Upper Saddle River, NJ.; Table 12.1, Copyright © 1990 by the American Psychological Association. Reproduced with permission. Caldwell & O'Reilly, (1990), Measuring person-job fit with the profile-comparison process, *Journal of Applied Psychology*, 75: 648–57. Reprinted with permission from D Caldwell. The use of APA information does not imply endorsement by APA; Figure 12.2, Copyright © 1943 by the American Psychological Association. Reproduced with permission. Maslow, A.H., (1943), A Theory of Human Motivation, *Psychological Review*, 50: 370–96. The use of APA information does not imply endorsement by APA.; Figure 12.7, Copyright © 1975 by the American Psychological Association. Reproduced with permission. Hackman & Oldman, 1975, Development of the job diagnostic survey, *Journal of Applied Psychology*, 60, 159–70, Reprinted with permission from R.J. Hackman. The use of APA information does not imply endorsement by APA.; Figure 12.8, Copyright © 1975 by the American Psychological Association. Reproduced with permission. Hackman & Oldman, 1975, Development of the job diagnostic survey, *Journal of Applied Psychology*, 60, 159–70. Reprinted with permission from R.J. Hackman. The use of APA information does not imply endorsement by APA; Figure 12.9 from Roe, R.A., Zinovieva, I.L., Dienes E, & Ten Horn, L.A., A comparison of work motivation in Bulgaria, Hungary and The Netherlands: test of a model, *Applied Psychology: An International Review*, (2000) Blackwell Publishing Ltd.; Figure 14.1 from Muhlemann et al., *Production and Operations Management*, 6th edition, 1992, Pearson Education Ltd; Table 14.1 from Schroeder, R.G. *Operations Management*, 4th edition, 1993, New York: McGraw-Hill. Material is reproduced with permission of The McGraw-Hill Companies.; Table 14.2 from Slack, N., Chambers, S., Harland, C., Harrison, A. and Johnston, R. (2004), *Operations Management*, 4th edition, Harlow: FT Prentice Hall.; Figure 14.4 from Muhlemann et al., *Production and Operations Management*, 6th edition, 1992, Pearson Education Ltd; Figure 14.5 Reprinted with permission from The Free Press Division, a division of Simon & Schuster Adult Publishing Group, from COMPETITIVE ADVANTAGE: Creating and Sustaining Superior Performance by Michael E. Porter. Copyright © 1985, 1998 by Michael E. Porter. All Rights Reserved.; Table 14.5 from Hill, T.J. (1991), *Production/Operations Management*, 2nd edition, London: Prentice Hall.; Table 14.6 from Slack, N., Chambers, S., Harland, C., Harrison, A. and Johnston, R. (2004), *Operations Management*, 4th edition, Harlow: Prentice Hall.; Table 14.11 from Slack, N., Chambers, S., Harland, C., Harrison, A. and Johnston, R. (2004), *Operations Management*, 4th edition, Harlow: Prentice Hall.; Table 14.13 from Slack, N., Chambers, S., Harland, C., Harrison, A. and Johnston, R. (2004), *Operations Management*, 4th edition, Harlow: Prentice Hall.; Table 14.14 from Schroeder, R.G., *Operations Management*, 4th edition, 1993, New

York: McGraw-Hill. Material is reproduced with permission of The McGraw-Hill Companies.; Figure 15.4 from Harry, M.J.S., (2001), *Business Information: A System Approach*, Pearson Education Ltd.; Figure 16.4 from Chadwick, (2001), *Essential Accounting for Managers*, Pearson Education Ltd.; Figure 16.5 from Chadwick, (2001), *Essential Accounting for Managers*, Pearson Education Ltd.; Figure 18.5 from Welford, R.J. (1998), The first five steps of ISO 14001 from *Corporate Environmental Management 1: Systems and Strategies*, reprinted with permission from Earthscan; Figure 19.5 from Freeman, C., & Hagedoom, J. (1992), *Globalisation of Technology*, reprinted with permission of C Freeman.; Figure 20.2 from Coulson, C. and Coe, T. (1991), *The Flat Organisation: Philosophy and Practice*: Chartered Management Institute, formerly the Institute of Management; reprinted with permission from the Chartered Management Institute.; Table 20.2 from Management ideas classified by personal impact from Huczynski, A.A. (1993) in Management Gurus, Routledge: Reprinted by kind permission of the author, Dr. A.A. Huczynski; Figure 20.3 from Coulson, C. and Coe, T. (1991), *The Flat Organisation: Philosophy and Practice*: Chartered Management Institute, formerly the Institute of Management; reprinted with permission from the Chartered Management Institute.;

In some instances we have been unable to trace the owners of copyright material, and we would appreciate any information that would enable us to do so.

SECTION A

MANAGING CHANGE

What is the manager's role? What is the main focus of management in the twenty-first century? What are the different levels of management responsibility? Why is it important for managers to be able to manage change? What are the differences between managers and leaders? What part does leadership play in management? How do the different theories of leadership apply to the management of organisations? What is the basis of the power of leaders? Is leadership necessary? Who is the customer? What are customer needs? How can organisations meet customer needs? Why is a consumer focus important? How relevant are these considerations in the management, leadership and success of organisations in the public sector?

This section sets the scene in terms of the manager's role in a time of change and the challenge of management in the twenty-first century. It considers levels of management responsibility and underlying styles and theories of management. Leadership is seen as an essential element in the management of organisations, and different styles and sources of power and control are analysed. Every manager has to focus on the organisation's customers through flexible management structures and strategies and this applies in practice to organisations in the private sector, in the public sector and in the voluntary sector.

CHAPTER 1

The management challenge

Outcomes

Having read this chapter, you will be able to:

- identify the manager's role in the twenty-first century;
- understand the management role and its challenges and responsibilities in the management of change;
- consider different levels of management responsibility;
- appreciate various ideas and theories about the role of the manager.

THE MANAGEMENT CHALLENGE

The manager's role

In the twenty-first century the world of work in which a manager operates is one of continuous change and the most important management skill is the management of change. Whether they are large or small, in the private, public or voluntary sectors, organisations have to deal with the consequences of ever more rapid innovations in technology, huge developments in communications, the decline and burgeoning of national economies and an increasing emphasis on global concerns with corporate responsibility and environmental policies. Organisations also have to face changes in legislation and political policies and upheavals in society and in cultural matters. At the same time the internal structures and cultures of businesses, public corporations and voluntary bodies have altered as a result of external changes and the need to increase output with the use of fewer resources. The importance of retaining a competitive advantage over competitors and the pressures of the marketplace mean that managers have to be creative and innovative to an unprecedented extent. In the first decade of the twenty-first century, change can be seen as the natural order of things so the concept of the most important management skill being the management of change arises from the fact that the really skilful part of a manager's job is setting up the method of working in the first place, and then renewing and refreshing these methods again and again.

The technological revolution heralded in the last decades of the twentieth century has arrived with a vengeance in recent years with the rapid spread across the population of the use of the Internet, mobile telephones and e-mail, while national economies such as Japan have become less prominent compared to those of China and India and concerns over global warming and the use of fossil fuels have given a new emphasis to corporate ethical, social and environmental policies. None of this has diminished the need for strategic management, the effective management of people and the management of functions and processes for getting things done. The management role is

> *'getting things done by other people'*   (Parker Follett, 1941)

so management can be described as

> *'the process of optimising human, material and financial contributions for the achievement of organisational goals'*   (Pearce and Robinson, 1989)

To be a successful manager at a senior level it is necessary to have an understanding of all areas of the business in order to be able to deal sensibly with every function as well as strategically with the whole enterprise. At a more junior level a manager has to understand all the areas of the business within the sphere of influence of a particular job role. This is why the typical MBA, aimed at people moving from junior or middle management roles to senior roles, has a syllabus which aims to widen an individual's knowledge and understanding and includes modules on finance and accounting, human resources, organisational theory, leadership, motivation, communication, corporate responsibility and environmental issues. Management can be defined as:

> *the process of achieving organisational goals and objectives effectively and efficiently through planning, organising, leading and controlling the human, material and financial resources available to it.*

An organisation's resources include the people working for it, its capital in terms of buildings, equipment, money, raw materials and products, and its customer base. A manufacturing company will have factories, machinery, vehicles, warehouses, sources of energy and a labour force. It will also have money in the form of capital and cash. A retailer will have shops and store rooms, communication and transport facilities, capital and a work force. A university has buildings which are variously equipped with machines and laboratories, desks and visual aids, capital and a range of academic and other employees. Managers bring 'enterprise' to the other three factors of production, land, labour and capital, in that managers plan the use of buildings, equipment and people, organise this combination, lead this process and control the results

At first glance a manager's role is to organise, supervise and control people so that there is a productive outcome to work. The manager's role is not the same as that of a supervisor although it may include supervision, it is not the same as monitoring or recording although it may also include these functions, it is a wider and deeper, more creative and innovative role. Organisations of one type or another are essential for productive work because they bring people together with raw materials and equipment in order to achieve a variety of goals. By combining people's talents and energy with resources, very often more can be achieved than by individuals working on their own. Organisations, whether they are companies, educational institutions, hospitals or football teams, will all have objectives and a purpose for being in existence and for continuing their work. These objectives or goals may be expressed in terms of profits, share price, market share, educational achievements, health or winning games. Every organisation will have a plan to achieve these objectives in order to make sure that they have the right people doing the right jobs with the best possible equipment at the right time. The complexity of the management role and what it involves is illustrated in Figure 1.1 opposite.

The idea of 'getting things done by other people' emphasises the fact that managers achieve organisational objectives by arranging for other people to perform whatever tasks are required and do not necessarily carry out these tasks themselves. This is obviously essential in a football team where even a player-manager must have other people to help the team to win. In industry one-person businesses can succeed by specialising in one aspect of a process, but major products and services are supplied by larger organisations because one-person businesses cannot produce a sufficient quantity of goods and services to meet consumer demand. It is a characteristic of developing economies that as the market for goods and services grows the importance of the one-person business declines relative to larger forms of organisation. The relatively 'old-fashioned' definitions emphasise the running of an organisation in terms of administration and control, which represents what can be described as an operational view of management. A more modern and dynamic view of management would suggest that it should be based on innovation and on satisfying the customer. This view suggests that people are imprisoned by their own experience and that in order to remain dynamic an organisation needs to change its structure frequently. The emphasis is not on running the organisation, although this remains an essential part of the management role, so much as on planning, developing and changing it.

Figure 1.2 suggests that all managers may be involved with the operational aspects of management but as they are promoted up the hierarchical pyramid, and they develop their careers, their role becomes increasingly one of planning, innovation and leadership. In fact these aspects of management are important in one way or another at all levels. Jim Kilts, CEO of Gillette, has suggested that

Figure 1.1 Management

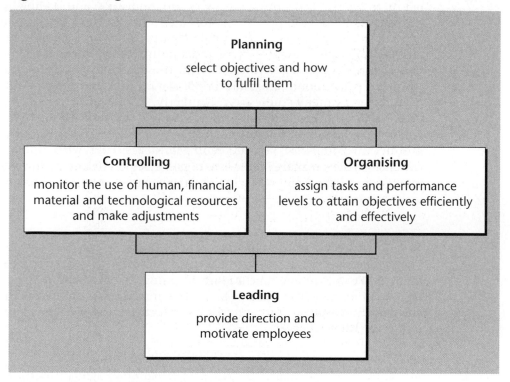

'*people always like to say that management made them do it. Well we are all management. If there is a problem, it's everybody's problem.*'   (Stern, 2005)

The idea that leadership is a lofty, inspirational matter removed from day-to-day management undervalues the art of management at all levels.

'*Managers are told that there is nothing wrong with strategy; the problem is that they are not executing it well. Managers end up as anxious task masters demanding performance, pushing targets at people.*'   (Binney *et al.*, 2005)

Figure 1.2 The management role

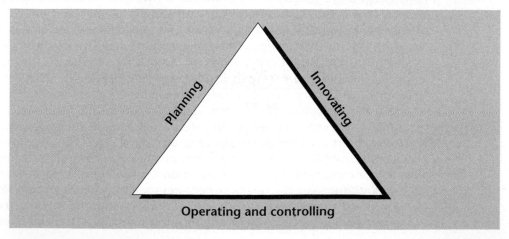

The role of a manager at a junior level may involve considerable attention to detail but there will still be scope for creativity and innovation and leading by example.

When technological progress is slow and other aspects of organisations remain constant for many years, perhaps the major part of a working lifetime, the important skills needed are supervisory and administrative in order to make sure that the established process continues. Under these circumstances operating and controlling are paramount and the work of the industrial foreman or supervisor has been found in many studies (e.g. Dunkerly, 1975 and Kerr *et al.*, 1986) to have included planning, scheduling and allocating work; monitoring output; checking equipment, health and safety; dealing with unforeseen staffing, equipment and production problems; record-keeping and assisting with operational work. However, when working methods and processes change every few years or pretty much constantly, then managing change becomes the most important management attribute.

The challenge

The management challenge is to maintain control over the processes of an organisation while at the same time leading, inspiring, directing and making decisions on all sorts of matters. The challenge for modern managers is to deal with this tension between operating the present systems, structures and processes and the need to change in order to survive.

> *'Management as it has been systematised and professionalised, has developed many axioms over the past century. But in the past twenty years, the stable conditions (large scale mass-production) that led to the slow emergence of these universals have blown apart.'*
> (Peters, 1987)

If this was true in 1987, it has become even more obvious in the first decade of the twenty-first century. The 'knowledge revolution' has eventually caught up with past predictions. Electronic commerce, including sales via the Internet, has become an increasingly ordinary part of everyday life. The number of broadband connections in the UK doubled in 2004 and has continued to grow. In the past, holiday planning has involved holidaymakers watching a travel agent look up flight times and availability and other aspects of the holiday on their computers with software packages not readily available to the booking public. Now anyone can access this information in the comfort of his or her own home. In the same way, instead of fighting the local Tesco car park and waiting in the checkout lines, shoppers can order their groceries via their PC screens. The 'dot-com' and e-commerce companies have arrived and managers and their organisations have to face this change.

Organisations, whether they are commercial companies or non-profit institutions, have to meet customer demands if they are to succeed. This is obvious with motor car companies and high street shops but is now also true in the non-profit sector for organisations such as schools, universities, hospitals and museums (see Chapter 4). As customer needs alter, so the business must change by anticipating customer wants, leading these where appropriate as well as responding to them. The emphasis today is on a focus on the customer, whether a consumer of goods and services, a patient needing health services, a student seeking a university education or a visitor searching for information in a library or a museum. All managers are concerned with leading their organisation, section, unit or team to enable work to be carried out successfully in response to the needs of their market. As society

→ Ch. 4

and the economy develop and as managers are promoted from junior to middle and senior levels, the requirement to be flexible, creative, innovative and able to absorb and communicate new ideas becomes of increasing importance.

This view of modern management suggests that it is about change, because in order to meet their objectives organisations need to focus on their customers through a marketing culture. This is as true of a professional football team as of a multinational company, a hospital trust or a small business. Management of a kind is required in the smallest task – in a one-person business, that one person will have to combine all the qualities of management as well as working at an operational level. Above all, in one way or another, the individual running a one-person business must satisfy the customers through the quality of the work and the service provided. The larger an organisation is then, the more specialised management can become with the separation of management functions, while at the highest level there will need again to be a convergence of specialised management skills, on a different plane, in order to develop organisational strategy (see Figure 1.3).

THE SCIENCE OF MANAGEMENT

→ Ch. 20
The examples of approaches to management in the nineteenth century and the first half of the twentieth century discussed in Chapter 20 indicate that management problems have not changed particularly, while styles and approaches have. These are very much dependent on circumstances, so that although managers may feel they have a better approach than their predecessors, in fact it is a different approach which may be better or worse according to the needs of the particular time. Operations research is a good example of this, developing out of the necessity in the UK to solve complex technical problems during the Second World War. At that time groups of mathematicians, scientists and engineers were brought together to solve such problems. The result was that significant technological and tactical

Figure 1.3 Levels of management

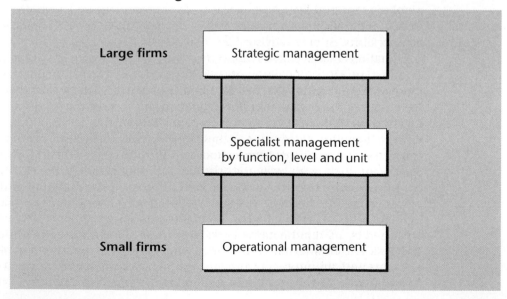

breakthroughs were achieved by this approach and after the war they were quickly applied to industry.

This management science approach has been characterised by solving problems through mixed teams of specialists from relevant disciplines who analyse the problem and suggest courses of action. Its main contribution to modern management has been in the development of models to help managers to analyse complex statistical data in order to obtain a greater understanding of a problem. It has produced an emphasis on decision making, on the use of quantitative models in planning and the evaluation of the effectiveness of decisions which has been greatly encouraged in the second half of the twentieth century by the development of computers.

Managers' roles change as they move up an organisation, so that at the junior level they are more concerned with the detail than with the overall picture. Distinctions have been made between the role of the foreman or supervisor and the junior manager or 'the first-line manager' (Betts, 1999; Owen, 2001). Supervisors engage with workers directly, immediately and face-to-face, junior managers often do so indirectly through the supervisors. Junior managers have delegated authority to take decisions at the operational level, while supervisors have responsibility but not authority. Lowe (1992) suggests that responsibility subsumes both accountability and control, so that a junior manager is both answerable and can make decisions. The supervisor has accountability without control, so is answerable but cannot decide. In practice these functional differences may be matters of degree and the description 'first-line manager' may include a whole variety of titles and roles. In the UK these functional distinctions are overlaid by distinctions of status so that supervisors and foremen can be considered to be 'non-commissioned officers' somewhere between the 'officer class' of managers and the 'ranks' of the workforce. In the management hierarchy, a junior sales manager may be heavily involved in selling or in supervising a small number of sales people. At middle management level a sales manager may control an area or a department, unit or section, organising and controlling a number of junior sales managers and having an input into planning the sales function of the organisation, into innovation and perhaps into sales strategy. The sales director will be mainly responsible for ensuring that the sales strategy of the organisation assists in meeting its objectives. There may, of course, be a number of intermediate levels or layers of management and a whole range of titles, so that, for example, many sales people are now called 'account managers' or 'product specialists' or even 'advisers'.

Operations management is concerned with matters which are in the control of an organisation. Operationally an organisation performs a transformation or conversion process where it adds value to a commodity or service. This means that the value of the output of the organisation is greater than the costs of the inputs and the process involved, so that whatever an organisation starts with in terms of 'raw materials' to process, it applies added value to these. For example, bakers start with raw materials consisting of ingredients such as flour and through their skill and with the correct equipment, such as an oven, they produce loaves of bread. At the end of the process the price obtained for the bread exceeds the cost of the materials and the baking process. Similarly, in the service sector, a holiday company starts with a destination in mind, seats on airline flights, hotel room bookings and a variety of excursions organised by its representatives and pulls these elements together into a package. This is sold to holidaymakers at a price which is greater than the cost of the various elements and the process of organising them. As a result an airline seat is transformed from a 'raw material' into an important element in a holiday.

There is usually a linked set of transformations or conversion processes between the beginning of the process and the final product, which together constitute a value chain (see Chapter 5). Operational management is involved in the organising, supervising and controlling of these processes. It is about routine, and it is specific and relatively short term making sure that people know what to do and are doing it so that the objectives of the organisation are achieved. Although senior managers and middle managers are concerned with these processes, it is the junior managers who spend most of their time heavily involved in organising, supervising and controlling (see Figure 1.4). As managers are promoted they become more involved in the strategy of the organisation, in innovating, risk taking and planning. While strategic management provides a sense of purpose (see Chapter 5), operational management provides for the organisation, control and supervision that enables this sense of purpose to achieve a concrete form.

→ Ch. 5

→ Ch. 5

Management science

These approaches, plus off-shoots and mixtures, can be identified in modern management practice. John Harvey-Jones (1993) has written that

> *'when I first started in industry in the fifties, attractions of work measurement and method study as a means of improving productivity seemed almost like a philosopher's stone.'*

During the 1960s 'there seemed to be a common belief that everything could be measured', while the '1970s were the period when we discovered that concentrating on method and systems somehow didn't seem to make the expected breakthroughs' and 'social science came back in fashion'. He has noted the optimism of the 1980s in contrast to the pessimism of the 1990s and has found it fascinating that 'management fashions seem to spread across the world with the speed of light, whereas

Figure 1.4 The management function

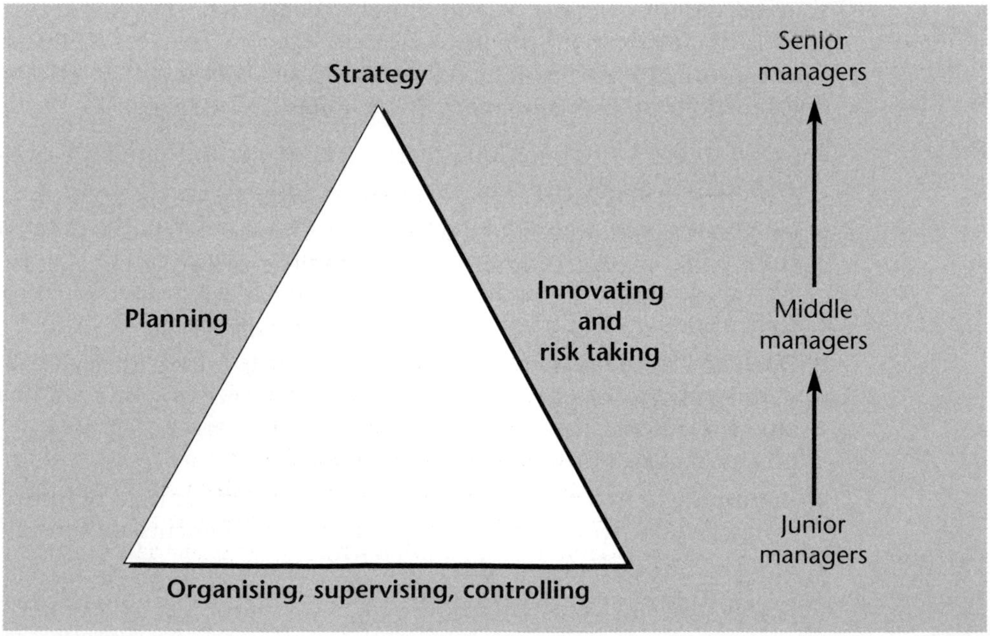

transferring technology appears to be an extraordinarily difficult task to achieve'. However, the popularity of measuring success through target setting has increased again in recent years and it can be argued that technological change has accelerated. Henry Mintzberg's classic study on *The Nature of Management Work* (1973) can be said to belong to the management science tradition because the largest section of the book consists of a discussion of programming managerial work by the use of management science and the downplaying of the importance of the manager as leader. Furthermore, the leadership role is seen in relatively administrative terms rather in relation to strategy, creativity and innovation.

An example of the rapid spread of management fashions is the emphasis on quality management in the late 1980s and early 1990s, which can be seen as another way of dressing up old ideas in new clothing. It can be argued that, like other management theories, quality management has been around a long time but it has to be discovered again by each new group of managers. In the same way, modern theories have included attempts to view the organisation as a single, integrated system, either through a systems approach or through a contingency approach, and these ideas are important in the understanding of modern management thinking and the role of managers.

The systems approach

The **systems approach** is based on the view that managers should focus on the role that each part of an organisation plays in the whole organisation, rather than dealing separately with each part. It takes into account the different needs of various functional management areas, such as production, marketing and finance. For example, the marketing department might want to be able to sell a large variety of products, while the production unit would prefer to have long production runs of a few items, and financial managers might be mainly concerned with keeping costs as low as possible. The systems approach means that managers have to discuss their various requirements in terms of the needs of the whole organisation. Production scheduling, for example, would only be completed once marketing and finance were in agreement with the plans. This interaction requires a high degree of communication and the breaking down of barriers between the various departments and functions of an organisation. The emphasis is on management awareness of:

- **Subsystems** – the individual parts that make up the whole organisation, for example a unit, department, company or industry.
- **Synergy** – emphasises the interrelationships between all the parts of an organisation, reflecting the concept that the whole is greater than the sum of its parts. This suggests that departments and units in a business are more productive when they work together than when they operate separately.
- **Open and closed systems** – reflect the extent to which an organisation interacts with its environment. Companies providing services to the public will normally be open systems, while those working within a larger organisation, such as component part manufacturers, will be more closed.
- **Boundaries** – in a closed system will tend to be more rigid than those in an open system, where boundaries with the outside environments are constantly changing.
- **Flows** – of information, materials and human energy which move through a system and are transformed in the process into goods and services.

■ **Feedback** – the process of monitoring information about systems in order to evaluate their operation.

This approach implies that management at all levels needs to be sensitive to the complexity of the organisation and accept a system which enables the organisation to work efficiently.

The contingency approach

This can be described as the 'golf club approach'. Like picking out the right golf club for a particular shot at a specific time on a particular day, the contingency approach to management problems suggests that different problems and situations require different solutions. Much depends on managers' experience with this approach, and it is understood that what might work well in one situation may not work in another. The task of management is to identify which technique will work in particular circumstances. In one case the solution to creating greater productivity may be to motivate employees by giving them greater responsibility; in another case, if the employees are relatively unskilled for example, it may be better to provide extra training and supervision as at least a preliminary step.

The contingency approach has developed through attempts to apply concepts drawn from the major schools of management thought. In applying these to solving management problems, advocates of this approach take the pragmatic view that no one approach is universally applicable. For example, on the one hand techniques used in scientific management, such as time study, may be used to investigate a particular problem; on the other hand, the ideas of the behavioural school may be involved in an inquiry into workers' motivation, perhaps followed by a quantitative analysis of the results. Jim Goodnight, the founder of SAS, the largest privately owned software company, has been quoted (Stern, 2005) as saying that 'managing by loitering' has kept him in touch with front-line activity ever since he started the business in 1976. 'I talk to key contributors (i.e. programmers) as much as I do to managers', he says.

The pragmatic view

Like a golfer selecting a club with full regard to all the variables such as distance, obstacles to be avoided as well as wind direction and other conditions, so will a manager need to consider the objectives of a particular action, the people involved, the equipment available and the internal and external conditions which prevail. The internal environment is the way the organisation works, its corporate culture, management structure and communication systems. Although golfers need to know their own capabilities and temperament in order to make a good start, they do not usually play as a team. A manager needs to take into account the abilities and temperament of his colleagues as well as his own. The external environment consists of the social, political and economic factors that affect an organisation, and a manager has to judge such matters as the movement of exchange rates and their effect on the international prices of company raw materials and finished products. Ethical considerations or green issues (see Chapters 17 and 18) may play a part in the organisation's market and the manager will need to consider the effect of such issues when making decisions on products and their marketing.

→ Chs 17 & 18

Managers also need to be aware of the relationship between the internal and external environments. Green issues may cause problems for the design and

production departments, but   , the
move to unleaded petrol in th   f car
engines and in the allocation   this
may occur again in the future   time
there are internal constraints   igers
must take into account in maki

- **Technological constraints** v   :om-
  pany in order to produce its   juire
  expensive capital equipment and it is difficult for them to change technology
  quickly to meet new demands. Car manufacturers need to have reasonable runs
  on their production lines in order to receive a profitable return on their investment. Small-scale engineering companies can use less specific capital equipment
  to produce special and individualised orders.

- **Task constraints** arise from the nature of the jobs performed and the skills of the
  workers involved. Assembly-line workers may be able to move to a different
  assembly line with a minimum of training, while finding it more difficult to take
  on more varied work.

- **Human constraints** reflect the competence of the people employed by an organisation and their motivation. A competent, well-trained and motivated workforce
  will exert fewer constraints on a manager than a less competent and poorly motivated workforce.

- **Organisational performance**, in that the ability of an organisation to compete
  effectively in its external environment depends on the organisational performance, including designing, producing, marketing and supplying.

- **The resource base**, including physical resources (buildings and production and
  service facilities), human resources (including employee competence, skills
  and attitudes) and financial resources (such as financial assets, financial control
  and systems).

THE ART OF MANAGEMENT

A synthesis

The management challenge is to answer the questions What are we doing? How do
we do it? and What do we do next? This is against the background of a rapidly
changing external environment and has in the foreground an increasingly well-
trained and educated workforce. The answer given by the contingency approach to
these questions is 'it all depends'. Each situation is examined to determine its
unique attribute before a management decision is made. This contrasts with earlier
approaches that tended to deal in universal principles which could be applied in
every situation. The modern management approach is to analyse the situation and
then to draw on the various schools of management thought in order to decide on
the most appropriate combination. This contingency approach helps managers to
be aware of the complexity in every situation and to take an active role in trying to
determine what would work best in each case. It calls for a bringing together, or
synthesis, of approaches and this throws a strong element of responsibility onto
management. While on the one hand managers are not encouraged to eliminate
unpredictable circumstances, on the other hand they are encouraged to consider all
contingencies and to be sufficiently flexible to take all possibilities into account.

Managers are now encouraged to recognise the ability of the people they manage and to push decision making as near as possible to the point of action. This process can develop 'flexibility by **empowerment**' (Peters, 1987) and it carries the contingency approach to what might be considered its logical conclusion. This suggests that the people who have to implement a decision should make it by analysing the situation and deciding on a course of action. Tom Peters believes that the empowering of people

> *'can most effectively be tapped when people are gathered in human scale groupings, that is, teams, or more precisely, self-managed teams'.*

This move to self-managed teams and decision making at the point of action makes it necessary for the integrative approach to management to come to terms with human relations management. The integrated approach developed through systems management and contingency management, which between them view the organisation as a single integrated body, at the same time including the diversity of self-managed teams.

In the 1980s William Ouchi (1981) observed that many of the most successful American companies displayed organisational behaviour similar to practices common in Japanese organisations. This included the emphasis on collective decision making and group responsibilities, on quality control based on periodic on-site meetings, and on the lifetime commitment to an organisation. On the other hand, he observed that the Japanese managerial style was borrowed from Western models of scientific management. He felt that an integration of these approaches would lead to management success. Scientific work methods could be incorporated into an integrative management theory and combined with human relations management. He felt that organisational goals could be achieved by making decision making a participatory activity for a greater number of employees, so that responsibility becomes a collaborative function as the product of group or team processes.

The corporate and national culture

If management can be seen as a synthesis of ideas, culminating in choices made in the end intuitively, then it can be described as an art. In golf, club selection may be based on scientific measurement, observation and experience but there is also an intuitive element which can turn a good professional shot into a great one. In spite of all the information the golfer may have, the very skilful golfer may have an immediate insight into the club and shot required in the circumstances which overrules the rational information available. This is the skill or art of the professional golfer, and this skill or 'feel' for a situation plays a part in the work of the professional manager and is set against the background of management theories.

→ Ch. 20 Exhibit 1.1 summarises the management theories that have developed over the last two centuries (for further analysis, see Chapter 20). This summary could be extended to include 2000+ with the influences of globalisation, technology and flexibility. Modern management is essentially about managing people as well as processes in a rapidly changing environment. There is a mass of information available to most managers in terms of costs, prices and market conditions, but in the end decisions may be based on a hunch or intuition. This is where experience and a feel for the particular process and people involved becomes essential, and this can be helped by the corporate culture of the organisation. Culture is an important factor in the art of management because for any organisation to operate effectively it must, to some extent, have a generally accepted set of beliefs and assumptions. These will usually have evolved over time and represent a collective experience without which managers would have to start from scratch each time they made a decision. This collective experience will be influenced by wider cultural perspectives so that managers have to be aware of the social, economic and political context they are working in, whether it is a region of the UK or an organisation in another country.

→ Ch. 19

Managers work in a national and social context, and different national cultures and social norms produce different views on how management should be conducted (see Chapter 19). In the twenty-first century management can be summarised as being involved in the global economy, based on technology and fluidity. A generalised view of global differences suggests that Japanese management, for example, is based on collective responsibility for the success of the organisation and, at least in the 'ideal' Japanese organisations, is also based on training for a wide variety of roles, lifelong careers and on trust and loyalty. In contrast, management in the USA is based on the use of systematic approaches to improving task performance, individualism, specific job roles and responsibilities, and the importance of market position. Other national business cultures challenge these models, so that the Arab style of management can be said to be based on strong social formalities where nepotism is expected and accepted and time constraints are not of primary importance.

China and Russia are both large countries with populations dominated by a single group (Han Chinese and ethnic Russian respectively). Both are undertaking pathways to capitalism and both have key roles in establishing international stabil-

Exhibit 1.1 Management theories

Scientific management:	
ADAM SMITH – BABBAGE – TOWNE – TAYLOR	1800–1914
Administrative management:	
FAYOL – WEBER	1900–1925
Behavioural theories:	
FOLLETT – BARNARD – MAYO	1900–1940
Management systems:	
OPERATIONS MANAGEMENT	
SYSTEMS MANAGEMENT	1940+
Contingency theories:	
PRAGMATIC MANAGEMENT – SITUATION THEORIES	1980+
Art of management:	
SYNTHESIS – INTEGRATION – ORGANISATIONAL CULTURE	1980+

ity (Michailova and Hutchings, 2006). They have both been ruled for years by a communist party with strong central planning but weak regulatory controls so that existing rules have been easy to violate and written contracts have had little value. Personal contacts and reciprocity within the boundaries of groups have substituted for reliable institutions. In other ways these two important countries have developed differently in recent years with China a rising superpower and Russia struggling to hold on to past glory. China has maintained central planning in coexistence with the gradual development of a market economy. Russia has rapidly replaced central planning with market-based mechanisms. International managers working with organisations in these countries have to recognise the differences between them as well as the similarities and, while developing interpersonal connections, recognise that they are within different commercial, social and political cultures.

The art of management can be characterised as reflection in action, so that managers' experience and understanding of the context in which they operate can be applied to the particular situations they face. They need to have a similar view to their colleagues of the nature of the organisation and the internal and external environments in which it operates. It is this organisational view of the world which helps to interpret the changes facing the organisation and the individuals within it. Changes tend to develop incrementally, decisions building one upon another so that past decisions mould future strategy. It is the management task to steer this process in the right direction, as well as being prepared to deal with the less frequent but more fundamental changes of direction that occur from time to time.

LEVELS OF MANAGEMENT

The art of management applies to all levels. Just as any job can be carried out well or badly, so can management at any level. While intuition is particularly important at the strategic level, applied experience is essential in the management of the most mundane task. An alert junior supervisor will quickly learn that there are various ways of achieving the same results from his or her subordinates. Although in any organisation managers can be distinguished by their functions and by their level of responsibility, the management skills they apply will depend on their actual role in the organisation. Attempts to produce flatter management structures may have reduced the number of stages in the hierarchy but have not greatly changed the underlying situation in most organisations. This remains pyramid-shaped with a relatively small number of senior managers at the top, a larger number of middle managers at the centre and an even larger group of junior managers supervising the majority of employees who are non-managerial (see Figure 1.5).

The 'typical' junior manager will be a supervisor of a unit or the senior member of a team. Junior managers are working at, or very close to, the operational level and may have titles such as foreman, team leader, coordinator, operational manager or, of course, supervisor. Their role is to coordinate the work of non-managerial employees and to have direct responsibility for machinery and materials. Junior managers are expected to be skilled at both overseeing work and doing it. They are able to supervise and to fill in when and where needed in order to maintain the smooth operation of the system. They have delegated authority (which may distinguish them from supervisors or foreman) to make decisions at an operational level.

Figure 1.5 Management levels

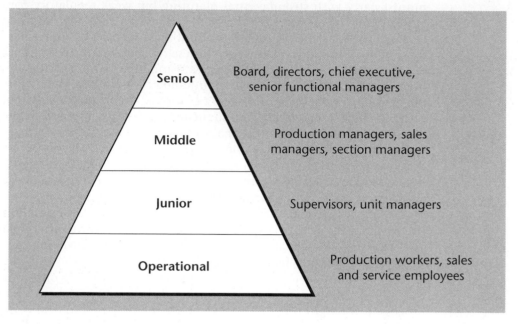

Middle managers are usually accountable for the work of junior managers and they in turn report to senior management. They will have a wider remit than the supervisors who report to them and spend much more of their time on management functions rather than in an operational role. They may step into an operational role from time to time but they may be managing areas of expertise in which they have some knowledge but not at an operational level. The manager of a large store may be able to take over from sales, at the till or in filling shelves but not necessarily in wordprocessing or in maintaining refrigerated units. At the same time, middle managers will have limits to their responsibilities, so that the store manager may not control pricing policy, advertising or training but may be involved in making sure that these policies are implemented.

Senior managers are the executives, at the highest level of the organisation, responsible for its overall direction and coordination and for directing its major activities. Senior managers are responsible for company-wide planning, organising, directing and controlling, and for providing strategic leadership to the company. They are also concerned with the demands imposed on the organisation by outside influences such as customers and suppliers. Above all, they are responsible for the overall direction and success or failure of the organisation. Within these three layers of management there may be numerous intermediate stages, particularly in middle management. Figure 1.6 shows a simplified management organisation chart.

Line management and functional management

Figure 1.6 depicts the formal line management relationship between members of an organisation but does not attempt to show their functional relationship. In practice there will be more or less formal networks of people on a functional basis, in some cases forming project committees, in other cases communicating across management lines in order to progress the work of the organisation. Some companies have

Figure 1.6 Management organisation chart

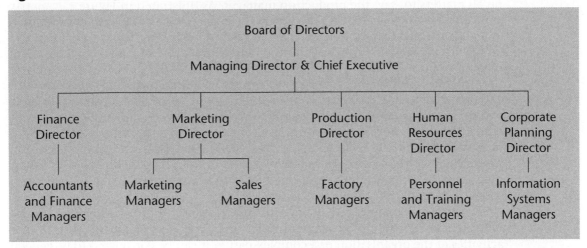

developed matrix structures to facilitate these communication networks, but in fact networks can create an informal matrix in any organisation.

Matrix structures (Figure 1.7) usually involve managers being responsible to more than one senior manager, so that for one part of their work they will be line managed by one manager and for another part by another. For example, the allocation of resources may be separated from the production process, so that a middle-ranking plant manager may be responsible to a marketing manager for the output and to a production manager for new materials. There may be responsibility to a third manager, say a human resources manager, for control of staff. It can be argued that this approach provides greater expertise in the various areas of work, but it lacks the

Figure 1.7 Matrix structures

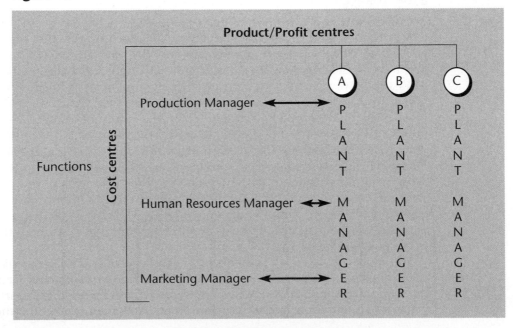

simplicity and certainties of a hierarchical structure where the plant manager reports on all matters to, say, the production manager. As illustrated in Figure 1.7, matrix structures are usually based on a division between a functional management role, such as marketing, and a project role, such as the production of a particular commodity.

Flatter management structures aim to reduce the layers of control and approval or veto over decision making. Peter Drucker (1988) has suggested that the ultimate flat structure is the factory manager in Nebraska who has himself as manager with 120 operatives on the production line without any intermediate managers. In large and complex organisations this very simple approach may be difficult to implement while retaining control and coordination, but the move towards fewer layers of management can help to speed up decision making and push the point of decision nearer the point of action. For example, companies can achieve one layer of senior management, one of middle and one of junior management, each with its own sphere of responsibility and decision making.

At every level, managers may have functional responsibilities or may be general managers responsible for a range of functions. Managers responsible for all the activities of the organisation or a complex part of it can be considered to be general managers. Most factory managers and shop/store managers are of this kind. They will line-manage people with a variety of skills and roles and will have some involvement in most of the organisational functions, such as finance, production, marketing and human relations. On the other hand, functional managers will be responsible for one activity within the organisation, such as marketing or finance. They will be responsible for line-managing staff within the same function. The marketing manager, for example, will be responsible for staff in sales, in promotions, advertising and public relations, and in market research. The market research manager will line-manage staff in data collection, statistics and information. In order to remain competitive, organisations have to find the structures which work best for them and reform these structures as necessary.

What managers do

It may be reasonably clear in an organisation who the managers are and the types and levels of responsibility they hold, but the question remains as to what they actually do. The theories of management provide some clues to what people in the past have considered to be the management job, while the level at which managers work also plays a part in what they do. Figures 1.4 and 1.5 indicate that managers move from a more operational role to one of planning and innovation as they move from junior to middle and senior management. Junior managers are likely to spend a large proportion of their time doing an operational job, whether it is production or sales. Depending on their exact role and the size of the unit they are managing, a greater or lesser proportion of their time will be spent on supervision, training and involvement with networks of other managers in the organisation. They may need to attend training sessions themselves in order to keep up to date, or they may be on a quality assurance committee or have regular briefing meetings with their line manager. A limited time will be spent on planning and this will tend to be about specific projects.

The middle manager will have much less of an operational role and will spend most of the time on management. This will include much more coordination and monitoring than supervision, although this is likely to remain an important part of the job. Organising, controlling and some planning are likely to be the main elements of the work. The large branch store manager will spend some time planning and preparing for the next day or week or month, a large proportion of time monitoring and supervising junior managers, and the rest of the time will act as a general manager involved in finance, purchasing, marketing, staffing matters and dealing with outside providers. His junior managers, in charge of particular sections of the store, will spend much more time tied down to their sections supervising all aspects of them.

Senior managers spend much of their time planning, organising and dealing with outside factors, including customers and suppliers. Henry Mintzberg, in a study on *The Nature of Managerial Work* (1980), found that all senior managers, in one way or another, have three independent roles:

- interpersonal roles
- informational roles
- decisional roles.

How these roles are performed depends on the structure and type of organisation and on the personality of the manager. Interpersonal roles arise from the manager's position in their particular company and from the extent to which they appear as a figurehead, or in terms of leadership and liaison. At times they will represent the company, either internally or externally, at presentations and with other companies, and at other times they will initiate more productive links between other managers and teams through liaison with them.

Senior managers will have an informational role because they become the focal point for receiving and sending information within the organisation and outside it. They monitor developments within the organisation, such as performance, as well as opportunities and threats outside the organisation, such as customer behaviour. They disseminate information in order to influence the actions of other people in the organisation, and they act as spokespeople and publicisers in representing the organisation to outside agencies. In decision making, managers strive to allocate resources in the most productive way to encourage innovation and change and to negotiate with other managers and groups within the organisation in order to develop it further. The way in which decisions are made in an organisation is an important indicator of the way it functions, whether it is relatively autocratic or democratic, and this in turn depends on the leadership role of senior managers and the resultant corporate culture (see Chapters 2 and 9).

→ Chs 2 & 9

How managers spend their time

As a clearer indication of what managers do, there have been surveys of how they spend their time. These show that at senior and middle levels, at least, time is spent in a range of activities depending very much on the nature of the organisation and the character of the individual. Exhibit 1.2 is a list of these activities in rank order. It should be remembered, however, that because a particular function does not appear on the list does not necessarily mean that it does not happen. For example, **management by walking about (MBWA)** may not exist in some managers' time allocation, but was stressed by Tom Peters and Robert Waterman in *In Search of Excellence* (1982) as an essential element in managerial success. No list will represent the full range of activities of an individual manager.

A 1997 survey of 258 chief executives carried out for the *Sunday Times* found that 79 per cent of those surveyed thought that the business, social and economic

Exhibit 1.2 How managers spend their time

- **Controlling**
- **Solving problems**
- **Planning**
- **Communicating informally and formally**
- **Communicating upwards**
- **Communicating downwards**
- **Attending meetings**
- **Reading**
- **Writing memos and letters**
- **Representing the company**

environment had created a culture in which cost cutting was the driving force for managers, instead of the development of the rounded skills needed to manage growth, expansion and innovation. Asked to name the most important management skills from a list of 11, the chief executives put leadership first, followed by vision, people management, communications and financial literacy. Although they said that a lack of management skills in their organisation had already prevented them from fully exploiting commercial opportunities, they were optimistic about the future because they thought that future managers would be better educated and trained and be more aware of competition.

MANAGING CHANGE

Descriptions of what managers do and how they spend their time provide only a partial view of a manager's actual role. Almost by definition, managers are a small minority of people in the employment of any organisation and therefore most people do not have experience of being a manager. Whereas managers have usually been through the operational stage and can to some extent transfer this type of experience to any operational area, it is more difficult for operators who have never been managers to understand the management viewpoint. On the other hand, of course, most people have some understanding of management processes because their work involves some of these processes, they have to manage their personal lives and their homes, and because they will experience the results of different management actions, approaches and styles. At a simple structural level there is often an understanding that work has to be managed, that someone has to make major decisions and that the organisation and individual jobs within it depend on management functions being performed.

The management of change in an organisation is an area of potential conflict because → Ch. 20 of these inherent issues of understanding and communication (see Chapter 20).

Management actions to facilitate change can easily be misunderstood because the procedures and processes already in existence appear to be perfectly good. These days the management of change is the most important management skill because it can be seen as a constant process of setting up working methods to meet changing circumstances. These 'changing circumstances' need to be understood by everyone. John Harvey-Jones (1993) has stated that change is easier to manage when there is an element of danger present in an organisation and there is an obvious need for change:

'It is impossible to change organisations which do not accept the dangers of their present way of doing things.'

Although the decision to implement change may be considered to be largely conceptual in nature, it takes effect in action and behaviour. Managing change is essentially about people and not concepts and ideas, while the results of change will be seen most clearly by most people in matters of detail. Faced with pressure for change, managers are likely to deal with the situation in ways which coincide with the culture of the organisation. This raises a particular challenge to management when the action required is outside the assumptions and beliefs of members of the organisation. Much change is incremental in that one change leads to another, and the main challenge to modern management is that the incremental steps are closer together than in the past. However, it is this increasing frequency of change which challenges the underlying culture of organisations – 'the way we do things around here'. For example, technological change may mean the gradual introduction of wordprocessors to replace typewriters, or the introduction of an automated assembly line with robots replacing the assembly-line jobs all at the same time. In the first case a few people will be left behind who are unable to make the change from typewriters to computers. In the second case all or most jobs will disappear, with perhaps a few new ones appearing in the form of maintenance or quality control. As a result of technological and scientific development 'the way we do things around here' may be altered overnight, but even in the most extreme cases the manager's role is to anticipate the change and prepare for it.

All change involves people and their working patterns and it can be argued that organisations can change only at the speed at which people in them are willing and able to change. Fundamental changes in attitudes take years rather than months, and the first part of the process involves a clear understanding that the status quo is no longer possible. This may be through dissatisfaction with the present position or fear of the consequences of adhering to it. For example, if competitors are clearly affecting the viability of the company then the present position can be seen as a threat and the need for change will be easily appreciated.

Change and organisational culture

→ Ch. 8

An organisation's **culture** can be defined as 'the way we do things around here' (see Chapter 8). It can be considered as a complex mixture of tangible factors that can be seen and touched, assumptions about how people should behave in the organisation and people's actual behaviour. Culture can be the basis of competitive advantage in markets because it may prove difficult to imitate. On the other hand it is also difficult to change and it can be argued that organisations are 'captured' by their own cultures in the sense of sharing more or less strongly a set of beliefs, customs, practices and ways of thinking and the development of ritual or accepted behaviour that they have come to share with each other through being and working together.

Tangible factors include the organisation's location, the buildings it inhabits, the decoration and layout of the workplaces. For example, so-called 'hot desking' has developed as a result of a particularly informal approach to work, and stand-up discussion around a tall table has developed as a way of encouraging meetings to be short and businesslike. There may be assumptions about when people arrive at work and when they leave and how many breaks they take. Although working hours may be set out in an employment contract, employees may be expected to work longer hours than those written down. The actual behaviour of employees may mean that although they are at work for long hours they take frequent breaks, so that the actual hours they work are similar to those of employees who are at work for a shorter time.

The ritual behaviour, symbols, myths and stories in an organisation can be analysed in order to study its culture. The way the founder of the company behaved may create stories and myths which persist in the company long after the founder has gone and continue to affect people's behaviour. In the same way, the style and actions of the present chief executive may set the tone for the company even if some of the reported incidents are in fact stories or myths. A very formal approach to working relationships by a boss may establish the style for everyone else, while an informal manner may encourage different behaviour.

Figure 1.8 illustrates some of the influences on **organisational culture**. Stories and myths that people in an organisation tell about what has happened in the past can provide a view of what they think is important. These may revolve around successes and failures, particular individuals and so on, and can indicate whether innovation or stability is important or whether company loyalty is highly prized. Symbols can indicate power structures in an organisation through car-parking privileges, or the

Figure 1.8 Influences on 'the way we do things around here'

size of offices for different people or functions. For example, if the head of the marketing function is a junior manager this may indicate the company's view of its importance.

The difficulty of managing cultural change in an organisation depends on the strength of the existing culture and the size of the proposed change. The NHS provides an example of an attempt to impose a new culture on a strong existing one and expecting a large change. The existence of a number of subcultures within an organisation will make change even more difficult. Strategic managers need to be sure that strategy requires shifts in values and assumptions or whether changes can be achieved within the present culture. Successful organisations tend to have a way of doing things which support their strategy. In order to achieve this managers can introduce a structure which encourages behaviours that do support organisational strategy. This includes the promotion and rewards structure and other policies which provide a clear message.

Organisations can perpetuate their cultures through a variety of **socialisation** mechanisms as well as more formal approaches (summarised in Exhibit 1.3). The **recruitment** process can be used to select people who will 'fit in' with the culture of the organisation and questions can be asked which help to create an awareness of what is important in the organisation. The **induction** process can be used in the same way to reinforce what is expected of the new recruit not only in terms of rules and regulations but also in terms of company policies and less formal expectations. Individuals will be at their most receptive to new ideas and ways of behaving at the early stages of their employment, and companies such as IBM have used this early stage to provide their new employees with something of their history and philosophy.

The **reward system** in an organisation sends a clear message to employees about what types of behaviour are expected and acclaimed by senior management. For example, if large bonuses are paid to teams rather than individuals, this will encourage team building and loyalty to the team. If bonuses are a small proportion of individuals' total remuneration, this may encourage a relatively cautious culture. At the same time if a company rewards the finance director to a much greater extent than the marketing director, this sends a message to everyone about the relative importance to the company of the two functions. Large corporations may have multiple reward systems reflecting the demands of different business situations or traditional differences between groups of employees. These systems may perpetuate

Exhibit 1.3 Factors in the management of cultures

- **Socialisation**

- **Recruitment policies**

- **Induction processes**

- **Reward systems**

- **Promotion policy**

- **Leadership**

- **Training and development**

multiple cultures, which means that managing cultures through reward systems may be difficult in large organisations.

Different salary systems can create or reinforce organisational cultures, so one way of managing the culture is to adjust the reward system. Where length of service is the most important criterion for salary increases, an organisation is likely to end up with large numbers of long-serving middle and senior managers, highly deferential to organisational norms and unlikely to show initiative or take risks. Where salary increases are determined by a rigid pay system, order and predictability will tend to become ingrained within the organisation. Where pay increases are a matter of discretion on the part of senior managers, the formation of cliques and self-serving activity may develop. If pay is linked to measured performance, such as the level of completed sales, conflict and antagonism may be encouraged.

In a similar way to the reward system, the **promotion process** can also influence the culture of an organisation. A policy of internal promotion will encourage loyalty and consistency while basic assumptions about the 'way we do things' are unlikely to be questioned. On the other hand, a policy of looking for external appointees is more likely to result in cultural diversity and can more easily lead to cultural change. The use of promotion to develop people and to indicate the organisation's commitment to its staff can contribute to an organisation with a common culture. In organisations with a highly competitive internal structure, promotions may be used to ensure that people with a particular viewpoint are in positions of influence.

Leadership is an important element in managing culture. Leaders can 'set a good example' in terms of their working habits. They can communicate important messages to employees, call meetings and shape agendas, and praise and reward members of staff who are considered to have worked well. Leaders can also act as barriers to culture change in that the leader may be the most resistant to change. For example, the founders of successful organisations may believe that they have a winning formula which they are very reluctant to change. The classic example is Henry Ford who had to be persuaded that the idea of 'a Model T car in any colour so long as it was black' was no longer a good idea when rival car companies began to produce cars of different colours.

Training and development may be used to try to introduce a change in the culture of an organisation. This approach involves explaining the reasons why a change is necessary, 'why things need to be done differently around here', and then trying to convince people so that this becomes part of their beliefs. This is particularly difficult unless all the other factors which can assist the management of culture are supporting the new approach. This means that, for example, the reward system, promotions and so on all point in the same direction in terms of cultural change. Above all, management leaders at all levels need to show by example the importance to them of the changes. Programmes of staff training, appraisal systems and coaching can combine to send a powerful message to everybody, but still may face the difficulty of overcoming basic beliefs and values. An example of the problems to be overcome is clearly seen where professionals are expected to start to run a business, in the way that doctors and consultants in the UK National Health Service and lecturers in the UK university system have been.

When faced with change in their organisation, it has been observed that people will often attempt to deal with the situation by searching for areas of change they can understand and cope with in terms of the existing culture. They will attempt to minimise the extent to which they are faced with uncertainty by looking for what is familiar. This will usually be as true of managers as of anybody else. Faced with change, managers will first seek a means of improving the implementation of existing strategy. They may start by tightening existing controls and making minor adjustments to the organisation. If this is not effective they may move on to further changes in line with the existing procedures.

The problem with this approach is that it is backward-looking. For example, managers may consider price changes or attempt to reduce the costs of production. These may be the right policies arrived at almost by chance rather than by considering the fundamental reason for change, which may be, for example, shifts in the expectations of customers and the need to alter the products and services provided for them. It may be that changes in price and reduction in costs are the correct decisions, but it may be that the company is producing the wrong product range or has not concentrated sufficiently on staff training in order to provide high-quality customer service.

Change should be forward-looking otherwise the organisation will gradually, perhaps imperceptibly, become more and more at odds with the environment in which it operates. Managers have to consider the type and quality of products or services that should be produced to meet the needs of their customers, and the level of service and backup required to encourage customers to make use of them. At the strategic level at least, managers need to look forward towards the changes that are necessary for the success of the organisation and then start to prepare people in the organisation to meet those changes. Major changes in the marketplace may occur as a result of competitors altering their policies and practices in one way or another – there may be a change in fashion among consumers or there may be a sudden shortage of materials. Managers can make piecemeal modifications in the operations of the organisation to meet the changes if they can be predicted to some extent. These may be sufficient in the short term but for more permanent change managers need to flag up situations in order to create a climate suited to more fundamental questioning of what is taken for granted. For example, this can be done by emphasising downturns in performance or by putting a spotlight on external threats and, at the same time, the need for change can be signalled by making internal organisational changes.

Forces for change

Organisations have both influences encouraging change and other influences acting to keep the organisation in a state of equilibrium. Those forces which oppose change can also be seen to be supporting stability and the status quo. In **forcefield theory** any behaviour can be seen as the result of an equilibrium between driving and restraining forces, with the driving forces pushing one way and the restraining forces the other. It can be argued that the performance that emerges is a reconciliation between these two sets of forces. For example, an increase in driving forces, say an autocratic style of management, may increase the level of active restraining forces, say distrust and resistance. This can mean that if managers attempt to initiate change by a series of orders and commands, this is likely to be met by either active resistance or more passive avoidance. It is not always easy to entirely avoid taking action which creates a strong counter-reaction. The extreme example is the closing down of a company, which can be accomplished while minimising disruption and hardship but, particularly in times of recession, may come very suddenly. Opposition to a sudden closure may take the form of some type of strike or legal action. However, these can be considered to be exceptional circumstances and most changes within an organisation can be managed in such a way that restraining forces are minimised. This process has been highlighted by Kurt Lewin (1951) in his work on forcefield theory (see also Chapter 14). He has identified multiple causes of behaviour which are summarised in Figure 1.9. Programmes of planned change can have the objective of weakening the restraining forces and supporting the driving forces in order to create a high level of performance.

→ Ch. 14

New technology, changes in raw materials supply and competition are among the factors which create a need for change, but these driving factors can also be seen in slightly different terms:

- time
- turbulence
- interdependence
- technology.

These terms summarise the reasons for change so that, for example, the time span for the communication of information has been radically reduced as the capability of IT has grown. Peter Drucker (1988) has referred to

> *'a shift from the command and control organisation, to the information based organisation – the organisation of the knowledge specialists ... it is the management challenge of the future.'*

The development of communication technologies and the power of the computer has enabled information-based tasks to be carried out more productively and more quickly and has necessitated considerable changes in business processes.

At the same time **turbulence** has been caused by rapid changes in politics, culture and society. Even in the most politically stable countries there are changes in policy, often as a result of economic pressures, necessitating considerable change in commercial and other organisations. Changes in exchange rates, trade regulations and educational and social policy will influence many organisations to a greater or lesser extent. At the same time there are cultural changes occurring, alternatives in

Figure 1.9 Forcefield diagram

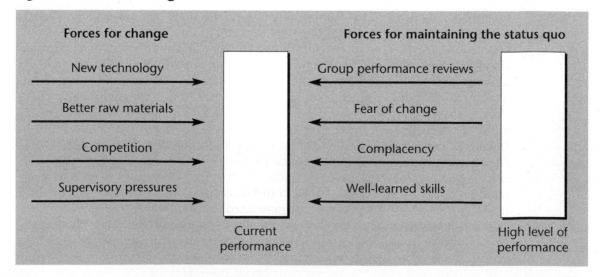

tastes and fashions which can create forces for change. For example, the fluctuations in oil prices since 1974 have had an economic consequence on many companies, while government policies on interest rates have affected the cost of borrowing and the return on investment. The growing number of 'dependants' (such as students and old-age pensioners) as against productive workers in the UK has led to the consideration of major changes in social policy.

Interdependence has increased with growing specialisation and attempts to improve productivity. Many companies have moved away from the idea of controlling all the sources of supply or sale they require or all the services they might need. The outsourcing of services has meant that a company may buy-in functions such as training or legal advice and rely increasingly on consultants. The company can then specialise on what it can do best, leaving other specialists to provide raw materials or sales outlets. For example, many companies outsource their cleaning and catering requirements as well as other specialist activities such as information technology, premises management and aspects of personnel management.

Technology has altered whole areas of work making some skills redundant while developing new areas. For example, automation has meant that some factories require more skills in terms of maintenance and quality control than in machine operation. The typing pool has been replaced by wordprocessors, photocopiers, fax machines and electronic mail. The need for quick responses, personally addressed correspondence and other forms of multiple or individual communication has been taken over by office machinery.

As a result of these forces, organisations require a dynamism which may be missing in the traditional culture, so that successful modern organisations do not simply respond to change, they see it coming and exploit the opportunities it creates. This requires a clearly articulated vision of the direction of the organisation and a strategy for change. It requires an ability to manage change and be able to intercept and respond to what is to come in the future. The challenge to management is to position an organisation so that it can move from its current state to its desired future state, and be able to do this again and again.

The process of change

It is possible to recognise certain characteristics in the process of change. These include uncertainty about the causes and effects of change, unwillingness to give up existing practices and awareness of problems in the change process. These characteristics arise from a natural reaction to deny that the change is necessary, to resist any change whatever its merits and, if necessary, to avoid changes when they are introduced.

Managers have to determine the actual causes of resistance to change and remain flexible enough in their approach to overcome them in an appropriate manner. There is a considerable degree of interaction between interdependent elements in any organisation and this has to be recognised. The structure of the organisation, the technology which is applied and the people working in it are highly interdependent and all three have to be involved in the change process. The task of the manager is to direct energy away from feelings of powerlessness and looking backwards and shift it towards seeing the opportunities for the future.

This is particularly important because in the process of change people feel that they are threatened by the future while they need to recognise the danger in the present position and the opportunity in the new one. The process may involve denial of the need to change and resistance to it, until the change is able to be explored when opportunities may be discussed and commitment created.

Figure 1.10 illustrates the transition that can take place in the change process, from denial and resistance to exploration and commitment. The challenge for managers is to help people through the process. People move from the familiar to the unknown and often experience a feeling of loss when they struggle to accept a new direction. This experience of loss can take a variety of forms:

- **Security** – people feel unsure of their position in the organisation and how it will change; 'we don't know where we stand'.
- **Competence** – they become worried about their ability to carry out new tasks; 'we don't know what to do'.
- **Relationships** – they may feel that familiar contacts will be lost with other employees, with managers and teams and groups; 'we don't know to whom we report'.
- **Territory** – they may feel uncertain about their work space or job responsibility; 'we don't know where we work or whether we can do this or not'.
- **Direction** – they lose a clear view of where they are going; 'why are we doing this?'

These feelings of loss are a normal part of the transition process. The management task is to acknowledge these feelings and attempt to allay them. This involves more than providing information because people in organisations will not necessarily alter their behaviour simply by being told. For example, many people have continued to smoke in spite of health warnings. People need support and encouragement and there is an important leadership role in the change process in creating a trust-

Figure 1.10 Transition

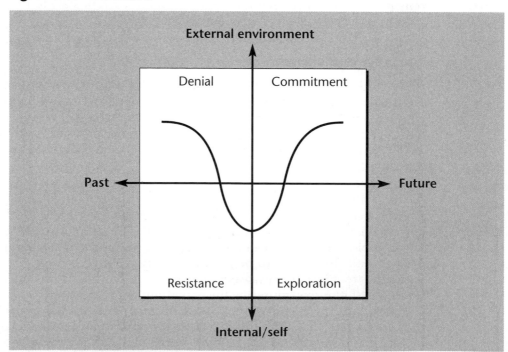

ing and supportive relationship. This requires considerable management skill and can place managers in an exposed position.

Managing change

The purpose of change is to move an organisation from its present point to a different one which is more desirable in meeting its objectives. In managing this process the gap between the starting point and the desirable conclusion needs to be identified. The usual steps are:

- **Vision** – a process of reminding everybody and clarifying to everybody the direction of the organisation; 'where we are going'.
- **Strategy** – outlining how this is to be achieved through the development of objectives and goals; 'how we are going to get there'.
- **Monitoring change** – progress is measured in order to observe and encourage change; 'this is how far we are now'.

Different stages of changes require different strategies. In the denial stage information has to be provided and time given in order to explain this information and suggest action. In the resistance stage managers have to have an acceptance of people's responses and encourage support. If people tell managers how they feel then the manager can be helped to respond effectively. In the exploration stage there can be a concentration on priorities, training can be provided and planning take place. There is then a commitment stage where long-term goals can be established with a concentration on team building.

The curve in Figure 1.11 can indicate the time taken by most people to move from one stage to the next. A deep curve can indicate a lengthy period of resistance

Figure 1.11 Managing change

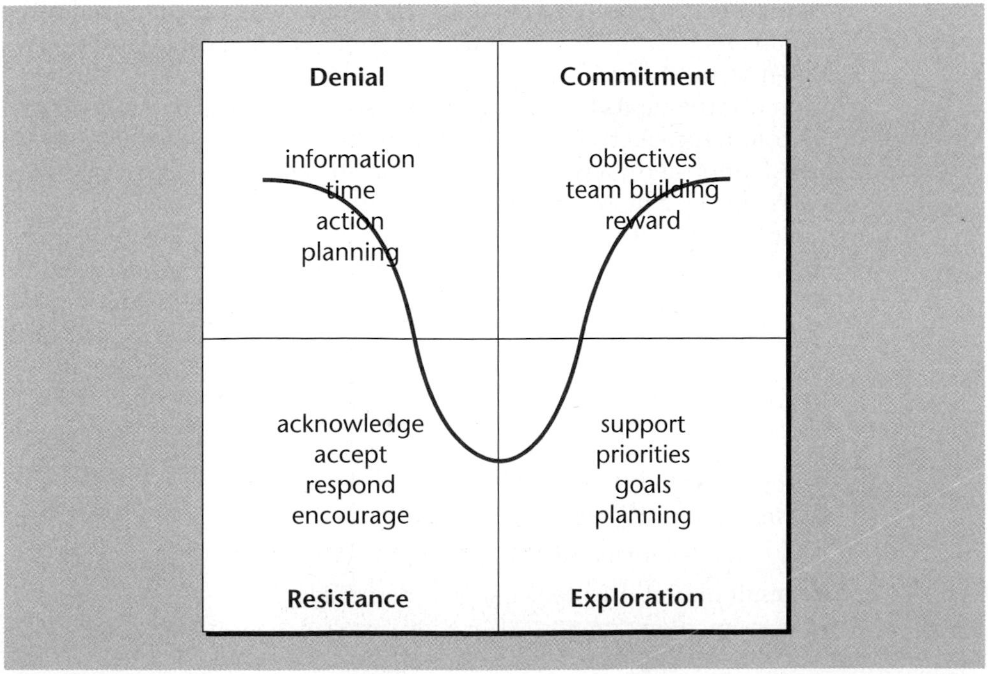

and exploration before there is a commitment. At one extreme there may be an intense period of denial and resistance, with people becoming angry or anxious, depressed and frustrated and a concentration on the impact the change will have on them personally.

Stress may appear during the exploration stage, with the expressed concern that the new system will be chaotic. Exploring new responsibilities and ways of doing things can mean that an understanding of a new system begins to emerge. Some people may experience what has been referred to as a 'Tarzan swing' in that they believe they have jumped to the final stage of commitment by swinging straight over resistance and exploration. This may be the result of a very persuasive manager or arise by concentrating on only one aspect of the change, perhaps particularly favourable to the individual. It may only be a short-term conversion which fades away over time and leaves long-term doubts. It may be better to work more slowly through the stages by developing a programme for change in order to establish long-term commitments.

The programme for change will include:

- **leadership** – from a person who provides a clear statement of the vision and objectives;
- **coherence** – agreement on the operational tasks and goals consistent with the strategic view;
- **communication** – the provision of clear and appropriate information to the relevant people about what is happening and why it is happening;
- **timing** – decisions on when to take action;
- **structure** – a structured approach which moves logically through an understanding of the forces for change to the agreement on the management of the change process.

This programme will inevitably contain traps for managers. Ignoring resistance to change or attempting to block it will tend to encourage resistance being felt more deeply and lasting longer. It can be argued that resistance should be sought out, taken seriously and the reasons for it should be discussed. Pushing too hard too soon on structural change or a change such as increasing productivity may prove to be counterproductive. Time to absorb the change needs to be provided in order to enable short-term responses, which may be emotional and negative, to fade and be overtaken by a more rational and positive approach.

This process is helped by involving people in planning for change and monitoring its progress. Active participation will help people to understand how the change will affect them and to come to terms with it. Employees need to be helped to say 'good goodbyes' to old practices, and resistance to change can be taken by managers as a sign that people have left the denial stage and are moving on. In this process it is essential that managers are clear about objectives and that these are SMART:

- **S**pecific about what is to be accomplished
- **M**easurable differences must be identified
- **A**ttainable targets should be established
- **R**esult output-oriented change is desirable
- **T**ime limits should be established.

There should also be a reward system for people attempting as well as accomplishing change. The rewards may be in the form of pay if this is appropriate, as for example if there is a change in contracts or job description, or in the form of status or recognition. A reward system can provide motivation but that can also be developed through leadership and encouraging involvement. People need to be part of the process which makes change work, for example by being a member of a team which decides on the detail of the change and by participation in task forces and quality circles.

Continuous change

People in organisations are often unwilling or unable to alter long-established attitudes and behaviour. A change in management style or attitude or a change in working practices may be seen as a violation of people's self-image or an indication of inadequacy. It is difficult to introduce change without suggesting a criticism of previous styles and methods. If it is suggested to a work unit that they should do things in a different way, they will immediately wonder what is wrong with their present operating method. There is an implied criticism, however diplomatically the suggestion is worded. If change can be perceived as a continuous process then it may be possible to avoid this problem, because it will become part of working practices.

If change is seen to be a short-term process then after a brief period of doing things differently people may return to their earlier practices. In order to avoid this a three-step model can be applied to the change process:

■ **Unfreezing** – the need for change is made so obvious that individuals and teams can easily recognise and accept it.

■ **Leadership** – managers foster new values, attitudes and behaviour through the process of identification and internalisation.

■ **Refreezing** – the new practices are locked into place by supporting and reinforcing mechanisms so that they become the new norm.

This process can be used to improve an organisation's response to continuous change. This can be seen as

> *'a top management-supported, long-range effort to improve an organisation's problem solving and renewal processes, particularly through a more effective and collaborative diagnosis and management of organisation culture.'*   (French and Ball, 1984)

This involves consultation right across the organisation, and one part of the change process is decentralising management by transferring ownership of the problem to the lowest possible level. Decentralisation, flatter management organisation and decisions taken at the point of action can increase both the ability to change and the speed with which change can be accomplished. Managers have to look at every way in which an organisation conducts itself in order to find the most productive and efficient processes.

Through this approach it is possible to institutionalise change so that it becomes a continuous process instead of a set piece every five years. This is the management view based on observation of Japanese management practices. For example, the concept of 'just-in-time' production involves close and flexible working between manufacturer, supplier and purchaser. Japanese car manufacturers can be seen as specifiers and assemblers rather than manufacturers in the old sense, whereas

General Motors in the USA has aimed at a high degree of vertical integration, controlling the manufacturing process from raw material to final product and customers. The 'just-in-time' process recreates the producer/customer relationship at every stage so that there is an urgency at each point. This may be a difficult feeling to transfer to departments and sections of a large organisation.

The Japanese have been determined to have continuous incremental development and believe that this is most likely where there is a direct link with the customer. In an organisation which is managed vertically, that is with a chain of control running from the raw material to the retail outlet, there is a vast amount of capital invested before the person nearest to the ultimate customer is reached. However strong the links may be in this chain, the final and crucial link with the consumer may not be sufficiently strong to control the weight of expectations of the rest of the company. In large, vertically controlled companies the people nearest to the ultimate customer may have difficulty in controlling everything that stands behind them. Rigidities tend to build up and pressures generate the wrong way. The 'just-in-time' philosophy may operate effectively in this type of organisation, but only if managers encourage close working between supplier and customer at every level and then leave them to resolve all the day-to-day problems, rather than pushing decisions up the line to others who will not feel the urgency of the situation.

THE MANAGEMENT CHALLENGE IN TIMES OF CHANGE

The management challenge is to fund, organise and control the efforts of an organisation to achieve particular goals, while at the same time identifying the need for change and implementing change though the development of an appropriate strategy. Changes in an organisation's environment may be reversible or irreversible. Irreversible changes are those that are permanent, or at least sufficiently long-term to require a fundamental change. The decline of the steel industry, for example, may in theory be reversible but this is so unlikely that it can be considered permanent. Acts of Parliament, such as those to alter the structure of the railway industry, are able to be repealed and amended but these are such long-term prospects that these alterations in structure can be considered fundamental. A reversible change may amount to seasonal or short-term alterations in conditions, which usually occur in the operating environment so that organisations can allow for them and alter their plans. Plans can be made for changes in the weather and particular events which will alter organisations' operational plans but may not result in fundamental change. Marks & Spencer, for example, experienced falling sales and profits in the early years of the twenty-first century as a result of fierce competition and the increased globalisation of supplies. Changes to meet these challenges saw a recovery in the company's fortunes in 2006 and 2007.

Kotter (2007) has suggested that efforts to transform organisations may fail because the steps taken to promote change have not been the correct steps or may have not been carried out in the right order. He has argued that there are eight steps which need to be taken in a particular order (Exhibit 1.4).

In one way or another, the changes introduced by the steps set out in Exhibit 1.4 need to lead to a point where the changes become part of the organisation's culture, so that they become 'the way we do things around here'.

Exhibit 1.4 Eight steps to transforming your organisation

1 Establishing a sense of urgency
- examine market and competitive realities
- identify problems and opportunities

2 Forming a powerful guiding coalition
- assemble a group with enough power to lead change
- encourage this group to work as a team

3 Creating a vision
- create a vision to direct the change effort
- develop strategies to achieve the vision

4 Communicating the vision
- communicate the vision by any means available
- encourage new behaviours by the example of the guiding coalition

5 Empowering others to act on the vision
- remove obstacles to change
- encourage non-traditional ideas, activities and actions

6 Planning for and creating short term wins
- plan and create performance improvements
- recognise and reward those involved in improvements

7 Consolidating improvements and encouraging more change
- use change successes to develop more changes in systems, structures and policies
- appoint, promote and develop employees who can implement vision
- reinvigorate the process with new projects and change agents

8 Institutionalising the changes
- make the connections between the new approaches and organisational successes
- develop the means to ensure further development and change

Source: Based on Kotter, J P (2007) 'Leading change: why transformation efforts fail', *Harvard Business Review*, January.

'Until new behaviours are rooted in the social norms and shared values, they are subject to degradation as soon as the pressure for change is removed.'   (Kotter, 2007)

Once change has been achieved, managers have to make sure that the conditions for further change and development are in place.

The Japanese approach is based on a need to continuously improve productivity faster than the competition. This can be seen as the challenge for all management in both the private and public sectors. In the public sector the challenge may be measured in different ways to those used in the private sector. Profit may not play a part, but measurement of activity against costs may replace monitoring of the return on capital invested. Income is now often linked to output and outcomes, while expenditure is firmly controlled and audited. Public sector managers are increasingly being asked to manage their organisations in a more commercial and effective way, exposed to competition and without any guarantee of survival. In many areas, public sector management is little different from that in the private sector with the same urgencies and pressures. This is exemplified by the increasing frequency of movement of managers between the two sectors. The contrasts between the private and public sectors are analysed in Chapter 4.

→ Ch. 4

Managers in both sectors have to face changes in the environment which require changes not only in the organisation but also in the internal content within an organisation. The Pettigrew *et al.* (1992) model, which suggests that organisational change depends on the why, what and how of change, can be applied to organisations (companies, institutions, 'bodies') in both sectors. This model was applied to research in the public sector (Hannagan, 2006) which supported the proposition that

> *'in order to be successful organizations needed to develop strategies which enabled them to cope with the environment in which they operated and changes to this environment.'*

This model identifies an external and internal context of change for organisations. A major change in the external context, such as an economic, social or technological upheaval, requires a strategic response by managers if their organisations are to be successful. Marks & Spencer, for example, attempted for some years to ignore the trend among rival clothing retailers to use Far Eastern manufacturers as a relatively cheap source of supply but competition from companies able to sell cheaper goods forced a change of policy.

In the Pettigrew *et al.* model, the internal context of organisations is seen as organisational structure, assets and resources and organisational culture, which set the broad context in which change occurs and which could also offer reasons for the need for change to take place. The content of change is a question of 'what' needs to take place in the structure and culture of an organisation for it to adjust to changes in order to be successful. The 'how' of change is then the processes by which changes are made in relation to planning and development, communication and consultation, and environmental assessment in terms of market research and marketing. Organisations need to develop an understanding of their environment, the markets they serve and the competition they are up against,

> *'they have to introduce policies, processes and structures within the organisation to enable them to compete successfully.'* (Hannagan, 2006)

The leadership and management of these processes is a critical factor in the success of organisations which need to react positively to strategic change in order to create a fit between the operation of the organisation and its new internal and external contexts. At the same time the challenge for managers is to encourage environmental assessment in order for an organisation to learn to adapt to fresh developments and new strategic change.

SUMMARY

■ The manager's role is greater than the process of organising people in order to achieve particular outcomes. While it includes this process, the real challenge is to manage change by leading and inspiring people.

■ Change has become a central factor because in order to meet their objectives organisations need to focus on their customers and their changing requirements.

■ Past and present theories of management provide ideas about the practice and process of management in order to decide on questions of organisation, control and planning.

■ Management skills are required at a variety of different levels, in different organisational structures and functional responsibilities, and these skills are clearly necessary for dealing with the complexities involved in the management of change.

Review and discussion questions

1 *What other differences are there between managers and leaders apart from those discussed in the case study below?*

2 *Are the main functions of managers involved with a reaction to change?*

3 *Is management a science or an art?*

4 *Are the same management skills required at different levels of management?*

5 *How far does forcefield theory help to explain the main influences for change in organisations?*

CASE STUDY

Managers and leaders

Manager versus leader personality

A managerial culture emphasizes rationality and control. Whether his or her energies are directed toward goals, resources, organization structures, or people, a manager is a problem solver. The manager asks: 'What problems have to be solved, and what are the best ways to achieve results so that people will continue to contribute to this organization?' From this perspective, leadership is simply a practical effort to direct affairs, and to fulfill his or her task, a manager requires that many people operate efficiently at different levels of status and responsibility. It takes neither genius nor heroism to be a manager, but rather persistence, toughmindedness, hard work, intelligence, analytical ability, and perhaps most important, tolerance and goodwill.

Another conception of leadership, however, attaches almost mystical beliefs to what a leader is and assumes that only great people are worthy of the drama of power and politics. Here leadership is a psychodrama in which a brilliant, lonely person must gain control of himself or herself as a precondition for controlling others. Such an expectation of leadership contrasts sharply with the mundane, practical, and yet important conception that leadership is really managing work that other people do.

Three questions come to mind. Is the leadership mystique merely a holdover from our childhood – from a sense of dependency and a longing for good and heroic parents? Or is it true that no matter how competent managers are, their leadership stagnates because of their limitations in visualizing purposes and generating value in work? Driven by narrow purposes, without an imaginative capacity and the ability to communicate, do managers then perpetuate group conflicts instead of reforming them into broader desires and goals?

If indeed problems demand greatness, then judging by past performance, the selection and development of leaders leave a great deal to chance. There are no known ways to train 'great' leaders. Further, beyond what we leave to chance, there is a deeper issue in the relationship between the need for competent managers and the longing for great leaders.

What it takes to ensure a supply of people who will assume practical responsibility may inhibit the development of great leaders. On the other hand, the presence of great leaders may undermine the development of managers who typically become very anxious in the relative disorder that leaders seem to generate.

It is easy enough to dismiss the dilemma of training managers, though we may need new leaders, or leaders at the expense of managers, by saying that the need is for people who can be both. But just as a managerial culture differs from the entrepreneurial culture that develops when leaders appear in organizations, managers and leaders are very different kinds of people. They differ in motivation, in personal history, and in how they think and act.

▶

Attitudes toward goals

Managers tend to adopt impersonal, if not passive, attitudes toward goals. Managerial goals arise out of necessities rather than desires and, therefore, are deeply embedded in their organization's history and culture.

Frederic G. Donner, chairman and chief executive officer of General Motors from 1958 to 1967, expressed this kind of attitude toward goals in defining GM's position on product development:

'To meet the challenge of the marketplace, we must recognize changes in customer needs and desires far enough ahead to have the right products in the right places at the right time and in the right quantity.

'We must balance trends in preference against the many compromises that are necessary to make a final product that is both reliable and good looking, that performs well and that sells at a competitive price in the necessary volume. We must design not just the cars we would like to build but, more important, the cars that our customers want to buy.'

Nowhere in this statement is there a notion that consumer tastes and preferences arise in part as a result of what manufacturers do. In reality, through product design, advertising, and promotion, consumers learn to like what they then say they need. Few would argue that people who enjoy taking snapshots need a camera that also develops pictures. But in response to a need for novelty, convenience, and a shorter interval between acting (snapping the picture) and gaining pleasure (seeing the shot), the Polaroid camera succeeded in the marketplace. It is inconceivable that Edwin Land responded to impressions of consumer need. Instead, he translated a technology (polarization of light) into a product, which proliferated and stimulated consumers' desires.

The example of Polaroid and Land suggests how leaders think about goals. They are active instead of reactive, shaping ideas instead of responding to them. Leaders adopt a personal and active attitude toward goals. The influence a leader exerts in altering moods, in evoking images and expectations, and in establishing specific desires and objectives determines the direction a business takes. The net result of this influence changes the way people think about what is desirable, possible, and necessary.

Source: A Zaleznik (2004) 'Managers and leaders: are they different?', *Harvard Business Review*, January, pp. 74–81.

FURTHER READING

Handy, C (1995) *The Age of Unreason*, **Random House Business Books.**
How organisations work and how managers and employees operate and need to operate in them.

Mintzberg, H (1980) *The Nature of Managerial Work*, **Englewood Cliffs, NJ: Prentice Hall.**
The classic discussion on the role of the manager.

Owen, J (2005) *How to Lead: What You Actually Need to Do to Manage, Lead and Succeed*, **Prentice Hall.**
A quick guide on how to succeed as a manager.

Tengblad, S (2006) 'Is there a "New Managerial Work"? A comparison with Henry Mintzberg's Classic Study 30 Years Later', *Journal of Management Studies*, **November, 43 (7).**
A discussion on how far the work of managers has changed in the twenty-first century.

WEBSITES

http://cgl.pathfinder.com/fortune/careers/1999/01/11interview.html
This provides information about successful managers, such as Jack Welch, the CEO of General Electric.

http://www.FT.com
The *Financial Times*, the world's leading international business newspaper.

http://www.clickMT.com
Management Today and the *Professional Manager*, two of the leading British management magazines.

Leadership in organisations

Having read this chapter, you will be able to:

■ describe leadership, consider its importance and identify the relationship between leadership and management in organisations;

■ analyse different theories of leadership as they apply to organisations;

■ examine styles of leadership and their impact on organisations;

■ understand leadership power, authority and control.

WHAT IS LEADERSHIP?

Definition

In all organisations, large or small, leadership is required in order for its objectives to be achieved. Good leadership can result in success, but poor leadership can result in failure, while the element of leadership can be provided by one person or by a team of people. An important part of the management role is to provide leadership of one kind or another because leadership is about providing direction for an organisation, making decisions on the methods and processes to achieve organisational objectives and helping to establish the 'style' and culture of an organisation – 'the way it operates'.

Leadership is the process of motivating other people to act in particular ways in order to achieve specific goals. The motivation of other people may be achieved in a variety of ways which affect leadership styles, and the way a person exercises leadership can be identified as a series of actions which are directed towards a particular objective. The emphasis is on action because, although leaders may exert influence through inspirational speeches, they are judged on what they do.

> *'Not the cry but the flight of the wild duck leads the flock to fly and to follow.'*
> (Chinese proverb quoted by Adair, 1989)

The word 'leader' derives from words meaning a path or road and suggests the importance of guidance on a journey. Both the word itself and the role of a leader are about looking forward, identifying the way ahead or steering others towards agreed objectives. This process means that leaders need to have followers and to share common goals with their followers. People following leaders give up, temporarily at least, their own ideas of the direction they should be going, in favour of the leader's ideas on this – they accede to the preferences of the leader in exchange for the rewards that they expect to receive as a result. The role of the leader is to convince them that this exchange is worthwhile – the greater the conviction, the higher the level of motivation there is likely to be and the more likely it is that the common objectives will be attained.

Leadership involves other people, who by the degree of their willingness to accept direction help to define the leader's status. Leadership also involves authority and responsibility, in terms of deciding the way ahead and being held responsible for the success or failure of achieving the agreed objectives. Although leadership is most clearly seen at times of high drama, it can arise in all sorts of situations when an individual takes charge and decides what to do next. It can be argued that people can exhibit 'qualities of leadership' in a variety of circumstances. These qualities are usually seen to be in the making of decisions and communicating them to other people in such a way that action is taken. At the same time, some people are referred to as 'born leaders', as though leadership is an inherent or even inherited quality. On the other hand, if leadership is seen as a process which can be analysed, and a series of actions which can be identified, then it can be learned, at least to some extent.

John Adair in *Great Leaders* (1989) suggests that

> *'the common sense conclusion of this book is that leadership potential can be developed, but it does have to be there in the first place.'*

The delegation of decision making in organisations means that it is essential for many people at all levels of management to have and to develop some potential for leadership. Management implies leadership, and in fact the success or failure of managers can be judged on their leadership qualities. If the manager's role is to achieve organisational goals then these are reached by showing people the way forward to find solutions and overcome obstacles. In a constantly changing social, economic and technological environment, leadership has become a more important attribute of management than in the past. In a more static environment, controlling and organising might be seen as more important than leadership for most managers, but this has changed. It is not just senior managers who need to look forward in order to foresee changes which are coming and to act accordingly. Team managers and supervisors also have to implement change at their own level, to understand it and to take their working colleagues and subordinates along with them. In an entrepreneurial role managers initiate and lead change in an organisation. In this role a leader sees opportunities and challenges and makes decisions to deal with them. This may involve introducing new products, changing the way products and services are sourced or in some other way introducing a change. The high street retailer Marks & Spencer had a difficult start to the first decade of the twenty-first century due to increased competition from low-cost, low-price stores and the falling popularity of their styles. The response by the chief executive and his team was to find cheaper sources of supply, introduce new designs, review the location of their stores and their offerings and to train their staff to provide the highest levels of customer service. These changes brought about a marked improvement in the company's fortunes.

Leadership can be seen as a subset of management in the sense that management is broader in scope as it is concerned with behavioural as well as non-behavioural matters, with people's behaviour as well as the allocation of material resources. In the UK the Department for Trade and Industry and the Department for Education and Skills established the Council for Excellence in Management and Leadership in the light of concern about UK productivity and a belief in the potential contribution of better leadership performance, and to help the country improve its stock of good quality leaders because, as they reported in 2002, they believed that leadership skills in the UK were in short supply. This idea of providing some kind of system for creating leadership qualities is the opposite of the view that leadership is an innate quality. Philip Green, the proprietor of Bhs, believes that he has achieved so much in his career due to instinct and an ability to remain focused (Blackhurst, 2005a).

It can be argued (see Massie and Douglas, 1977) that managers are concerned with bringing together resources, developing strategies, organising and controlling activities in order to achieve agreed objectives. At the same time managers, as leaders, have to select the goals and objectives of an organisation, decide what is to be done and motivate people to do it. Leadership can be seen as performing the influencing function of management, largely involved with establishing goals and motivating people to help achieve them. Looked at in this way, leaders decide 'where we are going' and influence people to take that particular direction, rather than describe 'how we are going to get there'.

> *'In leadership, the most important decisions you make are to get the right people. If they are right, everything falls into place.'*   (Allan Leighton in Blackhurst, 2005)

Allan Leighton has an impressive list of present and past leadership roles including being the youngest director in Mars worldwide, chair of Royal Mail, on the board of Leeds United Football Club, BSkyB, Lastminute.com, Selfridges and Bhs as well as being the chief executive who organised the takeover of Asda by Wal-Mart. He is quoted (in Blackhurst 2005) as saying that *'if you get good CEOs, you get good executives, who get good people beneath them. It really is that simple – and true'*. John Kotter (2001) argued that

> *'leadership and management are two distinctive and complementary systems of action. Each has its own function and characteristic activities. Both are necessary for success in an increasingly complex and volatile business environment.'*

Whereas management is about coping with complexity, leadership is about coping with change. Leaders set the direction, managers plan, organise and oversee the change.

The debate on the role of the manager against that of the leader is perhaps more a question of definition than substance, although inspired leaders are not necessarily good organisers and excellent managers may appear to be rather mundane in terms of leadership. In practice the most effective managers are also leaders, and the quality of leadership has become an increasingly important part of management ability. An organisation may be well organised and controlled, but without leadership it will be static and will not develop and progress.

> *'In order to be successful, organisations needed to develop strategies which enabled them to cope with the environment in which they operated and changes to that environment.'*
>
> (Hannagan, 2006)

and for the necessary strategic changes to be made leadership is required. An illustration of this is Allan Leighton's great pride in his involvement with Selfridges and its transformation from a dull department store into a modern, fashionable destination.

THEORIES OF LEADERSHIP

There are a number of approaches to understanding leadership, ranging from the traditional view that leaders are born and not made to the relatively recent view that leadership is more to do with the situation than to any universally desirable set of attributes.

Trait theories

The first systematic effort by researchers to understand leadership was the attempt to identify the personal characteristics of leaders. Their attempts can be termed as **trait theories**. It can be argued that there is a predisposition to consider leaders as naturally braver, more aggressive, more decisive and more articulate than other people, so that they stand out in terms of physical characteristics, personality and intelligence. One popular myth is that natural leaders are tall and stand above the crowd – like Charles de Gaulle or Abraham Lincoln. Alexander the Great was of medium height at a time when physical height was associated with superiority. When he first sat on the throne of Cyrus the Great it is reported that his servants had to replace the footstool with a low table. When he met some Persian emissaries they initially made their addresses to one of Alexander's staff who was the tallest man in the royal party. Alexander had other physical attributes which compensated for his lack of height – above all, he could inspire and motivate his soldiers.

The opposite popular view also exists, that natural leaders are below average height – like Napoleon Bonaparte or Mahatma Gandhi – and that they become leaders because they have to be more assertive than others. In fact, the results of studies on physical characteristics show that no physical traits clearly distinguish leaders from non-leaders. Some studies have shown that leaders as a group have been brighter, more extrovert and self-confident than non-leaders. However, although millions of people have these traits, few of them will attain positions of leadership. It is also possible that this is an example of a **self-fulfilling prophecy** situation, where individuals become more assertive and confident once they occupy a position of leadership, so that this trait may be the result rather than the cause of leadership ability.

Edwin Ghiselli researched the question of leadership personality traits for many years, while Fred Fiedler studied personality and intelligence traits. These researchers confirm the general conclusion that there are certain desirable traits in leaders, but the fact that an individual has some of them does not determine success. Ghiselli (1971) felt that the ability to supervise other people was important, along with intelligence and decisiveness. Fiedler (1971) concluded that successful leaders were more perceptive than their subordinates and were more psychologically distant.

A complicating factor in this trait theory is the question of cultural bias. If there is a bias towards tall leaders then most leaders will be tall because they are the ones who will be chosen. In the same way, the so-called 'glass ceiling' prevents women from becoming senior managers in some companies and therefore they do not emerge as leaders. When women do become senior managers research shows that they can be just as effective leaders as men. Even though an increasing number of people believe in equality of ability and opportunity, persistent and often subconscious social stereotyping can still continue to be an obstacle in the recognition of women as leaders. Research has also shown that male and female managers are judged to be equally effective by their subordinates (Donnell and Hall, 1980).

The research into personality traits, or a set of qualities that can be used to discriminate leaders from non-leaders, has failed to produce any consistent position. It appears that no trait or combination of traits guarantees that a leader will be successful (Wood, 2005).

The behavioural approach to leadership

When it became evident that effective leaders did not apparently have any distinguishing traits or qualities, researchers tried to understand how successful and unsuccessful managers behave differently. Instead of trying to find out what effective leaders were, research turned to trying to determine what effective leaders did. The questions asked in these studies were about how leaders communicated to their subordinates, how they attempted to motivate them, how they made decisions and so on. It was felt that if the effective behaviours could be identified then prospective managers who behaved in the more effective ways could be hired and current managers could be trained in such a way as to increase organisational productivity. The importance of arriving at this conclusion is that it meant that the correct actions and behaviour could be learned and training could be provided for leadership.

Research by Stogdill and Coons (1957) and others at Ohio State University during the 1940s concluded that there were two principal dimensions to leader behaviour. On the one hand there was a concern for people, and on the other a concern for production.

- **A concern for people** – this behaviour involves a manager's concern for developing mutual trust with subordinates. This was seen as an employee-oriented approach characterised by a manager's concern for employees. The manager's behaviour encourages mutual trust and two-way communication.

- **A concern for the task** – this behaviour involves a manager's concern for directing subordinates in order to achieve production targets. It is a task-oriented approach, where managers tend to be highly directive and emphasise completing a task according to plan.

The research discovered, as might be expected, that employee turnover rates were lowest and employee satisfaction highest under leaders who were rated highly in consideration for people. Conversely, high grievance rates and high turnover were associated with leaders who were rated lowly in consideration for people and highly in task orientation. However, it was not, of course, quite as simple as this. The researchers found that subordinates' ratings of their leaders' effectiveness depended not so much on the particular style of the leader as on the situation in which the style was used. For example, managers who worked in manufacturing and who exhibited high concern for task completion and low concern for people were rated by their supervisors as more proficient than more employee-centred managers. In service organisations, including hospitals and restaurants, the reverse was true so that the most highly rated managers were those with a high concern for people and a lower concern for task completion.

The management grid

The research into leadership behaviour has shown that it is multidimensional. One approach to this has been the management grid (Blake and Mouton, 1985) which identifies a range of management behaviours based on various ways that task-oriented and employee-oriented styles can interact with each other (see Figure 2.1). There are 81 possible interactions but to attempt to define every one would not be productive, so the researchers have described five extreme positions. Managers can then decide how close to any of these is their form of leadership.

- **Country club management** scores high on concern for people and low on concern for production. This management style may be based on a belief that the most important leadership activity is to secure the voluntary cooperation of group members in order to obtain high levels of productivity. Subordinates of these managers report generally high levels of satisfaction, but managers may be considered too easy-going and unable to make decisions.

- **Authoritarian management** scores a high concern for production and efficiency and a low concern for people. This management style is task-oriented and stresses the quality of the decision over the wishes of subordinates. Such managers believe that group-centred action may achieve mediocre results. They can be conscientious, loyal and personally capable but can become alienated from their subordinates, who may do only enough to keep themselves out of trouble.

- **Impoverished management** scores a low concern for both people and production. This management style does not provide leadership in a positive sense but believes in a laissez-faire approach, relying on previous practice to keep the organisation going.

Figure 2.1 The management grid

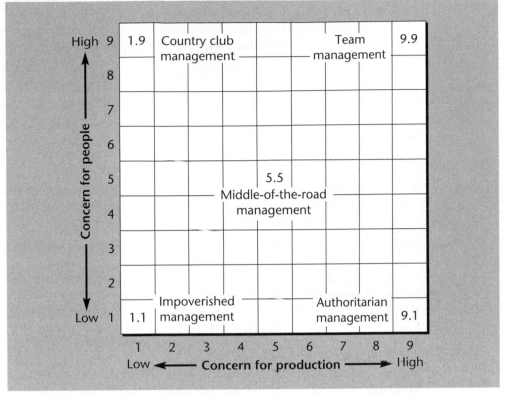

Source: R R Blake and J S Mouton (1985) *New Management Grid: The Key to Leadership Excellence*, Houston: Gulf Publishing Co. Adapted from R R Blake, J S Mouton, L B Barnes and L E Greiner (1964) 'Breakthrough in organizational development', *Harvard Business Review*, November/December, p 136. Copyright © 1964 by the Harvard Business School Publishing Corporation. Reprinted by permission of Harvard Business Review.

- **Middle-of-the-road management** scores a moderate amount of concern for both people and production. Managers applying this management style believe in compromise, so that decisions are taken but only if endorsed by subordinates. These managers may be dependable and support the status quo but are not likely to be dynamic leaders and may have difficulty facing up to innovation and change.

- **Team management** scores high on concern for both people and production. Blake and Mouton argue that this management style provides the most effective leadership. These managers believe that concern for people and for tasks are compatible. They believe that tasks need to be carefully explained and decisions agreed with subordinates to achieve a high level of commitment.

The contingency approach

Research into trait and behavioural approaches to effective leadership shows that it depends on many variables, in terms of individual personality, management style, corporate culture and the nature of the tasks to be performed. There is not one trait or approach which is effective in all situations. The contingency approach focuses on the situational factors which influence leadership.

Robert Tannenbaum and Warner Schmidt (1973) were among the first researchers to describe various factors which influenced a manager's choice of leadership style. They took into account the manager's need to note certain practical considerations before deciding how to manage. Also they recognised that managers had to distinguish between types of problems they should handle by themselves and those they should resolve jointly with their subordinates. They concluded that there were three main 'forces' on managers in deciding a leadership style:

■ **personal forces** – the manager's own background, experience, confidence and leadership inclinations;

■ **the characteristics of subordinates** – the manager's need to consider subordinates' relative willingness or unwillingness to accept responsibility and take decisions;

■ **the situation** – the manager's need to recognise the situation in which they find themselves in terms of corporate culture, their colleagues' style of work, the nature of the tasks to be performed and time pressures.

Tannenbaum and Schmidt combined these 'forces' into a leadership continuum (Figure 2.2).

This continuum suggests that a manager should consider a full range of options before deciding how to act, from a very autocratic leadership style to a very democratic one. Some problems, those for example which involve everybody, may be best dealt with through laissez-faire leadership. If all employees are accountable and influential in the decision-making process then the best role for the leader may be to follow a 'hands-off' approach.

The discussion of management style demonstrates another **self-fulfilling prophecy** in the sense that people will often react to a management style in such a way that managers will feel justified in their choice. For example, a leader may manage subordinates in an authoritarian style believing them to be low performers. This style may demotivate them, so that they do become low performers. A more democratic style may have encouraged greater initiative and high performance. This can affect the whole organisation because lower-level managers will model themselves on their superiors and attempt to manage in a similar way. Fleishman (1953) found that superiors who learned about new management styles in a human relations programme tended to change their actual behaviour if this was not consistent with their line manager's leadership style, and this was in spite of anything they learned on the programme.

Leadership and organisational culture

→ Ch. 4

The pressures to adopt a particular leadership style are also seen through the effects of corporate culture and peer expectations (see Chapter 4). Organisations have particular ways of doing things or place an emphasis on a particular measure of performance. For example, an advertising company may be fairly relaxed about working methods so long as the results are achieved. Leaders in this type of company may not be too concerned about how or when their employees work provided that their outcomes and results are successful. On the other hand a finance company may want to ensure strict accountability at every stage of its operation, so there is close supervision of subordinates by senior managers. The opinions, attitudes and behaviour of managers' peers can also affect leadership style in making

Figure 2.2 Leadership continuum

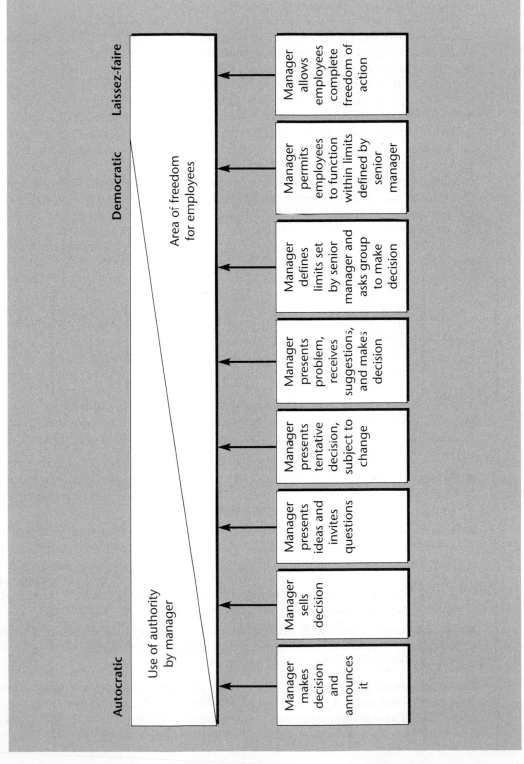

Source: Adapted from an exhibit from R Tannenbaum and W H Schmidt (1973) 'How to choose a leadership pattern', *Harvard Business Review*, May/June. Copyright © 1973 by Harvard Business School Publishing Corporation; all rights reserved. Reprinted by permission of Harvard Business Review.

managers either more cautious than they would be otherwise or more confident. If managers feel that they may be criticised for an employee-based approach then they may become more autocratic, whereas if they know that their peers favour the employee-based approach they may adopt this approach.

Power structures can influence how people behave in an organisation. The dominant group will usually be the senior management team, but marketing managers can have a powerful role in consumer goods companies and IT companies may rely heavily on individual and group knowledge. Organisational structures can also be an indication of dominant thinking in a company, with many layers of management suggesting a bureaucratic and controlled approach, while 'delayering' may not only be an attempt to cut costs but also to improve communications.

Organisational systems can be important in influencing culture. Control systems, for example, can be relatively 'hard' in that they have a financial implication or relatively 'soft' in encouraging people to behave in certain ways. Reward systems often provide a carrot and stick approach to organisational behaviour. At the same time the way in which information is available to people may be of significance. Information systems and learning systems can indicate whether the organisation has an open structure which encourages learning and development, or a more closed structure where information and learning are held by individuals or groups as a form of power.

Stories about the leader of an organisation with an insistence on good timing will influence attitudes towards timekeeping by all the employees, even if these stories are exaggerated. In practice, within a company different functions or departments may have different cultures which reflect both the people who work in it and expectations about it. For example, there may be a marked difference between the finance and the design departments with the people working for finance dressing relatively formally and with a clearly hierarchical structure, while the design department employees dress much more informally and operate on a consensus basis.

It can be argued that **successful organisations have 'a way of doing things', or culture, which supports their strategy and leaders have to take into account different organisational cultures.** The culture of an organisation will tend to consist of three layers:

- **Values** – these may be written down as part of the organisation's mission or vision statement. They are often vague statements of intent, such as 'serving the community' or 'conserving the environment'.

- **Beliefs** – these tend to be more specific in the sense that they may be about such matters as which suppliers the company is prepared to use. For example, a company like The Body Shop wants to have suppliers with good environmental and human rights records because of its policies in these areas, and companies such as Waitrose have what are referred to as 'fair trade' products which provide suppliers with a reasonable return.

- **Assumptions** – these are at the core of an organisation's culture. They are often difficult for employees to explain but they affect the day-to-day working of individuals and groups within the organisation.

The assumptions which are taken for granted are at the centre of an organisation's culture and, although these may not be articulated, they are understood by all the employees. These assumptions will be surrounded by beliefs which are more specific and values which may be strongly held but more difficult to put into practice.

In practice, the ability of leaders to organise, control and change their organisations will depend to a great extent on the culture that exists. There have been various studies which identify a range of cultures, none of which necessarily fit an organisation exactly but may provide an overall impression. For example, if an organisation is said to have a macho culture, it does provide an image of it even if it is not the whole story about the organisation. One way of describing cultures is to divide them into power, role, task and person cultures (Handy, 1993) (Exhibit 2.1).

A **power** culture is typically found in small entrepreneurial companies controlled by powerful figures. People in this culture share a belief in individuality and in taking risks, they believe that management should be an informal process with few rules and procedures. This type of culture suits people who thrive on political situations and are confident about the use of power.

A **role** culture is associated with bureaucracies where people's functions are defined in a formal way and they specialise in particular roles. People here share a belief in the importance of security and predictability and they equate successful management with rules and regulations. In this culture people will tend to be slow to change and they value security and predictability. The civil service is an example and banking is another, certainly in the past if not today.

A **task** culture is found where people focus on their job, or on a project, and share a belief in the importance of teamwork, expertise and in being adaptable. This is often the culture preferred by middle and junior managers because they know what they have to do and they can build up teams.

The **person** culture occurs where people believe that the organisation exists so that they can serve their own personal interests, for instance barristers and architects, and many other professionals.

Cultures tend to follow the life cycle of organisations, so that the power structure is often found in the early stages of a company's life when its structure is simple. In this stage there is a single source of power from which influence spreads throughout the organisation like a web. The internal organisation is highly dependent on trust, empathy and personal communications. Later the organisation will tend to change to the role culture as it grows and installs a functional structure, then it will develop a task culture to fit in with a structure based on sections and teams.

Another classification of cultures has been produced by Deal and Kennedy (1982) after the examination of hundreds of companies (Exhibit 2.2). They identified the **macho** culture which exists when an organisation is composed of individualists who are frequently called on to take high risks and receive rapid feedback on the quality of their actions and decisions. These cultures were felt to focus on speed and the short term and place enormous pressures on individuals because they are risk-taking cultures in which those who succeed have to take a tough attitude towards their

Exhibit 2.1 Handy's classification

- **Power** – individuality and powerful managers

- **Role** – bureaucratic and formal

- **Task** – focus on work and teamwork

- **Person** – serving personal interests

Exhibit 2.2 Deal and Kennedy's classification

- **Macho** – high risk, quick feedback

- **Work hard/play hard** – low risk, quick feedback

- **Bet-your-own-company** – high risk, long feedback

- **Process** – low risk, slow feedback

work and their colleagues. Many sales organisations cultivate this type of culture, which can be highly successful in high-risk quick-return environments, but they are unable to benefit from cooperative activity and tend to have a high turnover.

The **work hard/play hard** culture is a low-risk, quick-feedback culture which emphasises fun and action. Individual sales will not damage a member of staff and so production systems have many checks and balances built into them to neutralise the occurrence of big risks with rapid feedback on staff. These types of organisation are often customer-focused sales organisations or companies, like the fast-food chain McDonald's, which encourages competitions and systems of acknowledging good performance in order to maintain morale. These are often achievement cultures but they may displace volume for quality and concentrate heavily on the present rather than the future.

The **bet-your-own-company** culture exists in environments where the risks are high and the feedback on actions and decisions takes a long time. These companies invest in large-scale projects that take years to reach a conclusion. Decisions tend to be top-down, reflecting a hierarchical structure and a focus on the future. Employees are cooperative with colleagues and respect authority and technical competence.

The **process** culture is a relatively low-risk and slow-feedback approach. Employees work with little feedback and so they focus on how they do something rather than on what they do. There is often a rigid hierarchy with considerable emphasis on job titles and formality with relatively cautious employees who may be protective about their work and focused on technical perfection in the performance of their duties. Both the bet-your-own-company and the process cultures are slow to respond to change.

Another classification (by Scholz, 1987) divides cultures into five primary types (Exhibit 2.3). These are **stable**, **reactive**, **anticipating**, **exploring** and **creative**. A **stable** culture is one that is averse to risk, backward-looking and 'introverted' and does not accept change, while a **reactive** culture is one where risks are accepted, provided that they are small and it is also oriented to the present and accepts only minimal change. An **anticipating** culture accepts familiar risks, is still oriented to the present but accepts incremental change. An **exploring** culture is 'extroverted', oriented to the present and the future, operates on a risk against gain trade-off and accepts radical change. A **creative** structure is oriented to the future, and actually prefers unfamiliar risks and seeks novel change. These five culture types can be epitomised in terms of the slogans listed in Exhibit 2.3.

The problem with any classification of cultures is that organisations do not fit neatly into a particular type, although they may have dominant elements of one culture or another. Also, within organisations there may be different cultures so that often the finance department of a business is thought of as being a 'stable' or a

Exhibit 2.3 Scholz's classification

- ■ **Stable** – 'don't rock the boat'

- ■ **Reactive** – 'roll on the punches'

- ■ **Anticipating** – 'plan ahead'

- ■ **Exploring** – 'be where the action is'

- ■ **Creative** – 'invent the future'

'process' culture with a 'don't rock the boat' approach, the sales department may be considered to be more like an 'exploring' and perhaps 'macho' culture with a 'be where the action is' approach. The classification of culture does encourage consideration of this aspect of an organisation in strategic management, while the actual effect may depend on the relative strength of the culture. For example, the introduction of professional managers into hospital trusts has often created a clash between the professional approach adopted by the medical staff and the business-like approach which the managers introduced.

Around the basic assumptions and values in an organisation there are a number of views about such matters as attitudes to time and the working environment, innovation and learning, risks, power and control. For example, organisations need to be **learning organisations** so that the competencies of individuals, sections and the whole organisation are improved and maintained. This learning is in the sense that an organisation needs to learn faster than its competitors so that it can meet customer needs better. It can be argued that this is not only a major strategic advantage but perhaps the only sustainable long-term advantage. Working relationships are a feature of all organisations which can have a marked effect on the efficiency and effectiveness of their operations. In practice companies try all sorts of approaches to create the desired culture in organisational relationships. Such approaches include team-building techniques such as outward bound type courses, reorganising offices so that they are based on units of people working together (or are open plan or where there is some form of 'hot-desking') and longer-term programmes to encourage a productive interaction between individuals and groups.

Where people need reassurance and certainty there may be a strong culture or the culture that exists may appear stronger. For example, the doctors and nurses in a hospital trust may close ranks and emphasise the importance of medical considerations against those of business efficiency. Organisations with weak socialisation practices employing people on a part-time basis, such as supermarkets, will usually be weak in terms of both the degree of consensus and the degree of intensity in their culture.

Other organisations may evolve high consensus cultures which are not felt very deeply, so that a management is supported by all its employees but they would be likely to support another management if they were taken over. A high-intensity, low-consensus culture would be one in which the management was passionately supported by some employees, but by no means all of them. Japanese companies, which have employed people for life in the past and provide a wide range of benefits and strong socialisation programmes, are an example of companies with a high intensity and high consensus.

The main problem with thinking about the intensity of a culture or the degree of consensus in an organisation is that these are difficult factors to measure. However, when an organisation is subject to change for one reason or another, these factors do need to be considered. The change in the NHS over the last 20 years is a good example of this with clear cultural differences between the medical staff and the professional managers, with both having strongly felt, but different, views of the culture in which they would like to work. In these circumstances adjustments may be required by both groups.

The approach that suggests that various cultures require different leadership styles shifts the focus from the individual leader to the functions that leaders perform within an organisation. In order for any group to operate effectively, both tasks and problem-solving functions have to be performed and, at the same time, group-maintenance, team-building and 'social' functions are essential. It can be argued that any group of people needs to have leadership in both functions, so that on the one hand decisions are made, and on the other hand the ideas and feeling of the whole group are considered. *'Modern leadership research extends the focus between leaders and followers'* (Wood, 2005), so that while situational analysis suggests that individual leaders have a degree of flexibility in the style they adopt, critics (such as Pfeffer, 1977) emphasise the influence of the context in which leaders are working. The social functions can develop the cohesion of the group and may be carried out by encouragement and support, and by recognising the importance of all members of the group to its smooth operation. At the same time the recent emphasis on organisational vision and individual self-awareness has suggested that economically driven transactional leadership could be less important than transformational leadership where followers are moved *'to go beyond their self-interest to concerns for their group or organisation'* (Bass and Avolio, 1997).

The Situational Leadership® model

Hersey and Blanchard (2001) developed the view that leadership approaches depend very much on the readiness of others. They defined 'readiness' as the ability and willingness to perform a specific task. They contend that managers need to vary their leadership style to match the performance needs of their followers.

Hersey (2001) indicates that when an employee is not currently performing at a sustained and acceptable level that the leader should appropriately exhibit high task behaviour. However, there is more than ability to consider. If that person is also unwilling or resisting performance of the task (Figure 2.3 quadrant 1) they should only receive very low amounts of relationship behaviour from the leader and only in response to steps taken by the follower in the right direction. If that person, however, is not able but wants to do the task and genuinely is willing to try (Figure 2.3 quadrant 2) then the leader should not only provide high amounts of task behaviour but also high amounts of relationship behaviour that praises and supports positive steps in the right direction. As employees become more familiar with tasks and procedures of the organisation they may seek greater responsibility and the leadership style can become participatory (3). A point may be reached when a high level of delegation can be achieved (4).

The idea that the situation plays an important part in leadership style provides a dynamic and flexible view of leadership rather than a static one, which suits the modern approach to management and corporate culture.

On the one hand the manager can develop and encourage employees to take responsibility and become more 'mature'; on the other hand the employees' will-

Figure 2.3 Selecting appropriate styles

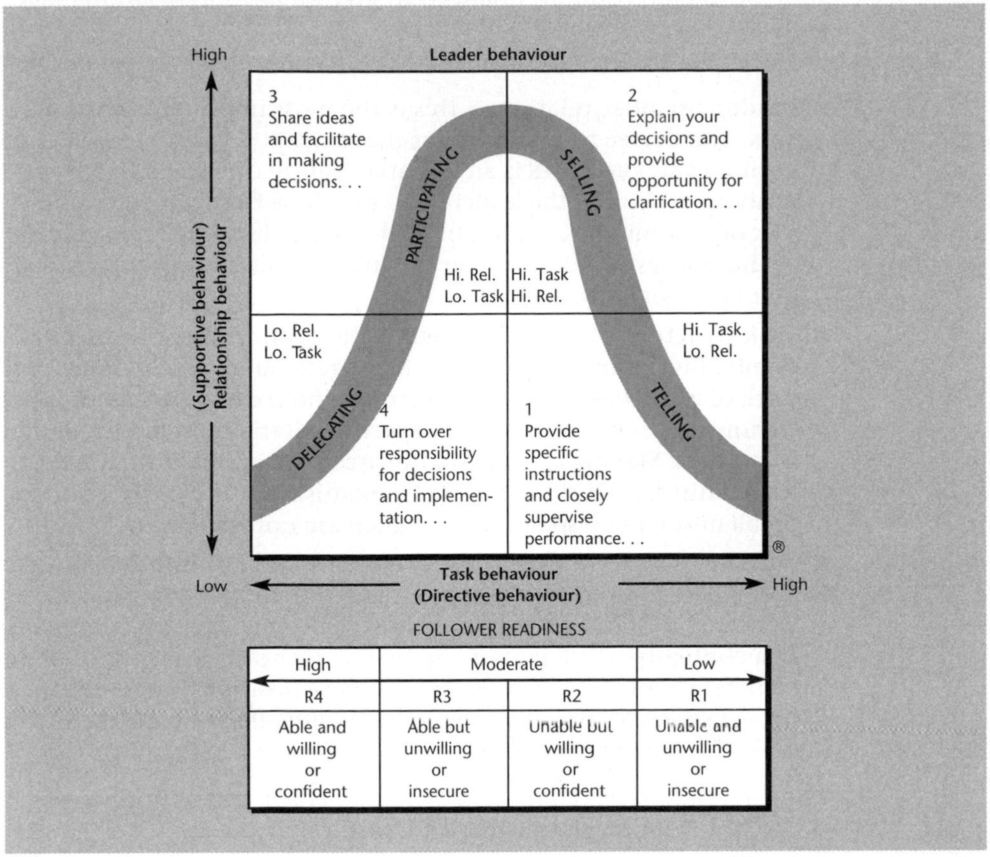

Source: P Hersey (1998) *The Situational Leader*. Reprinted by permission of the Center for Leadership Studies, Escondido, California.

ingness and ability to take decisions and manage themselves affect the leadership style a manager can adopt. The Situational Leadership® model does depend on managers' ability to be flexible in their leadership style. If they can be flexible then they can be effective in a range of situations. If not, then they can only be effective in a situation which matches their particular style. This argument emphasises the importance of the 'followers' to leadership, and the fact that the employees are an important influence on the style of leadership adopted in an organisation – they can be said to limit the power of a manager. The most effective followers or employees have characteristics which help the organisation to be successful. In a modern context this means that ideally they will be well behaved, responsible, energetic, committed and flexible. They will make sensible decisions in their sphere of control, and they will focus their energies. All this, of course, means that they may well succeed without strong leadership.

Research carried out by Fiedler (1971) was based on the view that managers have difficulty in altering the style which has helped them to achieve success, and that in fact they are not very flexible. It followed from this that trying to change a manager's style to fit the situation may be both useless and inefficient and, therefore, effective group performance could best be achieved by matching the manager to the situation or by changing the situation to match the manager. For example, an authoritarian manager can be selected to fill a post that requires directive leadership, or the job could be changed to give an authoritarian manager more formal authority over employees.

Fiedler argued that successful and effective leadership depends on three factors:

■ **Leader–member relations** – this is the most important factor in leader effectiveness. The degree to which leaders have the acceptance, confidence, support and loyalty of subordinates is an essential feature of leader effectiveness. When these relations are strong the leader has a firm base from which to influence the behaviour of subordinates. When the leader–subordinate relation is weak, the influence of the leaders is only through the impersonal authority provided by their position in the organisation.

■ **Task structure** – this is measured by the complexity or simplicity of the job to be carried out in an organisation. Managers have considerable power where the work of employees is highly structured and routine because it is possible in these circumstances to establish very specific criteria to enforce a desired level of performance. Managers will usually need to adopt a democratic, consultative leadership style if the work of an organisation is complex and employees have problem-solving responsibilities which are not routine.

■ **Leaders' position power** – the extent of formal or informal power which a manager is able to exert may be conferred on them by the organisation in which they work and the position they hold in it. The chief executives or managing directors of a company will have a great deal of authority because of their position in a commercial organisation. People in these positions can exert an autocratic style of leadership. Managers lower down the hierarchy of a company may have to be more democratic or laissez-faire.

The leadership styles contrasted by Fiedler (1971 and with Chemers, 1974) are similar to the employee-centred and task-oriented approaches. Fiedler's model, however, uses a simple scale to measure leadership style to indicate 'the degree to which a man described favourably or unfavourably his least preferred co-worker'. This was the employee with whom the person could work least well. Fiedler's theory was that managers who described their least preferred co-worker (LPC) in favourable terms were managers who had great concern for human relations. These are described as relationship-oriented leaders who are relatively permissive and considerate of the feelings of employees. On the other hand it is argued that managers who describe their LPC in an unfavourable manner tend to be task-oriented leaders who are less concerned with human relations and are relatively autocratic in their leadership style. These low-LPC managers want to achieve the completion of a task and the reaction of subordinates to their leadership style is of lower priority to them than the need to maintain production. This approach is a method of measuring the location of managers on the leadership style continuum.

In Figure 2.4 combinations 1, 2, 3 and 8 are most likely to prove successful for task-motivated leaders. The situation in combination 1 is very favourable to the leader and followers will accept directives in order to maintain their good standing with the leader. Although the leader's organisational power is diminished in combination 2, the strength of the leader's personal power, combined with the limited discretion allowed by a structured task, provide considerable opportunities for the task-oriented manager. In combination 3 the strength of the leader's personal and organisational power makes forceful leadership possible. In combination 8 the situation facing the leader is so unfavourable that a forceful, directive approach offers the most promising option.

Figure 2.4 Situational determinants of effective leadership

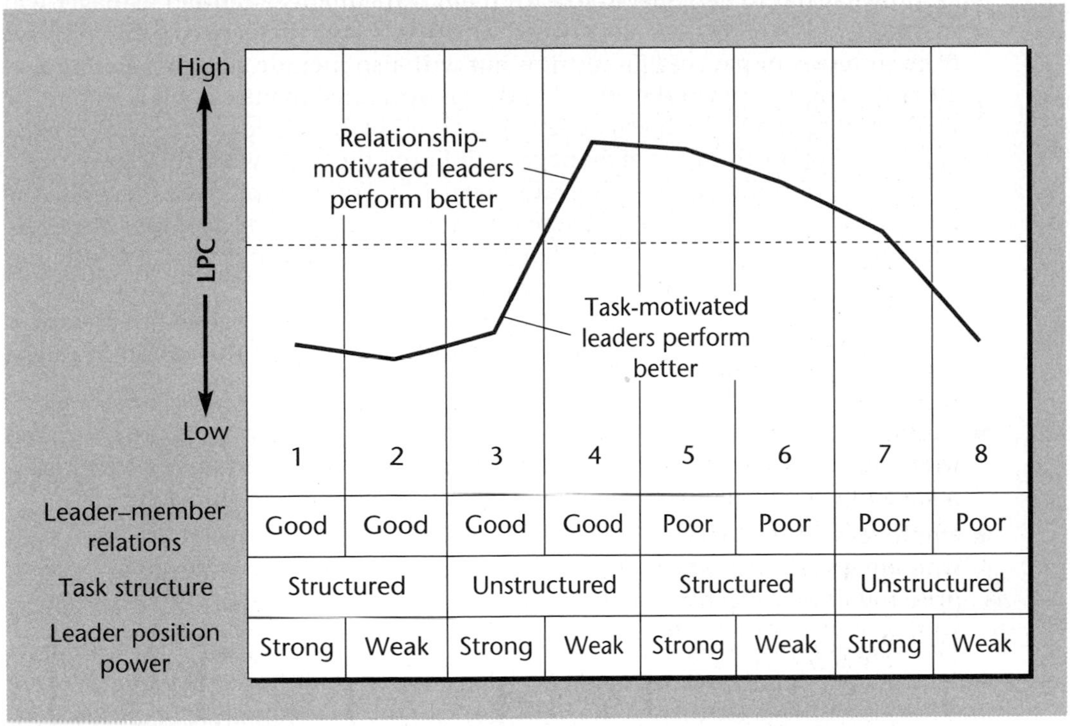

	1	2	3	4	5	6	7	8
Leader–member relations	Good	Good	Good	Good	Poor	Poor	Poor	Poor
Task structure	Structured		Unstructured		Structured		Unstructured	
Leader position power	Strong	Weak	Strong	Weak	Strong	Weak	Strong	Weak

Source: F E Fiedler and M M Chemers (1974) *Leadership and Effective Management*, p. 80, Copyright © Pearson Education 1974. Reprinted by permission of Pearson Education, Inc. Upper Saddle River, NJ.

In the other four combinations (4, 5, 6 and 7) a relationship-oriented style is likely to be most effective. These situations require a wide variety of skills and knowledge that can only be provided by encouraging the abilities of a number of people.

The path–goal theory of leadership

The **path–goal theory of leadership** was developed by Robert House (1971) and others as an approach to understanding and predicting leadership effectiveness in different situations. The theory focuses on the leader as a source of rewards and attempts to predict how different types of rewards and different leadership styles affect the performance of subordinates, based on the view that an individual's motivation depends both on the expectation and the attractiveness of the rewards available. The manager identifies the 'goals' and rewards which are available and the 'paths' to be taken to reach them.

In this process an effective leader:

■ identifies and communicates to subordinates the path they should follow in order to achieve personal and organisational objectives;

■ helps subordinates along this path;

■ helps to remove obstacles on the path that might prevent the achievement of these objectives.

The manager's leadership style will influence the perception of the rewards available and what has to be achieved to earn them. An employee-centred manager will offer a wide range of rewards and also be sensitive to individual needs. The rewards may be in terms of pay and promotion but will also include support, encouragement and recognition. On the other hand a task-oriented manager will offer a more limited set of rewards which will be less concerned with individual needs. However, people working for this type of manager will know precisely what they have to do in order to obtain the particular rewards available. For example, extra pay may be obtained for a clearly defined increase in productivity. It follows from the expectancy model of motivation that the 'best' leadership style for particular employees depends on the type of rewards they want.

So the path–goal theory suggests that the most effective leadership style will depend on the personal characteristics of employees and on the situation in the workplace. For example:

- employees who believe they have some control over their work situation and who are highly skilled may favour a participatory form of leadership which supports and encourages them and may resent an authoritarian approach;
- employees who believe they have little control over 'how things are done' and who are less skilled may prefer more directive leadership so that they can complete their tasks effectively and earn any bonus that is on offer.

This suggests that managers need to consider the characteristics of their employees and the work to be carried out before deciding on their leadership style. Vroom and Jago (1988) have criticised the path–goal theory as incomplete because it fails to take into account the characteristics of the type of decision with which they are faced and the situation in which the decision is being made. This can be seen as a further theory of leadership based on the level of participation between managers
→ Ch. 12 and employees. (See also Chapter 12.)

The participatory theory of leadership

Vroom and Yetton (1973) developed a model of situational leadership in order to help managers decide if and to what extent they should involve employees in solving a particular problem. They suggested that managers needed to ask themselves a number of questions before deciding on an appropriate leadership style.

- Is it necessary to make an objective decision with which employees may disagree?
- Do the managers have sufficient information or skill to solve the problem on their own?
- Is the problem structured?
- Is the acceptance of the employees critical for the success of the decision?
- If the decision was made by management would it be accepted by the employees?
- Is there likely to be conflict among employees about the best solution?
- Do employees share the achievement of the same objectives in solving the problem?

Once these questions have been answered it is then possible to select a leadership style, although there may be further choices to be made. Vroom and Yetton defined five leadership styles in terms of the degree of participation by subordinates in the decision-making process:

- **Autocratic I (AI)** – managers solve the problem or make the decisions themselves using available information.

- **Autocratic II (AII)** – managers obtain information from subordinates before making a decision and then decide on the solution to the problem themselves. The role of subordinates is to provide information for decision making, and they may or may not have been told what the information is for or what the problem is that needs to be solved.

- **Consultative I (CI)** – managers share the problem with the relevant subordinates individually and obtain their ideas and information. Managers then make the decision, which may or may not be influenced by the subordinates' opinions.

- **Consultative II (CII)** – managers share the problem with the relevant subordinates as a group and obtain their ideas and information. These may or may not be used in decision making.

- **Group participation (G)** – managers share a problem with subordinates as a group. The managers and subordinates together analyse the problem and consider alternative solutions. Managers act as coordinators in order to enable the group to reach a consensus, which is then accepted and implemented.

Depending on the nature of the problem, more than one leadership style may be appropriate because once managers have answered the questions they need to ask themselves the quality of the decision and its acceptance have been taken into account. Vroom and Yetton developed a 'tree diagram' or flow chart (Figure 2.5) to provide a guide to the process of arriving at an appropriate leadership style. Their research has shown that decisions consistent with this model have tended to be successful, while those that are inconsistent will tend to be unsuccessful. This research has been taken further to suggest that subordinates prefer their managers to make decisions consistent with this model.

When decisions have to be made quickly because of limited time, and the managers have sufficient information to make a decision, an autocratic style may in fact satisfy everybody. On the other hand if there are important problems to be solved in a situation where the subordinates have most of the information and it is important that they accept the choice of solution, then a participatory style of leadership is likely to be the most effective. In an emergency a leader makes quick decisions, often within an established framework or policy, while on long-term strategy the achievement of consensus may be more important with the leader's role being concerned with maintaining a focus on the problem and coordination of the process of arriving at a solution.

It can be argued that the effectiveness of decisions may depend on:

- the **quality** of the decisions
- the **commitment** made to the decision
- the **time taken** to make a decision.

There is a cost factor, certainly in terms of time, in making effective decisions which has to be balanced against the time lag between identifying a problem and solving it. Equally, taking a reasonable amount of time may help to develop the ability of other people to analyse problems and arrive at solutions. With fundamental and important decisions it is usually essential, in order to obtain the best results, for the people responsible for implementing the decision to feel that they have participated in arriving at it. Even if the final decision is not quite the one some people

Figure 2.5 Participative decision model

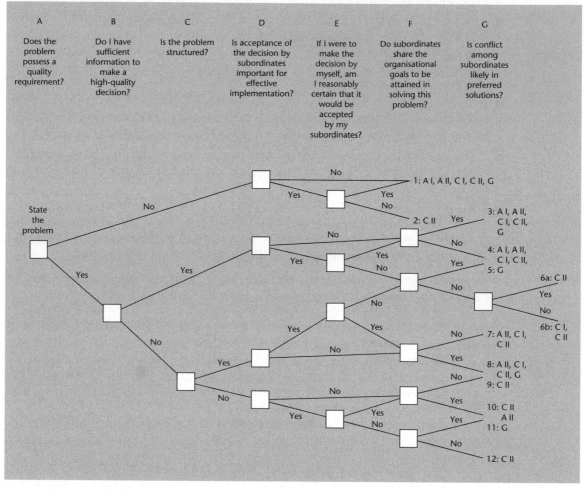

Source: V H Vroom and P W Yetton (1973) *Leadership and Decision Making*, Pittsburgh, PA: University of Pittsburgh Press. Copyright © 1973 by University of Pittsburgh Press.

would have chosen, if they have been consulted they may still be able to give it their full support.

By working through the questions A to G in Figure 2.5, managers can arrive at the appropriate level at which to involve their subordinates in the decision under consideration. For example, if managers are attempting to decide about buying a new piece of expensive equipment, they may answer 'Yes' to question A, 'No' to question B, 'Yes' to C, 'Yes' to D, 'No' to E, 'No' to F and 'No' to G. This path arrives at a CI/CII solution (6b) because the managers do not feel that they have sufficient information to make a high-quality decision (B) even though the problem has been structured (C), the acceptance of the decision by subordinates is important for effective implementation (D) and if the managers made the decision by themselves they are not sure that it would be accepted by subordinates (E), and at the same time the subordinates do not share the view that this expensive equipment is required (perhaps because there is a possibility that it might replace them in some way), however conflict among them over a preferred solution is unlikely. The conclusion might be that the suggested management approach is to share the problem with subordinates and obtain their views and any information they can provide. The managers can then make a decision, which may or may not be influenced by the subordinates' opinions (CI/CII).

Charismatic and transformational leadership

Charismatic leaders are able, through their personal vision and energy, to inspire followers and have a major impact on an organisation. This is all that matters in some views of leadership. Leadership qualities and abilities are not something to analyse, train and develop – from this point of view, either a person is a leader or not. This view of leadership suggests that it is a quality which is both mysterious and powerful and can act for either good or evil. **Charismatic leadership** can be identified in politics, war and industry, although whether leaders are charismatic or not is perhaps a matter of opinion. What Alexander the Great, Napoleon, Churchill, Hitler, Gandhi, John F Kennedy and Jim Jones had in common was their vision and their ability to persuade people to follow it. To their followers, charismatic leaders transform their lives in one way or another and they often do not want to ask too many questions about how this is achieved. Some of these leaders can also be described as **inspirational leaders** because they stimulate those around them to purposeful action without recourse to coercive power or authority, while others clearly do have a power base. The inspirational leaders generate a compelling vision which changes the way people look at the world around them and how they relate to each other. They can create situations where people come together in a common cause, ready to act. More objective analysis of the achievements of charismatic and inspirational leaders, usually identifies that the leaders had 'clay feet' and that there was a variety of complex factors combining to help them shine brightly for a time. In spite of these arguments, the fact remains that some leaders are able to exert great charisma and a transforming influence.

Max Weber, in the early part of the twentieth century, identified three forms of authority: traditional, charismatic and bureaucratic. According to Weber (1947) charisma is 'a certain quality of an individual personality by virtue of which he is considered extraordinary and treated as endowed with supernatural or exceptional forces or qualities'. In this sense charisma is a quality which is generated from inside a person, and it derives from the capacity of particular people to arouse and maintain belief in themselves as the source of knowledge and authority. A tragic

Exhibit 2.4 Jim Jones

In the early 1970s, Jim Jones, a pastor in the United States, created a devoted following in San Francisco called the People's Temple Sect. As a result of unwelcome interest in his activities in the USA, in 1974 Jones moved his sect to Guyana where he established a commune. Complaints of oppression within the commune led to a visit by a US congressman who was shot along with his companions.

As the investigation into this shooting closed in on him, Jones gathered together his followers and invited them to participate in a mass suicide. Most of them obeyed him without question, including parents who administered cyanide to their children. 914 people died in this tragedy, including over 240 children.

example of this was Jim Jones (Exhibit 2.4, see preceding page), who for a short time in the 1970s created a group of followers with blind faith in his leadership. A more recent example with some similarities to this was the leadership of David Koresh which led to hundreds of his followers dying at Waco in Texas in 1992.

Napoleon Bonaparte was considered to be a charismatic leader by the French nation of his day. Although the generals close to him recognised the mundane side of his character, they still considered that he possessed a magnetic attraction. Marshal Lannes was reported to have stated that 'I have always been the victim of my attachment to him', and Marshal Marmont wrote 'we marched surrounded by a kind of radiance whose warmth I can still feel as I did fifty years ago' (quoted in Adair, 1989).

The focus on leadership theory has moved from the attempt to identify the inborn traits of leaders through the study of the roles and behaviour of leaders, to the analysis of the leadership situation, work tasks and followers. The concentration on the individual leader has shifted. Although some charismatic leaders have personal characteristics which do make a difference in their organisations, the fact is that exceptional leaders are rare by definition. Not every organisation can have one but where they do exist they can be a powerful amplifier of organisational energy and performance. These qualities are not fully taken into account in the theories that have been considered so far. Perhaps it is a question of 'place and time', as suggested by the former British Prime Minister in Exhibit 2.5.

In analysing the concept of **transformational leadership**, Bernard Bass (1985) (see also Yukl, 1999 and Waldman *et al.*, 2006) contrasted two types of leadership: transactional and transformational. Transactional leaders determine what subordinates need to do to achieve their own and the organisation's objectives, then classify these requirements and help subordinates to become confident that they can reach their objectives. In contrast transformational leaders motivate people to do better than they would have expected by raising motivation and the importance of the value of

Exhibit 2.5 Leadership

'Great leadership comes in many different forms. From the steady determination and emotional appeal of a Winston Churchill to the gentler consensual style of a Stanley Baldwin. Both gave strong leadership, but they were leaders for different times and different circumstances. The British people needed a Churchill in War Years, but looked elsewhere when peace returned. As Carlyle observed, great leaders both lead and reflect the age in which they live.

It's the same in business. At one end of the scale is the colourful visionary with little taste for detail. At the other, the brilliant accountant, head full of figures, always looking at the costs and the fine point. Both have their place and their time.

But in my mind, there are two qualifications above all which I consider to be vital to good leadership. First, good leaders have the courage of their principles and clear, long-term objectives and goals. Second, good leaders never forget the people who work for them. The difference between passive obedience and active loyalty can make the difference between success and failure. From manager to messenger – they are all individuals with their own hopes, their own self-esteem and their own interest. A good leader remembers that and behaves accordingly.'

Source: John Major, British Prime Minister 1992–97, *Management Today*, November 1993. Reprinted with permission.

people's tasks within the organisation. These leaders go beyond transactional leadership by using their personal vision and energy to inspire their followers.

Richard Boyd (1987) has proposed that there are new skills required of leaders:

- **anticipatory skills** in order to provide foresight into a constantly changing situation;
- **vision skills** in order to lead the organisation towards the leader's or the general objectives;
- **value skills** in order to be in touch with employees' needs, both physical and spiritual, so that shared values and goals can be encouraged;
- **empowerment skills** so that power is shared;
- **self-understanding** in order for leaders to understand their own needs and those of their employees.

The question then arises of how far these skills can be taught. Peter Drucker (1992) has stated that

> *'more leaders have been made by accidental circumstances, sheer grit, or will, than have been made by all the leadership courses put together.'*

He suggests that heredity and early childhood experience may be the most important factors in leadership activity. Robert House (1971) considers that charismatic leaders communicate the imagination and energies of their followers. He suggests that they create an image of success and competence and set examples of the values they support through their own behaviour. They have high expectations of their followers and help to create the confidence that they can achieve high levels of performance. Charismatic leaders of this kind provide for a need to find meaning in a common cause. This can be said to reflect a desire for certainty in a commercial world which has become more complex over the years.

Peter Drucker (1992) has written that leadership has little to do with leadership qualities and even less to do with charisma:

> *'Leadership is not by itself good or desirable. Leadership is a means. Leadership to what end is the crucial question. History knows no more charismatic leaders than this century's triad of Stalin, Hitler, and Mao – the misleaders who inflicted as much evil and suffering on humanity as have ever been recorded.'*

The feature which distinguishes what Drucker terms the misleaders from the leaders is their goals. In this, charisma can become the undoing of leaders. He argues that it makes them inflexible, convinced of their own infallibility and unable to change, so that charisma does not in itself guarantee effectiveness as a leader. Drucker gives the example of John F Kennedy as perhaps the most charismatic person ever to occupy the White House, but who in fact achieved very little.

THEORIES X AND Y

One of the greatest contributions to the understanding of leadership has been the work of Douglas McGregor (1960) in developing Theories X and Y. He described the potential for leadership in terms of two opposing sets of assumptions that managers might hold about their subordinates. For the sake of simplicity these assumptions have been labelled **Theory X** and **Theory Y** to represent two extremes at opposite ends of a continuum.

Theory X managers tend to believe that people have an inherent dislike of work, regarding it as necessary for survival, and will avoid it wherever possible. Furthermore, these managers believe that people are lazy, prefer to be directed, want to avoid responsibility and are relatively unambitious. They have to be coerced, controlled and directed to make them work towards organisational goals. Above all, those managers who subscribe to Theory X believe that people want security. This means that these managers will be very directive in their approach to leadership and very strict and authoritarian with their subordinates. Organisational goals will not be agreed – they will be established, passed down from above and pushed through.

At the opposite end of the spectrum is Theory Y, which represents a much more optimistic view of human nature. Theory Y managers believe that people see work as a natural phenomenon, that they accept responsibility and in fact seek it. Furthermore, Theory Y managers believe that under the right circumstances people can derive satisfaction from their work and will work hard. They will help to achieve organisational objectives, provided that they both understand them and are rewarded for their efforts. This means that these managers will work cooperatively with subordinates in order to decide work objectives and the methods of achieving them. They will encourage the development of self-managed teams and the delegation of decisions towards the point of action. These managers believe in participative management and that the organisational structure, as well as its culture, can bring out the best in its employees by encouraging personal development and creativity.

Historically there has been a shift towards Theory Y approaches to leadership (see Exhibit 2.6). These developments remain patchy with companies using different approaches in practice, sometimes at odds with their declared policy. Within an organisation there may be differences as well, so that attempts by the senior managers to lead in a participative way may be partly thwarted by middle or junior managers who implement this policy in an autocratic way. On the other hand junior managers may attempt to encourage their subordinates to work as a self-managed team setting its own objectives and work schedules, while a dictatorial senior management may insist on particular objectives and work practices. In order to achieve a well organised, efficient Theory Y working environment, subordinates need to become accustomed to this kind of leadership so that they learn to take responsibility and make decisions.

It can be argued that in organisations where the workers are professionals, such as in teaching or in a science-based company, there is a good response to Theory Y leadership, while workers in unskilled jobs tend to work better under a more supervised Theory X approach. The reduction in unskilled work in recent years, added to the expansion of participation through self-managed teams and quality circles, belies

Exhibit 2.6 Management models

	MODERN		TRADITIONAL	
Theory Y	Participation Cooperation	Control Direction	**Theory X**
Work is natural	Communication Creativity	Orders Security	*Work is a necessity*

this differentiation. There is now the view that many people have in the past left their creativity and responsibility at the factory or office door and that leaders now want them to use these qualities and abilities as far as possible in the workplace.

The self-fulfilling prophecy

McGregor's research revealed that there was a **self-fulfilling prophecy** in leaders' views of their followers. His work showed that, to a large extent, subordinates behaved as their leaders and managers expected them to behave. This could mean either that managers were good predictors of behaviour or that employees responded to their managers' expectations. His research illustrated that when managers believed their workers would perform well, objective controls showed that they did; and when workers were expected to perform poorly, they did. This situation arises because leaders themselves behave in accordance with their expectations about their subordinates. When they thought their subordinates would perform well they supervised them, often without realising it, in a way that enhanced the likelihood of high performance. If leaders or managers have low expectations, then they tend to behave in ways which inhibit the performance of subordinates and demotivate them.

This can be seen very clearly when a new leader takes over a situation. When General Montgomery assumed command of the British Eighth Army in North Africa in 1942 during the Second World War, he found a dispirited army and senior officers who had little confidence in a new commander, their fourth within a year. He had to change this situation quickly and decided to alter the way that the officers were thinking. Instead of considering the next position to which the army could fall back, he encouraged a positive attitude which did not allow for retreat:

> *'We will stand and fight here. If we can't stay here alive, then let us stay here dead.'*
> (General Montgomery, quoted in Adair, 1989)

This was an uncompromising position but it worked. When a new chief executive takes over a company, he or she may be able to turn its fortunes around by an approach to leadership as much as by taking particular decisions. 'This is the way we will work' may be as important as 'this is what we will do'.

One of the most important tasks of a leader is to make decisions. Effective leadership requires the decisions to be both sound and practical, whether they are about the direction the organisation should take or the means by which it will make its way there. Just as there are Theory X and Theory Y leaders, so there are relatively autocratic or relatively democratic ways of making decisions. Some leaders will not tolerate any opposition to their decisions or the process by which they arrive at them. Other leaders will reach a decision by a process of consultation and discussion so that a consensus opinion emerges (see Figure 2.2).

To some extent these differences will depend on the personality and experience of the leader. Leaders' decision making will also depend on the confidence they have in their subordinates' development. Some leaders prefer to have absolute certainty about a decision, others can tolerate a degree of ambiguity. In delegating decision making to others a leader has to expect some uncertainty about how problems will be solved. In modern management situations, the role of managers as leaders will tend increasingly to be to encourage others to reach decisions on a wide range of issues.

The power of leaders

The power of managers over employees can be described as 'social power' because it is derived from the social interaction of leaders and their followers. This can be understood better by analysing this social power in more detail.

- **Coercive power** is a form of power that is often the main consideration in a general discussion on the subject. It is based on subordinates' fear of the leader and on punishment and threats, and is linked to the most extreme form of autocratic leadership.

- **Expert power** is based on the leader's possession of expertise, skill or knowledge and the recognition of this by others provides the leader with the power to make decisions.

- **Legitimate power** is based on the hierarchy of the organisation and the perception of subordinates that they should obey the orders of senior managers. On this basis the more senior the managers are the more legitimate power they have.

- **Referent power** is based on the charismatic power of leaders. People will accede to these leaders because they admire them and want to increase identification with them.

- **Reward power** is based on the leader's ability to provide rewards for followers. Subordinates support these leaders because of positive rewards such as pay, promotion and recognition.

- **Connection power** is based on a leader's relationships with influential partners, both inside and outside the organisation. Followers may want to remain on good terms with this leader.

- **Information power** is based on the leader's access to information that is valuable to other people. Followers want to share this access or to be involved with somebody who has such access.

Studies by Pearce and Robinson (1987), for example, have shown that the most effective managers today rely more on expert, referent and connection power than on coercive, legitimate, reward or information power. Leaders now tend to use personal power rather than positional power as management structures have become flatter and management practice more open. Information is now more widely shared and management is seen as a form of partnership in order to achieve agreed objectives.

Above all, leaders have to act – they have to perform and show results. There may be many ways of doing this but it can be argued that actions speak louder than words. When change becomes necessary in an organisation, the hardest problem may be to persuade people to agree on the causes of the difficulties. One way of doing this may be to emphasise the figures, another way may be to make an inspirational speech and try to cajole people to improve. Another way is to take action, in the sense of what Peters called 'management by walking about'. Another way of describing it is to break through the cognitive hurdle, the obstacle of what people know – what Kim and Mauborgne (2003) have called 'tipping point leadership' – the overcoming of political, resource, motivational and cognitive hurdles. Another way of describing this is to say that leaders need to be 'change agents', they need to put managers face to face with problems and customers.

The example used by Kim and Mauborgne was of William Bratton who, among other jobs, was Chief of Police of the New York Transit Police and then Commissioner of the New York Police Department (NYPD):

'When Bratton first went to New York to head the transit police in April 1990, he dis-covered that none of the senior officers rode the subway. They commuted to work and travelled around in cars provided by the city. Comfortably removed from the facts of underground life – and reassured by statistics showing that only 3 percent of the city's major crimes were committed in the subway – the senior managers had little sensitivity to riders' widespread concern about safety. In order to shatter the staff's complacency, Bratton began requiring that all transit police officials – beginning with himself – ride the subway to work, to meetings, and at night.'   (Kim and Mauborgne, 2003)

As a result of this, many senior officers in the Transit Police experienced for the first time the problems of the subway, which included jammed turnstiles, aggressive beggars, gangs of youths jumping turnstiles and jostling people on the platforms and 5000 people living in the subway system. When faced with the reality of fear and disorder in the New York subway, the senior managers could no longer deny the need for change in their policing methods. Bratton introduced zero-tolerance policing and in two years robberies were down 40 per cent in the subway, fare eva-sion was cut in half and more people used the system. There are still, of course, organisations which base their power on coercion and reward, and individual lead-ers who rely on these as the foundation of their power.

Leadership styles

The analysis of leadership suggests a range of styles, and research (Goleman, 2000) has shown that leaders who used styles that positively affected the climate in an organisation had decidedly better financial results than those who did not. Other factors were also found to be very important, such as economic conditions and competition, but the impact of leadership styles was felt to be much too important to ignore. The six styles identified were the coercive style, authoritative, affiliative, democratic, pacesetting and coaching (Exhibit 2.7).

The **coercive leader** requires immediate compliance in a drive for achievement. Decisions are taken at the top with little consideration for other people's ideas, so that initiative is stifled and people's sense of responsibility is eroded. Leaders with this style tend not to motivate people by showing them how their work fits into the organisational strategy, so that they may wonder if their job matters. This style is felt to work best when a sudden major impact is needed to alter the direction of an organisation by shocking people into a new way of working, but if it is used after the crisis has passed it will tend to have a negative impact on morale.

Exhibit 2.7 Leadership styles in a phrase

- **Coercive** – 'Do what I tell you'
- **Affiliative** – 'People come first'
- **Pacesetting** – 'Do as I do, now'
- **Authoritative** – 'Come with me'
- **Democratic** – 'What do you think?'
- **Coaching** – 'Try this'

The **authoritative leader** can mobilise people towards a new direction by having a clear vision for the organisation and by making it clear to people how their work fits into the organisational strategy. This means that people working for a leader of this type can understand why what they do matters and this maximises commitment to the organisation's objectives. The standards for success are clear and the rewards transparent while initiative and innovation can be achieved within the umbrella of the leader's vision and strategy. This style of leadership can be effective in many business situations, particularly when an organisation lacks a sense of direction. It does not work when a manager becomes overbearing or when a group of experts or peers are working together.

The **affiliative leader** encourages people to create harmony and tries to keep employees happy. The objective is to create strong loyalty, improve communications and the sharing of ideas and initiatives. It allows for innovation and risk taking and provides freedom for people to carry out their jobs in the way they think is most effective. This leadership style provides strong positive feedback and is highly motivating. It is particularly effective for team building and creating emotional links between team members by showing an interest in their personal lives and praising people at every opportunity. On the other hand the focus on praise and support may mean that poor performance is tolerated and people may feel that they do not have a guiding sense of direction. On its own it can be seen as a relatively weak form of leadership which may be effective when a group of experts or a group of friends are working together but otherwise needs to be combined with another style. Linked to an authoritative style, for example, a leader can provide a sense of direction and also be caring and interested in people.

The **democratic leader** tries to forge consensus through participation: the leader builds trust by listening to people's ideas and encouraging them to take responsibility by making or helping to make decisions. The main problem with this style of leadership is that crucial decisions may be put off while consensus is being built and people may feel that there is a lack of clear leadership. It works well to generate fresh ideas and where there are confident and competent employees and when it is combined with other styles. It can produce a very positive climate within an organisation but may need to be combined with an authoritarian style, for example to provide a clear strategy and direction.

The **pacesetting leader** sets high performance standards for everyone including the leader. This style requires good performance from everyone and does not tolerate poor performance and is obsessive about doing things better and faster. The problem with this style is that it can overwhelm employees so that they feel inadequate. They may become task oriented to an extent where initiatives are stifled as people try to do what they think the leader wants. The style works well when employees are self-motivated and highly competent and need little direction or organisation. Expert teams can work well with this leadership and it needs to be combined with other styles for wider success.

The **coaching leader** helps employees to identify their strengths and weaknesses and encourages them to establish long-term development goals. Coaching leaders rely on delegation and agree with employees about their role and responsibilities. They give employees challenging assignments and encourage initiative. This style focuses on personal development rather than on immediate work-related tasks and may be considered to be time consuming. It has a positive effect on the climate of an organisation because employees know that their work is known about and that feedback will be rapid – they know what is expected of them and develop a strong sense of commitment. It works well when employees are prepared for it because they want to improve their performance and realise that if they develop themselves it will help them to advance. This leadership style does not work well when employees are resistant to learning or changing their ways, or when leaders lack the talent to help employees.

In fact, leaders need to use different styles at different times and situations. The most effective leaders switch between leadership styles as needed, especially the authoritative, democratic, affiliative and coaching styles. To do this leaders have to be sensitive to the impact they are having on others and adjust their style in order to achieve the best results. In order to develop a range of styles, leaders have to increase the strength of their emotional intelligence in terms of improving their empathy, in building relationships and in communication. The situational theory of leadership suggests that the situation plays an important part in the leadership style which will be most effective, while the contingency theories suggest a continuum from more autocratic to laissez-faire styles as a range of options.

Leadership is often considered to be something special because it involves the ability to influence, arouse, inspire and transform (Bass and Avolio, 1994, Goleman, 2000) as well as the exercise of power in the setting of goals and objectives, the managing of cultures and the organising and motivating of people to get things done (Schein, 1985; Smircich and Morgan, 1982; Vroom and Yetton, 1973). These views suggest that there are particular qualities and abilities of leadership which not everyone has, as against the view that leadership is a form of work the skill for which can be acquired by training. It can be argued that leaders are skilled in managing performances, images and interpretations, and that they are familiar with the routines and patterns of works and that these skills can be taught. There are clearly aspects of the leadership role for which training can be provided – the managerial and routine aspects – but in the end a leader does need to exercise a high degree of *judgement* about what to do when, *understanding* of people and their motives, and *courage* to follow a course of action irrespective of its popularity, qualities which not everybody possesses.

Rooke and Torbert (2005) have argued that leaders are made, not born, and as a result they can transform themselves over a period of time. They identify seven leadership styles:

- the **opportunist** – wins in any way possible and may be good in emergencies and with sales opportunities;
- the **diplomat** – avoids overt conflict and helps bring people together;
- the **expert** – rules by logic and expertise and is useful as an individual contributor;
- the **achiever** – effectively achieves strategic goals and is well suited to managerial roles;
- the **individualist** – interweaves personal and organisational objectives and can be effective in entrepreneurial and consulting roles;
- the **strategist** – generates organisational and personal transformations and is effective in change leadership;
- the **alchemist** – generates social transformations and integrates material, spiritual and societal transformations.

It is possible for leaders to transform themselves from one style to another, for example from experts into achievers and into individualists, and from individualists into strategists. These transformations from one style to another can be encouraged by promotion, which can provide new opportunities, and by structural and process changes in organisations.

> *'The leader's voyage of development is not an easy one. Some people change little in their lifetimes; some change substantially ... those who are willing to work at developing themselves and becoming more self-aware can almost certainly evolve over time into truly transformational leaders.'*
> (Rooke and Torbert, 2005)

Is leadership necessary?

It can be argued that leaders only emerge in response to a perceived need by followers. At the same time the development of participative management and self-managed work groups may have reduced the need for leadership in the old sense. Manz and Sims (1987) have suggested that, although organisations provide individual employees with certain attitudes and values, people have their own value systems. Organisational control systems direct the behaviour of individual employees, but the influence is indirect because it is on the self-control systems and values that individuals bring to an organisation. This is illustrated in Figure 2.6.

Manz and Sims argue that the new leadership roles that emerge with the development of self-managed groups are more effective than the more formal and traditional roles. They defined 'self-leadership' as the ability of workers to motivate themselves to

Figure 2.6 Organisational control system

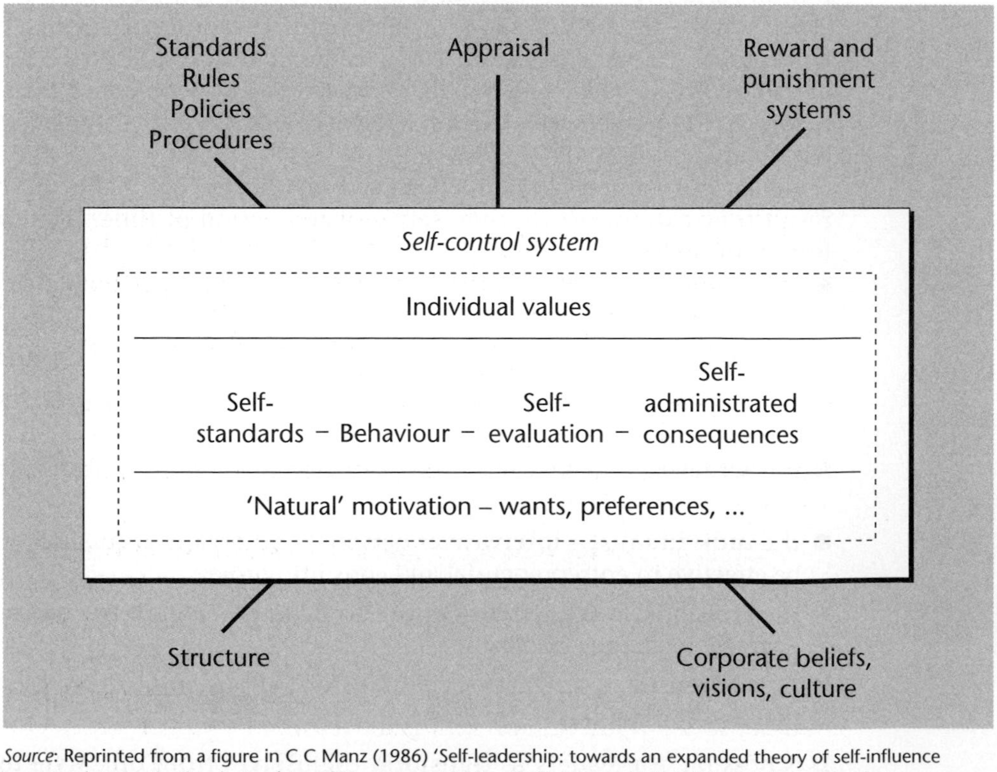

Source: Reprinted from a figure in C C Manz (1986) 'Self-leadership: towards an expanded theory of self-influence processes in organizations', *Academy of Management Review*, 2 (3). Copyright © 1986; all rights reserved.

perform tasks which are naturally appealing to them and those that are necessary but are not particularly attractive. They also suggest that this type of leadership encourages employee development and behaviour which does not deviate significantly from the organisation's behavioural standards. The creation of self-managed teams and groups requires the nurturing of a particular organisational culture which enables this process to work. It can be argued that leadership is still required to establish this situation and to provide the support necessary for this culture.

According to Charles Handy (1991), the modern organisation requires us

'to learn new ways and new habits, to live with more uncertainty, but more trust, less control, but more creativity.'

He argues that leadership remains as difficult to pin down as ever and it has to be seen in action to be recognised:

'The studies agree on very little but what they do agree on is probably at the heart of things. It is this: "A leader shapes and shares a vision which gives point to the work of others".'

The conclusion is that leadership is necessary, but new organisations in new situations need to be run in new ways. Flatter organisations mean that the traditional idea of constant upward movement by promotion into leadership positions with ever-increasing responsibility is no longer valid. There are fewer promotional posts and ambitious managers have to look at the horizontal rather than the vertical fast track. This means that they have a succession of different jobs at the same level, which gives them a wide view of the organisation and an opportunity to test their skills in a wide variety of roles. This has to be based on the view that a horizontal career is a good thing that prepares people well for the few senior management posts which do exist. Once the highest position is reached in an organisation, Porter *et al.* (2004) believe that a new leader may well be surprised by the realities and limitations of the job. They found that it is impossible for one person to run a large, complex organisation on their own because there are too many decisions to be made. Also it may be hard to know what is really going on because people approach the leader with caution, particularly if the news is bad. Orders have to be given with care or employees will be inclined to consult the leader to arrive at any decision and senior managers may feel that their decisions are being undermined. At the same time the organisation's leader is always sending a message in everything they do, including how they dress, what they do and what they say. All bosses have to report to somebody else, whether a board or a governing body, or even shareholders and customers, which means that they cannot simply 'do as they like'.

The questioning of the need for leadership puts an emphasis on the argument that leadership is not by itself good or desirable, it is a means to an end – that is to achieving certain objectives.

'Leadership is not the property of the leader – nor of the followers. It is what happens between people in a particular moment or situation. Leadership is a social process – the result of interactions between and within individuals and groups'

(Binney *et al.*, 2004)

The foundation of effective leadership can be seen as thinking through an organisation's mission, defining it and establishing it. A leader has to create trust in an organisation by articulating values and visions, leading by example and communicating with everyone involved. The role of the leader is to establish the goals and objectives and to monitor progress towards achieving them. As Peter Drucker (1992) has written,

'The leader's first task is to be the trumpet that sounds a clear sound.'

The second task of the leader is to accept that leadership is about responsibility rather than rank or privilege. Leaders accept responsibility for what happens in their organisations – in the words of a past US President, Harry S Truman, 'the buck stops here' – while allowing their subordinates to make mistakes and enjoy success. Peter Drucker argues that the third requirement of effective leadership is to earn trust. Without trust there are no followers and there is, therefore, no leader. Trust is belief in the vision of leaders and the conviction that they mean what they say.

Porter *et al.* (2004) have argued that new CEOs are faced with a number of challenges, or surprises when they become the senior employee of an organisation. These include the fact that the CEO cannot run the company alone, giving orders can be costly in terms of staff morale and other unforeseen consequences, it is always difficult to know what is really going on, the CEO is not the 'boss' who employed the CEO (the board) and, not least, the CEO is only human like everyone else!

It can be argued that leadership has little to do with charisma and much more to do with very hard work and being consistent. Real leaders demonstrate integrity, provide meaning, generate trust and communicate values. 'In doing so, they energise their followers, humanely push people to meet challenging business goals' (Bennis and O'Toole, 2000). As Peters and Waterman (1982) have described it:

'Leadership is many things. It is patient, usually boring coalition building. It is the purposeful seeking of cabals that one hopes will result in the appropriate ferment in the bowels of the organisation. It is meticulously shifting the attention of the institution through the mundane language of management systems. It is altering agendas so that new priorities get enough attention. It is being visible when things are going awry, and invisible when they are working well. It is building a loyal team at the top that speaks more or less with one voice. It is listening carefully much of the time, frequently speaking with encouragement, and reinforcing with believable action.'

Peters and Waterman believe that in almost every excellent company there is somewhere in its history an example of transforming leadership, most likely when the company was relatively small.

'Ask any group of business people the question, "What do effective leaders do?" and you'll hear a sweep of answers. Leaders set strategy; they motivate; they create a mission; they build a culture. Then they ask, "What should leaders do?" If the group is seasoned, you'll likely hear one response: the leader's singular job is to get results.'
(Goleman, 2000)

Sir Graham Day has stated that a world-class firm will have a world-class leader (see Exhibit 2.8). He argues that leadership addresses the questions of motivation, the objectives of working and the improvement of organisations.

In *Thriving on Chaos* (1987), Tom Peters argues that the leader at any level in an organisation must become an empiricist:

'That is, the firm must become a hotbed of tests of the unconventional. It must become an experimenting (and learning), adaptive change-seeking organisation.'

The organisation, it is argued, must ceaselessly send its people out to visit other interesting organisations of all kinds. The objective is for people to learn more and

Exhibit 2.8   World-class leaders

'I am very attracted by the words of Professor Abraham Zaleznik: "Leadership is made of substance, humanity and morality and we are painfully short of all three qualities in our collective lives."

There's the John Wayne, gung ho, follow-me attitude – but if there is no perceived reality or no human touch then it is unlikely to touch the constituents you want to lead. And without morality you may as well be Adolf Hitler. Leadership is the ability to change compelled performers into willing participants. If you only have a mandatory leadership, you have three negatives: pressure without motivation; process without substance; organisation without improvement. True leadership addresses those negatives. The attributes which ultimately matter are the abilities to communicate and inspire.

A world-class firm, regardless of size, will have a world-class leader. The CEO's ability and confidence in communicating his or her vision to all levels of the corporate hierarchy, and also to the community, will set him or her apart as an exceptional leader.'

Source: Sir Graham Day, *Management Today*, November 1993. Reprinted with permission.

to learn faster so that they can deal proactively with change. 'The organisation learns from the past, swipes from the best, adapts, tests, risks, fails, and adjusts – over and over.' Peters suggests that the core paradox is that all leaders at all levels must contend with creating and fostering internal stability in order to encourage the pursuit of constant change. He argues that this dichotomous task has not been imposed on leaders before. They must on the one hand insist on a clear vision, a way forward, and on the other hand insist on the constant testing of this vision so that it is expanded, contracted and eventually destroyed and replaced with a new vision. In this sense the role of the leader is simultaneously to promote stability and instability in the organisation.

Clive Woodward, the England rugby coach, is reported (Bolchover, 2005) to consider that leadership is transferable across disciplines, that passion for the job is essential and that tradition should never be followed for its own sake.

> *'If you have proved that you can successfully manage a team or an organisation in one industry, the chances are that you would fare equally well in another.'*
>
> (Bolchover, 2005)

Woodward emphasised the satisfaction of winning and being successful, while on the other hand

> *'to lead is to live dangerously. While leadership is often depicted as an exciting and glamorous endeavour, one in which you inspire others to follow you through good times and bad, such a portrayal ignores leadership's dark side: the inevitable attempts to take you out of the game.'*   (Heifetz and Linsky, 2002)

Once somebody 'raises their head above the parapet' to adopt a leadership position in the smallest undertaking or the largest, there are people who want to 'chop it off', to bring the leader 'down to earth' or 'down to size', to criticise and carp. For every person who is prepared to lead, there are dozens who will stand back and grumble.

'Many people who strive for high-authority positions are attracted to power. But in the end, that isn't enough to make the high stakes of the game worthwhile. We argue that, when they look deep within themselves, people grapple with the challenges of leadership in order to make a positive difference in the lives of others.'

(Heifetz and Linsky, 2002).

A practical view on leadership is provided by Jack Welch, the chief executive of General Electric. His company is one of the most successful companies in the world and he is seen by many as a management guru. He has admitted (in an article by Tony Allen-Mills, 2005) that he applies his management techniques to the servants in his home. He writes staff appraisals for the cook and the cleaner and talks to them about their work routines and their career goals: 'it doesn't do me any good if they are quietly seething about something'. In his book (Welch and Welch, 2006) he outlines the qualities and actions required of leaders. These include upgrading and improving their team at every opportunity:

'Think of yourself as a gardener. Occasionally you have to pull some weeds but most of the time you just nurture and tend. Then watch everything bloom.'

Leaders have to get under everyone's skin, exuding positive energy and optimism, they have to establish trust with candour, transparency and credit: 'your people should always know where they stand'. Leaders need to have the courage to make unpopular decisions: 'they are not a leader to win a popularity contest.' They need to be curious, to inspire risk taking and experimentation and they need to celebrate achievements.

So discussion and argument on leadership continue. Warren Bennis and Burt Nanus (1986) wrote that leadership remains the most studied and least understood topic in all the social sciences. They argue that, like beauty or love, we know it when we see it but we cannot easily define it or produce it on demand. They conclude that

'leaders articulate and define what has previously remained implicit or unsaid; they invent images, metaphors and models that provide a focus for new attention. By so doing, they consolidate a challenge provoking wisdom. In short, an essential factor in leadership is the capacity to influence and organise meaning for the members of the organisation.'

In looking at the relationship between management and leadership (see also Zaleznik, 2004), Bennis and Nanus (1986) suggest that

'managers are people who do things right and leaders are people who do the right thing. The difference may be summarised as activities of vision and judgement – effectiveness versus activities of mastering routine efficiency.'

As leadership is the function of setting a direction and introducing change, this requires the generation of energy and highly motivated behaviour. Ideally people are not pushed in the right direction by controls and regulations, they move in this direction through a sense of achievement, recognition and self-esteem. Successful leaders motivate people by communicating the direction and vision in a way which 'strikes a chord' with them, by involving them in the process of change and by recognising and rewarding success.

'The more that change characterises the business environment, the more leaders must motivate people to provide leadership as well. When this works, it tends to reproduce

leadership across the entire organisation, with people occupying multiple leadership roles throughout the hierarchy. This is highly valuable, because coping with change in any complex business demands initiatives from a multitude of people.' (Kotter, 2001)

Although military leadership does depend on control and regulation, ideally it also involves motivating people and sharing a vision. It is difficult to avoid military metaphors when discussing leadership because of the clear need for leadership in a military crisis. The link between the military and other spheres has been well summed up by General Sir Peter Inge in discussing his own views of the essential qualities of leadership (see the case study on pages 74–5). His list includes many of the qualities explored by other writers on the subject – personality, character, courage, willpower, knowledge and initiative.

SUMMARY

- It can be argued that management is largely concerned with leadership, because managers need to establish a sense of direction and to motivate people to move in that direction.

- The understanding of theories of leadership provides a basis for analysing leadership and management styles. This understanding is also a factor in the process of making decisions.

- The consideration of charismatic leadership helps to illustrate the power of leaders. Discussion of the need for leadership highlights the management tasks and objectives which are involved.

Review and discussion questions

1 *What is the connection between leadership and management?*

2 *How relevant are Theories X and Y to modern management?*

3 *Analyse the main considerations leaders need to take into account in making decisions.*

4 *Should the situation and the circumstances in which leadership is being exercised make a difference to the style of leadership?*

5 *What provides the power of leaders over their followers?*

6 *Is there a need for leadership?*

CASE STUDY

The qualities of leadership

The definition of a leader makes leadership sound simple: 'A person or thing that leads, or a person followed by others.' In fact, the more one exercises leadership or is led, the more one realises that the fundamental nature of leadership is very personal and is not susceptible to clear scientific analysis. A study of great leaders shows an enormous diversity in their style of leadership, personalities and in their ethos. This variety of personality, character and style leads me to believe that leadership is an art and not a science.

We, of course, have to recognise that leadership is not always inherently good and, indeed, many evil men have been very effective leaders. I will concentrate on good leadership in a democracy and, in particular, leadership within armed forces.

In this context, good leadership is perhaps best described as getting others to do often difficult and sometimes dangerous tasks willingly. However, leadership is required in all walks of life and, although the way that leadership is exercised and emphasis given to particular qualities may vary, I believe many of the essentials are similar. It was Field Marshal the Viscount Slim who said, 'When talking about leadership, one always comes back to the same basic principles.' I have to declare my hand and admit that he is one of my military heroes and his analysis of leadership and the way he exercised it are second to none. I lean on him very heavily in the points which follow.

Before turning to some specific qualities in a successful leader I would like to make one general point. I believe that it is fundamentally important for a leader to have a credo or belief in what he stands for and in the organisation, formation or body in which he is a leader. I suspect everyone has his own list of the essential qualities necessary in a leader. Here are mine:

- **Personality and character** – great leaders have the strength of character and personality to inspire confidence and to gain the trust of others. Clearly this is a personal thing but it can be developed by experience and training. I would emphasise that leaders do not have to be roaring extroverts to be successful. Some very charismatic leaders have been just quietly confident, although they had the ability to communicate.
- **Courage** – Field Marshal Slim said, 'Courage is the greatest of all virtues for without it there are no other virtues.' Although he was talking about both physical and moral courage, it was moral courage on which he laid the greatest emphasis. Indeed, I believe that moral courage is the single most important quality for a successful leader. It is the courage to do what you believe to be right without bothering about the consequences for yourself. The funny thing is that the more you use your moral courage on small issues, the easier it becomes to use it on big issues. Physical courage is, of course, the reverse and is more like a bank account. The more you use it the more likely it is to become overdrawn.
- **Willpower** – a leader has to learn to dominate events and never allow these events to get the better of him and this determination or willpower concerns not only rival organisations or, in the case of armed forces, the enemy, but equally colleagues and allies.
- **Knowledge** – this means knowledge not only of your profession but equally knowledge of the men under your command. Knowing them well and being known to them is vital if you are to gain their confidence. As a newly-joined platoon commander, after every one of my first few muster parades, the company sergeant major always asked me about a particular soldier. I was never able to answer him satisfactorily. Eventually, I plucked up courage to ask him what he meant and why he was asking me these questions. He said, 'I watch you on muster parade, Sir, and you inspect the men very thoroughly, their belts, their boots and their weapons, but you don't look them in the eye. Every morning you must look your soldiers in the eye and that will tell you how they feel and if they have a problem.' It was outstanding advice and done in a way that made me never forget it. Quite a psychologist.
- **Initiative** – this is, of course, a fundamentally important quality in any walk of life but nowhere more so than on the battlefield. I can do no better in this context than to quote Field Marshal Slim: 'Here one comes up against a conflict between determination, fixity of purpose and flexibility. There is always the danger that determination becomes plain obstinacy and flexibility, mere vacillation. If you can hold within yourself the balance between these two – strength of will and flexibility of mind – you will be well on the road to becoming a leader in a big way.'

In conclusion, I would add two final qualities. They are unselfishness and showing that you enjoy being a leader. In summary, to quote General Sir John Hackett: 'Successful military leadership is impossible without the leader's total engagement in the task in hand and to the group committed to his care for its discharge.' For all I know, this may be so not only in the military but in other spheres as well.

Source: General Sir Peter Inge, *Management Today*, November 1993. Reprinted with permission.

FURTHER READING

Bennis, W G and O'Toole, J (2000) 'Don't hire the wrong CEO', *Harvard Business Review*, May/June.
The importance of finding the correct chief executive to lead a company.

Binney, G, Wilke, G and Williams, C (2004) *Living Leadership: A Practical Guide for Ordinary Heroes*, Financial Times Prentice Hall.
A lively discussion of practical leadership based on interviews with chief executives.

Blackhurst, C (2005) 'Allan Leighton', *Management Today*, September.
The experiences of a CEO.

Goleman, D (2000) 'Leadership that gets results', *Harvard Business Review*, March/April.
A discussion on effective leadership.

Welch, J and Welch, S (2006) *Winning*, Harper Collins.
A world industrial leader answers questions.

WEBSITES

http://www.leadership-development.com
This is concerned with leadership development.

http://www.mailbase.ac.uk/lists/critical management
This is a source of critical discussion, reflection and information on management.

CHAPTER 3

Creating a consumer focus

Outcomes

Having read this chapter, you will be able to:

■ appreciate the importance of customer service;

■ explain the importance of flexibility in management structures in order to be able to meet the needs of consumers;

■ analyse the strategies required to meet consumer needs and to maintain a competitive edge;

■ judge the effects of the focus on the customer on the qualities and skills required in management;

■ understand new forms of organisational structure designed to meet customer needs.

THE CUSTOMER COMES FIRST

'At Asda, he'd (Allan Leighton, CEO of Asda) wandered around stores with a sticky label bearing the words "Allan, Happy to Help". Staff and customers told him all sorts of things they found irritating and could be improved and how fixing it would win their loyalty – from wonky trolleys, to bad signing, to wrong prices. The devil was in the detail, but that detail came from the only constituency that mattered.'

(Blackhurst, 2005a)

Organisations have changed and are changing as a result of a focus on the **customers**, and those which find themselves struggling to be successful often employ new managers to provide a fresh focus on customer needs and to lead them in a successful direction. It is now recognised that meeting customer needs is the foundation of any successful organisation and that the customers come first, second and third in organisational priorities. There may be pressure to improve shareholder value, to satisfy 'the board', to increase profits or to maintain and raise market share but it has become recognised that the secret to achieving any of these objectives is to satisfy the customer.

Customers have, of course, always been important. What has changed is the priority given to them and the urgency with which their needs are considered. It can be argued that customer service is now the only factor which distinguishes one organisation from another in the same business. At the same time, the customers have changed – they have become more demanding and they have more choice. It is these changes which have made a change in the role of managers imperative. For Allan Leighton (Blackhurst, 2005a) the key to improving the fortunes of Asda had been giving customers what they wanted, that is low prices. For most organisations their customers' perceptions are formed by contact with people representing the organisation. In order to provide an excellent service, these representatives have to have the power to make decisions without constantly conferring with a line manager. Employees have become responsible for a range of decisions which would have previously required management approval.

→ Ch. 17

This change was heralded by the so-called 'death of bureaucracy' identified by Warren Bennis (1966) among others. He argued that every age develops the organisational form appropriate to its time and that bureaucracy was appropriate to the first two-thirds of the twentieth century but not beyond that (see also Chapter 17). His view was that the order, precision and impersonal nature of bureaucracy were a reaction to the personal and capricious nature of management in the nineteenth century, remnants of which survived well into the twentieth century. Bennis recognised that there were new conditions developing in the last third of the twentieth century which had major implications for management. There was rapid and unexpected change in the position of most organisations, with increasing diversity which created a need for flexibility and new and specialised skills. This changing world was predicted by Alan Toffler in *Future Shock* (1970), a book which produced as much interest in its time as *In Search of Excellence* (Peters and Waterman, 1982) more than a decade later. At the same time the human relations approach to organisational management had emphasised the importance of leadership and communication, intrinsic job motivation and practices which facilitated flexibility and involvement.

The changes recognised by Bennis and Toffler have encouraged the view that there is no one best way to manage an organisation and that the appropriate method depends on the particular situation. This contingency approach has developed and expanded since the 1960s in response to competition and technology. W R Scott (1987) pointed out

> *'that previous definitions tend to view the organization as a closed system, separate from its environment and comprising a set of stable and easily identified participants. However, organizations are not closed systems, sealed off from their environments but are open to and dependent on flows of personnel and resources from outside.'*

Open organisations are characterised by uncertainty over the actions of others, such as customers, which leads them constantly to monitor these actions. They are also uncertain about the development of influences outside the organisation, for which they produce contingency plans. At the same time there are wide variations in the use of technology within organisations, even by those producing similar products or services, and in the speed of change and innovation. Organisations are also of different sizes and this has an effect on their management style. Some of the characteristics of open organisations and factors influencing their style are summarised in Exhibit 3.1.

Exhibit 3.1 Open organisations

Uncertainty over matters and events *outside* the organisation including:

- the actions of others;
- the inability ever to understand and control events fully;
- the uncertainty of forecasts (such as economic forecasts);
- the dependence on outside events (such as the changes in the membership of the European Community);
- the uncertainty created by other people's forecasts (such as views about the depth and duration of the recession in the UK and other developed economies of the early 1990s and in the Far Eastern economies in the late 1990s);
- the behaviour of customers and suppliers.

Development and innovations in technology:

- the use of different technologies by organisations producing different products and services;
- the use of different technologies by organisations producing similar products and services;
- the constant changes in technology owing to innovation.

Difference in size between organisations:

- it has become recognised that the structure and practices for the efficient organisation of large institutions may not be those most suitable for smaller ones;
- as organisations grow in size, more decentralised and impersonal structures may become appropriate.

Work at the University of Aston in the 1960s (Pugh and Hickson, 1976) found that size was the most important predictor of management style, so that the larger the organisation the more likely it was to adopt bureaucratic structures, while the smaller the organisation the more likely it was to adopt flexible structures. The increasing emphasis on the customer now points to the need for all organisations, large and small, to have a high degree of flexibility.

Contingency theories have moved a long way towards suggesting that management needs to be flexible and to apply the appropriate techniques to factors such as the size and situation of an organisation. Even so, it can be argued that the contingency approach does not provide a convincing explanation of how organisations do and should operate. It may be considered that organisational culture is not sufficiently taken into account and that it has become increasingly important for members of an organisation to take control of their structure and decision-making processes. Peters and Waterman (1982), for example, attempted to predict the way companies would need to organise and operate in the future based on what the best companies were doing at the moment or planning to do in the future.

Cath Keers has the role of customer director in the communications company O_2UK, a post which comes with a seat on the board and responsibility for creating the best customer and people experience (described in the article by Lucas, 2007). 'The first thing you have to do is really listen to customers and try to get beyond the obvious – and that is hard' she is quoted as saying in response to the way the company billed its customers. It was found that customers did not like the monthly invoices for their mobile telephones, not because of the design but because they had difficulty understanding what was 'on' and 'off' peak and what was 'in' or 'out' of their contract. This made them feel stupid or that they were 'being taken for a ride'. As a result the company simplified its contracts and introduced very flat rate tariffs.

> *'It's about looking at the emotional stuff that sits underneath the issues. The real insight for us was that we had to get much more transparency and clarity around how we contract with customers.'*   (Lucas, 2007)

Lucas (2007) describes how O_2 attempts to keep close to its customers by keeping at the cutting edge of what they really need in terms of technology.

> *'It has a team of people around the world – known as 'moles' – who hang out in cafes, bars or wherever it's happening and report back on shifts in consumer behaviour and trends in the way technology is being used.'*

The company sponsorship of the Arsenal Football Club and the England rugby team has given the company prime time publicity and it has also allowed it to 'treat' its customers and reward their loyalty by providing extra facilities at games of football and rugby.

O_2 also works on making employees feel valued as a critical part of serving their customers.

> *'It's about engaging people and making them feel they can make a difference. People are our biggest asset. They are O_2 – and we have to make sure they are feeling happy and secure because that will reflect in our customers' experiences.'*   (Lucas, 2007)

Keers describes her own passion and determination about her work and she believes in 'the shadow of a leader. If they don't see me doing it and living it, then why should anyone else?' Keeping close to the customer, a bias for action and recognising the importance of employees are some of the attributes of the so-called 'excellent companies' (Lucas, 2007).

IN SEARCH OF EXCELLENCE

Peters and Waterman carried out a study for management consultants McKinsey and Company of the 62 most successful companies in the USA. They were able to identify eight key attributes which organisations needed to manifest in order to achieve excellence. It can be argued that every one of these attributes is about people, and most of them focus directly or indirectly on the customer. Peters and Waterman argue that these attributes are largely opposed to the rational theories of management so popular in the past, whether they have been based on **scientific management**, bureaucratic control, human resource theories or a contingency approach. They argue that these rational approaches produced 'paralysis through analysis' to an extent where action stops and planning runs riot. Analysis may reach a point where it attempts to be precise about matters which are inherently uncertain, and at the same time the analysis of situations can become so complex that it becomes unwieldy. They suggest that a problem may arise where a 'correct' answer to a problem is identified irrespective of its application to the situation in question.

Peters and Waterman argue that past management techniques should be used as an aid to, but not as a substitute for, human judgement. They suggest that it is the freedom given to managers and employees to innovate and experiment with different solutions which distinguishes excellent companies from the less successful ones. In their study they identified the attributes which characterised most closely the distinct features of excellent, innovative companies – these are summarised in Exhibit 3.2.

In Peters and Waterman's view these core values may be concerned with such matters as the quality of customer service, or the importance of reliability. For example, they quote the McDonald's food franchise slogan, QSCV: Quality, Service, Cleanliness and Value. Excellent companies really do get close to their customers, while others just talk about it. The best organisations take customer service to extreme lengths in order to achieve quality, service and reliability. They listen to their customers by observing the customer view on product, quantity, quality and service and they claim to receive their best ideas for new products from listening intently and regularly to their customers. The excellent companies are

> *'driven by their direct orientation to the customers rather than by technology or by a desire to be the low-cost producer. They seem to focus more on the revenue-generation side of their service.'*

Rosabeth Moss Kanter (1989) has attempted to define what organisations need to be like in the future if they are to be successful. She believes that today's corporate elephants need to learn to dance as nimbly and speedily as mice if they are to survive in an increasingly competitive and rapidly changing world:

> *'If the main game of business is indeed like Alice in Wonderland croquet, then running it requires faster action, more creative manoeuvring, more flexibility and closer partnerships with employees and customers than was typical in the traditional corporate bureaucracy. It requires more agile, livelier management that pursues opportunity without being bogged down by cumbersome structures or weighty procedures that impede action. Corporate giants, in short, must learn how to dance.'*

Companies must be constantly alert and keep abreast of their competitors' intentions and their customers' needs, Kanter argues. Peters and Waterman (1982) have also illustrated the need for organisations to be alert and to be open to constant change. Although their ideas were very popular in the 1980s, some disenchantment

Exhibit 3.2 Excellent companies

Features of excellent, innovative companies:

■ A bias for action, rather than too much planning or waiting for something to happen.

■ Keeping close to the customer by learning from the people they serve and providing a high quality and reliable service.

■ Fostering autonomy and entrepreneurship through encouraging the development of leaders and innovators throughout the organisation and supporting creativity and risk taking.

■ Developing productivity through people by recognising that the main productivity gains could be achieved by employees rather than through capital investment.

■ Practising a hands-on, value-driven approach by concentrating on achievements rather than technological or economic resources or organisational structure.

■ 'Sticking to the knitting' by staying close to businesses that are already known and by following the approach that a company should never acquire a business it does not know how to run.

■ Organising a 'simple form' and 'lean staff' structure so that the organisation remains uncomplicated with relatively few top-level staff.

■ Maintaining simultaneous loose–tight properties: both centralised and decentralised, with autonomy pushed down to the shop floor and product development team, and centralisation around the core values.

→ Ch. 8 has occurred since because a number of the companies they used in arriving at the eight attributes for excellence experienced strategic setbacks (see Chapter 8 for the example of IBM). However, it remains important for organisations to consider these attributes in their strategy, while recognising that achieving them is not a guarantee of continued success where organisational environments and, in particular, customer needs change.

MANAGER 2000 PLUS

This theme of cooperation and collaboration has been developed by Robert Heller:

> *'Manager 2000 will practice cooperation and collaboration with everybody, inside and outside the firm, from colleagues and subordinates to customers and suppliers.'*
>
> (Heller, 1994b)

He argues that managers of the future have to be tolerant team players, putting the objectives of the team above the ambitions of an individual. This approach is encouraged by the devolution of power and delegation of decision making to self-managed teams at the point of production or customer service. Managers will work in organisations where the **hierarchical pyramid** is inverted, placing top management at the base and the customer at the summit (see Figure 3.1).

In this situation the manager's role is to support individuals and teams producing goods or supplying services directly to the customer. In placing the customer at the top of this pyramid, the objective is to provide the best in quality and service and through this process to find a competitive advantage. This in fact means 'keeping close to the customer' and finding out from them what they want in terms of quality and reliability.

'Managers 2000 plus', at all levels, will have to be involved in developing the potential of everybody around them. Hierarchical bureaucratic systems provided a framework for establishing and keeping the rules of an organisation, whether these were openly established or part of an accepted corporate culture. Heller argues that the horizontal principle is displacing the vertical principle in everything, from organisational structure to markets. The outcomes of business processes are all-important and innovation has become a necessity. The development of self-managed teams is perhaps less about empowerment, which suggests giving people the ability to manage work more effectively, than about enablement by ceasing to stop them from organising work effectively. In Rank Xerox, for example, the managing director is subjected to twice-yearly feedback from the 15 people who report directly to him, and the same applies to each of them and throughout the organisation. Everybody knows specifically what is expected of them and everybody is involved in deciding what they have to do.

It can be argued that organisations will be judged on their outcomes, and these will depend on looking at customer requirements with totally fresh eyes and reshaping the entire corporation in order to meet the redefined customer need:

> *'The "virtual corporation" seeks to meet customer needs in the shortest possible time by continual adaptation.'* (Heller, 1994a)

As a result of this it is argued that managers in the twenty-first century will not expect their jobs to be static because the business process will determine what is expected at any given time. They will advance in prestige and pay by moving from one successful assignment to the next, not by exchanging one title for another. More and more companies realise that a customer focus is the key to their future

Figure 3.1 The inverted pyramid

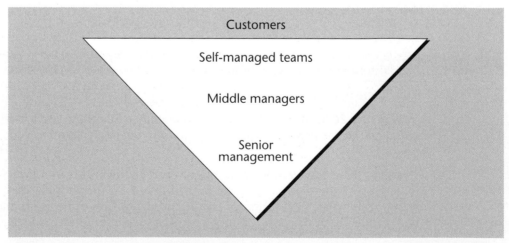

Customers

Self-managed teams

Middle managers

Senior
management

success. Whether the title of the person responsible for this includes words such as customer service director, marketing manager, brand manager or public relations officer, the realisation has developed that it is not sufficient to just install a new and better customer relations management system, it requires the whole organisation to be involved in the process. It is argued (in Gulati and Oldroyd, 2005) that organisations that move in the direction of an increased customer focus 'follow a surprisingly similar path, passing the same milestones and, in many cases, struggling with the same problems'.

They identify the main stages of this process as starting with the gathering of customer information in one place, which records each interaction a customer has with the company. In order to do this they have to identify their 'customers' and collect information in a uniform style so that it can be of use. Once customer information is assembled and organised, inferences can be drawn from it in order to improve company operations. This part of the process enables the organisation to gain insights into its operations from customers' past behaviour. It may then be possible to understand their likely future behaviour and to reach a point where it is possible to make a real response to customers' needs. This means that 'customer focus begins to define the organisation and pervade its every aspect' (Gulati and Oldroyd, 2005). Continental Airlines, for example, emerged from bankruptcy through the development of these stages to reach a customer focus which meant that it 'allows nearly all employees in the company access to its customer information – and it also provides them with access to the experts who can help them analyse and use it.'

SYNERGY

Synergy occurs when the whole adds up to more than the sum of the parts, so that every part of an organisation adds value to the whole. A priority for managers is to ensure that this is what actually happens in the business. In essence this means identifying and concentrating on the core business areas and removing all obstacles to their efficient and effective operation. Non-core activities are eliminated and concentration is focused towards the top of the inverted pyramid, at the point of contact with the customer.

The result of this 'search for synergy' is to create flatter, more responsive and less complex organisations. Non-core activities are 'hived off' and their functions contracted out or outsourced, or taken over by technology or by individual business units. For example, the company payroll may be computerised or contracted out to a specialised company and catering services may be outsourced to a national catering company or to a separate business unit. The objective is to increase productivity, flexibility and cost control by concentrating effort on the core business and making sure that all parts of this business are adding value to the whole organisation. One of the results of this has been a change in employment patterns:

> *'The job for life is a thing of the past, part-time and flexible work patterns and fixed-term contracts are becoming the norm. Managers must recognise this. To keep their options open, they need to grasp every available training opportunity.'* (Young, 1993)

In a survey of long-term employment strategies carried out in 1993 by the Institute of Management and Manpower plc, a move towards flexible working was identified. Over the previous five years it was found that 90 per cent of the UK's largest organisations had restructured and for 86 per cent this had resulted in job losses at all levels. Nearly 40 per cent expected to restructure again in the following year and 66 per cent over the next four years. As well as shedding permanent jobs, it was noted that employers were introducing greater flexibility into the working patterns of the staff who remained – 75 per cent of the companies predicted an increase in contracting out over the next few years.

This process of change has led to a flattening of hierarchies and a shrinkage in chains of command. In most organisations the terms of employment and the business itself are no longer disconnected, there is not sufficient slack in the economy to allow this. The new reality draws a very close connection between a person's job and the success or failure of their organisation.

THE ECONOMIC FOCUS

At a basic level there are two agents involved in any transaction, a consumer and a producer. In economic terms the consumers attempt to maximise their 'utility' or 'satisfaction' by purchasing goods and services which give the greatest value relative to the price charged for them. On the other hand the producer attempts to maximise profits by charging the highest price consumers will pay. In order to increase their profits producers have two choices. Either they produce goods and services which deliver better value to customers than those offered by competitors and thereby expand volume and sales, or they can reduce their costs in order to enhance the margin for profit on each unit of a commodity or service sold. The competitive element will, in economic terms, keep the market in equilibrium. If the price is too high relative to the cost of producing particular goods and services then other producers will find it profitable to enter the market in order to take advantage of the high profit margin. This will have the effect of lowering prices, as the supply of the goods and services increases relative to the demand for them. If the price is too low then production will be reduced because profits are not high enough, and as supply falls below demand then prices will rise.

These basic economic laws of supply and demand mean that to be successful companies need to provide goods and services that customers want, and to do so better and/or at a lower cost than their competitors (see the Case Study opposite). Unless an organisation has some form of monopoly position it will have to meet customer requirements better than its competitors in order to make a sale. Consumers will normally buy from a producer whose mix of product, price and service provides more value or satisfaction than that of its competitors. The only occasion when this will not be the case will be when consumers do not know what the competitors are offering or where there is no real choice. This lack of choice may be due to a monopoly position, where for example railways provide the only viable form of transport, or where there is a factor such as location, where for example there is only one major store within travelling distance which in practice limits consumer choice.

Strategic management can be said to be the understanding, planning and implementation of business policies based on these basic economic principles (see Chapter 5). It involves companies taking actions to direct their efforts towards the areas where customer value and competitive advantage can be achieved. It is in fact difficult for a company to decide how and where it should focus its efforts. Its marketing intelligence will help to do this, but this does involve answering complex questions about customer requirements, competitive response and relative cost

→ Ch. 5

CASE STUDY

Produced to price

I wrote an article in 1980 which explained why a contraction of manufacturing industry was an inevitable consequence of the growth of British North Sea oil production. This was my first encounter with manufacturing fetishists.

The article proved to be very controversial – it was, incidentally, right. Few critics focused on technical weaknesses in the argument. They said instead that what I was saying ought not to be true or, if true, ought not to be said.

I started to understand that for many people the role of manufacturing industry was an emotional issue rather than an economic one. 'Surely you don't think that an economy can survive on hairdressing and hamburger bars?' No, I did not, any more than I thought it could survive on steel and car production. But because I was not in favour of manufacturing industry, I was regarded as being against it.

It seems that it is impossible to be a disinterested observer of the share of manufacturing in national income – any more than it is possible to be a disinterested observer of Eric Cantona, or a test match between England and Australia.

The origins of manufacturing fetishism might be better explored by a psychologist or an anthropologist, but let me have a go.

Thousands of years ago people hunted, fished and made primitive implements. If a man was good at these things, his wife and children prospered; if not, they died. From this we have inherited the notion of a hierarchy of needs – food and shelter running ahead of chartered accountancy and cosmetic surgery. With it comes a notion of a hierarchy of importance for economic activities – agriculture and basic manufacturing running ahead of hairdressing and television programming.

All this ceased to have economic relevance, however, once technology advanced enough for it to be unnecessary to hunt and fish all day to get enough to eat – a state of affairs reached many years ago. Once primitive tribes achieved this, they started to add discretionary activities to the fulfilment of their basic needs.

The services that came into production then remain representative of the services we buy today. There was the priest, who warded off evil; the bureaucrat, who ruled over the tribe; the repair man, who sharpened the stones and the knives –

and eventually the insurance agent, who organised a scheme of mutual support for unlucky villagers whose cow died or whose house burnt down.

With the rise of a market economy came Adam Smith's division of labour. Specialist tasks were assigned to those best qualified to fulfil them. As Smith noted, the division of labour was limited by the extent of the market, and the growth in the geographical scope of markets has steadily increased the division of labour. But even in the early stages of discretionary expenditure, rewards became divorced from the place activities enjoyed in the hierarchy of needs.

You got paid only for goods that people wanted, but it soon became apparent that insurance and priestly services were among the things they did want. Given that what you produced was wanted, earnings reflected the scarcity of the talents needed to produce them, and your position in the power structure of the tribe. The first explains why the insurance and repair men did well, and the second accounted for the prosperity of the bureaucrat and the priest.

Those who are lucky enough to have that power or these rare talents have often felt embarrassed by earning more than those who work to satisfy more basic elements in the hierarchy of needs. Often, they also enjoy occupations that are less arduous and more fun. The embarrassment is rarely very great, and does seem to have diminished recently, but emphasising the importance we attach to these other supposedly more necessary, but less well-remunerated, activities is a means of assuaging it.

Whatever the truth of all this, none of it should provide a basis for economic policy or industrial strategy.

There is a slightly more persuasive version of the intellectual confusion that tends to the view that manufacturing is special. This suggests that manufacturing output is more important than services because manufacturing, unlike services, is sold to foreigners. Of course, many services are sold to foreigners and many manufactures are not, but there is some truth in the stereotype.

But the real weakness in this argument points the way to the correct answer to the valuation of different activities. If what matters is the tradeability of output, then why draw the line around the nation state? Why not draw it more broadly, or more narrowly? After all, neither the City of London nor a

▶

steelworks could survive on its own. You cannot drink derivatives or eat steel. They survive and are valuable because – and only because – they can persuade people outside their boundaries to value their output. The output is valuable, not because it can be sold to foreigners, but because it can be sold.

So the economic significance of an activity is not measured by its place in some objective hierarchy of needs. It is measured by what someone, other than the producer, thinks it is worth.

Source: J Kay, *Financial Times*, 13 June 1997. Copyright John Kay, economist. Reprinted with permission.

position. Managers' decisions are likely to be based on a mixture of market research, forward planning, political and cultural forces and what can be referred to as 'hunch' or even as 'vision'. Managers need to understand the criteria by which their existing and potential customers choose to purchase their company's products or services, and how they decide from which company to make their purchases. Within a company different groups of people may have a variety of ideas about customer needs and may emphasise different factors in relation to their products, such as technical quality, lower prices, prompt delivery, packaging or advertising.

CUSTOMER STRATEGY

Managers need to understand their customers in order to meet those customers' needs better. From an economic point of view customer demand will depend on a range of factors to do with costs, prices, preferences and **competitive advantage** (Exhibit 3.3).

Organisations need to know the specific requirements of each customer and whether these requirements can be segmented. If there are well-defined customer segments this can have important implications for both product design and marketing. Companies will attempt to segment customer requirements in an attempt both to satisfy as many people as possible on the one hand, and on the other hand in order not to have to tailor-make every item for each individual customer. In the production of a tailor-made suit, for example, there is an attempt to make it fit an individual customer 'perfectly', while 'off-the-peg' suits are produced in large quantities to fit a range of people segmented by such means as height, waist and chest measurements.

'Getting to know the customer' also involves being aware of how many different people are involved in the purchasing decision and the different kinds of requirements they may have. Even in a family the purchase of a suit for one of their

Exhibit 3.3 Customer strategy

To meet customer needs as well as possible a company needs to provide goods and services:

■ at lower cost;

■ at maximum customer satisfaction;

■ with competitive advantages.

members may give rise to sharp differences of opinion. In a company, purchasing may be viewed very differently by the product, finance and marketing managers. The finance manager, for example, may be particularly concerned about costs in terms of cost saving, while the marketing manager may consider costs in a rather different way, perhaps largely by comparison with competitors.

At the same time people will have different priorities in terms of the qualities they require in a product or service. These will include design, technical preferences, reliability and availability as well as price. The producers need to know how important these factors are to customers before they can decide which aspect to concentrate on improving. Without this knowledge it is very difficult for a manager to develop a strategy to obtain competitive advantage.

> *'The key element which distinguishes strategy from marketing is the explicit considera-tion of competitive advantage.'*   (Faulkner and Johnson, 1992)

Faulkner and Johnson, in their book in the Cranfield Management Research Series, argue that it is critical to know customer purchase criteria, and equally critical to understand how well a company meets these needs relative to those of its competitors. It is through an interaction of customer needs with competitor offerings that determines who will make the sale, and it is the company which meets customer needs better than its competitors which is likely to grow and be successful.

In order to monitor this competitive success, a company's products and services have to be based on a fundamental advantage in cost or skills. It is critical for managers to understand what the company costs are and what skills it has compared to competing companies. The skills available to an organisation will depend very heavily on its structure and organisation, its recruitment and retention policy and on staff training and development. Cost differences may arise because of the level of investment in equipment linked to the skill and productivity of employees. The scale of the operation may influence costs and the efficiency of management. Any structural skills or cost differences which are difficult for a competitor to replicate can be the basis of a competitive advantage if they result in an organisation being able to service customer needs better and at a lower cost.

It follows from this that organisations, in order to be successful, need to concentrate their efforts or activities in areas in which they have or can develop and maintain a competitive advantage in terms of cost and skills. It can be argued, for example, that the British motorcycle industry collapsed in the 1960s and 1970s because it failed to keep up with competitor improvements in terms of costs and customer needs, and that the success of the Japanese motorcycle industry was as a result of concentrating on both these factors.

As the economy develops, companies have to include consumer experience in their customer strategy. Largely as a result of increasing access to the Internet, consumers are able to learn about businesses on their own or through the collective knowledge of other customers. They now play an active role in creating and competing for value, they bring competence in the form of the knowledge and skills they possess and their willingness to learn and experiment. Prahalad and Ramaswamy (2000) have identified examples of this process in areas such as the software industry where 650,000 Microsoft customers were involved in testing a beta version of Windows 2000™ and sharing with the company their ideas for changing some of the product's features. Working with the beta software not only provided a test bed for Microsoft; it also helped many of the customers understand how Windows 2000™ could create value for their own businesses. It has been estimated that the R&D investment by these customers in co-developing the product has been more than $500 million worth of time and effort.

Other industries also involve their customers to a greater or lesser extent in the development of their products and services. For example, the availability of medical information on the Internet has meant that patients are able to increase their knowledge and shape their own health care. This has been recognised in the UK by the opening of NHS Direct to provide an immediate source of information for patients. In the tourist industry people are increasingly accessing travel information for themselves so that customers have access to knowledge similar to that of travel agents. Travel companies have, therefore, had to change their approaches and their products and services to take this into account.

Organisations have to learn to manage the variety of customer experiences in terms of the interface between a company and its customers, because the range of experience transcends the company's products and services. Managers have to develop products that shape themselves to the customers' needs rather than the other way around. The product has to be developed so that future modifications and extensions are based on the customers' changing needs and the company's changing capabilities. A computer user may in practice use it for two or three main functions, for example as a wordprocessor and for e-mail, so these functions need to be easily accessible for that particular user. Another may use it mainly for spreadsheets and to produce diagrams, charts and other illustrations, and for that user the priority is for this function to be easily accessible. These two users may change their needs over a period of time, for example to carry out research through the Internet, so the products they are using have to cope with these changing needs. Customers may find complicated menus annoying because they judge the product not by the number of functions it has but by the degree to which it provides the experiences they want.

Managers can help to shape customers' experiences by highlighting what is likely to be available next. This has to be a dialogue which makes sense to the consumer and is not so outside the consumer's experience that he or she ignores the developments. At the same time, because of the increasing access to information, customers are able to make greater demands on organisations. Managers can no longer assume that customers' knowledge of the product, prices and competing products is less than their own, so that in maintaining a competitive advantage for their organisation's products and services they have to take even more care than in the past to provide consumer benefits.

Customers can also be important in company growth. Zander and Zander (2005) argue that a firm's established customers are instrumental in generating ideas to enter new product areas, and that accommodation of their various needs result in the assimilation and creation of previously unexploited skills and resources. A study of the Hercules Powder Company's contacts with military customers for explosives, which was the firm's original and most important product line, appear to have led to the discovery and exploitation of demand for naval stores. Privileged access to information about the emerging needs of established customers provides an important basis for sustainable competitive advantage. It can be argued that this access depends on personal sales. As customers grow comfortable with the competence and reliability of a company supplying them with goods or services they also become more likely to assume the risks associated with adopting new products and services. This position of loyalty from existing customers is difficult for other companies to imitate. New firms will lack the insight into the particular needs of customers and this may limit their response to new product opportunities. A focus on the role of customers in company strategy and growth emphasises the idea of firms as open systems in depending on adapting to change among their customers and their external environment (see St John and Harrison, 1999; Stimpert and Duhaime, 1997; Farjoun, 1998; Prem and Butler, 2001).

One of the developments in meeting customer requirements in the twenty-first century has been the rise and rise of the 'third-age' consumer and the development of a 'grey advantage'. Nearly a fifth of the population of the industrial countries are above the traditional retirement age. The United States Census Bureau predicts that the number of Americans aged over 65 will triple to 70 million by 2030, or 20 per cent of the population, while the population over 65 in Japan is likely to be 27 per cent in 2020. In the UK the percentage of the population over 65 is anticipated to rise from 15 per cent in 2001 to 29 per cent in 2021, with 19 million people expected to be over the age of 60 in the UK by 2030. People are living longer, and with falling birth rates the older generations form a higher and higher proportion of total population.

Tempest *et al.* (2002) noted that 'longevity has not had too great an economic or social impact because the size of the working population has in parallel been significantly expanding.' However, this is changing and in the future a significant group of employees and customers will come from the older population. This presents both an opportunity and a challenge for organisations both in their employment policies and the focus on their customers. Already in the United States the emphasis in marketing cultures has shown a shift from 'being focused predominantly on youth, to being increasingly concerned with the needs and dreams of older adults' (Tempest *et al.*, 2002). The older age groups in many industrial countries already spend more on most products and services than the young. In the USA it is thought that by 2010 people in the 55–75 age range will outnumber those aged 25–34 by 18 million.

The expansion in the number of golf courses in the UK in the last decade is a reflection of this trend, while some companies, such as Saga, have capitalised on this segment of the market. Saga has expanded its services to reflect consumer demand to include travel, financial and other services aimed at the over 50s. Housing has been an important area of development for the consumer market with an increase in the number of senior citizens' apartment blocks and housing developments. The grey market is ripe for further segmentation and exploitation in areas such as health services and travel.

At the same time organisations can take advantage of the abilities and experience of older workers if they are prepared to be flexible in their employment practices. For example, they can offer gradual reductions in working hours, part-time work and shared jobs to match the physical and mental attributes of individuals.

'It is our belief that companies will best respond to the grey advantage agenda by customising their employment and market offerings to the individual, rather than expecting all workers and customers to conform to rigid offerings.'

(Tempest *et al.*, 2002)

In the public sector there have also been attempts to meet 'customer' needs. The UK Government established an 'e-government' target to make all government services available electronically by the end of 2005. The ambitious objectives have been to reduce National Health Service waiting lists, to reduce benefits fraud, to control civil service costs, to introduce identity cards and to introduce a 'longitudinal' database of citizens. In 2004 volunteers were invited by the UK Passport Office to receive cards bearing electronically encoded biometric information. This trial was designed to test iris scans, fingerprints and electronic facial recognition. To complement the identity card there has been work on a longitudinal database of work and benefits records by the Department for Work and Pensions in order to create a single record of every individual's history in employment, as benefit claimant and in retirement.

A national programme for information technology in the UK National Health Service has been designed to make an impact on frontline care with a national e-booking scheme that will allow doctors to reserve hospital appointments for their patients before they leave the doctor's surgery. While some of the public IT developments are controversial, this system is designed to be more patient-friendly than the present process. An online Government store has been established as a one-stop web shop to offer a variety of services to people, such as a system to provide easy access to car tax. This is a reflection of the explosion in online shopping which has removed the need to leave home to go to the local supermarket or travel agent, while computer search engines have replaced many of the functions of a reference library.

THE SUPPLY CHAIN

The objective of the supply chain for all companies is to deliver goods and services to consumers as efficiently and effectively as possible. Supply chain management involves managing the sequence of suppliers and purchasers covering all stages of processing – from obtaining raw materials, manufacturing the product or organising the service, to distributing the finished goods and services to consumers. Improvements to the supply chain are aimed at greater speed and cost-effectiveness, and in the quest for these objectives companies have introduced state-of-the-art technologies and employed experts to boost their performance. Some companies have teamed up to streamline processes, for example American clothing companies have formed a 'Quick Response' initiative. Lee (2004) has argued that when business is booming managers tend to concentrate on maximising speed, while when the economy experiences a downturn the priority changes to minimising supply costs. However, when an organisation's supply chain becomes more efficient and cost-effective it does not necessarily gain a sustainable advantage over its competitors. This depends on the agility of the reaction to change, so that an alteration in demand or supply is met successfully very rapidly. Also the successful supply chain has to adapt over time as market structures and strategies evolve and they align the interests of all the organisations in the supply network so that they maximise the chain's performance when they maximise their interests. 'Only supply chains that are agile, adaptable and aligned provide companies with sustainable competitive advantage' (Lee, 2004).

High-speed, low-cost supply chains are often unable to respond to unexpected changes in demand and supply because companies' centralised manufacturing and distribution facilities generate economies of scale and they are geared up to deliver container-loads of products to customers in order to minimise transportation time, freight costs and the number of deliveries. When the demand for a particular brand, pack size or assortment rises without warning, these organisations are unable to react quickly even if the items are in stock. There may also be problems with the launch of new products because demand will typically fluctuate, often with a slow start followed by a sharp increase in demand as 'early-adopters' buy the product, leading to a slowing down of demand until the main body of customers catch up with the availability of the new product.

Successful companies, such as Amazon, Wal-Mart and Dell create supply chains that respond to sudden and unexpected changes in markets:

> *'agility is critical, because in most industries both demand and supply fluctuate more rapidly and widely than they used to. Most supply chains cope by playing speed against costs, but agile ones respond both quickly and cost-efficiently.'*   (Lee, 2004)

They do this by promoting the flow of information with suppliers and customers, by building inventory buffers, by maintaining a stockpile of key components and also by having a dependable logistics system, developing contingency plans and crisis management teams. Successful companies also adapt their supply chains so that they can adjust to changing needs and structural shifts in the market. They do this by evaluating the needs of ultimate consumers, creating flexible product designs and determining where companies' products stand in terms of technology cycles and product life cycles. Successful companies also align the interests of all the organisations in their supply chain with their own, whether manufacturer, distributor or retailer. This is encouraged by providing incentives for better performance, by exchanging information and by laying down clear roles and responsibilities and providing an equitable share of risks, costs and gains.

> *'Great companies don't stick to the same supply networks when markets and strategies change. Rather, such organizations keep adapting their supply chains so they can adjust to changing needs.'*   (Lee, 2004)

THE 'NEW' MANAGER

→ Ch. 2

In Chapter 2, McGregor's (1960) model in terms of Theory X and Theory Y was discussed in relation to leadership. It can be argued that Theory Y will dominate management in the twenty-first century as organisations attempt to gain competitive advantage through developing employees' own motivation. Theory Y is based on the optimistic view of human nature that employees will help to achieve organisational objectives. This theory views the manager's role as working cooperatively with other employees in order to decide work objectives and methods of achieving them. Managers will encourage the development of self-managed teams and the delegation of decisions towards the point of action, and they will seek to develop people's own motivation by involvement in the organisation. In this process the 'soft' values, such as shared corporate objectives, become more important than the 'hard' values of control and direction (see Exhibit 3.4).

Exhibit 3.4 British Telecom's 'soft' values

- We put our customer first.
- We are professional.
- We respect each other.
- We work as a team.
- We are committed to continuous improvement.

The manager of the future has to 'live the vision' as well as being accountable for the performance of the organisation. The 'new' manager does less planning, organising and controlling and much more advising, enabling and encouraging. Jack Welch, the chief executive of General Electric in the USA, has been quoted as saying that the twenty-first century commercial wars are going to be won 'on our ideas, not by whips and chains'. Organisations should remove boundaries between jobs and empower people to 'encourage a learning culture' (Welch and Welch, 2006) and 'to unleash the energy of your workers'. Honeywell UK has developed self-managed manufacturing cells with full responsibility for product lines. The role of the manager in these circumstances is to advise self-managed groups, to ensure that they have the necessary resources and to encourage ideas and initiatives.

In an article entitled 'Survival Skills for a New Breed' (1993), Karen Clarke (the winner of a competition called 'Managing for Tomorrow') argues that

> *'the manager as we know him or her – decision maker, expert, boss, director – is extinct. The "new" manager has three roles – leader, coach and facilitator.'*

She argues that managerial success will be determined to an increasing extent by the ability to develop and position the organisation strategically and will be measured by staff performance. This means that managers have to accept the fact that they will no longer be the focus of attention but that they will be part of a team. It follows from this that rewards for managers will be based on the performance of the team. As leaders, managers will be looking at the wider picture, how the team fits into the plans for the whole organisation and how well it is meeting customer needs.

In these circumstances managers are responsible for establishing the boundaries and the culture in which people can work successfully and creatively. One of the 'new' management roles is to act as 'coach'. In this role, managers help employees to be successful and creative by ensuring that they understand the boundaries of their responsibilities and the resources available to them. The coach helps to build up confidence and trust and supports training and development to add to the skills of the team. Successful outcomes are then recorded and as individuals and teams increase in expertise they are given more freedom to organise their own work.

The 'new' manager is also a facilitator in the sense of encouraging new ideas and helping to carry them forward. There can always be a gap between plans and initiatives and their implementation:

> *'If words were deeds, the remaining 1990s would be the Years of the Customer – and 2000 would usher in a whole century of customer worship. But management science is the study of the gap between verbiage and action: the more lip-service the customer receives, the wider the gap is liable to grow.'*   (Heller, 1994a)

The manager has to act as a facilitator in closing this gap so that customers receive the benefits they want and come back for more. It has been estimated (by David Perkins of Loyalty Marketing Service) that typically it costs 80 per cent of the gross margin on an existing customer to obtain a new one. The manager has to make sure that the product or service is right first time and to research the scale and causes of customer loss. The manager as 'facilitator' has to recognise that although 'customers pay the bills, they do not pay the wages'. In other words, individuals and teams in organisations look inwards at colleagues as well as outwards at customers. Decisions on pay and promotion are made internally and it is essential that the correct organisational culture exists in order to enable confidence and trust to grow.

THE 'NEW' CULTURE

The rapid changes in the international marketplace have led to alterations in the corporate culture of even those organisations slowest to respond to culture change. Companies such as Delta Airlines and IBM, for example, had more or less official no-redundancy policies. The increase in international competition and the world-wide recession changed this, so that in the early 1990s there were layoffs at Delta and considerable downsizing at IBM. For managers as much as any other employees, the idea of a job for life has disappeared and the new contracts between many employers and their managers have become short term and based on mutual benefits. Apple Computers and General Electric, for example, have moved towards 'contractor charters' and away from the old-style long-term employment contracts (Egar, 1994).

These charters contract the services of a manager as long as the relationship is mutually beneficial. When forces outside the direct control of the company, such as the economy or competition, create difficulty for the company then the future of the contract may become open to question. There is an emphasis on the employee as a contributor rather than only a player, which means that the manager must find ways of adding value to the business and to grow and develop. The manager must become a 'learning person' within a 'learning organisation' which constantly changes, develops and grows. This form of contract or 'charter' complements flatter organisational structures where promotions are scarce and movement is more likely to be horizontal than vertical. These horizontal moves are into positions which add value to the organisation and provide opportunity for the individual to develop. Rewards tend to be based on performance outcomes rather than on factors such as age or length of service. This type of charter is based on a view that the organisation provides opportunities for individuals to develop and be rewarded as long as this process is adding value to the organisation.

This approach to working life tends to appeal only to flexible, enterprising self-starters and not to managers and employees who are looking for a job for life. The meaning of such words as 'commitment' and 'loyalty' is altered in these circumstances. People are committed to the organisation by adding value to its product and their loyalty is to the particular organisation which at a particular time provides them with the opportunity to develop and be rewarded for this. Under these conditions individuals have to take responsibility for their own development and career paths – they cannot expect this necessarily to be mapped out by the company for which they are working (see Chapter 20).

→ Ch. 20

> *'What people are increasingly working to acquire is the capital of their own individual reputation instead of the organisational capital that comes from learning one system well and meeting its idiosyncratic requirements. For many managers it might be more important, for example, to acquire or demonstrate a talent that a future employer or financial advisor might value than to get to know the right people several layers above in the corporation where they currently work.'*   (Kanter, 1989)

The 'new' culture promotes the idea of a shared destiny that develops collaboration and alliances and what could be described as 'enlightened self-interest'. In its most developed form this approach brings together all the stakeholders in an area of activity in a mutually beneficial alliance. Competitors can prosper together by increasing the overall size of the market, while managers, employees, shareholders, suppliers and customers can collaborate in obtaining the required levels of service and value. The original Rover and Honda collaboration contained elements of this approach in the same way as did the alliance between IBM and Apple Computers. The takeover of Rover by BMW in 1994 could be seen as not only a commercial development but also as the ending of the previous mutually beneficial alliance.

The obvious stakeholders in this form of alliance are shareholders, managers and employees who will share in the creation and distribution of wealth (see Exhibit 3.5). The customer can be a 'stakeholder' of such an alliance by being involved in the quality of the product or service. There is a need for two-way communication through customer surveys, complaints procedures, open meetings and the development of a 'consumer charter' expressing the level of quality and service customers should be able to expect. It is the role of the 'manager 2000 plus' to ensure that there is a high level of cooperation and collaboration with customers so that the latter can be involved in product and service development.

Exhibit 3.5 Alliances

Stakeholders in an alliance need to:

- create wealth and then distribute it;

- replace 'loyalty' with commitment to the creation of wealth;

- play an active part in wealth creation;

- invest in the future through technological and employee development;

- provide opportunities for managerial and employee development;

- take account of the realities of the marketplace;

- be prepared to accept change;

- help employees at a mutually beneficial time to return to the marketplace with transferable skills;

- encourage employees to accept responsibility for their development and their future.

NEW FORMS OF ORGANISATION

Charles Handy has argued in *The Age of Unreason* (1989) that there are fundamental changes taking place in organisational life. He suggests that companies are moving away from the labour-intensive organisations of the past to new knowledge-based structures. They will increasingly receive added value from their knowledge and creativity, and this is reflected in changing organisational structures. He acknowledges that companies are moving at different speeds and that the process is an evolutionary one, where they may take on some of the characteristics of a 'shamrock' organisation, which may or not be or become part of a 'federation' and will slowly evolve into a 'triple I' type of organisation.

The shamrock organisation

Handy suggests that the **shamrock organisation**, like the plant after which it is named, has three interlocking leaves in the sense that it is composed of three distinct groups of workers who are treated differently and have different expectations (see Figure 3.2).

A small group of specialist **core workers** form the first leaf. They are the nerve centre of the organisation in the sense that they are essential to its work and success. They are both specialists and generalists who run the organisation and control the technology which has replaced, to a large extent, much of the labour force. For example, a computer software or e-commerce company may have a small number of specialists at its centre providing the expertise on which the company is based.

The core workers are expected to be loyal to the organisation and to be flexible in meeting the challenge of constant change in both competitors' and customers' requirements. Core workers operate as colleagues and partners in the organisation, as opposed to superiors and subordinates. They are stakeholders in the company and in many ways they *are* the company. They expect to be rewarded for their achievements, rather than for any position they might occupy in the hierarchy. The role of the manager in this situation is one of coach, adviser and facilitator. There is considerable pressure on the core workers, 'a pressure which could be summed up by a new equation of half the people, paid twice as much, working three times as effectively' (Handy, 1989).

The shamrock organisation is small compared to its output. This is achieved by the use of technology on the one hand, and the contracting out and outsourcing, to individuals and other organisations, of work which was previously carried out by core employees.

> '*To get that three times improvement the smart organisation will equip their people with all the technological aids they need ... It will also expect those people to be smart, to be dedicated to their work (none of the leisure age here) and to be prepared to invest enough time and energy to keep ahead of the game, to go on learning, in other words, in order that they can go on thinking.*'   (Handy, 1989)

The second leaf, the **contract workers**, may or may not work exclusively for the company. Its constituents are contracted to carry out certain tasks for which they are paid a fee based on results, rather than on the time taken. The advantages of this arrangement are that it is cost effective because companies only pay for what they receive, it makes management easier because fewer people are on the payroll,

Figure 3.2 The shamrock organisation

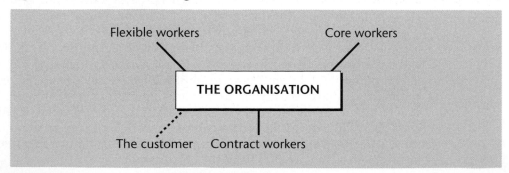

and when demand is reduced, it is the contractor who faces the problems rather than the company.

> *'Those organisations, although often smaller than the main organisation will have their own shamrocks, their own cores and their own subcontractors. It is a Chinese Box type of world. The individuals will be self-employed professionals or technicians, many of them past employees of the central organisation who ran out of roles in the core or who preferred the freedom of self-employment.'*   (Handy, 1989)

For example, the maintenance and cleaning of the offices of a computer software company may be contracted out, or it may employ contracted workers in a special call centre, either in the home country or abroad who may be paid on results, or there may be self-employed professionals who work from home for the company on contracted projects.

The third leaf of the shamrock organisation, the **flexible workers**, comprises a pool of part-time workers who are available for use by the organisation. These are people with relevant skills who are not in need of, or who cannot obtain, full-time employment but who are prepared to work on a part-time basis. They may be housewives who combine part-time work with raising a family, people who have retired early or people who prefer to have a variety of part-time jobs. They do not have the commitment to the company that core workers do but they enable the organisation to respond flexibly to changes in demand for their product or service. For example, a computer software company or e-commerce company may have a bank of part-time specialists who can be called on when required.

The shamrock organisation can have a large output, while being small in terms of direct employees. It can be organised with little bureaucracy and modern management practices. It can be extremely flexible in order to react to or anticipate fluctuations in customer demands. Core employees, in particular, can keep close to their customers and make sure that they satisfy their needs.

> *'The shamrock organisation, always there in embryo, has flourished because organisations have realised that you do not have to employ all the people all the time to get the work done.'*   (Handy, 1989)

Such organisations are also going further and realising that they do not necessarily need to locate everybody in one place. The development of technology enables an increasing number of people to work at a distance so that 'the early morning crush in the commuter train will one day be a thing of the past, or at least a twice-weekly chore'.

There is another form of subcontracting, through the **customer**, which Handy suggests could be a fourth leaf on the shamrock. This is the strong trend towards allowing the customer to do the work. This process is disguised as 'improving services', whether it actually does or not, and it creates a situation where the customer does work previously carried out by paid employees. Examples of this process include self-service in supermarkets, self-assembly furniture, cashpoints, carveries and buffet-style restaurants, self-service petrol stations, which may include payment at the pump, and so on. These examples all have self-service by customers in common. This saves the organisations vast amounts of money in terms of wages for staff to provide these services. The services can then be provided, if required, at an extra charge so that it is no longer part of the core of the organisation but is part of the contractual fringe. Self-service is marketed as a benefit to customers, when in fact its main advantage may be to the organisation.

The federal organisation

The **federal organisation** consists of a variety of individual organisations or groups of organisations allied together by a common approach and mutual interest. It provides a way for relatively small companies based on core workers to obtain the advantages of large companies:

> *'It allows individuals to work in organisation villages with the advantage of big city facilities.'*
> (Handy, 1989)

This enables organisations to enjoy the advantages of small, lean structures with the resources and power of big corporations. The drive and energy come from the parts of the federation rather than the centre:

> *'Federalism implies a variety of individual groups allied together under a common flag with some shared identity. Federalism seeks to make it big by keeping it small, or at least independent, by combining autocracy with cooperation. It is the method which businesses are slowly and powerfully evolving for getting the best of both worlds – the size which gives them clout in the market place and in the financial centres, as well as some economies of scale and the small unit size which gives them the flexibility which they need, as well as the sense of community for which individuals increasingly hanker.'*
> (Handy, 1989)

An example of this type of organisation is provided by Miles *et al.* (2000) in their description of Technical Computing and Graphics (TCG). This is an information technology company in Australia which is a federation of 13 small firms producing a wide range of technological products. They cooperate in searching for new product and service opportunities with the initiating firm acting as project leader for a new development.

Shamrock organisations retain their own autonomy in this system, while the federation provides a common platform for the integration of their activities. The federal organisation is concerned mainly with the future, in order to keep its members ahead of the competition. It seeks to maximise the innovative and creative potential of its members by specifying the central vision and quality standards and then encouraging innovation and initiative.

The management role in this situation is to provide an overall direction and then to develop opportunities for growth. At the same time the relatively small shamrock organisation members are able to maintain close links and alliances with their customers. Handy (1989) argues that

> *'organisational cities no longer work unless they are broken down into villages. In their big city mode they cannot cope with the variety needed in their products, their processes and their people. On the other hand, the villages on their own have not the resources nor the imagination to grow. Some villages, of course, will be content to survive, happy in their niche, but global markets need global products and large confederations to make them or do them.'*

The triple I organisation

Both the idea of the shamrock organisation and the federation can develop into what Handy refers to as the **triple I organisation.** This is one based on intelligence, information and ideas which form the intellectual capital represented by the core workers. The three Is equal added value because, as well as intelligence, they need good information to work with and ideas to build on if value is to be made from knowledge. These core workers will be

> *'expected to have not only the expertise appropriate to his or her particular role, but also be required to know and understand business, to have the technical skills of analysis and the human skills and the conceptual skills to keep them up to date.'*
>
> (Handy, 1989)

These are learning organisations, serving their customers as a result of their employees remaining at the leading edge of knowledge and skills. It is these types of organisations which require the changes in the role of the manager, concerned with performance more than formalities and acting as a coach, adviser and facilitator. There will still be mundane jobs in the organisation, but its heart will be a triple I operation otherwise value will not be added to pay for the support services. The specialists and professionals involved cannot be managed in the old ways, they have to be managed by consent and not by command, and they are obsessed with the pursuit of learning in order to keep up with the pace of change of quality because that produces long-term success. This concentration on quality is based on the organisation's customers and on providing them with the benefits they require.

THE INTERNATIONAL DIMENSION

Organisational change and alterations in the role of the manager are taking place across the world. Globalisation has encouraged companies to consider both their customer base and their organisation. Tesco is

> *'plotting an ambitious international expansion that could keep the company growing at the vertiginous pace it has enjoyed since 1997.'*
>
> (Davey, 2006)

Sir Terry Leahy, the CEO of Tesco, believes that China, India and America are the big areas for expansion in the future:

> *'If you are looking at the twenty-first century, these are the places to put your chips. Clearly, China and India are the growing markets, but actually you have to remember that the United States still accounts for a third of the world's GDP. The business has always been based around customers rather than being wedded to particular business systems or formats'*
>
> (Davey, 2006)

and it is this adaptability that is needed for success in international markets.

> *'We have sat down over the past three or four years and designed a format that is exactly right for the American consumer today.'*

In terms of organisational change, David Kilburn (1994) has noted changes in Japan for example. In many ways the Japanese style of management presents a paradox. The obsession for focus on the customer is one side of the equation, while the other side is what appears to be at least paternalistic if not autocratic forms of management. Japanese companies have been characterised by a strong loyalty to the company by employees – many employees join a company until retirement so that when they work with colleagues they are doing so on the basis that they will be working together for most of their lives. Japanese society has been described as more group-oriented than that of the USA or the UK, where the focus is more on individual achievement. The Japanese manager is essentially part of a team and will often not be able to hire or fire or restructure the team. The challenge to the Japanese manager is to motivate the team to achieve goals and to help them to develop their abilities. In the Japanese team many decisions are based on consensus and the manager's role is to lead the team towards this. This may take time, but once a decision has been made everyone will be behind it so that implementation will be relatively smooth. Managers will tend to have paternalistic and deferential relationships with their superiors. Pay is related to length of service rather than performance, with frequent on-the-job training in order to improve individual performance in achieving the strategic objectives of the company.

There are, however, signs that this traditional approach is changing. While it may still be true for the core workers there is now greater mobility between jobs, more restructuring in companies, with a reduction in the workforce through voluntary retirement. Observers have noted that subsidiaries and affiliates are being used to a greater extent and that the softer corporate values are being emphasised now compared to the harder values by concentrating more on staff training, developing skills and ensuring that all employees understand the organisation's values. Figure 3.3 illustrates the shift from the harder values of strategy, structure and systems to the softer ones of staff, skills and style. At the same time the paradox does continue in that the central selection of staff and control of training and development are still based on structure and systems. The slow growth in the 1990s has led to a need for flexibility and this is having an effect on Japanese companies as well as those in other countries. In comparison to Japanese culture it is argued that in the USA management styles are too individualistic for the changes taking place. The individualists have to be moulded into teams and the specialists have either to become generalists or be prepared to work with a range of people in these teams.

As well as the theories of organisational change put forward by such management gurus as Charles Handy, there is also the view that many of the changes are pragmatic. Customer demands are changing and companies alter processes and services in order to meet these demands.

> *'Lofty strategic concepts are in the trash can of history. For example, the old idea that every corporation should have a "vision" has been shelved by Microsoft, IBM and Chrysler, to name a few, and in its place these companies are improving efficiency across a broad front.'*   (Thakray, 1994)

Figure 3.3 Corporate values

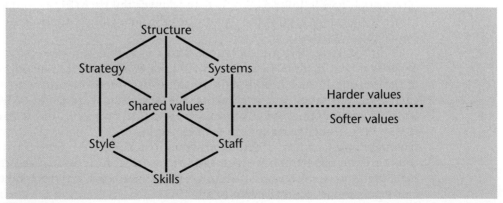

Peggy Salz-Trautman (1994) reports that it has been noted in Germany that tomorrow's manager will require broad-based skills and be able to work in teams. There are pressures on German companies to combine the solidity of industrial giants with the nimbleness of entrepreneurs. In other words the giants have to 'learn to dance'. These pressures include cut-throat international competition, causing the restructuring of companies, and the expanding services sector based on meeting customer needs. German managers have a long tradition of respect for technical expertise and attention to detail combined with a deep-seated respect for hierarchy and rank. Their managers of the future have to learn to be flexible and to embrace customer service in a wholehearted fashion. At the same time, companies such as Volkswagen AG recognise that the age of the charismatic individual leading the company is past and that the role of the manager has shifted to one of being a coach, facilitator and teamworker. The technology-oriented German company based on hard corporate values has had to shift towards the softer values based on customer focus.

The convergence of the world economy, brought about by vastly improved communication and seen in terms of both competition and cooperation, forces managers to adapt to new structures and fresh values or to see their organisations drown under a tidal wave of competition. In many companies, large ones in particular, management teams are likely to include several nationalities. Just as American managers have top positions in European companies (such as Rank Xerox UK) so many European managers have top positions in US companies (such as General Motors). For the 'international' manager, boundaries between nations are no longer important. What is important is looking at customer requirements with fresh eyes and reshaping the organisation in order to meet customer needs.

URGENCY

The objective of creating self-managed teams, concentrating on core workers and developing federations of relatively small companies, is to keep an organisation close to its customers. The focus is an obsession with strategic innovation so that the company is different to its competitors and better fulfils customer needs. These processes help to create a sense of urgency throughout an organisation because most people can relate directly to customer needs. The flatter organisation means that there is no hierarchy far removed from contact with customers and unable to relate to them. John Elliott, Chairman of Elliot Brothers Air Control and star of one of the Secret Millionaire television programmes on Channel 4, says he uses 'farmers' feet' instead of making appointments. 'Walking around is the best fertiliser', he says (Davidson, 2006), 'talk to people, listen, never tell them what to do, that undermines managers'. He ends the day in the customer call centre because it is the best source of information.

The process of division of labour and the expansion of separate functional departments in manufacturing, marketing, sales and finance developed a structure of senior, middle and junior managers in every function, and new departments, such as accountancy and **management information systems**, in order to manage them. Company time and effort was diverted into doing business with itself rather than with the outside customer. **Re-engineering** in the Michael Hammer approach (Hammer and Champy, 1993) means that instead of trying to improve coordination between departments organised into vertical functions, the organisation is structured into a collection of horizontal processes, each of which takes orders and delivers a product or service (see Exhibit 3.6).

Exhibit 3.6 Re-engineering

P	M	S	F		O	Dist/Mark/Sales/Fin	P	S
R	A	A	I		R		R	E
O	R	L	N		D		O	R
D	K	E	A	RE-ENGINEERED	E		D	V
U	E	S	N		R		U	I
C	T		C		S		C	C
T	I		E				T	E
I	N							
O	G							
N								

This horizontal principle shifts the focus of attention onto activities which are necessary to meet customer needs rather than on efforts to develop cooperation between internal departments. For many employees it leads to multiskilling and working in integrated teams which are empowered to make a whole range of decisions about the way they work. Employees are involved, or experience job enrichment, so that their talents are used more effectively in order that the organisation becomes more competitive. Managers move away from the authoritarian image to one of leader, facilitator and coach.

At Forte's Harvester restaurants, for example, staff teams devise their own publicity, carry out their own recruitment and track their own sales targets. Supervisors have been eliminated and the branch manager's role has changed to one of facilitator. The company mission, menu and image remain central issues along with decor and uniforms. Rover, Lucas and Rank Xerox have all moved towards re-engineered self-managed teams. However, Hammer and Champy estimate that 70 per cent of all re-engineering efforts fail, because top managers do not, in the final analysis, support it, or middle managers subvert its implementation, or because the change is not communicated sufficiently well to employees.

This process of re-engineering develops a sense of urgency by promoting autonomy and entrepreneurship at the point of interface with the customer. It can be argued that in a fiercely competitive marketplace it is no longer enough simply to satisfy customers. It is now necessary to go beyond this in order to exceed customer expectations time and time again. The organisation, it can be argued, has to become customer driven so that the entire company is saturated by the voice of the customer. In this situation the customer is the driving force behind the corporate vision, and it is the customer who defines quality in products and services.

SUMMARY

- This chapter is concerned with the changes in organisational structure brought about by a focus on the customer. Customer service has become a major issue in managing and organising companies and institutions. This has been highlighted by *In Search of Exellence* (Peters and Waterman, 1982) and other studies of successful organisations.

- These developments have created the need for different qualities and skills in management. This has been emphasised by the 'search for synergy' in the move to flatter, less complex and more responsive organisations. The economic focus also emphasises the requirement to provide for customer needs.

- Customer strategy involves achieving a competitive advantage in terms of cost and skills. The 'new' manager has to develop new roles in order to achieve and maintain this advantage as leader, coach and facilitator. Corporate culture has altered and become much more flexible so that managers face new challenges in the workplace and in their own careers. New forms of organisation have developed to reflect the increases in flexibility and the greater emphasis on customer service.

Review and discussion questions

1 *Can the concept of a consumer focus be applied to all organisations? What differences might arise in the application of the concept in different sectors of the economy and to organisations of different sizes?*

2 *How important are customer surveys in helping to meet their needs? Are there other ways of finding out what customers want?*

3 *How does the case study below illustrate 'management by walking about'? Can this approach be applied to other organisations?*

4 *Discuss the importance of knowing what competitors are doing and ways of checking on this.*

CASE STUDY

Tesco – Sir Terry Leahy

Starting as a shelf-stacker, Britain's most admired business leader has spent his whole career at Tesco, lifting it to fearsome market dominance. No charismatic general or smooth persuader, he bases his success on an ordinary man's extraordinary empathy with staff and customers.

In June, he went to a store in Royston and mucked in as a general assistant. Come on, this sort of thing – it's all for show, isn't it? 'Not at all, I enjoy it, I find it very satisfying. I'm learning as well. I want a better understanding of how these jobs are done.'

Leahy makes all his senior staff do it. Last year, 1000 store managers worked in other stores and 1000 staff from head office did the same. Top retailers will tell you how they visit stores and not just theirs but those of rivals, but Leahy takes trading places to a different level. Each week, he swoops on Tesco stores, wandering round, talking to staff and customers. And each week he tours a competitor. Does he ever go into the big Morrisons down the road? 'Every week. I talk to their staff. Some of them know me and show me round.'

Why can't he just put his feet up on his desk and bask in the glory of the soaring sales chart and the awards that adorn his office? 'I talk to people – I can smell how things are.' It's a party piece of his to tell you to brace yourself for the secret of successful retailing and then to say: 'It's this: never stop listening to customers and giving them what they want. It's that simple.'

On his way up the executive pole, he commissioned a survey of 250,000 Tesco customers, who said they wished Tesco would stop following Sainsbury and carve out its own identity. It was a pivotal point in Tesco's history, the moment when Tesco struck out on its own and left the rest of the industry trailing. It led to the Tesco Clubcard and Tesco Metro, the brand of smaller, high street stores, and to offering just about anything in the stores.

The sea change propelled Leahy to the top job. 'We've worked very hard over the years to organise ourselves from A to Z so we listen to customers.' Whether it's the Clubcard loyalty scheme or focus groups in stores or letters to him, Leahy puts them first. He answers every customer letter he gets personally. 'They really do matter. It's their values we live by.'

It's those values that tell him he's right to fight the farming and corner-shop lobbies, that Tesco customers vote with their feet. Some farmers who can't match the quality he demands and some corner shops that can't compete may go out of business, but so what? 'We're selling 50% more food than we did five years ago; we're the biggest customer of British farming there is and we've created 100,000 jobs in the last five years.'

Source: Extracted from C Blackhurst (2004) 'Sir Terry Leahy', *Management Today*, February, pp. 32–7.

FURTHER READING

Blackhurst, C (2005) 'Allan Leighton', *Management Today*, September.

Blackhurst, C (2005a) 'Philip Green', *Management Today*, October.
Articles about two leading CEOs who believe in putting the customer first.

Kanter, R M (1989) *When Giants learn to Dance: Mastering The Challenges of Strategy, Management and Careers in the 1990s*, Unwin.
A classic text on the importance of organisational flexibility and responsiveness.

Zander, I and Zander, U (2005) 'The inside track: on the important (but neglected) role of customers in the resource based view of strategy and firm growth', *Journal of Management Studies*, 42 (8).
A discussion on the importance of customers as a source of competitive advantage.

WEBSITES

http://www.benchnet.com
This provides examples of benchmarking.

http://www.motel6.com
http://www.basshotel.com/holiday-inn
These describe the competitive strategies of two hotel chains, Motel 6 and Holiday Inn.

CHAPTER 4

Managing in the public sector

Outcomes

Having read this chapter, you will be able to:

- explain the similarities and differences between management in the private and public sectors;

- expand on the consideration of organisational culture raised in earlier chapters;

- analyse the 'privatisation' of the public sector;

- discuss the importance of accountability, stakeholders and marketing in the public sector;

- comment on the movement of managers between the private and public sectors.

PRIVATE AND PUBLIC SECTOR MANAGEMENT

Opinions are divided between those who argue that the public sector is unique and operates under different conditions from the private sector and those who suggest that any differences between the two sectors have become increasingly blurred. There is no doubt that there are some differences between the two sectors and that any manager moving from an organisation in one sector to an organisation in the other sector has to take these differences into account and to adapt to the different cultures of the two sectors. In management terms there is a question of how great these differences are, how far the approaches to management adopted in one sector can be applied to the management of the other and how far there is a body of people with special skills in managing public sector organisations. In considering this question it should be noted that different countries have varying views as to the extent to which the public sector is seen as needing to learn from the private sector. It has been argued (Saint-Martin, 2000) that while in the UK there has been one-way traffic in ideas and techniques from the private sector into the public sector, in France this has been much weaker because of the social prestige of sections of the central state (such as the *grand corps*) which has retained control over valued technical knowledge, in particular accounting knowledge.

The starting point can be provided by consideration of the views of Socrates, who argued that

> *'whatever a man controls, if he knows what he wants and can get it he will be a good controller, whether he controls a chorus, an estate, a city or an army.'*
>
> (quoted in Adair, 1989)

Socrates did not see a difference between managing one kind of organisation and another kind; he did not believe that expertise in a particular area was a necessary requirement for management. He argued that the most experienced soldier was not necessarily the best person to lead an army. Rather, it was more important that the general leading the army had shown the ability to find the best experts in any field of activity, knew what he wanted to achieve and how to achieve it and had an eagerness to avoid defeat, to engage the enemy at the right time and to understand the importance of succeeding.

These arguments find modern expression in the headhunting of managers across industries, so that a chief executive may be sought who is not an expert in a particular industry but who has already proved the ability to be successful. It is seen in the appointment of generals and admirals to run charities or the appointment of majors and captains to be secretaries of golf clubs. These transitions do not always work because they depend on the ability of the manager to adapt to the culture and requirements of the new industry. A person who is successful in the disciplined world of the military services may find it difficult to adapt to a situation where control has to be achieved through different means. Similarly, a manager who has been successful in the private sector may find it difficult to adapt to the accepted norms of the public sector and vice versa. On the other hand there are many examples (see the case study at the end of Chapter 3) of managers who have worked their way up through one industry or particular company, where hands-on 'insider' experience may be felt to be of prime importance.

→ Ch. 3

Organisations are usually managed by people with experience in the industry, if not in the particular company. Large, long-standing companies, such as Shell Petroleum, tend to promote their senior managers from within, banks are usually headed by managers with long experience in banking, football clubs tend to be managed by ex-footballers, schools are managed by people who have been teachers. Ken Knight, Chief of the London Fire Service (in 2006), joined the fire service in 1966. His career has taken him to Surrey, Devon, the Home Office, Dorset, the West Midlands, the fire service inspectorate, the Channel Tunnel, Iraq, Zimbabwe and the USA.

> *'A leader has to make sure the direction is clear and people are following because they are inspired and excited, and not just curious – particularly at times of change when they feel unsettled.'*
> (Ken Knight quoted in Nowak, 2006)

This could as easily be a quote from the CEO of a private company as it is of the chief of a public sector service employing 7200 staff (of whom 5900 are operational firefighters) with an annual budget of £404 million.

Public sector organisations have, in the past, usually been managed by practitioners – for example, local authority chief executives have tended to be people whose whole career has been in local government, university vice-chancellors are usually people who have worked in the sector for many years, head teachers have usually been promoted from the classroom. 'Permeability' has increased between the private and public sectors, partly because of privatisation over the years, but intersector movement of managers does not happen as much as in the USA and there is still a tendency for 'each breed to stay in its own silo' (Cook, 2004). Since the 1980s in the UK, changes have occurred in parts of the public sector, for example in the National Health Service where hospital trusts have had specialist, non-practitioner managers appointed to run them. This has caused its own problems because the practitioners may feel that the 'non-practitioner' managers do not understand their problems. There are different views as to how far managers can be 'parachuted' into an organisation in an industry where they have little or no expertise because of their expertise in management in another sector. Socrates' viewpoint was that

> *'the management of private concerns differs only in point of number from that of public affairs. In other respects they are much alike, and particularly in this, that neither can be carried on without men, and the men employed in public and private transactions are the same.'*
> (quoted in Adair, 1989)

The chief executive of English Heritage is quoted (in Davidson, 2005) as saying

> *'there is a lot of misunderstanding in the private sector about how difficult and how tricky all these types of public sector jobs are, because there is often a fundamental lack of clarity about what you are trying to achieve in the organisation.'*

Before Simon Thurley became chief executive there were six chief executives in five years and he arrived just after a critical review where there was heavy criticism of the way the organisation operated. Ironically for a public sector organisation, the main criticism was that English Heritage was not making the most of its sites and was missing commercial opportunities.

SIMILARITIES BETWEEN THE PUBLIC AND PRIVATE SECTORS

It is hard to disagree with the view of Socrates that the process of management is concerned with the management of people and similar basic problems are raised whatever the form of organisation being managed. Rewards and punishments may be different and organisational cultures may vary but in the end people have to be organised and controlled. This view is based on the argument that management is a clear and distinct function – a science or an art – which is distinct from what is being managed. The opposite argument is that a knowledge of what is being managed is essential for good management, so that only people who have worked their way up through an industry should be a manager in an organisation within it – only university lecturers should become university managers, only medical practitioners should manage hospital trusts. It is argued that only in this way can the manager understand the intricacies of the organisation being managed and the difficulties of the people working in it (Exhibit 4.1).

In fact, of course, a manager is unable to have experience of all aspects of an organisation. Senior managers may have been promoted through the finance route, the production route, marketing, sales or human resources. At some point in the promotion ladder the specialist becomes a generalist having to understand the working of the whole section, department or company. In practice a manager who has moved from managing a specialist function will only have expertise in that one function and will have to develop the ability to manage wider areas of responsibility. It can be argued that working through an organisation in one capacity or another gives a feel for it which somebody from outside will not have acquired. This 'feel' involves an understanding of how the industry works, its customs and norms, the products and services it provides, its organisational culture. It can be argued that it is more difficult to pull the wool over the eyes of managers who have worked their way up a company or an industry because they have an insider's understanding of what is going on.

The increasingly volatile nature of careers of people in management has encouraged the view that management is a transferable skill, so that if you can manage in one area of activity you can manage in another. In practice, most people do become managers in the areas in which they have expertise and movement between industries and movement between the private and public sectors tend to be largely in specialist functions. Functional managers, such as accountants, information technology specialists, marketing or human resource experts, may move relatively freely between sectors but there has not been evidence of a free flow of more general managers. In terms of the private and public sectors this is partly explained by differences in pay and benefits but is also based on fundamental differences between the two sectors.

Exhibit 4.1 Similarities between private and public sector management

- The control of people
- Knowledge of purpose
- Achievement of an objective
- Practitioner experience
- Need for adaptation to new organisational cultures

DIFFERENCES BETWEEN THE PUBLIC AND PRIVATE SECTORS

The environment of public organisations is littered with considerations of accountability. Public opinion in general and interest groups in particular feel the need, and believe they have the right, to scrutinise the performance of a public sector organisation. Lobbying and interventions by elected officials and contractors are attempts to influence and control which have to be dealt with by negotiation and bargaining. These attempts at scrutiny and exerting influence on public sector organisations lead them to build buffers in the form of coalitions, advisory groups and bringing members of key groups into aspects of the management or governance of the organisation. Private organisations have fewer needs for these buffers and tend to have simpler, more traceable organisational arrangements. Public sector organisations are susceptible to greater and more open accountability than those in the private sector. Politicians, pressure groups, taxpayers and voters all have an interest in the performance of public sector organisations – they are all stakeholders and feel that they have a right to question performance. Private sector organisations also have stakeholders who have rights to question performance, but they will tend to be more circumscribed than in the public sector (Table 4.1) and to be focused on shareholders. If shareholder value is being sustained then a private company will not be scrutinised too closely.

Strategic management in public settings must identify the beliefs and demands of key stakeholders because the organisation is influenced by the views of opinion leaders, the manipulation of legislators and interest groups, and opposition to the activities of the organisation which can swamp the economic issues crucial for private organisations. How things are viewed and understood by **stakeholders** is important to any organisation, whether in the public or the private sector. But while in the private sector the views of the public may make themselves known largely through the market and through **shareholder** value, in the public sector these views may be applied directly to the organisation through representation on governing bodies or the boards of public corporations, or through advisory groups and other pressure groups. This means that decisions such as whether to offer new products or services or to modify existing ones have to pay particular attention to implementation as much as the apparent soundness of the proposed changes.

Table 4.1 Differences between private and public sector management

PRIVATE SECTOR	PUBLIC SECTOR
Profit motive	Service motive
Shareholder accountability	Stakeholder accountability
Market forces	Public value
Customer sovereignty	Patient, student, public needs
Goals	Ideals
Efficiency	Equity
'Bottom line'	Multiple goals
'Private' goods and services	'Public' goods and services

Whereas private organisations can test their efficiency and effectiveness by comparison with competitors or through the market and **customer** reaction, the beliefs of key stakeholders may override these tests in public organisations. The chief executive of English Heritage, Simon Thurley, is quoted (in Davidson, 2005) as arguing that his organisation has a series of statutory duties set out by parliament, overlaid by a series of political imperatives, so that whichever political party is in power tries to exert influence through the funding mechanism.

> *'If you are a quango, like us, you actually represent the interests of a group of people, and those people are all the people in the country who care passionately about their heritage and the historic environment.'*

English heritage has 6000 employees and a £172 million budget to promote conservation and preserve the castles, houses and gardens put into its care.

> *'So as chief executive of an organisation like that, it is sometimes very unclear whether you are trying to fulfil your statutory duty or trying to please the politicians, or trying to please your main constituency, or trying to do what the board says – and there are occasions when all four of those are facing in opposite directions.'*   (Davidson, 2005)

Public organisations have less freedom to add or delete services or to carry out other actions thought to be desirable and there may be constraints that limit spheres of action. In the past schools and colleges have had geographical catchment areas from which they could draw their pupils and students and hospital trusts have geographical areas of responsibility for patients, which have precluded marketing to find new customers. Public organisations may also have a stipulated set of services that they are expected to provide. Schools are expected to provide learning opportunities for particular age groups, hospitals are expected to provide health services, libraries to act as media resource centres. If these organisations move too far outside their specified area of activity they will have to satisfy their stakeholders that their new activities are legitimate and they may face both public and political opposition. This could be true, for example, if public sector hospitals became agents for pharmaceutical companies or schools became involved in the marketing of children's toys.

Private organisations can undertake proactive strategies which include divestiture or horizontal and vertical integration and acquisition. They can decide on the activities they carry out and they can decide not to be involved in particular activities on the basis of what the public will support sufficiently strongly for the organisation to make a profit. On the other hand public organisations are expected to provide particular services for reasons other than those indicated by the market. They may be expected to provide services as a result of tradition, because they are the only suppliers in an area or because there is felt to be a need. Although the freedom of action of public sector organisations such as hospitals and colleges of further education has been increased in the last two decades they will still be expected to provide a rounded service to their communities, in return for government financial support, because they may be the only suppliers of these services in the local area. They will alter their services on the basis of what activity is supported by the government rather than on economic grounds. Public sector organisations have to make changes on a more proactive basis than those in the private sector, usually involving an incremental move that balances opportunity and threat. However, if they are too proactive and involve too many groups then opposition may be crystallised, providing obstacles to action which may absorb efforts which could have been used to provide the new development.

OBJECTIVES IN THE PUBLIC SECTOR

Public organisations often have **multiple goals** that are both vague and conflicting. There is no '**bottom line**' that can be used as a proxy measure of success. Instead the demands of interest groups and manipulation by important stakeholders and third parties create a complex and confusing set of expectations that are frequently conflicting. Hospitals are judged using one set of standards by patients, another by medical staff and a third by their funding bodies. Funding bodies want efficiency targets to be achieved, patients want personalised care, medical staff demand improved resources. Goal ambiguity in public organisations makes performance expectations difficult to specify. Vague performance expectations mean that success cannot be easily recognised so that it is often difficult to identify and reward key contributors, while failure cannot be detected and corrected in a timely manner. There is often less urgency in public organisations than in private sector organisations because periodic elections, political changes and changes in rules and regulations interrupt public organisations' plans and projects.

Inertia can be encouraged in public sector organisations by having to 'bring up to speed' newly appointed individuals in **stakeholder** positions and to find out their agendas. A new minister in charge of prisons, for example, may have strong views on the penal system and may not understand the practical problems of the service. There may be disruption to the normal flow of activity and uncertainty about demands for the future which make it easy to rationalise inaction and this can lead to cautiousness, inflexibility and low rates of innovation. Hospitals are expected to produce quality performance in all their services, but there are problems in measuring 'quality' because the meaning of the term is both elusive and disputed. Consultants may be very concerned with procedures and results, patients with levels of care, hospital managers with the throughput of patients.

In the public sector strategic managers can use **ideals** in the place of **goals**. Ideals provide a picture of the desired future state of the organisation, giving concrete cues on which to build action. Ideals indicate best- and worst-case situations, with the worst case providing a floor on which to build and the best case a target towards which to plan. Ideals provide targets and offer ways to seek compromise among competing views that dictate what the organisation is (or is not) about. Strategic objectives in the public sector may be ill-defined and expressed in vague and abstract terms, such as 'serving the public', 'maintaining law and order', 'reducing inequality' or 'improving health'. Ideals may take the form of, for example, providing first-class health services for everybody. The introduction of targets, often linked to funding, has made some objectives more precise – for example, waiting list targets for hospital operations or pupil and student number targets for schools, colleges and universities. Attempts to measure levels of service and service quality have led to targets based on the 'outcomes' of educational services. It is a matter of opinion as to whether these targets go any way towards measuring quality. It can be argued, for example, that in order to meet outcome targets in education, establishments have reduced or 'dumbed-down' outcome levels (that is, examinations and assessment requirements have been made easier) so that while the numbers obtaining qualifications has increased the standard (educational level) has been reduced.

MARKET FORCES

The extent to which an organisation is in the public sector or the private sector can be measured by the extent to which it is open to **market forces** (Figure 4.1). The less market forces are allowed to affect an organisation the more clearly it can be said to be in the public sector. It can be argued that some goods, and particularly services, have to be provided by the state because they are in some way a collective need that private sector organisations cannot adequately provide. Defence and law and order are examples of these services. While it is possible to have private sector armies and private law enforcement agencies, examples of them are usually found in countries where the rule of law is weak or non-existent. In these circumstances the private armies carry out the wishes of particular warlords rather than the wishes of an established government. The same is true of private police forces. In practice there has been an increase, even in democracies, of privately employed bodyguards and security teams but they are still subject to the requirements of the law and the national police force.

Other **public 'goods and services'** include waste and refuse collection, street lighting, the provision of clean air, noise abatement, customs and excise services, immigration services and so on. The provision of these services cannot be left to the vagaries of the market, although parts of them have been 'privatised' by contracting private companies to carry out particular functions. Parts of waste disposal and refuse collection have been contracted to private companies, prison management has in some cases been taken over by private security companies, the supply of public utilities has been contracted out to private providers. These are all contracted out by government agencies and come under government scrutiny and monitoring.

Public service organisations are established in such a way that, whatever product or service they provide, their purpose is to be of **service to the public** rather than to produce a **profit** for their owners. Views on what can and cannot be provided by the public and private sectors have changed over the years, so that more and more of the activities which used to be provided by the public sector have been privatised in one way or another. While some products and services have been considered to be national assets, because they included a strong element of natural monopoly they needed to be under the direct control of the government. This view has changed so that contracts have been offered to private companies for particular services, public/private partnerships have been formed and public sector organisations have been increasingly exposed to market forces. In order to build the Millwall Fire Station, the London Fire Brigade formed a public/private partnership so that the fire station was included as part of a £60 million development with Cathedral Group plc. In the

Figure 4.1 Market forces and public goods and services

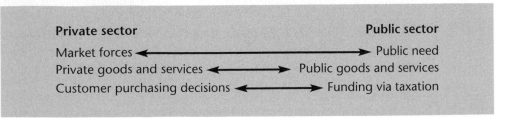

1940s and 1950s areas such as steel production, coal mining and railway services were nationalised to bring them under public ownership – however, since the 1980s denationalisation has placed most parts of these industries under private ownership.

The debate since the 1980s has shifted towards questions of how these products and services can be provided with greater **efficiency**, and developments such as the European Community have raised questions about national subsidies for particular industries. Both steel and coal production have been exposed to market forces and elements of the market have also been introduced into the provision of railways. Transport is an area which cuts across the private/public divide and is a rich area of debate. Roads are built and maintained by the use of public money, while there have been attempts to privatise the provision of railway lines. At the same time the production of cars and petrol comes under the private sector and the provision of railway services has been privatised under strict public scrutiny and government targets. Increasingly, private sector investment has been encouraged by governments in areas which have been provided by the public sector, with arrangements made for the private sector to receive profits from their activities. The national lottery has been a government-controlled initiative organised by a private profit-making company.

This blurring of the divide between the two sectors has meant that even areas of the public sector largely funded by taxation have been exposed to market forces. This has been the case with education and health services, with hospital trusts competing for funds and colleges and universities competing for students and the funds they attract. This has meant that whereas many of the public organisations involved in these areas were protected from market forces by regulations to ensure demand for their services, the removal of the so-called catchment areas for schools and colleges, for example, has introduced an element of competition to these organisations. At the same time there has been an encouragement to users of public services to adopt consumerist patterns of behaviour, coupled to the provision of information on performance and service standards.

Exhibit 4.2 'New public management'

The requirement for fundamental restructuring and reorientation of public sector services has been a constant refrain among policy makers in post-industrial economies over the past two decades. Motivated by political and economic pressures to enhance the efficiency and effectiveness of public sector provision, such restructuring and reorientation has been characterised by efforts to replicate private sector management practices and culture in public sector settings. Collectively these changes have been encapsulated in the catch-all term 'new public management'. Although the concept of the new public management has been critiqued as lacking focus and precision, at the core of this evolving new management ethos in the public sector is a change in the relationship between service providers and users. From being a relationship couched in terms of citizenship with myriad mutual commitments and obligations on the part of the citizen, it is increasingly expressed in consumerist terms, with emphasis placed on the primacy of the rights of service users, both individually and collectively.

Source: Laing, A and Hogg, G (2002) 'Political exhortation, patient expectation and professional execution: perspectives on the consumerisation of health care', *British Journal of Management*, 13 (2).

Competition inevitably involves some organisations succeeding and others being not so successful. The problems of public sector 'failure' have been politically important with the emphasis on corporate governance, targets and performance indicators and many national and local organisations have looked for effective turnaround strategies. The challenge has been to find ways to bring weak parts of public sector services up to the standards achieved by the best service providers. These services have included, in recent years, the areas of the health service, education, transport, criminal justice and social services. Boyne's (2004) research into the study of turnaround suggests that there has been little consideration of this in the public sector and very much more in the private sector. He found that private companies were more likely to recover from failure if they followed a combination of the following strategies:

- retrenchment
- repositioning
- reorganisation.

The most dramatic form of retrenchment is to withdraw from a market completely, but this is difficult, if not impossible, for a public sector organisation because it will be under a statutory obligation to provide a service. A social services department, for example, cannot withdraw from the provision of child care because it is not coping, it will have to look for another solution. This could include new management or expanding the role of other organisations, including those in the voluntary or private sectors. Another approach is to sell assets, with examples in recent years being health authorities, local authorities and the Ministry of Defence selling off buildings and land surplus to requirements. This approach may release extra resources to help make efficiency gains, although these can also be secured without reducing the size of the service through cost cutting.

Repositioning may also be more difficult in the public sector than in the private sector. The scope for market entry may be difficult for public sector organisations because of their statutory obligations. For example, social service security benefit offices cannot move into areas of banking, although the experience gained in this service in moving money might suit this form of diversification. However, public sector organisations are able to diversify within the limitations that surround them. For example, libraries have widened their offerings from dealing with books to include compact discs and the provision of internet facilities. Also, public organisations may reposition themselves by enhancing the quality of their existing services (for example, by introducing shorter waiting lists for hospital appointments and operations, or providing greater reliability in the timing of refuse collections) or by providing entirely new services in existing markets (such as online hospital appointments, or early screening and scanning for a number of conditions). Another form of repositioning available to the public sector is to improve the internal and external image of an organisation. Improving the organisational image may help to convince stakeholders and service users of the repositioning and improvement in the organisation.

Reorganisation is another strategy to help public organisations to improve performance (Boyne *et al.*, 2003; Pollitt and Bouckaert, 2000). This process includes new planning and budgetary procedures, changes in organisational culture, different styles of human resource management and the decentralisation of organisational structures. For example, in the further education sector new budgetary and planning procedures for colleges helped to encourage customer-driven, outward-looking approaches to the provision of their services (Hannagan, 2003 and 2006). This example also helped to emphasise the importance of leadership in the public sector (Hannagan, 2006), which has been further illustrated by the moving of superheads into failing schools and the transfer of senior managers from three-star to no- star hospitals in the National Health Service. Legislation, regulations and controls limit the flexibility of public sector organisations to turn failure into success compared to those in the private sector. This means that managing a public organisation is as difficult, although different, to managing a private company.

Public organisations lack an economic market that provides them with resources in the form of revenue. In the private sector the buying behaviour of people is the primary source of information indicating which products and services are or are not effective. Public sector organisations are dependent on oversight bodies for resources or reimbursement for services based on funding formulas. These formulas may be based to some extent on market forces, or they may be based on public policies or other considerations. They may allow public organisations to avoid efficiency and effectiveness considerations until these are raised by the oversight bodies – and budget allocations from these bodies may follow historical precedents creating incentives for organisations to spend at previous levels whether or not spending has produced useful outcomes. These 'oversight' or funding bodies make up the 'market' for many public sector organisations. Universities and colleges are funded on the basis of student numbers and other factors, such as staying-on rates for students and student success, which are established by the funding body and may be changed over time. This means that colleges and universities have to change their offerings to meet the demands of the funding bodies in order to maximise funding. The degree of '**publicness**' as against '**privateness**' of an organisation is illustrated in Figure 4.2.

Publicness, in the sense of how far an organisation is in the public sector, declines if direct charges can be made, just as privateness increases as direct market dealing develops. The extent to which an organisation is in the public or private sector is indicated by the strength of market signals, the extent of competition, financial arrangements and the availability of data to provide information about potential customers. Competition for customers can be limited in public sector organisations because they may be expected to collaborate with other organisations offering similar services. Competing for customers would be seen as creating a duplication of services which may be felt to be undesirable, and new competitors may be discouraged by regulatory bodies.

Figure 4.2 Degrees of 'publicness'

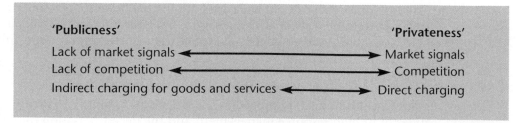

STRATEGIC MANAGEMENT IN THE PUBLIC SECTOR

It can be argued that strategic models that are competitive models are of little use in organisations with a significant degree of publicness because in the public sector strategy should be sought that enhances cooperation and collaboration. Strategic leaders in the public sector have to identify and appraise the historical context in which their organisations must operate. This is because issues arise from the tensions created by claims and counterclaims that characterise the beliefs of people who control public sector organisations and the demands of clients, politicians and professional and other stakeholders. Cumbersome mechanisms are needed in the public sector to deal with the logistics of consulting stakeholders and the public. Devices including governing bodies, advisory committees, task forces, public meetings and public announcements are used in order to determine expectations and refine understandings about what the organisation should do and how it should act.

Equity in dealing with clients and providing services may be more important than **efficiency** in the public sector, while efficiency dominates the concerns of the private sector. As publicness increases then efficiency and its comparatively clear cost-related goal become less useful and equity becomes more important. This means that an emphasis on efficiency may cause problems in the public sector. For example, libraries may find that the most efficient process is to keep books on the shelves, cut hours and limit the range of services, whereas most people want libraries to be open for long hours and want wide information services and encouraged book use. In these circumstances goals other than efficiency have to be established.

While **strategic management in the public sector** is undertaken to prompt action and discover agendas of activities that fit within political timeframes and to respond to consensual demands for change, private sector organisations use strategic management to provide an overview of activities and to slow activity rather than to prompt action. The concentration on efficiency means that strategic management in private organisations will be concerned with matters such as product viability. At the same time strategic planning in the public sector has to take into account the short-term considerations of politicians, who will tend to be looking for quick returns so that they can point to successes and achievements – they need to be confident about their ability to win the next election before they will look to the longer term. Public organisations may have a broader impact than private organisations in the sense that schools, for example, may be thought to be important in dealing with poverty, racism, child abuse, juvenile crime and other social problems – as well as their educational responsibilities. Everyone may feel they have an ownership stake in public organisations and so they are expected to show integrity, fairness, responsiveness, honesty and accountability to the public, while private organisations will have fewer implied obligations and people place fewer demands on them. The different priorities in strategic management in the public and private sectors is summarised in Table 4.2.

In the public sector, strategy may have to be developed with little support data. There may be limited information about markets and an unwillingness to divert funds into the collection of this information. At the same time it is difficult for public organisations to keep strategy and information secret. Outsiders may have a right to review and interpret information. Floating ideas to see what happens can be a problem in public settings, while strategy has to be devised in the face of public scrutiny. Demonstrations of involvement may be as important as good ideas and politics involves the managing of many stakeholders external to the organisation

Table 4.2 The different priorities of strategic management in the public and private sectors

PUBLIC SECTOR	PRIVATE SECTOR
Discover agendas	Product viability
Prompt action	Overview of activities
Equity	Efficiency
Meeting political/social obligations	Profit

who control or influence sources of money and whose support is essential. In private organisations politics seldom goes far beyond 'office politics' and coping with resistance to change.

Public sector managers have weaker power bases and less authority to alter or reshape the system they manage than private sector managers have. Autonomy and flexibility are generally lower in public organisations, making authority limits a key ingredient in defining publicness. For example, hospitals cannot promote service changes without the advice and consent of their medical staff, a group who may be more committed to their profession and to their particular service provision than to the organisation in which they are working. Consensus has to be established to accompany strategy formation. Encouraging effective performance by using incentives is much more difficult in public organisations than it is in private ones. It is generally more difficult to provide incentives in pay or other ways in order to enhance performance. In private organisations individuals' contributions to profit can be rewarded monetarily. Public sector employees may prefer job security, important tasks or power and recognition over financial rewards. Job security and promotion can only be given once and may not be available when a reward is needed, and linking people's performance to these rewards is more difficult than with financial rewards. Financial rewards can be tied to measurable performance in the private sector. Other means are needed to encourage productive behaviour in these circumstances and this calls for creativity in strategy formulation.

Strategy in any organisation can be seen as the process of achieving an essential fit between external threats and opportunities and internal competence. It can be defined as

> *'a pattern of purposes, policies, programmes, actions, decisions or resource allocations that define what an organization is, what it does, and why it does it.'* (Bryson, 1995)

It can be argued that strategic planning in the private sector is designed to slow down action in order to consider future actions, while in the public sector strategic planning is designed to prompt action. Strategy is often considered in terms of its military application: 'generalship or the art of conducting a campaign and manoeuvring an army' (Chambers, 1992), although this dictionary also describes 'strategy' as a 'long-term plan and a strategic position that gives its holder a decisive advantage.' In past battles a strategic position may have been to have the sun in the eyes of the enemy, or to face the sun and polish the army's shields so that the sun could be reflected into the enemy eyes – these strategic positions only provided a temporary advantage and a long-term plan was required. A more recent example was the government development of the Millennium Dome in London. It is an interesting structure, like a grounded flying saucer, but its contents in the millennium year showed little sign of an overall strategy beyond filling it in any way possible. There was a lack of a theme in the Dome's contents and in the longer run there was a lack of a plan about what to do with the structure after the millennium year. Porter (1996) came to the conclusion that

'strategy is creating fit among a company's activities [so that] if there is no fit among activities, there is no distinctive strategy.'

Whatever the activities of a public sector organisation, whether it is a police force, a university, a school, a hospital, a local council, an art gallery, a museum, a library or a broadcasting corporation, it needs a long-term strategy which involves a fit among these activities from which the organisation establishes a sense of purpose and direction.

THE PROBLEMS OF MANAGING IN THE PUBLIC SECTOR

It was reported in 2003 that the Ministry of Health was to appoint headhunters to

'seek high-powered managers to bring a harder hitting entrepreneurial culture to the boardrooms of the NHS in England.'   (Carvel, 2003)

It wanted young managers from the private sector to join the boards of hospitals and primary care trusts. At the same time the ministry announced a revolution to convert the National Health Service from a nationalised service into a network of competing providers, striving to give patients the best free health care. The start of this process was the establishment of so-called 'foundation hospitals' that are no longer under direct NHS ownership. The objective of moving private sector managers into the NHS and moving high-achieving hospitals out was to bring a decisive change in the culture of the NHS, which the Health Secretary believed was still locked in the attitudes of the 1940s.

The problems of private sector managers moving into the public sector has been highlighted by these initiatives. The chief executive of the NHS (Sir Nigel Crisp) was recruited from a private company and rose to become director of the London region of the NHS before promotion to the top job. He was understood to have known other private sector managers who took jobs in the NHS but who found the management style so alien that they left. In order to overcome this problem in this government initiative, recruits would be supported and mentored to help them in the new culture. Private sector managers have already been recruited or seconded to run central NHS facilities, including information technology and diagnostic and treatment centres. Also, a scheme has been introduced to build up a cohort of talented managers who could be placed in senior leadership roles in the NHS whenever they became available. The aim was to extend this approach into hospitals and primary care trusts which were the local bodies controlling most of the health budget in England.

A ministerial source was quoted as saying about the Health Secretary that

'he knows we have got to get out of the mindset that the only people who can be good managers are those who have come through the NHS route.'   (Carvel, 2003)

But Carvel, *The Guardian* Social Affairs Editor, recognised that this attitude was unlikely to win friends among public service professionals, who had experienced the failure of successive governments in their attempts to recruit from industry and the armed forces. It is likely that the most successful movement of managers from one sector to the other is in technical services such as information technology and accountancy, where the same or similar skills are required in both sectors. This may also apply to facilities management and human resource management, but the major obstacle remains the different mindset or culture of the two sectors. Changing mindsets is a notoriously difficult process and the problems arise in moving from the private sector into the public sector. The private sector manager arrives with a particular mindset into a situation where other mindsets are prevalent, and of course the mindset of managers from the armed forces will be different again.

An accountant who moved, after working for 30 years in private companies, to become the financial director of a further education college corporation felt that in this organisation, in contrast to the companies in which he had worked, managers did not have the on-the-job management training and development that they needed. He thought that in general, although the college had been independent of local authority control for some years,

> *'the mindset is still in local authority mode so that if there is any money left in the capital budgets bids are put in for it.'*   (Hannagan, 2003)

He was used to managers working out what they needed to deliver a product or service and then asking for it. He had found that entering the public sector after a long career in the private sector had been a

> *'cultural shock. In general people are better educated than in manufacturing industry, but everything becomes a debate, there is little discipline, everything is a debating society.'*   (Hannagan, 2003)

He also felt that there were limited sanctions in the public sector, so that while in the private sector 'if you do well you will earn a bonus and share options, if you do badly you are fired'. In contrast, he quoted the example of a senior member of his present staff who had made a serious mistake and had received a verbal warning. He thought that the college was poor at costing and that management information systems designed to help this process had developed slowly. As a result the college did not know which courses were viable and which were not, and even when a course was clearly unviable it was not closed down:

> *'an economic approach would mean that they were closed down, but where would local people go? They would have to travel long distances.'*   (Hannagan, 2003).

Mindsets can be seen as ways of working and expected ways of working, so that an officer in the armed forces may expect people to obey a command and will not expect much discussion. In the private sector senior managers will expect their orders and requests to be obeyed but will understand that these will have to fall within the job description of the employee. In the public sector an order or request may lead to a discussion about the reasons for it and its effects on the service. These differences arise because of the different organisational cultures that exist in various sectors of the economy. These so-called mindsets arise through exposure to particular organisational cultures and help to perpetuate them in the sense that a general view may be held that this is 'the way we do things around here' and this is 'the way we have always done things and should always do things' (see Chapters 1 and 2).

→ Chs 1 & 2

Doyle *et al.* (2000) have argued that the public sector was subjected to a variety of government-imposed changes in the 1990s based on 'managerialism' or 'the new public management'. These changes were multifaceted affecting funding, goals, structures, cultures and the role of management. While private sector organisations have implemented similar structural and cultural changes in the face of competitive pressures, these private concerns have not been directed to implement ideologically controversial changes based on shifts in government policy and priorities, or been subject to the gaze of the media, which may more readily publicise errors than successes. They also argue that the private sector has also not been constrained by powerful professional occupational groups, jealously guarded job demarcations, inflexible national pay systems, and rigid accounting and budgetary procedures.

ORGANISATIONAL CULTURE AND THE PUBLIC SECTOR

Meek (1988) thought that the concept of organisational culture could be

'a powerful analytical tool in the analysis and interpretation of human action within complex organisations.'

He argued that those intent on creating a healthy and successful corporate climate might concentrate on 'what is' in the pursuit of 'what should be', while corporate success could be more dependent on external influences of the marketplace than on internal interpersonal dynamics. He concluded that

'the assumption that a corporate culture can be created so as to unite members for the effective and efficient attainment of corporate goals flies in the face of almost everyone's experience of organisational life.'   (Meek, 1988)

His argument suggests that organisations are not one homogeneous culture, but multicultural. Although this can be seen in private sector companies, particular examples can be seen in public sector organisations such as tertiary education institutions and health services. For example, academics may have a greater allegiance to their profession than their institution and this could produce a conflict between the interests of the individual and the management of the institution. However, Meek did argue that there was a successful 'feel' about successful organisations and the difference between them and not so successful organisations went beyond explanations based on superior technology, efficient management and an advantageous position in the market. **Organisational culture** has been defined by Schein (1992) as

'a pattern of shared basic assumptions that a group learned as it solved its problems of external adaptation and internal integration, that have worked well enough to be considered valid and, therefore, to be taught to new members as the correct way to perceive, think and feel in relation to those problems.'

It is a complex mixture of tangible factors which can be seen and touched, such as an office space and its fixtures and fittings, assumptions about how people should behave in the organisation and people's actual behaviour.

'The culture of any group of people is that set of beliefs, customs, practices and ways of thinking that they have come to share with each other through being and working together. At the visible level the culture of a group takes the form of ritual behaviour, symbols, myths, stories, sounds and artefacts.'   (Stacey, 1999)

→ Chs 1 & 2

An organisation's culture is 'the way we do things around here' (see Chapter 1, pp. 15–17 and 23–7, and Chapter 2, pp. 46–52) and it may vary from office to office and department to department. In some offices the custom is to arrive at a particular time in the morning and leave at a particular time in the evening, in others the starting time is treated more casually and people feel they need to stay on as long as possible in the evenings to show how hard they are working. Some offices have traditional offices and desks, others are open plan with shared space and equipment, while others may have lounge areas, kitchens and mini-gyms. The factors which make up the culture of a group can be described as the TAB factors (Exhibit 4.3).

Group and organisational values and assumptions may be based on what has happened in the past, on leadership, on organisational structures and systems, on routine and ritual and power structures. The **assumptions** which are taken for granted are at the centre of an organisation's culture and are surrounded by **beliefs** which are more specific and **values** which may be strongly held but more difficult to put into practice (Figure 4.3). Peters and Waterman (1982) considered that organisations that were value driven were likely to be most successful, while Deal and Kennedy (1982) thought that organisations which shared strong and cohesive cultures were more likely to be flexible and cooperative and that transformation leadership could be a source of 'culture busting' to bring about strategic change. However, Pettigrew (1990) questioned to what extent cultures were in fact manageable because they were so embedded in organisations, and Newman (1994) suggested that culture prefigures the way in which strategy is made in a particular organisation. She thought that existing organisational culture would influence strategies that were developed in organisations and could blinker the perception of important strategic issues. She thought that change in the public sector involved radical changes to roles and boundaries within and between organisations so that fixed identities based on a profession, function or role were eroded and a sense of social purpose might clash with notions of progress.

Bryson (1995) argued that strategies were tailored to fit an organisation's culture, even if the purpose of the strategy was to change that culture in some way, and that the organisation's culture becomes more important during strategy formation because whatever patterns exist are typically manifestations of its culture. He argued that every organisation has an existing strategy, whether or not it is any good, which provided the pattern that supports its policies, decisions, resource allocations and other actions. This pattern, which was typically a manifestation of its culture, would need to be refined or sharpened or (less frequently) changed altogether for it to provide an effective bridge between the organisation and its environment. In the UK this environment began to change in the 1980s as public sector organisations had to become customer-oriented, entrepreneurial, innovative, flexible and responsive. Newman (1994) suggested that it was at this time that the public sector discovered 'culture' as a key dimension of change.

Exhibit 4.3 Organisational culture – the TAB factors

- Tangible factors – physical conditions
- Assumptions – expected attitudes and behaviour
- Behaviour – how people actually behave

Figure 4.3 Layers of culture within an organisation

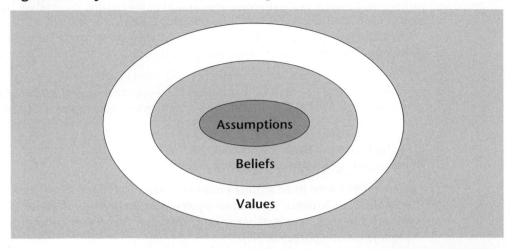

Newman argued that although there were elements of shared values in the public sector, in many cases cultures divided along departmental, functional or professional lines with different sets of values and practices. Consensus could be difficult in the public sector where conflict might arise between professional and old public sector values as against newly encouraged business and market-based values. She felt that assumptions based on the idea that culture was generated by, and centred on, the leader took little account of the complex dynamics in the public sector. She suggested that culture could not be separated from strategic change because the process of change was intimately intertwined with cultural norms and values. She argued that in the past those working in the public sector were able to operate within a framework of meanings about their role as public servants, with a sense of purpose based on doing good or benefiting society, and this was in exchange for a certain status and security. Strategic change produced conflicts over meanings, exposed conflicting values, created shifts in power bases and realigned groups. Individuals learned the rhetoric of new values and adopted new cultural symbols in order to defend or expand their power base.

Although organisational culture is an important element for the leadership of a public sector organisation to consider in the process of change, in extreme situations it may be swept aside because of an overriding priority. Accountability to the dominant stakeholder may be so important for a public sector organisation that the existing culture may be overridden in the need for change, in spite of the opposition of professionals. As a result of the 1992 Further and Higher Education Act, colleges of further education in England became corporate bodies limited by guarantee. Most of their funding came from a funding council and in order to achieve this funding they had to reach a number of targets in terms of student numbers and unit costs. In order to achieve these targets some colleges were prepared to put aside the organisational culture that existed (Hannagan, 2003, 2006). This raises questions on the views of Meek (1988) that culture was not an independent variable to be altered by the efforts of managers, it was something an organisation *is* rather than something an organisation *has*, although it supports Bryson's (1995) view that sometimes, although rarely, culture could be changed altogether in order for it to provide an effective bridge between the organisation and its environment. When the external pressures change dramatically, as was the case with colleges of further education in 1993, culture may have to change in order that the organisation can survive and clear environmental assessment and strong leadership become paramount for organisational success (Hannagan, 2006).

Organisational culture in the public sector is often strongly held but it has been challenged by developments in the last 20 or 30 years. A director of personnel stated that

> *'cultural change has been slow although it is easier with new staff, but staff who come to the college from industry soon become indoctrinated with the old culture.'*

(Hannagan, 2003)

In the report on their research in the UK National Health Service, McNulty and Whittington (1992) quoted a doctor as saying

> *'as a doctor I have three distinct priorities of loyalty. My first loyalty must always be to my individual patients. My second loyalty must be to my profession's standards and my third loyalty, and putting it third does not mean it is rubbish, is to whoever employs me at a particular time.'*

They identified conflicts between the organisation and the professional working in it in disputes over professional freedom and the preservation and development of professional standards so that cultural homogeneity (a feature of excellent organisations identified by Peters and Waterman, 1982) was difficult to achieve in public sector organisations. At English Heritage it was noted (in Davidson, 2005) that many of the employees of the organisation

> *'as is common in not-for-profit organisations – are passionate about what they do and don't want their working lives hemmed in. People work here because they love the job. They love the contact with the buildings and the opportunity to get involved with the sites, and the organisation is the vehicle that enables them to do that.'*

Public sector organisations have conflicting obligations which make it difficult to develop the homogeneous culture that may be possible in private organisations. Public sector values can be described as pluralistic in the sense that there are a range of loyalties and stakeholders.

A major difference between the two sectors is that the public sector has an obligation to provide a public service whether it is in terms of health, learning, conservation or law and order. Public sector organisations have a responsibility to satisfy social obligations in providing jobs, making 'good citizens' and ensuring publicly responsible behaviour, and they may also be seen to have an economic obligation in encouraging economic growth and providing economic leverage effects on the economy. At the same time public sector organisations are not profit-making and they cannot redefine themselves. They may be allowed to retain surpluses but they do not have an overriding objective to provide returns for their shareholders. They are not established in order to make profits and therefore their approach is more 'soft-edged' than a private sector organisation. Also they cannot change the whole nature of their operation in the way that is open to private sector organisations. They are established for a particular purpose, such as providing education or health services, and they have to continue to do this. They can diversify within this brief to some extent but they cannot change the main thrust of their activities. James Strachan, who has been managing director of Merrill Lynch and chairman of the Audit Commission, has been quoted as arguing that calculated risk can be a route to success in the public sector:

'It's important to change the culture, to alter the gross imbalance between the reward for success and the punishment for failure, which prevents people in the public sector putting their heads above the parapet.'   (Cook, 2004)

These are fundamental differences between the two sectors, which are reflected in their cultures. The private sector culture is a profit-driven one, where competition has to be met and the disciplines of the market apply. Organisational objectives are based around profit margins, share of the market and product and service viability and these concerns are passed down to individual managers and operatives. Jobs and remuneration depend on the success of the organisation. Individuals can be rewarded for the contribution they make to this success and they will lose their jobs if the organisation, or their part of it, is not successful. The public sector culture is a service-driven one where the needs of the people receiving the service have to be met and the disciplines implied by this apply. Organisational objectives are based around the successful provision of this service and the satisfying of various stakeholders, which include the public, and these concerns are passed down to individual managers and operatives. Jobs depend on stakeholder support for the provision of this service, while remuneration depends on historical precedents, bargaining power and by a concept of 'worth' based on public or other perceptions. Individuals may not be rewarded in a tangible form for their contribution to the success of the organisation, the reward may be in the form of satisfaction. There may be a concept of people following a vocation used in the sense of a 'calling' in which matters of remuneration are secondary to the provision of the service.

THE 'PRIVATISATION' OF THE PUBLIC SECTOR

Since the 1980s governments in the UK have tried to introduce elements of private sector culture into the public sector. The reason for this approach has been the increasing awareness of the cost of providing public services, pressures on national budgets and attempts to increase efficiency in the provision of public services. The actual situation of every service varies depending on the service they provide and the recipients of that service. For example, the ageing population of the country has put pressure on the National Health Service as the demand for services for older people has increased and the increase in the number of retired people means that fewer people are contributing to the National Insurance which pays for the service. At the same time medical advances have meant that more and more expensive procedures are now available at a cost, and there is simultaneously an increase in people's expectations of what they are entitled to receive. The cost of the NHS has risen and one way of meeting this rise has been to charge directly for an increasing range of services. The increased 'privatisation' of the public sector has been reflected in the increasing use of management consultants in the sector and the use of temporary management experts or 'interim managers'. The public sector provided 13 per cent of overall revenue for the largest consultancy firms in 2002 compared with 9 per cent in 2000, along with an increase in the use of interims to bridge gaps and improve quality. The increasing use of consultants in the UK was closely linked to the provision of accounting advice and associated information technology advice and, as was noted at the beginning of this chapter, accounting knowledge remained concentrated in one of the governmental *grand corps*.

Contractual arrangement such as Public Private Partnership (PPP) deals have been an approach to developing a link between public organisations and private companies. The London Underground's PPP arose from a simpler Private Finance Initiative (PFI) to establish contracts between the local authority-controlled London Underground and the two infrastructure companies Tube Lines and MetroNet. They were contracted to reduce lost customer hours and journey time and to improve the cleanliness and performance of the Underground service. London Underground's managing director has described the PPP contract as 'hard to manage, rigid and over-complex, but we just have to get on with it' (Saunders, 2006). The purpose of this type of public/private link-up is to provide private sector managers with space to use their knowledge, skills and experience, while retaining a publicly controlled means of holding the private companies to account, and while enabling private capital to be invested in public services. Christian Wolmar (who has written a book on the Underground) is quoted by Saunders (2006) as saying

'the PPP is just a daft way to procure. You can't issue 30-year maintenance contracts, there are just too many variables. Technology moves on, the kind of solutions we want when the contracts were drawn up may not be the ones we want in 30 years' time.'

However, these forms of contractual arrangement are being widely adopted for public projects on the railways, for hospitals, schools and universities. For example, the University Partnership Programme (UPP) involves universities retaining the freehold of a property while the buildings are operated by a commercial company. In 2002 Oxford Brookes University established a partnership to develop its student accommodation, with the UPP taking a 30-year lease on the site while the university retained the freehold. At the end of the partnership the site will revert to Oxford Brookes ownership for a nominal sum. Student accommodation, care homes and other public sector areas are seen as good areas in which to invest because they do not necessarily have the same fluctuations in value as properties and services in the private sector. While public sector organisations can free themselves to some extent of both expenditure and risk, private companies can make lucrative investments and profits. The CEO of Tube Lines has been quoted as saying that he would rather make a profit than not make one (Saunders, 2006), which illustrates the clash of cultures that can occur in these forms of partnership. Public sector managers can find that these contractual arrangements are a strong 'privatising' influence.

This introduction of private sector culture into the public sector has taken a number of forms and Exhibit 4.4 provides an example of 'privatisation' and the degree of free enterprise introduced, along with the controls imposed by a government-established and – controlled body. These controls included organisational objectives and the types of service which were to be provided.

Newman (1994) suggested that the public sector discovered 'culture' in the late 1980s as a key dimension of change, as public sector organisations had to become customer-oriented, entrepreneurial, innovative, flexible and responsive. Changes brought about by moves towards privatisation produced conflicts over meanings, exposed conflicting values, created shifts in power bases and realigned groups. Individuals learned the rhetoric of new values and adopted new cultural symbols in order to defend or expand their power base. Newman argued that strategy, culture and change interacted to produce tensions and ambiguities.

In further education colleges the pressure was to become more 'business like' after incorporation because they were working in a more competitive market and

Exhibit 4.4 The 'privatisation' of further education in England

In further education in England, the Further and Higher Education Act (1992) established further education colleges as public sector corporations with the power to employ people, earn and borrow money and decide how to spend their budgets. The dictionary definition of a corporation is '*a body or society authorised by law to act as one individual unit ... such as a company*' (Chambers, 1992). Further education corporations were like private companies in that they could employ people, borrow money, decide how to spend the money they received, decide how to use their assets, including their buildings, and decide how they achieved their strategic objectives. However, they did not have complete freedom to choose these objectives because they were established to a large extent by their stakeholders.

The chief stakeholder was the Further Education Funding Council (FEFC), which was superseded by the Learning and Skills Council in 2001. The council was the conduit for funds to flow from the government to the college corporations. In return for these funds, colleges had to provide part-time and full-time education for people over compulsory school age. At the same time the government established targets to be met by the corporation, including an expansion of 25 per cent in student numbers in three years, increased efficiency and an ability for the colleges to demonstrate that they were contributing to the economic success of the locality and the nation. Providing colleges met these objectives, they could earn money in other ways and spend their money in any way they wished. The clear mission of colleges was in terms of providing education and training services to people over the age of 16 mainly, but not exclusively, from their locality. Most of the funds they received were in practice tied to the provision of particular services required by the stakeholders. At the same time the governing body of each college became the corporation board while the principal became the chief executive.

had to become more productive and efficient in order to prosper. The gap between managers' and their need to meet efficiency targets, and practitioners and their professionalism was emphasised by these changes. Dunleavy and Hood (1994) suggested that traditionally the public sector was built on the idea of a highly distinctive public sector group and a dense grid of general procedural rules governing the conduct of its activities. The changes that occurred made the public sector less distinctive from the private sector in areas such as personnel policies, reward structure and methods of doing business, and also reduced the extent to which discretionary power was limited by uniform and general rules of procedure, particularly over staff, contracts and money. The direction of change was in terms of the reworking of budgets to make them more transparent in accounting terms, and viewing public sector organisations as a chain of principal–agent relationships with a network of contracts linking incentives to performance and disaggregating separable functions into quasi-contractual or quasi-market forms.

It can be argued (Dunleavy and Hood, 1994) that corporatisation falls short of full privatisation and is an unsatisfactory halfway house between the traditional structure of public administration and a system based on enforceable contracts and individual legal rights. As the central government planning role is eroded there could be a failure of guidance, administrative advice and outside expertise, while a narrow range of performance targets might cause managers to push through cost-minimising changes. There was also a risk of public services reflecting the interests of senior public servants rather that those of the service users, and public sector organisations might be reshaped in the format that suited the personal interests of senior managers. At the same time the service could be less accountable and accessible to the public, even if services were reformed with contrary aims and objectives. Big differences in pay levels between public and private sectors limited the degree to which really capable private sector managers with a strong track record could be brought into public bodies, so that a *de facto* public sector corps of managers remained in place.

There is evidence (Hannagan, 2003) that the incorporation model applied to further education did release pent-up forces of dynamism and entrepreneurship, ended ossified structures and encouraged innovation and competition. Structures were reformed, innovation was encouraged and competition had to be faced. However, Dopson and Stewart (1990) considered that public sector managers were cautious because accomplishments often went unrecognised, while mistakes were widely publicised and ridiculed. They questioned whether private sector management concepts could be transferred to the public sector and argued that public sector managers were likely to be less positive about new managerial practices than their counterparts in the private sector because of reduced public spending, the demands of central government for economies and low pay. Change created a demand for greater leadership at all levels, while traditional public sector managers were looked on more as administrators. At the same time private sector managers were more in control of the resources they needed to achieve their objectives than managers in the public sector.

NON-PROFIT ORGANISATIONS AND PROFITS

The pressure on public sector and other non-profit managers, such as those in charities, voluntary bodies and non-governmental organisations (NGOs) to adopt some of the methods and approaches of the private sector has also encouraged them to look for profit-making opportunities. Foster and Bradach (2005) argue that this search for profits is as much for social as economic reasons.

> *'The general enthusiasm for business, which reached a fever pitch during the booming 1990s, has had a profound impact on nonprofits and the institutions that support them. Like their counterparts in the commercial world, managers of non-profit organisations want to be viewed as active entrepreneurs rather than as passive bureaucrats and launching a successful commercial venture is one direct route to that goal. Board members, many of whom are accomplished business leaders, often encourage and reinforce that desire.'*

This argument has been very clearly supported in the UK by developments in the further education sector in the 1980s and 1990s. The 1985 Further Education Act allowed local authorities and colleges to set up companies and conduct commercial activities. As a result of this colleges established companies to take advantage of government grants and contracts and to be involved in entrepreneurial activity. For most colleges this activity was limited to little more than 2 per cent of college budgets (Hannagan, 2003) but in some cases it was carried much further to include involvement in leisure centres and shops and other areas of commercial activity.

For example, Bilston College saw an active role for itself in economic regeneration (Reeves, 1997). In a few cases, including that of Bilston College, this was an important element in the financial problems that some colleges experienced.

There has been some pressure on non-profit organisations to become self-sufficient, or at least to promote earned income as a means to sustainability in order to make them appear more disciplined, innovative and businesslike to their stakeholders. Foster and Bradach found in their research that there was a gap between the hype and the reality of the contribution of entrepreneurial activity to non-profit budgets.

> *'Earned income accounts for only a small share of funding in most nonprofit domains, and few of the ventures that have launched actually make money. Moreover, when we examined how nonprofits evaluate possible ventures, we discovered a pattern of unwarranted optimism. The potential financial returns are often exaggerated, and the challenges of running a successful business are routinely discounted.'*
>
> (Foster and Bradach, 2005)

Just as important as this consideration is that commercial ventures can distract public sector non-profit managers from their core mission and objectives, or even subvert these aims. There is a difference between a public sector organisation charging for some of its services directly or indirectly, or taking advantage of government grants, and operating in the profit-making commercial sector. Colleges and universities charge fees to students and provide commercial training facilities as an offshoot of the expertise contained within the organisation, hospitals may charge for private rooms or some of its services, doctors may charge for signing particular forms and so on, but these are relatively minor adjuncts to the main business of a university, a hospital or a surgery. These organisations could not survive without public funding and although charging for services and involvement in commercial activities may provide a proportion of their income, their whole structure and constitution, the rules under which they operate are based on their public funding. Public sector organisations tend to overlook or underestimate the operating costs of commercial ventures, including management costs, the cost of facilities and other overhead expenses and claims of profitability may ignore start-up costs and other expenses that face commercial operators.

The gap between the rhetoric and the reality of earned income from commercial activities in the non-profit sector may be the result of a lack of realism in evaluating the challenge of running a business. Public sector organisations have difficulty in this area because of:

- conflicting priorities;
- a lack of business perspective;
- an unwillingness to close down commercial activities.

Public sector managers are likely to carry over their employment and other practices into their commercial enterprises, even if these are not appropriate or viable. There may also be social and other objectives which conflict with the priority to make profits. Small businesses very often have a problem in clearly distinguishing between revenue and profit and this is true also of public sector managers. Indirect costs may be ignored or the cost of people's time, and the classic problem can arise that it is easy to sell products or services but it is more difficult to sell at a profit. When it is realised that an enterprise is facing financial problems then public sector managers may keep it going by putting more money into it rather than face failure.

Foster and Bradach (2005) give the example of a non-profit organisation that had the objective of providing teenagers with a safe after-school environment with Internet access, at no cost to itself. It found a building, received a government grant to refurbish it and was able to rent out parts of the building it was not going to use. However, the rental income did not cover the lease and maintenance costs so the organisation launched an additional income earning activity, an after-school café. The teenagers could not afford or were not interested in the offerings of the café and, rather than close the facility, the hours of the café were extended and it was opened for adults.

> *'The results are not yet known but the likelihood of success seems low. What remains is the picture of a well-intentioned non-profit venture, which had simply intended to offer Internet access to teenagers, on its way to building a large, money-losing conglomerate encompassing property management and food services.'*

(Foster and Bradach, 2005)

Earning income through commercial enterprises may be attractive to public sector managers because it can free, at least to some extent, the organisation from the strings attached to government funds so that the income can be used for whatever purposes the managers feel are important. However, public sector managers need to consider their priorities as much as the venture's financial potential.

MARKETING AND ENVIRONMENTAL ASSESSMENT

The differences between the two sectors can be particularly seen in such areas as marketing, environmental assessment and customer focus. The marketing function is critical to the private sector, leading to an emphasis on the relation of the company to its customers. Public sector organisations have many relationships with the public as customers, clients and citizens, so that as well as being concerned with market demand, a public sector organisation also has to be concerned with public need. Whereas the private sector organisation is accountable to the market, the public sector is accountable to a range of people and bodies and to the public at large. The public sector has to explain and justify its actions to a wider stakeholder interest than the private sector and pressure groups have a particularly significant influence because resources are both finite and limited and are distributed as an act of political will. This creates an immediate dilemma for the application of consumer principles. The public domain may be used to reconcile interests that may not be reconcilable and to meet aspirations that may not be capable of attainment, while the private sector organisation resolves such dilemmas by defining them out of its area of concern.

The fundamental dilemma of the public sector can be illustrated by reference to the British health services where the demand for health care always outstrips the supply of it. The level of demand has risen almost exponentially, while the willingness to pay has not. The developments in science and technology, social changes such as the ageing population, changing lifestyles such as those causing obesity, patterns of disease with a decline in some but an increase in others such as cancer and Aids, and changes in the economy, including levels of employment, all place pressures on the health services and the managers in the service.

Marketing is essential for the private sector because profits can only be achieved by meeting customer needs. Producing goods and services in the hope that people will want them is not a recipe for success in a competitive market. The 'privatisation' of the public sector has introduced competition into the market for some public sector organisations. In the research carried out by the author in the further education sector this was seen as one of the main causes of change in nearly 90 per cent of the colleges surveyed (Hannagan, 2003). The attitude to competition was a distinguishing feature of the colleges in this research, with the more successful colleges recognising the increased competition they faced after the barriers to it were removed at incorporation, while the less successful colleges wanted either to ignore it or believe that they could not do anything about it. The more successful colleges responded to competition by reacting to it either in an instinctive and unstructured way or through a structured approach to marketing, branding and a consumer focus (Hannagan, 2006). The evidence suggested that while the instinctive approach could be successful in the short run, long-term and steady success depended on well-organised market research, environmental assessment and customer care. Exhibit 4.5 illustrates the use of market research in the public sector.

In some areas of the public sector the importance of marketing has been recognised after 'privatisation', so that in the public utilities, for example, competition has encouraged organisations such as British Telecommunications, British Gas and the electricity boards to greatly enhance their marketing and customer care programmes. These are organisations that have been almost completely privatised, with share capital and profits replacing their public sector requirements. As in any organisation, whether in the public or private sector, the actual functioning of marketing and other aspects of management have to be adapted to the needs of the organisation and its market.

CONCLUSION

The two main differences between management in the private sector and the public sector are, in terms of accountability taken in a wide sense of the term, in the need to make profits and in the ability to decide on the nature of the business:

Exhibit 4.5 Marketing in the public sector

One view of marketing in a college of further education was that *'marketing is sticking adverts in the paper'*, another view was *'we know what we want, we provide the right courses and they can come and do them'* and *'we provide what they [students] want, because they don't know themselves'*. In contrast to these approaches, in another college of further education a director of marketing was appointed at a senior management level. She carried out detailed market research so that the college knew its customers in the form of students and potential students. She also carried out market research into the schools that provided the main supply of students, as well as into employers in the locality of the college and other organisations which could supply college customers or clients. She had segmented the college market and developed a brand for each segment, and she had developed a 'customer service' unit that staffed the college reception service and provided information and promotional materials. She had produced a detailed marketing plan and she had attempted to integrate marketing into the activities of the college, so that the marketing plan was felt in this college to be an essential element in its strategic management.

'Whatever the convergence between the two sectors, it can be noted that private sector organizations are responsible to shareholders for their profits, are governed by customer sovereignty and can choose their function and area of operation within these restraints. Public sector organizations on the other hand are responsible for their operation and solvency to their stakeholders, they have a duty to service public needs and to provide public value and their function and area of operation will be limited by statute.'
(Hannagan, 2006)

Private organisations are accountable to their shareholders and owners, and to their customers. Public organisations are accountable to the government or a government agency and to the public as well as to their customers. While they need to remain financially viable they do not need to make profits and they have to provide the service for which they were established. They have to meet public need and add 'public value' (Moore, 1995), so that the particular problem for public sector managers is in satisfying both the need for accountability and the need to provide a public service and this requires particular skill in the leadership of public sector organisations. Heymann (1987) explained that while public management was like business management in many respects, in one very important respect it was different, and that was that public managers were politically accountable. While Moore (1995) argued that the justification for managerial action in the public sector was the preferences that arose from representative processes, the aim of managerial work in the public sector is to create **public value**, just as the aim of managerial work in the private sector is to create private value.

If the privatisation of public sector organisations is taken to its logical conclusion, the organisation is moved into the private sector and has shares, but many organisations remain in the public sector with varying degrees of 'privatisation'. The degree to which this process impinges on the work and success of the organisation helps to determine the amount of private sector management function that it needs to acquire. The Institute of Public Policy Research has suggested that some public services could be improved by setting up public interest companies on the model of the NHS foundation trusts and housing associations. The distinctive feature of these companies is that, while they deliver a public service, they are independent of the state and do not have shareholders thus avoiding the difficulties of delivering complex public services through shareholder-owned companies in which public needs may conflict with those of the shareholders. In general, in terms of management the differences between the two sectors suggests that the managers working in them need to approach their tasks differently, although they are essentially carrying out similar functions.

SUMMARY

■ There are important differences between management in the public sector and in the private sector, as well as similarities. The process of management in both sectors is concerned with managing people so that as a result similar problems arise.

■ The major distinguishing factors in the public sector are stakeholder accountability, a service rather than a profit motive and the concept of public value rather than market forces.

■ As market forces and competition increase in the public sector, the degree of 'publicness' in public sector organisations decreases.

- Managers in the public sector have to take more account of political and social obligations than their counterparts in the private sector.
- Organisational culture is important in strategic management in both sectors, although there are differences because public sector culture tends to be service-driven, while private sector culture is profit-driven.

Review and discussion questions

1 *What are the differences between management in the public sector and in the private sector?*

2 *Why is stakeholder accountability so important in the public sector?*

3 *There has been a trend towards more 'privateness' in the public sector organisations in the UK in the last two decades. What does this mean and what is its importance?*

4 *What is meant by the concept of 'public value'? How does the concept of a 'customer' apply in public sector organisations?*

5 *Discuss the importance of organisational culture in public and private sector organisations and the differences between organisational culture in the two sectors.*

CASE STUDY

Creativity, leadership and change

When I arrived in the civil service nearly a decade ago one of my Benefits Agency directors said to me in my first week: 'You need to understand that the civil service is the culture of the written word.' I have often reflected just how right he was – and, of course, local government was not that different. The trouble is that words are of limited value. 'What I hear I forget, what I see I remember, what I do I know', which, roughly translated, means that no one was ever inspired by a memo. No one's life was ever changed by a carefully crafted paper to ministers. No one ever made a major creative breakthrough writing a report. Words can stultify creativity, slowing things down and encouraging the search for theoretical perfection at a time when you should be more concerned with momentum and action. Too much paper isn't just a costly frustration, it strangles creativity.

There is no better time to look forward with optimism than the start of a new millennium. To think afresh about how we want to modernise this country's public services. But it is time to look back too, and to ask ourselves what lessons have been drawn from the recent past. Just what have the past twenty years meant for the public services? Are there

lessons as we turn to the future? ... Looking back, I am ... struck by the way in which we seem increasingly to have assumed that the success of our economy, and indeed the success of our society and our public services, depends primarily on the success and profitability of the private wealth-creating sector. Certainly a strong dynamic private sector is vitally important; but success depends on coupling that with a vibrant creative public sector capable of anticipating and planning for change and facilitating economic success ...

Creativity is, by definition, an act of courage because it requires making connections which are out of the ordinary. This exposes you to potential ridicule and to above-average levels of risk. In the public sector, this is an additional problem because the prevailing climate is so risk-averse – partly because of an innate conservatism, partly because politicians tend not to relish unpleasant surprises and partly because the accountability frameworks are unsympathetic to risks which go wrong. In addition, my experience has been that telling public servants that they should take risks can open the floodgates to abdication and anarchy.

▶

On the other hand, we have to face up to the risk issue because it is the reason given by many public servants for eschewing innovation and creativity. Merely to exhort people to take risks is to leave them dangerously exposed. We need to help people to manage risk, which means helping to identify it, to develop a nose for it; it means helping them to develop the skills to define risk – is it financial, political or more to do with personal/individual credibility; and to assess the scale of the risk, whether in crude terms it is acceptable or unacceptable; it means ensuring people take reasonable steps to minimise risk. All of which may well take the form of getting alongside staff who are involved in creative activities and sharing the risk with them.

Finally, we, the leaders in the public sector, have a responsibility to help change the accountability frameworks so that they not only say they will look kindly on a well-managed risk which goes wrong, but that they actually do it. Whether or not someone is prepared to take a risk will depend upon the level of trust they are feeling. So certain organisations are likely to be organisations with high levels of trust, and creative teams are likely to trust their leader ... this suggests to me that organisations which will find creativity most difficult are organisations which are:

- hierarchical
- centralist
- prescriptive
- analytical/judgemental
- introspective/exclusive
- deferential
- risk-averse
- word bound
- controlling (people and resources)
- status-conscious
- poor listeners
- conflictual.

Regrettably, these words seem to me to have a pretty good match with the traditional public sector culture. Or to put it more positively – the kind of organisations most likely to be creative have fewer organisational levels, high management trust, active flow of ideas, effective idea management processes, routine future envisioning, managers who challenge, a balanced view of risk-takers, managers who delegate and managers who involve outsiders.

Source: Extracted from M Bichard (2000) 'Creativity, leadership and change', *Public Money and Management*, April/June. Sir Michael Bichard was Permanent Secretary at the Department of Education and Employment (DfEE) until 2001.

FURTHER READING

Bryson, J M (1995) *Strategic Planning for Public and Non-profit Organisations*, Jossey-Bass.
A discussion of strategic management in the public sector.

Cook, S (2004) 'Public attraction', *Management Today*, January.
An article on public sector culture and its effect on decisions in public sector organisations.

Dunleavy, P and Hood C (1994) 'From old public administration to new public management', *Public Money and Management*, Summer.
This article highlights the changes in public sector management that began in the 1980s and continue today.

Hannagan, T J (2006) 'Leadership and environmental assessment in further education', *Journal of Further and Higher Education*, November, 30 (4).
Describes research into an area of the public sector identifying important elements in the management of organisations.

Porter, M E (1996) 'What is strategy?', *Harvard Business Review*, November/December.
A classic study of strategic management in organisations.

WEBSITES

www.meb.co.uk/ijpsm.htm
Website of the *International Journal of Public Sector Management*.

www.publicnet.co.uk
For everybody interested in the public sector and its management.

www.blackwellpublishing.com
Website of the *Journal of Public Money and Management*.

www.cipfa-org-uk/
Website of the Chartered Institute of Public Finance and Accountancy (CIPFA).

www.statistics-gov.uk
National statistics online.

SECTION B

MANAGING STRATEGY

What is strategy? Why is strategic management important to managers at all levels? What is the difference between strategy and planning? What are the competitive forces affecting corporate strategy? How is corporate strategy implemented? What are the barriers to organisational planning and how can these be overcome? What is the importance of organisational development? How are business plans developed? What does quality mean in terms of industry and commerce? How are quality systems introduced and managed in organisations? Why is quality control important in terms of strategic management? How important is organisational culture in relation to strategic management? What is marketing? Why are marketing and environmental assessment essential for the management of strategy in all organisations?

Strategic management is concerned with the overall positioning and direction of an organisation and can be seen as a vital management activity of concern to managers at all levels. Modern management practices provide more opportunities than in the past for managers to be involved with the strategy of their organisations. Strategy can be developed through a process and through planning, although there is a difference between strategy and planning. A strategy to ensure total quality management is an important factor in meeting customer needs. Marketing and environmental assessment are essential in meeting customer needs.

CHAPTER 5

Managing a creative strategy

Outcomes

Having read this chapter, you will be able to:

- analyse the importance of strategic management;

- explain the role of planning in management;

- apply strategic management and planning to the process of developing corporate strategy;

- identify the factors influencing the corporate portfolio;

- analyse the competitive forces affecting corporate strategy.

WHAT IS STRATEGIC MANAGEMENT?

Strategic management consists of decisions and actions used to formulate and implement strategies that will provide a competitively superior fit between the organisation and its environment to enable it to achieve organisational objectives. It is about establishing a competitive advantage. It is not the same as strategic planning, although it may involve it, in that planning is associated with activity carried out a little apart from the line management of an organisation and reviewed at periodic well-defined intervals. Strategic planning tends to be associated with medium or long-term planning trends which are extrapolated for the key business variables and assumes a future point at which the organisation will arrive. This may inform support and act as a tool for strategic management, which is concerned with establishing a competitive advantage, sustainable over time, not simply by tactical manoeuvring but by taking an overall long-term perspective which directly influences line management. Strategic management is about achieving a sustained advantage for an organisation and positioning it correctly, while providing a yardstick against which it can measure its performance, as well as developing a plan of implementation and carrying out this plan.

Strategic management is about enabling an organisation to move from its present position to one it wants to be in to align it with its objectives and with the environment in which it is working. It can be considered to be the most complex task facing a manager because a strategic direction has to be established in an unknown future in the face of a range of choices, in a volatile and dynamic environment and involving everybody in the organisation. While strategic management is involved in all areas of management and the working of an organisation, it is not the same as day-to-day management because strategic management is concerned with issues affecting the fundamentals of an organisation while day-to-day, or operational, management may be concerned largely with keeping an organisation ticking over.

Operational management provides for organisation, control and supervision while strategic management provides a sense of purpose. Companies of all sizes – schools, universities, hospitals, charities and all other organisations – will have a purpose, whether it is to make profits, maintain market share, promote educational achievement, provide good health or to support particular groups of people. Operational management is essential because in order to achieve these purposes a variety of management functions has to be carried out. Strategic management emphasises the challenge to modern managers in maintaining dynamic roles in organisations, which requires great management skill given the speed of change in their environment.

→ Ch. 8

The PESTLE, STEP or SPECTACLES factors (described in Chapter 8) are the environment of an organisation – that is everything that influences its success or failure. These factors may include competition from other companies, uncertainty about raw material supplies, price fluctuations, government legislation and even natural disasters. The speed of change means that managers have to be prepared to constantly redevelop and reconstruct their company, so that as well as being operational they have to provide strategic leadership. They have to look ahead in a way which is more complicated than simply planning a journey in order to travel, or even just to arrive at a destination, because it involves taking into account constant changes in the organisation's working environment as well as changes in the organisation's personnel and competencies.

Strategic management is ambiguous and complex because the objective of a company may be very clearly defined but the way to achieve it may not be obvious. A company may have as its objective 'to increase market share' and this may be more closely defined by identifying a target percentage which the company hopes to achieve. The way to realise this objective may be obvious to start with but the reaction to these early moves and other changes in the environment may provide obstacles to its achievement. It is at this point that an underlying strategy is required, an approach that will enable the organisation to survive and prosper even after temporary setbacks.

In military terms, *strategos* is Greek for 'general', who is the strategist who plans the whole campaign, while the lower ranks of the army are the people who operationally make sure that troops and equipment are in the right places at the right time. Drucker (1961) has described strategy as

'the pattern of major objectives, purposes or goals and essential policies or plans for achieving these goals, stated in such a way as to define what business the company is in or is to be in and the kind of company it is or is to be.'

Strategic issues are attempts to answer such questions as: Who are our customers? Who are our competitors? What products and services should we offer? How can we offer these products and services most efficiently? These questions help to focus the attention of managers on how to position their organisation in relation to rival organisations. These decisions affect the long-term direction of the company and are usually concerned with gaining some advantage for the company.

Strategic decisions can be thought of as the search for an effective position for an organisation in relation to competitors in order to achieve an advantage. The 'position' is where the business sees itself in its market, which may be in terms of total market share, but also involves the '**positioning**' of each of the company products and services. This has to be based on a thorough analysis of the organisation's capacity to manage the five competitive forces (see page 159) identified by Porter (1998), so that when these change, the organisation's strategic position should be reviewed. When Charles Allen became the first CEO of ITV in 2003 he instigated a wholesale review of the organisation. 'I've got a sense of vision and desire as to what I want ITV to become,' he is reported to have said (Blackhurst, 2006). 'What we want to create now is a multimedia, multiplatform business. ITV has to reinvent itself.' His belief was that everything was moving in the direction of one home entertainment centre including TV programmes, computer games, Internet and communications. 'Four or five years from now, nobody will differentiate between the screens in their home, they will do everything.' Part of the repositioning of ITV involved management and structural changes along with a clear view that the crucial objective of the company was its share of the commercial market. 'I read that ITV is under pressure because "Dr Who" got nine million on the BBC, but the "X-Factor" was up against it and got eight million – that's 70 per cent of the commercial audience, which is terrific.'

→ Ch. 6

Strategy is concerned with the scope of an organisation's activities in terms of whether it concentrates on one area of activity or whether it is concerned with many. This is an indication of the organisation's boundaries, the number and range of its products and services (see Chapter 6). Tesco may be mainly a food retailer but it also sells clothes and other goods, and it has moved into financial services. Strategy is also about 'fit', which is the match between the resources and capabilities of the organisation and the opportunities open to it, and 'stretch', which is the process of innovation and development involved in finding new opportunities and creating a competitive advantage from the organisation's resources and competencies. Strategy involves matching the activities of an organisation to the environment in which it operates so that there is a 'strategic fit'. It is an attempt to identify the opportunities available and to tailor the strategy of the organisation to capitalise on them. There will also be an attempt to stretch resources and apply 'leverage' to them in order to create opportunities and to be in a position to exploit them (Exhibit 5.1).

Strategy involves identifying the **core competencies** that an organisation requires in order to optimise its ability to meet the opportunities and challenges it faces. The core competencies are those capabilities and skills which are necessary to underpin the organisation's competitive advantage. This is not only a question of making sure that the correct resources and competencies are available, but of identifying existing ones which can be used for creating new opportunities in the future.

Of course, managers may have a strategy without realising it. They may work on the basis that they do not have a strategy; they simply continue to do what they are doing now. This is, of course, in its own way a plan. The problem with a 'passive' strategy based on continuing to work as at present is that however successful this may have been in the past, and is now, it may not be successful in the future. 'Other things' will not remain 'equal'. On the one hand the external environment will change in terms of economic factors and political policies as well as technological development; on the other hand competitors will be searching for ways to expand their share of the market and internal problems may develop with key employees looking for more dynamic organisations or simply more money and career advancement.

Competition was a problem in the 1930s to the Ford Motor Company when it continued to produce its Model T in 'any colour the customer required as long as it was black', while their competitors produced more varied models which met customer requirements more closely. In the same way in the 1980s many computer companies experienced similar problems when what they had always produced was

Exhibit 5.1 Characteristics of strategic management

- Fundamental
- A sense of direction
- A sense of purpose
- Positioning
- Strategic fit
- Long term
- Looking ahead
- A search for competitive advantage
- Scope of activities
- Stretching and leverage

superseded. For example, the computer games company Nintendo took an early lead in the video games market when it expanded in the late 1980s. The company developed its Gameboy hand-held 8-bit games console which made it a major force in this developing market. It was then beaten into the 16-bit market by Sega which introduced its Mega Drive. Market share of the UK's video games in 1994 was 55 per cent to Nintendo and 34 per cent to Sega, but Sega claimed 70 per cent of the 16-bit market and, at this time, Sega and other companies were developing 32-bit video games. Nintendo has struggled to keep up with these developments – rather than concentrate on the 32-bit market it decided to move on to develop a 64-bit machine, Project Reality, and to 'leapfrog' into a technological lead.

Given the pitfalls of not having a strategy, or having a 'passive' one, managers need to have an active strategy, a way forward on which to base their decisions. A past chief executive of Sears, the largest retailer of drug and soft goods in the USA, has stated that

> *'business is like a war in one respect: if its ground strategy is correct, any number of tactical errors can be made and yet the enterprise proves successful.'*
> (General Robert E Wood quoted in Pearce and Robinson, 1989)

In this statement it is being suggested that even if the detailed actions are wrong they can be overcome where the overall strategy is effective. In other words, if travellers are on the correct road to their destination, a few diversions or stops may hold them up but will not prevent them from arriving where they want to be. If they do not know their destination, or they are on the wrong road, their chances of arriving in the right place are very limited, and in fact are governed by chance. In this sense strategy is a plan, a direction or a future course of action. It can also be seen as a pattern of behaviour over time and it can be described as an organisation's way of doing things or, for that matter, what it actually does. However, even this idea of aiming at a particular place or achieving particular objectives does not adequately describe strategy in terms of management. When organisations achieve a particular 'destination' it may be found that now they need to be in a slightly different place because they have moved on since the 'journey' started. A company may achieve the objectives it set itself two years earlier only to find that it arrives at a position it needed to be in a year earlier and now it needs to move forward again to keep up with the competition.

STRATEGIC OPTIONS

Strategic management is a method of defining the 'position' of an organisation, its objectives and how it expects to achieve them. In this process, organisations have to choose between broad strategies and the actions to be taken to achieve long-term objectives. These include options of retrenchment, growth or stability. A company may decide to reduce its size in terms of employees, production, assets and other factors. This decision may arise from a decline in demand for its products, changes in competition, the introduction of new technology or for some other reason. The **retrenchment** usually involves reducing business units, selling off parts of the business or, in the final analysis, the liquidation of the entire organisation.

In the recession of the early 1990s many companies reduced the size of their operations by using all these methods. **Outsourcing** areas of activity was a common process and enabled a company to relinquish ownership while retaining the service.

Re-engineering involves reducing the size of the labour force in order to reduce costs. Selling off parts of a company enables it to concentrate on what it considers to be its main core business. During this period Thorn-EMI, for example, reduced its training programme, sold off parts of its business and outsourced other areas. Rank Xerox UK decided to concentrate on its main business – photocopying and office documentation – and outsourced areas such as its information technology needs.

Stability involves a company attempting to remain the same size or grow in a very slow, controlled way. This 'pause strategy' often follows a period of rapid growth, when it is felt that time is needed to consolidate this expansion to make sure that it does not disappear. On the other hand, **growth** is often considered to be a company policy which will provide motivation and incentives to its employees and ensure its position in its markets. Increasing investment, product development, diversification into new markets and the acquisition of competitors are all processes for encouraging expansion.

In order to grow, a company may decide to follow a multinational policy by expanding into foreign markets. Developments such as those in Europe with the dropping of customs barriers in 1992 have helped to encourage this type of growth, as has the development of information technology and improved communications in the 1990s and 2000s. Globalisation is an important factor in the growth plan of some companies, particularly with the rapid development of consumer markets in countries like China, India, Russia and Brazil. Car manufacturers such as Ford have on the one hand tried to produce cars for particular markets such as North America and Europe, and on the other produced cars for a worldwide market with models such as the Focus and the Mondeo.

When organisations become complex and diversified, such as is the case with major national and multinational companies, strategy is very much the role of top management because coordination of the organisation's functional areas becomes crucial. Strategy at lower levels can be described as **operational strategy**. While overall strategy concentrates on effectiveness, that is 'doing the right things', operational strategy concentrates on efficiency, that is 'doing things right'. Strategic plans can provide guidance and boundaries for operational management and the two overlap in providing organisational strategy and the operational activity to achieve it. The grand plan represents the top-management view of the direction the organisation needs to take at any particular time. It provides a sense of direction which has to be implemented at all levels in the organisation if it is to succeed. This implementation requires a more operational strategy which ultimately arrives at a series of actions which need to be carried out in order to achieve it (Exhibit 5.2).

Exhibit 5.2 Characteristics of operation management

- **Organising**
- **Supervising and controlling**
- **Routine**
- **Short-term implications**
- **Operationally specific**

This operational strategy increasingly coincides with the organisation's marketing strategy because of the recognition that marketing provides the integration of organisational functions, and that without customers to demand its products and services an organisation does not have a *raison d'être*. Meeting the needs of customers is the first priority for any organisation, whether it is in the private or the public sector. Therefore the overall strategy in practice coincides with the marketing strategy. It is both informed by market research, in determining what should be done, and focuses on customer needs, in deciding how it is to be done. This is reflected in an organisation's formal, written strategic plan, which usually involves a series of stages moving from the relatively abstract to the very concrete, as outlined in Exhibit 5.3.

Exhibit 5.3 Corporate strategy

- **Mission statement or vision**   *What business are we in?*

- **Corporate objectives, goals and aims**   *Where do we want to go and how do we get there?*

- **Market research**   *Who are our customers and what are their needs?*

- **Audit of external environment**   *What are the threats and opportunities we face?*

- **Analysis of resources**   *What are our strengths and weaknesses?*

- **Marketing objectives**   *How do we achieve our objectives in marketing terms?*

- **Strategic plan**   *How do we match our objectives with our resources?*

- **Action plan**   *What do we have to do to achieve our objectives?*

A further stage can be added looping back to the beginning of the process in terms of monitoring and review.

THE STRATEGIC PLAN

The **strategic plan** of an organisation provides an idea of the overall direction of a company, the way it is planning to develop if it is able to control matters. This may be particularly difficult with growth and multinationalism. However, even retrenchment and stability may be difficult to achieve in practice. In a recession, stability may prove to be an optimistic aim, while attempts to sell off part of the business may prove difficult in practice. The actual strategy and the strategic intent of an organisation may be, in practice, different from the strategic plan because the written plan is produced at particular intervals of time and for a purpose, such as satisfying major stakeholders. Actual strategy and the management of it is constantly adjusted to circumstances and may be more or less focused than suggested in the written plan.

Increasingly, organisations have attempted to encapsulate the purpose of their activity, as much as the direction they wish to take, in a single short **vision** or **mission statement**. This statement represents the vision or mission of the organisation, or 'what it is about'. See, for example, the Ford Motor Company's statement of mission, values and guiding principles in Exhibit 5.5 (on pp. 144–5).

Mission statements are changed by companies from time to time in order to reflect adjustments by the company to markets and competition. The examples of mission or vision statements in this chapter are provided to illustrate the form they may take and may not be those in use by the companies now. The 'mission' might include the general direction the company is to take, but this may be expressed more clearly in the organisation's aims and objectives. In 1993 the airline British Midland described its mission in terms of improving service to meet customers' needs, 'allowing us to expand our business throughout Europe and, in doing so, generate the necessary profit to develop our company'.

A mission statement describes an organisation's basic purpose. A computer company, for example, may describe itself as providing low-cost, high-quality solutions to business problems. A record company may describe itself as being in the entertainment business, a retail company may describe itself as offering customers a range of high-quality, well-designed and attractive merchandise at reasonable prices. Cadbury Schweppes has described its task as building on its tradition of quality and value to provide brands, products, financial results and management performance that meet the interest of its shareholders, consumers, employees, customers, suppliers and the communities in which it operates.

A characteristic of mission statements is that they are succinct, distinctive and wide in scope. They are 'short in numbers and long in rhetoric' in the sense that they identify the organisation without providing a very specific approach to dealing with a target market. The mission statement outlines the present view of the organisation's purpose without restricting future possible development (see Exhibit 5.4). The computer company may wish to emphasise its width of possible work – it is not simply concerned with computer hardware or solving problems in information technology, it is concerned with using computers to solve business problems. The retail company may want to emphasise that it offers high-quality goods of all types at reasonable prices.

The mission statement of any organisation should answer the question: What business are we in? The National Children's Bureau, for example, has stated that it 'exists to promote and protect the welfare, interests and rights of all children in the UK on the basis of research and knowledge'. An engineering consultancy has described its purpose to be 'a leading engineering consultancy engaged in the management and execution of projects requiring the effective application of engineering technologies and physical sciences'. There can be little doubt about what these two organisations do and what business they are in. The National Children's Bureau's purpose is to look after the interests of children, specifically in the UK,

Exhibit 5.4 Mission statements

Mission statements focus on:

- **What business are we in?**

- **Who is to be served?**

- **What benefits are to be delivered?**

- **How are consumers to be satisfied?**

based on high-quality information. The Bureau is not concerned with the education or the health of children unless their welfare or rights need protecting in these areas. The engineering consultancy is clearly in engineering, and not other areas of consultancy and the application of engineering technology. In the same way British Airways has attempted to produce a mission statement that supports its slogan 'the world's favourite airline' and has in the past declared its mission to be 'the best and most successful company in the airline business'. In support of this statement British Airways has emphasised the importance of safety and security, of financial strength, of the need to provide services and value, to anticipate and respond quickly to customer needs, to be a good employer and to be a good neighbour concerned for the community and the environment.

Once an organisation identifies what type of business it is in, it needs to answer the question: What benefits do our customers seek? Customers may be seeking the benefit of a solution to business problems which they want solved in the most cost-effective way possible. Whether this involves computers and information technology may not be important, provided that the solutions are effective. The question – What is our business? – has to be defined in terms of the underlying need that the organisation is trying to serve. The engineering consultancy is offering the effective application of engineering technologies and the customers it serves will be looking for benefits in terms of these applications. The Ford Motor Company has made the quality of its products and services the number one priority in order to meet customer needs, to prosper and to provide a reasonable return to those who have invested in it. The statement reproduced in Exhibit 5.5 emphasises the importance of company employees, the quality of its products and the company's willingness to be judged on its profits. In order to achieve these profits, guiding principles are set out with quality and a customer focus at the top of the list. This was a statement for the company to live up to and it indicates its support for its major stakeholders in the form of its owners, its employees, its customers and its business partners. The statement provides an indication of the scope of the company's activities, automotive and financial products and services, and desired company approach to its work through social responsibility and equal opportunities.

Exhibit 5.5 Ford Motor Company's statement of mission, values and guiding principles

Ford Motor Company
Company mission, values and guiding principles

Mission
Ford Motor Company is a worldwide leader in automotive and financial products and services. Our mission is to improve continually our products and services to meet our customers' needs, allowing us to prosper as a business and to provide a reasonable return for our stockholders, the owners of our business.

Values
How we accomplish our mission is as important as the mission itself. Fundamental to success for the Company are these basic values:

■ **People** – Our people are the source of our strength. They provide our corporate intelligence and determine our reputation and vitality. Involvement and teamwork are our core human values.

■ **Products** – Our products are the end result of our efforts, and they should be the best in serving customers worldwide. As our products are viewed, so are we viewed.

■ **Profits** – Profits are the ultimate measure of how efficiently we provide customers with the best products for their needs. Profits are required to survive and grow.

Guiding principles

■ **Quality comes first** – To achieve customer satisfaction, the quality of our products and services must be our number one priority.

■ **Customers are the focus of everything we do** – Our work must be done with our customers in mind, providing better products and services than our competition.

■ **Continuous improvement is essential to our success** – We must strive for excellence in everything we do: in our products, in their safety and value; and in our services, our human relations, our competitiveness and our profitability.

■ **Employee involvement in our way of life** – We are a team. We must treat each other with trust and respect.

■ **Dealers and suppliers are our partners** – The Company must maintain mutually beneficial relationships with dealers, suppliers and our other business associates.

■ **Integrity is never compromised** – The conduct of our Company worldwide must be pursued in a manner that is socially responsible and commands respect for its integrity and for its positive contributions to society. Our doors are open to men and women alike without discrimination and without regard to ethnic origin or personal beliefs.

Source: Copyright © Ford Motor Company 1996. Reprinted with permission.

GOALS, AIMS AND OBJECTIVES

Once an organisation has decided on the business it is in, it can focus very clearly on its goals, aims and objectives. The corporate objectives of an organisation emphasise its direct aims, and in contrast to vision or mission statements these are precise statements of intent. They must be capable of measurement, by one method or another, in order to confirm whether or not objectives have been achieved. It is possible to distinguish between objectives, which fill out the abstractions of the mission statement in more concrete terms, and corporate goals and aims, which provide the operational detail that can lead to an action plan. Organisational goals and aims are objectives restated in an operational and measurable form, and most of the time very little distinction is made in the use of these three terms. While the objectives may be expressed in terms of the grand plan, combined with the goals and aims they will provide a concrete idea of the direction of the organisation and how it will get there.

The computer company with a mission statement concerned with solving business problems may have corporate objectives which state that it aims at a particular level of profitability and that it intends to obtain a particular percentage share of its market. Objectives are often expressed in terms of profit, market share, growth, or all three. Therefore, while the mission statement is a relatively abstract statement of the organisation's purpose, the corporate objectives, aims and goals are a combination of the grand plan (Where do we want to go?) and an idea of how to achieve it

(How do we get there?). The objectives will not only express the fact that the organisation intends to grow but also by how much and perhaps the main market or markets to be penetrated. For example, DHL Worldwide Express has specified the aim to 'become the acknowledged global leader in the express delivery of documents and packages'. DHL has also declared that leadership would be achieved by establishing industry standards of excellence for quality service and by monitoring the lowest cost position relative to the company service commitment in all markets of the world. These can be seen as specific market aims, leadership position and costing policy. The corporate objective is for DHL to become the global leader in its field. This objective would be achieved by establishing standards of excellence for quality services and by monitoring the cost position in all world markets, and provides a statement of what the company wants to achieve and an indication of how it will do this.

Corporate objectives can be seen either as primary or secondary objectives. **Primary objectives** are those which must be achieved if the organisation is to survive and succeed. These are often expressed in terms of profit, sales or market share, so that if a certain level of profit is not achieved the company will collapse. If certain levels of sales or market share are not attained then the company will not succeed and may be faced again with the ultimate problem of survival. **Secondary objectives** are a measure of the efficiency of an organisation. They are critical for success but may not affect survival for some time. They may be to do with customer care, product development, administrative efficiency, new office buildings and so on. In recent years many organisations, both in the private and public sectors, have raised the standing of such objectives as improving customer care from a secondary objective, which is only considered to affect survival over a long period, to a primary objective that will have a much more direct effect on levels of activity, profits and therefore survival. Whatever the priority given to particular objectives, it is important that they are clearly expressed, are measurable in one way or another and therefore realistic, with an assigned responsibility and a deadline for completion (see Exhibit 5.6).

An organisation needs to base its objectives on market research which should enable it to understand the customer's needs. The information arising from market research helps the organisation to be customer-oriented and to produce goods and services which meet customer needs. Market research will help to decide:

- customer needs at present;
- customer location and characteristics;

Exhibit 5.6 SMART objectives

Specific:	clearly and precisely expressed
Measurable:	so that there is confirmation of whether or not they are achieved
Agreed:	with those responsible for achieving them
Realistic:	so that they can be achieved
Timed:	with a deadline for achievement

- customer perceptions of the organisation's products and services;
- customer needs in the future;
- levels of customer satisfaction.

Managers have to ensure that the entire organisation is customer-oriented, otherwise one part of it may pull in a different direction. The mission statement, corporate objectives, goals and aims and the marketing strategy need to interact so that they are all directed one way. At the same time managers have to carry out an audit of the external environment. This 'environmental analysis' provides a systematic assessment of information about an organisation's strategic opportunities, as well as threats and problems which might prove to be obstacles to its development. This analysis enables managers to shape and evaluate strategic options and develop corporate strategy. In marketing terms, this is part of a SWOT (strengths, weaknesses, opportunities and threats) analysis. Opportunities may be discovered by revealing a part of the potential market that is relatively untouched. For example, a computer company may discover that while it has been concentrating on finding solutions to business problems in terms of products and finance there is a gap in terms of personnel and training functions. Clive Sinclair has invented products to fill perceived opportunities in the market such as portable computers, electric cars and powered bicycles, with more or less success.

Competition is the most obvious threat for most organisations. Market research identifies rival producers of goods and services. Most organisations are concerned with their market share and profitability and competing firms will have similar objectives. For example, McDonald's UK has described its purpose to be 'the United Kingdom's number one favourite quick service restaurant', led by the needs of its customers, committed to the welfare and development of its staff, with the provision of great tasting food in a relaxed, safe and consistent restaurant environment.

Matters such as competitors' product development and pricing policy will be taken into account in determining an organisation's own policies. For example, from time to time newspapers have entered into strong price competition. In 1994 *The Times,* in the UK, reduced its price to 20 pence while its rivals were priced at more than twice that level. This had a particular effect on the *Independent,* which attempted to counteract this pricing policy by reducing its own price to 30 pence. In 2003 the *Independent* produced a tabloid version of the paper as an alternative to its usual layout. This smaller issue was designed to be easier to read on commuter trains and in other crowded places and to compete on design rather than price with other broadsheet newspapers. Later in the year *The Times* followed this development with its own tabloid version.

Threats may also take the form of political, social, economic and technological changes. These may also represent opportunities, depending on how they affect the environment of the organisation. Tax changes, for example, may adversely affect a company or an industry. The changes in taxation on company cars in the UK, for example, have reduced their importance as a perk for managers and have altered the demand for particular cars. One change which illustrates this point was introduced in 1994. Instead of taxation being based on the cubic capacity of the car, it was based on its retail price. On the one hand this enabled larger-engined cars to be more widely sold to company car buyers but on the other hand car companies had to look very carefully at their prices and margins and those of their competitors.

Changes in government regulation and European Union laws may affect companies, particularly in matters such as environmental control and human resource legislation. At the same time the introduction of training grants and industrial development areas has provided opportunities for many companies. Social changes, such as the increase in leisure activities or the shifting age structure of the population, create opportunities for companies in the leisure business or for those which provide goods and services to pensioners, while presenting threats to companies producing goods for children. The development of technology presents opportunities to computer companies while representing a threat to companies whose technology cannot keep pace with that of competitors.

The marketing strategy of an organisation will depend on the analysis of its market position, and an evaluation of its external threats and opportunities and its internal strengths and weaknesses. The strengths of organisations may include location, product development, internal organisation, a skilled and dedicated labour force, good communications and image. Weaknesses may include the lack of financial resources, a small market share, a limited range of products and dilapidated premises. Of course many of the weaknesses represent opportunities for improvement and could therefore be turned into strengths. It will then hope to build on its strengths and opportunities so that it can meet its strategic objectives and achieve its vision. An example of this was IBM in the 1980s which considered its main strengths to be in the corporate market with the development of mainframes. It believed that its lack of direct retail experience with individual buyers constituted a weakness in terms of the new PC market. In comparing itself, through market research, with its competitors, it decided to enter the PC market by selling to business and corporate customers' gradually overcoming its weakness by licensing the sale of IBM PCs. At the time this appeared to be a sensible strategic marketing plan

→ Ch. 8   (see Exhibit 8.3 in Chapter 8).

STRATEGY

The **strategy** of an organisation involves matching its corporate objectives and its available resources. In this development of strategy, managers are concerned with reconciling the business that the organisation is in with the allocation of resources. The use of resources has to support the aims and goals agreed in the organisation and these in turn will determine the priorities in terms of resource use. If growth is a major element in the grand plan then resources are likely to be allocated to marketing and product development, while if contraction or retrenchment is the goal then more resources may be given to paying for the costs of redundancy payments, early retirement and the negotiations and consultations involved. This allocation process is concerned with the general purposes of an organisation, whether it is part of a grand plan, the overall objectives or a 'strategy' designed to keep the organisation in business.

While the overall strategy may be determined at a senior level, the detail may be better left to those as close as possible to the organisation's customers. This view is supported by Tom Peters (1992) in terms of strategy:

> *'I don't believe top management should be in the business of strategy setting at all, except as creators of a general business mission. Strategies must be set from below. (No, not "from" below. Set "in" below – i.e. by the autonomous business units, for the autonomous business units).'*

Strategy involves senior managers in establishing the overall purpose of the organisation and the objectives, aims and goals, while the question of tactics and approach to customers is decided at the level of individual business units. The strategic plan is the process of allocating resources in an organisation in order to achieve its strategic aims. This allocation will again be carried out at different levels, so that while resources may be allocated in a general way, detailed allocation will be left to business units or work teams. Of course, in many 'autonomous' business units the whole unit may prosper or fail depending on its relative success and this will depend on its own strategic plan and the success of its implementation. However, it remains the situation that the overall purpose of an organisation, its vision and values remain the responsibility of senior management. Changing this vision and these values is a slow process which requires the allocation of resources over a period of years.

Large companies, such as British Airways, have introduced staff training sessions, quality initiatives or corporate change programmes over many years in order to create different behavioural approaches in the company and to reinforce company values. Resources are allocated centrally to these programmes in order to promote developments which match the mission and corporate objectives of the company. For example, in the 1980s British Airways developed its 'Putting People First' and 'Managing People First' programmes in order to improve its service. It then evolved its mission statement ('to be the best and most successful company in the airline business') out of the purpose and success of its training programme (Exhibit 5.7).

It is possible to distinguish at least three levels of strategy: corporate, business and functional. **Corporate strategy** applies to large companies which are divided into a number of discrete and fairly autonomous units. Holding companies are typical of this type of organisation in which a number of companies are grouped together, usually for financial reasons such as the efficient allocation of capital and investment. Corporate strategy is the responsibility of the corporate head office with the fundamental issue being the reason for the different businesses being collected together.

Companies may be bought or sold by the holding company as their strategy changes, so at one time it may decide to extend its operations into new fields by buying companies outside its usual area of operation, at another time it may decide that the correct strategy is to consolidate on one industry or area of industry and sell companies that do not fit in with this strategy. Strategy may be based around investment, economies of scale or the sharing of core competencies and, in particular, decisions about the portfolio of businesses. In practice the corporation may adopt a hands-off approach to the individual companies or units under its control so long as they fulfil the corporate objectives.

At the level of **business strategy** the critical issues will be in terms of markets, critical success factors, the organisation of the business and overall competitive strategy. At the **functional level** the focus will be on departments or divisions of organisations. Most companies have some elements of a functional structure in which people concentrate on a particular specialism, such as finance, information systems, manufacturing and so on, and the overall business strategy has to be reflected and linked with the functional level strategies. This means that financial strategy, marketing strategy and human resources strategy have to reflect the overall company approach and may inform it as well as being shaped by it. The structure of a business needs to assist the business-level strategy in one way or another, otherwise responsibilities for parts of the strategy may not be picked up by the functional

Exhibit 5.7 British Airways

In November 1983 British Airways introduced a training programme called 'Putting People First'. The aim was to put 12,000 customer contact people through a two-day course to improve their customer service skills. The programme consisted of a mixture of presentations, exercises and group discussions in which staff reviewed their personal experience as customers of other service organisations. They also examined the implications for British Airways and were pressed to identify what they would do about these implications. The response to the training programme was mixed – some were sceptical, some saw it as a harmonising exercise, some dropped out and others were enthusiastic. But top management continued to support the programme demonstrating their commitment to customer service. The non-frontline staff began asking to be included and gradually the level of cynicism faded away. Staff began identifying the obstacles, confronting their managers with the fact that resources were insufficient to deliver the levels of customer care called for. The management responded to these issues and so encouraged staff to identify others.

Then in 1984 a programme for managers called 'Managing People First' was launched to change management styles. At the time management style was perceived to be dominated by sales and procedures and the aim of the training programme was to replace this with something more open and dynamic.

Other changes were made to reinforce the training programmes. For example, quality assurance and performance-related reward systems were introduced. The services being offered by the airline were also improved, demonstrating to staff that they would get the resources required to deliver better service.

It was only once the changes in behaviour were starting to show up as better service and greater customer satisfaction that mission statements were formulated in 1986.

Source: A Campbell, M Devine and D Young (1990) *A Sense of Mission*, London: Hutchinson.

units. At the same time it is possible for the functional units to interpret the business strategy in ways that suit them rather than reflecting the needs of the whole business.

At all levels strategic managers will be aiming to achieve a **sustainable competitive advantage**. A competitive advantage arises when a company receives a return on investment that is greater than the norm for its competitors for a period long enough to alter the relative standing of the company among its rivals. The product or service has to be sufficiently durable in terms of its life cycle to achieve the required return on investment and to enhance the reputation of the company. In due course competitors will succeed in imitating it and technological advances and social change can shorten product life, and an enhanced reputation can offset this to some extent.

A sustainable competitive advantage also depends on how easy or difficult it is for rivals to imitate or emulate the company offerings. A potential competitor will have to acquire the resources necessary to replicate the processes in order to develop a similar or better product, so if this is difficult the advantage can be more easily sustained. The development of strategy involves the identification of those factors which are critical in achieving an advantage. These critical success factors are those components of strategy where the organisation must excel to outperform competition. Managers have to assess the resources and competencies which have been built up through the delivery of the company's current and previous strategy, but a

Exhibit 5.8 Types of strategy

■ **Planned strategy**	a company decides on a way of proceeding or on a strategic plan
■ **Intended strategy**	a company decides to execute a pattern of decision making
■ **Deliberate strategy**	a company intends a particular strategy and it is accomplished
■ **Imposed strategy**	a company has strategy imposed by an outside agency
■ **Realised strategy**	a company strategy that has been accomplished
■ **Unrealised strategy**	an intended or deliberate company strategy which is not accomplished
■ **Emergent strategy**	where a company strategy is not intended but emerges over time

danger is that they may then favour new strategies that use these factors without taking account of the threats and the opportunities which may arise.

If there is too much reliance on factors that have produced success in the past there can be strategic drift in an organisation, where the actual strategy drifts further and further away from the strategy which is required for success (see Chapter 6). It may be possible for a company to exploit its unique critical success factors by taking advantage of new opportunities and 'stretching' its resources and competencies in ways which rivals find difficult to match. A company that has a good reputation in one area may move into new areas where its reputation will carry over. For example, Tesco has moved into areas such as clothing and finance based on its reputation for value in food retailing, the location of its stores and its ability to provide what people want.

→ Ch. 6

TYPES OF STRATEGY

The types of strategy are summarised in Exhibit 5.8 above. Strategic management is concerned with ensuring that there are sufficient core competencies to secure a competitive advantage. Strategy can be directed at improving and developing areas such as customer service, location, design and advertising skills if these are felt to be core competencies which can provide an advantage. In practice strategy is not always carefully **planned**, although (as in Exhibit 5.7) it may be. Strategy may be **intended** so that it does indicate the desired processes and direction for the business, deliberately formulated by strategic managers. This **deliberate** strategy will then be a systematic process of development and implementation.

'**Realised**' strategy is the strategy that a business is actually following in practice, which may be different from intended or deliberate strategy because although these may be planned they may not be implemented. However good the **intended strategy** might appear to be, it may be decided by managers that it will not be put into effect – the organisational culture may be in opposition to it so that for one reason or another it is not realised. The culture of the organisation may be opposed to it, stakeholders may block it or there may be power bases within the structure of a company which prevent the favoured form of strategy from being followed. Strategy can also be **imposed** on a business, for example as a result of overall corporate strategy or as a result of government legislation or regulation or in some other way. Antimonopoly legislation, for example, may limit a merger policy or environmental regulations may place obstacles to the favoured strategy of a company.

The development of strategy is most clearly seen in the distinction between deliberate and **emergent strategy** with the view that strategy can be formulated through complicated plans in a deliberate manner, or it emerges over time, step by step, in an incremental approach. Figure 5.1 illustrates the link between the various perspectives on strategy.

Figure 5.1 Forms of strategy

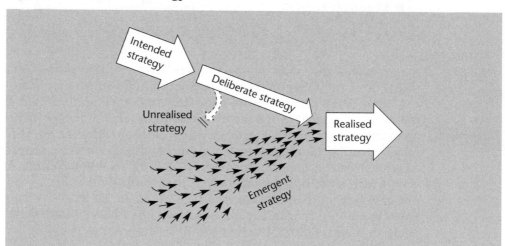

Source: H Mintzberg (1994, 2000) *The Rise and Fall of Strategic Planning*, Simon & Schuster.

Incremental strategy is a process of carrying out actions and gradually blending initiatives together into a coherent pattern. It is much more similar to the unstructured and unpredictable processes of exploration and invention than the orderly processes of design and production. This view of strategy sees planning as useful for routine tasks that need to be efficiently organised but less suitable for non-routine activities and innovation. Although 'planning' can mean simply a way of proceeding, it is often expected to involve preparing a written report, or a drawing or a tabulated statement.

TRANSFORMATION AND VALUE

Operationally a business performs a conversion or transformation process through which it adds value to a commodity or service, in the sense that the value of the output of the organisation is greater than the cost of the inputs and the process involved. Whatever the business, it starts with raw materials, whether these are goods or services, and, at whatever stage of production it is, the processes it applies to them add value. For example, a car assembly plant may start with raw materials of car body parts, engines, tyres, window glass, electrical components and so on, and by using the skill and competencies of the people working in the plant and its machinery and technology finished motor cars are assembled which are of greater value than the sum of all the components. Another example is provided by travel agents who start with the raw materials of access to flights, hotel rooms, excursions and so on and put these into a package which they are able to sell to tourists at a price which is greater than the cost of the various elements and the process of bringing them together for the consumer.

The 'value' of a product or service consists of the price plus the consumer surplus, which is a concept used by economists to distinguish between the price a consumer is prepared to pay for a product and the price the consumer does pay. Provided that the price of the product or service is below the value to the consumer it is likely to sell; if it is not then a sale is unlikely. This means that the package holiday is likely to sell to tourists if they feel that it is good 'value', that is if the cost to them is less than the price they are prepared to pay. Similarly a motor car retailer will buy a car from an assembly plant to sell on to a consumer if it is thought that the price they can sell it for is greater than the cost of buying it, advertising it and so on.

The conversion or transformation process usually consists of a linked set of stages of 'production' from basic raw materials to the final consumer. In the production of a motor car the basic raw materials are goods such as steel and rubber which are converted into car panels and tyres and passed on to car assemblers, from them to distributors and retailers until the finished new car is bought by the consumer. The 'value chain' passes through steel foundries, panel makers, car assemblers, distributors, retailers and consumers. This is a simple value chain because each link will in practice be involved with other value chains. For example, panel makers may receive their steel from a number of foundries and may pass on their finished panels to a number of assembly plants. They will also be involved in value chains which provide them with power, lighting and machinery.

Car assembly companies are in the same situation where, even in the simplest view of a value chain, they are receiving parts from a range of suppliers and passing on their finished cars to a number of distributors. All the value chains considered together can be said to form an 'industry', the motor car industry. A company in this industry will be in competition with other companies in that industry, as well as in a wider sense with other forms of transport and consumer spending in general. Businesses use a range of strategies to gain a competitive advantage over their rivals. They may try to make their product different from their competitors' products, with more features which add value to it. They may focus on a particular segment of the market in an attempt to provide exactly what it wants or they may form alliances of various types with competing companies, or with businesses further down or up the value chain. The actual environment in which strategy is developed will depend on the value chains of a business and the level of competition.

In deciding on a strategy, managers have to consider the risks involved in the sense of 'uncertainty', in that a particular course of action can lead to a number of possible outcomes. In this sense all courses of action carry risks, including doing nothing, because rivals will also be formulating strategies and there can be no guarantee that they are doing nothing. There are, of course, financial implications in alternative strategies and this is why doing nothing is often appealing. Innovation and change imply investment in design, testing, training, new plant and technology

→ Ch. 16
and usually increase the gearing ratio of the business – that is the ratio of the debt finance to shareholders' funds (see Chapter 16). Any alteration in strategy has to be accepted in one way or another by the business stakeholders, such as shareholders.

STAKEHOLDER STRATEGY

Stakeholders can be described as individuals and groups who are affected by the activities of an organisation. The most important stakeholders can be seen as those with the most to lose from the organisation's actions, but this does not always reflect their relative power. For example, the employees of a company may have most to lose from the success or failure of the strategies employed but financial backers may be the most powerful in actual decisions because they are in a stronger position to make or break the company. Strategies have to be developed taking into account the interests of stakeholders and their relative power.

All these stakeholders (Exhibit 5.9) have an interest in the company and may want to influence its future strategy. Managers have to reconcile the variety of interests that individuals and groups represent. Shareholders may be mainly interested in large dividends and a rise in the value of their shares, so they may be in favour of a strategy which maximises profits rather than the long-term development and growth of the company. Employees may be mainly concerned about the stability of their employment and the level of pay and other benefits, while the customers may be more concerned with the price of the goods the company produces, their quality and where they are available.

'Stakeholder mapping' is a process of analysing their influence on a company and how anxious each group is to impress its expectations on the organisation's choice of strategies. Strong unions may be able and be interested in exerting considerable pressure on the choice of strategy, but if the unions are weak then employees' interests may not be such an important pressure on the company. However, if particular employees are in short supply, perhaps because they have essential skills and competencies, their influence on strategic choice will be greater. Managers are faced with these and many other considerations when they choose strategies for their organisation. Strategic options are the broad choices open to a business and those that are selected are its 'strategic pathway'.

Exhibit 5.9 Typical business stakeholders

■ **Shareholders**	own the company and receive dividends
■ **Financial bodies**	fund companies and receive interest
■ **Employees**	provide labour and skills, and receive pay
■ **Trade unions**	organise labour and seek to influence pay
■ **Managers**	provide organisation and control, and receive pay
■ **Government**	legislates, regulates and receives taxation
■ **Customers**	consume the product and receive benefits
■ **Suppliers**	provide raw materials and receive costs

A strategic pathway consists of all the goods and services a company decides to offer, the quantities in which they are offered and their quality. Strategy is involved in the positioning of each product and service within its particular market and implies considerations of access to the resources and competencies required, sources of funds and the expectations of returns. Positioning is itself linked to questions of quality, price and design and considerations such as whether the commodity will be targeted at the luxury end of the market, the economy end or somewhere in the middle. A company will have a portfolio of offers of goods and services and strategic choices have to be made about each of these as well as the overall portfolio.

THE ACTION PLAN

Once the strategy has been agreed, managers need to decide on particular courses of action in order to achieve corporate objectives with the resources available. Detailed guidelines have to be developed in order to initiate and control action. The purpose of an action plan is to ensure that people responsible for accomplishing short-term and long-term objectives have clear guidance on what they need to do and how they are to achieve these objectives. Action plans also provide a mechanism by which top managers can satisfy themselves that what is being implemented is consistent with the intention of organisational strategy.

Action plans are concerned with turning priorities and organisational strategy into reality and they are linked to the use of resources in the form of both physical and human resources. They may show how many people are to be involved with a particular activity, the numbers of people and their skills and qualifications. Action plans also take into account how much money is available for a particular activity and the amount and type of equipment and premises required. In reflecting the organisation's strategic plan, action plans have a major impact on the successful implementation of these strategies in showing what actions are required and the timescale for completion.

At their simplest, action plans are lists of actions to be carried out by particular managers or operatives in order to achieve the requirements of the business unit. They are often the responsibility of operating managers in order to ensure that those responsible for implementing a strategy are also involved in developing it. They are usually accompanied by detailed budgets, which may act as a means of control as well as a means of communicating an action plan.

- Functional plans are produced to guide decisions and actions in the various functional areas of an organisation.
- Project plans are produced on a one-off basis in order to control specific programmes of work.
- Long-term plans, policies or procedures are used to establish guidelines for recurring activities.

These action plans can then be translated into detailed plans for individual employees or relatively small working units or teams. Corporate planning can mean that functional plans and policies become clear guidelines for individual action. In a sense the working position can be seen as a series of projects, each planned in order to control specific programmes of work and operating within policy guidelines. These project actions may be agreed by the self-managed team and the individuals within it, keeping within the policies established by corporate managers in order to achieve corporate objectives. For example, at its simplest the action plan of a salesperson may set out very clear actions and objectives in terms of the number of customers to be contacted, or the value of sales to be made in a particular period. The action plan may go further in establishing how the salesperson should function in terms of customer care, following up complaints and so on.

MONITORING AND REVIEW

The **strategic planning** process involves agreeing on a mission statement, deciding on corporate objectives, analysing markets and resources, auditing the internal and external environment, and arriving at an action plan. It is not, of course, a static process and once the framework is in place and is working it needs to be frequently reviewed in the light of any changes. Managers should review all aspects of the strategy constantly. At one extreme the action plan requires constant monitoring and adjustment, while at the other the mission statement may need to be altered only rarely. This should reflect the fact that, while the direction of the organisation should not be changing too frequently, the actions required to maintain that direction will entail frequent adjustment.

In reviewing the 'closeness of fit' between corporate actions and corporate direction and values alternative strategies may be considered. Managers look at existing strategies and can perform what is called 'gap analysis'. Here they simply attempt to determine whether a performance gap exists between what their existing strategy can be expected to accomplish realistically and the objectives that have been established. This can be in areas such as sales, productivity and profitability and also in areas such as staff training and development, customer care and in environmental issues. Where there is no gap managers can assume that the current strategy is probably the appropriate one. Where serious gaps are found to exist then managers will need to investigate these and look for alternative strategies. In extreme cases there may be a need for a significant change in the firm's strategy.

The monitoring and review process provides the loop back to all stages of organisational strategy and should provide a reminder that change and improvement are constant features of organisational life. The planning objective, in general terms, is an upward spiral of improved market information, better systems for competitor analysis and more efficient and effective use of resources. In monitoring the strategy and the strategic plan they can be matched against the corporate values and the guiding principles of the organisation. The review process can help to answer the question of how far the organisation's policies and actions coincide with and are supportive of its perceived values.

The values and guiding principles of an organisation are concerned with 'how it goes about its business'. As well as deciding what business it is in, what objectives it has and how it will achieve them, an organisation has to decide on its underlying values. These may be explicitly expressed (as in the case of the Ford Motor Company in Exhibit 5.5) or implied in the way in which business is conducted in an organisation. Usually this is expressed in terms of quality factors, customer care and employee development rather than in terms of corporate ethics, but social responsibility, equal opportunities and environmental issues may form an explicit part of the company philosophy.

THE STRATEGIC PORTFOLIO

→ Ch. 6

Every organisation consists of at least one and usually many more products and ser-vices. Between them these represent the 'business portfolio' (see Chapter 6). For example, in the case of automobile companies there are different models of car and various services provided in relation to cars. With travel agents their portfolio con-sists of a range of travel services which may include a number of different holidays. A company can be viewed as a portfolio of business investments which managers must balance by expanding investment in some, while reducing investment in others. Decisions have to be made by managers on the investment of resources in the vari-ous areas of the portfolio and their contribution to the business in order to provide the company with a competitive advantage. Most companies like to have a balanced mix of business units which are at various points in their respective life cycles.

One approach found to be useful in this process has been the **Boston matrix** (sometimes referred to as the Boston Consulting Group matrix or the growth–share → Ch. 8 matrix; see Chapter 8). The use of this for business units or product/service teams can help the corporation to define the questions: What business should we be in? What is our basic mission? How should we allocate corporate resources across the units and teams? The matrix analyses businesses along two dimensions, business growth and market share. Business growth measures how rapidly the whole indus-try is increasing in size, while market share measures the share a business unit has of this market compared to competitors.

Once it has been decided what the growth rate is in a market and the particular product/service market share, it is possible to allocate each unit to one of four quad-rants in the matrix (see Figure 5.2). The arrangement of business units that emerges within the matrix can provide managers with a means of establishing and describing

Figure 5.2 The Boston matrix: cash flows

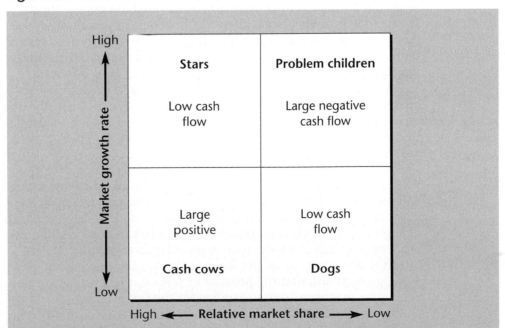

corporate strategy. In terms of balance, the desired grouping may be to have a number of units in each quadrant because there would then be a number of products and services producing a cash flow, with others requiring an injection of cash to move them from being 'problems' to 'stars' and with other units on their way out. This means that units in the lower part of the matrix, the so-called **cash cows** and 'dogs', could be used as a source of excess cash for investment in the 'problem children' (also referred to as 'question marks') and the 'stars' which represent the best opportunities for future growth and survival.

The allocation of individual business units to a particular position on the matrix helps managers to define strategic plans for the business with levels of activity consistent with corporate strategy. For example, 'cash cow' managers may be expected to produce relatively short-term profits, 'dog' managers may be expected to minimise expenditure and to reduce part of their operations to allow any available resources to be invested elsewhere, 'star' unit managers may be expected to increase market share with the help of investment in equipment and marketing, 'problem children' managers may be expected to review and evaluate the future potential of their business unit and to justify its continuation. It is, of course, crucial that a particular business unit is described accurately. For example, if a product or service has a low relative market share in a market with low growth then it should be described as a 'dog' and therefore be a likely candidate for 'divestment' by the company so that its resources can be reinvested in another product or service.

The growth–share matrix approach has been criticised because of the difficulty of describing some products/services and business units sufficiently accurately. At the margin, the difference between a subject for 'divesting' and a 'problem child' with potential for growth and development into a 'star' may be very small. It may be based on an estimation of market growth and the potential for future growth. It can be argued that the approach oversimplifies the situation in many organisations and that the terminology used in the matrix encourages this oversimplification. It does, however, provide an excellent starting point for analysing the position of business units and it would be an unwise corporation that did not use the portfolio approach in one way or another (see Exhibit 5.10). A range of variations on the Boston matrix have been developed, such as dividing the matrix into nine sections in order to define market share and market growth in more detail, but the basis of the process remains the same.

One of the frameworks used by managers in terms of portfolio strategy is life-cycle analysis. In this process business units' products/services are analysed and placed on a point against one of the four or five stages of the life cycle – introduction, growth, maturity (and saturation) and decline (see Figure 8.4). The typical situation is that managers are investing money in a product or service at the introductory stage, while expecting products at the mature stage to be cash cows and producing money for investment. Stars are likely to be seen in the growth stage where the market is still growing and there is an expectation that the product will achieve an increased share of the market. Dogs will usually be in the decline stage although they may be at another stage, such as introductory, but in fact be unsuccessful in terms of market share or as a result of a lower than expected market growth.

Introductory stage strategies focus on confirming that market growth and market share do exist and that the product or service is meeting customer needs. At the same time managers have to arrange for the financial support of the product at a time when investment significantly exceeds revenue. Growth stage strategy will focus on the size and potential of the market and opportunities to broaden the cus-

Exhibit 5.10 Portfolio analyses

Gillette Company

Gillette has several cash cows in its corporate portfolio. The most famous is the shaving division, which accounts for two-thirds of the company's total profits and holds a large share of a stable market. This division sells Ultra, Trac II, the Sensor shaving system, Good News disposable razor and new Sensor razor for women. In 1992 the company captured major control of the largest major blade company in China and access to that nation's vast population pool. The Oral-B laboratories division is also a cash cow with its steady sales of toothbrushes and other dental hygiene products. The stationery products division has star status. With a $560 million purchase of Parker Pen Holdings Limited, this division has become the world's largest marketer of writing instruments, which also includes Paper Mate, Flair, Erasemate and Waterman, and it shows potential for rapid growth overseas. Gillette's question marks are in the personal care division. A line of women's toiletries aimed at the European market failed, and Gillette's success with other lines – for example, men's Right Guard deodorant and Foamy shaving cream – have enjoyed only cyclical success. A new line of men's toiletries featuring a gel-based deodorant and a gel shaving cream was recently launched. If this new line fails to generate sales and market share, it may be assigned to the dog category, to which the Cricket line of disposable lighters was relegated. The Bic disposable lighter dominated the Cricket line so completely that Cricket became a dog and was eventually put out of its misery through liquidation. Gillette continues to experiment with new products and question marks to ensure that its portfolio will include stars and cash cows in the future.

Source: Excerpt from R L Daft (1994) *Management* (3rd edition), Orlando, FL: Dryden Press. Reprinted by permission of South-Western, a division of Thomson Learning.

tomer base. Managers need to strengthen the product/service appeal by developing such areas as brand identification, distribution outlets and price. At the maturity stage managers are faced with increasing competition and more resources may need to be invested in marketing and searching for new sales opportunities. In the decline stage managers will attempt either to monitor the business unit through a refocus of the customer base and cost cutting or employ strategies to enable the organisation to move out of that particular product/service while retaining resources to reinvest elsewhere.

COMPETITIVE FORCES STRATEGY

Michael Porter, a professor of economics and business strategy at Harvard Business School, has identified 'forces' that can be seen as the main factors which an organisation needs to take into account in order to exploit opportunities in its environment and to protect itself against competition. This has been referred to as the **competitive forces strategy** which provides a framework for the analysis of strategic management. He argued that five competitive forces exist in an organisation's environment (see Figure 5.3).

Figure 5.3 Competitive forces

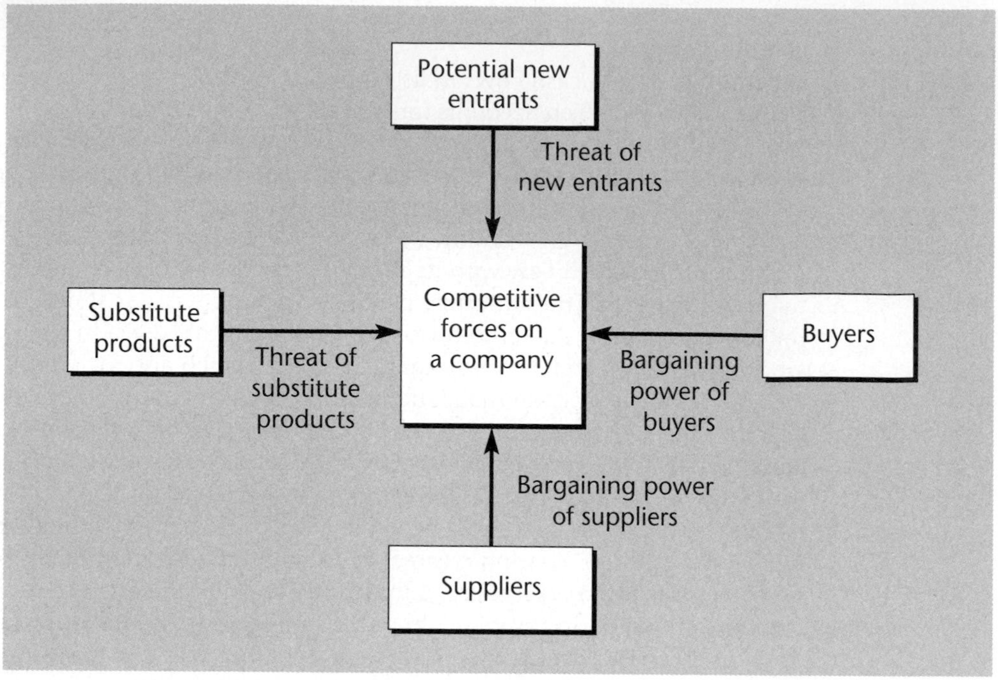

Source: Adapted and reprinted from M E Porter (1980) *Competitive Strategy: Techniques for Analyzing Industries and Competitors,* New York: Free Press. Copyright © 1980, 1988 by The Free Press, a division of Simon & Schuster.

- Potential new entrants have more difficulty in setting up in a high capital-intensive industry (such as motor cars) than in a service industry (such as an estate agency). Capital requirements and the scale are both potential barriers to entry.

- The bargaining power of buyers increases as advertising and consumer information create a situation where customers know about the full range of price and product options available. This is especially true when a company sells mainly to a few customers, such as is the case where manufacturers are supplying one or two retailers.

- The bargaining power of suppliers depends on the availability of substitute suppliers. A sole supplier will have great power.

- The threat of substitute products is most powerful where there are alternatives and substitutes for a company's product. Changes in opinions about the environment, costs and so on may influence the demand for these products.

- Rivalry among competitors may appear in terms of advertising, price and product differentiation, such as appeared in the 'cola wars' between Pepsi-Cola and Coca-Cola.

Porter suggested that a company could find a competitive advantage against these competitive forces either through differentiation or cost leadership, or by combining policies focused on a particular strategic target. For example, the **differentiation strategy** involves an attempt to distinguish the company's products and services from others in the industry. Product differentiation may involve product branding, adding distinct features or providing extra services. If a product is felt by consumers to be different from its competitors they may be prepared to pay high prices. Chanel No. 5 perfume, Mercedes-Benz cars and Rolex watches are all examples of this approach.

A **cost leadership strategy** involves reducing costs in order to undercut competitors' prices while providing a similar quality product. Companies such as Tesco and Kwik-Fit have followed this policy, while the John Lewis stores chain claims not to be undercut on price. These companies are in a good position to withstand a price war – customers have difficulty in finding lower prices and buyers will have little scope for price negotiations with suppliers. The low price acts as a barrier against new entrants and substitute products. A **combined strategy** involves the company using a differentiation or low-cost approach concentrated on a narrow target market. For example, some companies, such as Sun Alliance, have introduced low-cost insurance for the over-50s. The choice between cost leadership and differentiation will depend on which provide a greater competitive advantage. This will depend on the conditions in a particular industrial or business environment and when these conditions change then strategy has to change accordingly.

> *'In an initial phase, when an innovation has just been launched, it is possible to charge a premium price, but as competitors introduce similar solutions, price becomes increasingly important.'*   (Kald et al., 2000)

This suggests that over time strategy will change from an emphasis on differentiation to an emphasis on cost leadership.

Porter (1985) argues that combining the two strategies cannot last over a long period while earning an above average return and that management has to adapt an organisation's strategic position to match the development of its environment. He has argued (1996) (see the case study at the end of this chapter) that a sustainable strategic position requires trade-offs. Choosing a unique position is not enough to guarantee a sustainable advantage because a valuable position will attract imitation, either by matching the superior performance or by 'straddling'. The straddler attempts to match the benefit of a successful position while maintaining its existing position, but a strategic position is not sustainable unless there are trade-offs with other positions. Trade-offs create the need for choice and a purposeful limitation on what a company offers. They deter straddling or repositioning because competitors who engage in these approaches undermine their strategies and degrade the value of their existing activities, and positions built on systems of activities are generally far more sustainable than those built on individual activities.

The manager's role is to create fit among a company's activities and to integrate them so that the company does many things well. This requires trade-offs in competing in order to achieve a sustainable advantage, so that managers have to decide what not to do as well as what to do. Mintzberg (1987) and Miles and Snow (1978) have argued that strategies are the product of a large number of decisions which together form a clear pattern. This means that an organisation's reactions to change are adjustments to alterations in its environment rather than a clear change of strategy, but may represent a consistent pattern in the way an organisation relates to its environment. Mintzberg has called this a 'metastrategy', that is the underlying orientation of an organisation towards its environment and argues that while this may be modified over time it is seldom dramatically changed. Miles and Snow (1978) have classified organisations on the basis of the pattern of their reaction to changes in their environments and considered that this pattern was influential on organisational decisions on whether to concentrate on finding new markets or on

Table 5.1 The classification of business strategy

CLASSIFICATION	FEATURES
Defender	Stable domain, limited product range, competes through low cost or high quality, efficiency paramount, centralised structure
Prospector	Turbulent domain, always seeks new product and market opportunities, uncertain environment, flexible structure
Analyser	Hybrid, core of traditional products, enters new markets after viability established, matrix structure
Reactor	Lacks coherent strategy, structure inappropriate to purpose, misses opportunities, unsuccessful
Differentiation	Product uniqueness leads to higher prices, emphasis on marketing and research
Cost leadership	Low price, focus on high market share, standardised products, economies of scale
Focus	Focus on defined buyer group, product line or geographic market

Source: Summarised from M Kald, F Nilsson and B Rapp (2000) 'On strategy and management control: the importance of classifying the strategy of the business', *British Journal of Management*, 11 (3), September. Modified from R Simons (1990) 'The role of management control systems in creating competitive advantage new perspectives', *Accounting, Organisation and Society*, 15.

developing an existing market, while Porter classified organisations based on strategic positioning. Table 5.1 summarises these classifications.

Miles and Snow divided company reaction to change into four strategic patterns – defender, prospector, analyser and reactor to represent different patterns, while Porter's division was into differentiation, cost leadership and focus. Another classification was identified by Gupta and Govindarajan (1984) based on the strategic mission of organisations. These were build, hold and harvest. 'Build' is where the mission is to increase market share where there is low relative market share in, high growth industries. 'Hold' is where the mission is to keep existing market share, through quality improvements and marketing campaigns crucial for success where there is a high relative market share, typically in mature industries. 'Harvest' is where the mission is to maximise short-term earnings in situations where investments will decrease rapidly, although there is high relative market share, typically in declining industries.

STRATEGIC MANAGEMENT

In practice many organisations apply a range of strategies depending on changes in circumstances. In order to remain competitive and to survive managers need to be creative and innovative as well as using all the strategies available to them. Companies attempt to expand their markets by attracting new customers and by moving into national or international markets. Organisations develop their products by adding features or modifying design to remain ahead of the competition.

This is a process adapted by car companies in updating their models by making relatively small changes, adding features or producing special editions. Companies are facing changing customer demands and preferences, technological advances, global competitors and

> *'an even more complex new environment shaped by the increasing importance of information, the impact of technology, deregulation, the changing face of competition and patterns of employment, and the rise of knowledge as the key economic resource.'*
> (Herrmann, 2005)

Effective organisations not only attain 'fit' or alignment between themselves and their environment, capabilities and leadership, they also attain 'fitness' – that is the capacity to learn and change as circumstances alter. Organisational learning requires constant environmental assessment matched by continuous adaptation in leadership, internal structures and behaviour.

> *'To adapt successfully demands senior management with the courage and skill to lead a systematic organisational learning process that will "rejuvenate" the organisation reshaping its design, culture and political landscape.'*
> (Beer *et al.*, 2005)

This involves adapting strategy to changes in the environment and aligning the capabilities of the organisation with the new strategies, while also aligning organisational design, culture and leadership. The Peters and Waterman (1982) 'Seven-S' framework for successful companies encouraged managers to concentrate on strategy, structure and operating systems, while not ignoring shared values, the style of leadership and management, skills and staff. Changing the first three (the so-called hard factors) has generally proved easier than changing the last four (the so-called soft factors) because these all involve people and their attitudes. It usually proves much easier to change policies, organisational structures and working systems than to change people's points of view. People have personal and professional interests which may override the interests of the organisation, while changes raise questions about power and internal politics and career interests. Resistance to change may be reduced by good communication and leadership and a concern for motivation but people still resist change, particularly if it affects their values, skills and the way they are managed.

Beer *et al.* (2005) have suggested a number of barriers to overcome in the search for 'fitness' and alignment:

- unclear strategy and/or conflicting priorities;
- an ineffective top-management team;
- a leadership style that is too top down or, conversely, too laissez-faire;
- poor coordination across functions, businesses or geographic regions;
- inadequate leadership skills and development of down-the-line leaders;
- poor vertical communication.

Once environmental assessment has shown that strategic change is necessary then leadership and good management become all-important because without them there will not be a sense of purpose and direction to overcome these barriers to change.

Organisations use a number of other strategies in order to remain ahead of the competition. **Vertical integration** is a strategy with the aim of controlling channels of both supply and distribution. The company seeks to control its suppliers so that its supplies can be guaranteed at the lowest possible cost and at the quality it requires, and its distributors so that it is able to work closely with the final consumers. **Horizontal integration** is a strategy aimed at controlling competitors at the same level of production. A company may take over or merge with another company in order to acquire economies of scale, increased buying power and access to a wider range of consumers.

Diversification involves a strategy of spreading an organisation's activity beyond its main business. The main problem with this is that managers may find themselves working in areas where they have little expertise. Peters and Waterman (1982) have suggested that in fact managers should 'stick to the knitting' (see Chapter 2), in the sense of diversifying only into areas where managers do have expertise. This needs to be an area to which they can transfer an already acquired skill. Manufacturers may move increasingly into a related service area in which they have already been working on a small scale. For example, motor companies have moved into car leasing and car hire services. Restructuring strategy can include a range of approaches designed to reorganise the company in order to meet new challenges. Periods of recession cause retrenchment and possibly liquidation when a company is sold for its tangible assets, not as a going concern. On the other hand 'retrenchment' and 're-engineering' are often approaches designed to concentrate on the main business of an organisation by outsourcing or putting out to contract all those products or services which are not an essential part of the main business. Cleaning and catering services are among the most obvious of these but others include car leasing, information technology and advertising.

Strategic management can be seen as actions concerned with what an organisation should do in order to survive. Ralph Stacey (1999) has argued that the process is a highly complex one involving, as it does, a whole range of networks and control systems within an organisation of any size, and given the many unpredictable elements with which managers have to contend. He suggests that 'one approach to strategy is based on the idea that successful organisations are pulled to an identified future point'. In this case the task of management is to maintain the status quo until the future point is reached. Stacey argues that this is an impossible approach in practice and if it is applied it will fail.

> *'To succeed managers must practise the other approach, the one based on the idea that successful organisations are driven from where they are now to a destination that they create and discover.'*

Hamel and Prahalad (1989) have questioned the idea of 'fit' and the view that successful organisations adapt to their environment. In their study of successful companies in the late 1980s (such as Honda, Komatsu and Canon) as against the less successful ones (General Motors, Caterpillar and Xerox) they found that a distinguishing factor was the different mental models of strategy guiding their respective actions. They observed that less successful companies followed the conventional approach to maintaining strategic fit leading to a trimming of ambitions to those that could be met by available resources. Such companies were concerned mainly with product-market units rather than core competencies. Consistency was preserved through requiring conformity in behaviour and a focus on achieving financial objectives. On the other hand the focus of successful companies was on leveraging resources, that is using what they had in new and innovative ways in order to reach new goals. The main concern of these companies was to use their resources in challenging and stretching ways to build up a number of core competencies. Consistency was maintained by all sharing a central strategic intent.

→ Ch. 2

Hamel and Prahalad (1993) have supported the idea that organisational success arises from organisation-wide intention or strategic intent which is based on a challenging shared vision of the future leadership of the organisation. This is based on organisational learning, an obsession for winning, an understanding that competitive advantages are not inherently sustainable and that an organisation succeeds not by long-term planning but by achieving a broad, stretching and challenging intention to build core competencies. They argue that what distinguishes a small developing company from a larger developing one is not the smaller resource base but the greater gap that exists between the resource base and the aspiration of the company. This gap they refer to as 'stretch', so that the problem of large, established companies is not a lack of resource but insufficient ambition, a lack of stretch in their aspirations. They suggest that companies such as NEC, CNN, Sony, Glaxo and Honda are more united by the unreasonableness of their ambitions and their creativity in obtaining the most from the least than from any cultural or institutional heritage. They suggest that creating stretch is the single most important task of senior management.

The strategic role of managers, therefore, is not so much to stake out the future of an organisation but to help to accelerate the acquisition of market and industry knowledge. Managers use the resources they have to create requirements of the environment which they can meet, they push to achieve stretching goals and they aim to continually renew and transform their organisation. The creation of a 'learning organisation' is an essential element in modern management in both the private and the public sectors because, with improvements in the availability of information, competition has become more fierce rather than less so, and in order to cope with this successful organisations have to embrace new technology and new ideas. There is a sense of creative tension in strategic management because the development of a new direction and the concentration on stretch and leverage destroys the old certainties, and it is, therefore, at the forefront of the process of continuous change.

SUMMARY

- Strategic management is concerned with providing a purpose in order to establish the way forward for an organisation. It involves creating a sustainable competitive advantage for the organisation.

- The purpose of strategy is to enable an organisation to achieve its objectives in a well-organised and coordinated way. This is based on an effective understanding of customer needs and the integration of the marketing strategy into the organisational strategy in order to achieve the desired objectives.

- Organisational strategy is the process by which the vision or mission of an organisation is converted into an action plan. The purpose of the action plan is to ensure that everybody in an organisation understands the objectives of the organisation, their responsibilities in relation to them, the achievement of stretch and leverage, and how to put these factors into action in order to achieve the desired results.

- The action plan will include the formation of a corporate portfolio of products and services taking into account competitive forces. The whole process will need to be reviewed and monitored at regular intervals and then adjusted as necessary.

Review and discussion questions

1 *What is likely to be the result for an organisation of not developing a strategy?*

2 *Is the management of change an inevitable aspect of strategic management?*

3 *What processes can be used in developing organisational strategy from mission statement to action plan?*

4 *How important is competition as a factor in developing an organisation's product/service portfolio?*

5 *How should an organisation carry out the monitoring and review of its organisational strategy?*

CASE STUDY

Dare to be different

FT

If the theory of corporate strategy is a rising market, Michael Porter's stock has not quite kept pace. His reputation in the field, although immense, is based mainly on books published in the early 1980s. His best-known book, *The Competitive Advantage of Nations* (1990), is not primarily about corporations at all. But as professor of business administration at Harvard Business School, Porter is hardly out of touch. Nor, at 50, is he resting on his laurels. Much of his work lately has been on corporate strategy, and as he sees it, the discipline has taken some serious wrong turnings in the past decade. First, he says, the idea has grown up in some quarters that strategy is the same as operational efficiency. Companies need only employ modern techniques, such as total quality management or time-based competition, and the future will take care of itself. In reality, strategy and efficiency are fundamentally distinct. 'Operational improvement is doing the same thing better', Porter says. Strategy, by contrast, involves choosing. 'Choice arises from doing things differently from the rival. And strategy is about trade-offs, where you decide to do this and not that.'

The essence of strategy, in fact, lies in deciding what not to do.

'That is the manifestation that you have a strategy. It also collides with many messages that managers have been assimilating for some time: be close to your customer, and be customer-responsive. Strategy is the deliberate choice not to respond to some customers, or choosing which customer needs you are going to respond to.'

At this point, Porter introduces the second part of his thesis. If strategy does not consist of operational improvement, neither does it consist of focusing on a few core competencies. Real sustainable advantage comes rather from the way the activities of a company fit together.

'Any individual thing that a company does can usually be imitated. The whole notion that you should rest your success on a few core competencies is an idea that invites destructive competition. Successful companies don't compete that way. They fit together the things they do in a way which is very hard to replicate. You have to match everything, or you've basically matched nothing.'

An example he gives is the car rental business.

'The companies your readers will be familiar with are Hertz and Avis, and National and Budget. Those will be seen as the "successful" companies because they have strong brand images, and people see them at the airport when they're travelling around. It turns out that none of those companies has been very profitable, ever. They are all locked into an operational effectiveness competition, offering the same kind of cars at the same kind of airports with the same kind of technology.'

Compare that with Enterprise, a family-run company. 'They do very little consumer advertising, and have no on-airport locations. Their whole strategy is to provide cars for people whose car is stuck in the repair shop, or who have wrecked their car and are waiting for a replacement.' Enterprise has a lot of smaller locations, and will often deliver the car to the customer. The cars are older and kept in the fleet longer. It hires more educated staff, who sell to car-service companies or insurance agents. 'They've chosen not just to try harder, like Avis, but to do almost everything differently. They've made clear trade-offs. They've walked away from the business travel market at airports, and from meeting a lot of needs that rental customers have,' says Porter.

For most companies, Porter argues, this kind of thinking presents immense problems. 'To put it simply, managers don't like to choose. There are tremendous organisational pressures towards imitation and matching what the competitor does. Over time, this slowly but surely undermines the uniqueness of the competitive position.' In part, he says, this comes from a curious notion which has grown up over the past decade: that there are no trade-offs any more. 'People have come to think that you can achieve low cost and the highest quality, or high service and the lowest cost. They confuse moving to the frontier with where you are on the frontier.' This is because when a company has been badly managed, it is often possible to improve quality and cost simultaneously. 'But once you get to good process designs, you have to make choices again. This notion that quality is free has caused many managers to believe not only that they don't have to make choices, but that they shouldn't.'

All this leads many companies to destroy their own strategies. 'They start out with a clear position, and over time they're drawn into a competitive convergence where they and their rivals are all basically doing the same thing. Those kind of competitions become stalemates.'

Porter used to believe, he says, that the hard thing about strategy was understanding the external environment.

'I've now become convinced an equally hard part is coping with the internal forces which work against making clear trade-offs and strategic choices. This has led me to a new interest in the role of leadership in strategy. Most often, it's to make the choices. Strategy can't be delegated. Nobody in the organisation will appreciate these trade-offs except the leader. Once a strategy has been established, most of what leaders do is essentially to say "no": to screen the constant barrage of ideas and opportunities against the strategy, and see if they fit.'

In some industries, he argues, the competitors are clones – companies so similar they cannot even conceive of a different way of competing. The task then is to decide whether the economics of the industry are such that there are no opportunities for trade-offs.

'That's usually the key question. What if I only did that; could I do it better? What if I chose this technology and not that, or this customer group and no others? If you can do terrifically well at X by giving up Y, that gives you the basis for a distinctive position. If there's basically only one dominant way of competing, then you're the hamster running around on the wheel. If you're in that kind of industry, you have to configure your organisation for that kind of world. You're just going to keep trying harder. I argue those industries are worth avoiding.'

Some would argue that in an era of global competition, all industries will come to look like that. Porter disagrees.

'I don't think we're moving towards a hyper-competitive world in which there are no trade-offs. We're probably moving in the other direction. There are more customer segments than ever before, more technological options, more distribution channels. That ought to create lots of opportunities for unique positions.'

Source: Financial Times, 19 June 1997. Reprinted with permission.

FURTHER READING

Hannagan, T J (2001) *Mastering Strategic Management,* **Palgrave.**
A discussion, with many examples, of strategic management.

Herrmann, P (2005) 'Evolution of strategic management: the need for new dominant designs', *International Journal of Management Reviews,* **7 (2), June.**
How firms achieve sustainable competitive advantage.

Kald, M, Nilsson, F and Rapp B (2000) 'On strategy and management control: the importance of classifying the strategy of the business', *British Journal of Management,* **11 (3), September.**
A study of the relationship between business strategy and the design and use of management control.

Porter, M E (1996) 'What is strategy?', *Harvard Business Review,* **November/December.**
A classic debate on strategy.

WEBSITES

http://www.tdindustries.com/
Provides information on organisational mission statements.

http://www.the–body–shop.com
Information about The Body Shop and its policies.

CHAPTER 6

Developing an innovative business plan

Outcomes

Having read this chapter, you will be able to:

- describe the actions managers take in order to implement business strategy;

- analyse the processes of strategic planning to identify the functional role in achieving strategic objectives;

- identify the barriers to planning and methods of overcoming these barriers;

- explain the development of business plans and methods of forecasting future trends;

- explain the importance of organisational development.

FORMULATING A BUSINESS PLAN

Modern managers are faced with a situation in which change is the only 'constant' on which they can rely. One certainty in their lives is that things will not be the same in one year, three years or five years from now. The difficulty is to decide what these changes will be because it is hard to predict exactly when changes in technology will be widely adopted or when new technologies will be developed. Innovative technologies such as broadband, mobile telephones and e-mail were bought by the 'early adopters', people who like to be in the forefront of new technology, but it took longer before other people caught up and the 'laggards', people resistant to the charms of new technology, will still not own or use them. The timing of the full effects of globalisation and competition on particular organisations are equally, if not more, unpredictable. It can be argued that it is only by planning that the nature of the changes taking place can be fully charted and understood. In fact, managers take into account possible changes in deciding a course of action in the form of contingency plans. This is part of the process of turning business strategy into detailed plans of action. While the strategy sets the expected, proposed and desired direction and the objectives to be achieved, this has to be translated into activity which can be implemented and controlled. Exhibit 6.1 illustrates the importance a company can put on the meeting of objectives, while behind any success lies detailed activity in meeting its 'tough objectives' to satisfy its customers, shareholders and employees.

Exhibit 6.1 TRW Inc. of Cleveland, Ohio

Automotive, Aerospace, Information, Innovation
Tomorrow is here: We used to say 'Tomorrow is taking shape at a company called TRW'. While TRW has been helping to shape our world, we have also been working hard to streamline and strengthen our company.

We have set a course that aims to delight our three key constituent groups – customers, shareholders and employees – by providing each with superior performance. The facts demonstrate we are doing just that.

Several years ago, we set ourselves some tough objectives. We are meeting these objectives. Today, we are number one in our key markets. We are the world leader in occupant restraints, in steering systems, in certain automotive electronics markets, in advanced spacecraft technology, in defense communications and in consumer credit information, among others. We are also the world leader in complex systems integration.

Our businesses are in segments of industries that are outgrowing the markets themselves, and we are managing that growth for profit. Cost structures have been improved dramatically, and we are beginning to experience the benefits of our strategic investments over the past five years.

Further technology leadership, always a core TRW strength, is now helping to make us more competitive in all our businesses. Management is also stronger. Supporting a seasoned group of top managers we have a highly qualified, energetic and experienced team around the globe.

What are our priorities? Delivering on our commitments to customers, shareholders and employees. We are positioned for sustainable, significant increases in both sales and earnings. We are doing what we say we will do, and we will continue to deliver our promises.

Source: TRW Annual Report, 1994.

Strategy has to be operationalised into small action plans to be carried out by employees so that taken together these actions should achieve the objectives established by the business strategy. Much of this process is aimed at institutionalising the strategy so that it becomes part of the day-to-day work of the organisation; it has to become part of the culture of the organisation, 'the way we do things around here'. This process becomes overt and perhaps even obvious when an organisation is introducing major strategic change. For example, the British Airways customer service 'campaign' of the 1980s was designed to change the behaviour of its employees, so that in all their operations they put the customer first (see Exhibit 5.7, p. 150). This plan had the objective of creating major changes in behaviour. Many plans simply build on structures and accepted methods that already exist and are ingrained in the systems of the organisation.

Strategy, as applied to planning, is concerned with looking ahead.

'The maxim "managing means looking ahead" gives some idea of the importance attached to planning in the business world, and it is true that if foresight is not the whole of management at least it is an essential part of it.'   (Fayol, 1949)

Strategic management is certainly about decision making and action based on plans, and it is clear that this process needs to be managed so that plans can be seen as a drawing together of a set of independent decisions.

'Planning, of course, is not a separate, recognisable act ... every management act, mental or physical is inexorably intertwined with planning. It is as much a part of every managerial act as breathing is to the living human.'   (George, 1972)

In this way, planning can be seen as integrated decision making, in the sense of bringing together a series of decisions so that they relate to each other and form a rational whole to establish the action to be taken (see also Chapter 5).

→ Ch. 5   One of the major changes in organisations in the 2000s has been the need for flexibility in the workforce, which means an ability to change as circumstances alter and not to expect that present working patterns will last for ever, or even for very long. Technology has been a major factor in the pace of change and in the revolution in working methods and conditions for many people, and as a result of computerisation and information technology the working lives of many people have been completely altered. Managers often have difficulty in knowing how quickly these changes will take place and they may prove quicker or slower than expected. The demise of manual and electric typewriters was predicted for many years until quite suddenly wordprocessors made a clean sweep in a matter of a year or two.

Where an organisation is on course in terms of its strategic plans, the manager's role may be to fine tune the situation by making relatively small decisions on a routine basis in response to problems that arise or in an attempt to improve a business unit's performance. Minor problems can be solved immediately by management intervention while ignoring the effect of the decisions being made on other parts of the organisation. In contrast to these small decisions and minor problems, serious problems may demand planned management interventions in more than one area of the organisation. Managers have to recognise the effect on the various parts of the organisation and arrange for appropriate actions to be taken to satisfy the various areas affected and to monitor progress on the strategic plan.

WHAT IS THE PURPOSE OF PLANNING?

The major argument in favour of planning is in the coordination of decision making so that an organisation is moving in a well-focused direction. Without planning, the efforts of the organisation may not be well coordinated and managers and staff may be heading in different directions. Planning, whether this consists of an elaborate written document or a series of reports on agreed procedures, actions and understandings, also helps to ensure that the future is taken into account so that the organisation can control the situation it finds itself in as far as possible and prepare for unexpected eventualities. Daily routines can lead to the future being forgotten if everybody is too busy to consider medium or long-term problems. It can also be argued that planning is a rational form of management which enables organisations to acquire greater control over their future development.

In the past, scientific management, by emphasising the codification of routine tasks, encouraged the planning of operations. Mariann Jelinek (1979) argued that the equivalent of Taylor's work-study methods (see Chapter 20) in terms of strategy is a system of planning and control to establish a pattern which is not overwhelmed by operational details. Corporate strategy has

→ Ch. 20

> *'made possible for the first time concerted coordination ... and true policy for such organisations. So long as management is overwhelmed by the details of task performance, planning and policy will not occur ... that is, until what is routine is systematised and performance replicable without extensive management attention, management attention will necessarily focus on the routine. By the time of Du Pont and General Motors, the specification of task had moved from codifying workers' routine activities to codifying managers' routine activities.'*   (Jelinek, 1979)

The argument used here is that planning is seen as the key to the formulation of strategy. As organisations have become more complex, the need for plans and systems has grown. At its extreme this argument suggests that it is not people so much as systems that create the strategies, because systems are reliable and consistent while people are relatively unreliable.

> *'It is the responsibility of planning to make sure that the entire organisation knows very well what its customers' requirements are, what is the direction in which customer needs and customer expectations are changing, how technology is moving and how competitors serve their customers.'*   (Marquanett, 1990)

This quotation by the head of planning for Bell & Howell states that responsibility is held by planning rather than by planners. In his book on *The Rise and Fall of Strategic Planning* (2000), Henry Mintzberg seeks to demonstrate the fallaciousness of this approach. He argues that approaches based on formalisation, detachment and predetermination are not correct. The idea that a strategic plan can be translated into a system which accurately predicts the future is called into question. Forecasting is generally recognised as an uncertain science because all types of assumptions have to be made and a range of unpredictable forces may influence the outcomes. He quotes an earlier work in suggesting that

> *'The pressure of the managerial environment does not encourage the development of reflective planners, the classical literature notwithstanding. The job breeds adaptive information-manipulators who prefer the live, concrete situation. The manager works in an environment of stimulus–response, and he develops in his work a clear preference for live action.'*   (Mintzberg, 1973)

It is also the case that the less 'closed' the system, the more difficult accurate forecasting becomes. The Soviet Union attempted to create a closed and planned system under communism. This was of very limited success. Most managers work in much more 'open' systems where they are faced with the uncertainties of economic, social, political, technological and other change. Mintzberg concludes that too much planning may lead to chaos, but too little planning may also lead to chaos and more directly:

> *'Several decades of experience with strategic planning has taught us about the need to loosen up the process of strategy formation rather than try to seal it off through arbitrary formalisation.'*   (Mintzberg, 2000)

It is, of course, an unwise organisation that insists on keeping to its strategic plans in spite of changing circumstances. It can be argued that insistence on maintaining what had previously been a successful plan was the major cause of the collapse of the British motorcycle industry in the face of Japanese competition. This does not invalidate the whole planning process but does illustrate its dangers. Planning may have benefits even where plans have to be changed from time to time, and these changes themselves may be able to be made against a background of relative 'planned' stability.

It is possible to identify behavioural benefits in organisations where strategic planning is encouraged:

■ managers are in a position to detect problems and how best to resolve them;

■ alternative strategies can be considered in making decisions;

■ employees gain a better understanding of their organisation's strategies and may become more committed to them;

■ strategic planning can help to clarify everyone's responsibilities;

■ lower uncertainty about the future consequences of decisions can reduce resistance to change.

However, the dangers of a rigid adherence to planning need to be recognised. The plan may become inappropriate as factors such as competition and technology change, and a well-established plan may become so well accepted that it creates opposition to change. However a plan can help to support the 'sustainability' of strategic change, that is 'maintaining new working methods and performance levels for a period appropriate to the context' (Buchanan *et al.*, 2005). The opposite of this sustainability can be described as 'initiative decay', which arises where the gains from change are lost when new practices are abandoned or, as the National Health Modernisation Agency has described it, the 'improvement evaporation effect'. There is always a risk of this decay or evaporation when strategic changes are not sustained. Kotler (1995) among others has suggested that there are a number of categories of influence on sustainability:

■ **Individual** – how far do the individuals involved in change accept that anxiety and fear are natural responses to change and that the change can also provide a learning opportunity.

■ **Managerial** – the replacement of managers by new managers may result in initiatives not being supported because the new managers may want to introduce their own ideas. At the same time, managers have to be prepared to tackle difficult problems, some of which may affect the fundamental culture of the organisation, while accepting the need to change their own behaviour.

- **Leadership** – the original vision that created the strategic change may become obscure over time.

- **Cultural** – the sense of urgency about change may be dissipated because the change may not have become embedded in the culture of the organisation and there may not be clear links to levels of performance.

- **Political** – the team or teams who brought about the change may not be in a sufficiently powerful position to maintain momentum.

- **Temporal and processual** – there may not have been sufficient time for the strategic changes to become part of the culture of the organisation, while the change may be seen as a discrete, one-off issue rather than a stage on an extended process of implementation, spread and development.

Sustaining change can be assisted by institutionalising the changes so that they become part of the ongoing everyday activity of the organisation (Jacobs, 2002). This is more likely to be the case if the planned changes are consistent with the culture, practices and objectives of the organisation. At the same time individuals need to be committed to the change and be competent to carry out new tasks, or the same tasks in new ways, and need to be rewarded adequately. Another requirement is clear, consistent and challenging goals along with change agents who will support the changes and encourage internal support including support from trade unions and other employee organisations.

THE PLANNING PROCESS

Operational managers have to develop plans of one kind or another at the appropriate level in order to produce the actions required on a day-to-day basis to implement organisational strategy and the strategic plan, assuming this accurately reflects it. Each functional area of the organisation will need a plan, whether it is a written document or an agreed set of procedures and actions, to guide its decisions and actions. If the strategic plan has the objective of growth in a particular market then the sales and marketing division will have to decide how they are going to penetrate that market, or expand in it if they are already present. This may involve market research into customer needs, pilot promotions to test customer response and establishing outlets and channels of distribution. At the same time the production or service department will have to ensure that the product or service is adapted for the market and that suppliers will be available for the expected customer demand. The finance department will have to make sure that money is available to support an increase in output and increases in the marketing and sales expenditure. The personnel department will be involved in the appropriate recruitment of staff and the relocation of employees as necessary.

All the functional departmental plans have to be drawn together so that they operate smoothly in supporting each other. If the finance is not available at the right time, or if the production department cannot meet sales orders, then all the functional plans and the overall strategic plan will have to be reviewed to avoid chaos. In large organisations the importance of this coordination is taken to the point of establishing a separate corporate planning unit whose role is to make sure that all the various plans do fit together and support each other both in operation and in time. Where there is not such a unit then corporate planning will usually be the responsibility of a senior manager.

It is in the operation of these functional plans that marketing has its integrating function in matching customer requirements to the product or service. The marketing department will be close to the point of sale and customer service on the one hand, and on the other hand close to the design and production department. In Exhibit 6.2 the strategic plan is translated into functional plans for marketing, sales, production, personnel and finance.

Other functional departments and divisions, such as sites and buildings, transport, purchasing and supplies and administration will all need to have action plans which relate to the strategic plan and to the other functional plans. The sites and buildings department, for example, will need to discuss capital expenditure on new outlets for the company's products with the finance department. The finance department will be considering the financial control systems required by the new developments over purchasing and supplies, and any expansion in transport and distribution requirements.

Functional plans are usually developed to last for a relatively short period and they are then updated and possibly changed dramatically. However, they are designed over time. They can be distinguished in this way from project plans which are characterised by being designed for a one-off occasion which will not be repeated. This type of plan can be divided into programme plans and project plans, on the grounds that the programme plans are of greater complexity – however, it is often difficult to distinguish between these two types of activity. Whenever there is the need to plan for a one-off activity, whether it is to do with, say, health and safety training or building a new office block, it can be described as a project plan.

Exhibit 6.2 Functional plans

STRATEGIC PLAN: growth in a new regional market

FUNCTIONAL PLANS:

Marketing
- research into customer needs
- establishing possible outlets
- establishing channels of distribution
- carrying out pilot studies

Sales
- establishing contacts
- preliminary advertising and sales promotion

Production
- redesigning products as appropriate
- organising expansion of production
- arranging for increased supply of new materials
- coordinating transport and distribution requirements

Personnel
- recruiting new salespeople and administrators
- relocating employees to the new regional staff

Finance
- considering capital outlay
- supporting investment in design and production
- establishing cashflow plans
- paying wages for staff in new region

Project plans can be distinguished from functional plans in that they are established for a particular timeframe and they include more detail than is usually found in a functional plan. Once the plan has been implemented and the project is completed then the plans will be of little further use. Typical project plans are to build a new office block, design a one-off advertising campaign or develop an employee sickness policy. Once the block is completed, the advertising campaign has taken place or the sickness policy has been established then these plans have achieved their objective and they are of little further direct use.

A plan to build a new office block will often be produced by a project team consisting of people seconded temporarily, and on a part-time basis, from the various functional departments. There will be representatives from sites and buildings, finance, personnel and administration. They will produce draft plans to be considered by senior management and from these they will produce a brief for the architects and surveyors to translate into the detail of drawings and specifications. They will produce a schedule of activities to be completed by certain dates and a flowchart to show the sequence of events that should lead to the completion of the project. All of this has to be set in the context of the capital funds available and also in the context of the company's strategic views on the appearance of the office and the way it should function (Figure 6.1). A retail company, Tesco for example, builds its stores to an established design both externally and internally, so that the project plans for the building of a new store have to include these designs whatever the shape or location of the site.

Figure 6.1 Project plans: simple scheduling and flowcharts

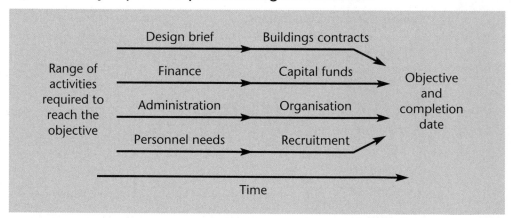

Managers will also produce policies and procedures which establish the boundary lines for making recurring decisions. These policies provide a framework for action, a reference point for employees in their actions. Design policy in an organisation may influence plans, while plans concerned with factors such as employee training may become policies to be applied in all cases. For example, it may become company policy for all staff to receive training in customer care. Policies are created in order to meet the objectives of the organisation and should, with other plans, help in the implementation of the strategic plan and company strategy.

BARRIERS TO STRATEGY

Strategy can be obstructed both by individuals establishing barriers to its success and as a result of the structure of the organisation.

There may be individual barriers because managers are more concerned with problem solving than long-term strategy and their focus is on day-to-day matters. This is more likely to be the case the closer managers are to the operations of an organisation because their daily tasks involve an action-oriented approach moving from one problem to the next. From their point of view strategic planning may be seen as an unnecessary luxury taking up valuable time which could be used to solve more problems and make more decisions. Individuals may also view strategy as a threat in that it may 'put ideas into people's heads' by encouraging them to think ahead. Managers may feel that the process of developing strategy raises the prospect of changing established methods and may raise more worries and concerns than it allays.

Strategic planning also requires a commitment to specific objectives and results, which may be commitments that managers are reluctant to make. This may be magnified by a lack of understanding about the purpose and process of planning by managers who have been promoted from the operational level without training in planning. At the same time the interaction of interests, conflict and power means that the process of change, decision making and planning can be political in nature. It can be argued that

> *'decision makers have different goals, form alliances to achieve their goals, and the preferences of the most powerful prevail.'*   (Elbanna, 2006)

People have conflicting experiences, preferences and interests which arise from different expectations of the future, so some may favour growth, others profitability, others stability above all. This leads to the view (Butcher and Clarke, 2001) that 'management is politics', that organisations consist of mutual interest and competing groups that sometimes come together to produce something worthwhile (see Chapter 9).

→ Ch. 9

> *'They are seldom uniform undertakings of rational, hierarchical coordination and action. Instead agendas constantly collide and align around different issues and managers spend most of their time dealing with this.'*   (Butcher and Clarke, 2001)

Barriers to strategic planning arise from these political influences because they can lead to limited open discussion and communication so that decision making may be divisive and time consuming. Political behaviour can lead to an incomplete understanding of environmental constraints and a concentration on internal factors. Stone (1997) has suggested that

> *'the term "company politics" refers to all the game-playing, snide, them and us, aggressive, sabotaging, negative, blaming, win–lose, withholding, non cooperative behaviour that goes on in hundreds of interactions every day in your organisation. Those who indulge in company politics do so in order achieve their personal agenda at the expense of others in the organisation. In this process, they demoralise and sabotage the company's success. Given their limited numbers, like one or two bad apples souring the barrel, they are disproportionately powerful.'*

Managers have to bring together people who have personal agendas and who are concerned about their self-interest so that these are harnessed in a positive and productive way. Organisational barriers may arise when there is little top-management support for strategy, or where there is support for strategic planning at senior management level but little support for this process being carried down to middle managers and the operational level. Even if there is support, the strategy and strategic plan may be too abstract or too statistical to be translated into operational terms. There is a danger that too much emphasis on planning will lead to very well-produced plans, expertly drafted but not in fact leading to implementation, so that operational activities ignore the plan and instead are based on the requirements of solving problems. Strategy needs to involve everybody concerned in both the process and in agreeing the objectives and the approach to implementation. Top-management support is essential if middle management and operational teams are to allocate time and effort to strategy and its implementation.

Environmental barriers may become important when complex and rapidly changing circumstances surrounding an organisation discourage strategic planning because any plans will have to be hedged around with contingencies. Strategy is produced provided that the economy remains stable, exchange rates do not change to any great extent, supplies of new materials can be guaranteed, government policy does not drastically alter and so on. Managers may feel that these factors, combined with increasing competition from rivals, make strategic planning a useless activity and that they should concentrate on counteracting the threats and challenges that the organisation faces. This is a 'passive' approach, or at best 'reactive', to the work of any organisation allowing other rival organisations and events to dictate its activity. Against this approach strategic planning can be seen as a 'positive' and 'active' setting of unique objectives and directions for the organisation to follow and to be defended as far as possible from outside interference.

This is not to ignore the importance of external forces on an organisation. There is a danger of overplanning, spending too long on the strategic planning process and sticking to strategies and plans that are no longer either viable or wise. Organisations at all levels require a sense of purpose and require strategies in order to keep up the momentum of moving in that direction, but they do not keep moving in a direction that proves to be a dead end (Exhibit 6.3).

Exhibit 6.3 Effects of strategic planning

Strategic plans can:

- promote the uniform handling of similar issues;

- establish control over independent action by establishing clear policies;

- ensure quicker decisions by establishing a framework for decision making;

- offer a predetermined answer to routine problems;

- counteract further resistance to change once the plan has been agreed;

- avoid making hasty and ill-conceived decisions;

- establish a time horizon for monitoring progress on developments;

- establish long-term, medium-term and short-term patterns of activity.

OVERCOMING BARRIERS TO STRATEGY

Strategic planning is part of every manager's role. Before managers can lead, organise or control a work situation they must decide what needs to be done, when and how it needs to be done and who will do it. Overcoming barriers to this type of planning is an important part of this process.

Top-management support is crucial to the success of strategic planning. Senior managers must not only support strategy but must be involved in it and be seen to be involved. Only then will middle managers and operational teams treat strategic planning as a priority by allocating time to it.

The need for strategic planning exists at all levels in an organisation, and this need is greatest at the top where it has the greatest potential impact on the organisation's success. Senior managers usually devote a majority of their time to strategy and their skill in doing this and in making sure strategies are implemented is how they earn their salaries. Even a small organisation needs to have a senior manager who plans and has a strategy, otherwise, although day-to-day problems may be solved effectively, events for which it is not prepared will catch up on the organisation.

Many barriers to strategic planning can be overcome by senior manager support and any organisation which does not have this support is facing great difficulty. The solution to this is through management training, as managers are promoted through the organisation, in order to provide time to consider the role and be given guidance on it.

Allocation of responsibility is an essential element of the planning process. Someone has to be responsible for the successful completion of the strategic plan, otherwise it will be nobody's top priority to achieve it. The chief executive of an organisation will be responsible for the success of the strategic plan and the success or failure of the organisation, while other managers, at the appropriate level, need to be identified as responsible for specific plans designed to meet the overall objectives. Reporting and appraisal systems, management by objectives and other organisation and control systems are all designed to support this process.

Consultation and communication procedures in this area help to reduce barriers to planning by involving a wide range of people in the process. If managers and other employees have been consulted in the development of strategic plans then they will feel some responsibility for their success and 'ownership' of their implementation. At the very least, people in an organisation need to be able to obtain and understand information relevant to planning and any plan with which they are concerned.

Training in planning skills and the implementation of the details of strategic plans encourages people to plan and use plans effectively. Individual barriers can be lowered by this process, particularly those associated with a lack of confidence in strategy and planning, fear of failure and unwillingness to relinquish established systems.

Self-managed teams as a form of organisational structure can encourage planning at the operational level. Managers and teams can feel committed to plans they have produced themselves or have helped to shape. Teams will often be able to contribute to wider plans so that a two-way process can be developed with strategic plans coming downwards and more detailed plans for implementation arising from the expertise and information of the self-managed teams. Their proximity to the organisation's customers and clients means that they are a valuable source of information in the development of a strategic plan, in monitoring it and in making adjustments to it.

Reward and encouragement for individuals and teams can be attached to the outcome of plans. This may be by a system of managing by objectives or by a performance-related pay structure where individual and team rewards are linked to the accomplishment of objectives established in the strategic planning process. These systems will increase the attention paid to planning and the commitment to it. Many reward systems have been organised more or less formally in this way with a bonus, productivity pay or performance-related pay system attached to meeting planned objectives (see Chapters 9 and 12).

→ Chs 9 & 12

Contingency strategy consists of preparing an alternative course of action in case the preferred course becomes either impossible or no longer desirable. Contingency planning has increased in importance as change and innovation have become a normal part of many organisations' environment. These plans provide a safety-valve for individuals or groups of people who have doubts about the ability of plans to work. They may be more prepared to try the plan when they see that there are alternative planned courses of action available.

The so-called worst-case scenario is an extreme example of this process and can be based on taking 'what ifs' to their logical conclusion. For example, posing the question 'What if competitors reduce their prices significantly?' may lead to careful consideration of how costs could be contained, how long the organisation could sustain a price war, the importance of producing a quality product so that the price war could be ignored and other possible courses of action. This approach can help to emphasise the importance of producing plans which are realistic and which clearly help to provide a competitive edge.

BUSINESS PLANS

As well as strategic planning being 'a good idea' essential for the development of an organisation and for judging its progress, it is also a necessity in many circumstances – essential in order that an organisation can obtain financial support. In this more narrow sense, business plans have been developed over many years as a major component of investment decisions. A company seeking a loan or investment will be required by potential customers to produce a business plan in support of its application. This will be used to convince outsiders that managers have carefully thought out the direction the business will follow in the future, that given their present resources and the proposed new investment then the company will be able to achieve its plans. Business plans may also be required in large organisations before a business unit can convince the parent organisation to invest in it.

Many small organisations will have little more than a business plan with which to convince the bank manager that the bank should lend them enough money to start up or expand their business. The plan has to enable the bank manager or other investor to assess the degree of risk and the quality of the people involved. This plan can convert a bright idea into a well-structured plan of action. A business plan can be seen simply as a more focused form of corporate plan:

> *'A business plan is a written statement setting out how the organisation making it intends to organise itself to satisfy the demands of its clients and thereby develop its business.'*   (Chartered Institute of Public Finance and Accountancy, 1992)

As well as a mission or vision – a statement of objectives and a clear view of strengths and weaknesses, opportunities and threats – a business plan must convince prospective investors that the planners have considered exactly who their customers are and what finance and resources are required in order to implement the plan. Customer needs can be ascertained by interviews and surveys which can determine the type of product or service they want and their views on the products or services available. This involves the production of qualitative information on customer views, expectations and perceptions, as much as quantitative information on how many customers buy a product or use a service. In terms of financial and resource planning there will need to be an attempt to forecast the future budget and trading position and an analysis of the effects of inflation, taxation and other factors. This includes a risk analysis to consider how 'risky' the assumptions are that have been made in the plan, and a sensitivity analysis assessing how sensitive the plan is to change. This process involves the 'what if' approach – What if the assumptions prove wrong? What if the environment changes? – and will also need to assess how great will be the impact of the 'what if' factors on the plan.

A new business may assume a growth in sales of 20 per cent a year based on their customer surveys, pilot sales schemes and the general growth of the market. What happens if the sales grow by only 10 per cent a year? Can the company survive on this or not? Similar questions can be asked about assumptions made on labour costs, raw material prices, changes in taxation, market growth rate, competitor activities and so on. While the usual barriers to planning exist with business plans, the fact that they are necessary in order to receive financial support removes the most obvious obstacles in terms of the purpose of planning. In large organisations there will be a number of planning levels (Figure 6.2) with each unit, cost centre or self-managed team producing its own business plan, both to convince senior managers of their viability and also to help inform functional and corporate planning. In small organisations the business plan may serve similar functions to the corporate and strategic plans of a large organisation.

Figure 6.2 Planning levels in large organisations

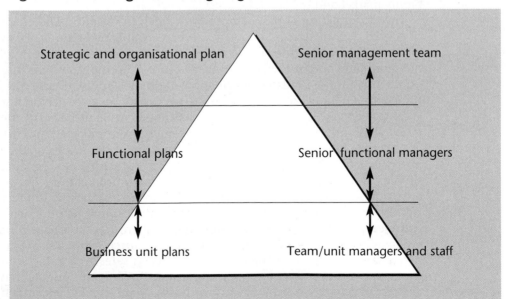

PLANNING TECHNIQUES

Forecasting is involved in all plans because, like strategy formulation, there will be an attempt to predict what will happen in the future. The fact that forecasts are sometimes proved wrong does not mean that they are useless. Perhaps the most obvious and notorious use of forecasting is weather forecasting. In the UK people may plan to have a barbecue at the weekend because dry, warm weather is forecast, but they will have as a contingency plan the possibility of moving inside if necessary. If it does rain on the night this does not prove the uselessness of listening to weather forecasts, simply that not too much reliance should be put on them in a country with a volatile weather system. If the forecast had been for continuous heavy rain then it would have been unwise to plan for a barbecue in the first place.

In fact most daily actions are based on some type of forecast which needs to be sufficiently accurate sufficiently often to guide present actions in a valid and purposeful way. While not too much reliance is placed on weather forecasts in the UK, in countries with a more stable weather structure considerable reliance can be placed on forecasts. In fact the most important use of forecasts is in order to arrive at the basic assumptions or premises on which the plan is based.

The reliance that can be placed on any particular forecast is a matter of managerial judgement, and this is an area where a manager's experience can play an important part in business success. Forecasting is used, for example, in estimating market trends and then making business decisions based on them. A simple example – if industrial and consumer surveys show that the market will grow in the next year, how does the organisation take advantage of this?

Forecasting is often based on **quantitative data**, for example that the market for package holidays will be 10 million holidaymakers next year. A common development of such data is to look at growth trends by taking past data and extrapolating it into the future. Not only can the general growth of package holidays be charted in this way, but also the growth or decline in the popularity of particular holiday destinations and the relative changes in different types of market, such as the family market and the singles market.

The extrapolating of past data is always open to variation and change as a result of altered circumstances and events. Where established data is not available or is unreliable then **qualitative** forecasting may be appropriate. This involves surveys, questionnaires and interviews asking for people's opinions and making judgements on the basis of the available information. Rating scales of various types can be used, for example asking consumers to note their views on a service on a scale of 1–10. Qualitative techniques are often used with new products because sales figures are unavailable and therefore potential consumers' opinions are particularly relevant. For example, once there are some sales figures about the most popular colours for a product then marketing can be based on them, but with a new product a consumer survey can be used asking potential customers to note colours in order of preference. Other qualitative forecasting techniques include the so-called Delphi technique where panels of experts are asked their opinions on a new product and the average of these groups of opinions are then used as a base for arriving at a judgement of the future of the product. Salesforce estimates are used by some organisations to predict the likely sales in each sales area and then to aggregate these for overall product forecasts. These and similar techniques all have the disadvantage of relying on subjective views but they are usually very much better than not doing anything.

Quantitative techniques are statistical techniques which are usually thought to provide more reliable information on future trends than can be arrived at by qualitative methods. Many statistics are already available to most organisations in terms of sales, turnover, marketing expenditure and so on. These can be analysed to produce ratios and trends which are very useful for planning.

Time-series analysis involves charting a variable, such as sales, over a period. The assumption is that the analysis of the past is a good predictor of the future. For example, if sales figures have risen over a series of months then it may be assumed that this growth will continue. Trends such as seasonal variation in sales and the rate of growth can be analysed in order to plan production and marketing as well as cash flow for the company. Figure 6.3 shows a five-year moving average of sales against the annual sales figure. The moving average shows a trend of rising sales over a 10-year period with regular fluctuations between the troughs and peaks occurring approximately every three years. At the end of the 10-year period, sales are beginning to fall again, and past trends would suggest that they will fall for a year or so before beginning to rise again. Past trends also suggest that the troughs will not be as deep as in years 2 and 6. In this extrapolation of the information, managers have to be very careful that they allow for the possibility that past trends will not be a good guide to the future, and do not become complacent in expecting these trends to occur in spite of any action they might take. In practice, managers need to try to prevent the downturn in years 9 and 10 and start to plan for this during the years of growth. For example, it may be possible to develop new products or to penetrate new markets in order to prevent what may appear to be an 'inevitable' fall in sales. A less optimistic strategy would be to prepare for the inevitable by, for example, cutting costs so that the organisation could weather the period of relatively low sales and wait for the next period of growth.

Correlation and regression modelling may be used to consider the effects of different variables on each other. For example, organisations need to know the results of marketing campaigns on sales. **Regression analysis** is designed to estimate one variable (such as the sales volume) on the basis of one or more other variables (such as

Figure 6.3 A moving average

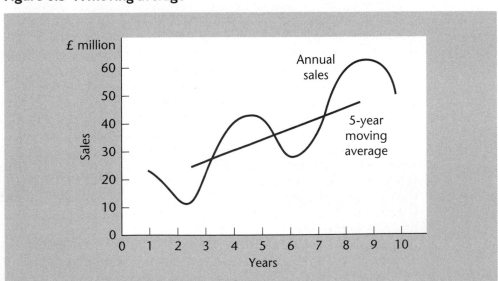

marketing expenditure) which are assumed to have some causal link with it. Correlation analysis compares two variables which are assumed to have an association with each other, so that a change in one will effect a change in the other. For example, an increase in advertising may be assumed to increase sales. While correlation analysis shows if there is an association between the two variables along with the strength of this association and its direction, regression analysis indicates the rate of change in one variable against the other. Between them it is possible to estimate, for example, whether increases in expenditure on advertising increase or decrease sales (i.e. the direction of association) as well as an indication of the amount of change in sales caused by a particular increase in advertising expenditure.

Linear trends can be shown by a straight line if there is in fact a linear relationship between the variables. A line of best fit can be calculated, which is the line closest to the two variables. A simple way of doing this is illustrated in Figure 6.4, while more complex methods include regression lines which aim to minimise the total divergence of the variables' coordinates from the line. This is an objective mathematical approach rather than the more subjective approach used in the scatter diagram in Figure 6.4.

Making a scatter diagram is a simple matter of plotting one variable against the other and then drawing a straight line as close to the points as possible. In Figure 6.4 there appears to be a positive correlation between sales and advertising, so that sales revenue rises as advertising expenditure rises and the relationship can be described as linear. It is important to note, however, that correlation does not prove causality. In other words the increased advertising expenditure may not have caused rising sales and vice versa. There may be a third ingredient which was of equal influence, such as a sudden growth in the market. The fact that there is a linear association between such variables does, however, provide a useful starting point for further investigation.

Linear programming is a more advanced statistical process used to determine the best combination of those resources and activities that are necessary to optimise an

Figure 6.4 A line of best fit

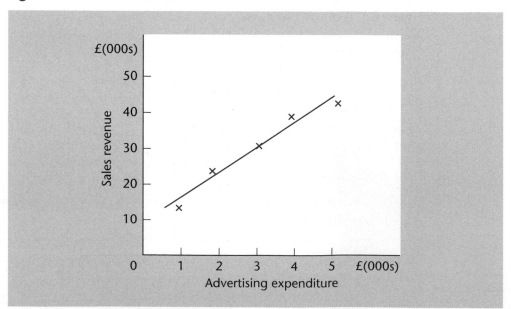

objective. For example, if the objective is to reduce costs then the constraints in doing this have to be identified – these may be resources, capacity or the time available to accomplish the objective. Both the costs and the items that represent constraints then need to be expressed in linear terms either algebraically or in graphic form in order to provide a means for the manager to reach a 'solution'. The manager in this case will usually be the operations manager (see Chapter 14).

→ Ch. 14

Scheduling techniques are designed to assist in the process of coordinating the activities of people and business units with the use of resources in order to achieve the completion of a specific task. For example, in the introduction of a new product the marketing manager needs to know exactly what customers want and the production manager needs to translate these demands into a design or a product. A schedule of a logical sequence of actions and the coordination of people and resources is required to start the production of a successful product. A range of computer models exist to assist in planning the successful flow of activity to reach the desired aim. Operations management has developed into an important part of any large organisation's functions.

The basis of scheduling techniques is the ability to plan activities to achieve a desired end and to reveal discrepancies between planned and actual achievement as the project progresses. If a gap appears between planned progress and actual achievement then managers can provide extra people and resources to fill this gap. For example, Gantt charts have been used for many years as a means of control – these have time charted on the horizontal axis and actions and tasks on the vertical axis (see Figure 6.5). Horizontal bars represent planned schedules and the time required for each task. In Figure 6.5 the filled bars show the actual progress against the outline bar which shows the time allotted (while the customer survey and design have been completed, production staff have only just begun to be employed). The use of colour coding can add to the complexity and the visual impact of such charts.

PERT (program evaluation review technique) is a long-standing technique which helps managers to schedule large-scale projects. It enables managers to create an

Figure 6.5 A Gantt chart

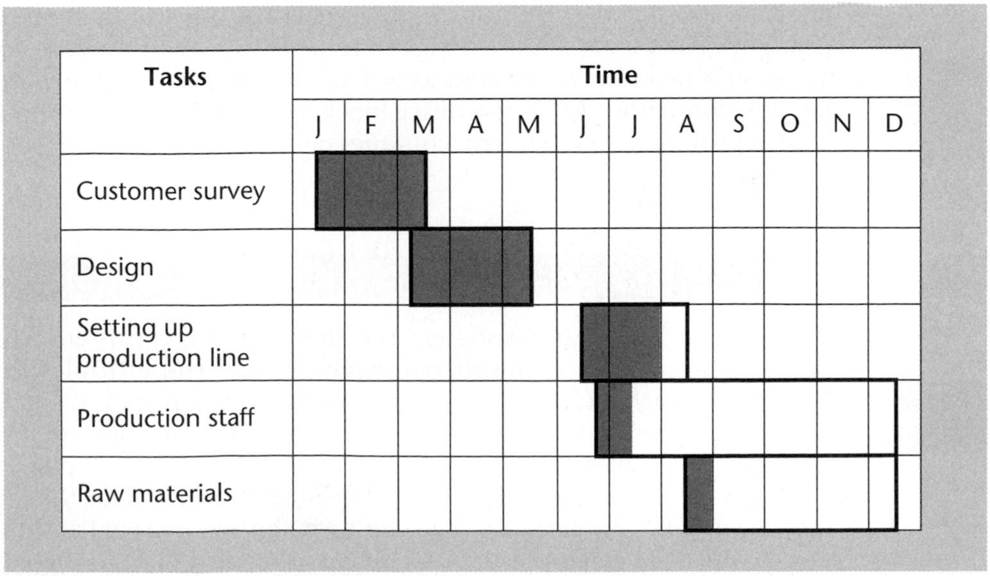

Tasks	Time											
	J	F	M	A	M	J	J	A	S	O	N	D
Customer survey												
Design												
Setting up production line												
Production staff												
Raw materials												

accurate estimate of the time required to complete a project. All the activities necessary for completion are identified, along with the events that indicate completion and the time required for each activity. This information is used to create a network diagram displaying all the activities, events and times that are involved from the start to the end of the project. The PERT diagram is then used as a control and monitoring device. For example, in the building of a new office block managers need to identify all the actions necessary to complete the project and construct a diagram to show the relationship between the different activities and events. A time is allocated for the completion of each activity and the sequence of activities is then tracked through to the completion of the project. Critical path analysis (CPA) is then applied to track the sequence of events which have to occur in a particular order within a given time for the completion of the project on the due date. In the case of a new office block, the concept and design will be the first stage along with the identification of finance and planning provision. Only when these factors have been identified and agreed can the building process actually start (see Figure 6.6).

Figure 6.6 A PERT analysis

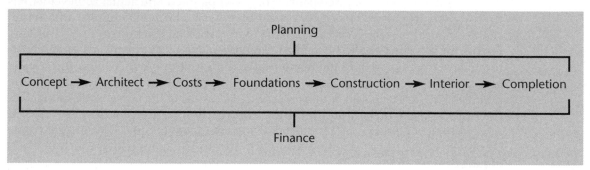

The critical path represents the least amount of time that a project can take from start to finish. This will be determined by such matters as the length of time required to obtain planning consent, the time required to lay foundations and so on. If an event on the critical path is delayed then this will hold up the entire project. Both PERT and CPA are designed to save time and therefore costs. They are based on actual time constraints as well as judgements about how long it takes to lay the foundations for a new office block, for example. They form the basis of a range of computer modelling techniques designed to assist managers in the planning process.

ORGANISATIONAL DEVELOPMENT

→ Chs 1, 2 & 8

Managing an organisation's strategy is easier when it is consistent with the organisation's culture, that is the shared values, beliefs and attitudes that shape the behaviour of each member of the organisation (see Chapters 1, 2 and 8). The priorities and attitudes of the strategy and culture have to coincide, and if this is not the case then it becomes very difficult to implement the strategic plan. For example, where public sector organisations have been privatised one of the main problems they have met is the market culture with which they are faced and the service culture to which the employees and consumers are accustomed. In these circumstances managers have to seek to change the organisation's culture. This is a slow process because it does involve attitudes and 'how we do things around here'. British Airways did this in the 1980s with their 'Putting People First' programme (see Chapter 5).

→ Ch. 5

Both the move to privatise UK public sector organisations and the effects of recession in the 1980s and 1990s have led to considerable discontinuities between strategy and culture in many areas. The old, cautious, traditional culture, based on 'jobs for life' and an established approach to clients and customers, has had to be replaced by a more aggressive competitive culture that promotes risk taking. Examples include British Airways, gas and electricity companies and hospital trusts in the public sector, and companies such as IBM in the private sector. In the 1990s IBM had to change their 'job for life' culture, based on a strong organisational cultural identity, to a less certain job situation for employees and a more aggressive approach to meet competition.

Doyle *et al.* (2000) found that in contrast with the private sector experience, recent organisational changes in the public sector have been:

- less well-monitored and coordinated and likely to lead to the loss of valuable knowledge and experience;
- less likely to be driven by an appropriately experienced manager;
- more pressured with less time to reflect and adjust, with high levels of 'burnout' and less likely to learn from experience;
- more likely to lead to middle management disillusionment and less likely to be seen as personally beneficial to the managers involved;
- more likely to have led to work intensification;
- more likely to have flattened the organisation hierarchy.

→ Ch. 4

The public sector has been subject to a variety of government-imposed changes since the 1990s (see Chapter 4) based on the 'new public management'. While the private sector has implemented similar structural and cultural changes in the face of competitive pressures, these have not been based on ideologically controversial changes based on shifts in government policy and priorities and has not taken place in the full gaze of the public and the media. In both the public and the private sectors, in order to bring organisational strategy and culture closer together, managers responsible for the change process will have to concentrate on people and their attitudes, perceptions, behaviour and expectations. **Organisational development (OD)** is the skilled application of behavioural science towards bringing about organisational change through people. It is a planned change, usually of the whole organisation, supported by senior managers. In large organisations it is an ongoing process which may be implemented through an OD manager and an OD department designed to improve internal relationships and problem solving and with the ability to deal with environmental changes.

Organisational development can help managers to address a range of organisational problems. The most obvious of these are when two companies merge or where one company is the subject of a takeover by another. In the process of merging the two companies' managers may concentrate on how well the products will fit together, or the marketing and management information systems, but fail to consider how closely they fit in terms of values, beliefs and practices. They may have quite different ways of 'doing things around here' which can greatly affect performance if it creates internal tensions. At the time of mergers and acquisitions managers may focus on finance rather than cultural differences, while in order to be sure of a smooth transition and integration, organisational development techniques need to be applied.

Another obvious source of potential behavioural problems in organisations is during a period of recession and decline. If the performance of the organisation leads to redundancies and reorganisation then tensions can develop which produce a lack of trust, and also stress. The same may be true during a period of rapid change when people are asked to work in different ways or to increase their productivity. Although the strategy may be clear, its implementation may be held up by conflicts created by the speed of change. In fact conflicts may be a managerial problem at any time in a successful organisation. For example, there may be a conflict between the product designers and the marketing team, both perhaps believing that they know what the customer wants.

There are a range of activities which can be used in organisational development to help to solve the problem.

- **Training** is the technique most frequently used to bring about change. In the British Airways case, the whole organisation was involved because this was an attempt to change behaviour and not simply skills.

- **Team building** can enhance the cohesiveness of both units and the whole organisation. For example, cross-organisational teams can help employees from different departments and units to understand each other's problems and to cooperate with each other.

- **Communication** can be improved between various parts of the organisation and regarding strategic plans and their implementation. Understanding the reasons for changes in working practices and values can help employees to come to terms with the changes. Consultation about the changes and their implementation can help both managers and other employees to understand and acquire ownership of the changes, particularly when they are as deep rooted as values and practices.

- **Survey–Feedback–Action (SFA)** techniques can be applied in order to encourage consultation and feedback. A questionnaire can be distributed to employees on such matters as working practices, values and organisation culture. After the survey is completed an OD consultant can meet with groups of employees to provide feedback about their responses and the problems that have been identified, and to discuss the way forward. For example, British Airways used the slogan 'The World's Favourite Airline' to show the standards to which they aspired.

→ Ch. 1

The process of achieving behavioural and attitudinal change involves unfreezing the situation, changing it and then refreezing it into the new mould (see Chapter 1). The unfreezing process requires a high level of communication and consultation in order to convince people that the changes are necessary. The immediate reaction of many people will be: How does this affect me? The so-called **SARAH** process will come into effect with shock at the changes being proposed and anger at the apparent rejection of the present, well-tried and apparently successful working practices (Exhibit 6.4).

Why do we need to change? What is wrong with the present system? Why are THEY proposing these changes? These are the kind of questions produced by shock and anger. This period of change is often associated with a diagnosis of the present situation and why a new one needs to be developed. A 'change agent' can be involved at this stage – this may be an OD specialist who performs a systematic

Exhibit 6.4 The change process

- Shock
- Anger
- Rejection
- Acceptance
- Help

diagnosis of the organisation and identifies work-related problems. The role of the specialist is to gather and analyse information through personal interviews, questionnaires and by observing meetings. The diagnosis helps to determine the extent of organisational problems and helps managers to unfreeze by making them aware of problems in their behaviour. The change agent may be an outsider who comes in as a consultant or the OD unit within an organisation.

As an ongoing process the survey–feedback–action technique can be used for upward feedback by which managers assess the senior manager to whom they report. The managers complete a questionnaire and the overall results are then discussed by the OD specialist with the senior manager. A meeting is chaired by the OD specialist with the senior manager and the reporting managers in order for them to express their views about their boss. This process can produce surprises for senior managers about how they are viewed by the people who work directly for them. This process of 'reverse appraisal' can be applied throughout the organisation starting at the top and working down to self-managed teams. In today's fast-changing work environment, managers need to update their diagnosis of the situation on a continual basis rather than only when major change is taking place. It does, of course, have particular importance at sensitive times, such as when mergers, contraction or, for that matter, rapid expansion is taking place.

The changing stage occurs when people begin to experiment with new behaviour and learn new skills in the workforce. This process is assisted by the intervention of OD specialists and others with specific plans for training and development of managers and employees. Training programmes will emphasise the new values and approaches, such as customer-first programmes, quality developments and 'investors in people'. Team building is encouraged, consultation on work practices and symbolic leadership activities are introduced. The rejection of change may be particularly vehement at the beginning of this stage, followed later by acceptance. In time, the people who have most strongly rejected the changes may be the ones who most wholeheartedly come to accept them.

The refreezing stage occurs when individuals acquire new attitudes, values and behaviours and are rewarded for them by the organisation. The OD specialist will provide help for everybody to change and an increasing number of people will look for help to adjust to the new values and approaches. The impact of new behaviours will be evaluated and reinforced. The reinforcement will be through training programmes, team meetings and the reward system.

The organisational development process suggests techniques which managers should apply continuously in organisations so that change is the accepted norm rather than an occasional and rare phenomenon. In this sense the use of terms such as unfreezing and refreezing suggests an end to the process before it starts again. In the altering of attitudes and behaviours it can be argued that, in fact, this is what often happens. While strategic change can be incremental, a step at a time, it is not always like this. The theory is that managers sense the changes required in the environment in which their organisations are working and gradually adapt to these changes through adjustment to the strategic plan and its implementation.

However, studies in the 1980s have suggested that managers resist change until a crisis occurs:

> *'Here managers resist changes that conflict with their predominant way of understanding their organisation and its environment, until some crisis makes it impossible to continue to do so.'*
> (Stacey, 1999)

This leads to **strategic drift** (Figure 6.7) because the organisation is carried forward by its own momentum, becoming more and more out of line with its environment. When this gap becomes too great then the organisation makes sudden adjustments.

Greiner (1972) has argued that strategic drift is virtually endemic in organisations in that they pass through a number of stages in order to sustain acceptable levels of performance. At each level they have to introduce major changes to the 'way they do things':

- **Growth through creativity** – the organisation grows through the creativity of a small group of people who manage in a highly personal style.
- **Growth through direction** – the organisation reaches a stage where it has to develop professional, functional management. This is often centrally directed and can develop into a restrictive hierarchy.

Figure 6.7 Strategic drift

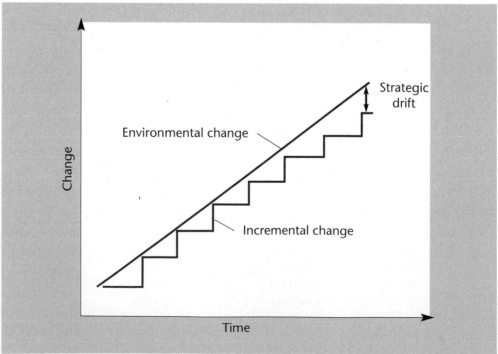

■ **Growth through delegation** – **delegation** and decentralisation help to resolve the crisis of a rigid hierarchy but may create divisions within the organisation.

■ **Growth through coordination** – systems may be introduced to encourage coordination and cooperation, but this may produce a crisis of bureaucracy.

■ **Growth through collaboration** – cultural change produces collaboration which is supported by teamwork.

Organisations may, of course, become stuck at one of these stages and not change their plans to grow further. The inability to change may stunt growth and the processes of corporate planning and organisational development are essential to assist this process through encouraging consultation, communication, training and the constant re-evaluation of strategic planning.

ORGANISATIONAL OBJECTIVES

Central to the implementation of the strategic plan is the setting of annual objectives. They are important because they establish precisely what must be accomplished each year in order to achieve an organisation's plan. In the process they establish the targets and objectives for managers, units and teams throughout the organisation. The annual objectives help to clarify managers' tasks and their role in the process of achieving the strategy and plans, and they can also provide a sense of purpose and motivation. They also provide a means of monitoring performance and to do this they should be measurable.

The development of annual objectives can reflect shifts in the strategic plan and can provide for incremental growth. If an organisation is skilled in corporate planning and organisational development then it can perhaps avoid a 'crisis' change with dramatic alterations in direction or values. However, if external factors outside the control of the organisation alter dramatically then it is difficult to avoid quite fundamental shifts in the corporate plan. The annual objectives can reflect this shift of position.

For example, government policy on the funding and governance of public sector institutions during the 1980s and 1990s has caused major changes in these institutions' ways of doing things and their approach to the future. UK government policy encouraged the rapid expansion of higher education in the early years of the 1990s and then suddenly cut back on this expansion in 1994. In the same way further education was encouraged to expand by 25 per cent in the period 1993–96 through the funding mechanism. Furthermore, the recession of the late 1980s and early 1990s caused private sector companies to re-evaluate their structures and organisation. Outsourcing of many services became common and there was a major shift to a group of core workers responsible for the core business of the company.

In order to implement annual objectives, managers have to develop a process to carry them through business units and to individuals. **Management by objectives (MBO)** was first proposed by Peter Drucker in *The Practice of Management* in 1955 and was very popular as a method of implementing strategic objectives in the 1960s and 1970s. Although it has fallen out of fashion as a system, many present-day methods are very similar to MBO in their approach and results. MBO describes a set of procedures that begins with objective setting and continues through performance review. Each person's major areas of responsibility are clearly defined in terms of measurable results, so that they can be used by employees in planning their work and by both employees and managers in monitoring progress. Performance reviews are conducted jointly over time and fresh objectives are established at appropriate intervals. The objectives identify the individual actions needed to fulfil the organisation's or business unit's strategy and annual objectives. Through this process MBO provides a method of integrating and focusing the work of all the members of an organisation on the strategic plan.

While this process involves objective setting by managers in line with the corporate objectives, Drucker emphasised from the start the importance of participation by all employees. He supported the ideas and principles of Douglas McGregor's 'Theory Y' (see Chapter 2) and felt that unless people were actually involved in their own objective setting then they could be half-hearted about the process. In more recent terminology, they need to feel 'ownership' of the objectives and the plans to meet them. This is of particular importance because of the autonomy usually provided in implementing plans. While it may be difficult to provide this autonomy for everybody in an organisation, managers, supervisors and team leaders are usually able to decide on the actions they need to carry out to achieve their objectives and those of the members of their team.

→ Ch. 2

The essential elements of MBO have been carried forward into a range of company and institution-based schemes of appraisal and performance review and evaluation, which have been developed under a variety of names to match particular organisational needs. The development of increasing autonomy in business units and self-managed teams encouraged the setting of objectives at these levels, with a feedback mechanism within the unit and team as well as on an organisation-wide basis. The advantages are seen in terms of improvements on past performance, particularly when individuals determine their own objectives and when there is feedback on performance.

In the 1980s and 1990s and into the twenty-first century the process of relating performance against objectives to the reward system has been extended through performance-related pay and target setting. However these systems have developed, the fundamental elements of MBO remain the focus on individual objectives and the feedback on their achievement. This focus has been considered to be a major motivator for many people in knowing what is expected of them and in their positive feeling of success when objectives are met. The participation of individuals in the process is essential to ensure that the objectives which are established are realistic.

INNOVATION AND ENTREPREURSHIP

'Much confusion exists about the proper definition of entrepreneurship. Some observers use the term to refer to all small businesses, others to all new businesses. In practice, however, a great many well-established businesses engage in highly successful entrepreneurship. The term, then, refers not to an enterprise's size or age but to a certain kind of activity. At the heart of that activity is innovation: the effort to create purposeful, focused change in an enterprise's economic or social potential.'

(Drucker, 1998)

All organisations face the challenge of innovation because their survival and growth depends on their capacity to renew their offerings, in terms of goods and services, and the way in which they create and deliver their offerings. The Chartered

Management Institute has described the relative weakness of the UK at innovation, the successful exploitation of new ideas, as 'well known but rarely understood' (Professional Manager, 2007). It is argued that innovation accounts for half of all productivity growth but while the UK is successful at basic science, or curiosity-driven research, it is less successful at turning the ideas of scientists and engineers into commercially viable products and services.

> *'The UK is becoming a focused-knowledge economy, where value lies increasingly in new ideas, software, services and relationships. In this environment, knowledge-based, innovative businesses such as biotechnology, pharmaceuticals, financial services, telecommunications, software and information technology are making an above average contribution to the UK's GDP and its competitiveness.'*

(Professional Manager, 2007)

New discoveries and inventions quickly replace what have become, temporarily, standard ways of doing things. The pace of change is illustrated by remembering that older people, even in developed countries, grew up without credit and debit cards, video-on-demand, cellular telephones, the Internet, the dominance of computers and so on. Organisations like Microsoft, Toyota, Nokia, Procter & Gamble and many others constantly search for an innovative edge. In this process most organisations in both the private and public sectors follow a similar series of activities:

■ **searching** – scanning the environment both inside the organisation and outside it for threats and opportunities;

■ **selecting** – deciding to which of these to provide a response;

■ **implementing** – translating the idea into something new and launching it;

■ **learning** – learning from this process so that it becomes part of the way in which the organisations operates.

This process involves creativity, that is 'new ideas', a new way of doing things. This may be a new product or service, a new management concept or a new delivery system. Creativity can be described as the generation of new ideas that meet perceived needs, ward off threats and respond to opportunities. Meeting needs is an essential element in this process, which again emphasises the importance of 'keeping close to the customer'. Adoption occurs when an organisation decides to go ahead with a proposed idea and implementation occurs when it is actually used. 'Venture' teams are formed in some organisations with the purpose of giving free reign to creativity, and they may be supported by 'a new venture fund' to provide employees with resources to develop new ideas, products and methods. At the same time 'corporate entrepreneurship' can be encouraged to support and develop new ideas and enterprising approaches.

Innovative ideas can arise from managers considering the kind of jobs which existing customers cannot get done or from the ways existing products are used which 'stretch' their use from what they were designed for. Looking at an organisation's 'non-customer' base, that is the consumers who do not use its products or services, may throw up new ideas. After all, the organisation's customers are presumably being satisfied, while those who are not customers may represent an important potential market. In some areas there may be 'bottled-up consumption' which can be released by new products or by adopting new methods. In the public sector Moore (2006) has suggested that innovation can increase public value in public sector organisations by:

- generating better methods for performing their core, basic function;
- exploiting the performance advantages that could be gained by abandoning a one-size-fits-all approach in favour of one that encourages customisation to meet the needs of varied circumstances and clients;
- use organisational capabilities to introduce new products and services to provide for different parts of their current services, or that meet needs outside the present service.

Drucker (1998) has pointed out that

'there are of course, innovations that spring from a flash of genius. Most innovations, however, especially the successful ones, result from a conscious, purposeful search for innovation opportunities.'

This begins with the analysis of the sources of new opportunities. These may arise as unexpected occurrences, through process needs, because of industry and market changes, as a result of demographic changes or new knowledge. Effective innovations usually start small, they do one specific thing:

'the elementary idea of putting the same number of matches into a matchbox (it used to be 50). This simple notion made possible the automatic filling of matchboxes and gave the Swedes a world monopoly on matches for half a century.'   (Drucker, 1998)

Successful innovations tend to be simple so that when they are implemented people exclaim on how obvious they are. Innovation is the foundation of entrepreneurship and is essential for sustained organisational success.

IMPLEMENTING AN INNOVATIVE BUSINESS PLAN

Change management is a relevant and necessary process at all organisational levels in order to implement an innovative business plan and achieve strategic objectives. This applies to individuals, teams, departments and corporations and involves the following ingredients (summarised from Doyle *et al.*, 2000):

- establishing corporate control over the timing, pacing and scheduling of change initiatives;
- establishing systematic and visible preplanning, monitoring and assessment mechanisms;
- developing effective stress-management procedures;
- adopting an innovative, focused approach to organisational communication;
- developing systematic mechanisms for capturing effectively the personal and organisational learning from change;
- introducing effectively resourced 'damage control' strategies to deal with increases in work, fatigue, burnout, self-interest and cynicism, and reduced loyalty, commitment and trust;
- introducing organisation-wide programmes for the development of change management expertise.

Developing a strategic plan involves these processes and the recognition of the barriers that prevent an organisation from implementing its plan and its strategy and from achieving its objectives. Beer *et al.* (2005) have identified seven organisational capabilities (the seven Cs) that research and experience have suggested are crucial to the implementation of most strategies:

- **Coordination** among teams, functions and departments ensures efficiency in working towards a common goal.
- **Competence** encompassing technical, functional, interpersonal and leadership skills that are dynamic and flexible in adapting to change.
- **Commitment** and accountability from each and every member is crucial if the organisation is to achieve its strategic goal.
- **Communication** (vertical, lateral and to stakeholders) enables clarity in what, why and how things need to be done.
- **Conflict management** helps to sustain healthy politics in the organisation.
- Encouraging **creativity** at all levels of the organisation enhances novel ways of solving problems.
- **Capacity management** matches financial and human resources (skills, knowledge) with the strategy.

Once there is a high degree of alignment and 'fitness' in the seven Cs then the organisation should be able to implement its business plan, achieve its strategic objectives and compete successfully. However, with the changes in the environment of organisations, maintaining fitness and alignment is a continuous learning process which requires feedback on performance and the constant appraisal of the internal structure and capabilities of the organisation.

Strategic management involves making decisions which will enable an organisation to achieve its organisational objectives. These decisions have to be translated into action in one way or another. In turning strategic policy into action, managers have to identify what is needed to realise strategic objectives, as well as recognising barriers to action that may arise and methods of overcoming these barriers. While forecasting and planning may be seen as activities which stand apart from operational management, plans have to be translated into actions. Business plans may be useful in describing how an organisation will be organised and how it will satisfy the needs of its customers but the success of these plans will be judged by how they are put into action, that is the way the organisation operates. Action plans need not only to show how objectives will be achieved but they need to be followed by employees at all levels in an organisation, in the way that a builder follows building plans. Action plans are concerned with turning objectives and priorities into reality and they provide a mechanism by which senior managers can satisfy themselves that what is being implemented is consistent with the intentions of organisational strategy.

SUMMARY

- Once an organisation has decided on a strategy the managers have then to decide how to implement it. Overall action plans have to be operationalised into smaller plans and tasks for employees to carry out. The role of management is to make relatively small decisions in order to fine-tune the situation to achieve the organisation's objectives. These may be drawn together by reference to an overall strategic plan.

■ The strategic planning process includes the development of plans at appropriate levels to produce the actions required to implement the strategic plan. The plans and actions of functional departments need to be drawn together so that the organisation operates smoothly. Marketing is the integrating function in matching customer requirements to the final product or service.

■ There are individual, organisational and environmental barriers to strategic planning which experienced management can overcome. Business plans establish how organisations intend to organise themselves to satisfy the demands of customers. This process is supported by forecasting techniques, both qualitative and quantitative.

■ Organisational development can help managers to deal with changes through staff training and development, team building and internal communication. If managers resist change or attempt to avoid implementing it, then strategic drift can occur.

■ Strategic objectives can be implemented by processes such as appraisal, review and performance-related pay. These systems focus on individual objectives and feedback on their achievement.

Review and discussion questions

1 *What are the main problems of implementing an organisation's strategy?*

2 *How are an organisation's strategic plans translated into detailed actions?*

3 *When is it appropriate to establish a project team? How will its operation differ from a more functional approach?*

4 *Outline the main barriers to planning. How can managers overcome these barriers?*

5 *What techniques are used in the development of business plans?*

6 *How important are performance measures in attaining an organisation's strategic objectives?*

CASE STUDY

Know your place

Standard Life and National Westminster are two businesses in the news. Each is an organisation with a great past behind it. Each of them has a name which commands envy and respect. Each of them has well-publicised problems. And, although the businesses and problems are very different, there is an important sense in which the issues they face are the same.

Banks, which were central to the British economy in the twentieth century, are products of the nine-teenth century. They came into existence in order to mobilise the small savings of individuals and lend them on to growing companies. Their effectiveness rested on the local knowledge of their managers. These managers were traditionally key figures in the local community. Their local knowledge gave confidence to depositors and allowed shrewd and informed assessments of the viability of the businesses the banks supported. There were some advantages to scale in banking. National coverage gave depositors confidence in the stability of the institutions which they trusted with their savings. An institution with branches from Carlisle to Camborne seemed likely still to be there when savers wanted their money back. The marble banking halls and grandiose head offices reinforced the sense of permanence.

And bigger banks were needed to handle bigger borrowers. By the 1920s the number of leading clearing banks in Britain was reduced to five. Midland, its roots in Britain's manufacturing heartland, was not just the largest bank in Britain; it was the largest bank in the world. Its rivals – Barclays, Lloyds, National Provincial and Westminster – were not too far behind. But around this time, the rationale for the banks' traditional collection of functions disappeared. Securities markets developed. That meant that you did not need to be a big financial services retailer to lend money to large corporations. And the skills involved in the two activities of retail deposit taking and business lending, once rather similar, had become quite distinct.

Nobody really noticed. As competitive pressures increased, the British banks followed the usual strategies of companies which do not really know what to do. They sought greater size by merger and internal expansion, and engaged in unfocused diversification into new businesses and new areas of the world. All of that was irrelevant, or worse. One final megamerger created the National Westminster Bank, but the government blocked further concentration. Banks discovered that it is easy to meet targets for growing your balance sheet so long as you are not too bothered about getting your money back. And they lost a packet buying stockbrokers and American banks.

Standard Life, too, had a golden era of success. It pioneered the retailing of equities to a mass market. That was not what the business said it was doing; in fact, if it had it would probably have been stopped. But by packaging equities as a life insurance product, it avoided restrictive regulation and secured effective distribution. There was not a long-term business there. It became easier, both legally and operationally, to sell shares more directly to individuals. And once that happened, there ceased to be a rationale for linking the three main things which Standard Life did: financial services retailing, investment management and the underwriting of risks.

Standard Life's response has been another stan-dard recourse for those with no easy strategic options: if you are not doing well enough at what you are doing already, try something else. Become a bank, or an investment management house. But there do seem to be quite a lot of well capitalised banks and successful investment management houses around already. What National Westminster and Standard Life have in common is that each embraces a range of functions which were sensibly undertaken together at a particular point in history, but for which the rationale of combination has now disappeared.

And each business has found that when you unpick the individual things they do, most of them are performed better by someone else. The banks found that their retail deposit services were upstaged by building societies, that their merchant banking arms found it difficult to match the resources and professionalism of specialist investment banks, and that lending to very large corporate and sovereign borrowers was so competitive that no one has made any money out of it, or is ever likely to.

British insurers learnt that their retailing capabilities were very limited in competition with people who had branch networks – or a red telephone; that their investment skills were inferior to those of specialist fund managers; and that their underwriting was outstripped in professionalism by continental reinsurers.

So what should businesses faced with these kinds of strategic dilemmas do? The main requirement is to identify which of the many activities such a business will be engaged in are ones in which it has an ongoing competitive advantage. What can you do that others cannot readily do as well? Lloyds did this in the 1980s when it understood that its strengths were in retail financial services and lending to small businesses, and quit the more glamorous but less profitable activities which required it to compete with every other bank in the world.

But sometimes strategic dilemmas have no solution. This is difficult for executives to accept, but not all questions have answers. Sometimes the proper job of managers is to preside over an orderly transfer of the activities they control to other businesses. This does not often happen quickly or without the costs and uncertainties associated with the takeover process. Perhaps it should.

Source: J Kay, *Financial Times*, 27 June 1997. Copyright John Kay, economist. Reprinted with permission.

FURTHER READING

Beer, M, Voelpel, S C, Leibold, M and Tekie, E R (2005) 'Strategic management as organisational learning: developing fit and alignment through a disciplined process', *Long Range Planning*, 38.
An analysis of how organisations adapt to new strategic circumstances.

Buchanan, D, Fitzgerald, L, Ketley, D, Gollop, R, Jones, J L, Lamont, S S, Neath, A and Whitby, E (2005) 'No going back: a review of the literature on sustaining organizational change', *International Journal of Management Reviews*, 7, September.
A review of how strategic change is maintained in organisations.

Doyle, M, Claydon, T and Buchanan, D (2000) 'Mixed results, lousy process: the management experience of organisational change', *British Journal of Management*, 11, special issue.
An analysis of management perceptions of strategic change and the change process.

Mintzberg, H (2000) *The Rise and Fall of Strategic Planning*, FT Prentice Hall.
The importance and drawbacks of strategic planning.

Porter, M E (1998) *Competitive Advantage: Creating and Sustaining Superior Performance*, Free Press.
A discussion of strategy and sustaining strategic change.

WEBSITES

http://learning.mit.edu/res/kv/index.html
Discusses the idea of the learning organisation.

http://www.carol.co.uk
Provides access to company reports.

http://www.nissan-na.com/smyrna/ind.html
Information about the Nissan company organisation.

CHAPTER 7

Controlling quality in organisations

Outcomes

Having read this chapter, you will be able to understand:

- the concept of 'quality' applied to commerce and industry;
- the application of this concept to all types of organisation;
- how a quality system can be introduced and managed within an organisation;
- the importance of focusing on the customer;
- the link between total quality and the management of change;
- the strategic importance of corporate objectives;
- the use of performance management;
- the differences between quality control and quality assurance;
- techniques such as 'right first time', 'just in time', and 'zero defects';
- the way in which quality can inform the whole approach to management.

WHAT IS 'QUALITY'?

'In today's competitive environment, ignoring the quality issue is tantamount to corporate suicide.'   (President of Hewlett-Packard, *Fortune*, October 1985)

In business and management terms there is an attempt to focus on a measurable concept of **quality** by concentrating on 'fitness for purpose'. A specification is supplied by the customer and the quality of the product is measured by how closely it conforms to this specification. It is based on the customer's perception of quality. In these terms quality can be defined as

'continually meeting agreed customer needs' or 'what it takes to satisfy the customer', or simply 'fitness for purpose'.

This last phrase has become a cliché, normally in the form of 'fit for purpose' and often without any clear idea of exactly what it means. In quality terms it means the closeness of the match between a product or service and the needs of the customer. In more general terms, quality is an elusive concept and the usual dictionary definition does not help to make it less so: 'That which makes a thing what it is, its attributes, its characteristics'. The 'quality' of a person may be measured by certain characteristics such as honesty and courage.

This approach involves values and judgements, while a statement such as 'the quality of a strawberry plant is that it bears strawberries' is value and judgement free – it is a statement of what the plant is. However, the fruit from different plants will be compared in size, colour and flavour and then may be graded into strawberries of different 'quality' in the more limited commercial sense of how well it satisfies customers and how well it sells. Supermarkets want their suppliers to provide strawberries, apples, potatoes and so on which conform to a particular size and appearance, while outlets such as farmers' markets concentrate more on taste, flavour and providing local produce.

In Helene Giroux's article on management fashions (2006), she charts the development of definitions and ideas about quality from

'if quality is perceived as merely meeting technical specifications ... only mediocre results will be achieved'   (Hoerschemeyer, 1989)

to

'quality means internal and external customer satisfaction.'   (Juran and Gryna, 1993)

'Currently, definitions such as "delighting the customer" and "satisfaction" are tossed about. The fact that these definitions are not measurable or expandable and are impossible to communicate has not changed many minds.'   (Crosby, 1997)

Earlier Crosby argued that manufacturing-based definitions have been misunderstood:

'Many writers have taken my definition of conformance to requirements, and twisted it as "conformance to specification". This creates a narrow, highly technical , manufacturing-orientated consideration.'   (Crosby, 1996).

A comprehensive definition is provided by Galgano (1994):

'Quality, therefore, includes the following: competitiveness; deliver; cost; morale; productivity; profit; product quality; quantity or volume; performance; service; safety; concern for the environment; the stockholders interest.'

Quality can be seen as an attribute of a product or service which ensures that it is attractive in the eyes of the customer. It is a relative property rather than an absolute one, in that a given product or service will be attractive to customers if it fulfils their expectations more fully than any other product or service under consideration. It means delivering the right product or service that is fit for the purposes required by the customer, at the right price, and at the right time and place. A company that produces and delivers a beautiful-looking car to a customer will not be considered to produce quality goods if the car does not work well. Whatever the costs involved, the materials used or the care taken in manufacture, the quality of the car will be considered poor if it is unreliable. A lawnmower that does not cut the lawn effectively is of no use to the customer whatever its price or however firmly the manufacturer describes it as a 'quality' or 'excellent' product.

WHY IS THE MANAGEMENT OF QUALITY IMPORTANT?

→ Ch. 3

The management of quality is important because of the need to focus on the customer and because meeting customer needs is the foundation of any successful organisation (see Chapter 3). Products and services have to be of a quality to meet customer requirements, as the quality of a product or service may be the distinguishing factor between the offerings of competing companies from which the consumer has to choose. Two products may serve the same purpose but if they sell for the same price and one is well designed and constructed from high-standard materials and the other is not then consumer demand is likely to be for the well-made product. This is even more likely to be the case if this product is more reliable and the company offers good after-sales service. If two restaurants in the same street charge similar prices for meals, but one provides slapdash service and the other looks after its customers, it is the one that provides a good service which is likely to be more successful.

'You get what you pay for' is a saying which suggests that the more you pay the better the quality of a product or service. Of course, this does not always follow but in consumer surveys there may be a distinction between the best product on offer in terms of quality and the best in relation to a balance between quality and price, or what may be called 'value for money'. The very highest quality may be expensive to achieve in relation to the material costs in the use of the very best materials and labour costs because of the time involved in ensuring high quality. However, whatever the costs and the price, the quality has to be sufficient to meet the requirements of enough customers to make the sale of the product or service successful.

→ Ch. 8

In organisational terms a lack of quality is likely to be a waste of resources through scrapped materials and wasted time as well as through rejection by consumers. Market research can help to identify what customers want (see Chapter 8), their purchasing behaviour and the requirements that organisations need to meet if they are to be successful. Quality-improvement programmes in organisations combine product improvement, the closer matching of customer needs, and process improvement. They not only result in a focus on quality matters but they can also create a demand for ever-higher standards, therefore making quality improvement an ongoing process.

The idea of managing the quality of products and services is important if not new, it can be traced through history (Juran, 1995).

'Many of the core principles and techniques of modern quality management were developed in the 1930s and 1940s and have been in use in the USA ever since – although maybe not as extensively as they could or should have been.' (Giroux, 2006)

The American Society for Quality Control was founded in 1946 and brought together quality practitioners. The interest in quality management increased rapidly in the 1980s as a result of American trade deficits and recession while Japan's exports were soaring and the Japanese economy booming. These differences between the two economies suggested that if American industry adopted the quality approach of the Japanese then it could prosper.

FOCUS ON THE CUSTOMER

If it is accepted that high quality is a measure of excellence taken from the customer's point of view then, although producers may grade their goods in terms of quality, whether the producers' view of the grading is upheld will depend on customer perception. If customers like their strawberries to be large, firm, red and sweet then fruit with those characteristics will be considered to be of the highest quality, and the producer of smaller, paler strawberries may not be able to convince customers of the high quality of their output, however sweet they may taste.

The focus on the customer means that quality is conceptualised in terms of the customer's perceptions. The organisation's objective is to identify customer requirements so that both the customer's and the organisation's needs are met. It is also the intention to meet these requirements first time and thus avoid the cost of sorting out problems. The process involves:

- **research**
- **specification and planning**
- **delivery**
- **review.**

→ Chs 5 & 6

This process focuses on the customer at key points and returns constantly to research (see Chapters 5 and 6) into changing customer needs (see Figure 7.1). When customer needs are identified, planning can take place into exactly what has to be delivered. The specifications and standards are determined so that priorities can be established to ensure that the product or service delivered is what the customer needs and that it meets customer perceptions. Although costs and price play an important part in this, most customers will pay what is necessary in order to receive what, in their view, is good quality. This in turn will generate profits as customers demand this product or service above others.

A customer can be defined as anyone who receives a product or service. This approach has been extended by many companies beyond the satisfaction of the external consumer in order to include the internal customer as well. One department in an organisation receives products or services from another department and passes these on to a third group. On an assembly line a commodity is passed along the line from one individual or team to another, each dependent on the other for the receipt of the commodity at the correct quality at the correct time, and aiming to pass it on with the correct added value and, again, on time.

The concept of the internal customer means that each process is viewed as a product so that evaluation takes place at once by the immediate customer or by the

Figure 7.1 Focus on the customer

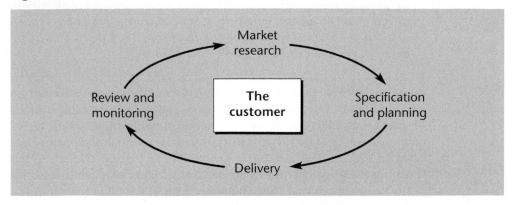

processor. This system will help to eliminate waste and reduce costs, while the overall objective will remain the satisfaction of the external customer. The product or service will be 'right first time' so that errors will be prevented through the need to satisfy the internal customer at each stage rather than through a final inspection.

TOTAL QUALITY MANAGEMENT

As companies have made a conscious effort to 'focus on the customer', **total quality management (TQM)** and other methods have been introduced to implement this. Total quality management is known by other names such as total quality improvement (TQI) or total quality control (TQC), or as strategic quality management (SQM), or simply as total quality (see Chapters 10 and 14).

→ Chs 10 & 14

It is possible to identify differences between total quality management and titles such as strategic quality management. How important these are remains a matter of opinion. Total quality management is often described as a 'value-based' approach to quality management; it may be seen as a goal which an organisation aims to achieve, or the idea of *total* quality may be considered unattainable. On the other hand strategic quality management can be described as both systematic and value based. It can be seen to suggest that the reason for improving quality is that it will have maximum strategic impact on the future of the organisation. Strategic quality management is designed as a practical and pragmatic framework in which the drive towards quality improvement can be sustained while not making claims on *total* quality. A counterargument to this is to consider the word 'total', in the context of total quality management, to mean that every part of an organisation is involved.

The approach can be recognised, whatever its title, by its objectives. Total (or strategic) quality management can be defined as:

> *'an intensive, long-term effort to transform all parts of the organisation in order to produce the best product and service possible to meet customer needs.'*

In some Japanese companies there is no such thing as total or strategic quality management – it is simply the way they operate and it does not need a title, although it could be described as 'right first time', in order to make sure that it happens (see Chapter 19). The management at the Toyota plant in Japan has stated that:

→ Ch. 19

'We estimate it will take you twenty years to be where we are now, and by that time we will have progressed further. We have moved from quality philosophy to measuring defects on an acceptable quality level basis to reducing our defect rate to below five to six parts per billion. Our last product recall was 1969 when we first started introducing what you know as Total Quality Management.'   (Atkinson, 1990)

Total quality management can be seen as a metaphor for the process and management of change, designed to realign the culture and working practices of an organisation for the pursuit of continued quality improvement. Initially the concept of quality tended to be considered in terms of narrow and specific techniques, such as quality circles (see p. 210) or statistical process (or quality) control (see pp. 219–222). The concept has developed into a pervasive one (see p. 221, the Taguchi method), touching every aspect of the organisation including suppliers and customers.

It can be argued that there have been phases in the evolution of TQM, starting with the idea that processes such as 'quality control', 'quality assurance' and 'statistical quality control' are all aspects of TQM that have to be managed. This phase may concentrate on methods and systems and lead on to the application of the concept of quality to people and the view that the management implications of quality are all-pervasive. This concentration on people may lead to the view that quality is about satisfying the customer and may move beyond the idea of providing what the customer thinks they want on to the idea of satisfying the latent needs of customers, providing them with goods and services and quality they had not fully realised they wanted.

In an organisation that practises total quality management, quality becomes the standard operating procedure and part of the culture (see p. 192 for a description of benchmarking). It is not simply a programme or project, but a way of life. It is proved by the quality of materials purchased from suppliers, the approach to defect control on the production line, the appearance of the building, the way problems are solved for customers, the way employees are organised and the organisation's internal communication system (see Chapter 10 for an analysis of organisational communication and TQM). This approach is founded on the premise that quality depends on individual effort and attitude. It is a rigorous, highly disciplined and skilled process which may challenge present practice and depends on a training programme throughout the organisation. Total quality management is predicated on a commitment to customer interests, needs, requirements and expectations, and on the commitment of everyone to the constant improvement of the quality of everything that the organisation does and provides for its customers (see pp. 220, 493 and 688 for a description of 'just-in-time' techniques).

→ Ch. 10

TQM is a strategic approach within an organisation which can provide an 'umbrella' under which a number of quality initiatives can be managed (see Figure 7.2). These are all part of a quality culture. The philosophy that supported this culture and the practical application of it originated through the ideas of Dr W Edwards Deming (1982, 1986), an American who provided the intellectual and practical drive behind Japan's post-war reconstruction. He encouraged Japanese companies to introduce total quality, and in particular to involve and consult with customers in an attempt to bring about continuous improvement of the product. Juran (1992) worked with Deming and concentrated on people-based management. He argued that, in a normal situation, the general attitude to maintaining and perpetuating current standards or levels of performance was good enough. He insisted that present performance in any function, at any level, can and should be improved

Figure 7.2 Total quality

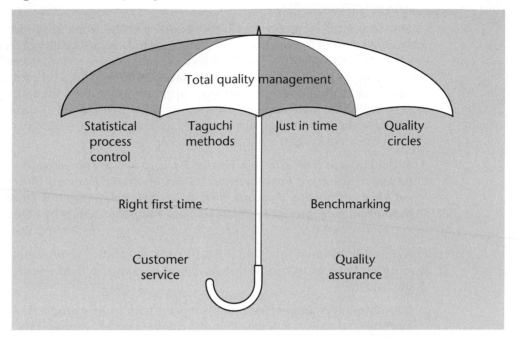

and that to achieve this improvement an organisation begins with identifying the internal obstacles that prevent people from doing the best they can and then eliminates them.

Philip Crosby (1978) has been another important influence on total quality, again with a focus on the people responsible for improving quality. Peters and Waterman expanded on these approaches in their book *In Search of Excellence* (1982). They found that many of the foremost 'excellent' companies were equally obsessed by quality and punctuality. They describe how the Caterpillar Tractor Company offers customers a 48-hour guaranteed parts delivery service anywhere in the world. If this guarantee is not met then the customer receives the part free. An article in *Fortune* magazine is quoted as stating:

> *'The company's operating principles are excellence of quality, reliability of performance, and loyalty in dealer relationships. Caterpillar has zealously pursued the goal of building a better, more efficient crawler tractor than anybody else in the world.'*
>
> (Peters and Waterman, 1982)

Another company highlighted by Peters and Waterman is McDonald's, whose theme is 'Quality, Service, Cleanliness and Value'. Founder Ray Kroc says, 'If I had a brick for every time I've repeated the phrase QSCV, I think I'd probably be able to bridge the Atlantic Ocean with them.' Quality is the priority because that is what McDonald's wants customers to enjoy every time they visit a McDonald's restaurant. All establishments are regularly monitored for QSCV and the results are linked to the manager's pay, while consistent failure to meet the McDonald's standards can lead to managers being sacked or the termination of the franchise. QSCV is applied not only to customer service but to all aspects of the business. The best ingredients are used in the food and cleanliness is insisted on. Peters and Waterman quote a former griddle tender as saying *'there was never an idle moment, whenever there was a slack time in the store, we were cleaning something.'*

The computer company Hewlett-Packard has the same approach to quality. Routine systems in the company are made to reinforce the quality objectives. These are built into the management-by-objectives programme so that everyone receives the latest quality information as well as data on orders, sales and profits. There is a 'quality web' throughout the company, appropriately called the LACE (lab awareness of customer environment) programme, in which Hewlett-Packard customers make presentations to company engineers about their own needs and their reactions to the products and services they receive.

'A Quality focus is ubiquitous in Hewlett-Packard because the employees don't seem to be able to separate it from anything else they are doing. If you ask them about personnel, they talk quality. If you ask them about field sales, they talk quality. If you ask them about management-by-objectives, they talk about quality-by-objectives.'

(Peters and Waterman, 1982)

Peters and Waterman found that quality and reliability were preferred by many leading companies to innovation or being first in the field. Hewlett-Packard is quoted again:

'The company is seldom first into the market with its new products. The company's marketing strategy is normally that of a counterpuncher. A competitor's new product comes on the market and Hewlett-Packard engineers, when making service calls on Hewlett-Packard equipment, ask the customers what they like or dislike about the new product, what features the customers would like to have ... and pretty soon the Hewlett-Packard salesmen are calling on customers again with a new product that answers their needs and wants. The result: happy and loyal customers.'

In these examples, and during the period of development of quality as the top priority for an organisation, it is apparent that total quality management involves the creation of an appropriate company culture – a climate based on 'never being satisfied' with the current quality of product and service in meeting customers' identified needs, requirements, interests and expectations. This search for opportunities for improvements can be referred to as total quality improvement. Not being satisfied with current inputs, processes, practices and outcomes encourages a system to be established covering research, analysis of needs, measurement of results and consideration of efficiency and effectiveness in order to improve what is produced and how it is produced.

Benchmarking is a process whereby a business compares its operations with those of similar organisations and, if it is able to, the best of its competitors. Companies have always benchmarked themselves with other companies in an informal way, although it is relatively recently that a formal and rigorous process has been introduced. The objective is to create and sustain excellence. The usual method is to select a business process to improve and to select a project team with the person responsible for the process in the business as team leader. The team develops a set of key process measures to compare with other companies' processes.

Comparisons are then made with companies within the same corporation, competitors and the best companies in other industries. Although some processes cannot easily be compared across industries, areas such as customer service can. It is then a question of obtaining collaboration from the target companies and investigating their processes. Whereas some of this investigation can be carried out at a 'distance' through documents and looking at delivery systems, benchmarking really requires visits to the target company – without them it is likely to be of little value. The investigation should reveal gaps between the company's processes and best practices. The team then develops an action plan to implement the improved process. It is at this stage that having the person responsible for the process as team leader, or as a member of the team, can prove a critical success factor for implementation.

The main areas to be benchmarked are usually those processes known to be inefficient or where there is some evidence that competitors or companies in other industries have better processes. The main advantages of benchmarking are the overcoming of a natural disbelief in the feasibility of improvements, making sure that improvement targets are high enough and helping to create a learning and outward-looking culture in the company.

In Figure 7.3 a competitive edge is achieved by encouraging the best possible utilisation of resources by a highly adaptable workforce in order to achieve corporate quality objectives. Competitive advantage is achieved and maintained within a framework of efficiency and effectiveness and acceptance of a process of continuous improvement. TQM as a 'metaphor for the management of change' is a process for encouraging the attitude that change is the usual situation, because through this comes quality improvement and success.

The keys to total quality management can be summarised as:

- measuring quality;
- incorporating quality objectives into strategic planning;
- obtaining the commitment of top management;
- forming teams in a structure of participative management;
- using resources efficiently and effectively;

Figure 7.3 Total quality improvement

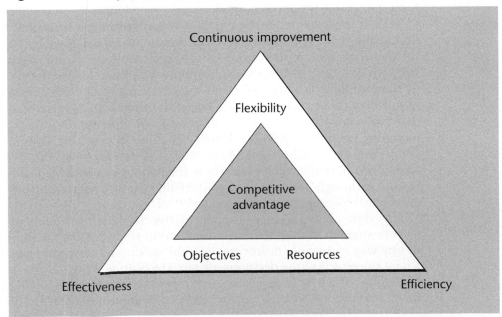

- **including suppliers and customers in quality improvement;**
- **building skills through training** (see pp. 354–7);
- **developing an attitude which welcomes change.**

This is perhaps summed up in Japanese management by *kaizen*, which is a continuous striving for perfection and, in quality terms, constant and continuous improvement. This includes all aspects of the organisation, such as staff training and development, product improvement, production and output improvement and attention to administration. At its best, this results in the output of high volumes of high-quality products supported by adaption and innovation.

IMPLICATIONS FOR MANAGEMENT

Total quality management impinges on every function in an organisation and will include marketing, product design, human resource development, financial resourcing, sites and buildings and estates management and so on. The cultural change required in most organisations in order to introduce and maintain TQM has to be led by senior managers. They need to be aware of and understand the principles and practices of total quality and be prepared to support it at every level. Particularly important is the need to ensure monitoring, measurement and evaluation of progress in all functions against identified and, if possible, quantified needs and specifications. Managers can use this evaluation in order to plan developments in TQM, as well as measuring the extent to which quality has been improved. The process can be applied inside an organisation as well as outside it in the sense that everyone has a 'customer' and is a 'customer' inside the organisation, relying on others' work and service and passing on work and service to others. Factual evidence can be obtained by monitoring progress against agreed objectives and this can inform the plans of each team in meeting its particular targets or objectives, which will in turn depend on other teams or individuals providing support in the form of high-quality goods or services.

TQM is implemented at the top of an organisation first because it is at this level that change can be initiated. Top managers require skills to enable them to change the way they work, so they can practise and promote quality management and then help others to acquire the necessary techniques and understanding.

The introduction of TQM through the whole organisation is a long-term strategy requiring a variety of approaches. For most organisations it is about the management of change and involves all aspects of human resources management, including leadership, problem solving, coaching, counselling, communication and team building. Training will be required at all levels, usually starting with those with a coordinating, supervisory or management role, but also concentrating on teams. Although TQM encourages consideration of factual information it also encourages 'people-based' management.

This style of management is participative, designed to enable people at every level to share in management decisions and in responsibility for them. This means in one way or another devolving decision making to the closest possible point to where the effects of the decisions are felt. Decision making may be delegated to an individual or a team. People are encouraged to identify and 'own' problems and their solutions, rather than passing them up or around the organisation. Teamwork becomes essential at an early stage if problems are to be identified and addressed and not hidden away. This approach focuses on corporate goals and teams identify with problems of specific relevance to their functions.

Teams need to know how their work relates to corporate goals and objectives so that they can understand the direction in which they are moving and can look for improvement opportunities. They need to have a clear idea of the resources at their disposal in order to achieve their particular objectives. It is then possible for the team to decide which members will carry out particular tasks, the methods to be employed, materials and equipment to use, and how and when to work. All of this puts great pressure on teamwork and on the team's responsibility for their own results (see Figure 7.4).

In the 1970s the Saab motor company broke away from the assembly-line system customarily used in car manufacturing and organised its workforce into teams working around each car. Teams could decide to rotate jobs and introduce other flexibilities into the way they worked so long as they achieved their target output at the requisite cost and quality levels.

Black & Decker adopted a total quality plan in 1980 to include every aspect of the business. A 'People Plan' was formed in order to 'free the people for their fullest contribution to business success'. To implement total quality the company formed 'quality circles' and after four years there were 35 successful circles in operation. In 1984 this development was reviewed and was considered to require rejuvenation. A new total customer service initiative was introduced which encompassed quality circles while focusing on 'excellence in everything we do'.

The Ciba Corning company also believes in total quality as a complete way of life affecting attitudes and commitments, 'a framework for bringing out the best in all employees'. The four principles underlying its approach are:

Figure 7.4 Introducing total quality management

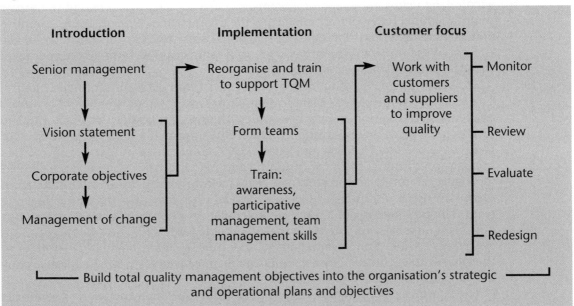

- meeting the requirements of customers
- error-free work
- managing by preventing errors rather than inspecting for error
- measuring by cost of quality.

These principles are delivered through a ten-point action plan which includes commitment from the top, communication, education and involvement for all employees. One approach to obtaining this involvement is the organisation of **quality circles**.

TEAM PROBLEM-SOLVING AND QUALITY CIRCLES

→ Ch. 9

Team problem-solving has been a major workplace innovation aimed at improving the variety and reliability of products and services (see Chapter 9). Issue handling in large organisations is an interactive process, because the issues are complex they require a range of informational inputs and they have widespread repercussions, while implementation is difficult. Using a group of people in order to solve these problems has the advantage that the group has more information and knowledge than a single individual and implementation is easier if the implementers are involved in the issue discussions. The problem with group discussions is that it can take longer to reach conclusions than an individual and the result may be a compromise rather than a clear-cut decision.

Teams are popular in organisations because they can develop an *esprit de corps*, because team members expect and demand that every member contributes to the team's objectives in one way or another. The team can make use of the different experience, skills and capabilities of its members, and at the same time the team approach facilitates cooperation and improves morale by increasing job satisfaction. While traditional teams were formed on a homogeneous functional basis, such as accounting teams and marketing teams, organisations have increased the use of multifunctional teams drawn from across the organisation. 'Project' teams comprise a wide range of people from different functional areas who can all contribute to the success of the project. When they work well teams can perform at a higher level than the same individuals working alone.

Teams are composed of individuals and have a formal or an informal structure. The increased popularity of team formation has made them the subject of study, particularly in relation to team dynamics, the way individuals interact and the influences of team leadership and structure. One approach to analysing the work of teams developed by Tuckman and Jensen (1977, summarised in Cartwright, 2002) is in terms of 'forming, storming, norming and performing' to which can be added 'dorming, reforming and adjourning'. These awkward terms are an attempt to summarise the processes through which the 'typical' team may pass, that is the 'life' of a team. The first meeting of a team can be crucial in establishing the way it works, how team members will interact, who will provide leadership and who might waste everybody's time. The 'forming' stage may involve team members introducing themselves to each other, establishing the team objective and the expertise contained within the team and its 'culture'.

The 'storming' stage represents the period during which the team experiences and settles conflicts so that progress can be made. Individuals will have their own agendas, they may jockey for position and they may take part in inappropriate behaviour. Either these conflicts are resolved or the team may be ineffective and break up. However, the storming stage can result in mutual respect being developed and greater openness established, so that the 'norming' stage is reached where working methods, rules and norms are agreed within the team. This may include a process for conflict resolution and allow the team to make progress towards its objectives. This can lead to 'performing' with the focus on achieving the team aims and goals. A 'dorming' team has reached a comfort point when it reaches a plateau and its performance stops improving, while a team which is disrupted may go through a 'reforming' stage where it experiences some of the earlier stages before it is fully operational. Finally, unless the team is formed more or less permanently, there will be an 'adjourning' stage where the team is disbanded because it has achieved its objectives, even if team members have established a bond which they want to perpetuate.

Belbin (1981) developed ideas about the role of individuals in teams. He argued that individuals had two roles – the first was a functional one related to particular competence and skills, while the other was more individual and personal, concerned with creativity, or attention to detail or sociability. Belbin identified eight team roles – a further role was added later:

■ coordinator

■ plant

■ shaper

■ monitor–evaluator

■ implementer

■ resource investigator

■ team worker

■ completer–finisher

■ (specialist).

The 'coordinator' or chairman is the individual who presides over the team and coordinates its efforts to meet its objectives. This is a person with the ability to focus on objectives and to understand and harness the skills and abilities of the team members. The plant is the team's source of original ideas, suggestions and proposals and may be 'planted' in a team to help to inspire it. The plant may be so full of ideas that the team's objectives are forgotten and the coordinator has to refocus the team. The 'shaper' is challenging, argumentative and impatient, while at the same time helping to shape the team's efforts and move it towards its objectives. The 'monitor–evaluator' is the analyst of the team assessing and evaluating the team's progress and acting as a critic rather than originating new ideas.

The 'implementer' is the team's organiser, turning decisions into manageable tasks. This individual will be the one who produces organisation charts and schedules and likes to have structure and order in the team's work. The 'resource investigator' is the team's communicator and will have lively, although sometimes short-lived enthusiasms, which may require focus, like the plant. The 'team worker' promotes unity and harmony in the team and provides loyalty and support, but may lack ideas and decisiveness. The 'completer–finisher' is concerned with detail and checking that everything has been done and nothing overlooked. This member provides a sense of urgency to meet deadlines, although may become bogged down in detail. The 'specialist' is a team role that has been added since Belbin's original work because there are times when teams need specialist input. A balanced team will include this cast of characters and while the clear absence of one of them can weaken the team, the presence of too many of one type can unbalance it. After all a team has been described (Katzenbach and Smith, 1993) as

'a small number of people with complementary skills who are committed to a common purpose, performance goals and working approach for which they hold themselves mutually accountable.'

One of the characteristics of total quality management has been the use of teams because TQM is process improvement and employee participation is an essential element of this. TQM involves encouraging employees to share ideas and act on what they suggest. One application of this approach has been the use of quality circles.

A quality circle can be described as

'a group who meet regularly, with management approval, to identify and solve their own work-related problems and implement their solutions to these problems.'

Small groups of employees, usually from the same workplace and under the same supervisor, volunteer to meet to identify problems and find solutions. They look at the problems that occur in their work area and that affect their own job. The group itself applies the solutions if it has the authority, otherwise management is presented with recommendations and decides on implementation.

Membership of quality circles is usually voluntary with a welcome for anyone who wishes to join and no official pressure for anyone to become a member. If the circle is successful, active and enthusiastic then it is expected that people will want to join. The supervisor of a work area will usually lead the circle. His or her role is to encourage volunteers to establish a group which he or she will chair because of previous experience and training in organising and running quality circles. The supervisor guides the circle in order to help it develop into a cohesive team and to focus on solving problems and improving quality. The circle will usually consist of between six and twelve members – large enough to generate a variety of ideas; small enough for everybody to be involved and have their say. If there are too many volunteers then either membership can be rotated or subgroups can be formed to consider particular tasks.

Management has to follow a 'hands-off' policy up to the point of implementation of a decision. Success depends on the members of a quality circle being assured that it 'belongs to them' and has not been formed by management. Management can be supportive and may suggest topics for consideration by the circle, but if it is any more heavy handed the role of members will be restricted. The most important consideration for management is to ensure that actions do follow any ideas or decisions reached by a quality circle, or to provide good reasons for not following up such ideas or decisions.

Quality circles were originally an American idea but were first practised on a wide scale in Japan. In order to compete with other industrial nations, Japanese industry realised in the late 1940s and 1950s that old ideas of management had to be discarded and that the initiative and skills of everybody on the workforce had to be harnessed. Emphasis was placed on training at shopfloor level and every effort was made to pass as much responsibility as possible to supervisors and operators. There was a particular emphasis on identifying quality problems at all levels and in all areas of companies.

In the late 1950s and through the 1960s Japanese companies introduced quality circles extensively, so that by 1980 it was estimated that there were over a million quality circles with ten million workers involved. It is significant that the literal translation of the Japanese term for quality circles is:

The gathering of the wisdom of the people.

The concept of the quality circle coincides with the culture of Japanese companies and builds on loyalty to the company. The 'family company' approach of duty to the company by employees allied with responsibility by the company for the welfare of its employees is well developed, while there is also a well-nurtured culture of it being in everyone's interest for the company to succeed, combined with peer pressure to encourage the success of a voluntary approach. Professor Ishikawa has suggested (1984) that quality circles act as a 'focus of perception' to identify personal pride and self-esteem with corporate achievement (see Chapter 14).

→ Ch. 14

Quality circles have been used across the world to draw on the expertise and knowledge of workers on the shopfloor in order to improve quality. They have been adapted by such companies as General Motors, Honeywell & Lockheed in the USA, and by Philips, Ford, Rolls-Royce and Marks & Spencer in the UK.

In many British companies, however, the culture has not been conducive to the development of quality circles. Where there is a strongly defended hierarchical structure, or sections and departments based on specialised expertise, the view that ideas from the shopfloor should be given priority is difficult to foster. At the same time the attitude that it is up to 'them' to solve problems may be strong at an operational level. Management/union dissension in the past has certainly discouraged the effective development of this kind of initiative.

It is clear that successful quality circles are not concerned with grumbles or complaints or irrelevant discussion of non-related subjects such as pay, personality conflicts or other grievances. The stress is on solving problems and producing action plans. For this approach to be understood and to be successful, the culture of the company has to be one which encourages participative management. If the culture has bred suspicion and secrecy, then grumbles and complaints may be at the top of the agenda. Quality circles are encouraged to discuss practicalities and not theories, so that positive results are produced rather than simply argument. One approach is to list problem areas and then to establish priorities and seek solutions by drawing on the skill and knowledge of the group. When problems are beyond solution by the group, specialists may be asked to join the circle for a number of meetings, or a subgroup may be established to investigate the problem in more detail.

Where the members of the quality circle have the power to make a decision they will carry it out, while on matters where they do not have authority they will make a presentation to the managers involved in the proposed change (see Figure 7.5). This may be a technical problem to do with the operation of machinery or equipment, it may be a staffing problem to do with skills or working times, it may be a question of the supply of materials, the purchase of spare parts, or it may be to do with costs and finance. The managers must then decide to take action or explain in detail the reasons for not taking action at this time. Managers also have to make sure that people do not identify too strongly with their particular circle when total quality has to be identified with the aims and objectives of the organisation as a whole. At the same time, some problems need to be solved on the spot rather than waiting for a quality circle meeting to sort them out.

Figure 7.5 Quality circles

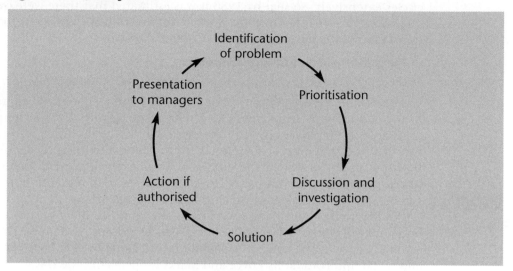

An enterprising quality circle will, of course, anticipate as many problems as possible and solve them.

ITT has provided an example of a solution discovered by a quality circle:

'It was standard practice to completely remove capacitors from the metal handling equipment to check for correct nominal capacitance. After this operation the capacitors were discarded. By purchasing hand held capacitance meters it is possible to take the equipment to the work and simply applying one terminal lead, measure the nominal capacitance while the remaining terminal lead is retained on the handling strip. This enables the capacitor to continue with the batch through the finishing operations. This change will result in a saving of more than $10,000 when it is fully implemented.'
(ITT *Circle News*, March 1981)

Managers play an important part in the success of quality circles. There has to be a commitment to the system throughout the organisation and one or two unsympathetic managers can ruin the whole process. Managers have to allow time and money for circle meetings and for preliminary training. They must be ready to attend presentations, to listen with an open mind to the proposals and to decide on their value on merit. Unions need also to be involved in the process so that their representatives understand what is happening. Unions will usually be supportive of the process because it involves the workforce more closely in the organisation and has the objective of improving job satisfaction. After all, quality circles have been described as 'a structured way of making management listen' by the Industrial Society.

FOCUS ON TOTAL QUALITY

Whether it is quality circles or another method of providing a focus on quality, the pursuit of total quality must be led from the front, by the chief executive, otherwise it may be considered as an afterthought. Deming (1982) put this another way:

'There is so much talk about involvement of employees, quality of work life, communi-cations and other poetic words. What is needed is involvement of management: get the management involved. Employees will become involved, the quality of life will improve, once management takes on the job of restoring dignity to the hourly worker.'

Combined with competitive pressures and the higher priority given to human resource management, the focus on quality encouraged reorganisation in many companies in the 1980s and 1990s. These developments have been away from the single, giant pyramid structures consisting of many different layers of management and grades of operative towards flatter structures often based on a total quality con-cept. Whole functions and levels have been eliminated in order to produce an organisation which is more flexible and speedier in response to market needs.

Waterman (1988) cites the Dana Company in the USA which in the mid-1970s had 14 layers of management between the chief executive and the staff floor. By the mid-1980s these layers had been reduced to five:

'At the extreme the company has one plant in Nebraska that employs 120 people – the organisation structure there is simple: 120 people, one plant manager, nothing in between.'

The key to this approach is often greater delegation. Many areas of decision making and accountability have been pushed down the organisation to be nearer the point where the decision takes effect. Senior management will adopt a more strategic role, setting broad objectives as a framework to ensure that all units are functioning effectively and working towards the corporate goals. The operational units are the closest group to their markets and they know best the requirements of the consumer. It is impossible for this level of delegation to work unless the practice and beliefs of management adapt to the new circumstances. There is a decline in supervision throughout the organisation as employees take on greater responsibil-ity. The role of the manager is to initiate new ideas and policies, to facilitate the work of the operational units and to monitor their progress.

In order to introduce this level of involvement there has to be a clear recognition that the purpose of this strategy is to increase mutual understanding and to improve the individual's contribution. This is a policy of openness, of encouraging individual creativity and initiative in the interests of the organisation.

In order to achieve this level of delegation it is necessary to:

- make certain that individuals understand what is expected from them in terms of their time at work;
- set the limits of delegation so that everyone knows the extent of their responsi-bility;
- train individuals so that they understand the aims and objectives of the dele-gated system and are technically able to cope with it;
- communicate the corporate business goals effectively so that everyone under-stands how these relate to them;
- enable a reverse flow of information to take place, from the shopfloor upwards, so that each manager knows the attitudes and aspirations of each person report-ing to them.

At the same time as this focus on the individual there has to be a clear under-standing of teamwork. In the introduction of total quality, teams are not the same as quality circles. The quality-circle approach is based on voluntary groups of employees considering particular tasks. Total quality management teams include everybody working in a particular area or function or in a cross-functional role. Individuals cannot opt out of this team or of meetings to consider the working of the group, or fail to take responsibility for their work. The team will be responsible for making sure that everybody contributes to its success and for discussing and implementing ways in which the whole team can improve performance. These teams may coincide with quality circles or the latter may form a separate system for considering quality – an alternative, perhaps task-oriented group. The usual process is for the functional team itself to become a type of quality circle on its own.

This process of delegating decision and responsibility to teams at the 'salt face' or 'firing line' is again not quite the same as a process popular in the 1980s known as 'team briefing'. These are meetings held at regular intervals when leaders bring their teams together to communicate what is happening at the workplace. In the team briefing system the priority is to achieve understanding of what people need to know because it affects their job – it is a systematic way of telling all employees about progress, policy, decisions, performance and future plans. It is not necessarily consultative and is not usually a method of encouraging two-way communication. Team briefing is a useful method of communication for management but it should not be confused with the purposes behind setting up teams in a TQM system.

The same is true of consultative committees, which are structured meetings of management and employee representatives, with the purpose of discussing management matters of common interest. They are a way of seeking the views of employees before management decisions are finally made or before they are implemented. They may be used whenever decisions affect employees, but they are not about negotiation on such matters as pay which requires once again a separate format of meetings. Consultative committees can play an important part in, for example, the management of change and can be a way of informing discussion on quality teams when managers are considering the initiation of new policies.

The Confederation of British Industry in *The Will to Win* (1980) stated that 'the system of giving the line employee more responsibility increases his/her job satisfaction and involvement'. In contrast the division of labour and scientific management, or 'Taylorism', have encouraged the analysis of work into constituent activities and given particular tasks to individual workers. The close definition of the worker's specialist role has meant that, at its extreme, workers respond by living up to the limited expectations of them by carrying out the tasks they have been given and no more or less.

Some organisations may have been paternalistic in their approach by not treating employees as adults – at the same time other organisations do not regard their employees as the prime source of their prosperity. With a limited view of their job, employees substitute habit for understanding and every change can, in Drucker's view (1968), represent to the employee 'a challenge of the incomprehensible and ... threatens his psychological security'. Drucker attacks scientific management for confusing analysis with action, for divorcing planning from doing. The successful companies 'hire a whole man or woman' and realise that 'with every pair of hands a mind comes free'. Ignoring the ideas of employees is epitomised by a General Motors' car worker in the USA whom Drucker (1968) quotes as saying:

> *'I guess I got laid off because I made poor quality cars. In 16 years not once was I ever asked for a suggestion as to how to do my job better. Not once.'*

In response to this many successful companies have introduced suggestion schemes. In the USA, IBM has said that its suggestion plan yielded ideas from 30,000 employees during 1985 which resulted in savings of more than $125 million. The company was happy to pay the employees $18 million in cash awards for these suggestions. While these schemes can be very effective, they have to fit into the overall company policy because it may be difficult to run financial inducements for ideas alongside voluntary consultation and a delegated team approach. If the company ethos encourages everybody to think in terms of constant improvement and enables people to communicate ideas, a suggestion box may not be necessary (see Figure 7.6).

Strategies designed to maximise the potential and actual contribution of every employee have to give considerable emphasis to communication and involvement policies. The move away from an organisation based on command and authority from the top, with limited and routine tasks at the bottom, has created a re-evaluation of the way companies communicate internally. It is no longer a question of ensuring that instructions are passed to the relevant people and then monitoring what happens. Communication is now seen as a means of improving understanding, of securing involvement through a free flow of information in order to create cohesion and mutual commitment on the part of all members of the organisation.

Managers rely on the capabilities of those carrying out the various tasks allotted to them. Managers have to ensure effective teamwork and cooperation and are responsible for coordinating, planning and monitoring to make sure that more flexible and less authoritarian structures nevertheless meet their objectives. This requires the listening skills of a facilitator able to anticipate and solve problems, to treat individuals sympathetically and with respect, and to identify the relative strengths and weaknesses of everyone involved.

Managers need to communicate the corporate business goals effectively to every team or group so that they are understood in sufficient depth and are related to the team and the individuals in it. This understanding must also include an appreciation of the external influences on the organisation, such as the nature of the competition, the impact of new technologies, the influence of government policy

Figure 7.6 Focus on quality

and the importance of markets and customers. Managers have to assess the level of understanding of these matters by teams and individuals. Surveys, meetings and discussions can help to do this and many organisations have found the most effective means of 'upward' communication to be a system of appraisal and performance review (see Chapters 4 and 6).

→ Chs 4 & 6

MEASURING QUALITY

The measurement of quality should not be thought of as a single and simple process, although in fact it can be if the one measurement that is used is profit. A simple indicator such as profit growth, market share or the return on capital invested can be used to judge how well a quality management system has worked and these certainly should be among the measures used. The problem is that taken on their own they do not indicate how they were achieved and, if successful, how they can be maintained. For this an analysis of the organisation is required with measurement taken at various levels.

At a strategic level, for example, in order to decide whether or not a performance management system has helped to put quality management into effect, it may be sensible to seek the answers to a number of questions:

■ Is there a strategic plan supported by senior managers which establishes the organisation's direction?

■ Is there a well-defined structure to support and develop a quality approach by managers, including a performance management system?

■ Are skills and techniques for quality improvement part of the training for managers and supervisors?

■ Are employees held accountable for on-the-job performance (see pp. 294–8 and 358–361)?

At the same time, there has to be a decision about what is to be evaluated. This can be achieved by a clear statement of overall objectives, plus objectives for every unit and team as well as individuals. At the operational level this will mean detailed production or service targets. At a more strategic level managers may prefer non-routine activities and those of short duration – they may prefer to be problem solvers rather than planners (see Table 7.1). This tendency can be offset by a participative process for establishing objectives and forms of evaluation so that managers can see the importance of longer-term objectives in establishing the context for detailed targets.

A manager needs to be both a problem solver and a planner and to be able to communicate the importance of medium and long-term objectives to employees at all levels so as to support the attainment of objectives and targets and measure performance against these.

In *Thriving on Chaos* (1987) Tom Peters identifies 12 attributes of a quality system, which in themselves represent a checklist against which an organisation's management can assess the stage it has reached in the development of such a system:

■ management is obsessed with quality;

■ the company has a guiding system or ideology;

■ quality is measured;

■ quality is rewarded;

Table 7.1 Planners and problem solvers

PROBLEM SOLVERS	PLANNERS
Short-duration activities	Advance planning
Non-routine tasks	Agreed systems
Emphasis on decisive action	Systems and schedules
Informal interaction	Formal, regular sessions
Effectiveness through authority	Roles of coach and counsellor
Low priority given to personnel task	Human resource management

- everyone is trained in techniques for assessing quality;
- there is a shift of managerial philosophy from adversarial to cooperative;
- it is recognised that there is no such thing as an insignificant improvement;
- there is constant stimulation to improve quality;
- there is a structure within the company dedicated to quality improvement;
- everybody is involved in quality management, including suppliers, distributors and customers;
- it is understood that costs decline as quality increases;
- it is recognised that quality is relative and improvement is never-ending.

QUALITY CONTROL AND QUALITY ASSURANCE

One of the 12 items on Peters' checklist suggests that quality improvement is never-ending. It is a relative value compared with the competition as perceived through the customer's eyes. It is an elusive concept because customer perception is itself difficult to predict. Peters argues that if you own a car in which some major part goes wrong, you may have a better view of its quality than if a number of small things go wrong. If the carburettor stops working or the gear box collapses you take the car to the garage and have the component repaired or replaced. If the service is efficient and problems do not recur then you can forget about the problem.

If the radio crackles, the door squeaks, the window sticks and there are a number of other small problems then they may not, even cumulatively, be worth the trouble of taking the car to the garage until the next service. Meanwhile they remain a constant reminder of the poor quality of the car. All these problems can be seen as a problem of quality control, which can be defined as being:

concerned with checking for errors during and after the process of manufacture.

Quality control often occurs at the end of the manufacturing process as a check to see if the commodity works. If it does not it is rejected and either scrapped or reworked. The problem with this approach is that there is heavy dependence on inspectors. This is expensive and obviously it is much better to identify the error at an earlier stage. **Statistical process control (SPC)** is a method of monitoring the conformity of a product to agreed specifications. By sampling units of the product, deviations from these specifications can be identified and adjustments made during the production process (see p. 688).

Modern control techniques are based on the idea of an 'error-free' or 'zero-defect' approach, or 'doing it right first time'. This concept arises because of the costs involved in correcting errors and the fact that the costs are usually greater the later they are identified. Under the TQM approach the team is made responsible for quality control, for reducing wastage and for ensuring that adjustments are made as soon as they are identified.

At a strategic level, quality can be built into the planning of the product or service. Juran and Deming worked extensively with the Japanese to enhance product quality through statistical methods. The first stage is to ensure that the product conforms to design specifications. The next stage is the use of SQC (statistical quality control) or process-control procedures in order to monitor quality during the production of the commodity or rendering of the service. Work teams or quality circles can decide and be delegated the power to decide how to reduce errors and 'do it right first time', while management has to support this process at every stage.

The Ford Motor Company introduced a slogan in the 1980s, 'At Ford, Quality is Job One.' A programme of quality control was introduced along with a new policy of participative management. The emphasis on achieving quotas was changed so that the quality of the product came first. Employee groups were made an important element in the quality control process rather than relying on a separate team of inspectors. Ford's President, Donald Peterson, stated his commitment to quality:

> *'The principles by which we will live and die, is that once we can do something well, we have to figure out how to do it even better.'*
>
> (Quoted by Stoner and Freeman, 1989)

A concept which builds on quality control is the 'just-in-time' (JIT) principle. This is concerned with improving production efficiency and reducing waste. It is a technique for minimising storage through careful planning and purchasing to meet the exact requirements of the customer, internal or external, and this is only possible if the product does in fact meet agreed specifications and suppliers cooperate fully.

It is at the strategic management level that decisions are made about total quality management and systems of quality control. The strategic approach includes:

- analysis of current position;
- choice of an appropriate starting point;
- implementation of policy, deciding what will be done, how, by whom and by when.

Quality assurance (QA) provides a framework for quality control and quality improvement. Quality assurance supports teams of employees with systems, resources and discretion appropriate to their unique contribution to the organisation to keep them in tune with progress of quality management and improvement. This aspect of management can help teams:

- understand quality characteristics;
- be realistic about the standards to be attained;
- undertake quality control through a measurement process, interpret the results and make or propose changes.

This process may be supported by a number of techniques such as QUEST (quality in every single task). This is the idea that everybody in an organisation is a 'customer' and 'supplier' and receives products and services from colleagues within the organisation.

The idea of service within the organisation enables each individual or group to undertake a **QUEST analysis**:

■ Who are my customers?

■ What do they demand from me?

■ In what way do I meet these demands?

■ How can I improve my service?

And

■ Who are my suppliers?

■ What service do I demand of them?

■ In what way do they meet these demands?

■ How can they improve their service?

KRA (key result areas) is a technique aimed at focusing on realistic outcomes for each team or individual. This may be by:

■ identifying a range of quality characteristics for the team which are consistent with the company's strategy;

■ agreeing realistic standards for each of these quality characteristics;

■ devising a system which can be measured and monitored.

The **Taguchi method** is based on the ideas of Dr Genichi Taguchi (1986) who developed his approach to improving quality engineering at a low cost. It helps to quantify the loss due to lack of quality of a performance characteristic, with the objective of identifying the real cause of a problem. It concentrates on the design of products, reducing variation of performance against the target specification. The Taguchi method depends on a management culture committed to TQM and it has, therefore, developed most successfully in Japan and the USA.

The concentration on customer specification has produced approaches such as the British Standard 5750 registration mark and its international counterpart ISO 9000. These do not establish a level of excellence for a product or service but they do provide:

a way of describing the capability of a system to produce goods or services to a specification.

Customers and potential customers should not expect BS 5750 to make a product the best available, and the registration mark is not a necessary prerequisite to total quality management. Quality is as much about 'doing the right thing' as 'doing things right', while BS 5750 is about 'doing things right'. It arises from the need in quality assurance to supply evidence to other organisations about a particular organisation's effectiveness.

These other organisations may be other companies being supplied with the product or service, government agencies, consumer organisations or any other group which perceives, rightly or wrongly, that the possession of BS 5750 or ISO 9000 is a kitemark of effectiveness, efficiency or quality. The UK has been the leader in this process of certification since a Government White Paper in 1982 required BS 5750 registration for nationalised industries and for public sector procurement generally.

BS 5750 places great emphasis on written evidence, documented systems and procedures. It is based on the status quo rather than on continual improvement, which is the main goal of TQM. The British Standard is a procedural system for companies to follow in order to set up and document an organisation's operational systems. The approach is designed to control each step in a process so that products or services match the specification. This type of process originally developed in industries where safety was a critical factor, such as aerospace, nuclear power and defence. This background is what has provided its particular approach – a very careful, closely audited step-by-step control for procedures. The procedures are established to meet a particular specification and then audited to ensure that they are being adhered to in detail. In the 1960s and 1970s the Ministry of Defence and the Central Electricity Board used their inspectors to visit potential suppliers to check that they could produce goods uniformly.

This is still the most important type of use for BS 5750, although some large companies (such as Ford and Marks & Spencer) 'inspect' potential suppliers and set their own operational and product quality standards which suppliers must meet. Some firms conduct their own auditing system in order to standardise procedures. None of these approaches should be confused with TQM.

INVESTING IN PEOPLE

For many organisations, people represent their largest cost – often 70 or 80 per cent of the total. In the UK an initiative which recognises this fact and has the goal of attaining quality in organisations has been 'Investors in People' (IIP). This rests on the premise that companies which have developed, or are developing, an awareness of quality acknowledge that people are the real key to achieving improvements. In a 'quality' culture people take ownership of their work and responsibility for the quality of their work. This arises from 'gap analysis', such as the gap identified by the Confederation of British Industry:

> *'The crucial importance of people to business success is now almost universally recognised by companies. But there is a huge gap between recognising this, and knowing exactly what to do about it.'* (Department of Employment, 1990c)

IIP is concerned with the contribution people can make to business success. By learning from the actions of those organisations which are already developing and using their people successfully, other organisations can adopt, and benefit from, an 'investing in people' approach.

IIP arose from the 1988 UK Government White Paper *Employment for the 1990s* which launched a partnership between business and government. The National Training Task Force was established and the Training and Enterprise Councils (TECs) and Local Enterprise Councils (in Scotland) were launched. A major priority of this initiative was to raise employer commitment to training by listening to businesses' ideas and needs, and looking at the people factors which made one organisation more successful than another.

Organisations' own agendas are centred around:

- productivity
- quality

- **focus on the customer**
- **flexibility.**

These priorities have given rise to operational and management practices such as TQM, and include customer care programmes, 'just-in-time' manufacturing and workplace teams. In all these practices people are understood to be the key to achieving total quality, and there is an emphasis on teams and seeing colleagues as internal customers, while being genuinely motivated to develop existing skills, develop new ones, accept the devolution of responsibility, make the best use of current or new resources and, if required, acquire new managerial skills.

The IIP approach aims to help organisations to improve performance through a planned approach to:

- **setting and communicating business goals;**
- **developing people to meet these goals;**

so that:

- **what people can do and are motivated to do;**
- **matches what the organisation needs them to do.**

This can be seen diagrammatically in Figure 7.7.

The objective is to encourage organisations to think consistently of their people as an investment and not a cost and act in a way which reflects this perspective. Organisations need to recognise people as a valuable business resource that can be used to create, protect or waste assets; that there are investment costs as well as benefits in this process; that the benefits will be greater than the costs; and that organisations will only benefit fully from investing in people if they start with clearly defined objectives and actions.

The actions required to improve quality through the IIP approach can be summarised in a form based on the UK IIP programme:

Figure 7.7 Investing in people

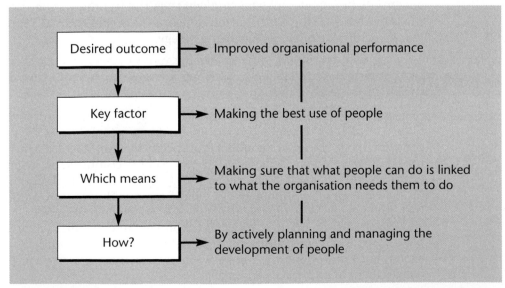

- Every employer should have a written but flexible plan which sets out business goals and targets, considers how employees will contribute to achieving the plan and specifies how development needs in particular will be assessed and met.

- Management should develop and communicate to all employees a vision of where the organisation is going and the contribution employees will make to its success, involving employee representatives as appropriate.

- The resources for training and developing employees should be clearly identified in the business plan.

- Managers should be responsible for regularly agreeing training and development needs with each employee in the context of business objectives, setting targets and standards linked, where appropriate, to the achievement of National Vocational Qualifications (or relevant units) and, in Scotland, Scottish Vocational Qualifications.

- Action should focus on the training needs of all new recruits and continually developing and improving the skills of existing employees.

- All employees should be encouraged to contribute to identifying and meeting their own job-related development needs.

- The investment, the competence and commitment of employees and the use made of skills learned should be reviewed at all levels against business goals and targets.

- The effectiveness of training and development should be reviewed at the top level and lead to renewed commitment and target setting.

In 1999 the UK Government introduced a White Paper called *Learning to Succeed*, which heralded another change in vocational education and training by establishing a Learning and Skills Council in 2001 to replace the previous funding arrangement and the Training and Enterprise Councils. The objective of the new skills body was to 'drive forward improvements in standards and bring together coherence and response' (HMSO, 1999) by putting the whole of vocational training under the Council so that the standards of skills and the lifelong learning required by the country in the twenty-first century could be achieved. Whatever the result of government initiatives may be, and whatever the techniques that may be applied, the importance of the contribution of people to organisational success remains a crucial factor in quality management strategy.

MANAGERS AND THE LAW

Managers need to understand the law as it relates to the operation of their organisations. The civil law is concerned with the rights of people, while the criminal law is concerned with the area of conduct that society will not tolerate. The basis of law in the UK is common law, that is the succession of decisions made by judges over the centuries. It is founded on precedents and not on Acts of Parliament and is based on the concept of reasonableness – what a reasonable person would conclude. So that, for example, a reasonable person would conclude that murder is unacceptable and is therefore an offence under common law. In consumer law, reasonableness plays a part when considering the legal rights of a customer, while a contract is any agreement enforceable by law between two or more consenting parties which obliges them to undertake certain acts.

Statute laws are those made by the Government and in the UK they have been passed by Parliament and signed by the Monarch. Every country has its own legal system and wherever an issue occurs then the legal system of that country, or a wider body such as the European Union, will generally apply. Depending on their role, managers will need to have some understanding of areas such as contract law, consumer law, employment law, health and safety at work and competition legislation in the countries in which they operate. When introducing a total quality management system particularly, as it affects consumers and employees, managers will need to make sure that any processes or procedures and the design of products comply with the relevant laws and regulations. Managers need to keep up to date with legislation that affects their business, it is part of the environment (see
→ Ch. 8
Chapter 8) in which their organisation operates.

CONCLUSION

Improving **productivity** and effectiveness means not only raising the quantity of output per unit, it also involves improving quality. A key to understanding the importance of quality management is the conviction that costs decline as quality increases. The opposite point of view is well rehearsed in all sorts of organisations and situations. A frequent approach centres on the point of view that 'of course we could improve the quality if we had more money and resources', and on the idea that 'you get what you pay for', based on the premise that the more you pay the better the quality.

There is, of course, some truth in these ideas and they may in fact describe the position very accurately in some situations. On the other hand, very often this is not the case. The increase in Japanese car sales in the 1980s and 1990s was based on producing cars which are 'fit for the purpose' – they are designed to fulfil customer requirements, they are reliable and they are relatively cheap. Their success has been based on providing what people want at a price they can afford. At the extreme it can be argued that a Rolls-Royce is a very carefully made car, which is reliable and of very high 'quality' or excellence, but its price puts it out of the reach of most people so that its quality will be compared with other 'handmade' cars and not with family saloons. Volvo has based the success of its cars on such factors as safety, reliability and longevity rather than price because it believes that these are the qualities that potential customers want. In fact, the important feature of its cars is that they are different and it is the difference in quality which the company relies on for its sales and profit.

If a company concentrates mainly on price, as for example cars produced by organisations in some eastern European countries, then there is a chance the relatively cheap car may not sell well because it does not have other qualities which customers require. The essential point is to produce goods which customers want at a price they can afford in a particular market, and the key to producing goods at a competitive price and with good quality is high productivity. The difference between the productivity of car manufacturers in Britain is considerable, with the most productive British workers employed by Japanese companies able to produce twice as many cars a year as the least productive British workers employed by British/American companies.

Differences between companies in terms of productivity arise as a result of greater investment in new equipment and technology, but as important as this are differences in management. The emphasis on quality, focusing of people's jobs, participative management, gaining the cooperation of unions, encouraging teamwork, setting clearly understood performance targets – these are all part of the difference. The lack of these aspects of management encourages expensive situations such as the rejection of products at the point of inspection, or eventually by the customer, the waste of materials, unnecessary expense on troubleshooters, wasteful hold-ups on supply lines and the maintenance of large and costly inventories to replace rejected products or parts. At the same time, if too much energy is expended on fighting internal battles within the organisation, either between management and unions or between different sections and departments, there is a dissipation of the effort required to fight the real external competition. The competitive edge is achieved by creating a positive and productive internal organisation while focusing on beating external competitors.

A 'quality first', 'right first time' approach means that customers are satisfied and stocks of spare parts and replacements can be kept to a minimum. If performance targets are the responsibility of the individual and team and the internal customer approach is prevalent then there is little need for inspection of the end product, supervision can be reduced to a minimum and a comparatively flat hierarchy can manage the company. All of this will save costs.

The TQM approach is based on the idea that managers are sure of their objectives within a broad vision, and for everybody in the organisation to have both a clear focus on their aims and goals and an understanding of the context in which they are working, as well as taking responsibility for work over which they have control. Accountability then becomes a question of peer pressure for most people within the 'internal customer' framework. Quality improvement within an organisation structured in this way is not delegated or subcontracted, it is a responsibility that everyone actively shares.

Management has a responsibility for leading this approach by providing the structural framework and by presenting an example of hard, productive and effective work. The Japanese suggest that management is a way of life which is a progression towards self-enlightenment. They perceive the human skills of imagination, personality, leadership and creativity as just as important as management skills, so that managers are engaged in creating a vision or mission to motivate the workforce. Quality management is concerned with how managers see themselves, what standards they set for themselves and how they motivate others. Out of this analysis should arise the appropriate structure for the organisation.

TQM is a business management philosophy which recognises that customer needs and business goals are inseparable. It pervades an organisation's culture, inspires commitment and encourages communication in all directions, based on work teams and quality systems which utilise resources effectively (see Figure 7.8). At its best, TQM can release a dynamic factor within an organisation which encourages success and profitability.

Figure 7.8 Total quality management

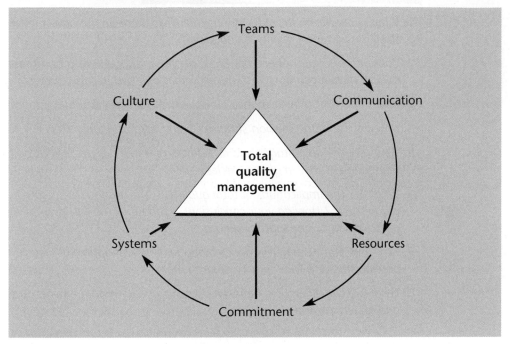

SUMMARY

- The management of quality is an essential feature in any organisation for maintaining a competitive advantage. It has always been a feature of industry and commerce in one way or another but since the 1940s it has become a priority interest of managers because of fierce competition in world markets. The Japanese needed to catch up and compete with the major industrial countries in the 1940s and 1950s, and by the 1960s they were doing this based on a total quality concept. UK managers in the 1980s, 1990s and into the twenty-first century have been in a similar position, finding themselves outcompeted in world markets, so that total quality has become an essential feature of their fightback.

- Underlying the quest for quality is the need to increase productivity by raising investment levels in high technology and by making the most of the workforce. This involves the delegation of decision making and responsibility in the process of achieving quality objectives. It also involves a concentration on training and development based on high expectations and increasing people's ability to deal with modern technology and participative management.

- Actions to achieve quality include the introduction of TQM programmes, focus on the customer and the development of techniques such as 'right first time' and 'just in time'. Performance management programmes and the investing in people approach are other ways of concentrating the attention of managers and everybody else in an organisation on the quality of their work and ultimately on the quality of products or services.

Review and discussion questions

1 What is meant by strategic management? Is there an important difference between strategic and total quality management?

2 Consider an organisation that has a quality management programme. Summarise it. How does it compare with the examples outlined in this chapter?

3 How important is participative management for a total quality programme?

4 How do vision and mission statements and corporate objectives link to TQM?

5 What are the advantages and drawbacks of quality circles? What part can management play in quality circles?

6 What are the implications of total quality for the management structure of an organisation? How do your conclusions compare to the situation in your own organisation or one that you know?

7 How important is a performance management and appraisal system as a prerequisite for a total quality programme?

8 What are the differences between strategic quality management, quality assurance and quality control?

CASE STUDY

British Aerospace

The Airbus Division is part of British Aerospace commercial division which handles work arising from the company's 20 per cent stake in Airbus Industries. Approximately two-thirds of the Airbus Division's payroll of 9000 is engaged in producing Airbus wingsets, while the other activities include a maintenance contract for the US Air Force.

Quality assurance has been developed in the Airbus Division over the last 22 years. Quality managers have progressively been introduced to replace inspectors, whose numbers have gradually fallen. A different philosophy of product quality has accompanied this change. Formerly, the aim was to produce 'engineering excellence' but now the goal is 'excellent engineering', a concept requiring a broader view of an item's function and with a higher priority for costs and the complexities of production. Essentially, the need is for excellent engineering at an affordable cost.

This has led to fresh approaches to all activities from design onwards. Statistical quality control methods still have some applications, but not as many as in mass-production flowline operations. Training has been a high priority from apprentices through to management. Stress is placed on topics such as customer orientation, the awareness of suppliers and what constitutes an affordable cost. There is an approved list of suppliers, with inspections every two years. This has been found to work well with large suppliers but not so well with smaller suppliers, and those with a proven record of high quality have come to be valued.

It has been found that growth at British Aerospace has enhanced quality rather than caused a decline in it. This has been put down to the scale of investment, the long production lines with increased volume and the concentration on quality as the top priority. Where amendments are made to production, a rule has been introduced that quality has to stay constant or improve. As a result, the larger the production lines, the more changes are made and the greater the number of quality improvements. This has been reinforced by the introduction of a total quality programme.

FURTHER READING

Creech, P B (1995) *The Five Pillars of TQM: How to Make TQM Work for You*, New York: Plume.
A discussion of the application of total quality management.

Crosby, P B (1996) *Quality is Still Free*, New York: McGraw-Hill.
An update on a classic book on quality management.

Giroux, H (2006) 'It was such a handy term: management fashions and pragmatic ambiguity', *Journal of Management Studies*, 43 (6), September.
A debate on the definition of quality control and how this has changed over time.

Hume, C and Wright, C (2006) 'You don't make a pig fatter by weighing it – performance management: the experience of the youth justice board', *Public Money and Management*, June.
An example of an approach to long-term sustainability and continuous improvement.

WEBSITES

http://www.severn-trent.co.uk
Provides information on how the Severn–Trent Water Company measures water quality.

http://www.tesco.co.uk
Information about the Tesco Internet Superstore.

CHAPTER 8

Marketing and environmental assessment

Outcomes

Having read this chapter, you will be able to:

- analyse the importance of marketing for all managers;

- discuss the fundamental relevance of marketing in all organisations;

- describe the basic principles and theories of marketing and the methods applied in marketing;

- understand marketing concepts which can be applied to the formation of a marketing plan and strategy in all forms of organisation;

- discuss the importance of market research;

- understand the importance of market segmentation and branding in providing a competitive edge.

MARKETING ORIENTATION

Organisational objectives have moved on from an overriding concern with technical excellence, costs and price to a consideration of customer service, quality and employee development. The development of the customer-oriented organisation (see Chapter 3) has made **marketing** a central activity in most companies and public sector institutions. The importance of the customer is recognised in the Chartered Institute of Marketing definition:

→ Ch. 3

Marketing is the management process responsible for identifying, anticipating and satisfying customer requirements profitably.

This consumer-centred view of economic activity can be traced back at least as far as Adam Smith's *Wealth of Nations*, published in 1776:

'Consumption is the role and purpose of all production; and the interest of the producer ought to be attended to only in so far as it may be necessary for promoting that of the consumer.'

Peter Drucker (1993) has defined marketing as

'the whole business seen from the point of view of its final result, that is from the customer's point of view.'

This illustrates the shift of marketing as a management function from a relatively low position in the order of priorities to a central one. Marketing has moved from being at best a second-tier activity, below production and finance, to being the integrating force represented at the top of organisational structures so that marketing is now a route to becoming a managing director or chief executive.

The position of the marketing function is often matched historically by the process by which companies raise the priority given to marketing. The nineteenth-century development of manufacturing industry was based on product-orientation with marketing hardly recognised as a separate activity. The early twentieth century saw the development of a sales-orientation based on the need to interest potential customers in the existing products and services which were increasingly threatened by competition. The second half of the twentieth century saw the development of increasing customer-orientation in all areas of the economy and society, based on determining the needs and wants of the customers and satisfying them. In the twenty-first century, providing what the customer wants and anticipating these wants are the vital factors which separate competitors.

This developing position in the overall economy has been reflected in particular sections of it and in particular organisations. The computer sales boom in the 1970s and 1980s was based on the development of products and programs, and it was only when computer companies met competition and found that selling their products became difficult that they turned to marketing in the 1980s and 1990s. Similarly, travel companies which had been successfully founded and expanded through selling cheap package holidays have had to adjust to customer demand for higher quality and more expensive holidays and those companies that have not paid attention to marketing have found it difficult to adjust. In the 1990s public sector institutions in the health service and education have been faced with the need to market their services as a result of changes to their corporate status and funding mechanisms, with the objective of making them more oriented towards consumers, patients, clients, pupils and students.

MARKETING AND SELLING

A **marketing orientation** is not the same as a sales orientation – although the two overlap, they represent different approaches to management within a company. Marketing is the whole process directed at satisfying the needs and wants of people through exchange. Selling can be seen as the culmination of this process, the point at which an exchange is agreed between supplier and customer. The two functions are separated in all but small organisations.

> *'When sales are disappointing, marketing blames the sales force for its poor execution of an otherwise brilliant rollout plan. The sales team, in turn, claims that marketing sets prices too high and uses too much of the budget, which instead should go toward hiring more sales people or paying the sales reps higher commissions.'*
>
> (Kotler *et al.*, 2006)

The marketing process comprises:

- finding out what the customer wants;
- developing products/services to satisfy those wants;
- establishing a price consistent with the requirements of the supplier and the perceptions of the customer;
- distributing products/services to the customer;
- agreeing on the exchange – selling.

At the point of sale the objective is to persuade the customer to take the step from wanting a product or service to actually purchasing it. Some goods will 'sell themselves' and customers will actively seek them out, but in most circumstances this is not the case. The more closely the commodity or service matches the customer's needs the easier it will be to close the sale, and this is most likely to be the situation where the organisation is customer-oriented. This selling function is the purpose of the sales team. Small organisations may not differentiate between the marketing and the sales function, for them they are one and the same role and the marketing that exists comes from managers, sales representatives and advertising agencies. As organisations grow they usually find the need to appoint marketing people to conduct market research, decide on the size of the market and to choose the best markets. At first marketing may be seen as an aspect of sales, as the people who organise the advertising and sales promotions. However, once the marketing function becomes involved with segmenting the market and developing brands then it becomes an important aspect of strategic planning, product development and finance and separate and different from the sales function.

The whole purpose of marketing is to provide a product/service that matches the customer's needs. In order to do this managers have to understand that customers are not so much looking for particular products or services as for benefits. Consumers are looking for goods and services to satisfy their needs and there may be a variety of ways of doing this. A gardener who wants to remove a branch from a tree may immediately reach for a saw. If, however, the branch could be removed with a simple cut in the bark followed by an injection then the sale of saws could decline. Computer companies are well aware of this fact because many of them owe their development and success to having a solution to a particular business problem. When another company has found a cheaper or simpler solution to this problem then the demand for the original solution will decline sharply. In these examples the consumers' need is to remove the branch of a tree, not for a saw; to solve a business problem, not for a particular computer program. In the same way when a consumer buys a loaf of bread the basic need is not for bread but to satisfy hunger and there are a variety of ways of doing this.

This view of consumer needs means that managers have to understand that they should be producing what can be sold rather than selling what can be made. This marketing concept changes the whole orientation of any organisation from one that produces what it is able to and then attempts to sell it, into one that produces what people want to buy. Managers have to determine the needs and wants of their target market and then deliver the desired satisfaction more effectively and efficiently than competitors. A selling orientation can easily concentrate on the needs of the seller rather than the buyer, and the need to convert the company's product or service into cash. The selling concept starts with the company's existing product and looks for intense promotion to achieve profitable sales, while the marketing concept starts with the needs and wants of the company's target customers and achieves profits through creating and maintaining customer satisfaction.

The sales team and the marketing team may have economic and cultural differences. Sales usually favours the lowest possible price because they can sell the product more easily and they have more room to negotiate, while marketing is concerned with revenue targets and wants to spend more on product development and promotion. Sales may consider that the money spent on promotion, such as full page advertisements in newspapers and television clips, would be better spent on increasing the quality and size of the sales force. Sales may consider that the product they are selling lacks the features required by their customers because their view of customer need may be based on individual customers, while marketing is more concerned with a product having wide appeal. Cultural differences arise because marketing people are analytical, data oriented and project focused and, from the sales force point of view, desk-bound. Sales people are people oriented, spending time with customers and building relationships their focus is on closing sales, while their marketing colleagues are focused on promotions and programmes. The marketing team is concerned with promoting customer awareness and brand loyalty while the sales team is more involved in purchase intentions and customer loyalty – a successful organisation has to bring them together into integrated focus.

It can be argued that all managers are involved in marketing, even when they are far removed from the marketing function or where their organisation pays little attention to marketing. Product/service design, advertising and promotion or the provision of customer service are all aspects of marketing, just as all managers help to create and promote an image of their company in the way they carry out the job. The marketing-oriented manager will attempt to make selling as superfluous as possible by understanding the consumer so well that the product or service 'sells itself'. Ideally marketing will result in a consumer who is ready to buy so that all that is needed to make a sale is for the product to be available.

MANAGERS AND MARKETING

A fully integrated marketing orientation will permeate the whole structure of an organisation and will influence the thinking and the actions of every manager (see Figure 8.1). Managers need to realise that while profits continue to be fundamental to business survival, they depend on the organisation satisfying the customer. This is the approach that provides a competitive edge.

Figure 8.1 The customer-oriented organisation

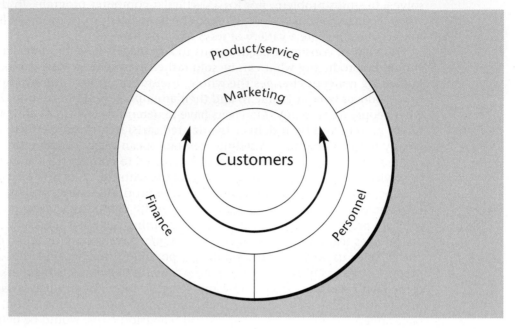

It is essential for any organisation to identify its customers if it is to improve its customer services and provide what the customer needs. The customer is usually identified as the person who pays for the product or service. Where there is no direct payment, such as in the public sector, the customer can be identified as the person who receives the service. There are different 'types' or 'levels' of customer because wholesalers can be considered to be customers of manufacturers and retailers to be customers of wholesalers. The 'final' customer is the person who eventually uses the product. It is this role which makes marketing an integrative function involving all areas of an organisation and everybody working in it (Figure 8.1). The marketing department is responsible for the technical aspects of a marketing policy but everybody is involved to a greater or lesser extent so that the whole corporate culture is affected, the image of the organisation and its strategic plan.

One of the greatest challenges for managers is to translate the words of mission statements, visions and corporate strategies into deeds. As the needs of customers change so the means of satisfying them have to change in response and adjust at least as quickly – where possible in anticipation.

KNOWING THE CUSTOMER

Managers have to decide about two fundamental marketing questions: What business are we in? Who is our customer?

What business are we in?

The answer to this may appear obvious and straightforward, but the examples of the saw manufacturer and the computer company illustrate the importance of arriving at a more fundamental answer. The computer company may describe its business in terms of information technology or computing or a software package, when it is in fact in the business of solving business problems through the application of technology. Once this is understood, the opportunities for the company open up and the meaning of 'sticking to the knitting' becomes clear.

It can be argued that when a company begins to ask what line of business it is actually in, it is beginning to identify marketing as an important management function. The next step is to appreciate the fact that marketing must permeate every area of the company. The question 'What is our business?' has to be defined in terms of the underlying consumer need that the organisation is trying to serve. A large retail store on the outskirts of a town may be trying to serve the shopping needs of a wide area limited only by the ability to get to it by car, while the corner shop situated in a residential location will be trying to serve the shopping needs of customers in an area defined by the ability to walk to it. In order to serve their customers they may both aim to carry a very wide variety of goods and to be open 'all hours'. However, the supermarket will be organised for regular but infrequent major shopping at relatively low prices, while the local shop will be organised for more irregular and more frequent shopping at relatively high prices. They will both survive while they are able to serve the needs of the consumers better than competitors. The local shop cannot hope to compete with the supermarket on price or variety but it may do so on its proximity to a group of consumers and its relative convenience.

Who is our customer?

The straightforward and obvious answer is that the customer is the person who pays for the product or service and it is possible to define the customer in these terms (see Figure 8.2). In fact, of course, the situation is more complicated than this. Some purchases are made for other people as gifts and although the person paying for the commodity is the customer who receives the benefit of purchasing a present, the final consumer is the person receiving the present. In the public sector there may not be a direct payment for a service, although payment may be indirect through the taxation and national insurance system. In this case the customer can be

Figure 8.2 The consumer

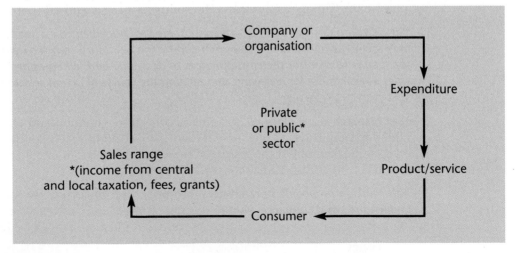

described as the person who receives the service whether it is health, education or leisure. Where children are involved in receiving a commodity or service, whether there is direct payment or not, the parents are also customers in that they may play a part in the payment and in the choices of their children who may be considered the 'primary' consumers.

Every organisation needs to know its customers, not only who they are but also what influences their purchasing decisions, the extent of their disposable income, the way they live, where they live and so on. Marketing depends on a detailed knowledge of customers and their needs so that the company or institution can meet these needs in the right place, at the right time and at the right price, and also anticipate fluctuations and changes in needs.

MARKET RESEARCH

After the acquisition of Hilton International by Ladbroke in 1987 there was concern that the Hilton name was being devalued in customer perceptions because it had been transplanted to other hotels. In 1988 an international market research survey was instigated under the direction of National Opinion Poll. The results were reassuring to the company because Hilton scored higher than its international competitors for both spontaneous and prompted awareness and as the first-choice chain of hotels. There were, however, some weaknesses identified by the research. The sub-brand Hilton National, created by Ladbroke from existing hotels, performed far less well in terms of awareness than the Hilton name; the Hilton International logo was the least well known of seven hotel logos tested; while Hilton was voted number one in brand image, prestige, business orientation and efficiency, it was seen as unfriendly with a hint of traditionalism tinged with complacency.

This research was followed up by Ladbroke in a 'Take me to the Hilton' advertising campaign in 1989 which was translated into nine languages and seen by about 54 million people. Further research in 1991 showed that many of the problems remained, which led to the company reviewing its brand positioning so that the Hilton International concentrated on international business travellers and wealthy tourists, while the Hilton National offered 'the Hilton experience' at affordable prices. Hotels have been reassessed and the Hilton National logo developed to emphasise the 'Hilton' connection. The company has recognised that

> *'far-reaching decisions can be taken by senior management on what to the outsider may seem like pure instinct. Research can be the necessary counter-balance. It offers the means to monitor the consequences of decisions and, when appropriate, it provides a mechanism for reviewing and refining the course of action selected.'*
>
> (*Marketing*, 28 January 1993)

Market research is the planned, systematic collection, collation and analysis of data designed to help the management of an organisation to reach decisions about its operation and to monitor the results of these decisions. It can be said to provide, in the words of the British Market Research Society:

> *'information on people's preferences, attitudes, likes and needs, to help companies understand what consumers want.'*

Strictly speaking, market*ing* research is concerned with the marketing *process* while market research is concerned with the measurement and analysis of *markets*. In practice the two terms are often used synonymously, although facts about the market are 'neutral' and objective, while the attitudes and opinions of customers have to be interpreted in order to help managers to make decisions. Market analysis is undertaken to determine the opportunities existing in a particular market and is about defining the market, describing it and analysing it. In this sense a market is the set of actual and potential consumers for particular goods and services. Managers are interested in:

- the size of the market for their products and services in terms of volume and value;
- the pattern of demand, including the economic, social, political and technical factors that might influence future demand and whether it is seasonal or cyclical;
- the market structure in terms of size and numbers of companies, income groups, sex and age distribution and geographic location;
- the buying habits of people (individuals as well as groups such as retailers and wholesalers) in the market;
- the market share of the company and how this compares with previous performance;
- past and future trends in areas such as population and national income;
- overseas markets that may present opportunities.

Managers need to be able to make predictions and decisions based on accurate information. While decisions can be made without very much information, a successful manager will want to have as many facts as possible before using judgement to make a decision. Market research enables decisions to be based on evidence and provides the basis for strategic planning and policy making.

The needs of customers in particular must be constantly monitored for managers to 'keep close to the customer'. It is important to know how satisfied customers are with products and services so that managers are able to introduce modifications or additions to satisfy customer needs more closely. The process will be a continuous one in order to keep up with or even ahead of changing needs (see Figure 8.3).

The questions that are to be answered to help managers make decisions have to be defined with as much clarity as possible in respect of the information that is required. The objectives of the research need to be established so that there is agreement about the expected outcomes. If, for example, a company needs to know its customers' opinions about a new product then the objective of the market research will be to establish these opinions as clearly as possible so that the product can be modified to match them. A sample survey may be used for this research, including a customer questionnaire and interviews. The results will be analysed and interpreted so that it can be presented to managers who will make decisions about the product. The research process will need to be monitored and as a result may be refined and the whole process will start again in order to see how well the modifications have been received by customers.

Figure 8.3 The research process

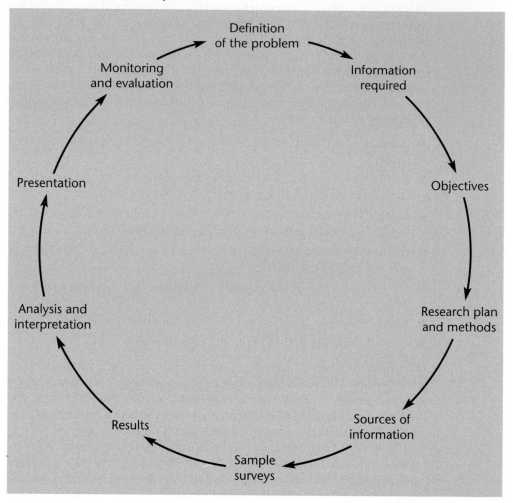

THE MARKETING PROCESS

Managers in any organisation must define the underlying need that it is trying to serve. This is reflected in the company mission statement or vision which describes the organisation's basic purpose. For example, a retail company may describe itself as offering customers a range of high quality, well designed and attractive merchandise at reasonable prices, while a computer company may want to emphasise the fact that it is not only about particular packages and products but that it concentrates on solving business problems. The corporate objectives will fill out the abstractions of the mission statements in more concrete terms and lead to the operational detail that results in an action plan.

In a marketing-oriented company, much of this process is informed by marketing on the grounds that there is no point in operating an organisation which is producing products or services which customers do not wish to buy. It can be argued that marketing analysis and planning begin and end with the customer. The starting point is to know about the organisation itself. This can be established through a

marketing audit, which is a formal review of everything that has affected or may affect the organisation's marketing environment, internal marketing system and specific marketing activities.

The marketing audit

A company's marketing environment (as distinct from, although including, environmental issues) consists of all the factors that are external to its own marketing system and that impinge on a successful exchange process with its customers. These factors can be collected into categories, sometimes referred to as the **STEP** (social, technological, economic, political) or **PESTLE factors**, which are:

- **Political**
- **Economic**
- **Social**
- **Technological**
- **Legal**
- **Environmental.**

Companies need to keep up to date with **political** changes that are occurring, not only in the countries in which they are operating but also across the world, because these will affect the work of the company in one way or another. For example, political disruption in the Middle East could result in reduced oil supplies and increases in the prices of petrol and other fuels. This could have a knock-on effect for the cost of transport which can affect the supply costs or distribution costs of even the smallest organisation. Changes in political parties and in governments can result in different policies being introduced which can affect companies in one way or another. The more managers understand about the political situations in which they are working, the more they are able to foresee and make allowances for effects on their organisation.

In a similar way managers need to keep up with **legislation** that affects their business. Health and safety regulations have to be met, European controls may have to be considered and pollution control may be the subject of new laws. There has been a growing interest in **environmental issues** and worldwide damage to the environment. The effects of different industrial sectors on the environment have been identified and vary considerably, so that, for example, it has been argued that oil companies can be environmentally damaging in their exploration for oil in the rainforests of the world, while the service sector has a less direct impact. Even in the service sector, of course, there are variations, so that tourism, for instance, can be polluting in environmentally sensitive areas of the world. This has encouraged the development of so-called 'eco-tourism' or environmentally friendly tourism.

Companies need to have a clear understanding of the **society** and the population to which their products and services are directed. As well as the size of the potential market there are questions of age distribution, sex distribution and income and education levels. As the population becomes wealthier or better educated, the range and quality of the goods demanded may change and companies have to keep up with these changes if they are to be successful. At the same time **economic** factors, such as levels of disposable income, will greatly influence consumer demand. For example, if disposable income falls then consumers will continue to buy necessities but will reduce spending on luxuries. In a recession house prices will fall and families may relocate less often so that demand for household goods will be reduced.

Technological changes have a major impact on most companies and can have an effect on the competitive edge of a company and make it either more or less cost-effective compared to its competitors. The rapidly expanding access to the Internet has altered the amount of information available to organisations' customers. Travel agencies, for example, have had to take into account the fact that tourists are now able to find out information on airline flights, hotels and excursions which is similar to the information they have in the agency; major stores, such as Tesco, have introduced Internet shopping as a part of their service to customers and there has been a huge expansion in the number of e-commerce 'dot-com' companies that have been established – often in competition with more traditional companies.

These external influences on an organisation's marketing environment do not, of course, fit neatly under these six headings. Environmental issues, such as pollution, are the subject of legislation and of social pressure; changes in taxation are political and have an economic impact; developments in technology can influence an organisation's costs and culture, and the whole way it works, and so on. All these 'external' influences on the market need to be understood by a successful company as well as information about its particular market and its own potential customers.

This gives rise to a further refinement of this consideration of the marketing environment which can be categorised as **SPECTACLES**:

- **Social**
- **Political**
- **Economic**
- **Cultural**
- **Technological**
- **Aesthetic**
- **Customers**
- **Legal**
- **Environmental**
- **Sectoral.**

As well as social, technological, economic, political, legal and environmental factors (covered in STEP, PEST and PESTLE), the influence of cultural, aesthetic, customer and sectoral factors in the environment of organisations is also taken into account.

Cultural factors can be defined as 'the way we do things around here', whether it is in an organisation, a particular society or region or a country. The importance of culture within organisations is discussed in Chapters 1, 2 and 4 while external cultural influences on organisations are considered in both Chapters 2 and 19. Organisations cannot operate in exactly the same way in other countries as they do in the UK and, even though they may have a high level of standardisation (as, for example, with McDonald's restaurants), they have to take account of people's customs, expectations and behaviour. Some of the early problems at Disneyland Paris arose from an attempt to transfer a North American culture directly to France. Automobile companies (such as Ford) have taken differences between countries to heart by producing different cars for different countries in order to attempt to match customer requirements.

→ Chs 1, 2 & 4

→ Chs 2 &19

Aesthetics can be thought of in terms of the appreciation of beauty or in terms of good taste; it can also be thought of in terms of image. There may be a difference between the image an organisation wants to project and the one it actually does project. The Body Shop, for example, attempts to project an environmentally friendly image but people also realise that it is a commercial company that has to make a profit. Promotional campaigns are designed in order to project and influence the image of an organisation but they do not always produce the expected result. Companies develop a reputation among consumers which they may find difficult to change. Marks & Spencer, for example, has attempted to alter its well established image in terms of its clothing products among consumers in order to compete with shops offering more trendy goods at cheaper prices.

→ Ch. 3

The importance of organisations understanding and reacting to **customer** requirements is analysed in Chapter 3. There has been a rise in 'consumerism' with an increase in the 'power' of customers and organisations have to meet customer needs if they are to survive in the long run. **Sectoral** factors are an essential element of an organisation's competitive strategy. Managers have to analyse the position of their organisation in the sector or sectors in which they operate, as well as the position of any actual and potential rivals, so that they can maintain a competitive advantage.

→ Ch. 18

The growing interest in **environmental** factors is discussed in Chapter 18. Organisations and their industries have a varied impact on the environment, so that it can, for example, be argued that oil companies' very business is environmentally damaging while the service sector has a less direct impact. However, the actual situation is complicated because, for example, the increasing demand for consumer goods has placed great pressures on resources and, as a result, on the environment. Managers face the challenge of meeting customer needs and integrating environmental considerations into their production and marketing plans.

SWOT analysis

Equally as important as this external business environment to a company's marketing plan is knowledge and understanding of its internal strengths and weaknesses. In marketing terms this process is known as a **SWOT analysis**:

- Strengths
- Weaknesses
- Opportunities
- Threats.

The SWOT analysis helps managers to focus their attention on the key areas within a company that need to be taken into account in producing a marketing plan. It highlights internal strengths and weaknesses from the customers' point of view as they relate to external opportunities and threats.

The strengths of an organisation may be in terms of proximity to its customers, its expertise, its ability to produce high-quality goods at low cost. Weaknesses will be the opposite of the strengths. A poor reputation, badly organised services and difficult communications may all be weaknesses of a company. The manager's role is to exploit the strengths of the company and to correct or compensate for the weaknesses.

The weaknesses of an organisation may give rise to opportunities, in the sense that the exposure of a weakness may be seen as an opportunity for development. A company that has been able to make a profit even though its customer care is poor can increase its profits and improve its position by taking the opportunity to improve its customer care. In terms of threats, competition is the most obvious for many companies and marketing is very much about maintaining a competitive edge. Other threats can be as a result of a fall in orders, increased import prices, changes in government regulations and changes in demand. The ability to meet and overcome these threats successfully is one of the strengths of a company and can separate those organisations which survive from those that do not.

THE MARKETING MIX

Once managers know the situation of their organisation in relation to its market, understand its internal and external position and have an idea of what their customers need then they can develop a marketing strategy. Managers have four major variables that can be controlled in order to arrive at their marketing strategy. These are the product or service produced by the organisation, its price, the way it is promoted and the place or places through which it is made available to the consumers. These are the **four Ps** which constitute the **marketing mix**:

- Product
- Price
- Place
- Promotion.

The marketing mix is the appropriate combination, in a particular set of circumstances, of the four Ps. It consists of everything an organisation can do to influence the demand for its products and services. Management has to make sure that the balance between these four variables is maintained or their marketing strategy will fail. What happens to one element in the marketing mix will have an effect on one or more of the others. For example, the quality of a product may be improved in order to meet customer demands but this may increase the cost of production and the price. However, another possibility is that the improved quality increases demand so that sales rise, with the result that there are economies of scale and lower unit costs which can be reflected in the price.

An effective marketing strategy will bring the four variables together in order to satisfy customer needs. To retain the competitive edge in a target market, managers have to develop and communicate the differences between their offering and those of competitors. The key to competitive positioning is to understand how members of the target market evaluate and choose between product brands. It may be on location, on price or on the way the product is sold. Managers must choose a marketing mix that will support and reinforce their chosen competitive position at an expenditure level they can afford. By this process marketing managers seek to achieve the optimum marketing mix for their company – that is the least amount of money and effort required to make a profit. The process of achieving this optimum marketing mix can be summarised as APPEAL:

- **Assess the needs of consumers**
- **Produce the right commodity or service**
- **Price the commodity or service successfully**

- **Ensure a high quality product and service**
- **Advertise and promote the product/service effectively**
- **Launch an efficient distribution system.**

Managers can manipulate and vary this process and the four Ps in order to improve the effectiveness of the marketing programme.

In terms of service marketing, it is possible to add **three other Ps**:

- **People**
- **Process**
- **Physical evidence.**

Including **people** as a factor in the marketing mix emphasises the importance of all those involved in the transaction of a service, including the customer and the person (or people) providing the service. The success of the service will depend on the relationship between the customer and the provider. The customer will have certain expectations and if these are not met by the provider then the service will not be a complete success. A holiday tour guide, for example, can provide minimal information to holidaymakers, or alternatively can suggest places to visit, arrange trips and provide support when problems arise. Some holidaymakers may be happy to be left alone, while others may want much more attention from the guide and be disappointed if they do not receive it.

The **process** is the actual interaction between all the people involved in the transaction. Training in service provision emphasises the importance of this interaction and the role of the provider in enabling the customer to receive the service in an efficient and effective way.

Physical evidence can range from the location in which the service takes place to the ticket or voucher with which the customer is provided. A flight ticket is the physical evidence that the traveller has purchased a seat on an aeroplane flight between two designated places, while a voucher may be the physical evidence that the holidaymaker has purchased a place on a guided tour.

The inclusion of these three extra Ps suggests that marketing must take them into account, particularly in the service sector. They emphasise that transactions are between people, that there is a process involved in each transaction and that consideration should be given to all the other aspects of the transaction.

PRODUCTS AND SERVICES

'A product is anything that can be offered to a market for attention, acquisition, use or consumption that might satisfy a want or need. It includes physical objects, services, persons, places, organizations and ideas.'   (Kotler, 1986)

This definition includes services and it is useful to realise both that they are 'products' in the broadest sense and that there are differences between them and physical commodities (see the discussion in the case study on p. 85–6). Whereas a commodity is tangible and its sale involves a change in ownership, a service is essentially intangible and does not result in the exchange of ownership. When a car is bought and sold, there is a change of ownership; when a holiday is bought and sold, ownership of the travel company, airbus or hotel remains unchanged.

Managers can view all commodities and services as solving consumer problems, and marketing as selling benefits rather than features – but, of course, features may be important if they help to provide benefits. For example, car salespeople may concentrate their sales drive on the special features their cars provide, while the ability of the cars to provide a reliable form of transport is taken for granted. The features help to differentiate one car from another but they will not serve any purpose unless the benefit of transport can be guaranteed. In fact, competition is often not so much about the product as about the value added to it in the form of packaging, services, customer advice, financing, delivery arrangements and so on. For example, Exhibit 8.1 illustrates the importance of packaging.

In considering their target market, managers need to take account of all aspects of it. These can be summarised by considering basic questions about the market which can be divided into the **six 'O's:**

- **Occupants** – which individuals constitute the market?
- **Object** – what do consumers wish to buy?
- **Occasions** – when do customers make purchases?
- **Organisations** – who is involved in the decision to purchase?
- **Objectives** – why do consumers buy particular commodities?
- **Operations** – how do consumers buy products and services?

Market research will help managers to understand their target markets so that their companies can produce the commodities and services wanted by the consumers in that particular market at a particular time. At the same time managers need to base their decisions on who is involved in purchasing and how and where consumers make decisions on purchases.

Making sure that the product or service is right for the consumer can be described as the single most important activity of marketing. If managers do not produce a commodity or service that consumers want, no amount of promotion or price incentives will encourage them to buy it, at least not more than once. In fact, managers will be aiming to satisfy the consumer so that demand is likely to be

Exhibit 8.1 Marketing: value added

In the run-up to Christmas 1993, Cadbury's decided to introduce a £5 million support package for 'Milk Tray'. This is one of the oldest and the best known mass-market brands and is the UK's biggest selling chocolate assortment brand. It had become squeezed by upmarket niche brands on one side and downmarket and own-label competitors on the other.

The support package was based on months of qualitative and quantitative research and was designed to increase the volume of sales by 20 per cent over 18 months. The revamp included the addition of two new flavours – truffle shell and praline fanfare – to reflect the company's view that consumers were being increasingly experimental in their tastes.

The big change was in the packaging for the chocolates, with a redesigned box to make it more upmarket with a cut-out lid, a separate choice card inside and a new tray design. The object was to make the product more 'feminine' and give it a more luxury feel.

repeated and other products or services of the company are also demanded. An important element of marketing is about reputation and recommendation. Personal recommendation is one of the most important ways in which a company's reputation and image are developed.

Ideally, managers will extend the features of the product or service so that they provide unique benefits not found in the competition. The concept of the 'unique selling proposition' includes the quality of design, style and service, reliability and cost. The successful development of this concept will help enhance customer loyalty. Loyal customers tend to be worth more to a company than new customers. The extra cost of replacing an existing customer with a new one can be as high as tenfold. Loyal customers are believed to spend more and to have a higher purchase frequency, and a satisfied customer is the best possible walking advertisement for any company.

The increase of competition in the 1990s was matched by rising customer sophistication, combined with price sensitivity, and has given impetus to consideration of 'relationship marketing' and customer loyalty.

> *'This more competitive environment will focus greater attention on the potential of existing customers. This will take two forms: an assessment of lifetime value and therefore the value of promoting loyalty; the possibilities of increasing the value of given customers through cross selling/upgrading programmes.'*
>
> (Henley Centre and Chartered Institute of Marketing, 1993)

The link between customer defections, or 'promiscuity', and profit offers an explanation for a move away from a culture where 'closing the sale' is of overriding importance, to one where encouraging customer loyalty is paramount. Customer retention (see Exhibit 8.2) can be defined as:

> *the number of customers present at the beginning of a period who remain as customers at the end of the period, divided by the number of those present at the beginning.*

Research from Bain and Company indicates that a business loses between 15 and 20 per cent of its customers each year (*Marketing*, 18 November 1993). In any business, the more satisfied the customer, the higher the retention rate.

Long-term relationships with customers are more profitable because:

- the cost of acquiring new customers can be substantial – a higher retention rate means that less marketing expenditure needs to be allocated to targeting potential customers;
- loyal customers tend to spend more;

Exhibit 8.2 Customer retention rate

1000 original customers, of whom 800 are retained:

$$\frac{800}{1000} \times 100 = 80\% \text{ customer retention rate}$$

1000 original customers, of whom 200 are retained:

$$\frac{200}{1000} \times 100 = 20\% \text{ customer retention rate}$$

- regular customers tend to place frequent, consistent orders and therefore usually cost less to serve;
- satisfied customers are the best advertisement for any business and are likely to introduce new customers to the company through word-of-mouth recommendations;
- satisfied customers are often willing to pay premium prices to a supplier they know and trust;
- retaining customers makes gaining market entry or share gain difficult for competitors;
- the information collated and held on loyal customers through database management allows the company to communicate regularly with them.

Sales can be increased by introducing tactical promotion and reactivating lapsed customers with specially targeted offers. The development of Air Miles to encourage customer loyalty has been spread across a number of products and is similar to long-term promotions such as petrol tokens. The objective of these promotions is the same – to encourage customers to buy products or services where they can obtain the petrol tokens or Air Miles.

For example, in 1989 Newey & Eyre became an Air Miles client when it launched a customer-loyalty programme. The national marketing manager stated, 'We felt that travel was still one of the most powerful motivators. We were also attracted by its flexibility and the fact that the perceived reward is greater than the cost.' Newey & Eyre is the largest electrical wholesaler in the UK and in spite of the recession it measured a growth in sales of 24 per cent in 1992. The company targeted a core group of customers from its more than 100,000 accounts and also provided Air Miles as an incentive for its own salesforce. The promotion was risk free in the sense that it secured incremental revenue. If a target was not reached then the customer was not rewarded with Air Miles.

In 1993 the magazine *Marketing* noted an increasing range of customer-loyalty initiatives. Examples have included Vauxhall's GM card, Diners Club, Asda, American Express, Argos Premier Points, Sainsbury's Homebase and British Airways Air Miles.

LIFE CYCLE ANALYSIS

Managers should understand the application of **life cycle analysis** in terms of the products and services for which they are responsible. This analysis can also be applied to the general rise and fall of companies. All products and services have a life cycle in the sense that, after they are introduced, they often pass through periods of growth, then relative stability and finally decline. This process can be mirrored in the fate of companies who do not take or are unable to take sufficient notice of the life cycle. Many of the original 'excellent' companies from the early 1980s declined as their products and services were overtaken by others. IBM is an example of this (see Exhibit 8.3), although it has survived successfully.

The performance of new products and services typically follows a pattern that includes five identifiable stages, each related to the passage of time and the levels of sales or demand (see Figure 8.4). The stages are:

Exhibit 8.3 The decline of IBM

In the early 1980s IBM controlled the newest and fastest growing technology and its name was synonymous with computing. By 1992 the company had experienced the largest ever loss recorded by any company anywhere.

IBM was one of Peters and Waterman's (1982) 'excellent' companies:

'With one act ... IBM simultaneously reaffirmed its heroic dimension (satisfying the individual's need to be part of something great) and its concern for individual self-expression (the need to stick it out).'

In a period of 10 years the company moved from being held up as an example of the success of capitalism to an example of its failings. It could be said that it was within its major strengths that IBM's weakness appeared. Its strength was based on an almost monopolistic position in the market for automated information. It was first with punch-cards and then with the mainframe and minicomputer.

As long as computers were the preserve of major corporations the IBM strategy worked, but with the development of the desktop personal computer this changed. IBM decided not to launch the desktop computer because it did not believe that anyone would want such an item and it was left to Apple Computers and other competitors to move into this market. IBM quickly followed, but without time to develop its own components it bought in chips from Intel and software from Microsoft. The launch of the IBM PC legitimised the desktop for corporations but also meant that other companies could produce IBM PC clones and Intel and Microsoft could sell their components to these companies. By 1994 there were 3000 clone manufacturers in Taiwan alone, helped in their success by the ability to network PCs to do much of the work of mainframes and minis.

In his book, *The Fate of IBM*, Robert Heller (1994) comments that IBM played a difficult hand badly, but in the end the new market was simply too big and the pace of change too fast for one company to remain in control.

- **Introduction** – a period of slow growth as the product/service is introduced.
- **Growth** – a period of rapid market acceptance.
- **Maturity** – a period of slower growth because the product/service has been accepted by most of the potential buyers.
- **Saturation** – a period when there are many competitors in the market which itself is no longer growing. This period can be combined with maturity.
- **Decline** – a period when performance starts a strong downward drift.

Of course, not all products and services follow this exact pattern and timescales can vary considerably, but careful analysis of the life cycle enables managers to focus on the appropriate marketing strategy for a particular stage in the life cycle of their products and service.

- **Introduction** – a new product or service may be a substitute for something else, either directly or indirectly. For a time, consumers may resist the new product while they consider that the old one still meets their needs. For this reason, and because the new product is not well known in the market, the demand will be slow in the introductory stage. The only exception to this is a fad or fashion

Figure 8.4 Product life cycle

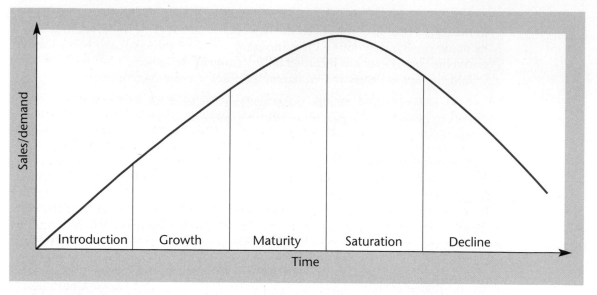

which may make an immediate impact. The marketing strategy for most goods when they are introduced will be to target the groups of people who are likely to be most interested. Previous customers are an obvious target. Computer companies producing a new product or introducing a new service will send information to their previous customers in the first instance. They will also attempt to attract the attention of the 'innovators' who find out about new products without help and who do not need much persuasion.

- **Growth** – the benefit of the new product/service will have become accepted by this stage. Production difficulties will have been overcome and development costs covered, so that usually the price can be reduced. Marketing strategy will usually involve a wider promotion to target new customers. Competitors will begin to enter the market during this stage. They spend money on promoting their product so the general awareness of it increases, helping to encourage further growth.

- **Maturity** – at this stage the product or service will have become widely accepted and competition will become the most important element for managers. Marketing may be aimed at an attempt to retain or assume the position of market leader or at challenging the leader by emphasising the advantages of the company's particular product.

- **Saturation** – sooner or later all the potential users of the product or service will have satisfied their demand for it, so that the market no longer grows. There will be plenty of suppliers competing in the market and this may lead to price wars. At the same time managers will search for new products and services to replace the old ones.

- **Decline** – as newer products and services are introduced, the demand for the old product or service will decline. Managers may decide to stop producing the commodity because it is felt to be better to invest in newer products. Advances in technology can cause the demand for a product to decline and changes in fashion or taste alter demand.

■ **Recovery** – it is possible for companies to recover, so that after a period of decline and heavy losses (IBM lost $16 billion between 1991 and 1993 – see Exhibit 8.4) a company may introduce changes which are sufficient to bring it back to an early stage of the life cycle. This company renewal may involve new products, internal restructuring or a fresh approach to marketing and sales which result in the company starting a new life cycle at the introduction or growth stage.

Life cycle analysis is observed quite easily in the development and decline of a new model of a motor car. At introduction, the marketing strategy is likely to include heavy advertising to encourage early demand. As the growth of sales develops, promotion will be designed to establish market share. The reputation of the product will become more important than in the introduction stage when innovators and 'risk takers' may be the main purchasers. Car manufacturers may emphasise matters such as reliability and security.

In maturity, an attempt will be made to retain market position against the competition, the emphasis may be on the quality of a well-established product and the features available in the car may play an important part in sales. Eventually the particular model of car will become relatively out of date compared with new models being introduced and saturation will have been reached with a decline in sales. As demand declines, car manufacturers and showrooms may attempt to boost sales by producing 'special editions', or promotions which may involve price cuts. Some car manufacturers have followed a policy of replacing their models in a particular price range before a decline in demand is too obvious. This could be said, for example, of Ford's replacement of the Cortina by the Sierra and then the Mondeo.

Exhibit 8.4 The recovery of IBM

Although IBM had experienced record losses by 1993, by 1997 the company had achieved a remarkable recovery. The appointment of a new chief executive, Lou Gerstner, in 1993 brought about one of the most remarkable corporate turn-arounds in US history. In 1997, for the first time in 10 years, IBM's market value topped $100 billion and its shares were trading at record levels. Shipments of PCs rose 27 per cent in 1996 boosting IBM's market share from 8.1 to 8.9 per cent and the absorption of the software company Lotus Development Corporation in 1995 proved unexpectedly successful. One view was that the culture of the two companies would clash and that IBM's software division would not be revitalised, but Lotus sales rose 60 per cent in 1996 to $650 million.

It has been reported that Lou Gerstner had little knowledge of computers when he joined IBM but he dismissed the idea that the company's problems were based on a lack of new products. His view was that the problem lay in the company's management and one fundamental change he made was to instruct the company sales force to find out what customers really wanted, rather than believing that they knew best and then giving it to them. At the same time the numbers of staff were being reduced from 300,000 to 215,000 and factories and research and development departments were closed. In 1997 two-thirds of IBM's revenue came from PCs and services and although the use of an IBM scoring system at the Atlanta Olympics ran into difficulties, the defeat of Gary Kasparov, the world chess champion, for the first time by IBM's 'Deep Blue' computer was a successful publicity stunt.

MARKET SEGMENTATION

Where clear differences can be identified, it is possible to group customers into market segments for marketing and sales purposes. The reason for doing this is to find the most promising opportunities for a company's talents, so that its strengths are utilised and its weaknesses are not important. Car companies specialise in certain features or in producing, for example, off-road or commercial vehicles.

Market segmentation is based on the characteristics of customers, such as:

- income
- age
- geography
- life style.

This segmentation may lead to 'niche' marketing where a relatively small producer may find a particular segment of customer need which is not otherwise satisfied. A specialised car manufacturer such as Morgan is an example of this in providing sports cars for people who want a 'traditional' performance sports car. The range of goods and services offered to specialist groups with particular interests is represented by the range of magazines available on newsagents' shelves. These cover a huge range of hobbies and interests from sports, to travel, property ownership, photography, computers, sex, cars, clothes and fashion, women's interests and so on. These are segmented not only by interest and life style but also by age and sex, so that there are the so-called 'lad's' magazines, men's magazines, women's magazines, children's magazines and further segmentation within these groups. Similarly, clothing retailers divide the products they offer into obvious segments such as men's, women's and children's and more subtly aim at particular income groups and lifestyle choices. Geographically, food retailers charge different prices for the same goods in different parts of the country, also depending on the state of competition in a particular area.

One characteristic in the consideration of market segmentation is the 20/80 principle, sometimes described as the 'Pareto effect'. Managers may notice that, for example, 20 per cent of customers account for 80 per cent of demand. Some car producers sell 80 per cent of their cars to fleet or company buyers who may account for only 20 per cent of their individual customers, while for other producers it may be the other way around. Another characteristic of this segmentation is 'branding'.

BRAND MANAGEMENT

A brand can be described as

'a product plus added values'.

One way of seeing a brand is as a bundle of functional, economic and psychological benefits for the consumer in that a brand will ensure a particular (and known to the customer) quality of product at an acceptable price and confirming or providing a particular image. Another way of looking at brand is as the associations and ideas attributed to a product or service by consumers. The clothing retailer Marks & Spencer, for example, has had the reputation for offering well made, middle of the road and reasonably priced products. When competitors introduced reasonably made, very cheap clothes in sharp, modern designs, the M & S brand became less popular. Recovery for the company has been based on confirming the quality image of the brand while competing on price and design. A brand name may become synonymous with the generic product, such as with 'Hoover', 'Kleenex', 'Biro' and 'Nylon'.

Another way of seeing a brand is as the 'added values applied to a product', that is mainly in terms of 'image' without this being applied to a particular product, but applied to a bundle of products. The Harley-Davidson image, for example, is well established through films like *Easy Rider* and the motorbike's American parentage. An article in the *Daily Telegraph* about the new Harley XR 1200 motor-bike, noted that

> *'the V-Rod was touted by Harley as the bike for those who liked the brand but not the bikes. By sticking more closely to the brand, the XR 1200 might just be that machine instead.'*   (Ash, 2007)

Separating the product from the brand in this way suggests that 'brand' can 'add value' to a range of products. The car manufacturer BMW has a reputation for producing quality motor cars and the motorcycles they produce carry the same brand, the same badge and the same 'added value'. When the supermarket chain Tesco moved into selling clothing, consumers would have expected similar principles of price and quality to apply to these products as already applied to its foodstuff.

Brands can be defined as

> *products and services plus added values that provide benefits to the consumer.*

Products branded with the retailer's name are known as 'own label' or 'own brand', in the USA 'private label'. In Cooperative shops, for example, there will be a choice of products, such as soup or jam, some of which are 'own label' or 'own brand' and some other brands. Brand names are critical elements in product differentiation and another way of defining 'brand' is

> *a name, design, label which is intended to identify the goods or services of one seller and to differentiate them from those of competitors.*

At one time most products were sold unbranded, that is they were sold out of barrels and cases. Into the 1950s flour, sugar and salt were still sold out of large bags or barrels, scooped out, weighed and poured into a paper bag or a twist of newspaper. Perhaps the earliest branding was carried out in medieval guilds where craftsmen were required to put trade marks on their products. A 'trademark' is a method of branding a product in the same way that cattle ranchers in the American west (and for that matter in many other places in many other ways) brand the cattle that belong to them with a symbol that differentiates them from cattle owned by other ranchers. In the past this branding was carried out with a hot iron, now it is more likely to be a tag or a microchip. 'Brand manager' is a distinct management role in many companies – a manager responsible for the planning, development and monitoring of a brand or a group of products, although the manager's title may be 'product manager' or 'market manager' depending on the job description and the company structure.

It is possible to consider marketing as managing the relationship between the brand and its various customers and, in these terms, building brand relationships is the key marketing function and 'brand equity' is the state of those relationships at any one time. Brand equity is the intangible asset and advantage associated with the brand. Branding has a number of advantages:

- the product is easily recognised and identified;
- it provides a strong link between advertising and other forms of promotion;
- it facilitates the introduction of new products, which can be introduced under an existing, well established and well regarded brand name (such as Heinz);
- a successful brand in one sector may be able to be carried over to other sectors;
- the seller's brand name and trademark can provide legal protection of unique product features which could otherwise be copied by competitors;
- brand loyalty, the attraction of loyal customers, will provide some protection from competition and help in future planning;
- good brands help to build the corporate image by advertising the quality of the company.

Whereas at one time an advertisement might be descriptive, in the sense of showing the product, once a brand is established a more abstract approach may be taken. The company easyJet has been branded as a cheap, simple, uncluttered and easy form of air travel. This concept has then been applied to other products such as cruising and mobile telephones. With its orange logo the company brand wants to convey a 'fun, straight talking, easy to get on with' life style so that a promotion for 'easyMobile' showed not a telephone but a mug, presumably indicating a relaxed approach. The sale of a product or service to a customer is not the end of a transaction, in fact the sale may represent the beginning of a consumer's relationship with a particular brand. If the first contact with easyJet is buying an easyMobile telephone, the consumer may judge the other offerings of the company on the basis of the 'ease' with which the telephone could be used against the fact that easyMobile was taken off the market at the end of 2006. No doubt with this in mind the company did conclude its rather rapid entry into and exit from the mobile market by providing for a relatively 'easy' transfer to another supplier.

It can be argued that a brand is a personality and establishes a relationship. When Heinz adds another product to its list, consumers who trust the brand will be prejudiced in favour of it (Volckner and Sattler, 2006). EasyMobile was sold on the basis of the personality of the owner – 'Stelios says: fun, straight talking, easy to get on with it. Your new easyMobile service is just like me!' (from the leaflet introducing the service). Successful brand extension is likely to depend on there being a good fit between the parent brand and the extension product so that they have similar characteristics (as in the example of the 'easy' brand). Also retailers have to accept the brand extension, encouraged by marketing support from the parent company through promotions and discounts. Brand extension has risks in that a new product that is unsuccessful may reflect badly on the parent brand. This is a major factor in the attempts by organisations to protect their names and trademarks. When other companies use a name or trademark which is the same as or very similar to the original one there may be 'brand dilution' or the blurring of the identity of the original brand (see Pullig *et al.*, 2006 and Exhibit 8.5).

Companies now actively manage customers as strategic assets through loyalty and relationship marketing because many customers are stable and can be 'segmented' on the strength of their sales history. This means that the marketing process can be seen as the management activity aimed at improving the relationships in the network, from the perspective of the brand, in order to improve brand equity.

Exhibit 8.5 Brand dilution

A dispute settled in the United States Supreme Court in 2003 concerned a small store selling lingerie and other 'adult novelty' items. It was called 'Victor's Secret' and shortly after opening the owners of the store were sued by the company 'Victoria's Secret' which claimed protection of its brand name under the Federal Trademark Dilution Act of 1995. The Supreme Court ruled that the 'senior', brand, Victoria's Secret, had to show evidence of actual dilution by the 'junior' brand, Victor's Secret, and that being able to show a mental association between the two companies and their products was insufficient. The court ruling found in favour of the junior brand.

It can be argued that this was an example of one form of brand dilution – tarnishment which can be described as a lowered evaluation of a senior brand due to a junior brand, so that there may be the attachment of a negative association to the senior brand. An example might be when the American Express slogan 'Don't leave home without it' was used to promote condoms by another company. Another form of dilution, blurring can be described as the gradual whittling away of the identity of the brand in the mind of the public due to the emergence of a junior brand. An example might be when the Lexis data service argued that the introduction of the Lexus automobile potentially added a new category association that would blur the meaning of the brand for consumers.

Source: Based on Pullig, C, Simmons, C J and Netemeyer, R G (2006) 'Brand dilution: when do new brands hurt existing brands?', *Journal of Marketing*, 70.

PRODUCT/SERVICE PORTFOLIO

Marketing is an essential factor in managers' decisions about the products and services a company will produce. As well as profits, managers are concerned with market share, because this is an indication of the extent to which a product can generate cash. In general terms the larger the market share that a product obtains then the more cash it can generate. On the other hand the greater the growth in the market the more cash is used to support the expansion.

This situation can be summarised by a classification known as the **Boston matrix**. Figure 8.5 shows the main categories of products or services used in this classification, which are given distinctive names to indicate their prospects:

- A **star** has a high market share and a high market growth rate. It will tend to generate as much cash as it uses and will be self-financing. In periods of economic expansion there will be a large number of stars – products and services which are in a growing market and have a large share of that market. Particular models of motor cars may fall into this category, along with household goods, popular holidays and so on.

- A **problem child** has a low market share but a high growth rate in a market that is itself growing. In order to increase market share it may require investment and promotion and it will therefore use cash even though it is not generating very much. These products and services represent a problem because managers must decide whether to stop producing them or whether their potential growth makes an investment worthwhile. For example, a computer firm may decide that it is worth spending money on developing and promoting one of its software

Figure 8.5 The Boston matrix

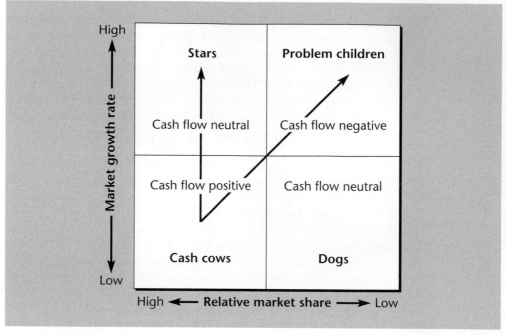

Source: Based on the Boston Consulting Group growth–share matrix.

packages because, even though the sales are relatively small at the moment, there is considerable scope for expansion. It may be felt that the low sales are due to limited promotion and product development.

- A **cash cow** has a high market share and a low market growth in a reasonably stable market. As a result of its established position, this type of product or service does not require developing or promoting and therefore cash is generated. A well-known brand of processed food may need little advertising, for example, and may still hold a large share of the market.

- A **dog** has a low market share and a low market growth, and in fact this type of product or service is likely to be a prime target for consideration for ending production. For example, a car model with poor and declining sales may cease to be manufactured because the cost of the people and equipment employed in producing it may be considered a poor use of resources compared with the alternatives.

Based on the Boston Consulting Group growth–share matrix

This analysis can provide managers with an indication of the type of policy they should follow for different products and services. The **product/service portfolio** of the company would ideally include a range of products/services at different stages. Cash generated by cash cows could, for example, be invested by company managers in stars or in selected problem children in order to make them into stars (the 'rising stars') as indicated by the arrows in Figure 8.5. The stars in turn could become cash cows as the need to promote and develop the product declines. Even some dogs can be saved from extinction by identifying segments of the market on which to concentrate, or by improving productivity in order to reduce costs. A car, for example, may retain a niche market even though its sales have fallen and with low production costs it may still be profitable. The British Leyland/Rover Mini is an example of this.

In considering marketing strategies managers will often be concerned with other aspects of the market, such as how far they are **penetrating** it in terms of reaching as many potential customers as possible, and how they can **extend** it in terms of opening new markets by finding new uses for the products or entirely new markets. Managers may also be concerned with **product development**, which means modifying or adding to the product or service in terms of quality and performance. They may want to **diversify** by both developing the product and extending the market. These elements comprise the **Ansoff matrix** which is illustrated in Figure 8.6.

With existing products managers will attempt to achieve increased **market penetration** in existing markets and also attempt to find new markets. They will look for product development and help to penetrate present markets, while aiming for new products or new uses for present products in order to diversify into new markets. Managers looking for market penetration and **market extension** in the computer industry began to look towards the so-called **SOHO** market in the middle 1990s. The 'small office, home office' developed as a potentially fast-growing area as the divide between work and leisure applications became blurred. Car manufacturers have found it possible to extend their market for four-wheel drive, off-road vehicles by developing more luxury products to sell as fashionable vehicles to buyers who may never leave the tarmac road but who wish to enjoy a rugged, outdoor image.

Ideally a company will produce a range of products which are at different stages of their life cycle, are stars and cash cows, and can be developed to further penetrate the market and extend it. It will do this by careful market research and developing new products to meet customer needs.

Figure 8.6 The Ansoff matrix

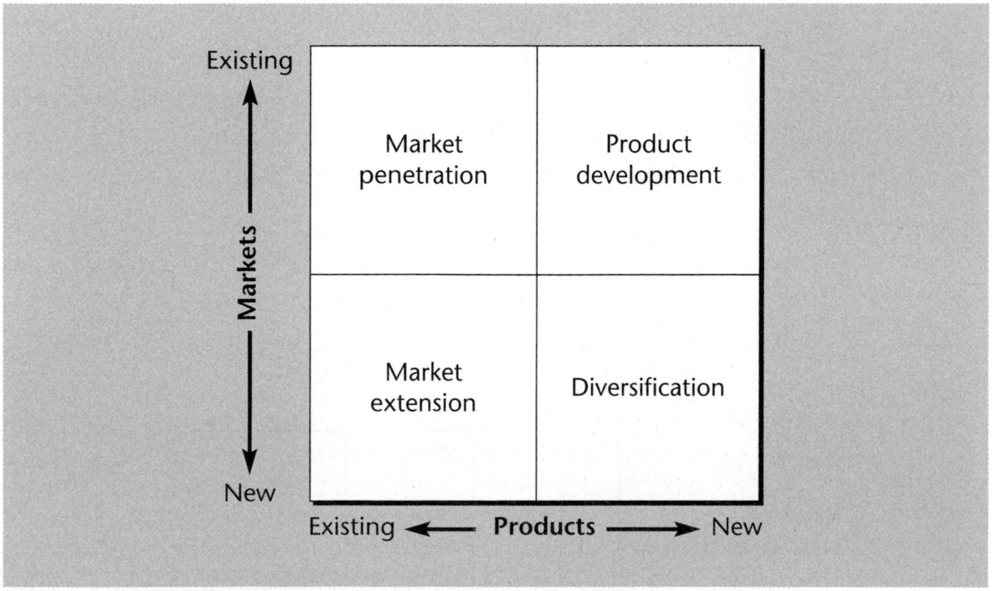

Source: Based on I Ansoff (1989) *Corporate Strategy*, Harmondsworth: Penguin.

PRICE, PLACE AND PROMOTION

Price

An organisation will need to decide the price of its products and services based on marketing objectives. Price must be consistent with the total marketing strategy for a product. There is little point in charging a low price for a luxury item or a high price for a commodity to be sold in a mass market. In fact price will depend very heavily on the supply and demand for the product (see Figure 8.7).

If supply is high and so is price (say, at point *a*) then demand will be low (at *x*). If supply is relatively low and so is the price (at point *b*), then demand will be high (at *y*). The equilibrium price (*e*) is where supply and demand are equal.

In practice, managers will want to keep prices as low as possible in order to encourage demand, while still retaining a high enough price to provide a good margin of profit on the sale of the product. In the introductory stage of the product life cycle the demand may grow very quickly and supply may be limited. At the same time price may not be a very important factor in consumers' decision making because they are anxious to be among the first to obtain the product. There is an opportunity for the organisation to charge relatively high prices to these 'innovators' and recover some of their research and development costs. The original personal computers, for example, were relatively expensive.

At the mature stage of the life cycle, the price of the product may be reduced in order to maintain or increase market share in what is likely to be an increasingly competitive market. In the saturation and decline stages, price will be manipulated

Figure 8.7 Supply, demand and price

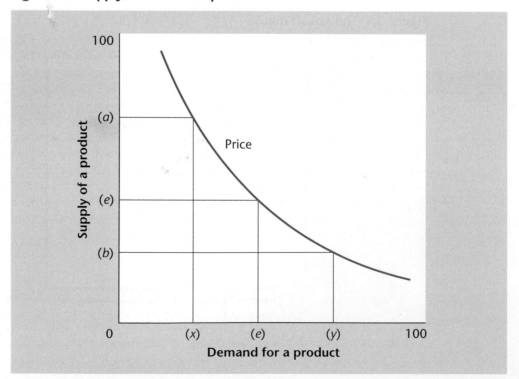

depending on market share and sales volume. It may be raised in order to create a cash cow within an established market, or lowered through sales promotions in order to extend sales.

A company will often attempt to position itself in terms of the price of its products in one or other area of the market. A car manufacturer, for example, may see itself in the luxury area of the market and target products and prices accordingly, while another manufacturer may be aiming at wide coverage of the mass market and produce a range of cars to appeal to different segments. Although a pricing policy may be a sophisticated process based on detailed market research and the consideration of a number of ratios, it is often based on a cost-plus process, on a consideration of competitors' prices or on 'what the market will bear'. One factor in these approaches is that there is less uncertainty over costs than there is about demand so that it is easy to arrive at a price by adding a percentage to costs. At the same time it is not necessary to make frequent changes to price in response to changes in demand. 'Loss leaders' are often based on a price which covers fixed costs such as equipment, capital and overheads, while variable costs, such as labour, are subsidised for a limited time by other sources of income.

Prices may be fixed slightly above or below those of competitors. For example, petrol stations often follow this pattern. Or price may be based on what it is felt people will pay, 'what the market will bear'. In a relatively expensive area, where salaries are high, the price of food, petrol and other goods may be higher than the same goods bought in a cheaper area. However, the village shop may decide to charge high prices because it has a 'captive' market, while the city store may be cheaper because it is surrounded by competition. In practice some products and services will have a far more price-sensitive market than others and managers need to take this into account in their pricing policy. At one extreme a company may have a monopoly, or near monopoly, of the sale of a particular commodity. In these circumstances the company can set whatever price it likes to match the desired level of demand. In more competitive markets, if a company puts a high price on its product then customers will not buy it because there are other suppliers. If an organisation lowers its price below that of other companies, competitors will lower their prices in order to compete.

Other things being equal, a high price will tend to reduce demand while a low price will tend to increase demand. However, demand may be very responsive to changes in price (that is, elastic) or relatively unresponsive to changes in price (that is, inelastic). In a situation where managers have products which are not sensitive to price changes, they can use a price-skimming policy by charging a high initial price in order to recover development costs and then lower prices as costs fall. When a product is more price sensitive, managers can introduce a low price to attract a large number of buyers and then raise prices to the normal level in the market hoping to keep its market share. This will be helped by selling the product or service in the right place.

Place

In marketing terms, the '**place**' is where the final exchange occurs between the seller and customer. Managers have to make decisions about where this exchange takes place, and how, and channels of distribution. Bank services, for example, were at one time usually provided across the counter, but in recent years they have moved to cash points and, increasingly, telephone banking. A distribution channel involves the process that brings together an organisation and its customers at a particular place and time for the purpose of exchange. This may be a shop, office or via a computer link. Simple distribution channels between manufacturers, retailers and customers vary in length and breadth (see Figure 8.8).

Managers must decide how to organise their distribution channel, in terms of the number of outlets, whether to use middlemen and the preferences of their customers. Logistics management is about having the correct product or service in the right place at the right time. This has changed in recent years as consumers have become 'unfettered' in the sense that customers have become detached from the channels that used to claim them. They have become more 'adversarial' shoppers in that they have been conditioned by discount stores and Internet offers to search for bargains more aggressively than in the past. Also, as customers have become more aware of how companies market to them, they have become more strategic, for example deciding when to book a holiday based on considerations of what time of the year the best deal will be available, or whether to book early or at the last minute. The consumer is now much better equipped with information and technology to make advantageous decisions, while on the other hand companies have discovered that their product quality, availability and pricing policy have become more transparent.

Figure 8.8 Channel length and breadth

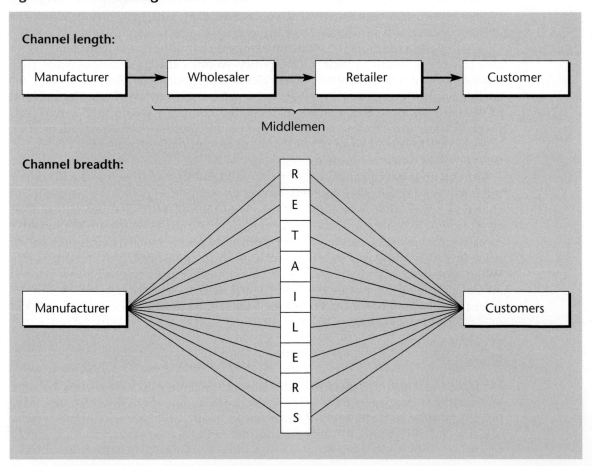

Meanwhile channels have proliferated with the expansion of such means of distribution as websites, catalogues and factory outlets. Nunes and Cespedes (2003) identify key sets of customer shopping behaviours:

- **habitual shoppers** tend to purchase from the same place over and over again in the same manner;
- **high-value deal seekers** know their own needs and surf the channels before buying at the lowest possible price;
- **variety-loving shoppers** gather information in many channels and then buy in their favourite, regardless of whether the price is the lowest available;
- **high-involvement shoppers** gather information in all channels, make their purchase in a low-cost channel and obtain customer support from the best source available.

Customers may behave one way for one purchase and in a different way for another purchase. They will typically progress through five predictable stages in the buying process. Potential buyers gain **awareness** of the product or service, then they **collect and consider** information about available alternatives. They evaluate the alternatives and arrive at a **preference**, they decide **where and how to purchase** and then consider what **after-sales service** may be required. In order to access customers, managers have to introduce a cross-channel selling strategy because the 'place' where the final exchange happens has changed and managers have to make use of a variety of channels to meet consumer preferences.

Promotion

Promotion requires communication with customers and potential customers. Not only do customers have to be able to obtain a product or service, they also must have heard of it. They need information about the product in order to decide whether they want it or not. At the same time most companies want to create a favourable image in order to maintain or increase levels of demand. This image will be developed through the nature of the product, the price, place and promotion. The image will be created by the marketing mix of those elements, and through publicity, public relations and advertising (see Exhibit 8.6).

This process of promotion will have the objective of encouraging consumers to reach a point where they 'demand' a product or service, that is 'the decision to buy'. The process of arriving at the final decision can be divided into awareness, knowledge, understanding, conviction and action. Consumers become aware of the fact that they have a need that must be satisfied, they discover that there are ways of satisfying it, consider the alternatives, make a decision and act on it by buying the product. This is the point at which customer requirements are satisfied and the marketing-oriented manager will have achieved a major objective. The image of the company is essential in encouraging the customer to return to it rather than go to competitors, and the manager, whether selling or producing the product or controlling the process, has a prime role in establishing this image. The whole process of customer care within a marketing orientation is very important in the development of an excellent company and in its success. The 'best' or optimum combination of product, price, place and promotion can be developed by a manager into a marketing plan and strategy for the organisation (see Chapter 5).

→ Ch. 5

Exhibit 8.6 Owners Abroad

In August 1994 the package holiday company Owners Abroad decided to spend £5 million on a new image. This was widely reported in newspapers and marketing journals, and a change of name was proposed to First Choice Holidays.

The plan was to streamline overlapping brands and save cash by targeting three distinct sectors of the holiday market. Household names such as Enterprise, Falcon and Sunmed would give way to First Choice, Sovereign and Freespirit. The company was keen to boost its share of the UK holiday market in the summer of 1995.

It was expected that fierce competition between top tour operators Thomson and Airtours would launch a price war offering big discounts on 1995 packages. The company proposed to introduce a massive advertising campaign to make sun-seekers more aware of Owners' brands. The main new brand name, First Choice, would cover family package holidays, while the successful Sovereign label would be kept to cover more expensive and exotic trips. But a special Freespirit grouping would offer holidays for the young, free and single featuring adventure breaks. The company believed that up to £4 million worth of holidays a year could be booked under this brand. It would aim to provide informal packages to childless adults who wanted more than a Club 18–30 break.

It was reported that Owners' new management was determined to build on the strong foundations which helped the company to defend itself from Airtours' hostile £290 million takeover bid in the previous year.

Strategic marketing

Strategic management includes marketing at every stage, because unless the customers of an organisation are satisfied and there is a demand for the product and services that it produces then it will not be successful. Strategy involves positioning an organisation and giving it a sense of purpose, and this has to include the needs of the marketplace. The marketing process can be seen as the 'nuts and bolts' of strategy because it is about positioning the company's products and services in their markets. Market research and competitor analysis provide the information that managers require in order to decide where to position products and services. If the company's traditional customers are moving upmarket because their disposable incomes are increasing then the company's products will need to match this move.

Organisations need to anticipate demand and how customer benefits will be best satisfied in the future. In the years 1999 and 2000 Marks & Spencer began to lose market share in retail clothing because the company did not anticipate the importance of its competitors and the demands of its customers. In 1999 reports in the financial press described the company as 'struggling' as its profits were reduced and its share price fell. Christmas sales were down by 3 per cent compared with the previous year, while competitors, such as Next, had seen Christmas sales rise by 18 per cent. The company attempted to regain its customers in the year 2000 by revamping its products, reducing costs by changing suppliers and cutting prices but by the end of the year there were reports of some stores closing.

The SWOT analysis provides a company with a picture of its particular strengths and the opportunities open to it, as well as its weaknesses and the threats to it. It can also provide a profile of the organisational competencies which can be compared to the marketing audit to analyse how far they match. In forecasting the required strategy for the future, technological changes have to be taken into account along with the social and economic trends, political and legal developments and environmental issues. In a similar way the formulation of strategy about how and where products and services are offered is an essential element of marketing strategy. The rapidly developing access to the Internet, for example, has revolutionised the 'place' in which a whole range of goods and services are offered to customers and bought and sold. It has also extended the available means of promoting a company's offering so that a whole range of organisations now have their own websites providing information.

The strategic manager's role is to exploit the strengths of a company and to correct and compensate for weaknesses. A market-oriented company will have marketing at its centre, integrating the work of all the other functions in the organisation and providing the information and analysis required for developing strategy.

SUMMARY

- This chapter describes and analyses the importance of marketing in the management of organisations. The development of a focus on customer needs has created a position where marketing is a central and integrating activity in management.

- The difference between marketing and selling is considered, as is the importance of market research, to be a foundation for meeting customer needs. The marketing process is essential for organisations to understand their position in relation to competitors.

- The marketing mix is the combination of product or service, price, place and promotion which together can form a marketing strategy in order to meet customer needs and maintain a competitive edge.

Review and discussion questions

1 *Why is marketing such an important function for most organisations?*

2 *Is there any difference between marketing and selling or are they the same activities described by different names?*

3 *What part can market research play in management decisions on product/service design?*

4 *How important is a marketing audit and SWOT analysis in the development of an organisation's marketing plan?*

5 *What is meant by a marketing strategy? Produce an outline strategy for a company, institution or club.*

6 *How is the price of a product or service determined? Is this an important element of an organisation's marketing strategy or are promotion, advertising, location and product more important?*

CASE STUDY

BMW and Fiat

This is the decade for centennial party time across the car industry. The celebrations for the combination of four wheels and an internal combustion engine, however, have been muted. A business that began about 100 years ago in Europe as a cottage industry often run by families is now run by consolidated multinationals, most of which suffer from the problem of global oversupply. Yet two of Europe's major car manufacturers remain under family control: BMW, an athletic stripling of only 86, and Fiat, which is really feeling every one of its 104 years.

The Quandt and Agnelli clans control two middling producers on the world scene, punching out about a million (BMW) and two million (Fiat) cars respectively. In Europe, Fiat has about 7.4% of the car market and BMW 4.3%. Size is no guarantee of success though. Whereas BMW, now with Rolls-Royce on stream, may be at its zenith in terms of the success of its products, Fiat is in severe distress.

BMW posted its biggest ever profit of Eu3.3 billion in 2002 (and is on target for new record profits, and sales, in 2003), while Fiat recorded a loss of Eu4.3 billion in 2002, the year its patriarchal boss died. The broader picture in Turin is grim. Since 1990, Fiat's share of the European market has halved and, worse, its share of the vital home market has plummeted from well over 50% in its heyday to less than 30% last year. What has gone right and wrong for these two dynasties, and how have they ended up in such contrasting states?

When Fiat boss Giovanni Agnelli – the founder's grandson – died last January, more than 100,000 mourners paid their respects as his body lay in state. His coffin was applauded as it made its way to Turin cathedral, and Italy's leading newspaper *Corriere della Sera* devoted its first 19 pages to his life and times. The funeral was attended by prime minister Silvio Berlusconi who, not for the first time in his political career, put his foot in it by arriving in an Audi. The mourners booed.

Agnelli, *l'avoccato* (the lawyer) as he was known, was a wastrel in his youth, but he squared up to his responsibilities once in the driving seat at Fiat. He became Italy's leading businessman, a lifetime senator and, for many, the uncrowned king of Italy. Agnelli enjoyed trysts with film stars, was a friend to the Kennedys, Henry Kissinger, Richard Nixon and the Rockefellers, and turned the family firm into an international conglomerate.

By contrast, the BMW godmother, Johanna Quandt, 76, is silent to the point of secrecy over her family's £12 billion controlling interest in the German carmaker. She has reputedly never given an interview, and neither have her children, and fellow shareholders, Stefan and Susanne. Collectively, their stake amounts to 46.6%. Stefan, now the largest single shareholder, is said to be next in line for chairmanship of BMW's supervisory board. Susanne, who worked at the Regensberg plant, changed her surname to Cant to avoid recognition.

Although the Quandts appear to take a relatively passive role in BMW, they hold the key to the firm's continued independence. That independence was rumoured to be under threat during the late '90s when, after the Rover ownership debacle, Ford began to take a close interest in the company.

But if Fiat is in serious trouble today, its position is not as dire as BMW's was in 1959. The German company struggled to get back on its feet after the war, its factories having been dismantled for war reparations. But by the mid '50s, it had launched a trio of cars: these were a motley bunch – the 501 and 502 (a huge limousine known as the Baroque Angel) were far too thirsty for that fuel-starved era, and the beautiful 507 roadster was an expensive flop.

To compensate in the short term, BMW built the tiny Italian austerity-chic Isetta bubble car under licence, in a deal similar to the arrangement it had with Austin in 1929 to build the first BMW car, the Dixi. BMW knew it had to produce a car positioned between these extremes, but struggled to find the money to do so. In 1959, on the brink of being taken over by Mercedes, it was saved by the acquisition of a major stake by Herbert Quandt, who celebrated by marrying his secretary Johanna. (The family shareholding dated back to the '20s and the historic publicity-shyness of the Quandts may be connected to the fact that Herbert's stepfather was Joseph Goebbels.)

Quandt's backing enabled the Neue Klasse 1500 to be developed, a quality, compact car whose character set the die for every BMW since – sporty saloon motoring for the middle classes. BMW recovered sufficiently to launch the smaller 02 series in 1966, which developed into the famous 2002. This was replaced in 1975 by the first generation of the 3 series that we know so well today.

Now a hugely successful model, the 3 series prompted accusations that BMW is a one-product company. It has long attempted to be more than that – its 2500 saloon, announced in the same year as the 02 series, was intended to take on the large Mercedes saloons – but it is only after several iterations of these big cars that it has got on level terms with Mercedes.

Today, BMW is fast filling all kinds of niches as the car market fragments to meet the demands of consumers who want their cars to be more individual. Besides the classic 3, 5 and 7 series, essentially the same saloon in different sizes, it offers coupé, estate and cabriolet versions of some of these cars, two four-wheel drives, a sports car and a big coupé. It is a well-planned, coherent range with brand values so strong that sales have weathered the controversy surrounding BMW's new design language – see the new 7, 5 and Z4 – almost unaffected.

BMW has rarely been short of Teutonic confidence. As its chairman Dr Helmut Panke said recently: 'We operate in the most promising segment of our industry – worldwide, the premium segments will grow roughly twice as fast as the mass segments in the last decade. We do not build, and will never build, boring cars.'

Among the masses, the Fiat story is never boring either. It, too, has enjoyed spectacular success at times. Fiat SpA – of which carmaker Fiat Auto is a part – is still Italy's biggest single conglomerate, with a turnover representing 4.8% of the country's GDP. It owns businesses ranging from newspapers to farm machinery.

The Fiat group has long been a diversified business – it was manufacturing commercial vehicles, marine engines and ball-bearings as long ago as 1902 – but for most of its history, car-making has been at the centre. Says Professor Garel Rhys of Cardiff Business School: 'Fiat had to create the industrial revolution in Italy.'

Where BMW's brand character is refined, aspirational, haughty and even arch, Fiat's brand character has its roots in the 1936 Topolino (little mouse), whose low price sped the motorisation of Italy. But the company's most famous car is the 1957 descendent of the Topolino, the Nuova 500, a cute, twin-cylinder bubble-like car of which more than 3.6 million were sold. It played a major role in the so-called 'economic miracle' in post-war Italy.

Fiat's failure to crack the market in bigger, more profitable cars goes some way to explaining why the company is in trouble. Whereas the margin on a BMW 3 series is a manufacturer's delight (and even more so on a 7 series), that on a Fiat Punto is tight. This failure has also led to an over-dependence by Fiat on one model. Today, that is the Punto, now in its second generation; before that it was the Uno – which rescued the company from another crisis in 1983. Before the Uno, it was the 127. Fiat also owns Lancia, which it bought for 10 lire in 1969, and Alfa Romeo, acquired in 1986, but its success with these brands has been inconsistent.

Fiat's car division was starved of money through the '70s, not least because the group was short of cash. At Agnelli's invitation, the Libyan government bought 10% of Fiat for $415 million, later adding another 4%, enough to win it two seats on the board. The arrangement persisted until 1986, when terrorist allegations surrounding Libya had the US blacklisting Fiat, and Agnelli had to raise $3.1 billion to buy the Libyans out. Investment was turned up again, but car design takes time and the new Uno did not appear until 1983. Fortunately for Agnelli, it was a great success.

Agnelli could not be accused of lacking vision. When he took control, many considered Fiat 'too big to be Italian, but too small to compete in Europe'. One of his greatest achievements was to make Fiat an international conglomerate, bringing together Case New Holland (the world's largest farm equipment manufacturer), Iveco trucks and the newspaper *La Stampa*. Yet a more committed approach to car exports might have proved a more valuable investment. Although Fiat had considerable success in Russia and central Europe, it had to withdraw from the US: unreliable products led to the joke: 'Fix It Again, Tony'.

But neither has BMW done everything right. In 1994, it embarked on a brand diversification strategy that was nothing short of startling – it bought Britain's troubled Rover Group. The objective was to provide the company with a portfolio of volume brands to complement its premium marque. So, it not only got the tarnished Rover badge, beloved only of the British pipe-and-slippers brigade, but also Land Rover, MG and Mini.

It knew it had bought a business in need of massive investment – which it provided on a scale not seen in decades – but it hadn't bargained on the infighting this provoked, both between BMW and Rover, and within BMW itself. At the Birmingham motor show launch of BMW's first Rover, the 75, boss Bernd Pischetsrieder heavily criticised the Longbridge plant with the intention of scaring the workforce into submission. It was a serious misjudgement.

Media analysts and workforce alike believed that BMW was giving up on the 'English Patient', and

Pischetsrieder and his number two, Wolfgang Reitzle, were forced to resign from the company on the same day in February 1999. BMW then took direct control, flying in planeloads of executives from Munich to Birmingham to 'purge' the place, seriously damaging morale. Little more than a year later, BMW disposed of Rover and MG to the Phoenix Consortium, and sold Land Rover to Ford. It retained the Mini brand and produced a successful updated version of the legenday marque.

Since ditching Rover, BMW's margins, sales and profitability have blossomed. It recently announced plans to sell 1.4 million vehicles annually by 2008 – only 400,000 short of its target when Rover was still on board. Its share price is buoyant, and mutterings that the Quandt family want out have ceased. But growth will come in large part from the forthcoming BMW 1 series, which will compete at the premium end of the Ford Focus segment. It was this very car that Pischetsrieder, and many others at BMW, felt was a stretch too far for the brand and would compromise its premium character. It was the reason for buying Rover.

Meanwhile, Fiat, to the surprise of some analysts, is intent on pursuing a strategy closer to BMW's, by concentrating on the car business. Umberto Agnelli, Gianni's younger brother, is in charge after a series of family tragedies. First, the highly regarded Giovanni Alberto Agnelli, who turned Vespa-maker Piaggio around, died of a rare form of stomach cancer in 1997 aged 33. Then Edoardo, Agnelli's son, committed suicide in 2000 after an unhappy life that included heroin addiction.

'Crazy Eddie', as he was known in New York, had become increasingly unhappy at seeing his younger relatives given preferment. In an interview with the left-wing daily *Il Manifesto* in 1998, he complained that 'part of my family has been overtaken by a baroque and decadent logic. Meaning no offence to anyone, we are approaching the gesture of Caligula, who made his horse a senator'. This was thought to be a reference to his now 25-year-old cousin John Elkann, the hot tip to take over the reins when he is fully groomed.

Many thought that Umberto, now 69, was keen to sell Fiat Auto. But he and chief executive Giuseppe Morchio concluded that it was car-making and the industrial businesses that generated by far the biggest chunk of Fiat's Eu55 billion turnover. In a programme of disposals in 2003, the Toro insurance company was sold, along with Fiat Avio and 51% of Fidis, Fiat's retail finance arm. The Agnelli family invested Eu250 million as part of a recapitali-

sation plan that has yielded Eu1 billion in total.

Shareholder GM did not subscribe to the recapitalisation, with the result that its 20% share has halved. Fiat's link with GM was forged in 2000, amid the possibility that Fiat might be sold to DaimlerChrysler in a $13 billion deal that would have given the Agnellis a 26% share in the German company. Umberto favoured the deal but Gianni did not, and Fiat remained in their hands. But it gave rise to the idea that Umberto wanted out of the car business; not so, says a Fiat insider – he just thought it a good deal.

The GM deal famously included a put option that could have forced the American giant to buy Fiat during 2004, but GM now argues that Fiat's restructuring invalidates the put. Fiat, which has sold its 6% holding in GM, argues otherwise, but the two have postponed the discussion for a year, not least because they have a highly successful joint venture covering purchasing and powertrain development.

Fiat claims it will recover without GM's money, with break-even during 2004, positive cashflow in 2005 and a 4% return on sales by 2006. The group also plans to launch 24 new models by 2010. This despite the failure to make redundancies on anything like the necessary scale and a shrinking European market pressured by discounting. Morchio also values Ferrari – part of Fiat SpA rather than Fiat Auto – as an R&D centre; although Fiat sold 34% of the company, it retains more than 50%.

If that suggests a Fiat wealthier than it appears, bear in mind that this company has many assets beyond car brands. With Iveco trucks, Comau – the global number one in automation systems for the auto industry – and Magneti Marelli, a car components supplier, Fiat has a turnover of Eu55 billion, Eu23 billion of which is accounted for by Fiat Auto. Despite being owned by Fiat, Italy's second-largest power producer Edison is not consolidated into the accounts. It's valuable and could also be sold.

Just as Fiat is more than cars, the Agnellis are more than Fiat. The family owns the supermarket chain La Rinascente, Juventus football club and even paper manufacturer Arjowiggins. The constitutional rules of these companies state that shares can be sold only to other family members, thus protecting the business. So, although Fiat has been in deep trouble, and has not left it behind, it has a substantial safety net.

But there's a lot of ground to be made up. Alfa Romeo is a great brand name, which during the 1960s was a model for BMW to emulate. Fiat saved it from the near-terminal effects of a cash drought during its state ownership, but poor after-sales service and a model range based on Fiat platforms has held it back.

Lancia was once great too, but has been allowed to atrophy and retreat to its home market. As to Fiat itself, there has been recent good news with the new Panda, which has just won the European Car of the Year award and has a fat order book. But if Fiat cannot make a success of small cars, it is doomed.

So both families have problems to address. *MT's* contributing editor and car observer Stephen Bayley has watched both companies for years: 'Family own-

ership of Fiat and BMW is only one contributor to their distinctive personalities. For good or bad, they reflect national characteristics: Fiat's strength and weakness was a distribution system based on village blacksmiths selling to customers with loyalties as fierce as *arrabiata*. BMW is a classic German Mittelstand business selling increasingly irrelevant technological *Bratwürst* to the image-conscious. Fierce competition threatens the first, changing taste the second. In future, it will be "family hold back" and let new products do the work.'

Source: R. Bremner (2004) *Management Today*, January.

FURTHER READING

Kotler, P (2001) *Kotler on Marketing*, **Free Press.**
How to create, win and dominate markets.

Kotler, P, Rackham, N and Krishnaswamy, S (2006) 'Ending the war between sales and marketing', *Harvard Business Review*, **July–August (special issue).**
How to bring sales and marketing closer together.

Nunes, P F and Cespedes, F V (2003) 'The customer has escaped', *Harvard Business Review*, **November.**
A discussion on the importance of the customer.

Raynor, M A (1998) 'That vision thing: do we need it?', *Long Range Planning*, **June.**
Argues the case for and against mission statements and vision.

Rein, I, Kotler, P, Stoller, M and Hamlin, M (2006) *High Visibility: Improving Your Personal and Professional Bid*, **McGraw-Hill.**
How to apply branding and other marketing ideas to individuals.

WEBSITES

http://www.benetton.com
This provides information on the importance of marketing and a knowledge of Benetton's wider strategy.

http://www.nestle.com
This profiles 'the world food company', Nestlé, and puts the company's wider operation in context.

http://www.statistics.gov.uk/statbase/mainmenu.asp
Information on UK statistics which can be used for market research

SECTION C

MANAGING PEOPLE

What is an organisation? What is the structure of organisations? How are they organised and controlled? How is the work of organisations monitored? Why is organisational communication an important part of management? What are the different types of communication? What will communications be like in the future? What is involved in human resource management? What are the differences between personnel management and human resource management? What are the current trends in the techniques for managing human resources? What is the importance of human resource management for the efficiency and effectiveness of an organisation? What motivates people at work?

Most people work in, or belong to, organisations and organisational theory helps people to understand and diagnose organisations. Good communication between people in all organisations is essential for success and there are a range of methods and models of communication. The developments of recent years, such as new technology and globalisation, have been described as a 'communication revolution'. People can be described as any organisation's most important assets and human resource management concerns the human side of enterprises. There are differences between personnel management and human resource management and they are both essential for efficient and effective organisations. This effectiveness depends on motivating people at work and there are many factors influencing motivation at work for managers to appreciate in organising people.

CHAPTER 9

Organisational theory and design

Outcomes

Having read this chapter, you will be able to:

- describe the process of organising;

- understand what an organisation is;

- analyse the structure of organisations;

- discuss organisational functions and coordination;

- explain the importance of division of work, delegation and authority;

- analyse performance management and management control.

ORGANISING

The work of all enterprises – large and small, public and private, working and recreational – has to be organised and controlled. The strategy and corporate objectives describe the purpose and direction to be taken, and the targets and the aims if the organisation is to be a success. Once the process of implementation and the action plan are agreed, managers have to organise the activities involved. **Organising** is the process of defining the tasks and activities to be carried out by a number of people to achieve particular objectives, while **management control** is the process of monitoring and adjusting these activities in order to achieve the greatest efficiency and effectiveness in meeting those objectives. In other words organising is deciding what is to be done and who is to do it, while control is making sure that it is done and done well. These are fundamental areas of the manager's role at all levels because it is through the process of organising and directing people and resources that the work of the organisation is accomplished. The control function loops back to the planning function as a review mechanism (see Figure 9.1).

Organising and controlling include all management functions because of the need to organise all of them, allocate resources and integrate everybody's work. Organisation lies at the heart of all activities; without it very little can be accomplished. It is, of course, possible to organise matters badly so that people and resources do not work together effectively. The management role is to organise activities in such a way that the efficiency and quality of an organisation's output and work are improved. When this is achieved people working together can accomplish more than the sum of their individual efforts, just as a football team can play far better with a high level of teamwork than it can if team members play as individuals. The process of organisation involves the allocation of responsibilities so that everyone knows what their task is and what resources they have at their disposal in order to accomplish this within a particular timeframe. This promotes accountability so that employees know to whom they are responsible for the completion of tasks – the structure of the organisation will establish these lines of responsibility.

Figure 9.1 The control loop

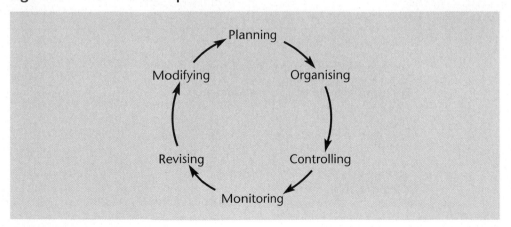

The structure also establishes the formal communication system, but it must be recognised that informal networks may create quite different patterns. The communication system should be efficient vertically, up and down, as well as horizontally and the organisation structure can assist this process. It should also reflect the needs of the organisation in terms of accountability and control. The management of an organisation can be seen as a series of stages moving from original concepts to actual practice, so that managers at different levels have to:

- determine the essential actions and tasks required to achieve the organisation's aims;
- divide these actions and tasks into assignments that can be carried out by departments, units or teams;
- divide these actions into assignments for each individual person;
- decide who is responsible for each action and task;
- organise the coordination of the work of each team or group.

The second and third division stages may be reversed, depending on whether the activities and tasks are grouped together before being subdivided into individual actions or afterwards. These stages describe the division of work within an organisation and the distribution of responsibility and authority (Table 9.1). Their operation may be determined by the structure of an established organisation, or may help to determine the structure for a new organisation. In practice, companies should alter their structures to meet the needs of their customers. If the gap widens between tasks and activities and the organisation's structure then tensions and inefficiencies are likely to arise. Therefore, if the work of a company changes to any extent, the structure has to be altered to reflect this. For example, suppose that a company is organised so that there is a separate business unit for each main product. If one of the products declines then that unit may need to be closed down or merged with another unit. If this is difficult because units and departments have become too inflexible, this can lead to great inefficiencies.

Table 9.1 Stages in organising

STAGES	ORGANISATION OF
Determine essential actions and tasks	Division of work
Divide action and tasks between teams and units	Structure
Divide actions and tasks into assignments for each individual	Action plans
Decide who is responsible for the completion of actions and tasks	Delegation
Arrange the coordination of the work of each team and department	Coordination

WHAT IS AN ORGANISATION?

Organisations can be shadowy entities, slightly opaque and obscure. Novels and movies have been produced with this as an essential element in the plot. Franz Kafka's *The Trial* (1994) is all about an individual becoming caught up in the impenetrable web of an organisation, while John Grisham's *The Firm* (1992) is about an individual who rebels against the expectations of a corrupt organisation. And then what about the organisations involved in *The Godfather* and in *The De Vinci Code*? These fictional examples are based on the difficulty of understanding organisations of various types and how they work and the sinister aspects of this. Joining a new company can be daunting because even if there is an induction course and the new entrant has been supplied with a management chart, this can only describe the bare bones of the organisation and at best show its structure on paper. The reality may be very different.

When somebody first enters a new job, the early days are likely to be taken up with meeting people, finding the way around and discovering who to go to for things they need. The view most people have of any organisation is likely to be the buildings and offices and an employee or two – the rest will be vague and unclear. Daft (2007) has described this as seeing 'the outcroppings' of organisations. In fact organisations are in touch with us every day, they are so common that they are taken for granted and if they are efficient and effective in providing products and services then people do not have to become too involved with an organisation beyond the delivery point.

It is when something goes wrong that people start to become involved in more detail. If a hotel room is unsatisfactory and the service is poor, customers start to get involved with the management of the hotel and to move up the management structure with their complaints – possibly questioning the ownership of the hotel and starting to wonder if it is part of a chain or a wider organisation. Organisations are all around us – most of us are born in a hospital; when we die our remains go to a church or a crematorium; our births and deaths, marriages and divorces are registered in a government agency; we are educated in schools, colleges and universities; we obtain our food from shops; we buy houses built by construction companies; we borrow money from a bank or building society; we travel with holiday companies; we work in an organisation; and so on. All these organisations have characteristics in common:

- they bring together resources to achieve desired objectives;
- they exist in order to produce goods and services efficiently and effectively;
- they create value for their owners, for customers and employees;
- they have to adapt to changes in their environment.

Unless an organisation produces goods and services efficiently and effectively it will disappear, and this is also the case if an organisation does not adapt to changes in competition, legislation and the demands for its goods and services. At the same time organisations have to create value for their owners (or they will move their investment somewhere else), for their customers (or they will obtain their goods and services elsewhere) and for their employees (or they will go to work for someone else). Organisations can also harness initiative and encourage innovation, they can create a demand for products and services and they can influence and shape people's lives. In practice organisations vary in size, scope and structure as well as in objectives. They can be huge globalised conglomerates, small family businesses or one-person operations. They may be publicly quoted companies owned by share-holders, private companies owned by one or a number of individuals or sole traders. They can be family owned businesses, cooperatives, franchises or partnerships. They may be public sector organisations 'owned' by the state, a quango, local authority or government department, or societies, clubs, churches and social groups.

→ Chs 4, 5 & 11

Organisations can be distinguished by size and ownership as well as by industry and objectives, and they can be distinguished by their stakeholders. Stakeholders are people or groups who have an interest in an organisation (see also Chapter 4, 5 and 11). In all organisations employees are stakeholders in that they have an obvious interest in it. Other stakeholders are the owners, creditors and consumers. In the private sector stakeholders can be individuals, shareholders, tax authorities, banks and other providers of finance, while in the public sector they can include the government, taxpayers and the 'public'. Stakeholders can include trade unions wanting to make sure that their members have good levels of pay and conditions of service, and communities with an interest in the activities of organisations in their area.

Stakeholders have expectations which organisations have to satisfy (see Exhibit 9.1), and organisations may find it difficult to simultaneously meet the needs of them all. Meeting the needs of customers may put pressure on the needs of suppliers, or because prices are kept low then wages may not meet the expectations of employees and trade unions. Companies like Wal-Mart in the USA and Tesco in the UK have been criticised for putting undue pressure on their suppliers in their desire for low prices and meeting customer needs. Another example is that increases in wages may reduce the profits available for distribution to shareholders. In the public sector the government targets concerning patient waiting lists have raised questions about levels of patient care. The managers of organisations have to meet the needs of all shareholders at least to a minimal level, while concentrating on its most important ones. This can influence the structure of organisations as well as the way they work, so that a private sector company may concentrate on its prof-

Exhibit 9.1 Organisational stakeholders and the returns they expect

The individuals:	
Owners and shareholders	profits and dividends
The government and the public	value for money, accountability, public satisfaction
Employees	pay, benefits, job satisfaction, management
Customers	customer satisfaction, value for money
The organisation:	
Creditors	returns on finance, creditworthiness, fiscal responsibility
Suppliers	revenue, fair trade
Unions	pay rates, employee benefits
The community	civil responsibility, social responsibility

itability in order to satisfy its shareholders, while a public sector organisation may concentrate on the requirements of the body that controls its income be it a government department, local authority or quango. A private company may concentrate its efforts on meeting the requirements of its shareholders, while a public sector organisation, such as an NHS Trust, may concentrate its efforts on meeting a requirement of the government, such as reducing patient waiting lists. These requirements, shareholder returns or government targets, can affect both the structure of the organisation and the way it works so that tensions can arise because other stakeholder expectations are not met.

Private sector organisations are either owned by one or more individuals or are owned by shareholders and all these stakeholders expect returns in the form of dividends and a share of the profits. Public sector organisations are owned directly or indirectly, depending on the arrangements which are established, by the government – and hence, in the sense that the government represents the voters, by the public. These stakeholders expect returns in the form of value for money, public satisfaction with the services provided and obedience to expectations and regulations. Employees have a stake in both private sector and public sector organisations, which is most clearly seen when a company closes down or a public sector organisation is disbanded. Employees, and the unions and staff associations who represent them, expect returns in the form of pay and benefits, job satisfaction and supervision and management in carrying out the tasks required of them. Over and above this, trade unions have expectations about rates of pay, employment benefits and levels of employment. Customers of all types of organisation have a stake in the organisations they use in that they depend on them for high quality, good value goods and services. Creditors have a stake in the creditworthiness and fiscal responsibility of organisations, while suppliers depend on organisations for the revenue for their goods and services and satisfactory trading arrangements. The community

→ Chs 17 & 18

has a stake in organisations' civil responsibility and social awareness (see Chapters 17 and 18).

ORGANISATIONAL THEORY

→ Ch. 20

Organisational theory is not a collection of facts, it is a way of thinking about organisations and ideas and theories about management and organisations. These have changed over the years (see Chapter 20 for a description of this). 'Scientific management' or 'Taylorism' developed towards the end of the nineteenth century, concentrated on how work was organised on the factory floor, while 'administrative management' considered the organisation as a whole. This developed into 'bureaucratic management' where the emphasis has been on designing an impersonal, rational basis for managing an organisation with clearly defined structures and lines of authority and accountability and the uniform application of standard rules. This has remained the basic structure of many organisations but in the last 30 years the pressures of increased competition, new technology and globalisation have created the need for more flexible structures. These have been based on increasing productivity through downsizing, structural re-engineering, the creation of the lean organisation, delayering, a focus on the customer, total quality management and motivating employees.

The relatively rigid structures of the past are no longer suitable for organisations faced with constant change. The correct structure for a company is contingent on

→ Chs 1 & 20

its situation, so to deal with a rapidly changing environment 'contingency theory' has of necessity become the contemporary organisational theory (see Chapter 1 and Chapter 20). Many companies are, in practice, in a state of flux, expanding or contracting, outsourcing, delayering, merging, acquiring, franchising, restructuring and reorganising. Whereas at one time people could expect to have a job for life in an organisation, now they may be on a relatively short-term contract, or work under no delusion that their job is there only until the next reshuffle of managers, or functions or structures. There has been a move from strict vertical hierarchies to more flexible, decentralised structures that emphasise information sharing, cooperation across all functions and up and down all operational layers with a premium on adaptability and flexibility. The modern organisational design attempts to

→ Chs 2, 3, 5 & 11

encourage a so-called learning organisation (see also Chapters 2, 3, 5 and 11) which is based on equality, open information, participation and, above all, a culture which encourages everybody to be involved in problem solving. Managing and organising is necessary for productive outputs to be achieved so that all organisations need a structure and design that fits with their objectives and their

→ Ch. 3

competitive environment (see also Chapter 3 for new forms of organisation such as 'the shamrock', 'the federal organisation' and the 'triple I').

ORGANISATIONAL DESIGN AND STRUCTURE

The outcome of a company's organising activities can be depicted in organisational design. The object of the design is to create an organisational structure which fits with its objectives, its resources and its environment because the structure describes the relationship between the different parts of the organisation and the people in it. It specifies the division of work, the hierarchy and authority structure, and the formal links that exist between people within the organisation. In practice, of course, there are cross-functional relationships, networks and informal links which are not described by a formal structure but may be of equal importance. A management or organisation chart is a diagram of an organisation's formal structure describing the functions, departments and positions of people within the organisation and how they are related.

An organisation chart usually consists of a line diagram showing the chain of command and official channels of communication (see Figures 1.6 and 1.7). A hierarchical structure will usually be described in terms of the organisation of line management and reporting, while a matrix structure will be described more in terms of relationships between units and people and processes of coordination. In order both to describe company structure and reflect the company priorities other forms of diagram may be designed, or more than one diagram may be felt to be appropriate. For example, in order to focus on the importance of customers, a diagram such as an inverted triangle (see Figure 9.2 opposite, above) may be felt to be appropriate.

In Figure 9.3, opposite, the teams and employees closest to the organisation's customers are at the top of the triangle in order to emphasise the supporting role of functional departments and senior management (see also Figure 3.1). Of course, much greater detail can be included in this type of diagram and it can simply consist of an inverted management chart. Figure 9.3 shows a more traditional chart with senior managers at the top, middle managers below them and operational staff at the bottom. At the same time the chart is divided into functional groupings with line management and responsibility flowing down the functions. It is difficult in this type of diagram to show functional links, coordination of projects and informal relationships. Some attempt can be made to do this by using dotted lines.

Figure 9.2 Inverted triangle

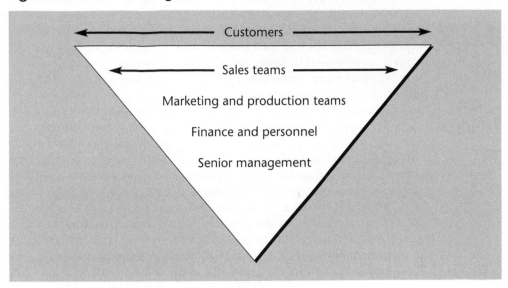

Figure 9.3 Organisation chart

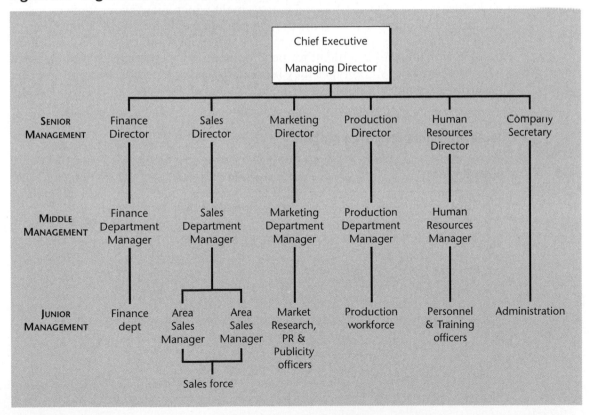

Functional structure

The functional structure illustrated in Figure 9.4 brings together all those engaged in related activities into one department. The production director and the production department are responsible for all the products manufactured by the company and the sales managers are responsible for all the sales of these products. This 'traditional' structure is often seen as the most logical method for dividing up the work of the organisation. It is used in small and medium organisations and in an adapted form it may be used in large organisations. However, the disadvantage of this structure becomes more obvious as an organisation grows in size (Table 9.2 summarises advantages and disadvantages).

This functional structure can bring together specialists and specialist equipment in order to develop high-quality products and services from their particular department. The staff in these departments can provide support for each other and their teamwork can help innovation to develop within their relatively narrow area. Line management control, leadership and authority are all very easily understood within this structure, and employees can develop considerable loyalty towards their department which may be more difficult to create for the whole company. This loyalty may develop some suspicion and even antagonism towards other departments. Other departments may be blamed when things go wrong or they may appear to be favoured by senior management and to receive more than their fair share of resources.

The advantages for managers and employees of a functional structure are that they can develop their expertise, they have a clear promotion path within the department and they can communicate easily with other people with similar backgrounds and working on similar tasks. These departments can develop a paternalistic form of leadership and management which may favour some people at the expense of others. At the same time the differences between the 'home' department and the others may be manifested in a variety of ways. Particular jargon may develop which makes it difficult for people from other departments to understand what is being said, stereotypes may be used to describe people working in other departments, company policies may be interpreted and put into practice differently

Table 9.2 Functional organisation

ADVANTAGES	DISADVANTAGES
Efficient use of specialised resources	Empire building and bureaucracy
Responsibility, authority and control are clear	Slow response to customer needs
Encourages specialised management	Narrow perspective and limited innovation
Promotes employee loyalty to small unit	Obscures responsibility for overall tasks
Clear promotion path	Limits scope for development of general managers and employees to move into new areas
Good 'vertical' communication	Poor networks and 'horizontal' communication

in the various departments and jealousies may develop over working space, equipment levels and so on.

Functional departments can encourage bureaucracy and empire building. The department may feel that it is more important the greater the resources it uses and the larger its staff. Managers and other staff may become reluctant to pass specialised information to people not in their department. There may be slow responses to changes in customer needs, particularly from those departments which have little contact with the final customer. Tasks which cut across departments may take a long time because they have to move sequentially from one department to another. This can be exacerbated by a lack of clear responsibility for such tasks with each department able to lay blame for any delay on another department. For example, all employees may be appointed through the personnel department and if it is slow in this process then other departments may have a long wait for salespeople or production workers. Genuine conflicts may develop over priorities so that, for example, new designs and innovation may not be seen as particularly important by the production department, whereas the marketing department considers that new designs are essential to meet customer needs.

As organisations grow in size, either by broadening their products and services or by expanding geographically, the disadvantages of a functional structure become apparent. It becomes more difficult to obtain quick decisions on actions because functional managers have to report to central headquarters in order to have decisions endorsed. At the same time, control over the departments becomes more difficult, and coordination may not be able to create a situation where the organisation's objectives can be achieved. These developments cause large organisations to consider other forms of structure to reflect their new requirements. The most extreme of these is the matrix structure.

Matrix structure

The usual matrix structure is designed to answer the main problems of the functional structure. It combines a vertical chain of command, through functions and departments or units, with a horizontal 'project', 'business unit' or 'product' team. The purpose of the matrix structure is to promote across the company groupings of people and skills to provide a team in order to produce a product or service. This lateral structure is led by a project or group manager who is expert in the team's assigned area of specialisation. The individual therefore has two bosses, a functional manager and a project or group manager. This is the basis for the use of the term 'matrix' which in mathematics applies to an array of vertical columns and horizontal rows.

An example of a matrix structure is shown in Figure 9.4 (see also Figure 1.7). Staff from production, marketing, sales, human resources and administration are divided into four project (or product/service) teams which consist of staff from all five functions under project managers who report to the chief executive. An individual employee in production, for instance, will be in a project team manufacturing a product and reporting to a project manager. The project manager is responsible for making sure that the team not only makes the product as specified but also markets it and sells it. Personnel, training or administrative staff may also be allocated to the team. The production employee will report to the production manager of the company, who will be responsible for initially allocating the employee to this specific project and also for the career of the employee in the organisation. The production manager is, in fact, the employee's line and functional manager, while the project manager is the task or activity manager.

In a similar way members of teams or units may have separate functional managers on a vertical scale, while the whole team moves together from one project to the next. Research teams in science and engineering often work in this way because the skills of the team may be complementary and essential for the completion of the task. At the same time the functional managers provide the specialist support and career path which may not be available through the team. In this way the matrix structure is intended to combine the advantages of functional specialisation with product or project specialisation. The matrix team works on relatively narrowly defined projects, while individuals retain the link with the functional structure of the organisation.

In some organisations a particular unit or section has a matrix structure, while the rest of the organisation has a functional structure. It has proved quite difficult in fact to organise on a full matrix in a large organisation, while small consultancies, research teams, advertising agencies and so on are able to work within this structure very easily. This is because an effective matrix structure requires a high degree of cooperation and flexibility from everybody at all levels. There must be open and direct lines of communication horizontally and vertically and a high level of confidence between managers and between employees. For these reasons matrix structures can work well where staff members have similar qualifications and share common goals, and where teamwork is more important than authority. Consultancies and research teams are good examples of this situation, and organisations such as advertising agencies may also operate in this way because everybody is working together on a variety of accounts.

Figure 9.4 Matrix structure

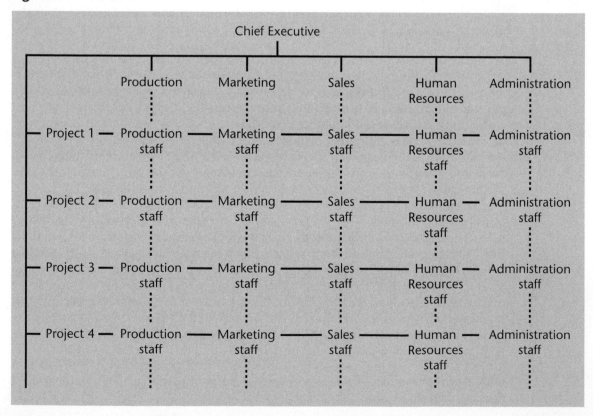

The matrix structure can be an effective means of bringing together people with the diverse skills required to solve a complex problem, such as in research teams and consultancies. It throws the focus on the project to be completed. This provides a common purpose with a well-defined objective for which the whole team or group can be responsible, while the functional structure can too easily fragment the clarity of this aim. By working together, people from various functions can understand the demands placed on other people from different areas of work. For example, preconceptions of marketing personnel about engineers can be overcome in this way, and vice versa. This understanding can produce a more realistic approach to each other's work. If the structure is sufficiently flexible and has not become rigid then it can help to keep down the costs of an organisation, because managers need only assign the number of people needed to complete a particular project (see Table 9.3).

Although the matrix structure may be easy to design and appears to have great advantages over the functional structure, it may be difficult to implement. Problems can arise over shared responsibility, the use of resources in common and the question of priorities. One manager may be played off against another by employees, so that the project manager, for example, is told that the functional manager has decided to pull an individual out of the team to work elsewhere. If this happens without proper consultation it can cause great problems for the project team.

Product, market and geographical structures

As a company diversifies so that its **products** and **services** penetrate a range of markets and expands to cover broad geographical areas, its structure needs to reflect these changes. The functional structure is usually felt to be inadequate for these circumstances. Functional managers can find themselves responsible for the production or marketing of numerous and vastly different products and services, and senior managers can become responsible for coordinating areas which are beyond their capacity to monitor and control. At the same time the matrix structure may not be suitable because it does not provide the necessary control over wide-ranging areas of work and too many people of different qualifications, experiences and backgrounds will be involved.

There are a number of different approaches to the problem of finding a structure to match the requirements of a company in this situation but the usual approach is to develop divisions or units which, unlike a functional department, resemble a separate

Table 9.3 Advantages and disadvantages of a matrix structure

ADVANTAGES	DISADVANTAGES
Focuses on end product	Requires excellent communications
Stimulates creativity	Encourages power struggles
Provides challenges	Risks duplication of effort
Enables flexibility in an organisation	Confuses lines of responsibility
Improves communication and understanding	Requires high levels of interpersonal skills
	May lead to more discussion than action

business. There is a divisional head who is responsible for the operation of the division and may be accountable for its profitability. However, unlike a separate business, the division has to conform to the company requirements and is accountable to it.

The company may establish the rules and policies for its divisions in connection with such areas as finance, training, personnel, advertising and so on. Some 'divisions' are given a high degree of autonomy in, say, a geographical area, so that they become satellite companies run as almost separate entities but owned by the parent company and responsible to it. For example, Rank Xerox UK plc is owned by the parent North American company but enjoys a high degree of autonomy within the UK and Europe. The creation of divisional structures has been advantageous in geographically distinct areas. A local company can produce products for its geographically local markets, it can develop marketing and sales techniques which are tailor-made for the local area and it can develop a culture which is sympathetic to the locality. For example, Ford UK produces motor cars aimed specifically at the UK and European markets and adapts its marketing and sales techniques to the requirements of these markets. Through this process the UK can be treated as a distinct market requiring clear focus in the approach to it.

Of course, these factors are true also where there are clearly different markets for the same product or service, or where a company is producing clearly different products or services for the same market. For example, many publishers have an education division for publishing educational and training books and a general or fiction division for publishing novels. This may be subdivided by age group, so that a children's book division concentrates on that market. Some books will cross the divisional lines and may be sold as a children's book by one division, as an educational reader by another and as a general work of fiction by a third.

A divisional-type structure (see Table 9.4) has the advantage of combining all the activities, skills and expertise required to produce and market particular products or a product in a particular marketplace. The whole process can be coordinated easily and the speed of decision making can be increased because divisional decisions are made relatively close to the point of implementation. Divisions are able to focus on the needs of their particular customers and managers have a degree of autonomy in meeting these needs. On the other hand, of course, there may be disadvantages to this structure. The interests of the division can be placed above those of the whole organisation. The division may not place organisational objectives in quite the same order of priority as the central organisation, and may place its short-term interests above the longer-term interests of the whole company.

Table 9.4 Divisional structure

ADVANTAGES	DISADVANTAGES
Focus on a product/service/market	May develop a conflict of interests
Clearly defines responsibilities and accountability	Possibility of a drift in meeting corporate objectives
Provides autonomy to managers	May produce neglect of long-term priorities
Provides supporting services from the centre to divisions	Central control may stifle local innovation

Divisional structures can lead to a conflict of interest between divisions which develop different objectives and priorities and it is the role of the central organisation to be responsible for coordinating the work of divisions. This is not the same as

→ Ch. 3

the federal organisation described in Chapter 3 (p. 97) where a number of separate organisations or companies come together out of mutual interest, although one of their objectives is to gain some of the advantages of a division of a large organisa-

→ Ch. 3

tion in terms of support. Chapter 3 describes changes to organisational structure brought about by greater flexibility in the labour force – this flexibility needs to be reflected in whichever management structure is chosen.

COORDINATION

Coordination is the integration of the activities of individuals and units into a concerted effort that works towards a common objective. In order to achieve this managers have to make sure that people, teams, units and divisions all work together towards a common aim. This requires a well-understood chain of command and span of management. It has been considered an essential feature of a chain of command for there to be 'unity of command' – that is, one person in charge. For example, Henri Fayol wrote in 1916 that

'a body with two heads in the social as in the animal sphere is a monster and has difficulty surviving.'   (Quoted in Fayol, 1949)

One of the major weaknesses of a matrix structure is that each employee will have two bosses and strong coordination will be required to prevent conflict. On the other hand it can be argued that strong command systems can be too rigid for the constant changes faced by organisations, and that managers require flexibility and excellent horizontal communication as well as the vertical communication promoted by a functional structure. The conflict arises, therefore, between unity of command on the one hand and the necessity to communicate between functions and other areas of expertise on the other. This has led to companies developing a variety of organisational designs, particularly in large and complex corporations.

As well as a clear 'boss', coordination requires a clear 'chain of command' in which authority is seen to start at the top and is scaled down through an organisation in an unbroken chain. In the traditional organisation chart (Figure 9.4) this means that most authority resides at the top of the pyramid and at successively lower levels it is dispersed among more people. This type of organisational design defines the formal lines of communication between subordinates and immediate superiors, and because there is absolute clarity about this it helps to reinforce the unity of command. For example, in Figure 9.4 a salesperson knows that an approach to the managing director will be through the area sales manager, the sales department manager and the sales director and, at the same time, directives will be passed down through this chain of command. It is of course essential that the salesperson can communicate with people in other functional areas without having to send a message up the sales chain of command and down the other functional chain of command. Discussion with, for example, a market researcher should be possible directly without involving the sales and marketing directors. This is the informal network that can be developed into cross-organisational project teams.

The span of command or **span of management,** or span of control, is the number of people or units for whom a manager is responsible. Choosing the correct span of control is important if an organisation's activities are to be successfully coordinated. If a manager is given too many subordinates to coordinate and control, the management of them may not be effective, while too few may not utilise the manager's abilities or may create a situation where there is very limited coordination. Attempts have been made to find an optimum span of management in terms of an ideal number of employees for a manager to control. The number recommended in recent times has often been around six, on the grounds that many more than this would mean that the manager could not spend sufficient time with each subordinate to provide effective monitoring and control. However, it has become recognised that in practice the appropriate span of management depends on the work to be carried out.

It is now argued that the organisation's need to coordinate should dictate the most productive span of management. For example, a narrowly defined role in financial management may require an equally narrow span of management because the need to coordinate the work of the function is small, while a widely defined role in marketing may require an equally wide span of management to include area marketing and sales managers, market research staff, advertising, public relations and communications staff. In fact, much will depend on the work to be coordinated and controlled. Where the work is routine and procedures are standardised, it may be possible for a manager to have a very wide span of management. For example, store managers tend to control a fairly large number of people because their work is largely routine, while management information systems (MIS) managers may have a narrow span of management because this is a capital-intensive area of work with the need for innovative solutions to company requirements. Once these solutions become routine then the span of control of the MIS manager can be extended.

At the same time, managers vary in their ability to manage a number of people. Some managers are better at controlling a small team with a focus on a particular area of work, while others are able to cope with a general management role dealing with a variety of people and controlling a wide area of work. The amount of time a manager requires to coordinate the activities of workers is a factor in this, while the nature of the marketing situation will also be an important influence. Some managers are given a range of tasks to complete, while others have a fairly simple list of objectives. At the same time the role of subordinates along with their competence and ability to work on their own will have an effect on the optimum span of management. The proximity of employees to the manager and the effectiveness of communication can also be factors in the span of management. A manager will usually have more difficulty in coordinating workers in different locations than in a single location but much will depend on the efficiency of internal communications (Table 9.5).

Table 9.5 Span of management

FACTORS INFLUENCING THE WIDTH OF CONTROL	RELATIONSHIP TO SPAN OF MANAGEMENT
Complexity of work activities	The more complex, the narrower the span
Variety of work activities	The greater the variety, the narrower the span
Quality of manager	The more talented the manager, the wider the span
Quality of subordinates	The more responsible and able, the wider the span

Frequently, as managers are promoted, their span of control widens. They will take responsibility for more areas of work with more variety and complexity. In order to be effective in these areas, many of which might usually call for a narrow span of management, managers need to be of a high quality.

ORGANISATIONAL DESIGN IN PRACTICE

Organisational design is the process of fitting the way an organisation works to its strategy in order to achieve the most successful possible performance. The way an organisation works includes a formal structure, its informal attitudes and culture, the way decisions are made and the reward systems. These are not static factors and they change in organisations all the time. Organisational design has to change with them if discontinuity is to be avoided. The effect of not changing is strategic drift (see Chapter 6, pp. 180–1), with an increasing gap appearing between the way the organisation works and its strategy. This can create tensions which will adversely affect performance. It is, therefore, important that:

→ Ch. 6

- as an organisation grows in size, the design is increasingly decentralised and managers delegate decision making to those parts of the organisation best placed to make these particular decisions;
- as an organisation changes its strategy, the organisational design remains consistent with this change;
- as the priorities as well as the products and services of an organisation change over time, organisational design reflects these changes;
- as technology changes, so organisational design changes because of alterations to information requirements and decision making.

Large organisations develop divisional and unit structures, while the move to focus on the customer has given rise to the development of self-managed teams whose role is to meet customer needs. The structure behind these teams is designed to be supportive (see the inverted triangle in Figure 9.3). Grouping of staff in teams or units may change as a result of alterations to the product/service portfolio, so that departmental barriers to people's or team's mobility have to be discouraged in order to retain flexibility. The introduction of new technology such as robotics, for example, has developed the need to consider the best form of structure in factories with fewer and perhaps more specialised staff.

Tension and discontinuity can arise because different parts of an organisation disagree over the purpose or direction of the organisation. The teams close to the customer, such as the sales teams, may be convinced that there is a need for a change in the design and packaging of the product, while the production team is convinced that the product is well made and to the specification required by consumers. Perhaps the salespeople view the company mission as being to 'serve the customer', while the production staff place much more emphasis on quality control and view the company mission in terms of 'producing a reliable, high-quality product'. In an organisation in which people are unsure of their mission and objectives there is a communication problem which may be to do with organisational design. The design may need to be more sharply defined with direction, purpose and responsibilities established very clearly.

Conflict arises in organisations as a result of differences in objectives as discussed in Chapter 8 with the conflict between sales and marketing and this can be exacerbated by perceived cultural differences, differences in location and differences in contacts with other functional areas and with customers. Conflict may arise over differences in power, or perceived power such as the level of control over resources, or the relative skills required in different tasks.

The organisational design should set out the decision-making process so that a senior manager does not have to make decisions lower down the organisation except in a crisis. It should establish levels of responsibility and spheres of control. It should define the division of work, areas of responsibility and delegation. These should not be matters of conjecture and doubt if an organisation is to work smoothly. This definition may be on relatively mechanistic lines so that the activities of the organisation are broken down into separate specialised tasks, with the objectives and authority for each individual unit precisely defined by senior managers. Or it may be more 'organic' in the sense that individuals work in groups, there is less emphasis on authority coming down the levels of management and more emphasis on communication across all levels of the organisation. In the constantly changing environment of modern management there is often an attempt to have a mixture of systems. The changes require flexibility and the ability of teams to react, while a feeling of stability may be promoted by a strong central system of delegation and overall objective setting.

Performance indicators have been introduced in order to establish a clear framework of accountability for an organisation (as well as for the individual – see later in this chapter) whatever its design or structure. For example, performance indicators in the public sector have been used to achieve greater control over public expenditure and greater value for money, to improve managerial competence as well as increasing accountability (Collier, 2006). This has been an element of the 'new

→ Ch. 4

public management' (see Chapter 4) that is oriented towards accountability in terms of results. This has been a 'top-down' approach in, for example, the police service with an emphasis on accountability rather than promoting learning and improvement. At the same time continually changing priorities to reflect political pressures do not enable an investment in infrastructure, personnel and training which could lead to long-term improvements in performance. When an organisation is presented with targets and performance measures, it will make sure that these are achieved, but just as 'you don't make a pig fatter by weighing it' (Hume and Wright, 2006) so the performance of an organisation is not necessarily improved by constantly measuring it.

DIVISION OF WORK

The **division of work** is the breaking down of tasks into component parts so that individuals are responsible for an activity or a limited set of activities instead of the whole task. The division of labour and specialisation have been recognised for a long time as an essential process in improving the productivity of an organisation.

For example, Adam Smith in *The Wealth of Nations*, published in 1776, described the vast increases in output which could be achieved by a division of work or division of labour. The illustration he used was in pin manufacturing. This relatively simple operation could be carried out by one person completing each individual pin or by a number of people working on parts of the production. He showed that 10 people working on their own produced 200 pins a day (20 each) but by dividing up the work they were able to produce 48,000 pins a day (4800 pins each). This remarkable difference was due to specialisation according to Adam Smith. The task of producing pins was divided into drawing the wire, straightening it, cutting it, grinding the point and so on. Each person specialised in one of these operations and because of this became expert in that particular operation. This enabled them to work much faster and more efficiently. They did not have to move from one operation to another and their skill in carrying out a single operation greatly increased.

→ Chs 1 & 20

This approach to the division of work was endorsed by Frederick Taylor and the supporters of scientific management (see Chapters 1 and 20). In practice it was applied to the work of textile factories in the late eighteenth and nineteenth centuries and to other manufacturing processes during the Industrial Revolution of the nineteenth century. In the twentieth century the application spread to service organisations such as McDonald's restaurants which have broken down the process of producing food into small steps. This process has considerable advantages, particularly in relation to efficiency and productivity:

- less skillful workers can be used, because the task has been simplified to a single operation or a few simple operations;
- training can be quick and relatively easy, because each person can be trained on a particular task without the need to develop a wide range of skills;
- proficiency is gained very rapidly, because the specialised task is repetitive and the worker has a great deal of practice at it;
- there is an increase in efficiency, because workers do not waste time moving between tasks;
- the speed of operation is increased;
- workers can choose to be assigned to the operation which best suits their aptitudes and preferences.

These advantages led to the assembly-line based factories which have characterised manufacturing from early in the Industrial Revolution to the present. Specialisation and the breaking down of tasks into simple component parts have enabled the development of mechanisation and the use of robots to replace people in many operations. Machines have been invented to take over the work of assembly-line workers so that labour-intensive industries have become increasingly capital intensive. Computers have been developed to control manufacturing processes so that monitoring progress and quality has also become mechanised. A similar process has been taking place in service industries and in management itself with the development of information technology.

At the same time this division of work and specialisation have given rise to problems and disadvantages as well as advantages:

- workers become skilled in only one operation and when that skill is no longer needed they have to be retrained;
- the mechanisation of many industrial operations has greatly reduced the demand for workers with limited skills and it is difficult to retrain workers to higher levels of skill if they do not have relatively high basic levels of education and training in the first place;
- constant repetition of a single operation is very boring and demotivating for many people;
- teamwork and creative innovation are not encouraged by this process;

- workers have to rely on a constant supply of products on which to carry out their particular operation and this may cause bottlenecks in production;
- workers are not motivated by a pride in the finished product or in the organisation because they perform such a small part of the overall production process.

In an attempt to overcome these disadvantages there has been a variety of schemes to establish different working systems to promote teamwork, pride in the product and quality. For example, the Saab Motor Company developed a system of producing its cars by teams of workers in the 1970s while other automobile manufacturers were using assembly-line processes. Each car was produced by a team working around an 'island' workstation with the component parts being supplied to the island for the team to assemble the car. In this system, if any faults were detected the whole team was responsible for their correction. Teamwork was encouraged in order to raise productivity, the team assembled a finished product in which they could take pride and they could carry out different tasks from day to day or week to week on the agreement of the team.

The traditional division of labour gave rise to the need for supervisors, progress chasers, foremen and quality control inspectors. The team process requires a team leader and the ability to access specialists such as maintenance engineers. Progress and quality will be controlled by the teams particularly if rewards are linked to output. This structure does require flexibility and wide skills in that an individual may be called on to carry out various tasks by the team. This can be described as 'job enlargement', where a number of routine jobs are within the worker's scope. The team approach also provides for job enrichment in that the team and each individual in it are given responsibility for deciding how the work is to be completed and how well it is carried out.

A central issue for managers is to determine the degree of specialisation appropriate to the effective completion of work. The narrower the scope of the job and the shallower it is then the greater the level of specialisation but the lower the employee's satisfaction may be. Work which is narrow in scope will consist of one or a very limited number of operations. If it is also lacking depth – that is, the worker has little control over it – it may be very boring. However, some people do prefer to have a limited, very predictable job which they can carry out without much thought. They know 'where they are' each day and do not have to face frequent changes. It can be argued that most people find this type of work boring and look for 'job enlargement' in terms of an increased number of activities related to their work, and job enrichment in terms of more autonomy over how they work.

Exhibit 9.2 provides a list of some of the characteristics of work which can help managers to decide on the content of individual tasks and to match the ability of individuals to particular areas of work. Work can be analysed in terms of the skill required to complete it, whether it can be divided into separate tasks or not, the degree to which an individual can decide on the job schedule, the extent to which the other people depend on the completion of the task and the type of feedback to be given.

A highly specialised job on an assembly line, for example, may require limited skill, no autonomy, be a small part of the whole process and receive direct feedback in terms of the number of operations completed. Attaching an item such as door handles on a motor car assembly line could have these work characteristics. The task would be very dependent on the supply of car bodies at the correct stage of readiness to work on and would in turn need to be carried out before the car is com-

Exhibit 9.2 Work characteristics

Skill	The variety of talents required to complete a task; work that requires initiative and creativity tends to be more skilled than work which is operational and repetitive.
Autonomy	The extent to which the individual who performs a task has the freedom to plan and schedule the work programme.
Dimension	The work involving completing a product may provide greater satisfaction and create a clearer job identity than that which is a small part of the overall process.
Significance	The extent to which work affects other people, either in terms of health and safety or in terms of the dependence of other people on the completion of the tasks involved.
Feedback	The extent to which an individual receives information about the effectiveness of completed work.

pleted. On the other hand a job such as product design requires a range of skills in matching the design to customer needs and company specifications, may have a high degree of autonomy in that the designer can schedule the work provided that deadlines are met, may at least involve seeing a product design through to completion, and be very significant in terms of the dependency of many people on the final design. Feedback would come in terms of the relative success of the design, perhaps measured by customer satisfaction.

Once the manager has decided on the nature of the work to be completed and has, as far as possible, matched this and the skills of the available workforce, then the operations and the work must be grouped in such a way that they can be effectively managed. One way of doing this is to form teams of people with complementary talents so that a whole task can be completed. The team may have a high degree of autonomy and may only be dependent on others at the beginning and end of its process. Individuals and teams will normally be grouped into departments, divisions or units.

DEPARTMENTALISATION

Whatever the unit of management is called, the process of **departmentalisation** is the grouping of jobs, tasks, processes and resources into logical units to perform an operation within an organisation. The term 'operation' is to some extent appropriate here because in managing a medical operation a group of individuals is brought together to complete a particular task. They form a team dependent on each other while the operation is being performed. It is possible for managers to organise the people in these teams into a department responsible for carrying out particular types of operation, or they can be organised into more specialised departments and brought together for a particular project. Departments can be function, product or market based.

The **functional approach** is the grouping of jobs and resources within an organisation so that employees performing similar tasks are in the same department. In most organisations there are functional departments which will include production, finance, human resources and marketing. The purpose of this arrangement is to bring experts and specialists together so that they can further develop their expertise, while the departmental manager has to understand and coordinate only a relatively narrow range of skills. However, it is possible that members of the department may lose sight of the organisation's overall business because they are concentrating on their own department and expertise. A functional departmental structure may cause bottlenecks when work has to flow from one to another and when each functional area has to make its own separate decisions.

The **product approach** is the grouping of jobs and resources around the products and services offered by an organisation. Products or services may be grouped together in relation to their particular needs. This may be based on geographical location, on marketing or on some other division which is considered advantageous. The product or products can become the central focus of the department and functions can adapt their roles to support it. Decision making can be facilitated by this focus and responsibilities can be clearly defined. However, each department will need its own functional specialists, which can be expensive, and the departments may concentrate on their own products or services at the expense of others produced in the organisation.

The **market approach** is the grouping of jobs and resources around the markets and customer groups identified by the organisation. The success of this form of departmentalisation depends on the ability to identify unique categories of customers and to focus on their particular requirements. One example of this exists in banks and other financial companies which are able to distinguish between individual customers, small businesses and large corporations. Departments based on markets are able to focus on the customers and to adjust rapidly to their needs. However, a high degree of coordination is required in order to make sure that this approach meets corporate objectives.

TEAMS

→ Ch. 7   Organising a team structure (see Chapter 7) is not necessarily an alternative to a departmentalised structure. Often departments will be divided into teams which bring together people concerned with a particular section of the department, or a particular group of customers or a project. A further layer of structure can be added by organising a number of teams into a section, with a number of sections in a department and a number of departments in a company. This enables tasks to be delegated to various levels but, with the move towards flexible organisations and delayering, the trend is more likely to be in establishing 'teams', whatever their actual title, reporting directly to a senior manager or via a middle manager to a senior manager. For example, a sales team may report directly to the sales director or via a sales manager who is responsible for the sales of a particular product or group of products and services.

→ Ch. 7   A team (see Chapter 7) is a group of two or more people who interact with each other for a particular purpose. Sports teams are the most obvious example but everyone who is working, apart from one-man businesses and sole traders, is likely to be in one or more teams whether they are formal or informal. Informal teams can arise through networking or social interaction. These teams may have a fluctuating membership and last for a relatively short time because membership relies on individual decisions. A formal work team will be established for a purpose, and although it is made up of individuals they will have a common objective which they will be responsible for achieving. A permanent work team will be part of the organisation's formal structure, while temporary work teams will include project teams, task forces, work groups. Teams can be divided in terms of their characteristics:

■ **structure** – supervised or self-managed;

■ **purpose** – problem solving, product development, task, project;

■ **membership** – based on functions, or cross-functional, multiskilled, across hierarchical levels;

■ **duration** – permanent, temporary;

■ **formality** – informal or formal.

A supervised team will have a team leader, probably a junior or middle manager, while a self-managed team operates without a manager but may have a chairman who can be temporary, or it may be a role that circulates between the team members. Project and problem-solving teams tend to be formed for a particular purpose, such as a project to plan and complete a building or arrange an event, or to solve a particular problem such as how to reorganise production to reduce costs. However a team is structured it is a dynamic organisation which develops and changes. Tuckman (1965) suggested that the four stages of development could (with a little strain on the words) be seen as forming, storming, norming and performing:

■ **forming** is when a group of people first come together as a team there is usually a degree of caution with people behaving according to what they think is acceptable behaviour;

■ **storming** is the stage when members of the team become less cautious and start to express their point of view – this can lead to conflict or the forming of alliances within the team;

■ **norming** is when the group learns how to work together and begins to appreciate each other's viewpoint and skills;

■ **performing** is when the group begins to work together to achieve their purpose, defining and sharing roles and really becoming an effective team.

→ Ch. 7 In *Team Roles at Work* (2003), Belbin has identified types of team member (see Chapter 7) in terms of their characteristics and qualities. Ideally a team would contain people who bring different skills and characteristics to it so that there is a balance. Research has shown that where this is not the case teams may fail to achieve their purpose. Belbin (2003) has identified the 'Apollo syndrome', for example, where teams composed entirely of highly intelligent individuals tended to be less successful that those with more representative members. Members of the Apollo teams tended to be adept at criticising each other and exploiting each other's weaknesses. Another role that can be added to a team is that of a specialist, who might be a temporary member of the team brought in to advise on a particular matter. The specialist's focus will be narrowly based on the needs of the team and expertise required. This may be to do with technology, or finance or about a particular product. Teams may also be 'virtual' in the sense that the advances in technology and high-quality communication systems allows teams to be formed of members from more or less anywhere and who may never meet.

AUTHORITY AND DELEGATION

Authority is the power related to each position within the organisation. It involves the right to give orders, make decisions and spend resources. In an organisation, authority provides a right to do these things supported by the structure of the organisation and which is understood by every employee when they join. The contract or job description will usually describe to whom the employees are responsible and for whom they are responsible. This means that employees accept orders and decisions and expect these to be carried out if they are agreed through the established structure.

Power is the ability to carry out an action, whereas authority can be seen as the right to do this. **Delegation** is the distribution of authority from a manager to a subordinate. **Responsibility** is an obligation to be liable for a task, decision or action. While authority can be delegated, responsibility cannot, so that a manager can provide a subordinate with the power to make a decision but still retains responsibility for it in the sense of being liable for the result. If the subordinate makes a decision which leads to a success then the manager can accept some of the praise; but if the decision leads to a problem then the manager is obliged to accept the blame. Managers are unable to simply pass all blame onto their subordinates because they have been responsible for the delegation of authority and if this has led to a problem this can be traced back to their decision to delegate.

Delegation of authority can only be successful when the subordinate has the ability, information and willingness to perform a task or make a decision. This can be supported by the organisational structure where clear lines of management and communication can enable the process to operate without difficulty. The position of an individual in the organisation endows that person with a particular type of power, sometimes referred to as legitimate power. Both power and authority can be different to this in that authority may arise, for example, out of respect for a person's expertise rather than their position, while power can arise from control over resources. An accountant, for example, may have the power to accumulate large amounts of clients' money without having the authority to do so. Managers may have the authority to make decisions in an organisation but may not have the power to carry them out because their subordinates do not respect their decisions and find ways of ignoring them.

The classical theory of authority is based on the hierarchical principle that authority flows down from the top of an organisation and is also dependent on the position held. When removed from this position the individual no longer has the authority associated with it. The opposite to this view is the 'acceptance' theory proposed by Mary Parker Follett (1941) and Chester Barnard (1938) (see Chapter 20). In this theory managers' authority depends on their subordinates and whether they do or do not choose to accept the managers' orders. Subordinates have the power to deny authority or to accept it. A different approach to this suggests that circumstances decide who is in authority and that this person will be different in different circumstances. For example, in an accident the first person on the scene may assume authority until the emergency services arrive, when the senior officer may take over. It follows from this that it may be the most knowledgeable person in a given situation who has authority, so that, for example, the managing director of a company may exert authority over a senior management meeting but will defer to the company accountant when there is a meeting on the financial accounts of the company or a meeting with the external auditors.

→ Ch. 20

In practice, authority is often a mixture of these theories in that while managers' positions in an organisation will greatly affect their range and depth of authority, these can only be exerted where they will be accepted. This acceptance may arise out of line management control because subordinates will depend on their senior line managers for reports and promotion, or out of respect for the judgement and experience of a more senior manager or as a result of a consensus. It is important to be aware how authority is exerted so that instructions are not confused, and so that as organisations become more democratic decisions increasingly arise from a consensus of what needs to be done.

Delegation arises because one manager cannot do all the work of the organisation. By delegating, the managers are able to extend their capability and capacity. They can take on new tasks while monitoring others delegated to subordinates. These more junior managers gain from the experience of taking on new tasks knowing that they can turn to the senior manager for help, and they can also build up specialised knowledge and expertise. While responsibility for a task is given to subordinates, the ultimate responsibility remains with the manager – this cannot be delegated. Authority to make decisions and use resources can be delegated and will be necessary for a task to be accomplished. If a task is delegated without the necessary authority then the subordinate will not be able to complete it. The subordinate will be accountable for the outcome of a delegated task to the manager, who will be accountable to a more senior manager and so on. To an extent authority flows upwards through an organisation.

→ Chs 1 & 2 Obstacles to delegation arise from managers' attitudes towards it or subordinates' reluctance to accept it, or because of factors related to the organisation and its culture (see Chapters 1 and 2). Managers may not want to relinquish authority to a subordinate, or they may feel that 'if you want a job done properly, do it yourself'. They may have concerns either that delegating may indicate they cannot carry out the job themselves, or that if it is carried out very well by the subordinates they will themselves appear to be less competent. Managers may feel that it is too time consuming to teach a subordinate how to carry out a task. Subordinates may lack confidence in their ability to complete a task and they may be afraid of failing in it. They may view delegation as simply being extra work, and they may not want to find out how to complete the task because it is easier to ask the manager. Some organisations are too small to provide much scope for delegation and in some it is not part of the 'corporate culture'. People may be assigned tasks which they are expected to carry out without recourse to delegation. The more centralised an organisation is the less delegation there is, because authority will not be widely distributed. In decentralised organisations authority is widely delegated between business units, departments and teams, or between people.

CONSULTATION AND NEGOTIATION

Sound human resources management policies help to foster good industrial relations. The culture of an organisation will be reflected in its industrial relations policy. This policy defines the relationship between management and employees over such matters as pay and working conditions, selection and recruitment, health and safety. Personnel managers and industrial relations officers are specialists in consultation and negotiation and may take a lead in the communications involved in the process. All managers, however, have a role in consultation and negotiation

→ Ch. 12
→ Ch. 1
(see Chapter 12) because of the importance of pay, working conditions, recruitment and redundancy in the process of change (see Chapter 1). Communication is an essential element of management and industrial relations, and consultation and negotiation are an important part of the work of all managers because of the manager's authority, credibility, access to information and responsibility for the allocation of resources.

Negotiation means that two or more parties meet in an attempt to reach a solution systematically. It is a structural attempt at logical problem-solving to identify and resolve a conflict or a potential conflict. Consultation is the process by which managers discuss matters of mutual interest with employees in an organisation. The actual purpose and process of consultation will depend on the culture of an organisation and the communication structures which have been developed in it. Levels of consultation will depend essentially on the prevailing management style (see → Ch. 2 Chapter 2). The 'leadership continuum' may tend to be autocratic, where managers rely on their authority, or democratic or laissez-faire, where there is much more freedom for employees' points of view. Consultation may provide:

- a communications channel in which management, having made a decision, simply informs employee representatives of the decision which has been made;
- a forum in which management seeks the views, feelings and ideas of employees prior to making a decision, while retaining the right to make that decision;
- a structure by which employees' views are made part of a joint decision-making process.

In small organisations the process of consultation and/or negotiation can be on an informal basis between individuals and managers, with each person effectively carrying out their own pay and conditions bargaining. In large organisations individual bargaining becomes impractical and systems are developed for classifying groups of employees into categories for pay and conditions purposes. Changes in levels of pay or in working conditions within categories or grades are negotiated by representatives drawn from employees or by representatives of a trade union. In many medium-sized and large organisations the usual process of consultation and negotiation is between management and unions.

The development of the unions has meant that conflict over pay and conditions can be guided into agreed channels with a process of discussion, consultation and negotiation. Basic pay and working conditions may be negotiated at a national level and the details at a local level. While the system may be a familiar process for both unions and management, the expectations of the two sides may differ considerably. Management will have priorities in relation to minimising costs and maintaining competitiveness or keeping within spending limits. Unions will be attempting to obtain the best pay and working conditions for their members. What is involved in the process of negotiation and the eventual arrival at an acceptable compromise is the 'structuring' or 'conditioning' of such contrasting expectations to meet on common ground (see Figure 9.5).

In this negotiating process both management and unions will start with an initial position which may be more extreme than they expect the other side to accept. At the same time each side has a fallback position which is the absolute limit to which it would consider being pushed by the other side. It is necessary to establish common ground between these two positions. This is an area within which each side will receive something of what it wants and will be prepared to make concessions in order to achieve it. Somewhere in this common ground there is a realistic position where agreement can be reached. When agreements are not reached then strikes and lock-outs may occur but in the end, if the organisation is to continue to operate, agreement has to be reached.

In this process managers need negotiating skills, patience and a clear view of their objectives. The goal of negotiation is to arrive at a position where both sides feel that they have won something, a 'win–win' situation. If one side feels it has lost heavily (a 'win–lose' outcome) the resulting agreement may be difficult to manage in the future because one side will be attempting to make up for its loss and dis-agreements may become frequent. Negotiating skills involve:

- testing and summarising what is being agreed to make sure that everybody inter-prets the substance of the agreement in the same way – an agreement has to work and ignoring even small points of dispute will make this very difficult;
- understanding the other side's need in order to discover and explore the common ground;
- communicating the reasons for a particular suggestion or action so that the other side knows what the motives are for a particular policy;
- assessing the process of negotiation to see if it could be improved.

Organisational culture will have a marked effect on the context in which these negotiations will take place. Open communication within an organisation can reduce the possibility of conflict arising and can develop trust and confidence between all employees. Where changes are being proposed they need to be dis-cussed in detail with all employees, explaining the need for them and consulting on alternative methods of implementation. Managers need to show that they under-stand the employees' concerns and to involve them in the process of change.

Figure 9.5 The process of negotiation

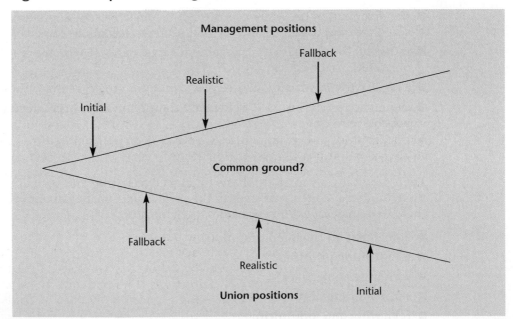

The history of industrial relations has seen rises and falls in the relative power of unions, reflected in their membership. In the UK, unions were strong in the 1960s and 1970s. In the 1990s the membership of many unions in the UK declined as a result of high unemployment, reductions in the labour force of many organisations and legislation controlling union activities. At the same time investment in the UK by overseas companies, such as Japanese-owned corporations, has been based on 'no-strike' deals with firm structures and systems for agreeing pay and conditions. The process for delayering and restructuring in many companies has often been accompanied by the development of self-managed teams at various levels, with the objective of placing more decision making in the hands of employees. In some organisations, particularly in Germany, employee and/or union representatives are members of the highest decision-making bodies.

The way that managers consult and negotiate in an organisation provides a clear indication of its culture. If senior management believes in and supports a process of open consultation with all employees, and promotes a situation where self-managed teams can make decisions about matters important to them, then the possibility of conflict within the organisation can be reduced. Where there is a cooperative approach the role of unions and negotiation can be viewed by managers as essential for the future success of the organisation.

PERFORMANCE MANAGEMENT

The process of managing organisations and control eventually comes down to the individual employee working in an organisation. Whatever the structure, the division of work, the level of coordination and the system of authority and delegation, the individuals have to know what they are to do and this has to be monitored. **Performance management** systems are designed to establish individual objectives which assist the achievement of corporate objectives and monitor progress on accomplishing them. The term 'performance management' means different practices to different managers but usually includes the following elements:

- the organisation has a shared vision of its objectives, or a mission statement or corporate objectives, which it communicates to its employees;
- individual performance management targets are set which are related to the organisational objectives;
- a regular, formal review is carried out to monitor progress toward these objectives;
- the review process is used to identify training needs, career development and possible rewards;
- the effectiveness of the whole process is evaluated against the overall performance of the organisation.

There is usually a strong emphasis on objective setting and formal appraisal and there is often a sequence of steps in the performance management cycle. Although these steps may have different names, they include:

- **agreement on the job description**
- **establishing priorities**
- **arriving at objectives**
- **setting a time horizon**
- **reviewing and monitoring.**

This process results in the assessment of the individual's performance and in 'coaching' in the sense of identifying means of improving performance through training and development and establishing career progression. Performance management can be defined as a method of improving business performance by focusing on key areas of activity.

→ Ch. 6

Performance management can be thought of as an extension of management by objectives (see Chapter 6). This system establishes objectives for an individual or a group and then judges performance on how well they have been achieved. The main problems with this approach are that sometimes the objectives are established by senior managers for their subordinates without any agreement, and that the coaching and counselling elements, felt to be so important in recent approaches, are left out. Although the objectives are supported by senior management, they are in some cases seen to be imposed with little help from above. In a well-organised process, managers will be helped to appreciate the value of their personal efforts and the way these efforts are expected to fit into the contributions to be made by those above and below. This approach can lead to a fully integrated appreciation of the links to corporate objectives (Figure 9.6).

Modern performance management places a very high emphasis on participation and on 'coaching' at all levels. The emphasis is on progression and development rather than measurement and control. Increasingly, it is seen as a fundamental support for total quality management. Drucker (1955) outlines the story of the three stonecutters to illustrate the point. When asked what they were doing:

> *'The first replied, "I am making a living."*
>
> *'The second said, "I am doing the best job of stonecutting in the entire country."*
>
> *'The third looked up and said, "I am building a cathedral." ' *

It can be argued that the first man knows what he wants from a day's work. He will give 'a fair day's work for a day's pay'. He will carry out his task but leave everything else to managers and supervisors. The second is a craftsman with his concentration on carrying out the best work possible within the limits of his craft. He will believe that

Figure 9.6 Performance management

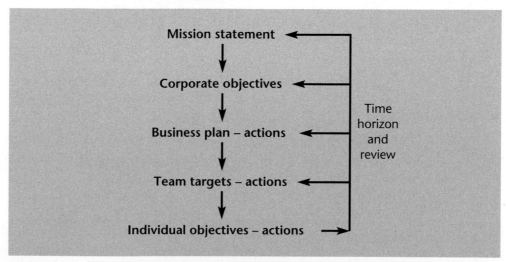

he is accomplishing something useful by cutting and polishing stones expertly but if, in fact, his work does not fit in with what is required for the building then it is useless. Managers may often find themselves in this position, working with great expertise on a particular function and developing habits which concentrate on the performance of the function rather than the objective of the whole business. Managers may, for example, appraise their subordinates according to their craftsmanship and promote and reward them accordingly. The third stonecutter does have a vision of the objectives of his work and of how his contribution fits in. He will not be content to carry out work which does not help to make progress in the building of the cathedral. He may suggest ways of improving the effectiveness of his work to ensure that the objective is reached. For Drucker, the definition of a manager is that 'in what he does he takes responsibility for the whole – that in cutting stone, he builds the whole cathedral'.

This situation cannot be achieved by maintaining occasional drives or campaigns on particular issues. An economy drive, for example, will usually not lead to efficiencies across the company but may lead to a cutback on staff and consumables where possible, which may not be in the most effective places for the company in the medium or long term. Managers need to take responsibility for their own work and to set objectives for themselves and their teams. They will take responsibility for their subordinates' performance in the same way that their line managers take responsibility for them.

In this form the management by objectives approach differs very little from modern performance management ideas: they both help to put into effect corporate objectives by directing attention to key areas of activity. One way or another managers need to assess their subordinates and to be assessed themselves by their supervisors (Figure 9.7). The appraisal process can judge people on:

- **what they achieve**
- **what they do**
- **what they are.**

In operating a performance management system managers will start by appraising themselves (see also pp. 358–61). This process begins with outlining the main tasks of the post and from this establishing a description of the job. This job description can then be agreed with a manager's immediate boss, that is the line manager. The next stage is to agree on the main priorities of the job in particular time periods, say

Figure 9.7 Management appraisal

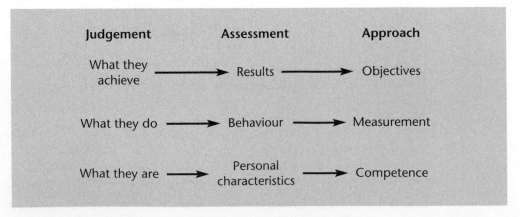

Judgement	Assessment	Approach
What they achieve	Results	Objectives
What they do	Behaviour	Measurement
What they are	Personal characteristics	Competence

three months, six months and a year. The line manager will need to make sure that this fits in with company objectives. Then the manager's objectives can be arrived at, again by agreement which is essential if the manager is to feel responsible for achieving the objectives. At the same time line managers will want to help to achieve these objectives in any way possible because they reflect their own objectives (Figure 9.8).

The objectives agreed by managers will take the form of actions to be completed within a certain period. They will be reviewed from time to time and may be altered in the light of changing circumstances by agreement between the manager and line manager. The process is not one of appraising for weakness, but analysing the situation. If the manager and his or her boss can agree on an area for improvement then this may be able to be helped through training. Alternatively it may be possible to focus the job on the manager's strengths so that personal characteristics and behavioural patterns can assist in arriving at achievements.

The whole emphasis of this approach is on the future, not on the past. It is all about performance and help, or 'coaching' to achieve good performance. The personality of the manager is less of an issue in this system, while the company can provide financial support and time for training if problems are identified or it is considered important to develop particular management techniques. Many companies provide training in subjects such as time management, assertiveness and report writing. The performance management system provides leverage points for integration with total quality management by encouraging policies, procedures and values which promote performance and ongoing activities based on a set of skills which facilitate high performance.

This process may or may not be attached to a salary review and performance pay. It may be thought to be more effective if it is linked to a reward system. However, performance is not the only criterion used in determining salary increases and promotions, and in many cases may not be the main factor. The accountability of one manager for the work of another and the focus on particular activities in order to achieve corporate objectives are the essential features of this process. The approach can be applied throughout the organisation with managers and supervisors responsible for their teams in achieving objectives, while the teams are, in turn, accountable to them. At a very operational level, where members of a team share or even interchange tasks, the team objectives and those of the individual may be indistinguishable.

Figure 9.8 Performance and management cycle

A well-organised and sympathetically implemented performance management system can build trust and improve communication in all areas of an organisation, and this can promote similarity in the high level of performance expectations – it can promote equity and recognise quality through financial and non-financial rewards. While executive support is necessary for total quality management, executive action is critical and performance management can provide the focus for this action down to the most operational level. The strategic plan emphasises the direction a company must follow to take advantage of opportunities and to reach medium and long-term objectives, while action plans make this a reality.

MANAGEMENT CONTROL

→ Ch. 14

Management control is necessary in order to monitor what people are doing, how they are doing it and what they accomplish. **Operational control** is at the level where managers are concerned with using physical, financial and human resources to accomplish organisational objectives (see also Chapter 14). **Strategic control** is at the level of factors which may affect the strategy of the organisation. This involves monitoring customers, competitors, suppliers, government policies, changes in technology and developments in the community. Managers face constant changes and this dynamic factor in the internal and external environment of organisations emphasises the importance of the link between planning and control. The time factor is important in this process because in the period between establishing objectives and accomplishing them changes can occur and will have to be taken on board. Well-designed controls enable managers to predict, monitor and adjust to changes. **Management control** can be seen as the process of monitoring and adjusting organisational activities in order to facilitate the accomplishment of organisational objectives. It is making something happen the way it was planned to happen.

The process of establishing objectives for individuals, teams and units through performance management helps to provide control, sometimes referred to as '**feedforward control**'. Performance management establishes what people are going to do and how they are going to do it. The attempt is made to predict problems and to consider ways of overcoming them in developing an action plan. **Concurrent control** is the process of controlling actions while they are being taken. The primary role of supervisors and foremen is to provide day-to-day, minute-to-minute control making adjustments as a process is taking place. Team leaders, operational and junior managers control tasks and activities as they take place, watching daily, weekly and monthly results, making decisions, fine-tuning the process so that the objectives can be achieved. As a new office block or factory is built, the plans will need to be adjusted and adapted while sight is not lost of the overall objective. The plans are agreed, drawings of the completed building are presented and the actions required to reach this point are established. When the foundations are dug out it may be that an unexpected layer of rock is discovered and decisions will have to be made to adjust the plans to deal with this problem. '**Feedback control**' concentrates on the outcomes of action. It is at this point that judgements are made about the original plans and the actions taken to turn them into reality. Feedback is a process of evaluating the success of the tasks and activities, the work of individuals and teams, and plans made for future development. For example, questions can be asked and answered regarding how well the building was planned, how well it was built, what problems arose during the construction and how well it is suited to its purpose.

The process of control starts with establishing standards of desired outcomes. These may be in numerical terms – an assembly line will produce a thousand units a day – or in financial terms – a retail store being expected to create sales of £10,000 a day – or in quality terms – a unit of production or a building has to be fit for the purpose for which it is to be used and meets expectations. Standards may include a time factor and may be measured by customer satisfaction or by some other qualitative method.

Once standards have been established, the next stage is to monitor progress through quality control and observation. Points of reference may be fixed in order to check on progress. The manager has to compare outcomes to the established standards, decide how much deviation is acceptable and sort out any problems that may arise. This process of comparing performance to standards is followed by corrective action. Functional managers will have their own monitoring and control systems. Financial control will be provided by the organisation's financial management to ensure that any project remains within the planned limits. Production and premises managers will control physical plant and premises, supplies and energy. Human resources managers use performance appraisal systems to monitor people's work. Operations management, management information systems, the process of decision making and financial management are all aspects of this control process (see Figure 9.9).

Figure 9.9 The control process

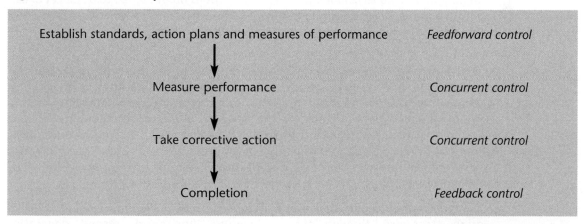

Establish standards, action plans and measures of performance — *Feedforward control*

↓

Measure performance — *Concurrent control*

↓

Take corrective action — *Concurrent control*

↓

Completion — *Feedback control*

ORGANISATIONS IN PRACTICE

These systems do not, of course, decide the performance of an organisation – they are an essential element in this performance and they monitor and control it. Performance is as much to do with people as with the physical assets on which they work. In the division of labour between capital, labour, raw materials and enterprise, all four have to be present and working together for anything to be produced. What is produced and how it is produced will depend on the materials and investment available and very heavily on the ability of the people who are available, their attitudes, creativity and competencies, and on how well the whole process is managed. Organisational identification (OI) has become an important concept in the area of organisational behaviour, in reflecting the underlying link or bond that exists between the employee and the organisation. In this OI is 'potentially capable of explaining and predicting many important attitudes and behaviours in the workplace' (Edwards, 2005) and can be a factor in improving organisational commitment (OC). While OI is concerned with what the organisation stands for and its image, OC relates to the way in which employees are treated.

→ Ch. 6

In practice, management can be described as 'politics' (see Chapter 6), the idea that organisations contain groups of competing mutual interest groups that may come together, or may be brought together, to produce something worthwhile. Organisations are seldom uniform undertakings of rational coordination and action, instead groups and individuals have different agendas and issues and managers have to deal with this.

> *'The term "company politics" refers to all the game-playing, snide, them and us, aggressive sabotaging, negative, blaming, win–lose, withholding, non-cooperative behaviour that goes on in hundreds of interactions every day in your organisation.'*
>
> (Stone, 1997)

Whatever the structure and design of the organisation the different agendas and groups may mean that people may achieve their own objectives at the expense of others and of organisational success. Organisational politics can be defined as 'those deliberate efforts made by individuals and groups to use power in pursuit of their own interests.'

> *'In the rational model of management, organisations are supposed to be places of corporate unity in which all employees work with consistent strategies cascaded down through the various levels and processes of the organisation.'*
>
> (Butcher and Clarke, 2001)

In fact most people have experience of working in or dealing with organisations where there is inadequate communication, discourteous treatment, management incompetence, discrimination in one form or another and corporate irresponsibility. Able managers have to recognise the practical problems that exist and to deal with organisational politics in order to make things happen. This means developing influential organisational relationships in all areas of the enterprise so that they understand the pressures that exist and develop them for a productive result. The problem in many organisations has been identified by Ghoshal (1997):

> *'Companies are trying to implement their sophisticated, multidimensional third generation strategies, through their delayering, horizontal, second generation organisations – but they are still trying to do that with first generation managers – managers whose personal sense of their roles and value added, and whose personal skills and competencies, have all been shaped by an earlier, outdated model.'*

While this was suggested in the last decade, it still applies in the present one where many managers have difficulty in keeping up with the speed of rapid globalisation, increased competition and surges in technology as well as in the changes in the composition and culture of the people they are responsible for organising and controlling.

SUMMARY

■ The role of management is to organise and control the tasks and activities to be carried out in order to achieve the strategic objectives of a company or institution. Without organisation, actions will not be taken in order to achieve these objectives and to ensure the quality of products and services produced.

- There is a variety of organisational structures which help to achieve these actions and companies need to adapt their structures in order to support and facilitate their operations. In the process of deciding on the structure of an organisation, managers need to consider questions of coordination, delegation and authority.

- Managers will have a particular span of control depending on the complexity of activities undertaken, the variety of work and the quality of managers and employees. Organisational design is the process of fitting the way an organisation works to its strategy in order to achieve the best possible performance.

- Work has to be divided between people, and jobs and tasks grouped into units in order to perform operations. In the end individuals in an organisation have to know their roles, and managers design performance measures in order both to establish individual objectives and monitor progress on accomplishing them. An appraisal process will assist this and enable management control to be focused at an individual level.

Review and discussion questions

1 *Why is management control important in any form of work? What purpose does it perform?*

2 *What is the function of organisational design?*

3 *What are the problems of a matrix structure as against a more functional design?*

4 *How does the span of management affect the role of a manager?*

5 *Is delegation an essential element of management or is it possible to manage without it?*

6 *Discuss the importance of management control and performance management.*

CASE STUDY

In search of a modern structure

Bertelsmann, the third largest media company in the world, is often held up as a model of corporate management in Germany. In spite of its size, however, it has always played up its origins as a small-town publisher and has maintained a decentralised structure.

The company has been one of the most noticeable examples of *Mittelstand* – small and medium-sized business – success. But now, principally as a result of sweeping change in the media sector, Bertelsmann is having to rethink its management structures, including the way in which its prized decentralisation works. Possible changes include the flotation of some of the group's businesses – a significant move for the

privately owned company. Originally a printer of hymnals and bibles based in the Westphalian town of Gutersloh, the company was rebuilt after 1945 by Reinhard Mohn, who expanded successfully into book clubs and general publishing. The money earned from these activities financed the acquisition of the majority of Gruner & Jahr, the magazine and newspaper publisher. Other acquisitions, in the 1980s, included the US companies Doubleday, the publisher, and record label RCA.

While the company has long outgrown the *Mittelstand* and Gutersloh – last year it had sales of DM21.5 bn (£7.5 bn) and net profits of DM905 m – Mohn sought to keep Bertelsmann, in spirit at least,

▶

close to its roots. Rather than opting for a monolithic structure, a web of *Mittelstand*-like entities was created in which managers are encouraged to behave as if they were running their own companies.

While Mohn, who stood down as chief executive in the 1980s, sought to retain the vigour of *Mittelstand* culture, he also tried to resolve the issues of ownership and generational change which often plague *Mittelstand* companies. He created a charitable foundation which owns the majority of the shares in the company, creating a structure which appeared to offer the best of all worlds. While retaining *Mittelstand* character in the group's subsidiaries, it eliminated some of the risks that go with family ownership and avoided the pitfalls of going public.

Recently, however, the decentralised structure has been called into question. Mark Wossner, chief executive, engaged consultants to canvass the most senior managers. The results gave him a shock: rather than basking in the independence, the man-

agers complained about the lack of synergies across the group. Says Wossner, who joined Bertelsmann nearly 30 years ago: 'Decentralisation brought all of us into this company. I would not have come here if I hadn't known I had the chance to run a company (profit centre) at a young age.' Wossner says the goal now is to create more 'cross-sections' in areas such as information technology within the group – without undermining the autonomy of managers. 'Back-office and infrastructure processes can be centralised. But the operational autonomy and the cultural and national approach in the different countries will be maintained,' he says.

For Wossner, the implementation of reforms also has a personal dimension, for he is due to stand down as chief executive next year. Before he goes he would like to leave his successor – thought most likely to be Thomas Middelhof, the board member responsible for the group's new media activities – with a reinvigorated structure.

Source: F Studeman, *Financial Times*, 27 June 1997. Reprinted with permission.

FURTHER READING

Beer, M, Voelpel, S C, Leibold, M and Tekie, E B (2005) 'Strategic management as organisational learning: developing fit and alignment through a disciplined process', *Long Range Planning*, 18.
A study of the need for organisations to create 'fit' and to develop organisational learning.

Belbin, R M (2003) *Management Teams* **(2nd revised edition), London: Butterworth Heinemann.**
A discussion of the role of teams in organisational structures.

Collier, P M (2006) 'In search of purpose and priorities: police performance indicators in England and Wales', *Public Money and Management*, June.
Public service objectives, priorities and performance indicators.

Daft, R (2007) *Understanding the Theory and Design of Organisations*, **Mason OH & London, Thomson South Western.**
A comprehensive study of organisational theory.

Desombre, T, Kelliher, C, Macfarlane, F and Ozbilgin, M (2006) 'Reorganising work roles in health care: evidence from the implementation of functional flexibility', *British Journal of Management*, 17 (2), June.
An account of the implementation of functional flexibility in the UK health service.

WEBSITES

http://www.hmso.gov.uk
The HMSO website with information about Acts of Parliament and other government publications.

http://www.pepsico.com
A description of the Pepsi-Cola company structure.

http://www.business.managementarena.com
Information about a range of business and management journals.

TYPES OF ORGANISATIONAL COMMUNICATION

In broad terms communication within organisations can be grouped under three headings – downward, upward and horizontal. These headings indicate the direction of the flow of information. A range of practices falls under these headings and they are illustrated in Table 10.1.

Table 10.1 Communication methods in organisations

METHODS	COMMUNICATION	
	Flow	**Goal**
Briefing groups	Downward	Team communication
Semi-autonomous work groups	Upward	Group responsibility
Chairman's forums	Downward	Information dissemination
Quality circles	Upward	Quality ethos Diagnostic improvements
Suggestion schemes	Upward	Diagnostic improvements

Source: Adapted from J Hyman and B Mason (1995) *Managing Employee Involvement and Participation*, London: Sage Publications. Reprinted with permission.

Downward communication

This refers to communication that flows from the top of the organisation and then cascades down through the hierarchical layers of its structure. This can be seen as the traditional approach to organisational communication where subordinates are simply given selected information. Their level of involvement in the process is limited and, to some extent, this can be regarded as a means of control as employees are given the 'company version' of events or information. Examples of such methods include team briefings, in-company newsletters and company reports.

Team briefings were originally developed by the British Industrial Society in the 1960s. They grew significantly in popularity during the 1980s in the UK and they could be found in blue-chip companies such as Jaguar and ICI. In some organisations there was trade union opposition to their introduction, some of whom felt their role in the company was being undermined by the organisation communicating directly to its employees. Briefings allow an organisation to pass information to its employees through section or department supervisors. It is essential, however, that the individual delivering the briefing has been trained appropriately so that the message is put across effectively. Typically the briefing will cover the four Ps:

- **Progress** – What is the aim of the briefing and the key points? What is the section doing? Was last month a good or bad month? What can be done to make next month better?

- **People** – Who has recently left or joined the company? What is the rate of absence among members of the department? Have there been any significant achievements by members of the section?

- **Policy** – Have there been any significant changes or new policies that the section needs to be made aware of?

- **Points** – Are there any other additional points that can be put across while the whole section is gathered together?

Overall the briefings allow managers to ensure that all employees are clear about what the organisation is doing. They also help to enhance employees' feelings of attachment to the company.

Upward communication

The direction of information flow is from employees upwards to the upper levels of management. The aim here is to make use of the knowledge and expertise held by individuals. Often such a process is related to quality issues, as typified by the total quality movement during the 1980s. It also allows employees to become more actively involved in the organisation. This permits an open and ongoing dialogue between individuals where people are able to question policies and procedures. Employees are also given the opportunity to provide feedback to managers to enhance organisational processes and so improve overall organisational effectiveness. Examples of such methods include surveys and staff **suggestion schemes**.

- **Staff suggestion schemes** – The aim of such schemes is to tap into the knowledge and creativity of the organisation's employees as a means of improving how the company operates. Individuals are encouraged to provide suggestions, usually in writing, to offer innovations or adaptations to what the company does. Typically these suggestions are evaluated by the company and successful suggestions are implemented and rewarded. Such schemes have a long history, with the first recorded scheme in the UK being at a shipyard in 1880, although they have been most popular in Japan where the idea of employees coming up with ideas is seen as being a normal part of employment.

  However, there has been renewed interest in suggestion schemes amongst many companies. In the UK, IdeasUK (the Association of Suggestion Schemes), the umbrella organisation for suggestion schemes, launched National Ideas Day in 2001. The aim of the day is to promote innovation and creativity among all employees and to encourage managers to actively support such schemes. Figures from the organisation show that in 2002–03 suggestions from employees in the UK saved companies £300 million. Perhaps the largest single saving was made at the Mini car manufacturing plant owned by BMW at Cowley in the UK where staff suggestions saved the company £10.5 million between 2002 and 2003. Some examples of current suggestion schemes are shown in Table 10.2.

  However, in a survey of 100 managers and HR professionals in 2004 by the Reed consultancy group, it was found that 1 in 10 believed that suggestion schemes were often ineffective. They suggest that to be successful any such schemes must be administered properly and have the support of senior management.

- **Attitude surveys** – surveys conducted among an organisation's workforce allow management to gain a better understanding of employees' views on a particular issue, or general views about the organisation. They also give employees the opportunity to voice their opinions on what the company is doing and how they feel about issues. A more recent development has been the use of attitude surveys

Table 10.2 Examples of staff suggestion schemes

ORGANISATION	SCHEME
J Sainsbury	'Tell Justin': employees can e-mail the chief executive, Justin King, with ideas – the scheme has had more than 7000 suggestions
Ministry of Defence	GEMS: winners are invited to a presentation by the Chief of Defence Staff
West Midlands Police Force	The scheme receives more than 30 suggestions a month
Marks & Spencer	Schemes rewards ideas up to £5000
Dubai World Trade Centre	The aim is to encourage and reward employee innovation
Bureau of Energy Efficiency (India)	'Jo Soche Who Paave': gives monetary rewards according to the financial benefit gained by the organisation

as a means for gaining feedback on managers' performance. For example, the UK based retail chain W. H. Smith uses a survey to gain feedback on managers' performance and the performance of senior management overall (Ainley, 1992). More recent evidence indicates that surveys are increasingly popular with organisations as a means of improving **employee engagement** – the extent to which individuals identify with, and feel committed to, their employer. Some examples of company staff attitude surveys are shown in Table 10.3.

Table 10.3 Examples of company staff attitude surveys

ORGANISATION	COMMENTS
Royal Bank of Scotland	Surveys all its 150,000 staff in 30 countries every year. Calculates an 'engagement index' based on their desire to say good things about the company, stay with the company and make extra effort
McDonald's	Conducts an annual employee attitude survey that has an 87% response rate among the workforce
Woolworths	Started in 1998, the company surveys all its employees twice a year to measure how engaged they are by asking questions about their job and communication

Source: Adapted from A Czerny (2004) *Woolworths Aims to Involve Staff People Management*, 30 June: 13; and M Emmott (2006) *Engaging Personalities*, available at: http:\\www.cipd.co.uk/cande/annual/conference/_daily_wed_005.htm.

Horizontal communication

This approach, also called lateral communication, involves individuals on the same level of the organisation, such as people in the same team or section or department, sharing information or knowledge. To be efficient companies need to make use of the 'hidden learning', or the **tacit knowledge**, held by individuals. Tacit knowledge refers to the knowledge and skills that people acquire in the course of doing their job. Companies need to create new knowledge, arising in part out of the tacit knowledge possessed by individuals. This new knowledge is developed through encouraging people to share their individual tacit knowledge with others in the organisation so that it becomes explicit knowledge (known by all). Others can then internalise this shared explicit knowledge and incorporate it into their tacit knowledge.

For example, in a study of the working behaviours of photocopier machine repair staff at the Rank Xerox company (Orr, 1990) employees were supposed to use manuals when trying to diagnose problems with the copiers. If the problem could not be solved then the normal procedure was to replace the copier. In reality, the repair staff felt that replacing machines was an admission of failure and so would try to repair any fault in the copiers. If they could not find a solution themselves they would contact each other to see if anyone else had come across a similar problem. The repair staff therefore created new knowledge in developing solutions that were not contained in the manual.

Quality circles

→ Ch. 7

Originally developed in Japan, **quality circles** are an extension of participative processes to remove obstacles to progress (see Chapter 7). The circles consist of small groups of 4 to 15 employees, usually doing a similar sort of work and reporting to the same supervisor. They meet regularly to identify and analyse work problems and provide solutions. Initially they were seized upon by American companies during the 1980s, who were seeking to match the quality of products produced by Japanese companies. In 1981 it was estimated that 750 companies and government agencies had established quality circles in the US. However, this figure is dwarfed by statistics from Japan which showed 140,000 registered quality circles in 1982 (Klotz, 1988). Subsequently they also became popular in the UK, particularly in the engineering sector.

Quality circles operate on the principle of *kaizen*, which translates as 'continual gradual improvement'. They have been found to enhance commitment to changes in work practices, and usually involve employees at all levels. They aim to improve productivity, improve quality and safety, reduce waste, improve communication between management and workers, create a problem-solving environment, increase job involvement and increase morale. By the late 1980s, however, quality circles had begun to decline in popularity. This happened partly because they were often introduced with little thought as to how they matched with companies' quality strategies and partly as they are quite limited in their use (Hill, 1991).

However, as organisations are driven to become more flexible and responsive to changes in the external environment, there is a need to facilitate the flow of information throughout the organisation. This means that communication becomes unidirectional as all members of the organisations have access to, and participate in, the spread of information.

Functions of communication

Within an organisation communication has several important functions:

■ **Information processing** – involves taking data from a variety of sources and in a variety of forms and turning it into meaningful information.

Others have looked at differences in communication within specific cultures. For example, Harris and Moran (2000) looked at the cultural characteristics of communication in Japan and found that:

■ indirect and vague communication is more acceptable than direct and specific references;

■ sentences are often left unfinished to allow the other person to come to their own conclusion;

■ the context of the communication is often vague to permit the other person to interpret the message in their own way;

■ the listener often makes signs and noises of acknowledgement while the other is speaking, but they are not saying 'yes' – merely indicating that they are listening;

■ business deals are often finalised and agreed during entertaining sessions that take place after formal discussions have taken place.

In attempting to ensure that communication is effective it is clearly important that individuals are sensitive to differences between the sender and the receiver. Differences that are culturally based can also have a significant impact on communication. However, much of the research into cultural differences in the communication process seems to rely on national stereotypes. There is, therefore, a risk that in attempting to react to possible cultural differences, an individual may attribute characteristics to an individual wrongly based on these stereotypes. Effective cross-cultural communication is therefore something of a balancing act between being sensitive to a particular culture's norms of behaviour and at the same time not applying broad generalisations to all members of that culture.

IMPROVING COMMUNICATION

Effective communication has the following characteristics (Dawson, 1996):

■ **Accuracy** – the message clearly reflects intention and truth as seen by the sender and is received as such.

■ **Reliability** – different observers would receive the message in the same way.

■ **Validity** – the message captures reality, is consistent and allows prediction.

■ **Adequacy** – the message is of sufficient quality and sent at an appropriate time.

■ **Effectiveness** – the message achieves the intended result from the sender's point of view.

One approach to improving interpersonal communication is through developing a greater understanding of the importance of **self-disclosure**. During communication.

> *'we make conscious and unconscious decisions about just how much information we will share with other people, how reciprocal the openness is, how honestly we react to incoming messages and how willing we are to own our own feelings.'* (DeVito, 1989)

Self-disclosure is important as it requires a degree of trust in the other person because they are being told something about you that they do not already know. This willingness to appear vulnerable is important as it helps to build a relationship with the other party. One way to understand the role of self-disclosure, and how it is involved in the communication process, is through using the Johari Window, originally developed by Joseph Luft and Harry Ingham (shown in Table 10.4).

Table 10.4 The Johari Window

	THINGS I KNOW	THINGS I DON'T KNOW
THINGS THEY KNOW	**Quadrant I** *ARENA* Open self	**Quadrant II** *BLINDSPOT* Blind self
THINGS THEY DON'T KNOW	**Quadrant III** *FACADE* Concealed self	**Quadrant IV** *UNKNOWN* Unconscious self

Source: Adapted from J Luft (1970) *Group Processes: An Introduction to Group Dynamics,* Palo Alto: National Press Books.

Harris (2002) explains the model's different sectors.

■ **Quadrant I: The area of free activity or public area** – this refers to behaviour and motivation known to self and known to others.

■ **Quadrant II: The blind area** – where others can see things in ourselves of which we are unaware.

■ **Quadrant III: The avoided or hidden area** – represents things we know but do not reveal to others (for example, a hidden agenda or matters about which we have sensitive feelings).

■ **Quadrant IV: Areas of unknown activity** – neither the individual nor others are aware of certain behaviours or motives.

When an individual encounters a new group or a new organisation, Quadrant I is very small so there is not much free and spontaneous interaction. As the group grows and matures, and the individual gets to know people, Quadrant I expands in size. This usually means that individuals are then able to be more like themselves and to perceive others as they really are. Quadrant III shrinks in area as Quadrant I grows larger. They now find it less necessary to hide or deny things they know or feel. In an atmosphere of growing mutual trust there is less need for a person to hide their thoughts or feelings. It takes longer for Quadrant II to reduce in size because usually there are 'good' psychological reasons to choose to ignore the things we feel or do.

These are several principles of change which can be identified within the Johari Window:

■ A change in any one quadrant will affect all other quadrants.

■ It takes energy to hide, deny or be blind to behaviour that is involved in interaction.

■ Threat tends to decrease awareness; mutual trust tends to increase awareness.

■ Forced awareness (exposure) is undesirable and usually ineffective.

■ Interpersonal learning means a change has taken place – so that Quadrant I is larger, and one or more of the other quadrants has grown smaller.

■ Working with others is facilitated by a large enough area of free activity. That means more of the resources and skills in the membership can be applied to the task at hand.

- The smaller the first quadrant, the poorer the communication.
- There is universal curiosity about the unknown area but this is held in check by custom, social training and by diverse fears.
- Sensitivity means appreciating the covert aspects of behaviour – in Quadrants II, III and IV – and respecting the desire of others to keep them so.
- Learning about group processes as they are experienced helps to increase awareness (larger Quadrant I) for the group as a whole as well as for individual members.

In an ideal situation communication would be most effective where one person communicates from their own open self to another person's open self. Where they do not know the other person, or they have suspicions about them, then they may choose to communicate from one of the other sectors. To improve communication an individual can reveal information about themselves and so attempt to move back into the arena, although this involves personal risk for the individual. Communication can also be improved by seeking to gain more information about others, which can often be achieved through feedback.

Listening and communication

Important considerations when looking at communication is the extent to which the person on the receiving end is listening and the extent to which they comprehend the message. Listening can be defined as

> *'the process whereby one person pays careful overt and covert attention to, and attempts to assimilate, understand and retain, the verbal and non-verbal signals being emitted by another.'*   (Hill and O'Brien, 1999)

However, there is more than one type of listening (Hargie *et al.*, 1994):

- **Comprehension listening** – this type of listening is apparent during fact-finding interviews or during a lecture. The focus is on listening for facts, ideas and key themes that it might be possible to use later.
- **Evaluative listening** – this is used when trying to gauge the merits of an argument that the other person is presenting, particularly if the other person is attempting to persuade. The aim is to try to identify the relative strengths or weaknesses in what is being said.
- **Empathic listening** – this is used when attempting to understand the perspective from which the other person is talking. It is important to communicate to the other person that you understand 'where they are coming from'. This type of listening is often used during counselling.
- **Appreciative listening** – most often found during leisure activities such as listening to music or poetry. The aim is to try to seek signals or messages that are wanted.

However, listening also requires that you understand the message that has been heard. Listener comprehension is a function of several factors, as shown in Figure 10.2.

Simply listening by itself is not sufficient, however, in attempting to ensure that a message is put across – there is a need to listen actively. During active listening, instead of simply playing a passive role and listening, the person on the receiving end sends back messages to the speaker to indicate that they are listening. There are

Figure 10.2 A model of listener comprehension

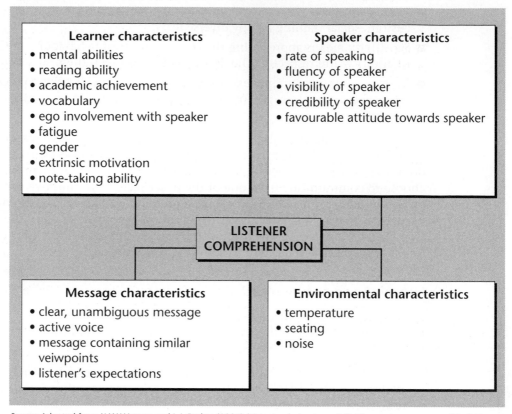

Source: Adapted from K W Watson and L L Barker (1984) 'Listening behaviour: definition and measurement' in R N Bostrom (ed), *Communication Yearbook*, California: Sage Publications Inc.

several possible strategies for demonstrating active listening (adapted from Robbins and Hunsaker 2003, and Harris, 2002) during interpersonal communication:

■ **Paraphrasing** – this involves providing a summary of what you think the sender just said to you. This serves to demonstrate whether or not you understood correctly what was said. It also allows the sender to check if they are being understood.

■ **Expressing understanding** – this is similar to paraphrasing but also takes into account the feelings and emotions that the sender puts into the message. By echoing those feelings correctly, the receiver further reinforces that they have understood the message.

■ **Asking questions** – by asking questions the receiver can clarify any areas where there is uncertainty and so ensure that they have decoded and understood the message in the way that the sender intended.

■ **Establish eye contact** – a lack of eye contact can indicate to the sender a lack of interest from the receiver.

■ **Display interest** – through gestures such as nodding the head and appropriate facial expressions (smiling at good news or something funny, for example) a receiver can indicate that they are actually listening to what is being said.

- **Avoid distracting gestures** – behaviours such as fidgeting or constantly looking at your watch suggest that you are not focusing on the speaker.
- **Ask questions** – interest can be demonstrated by asking the speaker to explain or expand on a point.
- **Avoid interruption** – the speaker should be allowed to complete their message.
- **Don't over-talk** – some receivers feel uncomfortable sitting and listening to a speaker without being able to contribute, but it is difficult to speak and to listen properly.

However, these should be taken as general guidelines only and, as indicated previously in this chapter, one should be aware of possible cultural considerations.

NON-VERBAL COMMUNICATION

In the communication process there are many means of putting across a particular message. Conversely, in attempting to understand a message there are a range of factors that can affect how that message is interpreted by those receiving it. One such important factor is non-verbal communication (NVC). This refers to all other forms of communication that do not involve verbal expression using words, and can be broken down into several categories:

- **kinesics** – communication through body movement;
- **oculesics** – communication through eye contact and gaze;
- **haptics** – communication through the use of bodily contact;
- **proxemics** – communication through the use of space;
- **chronemics** – communication through the use of time;
- **chromatics** – communication through the use of colours.

Research suggests that individuals learn from an early age how to use non-verbal signals as a means of communicating (Palmer and Simmons, 1995). As they grow older, people also learn how to integrate those non-verbal signals with their vocal communication to put across their message (Burgoon, 1991). This suggests that to understand communication it is essential to develop an awareness and understanding of both verbal and non-verbal signals.

Purposes of non-verbal communication

In a comprehensive review of the non-verbal communication literature, Hargie and Dickson (2004) argue that NVC serves the following purposes:

- to replace verbal communication in situations where it may be impossible or inappropriate to talk;
- to complement verbal communication, thereby enhancing the overall message;
- to modify the spoken word;
- to contradict, either intentionally or unintentionally, what is said;
- to regulate conversation by helping to mark speech turns;
- to express emotions and interpersonal attitudes;
- to negotiate relationships;

- to convey personal and social identity through features such as dress and adornments;
- to contextualise interaction by creating a particular social setting.

The importance of these different functions was demonstrated during the presidential election campaign in the United States in 1960. As part of the campaign the two main candidates – Richard Nixon and John F. Kennedy – agreed to a televised debate. During the debate Nixon received very poor ratings from television viewers, a result that many have subsequently attributed to two main NVC factors. Firstly, in the debate Nixon wore a dark grey suit, almost the same colour as the background used in the studio. In contrast Kennedy wore a dark blue suit. On television Nixon virtually blended into the background while Kennedy appeared to stand out. Secondly, Nixon appeared under the lights to have a 'five o'clock shadow' on his face while Kennedy looked clean-shaven. Analysts suggest that this made Nixon look untrustworthy, while Kennedy appeared more honest (adapted from Hargie and Dickson, 2004).

Research has also examined the effect of so-called 'background non-verbal communication' during public speaking – that is, NVC behaviours by one person while another is speaking during a debate or discussion. A group of individuals were asked to observe two speakers involved in a debate. While one speaker was talking, the other speaker was instructed to give off negative NVC signals, such as shaking his head and looking away, while listening. The researchers found that the more the person listening gave off negative NVC signals, the more the observers rated them badly, compared to the speaker (Seiter, 1999 and 2001). Seiter suggested this happened because the negative signals seen by observers were considered to be bad manners, or that it was inappropriate not to listen to someone who is speaking. This finding can be particularly important in the age of televised debates as viewers will often be shown pictures of individuals listening while their opponent is speaking.

Non-verbal behaviours can also be used when an individual wants to communicate something but finds that verbal communication is too direct, or the message may be unwelcome. This is a common feature of the Japanese culture where the speaker will often say what they think the other person wants to hear (*tatemae*), while sending more subtle non-verbal indicators of their real feelings (*honne*). For example, a business proposition may be rejected by saying 'I will think about it', while indicating with non-verbal signals that they are not interested (Marsh, 1996).

Kinesic behaviour (body language)

Kinesics covers all body movements that occur during communication and includes things such as gesture, touch, posture, facial expressions and eye contact. Body posture is often characterised as a method of being an effective communicator and research into height, for example, has generally found that taller people are perceived by others as being more impressive. Melamed and Bozionelos (1992) studied a sample of managers in the UK and found that height was a key factor affecting who was promoted within the organisation. Often people will try to make themselves taller – for example, by standing on a platform – when they want their speech to have more impact.

People will also often engage in postural echoing or mirroring – that is subconsciously copying the body language of another – during communication. This demonstrates interest in a conversation. Gestures can be difficult to interpret however as there is a strong cultural element involved. For example, in Russia if you are applauded by an audience it is seen as good manners to clap yourself. Gestures can often be combined with verbal communication to reinforce or emphasise a particular point. This technique is often used in public speaking by politicians when they may point a finger to emphasise their argument.

Ekman and Friesen (1975) group kinesic behaviour into five categories:

- **Emblems** – these are non-verbal acts that have a direct verbal translation such as the sign for 'peace'. They are frequently used when verbal channels are in some way blocked. A police officer directing traffic is an example of such communication.

- **Illustrators** – these are non-verbal acts that are tied to, or accompany, speech and help to illustrate what is being said verbally. Often these signs can have little meaning on their own. Teachers and other public speakers often use such gestures to emphasise important points.

- **Affect displays** – these are the facial configurations that reveal emotional states. They tend to occur subconsciously and are often unrelated to what is being said and can even contradict verbal speech. If they do contradict what is being said then this weakens the message. This also refers to other gestures such as hand movements that indicate mood or emotion: anger (clenched fist), embarrassment (hand covering the mouth) and boredom (hair preening). Such gestures tend to be spontaneous and so can be good indicators of how someone is actually feeling, even though they may be saying other things in their verbal communication.

- **Regulators** – these serve to maintain and moderate the flow of speech and listening. They mainly involve head and eye movements that can indicate attention or lack of it. When used incorrectly they can be seen as impolite. If they are used correctly they can help to indicate interest and to confirm active listening to what is being said. For example, when someone is speaking in public they will often drop their hands down to their sides to indicate to their audience that they have finished.

- **Adaptors** – these are entirely subconscious acts such as leg crossing, arm folding or shifts in posture. They can indicate anxiety, particularly if they are displayed frequently in a short space of time. However, as indicated above, they can be used as mirroring to indicate subconscious approval of the speaker.

There are also other gestures that have been identified as being important (Hargie and Dickson, 2004):

- **Head nods** – movements of the head can be used to replace speech or used in association with speech. This is particularly evident when two people are engaged in a conversation that involves asking or answering questions. Thomas and Bull (1981) found that before asking a question a person typically raises their head, and before answering a question the speaker turns their head away from the listener.

The body language movements used by individuals can also vary between different cultures, dependent to an extent on the norms of that culture. For example, in Brazil the gestures shown in Table 10.5 are frequently used.

Table 10.5 Non-verbal gestures in Brazil

GESTURE	MEANING AND FUNCTION
With the arm extended and the hand turned up or down, the fingers are flexed several times accompanied by the words 'psiu, psiu'	'Come here'
Closed fist held to the ear	To show that someone is speaking on the telephone
Finger and thumb of same hand rubbed together	Indicate that people referred to are intimate
Eyelid gently pulled downward	Either: 'Watch out, be careful, keep your eyes open' or 'Do you think I'm stupid enough to believe that?'
Fingers tapped under the chin	To show that a person doesn't know what they are talking about

Source: Adapted from M Guirdham (2002) *Interactive Behaviour at Work*, Harlow: Pearson Education.

Paralanguage

Paralanguage refers to vocalisations made by an individual that are not part of a recognised language. This covers four separate areas of non-verbal communication:

- **voice quality** – pitch, range, resonance;
- **vocal characteristics** – whispering, groaning, coughing;
- **vocal qualifiers** – momentary changes in volume or pitch;
- **vocal segregates** – pauses, interruptions ('ah', 'oh').

While they may appear to be a small part of speech they can be important as part of a conversation and in conveying a message. In fact some research has found that where technology replaces the need for face-to-face contact, and so removes the need for the 'ums' and 'errs', then the volume of communication between individuals tends to decrease (O'Conaill *et al.*, 1993).

Changing the volume or the tone of voice can also have a significant effect on how a message is interpreted. Kimble and Seidel (1991) found that a speaker who spoke loudly was perceived as more confident by listeners than someone who spoke quietly. Tone is particularly important in the Japanese language where there are different tones depending on who you are talking to. Intonation can also change the message by placing stress on a different word in a sentence. The process of changing the meaning of what is being said by altering where the stress is placed is referred to as 'prosody'. For example (Hargie and Dickson, 2004):

- **John's** lending me his CD – only John is giving the CD, no one else;
- John's **lending** me his CD – the CD is being lent, not borrowed or given;
- John's lending **me** his CD – the CD is only being lent to me;
- John's lending me **his** CD – the CD belongs only to John;
- John's lending me his **CD** – only the CD is being loaned.

The word in bold indicates where stress is placed when spoken.

However, sometimes not saying something can be just as important in attempting to communicate a message, and silence can play a key role. Like many aspects of non-verbal communication, however, silence can be interpreted differently in different cultures. In Japan it is usual to show respect for a speaker by remaining silent for a few seconds after they have finished talking, to indicate that you are thinking about what has been said (Yamada, 1997). In contrast, in Canada and the United States silence tends to indicate a lack of communication and long silences tend to indicate disagreement (McShane and von Glinow, 2003).

Proxemics

This refers to the spatial needs of people and their environment. At a general level this is referred to as 'territoriality', which is a geographical area that an individual feels they have some claim over. Hargie and Dickson (2004) identify four such territories:

- **Primary territory** – this refers to an area that is associated with someone who has exclusive use of it. For example, a house that others cannot enter without the owner's permission.

- **Secondary territory** – unlike the previous type there is no 'right' to occupancy, but people may still feel some degree of ownership of a particular space. For example, someone may sit in the same seat on the train every day and feel aggrieved if someone else sits there.

- **Public territory** – this refers to an area that is available to all but only for a set period, such as a parking space or a seat in a library. Although people have only a limited claim over that space, they often exceed that claim. For example, it is found that people take longer to leave a parking space when someone is waiting to take that space.

- **Interaction territory** – this is space created by others when they are interacting. For example, when a group is talking to each other on a footpath, others will walk around the group rather than disturb it.

The classic text about space in relation to the individual was written by Hall (1966), who identified a number of personal space regions – these are listed in Table 10.6

Table 10.6 Personal space zones

RANGE	DISTANCE	VOICE	IMPRESSION
Very close	3 to 6 inches	Soft whisper	Secret
Close	8 to 12 inches	Audible whisper	Highly confidential
Near	12 to 20 inches	Soft voice	Confidential
Neutral	20 to 36 inches	Soft voice/low volume	Personal
Neutral	4 to 5 feet	Full voice	Non-personal
Public	5 to 8 feet	Full voice	Public information
Across the room	8 to 20 feet	Loud voice (indoor)	Public information
Stretching limits	20 to 100 feet	Loud voice (outdoor)	Hailing distance

Source: E T Hall (1966) *The Hidden Dimension*, New York: Doubleday & Company, part of Random House.

An awareness of these different space regions can be important because individuals will feel uncomfortable if another person invades what is seen by them as an appropriate region. The context within which the interaction takes place may affect and distort the appropriateness of each region. For example, when eating a meal in a restaurant you may never have met the person serving the meal, but they can stand very close to you and this is seen as normal and acceptable. In contrast, when travelling on a train a stranger may sit very close to you and you may find this uncomfortable as 'your space' is being invaded. Within organisations people often behave in a territorial manner to gain, or protect, the territory that they already have. Objects such as furniture can be used to define boundaries. Furniture can also send messages – for example, when managers have bigger or better furniture than their subordinates.

Chronemics

Managers can use time as an effective communication tool. People can be kept waiting for a meeting or a meeting can be called at a time that means employees have to interrupt their normal work patterns. Research has identified two dominant time patterns that illustrate how individuals in different cultures can have different attitudes towards time (Gudykunst and Ting-Toomey, 1988):

- **Monochronic time schedule** (M-time) – time is seen as being very important and it is characterised by a linear pattern where the emphasis is on the use of time schedules and appointments. Time is viewed as something that can be controlled or wasted by individuals, and people tend to do one thing at a time. The M-pattern is typically found in North America and Northern Europe.
- **Polychronic time schedule** (P-time) – personal involvement is more important than schedules where the emphasis is on personal relationships rather than keeping appointments on time. This is the usual pattern that is found in Latin America and the Middle East.

A key feature of time as a form of communication is the extent to which time can be controlled by one party. This point is illustrated by Anderson (1999) who notes that

'Like money and property, the rich, the powerful and the dominant control time. By contrast, the lives of the less privileged are filled with waiting ... Waiting time decreases as status increases.'

Touch as communication

Touch as a means of non-verbal communication is widely used, but it is also bound by rules and conventions about what is acceptable. These boundaries over what is acceptable will also tend to change within different national cultures. Heslin and Alper (1983) suggest that touch serves four main functions:

- **Functional/professional** – in some professions a degree of touch, and some touching gestures, are seen as acceptable in that context but would be unacceptable if they occurred outside that context. For example, a doctor taking a patient's hand is seen as normal but carries no message.
- **Social/polite** – this can be a difficult area to understand as what is seen as being acceptable or 'normal' behaviour varies between different cultures. For example, in Western cultures shaking hands is an accepted form of greeting, but other cultures may find physical contact on a first meeting too intimate.

■ **Friendship/warmth** – such gestures are often used to demonstrate friendship or closeness between people and include hand-holding and linking arms.

■ **Love/intimacy** – in close relationships touch can play an important part in further cementing the relationship and in expressing feelings.

Rules about touch, however, will be affected by factors other than culture. Gender will also affect what is seen as acceptable. Generally men tend to touch less frequently than women, although this will vary in different countries. In the Middle East for example, males touching males is far more common than in Western countries.

Non-verbal communication in the selection interview

The areas of selection interviews and non-verbal communication have produced a significant body of published work during the last 30 years (Argyle, 1990). There is much work published relating to interview techniques – the methods that can be used, 'how to' techniques and video instruction. Research has also examined the effects of specific factors in the selection interview such as length of the interview, gaze duration and frequency, and interviewer background.

A significant element is the tendency for interviewers to make an immediate decision on first meeting a candidate. Although we often cannot remember someone's hair colour shortly after meeting them, we rarely forget the reaction that the person impresses on us – pleasant or unpleasant, agreeable or disagreeable. This would agree with the idea of the implicit theory of personality which suggests, for example, that someone who wears glasses is intelligent. Hartley (1999) comments that this effect can disappear quickly after talking to the person for a few minutes. The influence of non-verbal communication on the selection interview is shown in Figure 10.3.

Interpreting non-verbal signals

If one accepts that the interviewer notices the non-verbal communications of a candidate, it is less clear how they might be interpreted due to perceptual differences between individuals. People will not necessarily have the same perception of the same behaviour. Philosophers have for many years discussed the idea of perception and the ability to decode correctly non-verbal messages (Argyle, 1990). However, differences

Figure 10.3 Non-verbal signals in the selection interview

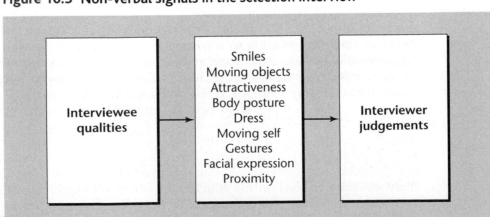

Source: P Hartley (1999) *Interpersonal Communication*, 2nd edition, London: Routledge. Reprinted with permission.

between interviewers based on perception and other factors such as differences in background (age, gender, culture) can also have an impact on the interpretation of NVCs. Much of the literature relating to bodily communication discusses the ability of the observer to interpret NVCs correctly (see for example Guirdham, 1990).

For example, one interviewer may consider the candidate to be attractive, and consequently perceive that he or she fits all the criteria – the so-called 'halo effect' described by Hinton (1993). At the same time another interviewer may not feel the same and rate the interviewee differently. Graves (1993) suggests that the personality and background of the interviewer can have a major impact on their interpretation of NVCs. The situation is further complicated by the nature of the interview. The interview situation may produce artificial answers and accounts. Responses given by interviewees may be interview-specific based on the time and the conditions under which the interview is carried out. Respondents, based on their subjective interpretations of both the questions and the situation, may respond with contrived or artificial answers.

All interviewers will arrive at an interview with a set of role expectations, that is an expectation of a set of behaviours to be exhibited during the interview from both parties. Even before the interview starts the outcome is influenced by the role expectancies held by the interviewer. This biasing will occur because

> *'in the construction of conceptions of the self and the other's role, the information that the actor initially possesses and brings to the interaction plays a crucial part. It is on the basis of this initial knowledge that the actor begins to define the situation and his own role in it, committing himself to a certain demeanour and deciding which aspects of the self he will present to his fellow participant. This will also be used to formulate his conceptions of the other's role, leading him to expect particular kinds of questions and responses.'*
>
> (Gilbert, 1980)

The situation is further complicated because both parties may make use of 'typifications'. When faced with an unfamiliar situation the individual will select a typification (an ideal pattern of actions and motives developed from previous experience) and attempt to understand the new situation in relation to this stored pattern. Often the individual will mentally search through a range of stored behaviour templates until they find a pattern matching the situation facing them. The interview is indexical as actions and statements occurring within the context of the interview are a product of that context. Individuals live in a world of multiple realities derived from these stored patterns or typifications, which are derived from the individual's memories of previous encounters. This may mean that what the interviewer perceives as responses relating to a particular interview may be wholly or partly responses from previous experiences and encounters recalled by the interviewee.

This perspective is similar to the views of Goffman (1990) who considers that all individuals will 'play a part' or 'give a performance' during everyday activities. It may not be possible, however, to ascertain an individual's objective perception of something. This is because the response they have will be a function of the role, or roles, the individual is playing at the time. During an interview, interviewees may attempt to play the role of what they perceive the interviewer would consider as being a 'good' candidate. In addition Goffman suggests that in certain situations there will exist 'regions' within which there will be an expected pattern of behaviour which individuals or groups will feel pressured to conform to. Within the context of a selection interview *both* participants could be said to be playing a role. The interviewee may make a value judgement about the type of behaviour they perceive the interviewer is looking for and attempt to construct 'good answers' along the lines they think are required, or that will show them in a positive light.

An added factor to consider when attempting to interpret and understand NVC signals is the presence of cultural differences. Although for some signals there seems to be a degree of commonality across cultures – with smiling, for example, several studies have found significant cultural differences. In some way this is similar to the situation found when speaking and someone may have difficulty understanding a particular accent. With NVC signals the same confusion can occur when people from different cultures attempt to understand someone else's signals (Marsh *et al.*, 2003).

In 1989 Colonel Qaddafi of Libya appeared in an interview on the American television programme *20/20*. He was interviewed by the show's host, Barbara Walters, who, after the interview had been completed, complained that Qaddafi would not look her in the eye during the interview and insisted on looking around the room. As a result she felt that he came across on screen as being untrustworthy. However, as a male from an Arabian culture, Qaddafi knew that correct behaviour for him is not to look a woman straight in the eye or continuously (Barnum and Wolniansky, 1989).

Guirdham (2002) offers a summary of non-verbal behaviours, how they can be interpreted and what they actually mean. This is shown in Table 10.7.

Table 10.7 Summary of non-verbal signals

NON-VERBAL CUE	HOW CUES ARE USUALLY INTERPRETED	WHAT THE CUES REALLY EXPRESS
Face at rest	Often thought to reveal personality and intelligence (but does not)	Age and ethnicity ranges, gender
Clothes, hairstyle, make-up	Used as major clues, conventions are important	Some attitudes and aspirations, image the person wants to project
Facial expression	As conveying mood or emotion	Emotions – especially fear, joy, anger, shock
Gaze	Conveys interest and attention – or lack of them	Interest and attention, looking up indicates end of speaking
Eye contact	Showing a desire to advance the relationship, sincerity – short bursts are distrusted	Shows interest – low amount indicates indicates dislike or awkwardness, used to express a range of feelings
Gestures	Convey arousal and animation – head nodding reinforces speakers, uncontrolled gestures (foot tapping) indicate impatience, hand over mouth or folded arms indicate defensiveness	Degree of involvement – can be deceptive
Handshake	Often assumed to reveal personality but this is unproven by research	Most people aware that handshakes are 'read' so gives few real clues
Changes in body language	Heightened emotion, more involvement	Heightened emotion, more involvement
Posture	Shows personality and attitudes	Affected by culture, not easily controlled, shows attitude towards the encounter
Voice and accent	National or regional origin, class, age, gender	National or regional origin, class, age, gender
Voice pitch	Shows personality and leadership qualities	Gives little away
Voice tone, speed	Shows friendliness, confidence, aggression	Degree of certainty, emotion or fatigue

Source: M Guirdham (2002) *Interactive Behaviour at Work*, p. 235, Harlow: Pearon Education.

TECHNOLOGY AND COMMUNICATION

Changes in technology have had a significant impact on communication with the growth of the Internet and the increased use of technology-based communication media such as e-mail, text messaging, mobile phones, video mobile phones and video-conferencing. A survey by Gallup in 1997 found that the average British employee received and sent 169 e-mail messages each working day. This growth in communication is affecting managers at all levels. The managing director of IBM (Belgium) recently stated:

> *'Everyday I answer about 30 telephone calls. I receive between 80 and 100 e-mails a day. It takes me about two hours to go through them. Every day I attend 5 to 10 meetings and I shake at least 10 different hands, aside from those of my employees. I give about 24 internal and 10 external presentations a year. My cellular phone is kept in the car so that I can remain attainable constantly. I also use the Internet at home every evening to stay informed of current events.'*   (Kreitner *et al.*, 2002)

E-mail

Since the sending of the first e-mail message in 1972 it has grown considerably as a means for communicating within the workplace. This has happened because e-mail is easy to handle, fast, cheap, easily stored and virtually universal. However, the downside to this ease of use and accessibility is that it is equally easy to make mistakes as the speed at which it is possible to compose or reply to a message, and the lack of face-to-face contact, mean that sometimes less care is taken with e-mail. People may say something in an impersonal e-mail that they would not say to a person's face or over the telephone. Senders may also not know about the etiquette involved when sending messages and so use inappropriate language or forget simple social norms that they might use in a conventional letter.

As e-mail replaces other means of communication, however, employees' work time is increasingly being taken up with dealing with these messages. A recent survey in the US found that 28 per cent of employees fall behind with their work due to the amount of time it takes them to handle daily e-mail messages (Swartz, 2006). In part this can be caused by individuals replying instantly to a message without looking at who is on a distribution list.

Communication in virtual teams

One example of the effect of developments in communications technologies has been the emergence of the virtual work team. 'Virtual teams' are groups of people who work interdependently with shared purpose across space, time and organisation boundaries using technology to communicate and collaborate. Virtual team members can be located across a country or across the world, rarely meet face-to-face and include members from different cultures. Many virtual teams are cross-functional and emphasise solving customer problems or generating new work processes. The United States Labour Department reported that in 2001, 19 million people worked from home online or from another location, and that by the end of 2002 over 100 million people worldwide would be working outside traditional offices (Pearlson and Sounders, 2001).

However, while technology allows individuals who are geographically separate to work as a team, the element of 'virtuality' presents different problems. The lack of face-to-face contact can have important implications for the development of trust within the team. Thus, a specific challenge for virtual teams, compared with face-to-face teams, is the difficulty of building trust between team members who rarely, or never, see each other (Kirkman *et al.*, 2002). However, they argue that building trust requires rapid responses to electronic communications from team members, reliable performance and consistent follow-through. Unlike face-to-face teams, where trust develops based on social bonds formed by informal chats, impromptu meetings or after-work gatherings, virtual team members establish trust based on predictable performance.

One of the side effects of advances in communications technology has been an increase in the possibilities for individuals to misbehave at work through computer viruses, erasing files and not saving files appropriately. The huge growth in use of the Internet, chat rooms and e-mail has offered opportunities for people to misuse such technology at work. For example, in 2001 the Ford Motor Company suspended three employees at the Dagenham plant in England for unauthorised use of the Internet. In January 2001 the insurance company Royal & Sun Alliance sacked 10 employees and suspended 70 others for forwarding material through e-mail that was considered inappropriate. However, perhaps a more damaging problem for organisations is employees who 'surf' Internet sites that are unconnected with their work during working hours. According to a survey in the *Computer Weekly* magazine, the average UK employee spends almost $3\frac{1}{2}$ hours a week looking at non-work-related sites (Bicknell, 2000). While Chen and Lindsay (2000) report the findings of a study by the Computer Security Institute involving 643 computer experts which found that 79 per cent of companies recorded employee abuse of Internet access privileges.

COMMUNICATING WITH DIFFERENT GROUPS

All organisations of reasonable size are made up of a range of different interest groups. On an informal level this can involve interest or social groups, while on a formal level it can involve trade unions and other employee representatives. Membership of trade unions has declined significantly in the UK since the start of the 1980s. However, at the same time as membership was in decline there was a move within organisations to adopting a human resources management (HRM) approach to people management. One consequence of this change was that whereas previously the only employees selectively involved with management in the organisation of a company had been trade unionists, employee involvement at all levels became standard management practice. And while it may appear that employees are being granted greater involvement in the organisation, it is often only selective involvement on the company's terms.

Employee involvement, especially in Britain, does not involve the sharing of power and authority, unlike other forms of industrial participation such as collective bargaining. Management retains their prerogative – the right to manage – and the initiative remains with employers to involve employees, or give employees the opportunity to be involved. Communication was traditionally characterised by formalised structures such as **joint consultative committees (JCCs)** and, more recently, works councils. These mechanisms served to provide a structure for dialogue between managers and employees. It is perhaps open to question, however, whether sometimes that dialogue is overstructured. In contrast, in mainland Europe communication within enterprises through collective channels remains more popular. This popularity is driven in part by continuing high levels of union membership and by the popularity of works councils.

In 1994 the European Works Council (EWC) Directive sought to impose on all member states the need to establish works councils, although the UK maintained an opt-out from the legislation. Under the provisions of the Directive any multinational that has at least 1000 employees within the Union, and at least 150 employees in each of two member states, must establish mechanisms for consulting and informing their employees. It is interesting, however, that in the directive there is no role specified for unions. There is much discussion, however, over whether works councils increase employee involvement and enhance communication within organisations. There is some evidence that the presence of councils did result in employees within those companies having a more positive attitude towards their employer (Addison and Belfield, 2002).

Works councils have also been popular outside Europe. In Japan there has been a long tradition of involvement and open communication between management and the workforce. For example in Korea, the Act of the Promotion of Worker Participation and Cooperation in 1996 sought to improve the role of councils and to improve employee participation. In contrast, in Taiwan and Singapore councils have been used by the state to undermine the position of unions under the guise of improving participation (Kim and Kim, 2004).

Clearly there remains a need for managers to be adept at consulting and negotiating with employees and their representatives through whatever forum or mechanism the company recognises – a view that is supported by the TUC in the UK who endorse the need for 'partnership' at work between organisations and unions.

Future issues

The future for communication within organisations has both predictable and unpredictable elements. Communication technologies will continue to develop allowing individuals to contact, and be contacted, more or less anytime and anywhere. The emergence and expansion of wireless connections through WiFi 'hot spots' will see a further step away from the need to be connected to an organisation. It is also likely that there will be a convergence of technology so that people will no longer need to carry a mobile phone and a laptop and other devices. From one perspective this means that communication will become even easier. However, this also means that perhaps there will be an even greater need to be aware of the communication rules in the virtual world.

Current thinking also suggests that the traditional organisational form, and so traditional ways of working, will continue to decline. Virtual teams and virtual organisations constitute a challenge to traditional management and communication approaches. Statistics also show that the number of people working from home continues to grow. Managers will increasingly have to manage and communicate with employees, colleagues, suppliers and customers they never meet face-to-face. So perhaps the key communication challenge for managers in the future is learning to understand and master this virtual communication.

CHAPTER 11

Human resources management

ROGER BENNETT, HELEN DAVIS AND LINDA GUNNELL

Outcomes

Having read this chapter, you will be able to:

- understand and explain the difference between personnel management and human resources management;

- recognise good practice in the fields of recruitment, selection and appraisal;

- appreciate the importance of human resources planning for the efficient management of enterprises;

- identify key legal requirements in relation to equal opportunities;

- assess the training needs of a business or large department;

- recognise the importance of employee participation, involvement and engagement;

- analyse the significance of current trends in the techniques for managing human resources.

NATURE OF HUMAN RESOURCES MANAGEMENT

Human resources management concerns the human side of enterprises and the factors that determine workers' relationships with their employing organisations. It is a wide-ranging subject that covers, among other things: management/worker communications; elements of work psychology; employee relations, training and motivation; organisation of the physical and social conditions of work; and, of course, personnel management.

Everyone who has control over others shares in human resources management. Accordingly, HRM is not a function that the individual manager can leave to specialists, although HRM professionals do play a vital role.

Human resources management and personnel management

On the ground, the terms 'personnel management' and 'HRM' are often used interchangeably by organisations. However, when first introduced the term was used, and is so used here, to indicate a *strategic* dimension, involving the total deployment of all the human resources available to the firm (Guest, 1987; Legge, 1989; Ferris and Buckley, 1996). Human resources management encompasses:

■ **The aggregate size of the organisation's labour force** in the context of an overall corporate plan – how many divisions and subsidiaries the company is to have, design of the organisation, etc.

■ **How much to spend on training the workforce** – given strategic decisions on target quality levels, product prices, volume of production and so on.

■ **The desirability of establishing relations with trade unions** – from the viewpoint of the effective management control of the entire organisation.

■ **Human asset accounting** – that is the systematic measurement and analysis of the costs and *financial* benefits of alternative personnel policies (e.g. the monetary consequences of staff development exercises, the effects of various salary structures, etc.) and the valuation of the human worth of the enterprise's employees.

The strategic approach to HRM involves the integration of personnel and other HRM considerations into the firm's overall corporate planning and strategy formulation procedures (Stroh and Caliguiri, 1998). It is proactive, seeking constantly to discover new ways of utilising the labour force in a more productive manner, thus giving the business a competitive edge. Practical manifestations of the adoption of a strategic approach to HRM might include:

■ incorporation of a brief summary of the firm's basic HRM policy into its mission statement;

■ explicit consideration of the consequences for employees of each of the firm's strategies and major new projects;

■ designing organisation structures to suit the needs of employees rather than conditioning the latter to fit in with the existing form of organisation;

■ having the head of HRM on the firm's board of directors.

More than ever before, human resources managers are expected to contribute to productivity and quality improvement, the stimulation of creative thinking, leadership and the development of corporate skills.

While some would argue that personnel management, when practised effectively, would have included all the above, there has been a new emphasis on the following since the term 'HRM' came into use:

- HRM is concerned with the wider implications of the management of change and not just with the effects of change on working practices. It seeks proactively to encourage flexible attitudes and the acceptance of new methods.

- Aspects of HRM constitute major inputs into organisational development exercises.

- 'Personnel management' has often been (necessarily) reactive and diagnostic. It *responded* to changes in employment law, labour market conditions, trade union actions, government codes of practice and other environmental influences. HRM, conversely, is *prescriptive* and concerned with strategies, the initiation of new activities and the development of fresh ideas.

- HRM determines general policies for employment relationships within the enterprise. Thus, it needs to establish within the organisation a *culture* that is conducive to employee commitment and cooperation. Personnel management, on the other hand, has been criticised for being primarily concerned with imposing *compliance* with company rules and procedures among employees, rather than with loyalty and commitment to the firm.

- 'Personnel management' has often had short-term perspectives; HRM has long-term perspectives, seeking to *integrate* all the human aspects of the organisation into a coherent whole and to establish high-level employee goals.

- The HRM approach emphasises the need:
  - for direct communication with employees rather than their collective representation;
  - to develop an organisational culture conducive to the adoption of flexible working methods;
  - to enhance employees' long-term capabilities, not just their competence at current duties.

Human resources management and competitive advantage

Research (Pettigrew and Whipp, 1991; Patterson *et al.*, 1997) has shown that the management of people makes a difference to company performance. The 1997 study confirmed that:

- The more satisfied workers are with their jobs, the better the company is likely to perform in terms of subsequent profitability and particularly productivity.

- Organisational culture significantly affects company performance. A culture of concern for employee welfare is by far and away one of the most striking predictors of increased performance.

- The practices which seem to be the most important in affecting performance are job design (in terms of flexibility, job responsibility, variety and use of formal teams) and the acquisition and development of skills (selection, induction, training and appraisal).

- HRM practices are more influential in how successful a company will be than either investment in research and development, the sophistication of the technology used, an emphasis on quality or even the use of competitive strategies.

HUMAN RESOURCES PLANNING

Definition of human resources planning

Human resources planning (HRP) is the comparison of an organisation's existing labour resources with forecast labour demand, and hence the scheduling of activities for acquiring, training, redeploying and possibly discarding labour. It seeks to ensure that an adequate supply of labour is available precisely when required. Specific human resource planning duties include:

- estimation of labour turnover for each grade of employee and the examination of the effects of high or low turnover rates on the organisation's performance;
- analysis of the consequences of changes in working practices and hours;
- predicting future labour shortages;
- devising schemes for handling the human problems arising from labour deficits or surpluses;
- introduction of early retirement and other natural wastage procedures;
- analysis of the skills, educational backgrounds, experience, capacities and potentials of employees.

Effective HRP should result in the right people doing the right things in the right place at precisely the right time. The process of human resources planning is illustrated in Figure 11.1.

HRP should help management in making decisions concerning recruitment, the avoidance of redundancies, training and staff development, and the estimation of the costs of employing labour. Sometimes redundancies can be avoided through the preparation of 'skills inventories' (i.e. detailed listings of all the competencies, work experiences and qualifications of current employees – even those characteristics not relevant to present occupations). The purpose of a skills inventory is to inform management of all the jobs that existing employees might be capable of undertaking.

Benefits of human resources planning

In preparing a human resources plan, management can coordinate and integrate all the organisation's HRM activities, avoiding duplication of effort and eliminating unnecessary waste (Schuler and Walker, 1990). Specific advantages to HRP include the following.

- The organisation will be ready to adapt future HRM activities to meet changing circumstances.
- Careful consideration of likely future events might lead to the discovery of better ways of managing human resources. Foreseeable pitfalls might be avoided.
- Measures to influence future events can be initiated by the organisation itself.
- Decisions concerning future HRM activities can be taken in advance, unhurriedly, using all the data available and considering all available options. This avoids decision-making in crisis situations with management unable to study all relevant issues judiciously and at length.
- Planning makes the organisation assess the feasibility of its HRM objectives critically.
- Labour shortfalls and surpluses may be avoided.

Figure 11.1 The human resources planning process

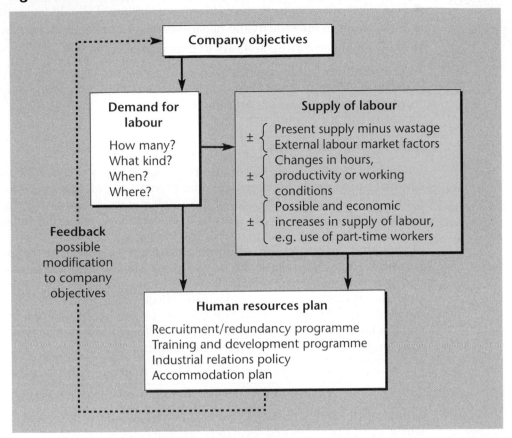

■ It helps the firm create and develop employee training and management succession programmes.

■ Some of the problems of managing change may be foreseen and their consequences mitigated. Consultations with affected groups and individuals can occur at an early stage in the change process.

■ Management is compelled to assess critically the strengths and weaknesses of its labour force and personnel policies.

■ Duplication of effort among employees can be avoided; coordination and integration of workers' efforts is improved.

PLANNING PROCEDURES

Principles of effective human resources planning

Certain fundamental principles should always be applied when preparing a human resources plan.

■ The plan should be as detailed as expenditure constraints allow.

■ Plans should not extend too far into the future – accurate prediction of the distant future is simply impossible.

- *All* alternative courses of action should be considered.
- Side effects and implications of the actions envisaged should be examined.
- Instructions to individuals and departments must be incorporated into the plan.
- Plans should be concise and easy to understand.

As the plan is executed its effectiveness in achieving stated objectives should be monitored. Differences between actual and desired positions must be quickly identified and remedial measures introduced.

Labour turnover analysis

Employees may be categorised according to age, length of service, occupation, educational background, job experience and promotion potential. **Labour turnover** is commonly measured by the ratio of the number of workers who left the firm during a certain period (normally six months or a year) to the average number of workers employed during the same period. If this is relatively constant over time then the organisation can predict the recruitment needed to keep all existing posts occupied. The problem is that if just one or two posts are filled and vacated many times during a particular period then the index becomes artificially high. For instance, if a single job is filled ten times in a year the effect on the index is identical to that of ten people leaving different jobs during that year. To overcome (partially) this problem the **labour stability index** can be used to show the extent to which employees with longer service are leaving the organisation:

$$\frac{\text{Number of employees with more than one year's service}}{\text{Total number of people employed one year ago}}$$

Note that this index does not reveal the average length of service of employees, which should be computed separately for each category of staff.

Another useful exercise is to compute the percentages of a group of employees – all of whom are hired on the same date – who are still with the firm after certain periods. Thus, for example, 10 per cent might have left by the end of one year, 25 per cent after two years, 70 per cent after five and so on. The firm can then predict how long, on average, it takes for, say, half of all workers recruited on a particular date to leave the firm. The exercise can be repeated for various occupational groups.

High labour turnover may be due to low pay, inadequate holiday entitlement, long working hours or other conditions of employment regarded by workers as unsatisfactory. Other causes include:

- **excessively monotonous work**
- **absence of promotion prospects**
- **bad recruitment and staff induction procedures**
- **ineffective grievance procedures**
- **poor communications within the organisation.**

High labour turnover is undesirable for several reasons. Recruitment and training costs increase, new entrants are relatively unproductive during the early stages of their service and additional demands are placed on the remaining staff. Morale is typically lower in organisations with high labour turnover. Note, however, that certain categories of employee exhibit, on average, exceptionally high labour turnover rates – notably young workers and those engaged in boring and repetitive duties. Also, workers are more likely to quit their jobs in rapidly expanding industries.

Steps in the HRP process

In drafting a human resources plan the organisation must consider the demand for labour, its potential supply (with corrections for its present misuse, overuse or underuse) and the external environment. By studying the interaction of all these factors it can then produce a plan showing how many and what kinds of employee are expected to be required in the future. The main points to be considered are as follows.

■ **The creation of an HRP group**, including the managers in charge of the main functions within the organisation.

■ **The statement of human resources objectives** in the light of the organisation's objectives by considering:
  – capital equipment plans;
  – reorganisation, e.g. centralisation or decentralisation;
  – changes in products or in output;
  – marketing plans;
  – financial limitations.

■ **The present utilisation of human resources**, in particular:
  – numbers of employees in various categories;
  – estimation of labour turnover for each grade of employee and the analysis of the effects of high or low turnover rates on the organisation's performance;
  – amount of overtime worked;
  – amount of short time;
  – appraisal of performance and potential of present employees;
  – general level of payment compared with that in other organisations.
  Note that for all the above accurate and complete personnel records are essential.

■ **The external environment of the organisation:**
  – recruitment position;
  – population trends;
  – local housing and transport plans;
  – national agreements dealing with conditions of work;
  – government policies on education, retirement, regional subsidies, etc.

■ **The potential supply of labour**, in particular:
  – effects of local emigration and immigration;
  – effects of recruitment or redundancy by local firms;
  – possibility of employing categories not now employed, e.g. part-time workers;
  – changes in productivity, working hours and/or practices.

FORECASTING AND THE HUMAN RESOURCES AUDIT

Human resources plans are predetermined responses to anticipated future events (Greenberg and Baron, 1997). It is axiomatic that possible future events must be predicted, so mechanisms for forecasting the future need to be devised. The demand for labour is a 'derived demand' depending as it does on the number and types of people needed to produce and distribute goods. Factors influencing the demand for a particular company's products include the rate of growth of total consumer spending, the intensity of competition (including competition from imported goods), changes in tastes and fashion, and possibly seasonal variations in levels of purchases. All these factors affect the volumes and characteristics of a firm's production and hence the labour it needs to employ. Unfortunately, accurate forecasting of such variables is notoriously difficult for several reasons, as outlined below.

- Many variables (tax levels, business laws, interest rates, consumer incomes, etc.) are determined by government and are thus beyond the organisation's control.
- Consumer tastes can change quickly and unpredictably.
- New technical inventions may occur.
- Competitors might alter their behaviour – fresh competition could emerge.
- Past events upon which forecasts are based might not occur in the future.
- Existing suppliers, distribution options, harmonious industrial relations, etc. could suddenly disappear.
- Technical difficulties (unreliable data, incorrect choice of statistical forecasting technique, etc.) might arise.

The longer the period of the forecast, the greater the likelihood of serious error. It is wise, therefore, to generate several different forecasts with a greater amount of detail the shorter the timespan involved, and each forecast assuming a different scenario of events. The accuracy of predictions should be monitored by comparing them with events as they occur, and sources of error (inadequate or incorrect data, faulty forecasting techniques, poor judgements by forecasters, etc.) should be identified. It is useful to know whether forecasts are on average persistently overestimating or underestimating actual performance.

The human resources audit and the final HR plan

Alongside its forecasts of the demands for various categories of labour, management needs to set out all its available information on the organisation's existing personnel, taken perhaps from a skills inventory (see p. 338) plus appraisal reports on the quality of employees' work. Analysis of this information might be set out in a separate document, the **human resources audit**, which lists the abilities, performance records and apparent potential of each of the organisation's departments and its employees. The aim of the exercise is to match the organisation's present and future human resources against current and forecast requirements thus enabling it to produce the final human resources plan showing in detail, by function, occupation and locations, how many employees it is *practicable* to employ at various stages in the future (Graham and Bennett, 1998). The following should appear in it:

- jobs which will appear, disappear or change;
- to what extent redeployment or retraining is possible;
- necessary changes at supervisory and management levels;
- training needs;
- recruitment, redundancy or retirement programmes;
- industrial relations implications;
- arrangements for feedback in case modifications in the plan or company objectives are necessary;
- details of arrangements for handling any human problems arising from labour deficits or surpluses – e.g. early retirement or other natural wastage procedures.

Short-term plans

Many organisations do not have the financial or managerial resources to forecast long-term HRP variables, or they feel that the nature of their business makes it impossible to look ahead for more than one year. Hence they might prepare short-term plans covering just the next 12 months. A short-term human resources plan is comparatively easy to put together because an organisation will usually make a production or marketing plan for a year ahead involving budgets, orders for new materials and components and sales quotas. From this can be derived the amount of **direct labour** in terms of labour-hours required in future and then, by dividing into this figure the number of available working hours, the number of workers can be obtained. Overtime and the average level of sickness absence and machine breakdowns must be taken into account when available working hours are calculated.

The amount of **indirect labour** may be estimated partly by fixed commitments and partly as a rule of thumb percentage of indirect to direct labour. From the total labour requirements a recruitment or redundancy plan can be derived, but the period is usually too short for any worthwhile training plan to be made.

An advantage of the short-term plan is the ease with which the forecast can be compared with the labour that was actually required and any discrepancies analysed.

RECRUITMENT

Recruitment is the first stage in the process of filling a vacancy. It involves the examination of the requirements for filling the vacancy (particularly in relation to job and person specifications), consideration of the sources of suitable candidates, drafting job advertisements and selecting media suitable to carry them, assessing appropriate salary levels for new employees, and arranging interviews and other aspects of 'selection' – the second stage in the staffing process (Cherrington, 1995). Selection requires the assessment of candidates by various means and the choice of the successful candidate. It is considered further in the section on selection and induction below.

Recruitment and selection procedures should be constantly evaluated for their:

- **cost effectiveness** – could you get results as good while spending less money on the process?
- **validity** – reliably attracting and selecting the most suitable candidates.

The recruitment process

The department in which the recruit will work must draft or revise a comprehensive job specification for the vacant position outlining its major and minor responsibilities, the skills, experience and qualifications needed, the grade and level of pay, the starting date, whether temporary or permanent, and particulars of any special conditions (shift work, for example) attached to the job. Then the vacancy is advertised in suitable media and/or recruitment agencies are approached.

External recruitment is expensive. It involves advertising, agency fees, distribution of application forms, preparation of shortlists, writing for references, interviewing, payment of travelling expenses, etc. If the candidate appointed is unsuitable or leaves within a short period then the entire procedure has to be repeated. The advantages of filling the vacancy internally rather than externally are:

■ better motivation of employees because their capabilities are considered and opportunities for promotion are offered;

■ better utilisation of employees because the organisation can often make better use of their abilities in a different job;

■ greater reliability as compared with external recruitment because a present employee is known more thoroughly than an external candidate;

■ that a current employee is more likely to stay with the organisation than an external candidate.

However, it should be noted that some organisations have a policy of always advertising externally because internal recruitment methods tend to reproduce the broad social characteristics of the current workforce, thereby continuing to exclude underrepresented groups, such as women or ethnic minorities.

Job advertisements

It has been estimated that about 10 per cent of all press advertising expenditure is devoted to 'situations vacant' advertising. There is no doubt that much of this huge sum is wasted, chiefly because so little research has been carried out compared with research in the field of product advertising. Many employers have been able to reduce their job advertising costs with no adverse effect on the quality or quantity of candidate response by experimenting with styles of advertisements, media and wording and keeping careful records of the number of replies received to each advertisement and the candidate who was eventually selected. The only reliable guidance about advertising comes from the person who receives and analyses the replies, i.e. the employer. Newspapers and advertising agencies, which often claim to advise on the style and size of advertisements, are not usually in a position to know and evaluate the response.

Job advertisements should aim at procuring a small number of well-qualified candidates quickly and as cheaply as possible. Note the high cost of placing job advertisements in newspapers. A single advertisement covering 140 mm × 2 columns (approximately one-eighth of a page) in one issue of a quality daily newspaper can cost £4000 or more, depending on the newspaper's circulation and the page position of the advertisement. Even a small advertisement in a regional newspaper can cost £700 or more. An advertisement which produces hundreds of replies is a disadvantage to the organisation because the employer will then be faced with the lengthy and expensive task of sorting out a few candidates for interview.

The advertisement can become the first stage in selection by describing the job and qualifications required so comprehensively that borderline candidates will be deterred from applying and good candidates encouraged. It is important to ensure that a job advertisement complies with the requirements of all discrimination legislation including age discrimination.

Headhunting

Very senior managers are sometimes recruited by a process known as 'executive search' or **headhunting**. Its advocates believe that the best candidates are not those who reply to advertisements or look for new jobs in other ways, but those who are successful in their present jobs and are not thinking of moving elsewhere.

On receipt of a commission from a client, the headhunter will search for potential candidates:

- in competing businesses – possibly obtaining their names from company reports, brochures, etc.;
- in the membership lists of professional bodies, trade association yearbooks, newspapers and magazines that mention successful managers in the relevant industry;
- through confidential headhunting networks.

Selected individuals are then approached discreetly and, following a discussion regarding the job and its remuneration, one or two of them are introduced to the client firm.

Advantages of headhunting are as follows.

- Headhunters should possess expert knowledge of the salary levels and fringe benefits necessary to attract good-calibre candidates. Also, they will analyse the vacancy and offer an opinion about the type of person required, will conduct initial screening, administer psychometric tests, etc. This saves the client many administrative costs and advertising expenses.
- Possibly, top managers who are already in employment will not bother to read job advertisements, newspapers and other conventional media and hence cannot be reached by these means.
- Senior managers who are prepared to consider a move sometimes make this known to leading headhunters, even though they would not openly apply to competing companies.
- If a targeted candidate does not want the job, he or she may suggest someone else who is equally suitable and who may in fact be interested.
- Recruiting firms are assured that candidates presented to them will almost certainly be well equipped for the vacant position.
- The anonymity of the recruiting organisation is preserved until the final stages in the procedure.

Criticisms of the executive search include:

- Headhunting is highly disruptive to successful businesses, which stand to lose expensively trained senior managers.
- It can be used to avoid equal opportunities laws on recruitment and selection.

- A headhunted individual might subsequently be enticed by other headhunters to leave his or her new firm after a short period. To avoid this some companies attach 'golden handcuffs' to senior management positions, i.e. they pay large cash bonuses which are only available to executives who stay with the firm a certain number of years.

- Arguably, headhunters rely too heavily on existing networks and trade contacts, creating thereby a glorified 'old boy system' which ignores good people from other sources.

- Headhunters' fees are far higher than those of conventional employment agencies (up to 50 per cent of the recruited individual's initial salary in some instances).

- The headhunter might acquire confidential information about the client company which could then be passed on to competing firms.

- Headhunters are not subject to the same long-term accountability as personnel managers employed within the business. Also they lack detailed knowledge of the client organisation's culture and operations.

EQUAL OPPORTUNITIES

The **Sex Discrimination Act 1975** sought to ensure that men and women and married persons be treated equally in employment situations. Thus, employers are not allowed to discriminate against either sex in:

- **selection procedures**
- **terms on which employment is offered**
- **access to opportunities for training or promotion**
- **fringe benefits**
- **deciding which workers shall be made redundant**.

Sex discrimination can be direct or indirect. The former means treating people unfavourably simply because of their sex – for example segregating women employees into separate departments and paying them lower wages. Indirect discrimination occurs when an employer applies a test or condition that puts one of the sexes at an unfair advantage. An example here would be a condition that all job applicants be over six feet three inches tall for work where the employee's height is not important. However, jobs where gender is a 'genuine occupational qualification' are exempt. Examples would be actors playing male or female roles, jobs in single-sex schools, hospitals or other institutions, and jobs where decency or privacy require employment of a particular sex.

While the law recognises discrimination in the form of sexual harassment, the courts have relied on European law to provide guidelines for what actually constitutes harassment. The 'Recommendation on the Protection of the Dignity of Women and Men at Work' (European Commission, 1991) carries a code of practice which defines sexual harassment as 'unwanted conduct of a sexual nature, or other conduct based on sex affecting the physical, verbal or non-verbal conduct'. An aggrieved employee may also take action under the Protection from Harassment Act of 1997. This Act was aimed at stalking but applies also to bullying and harassment in the workplace.

The Sex Discrimination Act makes it unlawful to discriminate against a person because he or she is married.

There is no ceiling on the amount of compensation that can be awarded to a person whom a tribunal considers has been directly or indirectly but intentionally discriminated against unlawfully.

The **Race Relations Act 1976** offers similar rights to 'racial groups' defined by colour, race, nationality or ethnic or national origins. A racial or ethnic group has been defined by the House of Lords as being identifiable by things such as a long-shared history, a common religion, a common language, a common geographical origin, a cultural tradition of its own, including family and workplace customs. As with the Sex Discrimination Act, there are exemptions.

Employment Equality (Sexual Orientation) Regulations 2003 protects everyone from direct and indirect discrimination, harassment and victimisation in employment and training on the grounds of sexual orientation.

Employment Equality (Religion or Belief) Regulations 2003 protects everyone from direct and indirect discrimination, harassment and victimisation in employment and training on the grounds of religion or belief.

Age Regulations came into force on 1 October 2006 and offer protection against discrimination in respect to age. See the section on age discrimination later.

The **Equality Act 2006** enabled the Commission for Equality and Human Rights to be established in October 2007.

Equal pay

The **Equal Pay Act 1970**, amended by the Equal Pay (Amendment) Regulations 1983, requires that men and women receive equal pay for work of equal value. All the terms and conditions of a woman's (or a man's) contract of employment must not be less favourable than that which would be issued to a member of the opposite sex. It is illegal to lay down separate rates of pay for men and women.

In 1996 the Equal Opportunities Commission published a code of practice on equal pay containing practical guidance to businesses concerning the elimination of pay discrimination between men and women. The code has sections covering, *inter alia*, the meaning of pay, implications of the law for employers, pay systems, the identification of discrimination and job evaluation and grading, plus a model equal pay policy. The code is admissible in evidence before an employment tribunal in any proceedings under the Sex Discrimination Act 1975 and the Equal Pay Act 1970.

Since 1 January 1984 any person has been able to claim equal pay relative to a member of the opposite sex employed by the same firm who does work of *equal value*, as determined by a job evaluation study. Hence, a woman, say, need not identify a man who is doing identical work for the firm on higher wages; she merely has to demonstrate that her job is *worth* the same in terms of its 'demands'. Such demands might relate to the effort, skill, responsibility assumed, working conditions or decision-making capacities required for effective performance.

Disabled workers

The **Disability Discrimination Act 1995 (Amendment) Regulations 2003** introduced new rights for disabled people in the areas of employment, education, public transport and access to goods, facilities and services. A National Disability Council was established to advise the government on eliminating discrimination against disabled people, and a code of practice was published containing a wide range of examples to illustrate how employers and others can comply with the Act. The code is not legally binding of *itself*, but is admissible as evidence in courts and industrial tribunals in order to establish whether discrimination has occurred. 'Disability' is defined as 'a physical or mental impairment which has a substantial and long-term adverse effect on a person's ability to carry out normal day-to-day activities'. Hence, a severe disfigurement represents a disability (though not if it results from tattooing or body piercing), as does anything likely to restrict an individual's mobility, manual dexterity, physical coordination, speech, hearing or eyesight, or perception of danger, or his or her capacities to learn or understand or to lift or carry everyday objects. However, addictions and antisocial behaviour do not entitle people to protection under the Act. Hay fever is also excluded (unless it aggravates another condition) together with behavioural tendencies towards theft, setting fires or exhibitionism. Specific provisions of the legislation are as follows.

- It is unlawful for an employer with 15 or more workers to treat disabled people less favourably than others unless there are justifiable reasons. Employers have to make 'reasonable adjustments' to working arrangements or environments where that would overcome the practical problems created by an individual's disability.

- No service-providing firm of any size may discriminate against the disabled, who have a legal *right* to be served. Thus, for example, a hotelier who pretends that all rooms are fully booked in order to refuse a booking from a mentally ill person is breaking the law.

- People letting or selling land or property must not discriminate against disabled persons.

- Colleges of further education are required to publish 'Disability Statements' to inform students about the arrangements they have made to help them to gain access to college facilities.

- A disabled person who feels that he or she has been unfairly discriminated against in employment or when applying for a job has a right of redress through an employment tribunal.

- New buses, taxis, trains and trams must satisfy minimum standards for access by disabled people.

Job applicants with criminal records

A person with a criminal conviction is not necessarily obliged to disclose this to a recruiting company, provided the conviction has been 'spent', i.e. a certain period has elapsed since the time of the offence.

The **Rehabilitation of Offenders Act 1974** contains a table of the time intervals that must pass by before a conviction becomes spent. For example, sentences of imprisonment are spent after 7 years if the sentence was for less than 6 months, or after 10 years for sentences of between 6 and 30 months. Fines become spent after various periods according to the level of fine imposed. A probation order is spent after 12 months. The periods are halved if the person involved was under 17 years of age when he or she was convicted.

However, some sentences can never be spent, notably life imprisonment (which in practice can mean that only a short period is actually spent in jail) and other periods of imprisonment for more than 30 months. Also, there are exceptions to the Act whereby candidates for certain jobs do have to reveal past convictions – namely, any form of work with young people under the age of 18, lawyers, chartered accountants, nurses, vets, dentists, medical practitioners, social and health workers, firearms dealers and prison officers.

Under the Act it is unlawful for an employer to deny someone a job solely on the grounds that the applicant has a spent conviction and, if the person is asked to declare on an application form whether he or she has a criminal record or is questioned about this during an interview, the applicant is legally entitled to 'forget' about ever having been convicted. If an employee is dismissed in consequence of a spent conviction being discovered then the dismissal is regarded in law as being unfair. Indeed, the employer may not reveal that the employee possesses a spent conviction to third parties (when writing references, for example). The justification for the Act is twofold:

- that in the absence of such legislation the possession of a criminal record would effectively debar the vast majority of petty criminals from obtaining employment, hence encouraging them to commit further offences;
- that criminal records are held only by people who have already been punished for their crimes, so that it is improper for such individuals to be punished again through not being able to get a job.

Age discrimination

From 1 October 2006 the **Employment Equality (Age) Regulations** made it illegal to discriminate because of age. This includes workers, employees, job seekers and trainees and includes discrimination against young and old – it applies to all discrimination according to age.

Direct discrimination occurs if someone is treated less favourably because of their age. Indirect discrimination means selection criteria, policies, benefits, employment rules or any other practice, which, although they have been applied to all employees, have the effect of disadvantaging people of a particular age unless the practice can be justified. Indirect discrimination is unlawful whether it is intentional or not (Age Partnership Group, 2006).

The TUC CIPD Guide to managing age discrimination (Flynn and McNair, 2007) states that age discrimination is bad for business. Not only is it unfair, it also wastes talent, experience and knowledge. This legislation is far-reaching in that it affects all areas of human resources management from adverting copy used in recruitment advertisements and interview questions in recruitment and selection procedures to all aspects of redundancy, retirement, pay, benefits, pensions appraisals and training which need to be reviewed to ensure that no age discrimination is present, as age discrimination is historically based in false assumptions and 'conventional wisdom'. The case law associated with this legislation is expected to develop over some time.

See the case study 'Don't get fooled again – you're not too old for the job' at the end of this chapter for examples of assumptions associated with age within the workplace.

Equal opportunities policies

Today many organisations have equal opportunities policies in which they formally state their commitment to equal opportunity ideals. These can cover age, politics and sexual orientation, as well as sex, race and disability discrimination. The advantages to having such a policy are that:

- top management is seen to endorse equal opportunity measures, creating an example to be followed at lower levels;
- as part of its policy the organisation might critically examine the sex, ethnic, age, etc. compositions of all its departments, divisions, occupational categories and levels of worker, exposing any unfair employment practices currently operating;
- the best candidates for jobs will (or should) be recruited or promoted regardless of their sex or ethnic origin, age or sexual orientation;
- discontent among existing minority-group employees may be avoided;
- it is less likely that the organisation will break the law.

Organisations sometimes publish extensive equal opportunity policy documents in order to placate existing minority group workers and/or external bodies (local authorities, government purchasing agencies, the Equal Opportunities Commission (EOC) or Commission for Racial Equality (CRE), etc.) but in fact have no commitment to equal opportunities whatsoever. They have no procedures for *implementing* their equal opportunity policy documents. This creates disillusion and cynicism among all concerned.

Both the EOC and CRE publish codes of practice setting out the steps to be taken to eliminate unfair discrimination in recruitment and other employment matters. The codes offer practical guidance on how personnel policies and procedures should be constructed in order to avoid discrimination, and how existing employees must be instructed about preventing contravention of the Act when interviewing, dealing with subordinates, selecting staff for promotion, etc.

SELECTION AND INDUCTION

Selection is the assessment of candidates for vacant jobs and the choice of the most suitable people. It involves matching the requirements of a job with the attributes of candidates (Boerlijst and Meijboom, 1989). This is facilitated by drafting a 'person specification' defining the background, education, training, personality and other characteristics of the ideal candidate. The person described may not exist but the process of drafting a person specification creates a standard against which candidates can be compared.

Schemes for categorising the various attributes required to perform certain types of work have existed for many years (Rodger, 1952; Fraser, 1954) and are usually presented in the form of a checklist describing the demands of the vacant job, as in the following example.

- **Physical aspects of the work.** Does the job require someone with exceptional strength or fitness (heavy lifting work, for instance), or a specific physical appearance, dress, speech or manner (e.g. for a position as a salesperson or receptionist)?
- **Need to communicate.** Some work involves regular contact with others. Workplace supervisors, salespeople, receptionists, training instructors, etc. need an external appearance, manners and communication skills that are not so important for socially isolated jobs (long-distance lorry driving, for instance). Jobs with social interaction require agreeable people who mix easily. Such jobs are unsuitable for hostile, aggressive individuals.

■ **Formal qualifications.** What is the minimum level of education and professional qualifications necessary for the job? It is important not to recruit people who are massively overqualified for the vacancy as they might quickly become bored and underperform, or leave the company. It is also important not to specify formal qualifications which are not strictly necessary, for example a GCSE in English when all that is required is an ability to write and speak articulately.

■ **Experience needed.** Should the person selected have personal experience of specific tasks, and if so for what periods and at what levels?

■ **Specific competences.** Does the work require a person with particular abilities such as mathematical competence, manual dexterity, or the capacity to think quickly, assimilate large quantities of information, exercise mental agility and interpret complicated issues? Employees who cannot easily withstand stress should not attempt harrowing or emotionally arduous duties.

■ **Personal ambition.** Repetitive production-line work is not intellectually stimulating; financial reward is probably the major motivating factor here. Other jobs present opportunities for creativity and self-development and thus would be appropriate for people with drive, enthusiasm, self-direction and personal ambition.

Note that organisations which specify unsubstantiated criteria that unnecessarily discriminate against one gender or members of ethnic minorities are open to legal challenge on the ground of indirect discrimination (see pp. 346 and 347).

Interviewing

The purpose of a job interview is to obtain information. Therefore, applicants should be put at ease as quickly as possible and hence into a frame of mind in which they will disclose the maximum amount of information about themselves. Uncomfortable, ill-at-ease candidates will not be as frank as those who are relaxed, confident and in full control of their responses. Accordingly, candidates should be interviewed promptly at the appointed time or, if delay is inevitable, apologies should be offered. Interruptions from telephone calls, secretaries, etc. disturb concentration and should be avoided.

The following rules should be followed when conducting interviews.

■ Opening remarks should be supportive and uncontroversial.

■ Questions which simply ask for repetition of information already provided on application forms should be avoided. Rather, the interviewer should seek supplementary information to probe the candidate's potential in depth.

■ Detailed note taking by interviewers is inadvisable because of its disturbing effects on the interviewee. Candidates should be assessed immediately after their interviews. Otherwise, important points in earlier interviews will be forgotten in the final end-of-session appraisal.

■ Open-ended questions such as 'what made you decide to do that?' or 'why did you enjoy that type of work?' are usually more productive in obtaining information than direct queries. Generally worded questions invite the candidate to discuss feelings, opinions and perceptions of events. Simple yes/no questions will not draw out the candidate's opinions.

■ Interviewers should not make critical or insensitive remarks during the interview.

■ Interviewers should not compare candidates with themselves.

- Only job-relevant questions should be asked.

- The 'halo effect' – assuming that because a candidate possesses one desirable characteristic (smart appearance or a good speaking voice, for example) then he or she must be equally good in all other areas – must not be allowed to influence the selection.

- 'Revealing' questions should not be asked. A revealing question discloses attitudes and beliefs held by the questioner. An example would be 'I like watching football, don't you?'

- Inappropriate criteria must not be applied. This could involve, for example, males who interview females associating attractive physical appearance with work ability, or appointing people the interviewer knows socially.

- Interviewers should not behave in a pompous manner. This wastes time and contributes nothing to the quality of the interview.

- Interview panels should be as small as possible. Over-large panels create unhelpful dramatic atmospheres and panel members might ask irrelevant and disconnected questions.

Testing

At best, selection tests are a useful complement to interviews. At worst, they are confusing and irrelevant appendages to the selection process. The purpose of an interview is to obtain information. Thus tests can be justified only to the extent that more and better information about a candidate is actually generated.

There are many serious problems involved in setting tests and correctly interpreting the results. Tests are particularly useful where interviews are not possible – for example, when large numbers of employees are to be engaged within a very short period, and for situations where candidates have no formal qualifications or experience of work, as in the case of recruiting school leavers who have no academic certificates. Advocates of selection testing claim that tests remove subjectivity in selection procedures. In principle, a good test should measure objectively the subject's abilities and characteristics. Moreover, an effective test will:

- **be cost effective to administer** – note that a single test can be given to a roomful of perhaps 40 or 50 people at each sitting, and only a couple of people will be needed to organise and invigilate the test;

- **measure precisely what it is intended to measure** – an intelligence test should assess intelligence, not learned responses; aptitude tests should indicate candidates' true potentials for undertaking the jobs for which they are being considered, not other occupations;

- **give consistent results when repeated** – only then can the results obtained from a single sitting be accepted as sufficiently reliable for appointment decisions;

- **discriminate between candidates** – good quality applicants should, if the test is working properly, obtain high marks and poor candidates should consistently fail. If candidates pass the test but then turn out to be incompetent then the test has not achieved its purpose;

- **rank the candidates** – the best candidate should obtain the top mark, the next best should get the second highest mark and so on;

- **be relevant to the job** – the characteristics exposed by performance in the test should relate directly to the job specification for the vacant post.

Induction

Once an offer of appointment is accepted then a contract of employment exists. The letter of appointment must include details of terms and conditions attached to the work – wages, working hours, holidays, sick pay, pension schemes, company rules, safety regulations, etc. Having considered all the terms and conditions, the recruit signs a document saying he or she understands and will abide by them. Subsequent breach of the contract will offer grounds for fair dismissal.

The high costs of recruitment will be wasted unless the new employee remains in employment and becomes productive as soon as possible. There is a high risk of the new employee leaving during the initial employment period:

> *'The induction period is activated during the pre-engagement process and is not complete until the employer and employee are reasonably satisfied with the employment relationship.'*   (Pilbeam and Corbridge, 2002)

The period of transition during which an **induction** crisis may occur varies widely. If an induction crisis occurs, the effect can be that the new employees decide that their decision to take up employment with the organisation was a mistake and results in their resignation. This means that the induction process must be seen as requiring more than a one-off induction training. The induction process allows for socialisation into the organisation's culture and helps to reduce the risk of early departure.

Part of the induction is the process of introducing recruits to an organisation and explaining their role within it, and usually begins with a guided tour of the building. Induction is important because impressions gained by new employees during this period can influence their perceptions of the organisation for many years to come. Good induction procedures also help employees to fit into strange and initially uncomfortable environments quickly and without fuss. Recruits should be welcomed personally by senior members of staff and then introduced to colleagues, supervisors and subordinates. Recruits may be given copies of the firm's organisation chart and an explanation of individual positions within it. Particular aspects of specific jobs can be discussed and, if appropriate, training arrangements made. Efficiency standards, expected output quality, security arrangements and so on will be detailed.

A crucially important aspect of the induction process is that of informing recruits where to go for help if they experience problems. Entrants should know who to approach and the correct procedures to follow. Appropriate contacts might be supervisors, personnel officers, higher managers or trade union representatives. In any event the recruit should know what to do if he or she:

■ has a problem with money or understanding the wage system;

■ has a medical problem;

■ feels that working conditions are unsafe;

■ does not get on with other people in the department;

■ has difficulty with the work;

■ is bullied or harassed;

■ has a complaint;

■ does not receive adequate training.

In addition to the direct induction process, other ways of aiding socialisation into the organisation include 'buddying'. The new starter is linked with an existing employee who is already settled within the same department. Having a ready-made colleague helps the socialisation process to proceed smoothly and gives the new starter an information source at his or her own level. Employees who act as buddies will need to be volunteers and have some training to ensure that they are clear about their role. Mentoring (see p. 357) can also be included within the induction process in addition to buddying.

Exit interviews

Employees deciding to leave the organisation present an opportunity to collect information on what motivated their decision. Analysis of this information can be used to improve retention and to develop a staff retention policy.

The timing of the exit interview will depend on the organisation and can range from the point of resignation to a later time, even after departure. The interview needs to be conducted professionally and with tact. In some cases a questionnaire is sent to the leaver to collect information. The response rate of this method of collection is reduced once the employee has left the organisation.

For employees who the organisation wishes to retain, an early exit interview can highlight reasons for the decision to leave. An offer can then be designed to retain the employee.

TRAINING AND DEVELOPMENT

The purpose of training is to improve employees' performances in their current jobs and/or to equip them for more demanding roles or a change in their role in the future. It is expensive – special instructors may have to be employed; external courses must be financed; internal courses require resourcing with materials, personnel and physical facilities. Moreover, there is no guarantee that trainees will actually benefit from participating in programmes. Employees are usually unproductive while undergoing training and there are many incidental expenses (hotel accommodation, travel, meal allowances, etc.).

Putting aside questions of staff morale, it might not make economic sense to spend enormous sums on training existing employees for higher-level work if competent people can be recruited cheaply from outside. Equally pointless is the (not uncommon) practice of training far more employees in a certain type of work than there are vacancies in that area. This policy, while ensuring a ready supply of qualified internal applicants whenever needs for a particular skill arise, causes high labour turnover as workers become increasingly frustrated at not being able to perform the work for which they were trained. Indeed, 'overtraining' policies can backfire, resulting in shortages of trained internal applicants for higher-level jobs (Schuler, 1992).

Training seeks to improve and develop the knowledge, skills and/or attitudes of employees. Apart from the benefits accruing to the individual worker (greater versatility, extra skills, etc.), many advantages accrue to the organisation. Employees become more flexible, the productivity and quality of work should improve, job satisfaction might increase (with consequent reductions in absenteeism and staff turnover rates) and the organisation need not fear the consequences of new technology.

The learning organisation

→ Ch. 3

The concept of the **learning organisation** is based on the view that if an organisation does not learn faster and keep ahead of its competitors it will not survive (see Chapter 3). If an organisation is considered to be a sum of its parts, including employees, the learning of these employees will enhance the organisation. The flaw in this argument is that it will only be true if the organisation values the learning and has systems that allow the learning to be shared through the organisation. This requires the organisation to nurture a culture that encourages learning, reflection and the sharing of its application of the learning within the organisation.

Encouraging learning in itself will not develop a learning organisation. Writers and researchers have presented varying views on the learning organisation:

> *'An organisation which facilitates the learning of all its members and continuously transforms itself.'*   (Pedler *et al.*, 1991)

And according to Senge (1990):

> *'the basic meaning of a "learning organisation" is an organisation that is continually expanding its capacity to create its future.'*

Links between the learning organisation and knowledge management can be drawn as they both highlight the importance to the organisation of continuous development to meet the changing needs of the external environment. The main differences are that the learning organisation focuses on the learning process and reflects on how the learning can be applied in the organisational context in the future. Double-loop learning occurs when the learning results in activities which modify and change the organisation's way of working. By contrast, in knowledge management the focus is on the availability and transference of knowledge that exists in the organisation, often centred on using computer systems for access.

Assessing training needs

Needs for employee training may arise from the introduction of new technologies or the organisation's diversification into different fields (Bernardin and Russel, 1993). Other causes of the need for training might be poor-quality output, high accident rates, high absenteeism or staff turnover, or unfavourable performance appraisal reports submitted by managers on their subordinates. Note, however, that any one of these might be caused by factors other than inadequate training.

Like any other business process, training can be very wasteful if it is not carefully planned and supervised. Without a logical, systematic approach some training may be given which is not necessary, and vice versa, or the extent of the training may be too small or too great. When the training is complete, validation will show whether it has been successful in achieving its aims and evaluation will attempt to measure its cost–benefit.

The systematic approach to training follows this programme.

1 The job is analysed and defined.

2 Reasonable standards of performance are established, perhaps by reference to experienced employees.

3 The employees being considered for training are studied to see if the required performance standards are being attained.

4 The difference (if any) between **2** and **3** is considered. It is often called the 'training gap', though it may be partly due to faults in the organisation, poor materials or defective equipment.

5 Training programmes are devised to meet the training needs revealed in **4**.

6 Training is given and appropriate records kept.

7 The performance achieved after training is measured. If the training programme has been successful then the performance standards set in **2** should now be achieved (validation).

8 An attempt is made to calculate the cost of the training and compare it with the financial benefit gained by the improved performance of the employees. The training programme may be revised if a method can be seen of achieving the same result at lower cost (evaluation).

Evaluation of training

For manual workers the success of a training programme might be quantified in terms of better productivity, higher quality of output, less absenteeism, lower staff turnover, greater adaptability, fewer accidents and less need for close supervision. Unfortunately, improved performance in many jobs is difficult to express quantitatively in the short term. And some skills acquired on courses undertaken today might not be used until some time in the future.

Training can improve workers' morale, create better interpersonal relationships, instil in employees a sense of loyalty to the organisation and provide other intangible benefits (Beer *et al.*, 1985). Note, however, that it is not sufficient merely to ask workers whether they feel more efficient as a consequence of attending a course; hard, objective evidence is also required. Courses which participants have particularly enjoyed (especially residential courses) may be popular not because of their intrinsic educational value but because of their holiday camp atmosphere, recreational facilities, friendships established among course members and so on.

The following procedure should be adopted when evaluating the effectiveness of training.

■ Ask the question, 'What difference would it make to the organisation's overall performance if the training did not take place?' If the answer is 'not very much' then critically reassess the value of the training.

■ Relate the outcomes of the training to the organisation's initial training objectives. Isolate divergences and explain why they occurred.

■ Interview people on completion of a course and ask them whether it was relevant to their work, whether it taught them things they did not previously know, whether it was too easy or too difficult, how well supported the programme was in terms of course materials, instructors, facilities, etc. and how they think the knowledge gained will help their future careers. Keep a written record of the answers and repeat the interview after at least six months have elapsed since finishing the course.

Management development

Management (and staff) development seeks to improve a person's overall career prospects rather than train him or her to perform duties necessary for the present job. Hence it normally comprises a series of planned training activities and work experiences designed to improve a manager's performance and equip him or her for higher-level work. Activities might include attendance on courses, job rotation, understudying (i.e. spending a short period as a personal assistant to a more senior manager), attachments to project committees and special working parties, and the completion of longer-term academic qualifications in the management field. Programmes may cover:

- background knowledge of the organisation, its trading environment, products, production methods, markets and personnel;
- administrative procedures, the legal environment, specialist techniques;
- management methods, analytical skills, organisation, delegation and control, time management;
- interpersonal skills, communication, leadership and coordination;
- creative abilities, decision making and problem solving.

Note that some organisations insist that managerial ability cannot be taught and that management training courses are therefore a waste of time. They argue that few courses contain material that is directly relevant and immediately applicable to real-life management situations, and that normal competition between managerial staff should ensure the 'survival of the fittest'.

In organisations which do train managerial staff, new approaches to training are increasingly common – they want to develop the initiative, self-reliance, leadership and interpersonal communication skills of managers as well as their technical abilities. An interesting recent development in the training field has been the increasing use of outdoor management training, which assumes the existence of direct parallels between the personal qualities necessary for successful management and those cultivated through participation in outdoor pursuits such as rock-climbing, canoeing, sailing or orienteering. The essential demands of these activities – planning, organising, team-building, dealing with uncertainty, direction and control – are the same, advocates argue, as those needed for management.

Coaching and mentoring

One-to-one coaching is increasingly being used as part of management development. The coaching can be targeted to achieve particular outcomes and the type and skill-base of the coach can be selected according to need. The coach needs to be a specialist having both coaching skills and the required knowledge base. Coaches can be used to consolidate learning following a training course, update business skills on a one-to-one basis, improve existing skills, recommend specific behaviours to develop or improve, reinforce on-the-job performance and to clarify performance goals and development needs. The coaching skills identified by Walton (1999) include listening and understanding, observing, giving feedback, understanding people, communication (written and verbal) and influencing.

Mentoring is not the same as coaching. A mentor is usually a senior employee who advises the more junior member of staff on personal and career development. It is essential that the mentor and protégé are not in a direct reporting relationship and that the relationship is quite separate from that which exists with a line manager. For a successful mentor–protégé relationship there needs to be mutual trust, regular meetings and confidentiality on both sides. The length of a mentoring relationship may have a fixed term or be open-ended. Mentoring can form part of an induction process.

PERFORMANCE MANAGEMENT AND APPRAISAL

→ Chs 9
& 14

Performance management is the integration of employee development with results-based assessment (see Chapters 9 and 14). It encompasses performance appraisal, objective-setting for individuals and departments, appropriate training programmes and performance-related pay. Appraisal of managers by their subordinates, peers and people in other departments (perhaps even customers) might also be included in the scheme (Philpott and Sheppard, 1992).

Target setting

An employee's targets could be stated in terms of achieving a certain standard (i.e. an ongoing performance criterion, such as a specified departmental staff attendance rate or the attainment of minimum quality levels) that is to be maintained indefinitely, or as an *ad hoc* goal (Fletcher and Williams, 1992). The advantages of bosses and employees jointly setting personal objectives are as follows.

■ It forces everyone in the department to think carefully about his or her role and duties, about why tasks are necessary and how best to get things done.

■ Targets are clarified and mechanisms are created for monitoring performance.

■ Crucial elements are identified in each job. This information is useful for determining training and recruitment needs.

■ Personal achievements of employees are recognised and can be rewarded appropriately.

■ Bosses and their colleagues are obliged to communicate. In consequence, bosses can quickly identify which employees are ready for promotion and the help they will need in preparing themselves for this.

■ Performance is appraised against quantified targets not subjective criteria.

■ There is forced coordination of activities – between departments, between junior and senior management, and between short-term and long-term goals.

The targets set should adhere to the following guidelines:

■ Targets should be precise, unambiguous and, if possible, expressed numerically. Targets can be expressed in quantities, lengths of time, money and/or percentages but generic objectives such as 'increase profits' or 'cut costs' are not acceptable.

■ Targets should relate to the crucial and primary elements of employees' jobs and not to trivial matters.

■ Targets should be consistent.

■ Each target should be accompanied by a statement of how it is to be achieved, by when, the resources necessary and how and where these will be acquired.

A good way to assess the usefulness of objectives is to ask whether they pass the **SMART** test, i.e. targets need to be:

■ **Specific**
■ **Measurable**
■ **Agreed between boss and worker**
■ **Realistic**
■ **Time related.**

Both parties should share a common perspective on the situation intended to exist after the achievement of objectives and on how soon results may reasonably be expected.

Appraisal

Managers frequently make *ad hoc* judgements about employees but are loath to discuss the grounds on which the opinions are based. Performance appraisal replaces casual assessment with formal, systematic procedures. Employees know they are being evaluated and are told the criteria that will be used in the course of the appraisal. Indeed, knowledge that an appraisal is soon to occur could motivate an employee into increased effort aimed at enhancing the outcomes of the assessment. Specifically, appraisal is the analysis of employees' past successes and failures, and the assessment of their suitability for promotion or further training. Its advantages include the following.

- Boss and employee are compelled to meet and discuss common work-related problems. Appraisees become aware of what exactly is expected of them and of their status in the eyes of their line managers.

- Appraisal monitors the feasibility of targets set by higher management, who receive valuable feedback on problems encountered when implementing policies. Thus it creates a cheap and effective early-warning system within the organisation's management information structure.

- It enables bosses to learn about employees and the true nature of their duties. Conducting appraisals helps a manager to remain in touch with the staff in the department. Unknown skills and competences might be uncovered. This data can be incorporated into the firm's human resources plan and hence assist in avoiding compulsory redundancies, in career and management succession planning, and in identifying needs for employee training (Kinnie and Lowe, 1990).

A successful appraisal is one that results in:

- reasonable targets which are mutually agreed, not arbitrarily determined;
- recognition of the employee's achievements;
- clear identification of obstacles to improved performance – organisational problems as well as individual difficulties;
- enthusiastic pursuit of measurable objectives;
- two-way communication between boss and worker.

It is important for appraisal to be seen as a staff development exercise, intended to be helpful to everyone concerned, and not as a form of restrictive control or disciplinary measure. The purpose, therefore, must be to assist both individuals and the organisation in improving their performances. Appraisal reviews are usually categorised into three types:

- **Performance reviews** – analyse employees' past successes and failures with a view to improving future performance.
- **Potential reviews** – assess subordinates' suitability for promotion and/or further training.
- **Reward reviews**, for determining pay rises. It is a well-established principle that salary assessments should be carried out well after performance and potential reviews have been completed, for two reasons:

- performance reviews examine personal strengths and weaknesses in order to improve efficiency. If salary matters are discussed during these meetings, they might dominate the conversation and discourage employees from being frank about their weaknesses;
- ultimately salary levels are determined by market forces of supply and demand for labour. Staff shortages can cause the firm to pay high wages quite independent of the objective worth of particular workers.

Self-appraisal and peer group appraisal

Appraisal might be more useful to the appraisee, and lead in the longer term to greater efficiency, if it is conducted either by the employee or by a colleague of equal occupational status. Such appraisals may analyse issues more critically than when people fear the career consequences of admitting mistakes. Appraisees state – using any of the methods previously discussed – how they regard their performance, the adequacy of the training they have received, the effects of alterations in job content, any perceptions of key objectives and future aspirations. They identify their own strengths and account for their failures and weaknesses suggesting ways in which the firm might better use their talents, skills and recently acquired experiences.

There are, of course, problems with self-appraisal.

■ Many people are quite incapable of analysing themselves. It is unusual for individuals to assess their own competence in other walks of life. At school, college and during the early stages of a career the individual becomes accustomed to being directed and evaluated by others. The transition of appraisee to self-assessor may require skilled and detailed guidance by someone already competent in appraisal techniques. Most appraisees in lower-level positions will have received no training in self-analysis or appraisal.

■ To the extent that appraisals form a basis for future career development, appraisees may overstate their successes while ignoring their failings.

On the other hand, employees are compelled to think carefully about the adequacy of their contribution, about barriers preventing improved performance, about their future and about the quality of their relationships with others.

Problems with performance appraisal

There are a number of problems with performance appraisal.

■ Dangers of favouritism, bias and stereotyping by managers who conduct appraisals.

■ Possibilities that inconsistent criteria will be applied by different managers when assessing the calibre of subordinates (Schneier *et al.*, 1991).

■ All the information relevant to a particular case may not be available.

■ Information may not be interpreted objective.

■ Assessors may seek to evaluate every subordinate as 'fair' or 'average' for all performance categories, perhaps to avoid controversy.

■ Assessors may focus on specific cases of outstandingly good and bad performance while ignoring the employee's average overall ability.

■ Appraisal systems require appraising managers to undertake extra work, which they may be reluctant to accept. Hence the process becomes a ritualistic chore to be completed as quickly as possible in a manner that causes the least comment from those affected by the scheme.

Douglas McGregor noted the great reluctance with which many managers undertake assessment responsibilities, preferring to treat subordinates as professional colleagues rather than as inferiors upon whom they are entitled to pass judgement (McGregor, 1957). Senior managers, McGregor asserted, dislike 'playing God'. Usually they are fully cognisant of their own biases and thus rightly seek to avoid situations where prejudice could arise. Also, subordinates may bitterly resent their personal qualities being commented on, seeing the appraisal as a patronising exercise designed to humiliate or to punish past inadequacies in their work.

Appraisal requires concentration, diligence and competence in the manager conducting the appraisal. Training in appraisal techniques is required, followed by substantial guided experience in their practical application. McGregor pointed out that:

■ few managers receive any instruction in appraisal methods;

■ even managers who are properly trained may not possess all the information needed to undertake fair appraisals – they may be out of touch with current working practices or unfamiliar with environmental problems affecting subordinates' work.

360 degree appraisal

The 360 degree appraisal has developed to overcome some of the problems highlighted above. This method collects feedback from a variety of sources in addition to the manager, including peers, customers, suppliers, senior and junior staff. If a balanced view is taken then the resulting appraisal will be more informed than feedback from a single source. Individuals' feedback will be coloured by their personal stance and this needs to be acknowledged.

The feedback process needs to be managed carefully. Special training is required for those involved in managing the process so that the information collected can be used to improve the overall work and behaviour.

The disadvantages of the 360 degree appraisal are that it is expensive, time-consuming and requires a high level of resourcing.

PROMOTION, TRANSFER, DEMOTION AND DISMISSAL

Promotion and demotion

Apart from improvements in pay and conditions of work, the most immediate incentives available to employees are opportunities for promotion. If the organisation has trained its staff adequately and ensured that employees' work experiences are sufficiently wide then internal promotion should be feasible. Thus external recruitment will be necessary only for specialist positions, or when no one within the organisation possesses appropriate qualifications for a post, or the organisation needs or wants to increase the diversity of its staff at all levels. Prospects of promotion often represent significant motivators (van Ham *et al.*, 1986). Promotion methods are worthy, therefore, of serious discussion.

The criteria used in selecting individuals for promotion may be based on ability or seniority. Ability-related systems accelerate the careers of staff who are exceptionally competent, whereas seniority-based procedures have the advantage of ensuring steady progression for all employees – and knowledge that promotion is reasonably assured can improve morale throughout the organisation. Promotion follows logically from training, performance appraisal, management development and management by objectives programmes.

People can be selected for promotion directly – management simply appointing chosen employees to higher posts – or vacancies can be advertised within the firm. Direct selection is quick, inexpensive and suitable where management knows the abilities of all its subordinates. Internal advertising is appropriate in organisations where several candidates of about the same level of ability might apply.

Unfair discrimination in promotion will upset and demotivate staff – it should be avoided at all costs. Organisations that operate in sensitive multicultural or multi-ethnic environments sometimes monitor the consequences of their promotion policies by checking whether certain groups are overrepresented among those who do not achieve promotion. Hence, if it is found that females, ethnic minorities or certain religious groups are prominent in the non-promoted category, reasons for this can be identified and remedial measures applied. Specifically, the following questions can be asked of any promotion system.

- What are the characteristics of non-promoted groups, and are there valid reasons explaining why individuals in these groups are not promoted?
- What contributions have non-promoted groups made to the work of the organisation? Have they been rewarded adequately for their contributions?
- Why do non-promoted individuals remain with the organisation?
- What help can be given to non-promoted groups in order to help them to qualify for promotion? What are the obstacles confronting non-promoted categories, and how can they be removed?
- What can management itself do to improve its knowledge of the backgrounds and difficulties experienced by non-promoted groups? How does management feel about these people?

A non-discriminatory promotion policy has numerous benefits. Internal personal relationships between managers and subordinates are improved and labour turnover will fall because able staff do not need to leave the organisation to do higher-level work. Efficiency should increase through use of the accumulated experience of long-serving employees in senior positions. Additionally, there is little risk of the promoted individuals possessing unknown deficiencies, as can occur with externally recruited senior staff. On the other hand outsiders can inject fresh ideas and apply new perspectives to existing problems – external recruits may be of much higher calibre than internal candidates.

Demotion is a move to a job within the company which is lower in importance. It is usually, though not always, accompanied by a reduction in pay. An employee may be demoted for the following reasons.

- His or her job may disappear or become less important through a departmental or company reorganisation.
- The worker may no longer be thought capable of carrying out his or her present responsibilities efficiently.

Unless the employee has requested it, demotion will probably have adverse effects.

- There will be less satisfaction of esteem and self-actualisation needs.
- The employee may show negative reactions to frustration.
- The employee may become a centre of discontent in the organisation.
- Other employees may lose confidence in the organisation.

An employee who resigns in consequence of a demotion may complain of unfair dismissal under a special category known as 'constructive dismissal' (see below).

Transfers

A transfer is a move to a job within the company which has approximately equal importance, status and pay. To manage human resources in a constructive way it is sometimes necessary to transfer employees to other jobs, sometimes because of changed work requirements and sometimes because an employee is unhappy or dissatisfied in the present job.

In some organisations it is the custom for the least satisfactory employees to be transferred from one department to another with the result that a transfer can be regarded as discreditable, particularly if it occurs at short notice and without explanation. An unhappy employee may therefore prefer to leave rather than seek a transfer.

In other organisations transfers are used as a means of developing promising employees by giving them experience in several departments. A few organisations advertise all vacancies internally and consider applicants for whom the new job would be a transfer rather than a promotion.

Transfers can increase job satisfaction and improve utilisation under the following circumstances.

- A transfer is regarded as a reselection.
- The need for a transfer is explained.
- Unsatisfactory employees are not dealt with by transferring them to other departments.
- Requests by employees for transfers are fully investigated.
- No employee is transferred to another district against his or her will.
- An employee transferred to another district is given financial assistance from the organisation to cover removal costs, legal fees, refurnishing, etc.

Dismissal

Dismissal means the termination of employment by:

- the employer, with or without notice; or
- the failure of the employer to renew a fixed-term contract; or
- the employee's resignation, with or without notice, when the employer behaves in a manner that demonstrates refusal to be bound by the contract of employment.

The last of these is termed **constructive dismissal**. It means the employer is behaving so unreasonably that the worker has no alternative but to quit.

Normally, an employer must give the employee notice of dismissal, as stated in the worker's contract of employment. Occasionally, however, dismissal without notice is permissible. This is known as **summary dismissal** and can occur when an employee's behaviour makes the fulfilment of a contract of employment impossible. Examples are theft, persistent drunkenness, violence, abusiveness to colleagues or customers and wilful disobedience or incompetence that immediately causes damage to the employer's business.

Many countries have statutes that govern how employees may be dismissed fairly. Under the Employment Rights Act 1996, employees covered by the Act as amended by an order made in 1989 (e.g. mostly those with at least one year's continuous service) may only be dismissed fairly for genuine redundancy or for:

- **gross misconduct** – for example refusal to obey reasonable instructions, dishonesty, persistent absenteeism, neglect of duties;

- **incapacity to do the job** – caused by such things as incompetence, illness (once the worker's contractual sick pay entitlement has expired), or the person not having the skills or aptitude for the work;

- **some other substantial reason** – for example going on strike, disruption of staff relations or a temporary job coming to an end provided the impermanent nature of the work was fully explained to the worker when the employment started.

'Redundancy' means that the organisation's need for employees to do work of a particular kind has ceased or diminished so that some have to lose their jobs. The criteria used to select individuals for redundancy must, by law, be fair and reasonable. Workers declared redundant are entitled to redundancy payments. The redundancy process is illustrated in Figure 11.2.

'Wrongful', as opposed to 'unfair', dismissal occurs when insufficient notice is given or there has been some other breach of the employment contract. It gives rise to a civil action for damages equivalent to the actual loss incurred. Wrongful dismissal may be claimed by any dismissed worker, regardless of length of service – so a worker who has been with the organisation for only a few days may be 'wrongfully' sacked.

Allegations of wrongful dismissal can be heard in a court or employment tribunal. A complaint for unfair dismissal goes to an employment tribunal, which can award compensation of up to £60,600 (2007).

The ACAS code on dismissal

Disciplinary procedures should be in writing, easy to understand and made known to employees and their representatives. The UK Advisory, Conciliation and Arbitration Service (ACAS) has issued an important code of practice on these matters which tribunals expect employers to abide by. This code recognises that the maintenance of discipline is a management responsibility but emphasises the desirability of involving workers' representatives when drafting procedures. In addition to the points outlined above, the main recommendations of the ACAS code are as follows.

- Employers should indicate the forms of conduct that are considered unacceptable, and in what circumstances. Rules should be particular rather than universal and justified in terms of the objective requirements of a job.

Figure 11.2 The redundancy process

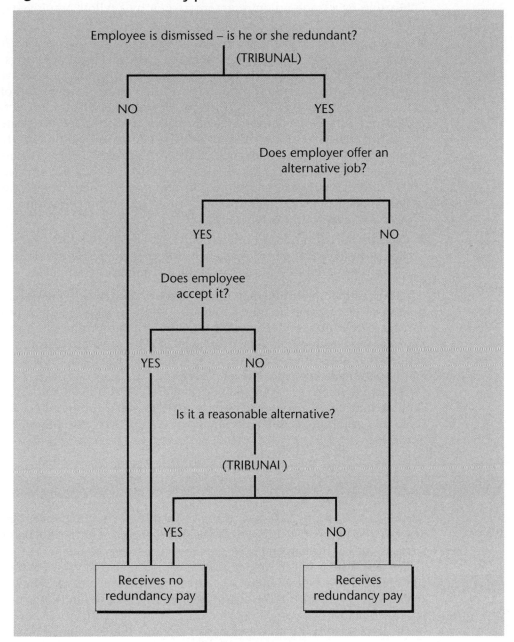

■ All workers should be given a copy of the organisation's rules and have them explained orally as part of an induction programme. Employees should be informed of the consequences of breaking rules, particularly those rules which, if broken, may result in summary dismissal.

■ All disciplinary procedures should be set out in writing and provide for matters to be dealt with quickly.

■ Only senior management should have the power to dismiss.

- The accused person should have the right to be accompanied at disciplinary hearings by a trade union representative or by a fellow employee of his or her own choice.

- Employees should not be dismissed for a first offence (except for gross misconduct). The code distinguishes between informal oral warnings for minor infringements of rules, and formal written warnings issued following serious offences. Formal warnings should set out the nature of the breach of discipline, the likely consequences of further offences and should state that the warning constitutes stage one of the formal procedure. If misconduct is repeated, a second and final written warning should be issued containing an unambiguous statement that a further recurrence of the offence will lead to whatever action (suspension, dismissal or some other sanction) has been determined. Assuming that the errant worker's behaviour does not improve then the next step is suspension or dismissal, accompanied by a written statement of reasons for the action taken and details of the right of appeal.

- The employer should take into account the employee's age, position, length of service and general performance and whether domestic problems etc. make it appropriate to reduce the severity of the disciplinary action taken.

Appeals should be considered quickly and be heard by a higher level of authority than took the original disciplinary action. Wherever possible the appeal should be considered by independent people who are not the immediate superiors of the manager who decided to dismiss the worker. The procedure should spell out the actions that may be taken by those hearing the appeal and enable any new evidence to be made known to the employee.

The Employment Act 2002 includes a section on dismissal and disciplinary procedures that details how disciplinary matters are to be handled. The standard three-step procedure is referred to in a new section 98A of the Employment Rights Act 1996.

ORGANISATIONAL CULTURE

Organisation cultures have been studied because of the differences between them. Schein (1985) describes three levels of culture, the most accessible being the visible artefacts, such as the corporate logo, and the physical environment of an organisation.

→ Ch. 4

The next level is not so easy to observe being the shared values of the members of the organisation (see Chapter 4). These are the beliefs and behavioural norms shared and agreed within the organisation as the 'way we do things here' and what is not acceptable.

The inner core is the unconscious assumptions that are shared by all members of the organisation that can only be found by discussion. If an organisation wishes to change its culture it will need to change all three levels.

Separate to organisational culture is organisational climate.

> *'Climate refers to a situation and links to thoughts, feelings and behaviours of organisational members.'*   (Denison, 1996)

The activities of human resources management can be used to support the existing culture in an organisation or as part of an organisational change programme. HR policies and procedures will affect the climate and can be used to support an attempt to change organisational culture.

EMPLOYEE RELATIONS

→ Ch. 9

This concerns how the relationship between employees and the organisation is managed (see Chapter 9). It includes relationships with trade unions, the management of workplace conflict, consultation processes and employee involvement and participation. Employee engagement can be viewed as the alignment of employees with the organisation's goals – this is also affected by how employee relations is managed.

Relations with trade unions and the management of workplace conflict will also be discussed in relation to employment legislation later in this chapter.

Trade unions

The period since 1978 has seen a decline in the level of union membership (Machin, 2000). The Employment Relations Act 1999 lays out a procedure for unionised employees' request for union recognition by an employer.

The culture, management style and organisational philosophy of an organisation will affect its view of unions – some organisations embrace unionisation whereas others resist it as strongly as possible.

Examples described in Gennard and Judge (2005) highlight the difference in tone between two types of organisations. For an organisation with a policy of not recognising unions for any employees or groups of employees, this arises from management policy, which is not to recognise a collective arrangement. In another organisation where there is no or low union membership the lack of union recognition may be because the employees have not chosen to join a union. The focus towards any potential unionisation appears quite different, although this cannot be confirmed until a situation occurs where unionised employees request union recognition.

The European Works Councils

The European Works Council (EWC) directive requires that an EWC be established in EU companies with at least 1000 employees and at least 150 employees in each of at least two member states. The directives give the EWC the right to meet with central management once a year. The directive also defines the areas requiring information or consultation as:

■ the structure, economic and financial situation of the business;
■ developments in production and sales;
■ the employment situation;
■ investment trends;
■ substantial changes concerning the introduction of new working methods, production processes, transfers of production, mergers, cutbacks or closures.

Employee involvement and participation

Employee involvement concentrates on the employee as an individual. Its focus is on developing a workforce that is committed to the organisation. The strategy is the *management* of staff rather than the control of staff.

Organisation programmes to encourage employee involvement include upward and downward communication, the active development of team working, quality circles and total quality working along with financial schemes to directly involve the employee with the increased profitability of the organisation such as share owner-ship schemes, profit-related pay and profit sharing, and representative participation.

Research conducted by Pecci *et al.* (2005) found that

> '*management's systematic sharing on performance targets relating from various aspects of the organisation can help to enhance employee commitment, and this in turn has a positive impact on labour productivity.*'

Employee participation centres on the involvement of employees with manage-ment in decision-making systems. The organisation relates to employees as a group communicating through staff representatives. This allows staff to feel part of the decision-making process. This may take the form of a staff–management joint con-sultation committee, worker representation on the company board, a trade union body or, in multinational organisations, the European Works Council.

Organisations that have systems for employee involvement and participation treat their employees as stakeholders in the organisation – in the same way that organisations see other stakeholders such as owners, customers, suppliers and the public. The culture of these organisations tends towards developing a partnership between the organisation and its employees.

Potential advantages of employee involvement and participation programmes for organisations are given in Gennard and Judge (2005).

■ Employees are better informed about their work tasks.

■ Employees are given increased intrinsic rewards from their work.

■ Employees enjoy increase job satisfaction.

■ Employee motivation is enhanced to achieve new goals.

■ Mutual trust and commitment are increased.

■ Labour turnover is reduced.

By empowering employees, the need for complex control systems is reduced which results in improved efficiency.

Employee engagement

Employee engagement describes a high level of commitment that can be developed between an organisation and its employees. It has been defined as:

> '*a positive attitude held by the employee towards the organisation and its values. An engaged employee is aware of business context, and works with colleagues to improve performance within the job for the benefit of the organisation. The organisation must work to develop and nurture engagement, which requires a two-way relationship between employer and employee.*'
> (Robinson *et al.*, 2004)

Employee engagement is more than job satisfaction – it describes the involvement that can be developed between an employee's values and commitment to the organisation's goals.

The term 'organisational citizenship' (CIPD, 2007) describes this combination of commitment to the organisation and its values plus a willingness to help out colleagues.

Three dimensions of engagement are outlined in the CIPD (2007) report as:

■ **emotional engagement** – to be emotionally involved in your work;

■ **cognitive engagement** – focusing very hard at work;

■ **physical engagement** – willingness to go the extra mile for your employer.

The successful development of employee engagement depends on how employees are managed, which means that the partnership between HR managers and line managers on managing employees and employee relations with the organisation are vital to achieving employee engagement.

In the annual report of the '100 Best Companies to Work For' sponsored by the *Sunday Times* (Brandon and Leonard, 2007) a link is made between employee retention and employee engagement. The report includes results from their research concerning where managers should focus to develop employee engagement:

- get employees on board and excited about the company and where it is going;
- keep them informed about the firm's progress and future plans;
- make sure you praise staff and give them feedback to acknowledge the level of their contribution;
- create a team atmosphere and make them feel valued, so they feel they can make a difference;
- give staff opportunities to grow and to develop with clearly defined targets and a distinct career path.

For the organisation there are a range of advantages of employee engagement – the staff promote the organisation as an employer of choice, show higher retention rates and engaged employees deliver improved business performance (CIPD, 2007).

THE FOUR Cs MODEL OF HUMAN RESOURCES MANAGEMENT

The **four Cs model** – commitment, competence, congruence and cost-effectiveness – was developed by researchers at the Harvard Business School as a means of investigating HRM issues in a wider environmental context than the mundane and instrumental tasks of recruitment and selection, training, appraisal, maintenance of employee records and so on (Beer *et al.*, 1985). According to the Harvard model, HRM policies need to derive from a critical analysis of:

- the demands of the various stakeholders in a business;
- a number of 'situational factors'.

Stakeholder theory

→ Chs 3 & 4

This asserts that since organisations are owned and operated by differing interest groups (**stakeholders**), management's main task is to balance the returns to various group interests (see Chapters 3 and 4). Examples of stakeholders are shareholders, different categories of employee, customers/users of the product, creditors (including banks), unions and (possibly) local or national government. Managers therefore need to be politicians and diplomats. They must establish good relations with each group, develop persuasive skills, create alliances, represent one faction to others, etc.

Stakeholder theory implies the recognition that each interest group possesses certain basic rights. Thus, for example, management should consider workers' interests as well as those of shareholders when making important decisions.

Stakeholders may or may not hold formal authority, although many will have invested something in the organisation whether this be work, finance or other resources. Accordingly, every investing stakeholder will expect a reward from the enterprise and normally will wish to influence how this is determined. Management must:

- identify the stakeholders in the organisation;
- determine the minimum return each stakeholder is willing to accept;
- seek to influence stakeholders' perceptions of the organisation – for example by persuading shareholders that a high dividend is not in a company's best long-term interest or convincing workers that a high wage settlement is not possible during the current year;
- identify key individuals in specific stakeholder groups and establish good relations with them.

Some stakeholders are simply groups or individuals who are affected by the organisation's activities, or who seek to represent certain 'constituencies' which cannot represent themselves, for example animals, the environment or overseas workers. Sometimes these have little influence and managers have to make moral judgements as to the responses they make to them. However, such groups can sometimes form powerful coalitions, excite the interest of the press or unsettle the organisation's staff – to the extreme detriment of the organisation!

Situational factors

These include the state of the labour market, the calibre and motivation of employees, management style (which itself depends in part on the culture of the local community), the technologies used in production and the nature of working methods (e.g. whether specialisation and the division of labour are required). Labour market situations are crucial to the analysis. The labour market comprises all the people seeking work and all the companies, government bodies and other organisations that require employees. Labour markets operate at regional, industry sector, national and (increasingly) international levels. There are submarkets for various categories of occupation, skill, educational background and other employee characteristics, and for different types of task.

Further situational factors that might be relevant are:

- the form of ownership of the organisation – and hence to whom management is accountable;
- the influence of trade unions and employers' associations;
- the laws and business practices of the society in which the organisation operates;
- the competitive environment;
- senior management's ability to coordinate and control.

Stakeholder expectations and situational factors need to be taken into account when formulating human resources strategies, and will affect HRM policies concerning such matters as remuneration systems, degree of supervision of workers, use of labour-intensive rather than capital-intensive methods, etc. An increase in the intensity of business competition may cause a firm to improve labour productivity, discard employees, restructure administrative systems and so on. A change in the age structure of the population can lead an organisation to hire more women. Rising educational standards may make it appropriate to redesign jobs in order to give workers more autonomy.

Outcomes to human resources management

According to the Harvard researchers, the effectiveness of the outcomes to human resources management should be evaluated under four headings: commitment, competence, congruence and cost-effectiveness.

- **Commitment** concerns employees' loyalty to the organisation, personal motivation and liking for their work. The degree of employee commitment may be assessed through attitude surveys, labour turnover and absenteeism statistics, and through interviews with workers who quit their jobs.

- **Competence** relates to employees' skills and abilities, training requirements and potential for higher-level work. These may be estimated through employee appraisal systems and the preparation of skills inventories (see p. 338). HRM policies should be designed to attract, retain and motivate competent workers.

- **Congruence** means that management and workers share the same vision of the organisation's goals and work together to attain them. In a well-managed organisation employees at all levels of authority will share common perspectives about the factors that determine its prosperity and future prospects. Such perspectives concern the guiding principles that govern the organisation's work – how things should be done, when, by whom and how enthusiastically.

  To some extent these perceptions may be created by management via its internal communications, style of leadership, organisation system and working methods but they can only be sustained and brought to bear on day-to-day operations by the organisation's workers. Staff should *feel* they possess a common objective. They need to experience a sense of affinity with the organisation and *want* to pursue a common cause. Congruence is evident in the absence of grievances and conflicts within the organisation, and in harmonious industrial relations.

- **Cost-effectiveness** concerns operational efficiency. Human resources should be used to the best advantage and in the most productive ways. Outputs must be maximised at the lowest input cost and the organisation must be quick to respond to market opportunities and environmental change.

Problems with the four Cs approach

The Harvard model suggests that human resources policies should seek to increase the level of each of the four Cs. For example, commitment may be enhanced through improving the flow of management–worker communication, while competence can be increased through extra training. Problems with the four Cs approach are:

- how *exactly* to measure these variables;

- possible conflicts between cost-effectiveness and congruence – especially if the drive for the former generates low wages;

- the huge variety of variables potentially relevant to any given HRM situation – often it is impossible to distinguish the key factors defining the true character of a particular state of affairs;

- the fact that sometimes a technology or set of working conditions makes it virtually impossible to increase the levels of some of the Cs – certain jobs are inevitably dirty, boring and repetitive, yet they still have to be done.

THE MANAGEMENT OF HUMAN RESOURCES

The modern approach to the management of human resources is to emphasise cooperation rather than conflict and to integrate HRM policies into the overall corporate strategies of the organisation. This requires senior management to:

- recognise the critical importance of harmonious relations with the workforce;
- relate HRM to the attainment of increased competitiveness, improved product quality and better customer care.

Well-constructed human resources policies are essential for the well-being of the firm and all efforts must be made to minimise the potential for conflicts between management and workers.

Strategic human resources management

The development of human resources management as a strategic function – strategic human resources management (SHRM) – brings the function into line with the other strategic functions of the business – finance and marketing. It acknowledges the contribution of the skills and knowledge of employees to continuing business competitiveness, together with the planning for future human resources needs.

Linking human resources management to the organisation's strategy is the basis of SHRM, so that human resources management underpins the business goals and vision of the organisation. To achieve this, HRM needs to be aligned horizontally so the major components (reward, resourcing, development, retention and employee relations) are aligned to achieve the organisation's strategy. The HR function must also be vertically integrated into the overall strategic plan.

The balanced scorecard

The **balanced scorecard** aims to link business areas of the organisation to its business strategy. Key measures are tracked and monitored. These measures have a direct link to the business strategy and are visible and applicable.

The key measures of the business in the main strategic areas are determined using cause-and-effect maps. Financial measures are seen as a major area in determining effective performance, but not as the sole area. Financial measures are important to shareholders but, unlike other areas of the business, they are short-term indicators. The balanced scorecard includes the monitoring of desirable long-term outcomes and performance drivers together with these short-term measures. They are used for setting targets. Having the same areas of measurement for all levels of the organisation, all employees can see how the objectives are linked to the organisation's goals.

The performance drivers selected for the balanced scorecard will be specific to the organisation and linked to customers, stakeholders, internal business processes and financial measures. This ensures that key business stakeholders – investors, customers and employees – are recognised.

The use of the balanced scorecard provides a system that helps to measure the effect of human resources management on the organisation's competitive success.

Role of the personnel department

In most, but not all, organisations human resources management is the responsibility of the personnel department. The personnel officer is often a generalist, since the variety of issues typically dealt with in a personnel department is so diverse that no one person can master all aspects of the job. Such a personnel manager requires a working, rather than a detailed, knowledge of:

■ the organisation, its products and the industry or sector in which it operates;

■ production methods and organisational structure;

■ pension schemes, wage and bonus arrangements;

■ law relating to employment;

■ the fundamentals of management theory and practice.

The mundane tasks of writing copy for job advertisements, organising training courses, keeping personnel records, operating wages systems, looking after health and safety at work arrangements, etc. are known collectively as the 'service function' of the personnel role. Other major personnel management functions are:

■ The **control function**, comprising:
  – analysis of key operational indices in the personnel field – labour turnover, wage costs, absenteeism and so on;
  – monitoring labour performance (staff appraisal, for example);
  – recommending appropriate remedial action to line managers.

■ The **advisory function**, whereby the personnel department offers expert advice on personnel policies and procedures:
  – which employees are ready for promotion;
  – who should attend a certain training course;
  – how a grievance procedure should be operated;
  – interpretation of contracts of employment, health and safety regulations, etc.

Evaluating the effectiveness of a personnel department

Effective personnel management should feed through into improved organisational performance, higher productivity among employees, better customer service and hence increased long-term sales (Burn, 1996). Measuring the value of the short-run activities of a personnel department, however, can be problematic. Specific difficulties attached to the evaluation of the personnel function are that:

■ since organisations operate in widely disparate commercial environments, wide differences in labour turnover, absenteeism, etc. are to be expected among firms engaged in similar lines of work;

■ personnel management is such a wide-ranging activity that it may not be appropriate to select just a handful of variables for appraisal.

Quantitative indices of a personnel department's work may be available in relation to:

■ unit labour costs compared to those in competing companies;
■ staff turnover;
■ absenteeism rates;
■ incidence of invocation of grievance procedures;
■ the proportion of the personnel department's staff that obtain professional qualifications;
■ number of days lost through strikes;
■ how long it takes to recruit a new employee;
■ successes achieved in the implementation of equal opportunities policies.

Subjective criteria include employee motivation, team spirit and willingness to accept change; the extent to which proposals emerging from the personnel department are accepted by senior management; the quality of relationships with trade unions; the calibre of job applicants responding to job advertisements; the usefulness of documents drafted by the department (job descriptions and person specifications, for example); and so on. Staff from other parts of the firm may be questioned in order to ascertain how they rate the personnel department in terms of such matters as:

■ how promptly it responds to requests for information or advice;
■ the quality of advice given by personnel department staff;
■ politeness and approachability of the department's members;
■ individual knowledge of technical personnel matters;
■ the department's overall contributions to the work of other sections.

Senior management may evaluate a personnel department's contributions on the basis of its ability to handle satisfactorily sensitive human relations problems arising from downsizing, organisational restructuring and the implementation of change. Also the personnel/human resources officer will be expected to make meaningful contributions to top management team decisions and to assist with strategic issues such as the formulation of mission statements, the determination of corporate culture, the facilitation of technological change and so on.

Decentralisation and devolution

Many personnel and HRM functions can be undertaken by managers in local units rather than through a central personnel department. Note that the individuals completing such duties in subsidiaries, divisions, etc. might *themselves* be personnel specialists rather than general line managers, although in practice this is rare because of the duplication of effort involved. The main problem with devolution of personnel and/or HRM work to non-specialist line managers is that they may be neither competent nor interested in personnel or HRM issues and may not be motivated to complete HRM duties properly, so that critically important personnel tasks are neglected. Bad HRM decisions lead to a poor corporate image, higher long-term costs and loss of output due to industrial conflict. Also line managers may focus all their attention on immediate and pressing personnel problems at the expense of long-term HRM planning, and it can result in HRM considerations not influencing strategic management decisions.

Effective devolution requires:

- the provision of backup services in relation to technical problems arising from contracts of employment, legal aspects of redundancy and dismissal, union recognition, etc. – an outside consultancy might assume this role;
- acceptance by everyone that line managers' workloads will have to increase following their assuming personnel responsibilities;
- the training of line managers in HRM techniques and concepts.

EUROPEAN UNION INFLUENCES

Following the UK general election of 1997 the incoming government announced its policy of positive engagement with the European Union and, in particular, that the UK would accept the European Social Charter. The latter originated during the 1987 Belgian presidency of the EU's Council of Ministers. It was put forward as a suggested device for ensuring that basic employment rights would not be eroded following the intense business competition expected to occur in consequence of the completion of the single internal market. Further objectives were to encourage EU governments to harmonise national employment laws and practices and to confirm the EU's commitment to an active social policy. The Social Charter was intended as a grand gesture towards the EU's labour force representing an unequivocal statement that *people* matter as well as business competition and that the interests of employees are just as important as those of firms.

The first draft of the Charter was published by the European Commission in May 1989 with the intention that each member state would implement its requirements at the national (rather than EU) level. Action would not be taken by the EU (via directives, regulations, etc.), provided the Charter's basic objectives could be effectively attained by member states or bodies within them.

Contents of the Social Charter

The basic rights to be established by the Charter were as follows:

- **Fair remuneration** – this would involve the specification of rules for establishing a fair wage.
- **Health, protection and safety at the workplace.**
- **Access to vocational training throughout a person's working life, including the right to retraining.**
- **Freedom of association and collective bargaining** – to belong or not belong to a trade union and for unions to have the right to bargain with employing firms.
- **Integration into working life of disabled people** – the provision of training for the disabled, accessibility to work premises, availability of special transport and explicit consideration of disabled people during the ergonomic design of equipment.
- **Information, consultation and worker participation in company decision making** – especially in enterprises that operate in more than one EU country.

- **Freedom of occupation, residence and movement of workers** – including equal treatment with regard to local taxes and social security entitlements.
- **Improvement in living and working conditions** – this embraces equality of treatment for part-time and temporary workers, controls on night working and requirements for weekly rest periods and paid holidays.
- **Social protection** – including adequate unemployment and other social security benefits.
- **Equal treatment of men and women.**
- **Protection of young people** – with a minimum working age of 15 years (16 for full-time employment) and a ban on night work for those under 18.
- **Reasonable living standards for senior citizens** – with a specified minimum income underwritten by the state.

There has recently been a wave of laws and regulations in the UK in the spirit of some of these basic objectives and, at time of writing, there are a good deal more in the pipeline. One effect of this may be to raise the profile of HR managers within organisations as employers seek to ensure that they keep within the new laws and regulations (many of which came into force very quickly, despite being quite complicated).

Some of the more recent acts and statutory instruments that organisations have been affected by are:

- Data Protection Act 1998
- Employment Relations Act 1999
- Public Interest Disclosure Act 1998
- Working Time Regulations 1998 and 1999
- Maternity and Parental Leave, etc. Regulations 1999
- National Minimum Wage Act 1999
- Part-time Workers (Prevention of Less Favourable Treatment) Regulations 2000
- The Regulation of Investigatory Powers Act 2000
- Fixed-Term Employees (Prevention of Less Favourable Treatment) Regulations 2002
- Employment Act 2002

The Human Rights Act 1998

This statute came into force in October 2000. It incorporates the provisions of the European Convention on Human Rights into UK law. Its articles include the right to respect for private and family life, and the right to freedom of expression. Courts and tribunals must now interpret law in a way that is compatible with the Convention. If this does not prove possible, UK law takes precedence. In fact, the British have been able to enforce their rights under the Convention since 1951, but only in the appropriate European court in Strasbourg.

Work–life balance

During the 1990s a culture of long hours and 'presentism' (being seen to be staying late at work) developed until it became the norm, and this trend has continued in recent years. This has resulted in an increasing tension between an employee's family commitments and work responsibilities. These changes have important considerations for the development of HR policies. Pressures pushing for improving changes in the work–life balance include compensation payments for stress caused by work pressures, an increase in the proportion of women returning to work following maternity leave, employees' expectation of work, the need to care for elderly adults and single-parent families. Flexible working patterns were initially highlighted to give firms a flexible workforce to meet changing customer requirements in Atkinson's flexible firm model (Atkinson, 1984). Political pressure from changes in European and UK law is also causing changes in the view of work–life balance. The best work–life balance depends on the individual's needs and it changes with the various life stages.

Government backing for improved work–life balance for families

The government launched an improved ACAS helpline service in January 2003. It is designed to give help and guidance on family-friendly employment rights for both employers and parents. New employment measures became law on 6 April 2003 giving parents with children under six years or disabled children under 18 years the right to request to work flexibly, and to have that request considered seriously.

Although there is no right to flexible working, a refusal may result in a claim of indirect sex discrimination, so that the employer would have to show an objective reason for justifying full-time working as a requirement and the refusal to permit part-time working (Willey, 2003). Maternity leave has been increased to 26 weeks paid and 26 weeks unpaid. Paternity leave has been set at two weeks' paid leave to be taken within eight weeks of the birth. Adoption leave has been set to mirror the provision of maternity leave and pay as closely as possible.

SUMMARY

■ Human resources are an organisation's most important asset and the effective management of human resources is a key determinant of an organisation's success. All managers who control others are necessarily involved in human resources management and thus require at least a rudimentary understanding of what the subject is about – its problems, possibilities and prospects, and how it relates to the organisation's strategy and management overall.

■ Human resources are much more difficult to manage than material resources, partly because conflict often occurs between the employer's and employees' wishes and partly because, to an increasing extent, employees try to share in making decisions about their working environment. Management must recognise workers' aspirations and harness and develop their innate abilities for the good of the organisation. Employees will not submit passively to manipulation or dictatorial control by management but more and more expect and demand some influence in the way they are employed. Research in the behavioural sciences shows that an appropriate response by management will benefit the organisation.

■ HRM is much more than the application within an organisation of a set of management techniques. It is concerned with the wider implications of the management of change and not just with the effects of change on working practices. It seeks proactively to encourage flexible attitudes and the acceptance of new methods.

Review and discussion questions

1 What is the definition of 'human resources management'? Explain the relationships between human resources management and personnel management.

2 Examine the training policies of an organisation. How effective are these policies and how could they be improved?

3 What are the reasons for an organisation promoting an awareness of work–life balance?

4 How do the strategies for employee participation and employee involvement vary? As an HR manager what steps would you take to encourage the development of employee engagement within an organisation.

CASE STUDY

Don't get fooled again – you're not too old for the job

How would you expect a distinguished 61-year-old man to behave? With restraint, perhaps, a certain decorum and calm? What you would probably not expect him to do is adopt a heroic, macho pose while windmilling his right arm through the air to the delight of the crowd standing in front of him.

But that was the image that confronted me on late-night television just over a week ago. The arm in question belonged, of course, to Pete Townshend, lead guitarist of The Who, and the crowd were the lucky few who had gathered in London's Roundhouse to enjoy the highlight of the BBC's recent 'Electric Proms' concerts.

The Who still perform their 1965 hit 'My Generation', written by Mr Townshend, which contains the famously defiant line, 'Hope I die before I get old' – a goal that, sadly, two of the original band members managed to achieve. The lead singer who delivers this line – with as much conviction as he did 40 years ago – is 62-year-old Roger Daltrey.

It is not only actuaries and pensions advisers who have had their expectations confounded by increased longevity. All of us are having to reassess our views on age.

For managers who may have begun their career with a clear idea about what the future held for them and knew precisely, given their age, where they stood in the corporate hierarchy, things have changed quite dramatically. Fiftysomethings face the prospect of being managed by people young enough (and perhaps disrespectful enough) to be

their children. But in other organisations, ambitious thirtysomethings may find their progress blocked by a tier of older, underperforming bosses who are clinging on for fear of being pushed out before their pension has grown to an acceptable level.

Businesses need to get much smarter about age, and fast. The demographics insist on it. And it is no use expecting government to sort out these problems for you. In any case, legislation has, so far, not proved terribly effective in bringing about what you might call cultural re-education in this area.

The US's Age Discrimination in Employment Act dates back to 1967, offering some protection to workers over the age of 40. The European age equality directive will be in force throughout the European Union only by the end of this year but its text was agreed in 2000 and it has been firmly on the agenda since that time.

In spite of all this law-making, traditional attitudes (and prejudices) about people's age and what it tells you about them are solidly in place. Research published last month by the Cranfield School of Management confirmed that age discrimination remains widespread, among UK employers at least. Preparation for, and compliance with, the new laws has done little to alter the view that, for example, younger workers are less reliable than their more seasoned colleagues, take more sick days and display less loyalty while older workers struggle with IT and new ways of working and are generally much more resistant to change.

There was a good example of inter-generational tension on display at last week's annual conference of the CBI, the UK's leading employers' organisation. George Osborne, the Conservative party's youthful shadow chancellor, received a distinctly unenthusiastic response from his largely grey-haired audience of business leaders.

But this sort of tension between the generations is a concern for some of the more thoughtful observers of the social and economic landscape. Noreen Siba, managing director of the International Longevity Centre, a London-based think-tank, argues that by failing to make better connections between the generations, whether at work or in the wider community, we risk polarising young and old, almost setting them up in opposition to each other, just at a time when we need to think harder about the financial implications of our ageing society.

Consider young graduates emerging from university today. They often have substantial loans to pay off while at the same time finding it hard to afford decent accommodation anywhere near their place of work. And pensions are a far-off, highly vulnerable commodity: they will probably have to work to the age of 70 before they can claim one. How unlike today's happy, golden generation whose homes are their fortune and whose index-linked final salary pensions are providing for a comfortable retirement.

This sort of discussion would have provided few surprises to Karl Mannheim, the Hungarian sociologist who published his essay 'On the Problem of Generations' in 1928. Mannheim understood how different generations could come to see themselves in conflict with each other. The outlook of individual generations might take the form of a collective response to major world events – wars or economic crises. But the neat historical lines drawn in the past by two world wars have been replaced by the more unpredictable responses of the boomer generation, whose attitudes and behaviour patterns vary so widely.

We should celebrate our increased longevity. Age should be seen more as an opportunity than a threat. But, at work, joining the dots between different age groups and managing that diversity for the benefit of the organisation are going to take leadership of a high order.

They are also going to require a serious shift in attitudes. Who says all those young graduates are going to be feckless, ill-disciplined and unwilling to work? Why do we presume older people have less to offer and that they have to be written off once the wrinkles and grey hair start to predominate? In a world of limited and diminishing natural resources, the waste of human talent we see today based on such prejudice is worse than a crime – it is a blunder.

Questions

1 *What are the assumptions in the workplace highlighted in this case study associated with age?*

2 *What do you think is the view of the author to managing age within an organisation?*

3 *As an HR manager you have been asked by your manager to design an 'age diversity awareness' training course. What aspects of the case study would you incorporate into the course and why?*

Source: Extract from S Stern (2006) 'Don't get fooled again – you're not too old for the job', *Financial Times*, 4 December 2006.

FURTHER READING

Beardwell, J and Claydon, T (2007) *Human Resource Management: A Contemporary Approach* (5th edition), Harlow: Pearson Education Limited.
This comprehensive text relates the historical context and academic theory to the development and practice of HR within organisations today. It includes sections on international HR and HR development.

Bloisi, W (2007) *An Introduction to Human Resource Management*, Maidenhead: McGraw-Hill Education.
A clear introduction to the essential topics of HR.

Foot, M and Hook, C (2005) *Introducing Human Resource Management* (4th edition), Harlow: Pearson Education Limited.
A practical review of the core HRM topics focusing on applications for the workplace.

Redman, T and Wilkinson, A (2006) *Contemporary Human Resource Management Text and Cases*, Harlow: Pearson Education Limited.
This text combines the theories underpinning the fundamentals of HR with a range of practical case studies that illustrate various aspects of HR.

Torrington, D, Hall, L and Taylor, S (2005) *Human Resource Management* (6th edition), Harlow: FT Prentice Hall.
A full, detailed and thorough text that combines the academic theory and practical aspects of HR.

WEBSITES

http://www.cipd.co.uk
Chartered Institute of Personnel and Development. Good source of information of a wide variety of HR issues. Some information only available to CIPD members.

http://www.hr2000.com/
HR Online. A popular and developing page which presents the services of a good range of HR consultants. Some 90 per cent is offered free.

http://www.acas.org.uk
Advisory, Conciliation and Arbitration Service (ACAS). Information and advice on employment law.

http://cre.gov.uk
The Commission for Racial Equality. Much useful information about relevant legislation, press releases, the benefits of ethnic diversity and the role of the CRE.

http://www.eoc.org.uk
The Equal Opportunities Commission. Clear explanations of relevant legislation, current issues, the role of the EOC and the latest press releases.

http://www.dti.gov.uk
The Department of Trade and Industry. Information on a wide range of issues affecting people at work.

www.disability.gov.uk
The Disability Rights Commission

www.tuc.org.uk
Source for both TUC/union issues and coverage of government policy/legislative developments and employment.

CHAPTER 12

Organisational motivation

DOMINIC COOPER

Outcomes

The objective of this chapter is to introduce the concept of motivation and explore ways of motivating people to perform for the good of the organisation. Having read this chapter you will be able to describe:

- the major work motivation theories;

- the psychological and situational factors that affect people's behaviour;

- the characteristics common to all motivation theories;

- the application of motivational concepts in the workplace;

- The constraints to motivating others.

CRITICAL MOTIVATION CONCEPTS

Motivation encompasses many concepts that can have different meanings to different people. In this chapter, the various critical concepts have particular meanings as described below.

- **Behaviour** refers to what people do. People infer others' motivation from their behaviour and actions. For example, an employee who works faster than others with the same workload and level of ability is often inferred to be more highly motivated.

- **Performance** refers to evaluating someone's behaviour against some predefined standard. Although most organisation theories simultaneously focus on performance and behaviour, employee behaviour often depends on situational constraints beyond many employees' control.

- **Situational constraints** are the first major determinant of people's behaviour. They create the working environment within which people have to operate. If equipment, manpower or other resources are not available in the right place at the right time then people behave much differently than when they are present. In turn, this affects performance. Broadly speaking situational constraints dictate what people are *allowed* to do in a given circumstance.

- **Ability** is the second major determinant of behaviour and refers to the capacity to perform in a given situation. In essence, ability refers to what people *can* do. This covers a wide range of personal attributes such as intelligence, knowledge, skills and behavioural competencies.

- **Motivation** is the third major determinant of behaviour. Motivation refers to what people *will* do given their ability, a supportive environment and the rewards on offer.

Each of these critical behavioural determinants could and does affect managerial assessments of employee performance. Managers often overlook **situational constraints** created by organisational shortcomings when assessing performance. Managers may also not recognise that employees do not always possess the **ability** to perform in the desired manner due to a lack of training. Some may not understand that people are not **motivated** to behave in the desired manner, perhaps because the levels and types of organisational rewards simply require too much effort to make them worth pursuing. Of course, all three of these factors may be in play at the same time, which this chapter hopes to make clear.

When discussing motivation we often mean 'why do people act in particular ways?' and/or 'how can I /we get them to act in certain ways?' Motivation actually refers to a psychological concept concerned with increasing the **direction**, **strength** and **duration** of people's work-related behaviours to influence the quality and quantity of people's performance output. Comprehending the distinction between these latter aspects is important in understanding the various motivation theories. **Direction** refers to the choice of activities people make in expending effort. Employees can, for example, choose to work carefully at one task but not another. **Strength** refers to the intensity of effort or energy employees might expend in pursuit of a job activity or task. Employees tend to expend more energy on tasks they find interesting and stimulating, compared to those perceived to be boring, mundane and/or repetitive. **Duration** refers to the persistence of people's motivation over time – that is, what people do in the face of obstacles, boredom or successful goal-achievement. Do they give up or continue? Blau (1993) assessed the motivation of bank tellers and found that the direction and strength of effort predicted the quality of their work performance. This illustrates that each of these aspects has direct implications for the way organisations attempt to motivate employees.

Because every employee is motivated to some end or other, it is nonsense to talk about an unmotivated person. In reality, employees are often simply directing their energies to achieve different aims. This type of behaviour tends to puzzle managers who often ask why it is that some employees do not direct and invest their energies in the desired manner. Broadly speaking this is often due to unclear expectations, a failure to align an employee's goals with that of the organisation, a poor history of recognising good performance and a poor supportive working environment. Often these factors combine to demotivate a previously motivated person.

Although financial inducements motivate some people in the short term, there are no magic formulae to motivate people to improve their performance over the longer term. People's motivation is dynamic: it needs constant nurturing. Importantly, one negative feature (e.g. a bullying manager) can outweigh ten positives features (e.g. an enriched job, etc.). Some of the factors proven to influence people's motivation are:

→ Ch. 2

- **a manager's leadership style** (see Chapter 2);
- **the degree of autonomy and authority allowed;**
- **the degree of managerial and organisational support exhibited;**
- **the amount of stress or distress experienced at work;**
- **the opportunities for growth and advancement;**
- **the amount of personal satisfaction people derive from their job;**
- **the magnitude of people's commitment to their organisation and/or career.**

Each of these factors is linked with specific work behaviours such as performance, absenteeism, tenure, turnover and organisational citizenship. In practice, attention to such factors is often overlooked simply because line managers are primarily interested in achieving short-term (e.g. monthly) production performance outcomes set by middle or senior management. However, this can create many motivational problems that surface in substandard performance.

Influencing factors

Many aspects of organisational life influence a person's behaviour and their motivation. It is well known that psychological attributes such as disposition, temperament, intelligence, ability and skill exert large influences on people's behaviour. It is less well known that approximately 80 per cent of people's behaviour is determined entirely by situational factors. This can be illustrated by a confident, dominant person's behaviour during a selection process at an assessment centre. During leaderless group discussion exercises, where each candidate's leadership potential was being assessed, one person was extremely forceful to the extent that he completely dominated the proceedings. Conversely, during the selection interview the person was quiet and deferential as he deferred to the interviewer's persistent questioning. Thus, the two different situations faced by the candidate altered the person's behaviour – in the leaderless group discussion, his disposition to dominate was allowed free rein, whereas the power relationships between the selector and candidate completely restrained the candidate's dominating behaviour. Importantly, a person's behaviour can also alter a situation. An extreme example might be that of the collapse of Barings, the British merchant bank brought about by Nick Leeson's fraudulent behaviour in the Tokyo stock markets in the mid-1990s. The types of situational factors influencing people's behaviour in the workplace are:

■ other people;
■ the type of work a person does;
■ the presence and quality of the management control systems;
■ the effectiveness of organisational communication systems;
■ the types and effectiveness of various reward systems;
■ the working environment (e.g. office or factory);
■ the size of the organisation;
■ the prevailing organisational culture.

In normal circumstances the most important situational features at work tend to be other people. This was aptly illustrated in the famous 'Hawthorne' studies conducted in the Hawthorne plant of the Western Electric Company in Chicago (Roethlisberger and Dickson, 1939) (see also Chapters 14 and 20). In the bank wiring observation room the work groups had established an output 'norm' averaging 6000 units per day. This 'unofficial' production norm was enforced by various methods. Workers would give each other verbal warnings or resort to physical violence to prevent 'rate-busting' (producing too much) or 'chiselling' (producing too little). Another behavioural norm was that inspectors should not be officious or pull rank on the workers. One inspector who violated this norm was ostracised by all the workers and subjected to vindictive pranks until he requested a transfer to a different department. This example reinforces the point that the situation people find themselves in, their personal psychological qualities and their ongoing behaviour all reciprocally interact to determine the way that work is done. These reciprocal relationships are illustrated by the framework in Figure 12.1, which is derived from social learning theory (Bandura, 1986).

→ Chs 14 & 20

In this triadic framework, behaviour is a function of both person and situational variables. Behaviour also exerts a reciprocal influence on both situational and personal factors. The reciprocal impact of each element on the others does not always take place immediately. A change in any one element may take time to exert its reciprocal influence on the other two. For example, the impact of changing the design of a job (situational) may immediately affect people's work-related behaviour, but not positively influence their motivation for six months or more. It is unfortunate, but true, that many good workplace improvement efforts are abandoned because of unrealistic expectations of immediate results that do not materialise. When trying to motivate others, it is clear that a manager must take all three elements of this framework and the time factor into account if the effort is to be successful.

Person factors

The extent to which person or dispositional variables reciprocally determine behaviour in organisations is illustrated with the psychological concept of **job**

Figure 12.1 Bandura's model of reciprocal determinism

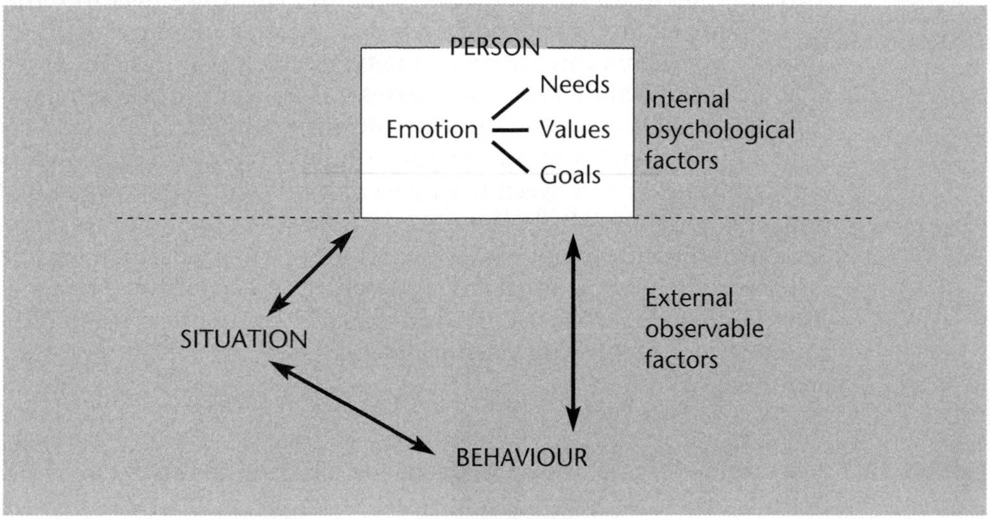

Source: Adapted from A Bandura (1986) *Social Foundations of Thought and Action: A Social Cognitive Theory*, pp. 22–5. Copyright © 1986 by permission of Pearson Education, Inc. Upper Saddle River, New Jersey.

satisfaction. This is an all-embracing concept that refers to job-related attitudes about various job-related characteristics, such as pay and reward policies, leadership behaviours, management styles, co-workers, etc. Attitudes about these factors are important because they are frequently the precursor of employee turnover. By way of example, Jenkins (1993) studied power plant workers and found that people's disposition to self-monitor their performance predicted their intention to quit. Job satisfaction predicted the turnover of those high in self-monitoring, whereas organisational commitment predicted the turnover intentions of those low in self-monitoring behaviour. Much of the research on job satisfaction has been concerned with showing the influence of situational and dispositional factors (see Warr, 1996). The work of Boudreau *et al.* (2001) provides a good example of this. They examined the role of personality and cognitive ability on the job search process of almost 1900 high-level US business executives. Situational variables used in the study were organisational success (whether or not the company achieved its strategic goals), salary levels and tenure (length of time in job). They discovered that extroverted individuals (disposition) experienced greater job satisfaction. However, in companies that had been successful in reaching their strategic goals over the previous two years (situational) these same people were more likely to search for new jobs. It was also found that cognitive ability was related to both salary and greater job search, suggesting that organisations need to recognise higher intelligence through greater compensation packages and letting these people know they are highly valued if they want to keep them. The case study outlined in Exhibit 12.1 further demonstrates how dispositional and situational factors might interact to affect performance.

Interested in job satisfaction, Arvey *et al.* (1989) provided other evidence to support the stability of personal qualities. This study involved the use of 34 pairs of twins reared apart from an early age. The results indicated that there is a significant genetic component to job satisfaction, as far as people inherit a tendency to view the world in an emotionally negative or positive way. Those who view the world in an emotionally negative way are less likely to be satisfied in their jobs than those who interpret events in a more positive way. This spills over into the way we view our working environment and affects our attitudes and motivation towards our job or work, and may even influence the type of work an individual seeks and finds. Evidence provided by Levin and Stokes (1989) confirms these relationships. They conducted a laboratory study with 140 subjects and a field study with 315 staff from a professional services company. In both studies, the results showed a small but significant link between negative emotions and job satisfaction. However, the presence of certain job characteristics exerted the largest effects on job satisfaction demonstrating that a motivating environment will exert much larger effects on performance than dispositional factors. Orpen (1994) confirmed this proposition with 135 employees from three financial services companies. He found that a lack of autonomy for highly motivated people adversely affected both job satisfaction and performance.

Exhibit 12.1 Interacting effects of dispositional and situational factors

Mount *et al.* (1998) investigated the relationship between people's disposition and jobs involving interpersonal interactions in the workplace. The study was based on the changing needs in the workplace where more jobs are becoming service-oriented rather than manufacturing-based, and on the drive in manufacturing towards teamworking. In both situations interpersonal skills are important to effective job performance: service-oriented settings typically involve an employee engaging in one-on-one interactions with customers and clients. The primary interactions in manufacturing are among co-workers in cooperative team-based situations.

The investigators analysed 11 studies that made use of the personal characteristics inventory (PCI), which utilises the 'big-five' factor model of personality and measures the constructs of:

- **conscientiousness** (e.g. responsible, dependable, persistent and achievement-oriented);
- **extraversion** (e.g. sociable, talkative and assertive);
- **emotional stability** (e.g. calm, secure and relaxed);
- **openness to experience** (e.g. imaginative, artistically sensitive and intellectual);
- **agreeableness** (e.g. good-natured, cooperative and trusting).

The jobs involved in the 11 studies ranged from counsellors, telemarketers and customer service representatives to teams of people involved in warehouse operations, production and delivery. The job performance of these people was rated by their own managers on two dimensions: overall job performance and the quality of interactions with others.

The initial analyses for all 11 studies indicated that the conscientiousness personality construct positively correlated with the job performance ratings in both service and manufacturing environments. This finding is consistent with much previous research that finds it a useful measure for predicting overall job performance in a variety of settings. When the 11 studies were analysed by service orientation or teamworking using the quality of interaction job ratings, it became apparent that emotional stability and agreeableness predicted job performance in teamworking. Conscientiousness and agreeableness predicted the job performance of those in service-oriented environments.

These results indicate that the type of work setting (one-on-one versus teams) interacts with people's disposition (personality) reciprocally to determine their job performance.

Source: K M Mount, M R Barrick and G L Stewart (1998) 'Five-factor model of personality and performance in jobs involving interpersonal interactions', *Human Performance*, 11, pp. 145–65.

Situational factors

Clegg and Wall (1990) demonstrated the influence of situational factors on behaviour and job-related attitudes in a British electronics factory. They showed that people's mental health was directly associated with the complexity of people's jobs – simple jobs were associated with poor mental health and highly complex jobs were associated with better mental health. Initial results suggested small differences between the two levels of mental health. When dispositional factors were considered, the differences became much larger. Those with lower levels of skill use, in a simple job, engaged in frequent daydreaming and consistently exhibited poorer levels of mental health. In contrast, those individuals who did complex jobs using a wider range of skills had much better levels of mental health. This study and others demonstrate the complexity of the interactions between person and situational factors. For example, Kohn and Schooler (1982) examined the relationship between disposition and choice of occupation. People who could view problems from many perspectives were attracted to jobs where they could use their intellectual skills. In turn, their intellectual skills improved because of the kind of work they were doing. The more these skills improved the more they tended to seek out even more intellectually demanding jobs. Similarly, Boswell *et al.* (2003) examined the organisational and job attributes important to job choice and the impact of situational features on graduate job-seekers' decisions. They found that company culture, challenging work, compensation package and geographical location influenced both accept and reject decisions. Advancement opportunities were also important to those who accepted, but not important to those who rejected, job offers.

The above demonstrates how person and situational variables interact to affect motivation, performance and other work-related behaviour. It makes sense, therefore, to ensure the compatibility of job demands with people's skills and abilities. The results of seven case studies (shown in Table 12.1) conducted by Caldwell and O'Reilly (1990) in a variety of organisations showed that where the person and the situation were well matched in terms of skills, abilities, job demands and so forth

Table 12.1 The effects of matching people to jobs

ORGANISATION	JOB	CORRELATIONS OF PERSON–JOB FIT WITH JOB PERFORMANCE
Consumer products	Production supervisors	0.98
Insurance company	Claims adjustment supervisors	0.60
Utility company	Senior finance managers	0.53
	Senior engineering managers	0.65
Computer manufacturers	Production supervisors	0.85
Computer distributor	Sales representatives	0.35
University	Departmental secretaries	0.53

Source: Caldwell and O'Reilly (1990) 'Measuring person-job fit with a profile-comparison process', *Journal of Applied Psychology*, 75, 648–57, American Psychological Association.

then motivation, performance and job satisfaction were also high. Conversely, work by Stadler (1994) and Balliod and Semner (1994) in a two-year study of turnover among computer specialists showed that where person–job fit was low, organisational commitment and job satisfaction were also low. In all instances, leaving was preceded by low job satisfaction. Only when changes in job design led to an improvement in job satisfaction did people stay with the organisation. Such findings are reinforced by work conducted in Australia, with accountants, bankers, occupational therapists and call-centre staff (BrKich *et al.*, 2002). They found that job fit was predictive of both job satisfaction and organisational commitment. This body of work demonstrates that job fit has a very strong impact on people's motivation and performance. Within everyday practical constraints, therefore, managers should do their best to ensure that the demands of a job match a person's skills and ability. Organisational change initiatives that introduce team working often provide such opportunities.

MOTIVATION THEORIES

Theories of motivation have been the subject of much debate since the early 1940s, and chronologically have broadly focused on:

- **genetic and hereditary factors** – e.g. **Maslow's hierarchy** of relative prepotency;
- **people's needs, personality and interests** – e.g. McClelland's managerial needs theory;
- **organisational justice and fairness** – e.g. Adams' equity theory;
- **incentives and rewards** – e.g. Vroom's expectancy theory;
- **behavioural change** – e.g. Luthans and Kreitner's organisational behaviour management;
- **the design of people's jobs** – e.g. Hackman and Oldham's job characteristics model;
- **setting targets** – e.g. Locke and Latham's goal-setting theory;
- **role modelling and self-efficacy** – e.g. Bandura's social learning theory.

Early work on motivation theory attempted to address the question of whether work motivation can make a difference to work performance or not. By the mid-1980s development work had shifted the emphasis to a more practical viewpoint by attempting to discover *how* the various factors of the different theories affect people's motivation and subsequent task performance. This focus on the more practical aspects led to each theory's effectiveness being assessed in terms of its usefulness to managers and practitioners. Such evaluations consistently rated behaviour management and goal-setting theory as the two most valid and effective work motivation theories, closely followed by expectancy theory, social learning theory and equity theory suggesting that positive reinforcements, goals, expectancies, social learning, participation and enriched jobs are the main factors that *actually* motivate people to perform well (Pinder, 1984).

In line with the triadic framework (Figure 12.1), the following addresses the major work-based motivation theories from two perspectives – from dispositional motivation theories and from situational motivation theories. Although none of them completely explains motivation, each serves to provide different, but complementary, routes to improve performance.

Dispositional motivation theories

Theories focused on dispositional factors are either **content** or **process** theories. Content theories concentrate on *what* motivates people by attempting to develop an understanding of fundamental human needs. Conversely, process theories concentrate on *how* motivation is aroused and maintained.

Content theories

Maslow's 'hierarchy of relative prepotency'

Abraham Maslow, an American psychologist, attempted the first classification of human needs to explain how people's motivation changes over time. As shown in Figure 12.2, Maslow (1942) asserts that human needs can be classified into motivating factors that influence people's behaviour at various stages of their lives. He described this as '**a hierarchy of relative prepotency**' but it is more often termed the 'hierarchy of needs'. In essence Maslow postulates that people have five basic needs and that their growth as people depends on satisfying each of them in sequential order. In order of importance these needs are:

1 **To be fed, clothed and sheltered** – basic physiological needs.
2 **To feel safe from threats** – safety and security needs.
3 **To be accepted by other people** – social needs.
4 **To feel valued by self and others** – self-esteem needs.
5 **To be self-fulfilled or successful** – self-actualisation needs.

Although it is a useful way of describing various types of motivator, the 'hierarchy of needs' is weak in several respects for workplace motivation.

■ **The five needs are not uniformly motivating** – at any given moment different people are likely to be striving to fulfil different need levels. This presents a problem for managers in that if each worker has a different hierarchy of needs then how does a manager provide motivators for all staff?

Figure 12.2 Maslow's hierarchy of relative prepotency

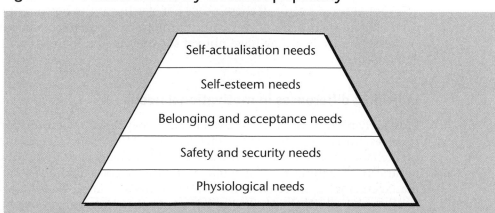

Source: A H Maslow (1942) 'A theory of human motivation', *Psychological Review*, 50, pp. 370–96.

■ **The model asserts that one motive should predominate at any one moment in time** – however, humans are more complex than this. For example, people work simultaneously to attain pay and rewards (security), social contact (belonging), status (self-esteem), etc.

■ **The hierarchy is difficult to relate to work processes** – people do not necessarily satisfy their higher-order needs through their jobs or occupations. Many prefer to satisfy their needs outside the workplace, for example through leisure activities.

■ **The hierarchy does not recognise situational factors** – the simplicity of the hierarchy does not reflect the reality that behaviour in the real world is shaped by situational pressures that are often beyond a person's individual control.

Hierarchical need theories propose that everyone's needs are organised in the same order, and that everybody strives for the same fundamental goals such as self-actualisation. Everyday experience suggests that people are more varied and complex than this and operate at many different motivational levels in these types of hierarchy. This can present many problems for employers as it is very difficult to satisfy all employees' needs simultaneously. Other problems reside in situational factors such as managerial policies and practices, an organisation's structure, the type of technology used and the external environment. Any motivational theory that proposes strong similarities between people can only lead to the conclusion that there is 'one best way' to manage and motivate others, which is simply not true.

Despite such problems, Maslow's theory remains popular with many human resource professionals, perhaps because it provides easy guidelines to follow. On this basis, managers should try to ensure that:

1 pay levels are commensurate with people's experience, skills, abilities and responsibilities so they can clothe, feed and house themselves comfortably;

2 the workplace is safe and there is a reasonable level of job security;

3 opportunities for socialisation are developed (e.g. teamworking) so people can interact with others;

4 people are recognised for their contribution to performance so they feel valued;

5 advancement opportunities are available to all.

Importantly, each of these increases people's work motivation. In practical terms, you should try to satisfy all these needs but starting at the bottom of the hierarchy first. After all there is not much point trying to motivate people by satisfying their 'self-esteem' needs if they have not yet satisfied the basic needs for food, clothes and housing.

Individual differences in motivational needs

Most early need theories were flawed because they failed to account for people's differences, an issue addressed by McClelland's (1961) 'managerial needs' theory. McClelland conducted research with over 500 managers from 25 different US corporations to determine just what motivates a good manager. He argues that managers possess three basic motivational needs – achievement, affiliation and power – each of which is linked to job satisfaction and competence in a number of occupations, particularly management (Medcof and Hausdorf, 1995).

Need for achievement

According to McClelland, the need for achievement (nAch), or the desire to do something better or more efficiently than before, is one of the keys to economic growth. Those high in nAch are people who prefer personal responsibility, positively enjoy competition, like to set, strive for and reach difficult goals, like to take calculated risks, like immediate short-term feedback on their performance and work hard until they attain excellence. Not surprisingly these people are often attracted to entrepreneurial roles. McClelland suggests that people high on this motive are likely to have grown up in environments that expected competence of them, gave them independence at an early age and evaluated them highly. People low on nAch are more satisfied when jobs involve little challenge but have a high probability of success.

A great deal of work on managers' achievement motivation show that companies whose executives have high achievement motivation produces better results. This is particularly true in an entrepreneurial rather than a bureaucratic organisation. For example, McClelland examined the motives of 51 technical entrepreneurs and calculated the growth rate of their companies in terms of the value of their sales. The growth rate of entrepreneur-led companies with high nAch was almost 250 per cent higher than companies led by entrepreneurs with moderate nAch. Other research (Cooper *et al.* 1994) reported that three of four studies found a positive relationship between nAch and the success of small enterprises.

Need for affiliation

During the course of his work, McClelland found that some major figures in industry did not score as highly on nAch as expected. He reasoned that a large part of working life in organisations was concerned with coordinating the activity of others, therefore the ability to relate to others was an important component of being a manager. He proposed that those who have this ability are high on need for affiliation (nAff), and that these people strive for approval from both their subordinates and superiors. Consequently, those high on nAff are sensitive to the needs of others. Such people are often found in people-oriented service jobs as opposed to managerial or administrative positions (Smither and Lindgren, 1978). It is suggested that there are two forms of nAff, one more managerially effective than the other.

The first, **affiliative assurance**, is best described as a striving for close relationships due to the perceived security that they provide. Such a person tends to look for continual approval and is anxious about possible rejection. In other words these managers want to be liked. They will expend a lot of energy on maintaining relationships at the expense of getting the job done. Generally speaking those high on affiliative assurance would rather hang on to team members than see them promoted, which may result in them showing favouritism towards some.

The second, **affiliative interest**, is best described as having care and concern for the feelings of others, but not at the expense of getting the job done. It is a concern for the legitimate needs and feelings of others while remaining focused on performance delivery, which is the type of affiliation that leads to greater organisational effectiveness.

Need for power

McClelland also discovered that good managers were high in interpersonal skills combined with a need to influence people for the good of the organisation by being in control of events, forcefully expressing opinions and being the leader. In other words these people had a greater need for power (nPow) than the need to achieve or need to be liked. A need for power, however, has both positive and negative aspects. The positive side shows itself as an interest in persuasion and interpersonal influence. The negative side shows itself as an unsocialised concern for personal dominance at the expense of others. The aspect that dominates is determined by the degree of self-control a manager possesses. Managers with a high degree of self-control will satisfy their need for power in socially acceptable ways via interpersonal influencing skills. These managers tend to be committed to organisational goals, want to serve others and, rather than dominate employees, they try to make them feel that they too have power. In contrast, managers who are more concerned with personal power show little sign of self-control and tend to exercise their power impulsively and in a haphazard manner. This inconsistency creates many difficulties for the manager's subordinates and can lead to major productivity problems.

Another important line of research arose from the work of McClelland – the leadership motive pattern. Achievement motivation is usually measured alongside the motives for power and for affiliation. McClelland noted that a certain pattern enabled people to be effective managers at the highest levels. For senior managers success tended to be associated with low levels of affiliation motive and a moderate to high need for power together with an ability to inhibit spontaneous impulses (i.e. good self-control). Lower-level managers' success was related to a combination of a high need for both power and achievement. Other researchers (see Exhibit 12.2) have found that those scoring highly on both nPow and nAch exhibited better managerial performance and a higher promotion rate than others. The opposite was true for those who scored low on these needs. As a whole, a manager's motivating potential appears to be predictive of effective managerial behaviour, which has obvious implications for personnel selection and placement practices (see Cooper *et al.*, 2003).

The importance of McClelland's work is the recognition that people have different needs. Although his findings are extremely useful for selection purposes, in line with other need theories, McClelland does not specify the motivational links between individual needs and actual performance. Indeed attempts to link nAch with performance have generally been unsuccessful. Matsui *et al.* (1982), for example, found nAch positively correlated with people's tendency to set goals, but nAch did not actually correlate with performance. Not surprisingly, the goals themselves were related to performance. Thus nAch appears to be indirectly related to performance, in that those high in nAch are likely to set goals. In turn it is the actual goals that affect performance (see the section on goal setting later in the chapter). This latter finding is confirmed in more recent work, using Alderfer's (1969) ERG needs theory which explored the link between existence, relatedness and growth needs, self-esteem and job performance in a South African study (Arnolds and Boshoff, 2002). Esteem and growth needs were clearly linked to performance intentions (goals). Self-esteem refers to the extent to which a person likes and views themself as a valuable and worthy member of society. Early work (Korman, 1970, 1976) suggested that those with high levels of self-esteem perform better than those with low self-esteem. Recent work appears to confirm this view. Judge and Bono (2001) meta-analytically reviewed the extant literature and found a significant relationship ($r = 0.26$) between self-esteem and job performance. This relationship was further tested with 124 insurance sales personnel by Erez and Judge (2001). They found self-esteem to be significantly correlated with sales volume, activity level, goal setting and goal commitment. However, the correlations were much larger for goal setting ($r = 0.33$) and goal commitment ($r = 0.49$). All self-esteem and nAch studies, therefore, indicate that those high in these attributes are more likely to set goals to increase their performance, and it is these goals that affect performance directly not the personal attributes *per se*. Instead, the personal attributes appear to affect the degree to which people commit themselves to goal achievement.

Such results indicate that managers should motivate others by setting a series of increasingly difficult task goals, in conjunction with the people concerned, to increase their commitment to achieving the goals. This will lead to much greater performance improvements over time. In turn, the more the person achieves a goal, the more the person will value themselves, which leads to higher levels of self-esteem and a higher commitment to achieving more difficult goals. The old adage 'success breeds success' is the underlying philosophy here. Other ways to increase self-esteem include managers communicating their confidence in the person's ability to achieve tasks (Rosenthal, 2002) and conducting 'self-esteem' workshops (e.g. Holstein, 1997). These can help employees to learn to think positively and conduct

→ Ch. 8 personal SWOT analyses (see Chapter 8) to identify their strengths and weaknesses with a view to identifying training needs so that they can take advantage of advancement opportunities and overcome any threats to career progression. Outward Bound courses are another approach known to increase self-esteem (Clements *et al.*, 1995).

Process theories

An alternative and complementary approach to understanding motivation lies in examining the psychological processes involved. Process theories acknowledge that:

- people have different competing needs;
- behaviour is a function of both the person and the situation;
- people are decision-making organisms;
- decisions are related to the link between behaviour and outcomes.

Exhibit 12.2 A test of McClelland's managerial needs model

Much of the early research on managerial motivation was conducted with the thematic apperception test (TAT), which involves people writing stories about a series of pictures. Unfortunately, this test was later found to be both unreliable and invalid. Because of these problems Stahl (1983) used the job choice exercise (JCE) to re-examine McClelland's concepts of managerial motivation. The JCE requires respondents to make 24 decisions about the attractiveness of jobs in motivational terms (i.e. nPow, nAch, nAff). In seven separate distributions the JCE was administered to a total of 1741 respondents including managers and shopfloor workers from a variety of industries, as well as students and air force cadets.

Examining the data in a number of different ways, Stahl showed that respondents who scored above 3.14 on nPow and 4.64 on nAch exhibited better levels of job performance, had a higher promotion rate than others and were more likely to be managers than shopfloor workers. The opposite was found for those with lower scores for nPow and nAch.

These findings supported the work of McClelland, who had asserted that 'power is the great motivator' for senior executives. Stahl, however, found that this also held for middle and junior managers. Thus McClelland's model of managerial needs appears to apply to all managerial levels.

Thus, as Figure 12.3 makes clear, process approaches recognise that there is a direct link between effort, performance and outcomes.

In essence, the process approach postulates that people only direct their efforts towards goals that they value. However, while the existence of a valued goal is a necessary condition for action, on its own it is not a sufficient condition – people will act only if there is a reasonable expectation that:

- their actions will lead to the desired goals;
- the benefits that flow from goal achievement are significant.

Expectancy theory

Vroom's (1964) **expectancy model theory** of motivation explicitly recognised the important role of these characteristics. The model states motivation is a function of the expectancy of reaching a certain outcome, multiplied by the value of the outcome for that person:

$$\text{motivation} = \text{expectancy} \times \text{value}$$

Vroom's theory predicts that outcomes with a high expectancy of achievement (e.g. sale of five cars a week) and highly valued rewards (e.g. extra commission) will direct people to exert much greater effort. Conversely, outcomes with high expectations (e.g. promotion) and neutral or even disliked consequences (e.g. working away from home) will reduce the amount of effort the person is prepared to invest, unless counterbalanced by highly valued rewards (e.g. increased pay, status and benefits). Similarly outcomes with relatively low expectancies of achievement (e.g. zero accidents on a construction site) and neutral valuations (e.g. no perceived personal benefits) will simply not influence people to perform. Expectancy theory is, therefore, hedonistic. People will only decide how much effort they are going to put into their work according to what they perceive they are going to get out of it and according to how much they value the potential outcomes.

More recent refinements (see Heckhausen *et al.* 1985 for an excellent review) have extended Vroom's original theory to include an instrumentality component based on a division of expectancy into two separate parts:

- the perceived probability of achieving the expected outcome;
- the perceived probability of actually being rewarded for achieving the expected outcome.

Instrumentality is concerned with the latter. The heart of the issue here is the extent to which good performance will actually be recognised and rewarded, and whether the rewards on offer adequately offset the costs and risks borne by an

Figure 12.3 **Expectancy theory relationships**

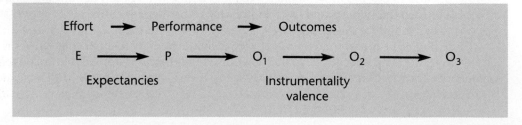

employee. For example, many initial positions offered to MBA graduates carry a low salary but possess greater opportunities for rapid advancement. Similarly, many positions offer very attractive salaries but little opportunity for advancement. A graduate offered both is likely to choose between them based on his or her perceptions that the likelihood of rapid advancement, with corresponding increases in compensation, is a reality. These refined versions are known as 'VIE models', where:

- **Expectancy** concerns the perceived relationship between the amount of people's effort and expected levels of performance. The question is 'Does greater effort lead to better performance?' Of extreme importance is not the actual relationship between effort and performance, rather it is what people believe. People must believe they can control job performance – if they do not then they will see no point in trying harder. Thus, the precise behaviours and outcomes constituting good levels of performance must be clear.

- **Instrumentality** refers to the perceived performance and outcomes relationship in terms of rewards and punishments. An important feedback loop is the probability of increased effort leading to increased reward (e.g. pay). Even if people conclude that greater effort on their part leads to better performance, if it does not lead to some valued and tangible reward this effort will not be sustained.

- **Valence** concerns the attractiveness of the rewards on offer. This aspect of the theory explicitly recognises that there are significant differences between people in terms of the outcomes they find attractive. If the rewards on offer are not highly valued, people may ask, 'Why bother?' The motivating potential of a reward, therefore, depends solely on the value a person places on it. If a reward (e.g. promotion) is highly valued then motivation is likely to be high. Conversely if a reward (e.g. promotion) is not valued then motivation is likely to be low. The notion of fairness may also enter employees' minds to the extent they will have a view of the level and kinds of reward that ought to be available for performing a particular type of work. The issue of equity (Adams, 1965) also enters into the way rewards are distributed in relation to performance and to any deprivations people may suffer in carrying out their work, such as working on a night shift. When people believe they are not receiving rewards (e.g. pay) commensurate with their experience, ability or effort then they work less hard (Hauenstein and Lord, 1989), become more selfish (Harder, 1992) and become dissatisfied with their jobs (Carr *et al.*, 1996). The important point here is that inequitable rewards lead to dissatisfaction, which weakens their motivating power.

Expectancy theory is useful as a means of identifying which rewards employees value for particular courses of action, rather than a means of translating motivation into performance. As such it shows that a person's level of performance varies in direct proportion to their need for achievement and anticipated satisfaction with any rewards offered. Although this sounds little more than common sense, it does draw attention to certain requirements for directing motivation, frequently neglected in practice. For example, managers should try to ensure that an employee's personal goals match those of the organisation by closer matching of the person to the job via effective personnel selection and human resources practices (see Cooper *et al.*, 2003). Similarly, managers must provide feedback in one form or another (e.g. praise) to employees so their efforts are seen to be acknowledged or rewarded. Other important implications for managers and organisations are listed in Exhibit 12.3.

Goal-setting theory

Goal-setting theory is one approach that successfully incorporates the notions of expectancy theory and many others besides. Inevitably, all attempts to motivate performance in the workplace include targets or goals in some form or other (e.g. vision statements, deadlines, etc.). First proposed by Ed Locke, an American psychologist, in 1968, at present goal setting is one of the most influential theories of work motivation applicable to all cultures. Numerous studies have established the influence that goal setting exerts on task performance. This research has repeatedly shown that specific goals, related to specific task requirements and accepted by employees, can control and improve virtually any type of measurable action (Locke and Latham, 2002). Indeed, Pinder (1984) stated:

> *'Goal-setting theory has demonstrated more scientific validity to date than any other theory or approach to motivation.'*

Core findings

Derived from both industry and academia, the central notion of goal setting is specific – difficult goals are the immediate, though not only, precursors of human action. Ninety per cent of all studies show a beneficial effect of goal setting on performance (e.g. Locke *et al.*, 1981). The core findings of this vast body of research show that:

- difficult goals lead to higher performance than moderate or easy goals;
- specific, difficult goals lead to higher performance than vague, broad goals or 'do your best' goals;
- feedback about goal-directed behaviour is absolutely necessary for goal setting to work;
- people need to be committed to achieving the goals.

Clearly the main aim of a goal is to place sufficient demands on people to motivate them to achieve higher levels of performance. However, on its own a goal is insufficient to motivate people. People must also be committed to goal achievement and be able to track their progress. The acronym SMART (Specific, Measurable, Attainable, Realistic and Time-bound) reflects such findings. By their very nature, specific and difficult but attainable goals affect performance by:

- presenting challenges that focus people's attention and actions on the specific task requirements leading to goal attainment;
- mobilising people's effort;
- boosting people's commitment to try harder and persevere until the goals are achieved;
- motivating people to search for the optimum performance strategy.

Specific goals

Specific goals remove any doubt about what is expected, enabling people to focus their attention solely on the activities specified. A goal-setting study conducted in a British manufacturing company demonstrated this effect (Cooper *et al.*, 1994). In an attempt to reduce accident rates, goals were set for specific unsafe behaviours in each of 14 departments. The results, illustrated in Figure 12.4, showed considerable reductions in accidents related to unsafe behaviours for which goals had been set. Conversely, accidents related to other safety behaviours, for which no goals had

conflicting goals. Indeed, a goal based on the minimum required is the typical choice, rather than the expected or ideal goal.

■ **Goal commitment** – how much people want to achieve a goal reflects their goal commitment. Commitment refers to a person's attachment to a goal, whether it is considered significant or important and how determined they are to reach it, even in the face of setbacks and obstacles. Acceptance of and commitment to goals are crucial factors in performance – as commitment declines, performance also declines (Erez and Zidon, 1984). Factors which enhance commitment fall into two broad categories: those convincing people that goal achievement is possible and important. Managers can play an important role in facilitating commitment to goals by persuading employees that the desired goals are both achievable and important. In addition, they should provide visible ongoing support. If they do not then the importance of the goal could be undermined resulting in goal rejection. Allowing and encouraging employees to participate in the goal-setting process improves commitment considerably. For many people, a goal set and delegated by others serves as a disincentive, which may lead to goal rejection. Some consistently argue that provided a goal is sufficiently difficult, delegated goals are as effective as participative goals for inducing high commitment and high performance (Locke *et al.*, 1988). A meta-analysis of the goal-setting literature revealed the potency of participative goals, rather than delegated goals, for improving a variety of task performances (Cooper, 1992). Tests of participative versus assigned goals in the UK construction industry by Cooper *et al.* (1992) found greater improved safety performance in the participation goal condition. Other meta-analyses confirm that participative goal setting positively influences goal commitment (Klein *et al.*, 1999).

Thus, the message from goal-setting theory is simple. A specific, challenging goal has maximum effect when:

■ the task is simple;

■ people have confidence in their ability to perform the task;

■ people are committed to the goal;

■ progress is measured;

■ regular accurate feedback is provided.

As these kinds of contingent factor make clear, goal-setting theory explicitly recognises the influence of person and situational variables. Illustrated in Figure 12.5, the reciprocal relationship between important goal-setting characteristics indicates how each might interact with and affect the others. For example, production goals will be affected by people's commitment to improving productivity, whether or not the production goals are in conflict with other organisational goals (e.g. productivity versus safety) and whether or not management is committed enough to provide the necessary support and resources for people to reach the goals (Cooper, 2006).

More recent applications of goal setting have developed the notion of **STRETCH targets** (Hamel and Prahalad, 1993), whereby completely unreasonable targets of such extreme difficulty are set that they appear absolutely impossible to achieve

→ Ch. 5

(see Chapter 5). The purpose of STRETCH is to completely revolutionise the way things are currently done. 'Thinking out of the box' or 'pushing the envelope' are commonly heard phrases encapsulating the thinking behind STRETCH targets. At first glance the notion of a STRETCH target appears diametrically opposed to the

Figure 12.5 Reciprocally determined model of goal setting

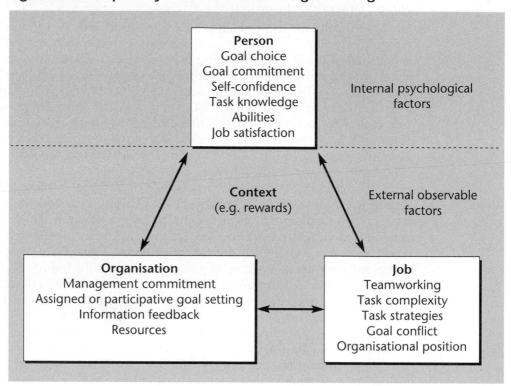

tenets of goal-setting theory, whereby an unattainable goal will reduce commitment and be rejected (Locke and Latham, 2002). In their exploration of goal-setting theory, Thompson *et al.* (1997) cite four successful STRETCH target case studies used to promote innovation, asset utilisation, reduced cycle times and performance improvements in the USA. In essence they concluded that goal-setting theory is correct. Situational factors account for the success of STRETCH in conjunction with a specific goal. STRETCH targets motivate if:

■ the change team is empowered and allowed to operate autonomously;

■ work structures (e.g. management systems) are changed to facilitate goal achievement;

■ the company fosters a culture of support and encouragement.

Changing jaded management practices and eliminating structural constraints determine the success of STRETCH targets. Rejuvenating demotivated workers to achieve STRETCH targets is dependent on this. Using STRETCH targets without considering situational aspects will lead to failure. This finding provides powerful evidence for the effectiveness of situational motivation theories.

SITUATIONAL MOTIVATION THEORIES

Behavioural psychologists, who take the view that situations direct and condition people's behaviour, provide extreme examples of the effects of situational influences. They propose that behaviour is a function of its contingent consequences –

reinforced behaviour will strengthen and continue. Behaviour that is punished, ignored or produces unimportant outcomes for the person will be less likely to occur. Thus, behaviourist approaches emphasise that people's behaviour is contingent on the types of reinforcement received.

The different types of consequences and their controlling effects on behaviour (shown in Figure 12.6) indicate that a positive reward strengthens and increases the probability of a person behaving in a particular way. In the workplace, for example, an employee praised by a manager for completing a difficult job within a certain deadline will be more likely to repeat that type of performance in the future. Conversely continuation of this type of good performance would extinguish were the employee's performance ignored. Similarly, avoiding a negative consequence can also strengthen the way people behave. For example, removing an aspect of a job that an employee dislikes (e.g. sitting on a committee) due to that person's good job performance would also reinforce that employee's behaviour. Punishing consequences, on the other hand, are purported to stop or decrease certain behaviours. For example, issuing a written warning to an employee for persistent lateness is a punisher meant to stop this type of behaviour. However, the influence of punishment and rewards on behaviour differs considerably. To be effective, a punisher has to fulfil two conditions – it mst be given immediately, and every single time the unwanted behaviour(s) occurs. For example, one reason why people continue to break the speed limit when driving is due to a lack of instant punishment every time they breach the limit. Similar factors operate in the workplace. If someone breaches rules and procedures and behaves incorrectly then more often than not co-workers and managers ignore it. Most times nothing bad happens. The lack of any punishing consequence teaches people that it is alright to behave incorrectly. Indeed, many undesired behaviours receive reinforcement in some way, perhaps from the time saved by taking a short cut, or making the job easier in some way. In contrast to punishers, positive reinforcement should be given every so often. Initially, give a positive consequence as soon as possible after the desired behaviour. To ensure that employees are clear about the linkages between the desired behaviour(s) and the positive consequence, give it only when the desired behaviour has actually occurred. Once established in the employee's repertoire, reduce the frequency of reinforcement (e.g. praise) over time. Many workplace incentive

Figure 12.6 Different reinforcers and their controlling effects on behaviour

Consequences		Effect on preceding behaviour
Positive reinforcement	'It's nice when it happens'	*Increase*
Negative reinforcement	'It's nice when taken away'	*Increase*
Punishment	'It's nasty when it happens'	*Decrease*
Extinction	'Nothing happens'	*Decrease*

programmes do not produce the desired result simply because the linkage between the desired behaviour and incentive (positive consequence) is not clear. Rather, managers give incentives for the outcomes of behaviour, not the actual behaviour. Recent research has shown that extremely high-performing companies habitually use praise and recognition to acknowledge desired behaviour (Townsend, 2001). Focusing solely on behaviour, this approach does not make use of any underlying psychological processes such as motivation or personality. Nonetheless, it successfully influences behaviour in a variety of work settings.

Organisational behaviour management

The behavioural approach outlined in the previous section is referred to as organisational behaviour management (OBM) when used in a strategic planned way. OBM has successfully improved a variety of work-related performances including absenteeism, productivity and quality in a variety of settings (Andrasik *et al.*, 1981; Stajkovic and Luthans, 1997). Key features of OBM, which significantly add to its success as a motivational technique, are:

■ its focus on current rather than past determinants of behaviour;

■ its emphasis on overt behaviour change as the measure for evaluating its effects;

■ its careful choice of the specific behaviours to be targeted;

■ its structured use of appropriate metrics to measure performance;

■ its use of reinforcers.

At the theoretical level behaviourist terminology describes the flow of these procedures as antecedents–behaviour–consequents (ABC model). **Antecedents** are described as 'controlling stimuli' that trigger or elicit observable behaviours (e.g. rules and procedures). **Consequents** are any events that follow as a direct result of the behaviour, and as such are described as reinforcers or punishers. For example, the ringing tone of a telephone would be described as an antecedent when it signals someone to pick up (behaviour) the handset to speak (consequent) with the caller. Speaking to the caller reinforces the behaviour of answering the phone. Although some might think the antecedent (e.g. ringing tone) is the most important aspect of determining behaviour, the consequent (e.g. speaking to the caller) has the most powerful influence. For example, if the phone rang repeatedly and nobody spoke each time it rang then it would not take long before people ignored the ringing phone. Using the ABC model allows managers to discover which antecedents and consequents are controlling which behaviours. When identified these are changed, so the target behaviours also change to what is desired (see Exhibit 12.4).

Antecedents

Managerial attempts to change employee behaviour often fail in practice because they focus almost exclusively on the antecedents of behaviour (e.g. rules, procedures, etc.) instead of the consequents (e.g. acknowledgment for good performance). Antecedents come *before* behaviour. They signal what is expected of people and largely communicate what the consequence(s) of fulfilling the expectations are likely to be. Although antecedents can influence behaviour on their own, they work much better when specifically paired with a consequence (e.g. Ray *et al.*, 1997). The factors known to increase the effectiveness of antecedents include:

Exhibit 12.4 Rearranging consequents

A psychology student working in a drugstore to pay her way through an American college noticed that some people completed their jobs faster than others. She examined the antecedents and consequences of each person's behaviour. She believed those people who worked faster rewarded themselves by doing a job they liked after completing a job they disliked (Situation A), and those who took longer did the nice job first followed by the job they disliked (Situation B). To test her theory, she observed the average length of time taken to complete certain tasks. The average timings for the different types of task were as follows:

TASK	AVERAGE TIMINGS IN MINUTES	
	Situation A	*Situation B*
Restock sweet shelves	20	35
Restock cigarette shelves	5	15
Vacuum floor	5	15
Dump rubbish	5	10
Clean store	45	90
Check in deliveries	30	60
Help pharmacist	50	60
Deliver orders	50	60
Totals	210	345

The average timings for each factor were found to be very different. Those rewarding themselves with a nice job after what was seen as a nasty job took 40 per cent less time than those people doing the nice job first followed by a nasty job. This effect is termed the 'Premack principle', after a researcher who had observed the same phenomenon in animals. With this principle it is possible for managers to identify tasks employees see as nice or nasty, and change the situation by rescheduling work so a nice job always follows a nasty job. In this way, a manager can easily rearrange the consequents of employees' behaviour without the use of incentives or other inducements, and increase production.

Source: R M O'Brien, A M Dickson and M P Rosow (eds) (1982) *Industrial Behavior Modification: A Learning-based Approach to Industrial Organizational Problems*, New York: Pergamon Press. Permission from Allyn and Bacon, © 1982 by Pearson Education.

- **Linkage** – explicitly link the antecedent to a consequence.
- **Timing** – the closer an antecedent is presented before the behaviour the more it will direct subsequent behaviour.
- **Specificity** – the more specific an instruction is, the more impact it will exert because it removes doubt about what is expected.
- **Importance** – the more important an antecedent is perceived to be, the more it will direct subsequent behaviour.

Increasing the managerial effectiveness of antecedents therefore requires that they are:

- important to achieve the desired behaviours;
- specific to the desired behaviours;
- explicitly linked with a consequence;
- presented immediately before the desired behaviours are performed.

Consequences

Consequences always come *after* behaviour. Importantly, behaviour may have more than one consequence *for an individual*. Some of these will also exert stronger reinforcing effects than others. For example, the consequences of finishing work early to attend a football match at Wembley may result in the person attending the match (positive) and seeing their team win (positive). Conversely they may have missed an important phone call that resulted in the loss of a sizeable sales order to another sales representative who did not leave early, which resulted in the loss of sales commission (negative). To a football fanatic, attending and experiencing the excitement of the match would provide a more positive consequence for leaving work early and outweigh the negative consequence of losing sales commission. This means that the next time this person's team played at Wembley they would probably leave work early again. A causal or neutral observer would most likely stay at work when other matches take place because the negative consequence of losing the sales commission would probably outweigh the positive consequence of watching the match. This scenario highlights the fact that the power of a consequence to influence behaviour is entirely dependent on whether or not the person values it (this accords with Vroom's (1964) expectancy theory). In practice this means that managers must not assume that other people will find a particular consequence as reinforcing as they might think. Some people find praise reinforcing, while others prefer awards, time off or money. Try to find out what each of your employees values.

Three features known to determine the strength of a consequent (reinforcer) are:

- **Timing** – the sooner a consequent follows behaviour, the more powerful it will be.
- **Consistency** –consequents certain to be received after behaviour are more powerful than uncertain consequents.
- **Significance** – positively valued consequents exert greater effects than negative (i.e. punishing) consequents.

So the more a manager can ensure that the consequents of behaviour are received immediately, are certain to be received and are seen as positive by the recipient then the more likely a desired behaviour will be repeated. Reid and Parsons (1996) demonstrated that employees prefer immediate feedback, indicating that feedback is an effective reinforcer that does not cost money. Consequents that are late, uncertain and negative will have little, if any, effect on behaviour. For example, an employee may never follow certain quality procedures (antecedent) because he or she is consistently (certain) rewarded by an immediate (soon) timesaving and extra production (positive) for non-compliance. To ensure that employees follow the correct procedures a manager must ensure that the consequents of following the correct procedures outweigh the consequents of not doing so (see Cooper, 1998). Because social rewards are one of the most powerful consequents known, a manager might try to address this problem by harnessing peer pressure and giving immediate positive feedback (e.g. praise) to those who behave in the desired manner. In some cases, organisations reinforce the very behaviours they are trying to eliminate.

Attempting to save money by reclaiming surpluses from annual departmental budgets and reducing the following year's budget allocation is a classic example. In these circumstances the organisation is rewarding managers who spend up to the budget limit, while simultaneously punishing thrifty managers! Allowing departmental managers to keep a certain percentage of budget savings for other work-related uses (e.g. updating computer equipment) is more likely to result in across-the-board savings. Exhibit 12.5 outlines how an OBM intervention reduced the number of MRSA cases in two intensive care units of a british health trust.

Recent innovations

Primarily due to the work of Bandura (1977) recent OBM applications have begun to incorporate the notion of social learning theory (SLT), whereby person, situational and behavioural variables reciprocally interact to determine people's behaviour. SLT incorporates many key notions, such as role modelling and self-efficacy, each of which may interact with each other.

Role modelling

There are numerous opportunities in the workplace for colleagues to observe, learn from and influence each other's behaviour at work. This is a powerful motivational technique for influencing behaviour and is called '**role modelling**'. Rakestraw and

Exhibit 12.5 Reducing MRSA cases with OBM techniques

A large hospital trust in the north of England was trying to reduce the number of cases of avoidable hospital aquired infections (HAI), particularly methicillin-resisitant *Staphylococcus aureus* (MRSA) in line with government targets. Two intensive care units agreed to pilot an OBM approach, in addition to conventional approaches such as patient screening and isolation, staff training and the development of improved policies and procedures.

A coordinator drawn from within the unit was trained in OBM principles to run the project on a daily basis. The clinical matron and senior unit managers assisted as project champions. After the training, frontline staff and line management came together to brainstorm and identify areas of concern. The unit as a whole agreed to target nursing documentation, patient charting and hand-washing behaviours. The unit coordinator developed a behavioural checklist to cover these topics that was agreed upon by all concerned. Trained health care assistants monitored these behaviours in the units for just 20 minutes per shift, at random times in each shift. Unit staff set improvement targets on the basis of the first week's observation results. Over the next 25-week intervention period, the observation data were analysed each week and summarised. This summary was used to give weekly feedback about progress to all unit staff at group meetings. Staff were involved in all aspects of the process including checklist development, observations, goal setting and regular performance feedback.

Compared to the pre-intervention rates, the targeted behaviours improved by 15 per cent with statistically significant reductions in MRSA of approximately 70 per cent over the next six months. Financial benefits included extra ICU bed capacity, reducing screening and laboratory costs, reduced eradication costs, lower overtime and agency staff costs, and reduced litigation liabilities.

This study demonstrated that OBM techniques, in conjunction with goal setting and feedback, can significantly improve performance in a medical environment at a relatively low cost.

Source: M D Cooper, K Farmery, M Johnson, C Harper, F L Clarke, P Holton, S Wilson, P Rayson and H Bence (2005) 'Changing personnel behaviour to improve quality care practices in an intensive care unit', *Therapeutics and Clinical Risk Management*, 1 (4), pp. 321–32.

Weiss (1981) showed that people who watch a high-performing role model (e.g. a trainee salesperson watching a company's top salesperson) imitate the role model's behaviour until thoroughly learnt. As the trainee gains experience he or she becomes more confident and more motivated to perform at a much higher level. Ultimately the trainee will perform better than the role model (the old adage 'the pupil becomes the teacher of the master' illustrates the principle here). Typically, we all engage in role-modelling behaviour in our first few days in a new company or workplace as we try to fit in – for example, by looking at the way people dress or the timing of rest breaks. This type of behaviour is common when someone is unsure how to behave in a certain situation. Usually we choose to model someone who is similar to us, is thought to be successful and to have status. Some forward-looking companies recognise this and provide mentors who take a special interest in new employees and guide them through the labyrinth of organisational life. While some research suggests that informal mentoring relationships are better than formal ones (Ragins and Cotton, 1999) it is important to ensure the mentor–employee fit is carefully examined (Mendelson et al., 1989). The better the relationship between mentors and mentees in a formal mentoring programme, the more mentees are motivated to work hard and be committed to their organisation (Orpen, 1997). In the medical field Wright and Carrese (2002) found that the attributes required of mentors were good interpersonal skills, a positive outlook, a commitment to excellence, growth, integrity and leadership.

Self-efficacy

This is very close in meaning to the expectancy concept in expectancy theory, and is defined as:

> *'how well one can execute courses of action required to deal with prospective situations.'*
> (Bandura, 1982)

However, self-efficacy is broader in meaning as it encompasses individuals' estimates of their total capacity to perform in a given situation, and therefore reflects a person's degree of self-confidence in performing a particular task. Much research has demonstrated very strong links between self-efficacy and a wide variety of work-related performance (Robertson and Sadri, 1993; Sadri and Robertson, 1993). This has shown that the more confident people are in their abilities, the more likely they are to set high goals and be committed to them. In turn, this results in high levels of performance (e.g. Locke et al., 1984). Renn and Fedor (2001) demonstrated these effects with staff from a customer call-centre that provided nationwide sales and service support for several hundred automotive retail stores in the USA. About a year before the study was conducted the company had instituted a three-pronged performance improvement programme, focusing on training, management monitoring of employee performance which resulted in both quantity (sales per hour) and quality (20 service quality behaviours) performance ratings, and the public posting of a league table containing the employees' ratings (i.e. feedback). During the study 150 employees completed a survey asking about the employees' perceived control over events (e.g. their sales quantity and quality), their propensity to seek feedback about their ongoing performance, how often they actually sought feedback and how they used the feedback to set their own improvement goals, and their perceived self-efficacy in relation to their work. Each individual's responses were correlated with their managerial performance ratings. The results indicate that self-efficacy is strongly related to personal control, feedback-seeking behaviour and the setting of personal performance goals. In terms of performance, higher levels of self-efficacy were more strongly related to quantity of sales than quality performance ratings. In contrast to these findings, Nicholson *et al.* (2000) showed that City of London equity traders with average levels of confidence performed much better than those with very high levels of self-confidence, whose annual bonuses were approximately £100,000 lower.

Although recent innovations have included person factors, OBM basically represents the systematic and applied use of the idea that situations determine the strength and direction of behaviour (motivation). Changes in the situation will bring about changes in behaviour. For many people, however, the most important aspect of the situation is the nature of the job they are required to do. For example, many manufacturing jobs involve closely supervised, machine-paced, repetitive tasks. Other jobs involve a great degree of autonomy and variety of work (e.g. university lecturers). The way that such job characteristics influence people's work-related behaviour and motivation is important. However, addressing these issues purely from an OBM perspective is unlikely to be successful. It may also require job design changes.

Job characteristics

A large stream of research has shown that the design of jobs can have an enormous impact on motivation, behaviour, productivity and **job satisfaction** (see Wall and Martin, 1987) and absenteeism (Rentsch and Steel, 1998). Two main approaches attempt to optimise the redesign of jobs. The first step is concerned with broadening the scope of people's work to introduce greater task variety. This generally takes the form of **job enlargement** or **job rotation**. Job enlargement strategies combine two or more specialised jobs so that the worker is able to use a wider range of skills. Job rotation increases task variety by moving people at regular intervals between different jobs. However, research shows these types of job redesign are inadequate – partly because enlargement attempts mainly focus on horizontal changes at the same organisational levels, and partly because simply adding two boring, repetitive, mundane-type jobs, or rotating people between them, is neither satisfying nor motivating. As succinctly pointed out by Herzberg *et al.* (1959):

> *'Adding one Mickey Mouse job to another Mickey Mouse job, adds up to an enlarged Mickey Mouse job.'*

Campion and McClelland (1993) provided support for this notion by showing that people's job satisfaction increases when they are allowed to make complex decisions, but decreases when more tasks of the same difficulty are simply added to enlarge a person's job. Recognition of such problems led to **job enrichment** schemes in attempts to make jobs more challenging rather than just more of the same. Job enrichment schemes add discretion and responsibility by vertically expanding the scope of a job while also providing some degree of autonomy.

Regarded as one of the most comprehensive frameworks for job redesign, Hackman and Oldham's (1975, 1976, 1980) job characteristics model (JCM) attempts to link the situational characteristics of a job with motivation. Maloney and McFillan (1995) provided a good example of this when they called for fundamental changes in the way the construction industry designs people's jobs to improve performance. As illustrated in Figure 12.7, the JCM suggests five job characteristics are important as they determine various aspects of employees' attitudes and behaviour.

According to the model, the design of a highly motivating job incorporates a high degree of several factors:

■ **Skill variety** – the degree to which a job incorporates a number of different activities and skills.

■ **Task identity** – the degree to which a whole piece of work is completed, rather than part of it.

■ **Task significance** – the extent to which a job exerts a substantial influence on the lives or work of others.

■ **Autonomy** – the extent of freedom and independence to make decisions.

■ **Feedback** – the extent to which feedback is provided about ongoing performance.

The theory proposes that skill variety, task identity and significance collectively influence the **experienced meaningfulness** (EM) of the work. Somebody low in EM is not likely to care much about the job and will therefore be less motivated to produce quality products or services. Similarly autonomy affects an employee's **experienced responsibility** (ER) – the extent to which people feel personal responsibility for the outcomes. For example, a finance director with high ER will be concerned to deliver a quality service to suppliers by personally ensuring that staff promptly process and pay invoices by the due date. Based on the notion of personal reward or reinforcement, feedback provides ongoing personal knowledge of how someone is performing. These characteristics are motivating only if people feel they are personally responsible for producing something worthwhile that they care about. In essence, the JCM posits the notion that more satisfying or motivating jobs are generally more productive.

Figure 12.7 Job characteristics model

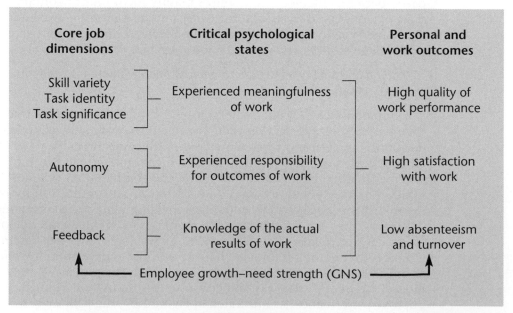

Source: Adapted from J R Hackman and G R Oldham (1975) 'Development of the job diagnostic survey', *Journal of Applied Psychology*, 60, pp. 159–70. Copyright © 1975 by the American Psychological Association.

Research shows that the model applies best to people with a strong need to grow and develop through the kind of work they do. For these kinds of people, improvements in the five core job characteristics will likely lead to greater productivity. However, people low in **growth–need strength** (GNS) are less likely to respond to such changes, perhaps because they do not feel they can cope with more complex demands.

Figure 12.8 shows some ideas for using JCM for job redesign to influence each of the five core job dimensions. Building on earlier models of job design, Hackman and Oldham (1975) suggest combining tasks to enhance both skill variety and task identity. Forming natural work groups could enhance task identity. Modern examples include quality circles or interdepartmental project teams within a matrix type organisational design (see Robertson *et al.*, 1992). Establishing client relations addresses people's social needs and enhances skill variety, the degree of autonomy, and provides opportunities for performance feedback. TQM organisations embracing the notion of internal markets provide many opportunities to establish client relations for jobs where this has previously been very difficult. Vertical loading, similar to job enrichment schemes, enhances people's autonomy as responsibility cascades down the organisation enabling people to make their own decisions. Indeed this is one of the central features of TQM systems, which advocates giving people responsibility and authority for identifying and solving quality problems. This reasoning is supported in a study by Kini and Hobson (2002) who found that empowerment (autonomy) of work teams positively impacted on TQM, in conjunction with clear expectations (goals) and performance monitoring (feedback).

Multiple feedback and/or communication channels assist people to monitor their performance so they can assess how well they are doing. As such, feedback fulfils many functions, not least of which is its motivational function. Exhibit 12.6 presents an example application of JCM in a British food manufacturing company.

Roe *et al.* (2000) integrated both Maslow's hierarchy of needs and Hackman and Oldham's JCM into a general model of work motivation (see Figure 12.9). The model postulates that situational characteristics lead to critical psychological states, which induce two main motivational factors – job involvement and organisational

Figure 12.8 Ideas for job enrichment

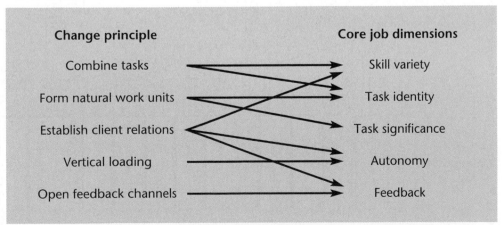

Figure 12.9 General model of work motivation

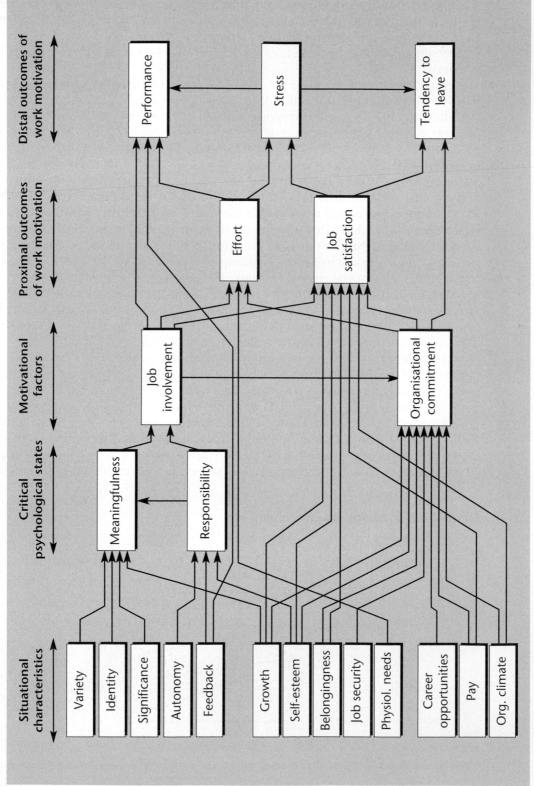

Source: Adapted from R A Roe, I L Zinovieva, E Dienes and L A Ten Horn (2000) 'A comparison of work motivation in Bulgaria, Hungary and The Netherlands: test of a model', *Applied Psychology: An International Review*, 49, pp. 658–87, Oxford: Blackwell Publishing Ltd.

commitment. In turn, these two factors lead to proximal motivational outcomes (effort and job satisfaction) both of which differentially affect levels of performance, stress and people's intention to leave the organisation. The model was tested with 565 Bulgarian, 614 Hungarian and 237 Dutch, blue-collar and white-collar workers. The model showed a remarkable degree of similarity across all three countries, although some differences related to the cultural context were also observed.

In practical terms, Roe's model indicates that incorporating Hackman and Oldams's five job characteristics into people's work will lead to greater job involvement. In turn this will stimulate greater effort, better job satisfaction, higher levels of organisational commitment and performance. On the other hand catering for Maslow's hierarchy of needs will induce organisational commitment and/or job satisfaction. Roe's model also indicates that effort is linked to performance and stress, while job satisfaction is linked to stress and an intention to leave the organisation. Thus people who find their jobs satisfying are likely to cope positively with levels of stress, which in turn enhances their performance. Conversely employees who are dissatisfied with their jobs are likely to experience debilitating levels of distress that increases their intention to leave. Interestingly feedback was the only situational characteristic directly linked to performance. This suggests that the provision of feedback is an absolute requirement for motivating people to perform.

Despite the claims made about the JCM *per se*, not all studies have succeeded in impacting either people's motivation or performance (see Boonzaier *et al.* 2001 for an excellent review of this literature). For example, Leach *et al.* (2003) showed that

Exhibit 12.6 The effects of job redesign

Kemp *et al.* (1983) redesigned jobs to introduce more variety and autonomy in a UK food manufacturing company. Employees in the existing jobs had little control over their work, and had little input to the decision-making process, as most decisions were made by the supervisors. The jobs were redesigned into semi-autonomous work groups consisting of 8–12 employees. Each group was allocated and was collectively responsible for eight different tasks within the production process. These tasks involved employees:

- allocating jobs among themselves;
- reaching performance targets and quality standards;
- recording production data;
- solving local production problems;
- ordering and collecting raw materials;
- delivering the finished product to the stores;
- selecting and training new recruits;
- managing their day-to-day activities.

Because the redesign process abolished the supervisory function, each of the teams reported directly to first-line managers.

Changes in the attitudes and behaviours of members of the redesigned jobs over a six-month period were compared to three control groups. Experimental groups reported an enhanced degree of autonomy and greater job satisfaction. Productivity also improved. A follow-up study two years later (Wall *et al.*, 1986) confirmed these findings.

Source: N J Kemp, T D Wall, C W Clegg and J L Cordery (1983) 'Autonomous work groups in a greenfield site: a comparative study', *Journal of Occupational Psychology*, 56, pp. 271–88.

empowerment could positively increase levels of job knowledge, although it does not always translate into either motivation or performance. Parker and Wall (1998) state that:

'it is not possible to redesign work successfully without considering the wider context.'

This timely reminder also accords with the work on STRETCH targets (Thompson *et al.*, 1997) and highlights that most applications of motivation theory cannot work without ensuring that the appropriate organisational support mechanisms are in place and functioning as intended.

SUMMARY

- One of the keys to effective work performance lies in an understanding of human motivation. This tour of motivation has examined the major theories and classified them according to person, behavioural and situational perspectives. Emphasising the links between disposition, behaviour, effort and the impact of situational constraints, this chapter has tried to make clear that there is no one best way to motivate others to maximise performance. Managers are well advised to use a combination of approaches best suiting the prevailing circumstances.

- Three elements common to all motivational approaches are goal setting, performance monitoring and feedback. Goal setting is the motivator for action, and performance monitoring is the means used to measure and evaluate performance to provide feedback, which in turn lets people know where they are in relation to the targets.

- The effectiveness of all motivation techniques are moderated by other factors such as individual differences in personality, confidence levels and ability, as well as the presence and quality of organisational support systems.

Review and discussion questions

1 *What are the practical implications of need theories?*

2 *How might you use expectancy theory to influence performance?*

3 *How would you apply goal setting to guarantee high performance?*

4 *How would you identify and use antecedents and consequents to motivate people to perform?*

5 *How should job redesign be approached to ensure that it motivates people to perform?*

CASE STUDY

RAC – rejuvenating employee motivation to increase customer satisfaction

The RAC employs approximately 4000 staff and is Britain's second largest motoring organisation, with around six million members. Their customer service centre at Bristol was moved from a city-centre location to a 'greenfield' site in 1995 and employed approximately 200 permanent staff. Union membership was less than 50 per cent and a number of competitor call centres had opened nearby. High overheads, inflexible working practices and new and existing competitors meant that the RAC came under increasing competitive pressures: they had lost three-quarters of a million customers in 1996. Membership retention was essential to long-term success, but customers increasingly made comparisons in terms of consistency, professionalism, responsiveness, accessibility and convenience. Service quality for existing and potential customers was seen as the key to achieving the group's business strategy of improving membership retention. External and internal audits showed that a serious lack of customer focus related to 240 external telephone numbers and 17 separate work groups dealing with different issues (e.g. sales, service, insurance and information). This often led to customers boarding a 'merry-go-round' and being passed from one part of the organisation to another, leading to poor membership retention.

The RAC set itself a series of objectives focused on the key aim of improving service quality and increasing customer satisfaction. The principal task was dealing with 80 per cent of calls at the first point of contact. The objectives were to develop a single call centre, change the call-centre culture by reviewing the management structure, modifying the reward and recognition system, and to increase flexibility by introducing multiskilling for staff. This meant, for example, that a new multiskilled position of customer adviser dealing with sales and service, replacing the old position of tele-administrator, was created for frontline staff. Customer advisers' performance was measured against minimum standards, which had to be met before a bonus was paid, using the following criteria:

- the number of calls per hour;
- the ratio of talk time to available time;
- an index of customer satisfaction;
- the rate at which calls were converted into sales;
- the average revenue for sales staff.

In addition to these quantitative measures, there were a number of quality standards such as close adherence to the scripted call structure and attendance. Other changes involved introducing a flatter and more integrated management structure with radically changed roles for team leaders. Team leaders had responsibility for ten to fifteen staff and were expected to spend around 80 per cent of their time with team members coaching, reviewing performance, providing feedback on individual and team performance and identifying training needs. Expectations of team leaders included leadership, building motivation and morale and introducing some 'fun' into the working environment by, for example, introducing spot prizes or raffles. Team leaders had to produce a daily report openly displaying performance measures for each employee in a format agreed by the team (feedback). Performance was averaged over the month and the standards of performance were perceived as clear and easy to understand. From March 1997 all the teams had names – such as 'The Untouchables' and 'The Pioneers' – which were chosen by the team members. The teams changed every year so team managers had new challenges and the teams themselves did not get stale.

Changes in HR practices led to high commitment management practices being adopted which reflected the demands of the external environment and customer expectations from an early stage in the establishment of the new site. For example, much of the responsibility for the day-to-day management of the recruitment process was devolved to line managers. The HR function trained and coached managers to select their own staff. An agreed recruitment procedure was used under the guidance and support of the HR function. The new call-centre structure necessitated a massive recruitment drive and involved the adoption of new and more sophisticated techniques, including radio advertising and telescreening, partly because of the need for cover and partly because of local labour market pressures. Traditionally the RAC employed many temporary staff in the call centre. The new philosophy was to reduce the reliance on temps and cut this down to a minimum for the summer peak period only (when around 30 per cent extra staff were employed on a temporary basis). Temporary staff received induction training and were expected to be skilled only in sales. Employed on less favourable terms and conditions than permanent staff, they were expected to abide by the new standards of performance. In the long term the aim was to have a pool of employees who varied their hours over the year, such as students who could work longer hours in the summer.

▶

The RAC recognised that training had been poor in the past and therefore established a new customer service training team. In addition, they developed new procedures to ensure that their customer advisers attained and retained the required performance standards to meet customer expectations. This included training for new products and computer systems carried out on the job during quiet times. This represented a change with the past, as the HR account manager noted, '*Traditionally you would see people reading a magazine when there was a break, even doing a bit of embroidery. But you wouldn't now – we are changing so much*'. Training for team managers was initially less adequate, partly because of the demands on their time made by their heavy workloads. Consequently they were slow to develop and foundered in their new roles. Once addressed with regular workshops, team managers' performance subsequently improved. Gradually the older, ineffective style changed, as one ex-supervisor explained: '*I was just managing the business not managing individual performance. I wasn't really involved with the development of people or identifying reasons why people were or were not performing*'.

Team bonding was encouraged by social events and there were constant attempts to make the work more fun and varied. These include additional rewards in the form of spot prizes or raffles (a prize might be a bottle of wine or a box of chocolates), themed dressing-up days, and *ad hoc* bonuses – one month, for example, each employee on the call centre floor received a bonus of £100 because the abandoned call rate was less than 5 per cent. There was also a suggestion scheme, called 'Bright Ideas', which was aimed at involving staff and encouraging them to think about ways of improving the business with raffle prizes for good ideas.

Before the reorganisation, terms and conditions of employment were inappropriate for the call-centre environment – salaries were low relative to the local labour market, there was no clear career progression route, there were additional payments for shift working and overtime was high, which, as the HR account manager noted, '*is a nonsense in a telephone environment where people have to be fresh and buzzy*'. The reorganisation resulted in the introduction of new terms and conditions, including a new reward package to reflect customer and business requirements. The new pay structure for customer advisers was designed to introduce common standards of performance, focus on high performance, integrate reward, development and performance to balance basic and variable pay and to reflect market rates (and thereby assist in the retention of staff). For customer advisers there were five layers, with progression based on per-formance and a variable incentive for overperfor-mance which could be up to 20 per cent of salary. With the exception of telesales staff, the new pay structure represented a pay increase of approximately 10 per cent in the basic and a maximum of 30 per cent in total earnings. Market research showed that the new pay rates compared favourably with other organisations in the locality.

A new team manager's salary including a bonus scheme based on team performance, which was considerably higher than the traditional supervisory pay, was also introduced alongside the new roles in July 1997. Team managers were set qualitative goals based on monitoring team members' calls and quantitative targets dependent on the performance of each team member. Individual team members had to achieve the minimum standards set for them before the team manager received their bonus. As one team manager noted, '*it doesn't matter how well your team is doing – if you are not nurturing them through the way you manage your team, then you don't receive a bonus*'. Other changes included a reduction in working hours for full-time staff from 40 to 35 hours and set rostered working hours. Under previous arrangements there was no attempt to match call volumes with the supply of labour. However, a new computerised system and the new working time arrangements meant that available resources were closely aligned to call volumes while extending the opening hours of the centre.

Performance improved from the beginning of 1997 with a 20 per cent increase in productivity (during a fairly stable pattern of demand) and the customer survey index was the highest ever achieved. Available time increased from 65 to 85 per cent and sales conversion rates of around one-third were achieved. There was no detrimental effect on sales in terms of volumes and revenue and there was also an increase in revenue for travel insurance. Labour turnover, which had averaged between 27 and 35 per cent over the three-year period prior to the changes, reduced significantly and fell to 8 per cent by the end of 1997 with absenteeism also halved.

The employee satisfaction index, based on MORI attitude surveys, also increased sharply. However, there was also evidence of high levels of stress, especially among team leaders. All team leaders interviewed felt positively about the new role despite having to work much harder. They considered they were more empowered, had greater responsibility, welcomed the opportunity to concentrate on people management skills and their pay was much better. Earnings increased for the majority of employees and pay compared very favourably with other call centres.

Training and development opportunities increased, there was more job variety and greater line management support. Morale and commitment among customer advisers improved and there was a greater feeling of job security. All staff welcomed the more open style of management – communications were felt to have improved, mainly because of the removal of supervisors, and customer advisers were more empowered in terms of dealing with customer complaints. In the words of one customer adviser comparing the new arrangements with the old, '*If I look back, when we first came out there was no motivation for me to come to work – no-one spoke to me, there was no team spirit, no training. Now there seems to be an air of we're going places. It's quite positive. Now I come to work, I enjoy it, I like to work on the PC, I like the advancement.*'

However, attitudes varied and some customer advisers considered the job to be more stressful and pressurised and the working day was now more strictly monitored and controlled. The main grievances, however, concerned the use of the call structure and the sales aspects of the job. All staff used the call structure although there was a lot of initial reaction against it. Some regarded the script as too rigid and felt threatened by using words written for them because it took away their individual personality. The sales side of the job was seen by some to be a disincentive to moving up because the new bonus scheme targets were much harder to achieve than before. Other frustrations of the new role concerned the new work stations, working bank holidays and the lack of privacy.

Questions

1   *Discuss what the RAC did to remove the quality improvement barriers highlighted by the audits and internal reviews in accordance with the various motivational theories.*

2   *What would you do to reduce the team leaders' stress and the staff's frustrations with the sales scripts and bonus scheme targets?*

Source: N Kinnie, S Hutchinson and J Purcell (2000) 'Fun and surveillance: the paradox of high commitment management in call centres', *International Journal of Human Resource Management*, 11 (5), pp. 967–85.

FURTHER READING

Dive, B (2002) *The Healthy Organization: A Revolutionary Approach to People and Management*, **Kogan Page.**
This book provides a wealth of information about the situational aspects of motivation, which links strategic attempts to motivate with operational and individual aspects.

Hayes, N (2001) *Managing Teams: A Strategy for Success*, **London: Thompson Learning.**
Uses much of motivational theory to develop organisational culture and teamworking, and can provide many scenarios for practical application.

Hinds, J M (1995) *Hinds Model of Company Success: How to Overcome Boredom Through Instant Teams and Transform Your Workplace*, **Millenium Books.**
Provides a useful antidote to the notion that applications of motivational theory are always successful.

Thomas, K (2003) *Intrinsic Motivation at Work: Building Energy and Commitment*, **Berrett-Koehler Publishers Inc.**
Provides a study of personal motivation at work. It explains why extrinsic rewards (wages, benefits, perks) are no longer enough to motivate people and details four intrinsic rewards that make work compelling – a sense of meaningfulness, a sense of choice, a sense of competence and a sense of progress.

WEBSITES

http://www.accel-team.com/motivation/index.html
Commercial website full of articles on motivation.

http://www.themanager.org/knowledgebase/hr/motivation.htm
A managerial self-help resource site containing interesting material and an original article by Maslow.

http://www.behavioral-safety.com
Contains practical information about OBM techniques to motivate people to comply with safety requirements.

http://www.siop.org/rvtirbin/shtml.dll/search.htm
Society of Industrial/Organizational Psychologists (USA). Type in 'Motivational Theory' as a search term.

http://www.zigonperf.com
Dedicated to human resources/performance management techniques.

SECTION D

MANAGING THE ORGANISATION

What is meant by management decision making? What are the key elements in the decision-making processes in organisations? What is operations management and how is it analysed? What is the transformation process within organisations? How are management, control and information related? What are the different forms of information in an organisation? How are the accounting and financial aspects of organisations controlled? Why should managers have an understanding of accounting and finance?

With increasing competition, managers have to make difficult decisions and they have to understand that there are different types of decision, as well as understand the processes and techniques involved. In order to satisfy customer needs, organisations have to operate successfully, which involves harnessing and transforming resources. Organisations use different forms of information and managers have to know about the relationship between the concepts of management, control and information. They also have to grasp modern developments in information processing. All managers have to have a reasonable understanding of accounting and finance so that they appreciate the financial position of their organisations and the financial aspects of their own activities.

CHAPTER 13

Decision-making processes in organisations

MIK WISNIEWSKI

Outcomes

Having read this chapter, you will be able to:

- explain the different types of management decision;
- identify the key elements of the decision-making process;
- explain the role of models in business decision making;
- apply some of the more common models useful to the business decision maker.

INTRODUCTION

Decisions, decisions, decisions

Talk to almost any manager in any organisation anywhere in the world and you will hear them comment on the increasing difficulties they face in making management decisions. Decisions have to be made more and more quickly; decisions have to be made more and more often; and decisions have to be made in increasingly complex and unpredictable situations. Coupled with this the risks associated with making the wrong decision have increased considerably. Make the wrong decision and your organisation may go out of business.

No matter whether the manager is involved in a private sector company, a public sector organisation or a non-profit organisation, his or her job has become increasingly difficult and complex. There are many contributory causes to this, of which Figure 13.1 illustrates some of the more obvious. All organisations must respond to a variety of strategic and operational pressures. Some of these may be internal to the organisation – the constant search for improved efficiency, for increased effectiveness and for the creation and strengthening of competitive advantage. Other factors may be largely external but generate pressure for change and decision making in their own right. These may include the following.

Figure 13.1 Pressure for change

Increasing competition

In the private sector competition is becoming increasingly severe. Markets that were thought secure now look vulnerable to competition from other domestic companies, from the Pacific rim economies, from the emerging market economies of what was Eastern Europe, from e-based competitors. Managers must decide how best to respond to this competition: which markets to compete in (and which not to) and on what basis to compete – price, quality, customer service, availability. In the public sector competition is also increasingly becoming the norm with more services having to engage in competition with the private sector to win contracts. Managers in these public sector organisations must make critical decisions on when and how to compete.

Changing nature of competition

The way in which businesses compete is also changing rapidly. Organisations must constantly strive to offer 'better' products and services than their competitors. The problem, of course, is deciding what changes to the product or service will be most valued by customers. Should a company reduce its price in order to compete? Should it keep the price the same but offer extended features to the product or service? Similar problems face managers in the public sector where better services must be balanced against declining budgets.

Increasing focus on quality and customer satisfaction

Customers in both public and private sectors have increasingly higher expectations in terms of product and service quality. With increasing choice, customers are able to favour organisations which deliver 'quality' products and services. Managers must decide how best to respond to this pressure and how to overcome the many problems that prevent quality products and services from being delivered.

Financial environment

Today's financial markets are global with sources of investment funding and opportunities for savings and investment no longer limited to domestic financial organisations. Couple this with the fact that many capital investments for business will cost billions of pounds and strategic alliances between different businesses – often competitors – become the norm. Consortia of organisations collaborate on ventures such as the Channel Tunnel and the development of new aerospace technology, and multiagency initiatives are commonplace in the public sector where no single organisation has the resources to develop an initiative alone. Decisions are required on who to form such alliances with and the detailed nature of such cooperative ventures.

Technology

Rapid technological change creates both opportunities and problems for managers. Technology can offer the potential for improved efficiency and related cost savings and the creation of real competitive advantage. However, an organisation needs to ensure that it invests in the 'right' technology. A few years – or in some cases, months – later and the business might find its technological investment outdated and inappropriate.

Rate of change

→ Ch. 1

As if these pressures were not problem enough for a manager, the speed at which change is taking place is actually increasing (see Chapter 1). Changes in technology, working practices, legislation, the competitive environment and so on take place with alarming frequency. Technological products such as computers, MP3 players and mobile phones have a life span measured in months, not years, before they are overtaken by more technologically advanced products.

A simple business scenario will be used to illustrate some of the points in this chapter and the increasingly difficult task of management decision making. A company operates a number of medium-sized hotels throughout Scotland: in Glasgow, Edinburgh, Aviemore and a number of other key cities and towns. The structure of the company is typical of many. Each hotel in the group acts as a profit centre and has a manager who is responsible for the day-to-day running of that hotel, although many of the routine decisions may be delegated to other staff. The managing director (MD) of the company has the responsibility for longer-term, strategic decisions relating to the future of the business. Consider many of the factors that will influence the business environment in which the group operates. Some hotels in the group may well face increased competition from other hotels, both in Edinburgh and perhaps other parts of Scotland, for the tourist segment of the market. Customers are becoming more articulate and demanding in terms of the levels of customer service and the overall quality levels which hotels provide. Changing patterns of business and leisure both offer opportunities and create problems for the business. An increasing number of tourists visiting Scotland offer the potential for increased business, as does the increasing foreign trade in which the Scottish economy is becoming involved.

Because of the extent and rate of the change pressures discussed earlier, managers in many organisations find that they have to make an increasing number of decisions: some of these are relatively minor and deal with day-to-day problems that arise. The hotel manager, for example, has to make routine decisions about the quantity of fresh food to order each day. Too much and the hotel's costs will escalate. Too little and there are obvious problems in terms of serving meals to customers. Others are more complex and may well affect the long-term future and success of the organisation. The MD may feel that, with an increasing number of foreign tourists visiting Scotland, the company should undertake an advertising campaign in selected foreign media (newspapers, magazines, TV, radio, websites) to attract customers. However, if the wrong media are used, in terms of market penetration, or the wrong countries are targeted then the consequences could well be adverse financial costs and lost business.

In a comparable development the consequences of these decisions take on increasing importance in terms of the future success of the organisation. Yet, at the same time as managers find themselves in a position of having to make more decisions, they also find that they have less and less time available in which to make a decision. That is, the timescale between recognising that a decision needs to be made and having to make a decision to resolve a problem or capitalise on an opportunity is becoming ever shorter. This is illustrated in Figure 13.2. Managers are faced with making decisions in situations of increasing complexity – there may be many different aspects to the situation that need to be considered carefully, decisions made in one area may well have consequences for other areas of activity, there may be legal implications for certain decisions, there will certainly be financial implications and so on. Additionally, with technological change the quantity of information available

Figure 13.2 Decision-making pressures

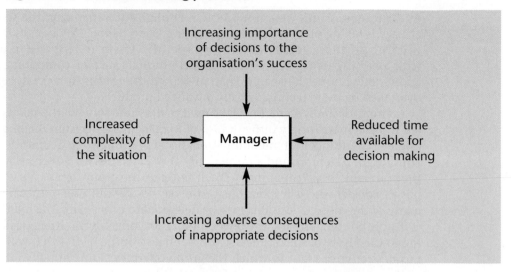

to managers steadily increases, making the task of deciding what is relevant and irrelevant more difficult. In the hotel group scenario a decision as to which countries in Europe to target as part of a promotional campaign might sound relatively straightforward. However, such a decision has to be put into the context of evaluating information about population trends, income and spending patterns, leisure habits, travel patterns and the like in a number of different countries.

Decisions are also becoming increasingly important to organisational success. There are no such things as trivial decisions in business any longer. Even apparently routine, day-to-day decisions may have long-term consequences. Equally the consequences of making decisions which later turn out to be wrong or inappropriate become more significant. With many decisions having major financial consequences for an organisation, getting it wrong might well send a company out of business. To compound these problems for the decision maker the time available to evaluate alternatives, to research the problem and to ponder what decision should be chosen is decreasing. Decisions typically must be made in a much shorter timescale. One illustration of this relates to decisions of financial institutions in terms of buying and selling foreign currency via the financial markets. Exchange rates are particularly volatile and decisions by key decision makers as to whether to buy or sell a particular currency and which currencies to deal in need to be made in minutes.

It is hardly surprising that considerable attention has been given both to examining the nature and methods of management decision making and to tools and techniques which can assist the manager in the decision making process. In the rest of this chapter we shall examine some of these in more detail.

TYPES OF DECISION

It will be worthwhile at this stage considering the different types of decision that managers face. There are many different ways in which we can categorise the types of decision that managers make, and one of the more useful of these is shown in Figure 13.3. Although any such categorisation is to some extent artificial, it is possi-

Figure 13.3 Decision types

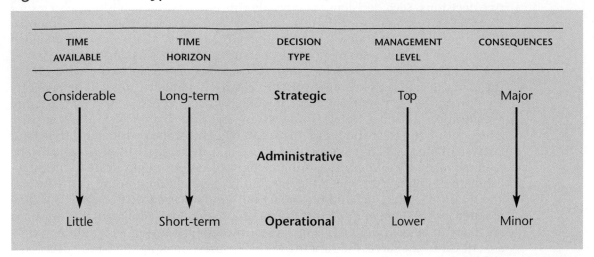

TIME AVAILABLE	TIME HORIZON	DECISION TYPE	MANAGEMENT LEVEL	CONSEQUENCES
Considerable	Long-term	**Strategic**	Top	Major
		Administrative		
Little	Short-term	**Operational**	Lower	Minor

ble to envisage three generic types of decision – at the **operational**, **administrative** and **strategic** levels. Naturally, the distinction between these types can be somewhat blurred at the edges – a series of apparently operational decisions, for example, could build into a strategic one. However, each type of decision is typically characterised by a number of features.

Operational decisions are typically routine, day-to-day decisions that will have little direct and immediate impact on the business as a whole, and may well be repetitive in the sense that such decisions have to be taken repeatedly, perhaps several times a year. Examples might be deciding how to deal with an individual customer's complaint, when to reorder office supplies and so on. Typically such decisions are governed primarily by predetermined 'rules' established by the organisation and will involve routine systems and procedures designed to help decision making. So, for example, there may be a formal procedure to follow in the case of a customer complaint or there may be preset guidelines as to when to reorder basic office supplies. Such decisions are typically taken by managers at the lower levels of the organisational hierarchy. Similarly on an individual basis the consequences of wrong or poor decisions will be minor (although a series of wrong decisions can build into major consequences). Managers typically have little time available in which to reach such a decision (and this is one of the reasons why predetermined procedures are in place) and are operating in a short-term time horizon.

At the other end of the spectrum there are what can be termed **strategic decisions**, which are more concerned with the achievement of corporate aims and objectives and long-term corporate plans. **Strategic decisions** may well involve determining which products/services to offer in the future and which to discontinue, which markets the organisation will compete in, on what basis the organisation will compete and so on. Understandably such decisions tend to be taken by the top layer of management in an organisation and will benefit from lengthy consideration, simply because they have major consequences for the future success of the organisation. Unlike operational decisions, strategic decisions cannot be taken by following a set procedure or a pre-established set of rules. Typically such decisions relate to situations that are more or less unique, or one-off, or where each situation needs to be considered on an individual basis.

In between these two types of decision we have what can be termed **administrative decisions**. Such decisions are typically concerned with establishing systems for control and organisation within the business, and may well relate to the administrative decisions that follow from key strategic decisions which will help establish systems and procedures to support the operational decision-making process.

To return to the hotel scenario, strategic decisions may relate to the expansion of the chain of hotels the company owns. Clearly such a decision will be taken by senior managers in the organisation, it will have major consequences for the entire organisation (opening hotels in the wrong locations may lead to the company going out of business) and senior managers will take some considerable time (and analysis) before making such a decision. Such decisions will also typically be required relatively infrequently. Administrative decisions might relate to the establishment of appropriate systems to ensure that a hotel functions properly. Payroll and financial systems will need to be set up, supplies and logistics systems will be required, as will human resources systems and so on. Such administrative decisions are likely to be taken by middle managers in the organisation and, although they are critical to the successful running of the business, making the wrong decision – about a particular supplier, for example – is unlikely to send the company out of business. Operational decisions will then be required by frontline managers responsible for the smooth running of the hotels on a day-to-day basis. The relevant manager – or perhaps an individual employee if operational decisions have been delegated – will have to make decisions about ensuring that the hotel bar is adequately stocked. Such decisions will be made frequently (perhaps daily) and clearly will need to be taken quickly. Such operational decisions may well be based on earlier administrative decisions. An automated stock control system, for example, may be in place to assist in such operational decisions perhaps by producing a daily report on yesterday's sales and today's stock levels.

Clearly not all decisions fit neatly into this – or any other – classification structure. Consider, for example, an organisation seeking to introduce an effective equal opportunities policy. Such a decision will have to be made by top management and will have major consequences for the organisation. However, it cannot really be called a strategic decision in the business sense of the word. It is also evident that it is not a decision for which procedures or systems can be applied. While such a classification system does not do justice to the complexity and variety of many managerial decisions, it does provide a useful framework for the different types of decision, their implications and for the roles of the different types of manager in an organisation.

THE DECISION-MAKING PROCESS

It will also be helpful at this stage to develop an overview of what can be described as the decision-making process. Consider the hotel scenario again. The manager of one of the hotels in the group has received a complaint from a guest that the requested morning newspaper has not been delivered. The manager has to decide what to do. While this may seem a relatively trivial decision problem – and one which is clearly operational in terms of our earlier framework – it will serve to illustrate the various stages of the decision-making process. One immediate decision that the manager should make is to apologise to the guest and try to rectify the immediate problem. This might solve the immediate – and obvious – problem but it is not clear what has caused the problem in the first place, nor whether the problem is likely to occur again in the future. There are various ways in which we can describe the process involved in decision making for this and any other decision situation. One of these is illustrated in Figure 13.4. (see also Chapter 8).

→ Ch. 8

Need for a decision

It is possible to begin at the stage described as 'need for a decision'. At some stage it will become evident to a manager that a decision is required relating to a particular situation. Such a decision might relate to a problem or crisis at the operational level, as in this case, or to dealing with a key strategic threat (a competitor lowering the price of their product, for example). It might also relate at a more strategic level to the realisation that an opportunity exists – for expansion, increased market share, enhanced competitive advantage. This stage seems a very obvious one but implies that both the organisation and manager have formal and informal monitoring systems to assess performance and standards and scan for opportunities. In the hotel scenario the manager becomes aware of the need for a decision at a relatively late stage – when the customer complains. This by itself indicates that the organisation does not appear to have appropriate information systems in place to resolve such potential difficulties as they are happening, or preferably before they can happen.

Problem definition

Once the decision-recognition phase has occurred then the problem-definition phase is reached. The manager needs to ensure that a clear definition of the problem (or opportunity) is provided. Again in the hotel context, the problem appears

Figure 13.4 The decision-making process

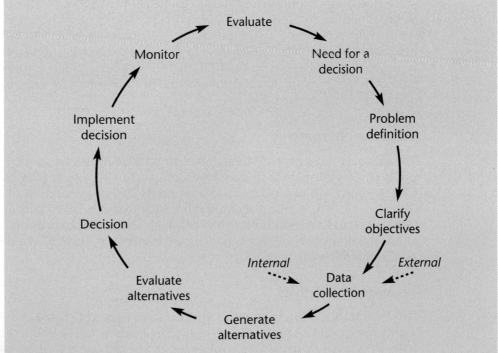

to be that a customer did not receive the ordered morning newspaper. But the manager needs to ensure that a clear, concise and accurate definition of the situation is produced. Did the newspaper not arrive at all or did it arrive late? Was the wrong newspaper delivered rather than the one the customer requested? Have other customers complained of the same problem? Did this happen just today or has it happened in the past? The manager must develop an appropriate understanding of what exactly the problem is, its extent and scope.

Clarify objectives

With such a definition the manager can then develop appropriate decision objectives – what the decision (still to be made) is intended to achieve. Clearly this, in part, will depend on the definition phase. A situation which has occurred only today with only one customer will have very different decision objectives from one which has occurred repeatedly over the last month with a number of customers. The objectives phase is a particularly important one, however. The manager must be clear about what a particular decision, or set of related decisions, is to achieve. Without this clarification the manager will not be in a position in the future to determine whether a particular decision that was made was effective or not.

Data collection

When the objectives have been clarified data must be collected about the problem. Again, this will depend on the scale of the decision situation. Such data may be collected from within the organisation or from external sources. For the hotel scenario management may collect data on the number of times this situation has arisen over the past month, whether the situation appears to occur at weekends or during the week, at times when the hotel is busy or when it is quiet and discussions might take place with both customers and staff to gain their perception of the scale and extent of the situation. Externally management may contact other hotels in the group to see if they experience a similar problem. Contact may also be made with the newsagent who supplies newspapers to the hotel to see what its records indicate in terms of the number of copies of different newspapers ordered and supplied. The data collected may be 'hard' data – factual or numerical – or may be 'soft' data – opinions of customers and staff.

Generate alternatives

The manager must now try to generate alternative decisions in the context of the problem or options which could be designed to resolve a particular problem. Clearly much will depend on the situation itself. The generation of such alternatives or options may take place through formal problem analysis using a number of techniques and decision tools (some of which are introduced later in this chapter). Other situations may call for a more creative approach, particularly when the situation is unstructured.

Evaluate alternatives

Once a number of alternatives or options have been generated then the decision maker must evaluate these. Clearly this must be done in the context of the 'clarify objectives' phase with alternatives evaluated in the context of how far they con-

results of the analysis do not provide the manager with a decision. What they do provide is additional information about the decision situation and the various alternatives that may be under consideration. They also provide an analytical framework for the manager to evaluate such alternatives. This is illustrated further with the second model we shall examine – the **payoff table**.

PAYOFF TABLES

It will be evident that one of the key characteristics of business decision making is that it takes place under considerable uncertainty. A manager must make a decision typically with incomplete knowledge about the situation or knowing that the future outcomes of decisions made now are uncertain. There are ways of examining these decision problems that can help clarify how decisions can be made.

This will be illustrated with a second scenario. The hotel group is considering its future direction and strategy. It has decided that there is the potential for increasing the number of business people from abroad who use the group's hotel facilities in Scotland. In particular it feels that concentrated advertising in selected markets in Europe would increase this type of business. What the group's managing director has in mind is an advertising campaign aimed at businesses wishing to develop commercial and industrial links with companies in Scotland. What the hotel will offer to these businesses is a special package deal. It will arrange air travel for foreign business people, a chauffeured executive car to collect them from the airport and take them to one of the group's hotels, and translation and interpretation facilities while they are in Scotland.

Three potential markets are currently under investigation – Scandinavia, Germany and Eastern Europe. The group has estimated that a suitable advertising campaign in each country (through TV, radio, the business press) would cost:

Scandinavia	£150,000
Germany	£200,000
Eastern Europe	£300,000

The financial director has indicated that the group has the financial resources to fund only one of these campaigns and the critical decision is: which one? Naturally the group expects a return for this expenditure through the increased business it attracts to its hotels. However, the situation is made difficult by the fact that the additional revenue generated will, in part, depend on the effectiveness of the campaign in each area. The group's marketing function has concluded that the overall effect of the campaign in each of the three areas could be classed as: low, medium or high impact. For each possibility they have quantified the financial return the group could anticipate from each area in terms of increased business. This is summarised in Table 13.1.

So, for example, if the group decides to campaign in Germany and the campaign has a low impact then it is expected the campaign will generate an additional £150,000 of business for the group. On the other hand if the campaign is focused on Scandinavia and the outcome is high then £250,000 of additional business is expected.

This scenario is typical of many situations that organisations have to face. The group is faced with a range of decision alternatives over which it has control (it can choose between them) but it also faces uncertainty in terms of the outcome of each of these alternatives. These future outcomes are referred to as 'states of nature' – they

Table 13.1 Financial returns from the campaign

AREA	OUTCOME (£000S)		
	LOW	MEDIUM	HIGH
Scandinavia	175	225	250
Germany	150	300	350
Eastern Europe	100	250	600

are outside the direct control of the group. However, they do include all possible outcomes and only one of them can actually occur. How does the group decide what to do *now*, given that it does not know the outcome from the campaign that will be achieved in the *future*? Table 13.1 shows only one side of the situation – the cost of the campaign must also be taken into account. This can be achieved by constructing what is known as a **payoff table**, which shows the net effect of each possible decision and each outcome. Table 13.2 shows the results when the campaign costs for each area have been subtracted from the expected returns shown in Table 13.1.

The payoff table can now be used to consider the attractiveness of alternative decisions. Clearly the decision made will be influenced by a number of factors other than the payoff table – how reliable the information is about the alternative decisions, how risky the various options are, how critical the decision is to the company's future and so on. One of the key factors, however, will depend on the organisation's attitude to these future states of nature. In the absence of any other information on the likelihood of each state of nature, we can consider a number of options.

The maximax criterion

Assume that the hotel group's senior managers take an optimistic view of the future outcome. If this were the case then they would choose the option which generated the highest possible payoff, since they feel that the 'best' state of nature will occur. Such an approach is known as the **maximax criterion** since we are searching for the *max*imum of the *max*imum payoffs. In this problem the maximax decision would be to launch the campaign in Eastern Europe since this – potentially – generates the highest payoff at £300,000 compared with the best possible payoff of £150,000 for

Table 13.2 Campaign payoffs

AREA	OUTCOME (£000S)		
	LOW	MEDIUM	HIGH
Scandinavia	25	75	100
Germany	−50	100	150
Eastern Europe	−200	−50	300

the German campaign and £100,000 for the Scandinavian. In general for this approach the maximum payoff for each option is found and then the largest of these chosen. This approach has the advantage of focusing on the best possible outcome from the alternative decisions under consideration.

The maximin criterion

The maximax decision is based on an optimistic view of the future in terms of the states of nature that could occur. However, the group may take a different attitude and consider the worst-case scenario – a pessimistic view about future outcomes. In such a situation the **maximin criterion** can be applied – the *maximum* of the *minimum* payoffs. The basic logic is to find the best decision given the assumption that the worst possible future outcome will occur. For each alternative decision the minimum (worst) payoff is found and then the largest of these chosen to find the most desirable decision. In this case this would lead to a decision to launch the campaign in Scandinavia since this is the largest of the minimum payoffs at £25,000 (the minimum payoffs being £25,000, –£50,000 and –£200,000 respectively). Such an approach ensures that management has taken the best decision if the worst outcome happens. However, it is also evident that the approach ignores the potentially larger payoffs from other decisions.

The minimax regret criterion

A third approach, the **minimax regret criterion**, uses the concept of opportunity loss or regret. Assume that the decision is made to launch the campaign in Scandinavia. Having committed itself to this course of action, management later observes that the impact of the campaign was high. With hindsight management realises that the decision made was not the best given the state of nature that actually occurred (even though when it made the decision it had no way of knowing which state of nature would prevail). The optimal decision for this state of nature would have been to campaign in Eastern Europe since this has a higher payoff given this state of nature. Effectively, the group has 'lost' £200,000 by making the decision to launch in Scandinavia. This figure is referred to as the **opportunity cost** – or **regret** – of the decision for that state of nature. The opportunity loss, or regret, associated with each possible decision and the various states of nature can be calculated using the same logic. This is summarised in Table 13.3.

Table 13.3 Regret

AREA	OUTCOME (£000S)		
	LOW	MEDIUM	HIGH
Scandinavia	0	25	200
Germany	75	0	150
Eastern Europe	225	150	0

Each column (state of nature) in the payoff table is considered in turn and it is determined, for that state of nature, what the optimum decision would be. So, if the campaign impact was low then the optimum decision would be to campaign in Scandinavia. If this decision had actually been made, the regret in financial terms would be zero, because it was the best decision given this state of nature. On the other hand if it had been decided to campaign in Germany then the regret would be £75,000 because a payoff of £25,000 could have been achieved, whereas the decision actually incurred a loss of £50,000. Similarly, if the decision had been made to campaign in Eastern Europe then the regret would have been £225,000. These calculations can be performed for the other two states of nature columns. This process can be repeated for each outcome in turn producing the data in Table 13.3.

For each of the decision options the maximum of these regret values is then obtained – that is £200,000 for Scandinavia, £150,000 for Germany and £225,000 for Eastern Europe. Each option is considered in turn and the maximum regret value shows the maximum opportunity cost associated with this option on the assumption that the worst state of nature happens. Management would then wish to make the decision where this maximum regret was minimised. This would be the decision to campaign in Germany because this has the lowest maximum regret at £150,000. The basic logic of the approach is to ask 'How much does the group stand to 'lose' from each decision if that decision turns out to be the wrong one?' Management then chooses the option where this potential 'loss' is minimised.

It is worth noting that in this scenario the three different approaches have led to three different options, with the decision made depending on the decision maker's view of the future. One of the benefits of this approach is that it requires the decision maker to consider and justify explicitly their view of future states of nature. One of its main drawbacks is that the three states of nature have been treated as being equally likely. Management needs to be able to incorporate such likelihood information into the decision-making process, which can be achieved by introducing the concept of **expected value**.

EXPECTED VALUE

It is clear that management is currently assuming that the three outcomes from the campaign are equally likely. This will not necessarily be a realistic assumption. Based on further analysis, market research or simply personal intuition and experience, management might feel that some of the outcomes are more likely than others. If this is the case, and such likelihoods can be quantified, then management will clearly want to take this extra factor into account when trying to reach an appropriate decision. Assume that the group has been able to quantify such likelihoods, referred to as **probabilities**, as shown in Table 13.4.

It can be seen that the probabilities of each outcome for Scandinavia and Germany are the same, but different from those for Eastern Europe. By convention a probability is shown as a value between 0 and 1, with 0 indicating something that can never happen and 1 indicating that it is certain to happen. For example, the low outcome has a probability of 0.2 for Scandinavia and for Germany: there is a 20 per cent chance that this is the outcome that will occur, compared with 40 per cent for medium and 40 per cent for high. For Eastern Europe, however, the probability of low is higher (i.e. this outcome is more likely to occur) at 50 per cent. Note that the total of the probabilities for each area individually total to 1 – that is, one of the three outcomes must occur.

Table 13.4 Probability of outcomes

| | OUTCOME (£000S) | | |
AREA	LOW	MEDIUM	HIGH
Scandinavia	0.2	0.4	0.4
Germany	0.2	0.4	0.4
Eastern Europe	0.5	0.2	0.3

Clearly management now needs to be able to use this additional information to help it reach a decision. The approach taken is to calculate the **expected value** (EV) for each of the alternative decisions. Consider the decision to campaign in Scandinavia. For this decision there are three possible states of nature, each with a payoff, and for each state of nature there is now a probability. It seems reasonable to use these probabilities to calculate a weighted average outcome for this decision. That is:

$$EV = (£25,000 \times 0.2) + (£75,000 \times 0.4) + (£100,000 \times 0.4)$$

That is, if we campaign in Scandinavia there is a 20 per cent chance of a £25,000 payoff, a 40 per cent chance of a £75,000 payoff and a 40 per cent chance of a £100,000 payoff. The calculation gives a figure of £75,000 as the expected value of this option – the alternative payoffs weighted by the respective probabilities. Care needs to be taken in terms of what EV represents. It is not a guaranteed payoff from this option. Rather it is a measure taking into account both the payoffs and their likelihood. The purpose of such EVs is to facilitate comparison between alternative decisions under such conditions of uncertainty. The EVs for the three alternative decisions are:

Scandinavia	£75,000
Germany	£90,000
Eastern Europe	–£40,000

Based on this information it would be logical to recommend that the campaign is launched in Germany since it has a higher EV. Note that the option for Eastern Europe actually has a negative EV – that is, its weighted payoff indicates a loss rather than a profit. Once again it must be stressed that making a decision on such a basis does not guarantee a positive payoff to the group. The state of nature that actually occurs in Germany could generate a payoff of –£50,000, £100,000 or £150,000. Overall, however, the German option is to be favoured since the weighted combination of payoffs and probabilities is higher than those for the other two options.

DECISION TREES

→ Ch. 2

It is also possible to examine this type of decision situation by constructing a **decision tree** which shows the relationship over time between decisions, outcomes, payoffs and probabilities (see also Chapter 2). The tree diagram for this problem is shown in Figure 13.7. The tree starts on the left. The box symbol (known as a **decision node**) is used to denote that at this point a decision must be made and the

Figure 13.7 Decision tree

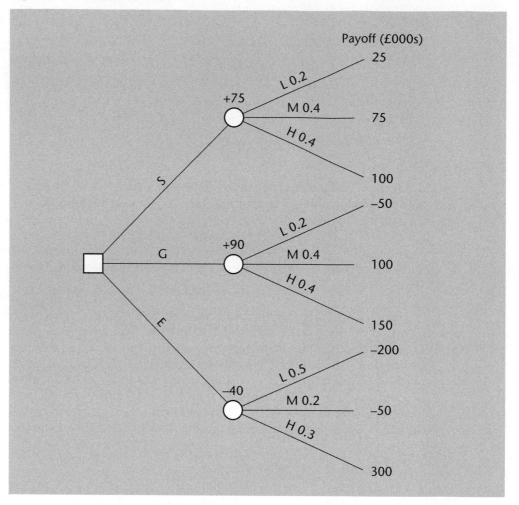

alternative decisions branch out from this node – to campaign in Scandinavia (S), Germany (G) or Eastern Europe (E). Each of these branches leads to an **outcome node** (represented by a circle) showing the states of nature – future outcomes from the decisions over which the decision maker has no control. In this example the node along each decision branch is the same – the campaign impact could turn out to be low (L), medium (M) or high (H). At the end of each branch there is a payoff – a total of nine possible payoffs in this problem. Information is then added on the payoffs, the probability of each outcome and the *EV*s of each decision branch. The decision maker now sees clearly the potential payoffs from each decision and state of nature combination. Also the *EV*s for each decision can be identified and used to assist in the decision-making process, as we have discussed.

Decision trees are useful ways of showing the outcomes and potential consequences of alternative decisions. They are also particularly useful in situations where a series of decisions may need to be taken over time and where subsequent decision options may depend on future outcomes. Consider an expansion of the existing scenario. One of the members of the hotel group's board of directors is still not convinced that the Eastern European option should be ruled out at this stage, particularly given that it offers potentially the largest payoff of the three (at £300,000). The director believes that if the company chooses this option for its promotion campaign and if the impact of that campaign is either low or medium in the future (leading to a negative payoff) then there is the possibility of a supplementary advertising campaign to try to boost business further. Some additional research has been conducted into this. If, six months after the initial campaign in Eastern Europe, the impact turns out to be low or medium then a supplementary campaign can be conducted at an additional cost of £100,000. If the initial impact is low then it is felt that this additional campaign has a probability of 0.3 of increasing the payoff by £300,000. However, there is a 0.7 probability that the additional campaign will have no further impact on payoff at all. If the initial outcome is medium then the supplementary campaign has a 0.4 probability of having a zero effect and a 0.6 probability of increasing payoff by £300,000.

Clearly the group needs to evaluate the effect of this additional option on the original decision. However, there is an additional difficulty. The finance department has indicated that it needs to know now – not in six months' time – whether the additional £100,000 will be needed for the campaign in order to ensure that the group's cash flow is not adversely affected. In other words the group cannot wait until it knows the outcome of the initial campaign before making a further decision. It needs to decide now what this second decision will be. It will be helpful if the additional information is summarised. For the Eastern European option we have:

INITIAL OUTCOME: LOW		INITIAL OUTCOME: MEDIUM	
Initial payoff	–£200,000	Initial payoff	–£50,000
Supplementary costs	£100,000	Supplementary costs	£100,000
Supplementary payoff:		Supplementary payoff:	
£0	(probability 0.7)	£0	(probability 0.4)
£300,000	(probability 0.3)	£300,000	(probability 0.6)

The part of the original decision tree relating to Eastern Europe has been updated to help decide what to do. Figure 13.8 shows the amended tree. The decision options relating to Scandinavia and Germany have been simplified to show only their respective *EV*s. If the Eastern European option is examined in detail it can be seen how the additional information is incorporated. The initial decision is one of three – S, G or E. For the Eastern Europe option there are the three original initial outcomes – low, medium or high. For the high outcome nothing alters in terms of probability or payoff. For low and medium, however, a second decision node is needed to help determine whether or not to launch a supplementary campaign. These options are shown as 'Supp' (supplementary campaign is launched) and 'No supp'. For the No supp option, in both cases, the payoffs remain as they were in the original problem. For the Supp decision option, however, there is a change. If the initial impact is low and the supplementary campaign is launched then there are two secondary outcomes – the supplementary campaign could lead to an increase in payoff or could leave the payoff unchanged. The respective probabilities and net payoffs are shown. It can then be seen that the *EV* of launching the supplementary

Figure 13.8 Amended decision tree (£000s)

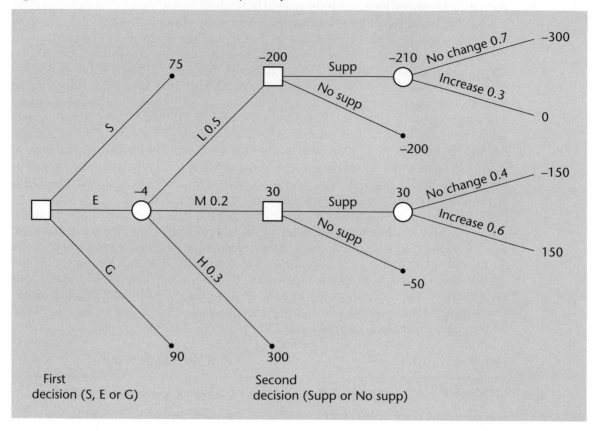

campaign *if* the initial impact is low would be –£210,000. This is actually a lower *EV* than the alternative decision of No supp. This implies that if management decides to target Eastern Europe (the initial decision) and if the campaign impact is low, it knows *now* that a supplementary campaign is not worthwhile. In other words management can predict now what a future decision would be relating to a particular set of outcomes based on the information given. For the initial impact of medium a similar process takes place. It can be seen that the *EV* of launching the supplementary campaign is £30,000 compared with the *EV* of not launching this campaign of –£50,000. Again management can predict a future decision. If it decides to campaign in Eastern Europe and if the initial impact is medium then a supplementary campaign should be launched.

However, does this affect management's initial decision to campaign in Germany and not Eastern Europe? This can be answered by working backwards through the amended diagram. The payoffs for each of the three initial outcomes are then –£200,000 (if the initial outcome is low the group would do nothing further), £30,000 (which has changed from the original –£50,000 because the group would now launch the supplementary campaign) and £300,000 (also unchanged). Using the original probabilities the *EV* for the Eastern European option is now –£4000. This is still negative and would not affect the original decision to target Germany. It can also illustrate how such an approach can be used to assess the present decisions that may have to be taken at some time in the future. Management does not have to wait for an outcome to occur before considering and choosing between alternative decision options – with the right information management can make that decision now and be ready to implement it should that particular outcome occur.

ISHIKAWA DIAGRAMS

→ Ch. 7

The next management technique useful in decision making is descriptive rather than quantitative. This is the **Ishikawa diagram** – alternatively known as the **cause–effect diagram** or the **fishbone diagram** (see Chapter 7). Originally developed for use in the area of quality management, organisations have found it equally useful in terms of wider problem solving and decision making. Consider the problem scenario we developed earlier, relating to customer complaints in the hotel about non-delivery of morning newspapers. An initial investigation has revealed that the problem is not a one-off, it has been happening for some time and a number of customers have experienced the problem. One of the difficulties the decision maker has in such a context is trying to determine the fundamental causes of the problem, the relative importance of each cause and possible relationships between causes. An Ishikawa diagram can help the decision maker by providing a framework to identify such causes and their relationships. The general format of the diagram is shown in Figure 13.9, although the approach is readily adapted to the exact situation under examination.

The diagram starts at the right-hand side with the observed effect. This is the issue, situation or problem that management is focusing on. The major causes, or contributory factors, relating to this effect are then identified and used to label the ends of each major branch as shown. One common approach is to consider five major factors – manpower (shortage of staff perhaps, inadequate training, poor communication between staff); materials (resources, quality of resources); machines; methods (work practices, data capture systems) and measurements. Factors which contribute to each of these major causes can then be determined and used to label sub-branches coming from each main cause branch, as in Figure 13.10.

The Ishikawa diagram is a method of focusing on the major factors causing a particular effect. It seems very simple and straightforward but is deceptively powerful

Figure 13.9 Ishikawa diagram: effect, causes and subcauses

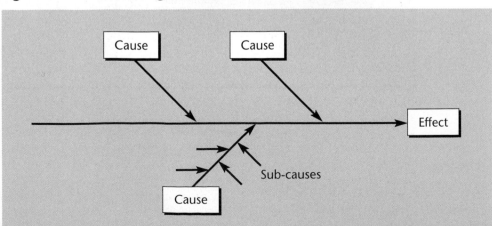

Figure 13.10 Ishikawa diagram: the five Ms

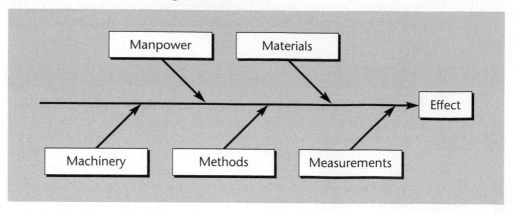

when used in the right way. A team approach to identifying causes is likely to be needed since most activities will involve a group of people rather than one individual. Figure 13.11 shows a completed diagram that might have been produced by the hotel manager after consultation with key members of staff.

On the manpower side, factors have been identified as understaffing in the hotel, key staff away ill, staff having an unclear idea as to who was responsible for providing this service, new staff not being told it was part of their duties. On the materials side, management has identified that on occasions the wrong newspapers are delivered to the hotel and sometimes not enough newspapers are delivered. On the methods side, it can be seen that orders are often sent late to the supplying newsagent (possibly linked to some of the materials causes), the room service staff (who take orders for morning papers from customers) do not communicate adequately with the staff who have to deliver the papers, occasionally the effect can be

Figure 13.11 Ishikawa diagram for the hotel newspaper problem

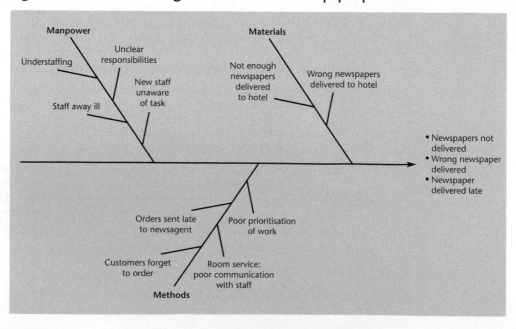

caused by customers in the hotel simply forgetting to place an order for a specific newspaper, and there can be a problem with staff prioritisation of this task among others that are expected of them (linked to one of the manpower causes). Note that the manager has decided to drop the machinery and measurement branches as being redundant to this problem analysis.

What the diagram provides is a focused analysis of key factors contributing to the problem. The manager now has a clear perspective on the contributing factors and can begin the process of prioritising between them and seeking solutions to them. In some cases there may be no direct solution. Understaffing, for example, may be a perennial problem if the company is exercising central control over local staff numbers. However, it is evident that improved training is needed for new staff to ensure they are aware of all their duties and it is also evident that communication needs to be improved between management, room service and staff, and also between the hotel and the supplying newsagent. Perhaps an agreement for the hotel to fax or e-mail its order last thing in the evening might help resolve some of these causes. Similarly a new system is needed to ensure that customers are aware of their need to order before a specific time.

The diagram demonstrates the potential in terms of assisting the decision maker. Whatever the possible solutions, the diagram allows management to assess the impact each solution could be expected to have on the effect. This by itself can be a valuable conclusion to reach. Improving staff training, for example, will not solve the entire problem given that there are other factors contributing to the problem that will not be solved by this initiative. Similarly, although the diagram is readily applied to effects in the guise of problems, it can also be applied to effects which indicate 'success'. If one feature of a product or service is seen as particularly successful then this method can be a useful mechanism for identifying the key factors that have contributed to this success with a view to replicating these factors for other products/services.

FORCEFIELD ANALYSIS

The techniques and models introduced so far are focused on the stages of the decision-making process that relate to the generation of alternatives and the evaluation of those alternatives. As has already been discussed, part of the management decision-making process involves the successful implementation of the decision made – making it work in other words. No matter how well designed the decision, a manager may well find in practice that once implemented the decision does not have the desired or expected effect.

Naturally there may be many reasons for this but **forcefield analysis** considers one aspect of such a situation (see Chapters 1 and 5). A decision situation – where some change is seen as necessary – can be visualised as comprising two mutually opposed forces: what can be described as restraining forces which resist the change implied in some decision, and driving forces which support or encourage change. The purpose of forcefield analysis is to help the manager to identify, in advance of decision implementation, what these critical forces are likely to be and to consider how best the restraining forces can be removed or minimised and how the driving forces can be strengthened. The approach in forcefield analysis is straightforward. Consider the decision situation shown in Figure 13.12.

→ Chs 1 & 5

Figure 13.12 Forcefield analysis

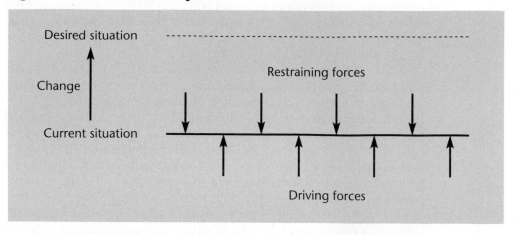

The current situation is shown as the solid line and the desired situation – after successful implementation of some decision – is shown as the dotted line. The gap between the two implies change. In the move to push towards the desired situation it is likely that a number of restraining forces will be encountered. These need to be identified individually and used to label each arrow line. A number of key driving forces can be identified in the same way. The next stage is to assess the relative strengths of each force – some will be stronger than others in either driving or restraining the change. The forcefield – and the current situation – can now be regarded as representing an equilibrium position, a position of balance. In order to push towards the desired situation management must either strengthen the driving forces to push the situation forward or weaken the restraining forces – or, of course, do both.

Consider another hotel scenario. In one hotel in the group the main reception desk is responsible for taking telephone bookings for accommodation from customers. Typically a customer will telephone the reception desk to make a booking, various details will then be entered into the computerised booking system and, at a later date, written confirmation sent to the customer. However, the hotel manager has recently become aware that an unacceptable number of errors occur in the input of customer details into the computerised booking system. In some cases this causes relatively minor problems – customers are greeted by the wrong name when they check into the hotel – in other cases it is more serious, for example the bill is sent to the wrong customer address. The manager has decided that a zero-defect target will be established – no errors of this kind will be tolerated.

Figure 13.13 shows the results of a forcefield analysis on the situation. A number of restraining forces have been identified and the relative importance of each shown in relation to the size of the arrowed line (with longer lines implying more importance). It can be seen that the effective implementation of the zero-defect decision will be restrained by inexperienced staff, inadequate equipment (with both poor screen layouts and antiquated equipment), physical difficulties caused by the layout of the reception area, and too many distractions when staff are on the phone and keying in details. Similarly a number of driving forces have also been identified including managerial pressure, the corporate objective of achieving customer satisfaction, planned modification to computer software and an initiative to allow reception staff some degree of job specialisation.

Figure 13.13 Forcefield analysis for the hotel booking problem

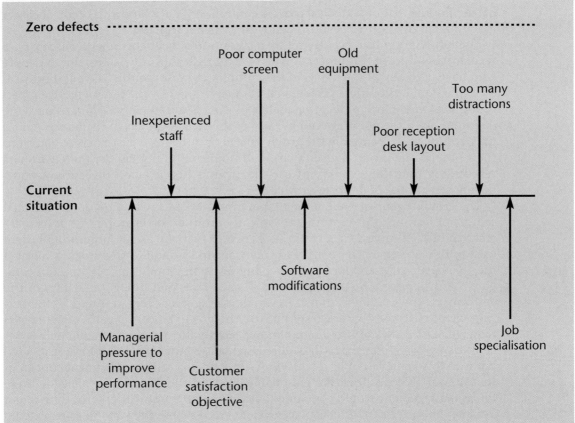

The decision maker can now use the analysis to evaluate how the restraining factors can be removed or reduced (indeed whether this will happen with some of the initiatives under way) and how to reinforce the driving forces. For example, the manager might decide to improve communications with reception staff so that they are fully aware of the importance of achieving customer satisfaction. Involving the reception staff in an evaluation of how the physical layout could be improved might help to resolve one of the restraining forces. A detailed proposal for additional capital expenditure to replace old equipment might be made to the group finance director. Whatever initiatives are taken, the forcefield analysis allows these to be focused on the key forces with a view to enhancing the successful implementation of the original decision to move towards a zero-defect situation.

STATISTICAL PROCESS CONTROL

The last technique introduced in this chapter is one which helps to close the loop of the decision-making process (Figure 13.14). As discussed earlier, an important part of this process is for an organisation to have methods and systems in place which periodically monitor and assess performance from a number of perspectives. Not only does this allow management to assess the impact of decisions already made, it provides them with a perspective on any developing situations which may require decisions at some stage in the future. One method that is useful in a variety of situations is that of **statistical process control** (SPC), also known as **control charts** (see Chapter 7). This will be illustrated with a further scenario.

→ Ch. 7

The hotel group has recently set up a system to collect customer feedback on a regular basis. Part of this process involves sending a short questionnaire to people who have used any of the hotels in the group in the last month. The questionnaire seeks the opinions of these people on a number of topics – the service received, perceptions of value for money, the quality of the restaurant service and so on. One question asks if the person would use any of the group's hotels in the future should the occasion arise. Naturally the group is keen to encourage customers to return to their hotels. The group has set a target of no more than 4 per cent of customers responding that they would not use the group's hotels again (because of poor-quality service, too high prices or whatever).

The group organises these surveys on a monthly basis with a randomly selected sample of last month's customers. Typically around 500 customer responses are received in each survey. Clearly the basics of a potentially useful monitoring system exist in this situation. There is a ready mechanism for monitoring progress towards the 4 per cent target and for identifying any worsening trends in this aspect of company performance. The principles of SPC are illustrated in Figure 13.14. On the vertical axis the variable is shown in which management has an interest – the percentage of customers who would not use the group's hotels again. On this axis management can establish a target or expected value for the variable, here 4 per cent. Using principles that will be discussed below, the upper and lower expected limits to this variable can be calculated. Within these limits management concludes that the variable is still within reasonable limits of the target value. Outside these limits management would conclude that the variable now differs from the target set. Such monitoring will take place over a period where the variable is repeatedly measured and its current value assessed against the target value.

Figure 13.14 Control chart

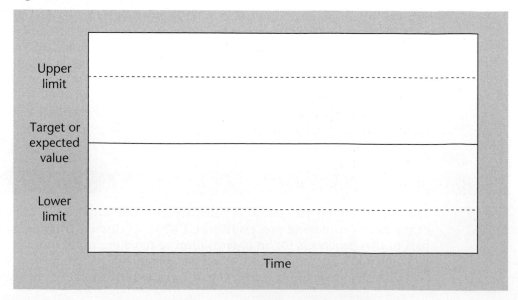

However, there does appear to be a slight difficulty in this process – this relates to the fact that the results in any one month will represent only a sample of customers and not all customers. For example, suppose management finds that last month 5 per cent of customers surveyed indicated they would not use the group's hotels again. Should the group conclude that customer attitudes – and possibly hotel performance – have worsened and are unacceptably higher than the target of 4 per cent? After all, it is based on only some customers. Perhaps a different sample of 500 customer responses would indicate a different result.

This scenario illustrates what is known as '**sampling variation**', which is a common problem for any organisation engaged in market research, opinion polls or customer satisfaction surveys. Sampling variation relates to the difference in results that might be expected simply by taking different samples of customers (or whatever is being measured). The subject area itself is very technical and the complete background required cannot be provided here. However, it is possible to introduce the general principles. At the heart of SPC lies what is known as the **sampling distribution**. All the group's customers last month can be defined as the statistical population (perhaps several thousand) and then it becomes clear that it would be possible to take many different samples of 500 customers from this population. Each sample would provide a result in terms of the percentage who would not use the group again. Some of these sample results would be the same and some would differ simply because there are different combinations of customers in the sample from the population.

It is possible to construct a frequency diagram showing the sample results and the frequency of these results. According to statistical theory a distribution like that shown in Figure 13.15 would be obtained. This shows the sampling distribution, which takes a typical symmetrical shape (known as the **normal distribution**). In the middle of this distribution is the result that would be obtained if all customers (the population) were asked. Most sample results (even though they are based on only 500 customer responses) will be similar to the population result. Relatively few sample results would be very different from the result obtained from asking the full customer population. In fact statistical theory allows for a further stage in predicting what these differences would be. Figure 13.16 shows the principles.

Using what is known as a **standard error** to measure variability, statistical theory predicts that 95 per cent of all sample results, where there is a normal distribution,

Figure 13.15 Sampling distribution of sample results

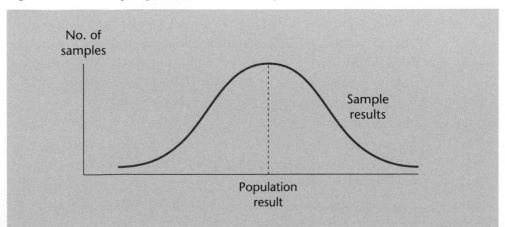

Figure 13.16 Sampling variation and standard errors

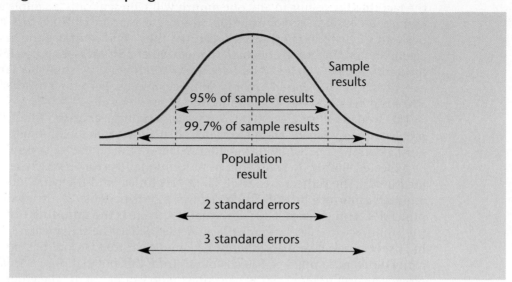

will occur within 2 standard errors (SEs) of the population result, while 99.7 per cent will occur within 3 SEs. This implies that, although it is only a sample result, it is possible to quantify how close it is likely to be to the population result.

The implications are straightforward. It is possible to treat the target figure of 4 per cent as the desired population result – i.e. no more than 4 per cent of all customers saying they would not use the group's hotels again. It is possible then to compare the result from any one sample of 500 customer responses against this target figure and use the 2SE and 3SE values as a measure. Put simply, if the target is being achieved then it can be anticipated (with 95 per cent confidence) that any sample of customer responses would be within 2SEs of 4 per cent, and with 99.7 per cent confidence that they would be within 3SEs of 4 per cent. But suppose a sample result was not within these 3SE limits? This would imply that the current population result was unlikely to be 4 per cent – it would imply that the target of 4 per cent set by the group is not being met.

The standard error can be calculated by using the following formula:

$$\sqrt{\frac{P(100 - P)}{n}}$$

where P is the assumed population percentage and n is the sample size. Here we would have:

$$\sqrt{\frac{4(100 - 4)}{500}}$$

$$\sqrt{\frac{4(96)}{500}}$$

$$= 0.876\%$$

and 2SEs would then be:

$$2(0.876) = 1.75\%$$
$$\text{and } 3SEs = 2.63\%.$$

This now provides a method for checking whether, based on a sample result of 500 customer responses, the group is meeting its target of 4 per cent or not. As long as the sample result is within 1.75 percentage points of the target (i.e. between 2.25 per cent and 5.75 per cent) it can be assumed that the target is being met. On the other hand if the sample result is outside the 3SE limit (i.e. outside the range 1.37 per cent to 6.63 per cent) then it is possible to be 99.7 per cent confident that the target is not being achieved. If it lies between 2SEs and 3SEs away from the target then a position can be adopted of seeing this result as warning that the target might not be being met. In the terminology of SPC the 2SE limit is known as a **warning limit** (warning that, if the sample result has exceeded this figure, then there would be a danger of not meeting the target), and the 3SE figure as an **action limit** indicating that management action is needed since, based on the sample result, the target is not being met. This is shown in diagram form in Figure 13.17.

This is a straightforward method for monitoring the target value based on samples taken every month. A sample result can be plotted on the control chart. If the result is within the warning limits then it is possible to reach the conclusion that the target of 4 per cent is being met. If the result is outside the action limits, then it can be concluded that the target is not being met and there is a need to take action accordingly. If the result is between the warning and action limits then it can be concluded that there are grounds for suspecting that the target is not being met, although it is not possible as yet to be positive about this. It is possible, under such circumstances, to arrange for another sample to be taken. Over time there would be a plot of the sample results. Not only would it be possible to monitor each month's result against the target, it would also be possible to observe any developing trends in the sample results. Figure 13.18 shows the principles.

The results of the last six months' samples are plotted. None of them breaches the warning limits so, on an individual basis, none of them is cause for concern. However, it should be noted that the last five months together show a definite upward trend in the sample results. It looks as if there is a slowly worsening attitude among samples of customers and this might be investigated before the next sample is taken.

Figure 13.17 Control chart with warning and action limits

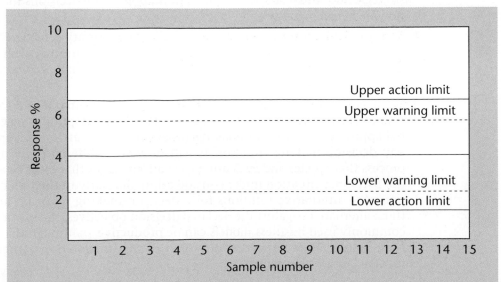

Figure 13.18 Control chart for six successive samples

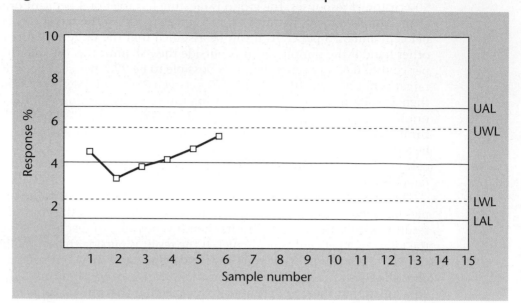

SUMMARY

■ Decision making forms an important part of any manager's workload, no matter at what level of management the individual operates and what the type or business of the organisation. Indeed it could be argued that decision making and problem solving are at the heart of a manager's role in any organisation.

■ The business environment in which such management decision making takes place is becoming increasingly complex, making the task of decision making that much more difficult. At the same time, and for many of the same reasons, the strategic and financial consequences of inappropriate decisions for an organisation are becoming greater.

■ The types of decision situations faced will naturally vary considerably from one organisation to another and from one manager to another. While decision-making approaches must be tailored to fit the particular circumstances, many decision situations have common aspects.

■ There is no panacea that can be offered to a decision maker as a foolproof and guaranteed method for decision making. However, adopting a logical and rational approach to a decision-making situation can be particularly productive. In any decision-making situation it will be worthwhile considering the wider process that applies and evaluating the various stages that must be addressed for the particular situation under consideration. Similarly in the task of generating potential alternative solutions for a decision-making situation and assessing those alternatives against the declared decision objectives, the use of a number of commonly used business models can be productive – although the output from such models must be seen as only part of the information-gathering process involved in decision making.

■ Such models are particularly valuable in decision-making situations where incomplete or inadequate information is available, where a number of alternatives are typically available and where uncertainty exists.

■ A number of these models have been introduced in this chapter but it must also be said that the last two or three decades have seen a veritable explosion of such models being developed and used. The subject area known as management science has provided many of these model developments and a number of texts are detailed in the references for further reading which introduce additional models of potential use to the decision maker.

Review and discussion questions

1 *From a management perspective what is the difference between decision making and problem solving?*

2 *Consider an organisation with which you are familiar. What is the organisation's attitude to risk? How does this affect its decision-making process?*

3 *As a manager facing a decision-making situation which has areas of uncertainty associated with it, is it possible to quantify such areas of uncertainty?*

4 *What are the key differences between management decision making and personal decision making?*

5 *Discuss how time affects the various stages of the decision-making process.*

6 *Consider the various decision-making support models introduced in this chapter. What factors would discourage managers from utilising the information derived from such models in the decision-making process?*

7 *'Decision making is the most important task for any manager.' Discuss this statement.*

8 *A manager in an organisation has been offered a considerable promotion. However, the promotion would involve moving to another part of the country.*

   a. *Using the decision-making process model consider how the manager would try to reach an appropriate decision.*

   b. *Draw a decision tree representing the decision-making situation.*

   c. *Assume the manager has decided to take the promotion. Draw a forcefield diagram to assess the critical factors which will affect the success of the move.*

CASE STUDY

Jaguar Cars

A Jaguar car. Instantly recognisable almost anywhere in the world and a global brand.

However, Jaguar has had a very chequered history over the last few decades and illustrates many of the issues relating to effective decision making discussed in this chapter. In the early 1980s the company came close to disappearing, with reducing market share, decreasing financial viability, outdated technology and working practices, and major product quality problems. With the introduction of new management it was able – painfully – to turn itself around and achieve improvements in efficiency, quality and profitability. Towards the end of the 1980s a worldwide recession emerged and the company again hit problems. In 1989 the company was bought by Ford Motor Company for around US$2.5 billion, with the new owner then having to find a further $700 million to help keep the company going in the short term.

Jaguar starkly illustrates the difficulties involved in decision making in today's environment. On the face of it, the company had tremendous potential. On the other hand it faced a number of major short-term problems. These included:

- the company was operating at a loss – it was estimated that in 1992 it actually lost $18,000 on each car sold;
- in motor industry terms it was very small, even when compared with its competitors in the luxury car market – Mercedes Benz, for example, had annual sales almost 20 times those of Jaguar;
- it was operating at below breakeven output – breakeven annual sales were estimated at 35,000; in 1993 Jaguar expected to produce and sell only 29,000 cars;
- worldwide there had been a dramatic collapse in the market for luxury cars;
- the company's cars had significant quality problems, particularly in relation to its major competitors, with, for example, a Jaguar car experiencing 75 per cent more defects than a Mercedes;
- many of the company's cars were relatively old models – however, the development costs of a new model were likely to run into the hundreds of millions of £s. In addition, such development would take considerable time.

The new management of Jaguar faced an array of interlinked problems as well as considerable uncertainty about markets, demand, customer loyalty and competitor strategy. It was also constrained by the desire to keep Jaguar as a unique product and not simply another variety of Ford car. A number of decisions were made to try to move the company forward. These included:

- immediate improvements in operating efficiency – assembly man-hours per car, for example, were reduced by almost 40 per cent in a two-year period, with a further 50 per cent reduction planned;
- significant quality improvements – with defects down by over 70 per cent on the XJ6 model alone;
- a major cost-reduction programme leading to a reduction in the workforce of almost 50 per cent;
- the introduction of, and development of, new models, but with decisions related to different timescales. In the short term the company decided to introduce a redesigned version of the XJ6 – which was a relatively quick and low-cost option – and longer term to invest in the design and the production of a totally new car aimed at the business executive market.

The decisions faced by the company's management in the 1990s were clearly a mixture of the strategic and the operational. At the operational level, decisions had to be made about how best to improve the company's immediate position. These needed to be made quickly and needed to have an immediate impact on the company's performance. While such decisions can be made relatively easily – relating to quality, productivity and operating costs – implementing such decisions effectively can be more problematic given issues of staff morale and uncertainty, and there is clearly considerable scope for some of the problem-solving techniques introduced in this chapter.

At the same time, a number of key strategic decisions were needed to try to ensure the company's long-term future. Such decisions related to the size of the company's customer base, the range of models available, its pricing policy and the location of its production base. Over time a series of related decisions emerged, and the sequential decision models introduced in this chapter clearly have a lot of potential in such a situation. As a short-term measure the company launched a redesigned version of the XJ6. In 1996 the company launched the XK8 sports car. The X200 executive saloon was launched in 1998 with further plans for the production of a family saloon, the X200.

The initial signs at the beginning of the twenty-first century were promising. Unit sales for Jaguar increased to just over 90,000 by 2000 and to just over 130,000 by 2002. However, Jaguar also recorded an operating loss in 2002 of around £300 million, around 50 per cent of the total loss recorded by Ford's luxury car division (which also included Land Rover, Aston Martin and Volvo). So, some 10 years later further decisions are needed – some by Jaguar's management and some by Ford's management given that Jaguar is part of the group.

Ford has invested an estimated £4 billion into Jaguar. This is a heavy investment and not to be written off lightly. However, Ford itself is now in financial difficulties and is undertaking a long-term strategic review of its own operations. One of the decisions is whether to retain Jaguar or to sell it off.

For Jaguar's management, although some progress has been made, some major challenges still have to be faced. The company has undertaken major cost-cutting in a bid to become more competitive but now faces a critical decision as to whether or not to move manufacture overseas to lower-cost economies. Uncertainties as to product quality then arise as do issues about customer perceptions given that the brand has been actively promoted through its 'Britishness'. There is also the issue that around half of Jagaur's recent sales have been in the US, a deliberate part of recent strategy. However, sales have been adversely affected by unfavourable exchange rates and by a shift among US customers to SUVs. Jaguar has also come under increasing pressure not just from its traditional competitors such as BMW, Mercedes and Audi, but also from volume car makers such as Toyota and Honda who see the top end of the luxury market as a profitable area for themselves.

Clearly further strategic and operational decisions are still needed reinforcing the point that organisations face a turbulent and ever-changing environment and that effective decision making becomes ever more difficult.

Questions

1 *What are the main strategic and operational pressures affecting Jaguar Cars over the last few years in terms of the external business environment?*

2 *What are the key strategic and operational decisions facing Jaguar?*

3 *Which of the models introduced in this chapter do you think would help Jaguar's management in the 1990s? In the mid-twenty-first century?*

FURTHER READING

Ackoff, R L (1978) *The Art of Problem Solving*, Chichester: Wiley.
A practical guide on the art rather than science of creative problem solving.

Dyson, R G and O'Brien F A (eds) (1998) *Strategic Development Methods and Models*, Chichester: Wiley.
Looks at decision making from a strategic perspective and introduces a number of useful tools and techniques.

Harvard Business Review (2001) *Harvard Business Review on Decision Making*, Boston, MA: Harvard Business School Press.
A collection of articles on decision making from the Harvard Business Review.

Juran, J M and Gryna, F M (1993) *Quality Planning and Analysis* (3rd edition), New York: McGraw-Hill.
Introduces a number of decision-making approaches aimed at improving product and service quality and customer satisfaction.

Moore, P G and Thomas, H (1988) *The Anatomy of Decisions*, Harmondsworth: Penguin.
Looks at the decision-making process and has a strong section on decision making under uncertainty.

Wisniewski, M (2006) *Quantitative Methods for Decision Makers* (4th edition), Harlow: FT Prentice Hall.
Reviews a number of quantitative techniques used in business decision making with case study examples.

WEBSITES

Many of the topics covered in this chapter come under the broad heading of either *management science or operational research*. Using either of these terms as the basis for a global search will find several million websites detailing the use of these techniques and their development. To get you started you might want to look at the following websites.

http://www.orsoc.org.uk/
The UK Operational Research Society.

http://www.uk.capgemini.com/services/consulting/or/success_stories/
Cap Gemini Ernst and Young's case study index of applications.

http://www.informs.org/resources
The Institute for Operations Research and Management Science.

CHAPTER 14

Operations management

RUTH BOADEN AND CLAIRE MOXHAM

Outcomes

Having read this chapter, you will be able to:

■ describe a framework for the analysis of operations management as one of the managerial roles within an organisation. It uses the analogy of operations as a transformation process, changing inputs into outputs;

■ explain the past, present and future context of the transformation process within the organisation;

■ show how the process may be classified and explain the impact of different types of process on the role of the manager;

■ demonstrate how the outputs from the process may be measured and consider the relevance of new ways of measuring;

■ examine the impact of the external environment on operations, with particular reference to the customer and the international context.

INTRODUCTION

The structure of the chapter reflects the theoretical basis around which it is built – that of **operations** being transformation processes where input resources are transformed into outputs. Following consideration of the past history and present organisational context of the process, future trends and means of classification are discussed. The role of the operations manager is also considered. Current and developing ways of measuring output are presented within the context of wider changes affecting operations. Finally the relationship between operations and the customer is analysed and some comment made on the implications of globalisation and multinational management on the operations manager. Five case studies are included to support and develop the key points raised in this chapter.

OPERATIONS MANAGEMENT AS A TRANSFORMATION PROCESS

Any organisation, whether it be a manufacturer, retailer, educational establishment, hospital or even government agency, exists to satisfy the needs of its customers or consumers – those who are the recipients of what is produced or the services carried out by the organisation (see Figure 14.1).

So within the context of an organisation what are 'operations'? An operation may be defined as

'a process, method or series of acts especially of a practical nature.'

In general, operations simply harness resources in order to produce something or to provide a service – they are part of every kind of organised activity within the

Figure 14.1 The closed loop of customer satisfaction

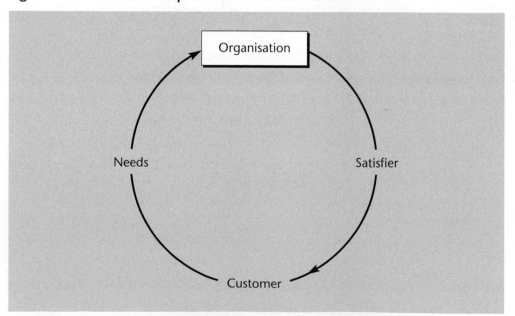

Source: K Lockyer, J Oakland and A Muhlemann (1992) *Production and Operations Management* (6th edition), Pearson Education Limited.

organisation. It is argued by some authors that **operations management** is an integral part of any managerial role (see Exhibit 14.1).

More specifically, operations can refer to a department or functional area within an organisation where certain resources are transformed into products or services by adding value to them. '**Operations managers**' therefore have to manage this process in some way.

There are several definitions of operations management which highlight the key features. Schroeder (1993) defines the key terms as:

> *'Operations managers are responsible for producing the supply of goods or services in organisations. Operations managers make decisions regarding the operations function and the transformation systems used. Operations management is the study of decision making in the operations function.'*

Harris (1989) uses a simpler definition which highlights all the key features of the task:

> *'operations management is the management of a system which provides goods or services to or for a customer, and involves the design, planning and control of the system.'*

Denzler (2000) defines operations management by 'what it does':

> *'Operations management is the business function that manages that part of a business that transforms raw materials and human inputs into goods and services of higher value.'*

Slack *et al.* (2006) discuss operations management in terms of process:

> *'operations and process management is the activity of managing the resources and processes that produce products and services.'*

Many authors view operations management as a transformation process, and this helps to highlight some of the key features of the task (see Figure 14.2).

Exhibit 14.1 Operations

■ A manufacturing company conducts operations in a mill, a foundry or a factory.

■ Banks operate from offices and branches.

■ Restaurant operations take place on chopping blocks, serving tables and takeaway counters.

■ Builders operate in offices where proposals are prepared and on construction sites.

■ University operations take place in lecture theatres, research laboratories, seminar rooms and on the sports field.

Source: Adapted from R J Schonberger and E M Knod (1994) *Operations Management: Continuous Improvement* (5th edition), Burr Ridge, IL: Richard D Irwin. Reprinted with permission from R D Irwin Inc.

Figure 14.2 The transformation process

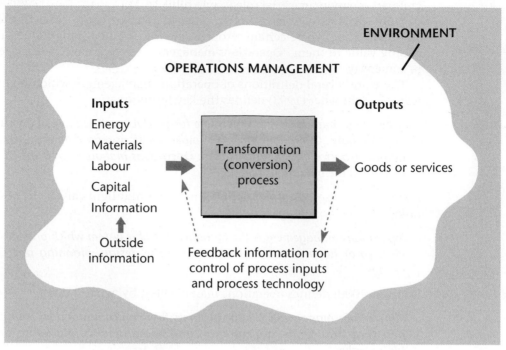

Examples of various operations classified in this way are shown in Table 14.1.
Slack *et al.* (2004) discuss the importance of operations management in terms of reducing the costs of producing products and services by increasing process efficiency, increasing revenue through good customer satisfaction and service quality, and by using innovation to reduce the need for investment in physical resources.

Table 14.1 Examples of operations classified as transformation processes

OPERATION	INPUTS	OUTPUTS
Bank	Cashiers, staff, computer equipment, facilities, energy	Financial services (loans, deposits)
Restaurant	Cooks, waiting staff, food, equipment, facilities, energy	Meals, entertainment, satisfied customers
Hospital	Doctors, nurses, staff, equipment, facilities, energy	Health services, healthy patients
University	Staff, equipment, facilities, energy, knowledge	Educated students, research
Airline	Planes, facilities, pilots, flight attendants, engineers, labour, energy	Transportation from one area to another

Source: Developed from R G Schroeder (1993) *Operations Management* (4th edition), © Copyright The McGraw-Hill Companies, Inc. 1993.

As part of the transformation process (see Figure 14.2) it is useful to make a distinction between **transformed** and **transforming resources** – those which are treated or transformed in a certain way and those which act upon the transformed resources (see Exhibit 14.2).

Exhibit 14.2 Transformed and transforming resources

Transformed resources:

- materials

- information

- customers

Transforming resources:

- facilities

- staff

Source: Adapted from N Slack, S Chambers, C Harland, A Harrison and R Johnston (2004) *Operations Management* (4th edition), Harlow: FT Prentice Hall.

One of the transformed resources is usually dominant in an operation – a bank deals with materials and customers but is primarily concerned with processing information. Manufacturing is primarily concerned with processing material but information is also very important. Classification of operations according to their predominant transformed resource is shown in Table 14.2.

Table 14.2 Operations classified according to primary transformed resource

PREDOMINANTLY MATERIALS PROCESSORS	PREDOMINANTLY INFORMATION PROCESSORS	PREDOMINANTLY CUSTOMER PROCESSORS
All manufacturers	Accountants	Hairdressers
Retail operations	Market research companies	Hotels
Warehouses	University research units	Hospitals
Postal service	Telecommunications companies	Theatres

Source: Adapted from N Slack, S Chambers, C Harland, A Harrison and R Johnston (2004) *Operations Management* (4th edition), Harlow: FT Prentice Hall.

In terms of the transforming resources, facilities may be high or low tech but are still important for any type of organisation. Staff will have various degrees of skill depending on the operation but reliability will be important in all cases. The role of staff in service operations is relatively more important than manufacturing because of the greater labour intensity of the **transformation process**.

THE CONTEXT OF THE TRANSFORMATION PROCESS: OPERATIONS STRATEGY

The interface between the transformation process and the environment is particularly important – both the environment within the organisation and the external environment must be considered. The relationship of operations to the environment is shown in Figure 14.3. Some of the aspects of these interfaces will be discussed in more detail when the role of the customer in operations is described.

Operations is generally considered to be a functional area – like marketing, etc. – rather than a basic discipline area of study – like economics, sociology, systems concepts, etc. It has traditionally been emphasised more in manufacturing because it is the major part of the organisation – in services, marketing is often considered to be more important. In terms of relationships with other functions within the organisation, the relationship between the marketing and operations functions is often considered to be the most crucial whatever the type of organisation. Lockyer *et al.* (1992) detail the relationship by defining a 'closed loop' which summarises all the key tasks involved in identifying and satisfying consumer needs (see Figure 14.4). The marketing role therefore covers stages (i) and (v) of this loop – identifying and forecasting, and distribution.

Figure 14.3 The relationship of operations to the environment

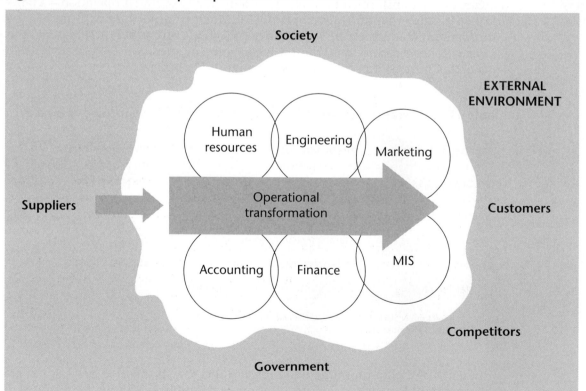

Source: R G Schroeder (1993) *Operations Management* (4th edition), Copyright © The McGraw-Hill Companies Inc.

Figure 14.4 From customer to customer – a closed loop

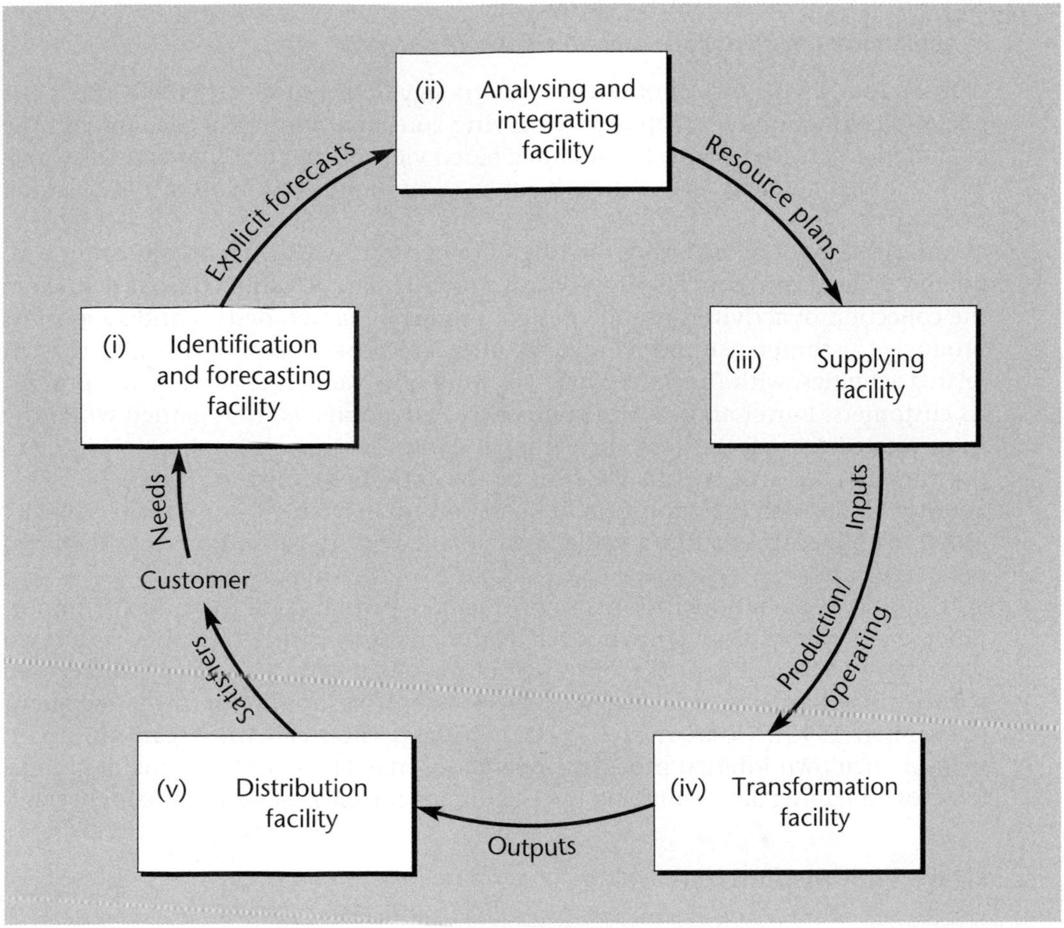

Source: K Lockyer, J Oakland and A Muhlemann (1992) *Production and Operations Management* (6th edition), Pearson Education Limited.

However, this approach may be criticised by those who believe that operations can offer competitive advantage to an organisation (e.g. Wheelwright and Hayes, 1985) and that customers and operations should be working more closely together. Other authors (Hill, 1993) believe that marketing strategy actually drives operations strategy following from the premise that customer requirements should drive the operations function. This is very much in line with the recent popularity of total quality approaches, which are identified by an increasing emphasis on putting the customer first, although this may be expressed in different ways (see Chapter 3).

→ Ch. 3

There has been a great deal of progress in the past five years in terms of developing the concept of operations strategy. This has arisen from the widespread adoption of the view that operations can offer competitive advantage to an organisation, be it manufacturing or service. One of the leading texts in the area (Slack and Lewis, 2002) defines operations strategy as

> *'the total pattern of decisions which shape the long-term capabilities of any type of operation and their contribution to overall strategy, through the reconciliation of market requirements with operations resources.'*

It argues strongly that the approach is applicable to both manufacturing and service organisations. It is concerned with the

'total transformation process that is the whole business.'

Slack and Lewis's model of operations strategy does not dictate the form of the operations function but proposes that giving consideration to the resources of the operation is consistent with the resource-based view of the firm that is increasingly well regarded and acts as a counterbalance to the traditionally dominant market perspective.

Another way of considering the role of operations within an organisation is to use the 'value chain' concept proposed by Porter (1985). A **value chain** is defined as the collection of activities used to design, produce, market, deliver and support its product. Customers, suppliers and the firm are broken down into discrete but related activities, with the value chain showing how value is created by the firm for its customers. Porter argues that competitive advantage is then gained when the value created exceeds the cost of creating it. 'Value' is what customers are willing to pay for and is created within the firm by the activities shown in Figure 14.5 This approach links with the definition of operations management proposed by Denzler (2000) who identifies adding value as the main activity carried out by the operations function.

It can be seen that operations is considered a primary activity and the importance of its role will be shown later in the chapter. While 'logistics' is shown separately by Porter it actually forms part of the broad definition of operations used within this chapter which includes the concept of supply chain management (Lamming, 1996). Cousins *et al.* (2007) discuss the need for organisations to manage their own internal processes (operations management) while maintaining a focus on obtaining and managing the best inputs for the organisation (supply chain

Figure 14.5 The firm chain value

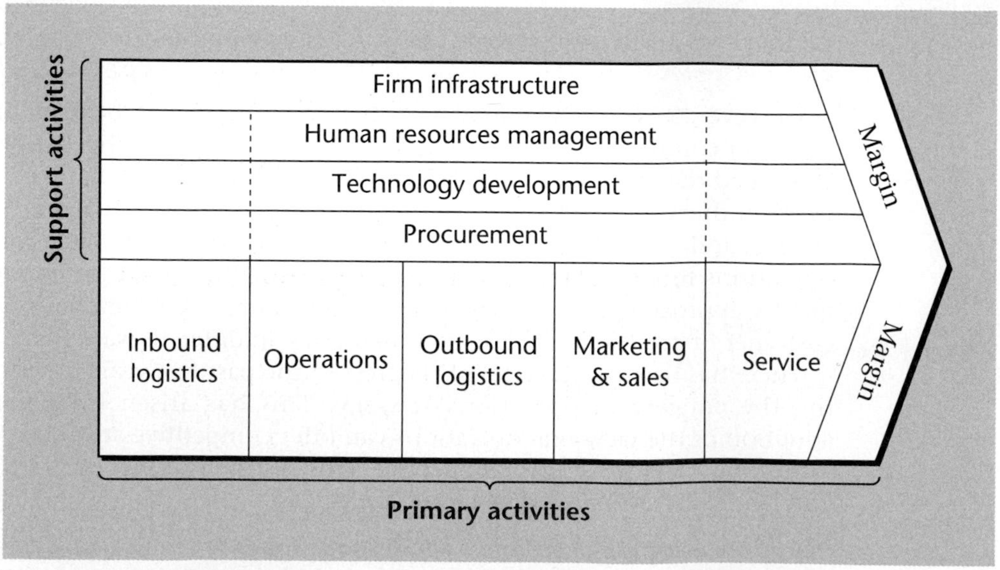

Source: Adapted from M E Porter (1985) *Competitive Advantage: Creating and Sustaining Superior Performance*, New York: Free Press, a division of Simon & Schuster. Copyright © 1985, 1998 by M E Porter.

management). Typical functions that might be included in such a broad definition of operations management include:

- purchasing
- production
- logistics
- maintenance
- goods receiving
- dispatch.

THE TRANSFORMATION PROCESS

Past history

In one sense operations management has existed as long as people have made things, although it was not recognised as such. Attention to 'production management' has been greatest in the past 200 years, and attention to operations management as a discipline only during the last 20 years or so. Operations management developed as a discipline because people realised that many different organisations were experiencing similar problems and whether they were service, manufacturing or public sector organisations did not make a significant difference.

It is not possible to give a strict chronological account of the way in which the area has developed but there are a number of major theoretical and practical contributions which have affected it (see Exhibit 14.3). Fuller accounts can be found in

→ Ch. 1   Fogarty *et al.* (1989) and Evans (1997) (see also Chapter 1).

Division of labour

→ Ch. 9   George (1968) argues that the concept of division of labour (see Chapter 9) can be traced back to the ancient Greeks (Plato's *The Republic*), where it was recognised that specialisation of labour on a single task can result in greater productivity and efficiency than assigning a number of tasks to one worker. This was also discussed by

Exhibit 14.3 Major contributions to the theoretical development of operations management

- **The division of labour – Adam Smith and Charles Babbage**
- **Standardisation of parts**
- **The Industrial Revolution**
- **The scientific study of work – Frederick Taylor**
- **Human relations – the Hawthorne experiments**
- **Decision modelling**
- **Technology**

→ Ch. 20

Adam Smith, author of the classic *The Wealth of Nations* (1776), who noted that output is increased by specialisation of labour (see Chapter 20). Workers become increasingly expert at one task, there is an avoidance of lost time due to changing to other jobs, and tools and machines can be added to improve efficiency. Charles Babbage (1832) noted that specialisation of labour makes it possible to pay wages only for the specific skills required. Division of labour is now being reviewed because of its effect on worker morale, turnover, job boredom and performance but it has been the foundation of many operations management techniques and methods of organising production systems.

Standardisation of parts

Manufacturing parts so that they are as interchangeable as possible is now commonplace in our society – for example, light bulbs of different wattage and shape but all with the same fitting. This was not, however, the case in the past and designing parts in this way is one of the major features of operations management which enabled increasing efficiency and specialisation of labour.

The Industrial Revolution

The Industrial Revolution took place during the late 1700s and early 1800s and was the time when machine power was substituted for human power. It was made possible by inventions such as the steam engine (invented by James Watt in 1764) and electricity. The demand for manufactured goods generated by the First World War (1914–18) aided the development of 'mass production' where very large quantities of goods were made using relatively high levels of automation. Society now appears to have shifted to a post-industrial period where manufacturing is not the primary source of income for many countries and services form the basis of the economy.

Scientific study of work

This method determines the best method of working using scientific principles – observing present work methods, developing an improved method through scientific measurement and analysis, training workers in the new method and continuing feedback and management of the work process. Taylor (1911) was the originator of these ideas and they gained widespread acceptance, although they have been criticised for being misapplied and used by management simply to 'speed up' workers without giving full consideration to their total range of needs. The scientific method is now seen by many as a means of exploiting workers and in opposition to newer methods of working which seek to take human needs into account.

Human relations

→ Ch. 12

Motivation and the human element in the design of work are vital and were highlighted by the Hawthorne experiments which indicated that worker motivation – along with the physical and technical environment – is crucial in improving productivity (see Chapter 12). The proponents of scientific management were forced as a result of these experiments to moderate their methods, which had placed an overemphasis on the technical elements of work design, and the concept of job enrichment was developed (Hackman *et al.*, 1975).

Decision models

Many of the traditional texts on production management concentrate almost entirely on the use of mathematical models to represent a production system in order to find optimal solutions within certain constraints. Examples of these models include the economic order quantity model used for inventory management and linear programming. Such models are still an important part of operations management but their limitations are now more clearly acknowledged, particularly in terms of their disregard for the human elements of operations and the limited range of assumptions on which many of the models had to be based in order to make them workable.

Technology

The application of computer technology has revolutionised operations management with computers being used for many planning and controlling tasks such as inventory management, production scheduling, costing and managing projects. Computers have been used for a number of years within the manufacturing process itself and this is still an important application. The advent of information technology in particular, where computer technology is used to store and process information, has been of particular significance within operations (Underwood, 1994). The Internet has enabled many organisations to increase the visibility of their supply processes (Cousins *et al.*, 2007) as it allows customers to select and purchase products via the web (for example, books and CDs) and to create bespoke service packages (for example, holidays) (Johnston and Clark, 2005).

PRESENT ORGANISATIONAL CONTEXT

Operations management plays an important role in any type of organisation, but different emphasis is placed on operations in manufacturing and service organisations. The differences and similarities between these types of organisation are important for operations managers since they need to understand clearly the nature of the organisation in which they are working and the relative importance of various aspects of operations management.

Operations can be classified in various ways. One useful classification is from Wild (1989), who identifies four different types.

■ **Manufacture** – where the physical output differs from the input: there is a change in the **form** utility of resources; *making something* – examples include car manufacture, food manufacture.

■ **Transport** – where the customer, or something belonging to the customer, is moved without any change in physical resources: there is a change in **place** utility; *moving something or someone* – examples include trains, distribution companies.

■ **Supply** – where the ownership of goods is changed without a change in form: there is a change in **possession** utility; *providing some physical goods* – examples include retailing, petrol stations.

■ **Service** – where the customer, or something belonging to the customer, is treated in some way: there is a change in **state** utility; *something happens to someone or something* – examples include dentists, the fire service.

It is not, however, always appropriate to assign an organisation solely to one category – most organisations have aspects of all of the above to varying degrees – but it is usual to be able to assign a primary category to an organisation and this will have implications for operations management.

It can be useful to distinguish between organisations according to the degree to which their transformation processes produce **goods**, i.e. tangible entities, or **services**, i.e. intangible entities. Goods are physical in nature and can be stored, transformed and transported. A service is produced and consumed more or less simultaneously but cannot be stored or transported (see Exhibit 14.4).

It can be argued that it is not appropriate to distinguish at all between manufacturing and service, but that there is simply a continuum of organisations with some having more emphasis on goods than others. However, most academics still maintain the distinction for the purposes of analysis and the UK government continues to issue economic statistics based on these classifications.

Even within service organisations there are difficulties of classification and the operations management implications vary. Schmenner (1986) has proposed the classification in Table 14.3 which is widely accepted. Degree of labour intensity refers to the ratio of capital to labour.

Schmenner goes on to discuss the implications of this classification for managerial roles and the points he makes are summarised in Table 14.4.

The major characteristics of services and their implications for operations management can be summarised as follows:

■ intangible output
■ variable, non-standard output
■ a service is perishable
■ high customer contact
■ customer participation
■ cannot be mass-produced
■ high personal judgement used by employees
■ labour intensity
■ decentralised facilities, near to the customer
■ demand varies greatly over a short period.

Exhibit 14.4 Goods or services

Primarily goods producers:
■ mines, chemical factories, oil refineries, farms, with little or no customer contact and not offering services as part of their marketing package.

Mixed production organisations:
■ most manufacturing companies, insurance companies and fast food outlets. All offer both goods and services. Manufacturing organisations often sell warranties and provide repair and after-sales service.

Primarily service producers:
■ dentists, management consultants, banks, educational institutions. Any tangible goods provided in connection with the service is incidental.

Table 14.3 The service process matrix

		DEGREE OF CONSUMER/SERVICE INTERACTION AND CUSTOMISATION	
		LOW	HIGH
DEGREE OF LABOUR INTENSITY	HIGH	**Mass service** e.g. retailing, banking, education	**Professional service** e.g. doctors, lawyers, accountants
	LOW	**Service factory** e.g. airlines, truck transportation, hotels, leisure resorts	**Service shop** e.g. hospitals, repair services

Table 14.4 Challenges for managers in service organisations

CLASSIFICATION	CHALLENGES
Low labour intensity	Capital expenditure Technology development Managing demand to avoid peaks and promote off-peaks Scheduling service delivery
High labour intensity	Hiring staff Training staff Developing and controlling methods of working Scheduling workers Controlling a large number of dispersed locations Managing growth
Low interaction/customisation	Marketing Attention to physical surroundings Managing a rigid organisation structure
High interaction/customisation	Managing cost increases Maintaining quality Dealing with customer participation in the process Managing the advancement of staff Managing a flat organisation Gaining employee loyalty

Intangible output

This describes the uniqueness of services more than any other aspect. Services are not a 'thing' that is produced but an activity that is experienced in some way, either by the customer directly or as a process carried out on possessions of the customer. The physical output from the process, therefore, does not exist in a tangible state and customer satisfaction is based on both the *process* (the service experience) and the *outcome* (the end result). There is often no clear boundary between process and outcome (Johnston and Clark, 2005) – for example, customers in a restaurant buy both the meal and they way it is served. Therefore service operations managers must manage the service process and the service outcome simultaneously.

Variable, non-standard output

The extent of this will depend on the exact type of service provided, as shown by Schmenner (1986), and in particular the degree of labour intensity, which makes quality control difficult. Quality is difficult to predict both for the organisation and the customer, and the reputation of the organisation is an important factor. Quality of service depends to a large extent, however, on the expectations of the consumer. With this in mind service operations, such as telephone call centres, use standard questions and processes when dealing with customer queries in an attempt to standardise the output of the customer service experience and manage customer expectation.

A service is perishable

A service is consumed instantly, for example using a hotel room or an airline seat, and cannot be stored, although consumers may enjoy the *benefit* for a long while afterwards – for example, a heart transplant.

This has a major impact on capacity planning, which is a key aspect of operations management. Periods of slack demand cannot be used to build stock to meet high demand in other periods, so capacity has to be varied. The large numbers of checkouts in supermarkets, not all of which are used at slack times, is an example of this. It is, however, expensive to build in extra capacity which may only be used at certain times, and it is not possible to hire employees at very short notice to cope with extra demand so they may have to appear as a fixed overhead rather than being varied with demand. In an attempt to make use of the available capacity, service organisations offer price incentives to encourage customers to move to less busy times. For example, train companies offer discounts for off-peak travel and restaurants offer cheaper 'early evening menus' from 5 to 7 pm.

High customer contact

Although this varies with the nature of the service (Schmenner, 1986), in general service organisations have a higher degree of customer contact than manufacturers – nevertheless this is changing even for manufacturing organisations. The customer may not be physically in contact with the provider, especially where technology is used, for example a telephone enquiry line, but in any case employee interaction is critical. In some cases organisations move 'messy' parts of the service process to places where they cannot be seen by the customer – sometimes referred to as back-room operations. This then allows the organisation to focus more on employee/customer interaction at the crucial point. Other organisations are proud to show all the parts of the operation to the customer – for example, McDonald's restaurants where all the kitchen operations are deliberately made visible, or Subway where the customer is part of the sandwich-making process.

Customer participation

The extent of customer participation depends on the type of service, and there may be a formal or informal relationship between the organisation and customer. It is a crucial factor in determination of quality and timeliness. Service operations need to guide the customer through the process using clear cues and visual management. For example, restaurants need to give clear cues as to whether it is self-service or has a table service to prevent customer confusion, frustration and ultimately dissatisfaction.

Cannot be mass-produced

This does not apply within the service factory quadrant of Schmenner's matrix and considerable benefits have been gained by service organisations applying mass-production principles to providing a service. For example, telephone call centres use technology to ask callers to select options on their keypad so that the service operation can quickly filter and meet the requirements of the high volume of customers. It is perhaps in this quadrant that operations management has had the greatest impact on service organisations. However, the customised nature of many services, such as medical treatment and legal advice, makes these types of service organisation very difficult to manage effectively.

High personal judgement used by employees

This is particularly marked in professional services – for example, lawyers and doctors who have a reputation for being the most difficult to manage. It applies to services which cannot be mass-produced and are often relatively labour intensive.

Labour intensity

This has implications for productivity (the ratio of output to input resources). Service organisations nearly always have lower overall productivity than manufacturing organisations. Where service organisations have substituted equipment for people (e.g. automatic cash dispensers in banks instead of going to the counter to obtain cash) or reorganised processes (e.g. self-service buffets rather than waiter service), there have been productivity improvements. People and equipment are not, however, always in opposition and may complement each other.

Decentralised facilities near to the customer

This is especially important where physical contact with the customer is involved and service location is critical to revenue for many organisations. It is not possible to ship services, because they have to be produced at the point of customer contact. In order to minimise variation between large numbers of locations there is a trend towards uniformity – many high streets look the same now – where all branches appear to be very similar and common procedures are used, with central common training.

Demand varies greatly over a short period

Relative to manufacturing organisations demand varies more often in service companies, with more of a random pattern (e.g. emergency services), and stocks cannot be made to help out. Some organisations try to alter demand (e.g. cheap off-peak offers), manage supply by building flexibility into operations (e.g. more checkouts open at busy times) or in some cases by ignoring variations (accepting that there will be longer queues at lunchtime). This third option is becoming less easy to justify as consumers are offered more choice and appear to be becoming more particular about service quality. The USA is an example of a society where service quality is now a crucial determinant of market position.

CURRENT INFLUENCES

Production management was important when the Western world was an 'industrial society', but the rise of service organisations and the decline of manufacturing have caused some people to question the relevance of operations. However, there are a number of reasons why operations management is considered to be increasingly important rather than in decline.

The resurgence of interest in operations during the 1980s was fuelled by the decline in the international competitiveness of Western industry, whose markets were taken over by foreign products and competition. The rate of productivity growth was also falling behind other countries, especially those in the Far East, and this was seen as being the province (and the fault) of the operations function. Whatever the 'solution' may be to the economic problems of the West (if, indeed, there is a single solution), increased investment, more research and development and changes in the approaches used to manage people all have to be put into action by operations managers and therefore affect the operations function.

Many of the fashionable ideas in management – total quality management (TQM), supply chain management (SCM), 'lean' thinking, business process re-engineering (BPR) and six sigma – not only affect but are centred around the operations function and focus on the process. Part of the appeal of such management techniques is the data-driven evidence-based approach to analysing processes. Many have also realised that focusing on, and improving, operations can increase efficiency (therefore reducing costs) as well as providing improved quality and service (which improves revenue). Slack and Lewis (2002) are clear that

> '"operations" is not always "operational" – operations management has an important strategic dimension.'

Some have not only seen operations as the key to future economic prosperity but also as a means of securing competitive advantage (Wheelwright and Hayes, 1985). It is clear that weak operations will affect the competitive position of the organisation, and as operations has become more closely linked to other parts of the organisation so its role in competitive positioning has become more important. At one time a good product, superior marketing or a technology which was difficult to imitate could make up for weak operations management. The role of operations is, however, different now:

> 'Superior operations management blends with superior design, marketing, accounting, supplier relations, human resource management and business strategy as an essential component of success. Weak operations management, on the other hand, tends to coincide with many other management weaknesses.' (Schonberger and Knod, 1994)

Current influences on operations include:

- customer-directed operations
- continuous improvement and quality
- lean and agile production
- integration with other functions
- globalisation of operations
- risk
- business ethics, corporate responsibility and the environment.

Customer-directed operations imply that operations have an external orientation so that they are well placed to meet customer requirements. However, customers may be

internal as well as external to the organisation – 'customer' can mean the next process as well as the final end user of the product or recipient of the service. The trend towards subcontracting and outsourcing of services has made it more difficult for organisations to control their external suppliers and contractors. However, the related growth of interest in supply chain management (Christopher, 1998) is a response to this influence and is becoming increasingly important. Strategic supplier selection is now seen by many as key to supporting an organisation's long-term objectives (Cousins *et al.*, 2007).

Continuous improvement and quality are influences that have increased in importance, not only as a result of increased emphasis on customer relationships but also because of the influence of Japanese manufacturers in the West (see Ishikawa, 1985). Many have described the changes in emphasis in Western organisations as a 'quality revolution' (Evans, 1997) and there is no doubt that a focus on quality is now a prerequisite for effective competitiveness in most markets. Although it originally started in the manufacturing sector, service quality is now a major focus for all organisations as it is often how customers differentiate between similar products and services. This is evidenced by the inclusion in this book of a whole chapter on quality management (see Chapter 7) which details its influence and highlights the strategic importance of quality management.

→ Ch. 7

Lean and agile production are influences that have become important as

> *'the goals of low cost and high productivity became "givens".'*   (Evans, 1997)

Lean production emphasises the reduction of waste and effective utilisation of resources in all aspects of the manufacturing process and utilises cross-functional teams, multiskilled workers, integration of supplier relationships and communications and flexible automation. Agile production focuses on the ability of the manufacturing process to respond quickly to changes in demand, in terms of volume and specification, and utilises lean production techniques to achieve this agility. Although the original applications were in manufacturing the concepts are also becoming accepted in service organisations, especially those where customer 'flow' is particularly important, for example hospitals, hotels and banks.

Integration with other functions is to some extent a result of some of the influences already described. However, it has also developed from the recent emphasis on business process improvement (Harrington, 1991) and business process re-engineering (Hammer and Champy, 1993). Counter to this influence is the increasing trend to decentralisation, although this can be alleviated to some extent by improvements in communications technology leading to 'virtual' organisations. Improved integration can enable reductions in total cycle time and facilitate a quicker response to customers thus improving customer service.

Globalisation of operations is inevitable as organisations compete internationally – many organisations describe themselves as competing in a global marketplace. However, the implications of such globalisation for operations has not always been simple, particularly where global companies are formed by mergers between organisations with very different operating procedures and organisational cultures (see Chapter 19). The characteristics of 'world class' manufacturers are well described by Schonberger (1996).

→ Ch. 19

Risk of technology failure, supplier failure and natural and man-made disasters can affect all operations. A focus on processes to prevent failures occurring, to minimise their effects and to continually improve is a key role for today's operations manager. Slack *et al.* (2006) use the terms *risk* and *resilience*:

> *'Risk is the potential for unwanted negative consequences from some event. Resilience is the ability to prevent, withstand and recover from those events.'*

Continuous improvement and quality techniques can be used to understand where risk or failure might occur and to improve and implement processes to prevent further occurrence.

Business ethics, corporate responsibility and the environment are key to all organisational functions including operations management (see Chapters 17 and 18). Recent legislation on emissions and the disposal of products at the end of their useful life has led to manufacturers being responsible for reducing waste and recycling, reusing or remanufacturing the products they produce. This has implications for product design and manufacture – two key operations management functions. A large number of computer hardware manufacturers provide a free recycling service for their customers. This service must be designed into the operations process.

→ Chs 17 & 18

Within the organisation it is argued that operations has an important role and, although this may be hotly debated by other functional areas, the argument proposed by Slack (1983) and developed subsequently by him and other authors, is based on facts rather than emotion. The case can be developed as follows.

Operations...

- concerns the management of most of the people within the organisation, either production workers or service personnel, and often represents 70–80 per cent of the total workforce;
- has responsibility for the effective use of the organisation's assets, both fixed assets and inventory (current assets), and therefore for the management of most of the organisation's funds;
- is responsible for most of the organisation's expenditure and has the largest budget allocation of any one function;
- is a pervasive activity (i.e. interacts with everything else);
- is the area in the organisation where many social and technological changes are taking place.

The role of an operations manager can be illustrated by the following two case studies which give accounts of what an operations manager does.

CASE STUDY 14.1

Operations management at United Biscuits

Andrew Hawley was sponsored by United Biscuits during his studies for his degree in business, and his early work experience with the company confirmed his interest in manufacturing operations: 'Where else could you be managing 50 people from the outset, in your early twenties? The satisfaction comes from being responsible for the performance of the plant and staff, seeing immediate results and – above all – from beating targets!'

Andrew had various roles in his first five years with the company; initially he was responsible for the day-to-day supervision of a factory, then he became a deputy factory manager of a small spe-

cialised plant, before moving to headquarters, where he is now responsible for aspects of operational and strategic planning.

'It is certainly a change being in a team of just six people after helping to manage a factory and I now face a whole new set of challenges. My hands-on experience of production has been invaluable for my current position. Without it, I wouldn't be able to decide on production systems and procedures three or more years in advance of implementation. The work is very diverse. Sometimes I am working to identify potential problems so that preventive mea-

sures can be implemented, and at other times I am involved in logistics projects aimed at integrating UB companies all over Europe, which will make enormous savings for the group. Many people have misconceptions about manufacturing and production management, they think that it is just about "doing" and is less stimulating and intellectually demanding than other disciplines. Nothing could be further from the truth in my opinion.

It has been my job at United Biscuits to ensure that all products leave our plant manufactured to our very demanding specifications. This involves not only responsibility for the process and the people, important though they are, but also for clear communication and

involvement with all of the other business functions to ensure that the business unit is run optimally. It is especially important to understand how production must be involved with the fundamental issues of cost, service, quality and innovation and to be able to create and manage change. Managers in the manufacturing role also have an important part to play in developing the business strategy, notably in coordination with the marketing department. In a real sense, when you're involved with manufacturing, every other discipline in the company is backing you, because you are the one that is producing exactly what millions of people are buying in the shops every day. This is, after all, what the company is there for in the first place!'

Source: N Slack, S Chambers, C Harland, A Harrison and R Johnston (1998, 2001) *Operations Management* , London: FT Prentice Hall. Reprinted with permission.

CASE STUDY 14.2

Operations management at a theme park

Alan Randell, the manager at Thorpe Park, Chertsey, arrives by 9 am, signs on, by radio, with Operations Control, and then calculates today's budgeted attendance – based on historic trading and present marketing initiatives. His estimate of 8000 was surpassed by the eventual attendance of 10,000. He then confirmed states of operations and ride-readiness. The maintenance staff arrive at 6.30 am and the cleaning department at 7.30 am. At 9 am all cast members (staff) have to be signed in and surveyed for their costume, hair length and entertainment presence. After checking with the admissions supervisor over kiosk state-of-readiness he decided to open 15 minutes early, at 9.15 am. By 9.30 there were already 436 parents and children inside.

After monitoring the turnstiles – he has entry operations responsibility as well as executive responsibility – he walks over the bridge.

'I saw Harley, the costumed character. Harley gave me five. It's a case of getting and delivering a level of adrenalin, happiness and smiles. I then went to see Snoopy's aerobics show. I'm looking to maintain Snoopy for the season. Then, the duty manager briefed me on cleanliness by Octopus Garden.'

There are almost 600 'cast', with 100 having a radio, so everything that's happening in the park

comes over and is known about immediately, whether it's inside No Way Out (the giant backwards turbobooster ride in pitch blackness), over the Flying Fish by Pot Bellies or on Miss Hippo's Jungle Safari.

'Back in my office I use the computer, which tells me how many fun-seekers are in the park, what time-segment they each arrived in, how that compares with yesterday and the same day last week – or any day in the last four years – and how much each of them paid, how they paid, when they paid …'

Thorpe Park is dedicated to a family market and a parent-friendliness profile, so the manager constantly monitors rides and adjusts cast levels to control queue lineage and foot-flow.

'So far today I've increased to three the waterbuses from Customs House. We've also had one nosebleed, a hand hurt on a fence and someone's been sick. After lunch – with this hot bright sunshine – I will be watching closely our key rides, the smash splashers, our wet, wet, wets: The Depth Charge, Thunder River and Logger's Leap. They'll be the hardest hit when the restaurants and food franchises' trade levels off. And at the Fantasy Reef pool I'll want to make sure the balance of younger children with older is acceptable, so we'll have extra monitors.'

Source: Developed from an interview by John Hind, *Observer*, 8 June 1997. Reprinted with permission.

THE PROCESS ITSELF

How can it be classified?

Operations management is about managing the transformation process, but there are a number of ways in which the process can be classified and these will affect the nature of the task. Process choice is important since it has implications for the way the system operates and it is not quick or cheap to change. This section will examine both manufacturing and service process types.

There are five major types of process for manufactured items:

- project
- jobbing, unit or one-off
- batch
- line
- continuous.

These are sometimes combined into three main categories: job/project, batch/intermittent and flow/mass. The exact terminology used will depend on the author of the book concerned and to some extent whether the book is of US or European origin.

Project

This type of process is used to produce a one-off item, for example a new building or film, or for a one-off service, such as a consultancy assignment. There is a sequence of operations but they are not usually repeated. The task is usually done at the customer's site (although not exclusively).

The major operations management task is to plan, sequence, coordinate and control the tasks leading to completion of the whole project – this is called project management. The process is usually relatively high cost and difficult to automate because of the lack of repeatability.

Jobbing, unit or one-off

This type of process is used for one-off or small-order requirements, with the product being of a smaller nature than for a project process, for example a purpose-built piece of equipment, designer dress, handmade shoes or bespoke computer system. The product is usually made in-house and then transported to the customer and commissioned before acceptance.

Batch

This process is used when similar items are required in larger volumes than for a jobbing process, and the products are produced in batches at intermittent intervals. The essential characteristic is that to provide another product/service the process has to be stopped and reset – the same equipment is used for a number of different products. Examples include car components, white goods, casting, a computer bureau that uses the same equipment for work from a number of different clients. General purpose equipment and highly skilled labour are used – this gives high flexibility but low efficiency with problems in controlling inventories, schedules and quality.

This is the type of process on which most production management texts have traditionally concentrated, and for which most methods have been developed. This is realistic because the majority of production is of this type, and probably a lot of service too.

Line

In this process a linear sequence of operations is used to make the product or service with equipment dedicated to that product or small range of products. The process is essentially repetitive where each product passes through the same sequence of operations. Examples include motor vehicle manufacturing, food preparation in McDonald's and some bank operations, for example cheque processing. The process is sometimes called 'mass' production, to distinguish it from continuous production. Line processes are very efficient but inflexible, as car makers have discovered to their cost. Customers are demanding more variety in products but manufacturers have found it difficult to satisfy this demand because their processes were established for large runs of similar products. The main sources of efficiency are the substitution of capital for labour wherever possible and highly specified labour tasks with a high degree of repetition.

Continuous

This is a variation of a line process, where several basic materials are processed through successive stages into one final product. It is usually more automated and standardised than a line process. The best example is petrochemicals but others include beer, paper and electricity production. The start-up cost of these processes is generally very high so they tend to be run continuously, or as near as possible, with little or no labour intervention. This process is not used in services because there is no labour content.

Classifying services

There are three major types of processes for services:

- professional services
- service shops
- mass services.

Professional services

These are often bespoke services with an emphasis on providing customer solutions. There is a high level of customer involvement and the professional service is knowledge and skills focused. This is similar to the project type of process. Examples include management consultants, lawyers, doctors and architects.

Service shops

This process provides a mix of front and back office activities to meet a range of customer requirements. The characteristics of this process are similar to those of jobbing or batch. Examples of service shops include banks, high street shops and hotels. This type of process is applicable for higher customer volumes than professional services but it offers less customisation.

Mass services

Mass services are applicable for high volumes of customers, for example call centres, and have similar characteristics to those of line or continuous processes. This type of process has low levels of customisation and is often equipment, rather than people, based. Examples include airports, supermarkets and rail services.

There are many different accounts of the various characteristics of the different classification of processes. Table 14.5 provides a summary of the manufacturing and service processes types and their major operational characteristics.

Table 14.5 Summary of process type and major operational characteristics

	JOB/PROJECT/ PROFFESSIONAL	BATCH/INTERMITTENT/ SERVICE SHOP	MASS (MANUFACTURING AND SERVICE)/LINE
Product aspects			
Product/service flow	None	Jumbled	Sequenced
Product/service variety	Very high	High	Low
Volume	Single unit	Medium	High
Labour aspects			
Skills	High	High	Low
Task type	Non-routine	Non-routine	Repetitive
Type of capital			
Investment	Low	Medium	High
Inventory/queues	Medium	High	Low
Equipment	General purpose	General purpose	Special purpose
Operations objectives			
Flexibility	High	Medium	Low
Cost	High	Medium	Low
Quality	More variable	More variable	Consistent
Delivery	Medium	Low	High

Source: Developed from T J Hill (1991) *Production/Operations Management* (2nd edition), London: Prentice Hall.

How should the process be arranged?

The type of process influences the layout of the operation.

'There is little point in having a well-sequenced process if in reality its activities are physically located in a way that involves excessive movements of materials, information or customers.'
(Slack *et al.*, 2006)

There are four common layout approaches:

- Fixed position
- Process
- Product/line
- Cellular.

Fixed position layouts

These require the equipment, machinery, plant and staff to move to the product or customer. In the case of manufacturing this is often because the product is too large to move, for example a bridge or building, and in services it may be because the customer is too delicate to move, for example in neurosurgery. The key issue for the operations manager is the scheduling and coordination of the resources during the project.

Process layouts

These are designed around the functional needs of the transforming resources (equipment, facilities, staff). This type of layout locates similar activities together.

For example, in a machine shop all the lathes are grouped together, as are all the milling machines etc. A library uses a process layout as all reference books, fiction, non-fiction and audiobooks are grouped in separate sections to meet the needs of a diverse range of users.

Product/line layouts

These locate people and equipment for the convenience of the transformed resources (materials, information, customers). The layout is designed to match the sequence of activities that is required to provide the product or service. Because the transformed resources flow along a 'line', high volumes of output are often achievable. This configuration is applicable for standardised outputs, such as automobile assembly or self-service buffets, as it permits little process variation.

Cellular layouts

These can provide the flexibility of a process layout and the efficiency of a product layout. The transforming resources necessary to meet the needs of one part of the operation are located in a cell. The internal layout of the cell may be arranged in any appropriate manner. After being processed in a cell, the transformed resources may move onto a subsequent cell. This configuration aims to match resources to product or service demand in order to reduce work-in-progress and throughput times. There are many examples of the utilisation of this type of layout in manufacturing. Service organisations are also adopting this technique, for example major supermarket chains are creating 'lunch cells' where customers can purchase sandwiches, drinks and snacks and then pay at a dedicated checkout rather than waiting in a queue in the main store.

Table 14.6 summarises the alternative layouts for particular process types. The type of layout that is ultimately selected depends on the objectives and constraints of the organisation.

Table 14.6 The relationship between process type and layout type

MANUFACTURING PROCESS TYPE	POTENTIAL LAYOUT TYPES		SERVICE PROCESS TYPE
Project	Fixed position layout Process layout	Fixed position layout Process layout Cell layout	Professional service
Jobbing	Process layout Cell layout	Process layout Cell layout	Service shop
Batch	Process layout Cell layout		
Mass	Cell layout Product layout	Product layout Cell layout	Mass service
Continuous	Product layout		

Source: N Slack, S Chambers, R Johnston and A Betts (2006) *Operations and Process Management,* p. 116. Harlow: FT Prentice Hall.

THE ROLE OF THE OPERATIONS MANAGER

There are many frameworks which attempt to describe what an operations manager does. The one presented here is based on that developed by Schroeder (1993) and has been selected because it is based around the concept that operations management is primarily a decision-making role. There are others who argue that operations is an integral part of any managerial role (e.g. Schonberger and Knod, 1994) and that, to some extent, every employee is a 'manager', at least of the immediate workplace (Scott Myers, 1991) including those who actually make the product or provide the service – first-line supervisors, department heads and general managers as well as technical experts. However, a narrower definition is more common and relates to those situated within the operations function itself. The involvement with day-to-day operations depends to a large extent on the level of the operations manager within the organisation, with lower-level managers having more detailed involvement. Job titles may include the following and can relate to lower-level supervisory roles right up to senior management and director positions:

- **Materials manager**
- **Purchasing manager**
- **Inventory manager**
- **Production control manager**
- **Quality manager**
- **Line manager**
- **Planning analyst**
- **Managing partner**
- **Customer service manager.**

Operations managers make decisions in five main areas:

- **Quality** – managing quality issues, controlling quality and improving it.
- **Process** – selecting and designing the transformation process, selecting and using the appropriate technology, layout of facilities.
- **Capacity** – forecasting demand, making decisions about facility location, planning at top and detailed levels, including project planning.
- **Inventory** – planning appropriate levels of inventory and methods of control, linking inventory to production planning and scheduling.
- **People** – managing the workforce, designing and improving jobs.

The decisions made by an operations manager are short-, medium- and long-term and involve all aspects of a manager's role – planning, controlling and staffing, (Fogarty *et al.*, 1989). The scope of operations management decisions can be summarised in four categories (developed from Fogarty *et al.*, 1989) where the various dimensions of decision making are combined (see Table 14.7).

A single decision may be made using criteria from any or all of the four areas and it should be noted that they are interrelated, so that decisions made in one area will affect other areas. An overall plan, strategy and direction are needed in order to determine the direction of the organisation. The overall goals can then be detailed to determine the actions and decisions needed in each functional area, including

Table 14.7 Dimensions of operations decision making

TIME PERIOD AFFECTED	RESOURCE MANAGED	DECISION AREA AFFECTED	MANAGEMENT FUNCTION
Long-range	Facilities	Capacity	Planning
Medium-range	Equipment	Materials	Execution
Short-range	Materials	Quality	Control
Present	Labour	Process	Organisation
	Information	Personnel	Staffing
	Capital		
	Energy		

operations management. Fogarty *et al.* say that typical operations management decisions include:

- a plant manager deciding the number of people of different skills that will be needed to meet the schedule for the coming year;
- a restaurant manager deciding the number of cooks, waiters and other staff that will be needed on each shift during the coming week, and then scheduling individuals to work those shifts;
- an analyst in a bank studying the processing of customers' cancelled cheques, searching for methods of reducing bottlenecks in the operation, reducing the flowthrough time and increasing productivity;
- a manager of a goods-receiving department studying methods of scheduling arrivals, assigning incoming trucks to unloading bays, unloading trucks, processing the necessary data, moving the items received to their proper location and eventually to their point of use.

The skills required for an operations manager are common with those of any manager, although there are a number of particular factors which are important. Most operations managers have a relatively high level of quantitative skill, which is useful in utilising the decision-making models which are a part of much operations management. A high level of interpersonal skill is also required because of the number of people involved. Many western education systems do not permit a wide enough range of interpersonal and behavioural skills to be developed if a high level of technical education is pursued, with the result that many operations managers are criticised for being technically capable but not managerially proficient. Attempts are now being made to address this at all levels of the education system.

Some of the typical tasks undertaken by an operations manager include:

- **management of a cost centre**
- **efficiency in the short and long term**
- **management of technology**
- **control of subsystems within the whole**
- **responsibility for money and work flow**
- **managing a process characterised by tangible outputs**
- **managing complexity.**

Management of a cost centre

An operations manager is responsible for a large proportion of the organisation's assets, and therefore controls a relatively large budget. While this does not necessarily require detailed accounting skills, a good understanding of financial matters is an asset.

Efficiency in the short and long term

Day-to-day activities have to be well controlled, but an operations manager also has to have a long-term view and must consider long-term trends too. The danger is to be only short-term oriented because that is the most pressing consideration. The operations manager's task has been described as:

> *'the task is problem oriented ... pressure is also a distinctive feature.'*

Management of technology

The operations manager may have to manage technology both within the product itself and within the process. It is increasingly difficult for operations managers to keep up to date with technological advances in any detail, and so they should attempt to understand the level of technology employed and its purpose, rather than the details of individual technologies which should be left to technical experts. Maintaining this balance and avoiding the temptation to get drawn into detailed technical issues are often difficult.

Control of subsystems within the whole

Operations managers will have a number of different groups reporting to them and may be responsible to several different functions. A balance between the potentially conflicting demands of the various groups is needed, making sure they all contribute effectively to the whole. The danger is that the performance of one subsystem will be optimised at the expense of the others.

Responsibility for money and work flow

Maintaining the balance between spending money and carrying out productive work is one of the major issues for operations managers. Table 14.8 shows that money is spent until the goods have been produced, and it is only at that point that the organisation may begin to get money back in (assuming a standard manufacturing process, not a project environment). In order to satisfy monthly accounting targets, operations are often put under pressure to 'get things out' at the end of the month so that money can come in, although this may not be optimal in terms of efficiency within the operations function. The link between commercial rules, negotiated by the accounting function, and the operation of the process is not always clearly defined.

Managing a process characterised by tangible outputs

Even in the case of services this will be true to some extent. Operations management is the management of the transformation process, which always has some form of output and which usually has at least some physical element. Because of the relative

Table 14.8 Money, work and material flow

MONEY FLOW	CURRENT ASSETS	WORK AND MATERIALS FLOW
Out	Raw materials and components	Materials/components bought from outside
Out	Work in progress	Labour and other materials/components added
Out	Finished goods	More labour and materials components added
In		Finished goods/services sold (cash sales)
In (eventually)		Finished goods/services sold (credit sales)
In		Payment made for credit sales

ease of measurement of the 'quality' or other features of the output, the short-term aspects of the operations management task are often given too high a priority. Coupled with the fact that operations is not always incorporated into corporate strategy, although it is argued that it should be (Skinner, 1969; Hill, 1993), there is a tendency simply to optimise the physical aspects of short-term performance.

Managing complexity

While this is true of any managerial task, the challenge for operations managers does not arise from the individual tasks involved, which of themselves can be quite tedious, but from combining the large number of these to make something which works well and is effective for the organisation as a whole. This task is summarised well by Schonberger and Knod (1994):

> '*Effective operations management blends the interests of customer, employee and manager, along with those of the public, shareholders and other stakeholders. Diverse resources, changing technologies and hard-to-predict demands add to the challenge. Human ingenuity, diligence and the right management tools are required to blend all the interests properly.*'

A typical day in the life of an operations manager is given in Case Study 14.3.

CASE STUDY 14.3

A day in the life of an operations manager

Sue Jones is the operations manager for the UK plant of Estech Ltd – a medium-sized company that manufactures and repairs marine seismic equipment used by oil companies engaged in offshore oil exploration. The main activity is the manufacture and repair of hydrophonic cables towed by seismic survey ships. Each cable is made up of sections and costs about £500,000. Repair and technical support arrangements are vital given the hostile nature of the marine environment.

The plant is divided into two main areas – cable manufacture and repair, and technical manufacture and repair. Each area has a manager who is responsible to Sue, who currently has 40 people working for her. She is directly responsible to the managing director for all aspects of production, repairs, logistics, quality, site facilities and research and development.

▶

8 am In the factory
The main factory starts at 7.30 am and Sue walks round the plant for half an hour talking to people, including John Butler, the filling shop supervisor. The previous day there were problems with one of the machines and Sue wants to check progress.

8.30 am Sue's office
Jim Edwards, the quality manager, appears at the office door to report that problems with the delivery of a key component have been sorted. Five minutes later it is the site facilities manager who calls. Sue operates an 'open door' policy and consciously sets this time aside for 'mopping up' problems from the previous day.

9 am Cable and repair manager's office
Sue joins the daily meeting of the production team. During the night Sue received a telephone call from the MD who had in turn received a call from the leader of a seismic survey team on board a survey ship off the coast of Nigeria. He had damaged three of his six cables in a collision and is anxious to get the damage repaired. This morning's meeting has to consider the feasibility of getting the damaged sections repaired within the next two weeks as the MD promised. Sue's task is to assess the situation with all those directly involved and with them arrive at a decision.

Not only does the team have to consider what is technically possible, it has to think through the consequences of rescheduling work. Fortunately two of the jobs being done this week are routine ones put into the schedule because there was a gap between two high-priority jobs. After much discussion, the consensus is that the Nigerian job can be fitted in. Staff are going to have to reschedule their work and there will have to be some overtime, but the client is going to get what he wants.

9.45 am Sue's office
The next hour and a half are devoted to work on ongoing projects. These include negotiating the technical requirements of a major new potential customer, the development of a new product and the evaluation of a new supplier.

11 am Reception
Sue meets two visitors from a potential new customer. After a tour of the plant she joins them in a meeting with the cable repair manager and two technicians.

1 pm Canteen
Lunch and an opportunity to talk to two new members of staff about their training course.

2 pm Sue's office
She makes some phone calls and prepares some faxes, as well as holding a meeting with the management accounts manager. The board has requested that the monthly production report should be available seven days after the month end rather than 14 days as at present. The meeting is to explore what needs to be done in order to meet the request. Once this meeting is over, Sue checks her 'things to do list'. The human resources manager has requested a job specification for a new technical post which has to be ready the following day.

4 pm The factory
The job specification is still not complete. Sue is back on the shopfloor to check progress on the Nigerian job. All the schedule revisions have been sorted out and work will start in two days' time when the damaged cables arrive back in the UK.

4.15 pm Sue's office
Sue takes stock of the day. The job specification is still incomplete. She checks the 'things to do list' again. She has an appointment with the R&D manager at 5.00 pm. There are some minor administrative tasks that can be put off to the end of the day so Sue decides to finish the job specification immediately.

5 pm R&D manager's office
At the meeting Dr Broadley, the R&D manager, is anxious that a new piece of equipment be purchased to facilitate his work on an enhancement to one of the company's major products. Sue agrees to take the matter up with the MD.

5.15 pm MD's office
Sue goes to see the MD and they review the day's events, particularly their success in fitting in the repair job for Nigeria, and the R&D manager's request for new equipment. They agree to investigate this further.

5.30 pm Sue's office
Sue dictates three letters and a couple of memos for the following day, sorts out the few remaining items left on her desk ready for tomorrow, and locks up and leaves.

Source: Developed from D Waters (1996) *Operations Management*, Reading, MA: Addison-Wesley Longman.

THE OUTPUTS

Productivity as a performance measure

Measuring performance is one of the most important aspects of operations management and has received a great deal of attention during the past few years. In order to make any improvements to the functioning of the transformation process there must be methods for measuring its current effectiveness. This section considers the traditional measures of performance, and the subsequent section discusses more recent developments.

Productivity is the broadest measure of operations management performance, but perhaps the least enlightening. All it does is assess how resources are utilised and managed to achieve a set of desired results. Productivity is defined as the ratio of output to input:

$$\frac{\text{output}}{\text{input}} = \frac{\text{results achieved}}{\text{resources consumed}}$$

An increase in productivity can, therefore, result from *either* an increase in output *or* a decrease in input. However, the problems of measuring output and input in the same units, and the debate about whether the resulting ratio has any real meaning, has led to productivity being considered in relative terms – considering *changes* in the ratio, comparing results in one period with those in another. A productivity index is often used, in which one period is given a value of 100 and then values in subsequent periods compared to that base.

Productivity has been a popular measure for many years, primarily because it is directly linked to profit and has, therefore, attracted a good deal of senior management attention. If a percentage increase in sales is compared with an equivalent percentage increase in productivity then there is a very different effect on profit (see Table 14.9).

While this analysis fails to indicate the relative amount of effort required to achieve the same percentage change in sales and productivity, it does demonstrate the link between productivity and profit which has for so long attracted the attention of senior managers. However, measuring productivity in services is not as simple because the outputs are not as easy to identify and measure. Although there are techniques that can help to develop this concept within services (data envelopment analysis being one example – see Charnes *et al.*, 1978) the results of using productivity can be misleading.

Partial productivity measures relate the value of output to the value of one of the inputs. For example,

$$\text{labour productivity} = \frac{\text{output (£ value)}}{\text{labour hours (or costs)}}$$

Labour productivity has been the most common measure, especially in manufacturing, but it oversimplifies the basis on which operations should be assessed and is misleading. It was used because it is relatively easy to calculate, because labour was a significant factor of production when productivity was first conceived, and because labour cost was seen as more inherently variable than material or capital. However, the relatively low proportion of total cost represented by labour cost in most manufacturing organisations today makes this measure unrepresentative. This

Table 14.9 Impact of changes in sales and productivity

	BEFORE CHANGES	AFTER 10% SALES INCREASE	AFTER 10% INCREASE IN PRODUCTIVITY
Sales	£100	£110	£100
Variable costs	£70	£77	£63
Fixed costs	£20	£20	£20
Profit	£10	£13 (+30%)	£17 (+70%)

relative proportion of costs attributable to 'staff' in various industries is shown in Table 14.10 and it should be borne in mind that this will include indirect labour too (that allocated to overhead rather than that which varies with the volume of business being done).

An alternative measure of performance developed more recently is **added value**:

$$\text{Added value} = \text{sales reveue} - \text{material and outside service costs}$$

$$\text{Added value index} = \frac{\text{total employment costs}}{\text{added value}}$$

This is particularly useful for measuring managerial performance, since it is less affected by factors external to the manager's control (e.g. inflation) than is profit, and focuses on employee productivity which is a major managerial task.

NEW WAYS OF MEASUREMENT

Using productivity as a measure of operations performance has been criticised for focusing on the short term, lacking strategic focus and not supporting continuous and quality improvement. These limitations, coupled with the trends in organisations and the environment which have led to a greater focus on customer needs, have resulted in new ways of operations performance evaluation being developed

→ Ch. 7

(see Chapter 7). Productivity is no longer seen as a single measure, although it may be used in conjunction with others. It is now generally accepted that the main criteria to be used for evaluating operations management are:

- **cost** – of the transformation process;
- **quality** – of product or service;
- **delivery** – to customer, sometimes divided into delivery speed and delivery dependability;
- **flexibility** – of process.

Many of the trade-offs which are regarded as an inherent part of operations management are related to these factors. They lead to five major performance objectives (Slack *et al.*, 2006):

Table 14.10 Composition of total cost

	STAFF	TECHNOLOGY, FACILITIES & EQUIPMENT	MATERIALS/ BOUGHT-IN SERVICES
Hospital	45%	35%	20%
Car manufacturing plant	25%	15%	60%
Bus company	52%	40%	8%
Supermarket	10%	25%	65%

- doing things RIGHT   → the QUALITY advantage
- doing things FAST   → the SPEED advantage
- doing things ON TIME   → the DEPENDABILITY advantage
- CHANGING what you do → the FLEXIBILITY advantage
- doing things CHEAPLY   → the COST advantage

An organisation may want to achieve all or just one of these, although generally it is not possible to develop action plans which support all of them simultaneously.

Quality

Quality is fundamental and visible and leads to internal benefits such as reduced cost (because less time is spent in correcting mistakes and putting confusion right) and increased dependability (because people have more time to concentrate on being good at their job, and therefore become more reliable at doing it). See Exhibit 14.5.

Exhibit 14.5 What does quality mean?

In a hospital?
- patients receive the most appropriate treatment
- treatment is carried out in the correct manner
- patients are consulted and informed
- staff are friendly and helpful.

In a car manufacturing plant?
- all parts made to specification
- all assembly to specification
- product is reliable
- product is attractive.

In a bus company?
- buses are clean and tidy
- buses are quiet and fume free
- timetable is accurate and easy to understand
- staff are friendly and helpful.

In a supermarket?
- goods are in good condition
- store is clean and tidy
- decor is appropriate and attractive
- staff are friendly and helpful.

Source: Developed from N Slack, S Chambers and R Johnston (2004) *Operations Management* (4th edition), p. 45. Harlow: FT Prentice Hall.

Speed

This is to do with how long customers have to wait to receive products or services (see Exhibit 14.6). Increased speed reduces inventories (stock), since less material is needed for buffering, and also reduces risks. There is less reliance on forecasting with more opportunity to make what the customer actually wants.

Exhibit 14.6 What does speed mean?

In a hospital?
- time between requiring and receiving treatment
- time for test results to be returned.

In a car manufacturing plant?
- time between dealers requesting a vehicle and getting it
- time to deliver spares to service centres.

In a bus company?
- time between customer setting out and reaching their destination.

In a supermarket?
- time taken for total transaction from selecting goods to leaving store
- availability of goods (are they on the shelf?).

Source: Developed from N Slack, S Chambers and R Johnston (2004) *Operations Management* (4th edition), p. 47. Harlow: FT Prentice Hall.

Dependability

This is concerned with doing things in time so that customers receive their product or service when they were promised (see Exhibit 14.7). Dependability saves time – less time has to be spent on sorting out problems and therefore there is more time to spend on direct productive work. It also saves money, where other resources have to be diverted to make up for problems, and gives stability in the operations. A level of trust is built up where things are reliable and this will be lost when dependability is reduced.

Flexibility

This is to do with being able to change the operation in some way – what it does, how it does it or when it does it. There are four main types of flexibility:

- **product/service** – different products or services;
- **mix** – a wide range of products/services;
- **volume** – different quantities of products/services;
- **delivery** – different delivery times.

Further details about flexibility can be found in Slack *et al.* (2004). Examples of flexibility in various types of operation are shown in Table 14.11.

Exhibit 14.7 What does dependability mean?

In a hospital?
- proportion of appointments cancelled
- keeping to appointment times
- test results returned as promised.

In a car manufacturing plant?
- on-time delivery of vehicles to dealers
- on-time delivery of spares to service centres.

In a bus company?
- keeping to the published timetable at all points on the route
- availability of seats for passengers.

In a supermarket?
- predictability of opening hours
- proportion of goods out of stock
- keeping to 'reasonable' queueing times
- availability of parking.

Source: Developed from N Slack, S Chambers and R Johnston (2004) *Operations Management* (4th edition), p. 50. Harlow: FT Prentice Hall.

Flexibility has a number of internal benefits. It speeds up responses (for example, when emergencies arise in a hospital); it saves time in changing over from one task to another; it maintains dependability where resources can easily be swapped to other tasks in order to fulfil overall promises.

Table 14.11 Examples of flexibility

TYPE OF FLEXIBILITY	HOSPITAL	CAR MANUFACTURING PLANT	BUS COMPANY	SUPERMARKET
Product/service	Introduction of new types of treatment	Introduction of new models	Introduction of new routes	Introduction of new goods or promotions
Mix	Range of available treatments	Range of product options	Number of locations served	Range of goods stocked
Volume	Ability to adjust number of patients treated	Ability to adjust number of vehicles manufactured	Ability to adjust frequency of services	Ability to adjust number of customers served
Delivery	Ability to reschedule appointments	Ability to reschedule manufacturing priorities	Ability to reschedule trips	Ability to obtain out-of-stock items

Source: Developed from N Slack, S Chambers, C Harland, A Harrison and R Johnston (2004) *Operations Management* (4th edition), p. 52. Harlow: FT Prentice Hall.

Cost

This is still the major objective for many organisations which believe that they compete primarily on cost, although many customers do have other considerations. Cost is incurred in three main areas:

■ staff costs

■ technology, facilities and equipment costs

■ material costs and bought-in services.

The breakdown of total cost is, however, very different in different types of organisation, as shown in Table 14.10. All the other objectives act on costs, via the internal effects described earlier, so cost improvement can be obtained from improving the other objectives.

Trade-off and the relative importance of performance objectives

The conventional view is that improvement in one aspect of performance can only be achieved at the expense of performance in another area:

> *'Most managers will readily admit that there are compromises or trade-offs to be made in designing an airplane or truck. In the case of an airplane, trade-offs would involve matters such as cruising speed, take-off and landing distances, initial cost, maintenance, fuel consumption, passenger comfort and cargo or passenger capacity. For instance, no one can design a 500 passenger plane that can land on an aircraft carrier and also break the sound barrier. Much the same thing is true in manufacturing.*
>
> (Skinner, 1969)

This has, however, been challenged by organisations which give the 'best of both worlds'. For example, quality and cost used to be seen in opposition so that improved quality could only be had at greater cost, whereas now it is recognised that improved quality may actually reduce cost.

Constraints on improvement may be technical or attitudinal. For example, if the attitude about quality changes from 'screen the bad products out' to 'stop the mistakes being made in the first place', then the quality/cost trade-off becomes irrelevant. This has happened in many of the 'world-class' organisations.

The long-term aim of operations managers has to be to change those things within the operation that cause performance of one aspect to deteriorate as the other improves – i.e. to change the constraints on the operation in total, rather than merely altering one aspect. Weak companies appear to embody the trade-off mentality in the way they operate, and suffer as a result. Companies attempting to improve can develop immunity to some of the trade-offs, many having started with eliminating the cost/quality trade-off. 'World-class' companies aim for improvement in all areas and have largely eliminated trade-off obstacles.

The way in which the relative importance of performance objectives is determined is crucial to the link between operations objectives and overall strategy.

> *'It is essential to define and monitor performance measures in order to track progress in implementing strategic initiatives and accomplishing strategic goals and objectives'*
>
> (Poister, 2003)

Targets are often aggregated together or balanced with each other, perhaps using an approach such as the balanced scorecard (Kaplan and Norton, 1996). Private sector organisations need to demonstrate a high level of economic performance to shareholders. However, because public sector organisations, including local government and schools, operate without market competition performance measurement is often used as a substitute for market pressures (Moriarty and Kennedy, 2002). The demonstration of performance is therefore crucial to an organisation's survival. The choice and level of aggregation of performance targets will determine their strategic relevance as well as their ability to diagnose operations problems. This is shown in Figure 14.6.

Figure 14.6 Performance targets can involve different levels of aggregation

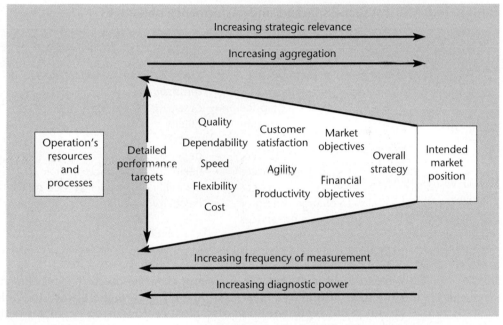

Source: N Slack and M Lewis (2002) *Operations Strategy*, Pearson Education Limited, Figure 11.4.

THE EXTERNAL ENVIRONMENT

Operations management and the customer

Customers are important for any organisation and it has already been shown that interaction between the operations function and the customer has increased in the past few years, and is likely to continue to do so (see Chapter 3). It is therefore important to consider the points at which the customer influences operations performance.

→ Ch. 3

It has already been shown that the customer will have needs which should be met by the organisation. However, the needs of the customers themselves may have a number of components:

- a statement of recognised need
- an expectation of the way in which that need should be met
- an idea of the benefits of having that need met.

It can therefore be seen that 'customer requirements' are not simply concerned with the product or service provided but also the way in which the operation is carried out and the expected effect on the customer.

> *'Products are* **what** *we produce, service is* **how** *we provide them.'*   (Evans, 1997)

This is of particular importance for operations managers.

Customers have a direct influence on performance objectives through critical success factors – the key things by which the customer decides whether the organisation and its products are suitable for its needs. The link between these is shown in Exhibit 14.8.

Exhibit 14.8 Critical success factors and performance objectives

CRITICAL SUCCESS FACTORS		PERFORMANCE OBJECTIVES
If customers value these things ...		*then the operation will need to be good at these things ...*
price	→	cost
quality	→	quality
fast delivery	→	speed
reliable delivery	→	dependability
innovative products and services	→	flexibility of product/service
wide range of products and services	→	flexibility of product/service mix
the ability to change timing or quantity of products or services	→	flexibility of volume and/or delivery

Source: Developed from N Slack, S Chambers and R Johnston (2004) *Operations Management* (4th edition), p. 72. Harlow: FT Prentice Hall.

While it is difficult to generalise about customer needs it has been shown that, in broad terms, customers appear to have the requirements shown in Table 14.12.

These do not represent trade-offs. Most customers do not want better quality at the expense of lower costs – they want better quality *and* lower cost! They want continuous improvement in all aspects.

However, it is also important to be able to distinguish between critical success factors – not all are equally important for all customers. One way of doing this is through order-winning and order-qualifying criteria (Hill, 1993).

Table 14.12 Customer requirements

HIGH	LOW
Quality	**Costs**
Flexibility: to change volume, specification, delivery	**Lead times:** getting shorter all the time for new products and processing ongoing demands
Levels of service	**Variability:** most customers prefer no variability at all

Source: Developed from R J Schonberger and E M Knod (1994) *Operations Management: Continuous Improvement* (5th edition), Burr Ridge, IL: Richard D Irwin.

■ **Order-winning criteria** are those things which significantly contribute to getting an order against competitors in the same market. They are the most important in terms of defining competitive position – raising performance in an order-winning factor will either result in more business or improve the chances of gaining more business.

■ **Order-qualifying criteria** are the aspects of performance that have to be above a certain level in order for the product/service even to be considered by the customer. They get the product into the market or onto the customer's list.

Table 14.13 shows the characteristics of two product groups produced by the same company, the ways in which they differ and the impact this has on order-qualifying and order-winning criteria.

Table 14.13 Comparison of critical success factors and performance objectives

	PRODUCT GROUP 1	PRODUCT GROUP 2
Products	Standard electronic medical equipment	Electronic measuring devices
Customers	Hospitals/clinics	Other medical equipment companies
Product specification	Not high tech but with periodic updates	Most types are high performance
Product range	Narrow – four variants	Very wide with some customisation
Design changes	Infrequent	Continual
Delivery	Fast – from stock	On-time delivery important
Quality	Means reliability	Means performance
Demand	Predictable	Unpredictable
Volume per product type	High	Medium to low
Profit margins	Low to medium	Medium to very high
Critical success factors	↓	↓
Order winners	*Price* *Product reliability*	*Product specification* *Product range*
Order qualifiers	*Delivery speed* *Product performance* *Quality*	*On-time delivery* *Delivery speed* *Price*
Less important	*Product range*	
Internal performance objectives	↓ *Cost* *Product/service flexibility*	↓ *Quality* *Mix flexibility* *Dependability*

Source: Developed from N Slack, S Chambers, C Harland, A Harrison and R Johnston (2004) *Operations Management* (4th edition), p. 74. Harlow: FT Prentice Hall.

Another way in which the customer influences operations indirectly is through the pattern of demand which enables the organisation to decide whether to **make to order or make to stock**. The decision will be related to the type of process employed, but not always directly. This is a key decision for every organisation with advantages depending on the product and the market.

A make-to-order organisation responds to a customer order before starting manufacture. However, it may manufacture kits or sub-assemblies before customer orders are received, in order to be able to deliver within an acceptable leadtime. A **make-to-stock organisation** does not assign orders to individual customers during the production process. Table 14.14 shows the impact of these two options on performance objectives and the major operations problems.

While the general principles concerning improvement of relationships with both suppliers and customers are valid for all organisations, it can be seen that operations will have a very different relationship with external agents, depending on the nature of the process employed within the organisation and the performance criteria that are specified (Cousins *et al.*, 2007)

Table 14.14 Characteristics of make-to-stock and make-to-order environments

CHARACTERISTICS	MAKE-TO-STOCK	MAKE-TO-ORDER
Product	Producer specified Low variety Inexpensive	Customer specified High variety Expensive
Objectives	Balance inventory, capacity and service	Manage delivery lead times and capacity
Main operations problems	Forecasting Planning production Control of inventory	Delivery promises Delivery lead time

Source: R G Schroeder (1993) *Operations Management* (4th edition), New York: McGraw-Hill. Copyright © The McGraw-Hill Companies Inc.

GLOBALISATION AND MULTINATIONAL MANAGEMENT

Operations management is the same in principle wherever it is practised. However, there are differences in emphasis in different parts of the world which are argued to have implications for differences in productivity and organisational performance, especially between the West and the Far East. There is also an ongoing debate about the extent to which the national culture affects the decision-making role of the operations manager and the methods which may be employed.

The global nature of business is now widely accepted and yet its implications for operations have not always been thought through. Schroeder (1993) distinguishes between three types of international firm:

■ **Global** – marketing a similar product throughout the world, with a worldwide scale of operations.

- **Multinational** – marketing and producing products in various countries suited to local tastes. It is usually organised with separate divisions or independent foreign subsidiaries in each country.
- **Export** – products are shipped to various countries from a domestic facility. It may use agents for marketing abroad.

Schroeder argues that each type of firm still has a place because each can compete on different things. A global firm is well placed to gain economies of scale and compete primarily on price. A multinational firm can differentiate its products for the relevant local markets, as well as differentiating service, quality, responsiveness to customer demands or other factors that may have local importance.

The main issues to consider in developing an understanding of international operations strategy are as follows:

- **Location of operations to form an international network** – this is a cost issue but also has to take into account cultural issues and legal considerations, as well as potential markets.
- **Management of the network across national boundaries** – technology has had a beneficial effect on this but there are still issues to be considered.
- **Development of different operations practices within different countries** – this seems to be inevitable, however central the control of the organisation is. The social, political, demographic and economic environments all have a significant effect on the development of these practices.
- **Transfer of practices from one country to another** – this is a key issue for the West at present as organisations try to implement Japanese-style practices. Many companies have found that the practices are applicable but that they need some modification. The more similar the cultural and economic context then the easier it appears to be to transfer operations practices successfully.

There is a set of common principles which appear to be followed by the leading 'world-class' manufacturers in Japan, Germany and the USA. All these principles relate to the operations function. Authors differ as to the exact wording of these principles (e.g. Schonberger, 1996) although Schroeder (1993) broadly summarises them as follows:

- **Put the customer first** – to be followed by everyone, not just the salesforce.
- **Be conscious of quality** – quality has to be thought into every product and every aspect of performance has to be seen through the customer's eyes.
- **Involve employees** – seeking consensus and input from everyone and developing mutual trust and respect.
- **Practise just-in-time production** – striving to reduce waste in all forms, including inventory, space, errors and overheads.
- **Emphasise appropriate technology** – includes technological innovation but also the use of technology where appropriate.
- **Emphasise the long term** – where the short-term interests of shareholders are promoted at the expense of long-term investment then organisations struggle on a world-class scale.
- **Be action oriented** – world-class companies are relatively small and decentralised with relatively flat organisation structures.

→ Ch. 19   Chapter 19 provides a detailed analysis of the management implications of globalisation and multinational management.

SUMMARY

- This chapter shows that operations management can be considered as a transformation process where inputs are transformed into outputs. This is a good basis for an analysis of the influences on and functioning of operations.

- Operations management has developed from, and been influenced by, a variety of factors from a number of academic disciplines.

- The relationship between the operations function and other functions within the organisation depends on the type of organisation – that is, the extent to which an organisation produces goods or services. This will also affect the nature of the operations management task, in particular the emphasis placed on various factors of operations management.

- The major trends affecting operations include an increased emphasis on the customer, continuous improvement, involvement of everyone in the organisation, integration with other organisational functions and globalisation of organisations.

- The operations process may be classified according to volume and type of product or service produced, and this will have an impact on the role of the manager.

- The outputs from the process can be measured using a traditional ratio of input to output resources but this is limited in applicability. New ways of measuring focus on the effectiveness of the five operations performance measures: quality, cost, delivery speed, delivery dependability and flexibility, and link measurement to strategy.

- Customers and their requirements are increasingly important in determining how operations are managed. It is important for the organisation to develop an understanding of the needs of the customer and the ways in which customers judge the suitability of an organisation, product or service.

- The context of globalisation has also become increasingly important, particularly with the increased market share gained by Japanese manufactured goods along with mergers and acquisitions and rapidly developing economies such as those of China, India and Brazil. Although it is not clear whether operations techniques are fully transferable across national boundaries, it seems that national culture may affect their implementation.

Review and discussion questions

1 *What is 'operations management' and what is meant by the 'transformation process' in an organisation?*

2 *How do the characteristics of services differ from those of products?*

3 *How does the operations manager carry out his or her role?*

4 *How can the performance of the transformation process be measured?*

5 *Why are both customers and the external environment important in operations management?*

CASE STUDY 14.4

DuPont

DuPont's May Plant in Camden, South Carolina employs approximately 125 people and produces roughly 69 million pounds of textile fibre each year. The textile area includes production, shipping, inspection and testing. Textile fibres are produced in a continuous spinning operation. After fibre is wound on a spool, it is placed on a special buggy that holds many spools. The buggies are wheeled to a test-and-inspection station. Finally, the product is grouped, packaged and shipped. Spinning machines cannot be shut down without incurring tremendous start-up costs. Even slowing production will adversely affect product consistency and quality. Those facts complicate the job of the plant managers, who faced many problematic issues. The quality of work life for operators, supervisors and area managers was poor, with many safety problems. There were constant telephone calls from customers about delivery schedules, calls that were often unpleasant and at times confrontational. Customers' orders were not being met in a timely way. Other problems were product shortages, excessive backlogs, high inventories and lost or misplaced yarn. Product-quality variation and production yields were unacceptable. There was ongoing pressure from the marketing group, as well as from plant executives, to stem the flow of customer complaints.

Employees, supervisors and managers were eager for change. One area supervisor had been exposed to world-class operations management principles and prompted the journey towards successfully and permanently resolving the problems. One step was to lock up many of the buggies except when needed for an emergency. With fewer buggies in operation, bottlenecks became acutely visible, and the sources of problems were more quickly identified and corrected. The result was a smoother flow of product through the facility. Jobs were simplified and a visual control system was adopted. In the new system, buggies were placed only in small marked-off spaces, which limited the amount of inventory and flagged problems. Even forklifts had specific parking places to enable easy identification of the ones that were leaking fluid and posed a safety problem. Employees measured the time it took for products to move through the facility and backlogs at each workstation, plotting the results so that deviations could be identified quickly and corrected. Extensive on the job education and training, supplemented by meetings and individual coaching and counselling, helped to involve all employees in the improvement efforts.

As a result of those initiatives, work-in-process inventory was reduced an astounding 96 per cent, working capital declined by $2 million; employee suggestions increased 300 per cent, and product quality improved 10 per cent. Most of the results were achieved within the first three months after implementation of the changes.

Source: J R Evans (1997) *Production/Operations Management: Quality, Performance and Value*, St Paul, MN: West Publishing Company. Reprinted with permission of South-Western, a division of Thomson Leaning.

CASE STUDY 14.5

The Ritz-Carlton Hotel Company: service through people

The Ritz-Carlton Hotel Company is one example of an outstanding service company. In 1992 it became the first hospitality organisation to receive the Malcolm Baldrige National Quality Award. The hotel industry is very competitive, one in which customers place high emphasis on reliability, timely delivery and price value. The Ritz-Carlton focuses on the principal concerns of its main customers and strives to provide highly personalised, genuinely caring service. Attention to its employees, processes and use of information technology are three of the many strengths of the Ritz-Carlton that helped it to receive national recognition.

The Ritz-Carlton's company philosophy is 'Ladies and Gentlemen Serving Ladies and Gentlemen.' Its credo states, 'The genuine care and comfort of our guests is our highest mission.' The company's 'three steps of service' are (1) a warm greeting in which

▶

employees use the guest's name, (2) anticipation of and compliance with the guest's needs, and (3) a warm farewell, again using the guest's name if possible. A Ritz-Carlton employee will not point a guest in a desired direction; he or she will lead the guest to the desired destination. In attending to complaints, employees must respond within 10 minutes and follow up with a phone call within 20 minutes to make sure the customer is satisfied. The employees have the responsibility to solve problems, and they are given considerable latitude and authority in doing so to ensure total customer satisfaction. Any failure, such as not having a room ready on time, requires complimentary cocktails, an amenity sent to the room and a letter of apology.

Employees are empowered to 'move heaven and earth to satisfy a customer', to contact other employees, to help resolve a problem swiftly, to spend up to $2000 to satisfy a guest, to decide the business terms of a sale, to become involved in setting plans for their work area and to speak with anyone in the management hierarchy about any problem.

The company's objectives are to improve the quality of its products and services, reduce cycle time, and improve price value and customer retention. At each level of the company, teams are charged with setting objectives and devising action plans, which are reviewed by the corporate steering committee. Such an approach ensures that (1) all teams are aligned around a common vision and agreed-upon objectives, (2) all employees are encouraged to think beyond the demands of daily activities, and (3) continual communication is maintained among the diverse functions that make up the company. To provide the personalised service demanded by the company's customers, the human resources function works in close coordination with all other functions. All hotels have a director of human resources and a training manager, both of whom are assisted by the hotel's quality leader. Each work area has a departmental trainer who is charged with the training and certification of new employees in that unit. The Ritz-Carlton uses a highly predictive 'character trait recruiting' instrument to determine a candidate's capability to meet the requirements of each of 120 job positions. New employees receive two days' orientation by senior executives to demonstrate methods and instil the Ritz-Carlton values. Three weeks later managers monitor the effectiveness of the instruction and make necessary changes in a follow-up session. Later, new employees must pass written and skill-demonstration tests to become certified in their work areas.

Every employee receives instruction designed to make him or her a certified quality engineer capable of identifying wasteful complexity within his or her work. In all, employees receive more than 100 hours of quality education to foster premium service commitment, solve problems, set strategic quality plans and generate new ideas. And every day, in every work area, during every shift, a quality line-up meeting of employees occurs for a briefing session.

Customised hotel products and services, such as meetings and banquet events, receive the full attention of cross-functional teams. In the process of designing and delivering customised services, all internal and external suppliers become involved as early as possible, production and delivery capabilities are verified prior to each event, samples are prepared and critiqued by event planners, and 'after-event' assessments are conducted for continuous improvement.

The Ritz-Carlton applies information technology to capture and use customer satisfaction data and other important data in real time. Its information systems enable every employee to collect and use data on a daily basis, including online guest preference information, quantity of error-free products and services and complaints indicating opportunities for improvement. A guest-profiling system that registers the individual preferences of 240,000 guests who have stayed at least three times at any of the hotels gives front-desk employees immediate access to such information as whether a guest smokes, whether he or she prefers wine or a rose in the evening, and even which kind of pillow is preferred.

Those are only a few of the key operations management activities practised at The Ritz-Carlton. The results are impressive. Customer satisfaction is upwards of 95 per cent. Employee turnover is only 48 per cent, versus an annual industry average of more than 100 per cent. The number of employees needed per guest room during pre-opening activities of a new hotel was reduced by 12 per cent. Within a three-year period, the Ritz-Carlton reduced the number of hours worked per guest room by 8 per cent. Housekeeping cost per occupied room was reduced from $7.90 at the end of 1991 to $7.30 at the beginning of 1992. The time required to clean an average room has decreased from 30 to 28.5 minutes. Even elevator waiting time has been reduced by 33 per cent. Departmental profits per available guest room are nearly five times the industry average. One lesson the hotel has learned is to never underestimate the value of even one idea or improvement effort.

Source: J R Evans (1997) Production/Operations Management: Quality, Performance and Value, St Paul, MN: West Publishing Company. Reprinted with permission of South-Western, a division of Thomson Learning.

FURTHER READING

Cousins, P, Lamming, R, Lawson, B and Squire, B (2007) *Strategic Supply Management: Theories, Concepts and Practice*, Pearson.
Provides a complete overview of supply chain management.

Johnston, R and Clark, G (2005) *Service Operations Management* (2nd edition), Harlow: FT Prentice Hall.
A comprehensive book focusing purely on operations management in service organisations.

Slack, N, Chambers, S and Johnston, R (2004) *Operations Management* (4th edition), Harlow: FT Prentice Hall.
Provides complete coverage of the concepts of operations management and includes case studies.

Slack, N, Chambers, S, Johnston, R and Betts, A (2006) *Operations and Process Management*, Harlow: FT Prentice Hall.
Focuses on the key process issues of operations management and includes case studies.

WEBSITES

General resource pages
There are a number of general resource pages for operations management on the Internet, including:

http://www.bized.ac.uk/fme/5.htm
The operations management page on the Bized website (http://www.bized.ac.uk/). Bized is a unique business and economics service for students, teachers and lecturers. Studying operations management on the Internet can be of great value. Understanding where to access the best resources, and the nature of rapidly changing operations technologies and methodologies, is very important both to students and to operations practitioners. Visiting operations management websites will give a solid introduction to latest technologies to both students and executives of operations management. This site is UK-based.

http://bradley.bradley.edu/~rf/opman.html
Ross L. Fink's operations management homepage – this site has a wide variety of links providing information related to various operations management topics. It is US-based and very comprehensive.

http://www.sussex.ac.uk/Users/dt31/TOMI/
The technology and operations management pages, formerly called Twigg's Operations Management Index, provide comprehensive information on hot topics, conferences, professional organisations, books and journals, academic departments and other Internet resources.

Interactive pages
Operations management lends itself well to interactive web pages and these are now exploited in a variety of ways.

http://bradley.bradley.edu/~rf/plantour.htm
The links contain interactive plant tours. These websites are developed by organisations to allow individuals an opportunity to see their operations. Most of these sites are for manufacturing facilities. However, a few are for service operations.

http://www.cbpa.drake.edu/bmeyer/POOL/index.html
Principles of operations online laboratory. This site is designed as an aid to learning concepts in operations management (OM). The observatory provides video clips and image files of people at work. You can study their methods, time their operations and devise ways to improve their processes. The experiment stations contain simulations that you can use online to learn about concepts in OM. The software tool chest contains computer programs and spreadsheet templates for common OM problems.

Publishers' sites
Many of the main publishers of business and management textbooks also provide pages of links to other subject resources that are useful whether or not you use the textbook that they publish.

http://www.mhhe.com/omc/index.html
Irwin/McGraw-Hill: the OM Center. A website of resources supported by the publishers Irwin/McGraw-Hill but drawing on much wider resources. Resources include Company Tours, BusinessWeek OM articles, OM publications online, OM organisations, OM software, OM newsfeeds and a video library. OM Center is designed to be a fast-loading informational site with minimal glitter and glitz that would slow it down. It is marketed as *the* source for a faculty looking for pedagogical support or references and for students seeking current OM information. Links are limited to those only providing useful information. If a commercial site offers educational value, the site aims to link to it, but does not endorse products or services of any firm, except for Irwin/McGraw-Hill.

http://vig.pearsoned.co.uk/catalog/academic/course/0,1143,341415,00.html
This is the main page for access to the support sites for all operations/project management books published by Pearson Education. Students can explore a collection of resources correlated to a book's table of contents, including a study guide, multiple-choice questions and web links. Many have links to companion websites.

http://www.palgrave.com/products/Results.aspx?bty=&src=br&sma=P011&smi=0140
OM texts published by Palgrave are listed here and many have companion websites.

Academic networks
These websites contain many links to other sites of interest to those studying OM, including the leading journals in the area;

- European Operations Management Association – **http://www.euroma-online.org**

- Academy of Management Operations Management Division – **http://om.aomonline.org/**
- Production and Operations Management Society – **http://www.poms.org/**
- Service Operations Management Association – **http://soma.byu.edu/soma/**

CHAPTER 15

Information technology and control

MIKE HARRY

Outcomes

Having read this chapter, you will be able to:

- identify the different forms of information used in organisations and business;

- establish an understanding of a systems view of the relationship between the concepts of management, control and information;

- use the understanding of this relationship to identify the role of the management information system in organisation and business;

- critically assess other views of information and management;

- establish present and future management implications of specific forms of information and communications technology-based information systems.

CASE STUDY 15.1

i2010 – a European information society for growth and employment

'i2010' is a European Commission strategy, aimed at an integrated approach to the information society and to audio-visual media policies in the EU. It is part of a much wider strategic process that began with a meeting of the European Council in Lisbon, in March 2000. This launched the Lisbon Strategy, which aimed at making the European Union the most competitive economy in the world and achieving full employment by 2010. The strategy rested on three pillars, which included an economic pillar where an emphasis is placed on the need to adapt constantly to changes in the information society and to boost research and development.

'eEurope – an information society for all', is part of the Lisbon Strategy which states that the European Union should become, by 2010, the most competitive and dynamic knowledge-based economy in the world. The main objectives of the initiative are the following:

■ bringing every citizen, home and school, every business and administration, into the digital age and online;
■ creating a digitally literate Europe, supported by an entrepreneurial culture open to information technology;
■ ensuring that the information society is socially inclusive.

eEurope 2005 was essentially focused on the deployment of broadband access at competitive prices, network security and better use of information technology by public bodies (eGovernment). Launched in June 2005, the i2010 initiative is a new strategy framework of the Commission in the field of the information society and the media. i2010 is the first Commission initiative adopted in the context of the revised Lisbon Strategy and the partnership for growth and employment.

i2010 interprets the three eEurope objectives in the form of three priorities for Europe's information society and media policy; to be achieved by 2010:

■ creating a Single European Information Space;
■ strengthening innovation and investment in information and communications technologies (ICT) research;
■ achieving an inclusive European information and media society.

'A Single European Information Space' means offering affordable and secure high-**bandwidth** communications, which will encourage new services and on-line content. This will require enhancing devices and platforms that 'talk to one another'; and making the Internet safer from fraudsters, harmful content and technology failures. In support of these aims, the Commission intends to review the regulatory framework for electronic communications, including defining a strategy for efficient spectrum management, and creating a consistent internal market framework for information and media services.

In order to boost 'innovation and investment' in ICT research, the Commission aims to increase EU ICT research support by 80% by 2010 and inviting Member States to do the same. The Commission also aims at making specific proposals on an developing tools to support new patterns of work that enhance innovation in enterprises and adaptation to new skill needs.

'An inclusive information society' means offering high-quality public services and improving quality of life by making ICT systems easier for a larger number of people to access and use. Since this also implies that people have the knowledge and skill, as well as access to technology, it means addressing issues such as equal opportunities, ICT skills and regional divisions. Proposed projects in support of inclusivity and improved quality of life include initiatives relating to caring for people in an ageing society, safer and cleaner transport and digital libraries to encourage cultural diversity.

Source: http://ec.europa.eu/information_society/eeurope/.

CASE STUDY 15.2

The Charity Commission

Charity can be very simple when there is one person who gives, and another who receives. We open our wallet and give money, or a helping hand, to the one in need. But once we decide to cooperate with others in being the givers, or we aim at supporting large numbers of people over time, then charity becomes more complex.

Those in need have to be identified, and their needs have to be understood. Who are they? Where are they? What do they need? When do they need it? Then there is the question of the potential givers. Who are they? What causes do they want to support? What do they need to know about the charity? What, or how much, can they afford to give? At this point, the practice of charity becomes an activity, or 'business', that needs to be managed.

The term 'charities' is used to describe organisations that aim to achieve the complex business of connecting donors to those in need. They range from small groups meeting local needs, with few resources, to publicly well-known major charities with budgets of millions.

In the UK, and other countries, an extra complication can apply. For many years, governments of various political persuasions have encouraged charitable giving. They have done this by exempting income given to charity from tax. So if a taxpayer gives money to a charity, the tax that the taxpayer has paid on that money is given back to the charity by the Government.

Since there are large numbers of donors, and amounts of money, involved in this process official bodies have been set up to ensure that charities operate legally, for the public benefit, and independently of Government or commercial interests. The Charity Commission for England and Wales is one example of such a body. It is established by law as the regulator and registrar of charities in England and Wales.

Most charities in England and Wales have to register with the Charity Commission. Their legal obligations then depend on their size and resources. For example, charities with yearly incomes over £10,000 have to send their accounts and report every year, and information about them is published on the Charity Commission website. The aim is to help people to inform themselves about the individual charities. Charities that have seriously defaulted on these legal obligations have their details published on a 'defaulting charities' finder facility on the website.

The website provides guidance to 24,000 charities each year (12 million hits per year) and a telephone contact centre covers 250,000 calls per year.

Source: www.charity-commission.gov.uk – last accessed on 13/06/07.

ISSUES IN BUSINESS AND MANAGEMENT INFORMATION

The two deliberately different case studies have been chosen in order to raise a wide range of issues. But we shall also see that apparently different business and management situations can often share characteristics once we look beyond words and labels. We begin with two important issues:

■ What views can be taken of the nature of **information** in this age of **networked** global information and communications technology?

■ How does the view taken of information affect our view of what constitutes business and management?

The important conclusions that can be demonstrated by analysing these issues are that:

■ information is a *rich* concept;

■ the nature of networked information systems has changed the *concept* of business and management systems that was held before the revolution in information and communications technology (ICT).

The case studies chosen for this chapter might seem different from what could have been expected under the heading of 'business' or 'management'. A case involving the problems associated with managing a large organisational computer network or database might have seemed more appropriate. Such a view would have chosen supply chain management for a large retail chain or business-to-business electronic commerce as a context for business and management information.

There is an important false assumption behind such a view, which is revealed by the wide range of appplications covered by the eEurope initiative outlined in the opening case study, and by comparing it with the operations of a small charity. To assume that a large database is a more relevant example for the subject of information and management than, say, a small charity recording its accounts on a laptop implies two false assumptions.

- The complexity of an organisation can be equated to its size – according to this view, the issues at a European level must be more complex than those at a personal level.

- The separation and classification of activities into different functions – like social, educational, political, business, or management – is likely to remain the same after the advent of information and communications technology as it was before.

Even a simple everyday example can show that the first assumption, equating complexity with size, is false. The plumbing system of a house takes up more space than a human being, weighs more and contains more energy but it is easier to make water come out of a tap automatically than to make an individual human being give out sympathy, money or secret personal information; and much less easy to get a human plumber out on Christmas Eve!

The quality that makes human beings more complex than water systems is **richness**. Richness is not determined by size but by the *variety* of components contained in a particular *whole* and the degree of *complexity* of their *interaction*. This chapter will, therefore, cover important management information issues in the context of large organisations as well as small ones.

The falseness of the second assumption is shown by the very reason that the European Commission set up the eEurope initiative. The Commission had noted that, although Europe enjoyed one of the highest levels of education in the world and had the necessary investment capacity, it lagged far behind in the use of information and communication technology. **Boundaries** that used to be set by *physical* separation or *labels* are no longer a reliable way of looking at the world after the advent of global connection through information and communications technology. The **Internet** redefines boundaries. Businesses which require that both their employees and their customers have the skills to sell and buy over the Internet can no longer see education as some separate object of no interest. Similarly an education system that hopes to produce citizens who will live in the world of global connection cannot work in isolation from the context and procedures of information and communications technology.

The richness of information as a concept

To show the richness of information as a concept, this section will consider in more detail some of the different views that can be taken of it, regardless of the size of organisation involved. Whether in the whole of Europe or in a local charity, as well as many other organisations big and small, information might been seen as:

- **data** organised into a particular **structure**;
- the output of a **process** applied to other information or data;
- a means of **communication** between a sender and a receiver;
- a form of **knowledge**;
- a source of clarification and reduction of uncertainty;
- a possession which gives **power**;
- something of **interest**;
- **intuition**, with no obviously immediate logical source.

Examples of information as data organised into a particular **structure** can be seen in any business document. An entry like 'Quantity 10, Price £23.50' contains the same individual characters and figures as 'Quantity 23, Price £10.50' but the information represented is different in each case. The particular structure used to organise data gives it an overall meaning called 'information'. The study of the concept of a database (later in this chapter) will show that a major property of a **database management system** is the ability to assemble data in the particular structure required by the user to produce information needed. In the Internet context there is a potential database of many terabytes but how this is organised in terms of structure and connection greatly affects how far it is information, rather than confusion.

Information can also be seen as the output of a **process** applied to other information or data. The previous invoice example would also need to contain information about cost. This is easily obtained by multiplying the quantity and price but such a trivial example is just one instance of the whole concept of data processing. From this viewpoint any information system can be seen as a kind of information factory that uses raw material called data and transforms it into a product called information. This chapter considers some of the different forms of transformation an information system has to carry out. The important implication for management, however, is that it is the customer who uses the product of this information factory, whether it be in paying an invoice or scanning the Internet.

Information implies **communication** between a sender and a receiver. Unread, unused or unknown information is a managerial nonsense – words have to be spoken, documents sent and electronic data transmitted. The vast potential of the information on the Internet will be of little use to the citizens of Europe if it remains undiscovered and uncommunicated. Ensuring such communication will require both information and communications technology and the human relations skills of teachers. It is important to realise that a glance or a nod can also be the communication of information, and now that we have web cameras the glances or nods may be electronic. This chapter will show how an information system needs to deal with the communication of both hard and soft information.

Information as a form of **knowledge** is implied by phrases like 'to know' and 'being informed'. The eEurope initiative recognises that the success of the European economy will depend on the ability of consumers and citizens to use information and communications technology. However, the technology itself can give the user some of the knowledge needed to use it. Issues like this will be explored further later in the chapter under intelligent and expert systems and the concept of a knowledge base.

The concept of information as a means of **clarification** and **reduction of uncertainty** follows from the view of it as a form of knowledge. A major policy reason for setting up the Charity Commission website was to inform charities of their legal obligations. In particular this needed to deal with the duties of trustees and the management of finances. Since it is unlikely that businesses and customers will trade over the Internet if they cannot be certain that they are protected against insecurity in its operations or fraud, so the eEurope initiative to support research and development in these key areas is an attempt to reduce uncertainty.

When instigating eEurope, the European heads of state talked of creating 'the most competitive and dynamic knowledge-driven economy in the world'. They clearly saw information as a source of **power**. The strength of the European economy was no longer just seen as depending on the capacity to manufacture and sell – it should be 'knowledge-driven'. The need for charities to raise funds makes it essential for them to identify and interest potential donors. The exploitation of information and communications technology is a major factor in empowering charities to do this. Television and radio adverts, websites and mail shots from a database of potential donors all involve the use of information and communications technology. Nor is the information flow just one-way from charity to donor – information technology also enables the analysis of donors and social groups to identify the 'market' for charity promotions.

Information as a source of **interest** can be illustrated with the example of a potential donor viewing a television appeal for, say, providing clean water facilities for people in a developing country. The donor may not have been aware that many people have to walk great distances every day just to acquire clean water. So far, interest has been aroused but at that point no management activity is involved. However, once information is also seen as a reducer of uncertainty and a source of power then it is also likely to become of interest to managing what we do. An important reason for anything but ephemeral interest in information is that we learn something from it that we can use in the future. In the example of the donor, who is deciding what to do with, or who is managing, his money, the curiosity aroused by the television appeal could have been the first stage of selecting a charity and deciding what to give. Similarly, in a wider picture, for the European Commission it was not just idle curiosity that made it interested to find that the uptake of the Internet in Europe had remained comparatively low in the late 1990s – once interest was aroused then the desire for action followed.

Information as **intuition**, with no obviously immediate logical source, can be used to question many of the views of information we have considered so far. 'Body language', 'It's not what you know but who you know', 'How come you so clever, me so rich?' are all quotes and phrases from a view of management which thinks that formal views of systems ignore what really goes on in management with its human component. The enthusiasm for adapting to the world of the Internet may be shared by the European Commission and a small local charity, but, in the end, this enthusiasm cannot be based on logic alone. There is no reliable formula for predicting the future. An important ingredient of the commitment to exploiting information and communications technology is an intuitive belief that the future lies in this direction. Real management information also includes a similar soft, intuitive component and any overall view of information must take account of this.

Changing concepts of the boundaries of business and management systems

Imagine the following scenes in a video. The first shows two Indian teams playing cricket. The camera pulls back from the match to reveal that the teams are playing in California, USA. The members of the teams are Indians who have moved to the USA to work as software engineers for an organisation in California.

Now for the second scene – it also shows two Indian teams playing cricket. Once again, the camera pulls back from the match to reveal that the teams are now playing at home in their own country. These team members also work as software engineers for an organisation in California.

What is the difference between these two scenes? The answer is quite simple – the second scene shows what is possible after the advent of the Internet. In today's globally connected world an Indian software engineer can be as much in contact with a Californian information system as someone on a local area network. It is no longer automatically necessary for someone to be physically present in an organisation in order to be connected and part of the working system. These two illustrative scenes have their basis in fact. India, as a country with strong software engineering skills, is serving many organisations throughout the world without its software engineers necessarily having to leave their country.

Consider two more scenes. In the first a television news producer is assembling a programme using a networked computer system that stores sound, pictures and videos of current news reports. The producer can use this system not only as a source of her material, she can also use its software to assemble and schedule selected material into a complete news programme. All that is then required is a newsreader and a time slot and the news programme can go on air.

Now consider a second scene. A person who used to pay a TV licence fee now pays a subscription fee for access to the networked computer system over the Internet. He doesn't need a producer to tell him what he may see of the news; he doesn't need a newsreader to read what he can read for himself; and he doesn't need to be told what time of the day he must do it. The boundaries between the roles of news provider, editor, reader and viewer have changed and been blurred by information and communications technology. In the second scene the 'producer' is the viewer.

Making sense of business and management information

The richness of information and the changing roles and boundaries resulting from the new information and communications technology mean that older ways of viewing business and management information do not always work in the new world of multimedia and the Internet. However, not all business and management information is on the Internet. Despite the dramatic developments in information and communications technology, much of the information used by business and management is being processed by internal computer systems and frequently uses manually produced documents.

What is needed, therefore, is a view of information that is relevant to *all* the different kinds of information systems. Such a view ought to be able to:

■ look behind *how* management is described by titles and labels to see *what* management actually does;

■ look behind *how* information is communicated, processed or recorded to see *what* the information is and what management uses it for.

The distinction between the 'how' and the 'what' of management and information is sometimes described as the distinction between the *physical* and the *logical*, or between the *concrete* and the *abstract*. The next section presents a relationship between:

- **information systems**
- **control systems**
- **management systems**

with the aim of revealing how all forms of business and management information can be related to a common, consistent model.

INFORMATION, CONTROL AND MANAGEMENT SYSTEMS

The title of this chapter is *Information Technology and Control in Organisations*. In fact, information and communications technology never controlled anything. What leads to control is the incorporation of information and communications technology into the organisation as a whole system, and its use by human beings. In this section we shall explain this relationship.

Figure 15.1 shows the relationship between information, control and management systems. In terms of hierarchical structure an information system can be seen as a subsystem of a control system, and a control system as a subsystem of a management system. To explain this relationship further, the meaning of the word '**system**' needs exploring, followed by an explanation of the particular examples of management, control and information. For the application of systems thinking to business and management information see Harry (2001).

Properties of systems

Anything called a system in this chapter will be characterised by the following features.

Figure 15.1 Information, control and management systems

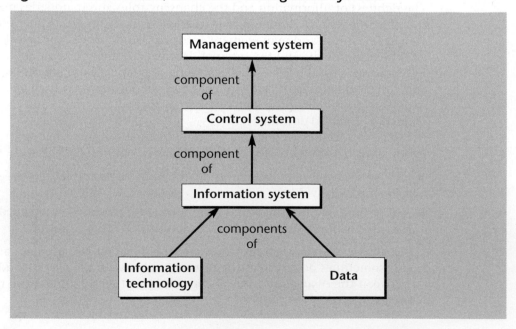

- **An assembly of two or more *components*.** Thus a computer system might consist of a keyboard, screen, a tower containing the disk drives and central processor and a printer. If an organisation like the EU is viewed as a system it would also include human, financial, material and political components, as well as IT systems connected by networks. Components may be physical or concrete. For example, equipment is concrete, information or money is abstract.

- **The components will be *connected* together in some fixed set of relationships called a *structure*.** The components of a computer system have to be connected up correctly for it to be a system rather than a chaotic heap. Similarly the very word 'organisation' implies appropriate forms of relationships between people, facilities, equipment and resources. The connections, like the components, may be abstract. Thus membership of an organisation (like the EU) or the association of information with an individual, like the value of a charity donor's gift, is a logical rather than a physical connection.

- **The components within this structure will *interact*.** Once the components of a computer system are correctly connected together, they are able to send electrical signals to each other. Once someone becomes a member of an organisation, he or she communicates with other people, uses equipment and interacts in many ways.

- **The interaction of the components will result in the system carrying out various *transformation processes*.** A computer system will transform input data on, say, hours worked by employees into output information such as wages to be paid. Transformations may also be concrete or abstract. Thus building a new university computer facility physically transforms rooms and equipment into a computer lab, but when the EU Council of Ministers passes a resolution that transforms a proposal into a policy the transformation is logical or abstract.

- **The result of all the above properties will be that a system can be viewed as a *whole* with its own *identity* and *emergent properties*.** Once a computer system is up and working then it can do things as a whole system which are not achievable by the separate parts. What eEurope calls an 'information society for all' will only emerge when all the facilities and human skills come together as a result of learning and investment. What a charity might call 'famine relief' requires that food, transport and people all come together in a coordinated way, at the right place and at the right time.

- **The particular view of the system thus presented will be someone's concept.** A school pupil, an EU commissioner, a national politician, a schools inspector and an employer are all likely to have different views of an educational system designed to create 'an information society for all'.

These six features of any system will be referred to and developed as they apply to the particular examples of management, control and information systems, as in Figure 15.1.

Management and control

The following tentative definition of management, originally from Harry (1990), can be used as a starting point:

> *'Management is an activity which aims to achieve something desirable to those who manage.'*

How might this apply to our two cases? The EU Council of Ministers wants to create an information society for all. The UK Government, through the the Charity Commission, wants to ensure that charities are run honestly and effectively. Hence, both of these organisations had something desirable they aimed to achieve.

These examples of 'something desirable' can be used to establish the concept of control as an essential component of management. Control is often taken to imply a particular management style. It may be used with another concept, **hierarchy**, to signify a rigid, authoritarian approach to management. Such a use of the two terms implies a stereotype 'boss' who 'controls' by 'giving orders'. In this chapter control refers to a concept and not a particular management style. Control is a property that 'emerges' (see 'emergent properties' above) when all the necessary components are brought together as a system.

This distinction between a concept of what something is and how it is done can be expressed as the difference between the whats and the hows we introduced above. *What* the EU wanted to create was an information society for all. *How* it decided to create such a thing could have involved many different methods. Originally, the European Union decided to provide all schools with an Internet connection by the end of 2001. Now we might feel that the EU may have thought it better to have delayed the universal installation of hardware until the advent of successful wireless technology. Instead of working through schools, it could have been more ambitious and worked through homes. It could have given remote regions or disabled people priority. Just as there can be many routes leading to the same destination, there can be many different *hows* leading to the same *what*.

The stereotyped view of control, explained above, is restrictive because it fails to recognise the choice of ways of exerting control. The concept of control, therefore, needs further explanation to show why it is the link between the concepts of information and management.

The main components of a control system

A standard model of a control system (Harry, 2001) has the following components.

■ **Defined goals** – what is regarded as 'something desirable to those who manage'. **Goals** may be hard and soft. 'The Commission aims to increase EU ICT research support by 80% by 2010' is a goal that can be defined in terms of specific figures for the amount of money and the date of expenditure. Hard goals are those which can be assessed by objective criteria, like money or years. However, a charity's goal of providing for 'those in need' is not objectively definable. For such a goal, success of achievement depends on the subjective interpretation of what 'needs' we consider important. Soft goals are those whose interpretation and definition depend on the values or world view of those concerned.

■ A **transformation process** – capable of achieving the defined goals. It may be concerned with concrete or abstract transformations. Concrete transformations are concerned with physical changes, like delivering food to a hungry person. Abstract transformations are concerned with conceptual changes, such as the change of ownership of money when a donation is made by credit card over the Internet. From a management viewpoint, whatever the transformation process its output should conform as closely as possible to the system's goals.

■ **Environmental disturbances** – may interfere with the workings of a transformation process and divert it from its goals but are not part of the control system.

They are, however, the reason for its existence. Changes in the number of citizens or businesses online, or of the enthusiasm of the European public for information and communications technology will affect what modification of inputs the EU will make to the particular process being controlled. More connections online might need more expenditure, less enthusiasm might require better publicity. The occurrence of a disaster, like the Asian Tsunami, will require dramatic changes in the inputs to some charities.

■ A **sensor** – to enable the controller to register the outputs of the transformation process. The sensor is a concept: in practice it can be a particular person, a group or a piece of equipment. Thus it may be a charity worker opening an envelope and recording a donation on paper, a charity website electronically recording the number of hits or the EU Commission gathering information about the workings of the current regulatory framework for electronic communications.

■ **Feedback** – which communicates the values of the outputs registered by the sensor. If we seek to control, it is not sufficient to observe. The observations have to be communicated to those who need them to make control decisions. Thus the charity worker, having recorded the donation, must ensure that it appears in the accounts of the charity. If a charity website has recorded the number of hits electronically this information may be forwarded to those who have to make decisions on the basis of its success. Once the EU Commission has gathered information about the workings of the current regulatory framework for electronic communications, then it can use the results to plan future modifications to legislation.

■ A process called the **comparator** – to compare the values of the outputs from the transformation process with the goals we wished to achieve. Thus donations to a charity will be compared with its needs targets to see if more vigorous campaigning is needed, hits on a website enable us to see how effective it is or workings of a regulatory framework can be compared with the outcomes originally intended when it was legislated.

■ An **actuator/effector** – to adjust the inputs to the transformation process with the aim of bringing its outputs back towards the goals. Thus a new campaign may be started or not, a website may be redesigned or not and legislation could be modified or scrapped altogether.

The terms in bold are the components of the model of a control system illustrated in Figure 15.2. This model has its origins in engineering and cybernetics but we are interested in its role of connecting management and information systems. If we did not make the distinction between the concept and implementation of control then there would be the danger of assuming that controlling systems which included human beings are no different from controlling a central heating system or a bathroom shower. (Both of these examples are commonly used in textbooks to illustrate control systems.) In this chapter no such assumption is made. A voluntary worker in a charity and a lawyer working for the EU can both have roles as a control system's comparator and actuator, but we would not necessarily want a charity worker to draw up legislation.

The information system as a component of the control system

An important feature of Figure 15.2 can now be noted. The loop that runs from the sensor to the actuator/effector consists of components that are all dealing with **information**. This feature represents one of the important links that the control

Figure 15.2 A control system

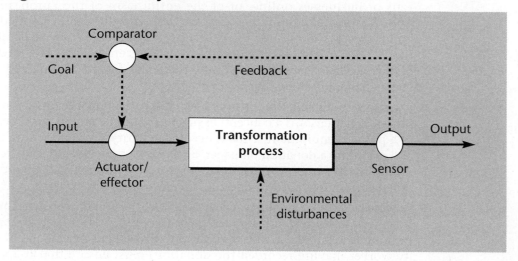

system makes between the wider management system and the information system. Looking further into the control model we can see that three types of information are needed for any working of a control system:

- information about the **state of the process** being controlled at any particular time and its behaviour over a period – this will come from the sensor monitoring the process outputs;
- information about **environmental disturbances**;
- information about the **goals** which the process being controlled should attempt to achieve.

Generally, all of the components of the control system which are concerned with the input, processing, storage and output of information can be seen as making up a subsystem of the control system itself. Because the transformation processes of this subsystem are exclusively concerned with information it can be sensibly called an information system.

There is one important feature missing from this view. Figure 15.2 tells us nothing about where the information about goals comes from. A complete view of an information system, therefore, must also include the process of **goal setting**. Figure 15.3 shows how this can be done.

Goal setting can be explained by viewing a control system as a **hierarchy**. When seeking to control a process – whether it is charitably 'providing for those in need' or creating an 'information society for all' – those in control must refer to goals such as shelter provided for the homeless or the take-up of information and communications technology by EU citizens. However, as the needs of victims of disaster or famine can change, so can the forms of information and communications technology available and the relevant skills needed by citizens and businesses. In these circumstances, goals have to be reviewed and sometimes changed. Thus the goals for eEurope 2005 had to be different from those of 1999 in order to take account of EU enlargement. In turn, while eEurope 2005 was essentially focused on the deployment of broadband access and better use of information technology by public bodies, i2010 had to take account of newly emerging issues such as global warming (cleaner transport) and an

Figure 15.3 Goal setting

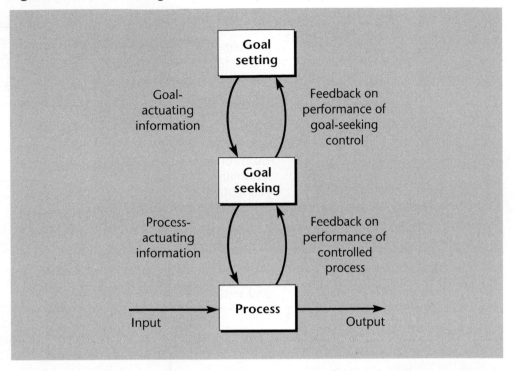

ageing population. Generally, changes in the **environment** of the organisation which is being managed will require modification of its goals.

This modification of goals, or goal setting, is itself a control process which seeks to control the control system modelled in Figure 15.2. The way it does this involves a similar sequence or loop from sensor to actuator as before. Figure 15.3, therefore, shows that a complete control system is a hierarchy of two components or subsystems:

■ **Goal-seeking control** – attempting to control a particular process, like the behaviour of charities or citizens' exploitation of information and communications technology in the examples above.

■ **Goal-setting control** – setting and modifying the goals used by goal-seeking control in response to changes in the environment. In the eEurope example this resulted in at least three modifications to the programme between 1999 and 2005.

Examples of goal-seeking and goal-setting functions in business organisations are shown in Figure 15.4. The terminology used is that of Harry (2001). It is essential to see this model as *descriptive* rather than *prescriptive*. The model shows *what* the components of control are. It does not show *how* they may be implemented since that will depend on the nature of the organisation and its management.

Forms of goal setting in the control hierarchy

The need for a goal-setting control component in the whole control system adds to the role described for the information system so far. Goal-setting control requires:

Figure 15.4 Goal seeking and goal setting functions

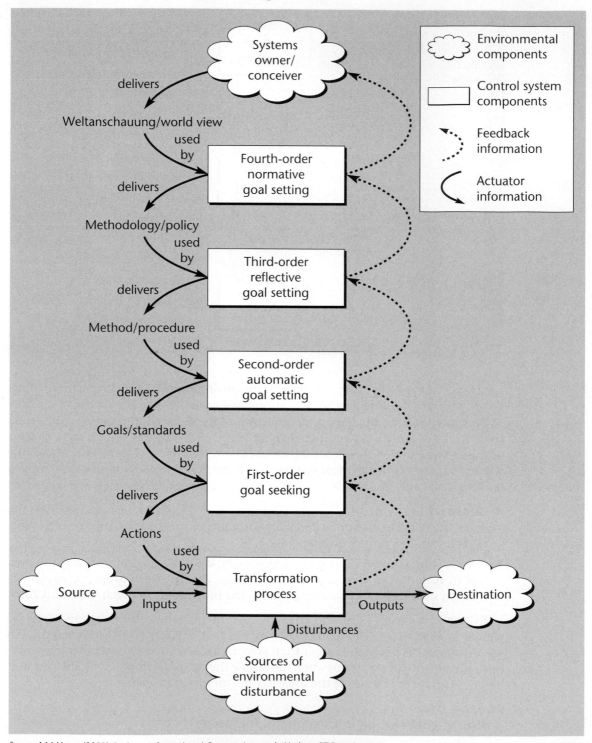

Source: M J Harry (2001) *Business Information: A Systems Approach,* Harlow: FT Prentice Hall.

- the ability to **store** information received as feedback on the behaviour of the goal-seeking component of the control system;

- the ability to **analyse** this information and learn from it;

- access to information about the **values** or **world view** of management, which will enable goal setting to select goals which reflect the norms and values of management.

The ability to store information can be seen to be essential in considering, for example, the setting of goals in the context of establishing a disaster relief programme by a charity or deciding on a famine relief programme. How much money is needed to equip a community with emergency housing? How long will it take? What skills and equipment are needed? How much time should be allocated to complete the programme? What can be learnt from past experience?

The answers to questions like these enable the management of governments or organisations to set their goals. Maybe last year's charity budget was not enough. Perhaps it was because too much money was was wasted on a fund-raising activity that was ineffective. Answers will only be possible if past experience is available as *stored information* available to the learning process – a record is needed of successes – mistakes and their outcome if learning is to happen.

But storage alone is not enough. Learning implies the ability to reflect and analyse the experience which is recorded. Raw data on the money spent over a period only becomes information after such actions as comparing times and costs, calculating trends and looking at the whole picture presented by the data.

Even when data have been stored and analysed in this way, something else is needed if goals are to be set or modified. In the context of a charity aiming at disaster relief, analysis of data stored on money raised may tell us about such things as the effectiveness of different forms of fundraising, the response of different sectors of society or the impact of different types of disaster. What it will *not* tell us is whether one charitable cause is worth more of our attention than another, what proportion of our money ought go to which cause or whether one method of fundraising is more ethical than another. Such choices can only be made on the basis of a management policy which will, in turn, reflect the values and norms which come from the *values* or *world view* of the organisation concerned.

Goal setting, therefore, requires the information system to deal with a mix of hard information – on such things as costs and number of people – and soft, normative information about policy or values. Whether the physical implementation of the information system in any organisation explicitly recognises the normative component or not does not prevent it from being present. Failure to recognise that all goals reflect certain values does not prevent them from doing so. The eEurope strategy is loaded with assumptions about the desirability of technological progress; yet is progress automatically good? Every charity assumes that its cause is good but would everyone agree?

A good model of an information system should, therefore, explain the relationship between the different forms of information that it has to deal with and the role that they play. Figure 15.4 represents one attempt to do this. The model distinguishes three components in the complete process of goal setting:

- **normative**
- **reflective**
- **automatic.**

It was shown above that there is a **normative** component in goal setting because goals reflect values. Whether this reflection is conscious or occurs by default, a normative component is nevertheless present in the goal-setting process. In the eEurope case, for example, goals expressed in terms of the take-up of information and communications technology reflected norms about the desirability of progress and universality.

The **reflective** component in goal setting seeks to produce a method or procedure that can be used to set goals conforming to normative values. Thus, if the norm of 'an information society for all' means equipping schools with information and communications technology then reflective goal setting will deliver a method for doing this. Once the method has been set, automatic testing and calculation can be used to produce a decision about how much of the various types of equipment ought to be installed in each school.

From this review of information, control and management systems the following central conclusions can be drawn.

- The information system of an organisation is more than information and communications technology and paperwork. All forms of information that are used to set goals and help management to achieve them should be considered as business and management information.

- Ignoring the existence of relevant information, on the basis that it is difficult to quantify or computerise, will merely mean that it continues to play a role in an unmanaged way. Since all forms of information interact through the control system, unmanaged information will distort the workings of the formal system.

DATA PROCESSING AND DATABASE MANAGEMENT

Designing and developing information systems

The relationships shown in Figure 15.4 have important practical implications for the design and implementation of computer-based information systems. Figure 15.4 shows the information system as a translator of management values into specific goals expressing what the organisation seeks to achieve through its operations. There is no such thing as 'the' information system. For each organisation, the particular information system that it uses, including the computer-based technological component, will reflect the values of the wider management system. This relationship may not be formalised but, as noted above, ignoring the existence of relevant information on the basis that it is difficult to quantify or computerise will merely mean that it continues to play a role in an unmanaged way. In such cases of neglect, the values will be those of accepting accident, anarchy or blind politics as a means of implementing management goals.

If the information system is consciously to reflect the values of management then it should be designed top down. The phrase 'top down' should be understood in terms of the concept of systems hierarchy. The top of this hierarchy is not senior management or the 'bosses' but the whole organisation and its needs. The phrase 'top down', therefore, refers to the concept of using the norms of the whole organisation as a basis for establishing goals and thereby defining the role of the information system in the context of Figure 15.4.

Designing the details of a computerised information system can only follow the establishment of its organisational context. In forming the eEurope programme the

EU could only decide on the design of a programme for promoting eEurope after it had decided its political position in the new world of information and communications technology and the Internet. The details of how something should be provided can only follow a decision on what values the process should reflect.

An historically mainline view like that of Olle *et al.* (1988), which continues to be relevant, sees four major stages in information systems development.

- **Information systems planning** – determining the information requirements of the organisation and its business objectives. Also checking any existing information strategy and objectives.

- **Business analysis** – analysing the business or organisational activities that may be covered by the information systems' development process and the properties of any existing information system.

- **Systems design** – the prescriptive or definitive activity that identifies the components of the system to be constructed and describes what they must do.

- **Construction design** – how the system design of the previous stage is to be constructed.

Approaches following a version of this sequence are top down because they first establish what the business or organisation does, then its information needs, and only finally the detailed design and construction of the computer-based information system. Note also that these last two stages follow the top-down sequence of 'what they must do' preceding '*how* the system is to be constructed'.

Scheduling the information system

The discussion of sensing and feedback above showed that they were concerned with information about the behaviour of the process being controlled and its state at any particular time. This implies that the sensor in a control system can monitor both static and dynamic properties of the process being controlled. For example, checking the take-up of a new type of information and communications technology over the EU will not only reveal how far it is being used at any time, but also how the level of use increases over time. The same can be said about checking the financial position of an organisation. The sensor can give the financial assets and liabilities at a particular point in time. Over a period of time it can also show their net movement. The balance sheet and the profit and loss account are thus examples of the static and dynamic properties of a controlled process.

Another feature of control is the feedback loop. This raises another important issue about sensing outputs – how frequently should the sensing and feedback take place? Our previous example of the balance sheet and profit and loss account illustrates this point. A worried shareholder might wish that accounts for shaky companies came out every month. Busy self-employed people can find that the annual task of producing formal accounts, just to satisfy government legislation, comes round frequently enough.

In practice, managing an information system must find a balance between:

- **real-time systems** – which continually sense the outputs from controlled processes;
- **batch-processing systems** – which store the information about the outputs from a process over a period of time. Only at the end of this period will it complete the feedback, comparison and actuation loop to modify the inputs to the controlled process.

The particular way in which this balance is made will depend on costs. Figure 15.5 illustrates the principle. One set of costs is associated with the operation of the information system itself. These tend to be higher for systems which operate high-frequency or continuous feedback. The other set of costs is associated with the increase in error or bad management decisions which come with older, dated information. This tends to be associated with low update frequency or batch-processing systems. The relationship between frequency of feedback and the total costs of operating the system will have a minimum, representing the balance between the two cost types.

In practice it is very unlikely that an exact minimum cost frequency can be calculated. It is possible, however, to use the principles illustrated in Figure 15.5 to identify which costs need to be assessed before making management judgements about the kind of information technology needed to support an information system. Some examples will illustrate this.

The first examples are concerned with computer-based information systems with a need for very frequent or near continuous feedback. As shown, these will be expensive to operate. Real-time systems are the extreme example of this. Every time there is any change in the business process that is being controlled, information about the change is immediately taken up by the computer system and then processed. Common examples of real-time systems are:

- airline and hotel chain booking systems;
- banking and financial trading systems;
- large-scale electronic point of sale retailing/stock control systems as part of a supply chain.

These systems all require recorded information to be up to date. A booking system that could only tell whether there were any seats on a plane flight last week would lead to business suicide. Similarly records of vacancies in hotels, the price of stocks and shares and the availability of goods from a central warehouse all require information on the state of the organisation as it is *now*.

Such systems are expensive to operate because the control loop joining the sensor with the rest of the information system is in continuous operation. In practice such systems are likely to be based on a telecommunication network that can immediately transmit data on enquiries, bookings, sales, etc. to a computer system

Figure 15.5 Costs and information systems management

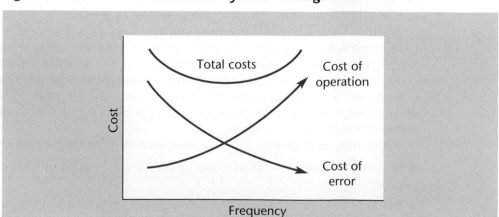

that continuously updates records. It also implies elaborate security and backup functions to ensure that the system cannot be switched off by failure, in addition to 24/7 manning by human operators who have to be paid.

The expense of a real-time system is justified by the need to avoid the high cost of potential error. In terms of Figure 15.5, organisations needing real-time systems are those whose cost of error is at high levels for all but the highest frequencies. It's hard to imagine an airline that could work with booking information that was a week out of date, or a supermarket getting by with last month's stock figures. Organisations like these need information updated every second, and this need pushes the total cost curve minimum position towards high frequencies.

Many businesses do not require such up-to-date information. The costs of information being old are not so vital. If employees are paid weekly on the basis of hours worked then it doesn't matter if there is no available running total during the week. All that is needed is to collect the daily hours data during the week and process them as a batch. The same goes for many monthly business accounts. Documented records of sales are kept as they occur, but updating the account and issuing statements is only required at the month end.

Figure 15.5 implies that batch processing is more likely where the cost of error associated with aged information falls away rapidly at all but the lowest frequencies. Provided that we vet potential customers for creditworthiness, little is gained by operating a weekly rather than a monthly accounting system. The total cost curve for batch processing will therefore be one where the rapid decline of error costs with increased feedback frequency makes the minimum total cost correspond to low frequency feedback. This low frequency can often mean that only simple information technology is needed – the system may be manual or contracted to a computer agency.

Exploiting the information resource

One view of information considered above was one of data as the structured building material of information. This stock of material can be described as a **database**. This can be managed by software to produce the information needed by the user. Such a system of controlling a database is called a **database management system** (DBMS).

To understand the relationship between the data stored and the information produced by a DBMS consider the following:

- What do the terms **file** and **record** mean in the context of information systems based on contemporary information and communications technology?
- If the the two terms mean something different, how can this difference be shown to be important in terms of its implications for managing information systems?

The first question can be answered by distinguishing the *physical* and *logical* views of data and information. Recalling what was covered in our review of the properties of systems earlier, a logical view of information or data is concerned with *what* it is, and a physical view with *how* it is recorded, accessed or transmitted.

In everyday use, a 'file' is seen as a source of information about a number of people or things, present as a series of 'records'. Records and files are often seen in physical terms. Thus a file might be a box with the records as individual cards inside. In a computer system the records might be areas of magnetic patterns on a disk. However implemented, the physical view sees the connection between records in a file, and of data in the record, as physically connected on the recording.

The first computer-based systems took a physical view of records and files. The result has been that, ever since, computer-based files and records have often been subjected to the same restrictions of access as individual physical filing cabinets in separate departmental offices. Thus the sales file is seen as a set of documents for the sales department, the personnel file as a set of documents for the personnel department and the parts file is out at the moment because the production manager has just borrowed it! And we should not assume that such backward images are not still alive. I suspect that your computer, like mine, still uses images of folders and documents to represent what are very different electronic concepts.

Modern computer-based applications of database management no longer require us to think in these terms. Instead, the data used by a DBMS can be seen as a resource that can be 'mined' by the system. Harry (2001) uses the analogy of two types of coffee machine to explain the difference. The first kind of coffee machine has separate columns containing plastic cups already filled with the ingredients. The second kind does not have ready mixed combinations – instead, it mixes ingredients to order.

Manual filing systems are like the first type of machine in that the data 'ingredients' are stored ready-mixed. Thus the personnel file will have all the data about name, age, address, status, tax coding, etc. arranged together to form a record on a card. For a DBMS, what is physically recorded is not data structured into records but individual items of data. When the user asks for a record, the data items making up the record are assembled by the DBMS. This means that neither the computer nor its recording devices actually contain the records in their physical form, any more than our second type of coffee machine contains the various drinks. Instead a database has the potential to produce any kind of information 'drink' in the form of a record of data items assembled by the DBMS. An example of this is a software package like SAP R/3 (see the case study of the end of chapter) that provides the ability to produce a wide range of tailor-made reports to users and managers at various levels and in different roles.

Figures 15.6 and 15.7 show these two views of accessing and processing data. Figure 15.7 shows that a database system has two main components:

- **the database**
- **the database management system.**

The database consists of stored data and metadata, which define the characteristics of the stored data. The database management system is the software that can assemble the data into the form required by the user, rather as the second kind of coffee machine can assemble white/black coffee with/without sugar, etc.

A DBMS makes it much easier to support the different information needs of the different functions of management, without special programming. The older, file-based view meant that data were physically stored in a way that made it easy to meet the needs of the particular department that used the file. Thus, order processing would store data about a particular customer in terms of who the customer was and what he/she had bought in a particular month, so that the computer program could process them to produce monthly accounts. If the marketing department wanted sales analysed by, say, classifying products sales against postcodes, the reply might have been 'We need to write a special program.'

For current computer systems practice this last example is misleading. It implies that the restrictions of the old, physical, file-based system are now past. In fact the

Figure 15.6 File processing system

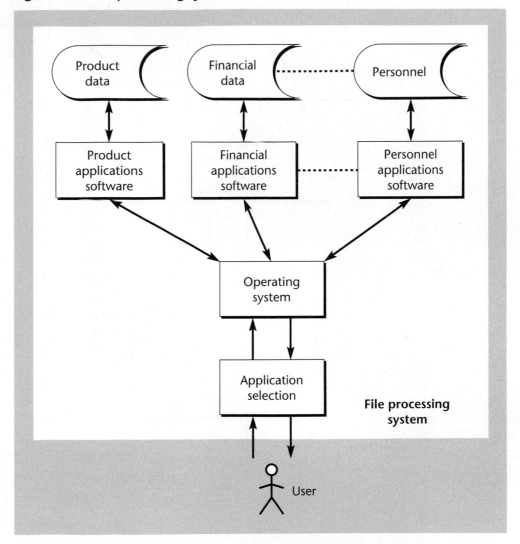

managers of many current computer systems still regard a request for non-routine output as 'special' or 'difficult'. A true DBMS presents no such problem and the 'difficulties' may well be the result of information technology specialists defending their empires.

The software used by a DBMS can take different forms depending on the type of user. There are now several common forms of high-level software which are designed to help non-technical users to query and process a database. The term 'high level' can be understood as a systemic concept. High-level software communicates in terms of *whats* rather than *hows*. In particular, declarative or fourth-generation languages enable users to state what they want from the database using English-like statements. A near universal example of this is SQL (sometimes called 'sequel'). Various Microsoft, Oracle and Linux database applications use SQL. Even easier forms of software use graphics on the computer screen – icons, menus or some combination of them.

Figure 15.7 Database system

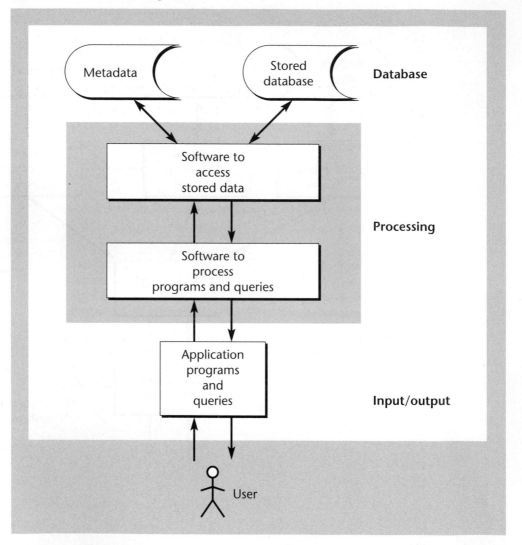

The use of a DBMS has important implications for management:

■ The principles for defining the contents of a database and the process of constructing it should reflect the needs of the wider management system. This means that any method for the development of a database system will include initial stages that analyse the needs of the business or organisation. This confirms the statements made about information systems development above.

■ The management structure which controls the setup and use of the database should reflect user need rather than computer specialist convenience.

The view of the control system in Figure 15.1 as the link between management and information shows why a DBMS has more potential in management terms than the older, physical, file-based systems. It was shown that information used for goal seeking control also needs to be stored and analysed by higher-order control to set these goals. If this process of analysis required specially developed computer programs then all the higher-order functions of management, such as marketing, etc. (Figure 15.4), would represent a special, expensive problem for the information system. In practice a modern DBMS should make this concern an irrelevance – whether it does or does not is a management-information issue, not a technical issue.

MANAGEMENT INFORMATION SYSTEMS, DECISION SUPPORT SYSTEMS AND EXECUTIVE INFORMATION SYSTEMS

The terms **management information systems** (MIS), **decision support systems** (DSS) and **executive information systems** (EIS) frequently occur in books about information systems and they are usually considered as different forms of information system. Turban *et al.* (2006) is an example of a popular text that does this. This section will consider what features are supposed to distinguish these three types of information system, and use the management, control and information systems relationship to show that they are interrelated, overlap and form component functions of the whole information system. It will also show that they are neither new concepts nor conceptually very different, as implied by Turban *et al.* (2006).

Management information systems

The term **management information system (MIS)** is generally used to refer to the information system which deals with the control of so-called 'routine', 'structured' or 'day-to-day' operations. In many popular texts the distinction between the MIS and DSS or EIS is made in terms of a classical view of management hierarchy. Figure 15.8 illustrates a version of this view.

Whatever its relevance or usefulness, Figure 15.8 is neither a systems view of management nor of the systems concept of hierarchy. It represents management functions in terms of who does them or how they are carried out. It usually does this in terms of people's job titles, like 'operator' or 'senior executive'. In contrast

Figure 15.8 Classical view of management functions

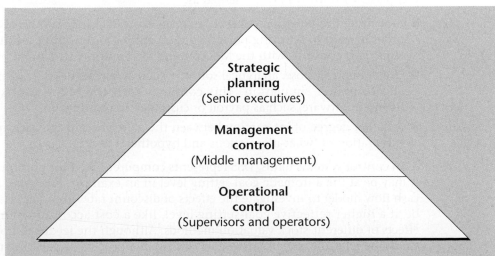

Strategic
planning
(Senior executives)

Management
control
(Middle management)

Operational
control
(Supervisors and operators)

the systems view considers what functions are – regardless of how they are implemented – and hierarchy as levels of conceptual aggregation.

Figure 15.9 shows a view of MIS which conforms to the classical view of management hierarchy and the role of information systems within it. Its functions may be summarised as follows.

■ **Reporting on summaries of basic transactions and exceptions from plan** – in control systems terms, feedback on deviations from the process goals.

■ **Using simple analytical tools** – implies that the MIS will use standard programs which merely require the user to answer set questions like 'how many hours worked?' or 'what is the stock level?'

■ **Solving structured, repetitive problems** – implies that the 'lower-order' employees of the hierarchy of Figure 15.8 process information without the need to make decisions affecting management or strategic functions.

■ **Producing routine reports** – in terms of control systems hierarchy, this implies batch processing of stored feedback, with the implication that this material may be used for goal setting. The term 'routine' could falsely suggest that the advent of a crisis in an organisation has never led to a special request from such 'routine' functions as sales order processing for special reports, like an immediate analysis of some defaulting customer's account. In fact, most forms of MIS take this in their stride if working with a modem database system as above.

Note also that a conventional picture of MIS, like that in Figure 15.9, gives no indication of how the system might be modified or even redesigned. Conventional views of information systems would see this as the separate specialist task of some function like 'systems analysis and design' which would manage the systems development issues discussed above.

Decision support systems

While the MIS controls routine operations using structured data processing methods, the decision support system (DSS) is seen as supporting decisions on 'less routine issues' and solving 'semi-structured' problems. The main features of DSS compared with MIS can be presented as:

■ Modelling the potential effects of management decisions on the organisation in order to help in selecting possible opportunities and finding solutions to problems. This contrasts with the MIS concern with routine, structured procedures.

■ Use of multipurpose, analytical software such as spreadsheets, statistical packages and computer simulation. This contrasts with the MIS use of specific task-oriented software, such as payroll or customer accounting.

■ A higher degree of interaction between the software and the user, including the exploration of 'what-if' questions and hypothesis testing.

In control systems terms, DSS represents computer-based support for goal setting. It may be at the automatic goal-setting level in an example, like using a discounted cash flow model to investigate the effects of discount rate on project viability. It can be at a higher reflective goal-setting level, like a cost accounting analysis of the effects of different stock valuation methods. Although the feedback from using DSS would be relevant to normative goal setting, the process of deciding norms is still an exclusively human province.

Figure 15.10 Expert system

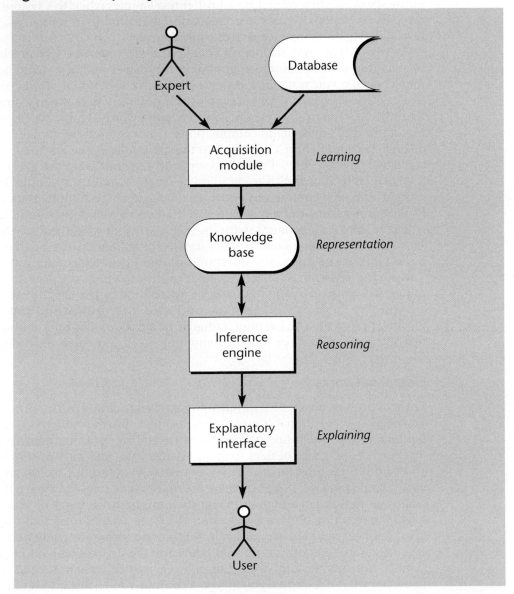

written word could substitute for the spoken word. Hence, computer-based word-processing extended the abilities of the typewriter. Like the typewriter, however, word-processing depends on the keyboard to transcribe human use of words into machine use. Given that speech is not the transmission of individual letters, and that the QWERTY keyboard may have been deliberately designed to be hard to use, the ability to speak directly to a computer system could enable a better integration of the machine and human components of an information system. **Speech recognition** is the attempt to do this.

Speech recognition can work at increasing levels of complexity. At the simplest level the computer system can recognise particular words. A more sophisticated system distinguishes between speakers of the same word. Thus most speech recognition software has a learning mode, where the software compares the sound of the speaker with a set script. A further level comes when the system can understand the meaning of words in combination, like phrases or sentences. The highest level is where the system recognises equivalents.

An example of these distinctions would be a cash machine system which tried to work in response to a spoken request for money. The simplest system might ask how much money you wanted and could recognise individual words like 'fifty' or 'twenty-five'. The next level of complexity would be where the machine could distinguish between two people speaking the same words. The system might be more useful if it could understand combinations of words. Thus 'withdraw fifty' could be distinguished from 'have I got fifty?' At the highest level, the machine would understand that 'give me fifty', 'I'd like fifty' and 'fifty pounds please' were equivalents.

This final level of speech recognition begins to demand a machine that not only recognises speech but starts to understand language. Even if it had not come across the particular format of a question like 'Can you give me fifty pounds please?' it would be able to communicate with the user to find out what the new request meant. To do this the machine would have to start learning from experience. It might do this by using its recognition of a questioning tone in the voice, the use of the word 'please' and knowing what 'fifty pounds' meant to guess at a meaning of the new phrase. The particular form of questions understood by the machine would then be governed by the responses of the user and what it recognised and understood. The machine would then be learning, rather as humans do. Attempts at building such a machine have led to a new form of computing based on **neural networks**.

Neural networks

These represent a way of computing that tries to work in the human way just described. A conventional computer-based expert system would try to capture experience at image recognition or speech understanding by using the two components discussed above – a list of rules (or a knowledge base) and ways of concluding inferences from these rules (or an inference engine). When trying to recognise a face or understand language, however, there are no obvious rules that make it easier for a computer to do than a human being. How might a computer be made to understand the meaning of the word 'game'? Deciding a set of rules that was anywhere near complete would be very difficult, yet humans use words easily from childhood, and images too – I look out of the window and see six trees which I can distinguish from all the other features, including an excavator and a hen. A child could do the same, but what rules would you give to a computer to enable it to do this?

Neural networks do not work by storing up increasingly complex combinations of rules. Instead they store the results of individual experiences in a network of interconnections which form one whole experience. Thus a boy decides that something is a tree because his senses' experience of it sufficiently matches the whole of his past experiences of trees, rather than because his brain uses a 'computer program' from its store of rules to test out the data coming from the boy's senses. Every time someone has such an experience, however, the totality of the experience of a tree may be modified – like the first time a tree is seen with copper rather than green leaves.

From this, the following conclusions can be drawn in relation to business and management information.

■ Expert systems and other forms of so-called machine intelligence are already useful for some management information systems which can work on the basis of diagnostic rules. Examples of these are in technical, legal and administrative areas where what is required can be translated into how its occurrence can be tested.

■ Attempts to make machines emulate human management behaviour in dealing with more complex forms of information – like those which deal with interpretation, interest, power or intuition – may be possible using neural networks in the future, but at the moment this is still new technology with an unclear future. Complete integration of human and computer systems is still to come.

A CONTINUING REVOLUTION IN INFORMATION AND COMMUNICATIONS TECHNOLOGY?

The title of this section discusses two questions:

■ Is there really a continuing revolution? If so, where is it occurring?

■ What are the causes of this revolution?

A continuing revolution?

Words often get devalued by frequent use. Five hundred years ago the word 'naughty' was a description that might have been given to someone who deserved to be hanged. These days 'naughty' is used by TV adverts to cover the idea of eating chocolate in the bath. Given the continuing tendency to devalue words by exaggeration, should there be caution when the developments in information and communications technology at the start of the twenty-first century are described as a 'revolution'? The answer lies in the previous distinction of *whats* and *hows*.

When faced with something new, many people try to relate it to something that they already know as a first step to understanding. Examples of this can be seen in the names used by previous revolutionary technologies. Many of the words used to describe the steam engine and the railway such as 'carriage' or 'track' came from the pre-industrial era. The locomotive that pulled the carriages was thought of as an 'iron horse', and it is no coincidence that for nearly 100 years the iron horse continued to pull the carriages from the front, just as the horse itself had done. Only in the second half of the twentieth century did a recognition of what the motive power of a railway train does break away from how the horse did it before. The sources of motion in modern trains may be at the front, the back or underneath the vehicles they propel. They can push as well as pull and can work as efficiently backwards as they do forwards. The danger of using old 'hows' to understand new ways of doing things is that the 'whats' are obscured and potential new 'hows' are therefore also hidden. As long as the railway locomotive was tied to the how-notions of the horse, new ways of implementing the 'what' of motive power were inhibited.

Examples of carrying-over old ideas are easy to find in information technology. One important example is that of graphical user interfaces (GUIs), like Microsoft Windows. These aim to make computers accessible to people who are not computer specialists by presenting them with a screen dislaying little symbols, or so-called 'icons'. These icons represent objects or actions which the user would like to control using the mouse as a pointing device.

GUIs seem to be very friendly and helpful but they are a good example of the dangers as well as the advantages of carrying over old technological views into new fields. For example, to see what is recorded in a file the user points the mouse at an icon that looks like a folder that might be used in a traditional paper-based filing cabinet system. When the button on the mouse is clicked, the contents of the file appear on the screen. If the file and its contents are no longer relevant then they can be scrapped by clicking on an icon that looks like a wastepaper basket.

Although this imagery (*icon* is the Greek word for image) is helpful for a user who wants to interpret the new technology in terms of the old, it is very misleading about what actually happens. Clicking on an icon to supposedly withdraw a 'file' from the 'filing cabinet' is nonsense. Withdrawing an actual paper file from a real-life filing cabinet means that the cabinet no longer contains the file. The sort of conversation that might take place in the office would be: 'Where's the file?' 'I don't know, someone has it out at the moment.'

On a computer-based system, calling the file up on to the screen actually calls up a copy. The original information is still there, recorded on the computer disk. If the computer in question is just one of many PCs on a network, users can have a copy whenever they like regardless of what all the other users are doing. The icon-based GUI concept of a 'file' or 'folder' in a 'filing cabinet' is therefore very misleading. Everybody who wants one can have a copy of what is in the file, and the file itself is still safely in the cabinet. In terms of an Internet connection this has dramatic implications for the virtually costless copying and reproduction of information, impossible with physical paper documents.

It is also worth noting how misleading the images of files, folders and filing cabinets are in their implications for data security. If someone steals a folder from a real filing cabinet, a quick check will show that it is missing and that theft has occurred. 'Removing' a folder from an electronic filing cabinet leaves no such gap, and a whole family of software dedicated to forming 'firewalls' has grown with the Internet to prevent secret 'burglary' of information from computers connected to it.

To appreciate how far new technology can be considered to be a revolution, therefore, requires a distinction of the logical and physical properties of systems. In as far as new technology is used to provide new hows for old whats the revolution is merely one of degree, like faster calculations or more efficient storage, but if new technology means new whats, it can be revolutionary indeed.

Thus if potentially unlimited copies of a file can be accessed by users on a computer network without the removal of the original data, the concept of access to information is something new compared to the old physical access to a filing cabinet. If the networking of computer systems and telecommunications means that an Australian and a Norwegian can have the same near-instant access to that data then the concept of the location of information is completely changed. It is the breakdown of the old physical restrictions, like the location of information, that is the real revolution, not just faster ways of doing what we did before.

There are, therefore, two ways of answering the question as to whether developments in computer-based information systems amount to a revolution. If a revolution implies new ways of doing old things then recent developments in information and communications technology do not amount to a revolution. Indeed, modern systems will still require traditional components such as printed sheets of paper, handwritten signatures and sticky labels. If, however, the whole that emerges from the combination and interaction of the new with the old is considered, the word 'revolution' is justified. The principal areas where this continues to occur are:

- **Communications** and **networking** – these are the physical means of implementing the systems principle of connecting parts into a whole, which will have its own new emergent properties. Thus whatever the attempts by politicians to retain or remove boundaries, there is a *de facto* world information system for many types of information.

- **Multimedia integration** – the development of network integrated information and communications technology systems that cover the five human senses, thus extending information well beyond what can be expressed by printed language and numbers. A good example of this can be seen when we compare the modifications to the aims of eEurope over the years since 1999. The emphasis has moved on from concern with computers to a much richer view of the different forms of information and communications technology that mingle and merge the various media.

- **Intelligent learning systems** – these are likely to emerge dramatically as the Internet removes physical barriers to information, multimedia integration removes barriers between types of information and artificial intelligence systems exploit the integration of both.

Communications and networking

It is very important to realise that all networks, including the Internet, are **systems** with all the properties that implies. Thus the Internet, like any other system, has its abstract as well as its concrete components. People who have decided to get connected to the **Internet** find that they do not just need to buy a modem to physically connect their computer, whether by wire or wireless – connection also requires the appropriate software which is able to use the appropriate **protocols**. Thus the 'http://www' to be found at the start of a website address is a coding to indicate that the communication is intended to make a link with information on the web rather than one of the other facilities on the Internet. Hence, connection has to be made logically as well as physically.

Like any other system, description of the structure, processes or other properties of the Internet will be a reflection of the values and actions of the particular user concerned. The user is a component of the system who interacts with it and it is the result of this interaction that determines the behaviour and output of the whole. Any view of the Internet that sees it as a set thing which delivers particular certainties to a passive user is a misconception.

What effects is the Internet having on business and organisational management? The following are particularly evident:

- **distortion of physical geography**
- **globalisation of information**
- **reduction of systems lags**
- **re-evaluation of information technology**
- **rethinking of conventional thinking about control.**

Distortion of physical geography is the shrinking effect that the Internet has on distance. The Internet can take a manager as close to information and people halfway around the world as those in the same town. Telephones, radios and televisions have been doing this already but telephones are mainly audio, one-to-one machines, and radios and televisions are not interactive. The Internet covers a combination of everything that these other forms of information technology can do plus other new things such as the communication of software.

The Internet generally, and the web in particular, are leading to a **globalisation of information**. For example, someone in Britain wanted to buy a small amount of US treasury bills. On consulting a UK stockbroker, the person making the enquiry was informed that this is both a complex and expensive business, and that anyway it is only worthwhile for amounts above $35,000. However, a quick visit to the US Treasury site on the web revealed that small amounts of stock can be easily bought at little expense and that, furthermore, an application form for the stock can be downloaded directly on to the enquirer's computer. Applying the lesson of this experience to professional, business and management activity generally implies that protecting knowledge-based competitive advantage will become more difficult in the future.

Reduction of systems lags refers to the role of the information system as a component of control, as illustrated in Figure 15.8. The widespread and continuous connection that now exists between most of the major world information systems in business, economics and finance means that the world never sleeps and that much information spreading is almost instantaneous. Consequently managers, as operators of control systems, can pick up and respond to environmental disturbances much more quickly than in the past. Whether this leads to more or less stability in markets is a complex point that cannot be covered here but it can be said that it leads to more extremes, in the sense that it magnifies existing tendencies.

But the most important impact of the Internet on management is the **re-evaluation of information technology**. If, as above, connection to the Internet puts the user at a terminal which has access to all the other computers and data on the Internet then that user is effectively using a *global computer* (see Harry, 2001). If the wide variety of forms in which this information can be accessed is also included, such as text, live voice, audio, video, e-mail, newsgroups and software, then the present forms of information technology are likely to become quickly redundant. It would be very surprising if, by 2010, televisions, computers, telephones and radios are still completely separate bits of equipment. Video phones are only the first step. Instead new forms of information technology (the 'hows') are likely to combine many of the logical roles (the 'whats') of existing information systems.

Rethinking of conventional thinking about control refers to the concepts covered in the section on control in this chapter. Control is a *concept* not a management method. The Internet is clearly under control because it works systematically and enables millions of users to interact in an orderly and controlled fashion. But who controls the Internet? The answer is that no one, single body or person controls it. Instead control is an *emergent property* that comes from people and information and communications technology conforming to standards and protocols that bring *structure* to the system. Reference to the earlier section on systems concepts will refresh what the terms in italics mean.

Multimedia integration

When discussing the Internet we referred to its role in the distortion of physical geography. In fact all forms of networking have this potential in that they remove or alter barriers. For example, two people located at two different sites, but in e-mail contact through a company area network, are more 'in contact' than two people at opposite ends of the company car park. However, separation and barriers are not just a question of distance. For people or electronic machines to communicate they must be able to use the appropriate language or protocols – they must have the appropriate *abstract* or *logical* connection, as we saw above.

Two particular ways in which this is occurring are through the development of **personal area networks** (PAN) and **wireless information devices** (WID). The idea of a personal area network is to integrate various personal electronic devices such as the mobile phone, electronic organiser and music player. Once connected so that they can interact, these become portable networks. Any such connection is likely to be most convenient if it is wireless, and radio technologies such as WiFi and Bluetooth are perhaps the best known developments to date in this area. Besides integrating at a personal level, like sharing a headset, the wireless connection enables access to nearby fixed devices like printers. Also the connection of the mobile phone with the electronic organiser enables the PAN to be integrated with the Internet.

Emerging wireless information devices take this concept a step further by integrating the devices themselves. The term 'teleputer' has been coined by George Gilder to describe the 'do it all' device which, before 2010, will bring about 'the convergence of the mobile phone, PDA, personal application execution machine, corporate systems access, camera, torch light, web browser, video game player, GPS device, MP3 music storage and player, broadcast and on-demand TV, RFID (radio-frequency identification) tag, proximity card for grocery bill payment and highway toll payment, and even more as fuel-cell batteries provide more energy storage. Driven largely by demand for personal convenience, this will be partly funded by personalised context-based advertising.

The key to understanding any of these developments is to remember that connections and boundaries are abstract systems concepts that may be manifested in changing technological ways. Developments in information and communications technology will continually require us to recognise what is going on behind the jargon and the labels.

Intelligent learning systems

As we saw earlier, information is a property that emerges when data items are brought together. Any arithmetic growth of available stored data leads to geometric growth of potential information since data can be combined and manipulated in just about any way needed by the user. The connection of databases over networks, whether within organisations, between organisations or over the whole Internet, means that many new forms of information are now available.

Data about, say, the sales of one particular product to one particular segment of one particular market at one particular time may reveal useful management information for that product. If, however, we consider data about many products and many market segments over time then we are likely to learn many additional things about products and markets that only emerge in a wider strategic context. The process of discovering such emergent information by analysing large amounts of data is already established – it is sometimes called **data mining**.

The ability to deal with large amounts of data, with the hope of discovering emergent information, depends on the ability of the processes used. This becomes possible through the application of artificial intelligence based on the neural network structures considered earlier. In particular, such abilities to learn will push information and communications technology into the higher information and control levels of decision making and goal setting of Figure 15.4. Thus it may be the information and communications technology systems that, *without prompting*, suggest desirable goals or take over making high-level decisions. In this situation, as has been emphasised throughout this chapter, it is for the humans in management to decide how far such potentials for the application of information and communications technology should be realised. But how far is this within our control?

What are the causes of the ICT revolution?

In *The Soft Edge: A Natural History and Future of the Information Revolution*, Paul Levinson (1997) explores the ideas of *'technological determinism'. Hard* determinism is the view that technology contains within itself the means of determining how it will be used by human beings. *Soft* determinism is the view that technology can only influence how it will be used. Levinson seems to go even further by arguing that technology and human society evolve in partnership, and that if technology is not amenable to human needs then it will die off. Successful technology is therefore absorbed into human society by a natural selection process.

This view contrasts with earlier technological pessimists such as Postman (1993) who sees technology as a dehumanising overlord outside human control.

SUMMARY

- The effect of developments in modern information and communications technology on management requires a rethinking of the implications of words such as **information** and **system**, as well as the word **management** itself. Innovations in technology not only affect how management operates to achieve existing goals, it also opens up new potential for what management can hope to achieve.

- The key to understanding the effect of information and communications technology on management is a recognition of the key role of the concept of **control** as the important connection between what management seeks to achieve and what the information system must deliver.

- An analysis of this requirement shows that information is more than the output of the workings of technology. A true information system also recognises the role of human beings and the organisational environment – good and bad motivation, honesty and cheating, successful and failed communication, etc. will still have the same effects as in the past and will call for skills in human management.

- A balanced view of the role of the information system in management must also recognise that a supposed 'revolution' resulting from information technology developments is not as new as it might first appear. Instead enduring principles may be interpreted in new technological ways.

Review and discussion questions

1 *This chapter discussed the richness of information as a concept. Take the list of data structure, process, communication, etc. on p. 503 as a starting point. Select a familiar or documented organisation and list examples that can be found to illustrate the views listed? Are there other aspects of information that build on its richness as a concept?*

2 *What effects does the presence of human beings have on the concept of control when it is applied to the management of organisations?*

3 *What different uses are made of the word 'network' in different business situations?*

4 *Are senior managers or directors principally concerned with strategy rather than operations? Choose a familiar organisation and consider how it behaves when faced with a public crisis. Discuss this issue.*

5 *What can information and communications technology do better than human beings? What can human beings do better than information and communications technology?*

6 *What management functions can information and communications technology systems perform better than humans?*

7 *What do you consider to be the most important potential developments in information and communications technology in the twenty-first century? Why do you consider them to be important?*

CASE STUDY 15.3

The SAP Story (www.sap.com)

In 1972 five former IBM employees started a company called 'Systems, Applications, and Products in Data Processing'. Their aim was to develop standard application software for real-time business processing. Over the next 35 years, SAP evolved from a small, regional enterprise into an international company which now employs over 39,000 people.

The first major development was the completion of a financial accounting software product which then became the basis for other real-time data processing components in what later came to be known as the 'R/1 system', where 'R' stands for 'real-time'. Subsequent developments produced SAP R/2, then SAP R/3.

During the 1980s, 50 of the 100 largest German industrial firms became SAP customers, and the company began a process of international expansion. Subsidiaries were founded in Denmark, Sweden, Italy and the United States with SAP R/2 having been developed to handle different languages and currencies. In the 1990s SAP R/3 was released, and by 1996 the company had gained 1089 new SAP R/3 customers with SAP R/3 being installed in more than 9000 systems worldwide. By 2005 the company claims that 12 million users work each day with SAP solutions. There are now 100,600 installations worldwide, more than 1500 partners, over 25 industry-specific business solutions and more than 33,200 customers in 120 countries. SAP is the world's third-largest independent software vendor.

SAP R/3 has three main functional modules which cover the main classes of business activity: financial, human resources and logistics.

The financial function module includes standard components such as financial accounting, cost control and investment and treasury management; as well as specialist applications such as the management of real estate and rent. At the executive level

▶

there are opportunities for controlling the enterprise through business planning and budgeting, profit centre accounting and the use of an executive information system.

Human resources provides the narrower functions of payroll, time and travel management and benefits administration. But human resources are not only seen in such financial terms – there are also opportunities to manage personnel planning and development through the management of training and other events.

SAP's view of 'logistics' is wider than the more usual meaning of managing storage and distribution. Sales, production planning and control, materials management, quality control and plant maintenance are all covered by the SAP logistics module. As well as these continuous activities, support is also provided for project management.

SAP R/3 also provides the ability to produce a wide range of tailor-made reports to users and managers at various levels and in different roles.

At this point in our review, it may seem that SAP R/3 is every manager's answer to everything. But the success of any software depends on how it is implemented and applied. In their paper (www-i4.informatik.rwth-aachen.de/~jakobs/siit99/proceedings/Al-Mashari.doc) Majed Al-Mashari and Mohamed Zairi review some of

the potential problems and pitfalls which may come from poor, or irrelevant, implementation. As they say, 'a fully integrative perspective has to be adopted. Conversely, the narrow focus on technical elements, at the cost of social and organisational components, has proved to be a major cause of failure.'

Questions

One of the major issues that comes from the existence of what looks like a ready-made solution like SAP R/3, is that of adaption. *Does the business re-engineer its processes to adapt to existing software 'solutions'? Or must the software be re-engineered to adapt to the 'problems' of the business? This issue of how we match the means of control to the thing controlled is one we cover in this chapter. Does the near-universal availability of SAP mean that businesses and organisations may be tempted to distort their operation to fit the use of SAP; so that the information and communications technology 'tail' wags the organisational 'dog'?*

1   *How adaptable is SAP R/3 to the needs of a particular organisation?*

2   *Does the structure of the components of SAP R/3 imply a particular management structure in the using organisation? Consider this in relation to the concepts of control hierarchy covered in this chapter.*

FURTHER READING

Practice:
Lan, Y-C and Unhelkar, B (eds) (2005) *Global Integrated Supply Chain Systems*, Idea Group.

Laudon, K C (2006) *Management Information Systems: Managing The Digital Firm*, Academic Internet Publishers Inc.

Modahl, M (2001) *Now or Never: How Companies Must Change Today to Win the Battle for Internet Consumers*, Texere Publishing.

Turban, E, Leidner, D, McLean, E and Wetherbe, J (2006) *Information Technology for Management:Transforming Organizations in the Digital Economy* (5th edition), New York: Wiley & Sons

Webster, F and Puoskari, E (eds) (2003) *The Information Society Reader*, Routledge.

Principles:
Chopra, S and Meindl, P (2001) *Supply Chain Management*, New Jersey: Prentice Hall.

Harry, M J (2001) *Business Information: A Systems Approach*, Harlow: FT Prentice Hall.

Schoderbeck, P, Schoderbeck, C G and Kefalas, A G (1990) *Management Systems*, Homewood, IL: BPI Irwin.

WEBSITES

http://pespmc1.vub.ac.be/CSTHINK.html
An excellent source for books, papers and journals that give the theory, history and current sources of systems thinking and a systems approach to management. Last modified 03/12/04 and accessed 22/12/06.

http://www.becta.org.uk/
Up-to-date information on the application of information and communications technology in education. Accessed 23/12/06.

http://www.cabinetoffice.gov.uk/e-government/
The UK 'eGovernment' unit. Up-to-date information on the application of information and communications technology in government and business 'ensuring that IT supports the business transformation of Government itself so that we can provide better, more efficient, public services.' Accessed 23/12/06.

http://web.engr.oregonstate.edu/~funkk/Technology/critiques.html
A pejorative website that claims that, beside its intended good consequences, technology always has unforeseeable bad effects and that technology may be out of human control. Accessed 3/02/07.

http://ec.europa.eu/information_society/eeurope/
The EU perspective on promoting information and communications technology in business and society. Accessed 23/12/06.

http://www.gildertech.com/
The Gilder Technology Report is a monthly technology investment newsletter that reviews developments in ICT 'that are reshaping the global economy'. Accessed 01/02/07.

http://www.sap.com/sbs/index.epx
Although this is an unashamedly commercial site, which pushes the company product, it does give a wide view of how networked information and communications technology is applied. Accessed 23/12/06.

CHAPTER 16

Financial control and accounting

VIRA KRAKHMAL AND LESLIE CHADWICK

Outcomes

The purpose of this chapter is to provide management, particularly non-financial managers/executives, with an understanding of the areas of accounting and finance to enable them to fulfil their strategic role more effectively. It is not the aim to convert the reader into an accountant or to become too involved in the 'number-crunching' aspects of the subject.

It is important for management to gain a reasonable understanding of accounting and finance, which it is hoped will help them to appreciate the data which is generated and its limitations.

Having read this chapter, you will be able to:

■ comprehend major aspects of accounting, legal and regulatory framework;

■ understand the accounting-standard setting process developed in the UK and the reasons behind the establishment of International Accounting Standards;

■ describe briefly the areas of activity covered by financial accounting, cost and management accounting, financial management and auditing;

■ illustrate how the net profit before tax is computed and appropriated, i.e. shared out;

■ understand balance sheet information, in particular the capital employed and what it consists of, and the employment of capital – e.g. fixed assets and working capital;

■ appreciate what a cash flow statement includes to help explain why cash movements have occurred;

- spell out some of the ways in which 'creative accounting' can affect the reported figures in an organisation's accounts;

- look at accounting ratios which cover profitability, liquidity, efficiency, capital structure and investment, and understand what they are describing and possible reasons for fluctuations;

- show how to calculate particular ratios;

- appreciate that there are different ways of incorporating overheads in the cost of products and services;

- understand techniques that enhance decision-making processes;

- provide an understanding of the principles of budgetary control;

- demonstrate how a cash budget is prepared and its purpose;

- explain briefly what is involved in the preparation of capital budgets for both income and expenditure;

- recognise the dangers to an organisation which can result from the behavioural aspects of budgeting;

- describe the duties of the external auditor relating to capital expenditure;

- show how standard costing helps to control both price and quantity via variance analysis;

- provide an appreciation of what financial management involves – e.g. the sources of finance, leasing, gearing, the cost of capital and capital investment appraisal;

- appreciate the significance of economic valued added, market value added, free cash flow;

- briefly explain the following methods of capital investment appraisal – payback, average rate of return, net present value method, internal rate of return and discounted payback.

INTRODUCTION

From a review of Figure 16.1, it can be observed that there are four distinct but related subject areas, which are:

- legal and regulatory framework
- financial accounting which incorporates financial management
- cost and management accounting
- auditing, both internal and external.

All four areas depend on the same pool of data. It should be noted that the responsibility for these activities will devolve to one or a number of persons depending on the size of the organisation. For example, in a small company one qualified or semi-qualified accountant could be responsible for everything.

LEGAL AND REGULATORY FRAMEWORK

Companies Act

Since the Companies Act 1947 was passed, companies incorporated in the United Kingdom have been required by law to publish annual audited accounts containing a large number of disclosures relating to the company, its accounting and operations. However, before the Companies Act 1981 most of the detailed rules were to be found in the accounting standards rather than the law. The implementation of the EU Directives in 1981 and 1989 meant that detailed rules on accounting layout and measurement are now included in British law. The Companies Act 1985 now details the minimum information that must be both disclosed in the accounts and subsequently filed at Companies House. All companies have a legal requirement to prepare accounts that are 'true and fair' and, with the exception of very small companies, that have been audited by an independent accountant. The Act also requires that the accounts include a director's report, a profit and loss account, a balance sheet, an auditor's report and notes to the accounts.

National accounting standards

The accounting rules are called the Accounting Standards and are set, in the UK, by the Accounting Standards Board. The accounting rules that were issued before August 1990 are called Statements of Standard Accounting Practice (SSAPs) but subsequently they have been called Financial Reporting Standards (FRSs). The UK accounting rules cover things that would be set in law in many other countries. They clarify the way that profit should be measured, how assets and liabilities should be valued, and require additional information to be disclosed in the notes to the accounts.

International accounting standards

Companies seeking capital outside their home markets and investors attempting to diversify their investments internationally faced increasing problems resulting from national differences in accounting measurements, disclosure and auditing.

Figure 16.1 Accounting and finance

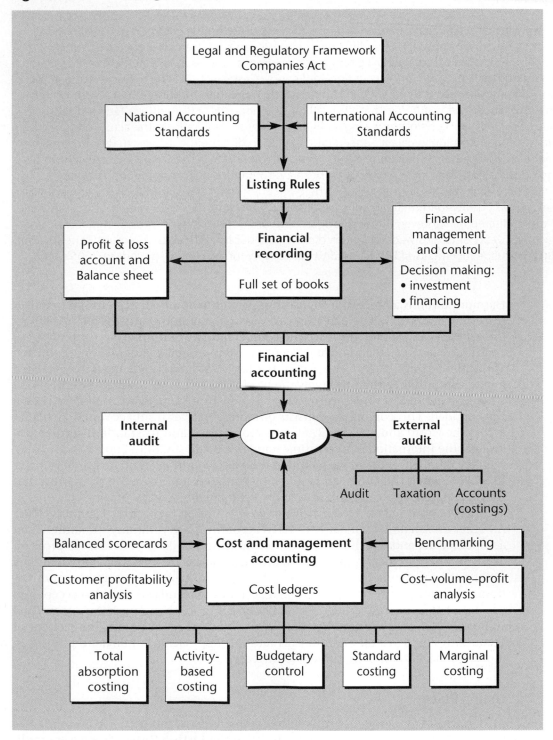

Exhibit 16.1 Pension cost

The provision of occupational pension schemes for employees is now common practice in the UK and in many other countries. Expenditure on pensions can be extremely significant, adding 20 per cent more to the cost of employee remuneration. Prior to the issue of Statements of Standard Accounting Practice (SSAP) 24 (Accounting for Pension Costs) in 1988, the treatment of pension costs in financial statements was subject to very little regulation through either law or professional guidance. The result was that, in general, the financial statements failed to disclose a realistic figure for the costs of employing staff in that they did not indicate the actual costs of the pensions and, accordingly, balance sheets often failed to disclose the liability that the company faced in discharging its obligations. Many thought that SSAP 24 was a major step forward in bringing some degree of order to what had been a disorganised field of accounting activity.

Despite, or possibly in part because of, the pioneering nature of SSAP 24, many companies believed that it suffered from a number of conceptual weaknesses and allowed reporting entities too much discretion. However, it took a long time to bring forward an improved standard. Only after many years of extensive deliberation did the ASB publish FRS 17 (Retirement Benefits) in 2000. The full requirements of FRS 17 became mandatory for accounting periods in 2005.

Harmonisation is a process of increasing the compatibility of accounting practices by setting limits on how much they can vary. Harmonised standards are free of logical conflicts and should improve the comparability of information from different countries. The history and development of international standards for accounting and auditing trails back all the way to the late 1960s, but never have they reached greater prominence than today as the world moves closer towards international convergence. In 1973 the International Accounting Standards Committee (IASC) was founded. This committee consists of representatives from accountancy bodies across the world and later the IASC was reorganised and its standard-setting arm become the International Accounting Standards Board (IASB) in 2001.

A key moment in the move to International Accounting Standards (IAS) came in June 2002 when the European Council of Ministers approved the regulation that would require all EU companies listed on a regulated market to prepare accounts in accordance with IAS for accounting periods beginning on or after 1 January 2005. All other international standard efforts in accounting are voluntary in nature. Their acceptance depends on those who use accounting standards. There is no problem when an international standard and national standard are the same, but when they differ national standards usually come first (take primacy). For example, multinational companies may use international accounting standards and also accept and use national standards. When companies adopt more than one set of accounting standards the result is often that they must issue one set of reports for each set of accounting standards they adopt. This multiple approach to financial reporting by multinational corporations is likely to increase.

Listing Rules

Although all companies are subject to Company Law, publicly listed companies have to abide by additional regulations called the **Listing Rules**. These were traditionally established by the stock exchange itself but are now administered by the Financial Services Authority (FSA) and effectively have the force of law.

The Listing Rules dictate such matters as the contents of the prospectus on an Initial Public Offering (IPO), ongoing obligations such as the disclosure of share price sensitive information, and communications on new share offers, rights issues, and potential or actual takeover bids for the company. The Combined Code on Corporate Governance is also now the responsibility of the FSA but it has advisory rather than legally binding effect.

The UK's listing regime is aimed at ensuring an appropriate level of regulation, while retaining and reinforcing all the features which contribute to the flexibility and transparency of the UK's capital markets. The new Listing, Prospectus and Disclosure Rules took effect in 2005 replacing the UK Listing Authority Sourcebook. The Listing Rules focus on eligibility requirements, listing application procedures and ongoing obligations of listed issuers. The Prospectus Rules (mainly driven by the EU Prospectus Directive) govern the circumstances in which a prospectus is required along with its contents and applicable procedures. The Disclosure Rules reflect the implementation of the EU Market Abuse Directive and govern disclosure of market information by companies, directors and senior management. Taken together, the three elements of the new regime represent a major regulatory environment in which UK listed companies operate.

Sarbanes-Oxley Act

Signed into law by the United States President George W. Bush in 2002, the Sarbanes-Oxley Act (SOX) represents the most dramatic change to federal securities law in the United States since the 1930s. SOX applies to all publicly traded companies and is the US federal government's response to accounting scandals involving businesses.

The purpose of the Act is to ensure that the board of directors of publicly held companies take responsibility for both receiving accurate information about the company finances and reporting accurately on those finances to the public. The most important part of the SOX establishes the Public Company Accounting Oversight Board which is charged with overseeing, regulating, inspecting and disciplining accounting firms in their roles as auditors of public companies. SOX also covers issues such as auditor independence, corporate governance and enhanced financial disclosure. It is considered by some as one of the most significant changes to United States securities laws.

SOX applies to US public companies and their global subsidiaries, and from 2005 it also applies to any foreign company whose shares are traded on the US stock exchange and to the companies that are contemplating such a listing. The US Securities and Exchange Commission (SEC) have extended the deadline for non-US companies to comply with Sarbanes-Oxley Act to 2006. The delay allowed most UK companies a full financial year to deal with the International Financial Reporting Standard (IFRS) and the new listing regime in the UK before full compliance with SOX.

FINANCIAL ACCOUNTING

Financial accounting involves the design and management of the recording system, manual or computerised, for cash and bank balances, receipts and payments, and various assets and liabilities. In addition to the production of internal accounts another principal output is to be found in the company's annual report and accounts, published for external reporting purposes, which includes:

- a profit and loss account
- a balance sheet
- a directors' report
- a cash flow statement
- a financial analysis consisting of appropriate ratios and statistics.

How do we compute the profit and loss?

Exhibit 16.2 shows a specimen **profit and loss account**, which may also be called an income statement, prepared for internal reporting purposes. This will be used to illustrate how certain figures have been arrived at.

The way in which the profit or loss (P&L) is computed is governed by the application of accounting concepts and accounting policies. The *figures which appear in Exhibit 16.2 will have been computed along the following lines.*

Sales

The sales figure will include all cash and credit sales for the period covered by the accounts irrespective of whether or not the cash has been received from the sales on credit. This is known as the realisation concept. Any amounts which are owing from credit customers at the end of the period will be shown as 'debtors' or 'accounts receivable' in the **balance sheet**. Note that in the UK, for a company registered for VAT, the sales figure excludes VAT.

Cost of sales

Cost of sales is computed by adding the opening stocks to the stock purchased during the period (the purchases), and then deducting the closing stock.

The opening stock of finished products, work-in-progress, raw materials and fuels could be described as 'the previous period's deferred expense'. This is an example of the **matching concept**. The stock will be accounted for as an expense in the period in which it is sold. Until it is sold it will be carried forward to the next accounting period as the closing stock.

The purchases figure is computed in the same way as the sales figure – that is, it consists of all of the purchases for the accounting period, both cash and credit, even though certain of the suppliers of goods/materials on credit have not yet been paid. Amounts which are still owing to suppliers at the end of the period will be shown as 'creditors' or 'accounts payable' in the balance sheet.

The opening and closing stocks of work-in-progress will, in addition to the material costs, include the labour cost plus a share of the overhead costs – such as rent of factory, insurance of machinery, etc. The principle which governs the way in which the stocks of finished goods and work-in-progress are valued is consistency. However, companies can and do change their accounting policies. If they do change them, they must **disclose** the fact in their annual report and accounts which are prepared for external reporting purposes.

Gross profit

The **gross profit** is the difference between the sales figure and the cost price of the sales. It is sometimes referred to as the 'mark up' when expressed as a percentage of sales or cost.

Exhibit 16.2 Le Caylar plc: profit and loss account for the year ended 30 June 20X8

20X7		Profit and Loss Account:	20X8	
£000	£000		£000	£000
	8 000	Sales		9 800
	4 420	*Less* Cost of sales		5 712
	3 580	**GROSS PROFIT**		**4 088**
	56	*Add* Other income and discounts receivable		64
	3 636			4 152
		Less Expenses (such as motor expenses, stationery, office salaries, directors' remuneration, interest on loans & debentures, bank interest & charges, and adjustment to the provision for bad &		
	1 603	doubtful debts, depreciation of fixed assets, etc.)		1 702
	2 033	**NET PROFIT BEFORE TAX**		**2 450**
		Appropriations:		
	265	*Less* Taxation		310
	1 768	*Net profit after tax*		2 140
	200	*Less* Transfers to general reserve		300
	1 568			1 840
		Less Ordinary share dividends:		
300		Interim paid	300	
900	1 200	Final proposed dividend	1 200	1 500
	368	*Retained*		**340**
		Add Profit & Loss a/c: undistributed profits		
	4 892	balance brought forward		5 260
	5 260			5 600

Other income

Other income received, such as rent from letting some of the premises, is accounted for per period. Thus if the accounting period is 12 months, and the property is let for the whole of that period, all the rent receivable for that period should be included even if it has not yet been received. Any amount of rent receivable owing would be carried forward as a current asset, i.e. as a rental debtor.

Discounts receivable

Discounts receivable are not discounts for bulk orders, they are discounts which are given by the suppliers of the goods and services received on credit (i.e. from creditors) for prompt payment of the amounts owing to them.

Expenses

The various expenses will be for the accounting period. Any amounts owing which are applicable to the period will be included and then shown as an accrual in the current liabilities section of the balance sheet. In the case where an expense includes an amount which has been paid in advance for the next accounting period, the amount of the prepayment will not be included as an expense for the current accounting period. It will, however, be carried forward to the next accounting period as a current asset in the balance sheet. It will then be charged as an expense in the next accounting period.

Provision for bad and doubtful debts

Provision for bad and doubtful debts is a slice of the profits which ought not/cannot be taken as profits. It represents the value of sales included in the earlier recorded sales figure which are expected to be bad or doubtful.

Depreciation

Depreciation of fixed assets – i.e. those assets such as plant and machinery, fixtures and fittings and equipment that are bought to be used in the business over several years and not for resale – are depreciated to spread their cost over the useful life of the asset concerned. They are depreciated according to the method which is stated in the company's depreciation accounting policy which, for example, could read 'plant and machinery is depreciated according to the useful life less the anticipated residual value' or 'on a straight line basis, based on the useful life of the asset'.

Interest payments

The figure here is made up of all the **interest payments** for the period under review made by the company on borrowings in the form of:

- bank loans
- overdrafts
- **debenture interest** (see sources of finance for more information about debentures).

Directors' remuneration

Directors' remuneration includes all the salaries, fees, bonuses, etc. due or paid to directors for the period in question. It can be particularly interesting to note how information about this is shown in the annual reports and accounts of companies.

Net profit before tax

A more accurate description of this figure would be gross profit plus other income less all expenses, including any adjustment to the provision for bad and doubtful debts, depreciation, interest payable (other than dividends) and directors' remuneration. A knowledge of what the net profit before tax figure represents is important and useful when looking at financial analysis regarding profitability ratios.

The profit and loss appropriation account

Appropriations in the profit and loss account show how the net profit before tax is shared between taxation, dividends for shareholders (both for ordinary shareholders and preference shareholders), transfers to reserves and 'ploughed back' as retained earnings. The retained earnings (undistributed profits) for the period will be added to the cumulative balance brought forward from the last period and shown in the balance sheet as a reserve under the heading of retained earnings, undistributed profits or profit and loss account balance. This problem of having a number of names to describe the same item happens time and time again within accounting terminology and is something that the reader should be aware of.

Materiality

Before looking at the next item, it is important to know about another concept which may occasionally conflict with other concepts because of the way in which it is applied. It is the concept of **materiality** and dictates that where, for example, a fixed asset has such a low value then it may be charged to the profit and loss account as an expense of the period in which it was purchased. However, what is significant in terms of value is dependent on the judgement of whoever has to make that decision. Thus, the same expense or income item, even in the same company, could be treated differently by different individuals. Finally it should be noted that the application of concepts such as materiality is affected by the taxation system – for example, is the item a repair and renewal and chargeable as an expense in the profit and loss account, or is it a fixed asset that needs to be written off over a number of years?

What is a balance sheet?

A balance sheet is *not* an account; it is simply a statement of assets and liabilities extracted from the accounting records at a particular moment in time. It has been likened to a snapshot taken at a moment in time portraying the financial health of the organisation. This means that if another balance sheet is prepared within a few days, or a week or a month, the position could have changed dramatically. A balance sheet today may be a picture of health; a balance sheet tomorrow, a picture of woe!

Assets are cash and bank balances or items which have been purchased (on cash or credit) such as machinery, stocks of raw materials and investments, or amounts owing to the company, for example by customers (debtors) who have been sold products or services on credit. A quick definition of assets is 'what the company owns'.

Capital and liabilities, in the form of share capital, loans and amounts owing by the company to suppliers (creditors), represent a claim on the company. In brief, capital and liabilities are 'what the company owes'.

Why is capital shown as an amount owing? The answer to this is quite logical. Capital represents an investment in the company by shareholders and loan creditors. It is, therefore, an amount which is owing by the company to them. In the event of being wound up the company, if it has sufficient funds, will repay all its debts including the share capital.

From a review of the balance sheet in Exhibit 16.3 it should be clear that the 'capital employed' section shows where the financing has come from (e.g. share capital, reserves, etc.) and the 'employment of capital' section shows how this has been used (e.g. to buy fixed assets and current assets). It also shows, in the calculation of working capital, that current assets are partly financed by the current liabilities (e.g. creditors).

Capital employed

Share capital

■ **Authorised share capital**. The description which appears on the balance sheet is a statement included for information purposes only. The authorised **share capital** is the maximum amount of shares which the company can issue, as directed by its Memorandum and Articles of Association (the document which governs its constitution, e.g. it defines the rights of shareholders).

■ **Issued ordinary share capital**. The **ordinary shares** usually have voting rights assigned to them. They are described in a number of ways, for example:

– **£1 ordinary shares** – this is their **face** or **par** value; any amount received in excess of this 'nominal' value of £1 is called the **share premium**.

– **Fully or partly paid** – where the full amount on shares has not been received, including any share premium, this is described as **calls**. The call for further cash will be made under the terms of the share offer. The holders of ordinary shares, in addition to attracting capital gains (or losses) on their shares, will also receive a **dividend**.

Preference share capital

These are usually:

■ **fixed interest bearing in terms of their dividends** – for example 6 per cent preference shares;

■ **cumulative** (unless otherwise stated) – which means that if their dividend is in arrears then it will be carried forward to be paid in the future;

■ **redeemable** – at some future date;

■ **non-voting shares** – unless their dividend is in arrears.

Note that there are no preference shares in Le Caylar plc's balance sheet.

Reserves

Some of the **reserves** which you may come across are:

■ **Share premium account** – you may recall that this is the amount by which the share price exceeds the par value (also called **face value** or **nominal value**). For example, if ordinary shares with a par value of £1 each are issued at £2.60 each, the balance sheet will show the number of ordinary shares issued valued at £1 each as ordinary share capital, and the number of shares issued multiplied by £1.60 each as share premium in the reserves section. The uses to which the share premium may be put are restricted in the UK to those specified by company law.

Exhibit 16.3 Le Caylar plc: balance sheet as at 30 June 20X8

20X7			20X8	
		Authorised share capital		
		50m £1 ordinary shares		
£000	£000		£000	£000
		CAPITAL EMPLOYED:		
		Issued share capital		
	20 000	20m £1 ordinary shares (fully paid)		20 000
		Reserves		
2 500		Share premium	2 500	
4 400		General reserve	4 700	
5 260	12 160	P & L a/c (undistributed profits)	5 600	12 800
	32 160	*Ordinary shareholders' funds*		32 800
		Long-term debt		
4 000		Long-term loan (10%)	4 000	
nil	4 000	8% debentures	12 000	16 000
	36 160			48 800
		EMPLOYMENT OF CAPITAL		
	23 000	*Fixed assets* (net of depreciation)		31 000
		Working capital: (A) – (B)		
		Current assets		
9 400		Stocks	12 188	
		Debtors (after deducting provision for		
6 200		bad & doubtful debts)	8 640	
400		Prepayments	450	
2 100		Bank balances	2 600	
16		Cash in hand	22	
18 116			(A) 23 900	
		Less current liabilities (due within 12 months)		
3 556		Creditors	4 300	
235		Accrued expenses	290	
265		Taxation owing	310	
900		Proposed dividend	1 200	
4 956	13 160		(B) 6 100	17 800
	36 160			48 800

- **Capital reserve** – this may have arisen on the revaluation of freehold property or on the acquisition of a subsidiary company. (There was no capital reserve in Exhibit 16.2.)

- **General reserve** – this is the cumulative amount of profits which have been appropriated to date (in the profit and loss appropriation account). The transfers are made at the discretion of the directors, probably because the profits represented by the transfers have been reinvested long term within the business (e.g. buying fixed assets) and cannot therefore be regarded as freely distributable as dividends to shareholders.

- **Profit and loss account balance** (or **retained earnings** or undistributed profits) – the cumulation of all the remaining profits which have been 'ploughed back' and reinvested in the business to date. The amount which is 'ploughed back' each year is shown in the profit and loss appropriation account. It is the net profit before tax, less tax, less transfers to reserves and less dividends for the period which have been paid or proposed.

- **Long-term debt** or **long-term liabilities** – items which appear under this heading represent loans or debentures from banks or other financial institutions:
  - **loans** may be **secured** or **unsecured** with **fixed** or **variable rates of interest**. Many types are now on the market, e.g. some loans even allow repayment holidays;
  - **debentures** are a specialised type of loan (usually secured by a charge on the assets) and repayable between certain future dates. Trustees are usually appointed to protect the interests of the debenture holders.

Employment of capital

Fixed assets

Fixed assets are purchased to be used in the business and are not intended for resale – for example freehold land and buildings, plant, machinery, equipment, fixtures and fittings and motor vehicles. They are shown at their historic cost (or revaluation) less depreciation computed in accordance with the company's depreciation accounting policy. You may be a little confused with the way in which fixed assets appear. This should not be a problem because they tend to be shown at their original cost (or revaluation if there has been one) less the cumulative depreciation to date, i.e.:

cost of fixed asset – cumulative depreciation to date = net (or net book value).

Investments

This asset can be made up of the **investments** made by the company in the shares of other companies or government stocks. They are usually shown at their cost with a note of their valuation at the balance sheet date. (Exhibit 16.2 did not have any investments.)

Working capital

WC = CA – CL, meaning **working capital** is the difference between the current assets and the current liabilities, e.g. £17,800 in 20X8.

- **Current assets** are made up of:
  - **stocks** of raw materials, work-in-progress and finished goods;

- **debtors** which are amounts owing from sales of goods and/or services to customers on credit, less any provision for bad and doubtful debts, if any, to value the debtors at a more realistic figure;
- **prepayments** which are amounts paid for various goods and services which will benefit the next or future accounting periods, e.g. rent, insurance, advertising, etc. paid in advance;
- **bank balances;**
- **cash in hand** including petty cash balances.

■ **Current liabilities** consist of:
- **creditors** for goods and services which have been supplied to the company on credit, i.e. amounts owing to suppliers;
- **accruals**, expenses included in the profit and loss for the period but which have not yet been paid – for example invoices for the servicing of company vehicles, stationery, accountancy fees and so on;
- **taxation**, the amount owing to the tax authorities;
- **proposed dividends**, the dividend which has yet to be paid to the shareholders for the period in question. Where companies have already paid an 'interim dividend' this figure will represent the amount of the 'final dividend'.

There are many other items which could appear – for example assets such as 'patents' and 'trademarks' and liabilities such as 'convertible loan stock' (these are loans that can at some future date be converted into ordinary shares).

Cash flow statements

The format for the **cash flow statement** which is currently used in the UK is prescribed by a financial reporting standard (FRS 1). The cash flow statement is sometimes also described as a 'funds flow statement' and gives an indication of the reasons why cash movements have happened during the accounting period under review.

A typical cash flow statement will include:

■ **net cash flow from operating activities**

■ **returns on investments, and the servicing of finance** – for example dividends paid and received, interest paid

■ **taxation**

■ **investing activities** – for example the purchase and sale of fixed assets and investments

■ **financing** – for example funds from an issue of share capital, loans received or repaid.

Creative accounting

However, it should be appreciated that accounting is not an exact science and that it does have several limitations, some of which are as follows.

■ The information included in the profit and loss account and balance sheet has been arrived at by individuals employing their own personal interpretations/judgement of the accounting principles and concepts. They may also have been prepared with the taxation aspects in mind.

■ **'Window dressing'** may have taken place to show a position which is not typical of that which existed throughout the period. For example, because of a special effort at collecting debts, the debtors figure may be much lower than the level which existed throughout the period. Window dressing can and does affect the ratios which are calculated, in many instances quite significantly. Other examples of window dressing are running down stocks, changing accounting policies, revaluations, etc.

■ 'Off balance sheet financing'. Many companies nowadays have many fixed assets which do not appear on their balance sheets. This is because certain fixed assets are hired, rented or leased, such as machinery, office equipment, etc. This makes it very difficult when it comes to inter-firm comparisons using **ratio analysis**.

FINANCIAL ANALYSIS

A study of the various ratios over time for one's own organisation with those of other organisations and/or industry figures can provide management with much 'food for thought'. They can help indicate areas of activity which need investigation and provoke questions.

There are many ratios, books full in fact, and it is impossible to cover all of them here. Using Exhibits 16.2 and 16.3 of Le Caylar plc, a number of the ratios, which the non-financial manager/director/executive may find useful, are illustrated below (all amounts in £000).

Profitability

Gross profit to sales percentage

	20X7	20X8
$\dfrac{\text{Gross profit}}{\text{Sales}} \times 100$	$\dfrac{3\,580}{8\,000} \times 100$	$\dfrac{4\,088}{9\,800} \times 100$
	$= 44.75\%$	$= 41.71\%$

This shows the company's average mark-up on the selling price. The reason for the fall in 20X8 could be that the margins are being cut to reach sales targets and increase market share, or that certain lines are being sold off at well below the average mark-up.

Net profit before tax to sales percentage

	20X7	20X8
$\dfrac{\text{Net profit before tax}}{\text{Sales}} \times 100$	$\dfrac{2\,033}{8\,000} \times 100$	$\dfrac{2\,450}{9\,800} \times 100$
	$= 25.41\%$	$= 25.00\%$

One way of looking at this is to show how it explains the profit generated for each £1 of sales. Both years generate around 25p for every £1 of sales made. Movements in this percentage are caused by fluctuations in gross profit, expenses, depreciation, directors' fees, interest payments, etc. It can be said that it provides an indication of what is happening to the overheads. From these figures, it looks as though the company has managed to control its overheads more effectively. Despite a dip in the gross profit percentage, the net profit percentage is almost the same even though the company has operated at a higher level of activity.

Net profit before interest and tax as a percentage of the capital employed (return on investment)

	20X7	20X8	
Net profit before tax	2033	2450	
Add Interest on loan (10%)	400	400	
Interest on debentures	–	960	(Full year assumed)
	£2433	£3810	

$$\text{20X7} \qquad \frac{2433}{36160} \times 100 = 6.73\% \qquad \text{20X8} \qquad \frac{3810}{48800} \times 100 = 7.81\%$$

This is a very good measure for looking at the productivity of the capital employed. It looks at the net profit before interest and tax (NPBIT) as a percentage of the capital invested irrespective of where that capital came from, e.g. share capital, reserves, loans, etc. It therefore gives an **overall return on the capital employed**.

Although the return is improving for Le Caylar plc, it is less than the cost of the new borrowing. The debentures are at 8 per cent. One possible explanation is that the company was fighting for survival at a time of difficult trading conditions/recession. It is to be hoped that the new investment, indicated by the increase in fixed assets, will benefit future trading periods.

The interest calculations are computed by referring to the information given in Exhibit 16.3, the balance sheet.

Liquidity

To compute some of the **liquidity ratios** for both years more information is needed for 20X6, which is:

	20X6
Stocks	8600
Debtors	5200
Creditors	2944

Current ratio

The **current ratio** is the ratio of current assets to current liabilities, and measures the company's ability to pay its debts as the debts become due:

$$\text{20X7} \qquad\qquad \text{20X8}$$

$$\frac{18116}{4956} = 3.66 \qquad\qquad \frac{23900}{6100} = 3.92$$

For every £1 owing, the company had £3.66 cover in 20X7 and £3.92 cover in 20X8. The increase looks as though it could be caused by the significant increases in stocks and debtors which tie up more capital. This could also provide another reason for the poor performance in the productivity of the capital employed, i.e. the return on investment.

Acid test

The acid test is computed as above but excludes stocks as they are not classed as being as liquid as the other current assets. It may also be described as the ratio of liquid assets to current liabilities.

20X7	20X8
$\dfrac{8\,716}{4\,956} = 1.76$	$\dfrac{11\,712}{6\,100} = 1.92$

The rule of thumb for this ratio is one to one, but in practice companies do tend to manage on less. An acid test of around 0.85 is not untypical. The company had cover of £1.76 in 20X7 and £1.92 in 20X8 for every pound that is owed. In the words of the **Boston matrix**, it would no doubt be classified as a 'cash cow' – not much growth in turnover but with a lot of cash. It does have a lot of capital tied up in debtors and large amounts in the bank.

Efficiency ratios

Average collection period

The average collection period shows how long it takes to collect the amounts owing from debtors. It can be computed as follows:

$$\frac{\text{average debtors (i.e. opening plus closing debtors divided by two)}}{\text{sales}} \times 365 \text{ days}$$

20X7	20X8
$\dfrac{5\,700}{8\,000} \times 365 = 260 \text{ days}$	$\dfrac{7\,420}{9\,800} \times 365 = 276 \text{ days}$

It would appear that the company's credit control is very poor and getting worse, and that it is allowing its debtors far too long a time in which to pay. Periods of around 45 days or 60 days are quite typical of certain industries and 90 days is not uncommon. Again, because of adverse trading conditions and increased competition, the company may have been forced into giving more than generous credit terms.

Average credit period

The average credit period shows how long it takes to pay the suppliers of purchases on credit. This would be computed in the same way as the average collection period, if possible using the following calculation:

$$\frac{\text{average creditors (i.e. opening plus closing creditors divided by two)}}{\text{purchases on credit}} \times 365 \text{ days}$$

At this point it should be noted that information about the amount of sales or purchases on credit is not always available. If that is the case, just use the total sales figure or total purchases figure.

Rate of stock turnover (or 'stockturn')

Here the computation uses the 'cost of sales' if available; if not then the sales figure can be used. It represents how many times the average stock held is sold in a given period and can also be converted to give the average time that it remains in stock before being sold. One way of calculating it is:

$$\frac{\text{average stock}}{\text{cost of sales}} \times 365$$

20X7	20X8

$$\frac{9\,000}{4\,420} \times 365 = 743 \text{ days} \qquad \frac{10\,794}{5\,712} \times 365 = 690 \text{ days}$$

Holding stocks for long periods is expensive in terms of the amount of capital tied up, interest payments and other holding costs. The company needs to make a very careful review of its stock control area – stocks would appear to be tied up for periods which are far too long. Certain companies have been known to carry on producing stock even though their market for certain products is in decline!

Capital structure

Gearing

Gearing (also called **leverage**) is an indication of the relationship between the **long-term debt** and the equity (equity defined as ordinary share capital plus the reserves). One way of expressing this relationship is:

$$\frac{\text{long-term debt}}{\text{equity} + \text{long-term debt}} \times 100$$

20X7	20X8

$$\frac{4\,000}{36\,160} \times 100 = 11.06\% \qquad \frac{16\,000}{48\,800} \times 100 = 32.79\%$$

In 20X7 the company could be described as 'low geared', i.e. it has a low proportion of long-term debt (sometimes just called 'debt'). The debentures issued in 20X8 have caused the company to become more 'highly geared'. In times of poor trading conditions it is the more highly geared companies that are at risk of going out of business because of their obligations to make loan repayments and pay interest at regular intervals on their debentures/long-term loans. Note that what is high or low gearing will depend on the industry/type of business concerned. Gearing has been described as 'using debt to increase the wealth of ordinary shareholders' – that is, if the project concerned generates profit, after the payment of the interest on the long-term debt, any excess belongs to the ordinary shareholders.

Investment

Earnings/shareholders' equity (return on equity)

This is computed as follows:

$$\frac{\text{net profit after tax (less preference dividend, if any)}}{\text{equity (i.e. the ordinary shareholders' funds)}} \times 100$$

20X7	20X8
$\dfrac{1\,768}{32\,160} \times 100 = 5.50\%$	$\dfrac{2\,140}{32\,800} \times 100 = 6.52\%$

This provides an indication of the return that is being earned on behalf of the ordinary shareholders. There has been a slight improvement. It would be hoped that this will grow in the future as a result of the higher gearing and the increased investment in fixed assets.

Earnings per share (EPS)

The amount which each ordinary share is producing is calculated as follows:

$$\frac{\text{net profit after tax (less any preference dividend, if any)}}{\text{number of ordinary shares}}$$

20X7	20X8
$\dfrac{1\,768}{20\,000} = 8.84$ pence per share	$\dfrac{2\,140}{20\,000} = 10.7$ pence per share

This would have to be compared with a 'yardstick' such as the earnings per share of the industry or various competitors.

COST AND MANAGEMENT ACCOUNTING

Cost and management accounting is involved with satisfying the information needs of management. It is there to assist management with decision making, for example planning the organisation's economic performance, controlling costs and improving profitability. However, it should be noted that the information provided by the management accounting function is just one component part of the decision-making jigsaw. There are other factors to take into account, for example non-financial factors such as the ease of maintenance, servicing arrangements, importing problems, standardisation, etc. One of the most difficult problems which the management accountant has to deal with is how to account for overheads. Overheads comprise the indirect expenditure – that is, expenditure which does not directly form part of the product or service.

There are three approaches which can be followed. These can be described briefly as:

■ **Total absorption costing** – this method shares up the production overheads between departments/locations (cost centres) and then charges them to the products via a predetermined rate per direct labour hour or machine hour or some other basis (absorption rate/recovery rate), the aim being to recover the overhead expenditure in the product costs.

- **Activity-based costing** – in effect a more sophisticated total absorption costing method. The overheads are shared up according to 'cost drivers'. A cost driver is the activity which causes the cost to be incurred, for example the number of setups, the number of purchase orders, etc.

- **Marginal costing** – only the variable overheads, those which vary directly with the production of the product, are included in the product costs. The fixed costs are not included in the product costs and are treated as 'period costs' – they are written off as an expense of the period to which they belong.

The bulk of what is reviewed here regarding management accounting are techniques for enhanced decision making, i.e. cost-volume-profit analysis, customer profitability analysis, benchmarking and the use of balanced scorecards.

In order for management to control costs, budgets and standards must be set for each element of cost, i.e. materials, labour and overheads.

Standard costing and budgetary control are modern techniques which measure actual costs against predetermined standards/budgets. By analysis of the variances between actual and standard/budget, they provide managers with a means of continuous control so that they can take appropriate remedial action, as indicated in Figure 16.2. The same principle may also be applied to sales and other sources of income.

Figure 16.2 The three phases of predetermined cost control

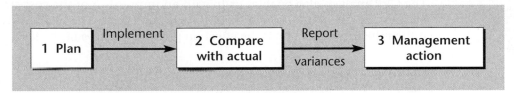

The variance reports mentioned would be designed to highlight variances which are adverse and of significant value and include an explanation as to why the variance has occurred.

Cost-volume-profit analysis

The objective of cost-volume-profit (CVP) analysis is to establish what will happen to the financial results if a specified level of activity or volume fluctuates. This information is vital to management because one of the most important variables influencing total revenues, total costs and profits is output or volume. Broadly, costs can be analysed between those that are fixed relative to the volume of activity (e.g. rent, insurance, staff salaries) and those that vary with the volume of activity (e.g. raw materials, customer services costs). If, in respect of a particular activity, the total fixed cost and the total variable cost per unit for a period are known then it is possible to produce a breakeven chart. These illustrate how costs relate to changes in the volume of business – see Figure 16.3. They also enable us to identify:

- fixed, variable and total costs, and total revenues;
- the breakeven point in sales volume;
- Profits or losses above and below target sales within a relevant range.

Figure 16.3 Breakeven analysis chart

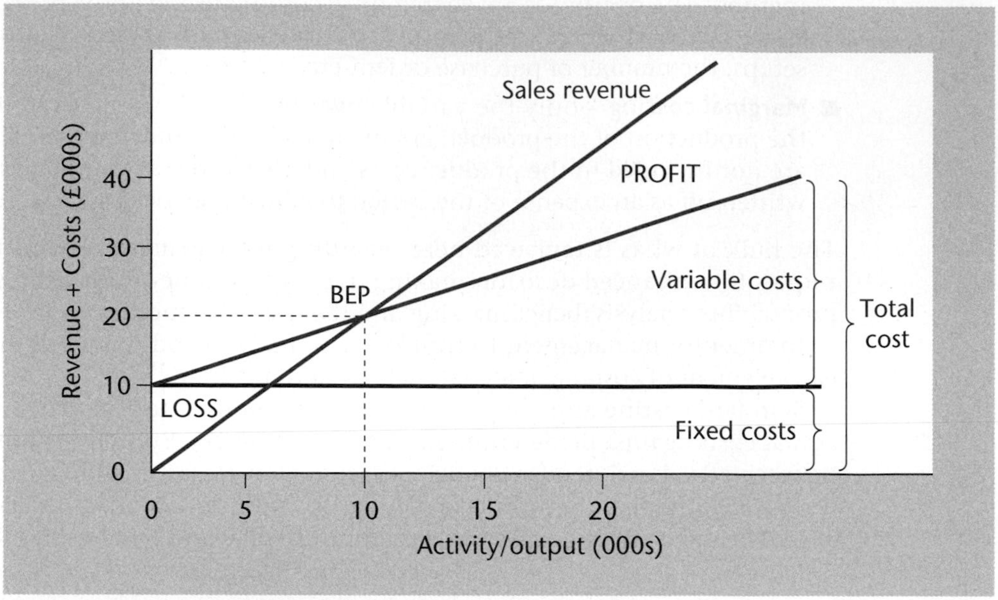

The CVP analysis also enables us to gain an impression of the cost structures of a business, i.e. the proportion of fixed costs to total costs. The higher this proportion is then the more dramatic is the effect on profit of changes in the level of demand.

Customer profitability analysis

Many costs in a company are customer, not product, driven. These cost drivers include supply and delivery patterns, customer locations, quality, after-sales service levels, sales and promotion effort and the level of discounts allowed. Given the modern emphasis on the need to be customer focused, this can lead to the profitability requirement being overlooked. Customer profitability analysis involves the identification of revenues, costs and profit by individual customer or customer group. If costs are shared out by customer rather than over product lines, it could result in some customers being identified as unprofitable.

The aim of customer profitability analysis is to identify low volume and low margin customers and either stop doing business with them or modify the service provided to them. However, even if the unprofitable customers have gone, the existing fixed costs are reapportioned over fewer customers, which may then indicate another loss maker, and so on until no customers remain. Therefore, in some cases there may be a need for keeping the business even if it is loss making. The customer may be new or growing and may be likely to place more profitable orders in the future. Also, it is important to distinguish between profit and contribution. A customer may appear to be unprofitable merely because of the costing method used and yet be making a positive contribution. Advocates, for example, argue that activity-based costing provides a better basis for calculating customer profitability than traditional product and service costing approaches.

- **the stage of setting objectives and formulating policy** – e.g. discussions about how to achieve the objectives;
- **the budget preparation stage** – e.g. in order to keep to the budget timetable and to set sensible targets;
- **the control stage** – e.g. the way in which information is to be reported and acted on;
- **the monitoring stage** – e.g. monitoring the environment to detect changes in basic assumptions, and reviewing and revising to cope with changing circumstances.

Cash budgets

Cash budgets (also called **cash flow forecasts**) attempt to predict what the cash and bank balances will be for a specified period – usually between three and 12 months. The movement of cash is recorded when it is expected to come in or go out. This involves taking into account the average period of credit granted to customers (i.e. debtors) or that allowed by suppliers (i.e. creditors). It does not matter about the period covered by the expenditure (e.g. rent paid or dividends paid), what does matter is the date on which the expenditure is expected to be incurred in cash. Certain items which affect the measurement of the profit or loss in the P & L account do not affect the cash budget. For example:

- **depreciation** is a non-cash item – the money moves when the fixed asset is paid for;
- **stocks** of raw materials, work-in-progress and finished products;
- **accrued expenses** – i.e. expenses belonging to the period but still outstanding at the end of the period;
- **prepaid expenses** – any cash involved for these will all have gone through the cash budget and no adjustment will be made as the cash has already moved;
- **provisions** – for bad debts are non-cash items;
- **taxation owing** which will be paid in the future;
- **transfers to reserves** – no cash moves, it is just an appropriation of profits;
- **proposed dividends.**

The purpose of the cash budget is to:

- make sure that cash is **available as and when needed**;
- **highlight shortages** so that early action can be taken – for example internal action to delay certain payments, put back certain investment plans or hold discussions with the bank;
- **highlight surpluses** in order to put them to work – for example investing them in the short term, or switching them to a bank account which provides a better return. This activity is known as the **treasury function.**

It can be observed from the cash graph in Figure 16.6 that area 'A' indicates a period of around four months when the company has surplus funds. Simply to leave it in a bank current account would be considered poor financial management – the balance could be earning a better return elsewhere. The critical position identified by area 'B' arises when the bank balance falls below the agreed overdraft limit. Because this position has been estimated and identified well before it is anticipated to happen, there should be time enough for management to decide on the appropriate form of action. It may be possible to take internal action without having to apply to the bank for a loan or an increase in the overdraft limit.

Figure 16.6 The cash gap

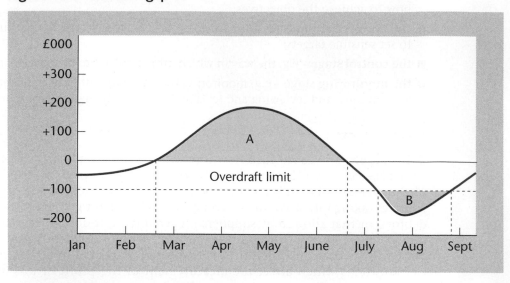

A very brief specimen layout of a cash budget is provided in Figure 16.7. The analysis provided could, however, be much more detailed.

Figure 16.7   A cash budget

20X7	Opening balance	INFLOWS Sales	OUTFLOWS Purchases	Labour costs	Overheads (rent, etc.)	Dividends and tax paid	Fixed assets	Closing balance
Jan								
Feb								
Mar								
Apr								

CAPITAL BUDGETS

The **capital budget** (*see* Figure 16.8) spells out the organisation's future requirements in terms of:

■ **fixed assets** – e.g. buildings, plant and machinery, equipment;

■ **working capital** – e.g. to finance an increase in the holding of raw materials;

■ **investment in securities** – e.g. shares in UK companies;

Figure 16.8 Capital budgets

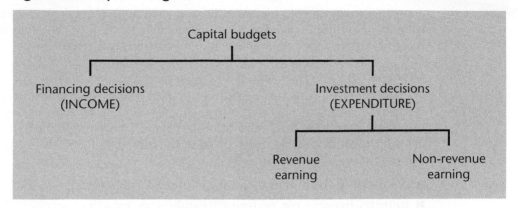

- redemption of preference shares and debentures;
- repayment of loans;
- forms of finance to be used and their timing.

The capital budget will be subdivided into short-term and long-term plans. These plans will need to be carefully monitored and action taken to combat the effects of changes in the perceived environment. (Capital investment appraisal is covered later on in this chapter.)

Capital budgets: finance

The planned requirements in terms of expenditure must be financed from internal or external sources. Although the financing decision is closely related to the investment decision it is in fact a quite independent decision. The capital budget relating to the financing requirements will be drawn up to cover:

- **the amount** required to cover the budgeted expenditure;
- **the timing** of the expenditure – in this respect the cash budget is a very important tool as it indicates when the cash is needed;
- **the type of finance** to be used – e.g. debt, equity or internal financing such as retained earnings.

It is most important to keep a watchful eye on what is happening in the capital markets. The possibility of refinancing existing borrowings should not be ignored. Refinancing could well save an organisation (be it in the public or private sector) a great deal of money. It is imperative that alternative courses of providing fixed assets are considered, such as rental, hire purchase, leasing, hiring, sale and leaseback.

Capital budgets: investment

Management has the onerous task of seeing that all the personnel who should be involved with the preparation of capital budgets are in fact actively involved. The preparation of the capital budgets for revenue-earning and non-revenue-earning investments could well be along the following lines.

Timetable

A timetable will need to be drawn up and circulated in good time, giving dates for submission of proposals, meeting dates for consideration of proposals and the final meeting date at which the budget should be approved.

Coordination

The person responsible for coordinating all the budgets, usually the accountant, must ensure that all personnel concerned know what is expected of them. The coordinator should also make sure that appropriate data and information are made available to all those who are involved in the capital budgeting preparation process.

Such information may include:

- **details of environmental change** – internal and external;
- **industry figures** – e.g. performance indicators, growth in sales;
- **the revenue implications of capital expenditure** – e.g. the recurring annual costs associated with a particular fixed asset;
- **the company's policy on credit, stock and the replacement of fixed assets;**
- **grants available** – e.g from UK and EU sources;
- **taxation implications.**

In order to obtain the cooperation and participation of those involved it is essential that there is clear and effective communication.

Assessing the needs

To a large extent the needs in terms of plant, machinery, equipment and fixtures will be determined by the other interrelated budgets.

Submitting proposals

Departmental managers, knowing what is required of them, will need to formulate and submit their proposals. In the case of revenue-earning capital expenditure their needs will no doubt be based on:

- **matching** the needs of the other functional budgets;
- **replacement** of existing assets.

It is important for management to formulate a replacement policy for revenue- and non-revenue-earning capital expenditure. For instance, executive cars and IT equipment could be replaced every three years, while certain machines could be replaced every five years. A replacement schedule may be drawn up containing details of the fixed assets which are to be replaced (e.g. estimated residual values) and their proposed replacements. The policy must be flexible and reviewed at regular intervals.

For non-revenue-earning capital expenditure the managers concerned should provide those who have the final say with satisfactory justification for the expenditure. Organisations spend a great deal of money on items that are non-revenue-earning, such as fixtures and fittings and office equipment.

Search

When submissions have been received a search should take place to reveal other alternatives which were not pointed out at the time of the original submission.

Preliminary vetting

The managers concerned will look carefully at all the proposals and obtain further information if necessary. They will then decide which proposals will go through to the next stage of the exercise. Rejecting some proposals at this stage will avoid wasting valuable time and effort later on.

Evaluation

The evaluation of the revenue-earning capital budgets will take place using, for example, capital investment appraisal. Various factors such as price, quality and reliability will have to be taken into account when assessing alternative non-revenue-earning capital expenditures.

Presentation

The results of the evaluation will be presented to management in an appropriate format. Meetings may be arranged to discuss the proposals further with the staff concerned.

Selection

After careful consideration of the information contained in the evaluation, plus any further information, management will meet to decide and approve the capital expenditure budget. This may be subdivided into short-term, medium-term and long-term capital budgets.

Communication

The process does not end with selection. It is also important to inform the appropriate personnel of the decisions which have been reached and to thank them for playing their part in the budgeting exercise. The budgets may be reviewed and revised several times before they are finally accepted and approved.

Capital allocation

When faced with the task of allocating **capital expenditure** between the various departments and cost centres the following points should be taken into account.

■ Is capital expenditure over the last few years a good guide to what will be expected next year? This approach tends to look backwards and not forwards and goes against the principles of sound budgeting. The information relating to past allocations is just one very small part of the mass of information required. If historic capital expenditures were acceptable as a basis for fixing future allocations this would encourage spending on unnecessary projects. Justification of projects is therefore of paramount importance.

■ Across-the-board cuts in capital expenditure do not make any sense. This kind of compromise has the effect of cutting the essential as well as the not so essential projects.

■ It is important that needs are assessed, expenditure justified and projects and alternatives considered and carefully appraised.

Zero-based budgeting

Zero-based budgeting (ZBB) has been found to be particularly useful for non-revenue-earning capital projects and for service and support areas. It forces managers to justify and rank their programmes/projects. Top management can then screen and review the proposals and after careful consideration decide which will go ahead. It is claimed that ZBB promotes a much more efficient allocation of the scarce resources of an organisation.

Capital expenditure: the role of audit

It is the duty of the external auditor to verify:

- the existence
- the ownership
- the basis of valuation

of fixed assets and investments.

The external and internal (if any) auditors are particularly concerned with internal control systems governing the purchase of fixed assets. They will look most carefully to see that the purchase has been correctly authorised by the appropriate personnel. Their role also extends to preventing and/or detecting errors and fraud in this area and thereby reducing/eliminating losses.

Capital budgets: conclusions

Success in the area of capital budgets depends on a number of factors, some of the principal ones being as follows.

- It is essential for there to be adequate and effective coordination, cooperation and communication between all those involved in the budgeting process.
- Time should be devoted to a full and frank discussion of the proposals and alternatives.
- The process should involve the appropriate personnel concerned.
- Thought is needed to secure control over the capital budgets and authority should be laid down and clearly defined – for example the authority to order up to a certain value of materials and the authority to sign orders.
- All the personnel concerned should be educated regarding the benefits of budgeting and the way in which capital budgeting decisions are made within their organisation.
- As with other budgets, provision should be made for the monitoring and comparison of budgeted and actual results. Reasons for variances should be investigated and, where appropriate, remedial action should be taken.
- The plans should be flexible enough to alter as changes in the environment dictate.
- The interest of directors (and managers) in contracts should be established, recorded and taken into account.
- The internal and external auditors have a part to play in the control of capital expenditure – their help in devising internal control systems should not be overlooked.

■ Another approach worth looking at is zero-based budgeting, which challenges managers to rank and justify their proposals.

■ Behavioural factors cannot and should not be ignored.

■ It is important for the whole capital budgeting process to be planned and timetabled, so that it can be ready for implementation on time.

Behavioural factors

Behavioural aspects of budgeting can significantly influence capital expenditure decisions and budgeting in general.

Seats of power

Certain individuals and/or groups within an organisation may be able to exert considerable influence over the outcome of proposed capital expenditure. This could lead the organisation in a direction which conflicts with its corporate objectives. For example, it could destroy itself by going overboard with the development of a new product. The power referred to may be by political access (i.e. access to top management) or by voting rights on committees.

Empire builders

Empire builders within an organisation can involve it in unnecessary expenditure. Actions by such individuals and/or groups may fulfil their own personal objectives but these may run counter to the organisation's corporate objectives. In such cases the organisation could well find itself with a high proportion of surplus assets such as plant, equipment and buildings.

Gatekeepers

Gatekeepers are personnel who sit on important information flow junctions. They are in a position to regulate the flow of information and so are in a position to determine what the various levels of management may or may not see.

Beat the system

Individuals or groups may be able to 'beat the system' – they may even take a pride in doing so. For example, a company places a limit of £10,000 on the ordering of capital equipment. Above this limit additional authority is required. The personnel beating the system simply buy a machine for, say, £11,500 by making out two orders, one for, say, £9000 and the other for £2500. This does happen in the real world and efficient internal control systems and audit procedures are called for.

The know-all

Managers have been known to buy expensive equipment without realising that the equipment concerned would only work if certain additional equipment was also purchased. Had they discussed this with their subordinates then they might have avoided making such disastrous and expensive decisions. In one case, although the subordinates were not consulted, they knew of the decision by their know-all manager to purchase a fixed asset. They all remained silent even though they knew there would be problems, and were pleased when things went wrong! This highlights just how important *participation* is and that meetings to discuss investments in fixed assets can save a great deal of time and money.

STANDARD COSTS

Definition

A standard cost is an estimated cost, prepared in advance of production or supply, correlating a technical specification of materials and labour to the prices and wage rates estimated for a selected period, with the addition of an apportionment of the overhead expenses estimated for the same period within a prescribed set of working conditions.

The advantages of **standard costing** are:

■ it provides management with regular and timely reports on matters which are not proceeding according to plan or expectations thus enabling corrective action to be taken;

■ it ensures control of all factors, whether related to expenses or output, which affect production costs;

■ it looks at both price and quantity variances when it reviews performance;

■ cost control is exercised in standard costing via variance analysis.

Figure 16.9 illustrates how standard costing fits into the cost control picture. The feedback loop is important and indicates that standards must also be monitored so that any necessary amendments can be made.

Figure 16.9 Cost control using standard costing

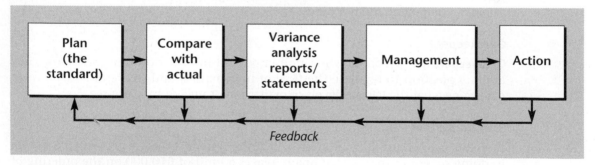

Calculation of the variances

The cost (total) variance is the difference between the standard cost (for the actual level of activity) and the actual cost. This can be subdivided into two subvariances, as shown in Figure 16.10.

Figure 16.10 The cost variance

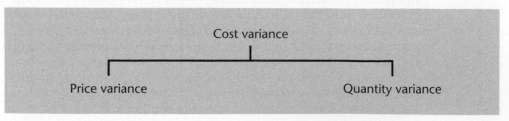

The labour variances (see Exhibit 16.4) are the labour rate variance and the labour efficiency variance. The materials variances are the material price variance and the material usage variance. The division into both price and quantity variances is an aid to control – for example, if the labour force is taking longer to produce products than the time allowed this can be investigated/discussed with appropriate personnel.

It can be observed from the calculations in Exhibit 16.4 that both subvariances add back to the cost (total) variance. What really matters is the reporting side and the decision as to what form of corrective action will be taken.

Exhibit 16.4 Labour variances

	LABOUR OR WAGES VARIANCE	LABOUR RATE OR WAGE RATE VARIANCE	LABOUR EFFICIENCY VARIANCE
	£	£	£
Actual hours @ actual rate (1950 @ £8.40)	16 380	16 380	–
Standard hours @ standard rate (2000 @ £8)	16 000	–	16 000
Actual hours @ standard rate (1950 @ £8)	–	15 600	15 600
	£ 380 (A)	£ 780 (A)	£ 400 (F)

SUMMARY (PROOF)	£	
Labour rate variance	780	(A)
Labour efficiency variance	400	(F)
= Labour cost variance	£380	(A)

(A) = Adverse (F) = Favourable

FINANCIAL MANAGEMENT

Although **financial management** was shown as being part of the financial accounting side of the business in Figure 16.1, it has developed over the years into a specialist area in its own right. Whether or not the financial management function is carried out by a financial accountant or a management accountant will depend to a large extent on the size of the organisation. Financial management covers numerous areas such as sources of funds, cost of capital, capital structure, the value of companies, dividend policy, capital investment appraisal, etc. It is considered that all managers/executives should know something about capital investment appraisal. However, first a brief insight into some of the other areas of financial management will be given.

Sources of finance

Managers, especially on the financial side of an organisation, are particularly involved with the raising of capital and the management of the financial structure.

Capital can be obtained from a multitude of places. The charges for capital will reflect the timespan concerned and the risk to the institution which is providing the finance. It must be remembered that in addition to paying the interest on certain types of finance (e.g. loans and debentures) there is also an obligation to repay the capital at some future date.

Finance is always available but at a price. Matching the time span over which finance is repayable with the life of the project or investment is worth considering. There are numerous sources of finance but internal sources – such as retained earnings, selling surplus assets, improved credit control, etc. – must not be overlooked.

In addition a careful watch needs to be kept on what is available through government agencies and the EU. These sources change quite frequently, hence the need for regular monitoring.

The lease or buy decision

An alternative to outright purchase of a fixed asset is **leasing**. It enables firms to acquire various fixed assets such as premises, plant, machinery, fixtures, equipment and motor vehicles. With a lease the lessor retains ownership of the asset, although at the end of certain leases ownership may pass to the lessee. The lessee agrees to meet certain conditions, for example to pay a rental at specified intervals, to keep the asset in good condition, to carry out regular maintenance and to insure the asset.

Leasing tends to be encouraged by tax implications, high interest rates and cash shortages. It frees an organisation from having to find a large lump sum and the costs of acquiring and servicing such a sum.

It can be said that, in relation to machinery and equipment, leasing provides a 'hedge against obsolescence'. Leases are negotiated for a number of years, at the end of which the asset in question may be returned and another asset leased. This enables the organisation concerned to keep pace with developments in new technology without being burdened with machinery and equipment which are out of date.

Capital structure and gearing

The term **capital structure** is generally used to describe an organisation's more permanent and/or long-term financing – e.g. ordinary shares, preference shares, long-term debt and reserves.

Gearing (known as **leveraging** in the USA) refers to the relationship between the long-term debt (i.e. debentures and long-term loans) plus preference shares, if any, and the equity (i.e. issued and paid-up ordinary share capital plus reserves). However, certain gearing calculations include the preference shares with the equity. If the proportion of long-term debt to equity is high then the company is described as being *highly geared*. If the position is reversed then the company is classed as *low geared*. However, to state with authority whether or not a company is high or low geared, one must look at the gearing ratios for the particular industry in which the company operates.

There is a greater possibility of increasing the return on net worth and the stake of the ordinary shareholder if the company is highly geared and trading conditions are favourable. Conversely, when trading conditions are poor then a highly geared company stands to make low returns because of the obligation to pay interest. It is this obligation to pay interest and in certain cases to repay the capital within a specified period (e.g. on a long-term loan) that increases the risk to the company. The interest (e.g. on debentures) must be paid whether or not the company makes a profit.

The cost of capital

The **cost of capital** cannot be ignored because all capital does have both a cost and an opportunity cost. When selecting a discount rate for capital investment appraisal purposes, many authorities favour the use of the cost of capital figure. However, there are a number of different cost of capital figures which could be used. A full discussion of this subject is outside the scope of this chapter. Investors are only likely to invest in a business if the return is commensurate with the risk involved.

Economic value added

A relatively recent tool that companies are using to measure performance is economic value added (EVA), something economists call economic profit. Basically EVA is after-tax operating profit minus the total annual cost of capital. It is a measure of the value added to or depleted from shareholder value in one period. A positive EVA requires that a company earn a return on its assets that exceeds the cost of debt and equity, thus adding to shareholder value. EVA is an actual monetary amount of value added and it measures changes in value for a period. The capital charge is the most distinctive and important aspect of EVA. By taking all capital costs into account, including the cost of equity, EVA shows the amount of wealth a business has created or lost in each reporting period. EVA has the advantage of being conceptually simple and easy to explain to non-financial managers because it starts with familiar operating profits and simply deducts a charge for the capital invested in the company as a whole, in a business unit or even in a single plant, office or assembly line. By assessing a charge for using capital, EVA makes managers care about managing assets as well as income and helps them to assess the trade-offs between the two properly. This broader, more complete view of the economics of a business can make dramatic differences.

Market value added

Market value added (MVA) measures the amount of wealth that a company has created for its shareholders since the start of the company. It compares the amount of cash that investors have invested in the business with the present value of the cash they can expect to take out of it. Every company's most important mission is to maximise MVA because there is also a direct link between EVA and share price. This value is the difference between the current market value of a company and the capital given by investors, which includes both shareholders and bondholders. If the value is higher then the company has an added value, if it is lower then it has a lesser value. In short an MVA is the total of all the capital that is held against the company, which also includes the market value of debt and equity. If the value is higher then the shareholders are definitely profited.

Free cash flow

Free cash flow can be very useful in assessing a company's financial health because it strips away all the accounting assumptions built into earnings. A company's earnings may be high and growing, but until you look at free cash flow it is unknown if the company really generated money in a given year. When companies report their earnings, these are reported on an accrual basis according to generally accepted accounting principles (GAAP). These earnings are usually not based on cash receipts. For example, a company may make a sale in one month and not receive payment until a few months later. The company does, however, have to make new investments to remain competitive but these investments are often not completely reflected in the reported earnings.

Free cash flow is the amount of cash that a company has left over after it has paid all its expenses, including investments. Negative free cash flow is not necessarily an indication of a bad company, however, because many companies put a lot of their cash into investments, which diminishes their free cash flow. But if a company is spending so much cash then it should have a good reason for doing so and it should be earning a sufficiently high rate of return on its investments.

CAPITAL INVESTMENT APPRAISAL

The planning, control and investment of capital projects

The planning, control and investment of capital involve attempting to answer numerous questions many of which are open-ended, subjective and not easily defined. Some of the key questions are:

- **Which source of funds should be used for financing a particular investment?** This involves considering factors such as the cost of capital, the term (e.g. long term or short term), repayment arrangements, legal aspects, etc.

- **What is the cost of capital?** In determining this it will also be necessary to establish which cost of capital figure should be used (e.g. weighted average cost).

- **What should the expected (ROI) return on investment (return on capital employed) be?** It is very difficult to define an adequate return and the amount anticipated will vary between firms and industries. ROI is very important from the viewpoint of the providers and users of the funds.

- **In the area of capital investment appraisal which discount rate should be used?** A number of alternatives could be selected and deemed appropriate – for example the cost of capital or the anticipated returns on projects commensurate with the risk involved.

- **In deciding on an investment of capital, how will the risks involved in the project be assessed and taken into account in the computations?** This very broad area is the subject of constant debate and features regularly in the financial press. Uncertainty may be handled by probability approaches to likely results, to give the best and worst and most likely outcomes.

- **Why should the company opt for a particular capital structure?** Following on from this one could also ask: Which capital structure would be most appropriate for the company now and in the future?

■ **How much working capital should a firm have?** Cash flow and profitability do not go hand in hand. It is vital to the long-term survival of a business to be able to pay debts as they become due.

The essential elements of a system for planning and evaluating capital investments are illustrated in Figure 16.11, and are as follows:

■ **Objectives** – all projects should be in line with the objectives and/or the policy of the company concerned. In particular the company's objectives relating to the required return on capital employed should be clearly stated.

■ **Data collection and analysis** – data has to be collected, classified, analysed and presented in a form appropriate to the needs and understanding of the user. A key decision to be made is the method/s by which the investment is to be appraised (e.g. discounted cash flow).

■ The **management information system** – the provision of relevant and appropriate information to management can most certainly enhance the decision-making process. An effective management information system is, therefore, a prerequisite for efficient planning and control. The quality of the information will help determine the accuracy of forecasts relating to future performance. However, it is possible to provide management with too much information, and *information overload* tends to weigh them down. The quality of the information, rather than its quantity, is therefore closely linked to the quality of decision making (see Chapters 13 and 15).

→ Chs 13 & 15

Figure 16.11 The capital investment decision

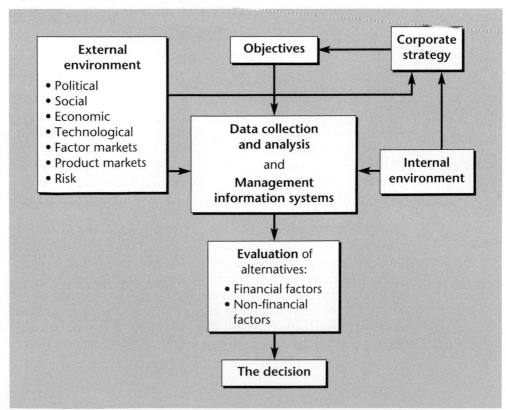

■ **Monitoring the external environment** – the external environment in which a firm operates is diverse and complex. It must be monitored continuously to reveal threats and opportunities which could, at a stroke, change the whole nature of the firm's activities and capital investment programme, e.g. political instability in the country of a major customer (see Chapter 8).

→ Ch. 8

■ **The internal environment** – a firm cannot ignore its own internal environment, the analysis of which should indicate strengths and weaknesses, for example in industrial relations, idle capacity, etc. The acceptance by workers of new plant or new processes can be of prime importance (see Chapter 9).

→ Ch. 9

■ **Evaluation** – in addition to the financial factors which have to be examined, management must also take various non-financial factors into account, for example availability of spare parts, flexibility, standardisation, etc.

A decision to go ahead with an investment does not end the story. The investment should be monitored carefully and changes in the environment cannot be ignored. Companies must be able to adjust rapidly to meet changes in circumstances if they are to survive and prosper.

The real value of a business is the sum of the value of its *existing* assets plus the value of its *future* investment opportunities. Existing assets represent prior investment decisions, the consequences of which (in terms of profits and cash flows) are still with us. Future investment opportunities represent the scope a business possesses for making profitable investment decisions in the future. The investment potential will vary from firm to firm and industry to industry and will depend, to a large extent, on:

■ management's ability to generate, select and execute investment projects;

■ its capacity to raise funds to finance investments;

■ corporate strategy.

The problem of data

The key to good investment decision-making rests with the quality of information on which an investment project is evaluated. The actual method of appraisal is of only secondary importance compared with the vital issue of the reliability of the underlying estimates and assumptions. At best the data is often a reasoned estimate; at worst it may be little more than a guess. It is of little benefit to introduce sophisticated appraisal techniques unless the degree of accuracy they suggest is matched by the quality of data supporting the analysis.

The methods described in this chapter all depend on the predetermination of the cash flows. Thus one should always be aware that the cash flows used in capital investment appraisal are only estimates. The cash flows which are to be used should be relevant/incremental cash flows – that is, if the expense or revenue arises as a direct result of the project going ahead then it is a relevant cash flow. If the expense or revenue would happen whether or not the project goes ahead then it is irrelevant – for example the costs of a feasibility study and certain fixed costs. As with cash budgets, depreciation is a non-cash item and so is not included in the cash flows.

EVALUATION METHODS

Methods which do not take the time value of money into account

Payback

This method calculates how long it takes the cash flows generated by a specific project to recover the initial cost of the investment. Those who use this method of evaluation prefer projects which repay the cost of the initial investment in the shortest time. In estimating cash flows, the earlier cash flows are likely to be more accurate than the later ones.

Average rate of return (unadjusted rate of return)

This return on investment method expresses the average cash flow per year as a percentage of the initial investment. Although it is simple to calculate, it must be pointed out that it does ignore the timing of the cash flows – that is, it averages the cash flows over the life of the project, when in fact they could fluctuate quite significantly from year to year and within each individual year.

Methods which do take account of the time value of money

Both the payback and average of rate of return methods suffer because they ignore the **time value of money**. The timing of the cash flows – the year in which the money comes in or goes out – can have a dramatic impact on a project. The time value of money means that £1 tomorrow will be worth less than £1 today. Thus cash flows which are to be received in the future are not worth as much as they are now. The following methods are preferable because they do take into account the time value of money.

Net present value method

To find the **net present value** (NPV) each of the cash flows is multiplied by the appropriate discount factor using discount tables, for example the present value of £1 table. These are then added up and the initial investment deducted. If the resulting NPV figure is positive then the project is worthy of consideration; if the NPV is negative then the project should be rejected because it is not a wealth-creating opportunity. Note that when using this method, if all the cash flows are identical then the present value of an annuity of £1 table could be used and would save calculation time. Note also, however, that the selection of the discount rate is at the discretion of the selector.

Profitability index

The **profitability index** is the present value of the cash flows divided by the initial cost of the project and is useful for comparing two dissimilar projects.

Internal rate of return or yield method

The **internal rate of return (IRR)** is the discount rate which will produce an NPV of nil – that is, the cash flows discounted less the initial cost of the machine/equipment/project is equal to zero. Therefore, projects with an IRR greater than the cost of capital are worthy of consideration.

Discounted payback

This method simply calculates the payback using the discounted cash flows.

Taxation aspects

Taxation allowances must be included in the cash flows for the period that benefits from those allowances. Tax payments must be included in the cash flows for the period in which they are to be paid over. Thus care needs to be exercised in taking the tax factor into account by considering the various time lags – for example the tax on the income from year 1 could be paid in year 2 and so on.

Non-quantitative aspects

Frequently the cost or benefits arising from a particular investment decision are difficult, if not impossible, to quantify. Yet non-quantitative aspects should not be ignored. There is a real danger of accountants being so preoccupied with the financial aspects of capital investment appraisal that they may tend to ignore other important factors. Such non-quantitative factors include:

- **efficiency of servicing**
- **reliability**
- **risks associated with buying from overseas**
- **desire for technical superiority**
- **flexibility.**

SUMMARY

- Major aspects of the legal and regulatory framework of accounting were introduced by covering Companies Act, national accounting standards, international accounting standards and listing rules.
- In financial accounting the profit and loss account and balance sheet were reviewed together with the terminology associated with them – e.g. prepayments, depreciation, assets and liabilities – and the way in which the figures are arrived at. In addition, their limitations were highlighted – for example, the way in which 'creative accounting' can affect the figures.
- Financial analysis was also introduced via a selected number of ratios such as profitability and liquidity ratios, and some possible explanations for movements in them were provided.
- The management accounting area covered decision-making techniques, budgetary control and an introduction to standard costing. In budgeting the key words should act as a reminder of the principles of good budgeting practice. They are:
  - preparation in advance
  - control by responsibility
  - setting targets
  - participation

New management puts strategy to banks

Queens Moat plans to form core hotel chain

The essence of the business strategy Queens Moat Houses has put to its bank is a plan to form a core chain of 50 UK hotels, which will be rebranded and form a base for eventual expansion.

The new management expects to be ready to launch this chain by the first quarter of 1995. The 50 hotels are expected to contribute 80 per cent of budgeted trading profits for 1994.

The new chain, a name for which has yet to be chosen, will be 'leading, three-star-plus' hotels, each with more than 100 rooms, located in or near city centres, and having a restaurant and bar.

QMH believes these can achieve 'substantial increases in both trading profits and cash flows'. The operational gearing in hotels is such that profits can rebound sharply once occupancy and room rates are moving upwards.

The rest of the group's hotels, another 53 in the UK and 86 in continental Europe, will not be put up for sale immediately. They will run for profit with the aim of maximising their value either through eventual sales or as additional security for the group's lenders.

Hotel sales in the present climate – with large numbers of UK hotels in receivership and the market in continental Europe worsening – are unlikely on a large scale although some, such as the Dutch hotels, are up for sale.

At the same time, the financial restructuring will give the group a balance sheet more appropriate to its operations. This will involve a substantial debt for equity swap, cutting the interest charges QMH must service from its operation and giving the banks con-

trol of a majority of the equity. The exact size of the swap has yet to be decided but it is certain the existing shareholders will be substantially diluted.

Bankers who have seen the business plan say the new management team has put forward 'sensible projections' which indicate a beginning of a recovery in UK profits in 1993 and 1994, with a larger rise later on. Profits from continental Europe are still under pressure.

In the UK, occupancy rates began to pick up in late May and early June, QMH said yesterday, although room rates were still under pressure. A rise in room rates is expected in 1994, however.

UK hoteliers were increasingly confident that the down-turn had ended, Mr Trevor Ward, a director of the Horwath hotels and leisure consultancy, said yesterday. The consultancy's quarterly survey in September found that nearly 80 per cent of hoteliers questioned believed recovery had started, compared with 57 per cent three months previously. Over 80 per cent, however, believed full recovery was a year or more away.

Mr Maurice Segal, chairman of Expotel, a large reservations agency, said yesterday that QMH appeared to be trading reasonably well but that room rates for the industry were still lower than last year.

The plan assumes some revival in hotel prices in the longer term, which could even repay the group's loans in full. One banker said yesterday, 'if the banks sit tight the restructuring has to be better than receivership'.

Source: M Urry and M Skapinker, *Financial Times*, 31 October 1993. Reprinted with permission.

Valuations 'altered to inflate QMH profit'

The thorny issue of hotel valuations was put under the spotlight in the High Court yesterday as four former directors of Queens Moat Houses were accused of manipulating valuations to inflate profits artificially.

The four men, including John Bairstow, the former chairman, were all sacked in 1993 in the wake of the suspension of QMH shares, and are now suing the company for unfair dismissal.

In the run-up to the start of the trial this week, Mr Bairstow and his colleagues – Martin Marcus, David Hersey and Allan Porter – had tried to argue that a controversial £922 million property writedown instigated by current management was largely to blame

for the financial mire in which QMH finds itself.

Michael Burton, QC, for QMH, continuing his opening remarks, cited valuations as one of the tools used by former directors to cover up profit shortfalls. He estimated that up to £60 million of the £90 million pre-tax profit reported in 1991 had been 'either non-existent and artificially created or, at the very least, should have been separately disclosed' as exceptional items.

He cited the example of London's Sloane Club, which was valued at £17 million when QMH acquired it in 1990 as part of Norfolk Capital Hotels. As a result, Mr Burton said, when the hotel was sold on in 1991, the company should have booked a loss on the transaction of £3 million.

'In fact, it appears that the £17 million was revalued to £15 million, then, just before the interim report at the end of June 1991, it was devalued again to £9.5 million.'

But, according to Mr Burton, that was not the end of the matter, as the directors then decided to use yet another valuation, this time the £3.8 million that the Sloane Club had originally cost Norfolk Capital in 1988. 'When it came to the end of the year they needed some more profit to be found, and squeezing as much as they could out of a pint pot,

they had a rethink on the Sloane Club transaction, and at the year-end what should have been a loss of £3 million had become a profit of £10.2 million.'

Mr Burton, who this week has outlined how sale and leaseback deals and incentive management schemes were also used to inflate profits, said that Mr Bairstow and the other three men had failed in their duty to disclose such one-off profits in the report and accounts, choosing instead to disguise them as trading profits.

The case continues.

Source: D Walsh, *The Times*, 10 October 1997. Reprinted with permission.

Incentive plan 'used to falsify QMH profit'

Former directors of Queens Moat Houses used an incentive management scheme to falsify profit figures and paint a positive picture of the company's worsening financial performance, the High Court was told yesterday.

The controversial scheme, under which some hotel managers paid an agreed annual fee to QMH head office and pocketed any additional profits, is at the centre of a case for unfair dismissal brought by John Bairstow, former chairman of QMH, and three other former directors.

The four men, all of whom were sacked after trading in the company's shares was suspended in April 1993, were accused yesterday of misleading the market to expect profits of between £80 million and £85 million when they knew this could not be achieved. The accounts produced after their departure showed losses of £1.04 billion after a £922 million property writedown.

Michael Burton, QC, for QMH, said the problem with the incentive management scheme was that the annual fee paid by hotels was booked to group profits in the year the contract was signed, even though the money was normally paid in 13 monthly instalments

the following year. This 'front-loading' had led to the double-counting of profits from hotels transferring from the management to the incentive scheme.

'The mischief of that,' Mr Burton said, 'is that if you have a hotel which is in the managed sector from January through to October, and then have 12 months' worth of the next year in the form of the incentive fee, you thus get yourself 20 months' profit in one year.' He alleged that hotels were deliberately signed up to the scheme towards the year-end to bolster current-year profits.

Even when the recession had made it difficult for some managers to pay the annual fee, the company had often persuaded them to renew their contracts so the fees could again be booked to profits. He further claimed that to avoid profits being too heavily weighted towards the second half, interim results had been boosted by the addition of a proportion of the front-loaded fee the company expected later in the year, completely falsifying the profit figure for the year.

The case continues.

Source: D Walsh, *The Times*, 7 October 1997. Reprinted with permission.

Queens Moat auditing under scrutiny

The near collapse of Queens Moat Houses (QMH), the hotels group, in 1993 is to be investigated by the accountancy profession's disciplinary scheme.

Chris Dickson, the former Serious Fraud Officer lawyer who is executive counsel of the accountants' Joint Disciplinary Scheme, is to investigate both the company's controversial accounting policies and

shares dealings by Martin Marcus, a qualified accountant and former deputy chairman of QMH. Mr Dickson will then decide whether the case should be heard by an independent tribunal.

'The case will revolve around the accounting policies adopted by the company and the extent to which the auditors waved them through.'

The company's then auditors, Bird Luckin, will come under scrutiny, with Maurice Hart, a partner of the firm and a non-executive director of QMH, expected to be central to the investigation.

QMH's accounting policies at the start of the 1990s have been called into question, in particular, an incentive scheme for managers which allegedly enabled future profits to be brought forward.

Similarly, the group allegedly had not been charging depreciation on its portfolio of hotels, further inflating profits.

However, a statement from the Joint Disciplinary Scheme said the referral of the matter to it by the Institute of Chartered Accountants in England and Wales 'should not be construed as meaning that a view has been formed that a prima facie case exists against any member or member firm'.

The company is currently embroiled in a long-running trial at the High Court involving former directors. The four men, including John Bairstow, QMH's founder and former chairman, are claiming wrongful dismissal.

The hearing, which started last October, is scheduled to conclude some time next month, although a decision is not expected until much later this year.

Source: D Walsh, *The Times*, 16 June 1998. Reprinted with permission.

Judge orders former QMH directors to pay back £42m

John Bairstow, the founder of Queens Moat Houses, and three other former directors face bankruptcy after the High Court ordered them to repay £28 million of unlawfully paid dividends – or £42 million after adding interest.

Mr Justice Nelson, who in July rejected their claim for wrongful dismissal, ruled that the hotel group's 1991 full-year accounts had not given a true and fair view and that there had been insufficient distributable reserves to pay a dividend to ordinary shareholders.

He added: 'None of the claimants were acting honestly or reasonably. I am not satisfied that any dividends – save for preference dividends – would have been paid if the accounts had shown a true and fair view.' Upholding QMH's counterclaim, he ordered the repayment of £27.7 million to the company plus interest of about £14 million.

The judge also found that the 1990 accounts had shown insufficient reserves and that the men were in breach of duty in paying a dividend totalling about £30 million.

However, he ruled that it would not have to be repaid as they acted 'honestly and reasonably' in authorising the payout. He deferred a decision on what proportion of QMH's legal bill of £6.5 million they will be liable for. Even so, the £42 million they must pay dwarfs the combined assets of about £3.5 million declared to the court. Mr Bairstow, who has built a personal fortune of about £3 million, will be forced to sell his Essex mansion and other properties.

Speaking outside the court, a surprisingly sanguine Mr Bairstow said the ruling called into question the whole issue of directors' responsibilities and the role of advisers in signing off accounts. 'What it amounts to is that the director of a public company cannot rely on external accountancy advice, auditors' certificates or other professional advice, because ultimately they will themselves be held liable for any subsequent problems.'

Mr Bairstow, who has yet to decide whether to apply for leave to appeal, added: 'The only beneficiaries from what happened were the shareholders, who got a dividend which would have otherwise gone to the banks under the financial restructuring undertaken by the new management.'

Mr Bairstow – together with Martin Marcus, deputy chairman, David Hersey, finance director, and Allan Porter, deputy finance director – were sacked in the wake of the suspension of trading in QMH shares in March 1993. The subsequent restructuring resulted in a £922 million writedown of assets and a resultant £1 billion loss.

In his damning judgment in July, Mr Justice Nelson found that the four had attempted to prop up the company through 'dubious transactions, doubtful accounting policies, the creation of artificial profit ... and the making of false statements to analysts.'

Source: D Walsh, *The Times*, 24 September 1999. Reprinted with permission.

▶

JDS takes Luckin case

The English ICA has transferred its investigation into the role played by auditor Bird Luckin in the £1bn losses suffered by hotels group Queens Moat Houses to the senior accountancy watchdog, the Joint Disciplinary Scheme.

The investigation, which has faced increasing criticism for a series of delays since the company nearly crashed in 1992, will be taken up by JDS head Chris Dickson.

Fifteen-partner firm Bird Luckin was sacked by Queens Moat in June 1993 after the troubled company had been forced to reveal large-scale accounting irregularities that led to the suspension of its shares on the Stock Exchange and property writedowns worth more than £800m.

Since then the institute has waited for the results of a major Department of Trade and Industry investigation, led by Binder Hamlyn senior partner Adrian Burn and barrister Patrick Phillips, before launching its own probe.

Binder Hamlyn has run up bills of more than £2.5m since taking on the investigation. A report has yet to be published.

Chris Dickson said a prima facie case has yet to be established in the case against any members, but he would be looking into the 'discovery of serious accounting issues in relation to Queens Moat Houses plc group which led to prior year-end adjustments in financial statements for the year ending 31 December 1992'. He added he would also be questioning a member of the institute who was a director of the company about his sharedealings at the time.

Four chartered accountants sat on the company's board: Martin Marcus, deputy chairman and joint managing director; finance director David Hersey; deputy FD Allan Porter; and Maurice Hart, an ex-senior partner of Bird Luckin.

Source: P Inman, *Accountancy Age*, 15 October 1998.

FURTHER READING

Attrill, P and McLaney, E (2001) *Accounting and Finance for Non-specialists*, **Harlow: FT Prentice Hall.**
The book provides an introduction to accounting and finance. The text does not focus on the technical aspects but rather examines the basic principles and underlying concepts of accounting for decision making.

Attrill, P and McLaney, E (2002) *Management Accounting and Finance for Non-specialists*, **Harlow: FT Prentice Hall.**
The book is directed at non-accounting readers and those who are studying independently. The book is useful as an introduction to the principles of management accounting.

Chadwick, L (2000) *Management Accounting: Elements of Business* (2nd edition), **London: Thomson Learning.**
This book is intended as an introductory management accounting text and establishes the vital importance of accounting as a management tool. The book is written in a stimulating, accessible style. It includes step-by-step examples, question and answer sections, multiple-choice texts, lists of key works and self-assessment exercises.

Chadwick, L (2001a) *Essential Financial Accounting for Managers*, **Harlow: FT Prentice Hall.**
This book focuses on the core essentials of accounting, such as understanding what a balance sheet is, how to understand a profit and loss account, explanations of

accounts (why profits have gone up, and cash and bank balances have gone down, etc.) and limitations of the information produced.

Chadwick, L (2001b) *Essential Management Accounting For Managers*, **Harlow: FT Prentice Hall.**
The book introduces a good grasp of the management accounting terminology. It helps learning to understand how the figures have been arrived at and how to use management accounting information to make business decisions. In addition the book provides the limitations of the information produced and how this information, and systems and techniques may affect people.

Chadwick, L (2002) *Essential Accounting and Finance for Managers*, **Harlow: FT Prentice Hall.**
This book focuses on critical analysis and interpretation of accounting. It takes readers beyond the beginner/non-specialist level and helps them to apply finance with accounting tools and techniques to the real world of business.

Dyson, J R (2007) *Accounting for Non-Accounting Students*, **Harlow: FT Prentice Hall.**
This is a comprehensive and wide-ranging textbook on the theory and practice of modern financial and management accounting. It provides a framework for the understanding of accounting and an appreciation of the purpose of various accounting practices.

Horngren, C, Sundem, G and Stratton, W (2006) *Introduction to Management Accounting* (13th edition), London: Pearson.
This text offers a relevant, real-world decision-making approach to management accounting. Readers can develop a solid understanding of costs and cost behaviour and the use of cost information for planning and control decisions.

Weetman, P (2006) *Financial and Management Accounting: An Introduction* (4th edition), Harlow: FT Prentice Hall.
This provides readers with a clear and well-structured introduction to financial and management accounting. This edition retains all of the classic features, particularly its clarity of expression within a sound conceptual framework.

WEBSITES

www.frc.org.uk
For the Financial Reporting Council.

www.iasb.org
For the International Accounting Standards Board.

www.fsa.gov.uk
For the Financial Services Authority.

www.itbp.com
For the virtual school of accounting.

www.ft.com
For the Financial Times website.

www.thisismoney.co.uk
For sources of finance.

www.drury-online.com
The leading author in Europe on management accounting.

www.pearsoneduc.com and www.booksites.net
To help search for other textbooks on various subjects.

In addition, why not look at the websites of a number of companies?

SECTION E

MANAGEMENT ISSUES

What is meant by business ethics? Why are ethical values important to managers? What are the ethical responsibilities of corporations? What internal and external factors influence a corporation's ethical stance and internal values? What is meant by 'environmental issues' in relation to organisations? What pressures do these issues place on industry? What constitutes an environmentally friendly product or operation? What management strategies can improve an organisation's environmental performance? What differences are there between the management of business operations in a domestic setting and in a multinational setting? What is meant by globalisation? What strategies enable foreign organisations to maximise their advantages in foreign markets? How do multinational organisations operate? What skills are required in management? How do management careers develop? Why should managers be interested in management theories? How far have present ideas on management built on those of the past? How do managers deal with changes in their environment?

It can be argued that all corporate decisions are linked to a set of business ethics and to ethical values and that the structures and procedures which define the ethos of an organisation can predict the prospects for corporate performance. Corporations have ethical responsibilities and they have internal values which are influenced by both external and internal factors. There has been a growth in public interest and awareness of environmental issues and this places pressures on industry. Different industrial sectors have varied effects on the environment. Management strategies can improve an organisation's environmental performance. Management in a multinational setting differs from business operations in a domestic setting. There are management strategies which enable foreign organisations to maximise their advantages in foreign markets. Management careers evolve through a series of stages within which managers need to acquire a range of skills. Present management practices have built to some extent on past experience while managers today need constantly to adapt to changing circumstances.

CHAPTER 17

Ethical values and corporate social responsibility

Outcomes

Having read this chapter, you will be able to:

- argue that all corporate decisions are linked to a set of business ethics;

- explain why ethical values are of importance to managers;

- analyse how far the structures and procedures which define the ethos of an organisation can predict the prospects for corporate performance;

- understand the importance of public interest and the relationship of an organisation with stakeholders;

- explain the ethical responsibilities of corporations;

- outline the internal and external factors which influence a corporation's ethical stance and internal values.

ETHICAL VALUES

Corporate social responsibility (CSR) is now on the global policy agenda, with the last 20 years having seen great strides forward in CSR. Domestically and internationally governmental, business and other organisations are getting involved with CSR initiatives. At the European and UK domestic levels, the European Commission adopted a new strategy on CSR in 2002; and in the same year the UK government published its second national CSR report. The UK government has also now appointed a minister for CSR. International organisations such as the United Nations, the International Labour Organisation (ILO) and the Organisation for Economic Cooperation and Development (OECD) have also taken the lead. Initiatives such as the UN Global Compact, the ILO Declaration on Fundamental Principles and Rights at Work, and the Tripartite Declaration of Principles Concerning Multinational Enterprises and Social Policy, and the OECD voluntary guidelines for multinational enterprises now dominate the corporate agenda, thus making CSR important for organisations of all kinds, large and small alike (Hopkins, 2003).

Although CSR remains a relatively new line of study, its roots undoubtedly go back to some of the key philosophical debates over ethics, values, equity and equality (Smith, 2003). The emergence of business ethics and responsible action on the corporate agenda is, however, more a function of the growing awareness of the social, political and environmental impact of the modern industrial enterprise. Many of the shifts in political attitudes towards firms, for example, reflect serious abuse by specific companies and specific business leaders. The misappropriation of pension funds, repression of workers in the Third World, environmental incidents and even the bribery and corruption associated with deals to gain large government contracts are all issues which have hit the headlines over the last few years.

The importance of ethical values and business ethics to managers arises partly because of changes in an approach to work and partly as a result of an increasing understanding of managerial responsibility. What has been described as the 'counter revolution of our time' (Phelps-Brown, 1990) has been a move towards embracing individualism and away from collectivism and the welfare state. Rising standards of living have enabled more people to make lifestyle choices and improving educational opportunities have freed people from previous constraints on work opportunities. As a result managers are much more concerned than in the past about choosing morally justified forms of work, while they are also faced with moral questions in such areas as advertising policy and environmental issues.

Also, managers have increasingly recognised that the establishment of their authority, as distinct from the power bestowed by their hierarchical position, has to include an understanding of the responsibility their role involves. Managers have been described as a 'barbarian elite' (Anthony, 1998), in the sense that they are part of an elite which carries authority, whereas barbarians are respected only because of fear of their power. Managers have to acquire moral authority in the way they carry out their role so that their authority is respected and not simply feared.

Warren and Tweedale (2002) have emphasised that the development of business ethics occurred earlier in the USA than in the UK. They pin-point that the take-off of business ethics as an academic discipline occurred in the USA in 1974 when the first national conference on business ethics was held at the University of Kansas. A committee for Education in Business Ethics (CEBE) was set up and reported in 1980 on guidelines for the curricula of business ethics courses. The Federal Government has passed legislation that encourages corporations to engage actively in business ethics training, which has itself encouraged the growth of a large ethics consultancy industry. Warren and Tweedale (2002) argue that business ethics has been pioneered in the USA mainly because it has had three powerful sponsoring institutions: 'corporations, churches and the state'. In the UK only the first of these three sponsors has taken a serious interest in the subject.

It can be argued that all corporate decisions are linked to a set of business ethics and that by considering the structures and procedures which define the ethics of an organisation it ought to be possible to say something about the prospects and preconditions for corporate performance. However, the systematic treatment of business ethics has been neglected in most advanced economies. Within the social sciences the study of political economy, for example, has been replaced by economic science and positive economics and this has placed an emphasis on theories of optimisation rather than wider corporate and social responsibility at the firm level. Western economies, in particular, have developed along particular paths with an emphasis on industrial growth, productivity, efficiency (defined in narrow monetary terms) and performance (usually defined by profits and increases in share prices) and to the development of a narrow, profit-centred corporate ethic.

There are those who suggest, however, that social responsibility and environmental considerations can no longer be ignored in the context of an ethical (and indeed efficient) approach to doing business. Hartley (1993), for example, suggests that the interests of a firm are actually best served by paying scrupulous attention to the public interest and by seeking a trusting relationship with the various stakeholders with which a firm is involved. In the process, society is also best served because the firm is forced to consider a whole range of competing objectives and to move away from activities which are derived from short-term performance indicators. These various stakeholders the firm must consider are its customers, suppliers, employees, shareholders, the financial institutions, local communities and government. The stakeholder concept stresses the idea that a company has responsibilities to all these groups (even though they will have unequal amounts of power) and will be involved in balancing the often competing demands put upon it. A company's ethical stance will therefore be influenced both by internal values and by pressures exerted on it from external sources. Such pressures have grown as stakeholders have become more interested in the activities of business and as information availability and communications technology have increased.

Windsor (2006) has discussed CSR in terms of two competing approaches which share the themes of improving general welfare and accepting compliance with public policy. The two approaches are a concern with **general welfare** through an ethical conception and a concern with **private wealth** through an economic conception. Whereas the ethical conception looks to corporate self-restraint, expansive public policy and corporate altruism, the economic conception looks to fiduciary responsibility, minimalist public policy and customary ethics. These two approaches are linked, by Windsor, by a corporate citizenship conception based on political influence, the importance of corporate reputation and strategic philanthropy. Organisations may move towards the ethical conception because of a need to maintain an acceptable corporate reputation, while the economic conception may be modified by the adoption of a strategic philanthropy. Ethical responsibilities lie between mandatory compliance, both legal and economic, and desirable philanthropy. Society and many stakeholders expect ethical behaviour by organisations beyond mandatory compliance.

It can be argued that if the financial performance of a business and its social performance both rise, this is a gain all round and corresponds to Adam Smith's expectation (in *The Wealth of Nations*, 1776) of what happens with the operation of the 'invisible hand' of supply and demand in a free market economy. If both financial performance and social performance decline there are clearly problems, while if financial performance rises and social performance declines there is a conflict between financial and social responsibility, although social welfare may rise in the long run. A decline in financial performance and a rise in social performance also indicates a conflict which can result in a long-term decline in social welfare.

Milton Friedman (1963) has argued that the social responsibility of business is to maximise profits within the bounds of the law, in free competition without fraud or deception:

> *'If businessmen do have a social responsibility other than making maximum profits for stockholders, how are they to know what it is? Can self-selected private individuals decide what the social interest is? Can they decide how great a burden they are justified in placing on themselves or their stockholders to serve that social interest?'*

Husted and Salazar (2006) have suggested that social investment by a company may arise from two types of motivation: **altruism** and **egotism**. They quote an example of corporate altruism:

> *'Merck announced in 1987 that it would donate Mectizan, a drug to combat river blindness, to people in third world countries affected by the disease. The Merck decision has provided some benefits such as increased employee pride as well as community recognition. However, at least ten years later, it was still not clear whether Mectizan would provide a long-term payoff for Merck.'*

An egotistical approach cannot avoid social welfare because businesses take resources from society in terms of land, labour and capital. A company's actions will have results for the company itself and for society. If a company causes pollution it may be fined and shut down. If it is indifferent to the poverty that surrounds it then the problem of social instability may increase its costs. If it ignores poor educational standards then its productivity may be affected. Although it is not necessarily easy for firms to increase profits for stockholders at the same time as developing their social output, Husted and Salazar (2006) argue that more companies are seeking ways to achieve both profitability and social performance. They give the example of Bank-Boston (Fleet Boston Financial Corporation) and its development of the First Community Bank (FCB) (now Fleet Community Bank) as a way of reaching groups of low-income areas that have traditionally been marginalised by consumer banking. FCB has successfully brought new clients into the banking system and

> *'now consists of 47 branches with over $1.5 billion in deposits. Not only has FCB contributed to regional economic development in these areas, it has also become a profitable institution within the Fleet Boston group. In addition, it has provided a laboratory for the bank in the development of such innovations as multilingual ATMs, products for newcomers to banking, equity investments in the inner city and community development officers.'* (Husted and Salazar, 2006)

Although there has been an increase in interest in business ethics, the global dimension of many businesses has raised conflicts between their financial and welfare interests which Windsor (2006) illustrates in terms of legal procedures:

'Unnamed plaintiffs, citizens of Myanmar (Burma), sued in US federal court arguing that Union Oil of California bears liability for alleged human right abuses by the Myanmar government. Unocal was a passive minority investor in a pipeline built and operated by a Myanmar state enterprises and a French firm to transport natural gas from the Andaman Sea to Thailand. The state enterprise and the French firm have been dismissed from the case for want of jurisdiction. The suit against Unocal was dismissed and then reinstated on appeal. The suit was ordered to trial. The essential argument alleges that Unocal knew what its Myanmar partner would likely do (if the alleged facts are true) and invested for financial gain in disregard of that knowledge. Both international law and federal common law forbid slavery or near equivalents, and plaintiffs allege slave-like abuse in Myanmar's role in the pipeline. Unocal eventually settled out of court.'

(Windsor, 2006)

At the same time it has been argued that business 'ethicists' (those interested in the ethical behaviour of businesses) have

'occupied a rarefied moral high ground, removed from the real-world problems of the vast majority of managers. They have been too preoccupied with absolutist notions of what it means for managers to be ethical, with overly generalised criticisms of capitalism as an economic system, with dense and abstract theorising and with prescriptions that apply only remotely to managerial practice'

(Stark, 1993)

BUSINESS ETHICS

Providing some sort of definition of **business ethics** is difficult because it will depend on both the values of individuals working in the organisation, and particularly on the culture created by the individual ethics of senior management and on any codes of conduct which formally exist within the organisation or standards adopted from external agencies. One single ethical code is not observed in all parts of society but different codes in different places and at different times, and this is replicated within any organisation. It is possible to distinguish between 'personal value systems', which individuals will bring to the workplace, and a 'formal business code', which may exist in some businesses through an explicit set of rules (Burke *et al.*, 1993). Perhaps more importantly there is the 'actual value system', which is the moral climate experienced by staff in their daily business lives and which will determine the behaviour of the organisation as a whole, and a 'necessary value system', which is the minimum level of ethics (often equated with legal requirements) that has to exist for the organisation to survive.

In a pluralistic society social cultural and organisational power structures will tend to interact with these value systems. Such interaction may bring about a consensus or norm in certain areas of business activity, but it may also result in conflict where the ultimate outcome will depend crucially on the balance of power. One of the phenomena seen in the last few years is a shift of some of that power towards the consumer and the general public, and this has renewed the interest in business ethics and corporate responsibility. **Ethics** is the science of morals, the branch of philosophy which is concerned with human character and conduct – it is a system of morals and rules of behaviour. A working definition of **business ethics** is

'a set of moral principles and values in business activity and business organizations which interact with society and which vary between organisations, countries and over time.'

Ethics tends also to be culturally specific. In some societies what may be considered as unethical by others may be felt to be completely normal. This can include areas such as child labour, environmental issues, attitudes to women working or health and safety issues. An issue which causes problems for those advocating stronger codes of business ethics is that not all desirable ethics are mutually consistent. In those circumstances judgements have to be made based on valuing different ethical actions. Outcomes will be determined by power structures and dominant ideologies will tend to arise. Such ideologies are, nevertheless, often a product of compromise and may not necessarily be first best solutions.

The study of business ethics is not new. In the nineteenth century, utilitarian reformers highlighted the need for ethical principles to be part of the free enterprise system. Currently, the literature on business ethics, and on ethics generally, is vital and growing. A key issue, however, is that there are many dilemmas where major principles, held to be moral imperatives, can in some circumstances be incompatible. There must, therefore, exist some sort of hierarchy which places more emphasis on one principle than another – so that recently there has been the movement of social and environmental considerations up that hierarchy, for example.

Ultimately it is organisation which dictates the hierarchy of different principles. The various levels of organisation, from whole economic and political systems via institutions and organisations to individual relationships, suggest particular hierarchies of principles (Donaldson, 1989). These hierarchies obviously shift over time and between different economic and political systems. They can be influenced, although that, in turn, will depend on power relationships. Many principles of business ethics might be considered somewhat abstract. A key issue, therefore, is how commonly accepted principles (such as improved environmental performance at the organisation level) can be translated into practice. This has to be done via codes (legal and self-regulating), education, communication and information but these vehicles for change are themselves open to manipulation by those with power and the best principles are not always translated into best practice.

When ethical outcomes are discussed, words such as 'moral', 'ethical', 'good', 'efficient', 'rational', 'effective', 'fair', 'best' and 'improved' all come to mean different things in different circumstances. The meanings, connotations and overtones of words and phrases are often deployed in the conflicts and struggles for supremacy. The language of management is rich in emotive and ideological content and, therefore, what organisations and managers say they are doing must be treated with healthy scepticism. Stark (1993) has contrasted the success that ethical considerations have had in professions other than management, such as medicine and law, 'in providing real and welcome assistance to their practicitioners'. However, management is not a profession such as medicine or law and the challenge is to

> *'make business ethics seem relevant to business, since there is no natural niche for it as an ethics for a recognised profession of business'*   (Sorell, 1998)

and to fit it into a British moral and political tradition.

According to Donaldson (1989) there has been a relative neglect of the systematic handling of values in business which has been self-conscious. The consequences of the neglect can be seen both in anxiety about industrial performance in the West and a rise of concern about moral or ethical issues. A patchy awareness of the problem is to be seen in the sporadic (and at times piecemeal) nature of attempts by governments to regulate industry. This is well illustrated by the uneven growth in environmental legislation in the West and the continued growth of *ad hoc* codes of conduct in this area.

All organisations operate an ethical code, whether they know it or not. This may not be at all times consistent but it is based on codes of conduct embedded in company culture and through the actions and decisions of senior management. Those codes will also be influenced by society's norms and, in the business world, by institutions and practices which stress the need to create wealth measured in quantitative financial terms. For any business which wishes to survive or to avoid hostile takeover, the system necessarily pushes profits to the top of the corporate agenda and pushes other issues down the agenda. So-called ethical businesses – that is companies founded with a social conscience – have a long history in the UK. They date back over two hundred years and include building societies, retailers, food and confectionery manufacturers, cooperative stores, credit unions and trustee savings banks. There are such companies as Cadbury, the John Lewis Partnership, Sainsbury and the Cooperative Wholesale Society. Many were established with mutual or cooperative ownership. On the other hand there are many descriptions of examples of corporate crime such as insider dealing and fraud by Kynaston (1999) and Michie (1999), Raw *et al.* (1971, 1977) on Slater Walker and the IOS, Sampson (1977, 1982) on banking and arms dealing, ethical problems raised by asbestos (Tweedale, 2000) and a number of books on the problems of Enron (Fox, 2004, McLean and Elkind, 2004, Eichenwald, 2005) and on other corporate problems such as Markham (2006) and Armour and McCahery (2006).

There is no business practice, action or statement that cannot have an ethical dimension. Businesses serve a variety of purposes for different stakeholders. Therefore, it can be argued that as a necessary condition business activities are justifiable only in so far as they can be shown to meet the legitimate requirements of stakeholders. However, these requirements can be, and often are, in conflict and can change over time. We have major problems in identifying requirements and reconciling them. Moreover, we have suggested that the principles, ideals and moral values on which stakeholders' requirements are based can be, in themselves, contradictory. The traditional way of resolving these issues is for the organisation to assume primacy over individuals, allowing it to pursue objectives dictated by senior management, subject to financial constraints imposed by owners and lenders. Thus organisations often adopt their own identity and culture and often exist outside the democratic framework. But we must realise that business ought to be a means and not an end, and it is a means for satisfying the requirements of all who have a legitimate claim.

It might be argued that any philosophy or course of action that does not take the public interest into consideration is intolerable in today's society (Hartley, 1993). Today's firms face more critical scrutiny from stakeholders and operate in a setting which is becoming more regulatory and litigious than in the past. The notion of public trust is also becoming more important. A clear measure of how far there has been a move towards a more responsive and responsible business climate is indicated by the fact that if a firm violates public trust then it is likely to be surpassed by its competitors, who will be eager to please customers by addressing their wants more accurately. Moreover, while the overwhelming majority of business dealings are non-controversial, any abuses increasingly receive considerable publicity harming the image of business. Once a company's image has been damaged, it often takes a long time to reverse that damage.

In order to remain economically active, organisations need to learn from their mistakes or from those of other organisations. They need to take care to avoid situations and actions that might harm their relationship with their various stakeholders. In the worst of all cases, where an organisation faces a catastrophe suddenly and without warning, its whole market image and business strategy can be destroyed. Examples of such events are increasingly commonplace. For example, in the case of Union Carbide, when one of its chemical plants in Bhopal leaked 40 tons of toxic chemicals, the event had (and continues to have) a profound effect on the reputation of that company. Although the company quickly rushed aid to the victims it was bitterly condemned for complacency and the loose controls that permitted the accident to happen in the first place.

→ Ch. 18

Environmental considerations are only one of many issues which might be included under the umbrella of business ethics (see Chapter 18). They nevertheless constitute an issue which has grown in importance. As a result of the many accidents and growing environmental damage caused by organisations there have been increasing demands from consumers for firms to operate more ethically in this area. The consumer movement has fundamentally shaped and contributed to the significant increase in legislation and regulation at all levels of government. This has been aimed at preventing abuses in the marketplace and in the environment and, therefore, environmental management strategies are increasingly commonplace in leading organisations around the world. To date, however, environmental considerations have not been given enough attention within the framework of business ethics because dominant ideologies are being shaped more by short-term financial considerations than by the need to do business in a sustainable way.

ETHICAL MANAGEMENT IN THE PUBLIC SECTOR

The ethical dimension of management in the public sector may be taken for granted because concepts of integrity, probity, accountability and impartiality are expected features of the qualities and job descriptions of civil servants and public sector professionals in areas of service such as education and health. At the same time, once the profit motive has been removed, it can be argued that Windsor's (2006) 'economic conception' no longer applies and the 'ethical conception' can become paramount. However, in any circumstances where money is being handled or power is being exerted there are opportunities for bribery and corruption and also the temptation to make unethical decisions. In fact public opinion surveys do not identify a lack of trust of public sector professionals, while this is much more the case in the UK in terms of elected politicians (Lawton, 2006).

→ Ch. 4

There has been considerable change in most aspects of public policy and management over the last two decades so that public sector professionals carry out their duties in very different circumstances from the past (see Chapter 4). The adoption of a so-called 'marketing approach', devolved management responsibility, the creation of business units and cost-centres, public/private partnerships and contracts, the outsourcing of public service functions and a 'customer', client, consumer focus have all raised questions of public value and public welfare. The 'new public management' of recent years has encouraged a more 'businesslike' approach to the provision of public services based on targets and accountability, with funding bodies, controllers and ombudsmen putting pressure on public sector managers to meet certain standards and levels of service.

The emphasis in public sector organisations has inevitably moved to meeting the targets on which their funding depends and this can put pressure on the ethical conception. At the least it can mean that public welfare is skewed to equal the targets and levels of service established by the government agency. When a private company is running a prison for the prison service, for example, if the main criteria for success is based on the number of prisoners it is able to house then this may become the focus of effort at the expense of levels of service or the training of prison officers. If the main target for a hospital trust is to reduce waiting lists then considerations of service levels may be put under pressure. If funding levels are based on the number of students then colleges and universities may see recruitment as their main priority over their ability to provide an excellent service. At the least these approaches put pressure on public sector managers. It may be possible to meet targets and meet the best ethical standards but if cost cutting, value for money and achieving targets become the priority then previous ideas of 'professional standards', quality and levels of service may be modified or lost.

'The manager in the public services is a complex person of many roles with mixed motives and mixed purposes' (Lawton, 1998). Public sector organisations are basically those funded by the government and its agencies. They do not have to worry about achieving shareholder value or making a profit, but they do have to worry about balancing their books, achieving levels of funding and satisfying the needs of a variety of stakeholders who may have different objectives. Employees may be mainly concerned with job stability, pay levels and ideas about professional service levels; unions mainly with pay and conditions of service; the people who receive the service with the speed and level at which it is offered; and the funding agency with cost efficiency and value for money.

More than is the case in the private sector, public sector organisations are concerned not only with goals and objectives but also with ideals. In the provision of a national health service in the UK, for example, the underlying ideal is to provide comprehensive health services of a high quality that are free at the point of delivery for everyone. When this is financially impossible then choices have to be made and ethical considerations start to come into play. Questions arise as to whether everyone should receive any treatment that is medically available, or whether some treatments are too expensive; or whether groups such as old people, habitual smokers or the obese should receive the same levels of treatment as everyone else.

> 'A feature of the public service in the UK, particularly for civil servants at central government level, has been the importance of tradition and continuity over time, enshrined in the principles of public life of selflessness, integrity, objectivity, accountability, openness, honesty and leadership, as articulated by the Committee on Standards in Public Life.'
>
> (Lawton, 2006)

These seven principles of public life were enshrined by the Nolan Committee in its first report on standards in public life in 1995. However, the extent of corruption, malpractice and political patronage have been a matter of concern in the UK and elsewhere. For example, the response to Hurricane Katrina in the USA in 2005 by federal, state and city officials raised the issues of political patronage, the ability of public officials to provide ethical leadership and uphold public interest. The so-called 'cash for honours' inquiry running through 2006 and 2007 has raised ethical questions about the funding of political parties in the UK.

Ethical issues are all around those who work in every organisation, whether it is a local football team, a multinational company, a school or a local authority, and

> 'those working in the public services are working within organisations which exist to fulfil social and ethical purposes. While accepting that organisations have a history and a fabric made up of practices and traditions that are greater than the sum of the individuals working within them at any one time, it is still individuals acting on behalf

of the organisations that make decisions concerning other individuals. We cannot hide behind roles: if we are told by a senior manager to massage statistics, to bend the rules in favour of one client or contractor, to dilute the quality of what we produce because of the demands of cost-cutting, we can take a stand.' (Lawton, 1998)

Lawton argues that individuals can make a difference, they have to live with the consequences of their actions and account for them to the public. While in the private sector accountability to the public is claimed through shareholders and customers, in the public sector there is a direct link between managers and the public whether it is through a trust board, school governors or electors, or through patients, pupils and the general public.

INTERNATIONAL AND CULTURAL DIFFERENCES

Ethics might be viewed as a subset of culture and where cultural differences exist across borders there are likely to be differences in ethics which are culturally defined. 'Culture difference' is a term frequently used to explain behavioural and other differences when doing business in foreign countries. However, it is a concept which has received scant attention and although most people would have ideas about the generic implications of different cultures, whether or not they really understand the specific features is more questionable.

→ Chs 1, 2 & 4

Kroeber and Kluckhohn (1952) provide the following definition of culture (see also Chapters 1, 2 and 4):

'Culture consists of patterns, explicit and implicit, of and for behaviour acquired and transmitted by symbols, constituting the distinctive achievement of human groups, including their embodiments in artifacts: the essential core of culture consists of traditional (i.e. historically derived and selected) ideas and especially their attached values; culture systems may, on the one hand, be considered as products of action, on the other as conditioning elements of further action.'

This somewhat complex definition brings with it a number of important distinguishable factors.

- Culture is not innate, but learned. In other words people are not born with an understanding of culture. It is something acquired through the socialisation process.

- It is shared, communicated and transmitted by members of a social set and defines the boundaries between different groups. This point is linked with the first since it is through reinforcement within a social group that culture is learned.

- Various elements of culture are interrelated. Attitudes and beliefs may, in turn, be related to religious and/or ethical ideologies, and ethics and ideologies may be adopted which match attitudes and beliefs resulting from experience and socialisation.

Corporate social responsibility and business ethics are very much interrelated and the behaviour of the organisation with respect to these issues will depend on shared cultures within social groups, the organisation of the business (which itself will tend to have a corporate culture) and countries (or regions). It should also be recognised, however, that culture changes over time – which explains some of the swings towards and away from issues of corporate responsibility which we have seen over the past four decades. Such change can be gradual or extremely swift. Changes in the treatment of and attitudes towards women and their abilities in the workplace is something which has developed gradually. However, there have been rapid changes in attitudes surrounding sexuality as a result of HIV and a greater awareness of the problems caused by global warming following obvious changes in the world's climate.

Differing ethics across national boundaries will be fundamentally related to values and attitudes. Values are often considered to be the standards by which things may be judged and serve to shape people's (and organisations') beliefs and attitudes (Welford *et al.*, 2001). This is probably the most elusive element of culture as values and attitudes only become apparent through communication and interaction. Ethics, which will be part of these values, will therefore often have to be discovered, and where there are additional barriers to understanding (e.g. different languages, legal frameworks and customs) such discovery is very difficult. However, not to attempt to identify the values and ethics of a business means that a trading partner may well find itself in trouble if such values and ethics are not congruent.

Culture, therefore, helps to define not only individual attitudes and behaviours (including those of managers) but also business norms. It is difficult to isolate the business culture in a country from that appertaining to the people and their society. Both feed off each other and similar patterns can be observed between the systems and networks at both an individual and a commercial level. However, the ethics and attitudes held by an organisation will not simply be the sum of all individual ethics within it – that would be to ignore the differing amounts of power which various stakeholders have to influence corporate culture. Equally, the politics and economic policies of a country cannot really be isolated from the framework within which the organisation operates, and organisations often find it useful to change their corporate priorities (and thus their ethics) when political power shifts externally.

Conducting international trade, therefore, requires organisations to manage across cultures, within a wider array of ethical considerations and where the notion of corporate responsibility may be very different indeed. Mole (1990) defines culture as 'the way we do things round here' recognising that people and organisations in different countries, as a result of their specific cultural backgrounds, behave differently and that to analyse the situation any further is extremely difficult. Therefore, operating across borders requires respect and a basic understanding of political, economic, legal, professional and ethical norms. At the management level, business cultures and those pertaining to the individual interact to dictate the behaviour of managers within the work organisation. Failure to adapt approaches to the nuances of behaviour and attitudes in different countries can cause expensive mistakes.

As business becomes increasingly internationalised there is an increasing likelihood of encountering business partners from very different cultures, who subscribe to radically different ethical systems. The fact that there are different management cultures with different value systems means that there are no easy solutions to ethical dilemmas in international business. Many would argue that the simplest and most practical approach to ethical problems is to adopt moral relativism. In its simplest form this means adopting local values and ethics when doing business in any particular location. This may be acceptable when it is the Western business executive who must be prepared to forgo alcohol in countries where it is shunned. However, it might also mean going along with the practice of bribery in countries where this is the norm, indeed it could even be argued that bribery is not as insidious in these countries as it is in the West, since it is regarded as quite a normal way to supplement rather low wages.

However, there is a serious problem with adopting a stance based on cultural relativism. If it is desirable for Westerners abroad to adopt the prevailing norms in the countries in which they do business, then the same might have to apply in the reverse situation. In other words immigrant workers, for example, would be expected to adopt Western norms of behaviour, dress and customs. There would be no room for the Jewish sabbath or regular prayer breaks for Muslims. But such a stance would run counter to ideals of religious (and other) freedoms which are inherently bound up with respecting the individual (Chryssides and Kaler, 1993).

CODES OF CONDUCT AND STANDARDS

Although there has been an increasing amount of regulation covering a range of social and environmental issues, there is still more emphasis put on market-based and voluntary measures. Coupled with this, previous deregulation measures, introduced by more right-wing governments to appease industry, have continued to result in more emphasis being put on voluntary codes of conduct and standards. The design and definition of voluntary codes and standards are, therefore, important to consider.

Codes of conduct defined within an organisation, or imported from elsewhere in the form of standards, are usually associated with practical sets of rules and guidelines. They tend to be expressions of mixtures of technical, prudential and moral imperatives. They influence behaviour and, therefore, ethical outcomes. However, standards which are externally driven are typically expressed in a form that is well protected from discussion, expressing aims in matter-of-fact language (Donaldson, 1989). In turn, therefore, a standard carries with it a dominant ideology which, because it is standardised, has a multiplier effect and increasing weight if the standard becomes a norm.

The adoption of codes of conduct and standards within any organisation necessarily raises a number of questions. The most obvious one concerns the type of subculture that a code brings with it. Does it represent a piecemeal attempt to placate demands from pressure groups and consumers or is it a more serious attempt at ethical behaviour, for example? There is also a question of how effective the codes are in promoting what they stand for. Taken together these questions provide a measure of the extent to which the standards are genuine and operational, rather than cynical and self-deluding.

Codes of conduct which become accepted across firms in an industry, or even across industries, are very powerful and they are often written into contracts between organisations. There may be a view that a code promoting some sort of social commitment or environmental improvement is a step forward and that organisations that follow others in adopting such standards should be congratulated, but more analysis of the content and purpose of such a code is necessary before that conclusion can be reached. Some codes push employees and customers into a set of values which verge on indoctrination. Stakeholders in those sorts of situation come to possess what Marxists see as false consciousness. In addition the fact that a code of conduct is widely accepted does not guarantee that the values within it are not restricted or inconsistent.

There is very little research on the generation, operation, monitoring and amendment of codes of conduct. However, it is argued forcefully by Donaldson (1989) that because codes tend to be expressions of mixtures of technical, prudential and moral imperatives, and because they tend to vary in the extent to which they are or can be enforced, they cannot be regarded as the major vehicles for identifying and encouraging the practices which will raise the level of values in business and industry. Moreover, codes and standards are defined outside the normal democratic framework which determines laws. They are constructed by agencies (often professional bodies or representatives of senior management in industry) with their own motivations, values and interests. On this subject Donaldson and Waller (1980) point to a statement of Bernard Shaw when he asserted that professions can be conspiracies against the laity and that their codes, it may be added, are widely held to be primarily aimed at the protection of the members of the profession rather than the public. Much the same accusation might be levelled against industry standards. Moreover, the matter of the development of codes and standards is bound up with the matter of enforcement. Codes which are not enforced or fail to deliver their expected outcomes, for whatever reason, might be thought of as little more than cynical expressions of pious hopes.

Much of what has been discussed here can be illustrated by reference to the Responsible Care Programme, which in itself provides a standard for firms operating in the chemical industry to adopt. It is a voluntary code where performance is measured in terms of continuous improvement. Responsible Care is unique to the chemical industry and originated in Canada in 1984. Launched in 1989 in the UK by the Chemical Industries Association (CIA), the cornerstone of the system is **commitment**. Chief executives of member companies are invited to sign a set of guiding principles pledging their company to make health, safety and environmental performance an integral part of overall business policy. Adherence to the principles and objectives of Responsible Care is a condition of membership of the CIA. All employees and company contractors have to be made aware of these principles. The guiding principles also require companies to:

- **conform to statutory regulations;**
- **operate to the best practices of the industry;**
- **assess the actual and potential health, safety and environmental impacts of their activities and products;**
- **work closely with the authorities and the community in achieving the required levels of performance;**
- **be open about activities and give relevant information to interested parties.**

A company operating the Responsible Care Programme is required to have a clear corporate policy and the communication of this is seen as vital. The key principle being used in the Responsible Care Programme is self-assessment. However, the CIA does assess the effectiveness of the programme across all firms by collecting indicators of performance from them. Companies are encouraged to submit six classes of data to the association. Individual company data are not published but a national aggregate figure is published annually. This shows industry trends and enables individual companies to assess their own placing accordingly. The six indicators of performance are:

- **environmental protection spending;**
- **safety and health (lost time, accidents for employees and contractors);**
- **waste and emissions:**
  - discharges of 'red list' substances
  - waste disposal
  - an environmental index of five key discharges by site;

■ distribution (all incidents);

■ energy consumption (total on-site);

■ all complaints.

A key element of the Responsible Care system is the sharing of information and participation of employees and the local community. Local Responsible Care 'cells' operate for the exchange of information and experience between firms. Employee involvement is also welcomed and the CIA has established training programmes which set targets for appraisal. Firms are encouraged to have community liaison groups and initiatives recognising the continuing need to forge improved relationships with the public.

However, in its 1993 report on the Responsible Care Programme (ENDS, 1993) the CIA was implicitly forced to admit that the programme was not functioning in accordance with its aims. The main reason for this was that sites claiming to adhere to the Responsible Care standard were simply not observing its principles. Over the three-year reporting period only 57 per cent of firms made returns for all three years, and only 74 per cent made any returns at all. Even more importantly, the third indicator of performance deals with waste and emissions, where firms are supposed to report an environmental index by site designed to give a composite picture of gaseous, liquid and solid releases. Only one-third of all the firms supposed to be operating Responsible Care reported this data in full, and of those over 30 per cent reported a worsening environmental impact. In 1997, although these statistics showed some improvement, it was still the case that many companies claiming to operate a Responsible Care Programme were still not adhering to all its principles.

Codes of conduct are, therefore, nothing if they are not adhered to and voluntary approaches often slip down a list of priorities when other pressing issues arise. While some chemical companies are clearly committed to improving their health, safety and environmental performance, it seems that not all are adhering to the spirit of Responsible Care. Indeed while some make efforts to follow the guidelines of the programme, many more treat Responsible Care as a smokescreen. Many of those managers in the chemical industry who appear confident of their procedures for improving environmental performance are certainly either suffering from the false consciousness which was suggested earlier or are making much more cynical attempts to hide their environmental impact in an attempt to hang on to market share and profitability.

THE CONTRIBUTION OF ETHICS TO MANAGEMENT STRATEGIES

'Ethics' refers to standards of right conduct. Unfortunately there is often incomplete agreement as to what constitutes ethical behaviour. In the case of illegal and exploitative activities there is not much dispute. But many practices fall into a grey area where opinions may differ as to what is ethical and what is unethical and unacceptable. One possible example of environmental strategies which fall into that grey area relates to the eco-labelling of products and claims associated with the environmental friendliness of a product. There are examples of firms using tactics to persuade people to buy, often misleading customers into thinking they are getting a product which will not harm the environment and exaggerating advertising claims. Unfortunately some business organisations have decided to 'walk on the edge' of ethical practices (Hartley, 1993). This is a dangerous strategy because the dividing line will be different for different people and groups. Moreover, what society once tolerated as acceptable behaviour may rapidly become unacceptable and organisations which choose to position themselves so close to criticism will end up battling with time. To a large extent business ethics are firmly on the agenda and it is now expected that much more ethical conduct should be the norm, whereas previously questionable practices had been regarded with apathy or ignorance.

It is now no longer justifiable to see business ethics as directly connected with the law and 'necessary value systems' are inappropriate. The relationship between ethical conduct and the law is sometimes confusing. Naïve businesses might rationalise that actions within the law are, by definition, ethical and perfectly justifiable. But an 'if it's legal it's ethical' attitude disregards the fact that the law codifies only that part of ethics which society feels so strongly about that it is willing to support it with physical force (Westing, 1968).

Many organisations assume that the more strictly one interprets ethical behaviour then the more profits suffer. Certainly the muted sales efforts that may result from toning down product claims or refusing to buy raw materials that result in the exploitation of indigenous populations may hurt profits. Yet a strong argument can also be made that scrupulously honest and ethical behaviour is better for business and for profits. Well-satisfied customers tend to bring repeat business and so it is desirable to develop trusting relationships, not only with customers but also personnel, suppliers and the other stakeholders with which an organisation deals. Ethical conduct is not incompatible with profitability but it can change time scales because it is more compatible with maximising profits in the long run, even though in the shorter term the disregard of ethical principles may yield more profit.

There are particular areas where the issue of corporate responsibility is seen as being important:

- profits and growth
- the dominance of competition
- expediency and indifference
- dominant ideology and business strategy.

Profits and growth

In most organisations career development and higher salaries depend on achieving greater sales and profits. This is true not only for individual employees and executives but for departments, divisions and the entire organisation. The value that stockholders and investors, creditors and suppliers place on a company depends to a large extent on growth. In turn the dominant measure of growth is increasing sales and profits. The better the growth rate then the more money is available for further expansion by investors and creditors at attractive rates. Suppliers and customers are more eager to do business. Top-quality personnel and executives are also attracted more easily.

In particular the dominant drive would seem to be towards profits and profit maximisation. This is justified by economists such as Friedman (1963) whose view neglects the responsibility that all actors in society have to benefit society in terms which are wider than the narrowly based performance measures that he adopts. The emphasis on quantitative measures of performance and on growth, in particular, has some potential negative consequences. It tends to push social issues down the corporate agenda. An emphasis on growth becomes all-pervading and social and environmental objectives (which may or may not exist) are compromised. Moreover, with a dominant growth strategy people are not measured on the basis of their moral contribution to the business enterprise. Hence, they become caught up in a system which is characterised by an ethic foreign to, and often lower than, the ethics of human beings (Holloway and Hancock, 1968), which tends to devalue the role of the worker and of those involved further down the supply chain, so that when it comes to the consideration of the effect that the production and processing of raw materials might have on indigenous Third World populations, very little weight is attached to the needs and aspirations of these peoples.

According to Bloom *et al.* (1994), in a wide-ranging survey of European directors, companies are perceived by their leaders as always needing to act within a social as well as an economic context because of the range of stakeholder pressures. All shareholders, suppliers, employees, clients, creditors, local communities, etc. have legitimate interests in the future of the company and this influences decision making and planning. As a result many directors implicitly wish to take a longer-term perspective on their activities but are hindered from doing so because of the shorter-term demands of shareholders and stock markets.

Many senior managers come to realise, however, that profit maximisation measures are not the only measure of success in a company, and nor should they be the central aim or starting point of business strategy. Profit comes as the product of success, and success, in turn, depends on creating an organisation where all the interlocking elements work well together and function appropriately. For example, paying workers the lowest possible wage, making them work in poor conditions and treating them in a patronising way are more likely to lead to conflict than to cooperation. Such conflict will lower productivity and profits. Moreover, a strategy producing maximum profit today may not be consistent with maximum profit tomorrow. That will depend on the investment strategy of a company and that, in turn, requires managers to create a durable company which can survive competing pressures from all its stakeholders.

Because of the nature of capital markets, however, Bloom *et al.* (1994) report that many British directors are caught in a trap. In the UK about 80 per cent of company shares are quoted on the stock market compared with under 50 per cent in Germany and less than 20 per cent in Italy. Because of pressure for dividends from shareholders and the threat of hostile takeover if profits (and therefore share prices) fall, managers do not have the breadth of movement to think about longer-term issues. Shareholders have a very important role to play in allowing companies to operate on the social dimension. They are just one stakeholder but their ownership of shares and, therefore, the ownership of part of the company often means that their position is firmly at the top of the pile of stakeholders. This, perhaps, requires careful thought about what ownership really means. Shareholders provide money to companies for reasons which they choose, but they can get out of their commitment to the company more quickly and easily than an employee or a supplier can. Some see shareholding as rather more analogous with horseracing than anything else. When a horse is backed in a race the backer puts money on that horse hoping for some sort of return if it does well, but the backer does not own a bit of the horse. If the backer did own the horse it would require much more of a commitment than simply providing the money and sitting back. If the horse was flogged and abused in order to win a race then the owner would be accountable for its ill-treatment. In the corporate sense, therefore, not only must the rights of ownership be considered but also the responsibilities and obligations of ownership.

That is not, however, to devalue economic performance. Often economic performance, motivation and commitment are the basis of a company's capacity to perform in a social dimension. For larger companies the need to operate on a social scale is increased because of the magnitude of their decisions. Whereas small firms will have little impact on social structures around them, a large firm deciding to lay off large parts of its workforce, for example, will have a much bigger influence. Moreover, companies operating on an international scale (particularly those which are essentially transnational) will have an enormous social impact. They will have a complicated network of stakeholders to deal with, including governments, international agencies, workers and customers with very different cultures and often powerful pressure groups.

The dominance of competition

An intensely competitive environment, especially if coupled with a firm's inability to differentiate products substantially or to cement segments of the market, will tend to motivate unethical behaviour (Hartley, 1993). The actions of one or a few firms in a fiercely competitive industry may generate a follow-the-leader situation, requiring the more ethical competitors to choose lower profits or lower ethics. Moreover, in a fiercely competitive environment the objective of the business organisation is dominated by the need to increase market share, to stay one step ahead of competitors, and therefore to adopt isolationist and independent strategies. To succeed in the marketplace, businesses feel the need to cut costs, to downgrade other objectives which might be perceived as expensive and to cut corners where possible.

That is not to suggest that competition is bad but that its dominance does mitigate against the opportunities which can be brought about through cooperation. Moreover, wider social issues are often overlooked because they are perceived as adding to costs with any benefits being somewhat intangible. The blind belief that competition is always in some way superior to other models means that alternative arrangements – such as cooperative strategies, public sector monopolies, not-for-profit organisations and local purchase and trading schemes – are often devalued. Yet these alternatives often provide for outcomes which may be ethically, socially and environmentally superior.

Expediency and indifference

The attitude of expediency and indifference to customers' best interests accounts for both complacency and unethical practices. These attitudes, whether permeating an entire firm or affecting only a few individuals, are hardly conducive to repeat business and customer loyalty. They are more prevalent in firms with many small customers and in those firms where repeat business is relatively unimportant. To take an example, such attitudes also have an impact on environmental issues. They tend to mean that corners are cut and due care is not taken to protect the environment. They tend to increase the unnecessary use of resources and generate excessive waste, and to mitigate against the adoption of systems and procedures which can prevent accidents and environmental damage. Moreover, indifference and apathy tend to mitigate against accepting the responsibility which every individual and every organisation has in protecting the environment now and in the future.

Welford (1994) demonstrates that in the context of environmental issues managers often have higher environmental ethics for themselves and their families than they do within the workplace. Whereas they are often complacent within the workforce, they see environmental improvement more generally as important to their own quality of life. This clear contradiction represents a 'free-rider problem'. While they want to see environmental improvement, they are unwilling to adjust their own behaviour in their workplace to achieve that, relying only on other people to make the changes required to improve overall environmental performance. Such indifference to the real importance of everyone working together is explained by an unwillingness to spend the time and effort to consider what improvements managers might make themselves. Other priorities (often associated with profitability) are allowed to provide the excuse for inaction.

Dominant ideology and business strategy

Significant evidence exists that management trends which become popular exert a strong influence on the ongoing techniques of corporate management. New concepts which are successfully implemented in certain organisations become accepted, become dominant and, even when they are inappropriate, become the norm (Mintzberg, 1979). DiMaggio and Powell (1983) offer three explanations for this phenomenon. First, organisations will submit to both formal and informal pressures from other organisations on which they depend. Second, when faced with uncertainty organisations may model themselves on organisations which have seemed to be successful and adopt the sorts of technique which they see being introduced. Third, normative pressures, which stem from a degree of professionalism among management, can cause the adoption of 'fashionable' management techniques. Universities, training institutions, standard setters and professional associations are all vehicles for the development of normative rules. These are precisely the trends seen in contemporary approaches to corporate responsibility, which are often piecemeal and sporadic. This piecemeal approach is becoming the accepted ideology because it is being adopted by leading firms, espoused by academics and legitimised by standard setters and policy makers.

The attitudes, values and actions of senior management will tend to form the culture in any organisation. In particular the chief executive will tend to be very important in influencing the behaviour of the next tier of executives, and on down the line to the shopfloor employees. We know that senior managers will tend to have a contagious influence and too often they will have a vested interest more in short-term performance than in acting ethically. Acting ethically and in a socially responsible manner, therefore, often requires culture change from the top down. Related to the top executive's influence over a company are the often mechanistic management systems and structures which so often exist in the most inflexible organisations. These are in place because they are easy to control but such structures will often stifle creativity. Moreover, any discussion relating to values will be second to structure and this will too often define the firm's immediate interests as regards short-term performance. Customer and employee safety, integrity and environmental protection will be secondary considerations.

While senior management itself may not be directly involved in unethical practices, it often promotes such behaviour by strongly insisting on short-term profit maximisation and performance goals. When these goals are difficult to achieve, and not achieving them can be met with severe penalties, the climate is set for undesirable conduct – deceptive advertising, overselling, adulterated products, inappropriate waste management practices, negligence towards environmental standards and other unethical behaviour. A clear alternative to the mechanistic, management-dominated approach is to encourage the participation of the workforce and make them feel valued. This in turn encourages commitment to the organisation and better work practices and avoids problems associated with apathy and indifference (Welford, 1992).

STRUCTURAL BARRIERS TO ETHICAL BUSINESS AND CORPORATE SOCIAL RESPONSIBILITY

The very nature of the contemporary capitalist structure which stresses competition, the maximisation of profits and the reduction of costs acts as a fundamental barrier to the adoption of ethical practices in business. In many markets, particularly where oligopolistic structures exist, strategies may be adopted which are based on tacit collusion, where firms will follow dominant market leaders. It is often perceived that unless such a strategy is adopted then firms will be at a competitive disadvantage and their viability may even be threatened. Therefore, what becomes accepted business practice, by dominant companies, tends to permeate a whole industry so that the dominant ideologies associated with the most profitable companies perpetuate themselves and set the tone for business strategies. In these circumstances it is market share and financial performance which come to dominate other measures of the success of the company.

On the other hand, in times when demand falls or when any organisation finds itself in a very competitive situation, financial indicators remain dominant and cost cutting often prevails. However, we know that in two major catastrophes, Bhopal and the Alaskan oil spill, cost cutting severely affected safety measures and contributed greatly to the gravity of the problem and the consequent handling of it (Hartley, 1993). Whatever the market structure, therefore, success is measured first and foremost on principles of financial management and wider ethical considerations are sidelined. The overemphasis on money, dictated by the economic system, therefore represents a barrier to the adoption of real corporate responsibility.

According to Donaldson (1989), however, the most serious barriers to improvement are not in the nature of people or business and industry but are attitudinal. There is, therefore, a need to change attitudes via a change in the culture of an organisation. Central here is a commitment towards improved ethics. Many studies have demonstrated the ease with which the commitment of employees can be gained through methods associated with behavioural science (Luthans, 1985). While such techniques are sometimes criticised as being potentially manipulative, they hold great potential for increasing ethical behaviour. A 'bolt-on' morality is not being sought (so common with codes of conduct and standards) but a genuine attempt at introducing real ethical improvements.

This inevitably leads to considering whether current bureaucratic structures in society and industry are conducive to the introduction of systems which promote ethical behaviour. The stunted development of any consideration of alternative forms of bureaucracy provides us with a major challenge for the future. There is a need for more innovation and imagination on the part of management. Cooperative and participative forms of industrial organisation have, for example, often been seen as appropriate only to alternative small artisan operations or have been a last-resort attempt at rescuing businesses which are due to close for commercial reasons. Ethical concerns are a challenge to look more closely at developments associated with industrial democracy and alternative industrial arrangements. The bureaucratic habits of hierarchy and the narrow distribution of power may not, in the end, be conducive to a sustainable future.

OPERATIONAL BARRIERS TO ETHICAL BUSINESS AND CORPORATE SOCIAL RESPONSIBILITY

Businesses are also prevented from acting in a more responsible way by ideologies relating to product responsibility, promotional activities and international trade which are based on custom and practice rather than any real evaluation of ethical considerations. There is an accepted code of conduct in each of these areas which, once again, stresses short-term performance, perceives change as being costly and fundamentally devalues the rights of individual human beings. It is worth examining each of these issues in turn.

Product responsibility

The traditional view of a product is that once it is sold the responsibility for its safe use and disposal passes to the consumer. That cut-off point means that firms often do not consider the wider impacts caused by the use and disposal of their product. More forward-looking companies are now accepting that the product which they produce is fundamentally their responsibility from cradle to grave. The most advanced companies have introduced product stewardship procedures to ensure that a product is used correctly and disposed of in an environmentally friendly way. However, this approach is yet to be found throughout industry, where the dominant ideology seems to stress the idea that property rights imply responsibility so that as soon as such rights are transferred through the sale of the product, the company no longer has a duty of care against environmental damage.

Promotional activities

Promotional activities are designed to increase sales and are judged on the basis of so doing. Too many experiences of marketing strategies, to date, have been associated with exaggeration and deception. There is a temptation in marketing departments to overemphasise a product's attributes. Unfortunately, moderation is not always practised – mild exaggerations can multiply and become outright deception. With many products false claims can be recognised by customers, who refuse to buy the product again, but where such claims cannot be easily substantiated then false claims are harder to detect. Nevertheless, pressure groups and competitors are always willing to expose unreasonable claims and this damages not only product sales but also the reputation of the firm. Advertising statements, if well presented and attractive, should induce customers to purchase the product, but if the expectations generated by advertisements are not realised then there will be no repeat business. Repeat business is the very thing most firms seek – a continuity of business, which means loyal and satisfied customers.

International trade

Many companies today do business worldwide and source their raw materials from a range of countries. Although this presents great opportunities it also poses some problems, some ethical dilemmas and many opportunities for abuse. Unethical practices have a critical effect on the image of companies at home and abroad. Union Carbide's acceptance of lower operating standards in its Third World operations led to the Bhopal accident. The lesson to be learned is that standards and controls must be even more rigidly applied in countries where workers and managers may be less competent than they are in more economically and educationally advanced countries. A major ethical question also revolves around the sourcing of raw materials from parts of the world where indigenous populations are adversely affected. The drive for low-cost inputs leads to the exploitation of such people and the abuse of their land, and attacks their fundamental right to lead their lives as they would wish.

CORPORATE SOCIAL RESPONSIBILITY AND THE DEVELOPMENT OF AN ETHICAL ORGANISATION

It is commonly claimed that there is an inevitable trade-off between profit and ethics or morals and that the ultimate constraint to improved ethical behaviour is the need to show an acceptable rate of return on investment. The counterclaim is that behaving responsibly is good business and that taking an honest and ethical approach to industrial activities will lead to satisfied customers and repeat business. There are two problems with both of these arguments. First, they implicitly assume that ethics can be measured and thereby characterise the 'ethical firm' or provide lists of good or bad practices, whereas the notion of the ethical firm is difficult to describe and attempting to do so may be fruitless. Second, both arguments implicitly assume an underlying business structure where the primary outcome is profitability, although there are alternative models.

Alternative ideas and alternative structures can be achieved through quite marginal changes but they can bring about much improved outcomes. For example, there are key procedures associated with reforms in the workplace which firms can adopt that will push them along the path of more ethical behaviour. This revolves around issues of industrial democracy, respecting the values of everybody associated with an organisation and allowing diversity to exist. More open procedures and less hierarchical bureaucracy in decision making could be developed within organisations. This in turn needs to be linked to an ethical awareness-raising campaign, both within and external to the firm, helping to raise the overall ethical profile.

Argyris (1964) argues that firms typically place individuals in positions of passivity and dependency that are at odds with the needs of mature individuals. Bennis (1972) and Burns and Stalker (1963) go further in suggesting that bureaucracies are too inflexible to be able to adapt to changes in increasingly volatile and discriminating markets (see also Chapter 3). Traditional bureaucracies promote decision making to the top of the organisation and the results are subsequently handed down. Because of the narrow constituency involved in the decision-making process, they may not only be suboptimal decisions but may also be severely at odds with the values of a workforce. Bureaucracies hold within themselves methods of con-

→ Ch. 3

trolling and channelling information. Those with power in the bureaucracy will go to great lengths to ensure conformity to internal codes, and they have a range of sanctions available to them for persuasion and enforcement. Such codes may be at odds with more ethical behaviour. Flatter hierarchies, participative decision making and increased self-determination by workers are initial steps to begin to resolve such problems.

If increased industrial democracy better enables firms to act in ethical ways and if the many advocates of participative arrangements (e.g. Welford, 1989) are right in suggesting that participation improves productivity and performance, then it needs to be considered why there has not been a manifestation of this form of industrial organisation. Any movement towards some form of corporate democracy is taking place slowly and in a piecemeal fashion, but it might be accelerated if legislation which more freely permitted different styles of participation and democratic processes were to be introduced, thus doing away with the restrictive structure of authority and responsibility required by law which often inhibits moves in this direction.

Allen (2007) argues that one way to be ethical is to provide intrinsically positive products or services, such as organic food or recycling, but he goes further in suggesting that regardless of core activities any business can be run in an ethical way. He considers that being ethical is about 'fairness' and it is up to each manager to decide what feels right for their organisation. 'You should always retain a set of core ethical values that are not to be compromised' (Allen, 2007), while all business decisions have an impact on the wider world and can be made ethically. Reeves (2005) describes 'ethicality' as a growing business issue:

> *'Ethics officers are popping up in many corporations. Ethical investment is an established niche in the capital markets.'*

Reeves (2005) divides consumers into three groups. There are those who know about ethical businesses and who realise that small, and what may be largely 'cosmetic', ethically directed alterations in company's policies do not mean that the whole organisation has moved in this direction. There are those who know about ethical products and services but are not concerned whether companies are being ethically correct or not. They want businesses to 'stick to their knitting of generating wealth'. The third, and largest, group does not care who makes what and on what ethical basis. Reeves discusses the launch of a fair-trade coffee by the company Nestlé:

> *'Although the new line of fair coffee has the Fairtrade kitemark from the Fairtrade Foundation, the World Development Movement said that the launch "is more likely to be an attempt to cash in on a growing market or a cynical marketing exercise than represent the beginning of a fundamental shift in Nestle's business model."'*

He argues that Nestlé has made a cautious move into the fair-trade market as a result of modest shifts in consumer demand and he asks the question 'whose fault is it that only 3% of the market in instant coffee is fair-trade?' He argues that if consumers increased their demand for coffee with this label then this proportion would change:

> *'The problem with ethical business, or corporate social responsibility, is that it all too often expects businesses to live in the world as we would wish it to be – full of ethical consumers and clients – rather than as it really is: full of demanding shareholders and profit targets.'*
> (Reeves, 2005)

Meanwhile the ethical business movement has developed and expanded. For example, Fairtrade was established in 1992 in the UK by a group of development agencies and charities as an independent product certification label. Its label has been supported by a number of well-known companies including Marks & Spencer and the Co-op in connection with a number of products including coffee, chocolate and bananas. Growing awareness of global poverty, concerns about food sources and rising prosperity have helped to promote the issue and Fairtrade enjoyed a 265 per cent growth between 2002 and 2007. Cafedirect is the UK's largest Fairtrade coffee company and the chief executive, Penny Newman, who was previously at Body Shop, describes the Body Shop founder, Anita Roddick, as an inspirational role model. The Fairtrade label promises a fair price to farmers agreed by the Foundation but Penny Newman has stressed the need to make profits.

> *'"If you want to change the trading system, you've got to be on the same terms as the conventional system. You need to make a profit; it's what you do with the profit." She launched a range of "gourmet" coffees to combat the impression that so called ethical products made you feel good but did not taste good. She focused on talking to producers about using the money to improve the product "You can't just rely on the argument that people should move into Fairtrade because it's the right thing to do."'*
>
> (Martinson, 2007)

At the same time Marks & Spencer have introduced the new 'M & S Ethical Fund' with the tag line 'Nobody can guarantee your investments will always do well. But we can assure you they'll always do good' (Guardian, 2007). It states that the new Ethical Fund 'allows you to invest with a clear conscience' with the objective of providing long-term capital growth by investing in predominantly UK companies that meet the social, environmental and ethical criteria of making a positive contribution to society. 'We're determined to avoid investing in companies primarily involved with armaments, the fur trade, gambling, tobacco, pornography and those that conduct or commission animal testing for cosmetic or toiletry purposes or make use of child labour.' In 2007 there were 90 different ethical ISAs on offer to UK investors and they were at the top of the performance tables over the previous year.

Corporate social responsibility has clearly moved into a central place in organisations' agendas, but Porter and Kramer (2006) claim that although many companies have done much to improve the social and environmental consequences of their activities, these efforts have not been as productive as they could be. They argue that this is because they tend to 'pit business against society, when clearly the two are interdependent' and because companies are encouraged to think of CSR in generic ways instead of in the way most appropriate to each firm's strategy. Also the development of CSR has been based on the arguments of moral obligation, sustainability, stakeholder support and reputation, all of which focus on the tension between business and society.

> *'Corporations are not responsible for all the world's problems, nor do they have the resources to solve them all. Each company can identify the particular set of societal problems that it is best equipped to help to resolve and from which it can gain the greatest competitive advantage.'*

At the same time Porter and Kramer argue that

> *'when a well-run business applies its vast resources, expertise, and management talent to problems that it understands and in which it has a stake, it can have a greater impact on social good than any other institution or philanthropic organisation.'*

These approaches help to bring together the ethical and economic issues raised which otherwise can be seen as opposing forces in relation to corporate social responsibility.

SUMMARY

- Corporate social responsibility is now on the global policy agenda with the impact of recent initiatives being that companies are increasingly being faced with the challenge of integrating ethical considerations into their production and marketing plans. There is always an incentive, however, for profit-maximising companies seeking short-term rewards to opt out of their ethical obligations concerning CSR. What is required, therefore, is a thorough re-examination of business ethics within any organisation and a change in ideology towards an acceptance by industry of its moral and social responsibilities.

- Perhaps one of the most important lessons which business organisations are beginning to learn relates to the desirability of seeking an honest and trusting relationship with customers (as well as with their other stakeholders). Such an ethical relationship requires concern for customer satisfaction, widely defined, and fair dealings. Objectives should be written in ethical terms and stress loyalty and repeat business. Such a philosophy and attitude must permeate an organisation. It can easily be short-circuited if a general climate of opportunism and severe financial performance pressures prevail.

- Ethical management in the public sector cannot be taken for granted, particularly with the development of a more 'business-like' approach and the 'new public management'.

- An honest and trusting relationship should not be sought with consumers or final users alone. It should characterise the relationship between sales representatives and their clients, which suggests no exaggeration or misrepresentation, greater efforts at understanding customers' needs and better servicing. It may even mean forgoing a sales opportunity when a customer's best interest may be better served by another product or at another time. The trusting relationship suggests repudiating any adversarial stance with employees, with suppliers and, beyond this, with all the communities in which a firm does business. Firms need to throw away ideologies based on financial performance alone and consider their corporate relationship with society. Such a relationship requires sound ethical conduct. It should foster a good reputation and public image.

- It has been argued that the competitive nature of markets is often a barrier to responsible corporate performance and creates isolationist strategies. Unethical and unilateral actions may result in an initial competitive advantage but may hurt a firm's overall image and reputation in the longer term. To have a coherent social strategy firms need a consistent set of business ethics and need to measure their performance using a range of longer-term indicators. The notion of stakeholder accountability also reminds us that it is really not possible to separate ethical considerations from other issues such as the treatment of women and minority groups, the treatment of animals and the protection of indigenous populations. A set of ethics alone will not necessarily lead to better business practices, however. What is also needed is a fundamental re-examination of dominant ideologies in the business world and culture change which is capable of challenging accepted wisdoms.

■ The rise of organised pressure groups and interest groups makes it doubly important that managers consider the arguments of all stakeholders in a decision's outcome. Since these groups publicly promote their causes in a single-minded way and do not, therefore, have the competing objectives so often faced by management, they have an advantage over the traditional company in the strong message which they can convey. Decisions taken in isolation by an elite group are therefore far more likely to result in suboptimal outcomes.

■ The major issues and arguments surrounding business ethics and CSR are not so much substantive but more associated with procedures and received 'wisdom' associated with structures and hierarchies. It has been argued that these barriers to improved ethics can be overcome through the removal of such traditional structures. There needs to be careful thought about putting a new emphasis on stakeholder accountability and a move towards new democratic forms of organisation within the workplace. The tension between business and society can be reduced by encouraging businesses to focus their development of a corporate social responsibility on the problems that they understand and in which they have a stake.

Review and discussion questions

1 *What is the link between corporate social responsibility and business ethics?*

2 *Is it enough for business ethics to be defined so as to meet the legitimate needs of stakeholders?*

3 *How do differences in cultures often found in different countries make the role of the manager more difficult?*

4 *Do you consider that codes of conduct and standards simplify ethical dilemmas or simply reinforce accepted ideology (which may actually be unethical)?*

5 *What do you consider are the biggest barriers to improving corporate social responsibility?*

6 *Is it always unethical to offer bribes when doing business internationally?*

CASE STUDY 17.1

Shell to face shareholder vote on ethics

Shell Transport & Trading, the UK arm of the Anglo-Dutch oil group, is facing a potentially embarrassing battle with some institutional shareholders over a resolution they have put down for the annual meeting in May. A group of shareholders holding just under 1 per cent of the company is calling on it to improve accountability by establishing new procedures for dealing with environmental and human rights issues. Pirc, the corporate governance consul-

tant advising the shareholders, says the Shell resolution is the first of its kind in the UK. In the US, public companies regularly face resolutions from shareholders about environmental and social concerns.

The Shell shareholder group includes 18 public and private pension funds, five religious institutions, an academic fund and individuals from a pressure group called the Ecumenical Committee on Corporate Responsibility. They say Shell's reputation has been damaged by controversies such as the aborted plan to sink the Brent Spar oil storage rig at sea and its environmental and human rights record in Nigeria. Their statement supporting the resolution says: 'Shareholders have a responsibility as owners to ensure that companies have structures and policies in place to enable them to operate to the highest standards, and that companies should disclose to shareholders progress made in achieving improvements in performance. We believe that this resolution will help Shell accomplish these goals.'

In particular, the group wants a named member of Shell's committee of managing directors to take charge of environmental and corporate responsibility policies. It also wants Shell to agree to an external audit of these policies, and to publish a report to shareholders before the end of this year on its operations in Nigeria, which have been the focus

of pressure group campaigning for several years.

Shell has denied allegations from pressure groups that it has contributed to pollution of the environment in the Niger delta region and has assisted the Nigerian government's alleged persecution of the region's Ogoni tribe. Shell Transport & Trading, a UK quoted company, and Royal Dutch Petroleum, quoted in The Netherlands, own the Royal Dutch/Shell group on a 40:60 basis. The company confirmed that the resolution had been lodged and that shareholders would be voting on it at the annual general meeting. 'We are considering our response to it at the moment,' the company said, adding that the issues in the resolution were being covered by a company review of its Statement of General Business Principles, which deals with environmental issues.

Source: Financial Times, 24 February 1997. Reprinted with permission.

CASE STUDY 17.2

The UK Government's CSR strategy and web-based activity

The UK Government CSR strategy

The UK Government has provided a commitment to encourage the development of CSR and the following provides a summary of the national vision, strategy and priorities and keynote action areas, as outlined in the UK Government's Department of Trade and Industry, *Business and Society: Corporate Social Responsibility Report 2002*. This report can be downloaded from http://www.societyandbusiness.gov.uk, which is the UK Government's corporate social responsibility website.

Vision

The UK Government's vision for corporate social responsibility is: to see private, voluntary and public sector organisations in the UK take account of their economic, social and environmental impacts, and take complementary action to address key challenges based on their core competences – locally, regionally, nationally and internationally.

Strategy

The UK Government's strategy for advancing its vision is to:

- promote activities that bring economic, social and environmental benefits;
- work in partnership with a range of organisations, including the private sector, community bodies, unions, consumers and other stakeholders;
- encourage innovative approaches and good practice in CSR;
- define minimum levels of performance; and
- encourage awareness, trust and healthy public dialogue on CSR.

The UK Government's CSR strategy is tied to its strategy for sustainable development, with its aims of social progress, protection of the environment, prudent use of natural resources, and economic growth and employment.

Priorities and keynote actions

The UK strategy addresses five priority issues and identifies key action points in each area, with these being to:

- Raise the profile and highlight the importance of CSR. *Action: The Government states that it will take full account of opportunities to increase the adoption and reporting of CSR (see http://defra.gov.uk for*

▶

the New General Guidelines on Environment Reporting) as part of a continuing review of intelligent regulation and fiscal incentives.

■ Make responsible behaviour considerations integral to the decision-making processes of organisations.
Action: The Government states that it will take steps to establish CSR within the mainstream decision-making of organisations, with a strong focus on the following areas: the environment, neighbourhood renewal, adult basic skills and international developments (see http://www.societyandbusiness.gov.uk for further details).

■ Assist the involvement of small and medium-sized enterprises (SMEs) in CSR initiatives.
Action: The Government states that it will create a step change in the consistency and quality of CSR guidance to SMEs by stimulating a joint approach among their key advisory organisations (see http://www.societyandbusiness.gov.uk for further details).

■ Promote greater transparency in CSR reporting and awareness.
Action: The Government states that it will consult widely with all stakeholders to ensure that greater transparency and clarity is brought to the current confusing set of reporting models and codes of practice (see e.g. http://www.unglobal compact.org, http://www.ilo.org, http://www. ftse4good.com and http://www.oecd.org for a range of such initiatives).

■ Promote and facilitate good practice in CSR internationally as well as domestically.
Action: The Government states that it will support the development of the Ethical Trading Initiative (see http://www.ethicaltrade.org for further details) and other international, as well as national, work on best practice.

These keynote policies are supported by steps to improve the impact and example of the Government's own activities, including consideration, within the policy and legal framework, of departmental and public procurement practices.

Web-based activity instructions

Please read the case study above and consult the UK Government CSR website (http://www.societyandbusiness.gov.uk) before completing the activity. Consulting the additional web links provided should also assist you.

The task

Drawing on the UK Government strategy for CSR:

■ consider how the UK Government defines CSR;
■ outline further the UK Government's vision and strategy for CSR; and
■ discuss the difficulties that the UK Government might encounter when implementing its strategy and in particular the priority/keynote action areas identified.

Source: Department of Trade and Industry (2002) *Business and Society: Corporate Social Responsibility Report 2002*, London: DTI.

FURTHER READING

Crane, A and Matten, D (2003) *Business Ethics*, Oxford: Oxford University Press.
A comprehensive discussion of business ethics.

Lawton, A (1998) *Ethical Management for the Public Services*, Buckingham: The Open University Press.
The ethical dimension in the public sector.

Markham, J W (2006) *A Financial History of Modern US Corporate Scandals: Enron to Reform*, M E Sharpe.
Examples of US corporate scandals.

Porter, M E and Kramer, M R (2006) 'Strategy and society', *Harvard Business Review*, December.
The link between competitive advantage and corporate social responsibility.

Windsor, D (2006) 'Corporate social responses: three key approaches', *Journal of Management Studies*, 43 (1), January.
Discussion of corporate ethics and corporate social responsibility.

WEBSITES

http://defra.gov.uk
This is the website of the UK Government Department of Environment, Food and Rural Affairs. Of particular interest are the new General Guidelines on Environment Reporting, developed in partnership with the Department of Trade and Industry (DTI) and the Confederation of British Industry (CBI). These guidelines explain in a comprehensive way the basics of how to produce an environment report and suggest contents and key indicators to report against.

http://ethicaltrade.org
This is the website of the Ethical Trading Initiative (ETI) which was set up in 1998. Corporate members of the ETI include major high street names with a combined annual turnover estimated to be almost £100 billion. These businesses address supply chain issues such as working hours and the 'living wage', rights-based and related issues.

http://europa.eu.int
This website provides access to the European Union's corporate social responsibility Green Paper (published in July 2001) the consultation documents and the 250 responses received.

http://ilo.org
This website provides access to the 1988 Declaration on Fundamental Principles and Rights at Work of the International Labour Organisation (ILO). This establishes internationally agreed core labour standards and provides commitments to eliminating the worst forms of child labour, slavery and forced labour, and to uphold workers' freedom of association and the right to work free of discrimination. This website also provides access to the ILO Tripartite Declaration of Principles Concerning Multinational Enterprises and Social Policy (1977, amended 2000). This sets out guidelines for action by governments, multinational enterprises and workers' and employers' organisations.

http://ftse4good.com
This is the website of the FTSE4Good which was introduced by the FTSE in May 2001. Of particular interest are the four socially responsible investment (SRI) indices covering UK, European, US and global companies. These are used to list companies which demonstrate responsible behaviour on human rights, the environment and society. An independent committee of 14 international experts undertakes a review of the indices every six months, with the scheme being supported by UNICEF.

http://oecd.org
This is the website of the Organisation for Economic Cooperation and Development (OECD). Of particular interest are the voluntary guidelines for multinational enterprises which set out government expectations of business behaviour globally in areas such as environment, labour and disclosure. Although voluntary they do contain a mechanism whereby concerns about the activities of multinationals can be brought to the attention of signatory governments.

http://www.societyandbusiness.gov.uk
This is the UK Government's corporate social responsibility website. Of particular interest is the Department of Trade and Industry, *Business and Society: Corporate Social Responsibility Report 2002*.

http://unglobalcompact.org
This is the website of the UN Global Compact which was launched in July 2000. This encourages companies to build human rights, labour and environmental principles into their business strategies for the developing world. Many leading companies, such as Shell, BP, Rio Tinto, BG Group and Unilever, have signed up to the Compact.

Environmental issues in organisations

Having read this chapter, you will be able to:

- explain why there has been a growth in public and corporate environmental awareness in recent years;

- explain the strategic and functional issues which environmental issues place on business;

- discuss a range of management strategies to improve a company's environmental performance;

- outline the components of the environmental management systems ISO 14001 and the Eco-Management and Audit Scheme (EMAS) Regulation;

- discuss the concept of product stewardship and the EU's eco-labelling regulation;

- identify how organisations can benefit from environmental management.

ENVIRONMENTAL MANAGEMENT

Over the last 40 years there has been a growing interest in the environment, or more specifically in the damage being inflicted on the environment by human activity worldwide. In Europe the process of integration has brought the transnational nature of the environmental problem to the forefront of the social, political and corporate agenda. Environmental problems and issues such as the hole in the ozone layer, climate change and global warming are the result of not one country's action but that of many. Acid rain, which is polluting rivers and lakes and damaging forests, often emanates from one country and is deposited in another.

The effects of different industrial sectors on the environment vary enormously. At one end of the spectrum might be multinational oil companies, whose very business is environmentally damaging, and at the other end might be retailers and the service sector, who have less of a direct impact on the environment – although, in most cases, they could still make environmental improvements through recycling and improved transportation policies. There is still much confusion for both consumers and companies about what constitutes an environmentally friendly product or operation, and the 'green revolution' to date has provided few answers, although many misrepresentations, particularly in the area of product marketing, have been exposed.

At the root of some of the environmental problems is the growth in consumerism and materialism. The notion that 'the consumer is king' may drive the market mechanism but the overemphasis placed on the satisfaction of customers' wants in the developed economies of the world has had a profound effect on the planet's ability to sustain life and on biodiversity. It is generally accepted that the world cannot go on using the resources of the planet at the present rate. But there is a 'free-rider problem' at work – everyone thinks that something should happen to mitigate the problem but many people just assume that everyone else will do it, and anyway their individual impact is minute so it will make no difference to the environment. This is illustrated by Exhibit 18.1.

Everything that consumers, companies and other institutions do will have some impact on the environment, but for *sustainable* development the emphasis needs to be on the strategies that organisations can follow to improve their environmental performance. Even substances which, in their final form, are environmentally benign may have been unfriendly in their manufacture, especially if that manufacture was

Exhibit 18.1 Packaging in the UK

'Now we know buying fruit and vegetables packed in unwanted plastic – destined for landfill sites – is not just environmentally unsound, but expensive'
(*Evening Standard*, Comment 18 April 2007)

The paper's report suggests that packaging adds 20 per cent to the cost of fruit in Waitrose, bearing out the Women's Institute finding that packaging adds about £8 to every £50 spent on food. The answer was to buy loose and for retailers to reduce packaging: 'most fruit, after all, comes ready-wrapped by nature.' A green pressure group, WRAP, was reported to be drawing up plans for industry-wide labelling on packaging disposal, while a spokesman for Waitrose declared that 'reducing packaging is a key priority for us and we have reduced the weight of product packaging by 33 per cent since 2000.'

energy-greedy. They may have been produced using non-renewable resources and may also pose problems after they have been used and it comes to their disposal. If a 'cradle-to-the-grave' view of products is taken, where their environmental impact is examined through their life cycle from raw materials and through usage to disposal then there are few, if any, products which will fail to have a negative impact on the environment. The key question, therefore, is not how environmental damage is completely eliminated but how it is reduced it over time, and how a state of balance is achieved such that the amount of environmental damage is repairable and therefore sustainable.

Industry, particularly in the developed world, must increasingly take into account the costs of the effects of its operations on the environment as opposed to regarding the planet as a free resource. In the past, few companies counted the costs of the pollution they discharged into the atmosphere and the debate has now turned to legislation aimed at forcing companies to comply with certain standards and taxing those which pollute. The so-called 'polluter pays' principle is now central to legislation in the developed countries. The implication here is clearly that prices will rise for consumers as organisations experience increased costs associated with environmental improvements. Lower energy consumption and more efficient use of resources are obvious targets for improvement and should not conflict with industry's aims, since their attainment can actually reduce costs. Many materials are already recycled and a thriving, and at times profitable, recycling industry has been established across Europe (see Exhibit 18.2).

Many of the products now considered to be environmentally hazardous were, at the time of their discovery, regarded as an invaluable resource. The best example of this has been the use of chlorofluorocarbons in refrigerators, which have since been found to be a major ozone-depleting agent. Predicting a product's long-term impact on the environment is a difficult process and, until recently, has rarely been done. This will change as firms are forced to consider cradle-to-grave management of their products and as the benefit of doubt is increasingly given to the welfare of the planet. Moreover, industry has a responsibility to ensure that its products are less harmful to the environment and there is a need to push along a very steep environmental learning curve.

Many governments across Europe have been implementing increasingly stringent environmental legislation. At the level of the European Union there has been an emphasis on the provision of information about products and processes to the public. However, a common problem is that the statutory bodies which do exist with

Exhibit 18.2 Organisational commitment in the UK

> *'As a responsible member of the business community we are working to reduce our impact on the environment. Climate change is one of the greatest challenges of modern times and the Society has and will continue to take action to tackle climate change by reducing our carbon emissions.'*
>
> (The Coventry Building Society TLC,
> Annual General Meeting report, 2007 *Investing in Your Future*)

Practical steps to do this included purchasing greener electricity, working with the Carbon Trust to identify ways of reducing energy consumption, recycling waste paper and printer cartridges and where possible using paper that 'comes from greener sources'.

responsibility for monitoring the environmental performance of organisations have limited resources and powers in most cases. Organisations themselves have often been shown to be ignorant of current environmental legislation, particularly with regard to EU environmental directives and legislation on issues such as waste disposal, air pollution and water quality. However, such ignorance is not an excuse for non-compliance. Moreover, non-compliance which can be attributed to negligence can not only result in fines but occasionally in imprisonment for company directors.

In the USA the Environmental Protection Agency (EPA) is an independent environmental body with significant power. In 1980 the US Congress passed the Comprehensive Environmental Response, Compensation and Liability Act, better known as 'Superfund'. Under the provisions of the Act, companies must report potentially toxic spills and releases greater than a clearly defined minimum. Violations of this are criminal offences with penalties of up to one year in jail and a significant fine. Superfund also deals with uncontrolled hazardous waste sites where previous or present owners and operators of a site must help to pay for whatever remedial action is necessary. If the previous firm has gone out of business, the EPA has often managed to obtain funds from the companies which sent the waste there for treatment or disposal in the first instance. In the UK, by contrast, local authority regulators and pollution inspectors all adopt an approach of constructive engagement with companies rather than fining them in the first instance for pollution violations.

The rapid growth of public environmental awareness in recent years has placed new pressures on industry. These pressures can take many forms as individuals collectively exercise their environmental conscience as customers, employees, investors, voters, neighbours and fellow citizens. However, whether it is due to intellectual fatigue with environmental issues, a lack of conviction that an individual's own actions will have an impact or a reluctance to reduce private consumption for public welfare, it seems that many individuals prefer to pass their responsibilities on to those parties that they feel can make a significant impact. The two major parties that the public perceive as being able to make a difference are government and industry. Given the public's inherent reluctance to reduce its own levels of consumption, it is apparent that government and industry must respond in order to protect the environment effectively.

In this area of management there are frequent changes in regulations, legislation, treaties and agreements and in the details that apply to particular industries; the regulations and agreements discussed in this Chapter are examples of these.

USING THE PRICE MECHANISM TO ALLEVIATE POLLUTION

The use of the market mechanism to distribute goods and services in the West, with its consequent stress on property rights, has contributed to the environmental degradation which we have experienced. Much of the environment (particularly the air and atmosphere) is treated as a free good since no individual owns it and there are no assigned property rights to it. Firms and consumers have therefore made excessive use of environmental resources both as an input and as a source of output (or sink). This is illustrated in Figure 18.1.

Suppose that a firm produces a good and in the process of doing so it pollutes the air around it. Traditionally, and ignoring legislation which might or might not exist, the firm can do this freely since no one owns the air. Assume that the demand for the product is D_1 and the production and marketing costs of the firm imply that it is willing to sell along a supply curve given by S_1. Essentially S_1 is drawn based on only the private costs of the firm, that is, those which it must pay

Figure 18.1 Using the market mechanism to deal with environmental damage

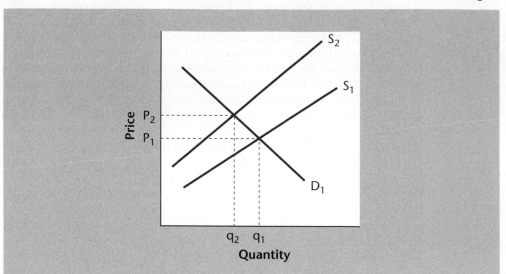

in a monetary form, but the pollution caused to the local community imposes a cost on them and on society as a whole. If the firm was required to internalise those costs either by paying a tax-to-pollute based on an estimate of the social cost that that pollution caused (the tax might subsequently be used to clean up the pollution), or by the use of legislation banning the pollution (meaning that the firm would have to invest in a new non-polluting process) then its own costs would rise. The firm's willingness to supply at any particular price would be reduced and S_1 would shift backwards to S_2. The equilibrium in the market would shift from P_1q_1 to P_2q_2. Thus less of the good would be produced and at a higher price.

The premise on which most developed countries' environmental legislation has largely been based is the 'polluter pays' principle. In other words this is a notion that public money should not be used in clearing up or avoiding pollution but, as described above, the polluters themselves should face those costs. From a welfare point of view, the difference between a firm compensating a local community for the pollution it creates and the community paying the firm not to pollute is purely distributional, but from an ethical perspective it is often argued that the 'polluter pays' principle is superior.

The sort of analysis described by Figure 18.1 can be extended to the economy as a whole. Since most processes will impose at least some negative impact on the environment, the fact that the environment has not been properly costed and treated as a free good over time has meant that too many goods have been produced. Moreover, it can be argued that mass-production techniques which have enabled firms to produce more and more goods and to charge lower prices have been particularly damaging.

SUSTAINABLE DEVELOPMENT

The belief which lies behind the concept of sustainable development is that there is a trade-off between continuous economic growth and the sustainability of the environment. Over time, growth causes pollution and atmospheric damage. The concept of sustainable development stresses the interdependence between economic growth and environmental quality. It is possible to make development and environmental protection compatible by following sustainable strategies and by not developing the particular areas of economic activity that are most damaging to the environment.

The Brundtland Report (World Commission on Environment and Development, 1987), commissioned by the United Nations to examine long-term environmental strategies, argued that economic development and environmental protection could be made compatible but that this would require quite radical changes in economic practices throughout the world. They defined sustainable development as:

> *'development that meets the needs of the present without compromising the ability of future generations to meet their own needs.'*

In other words mass consumption is not possible indefinitely and if society today acts as if all non-renewable resources are plentiful then eventually there will be nothing left for the future. More importantly than that, however, mass consumption may cause such irreparable damage that humans may not even be able to live on the planet in the future.

The challenge that faces the economic system is how to continue to fulfil its vital role within modern society while working towards sustainability. Complying with the principles of sustainability cannot be achieved overnight. However, both for entire economies and for individual businesses there is hope that it can be achieved within the time scales which appear to be necessary if environmental catastrophe is to be avoided.

According to Welford (1993), sustainable development is made up of three closely connected issues and associated conditions.

■ **Environment** – this must be valued as an integral part of the economic process and not treated as a free good. The environmental stock has to be protected, which implies minimal use of non-renewable resources and minimal emission of pollutants. The ecosystem has to be protected so the loss of plant and animal species has to be avoided.

■ **Equity** – one of the biggest threats facing the world is that the developing countries want to grow rapidly to achieve the same standards of living as those in the West. That in itself would cause a major environmental disaster if it were modelled on the same sort of growth as experienced in post-war Europe. Therefore, there needs to be a greater degree of equity and the key issue of poverty has to be addressed, but it seems hypocritical for the West to tell the Third World that it cannot attain the same standards of living and consumption.

■ **Futurity** – sustainable development requires that society, businesses and individuals operate on a different time scale than that which currently operates in the economy. While companies commonly operate under competitive pressures to achieve short-term gains, long-term environmental protection is often compromised. To ensure that longer-term, intergenerational considerations are observed, longer planning horizons need to be adopted and business policy needs to be proactive rather than reactive.

The Brundtland Report concludes that these three conditions are not being met. The industrialised world has already used much of the planet's ecological capital and many of the development paths of the industrialised nations are clearly unsustainable. Non-renewable resources are being depleted, while renewable resources such as soil, water and the atmosphere are being degraded. This has been caused by economic development but in time will undermine the very foundations of that development.

Like the Brundtland Report, more recent initiatives by the United Nations, including the Earth Summit held in Rio in 1992 and the World Summit on Sustainable Development (Rio+10) held in Johannesburg in 2002, call for development which is environmentally and socially sustainable rather than the current situation of unplanned, undifferentiated growth. This means reconsidering the current measures of growth, such as gross national product (GNP), which fail to take account of environmental debits such as pollution or the depletion of the natural capital stock. While concern about the depletion of materials and energy resources has diminished since the 1970s, there is nevertheless concern surrounding the environment's capacity to act as a sink for waste. For example, bringing developing countries' energy use up to the level of the developing world's would mean an increase in consumption by a factor of five. Using present energy-generation methods the planet could not cope with the impact of sulphur dioxide and carbon dioxide emissions and the consequential acidification and global warming of the environment.

One major obstacle preventing sustainability from being achieved is the overall level of consumption. However, Western consumers are apparently reluctant to significantly reduce their own levels of consumption. While governments are increasingly adopting economic instruments such as taxes, subsidies and product-labelling schemes to reduce and channel consumption towards more environmentally friendly alternatives, industry itself must be encouraged further to increase environmental efficiency.

Sustainability challenges industry to produce higher levels of output while using lower levels of input and generating less waste. The problem that remains is that while relative environmental impact per unit of output has fallen, increases in the absolute level of output, and hence environmental impact, have more than offset any gains in relative environmental efficiency. However, if we examine the ways in which environmental efficiency has been improved then we can begin to understand some of the key practical elements with which sustainability may be better promoted.

CORPORATE RESPONSES TO SUSTAINABLE DEVELOPMENT

Organisations are faced with a challenge of integrating environmental considerations into their production and marketing plans. There is always an incentive, however, for profit-maximising firms seeking short-term rewards to opt out and become a free-rider (assuming that everyone else will be environmentally conscious such that their own pollution will become negligible). However, European Union environmental legislation is increasingly plugging the gaps which allow this to happen and firms attempting to hide their illegal pollution are now subject to severe penalties. In many cases individual company directors can also be prosecuted and imprisoned for negligence which leads to environmental damage. Even before then businesses should recognise that it is not only ethical to be environmentally friendly but, with the growth of consumer awareness in the environmental area, that it will also be good business.

Organisations clearly have a role to play in the development of substitutes for non-renewable resources and innovations which reduce waste and use energy more efficiently. They also have a role in processing those materials in a way which brings about environmental improvements. For many products (e.g. cars and wash-

Exhibit 18.3 Company commitment in the UK

'Five years. Five commitments. One world. And 100 things we want to change'.

■ *Climate change* – we'll aim to make all our UK operations carbon neutral within five years. We'll maximize our use of renewable energy and only use offsetting as a last resort. And, we'll be helping our customers and suppliers to cut their carbon emissions too.

■ *Waste* – we'll significantly reduce the amount of packaging and carrier bags that we use and find new ways to recycle materials. By 2012 we aim to ensure that none of our clothing or packaging need end up as landfill.

■ *Sustainable raw materials* – from fish to forests, our goal is to make sure our key raw materials come from the most sustainable sources available to us, protecting the environment and the world's natural resources for future generations.

■ *Fair partner* – by being a fair partner we'll help to improve the lives of hundreds of thousands of people in our worldwide supply chain and local communities.

■ *Health* – we'll continue to expand our healthy eating ranges and help customers and employees to choose healthier lifestyles through clear labelling and easily accessible information.

Source: Marks & Spencer plc, *the Guardian*, 19 March 2007

ing machines) the major area of environmental damage occurs in their usage. Organisations often have the opportunity of reducing this damage at the design stage, and when new products are being developed there is a whole new opportunity for considering both the use and disposal of the product. According to the American Marketing Association (Luo and Bhattacharya, 2006) as many as 90 per cent of 'Fortune 500' companies (i.e. the foremost American companies) have explicit corporate social responsibility initiatives. The increasing importance of CSR in practice has been seen in marketing studies which found that these programmes have a significant influence on several customer-related outcomes (Luo and Bhattacharya, 2006). Specifically, CSR affects consumer product responses, customer-company identification and customers' product attitude directly or indirectly and it can contribute positively to market value.

Given the internal and external demands to improve the environmental performance of organisations, those that achieve high standards of environmental performance will benefit in a number of ways. In order to realise this competitive advantage organisations must seek to develop management strategies which will improve their environmental performance and address the environmental demands placed on them by government, the EU and stakeholders. By incorporating the increasingly important environmental dimension into the decision-making processes of the organisation, managers can seek to reduce costs and exploit the opportunities offered by increased public environmental concern within a dynamic marketplace (see Exhibit 18.3). Such a strategy must be proactive and honest. It may also involve a degree of education and campaigning, such as that undertaken by The Body Shop – but more than anything it must be ethical.

The general principles of such a strategy are embodied within the International Chamber of Commerce (ICC)/World Business Council for Sustainable Development (WBCSD) *Business Charter for Sustainable Development*. The key elements to this strategy are embodied in 16 'principles for environmental management' – organisations are encouraged to endorse these following aims.

- **Corporate priority** – to recognise environmental management as among the highest corporate priorities and as a key determinant to sustainable development; to establish policies, programmes and practices for conducting operations in an environmentally sound manner.

- **Integrated management** – to integrate these policies, programmes and practices fully into each business as an essential element of management in all its functions.

- **Process of improvement** – to continue to improve corporate policies, programmes and environmental performance taking into account technical developments, scientific understanding, consumer needs and community expectations, with legal regulations as a starting point; and to apply the same environmental criteria internationally.

- **Employee education** – to educate, train and motivate employees to conduct their activities in an environmentally responsible manner.

- **Prior assessment** – to assess environmental impacts before starting a new activity or project and before decommissioning a facility or leaving a site.

- **Products and services** – to develop and provide products and services that have no undue environmental impact and are safe in their intended use, that are efficient in their consumption of energy and natural resources and that can be recycled, reused or disposed of safely.

- **Customer advice** – to advise and, where relevant, educate customers, distributors and the public in the safe use, transportation, storage and disposal of products provided; to apply similar considerations to the provision of services.

- **Facilities and operations** – to develop, design and operate facilities and conduct activities taking into consideration the efficient use of energy and raw materials, the sustainable use of renewable resources, the minimisation of adverse environmental impact and waste generation, and the safe and responsible disposal of residual wastes.

- **Research** – to conduct or support research on the environmental impacts of raw materials, products, processes, emissions and wastes associated with the enterprise and on the means of minimising such adverse impacts.

- **Precautionary approach** – to modify the manufacture, marketing or use of products or services to the conduct of activities consistent with scientific and technical understanding, to prevent serious or irreversible environmental degradation.

- **Contractors and suppliers** – to promote the adoption of these principles by contractors acting on behalf of the enterprise encouraging and, where appropriate, requiring improvements in their practices to make them consistent with those of the enterprise; to encourage the wider adoption of these principles by suppliers.

- **Emergency preparedness** – to develop and maintain, where appropriate hazards exist, emergency preparedness plans in conjunction with the emergency services, relevant authorities and the local community recognising potential cross-boundary impacts.

- **Transfer of technology** – to contribute to the transfer of environmentally sound technology and management methods throughout the industrial and public sectors.

- **Contributing to the common effort** – to contribute to the development of public policy and to business, governmental and intergovernmental programmes and educational initiatives that will enhance environmental awareness and protection.

- **Openness to concerns** – to foster openness and dialogue with employees and the public, anticipating and responding to their concerns about the potential hazards and impacts of operations, products, wastes or services, including those of trans-boundary or global significance.

- **Compliance and reporting** – to measure environmental performance, to conduct regular environmental audits and assessments of compliance with company requirements and these principles; periodically to provide appropriate information to the board of directors, shareholders, employees, the authorities and the public.

This Business Charter for Sustainable Development is one of the most widely supported business and environment charters, with over 1500 signatories worldwide, including leading companies such as Shell, BOC, British Airways, ICI, British Gas, Samsung, General Motors and Ford. Many of these companies have implemented the charter's recommendations within existing environmental initiatives and management systems.

THE EUROPEAN INTEGRATION PROCESS AND CORPORATE ENVIRONMENTAL MANAGEMENT

The original Treaty of Rome was concerned with stimulating economic growth and made no specific reference to the environment. Since then, however, EU environmental policy has developed in line with general concern in Europe and the deteriorating environmental position in which Europe finds itself. By 2003, over 300 pieces of environmental legislation had been passed covering pollution of the air and water, noise pollution, chemicals, waste, environmental impact assessment, the prevention of industrial accidents and wildlife protection. Exhibit 18.4 outlines the principal EU landmarks up to 2003.

However, few member states have been able to enforce EU legislation fully. Denmark is probably the only country with a consistently good record and the southern European countries have consistently bad records. Once again, this highlights the emphasis often given to economic growth rather than environmental protection, with the primary aim of countries such as Spain and Portugal being the attainment of similar living standards to the rest of the Union.

The Single European Act gave environmental policy a boost, stating that there is not only a need for such legislation but that the laws should meet three key objectives:

- **preservation, protection and improvement of the quality of the environment;**
- **protection of human health;**
- **prudent and rational use of natural resources.**

These objectives must be met by applying four principles:

- **prevention of harm to the environment;**
- **control of pollution at source;**

Exhibit 18.4 Examples of important EU landmarks

1967 First Environmental Directive, on classification, packaging and labelling of dangerous substances (67/548)

1970 Directive establishing framework for measures to combat air pollution from motor vehicles (70/220)

1973 Launch of first European environment action programme 1973–76

1979 Birds Directive, on the protection of birds and their habitats (79/409)

1980 Directive laying down minimum standards for drinking water (80/778)

1985 Directive on Environmental Impact Assessment (85/337)

1990 Directives to limit the use and release of genetically modified organisms (GMOs) (90/219 and 90/220)

1991 Maastricht Treaty Article 6 lays down that all EU policies and activities must integrate environmental protection

1992 Habitats Directive, on the conservation of natural habitats and wild flora and fauna (92/43)

1994 European Environment Agency established

1999 Start of Green Week, the annual EU environmental conferences

2000 Framework Directive for European policy on water (2000/60)

2001 Launch of the Sixth Environmental Action Programme 2001–10: Environment 2010, Our Future, Our Choice

2002 Ratification of the Kyoto Protocol on Climate Change

Source: European Commission (2002) *Choices for a Greener Future: The European Union and the Environment*, Brussels: European Commission Directorate-General for press and communications.

■ the polluter should pay;

■ **integration of environmental considerations into other European Union policies** (all EU policies are now required to take the environment into account).

The Internal Market Programme has added a new note of urgency to environmental problems. The relationship between economic growth and the environment has returned to centre stage. Clearly, there exists a major opportunity with industrial and legislative restructuring to put into place the appropriate financial and regulatory mechanisms that would make the internal market environmentally sustainable. The extent to which this happens will be seen over time, but the Single European Act also provides the necessary constitutional basis for a forceful environmental response. Perhaps the strongest part of this is the requirement that policy makers should make environmental considerations a component of all the European Union's other policies.

In 2001 the European Union introduced its Sixth Environmental Action Programme setting out priorities for action, practical objectives and the means to achieve them in the areas of climate change, nature and biodiversity, environment and health and quality of life, and natural resources and waste. The Sixth Environmental Action Programme provides the environmental component of the European Union's strategy for sustainable development until 2010, with the objectives being set out in Exhibit 18.5.

The First Environmental Action Programme, launched in 1973, set out a number of principles which have formed the basis of environmental action in the EU ever since – these remain important when examining the strategic aims of EU environmental policy more broadly. The aims are set out in Exhibit 18.6.

Exhibit 18.5 Objectives of the EU's sixth environmental action programme

■ To stabilise the atmospheric concentrations of greenhouse gases at a level that will not cause unnatural variations of the earth's climate.

■ To protect and restore the functioning of natural systems and halt the loss of biodiversity in the European Union and globally. To protect soils against erosion and pollution.

■ To achieve a quality of the environment where the levels of man-made contaminants, including different types of radiation, do not give rise to significant impacts or risks to human health.

■ To ensure that the consumption of renewable and non-renewable resources does not exceed the carrying capacity of the environment. To achieve a decoupling of resource use from economic growth through significantly improved resource efficiency, dematerialisation of the economy, and waste prevention.

Source: European Commission (2001) *Environment 2010: Our Future, Our Choice*, Brussels: European Commission.

Exhibit 18.6 The EU's environmental principles

■ Prevention is better than cure.

■ Environmental effects should be taken into account at the earliest possible stage in decision making

■ Exploitation of nature and natural resources which causes significant damage to the ecological balance must be avoided. The natural environment can only absorb pollution to a limited extent. Nature is an asset which may be used but not abused.

■ Scientific knowledge should be improved to enable action to be taken.

■ The 'polluter pays' principle – the polluter should pay for preventing and eliminating environmental nuisance.

■ Activities in one member state should not cause environmental deterioration in another.

■ Environmental policies of member states must take account of the interests of developing countries.

■ The EU and member states should act together in international organisations and in promoting international environmental policy.

■ Education of citizens is necessary as the protection of the environment is a matter for everyone.

■ The principle of action at the appropriate level – for each type of pollution it is necessary to establish the level of action which is best suited for achieving the protection required, be it local, regional, national, EU-wide or international.

■ National environmental policies must be coordinated within the EU without impinging on progress at the national level. It is intended that implementation of the action programme and gathering of environmental information by the proposed European Environment Agency will secure this.

Source: Official Journal of the European Communities: C112, 20 December 1973.

The main activities of the EU in the environmental policy arena, until 1987, were centred on the application of nearly 200 command and control directives in areas as diverse as lead in petrol and aircraft noise. More recently, realising that environmental policy is of little use unless enforced, EU environmental policy has given increased emphasis to the improved enforcement of existing legislation, with this being an important component of the Sixth Environmental Action Programme. Emphasis has also shifted from the use of traditional command-and-control instruments in environmental policy to the application of economic market-based instruments such as the proposed carbon tax and voluntary initiatives such as the eco-labelling and eco-management and audit schemes (see later in this chapter). The aim of such measures is to encourage change in all sectors of industry and society in a more general way than can be achieved through the use of tightly defined legislative instruments. Economic instruments and voluntary measures are seen as complementing rather than substituting for the more traditional application of command-and-control measures.

The EU view of the future of environmental policy and its interface with industrial development is clear. With over 400 million inhabitants the European Union is the largest trading bloc in the world and so is in a critical position to take the lead in moving towards sustainability. The Commission accepts that tighter environmental policy will have an impact on the costs of industry. However, a high level of environmental protection has increasingly become not only a policy objective of its own but also a precondition of industrial expansion. In this respect a new impetus towards a better integration of policies aiming at consolidating industrial competitiveness and at achieving a high level of protection of the environment is necessary in order to make the two objectives fully mutually supportive.

These views are given more substance within the Sixth Environmental Action Programme, and a number of specific measures relating to industry are included. Perhaps most importantly, the commitment of the EU to strengthen environmental policy is underlined. The EU shares the view that urgent action is needed for environmental protection and that many of the great environmental struggles will be won or lost in the next ten years. Further, it states that achieving sustainability will demand practical and political commitment over an extended period and that the EU, as the largest trading bloc in the world, must exercise its responsibility and commit itself to that goal.

For industries and companies that are facing a rising tide of environmental legislation, it is essential that attempts are made to find out about and then positively address the legislative pressures which they are under. However, the Sixth Environmental Action Programme primarily focuses on the improved enforcement of existing legislation as a key objective rather than the adoption of new legislation. To some extent this should allow industry to take stock of the rapid increase in environmental legislation that has taken place in recent years and to focus on achieving compliance with existing legislation. Despite the stated objective to concentrate on the effective implementation of existing policy, there are many pieces of environmental legislation in the EU policy pipeline which are awaiting final adoption. Many of these measures have fundamental implications for business and it therefore remains essential to track forthcoming legislation.

Furthermore, the Sixth Environmental Action Programme reiterates the aspiration that environmental policy should be fully incorporated into all other European Union policies (sometimes known as 'mainstreaming'). Therefore, while it may become easier to track the development of policies which are explicitly environmental, it will become more difficult to monitor the development of environmental policy throughout the activities of the Commission as a whole. The European Environment Agency now collects data and monitors compliance throughout the European Union and disseminates information to all interested parties. It is being proactive in encouraging all firms (including smaller enterprises) to take environmental issues more seriously.

The strategic significance of the EU's views cannot be overstated. By taking a long-term, EU-wide perspective and accepting that industrial competitiveness is enhanced by tight environmental legislation, the policy framework within which all European organisations must participate will reflect these views. Some organisations, some regions and some nations will benefit. If the views of the EU are correct then the economic prospects of the European Union as a whole will benefit and the environment will certainly benefit. However, realising these benefits will not be automatic at the organisation level and strategic planning and proactive responses to the changing policy climate are imperative if success is to be secured. Information must be gathered, its implications assessed and the necessary action taken in a systematic and integrated way.

Tackling environmental problems always requires a concerted and cooperative effort. In the EU success will depend on the extent to which member states are politically committed to the environmental philosophy and the extent to which they are willing to cooperate. The balancing of the economic growth/environment trade-off is likely to determine the Europe-wide success of any policies but there also need to be concerted and cooperative political motivations. It can be argued that the attainment of an effective and concerted environmental policy in Europe will require political and economic union. However, since the EU and national governments legislate over environmental protection and police offenders, significant environmental improvement will only be attained with the cooperation and commitment of producers. There is, therefore, a need for firms to institute environmental management practices.

CORPORATE ENVIRONMENTAL MANAGEMENT STRATEGIES

Most companies have realised that environmental issues need to be addressed for a number of reasons, including consumer pressure, potential cost savings, legislation and ethics. Larger companies are in turn putting pressure on supply chains, insisting that their smaller suppliers also respond to environmental issues. There is, therefore, growing interest in the area of corporate environmental management. Environmental considerations are likely to be a source of quite profound changes in business practices. With this in mind, there are a number of important questions which organisations should ask themselves.

- Is the organisation meeting its existing environmental commitments?
- Is the organisation adhering to environmental legislation, and what will be the impact on it as environmental legislation becomes more stringent?
- Is concern for the environment integral to each of the organisation's operations?
- Do managers and workers see environmental improvement as a goal and in what ways are personnel being encouraged to be more involved?

- Does the organisation have the capacity to evaluate the environmental impact of its processes and products, including packaging and distribution channels?
- Are there new product opportunities which the organisation could exploit which would have less negative environmental impact?
- How vulnerable is the organisation to environmental changes such as climate change?
- What financial and organisational constraints are there which might prevent environmental improvement from taking place?
- How are the organisation's competitors placed in terms of environmental accountability, and can the environmental performance of the organisation be turned to a competitive advantage?
- Does the organisation have a systematic approach to management which can be used to integrate environmental issues?

The answers to these questions provide the organisation with the basis of a strategic plan for the environment. An environmental policy can be developed from these questions and it can be circulated to the organisation's personnel, suppliers and vendors and to the public. The environmental policy sets out the context for future action. There is no single model and the policy will reflect an organisation's structure, location, industrial sector and business culture. If such a document is published then it is important that it is adhered to, thereby providing an all-important environmental ethos around which the organisation must operate.

All aspects of an organisation's operations – from accounting and purchasing to product design, manufacture, sales, marketing, distribution and the use and disposal of the product – will have an impact on the environment and the environmental policy should reflect a recognition of this. The policy needs to be comprehensive and detailed but it should not contain statements or targets which the organisation cannot hope to achieve. This will do more harm than good if exposed. The content of different policies will vary and be influenced by the activities of the particular organisation. However, there are some general principles which can be applied to the content of the policy statement.

- Adopt and aim to apply the principles of 'sustainable development', which meet the needs of the present without compromising the abilities of future generations to meet their own needs.
- Strive to adopt the highest available environmental standards in all site locations and all countries, and meet or exceed all applicable regulations.
- Adopt a total 'cradle-to-grave' environmental assessment and accept responsibility for all products and services including the raw materials used and the disposal of the product after use.
- Aim to minimise the use of all materials, supplies and energy and wherever possible use renewable or recyclable materials and components.
- Minimise waste produced in all parts of the business – aim for waste-free processes and where waste is produced avoid the use of terminal waste treatment, dealing with it, as far as possible, at source.
- Render any unavoidable wastes harmless and dispose of them in a way which has the least impact on the environment.

■ Expect high environmental standards from all parties involved in the business, including suppliers, contractors and vendors and put pressure on these groups to improve their environmental performance in line with your own.

■ Be committed to improving relations with the local community and the public at large and where necessary introduce education and liaison programmes.

■ Adopt an environmentally sound transport strategy and assess the general infrastructure of the organisation.

■ Assess, on a continuous basis, the environmental impact of all operations and procedures through an environmental audit.

■ Assist in developing solutions to environmental problems and support the development of external environmental initiatives.

■ Preserve nature, protect ecological habitats and create conservation schemes.

■ Accept strict liability for environmental damage, not blaming others for environmental damage, accidents and incidents.

Environmental policies should identify key performance areas and form a sound basis for setting corporate objectives. They need to be detailed enough to demonstrate that the organisation's commitment goes beyond lip service. A clearly defined environmental policy should be implementable, practical and relate to the areas in which the organisation wishes to improve its environmental performance. In particular, when designing an environmental policy the organisation needs to think hard about how it is going to quantify its objectives and measure its environmental performance.

For a policy to be implemented personnel with special responsibilities for environmental performance will have to be found. Many organisations in Europe have discovered that the best way to achieve this, in the short run, is to appoint a main board environment director. This person will be there to champion the environment and will need some very important personal skills as well as legitimacy. Such legitimacy is often achieved by the publication of the organisation's environmental policy.

There are three very clear roles which an environmental director can take on:

■ **taking a strategic view** – promoting minimal environmental impact from products and processes and developing an integrated and comprehensive approach;

■ **raising the profile of the environment** – coordinating educational efforts within the organisation, developing partnerships with customers, other organisations (particularly suppliers), environmental pressure groups, legislators, the EU and national government.

■ **putting policy into practice** – establishing monitoring systems and environmental audits, establishing environmental improvement plans, involving all personnel and making them accountable and responsible for the environmental performance of their business, and taking anticipatory action which is central to good environmental performance.

The initial stage in the implementation of an environmental approach at organisation level must be for the organisation to establish exactly how well or how badly it is performing environmentally. Moxen and Strachan (1998) indicate that an increasingly common way of achieving this is to undertake an environmental audit – this is often the first step in 'greening' an organisation.

ENVIRONMENTAL AUDITING

The first **environmental audits** can be traced back to the USA where corporations adopted this methodology during the 1970s in response to their domestic liability laws. Such audits are now common among European businesses. Many banks and other financial institutions are insisting on companies undertaking environmental audits in order to reduce future environmental liabilities (Welford, 1998). Environmental audits are usually carried out by teams which include lawyers, economists, engineers, scientists and environmental generalists drawn from industry, government and consultancy.

Environmental auditing is a check both on the environmental performance of an organisation and on the performance of the management system (see below) which should be designed to bring about improvements in that performance. In the first instance the organisation needs to establish a baseline against which to measure future audits, commonly referred to as the **environmental review**. The environmental review follows many of the procedures of an audit, as laid out below. However, strictly speaking, an audit measures the attainment or non-attainment of some target objectives, whereas the environmental review simply provides an initial assessment of the environmental performance of the organisation.

The environmental audit consists of a regular, independent, systematic, documented and objective evaluation of the environmental performance of an organisation. It should measure how well organisations, management and equipment are performing with the aim of helping management to safeguard the environment. It also provides management information which can be used in the control of environmental practices and in assessing compliance with organisation policies, which include meeting regulatory requirements. It should be stressed, however, that within the task of environmental management there is a role for everyone in the organisation.

The overall aim of environmental auditing is to help safeguard the environment and minimise the risks to human health. Although auditing alone cannot achieve that, it is a powerful managerial tool. The key objectives of the environmental audit are:

- to determine the extent to which environmental management systems in an organisation are performing adequately;
- to verify compliance with local, national and European environmental and health and safety legislation;
- to verify compliance with an organisation's own stated corporate policy;
- to develop and promulgate internal procedures needed to achieve the organisation's environmental objectives;
- to minimise human exposure to risks from the environment and ensure adequate health and safety provision;
- to identify and assess risk resulting from environmental failure;
- to assess the impact on the local environment of a particular plant or process by means of air, water and soil sampling;
- to advise an organisation on environmental improvements it can make.

There are a number of benefits to organisations in undertaking an environmental audit. These include assurances that legislation is being adhered to and the consequent prevention of fines and litigation, an improved public image which can be

Figure 18.3 The European EMAS cycle

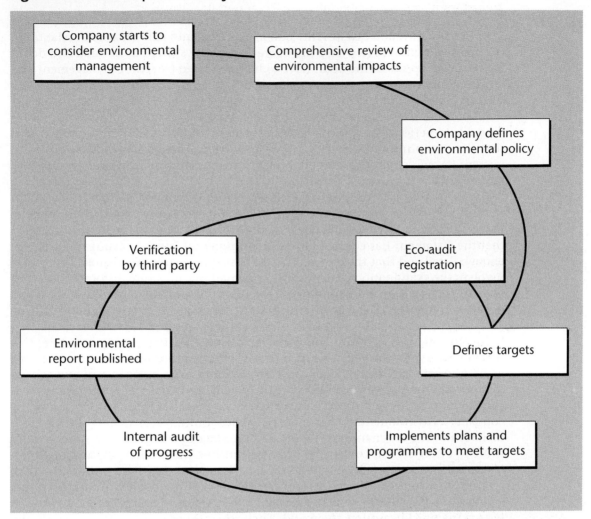

- put into place plans and systems to achieve these targets and include provisions for their constant monitoring;
- periodically audit to assess progress;
- report the audit findings to the public and have these findings verified by a third party;
- set new targets for further progress and repeat the procedure.

There is a need to establish systems based on the environmental review which:

- assess and manage the environmental impact of activities;
- manage the use of energy, raw materials and water;
- minimise waste;
- consider the selection and design of products and processes;
- prevent accidents;

■ include staff in consultation and provide motivation and training;

■ inform and involve the public.

Essentially the audit assesses this system and evaluates performance in relation to the environmental review and the operation of the system as defined and documented. The results of the audit have to be considered by senior management and any necessary revisions to the company policy, objectives, targets, action plans and systems made.

All of these steps can be internal to the company if there is sufficient expertise available to perform the various tasks adequately. Indeed the intention of EMAS is that the discipline of having to follow these steps should help the company to manage its own environmental performance better. However, there are also important external aspects to the scheme.

EMAS requires that an external environmental statement is prepared based on the findings of the audit or initial review. Validation of this statement must be made by external accredited environmental verifiers. The validation will confirm that the statement has covered all the environmental issues relevant to the site in enough detail and that the information presented is reliable. The validation process involves the examination of relevant documentation, including information about the site, its activities, a description of the environmental management system and details and findings of the environmental review or audit. This would normally be followed by an inspection visit to the site and preparation of a verifier's report.

In order to join EMAS a company has to be able to demonstrate that this sequence of events has taken place and that sensible targets have been set towards which the company should make progress. The approved independent and accredited environmental verifier (AEV) will have checked that the audit process was carried out properly and that the environmental report is a true and fair view of the company's environmental performance. Application can subsequently be made for inclusion in the eco-management and audit register of companies. In order to continue to be registered, companies have to continue the EMAS cycle and maintain commitment to improving environmental performance. Any lapse will result in the removal of a company's name from the register. EMAS now has an international equivalent – ISO 14001 – which, although not identical to EMAS, is a standard that is growing quickly around the world. The principles of ISO 14001 are largely the same as EMAS but it contains no requirement for public reporting.

THE ISO 14000 SERIES

The International Organisation for Standardisation (ISO) has developed a series of 'Global Green Standards' and these are summarised in Figure 18.4. The first component of the ISO 14000 series was published in 1996. When compared to other international standards developed by ISO, ISO 14001 was published relatively quickly. This represents the influence that the British Standards BS 7750 environmental management system and the European Council of Ministers' eco-management and audit scheme (EMAS) Regulation had on its development, and also that of the quality management system ISO 9001. Annex B of the ISO 14001 Specification Document (BSI 1996) describes the links between ISO 14001 and ISO 9001. Organisations that have ISO 9001 in place often use this as a basis to implement ISO 14001.

Figure 18.4 The structure of the ISO 14000 series

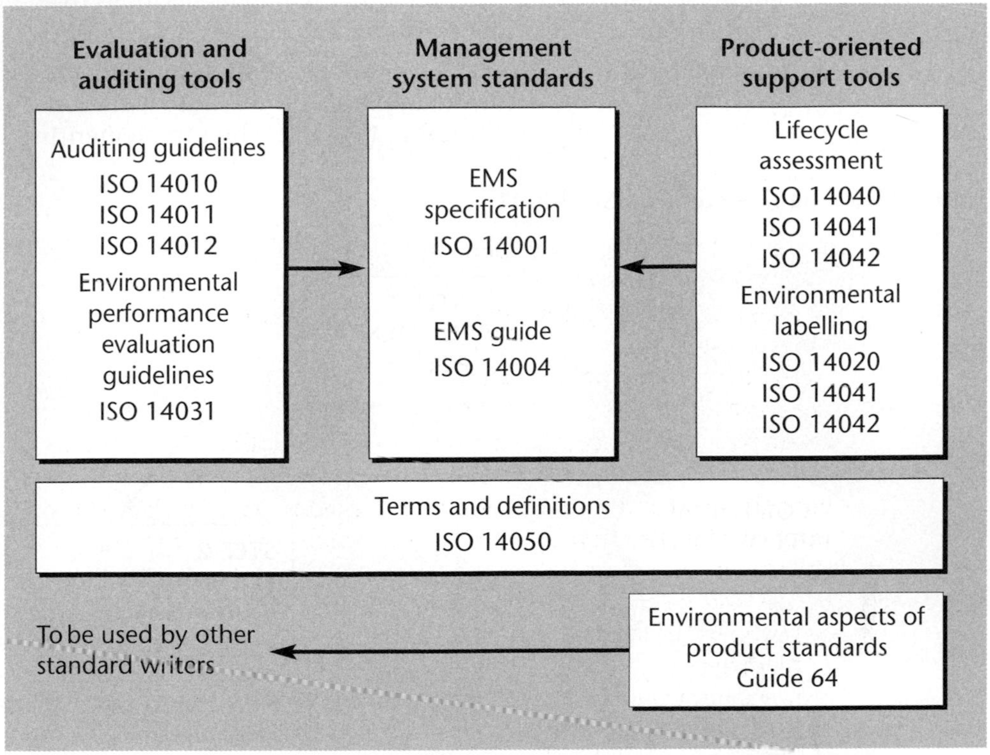

Evaluation and auditing tools	Management system standards	Product-oriented support tools
Auditing guidelines ISO 14010 ISO 14011 ISO 14012 Environmental performance evaluation guidelines ISO 14031	EMS specification ISO 14001 EMS guide ISO 14004	Lifecycle assessment ISO 14040 ISO 14041 ISO 14042 Environmental labelling ISO 14020 ISO 14041 ISO 14042

Terms and definitions
ISO 14050

To be used by other standard writers ← Environmental aspects of product standards Guide 64

Source: BSI British Standards (1996) *Environmental Management Systems Handbook: A Guide to the BS EN ISO 14000 series*, London: BSI.

ISO 14001 provides a blueprint for the development of an environmental management system, with its overall aim being to support environmental protection and prevention of pollution in harmony with socio-economic needs. Those organisations that wish to demonstrate continual improvements in environmental performance are recommended to certify their environmental management systems to ISO 14001. ISO 14001 consists of five core components, with Strachan *et al.* (2003) noting that these represent the main steps to implementing this strategic environmental management system.

1 **The environmental policy** – senior management must produce an environmental policy statement. This needs to set out an organisation's intentions in relation to its environmental aspects and must contain a commitment to continual improvement, the prevention of pollution and compliance with relevant environmental legislation. The policy statement must be appropriate for the nature, scale and environmental aspects of the organisation, set a framework for objectives and targets, be documented and be made available to the general public.

2 **Planning** – an organisation must then set itself appropriate objectives and targets in relation to the environmental policy and devise an appropriate action plan to meet them. During the planning stage an organisation must identify what ISO 14001 refers to as 'environmental aspects', with this defined as being elements of an organisation's activities, products or services that can interact with the environment. An organisation is recommended to undertake an environmental

review to establish its aspects, with other issues included in the planning component of ISO 14001 being legal and other requirements, objectives and targets and
the environmental management programme.

3 **Implementation and operation** – an organisation must then establish the various elements necessary for the implementation and operation of the plan. ISO
14001 offers a blueprint for doing this and when implementing ISO 14001 an

Figure 18.5 The five steps of ISO 14001

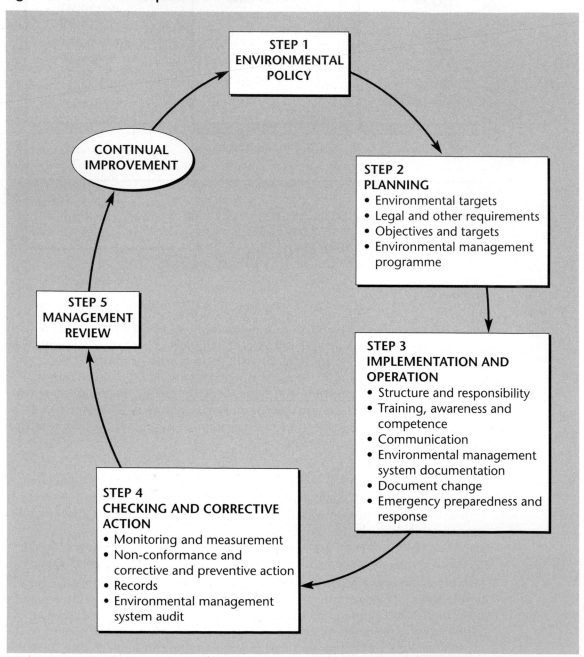

organisation must consider the following issues – structure and operation; training, awareness and competence; documentation and control; operational control; and emergency preparedness and response.

4 **Checking and corrective action** – having implemented the management system, an organisation must then check to ensure that it has been successful in meeting its environmental objectives and targets. If these have not been met then corrective action is needed. The management system must be audited periodically.

5 **The management review** – senior management must periodically review the management system to ensure its continuing effectiveness and suitability. Changes must be made to reflect the changing context of the organisation and the commitment to continual improvement made in the environmental policy statement.

The components of ISO 14001 and their sub-elements are brought together and are shown as a model in Figure 18.5. Since the launch of ISO 14001 approximately 20,000 companies around the world have implemented the initiative, with another reported 80,000 now in the process of doing so. Those companies which have implemented ISO 14001 have done so for a number of reasons. Some of the external drivers and benefits are third party assurance and recognition, market access, regulatory relief, improved investor confidence and enhanced public image and community relations. The internal drivers and benefits are reduced incidents and liability, cost savings and improved efficiency and improved business performance. However, many commentators, such as Strachan *et al.* (2003), have voiced their concerns over the difficulty and cost of introducing ISO 14001 and have indicated that ISO 14001 requirements are too sophisticated and do not add value in small and medium-sized enterprises.

PRODUCT STEWARDSHIP AND ECO-LABELLING

Product design managers are increasingly examining ways in which the total life cycle of a product can be managed to ensure that potential environmental damage is minimised. In other words they are looking to create an enclosed resource loop where waste is recycled, and even the product itself is recycled at the end of its use. Natural ecosystems operate in a similar fashion so that the waste from one process feeds into another as a nutrient. Traditional environmentally damaging production and consumption work more in a linear way, such that inputs and outputs are not connected and possible environmental improvements are missed. One alternative is cradle-to-grave management where organisations have to recognise their wider responsibility and manage the entire life cycle of their products.

Many organisations are recognising their responsibility in this area in terms of what has been termed 'product stewardship'. This involves:

- examining the design of a product and considering how efficient it is;
- considering the energy sources, raw materials and components used in the product and deciding if they can be replaced by alternatives which are more environmentally friendly;
- examining the production process itself and considering whether a more energy-efficient and less polluting process innovation might be found;
- re-examining the disposal of the product and the waste from its production in terms of recycling and returning the used materials to the production cycle after use;

■ reconsidering the after-sales service and packaging of the product and ensuring that adequate information is provided for its safe and energy-efficient use and environmentally friendly disposal of waste caused by consumption of the product.

It is relatively easy for organisations to target their internal systems and make changes to improve the environment. The part of cradle-to-grave management probably hardest to achieve is the return of materials from the consumer-waste stream. For example, only 2 per cent of consumer-used plastic is recycled in the EU because of a lack of an effective collection infrastructure combined with under-developed markets for recycled plastics. One solution is for companies to take action and to construct their own recycling infrastructure. Many environmentalists would like to see the reintroduction of deposits on glass bottles for example.

Over time, eco-labelling schemes have been devised in a number of countries in an attempt to promote the use of production methods which are less harmful to the environment. The first such scheme was introduced in the Federal Republic of Germany in 1978. Canada, Japan and Norway established their own schemes in 1989. The schemes were also introduced to prevent spurious environmental claims. Germany's Blue Angel eco-labelling scheme is probably the world's best established programme. Launched in 1978 by the German government, it now has almost 4000 products carrying the label. The organisers of the scheme claim that 80 per cent of German households are aware of the scheme and that it receives widespread support from manufacturers. Like the EU scheme, the label is not restricted to domestic-made goods. The Japanese multinational Konica was the first company to win a Blue Angel label for use on a photocopier for example. Many firms are aware that they cannot be without the Blue Angel award because the public sector and many large German companies will make every attempt to buy only products which carry the label.

The objectives of the EU's eco-labelling Regulation, agreed at the end of 1991, are to promote products with a reduced environmental impact during their entire life cycles and to provide better information to consumers on the environmental impacts of products. These must not be achieved at the expense of compromising the product or workers' safety, or significantly affecting the properties which make the product fit for use. The EU scheme is designed to reduce confusion by providing an authoritative and independent label to identify those goods with the lowest environmental impact in a particular product group. That is not to suggest that those products are environmentally benign, simply that their environmental performance is superior to products in the same group which do not have a label. The scheme should also encourage the production and sale of more environmentally responsible products and so alleviate the impact of consumption on the environment.

The label should affect all the businesses along a supply chain, even if some suppliers cannot use the label themselves. This is because suppliers will have to provide detailed information about their own components and their manufacturing process in order that the suppliers of the end product can apply to use the eco-label, on the basis of a life cycle assessment. Thus, in time, the label may become a minimum standard specified by an increasing number of buyers who practise green procurement policies.

All products, excluding food, drink and pharmaceuticals, are potentially eligible for an eco-label if they meet these objectives and are in conformity with the EU's health, safety and environmental requirements. Products comprising substances or preparations classified as 'dangerous' under EU legislation will also be barred from receiving an eco-label, along with any product manufactured by a process likely to cause significant direct harm to humans or the environment.

The EU scheme, issued as a Regulation, applies directly to all member states and is EU-wide. It is a voluntary scheme and self-financing. It assesses individual products and their manufacturing processes so that a multiproduct organisation will have to make multiple applications if it wants all of its products to have eco-labels. The criteria for the award of an eco-label are ever tightening, so that on application for the renewal of an eco-label producers cannot assume that just because their environmental performance has remained unchanged it will be awarded the label again.

Judgement of the products must be made on the basis of a cradle-to-grave analysis or life cycle assessment (LCA). The assessment matrix in Exhibit 18.7 must be used in setting criteria for the award of an eco-label. This will require account to be taken, where relevant, of a product group's soil, water, air and noise pollution impacts, waste generation, energy and resource consumption and effects on ecosystems. These impacts must be assessed in the preproduction, production, distribution, use and disposal stages. The criteria established for the award of an eco-label within a product group must be precise, clear and objective so that they can be applied consistently by the national bodies which award the eco-labels.

National competent bodies, which are independent and neutral, award eco-labels for products. They are made up of representatives from industry, government, environmental pressure groups and consumer groups and the body has to reflect the full range of social interests. These bodies act as a kind of jury assessing the environmental performance of the product by reference to the agreed general principles and specific environmental criteria for each product group.

Exhibit 18.7 EU eco-labelling scheme indicative assessment matrix

Environmental fields	Product life cycle				
	Preproduction	Production	Distribution	Utilisation	Disposal
Waste relevance					
Soil pollution and degradation					
Water contamination					
Air contamination					
Noise					
Consumption of energy					
Consumption of natural resources					
Effects on ecosystems					

The use of an eco-label is not necessarily open to any product. The first step is to get a particular product group accepted as suitable for the award of a label. It may be the case that a particularly polluting group of products (e.g. cars) will not be open to such an award. Requests for the establishment of new product groups may come from consumers or industry itself and are addressed to the competent body in the member state. The competent body, if it so wishes, can ask the Commission to submit a proposal to its regulatory committee. In any event the Commission will consult with interest groups and take advice from a range of sources. If it is decided that a particular product group will be open to the award of an eco-label then this will be announced in the *Official Journal of the European Communities*. This process is outlined in Figure 18.6.

Following applications from manufacturers or importers of a particular product for the award of an eco-label, the national competent body has to notify the Commission of its decision relating to the award of an eco-label enclosing full and summary results of the assessment. The Commission will then notify other member states and they usually have 30 days to make reasoned objections to the recommendations. If there are no objections, the award proceeds and a contract to use the label for a specified period is drawn up. Lists of products able to use the eco-label are published. In the case of any objections and disagreement, the Commission, acting through its advisory or regulatory body of national experts, will make the final decision. This procedure is summarised in Figure 18.7. Companies applying for an eco-label have to pay a fee to cover administration costs and a fee is also charged for the use of the label if awarded. Companies which succeed with their applications can only use the eco-label in advertising the specific products for which it was awarded.

Figure 18.6 Selection of new product groups

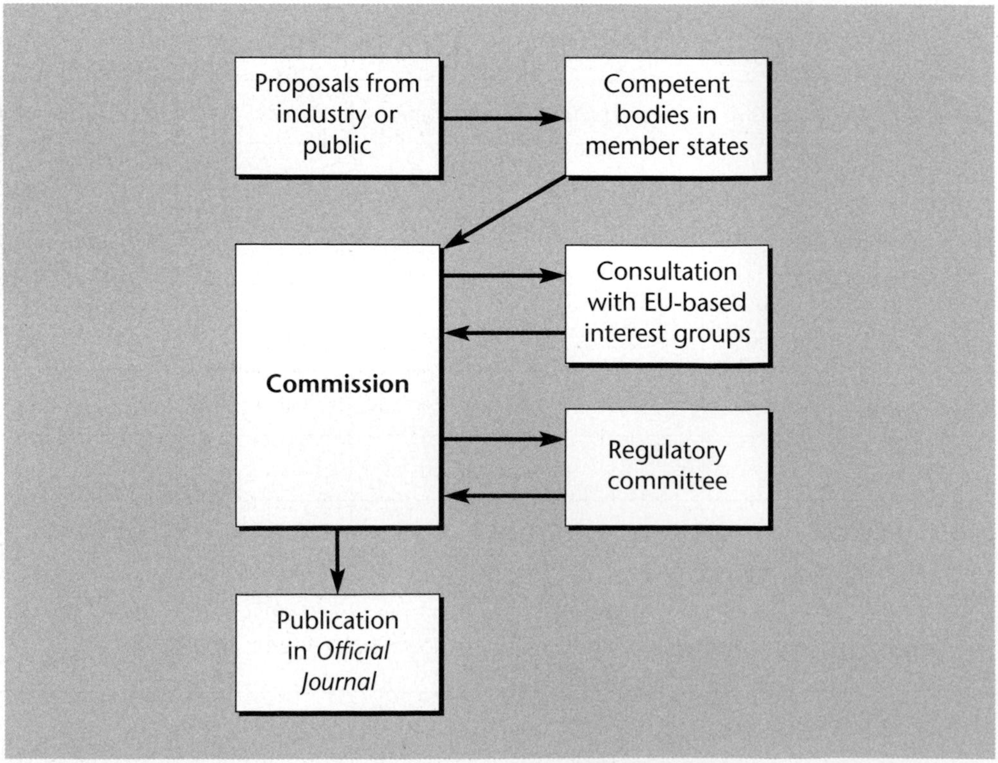

Figure 18.7 Award of an eco-label to individual products

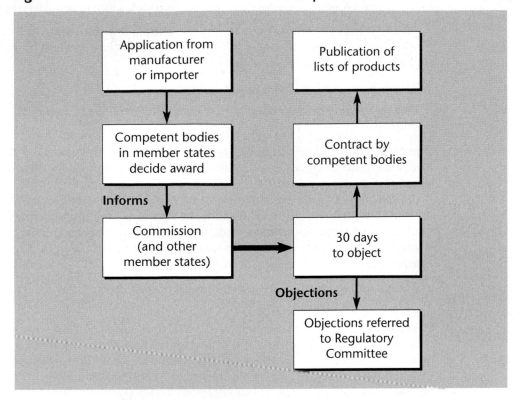

GREEN ISSUES AND FUTURE DEVELOPMENTS

The British government had a Kyoto commitment to reduce greenhouse gas emissions by 12.5 per cent on 1990 levels between 2008 and 2012. It was reported in the *Guardian* newspaper (27 March 2007) that while the government was on track to meet this goal, it would be more difficult to meet a separate domestic pledge to cut CO_2 by 20 per cent by 2010. The UK was reported to be the first country to introduce a national scheme to trade greenhouse gas emissions and it was pushing for a linked-up global market. Launched in 2002 the UK's carbon trading system aimed to reduce emissions by rewarding companies that introduced new 'greener' technology.

Meanwhile, since the turn of the century newspapers and magazines have been littered with reports of organisations polishing up their environmental credentials (Exhibit 18.1 and Exhibit 18.2). Annual reports are also being used to confirm companies' corporate social responsibility policies (Exhibit 18.3). In its Annual Report for 2005, the energy company International Power reported that

> *'as with any large industrial process, the environmental impact arising from electricity generation is now subject to international – as well as national, regional and local – scrutiny and regulation. Our continuing obligation is to manage our growing portfolio of assets so as to reduce the environmental impact of our activities.'*

The report also states that the company stakeholders, employees, shareholders, suppliers, regulators and host communities expected the company to continue to be known throughout the world as a responsible, efficient and successful company.

However, the term 'green' has been questioned generally because it has been overused and 'open to use for our own purposes' (*Sunday Times*, 21 January 2007):

'It seems that everything must still be green, from organic cotton baby clothes from Green Baby, to funerals where the deceased is buried in woodland to the cheeping of birdsong in a biodegradeable coffin.'

This article, by Rachel Johnson, continues:

'yes, everything is either green or low carbon or low impact, and if it's not green it's organic.'

She argues that changes in policy are not driven solely by legitimate anxiety about the planet, the species or our children's children but also by capturing market share. Wal-Mart, Marks & Spencer and Tesco have all taken initiatives to be 'green', while Asda has been reported as wanting to be Britain's greenest grocer. Wal-Mart has moved to switch the entire group to using renewable energy, to achieve zero waste and to sell sustainable products. Asda has been cutting the use of road transport and switching to rail transport, buying local produce and aims to recycle or reuse all its waste by 2010. However, Friends of the Earth think that

'there is still a long way to go before supermarkets can call themselves green companies'   (*Sunday Times*, 21 January 2007)

Meanwhile, oil companies such as ExxonMobil and Shell have been criticised by trade unions and environmental campaigners because of their huge profits while being two of the biggest carbon emitters in the world. Exxon's net income in 2006 was reported to be the largest ever recorded in US corporate history. The chairman of Shell UK , in an article in *Management Today* (February 2007) argued that for many years Shell had advocated using the power of markets to tackle climate change. This process should include businesses providing input into the policy for carbon mitigation, innovation in product portfolios and the use of renewable sources of energy. At the same time within the company there should be a promotion of the desire of employees to see their company respond to the changing needs of society, providing people with an opportunity to deploy their creative professional skills and 'sticking to market incentives that will drive the innovation and change needed in the global energy system. With the right commercial framework and the right frame of mind, business can deliver.'

It can be argued that environmental damage is inherent in the structures of modern societies because of rates of consumption. Globally developing countries are moving in the same direction so that, for example, China's economy is booming and its growth is in a dirty, polluting fashion. However it is the people in developed countries who are encouraging this rapid growth by demanding cheap manufactured goods. The Kyoto Protocol, signed in 1997, officially came into force on 16 February 2005 following ratification by more than 55 countries that together produce more than 55 per cent of the world's greenhouse gas (GHG) emissions. Under the Protocol, signatory countries have to reduce their emissions of GHG by an average of 5.2 per cent from their 1990 level by 2012.

'Developing countries such as China and India have no constraining obligation with respect to the Protocol. The absence of specific requirements for these developing countries that account for an increasing proportion of global GHG emissions has fuelled opposition to and criticism of the Kyoto Protocol, especially in the US.'   (Boiral, 2006)

While controversy surrounding the Protocol and its complexity have led to delays and long negotiations in framing the international measures to be applied, the emergence and strengthening of international and local mechanisms for GHG reduction has encouraged organisations to consider environmental issues seriously. Kyoto allowed signatory countries to trade emission credits between themselves. Since January 2005 the European GHG trading scheme has allowed companies to buy or sell emissions credits so that large industrial emitters that have succeeded in reducing their emissions below quota levels can sell such permits and take advantage of the trading system, while those who have exceeded their quotas will have to buy GHG emissions permits. Emission credits can also be earned by countries and companies investing in other industrial countries and in developing countries to reduce GHG emissions. Large polluting companies can earn emission credits by investing in reforestation schemes – that is, by the use of 'carbon sinks'.

The economic and strategic impact of climate change will depend on capital asset management, the global competitiveness of countries, the anticipation of institutional change stemming from the Kyoto Protocol and the ability of the market to take advantage of the emergence of new opportunities related to climate change policies (Hoffman, 2002 and 2005). Hoffman argues that companies can benefit from voluntary GHG reductions through:

- operational improvement;
- anticipating and influencing climate change regulations;
- accessing new sources of capital;
- improving risk management;
- elevating corporate reputation;
- identifying new market opportunities;
- enhancing human resource management.

There continue to be arguments between the view that environmental actions are a cost source for organisations and the view that benefits can arise from green initiatives. Economic issues reflect the financial risks of environmental actions against market opportunities and competitive advantage. Political issues arise from regulations, subsidies and tax changes, while social issues arise from organisational image, employee views and external pressures. Scientific and technical issues arise from innovation opportunities, research and development and data on green issues. Environmental issues have been used as a criteria for evaluating performance in financial markets and assessing good governance.

'Owing to the growing number of studies demonstrating the gravity of global warming and calling for the adoption of a precautionary principle, the decrease in the scientific uncertainties often raised by those who oppose the Kyoto Protocol means that this pressure is all the more likely to increase.' (Boiral, 2006)

SUMMARY

■ Governments will increasingly seek to make the polluter pay and one consequence of this is that some industries and products may simply disappear. Ultimately, however, the success of environmental improvement will be determined largely by the responsiveness of business.

■ That is not to suggest that legislation is a bad thing. Indeed it can act as the impetus to an organisation thinking about instituting proper environmental management. In addition, increasing legislation and government expenditure to increase environmentally related expenditure might be seen as a win–win situation. It stimulates the economy without leading to the pollution problems often associated with growth. Moreover, a shift in expenditure from the military to promoting security on the environmental front is possible.

■ The environmental revolution has been gathering momentum and speed since the 1960s and developed rapidly in the 1980s and 1990s. Environmental considerations are likely to form an integral part of commercial normality and, indeed, competitiveness in the twenty-first century. Definitions of business success are likely to include the assumption of a zero impact on the environment at the very least.

■ A competitive advantage can be achieved not merely by keeping abreast of environmental developments but also by initiating change within an organisation and responding with new environmentally friendly products and production processes.

■ Indeed growing consumer awareness and environmental pressure groups are likely to ensure that organisations that do not take action on the environmental front will lose market share and, with increased competition, environmental management will provide organisations with a competitive edge.

Review and discussion questions

1 *In general, how can an organisation turn an expensive environmental management policy into a competitive advantage?*

2 *How would economic theory suggest that a pollution problem is tackled?*

3 *Is a sustainable development model of economic development possible?*

4 *In what ways does European integration help to control pollution? What sorts of steps are being taken in the EU?*

5 *How can industry be encouraged to institute environmental management systems?*

6 *How is the adoption of the Kyoto Protocol influencing the adoption of green policies in organisations?*

The Body Shop International

Background

The Body Shop was founded in March 1976 when Anita Roddick opened her first shop in Brighton. Before 1976, working for the United Nations, she had travelled around the world and met people from a number of different cultures. Observing how people treated their skin and hair, she learned that certain things cleansed, polished and protected the skin without having to be formulated into a cream or shampoo. When she started The Body Shop, Anita Roddick aimed to utilise these raw ingredients such as plants, herbs and roots in products which would be acceptable to consumers. Only six years later she was described by the International Chamber of Commerce as 'the inventor of sustainable retailing' (Williams and Goliike, 1982).

The first shop was basic and at first sold only 15 lines. They were packed in different sizes to fill up the shelves and to give the customer an opportunity to try a product without buying a large bottle. A refill service operated which allowed customers to refill their empty bottles instead of throwing them away. Although this was clearly an environmentally friendly strategy, it was also initially implemented to cut down the costs of packaging.

Today, The Body Shop's principal activities are to formulate and retail products which are primarily associated with cleansing, polishing and protecting the skin and hair. The underlying aims are to conduct that business ethically, with a minimum of hype, and to promote health rather than glamour. Naturally based, close-to-source ingredients are used wherever possible and ingredients and final products are not tested on animals (Wheeler, 1992). Packaging is kept to a minimum and refill services are offered in all shops. Packaging, in the form of plastic bottles, can be returned to shops and is recycled into accessories.

The Body Shop's full range now contains over 300 products. The organisation trades in over 40 countries and employs around 6000 people, either directly or in franchises. Senior management in the organisation is committed to the encouragement of positive change. The aim is to establish a new work ethic that will enable business to thrive without causing adverse damage to the environment, at both the local and global level. There is an emphasis placed on not selling products which have an adverse effect on sustainability, i.e. those which consume a disproportionate amount of energy during manufacture or disposal, generate excessive wastes, use ingredients from threatened habitats, which are obtained by cruelty, or which adversely affect other countries, especially the developing countries.

Environmental strategies are at the centre of The Body Shop's approach to business. Moreover, the organisation has been so successful in raising the profile of the environment both within and external to the business that it is endlessly cited as being the leading business, worldwide, in this field. Even though the organisation itself would argue that there is still more to be achieved, this case study examines the practices and systems which have enabled The Body Shop to reach this leading position.

Commitment and policy

One of the most apparent characteristics of The Body Shop is its commitment to environmental and social excellence. This is often attributed to Anita Roddick herself. While many of the principles are hers, the truth is that commitment exists not only at board level but throughout the whole organisation. Everybody is encouraged to contribute to environmental improvement. The ultimate aim of The Body Shop is to include environmental issues in every area of its operations but, at the same time, the organisation rejects environmental opportunism which has often paralleled the green marketing strategies of more cynical firms.

At first, The Body Shop did not commit itself to a formal strategy or programme of environmental improvements. Action was taken when environmental problems were identified. This approach tended to increase employee involvement and reduce bureaucracy. However, with the continued growth of the organisation, it has been necessary to move to a more systematic approach, setting targets and planning for environmental improvement.

The overriding factor for The Body Shop is the perception of a moral obligation to drive towards sustainability in business (Roddick, 1991). It is impossible to measure progress towards this ideal without a detailed policy statement followed by a systematic process of data gathering and public reporting. Hence, auditing activities are considered absolutely essential to the company's long-term

▶

mission to become a truly sustainable operation. In other words, it aims to replace as many of the planet's resources as are utilised. That fundamental aim translates into a wish to play a full part in handing on a safer and more equitable world to future generations. The fundamental basis of this goal is a commitment to the broader concept of sustainable development. It is the strong belief of The Body Shop that the moral burden of achieving sustainability in business should become the principal driving force behind business in the future.

Social and environmental auditing

The only real way to achieve environmental improvement is to take a systematic approach to achieving its aims through an appropriate management structure and periodically to assess or audit progress, measuring the extent to which targets and basic objectives are being met. For that reason social and environmental auditing has a very high profile at The Body Shop. It involves all staff and managers in continuous data collection, frequent reviews of priorities and targets (on a department-by-department basis) and an annual process of public reporting of results.

In parallel with the necessity for environmental auditing, there is a need to put in place management systems capable of achieving targets and adhering to environmental policy. The Body Shop maintains a very decentralised system of corporate environmental management. A corporate team of social and environmental audit specialists acts as a central resource for networks of environmental 'advisers' and coordinators in headquarters departments, subsidiaries, retail outlets and international markets. Advisers and coordinators are usually part-time, fulfilling their role in social and environmental communications and auditing alongside normal duties.

The Body Shop carries out its environmental auditing in line with the EU eco-management and audit scheme, publishing social, environmental and fair trade reports which lay out its annual report to the public on its environmental and social performance.

In 1996 The Body Shop carried out and published its first full social audit of its activities. The approach was to assess the environmental, social and animal protection performance of the company, by reference to the opinions and perceptions of a range of stakeholders. This move widened the environmental auditing methodology previously adopted by The Body Shop and included a range of social issues. This is fully consistent with the moves towards incorporating wider aspects of sustainable development into the organisation and is now being replicated by a number of other companies. Although there have been many changes at The Body Shop in terms of reorganisation, social and environmental issues continue to differentiate the company from many of its competitors, and are often seen as a source of competitive advantage.

FURTHER READING

Adams, W M (2001) *Green Development: Environmental and Sustainability in the South,* Routledge.
A discussion of sustainable development.

Boiral, O (2006) 'Global warming: should companies adopt a proactive strategy?', *Long Range Planning,* 39.
A global approach to anticipating the possible impact of global warming.

Claus-Henrich, D and Ergenzinger, R (2005) 'Enabling sustainable management through a new multidisciplinary concept of customer satisfaction', *European Journal of Marketing,* 39.
Sustainable development and customer satisfaction.

Kotler, P and Lee, N (2004) *Corporate Social Responsibility: Doing the Most Good for Your Company and Your Cause,* New York: John Wiley & Sons
Corporate social responsibility and environmental management.

Luo, X and Bhattacharya, C B (2006) 'Corporate social responsibility, customer satisfaction, and market value', *Journal of Marketing,* American Marketing Association, 70, October.
Corporate social responsibility and market value – the contribution of CSR to the 'bottom line'.

WEBSITES

http://www.corporateresponsibilitygroup.com/what/core.htm
This is the website of the Corporate Responsibility Group. It includes 50 of the UK's leading companies which are committed to a responsible approach to business practice.

http://www.emas.org.uk
This is the website of the UK EMAS body providing information about EMAS.

http://www.europa.eu.int
This is the website of the European Union with information about the EU's sustainable development strategy.

http://www.iso.ch
This is the website of the International Organisation for Standardisation giving information about the ISO 14000 series.

http://www.sustainable-development.gov.uk
This is the website of the UK Government with information about the UK Government's sustainable development strategy.

http//www.foe.org
Friends of the Earth website.

http//www.greenpeace.org
Greenpeace website.

CHAPTER 19

Globalisation and multinational management

KATE PRESCOTT AND DAVID EDELSHAIN

Outcomes

Having read this chapter, you will be able to:

■ understand the differences between the management of business operations in a domestic setting and in a multinational and global setting;

■ explain the problems faced by organisations in foreign markets;

■ analyse the management strategies which enable foreign organisations to maximise their advantages in foreign markets;

■ compare the wide range of management practices in multinational organisations;

■ understand the complex task of management in a global economy.

MULTINATIONAL MANAGEMENT

An obvious question to ask in relation to multinational management is: How does it differ from management of business operations in a domestic setting? There are four key issues which must be addressed to provide an answer:

■ Understanding and reacting to change in the global environment.

■ Cross-cultural management.

■ Managing flexibly and creatively in today's dynamic business setting.

■ Drawing on the knowledge and skills of the worldwide management arena in order to develop 'best practice'.

As well as the consideration of these four factors in providing an understanding of the complex task of multinational management, one of the most significant changes in international business in recent years has been the rise in the incidence of international activity by small enterprises. Along with discussion of the challenges to multinational enterprises (MNEs), the managerial demands on small and medium-sized enterprises (SMEs) need also to be considered.

The process of international management does not take place in a vacuum – success depends on adapting to the diverse environments in which businesses operate. For managers this is a highly complex task, not least because human beings, by their very nature, often feel uncomfortable or dislocated when operating outside their own cultural domain.

Setting a context

The challenge of international management is fitting strategic development to a continually evolving marketplace. Before embarking on a discussion of what this means in practice, it is useful to establish some parameters and terminology which explain different stages of development and current trends in the strategic activities of international operators.

There are four basic strategies which firms may employ to enter and compete in the foreign market. The choice of type depends critically on the extent to which firms wish to focus on cost reduction or local responsiveness. The choice must also depend on the linkages between the different constituent businesses and products that a firm may have because many international firms are multibusiness and multiproduct (see Calori *et al.*, 2000). The four strategic options are **international** strategy, **multidomestic** strategy, **global** strategy and **transnational** strategy.

International strategy

Here firms transfer skills and advantages, usually developed domestically, to overseas markets where there is the potential to secure differential advantage. Product development tends to be centralised and tight control and coordination come from the centre. In foreign markets, firms typically establish sales and marketing activities, and sometimes production.

This strategy is useful where firms are attempting to exploit their core competence internationally without pressures for local responsiveness and cost reduction, an example being McDonald's. For them the focus is on exploiting their brand and image. Customisation of products is less important (although elements of the product range are adapted from market to market) and duplication of business in different centres is not damaging to profitability as economies of scale are not critical to success.

Multidomestic strategy

With a multidomestic strategy the focus is on maximising local responsiveness. Unlike international firms these organisations customise both their product and marketing strategy extensively to suit the local needs of the market. This usually means not only local production and sales and marketing, but also local product development and R&D centres designed to support market-specific rather than international activity. A structure of this type typically gives rise to a high cost base, although this can be compensated for by adding value to local products through targeted differentiation and marketing.

A major problem facing multidomestic firms is control. With different divisions pursuing their own objectives, this can mean the creation of decentralised federations through which it is difficult to transfer skills and information.

Global strategy

A global strategy is one in which firms exploit experience-curve effects and economies of scale. Production, marketing and product development activities are concentrated in a smaller number of advantageous locations (e.g. low-cost production centres or regionally based marketing centres). The extent of customisation tends to be limited as this raises costs through duplication. Instead firms exploit cost advantages, often competing aggressively on price.

This strategy is inappropriate where the demands for local responsiveness are high. Today, this option is therefore only really available to firms where there is an option to develop a common worldwide product, often only the preserve of industrial goods companies. For many consumer goods companies there remains continued pressure to adapt to local market conditions, customising products and strategies.

Transnational strategy

For two decades now the highly competitive nature of world markets has meant that firms have been exploring strategies which allow them to reap the benefits of both cost minimisation and local responsiveness and to exploit competences which are developed in all business centres worldwide (Hedlund, 1986). While this is obviously the ideal it is far from a straightforward approach to international development – rationalising the demands for cost minimisation (which dictate more centralised business operations and larger-scale operating units) with those for local responsiveness (which dictate customisation and duplication) is a highly complex task and one which demands a high level of flexibility.

The only way of achieving such a complex mix is to split businesses into a series of constituent functions which are variously centralised and decentralised. For example, a firm may choose to concentrate its R&D and production operations in a small number of regional sites (maybe one in the Americas, one in Europe and one in Asia Pacific) while at the same time dispersing sales and marketing activity to each target market to ensure maximum local responsiveness.

Some of the first moves made in this direction were by the Japanese in the early 1980s. Multinational giants such as Honda and Canon fostered the idea of the four-headquarters system. This involved establishing their major regional research, production and marketing centres in the three main areas of the global triad (America, Europe and Asia Pacific), each responsible for adapting business to regional needs. These were then supported by an all-embracing corporate headquarters which coordinated the transfer of competences and skills between regions as well as establishing global policy and corporate identity. Within each region, local adaptation is also made possible by the establishment of market-based sales and marketing centres. Today there is evidence of transnational strategy (or at least elements of such an approach) across a wide range of producers including Nestlé, Unilever, Caterpillar and Ford.

These four different approaches to international expansion incorporate a number of key issues which will be revisited later in the chapter:

- managing the diversity of global regions and markets;
- selecting appropriate strategies which take into consideration market and product characteristics (these include market entry strategies as well as those concerned with internalisation versus externalisation of business operations);
- centralisation versus decentralisation and standardisation versus adaptation;
- establishing strategies and structures which are flexible and responsive to change;
- learning and developing systems for best practice.

On the first of these issues it is important to understand how international managers are reacting to change in the global environment, managing across different international cultures and coping with commonality and diversity between markets.

THE CHANGING GLOBAL ENVIRONMENT

Globalisation

There are disagreements about the meaning of the term 'globalisation' because of the difficulty of understanding a complex, 'globalised' world. It is more than simply the homogenisation of cultures, markets, production structures and fashions as a result of technological innovations in communications and transport. It can be described in terms of the changing relationship between governments and big businesses and the span of operations of an organisation. In the case study at the end of this chapter it is argued that it is now recognised that

> *'a formerly international political economy, constructed around the building blocks of national economies, politics and societies, and multinational forms of corporate organisation, is being transformed to create new, quantitatively different forms of supra-national organisation.'*
> (Hudson, 2002)

Companies looking for the cheapest source of supply for the production of their goods look around the world rather than just around their own national economy. When Japan, Taiwan and South Korea could produce goods more cheaply than anyone else businesses looked towards them, when their costs began to rise businesses turned their attention to China and India. The developments in technology mean that services as well as goods have begun to be sourced on a worldwide basis. The growth in call centres in India has been an example of the global outsourcing of services. The sale of services, advice centres and backup services, data processing, secretarial and administrative functions and so on for the UK market have been located in India because of lower wages, the availability of well-educated employees and the wide knowledge of English.

The interest in global warming and environmental management along with the pressure on organisations to adopt policies of corporate social responsibility has had worldwide implications with considerable repercussions for globalisation.

Regionalisation

'Regionalisation' has become an increasingly important feature of the global business environment since the Second World War, although the constructs on which regional integration are based (principally free trade) are far from new. Adam Smith, writing in the eighteenth century, noted that the greatest economic benefits accrue from free trade, the 'invisible hand' of government trade policy serving only to distort the process of industrial specialisation which allows countries to utilise their resources to best effect. In 1947, as countries moved to forge greater global cooperation in an effort to put the adverse experiences of the Second World War behind them, the General Agreement on Tariffs and Trade (GATT) was formed with the intention of reducing/removing tariffs and quotas between countries on a unilateral basis.

GATT and free trade

Through 11 multilateral rounds on tariff negotiation, the achievements of GATT had been considerable, extending in the Uruguay round of talks to concerns of trade in services on a global basis. However, many critics now argue that the role of its successor – the World Trade Organisation (WTO) – has been undermined. In particular they note that, as international business flows in the modern world have grown more complex, trade policies and protectionist measures have become more concerned with non-tariff barriers which are less easy to detect and far harder to control.

Trading blocs

Compounding the problems of GATT, and now the WTO, has been the development of regional trading blocs, the single European market being the most publicised and far-reaching. Although the more recent signing of the North American Free Trade Agreement (NAFTA), including the USA, Canada and Mexico, and ongoing talks concerning greater unification of Asia Pacific countries demonstrate the importance of regionalisation in the global 'triad' (the three leading regions of the developed world), the most notable feature of trading blocs is that they promote free trade on the 'inside' (between participating member states), although external protectionism can be (and often is) a central tenet of supporting government policy. It is only necessary to look to the accusations by the Japanese and Americans of the Europeans creating an impenetrable 'fortress', or the efforts of the USA to reduce Japan's trade surplus with the USA and the concomitant threat of increased protectionism, to understand that many of the trade deals currently being forged are between the triad members – the Americas, the Asia Pacific region and Europe. This has led to a re-emergence of 'bilateral bargaining' in trade negotiations, for example in relation to steel and bananas, which GATT was so anxious to eradicate in the post-war era (Welford and Prescott, 1996).

The desire for countries to affiliate themselves in large economic groupings stems from the belief that large, unrestricted markets lead to intensified competition and thus provide an impetus for improved efficiency. While the term 'efficiency' is often used loosely, here it specifically refers to both static effects (those arising from immediate cost-saving strategies) and dynamic effects (those accruing from better innovation and product development). From the perspective of the European

to liaise with other industry players while nevertheless shielding their unique advantages from them.

For smaller firms, with fewer resources to dedicate to technological development, the challenges are more severe. Failure to keep abreast of technology may ultimately result in their demise but investment in R&D may be considered too high risk. Nevertheless, as there is no documented proof that large firms are more successful innovators than small firms, there is no size limit on firms allowed to bid for government support. Alternatively small firms may be best served by concentrating their efforts on product development, refining technologies for specific market niches or licensing in technologies with market potential.

Political change

The opening up of communist countries to Western businesses and the adoption of capitalist principles by many previously centrally planned economies has, albeit haltingly, extended business opportunities on a global scale. The initial rush for developed country multinationals to establish a presence in the newly emerging markets, be it via joint venture or foreign direct investment, has met with mixed fortune and has led to greater caution and tempered optimism. China, India, the Czech Republic, former East Germany, Brazil and a whole host of other 'best' emerging markets have become the focus for international operators seeking long-term growth and development.

Although many of these regions are far from ensuring long-term political stability, as the Asian financial crisis that began in 1997 has illustrated only too well, their growing liberalisation, deregulation and genuine openness to companies from developed countries (and their technologies) have changed the orientation of many businesses. Even where corporate governance needs substantial upgrading and opportunities may not turn out to result in short-term profit, the search for first-mover advantages and the belief that countries such as these will offer up vast consumer markets in the future make them attractive to today's investors.

Management challenges

Entering these new countries and servicing the needs of customers pose a number of serious challenges to international firms.

■ Dealing with new cultures, some of which are still dominated by communist ideals and work practices that can make the establishment of efficient business systems difficult. Employees who fail to understand the importance of productivity, partner companies for whom the concept of marketing is alien, bureaucratic rules, black-market economies, cronyism and corruption all need to be understood and catered for.

■ Cooperative business solutions are often the only means of entry, either to reduce risk or to secure access where governments place restrictions on foreign ownership. Hence some companies need to develop new internal skills to manage cooperative rather than competitive business operations.

■ Changing the balance of world business operations. Emerging markets in the East (particularly India and China), with their large populations and extensive natural resources, mean a further shift in economic activity towards the Asia Pacific region despite the greater uncertainties of doing business there. This will inevitably change the balance of world business and force companies to reassess their own international balance and coverage.

International money markets

The achievement of monetary union in 'Euroland' in the single European market in 1999, although beset by problems as a result of national sovereign concerns, has received a lot of support from European managers. The main reason for this is that a common currency in Europe has allowed firms to plan with greater certainty, as European business transactions have largely been removed from the uncertainties of exchange rate fluctuations.

In recent years, flexible exchange rates have come to characterise international business transactions. This means that the value of any currency for international traders is the price at which the currency is traded in the open market. Consequently international business traders are subject to sometimes dramatic changes in domestic and foreign economic conditions which have an important impact on the price competitiveness of goods traded abroad. With exchange rate fluctuations difficult to predict, there is always the risk that exchange rate movements eradicate profits between agreement of terms for exporting contracts and final payment. Nevertheless, exchange rate movements can confer as much advantage as they can pain. Multinationals, paradoxically exposed to a greater mix of currencies of input or supply and of output or demand, are at much less risk. They often find that as a result of globalisation pressures they are much more naturally hedged than the simple exporter or importer, whose reliance on operational techniques and financial instruments may still leave their currency imbalances unsolved (see Edelshain, 1995).

Such is the case for small firms, usually dealing in fewer overseas markets and thus spreading their risk more thinly, for whom adverse movements in exchange rates can be critical. Recurring risks can only be minimised at the cost of taking out 'insurance' – forward exchange protection provided by banks (at a price) can only eliminate each transaction risk to ensure that the final payment matches the agreed price at the time the contract was signed. Risk to its future business, its economic exposure, remains. For larger firms, establishing overseas facilities may prove a more favourable alternative. This means that activities are undertaken in the foreign country (and currency) and that cash flow and profits can be converted into the domestic currency only when exchange rates are favourable.

A fixed exchange rate (sought through the European Exchange Rate Mechanism) and the single European currency eradicate most (but not all, as there is still exposure to non-euro competitors) such problems for European business operations in Euroland, further facilitating the potential to operate unhindered in a wider European market. Many economists believed that European firms would only reap the full benefits of economic union once the single currency had been fully established, putting them on a par with their American and Japanese counterparts who are able to conduct business in large domestic markets in a single currency. However, a proviso must be that the euro replaces the US dollar as the currency of many current European business transactions and it is still uncertain whether these benefits have yet been captured.

CROSS-CULTURAL MANAGEMENT

The terms 'culture' and 'cultural difference' are used liberally by international managers, although the reality of what these concepts mean in practice is likely to be far less widely understood (Figure 19.1 shows the main elements of culture). As soon as any organisation begins to sell its products and services outside its own domestic market, indeed to set up an operation in a local market to do so, it will be exposed to a different cultural environment with its own distinct norms and behaviours. Ultimately, cultural sensitivity can mean the difference between success and failure. Ricks and Mahajan's (1984) analysis of 'blunders' in international marketing examines a number of cases where firms (even leading multinational players) have failed to understand fully local market nuances with disastrous results. For example, General Motors' promotional campaign in Belgium centred on a slogan of 'Body by Fischer', which in translation read 'Corpse by Fischer'; the same company launched a brand of car in Puerto Rico called the 'Nova', which in the local language sounded like 'no va' – it does not go; Goodyear Tyre and Rubber Company made illegal claims of superiority about its products in West Germany because it did not take account of local legal requirements; and General Mills allegedly targeted its advertising in the UK at children, which was considered unethical. Mistakes of this kind can prove costly and may also damage the reputation of the firm in the marketplace. Equally damaging can be an ethnocentric approach to the way one's staff in foreign branches and subsidiaries are managed. Perlmutter (1969) has highlighted the danger of doing everything the way it is done in the home or head office country, as

Figure 19.1 Emerging areas of technology

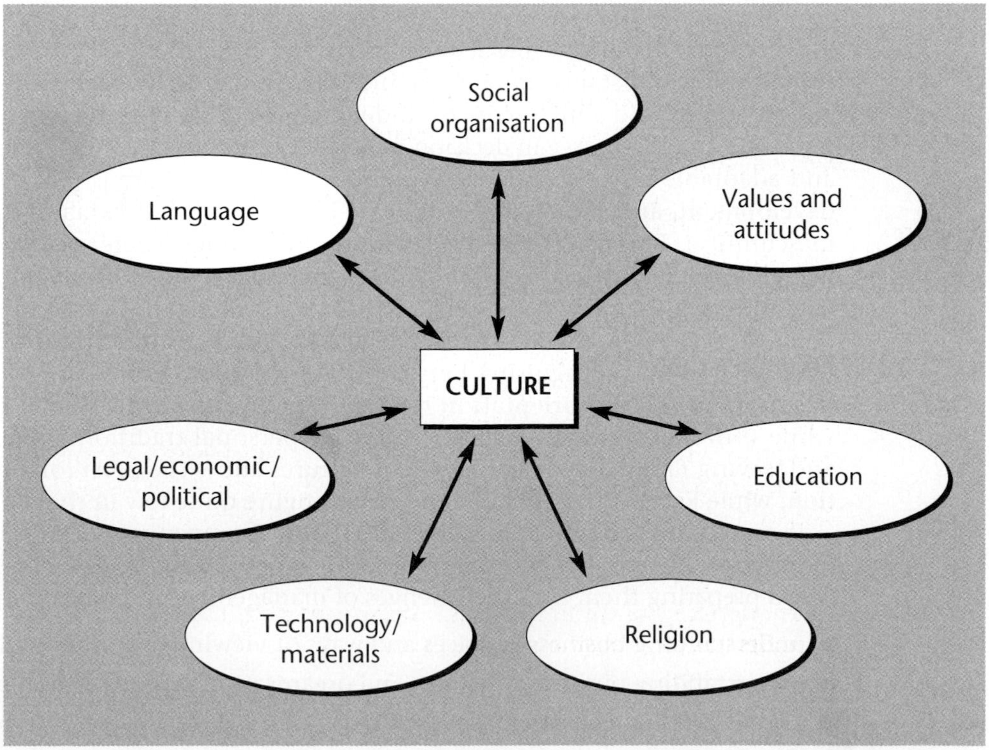

distinct from the way they do it locally or anywhere else in the world where they may do it better still. Remembering that we employ self-reference criteria in evaluating other cultures, taking cultural management seriously is, therefore, a prerequisite to doing business abroad if a firm wants to ensure long-term growth and survival.

Defining and categorising culture

One of the most notable studies of the relationship between national cultures and values in the workplace was undertaken by Geert Hofstede between 1967 and 1973. Based on research of 116,000 business personnel from over 17 countries, he identified 11 clusters of countries along his four original key dimensions (Hofstede, 1983).

- **Power distance** – focuses on how society deals with inequalities between people in physical and educational terms – countries with a high score (between 0 and 100) are those which feature broad differences between individuals in terms of power and wealth.
- **Uncertainty avoidance** – index relates to the extent to which countries establish formal rules and fixed patterns of life (such as career structures).
- **Individualism** – at the high end of the scale are those societies where ties between individuals are very loose, as opposed to those societies where individuals are born into 'collectives' which support and foster development in return for loyalty.
- **Masculinity** – the more 'masculine' a society then the more it values outcomes, assertiveness and materialism. Less concern is shown for quality of life. 'Femininity' relates to process, to caring and concern for people.

Figure 19.2 highlights the relative positions on a four-dimensional matrix for a range of countries. It clearly demonstrates that there are broad differences along the four dimensions between the highlighted countries, differences that need to be taken into account when managing across borders. For instance, the UK displays low scores for both power distance and uncertainty avoidance, an average score on the masculinity index and a high score for individualism. This suggests a society in which negotiation figures large in decision making (low power distance), rules are flexible and adaptable (low uncertainty avoidance) and great store is placed on personal development, and success and entrepreneurship (high individualism and medium masculinity). This compares with a country like France where society is based on a pyramidal hierarchy held together by tight rules and unity of command, or Germany where personal command is largely unnecessary as rules settle everything.

More recently Hofstede has also added a fifth dimension to his research – **time-frame**. Here he distinguishes between long-term and short-term orientation of business. **Long-term orientation** relates to such values as thrift and perseverance, while **short-term values** include respect for personal tradition, social obligations and 'saving face'. Generally East Asian cultures show the most long-term orientation, while European and American cultures figure quite low in the rankings.

Research, by those like Hofstede (1983) and Trompenaars (1993), has provided managers with insights into different business behaviours and practices around the world preparing them for the challenges of management in terms of:

- understanding business practices and ways of viewing business development;
- understanding business structures and organisation from a cultural perspective;
- understanding what motivates people in terms of their career and personal aspirations.

Figure 19.2 Cross-cultural comparisons

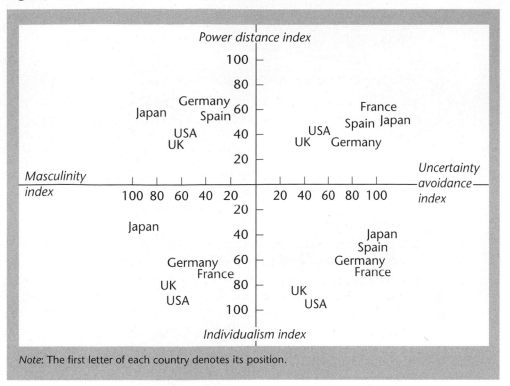

Note: The first letter of each country denotes its position.

It may be argued, however, that Hofstede's five dimensions provide an oversimplistic view of cultural difference between the markets of the world and fail to give much insight into the workings of society as a whole. Here, other alternatives need to be considered. The model depicted in Figure 19.1, which suggests a number of cultural elements for analysis, provides an alternative that extends understanding beyond the business world to customers and markets.

Cultural analysis of this nature allows managers to identify commonalities and differences between countries, and thus to develop clusters of countries for targeting sales and marketing activity. Examples of such clustering are provided in Figure 19.3. This is based on work undertaken by Vandermerwe (1993) on similarities and differences between demographics, economic variables and lifestyle characteristics of the member states of the European Union. Interestingly, her findings show that clusters are not necessarily based on geographic boundaries. She also goes on to suggest that other 'clusters' need to be considered by European managers:

■ mass clusters with common consumer needs;

■ niche clusters where consumers have similar but not identical needs;

■ local and specialised clusters.

The management challenge, then, is not simply to be aware of the individual cultural elements of each society but in understanding and managing the extent and nature of diversity between different cultures.

Figure 19.3 European 'cultural clusters'

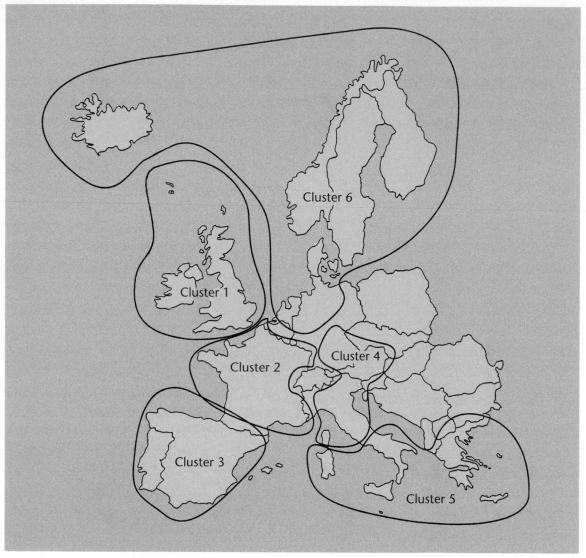

Source: S Vandermerwe (1993) 'A framework for constructing Euro-networks', *European Management Journal*, 11 (1), March.

Managing diversity

Nations and societies are not the same – each has features which make it unique and distinct from both immediate and distant neighbours. This diversity poses a serious challenge to international managers who not only have to understand different needs, wants, business and buyer behaviours in different clusters, but also have to integrate this diversity into an holistic strategy.

It has been argued (Bloom *et al.*, 1994) that Europeans are better than their international counterparts at dealing with diversity. Because business in Europe has been developed across a wide array of diverse national cultures, mechanisms for integrating diversity have been central to competitive success. This compares with the Japanese who developed their businesses in a highly homogeneous market and with the Americans who have sought to integrate diverse cultures into a uniquely identifiable and all-embracing 'American' norm. As a result it is not surprising that American and Japanese management models typically highlight diversity as a problem while Europeans consider it a way of life.

This kind of thinking has led to distinct differences in approach to international strategic development across the world. Porter (1991), perhaps idealistically, suggested:

'One of the things that Europe 1992 integration will do is hasten the process by which larger European companies move from confederations of subsidiaries to become truly integrated, worldwide competitors. For each product line, there will be a clear home base, with some or many outside the home country. European companies have tended to do well in businesses that are essentially a collection of national markets but not so well in the truly global arena.'

In other words, the Europeans' tendency to deal with diversity by focusing on differentiation and local market adaptation, while attractive in the past, is less desirable in the European (and global) markets of today, where greater commonality between regions and potential for more standardisation and integration of business practices are not only possible, but desirable.

Brian Goldthorp, Director of Personnel at Trafalgar House, confirms this line of thinking:

'But the reverse side of the coin is that when we look at parts of the world where these pressures of diversity are not as overwhelming as they are in Europe, we continue to concentrate on dealing with differentiation, so Europeans are less successful there. American and Japanese corporations show the reciprocal traits. They are enormously good where there are products and strategies of an undifferentiated kind.'

(Bloom *et al.*, 1994)

Aside from advantages of local responsiveness, other benefits accrue from a differentiated approach to strategic management across cultures – an ability to work successfully in other cultures and adapt to the nuances and norms of different societies. Japanese managers often find this difficult as a result of their 'sheltered' development in a homogeneous society. The literature is now awash with examples of the serious problems experienced by Japanese companies attempting to introduce Japanese management practices into the West. Their approach is to persuade people that the Japanese way is the best, even if some of the practices run counter to local cultural norms and practices. Americans, on the other hand, tend to be more dogmatic – they impose structures and rules and demand change from local employees.

The message seems to be that managers need to extend their 'toolkit'. They need to be made aware of the different strategic options available to them so they can devise the most appropriate fit between strategy and diverse market structure. This may mean shifting towards a more transnational strategy – balancing differentiation (local adaptation) and standardisation (centralisation into larger units), simply looking for parts of the business where change of this kind is appropriate, or consolidating the chosen approach (global or multidomestic) to suit the needs of the product market.

Cultural change

All of the above takes place against a backdrop of change. Culture, whether national or business-based, is a dynamic phenomenon – norms and practices are continually adjusting and changing. However, there is little agreement on whether such change is bringing markets closer together or breaking them apart into smaller niche segments.

Some industry observers argue that culture is becoming increasingly homogeneous on a global scale. Certain global products have become widely accepted, partly because they appeal to large, cultural subgroups which show a degree of standardisation on a global scale. Coca-Cola, Levi jeans and Reebock training shoes, McDonald's hamburgers and Swatch watches have broad appeal to the youth 'subculture'. Products of this kind suggest that there is scope for global standardisation, although in all these cases the way in which the product is managed at a local level shows a degree of differentiation on a market-by-market basis as a result of local country cultural conditions. Such adaptation may include:

- product/servicing adaptation to cater for different needs and wants and competitor activity;
- adaptation of promotion and advertising such that the message is relevant to local customers and meets with local legislation and standards;
- adaptation of channel decisions due to different buying behaviour;
- adaptation of recruitment policies in line with local educational systems and standards;
- adaptation of pay and remuneration to ensure staff motivation;
- adaptation of price to fit with local conditions.

Others point to the way in which cultural groups are becoming more distinct from each other:

'In Coca-Cola we're seeing a dichotomy taking place in business today. Some of the customers of the Coca-Cola system in Europe, such as large international companies, are becoming more European. Many of them want one programme for Europe.

On the other hand, the consumer is becoming more local, in our view. We are advertising Coca-Cola in Barcelona today in two languages – Spanish and Catalan. It is a recent phenomenon and we see it taking place in Scotland, Wales, the French regions, the German Länder ... People are becoming more culturally attuned with their localities and marketeers have to recognise it and be prepared to deal with it.'

(Ralph Cooper, President of Coca-Cola's European Community Group in Bloom *et al.*, 1994)

It is clear that Levitt's (1983) prediction that intensified competition and technological development would lead companies to operate globally, ignoring 'superficial' national differences, is unlikely ever to apply to all firms in all industries across the world. This is particularly so when growing consumer wealth allows consumers to be more discriminating.

While we may be seeing the emergence of a 'global village' in terms of our awareness of our neighbours, this does not automatically suggest that neighbours will seek to become like each other. With evidence apparently to prove both sides of the debate the only conclusion can be: 'it depends'. While, from a management point of view, this is far from satisfying as it provides few guidelines and prescriptions, it is important to consider the strategic management challenge as one which incorporates a review of individual markets, products and timeframes (Halliburton and Hünerberg, 1987).

MATCHING STRATEGIES TO THE INTERNATIONAL ENVIRONMENT

International firms have at their disposal a wide range of strategic options from which to draw. At a generic level firms may choose between exporting, licensing and other contractual arrangements and foreign direct investment, although at an operational level each of these alternatives offers up a wide range of strategic alternatives. It is beyond the scope of this chapter to explore fully the nature of these alternatives but see Dunning (1988) who does so. What is important, however, is understanding some of the key differences and managerial considerations.

Understanding decision-making criteria

To return to the argument outlined above, the dynamic and diverse global business environment of today makes it difficult to prescribe generic solutions to management challenges. Much depends on the nature of the market, the product and the firm itself. Failure to make pragmatic decisions about the best 'fit' of strategy to market conditions is likely to result in managers missing the best opportunities for exploiting their advantages in foreign markets. This involves managers considering a wide array of both internal and external factors and choosing the most appropriate strategy in each instance.

External factors include:

- **host market factors** – size, growth, competitive conditions, distribution, infrastructure;
- **host market environment** – political, economic and socio-cultural conditions;
- **host market production factors** – availability, quality and costs of inputs;
- **domestic market factors** – competitive conditions, growth, government policies and internal factors.

Internal factors include:

- **product factors** – product technology, differentiation, service provision and potential for global standardisation;
- **company resources** – management, capital and technology, and overall commitment to international business.

Assessing the most appropriate means of entering and servicing the market along each of these dimensions is likely to result in a number of different options being appropriate for a variety of reasons. Managers therefore have to decide on a final strategy based on firstly their overall objectives for growth and development, and secondly the weighting of factors in their own industry's competitive development.

For instance, the company has to decide on both the long-term and short-term objectives for entering a particular market. If, for instance, the company's objective is merely to sell off excess capacity in overseas markets then it is unlikely that foreign investment will prove attractive. If, on the other hand, the company is looking to establish a committed presence in the market then it may wish to invest significant resources in establishing a strong market presence. In terms of weighting factors, in some industries certain factors emerge as being more critical than others. Take, for example, the retail financial service industry – with many markets being mature and in a state of overcapacity, foreign direct investment, attractive in terms of local presence and closeness to customers, is both expensive and limited in its potential to secure significant market penetration. Gaining access to established distribution networks through alliances (or possibly takeover of existing organisations) is the priority and thus distribution conditions should be highly weighted in making the final decision.

It is clear from this very brief overview that the decision-making challenge facing international managers, with regard to market entry, is highly complex requiring high levels of research and detailed analysis. This is explored more fully in Grant (2002). More often than not, however, firms base their decisions on imperfect information because information is either too expensive to gather or not available, or decisions need to be made quickly if firms are to take advantage of available opportunities. For many managers, then, the reality of international decision making is strategic adjustment, considering changes in operational modes, which mean either shifts between generic modes of market servicing or intermode shifts, such as from exporting via a sales representative to exporting via a wholly owned subsidiary. These decisions are usually made in line with the ongoing experience of the firm – the learning curve – wherein additional knowledge about the market and the product's experience in that market gives better information on which to base strategic decisions.

Consequently foreign market servicing decisions are dynamic. Continual assessment and reassessment is essential if firms are to adjust to changes in both internal and external conditions.

Exploiting compensating advantages

Firms entering foreign markets are often at a disadvantage *vis-à-vis* indigenous companies as a result of their lack of understanding of the local market. The pioneering work of Hymer (1960), which is often considered to be the foundation of current international business theory, proposed that market entrants require some form of compensating advantage to compete successfully with local firms, which possess innate strengths. Such advantage may include proprietary technology (raising the emphasis of technology development and management), preferential access to capital, superior marketing skills, absolute cost advantages, economies of scale or product differentiation.

Firms exporting to the foreign market are usually at a disadvantage compared to local organisations because of their distance from the market. This has two effects – it makes it difficult to monitor market conditions; but, perhaps more importantly, it also raises doubts in the mind of the consumer about the firm's ability to deliver on time and to provide appropriate service and backup. Local agents and distributors can act as a surrogate presence in the market alleviating these problems, although the question for consumers remains: Why should I buy from a foreign firm if a local organisation can equally satisfy my needs? Managers must therefore concern themselves with positioning the product (through differentiation) and promoting it in such a way that there are perceived advantages in purchasing a foreign alternative.

Firms undertaking licensing and other contractual arrangements avoid the problems of 'foreignness' because local firms act as representatives in the local market. Indeed, as products are produced locally, consumers may be unaware of the fact that the technology or brand belongs to a foreign firm. The main concern with licensing (and joint ventures) is that the agreement will give rise to a competitor. Because the company is imparting knowledge and/or expertise to a third party there is the possibility that the company's comparative advantage will be eroded through transfer and this will subsequently be used against it on termination of the contract. Patents and trademarks may provide a degree of protection. Alternatively firms may consider providing partners with a 'secret ingredient' supplied to the third party through a tied purchase agreement, where the licensee or joint venture partner is contracted to obtain certain components from the licensor. Some antitrust authorities, however, rule against such agreements as they see them as being anticompetitive.

Within licensing and other contractual arrangements, therefore, the key managerial decision is not so much what returns will be produced in the short term, but the long-term implications of technology transfer. If the firm's compensating advantage is its proprietary technology, sharing technological information should usually be avoided.

Foreign direct investment gives firms the ability to establish a local persona and compete on a more equal level with indigenous firms. Indeed many of the long-established multinational enterprises in global markets have carved out a global rather than a home-country persona which gives them complete acceptability in foreign markets.

The issue of government procurement requires some attention in relation to foreign direct investment. In some industries, governments are the major purchasers of goods and services (e.g. the defence industry and pharmaceuticals). There is a natural tendency for governments to purchase goods and services from local firms to the exclusion of foreign organisations, regardless of price and quality differentials, because of the benefits of lower transport and trading costs, better after-sales service and quicker delivery. There are also social benefits in terms of supporting employment, assisting ailing industries, bolstering new emerging sectors and ensuring that profits are earned locally. Firms operating in these industries, therefore, have little choice but to locate activities in the target market. Failure to do so is likely to result in their exclusion from public procurement contracts and an inability to penetrate the market.

Internalisation versus externalisation

Taking the three generic modes it is possible to suggest that exporting and foreign direct investment differ from licensing in that production is internalised – that is, carried out by the firm itself. In the case of licensing and other contractual relationships, however, production (and possibly other complementary functions) are 'externalised' and are carried out by a third party. In many ways this is an oversimplistic way of categorising strategies as it only relates to the nature of the production process and ignores other business functions such as sales and marketing and distribution. Taking this wider perspective it is possible to suggest various forms of exporting via intermediaries which also include elements of externalisation, and licensing which involves the supply of critical components to the licensee firm and involves a degree of internalisation. What is important, therefore, is not an attempt to categorise various strategic alternatives but an understanding of the managerial challenge in terms of balancing advantages from internalisation and externalisation – weighing up relative costs of administration against those of conducting transactions, in undertaking business activities within the firm or relying on third parties conducting various value chain activities.

Critical to the management consideration in this respect is the concept of control. Internalisation of activities implies full control over business functions. This is often believed to be a source of advantage as it gives managers free choice over strategies and operational decision making, which can be hard to achieve when working with a third party. Nevertheless, firms have to trade off the additional costs incurred in gaining control, both in terms of ownership of business facilities and the ongoing costs associated with day-to-day management of a full range of business functions, against the benefits of ownership.

This assumes that success is critically dependent on control which may not always be the case. Take the example of a firm exporting via a host country distributor. In an effort to ensure that the foreign intermediary maximises business on the exporter's behalf, the firm may set targets and quotas, offer rewards for meeting specified sales volumes or impose sanctions if targets are not met. In this way the firm may seek to 'control' the intermediary. Alternatively the firm may choose to cooperate with the intermediary, providing additional support such as sales and service training, and providing targeted promotional literature.

Research by the Industrial Marketing and Purchasing Group (Valla, 1986) underlines that for more than two decades the idea that cooperation in such circumstances is preferable to control has been recognised. Here, better results stem from investing more human resources into the operation, basing staff from the supplier organisation in the target market to assist the intermediary, demonstrating positive commitment and encouraging the agent to work harder on the principal's behalf. Similarly, encouraging personnel to become involved with their counterparts in the customer organisation at various functional levels strengthens the bond between supplier and final customer and raises the level of trust and understanding. Here bilateral relations between supplier and intermediary are extended to 'tripartite' relations, where the manufacturer is also in direct contact with the final customer, working in conjunction with the intermediary.

The success of Japanese firms in the car industry provides a further example of cooperation rather than control. Rather than integrate backwards and 'internalise' component manufacture, Japanese firms prefer to establish close working relationships with their suppliers – a cooperative solution rather than an attempt to derive full control. The success of this kind of practice has led Western car manufacturers to follow suit, the industry now being characterised by car assemblers (the leading manufacturers) extending their power through close business linkages rather than ownership of diverse business functions.

What ownership does afford, however, and the focus of Japanese foreign direct investment in the USA in setting up or acquiring distribution companies underlines this, is internalisation of information and more direct lines of communication between the market and the decision-making locus of the organisation. In this respect intermediaries may be seen as either facilitators or bottlenecks for information gathering. Where working relationships are good, the third-party organisation is more likely to collect and pass on critical information, although there is a limit to the amount of time and attention it is able or prepared to dedicate to such a function for one manufacturer which may contribute only a small part to its total business portfolio. This has led, in many instances, to firms establishing sales and marketing offices in foreign markets, not only for the purpose of handling contracts in the overseas market but in order to have an operation 'on the ground' that is able to monitor changes in market conditions and demand patterns. This points to the splitting up, in locational terms, of various business functions in the value chain.

Centralisation versus decentralisation

It is also possible to distinguish between the three generic modes of foreign market servicing in terms of the location of business activities. With manufacture, licensing and foreign direct investment involve manufacturing in the host country, while exporting involves manufacturing in the domestic market or another manufacturing base outside the target market. Once again, however, this oversimplification ignores the tendency for firms to internationalise different parts of the business rather than all elements of the value chain.

The critical managerial decision here is between centralisation and decentralisation. Centralisation assumes that advantages accrue from conducting business in large-scale centres where economies of scale can be achieved in a variety of business functions. Decentralisation, on the other hand, assumes that greater advantages arise from conducting business in the host market where adaptation to the local environment and greater decision-making flexibility through local autonomy permit a higher degree of local sensitivity.

Within the European Union many of the cost-saving benefits ascribed to unification are seen to come from economies of scale, which suggests centralisation is the key challenge. This need not, however, mean single-site production locations. Plant economies can be achieved through specialisation, individual manufacturing units concentrating on single products, or on a narrow range of the company's portfolio which allows the removal of effort duplication and thus greater plant efficiency. McCains, the Canadian frozen food manufacturer, has followed this approach in its European operations and the UK pharmaceutical firm, Glaxo, has taken advantage of the liberalisation of the American market through the NAFTA agreement to reorganise production in its Mexican, American and Canadian plants on a product-specific basis.

A trend may, however, be observed in terms of decentralisation of sales and marketing activities. While cost-saving and plant economies may be attractive in production, closeness to the market and local responsiveness dominate in sales and distribution. Management can no longer consider the business as an amalgam of functions. These need to be unbundled and decisions made separately concerning their centralisation or decentralisation if a balance is to be struck between the advantages offered by both approaches.

This means looking beyond simple taxonomies and classifications and finding creative solutions to problems. Take the case of Lucas Girling, part of the Lucas Engineering Group, manufacturing motor braking systems. As closeness to customers is paramount (because of the cooperative alliances established in the car industry) the company has little choice but to manufacture in close proximity to the major car assemblers. At face value this dilutes the potential for economies of scale necessitating the establishment of many global production centres, with a degree of duplication of effort. However, through the adoption of 'flexible specialisation' and computer-aided manufacturing its plants are small (employing between 40 and 50 employees) and capable of batch-sized production. Thus, even with decentralisation, it is able to achieve adaptability and efficiency.

Standardisation versus adaptation

Standardisation of products also gives the potential for economies of scale. However, global standardisation is not possible for many products as they need to be adapted to cater for local market conditions and, in particular, for that country's cultural nuances. Where product adaptation is necessary the attraction of centralised production diminishes, as the downtime in production required to change machinery over from one product to another can be outweighed by the benefits of establishing dedicated manufacturing facilities in the target market.

The decision to standardise or adapt involves a trade-off between the costs and benefits to the firm. In essence managers have to decide whether the cost savings from producing on a large-scale basis outweigh the profits resulting from local market adaptation (which may involve the establishment of local manufacturing plants). This decision is determined by a number of factors:

- **the nature of the product** – it is generally agreed that industrial products are easier to standardise than consumer products, the latter being greatly influenced by cultural tastes;
- **legal requirements** – product, packaging and labelling standards which often differ markedly on a country-by-country basis;
- **physical conditions** – such as climate, living conditions and income;
- **competition** – which will dictate market positioning and differentiation.

What also emerges is that the standardisation versus adaptation issue impinges on the decision to centralise or decentralise manufacturing and, taken together, these two issues combine to explain the overall strategic orientation discussed above: international, multidomestic, multinational and transnational.

Business organisation

Business organisation is seldom something which is planned – typically it evolves as a firm grows and diversifies. Structures emerge out of strategic decisions regarding the nature of products and services, and the geographic coverage of the firm in the international marketplace. Through this evolutionary process there are four different 'ideal' types of organisational structure the firm may employ – an international division structure, a product division structure, a geographic division structure and a matrix structure. Each of these is depicted in Figure 19.4.

International division structure

Small firms expanding abroad for the first time, as Swedish research (Johanson and Vahine, 1977) has uniquely confirmed, tend to establish an export office or an international division staffed, in the first instance, by a small number of personnel responsible for all international business dealings (i.e. all products in all markets). As the scale and scope of international activity grows, the export focus of this division may change to one that supports international production effort. This production may be organised on a country-by-country basis (a full range of the portfolio being produced in each target market) or a product basis (different products being produced in different centres). But, while Davis (1992) reported that 60 per cent of all firms that have internationalised have first adopted this structure, other research has consistently failed to identify any one pattern of internationalisation.

There are some problems associated with this kind of structure. First, it creates conflict between national and international decision making. It is not uncommon for the international division to have less say in corporate policy making, even when it contributes more to the overall business, simply because it was 'added on' at a later stage

Figure 19.4 (a) Product division structure with separate international division; (b) Global product division structure; (c) Global geographic division structure; (d) Simplifed global matrix structure

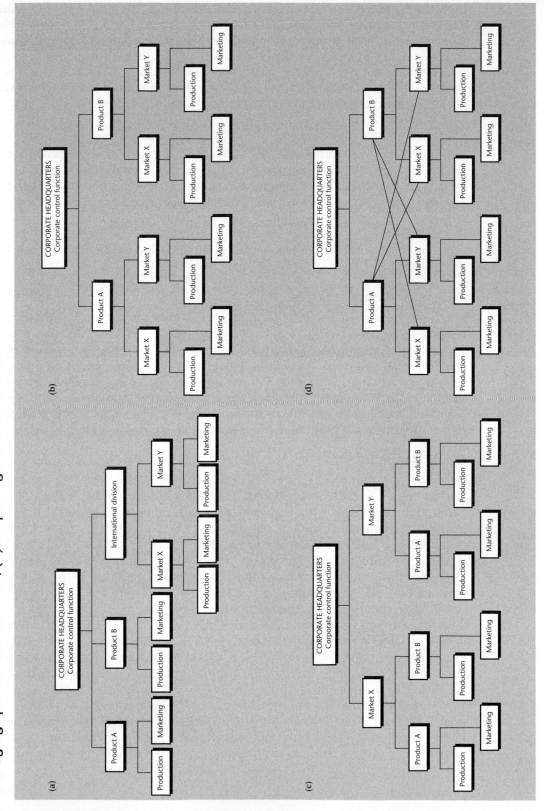

in the company's development. Second, it is difficult for the head of the international division to rationalise the demands of different countries and/or products. Third, it does not provide opportunities for coordination between domestic and international activities. This can make global product development difficult to achieve and global production planning, based on experience curve and locational economies, hard to manage. As a result of these limitations firms expanding internationally often shift to one of the international organisation structures outlined below.

Product division structure

This is usually a structure adopted by companies that have a diverse product portfolio. The headquarters is responsible for supporting and managing each product on a worldwide basis in terms of design, value adding, sales and promotion. The great advantage of this kind of structure is that it allows a company to focus on global efficiencies within disparate product divisions, locating production in low-cost centres and generating efficiency through product focus. The main disadvantage of such an option is that it can hamper the ability of the company to be responsive at a national level.

Geographic division structure

The focus here is on adapting to differences between countries and geographic regions. Different divisions are set up in geographic centres and decision making is regionally rather than internationally centralised. This structure tends to be used where companies have a low degree of diversification but are intent on maximising advantages from local adaptation. Geographic areas are often self-contained with their own R&D, production and sales and marketing. The main advantage of this approach is the ability to maximise local responsiveness, although this may be traded off against a higher cost structure, as duplication is commonplace.

Global matrix structure

The above description suggests that a geographic division structure better suits a multidomestic focus, while a global product division structure is appropriate for firms pursuing global or international strategies. But what is appropriate for firms attempting to pursue a transnational strategy? The global matrix structure offers the potential to derive the benefits from both the geographic and product division structures outlined above. The theory suggests that decision making is organised along two dimensions – product and market – based on a process of cooperation, consultation and compromise.

While, in theory at least, the matrix structure looks to offer distinct advantages, in practice these advantages are far from easy to realise. Consensus decision making is hard to achieve, particularly as there is inherent conflict between local adaptation and the generation of scale economies. Attempts to reach consensus can severely slow down the decision-making process and limit the degree to which the firm is responsive to the dynamics of the market.

As a result 'matrix' organisations of the 1990s have emerged from attempts to evolve flexibility rather than from wholesale adoption of new structures. The matrix structure involves the establishment of networks, the splitting up of businesses into constituent functions (production versus marketing versus R&D) and the establishment of interfunction/intercountry project groups.

Research on managing the multinational enterprise points to the development of global 'heterarchies' characterised by multiple centres of control (functional, geographic or product-based) coordinated through normative means:

> *'Corporate culture, management ethics, style and similar concepts become critical in understanding why a heterarchy does not break down into anarchy.'*
>
> (Hedlund and Rolander, 1990)

A multinational company might, therefore, have various 'headquarters' around the world – an administrative HQ in its domestic market; a financial centre in London; an R&D centre in Germany (a centre of excellence for technological development); and manufacturing headquarters in the three triad regions (the Americas, Asia Pacific and Europe). Certain Japanese multinationals, such as Canon and Honda, have developed what has been termed 'the four headquarters system' which involves establishing regional headquarters in Japan, Asia, the USA and Europe. The aim is to satisfy local requirements while at the same time exploiting the strengths of being a worldwide producer.

The main advantage of the heterarchy is its flexibility. It allows managers to concentrate on different functional areas of the business independently (and perhaps at different times) and permits a high degree of diversity in strategic development giving subsidiaries scope to develop local business operations in a way which is appropriate to local conditions. Flexibility also extends to the development of cooperative agreements with other organisations which may be decided at a functional rather than corporate level. The obvious question, though, is how does this highly diverse and geographically dispersed organisation integrate? The answer lies in the sharing of information between the various parts, now possible with modern technology, which means that experiences of one division in one part of the world can be shared and drawn on by divisions elsewhere. The domestic head office therefore becomes a conduit for information transfer and a coordinating mechanism for the company's objectives and overall direction. No longer is it a decision-making machine – it is a facilitator for a global business network.

Organising for technological development

With technology change featuring so largely in the emerging global business environment, the challenge of managing technological development deserves some comment. Up until relatively recently many multinational companies took the decision to centralise their global R&D activities for a variety of reasons. First, there was the need to control the development of new technologies on which the company's future competitiveness might rest. Second, there were economies of scale in R&D where very large amounts of resources can be concentrated into single centres with no duplication of effort. Finally, there was the fear that foreign research departments might be a source of leakage of ideas and knowledge.

Changes in the global environment and the carving up of the world market into three leading global centres, many yielding 'centres of excellence' in research in particular industries, has changed the thinking of technology managers in many multinationals. Decentralisation of R&D functions has begun to feature in the strategies of global firms as they seek to derive maximum advantage from a global organisation. The following outline of various types of R&D organisational development, derived by Bartlett and Ghoshal (1990), explains this thinking.

- **Centre for global** – the approach typically followed by multinationals (outlined above). While there are advantages in terms of control and scale economies, this approach runs the risk of being insensitive to local market demands in the leading markets of the world.

- **Local for local** – an approach that suggests conducting research in all target markets so that the technologies which are developed match local market demands. While beneficial in terms of local adaptation, the approach implicitly involves duplication of effort and a tendency for subsidiaries to 'reinvent the wheel' in an attempt to maintain the local autonomy.

- **Locally leveraged** – under this arrangement managers can take the most creative and innovative developments from the various subsidiaries and share them with other subsidiaries worldwide. The main disadvantage is that there are frequently impediments to transferring products from one market to another – particularly cultural differences and local market demand conditions.

- **Globally linked** – promoted by Bartlett and Goshal as the optimum solution to the technology development challenge, this approach involves the establishment of flexible linkages between research teams from various global centres. Structures of this kind allow companies to exploit synergies in technology development at the same time as exploiting local leverage advantages. The major drawbacks to this approach are the cost of coordination and the complexities of managing the linkages on an ongoing basis.

None of the approaches, therefore, emerges as adeptly suited to the changing global environment. Each has its advantages and disadvantages. This points to managers developing flexible systems which allow them to maximise a variety of advantages from the different approaches, while at the same time minimising the costs and managerial complexities. This may mean having major centres for R&D in a number of key global locations, with a series of local R&D support offices acting more as idea-generating centres than capital-intensive research laboratories.

International strategic development of small firms

The literature on business start-up has typically suggested that companies should concentrate their activities on securing a defensible domestic position before exploring international opportunities. The belief is that small firms should start in a national region, roll out to the national market and then cherry-pick opportunities in the international arena, but how appropriate is such a prescription for a small firm in the twenty-first century which has developed an innovative technology and whose marketplace is a niche which extends beyond national borders?

Today many global industries sport the features of a global oligopoly. At one end of the scale a small number of large multinationals (often no more than one from each developed nation) compete globally on differentiation rather than price, and at the other end a large number of small, specialist niche players satisfy the needs of small customer groups. With intense competition these niches are tending to get smaller and smaller, and firms are therefore forced to target their activities more closely towards ever more specialised customer groups. This often means that national marketplaces are not of a sufficient scale to support the activities of small, specialist firms which are therefore forced to internationalise, often early on in their development cycle.

These firms, lacking the financial resources to consider large-scale investment, are forced to explore creative solutions to their international expansion and development. This often leads them to work cooperatively, either with distributors or partner-manufacturers, or to establish small-scale offices (often staffed by only one person) in key markets where it is essential to have eyes and ears to the ground.

While many of the problems of standardisation versus adaptation, internalisation versus externalisation and coordination remain the same for small organisations, they face a series of other challenges:

■ cash flow management – which has implications of adding resources to support international expansion;

■ financial management and the high risk of non-payment – whereas large firms can cross-subsidise, small firms are vulnerable and so have to seek protection through the purchase of, often expensive, insurance products;

■ strategic vision and international capabilities – with a small workforce much depends on the vision and ability of the chief executive.

It is arguable, therefore, that small-firm managers need to be better prepared than their large-firm counterparts. For them survival may rest on them successfully exploiting opportunities in a diverse array of markets worldwide, which stretches their resources and demands very high levels of cultural sensitivity and diversity integration.

Business cooperation

One of the issues highlighted above was the importance of flexibility in strategy development. Firms need to be able to react quickly to changes in the marketplace and emerging trends in business development. It is possible to argue here that firms with extensive fixed assets may find themselves at a disadvantage. Take, for example, a firm that has integrated backwards and internalised its sources of supply. Although this means guaranteed inputs into the production process, it limits the extent to which the organisation can shop around for the cheapest components and materials, or those incorporating the latest technological breakthroughs. In other words it limits the extent to which the firm can react to developments in the market. The alternative position, buying on the open market, may, however, be equally unsatisfactory – there is no control over the flow of supply or the price of the inputs. The solution being sought by many firms is to consider cooperation rather than internalisation. Similar trends are also being witnessed further down the channel when working with distributors and retailers.

Cooperation is not, however, restricted to relationships within the organisation's value chain. More and more organisations are combining their resources to solve common strategic problems, be it in the area of product development and R&D or production, business development or marketing. Such relationships with other organisations not only mean sharing knowledge and skills, but also the ability to switch allegiances and the nature of alliances when market conditions change.

Technological collaboration

The recent trend towards greater cooperation in business may be partly adduced to rapid changes in technological developments, as outlined above. With shortening technology life cycles and, therefore, the marketable 'life' of products, managers are increasingly looking to lower costs of R&D and to ensure rapid returns on their investment in the marketplace. The latter is often achieved through rapid internationalisation of new product developments, whereas the former is increasingly causing firms to share the costs and risks of technological development with other competitors in the industry. This trend has been further reinforced by the rising costs of R&D, which in some developed markets have outpaced rates of inflation by as much as 10 per cent. In some sectors, therefore, even the largest multinational enterprises are finding it difficult to fund major research initiatives on their own. This is spawning a large number of industry linkages and cooperative arrangements for the development of new primary technologies.

At face value this may appear to be tantamount to 'collusion', diluting the impact of free trade and restricting competition. However, the position in the value chain of many of these collaborative linkages suggests otherwise. As the research process is distinct from the marketing of products, firms may collaborate on upstream activities but compete aggressively in the marketplace. A further feature of such collaboration is the setting of industry standards. In the consumer electronics industry, for example, firms will not have forgotten the case of the video cassette recorder where the VHS technology introduced by Matsushita 'cannibalised' the Sony Betamax technology and led to Matsushita controlling approximately 45 per cent of the world VCR market in 1983. With this in mind Philips entered into an alliance with Matsushita in 1992 to manufacture and market the digital compact cassette which Philips had developed. It hoped that the global power of the joint company would eliminate market competition provided by Sony's 'mini-compact disc' technology, the sharing of the risk and the pooling of global resources giving it extensive global spread through which such an international standard could be set.

Collaboration and market entry

Linkages between firms are not, however, restricted to technology development. Intensified competition brought about by free trade initiatives means that many mature, developed markets can be difficult to enter. Strategic alliances between firms can serve as a useful means of securing market access as well as bypassing the cultural difficulties of being a foreign firm operating on alien soil. Furthermore, entering into an alliance with a partner in this way can be an effective way of side-stepping head-to-head competition. It also provides firms with an important means of learning about the foreign market. The significance of the learning curve in international business activity cannot be overstated. When operating in a foreign market for the first time, foreign firms are often at a disadvantage *vis-à-vis* local indigenous firms as a result of their lack of understanding about local cultures and business practices. By entering into an alliance with a local player there is a form of 'quasi-internalisation' of market knowledge and development, critical information being passed from the local organisation to the international entrant.

Many Western firms have used the joint venture route as an important means of securing a strong foothold in the Japanese market. Typically Japan is seen as a 'black box' to Western managers, its culture and business practices differing markedly from those pertaining to Western nations. Lowering the risk of failure through joint ventures and using the strategy as a pre-emptive stage in developing wholly owned manufacturing facilities in the Japanese market has been a popular development route for Western firms attempting to consolidate their activities in Japan.

Collaboration and vertical integration

Alliances have also become popular between manufacturers and their suppliers. This may arguably result from the well-publicised success of Japanese firms, which have developed very strong cooperative links with their suppliers, although the rapid technology change must also play a part. In order to ensure that suppliers and manufacturers are continuing to move in the same direction, joint research programmes can facilitate component development and ensure an automatic 'match' between the demands of the producer and the products of the supplier. Once again the car industry provides a good example of this in practice. Component suppliers are no longer seen as being separate from the automobile production process – they are involved throughout the research, development and commercialisation process in order that the elements of the final vehicle fit the standards and specifications outlined by the car designers and manufacturers.

Industry networks

Emerging from the various forms of cooperation and alliance are a number of complex industry networks where firms are linked together through both formal and informal contracts. Figure 19.5 outlines the nature and scope of such a complex network in the information technology sector. It clearly shows that there are very few firms in the industry which remain insular as regards the process of cooperation. The number of alliances between firms also gives rise to the notion that many of them are 'project based' – entered into in order to develop a solution to a specific problem. This contradicts the traditional view of joint ventures which implies long-term commitment and cooperation and highlights the changing nature of modern-day alliances, which tend to be more fluid and flexible. The main implication here is that firms which remain on the outside are likely to be left out of the technological changes, market developments and vertical business agreements which are now characteristic of many industrial sectors. They are thus likely to fall behind their competitors and find it difficult to stay abreast of the dynamic changes taking place. Failure to embrace the challenges posed by industrial cooperation may therefore cost companies dearly.

Managerial challenges

Joint ventures may prove as attractive to small firms as to their larger rivals. However, the risk for small firms is being taken over by the more powerful partner. Small organisations dealing in innovative products are a rich source of new technology introduction for larger firms, joint ventures serving as a pre-emptive stage in acquiring the technology (and the firm).

For all firms, successful joint ventures usually necessitate a shift in company 'culture'. Companies generally grow on the basis of their ability to compete and to develop strategies allowing them to gain a strong market position at the expense of leading rivals. However, as the global market environment is becoming increasingly competitive in terms of market entry and development as well as technological innovation, success in some business sectors is becoming more and more reliant on striking a balance between competition and cooperation, rather than simple organic expansion. Nevertheless, it must be stressed that joint ventures are not a 'quick fix' for firms attempting to develop their international activities. While

Figure 19.5 Alliances in the information technology sector (1985–9)

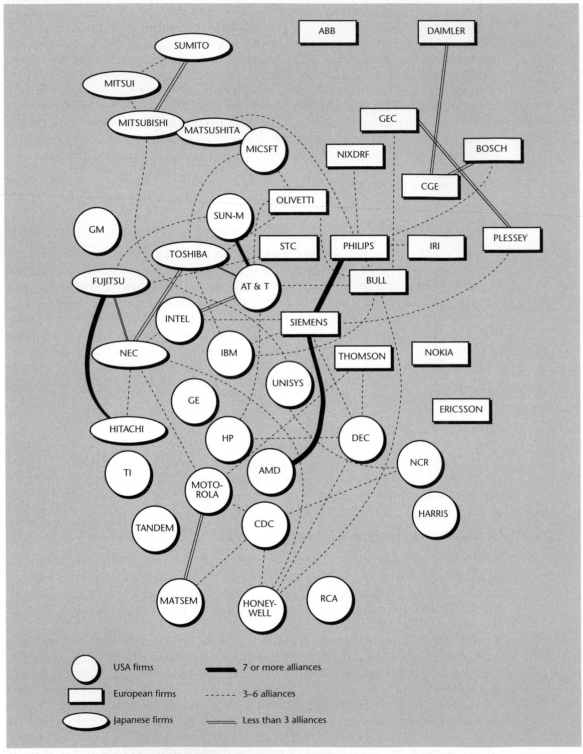

Source: C Freeman and J Hagedoorn (1992) *Globalisation of technology*: working paper, Maastricht Research Institute on Innovation and Technology. Reprinted by kind permission of the authors.

many firms have found that entering markets through established distribution networks of competitor firms can provide rapid access to markets and easy assimilation of cultural differences, the longevity of joint ventures is thrown into question by the documented high failure rates resulting from the difficulties of managing joint operations on an ongoing basis (Doz *et al.*, 1990). Conflict between partners is common in joint alliances due to a number of factors:

- the ongoing desire to suboptimise – this can result in a failure to share information or overpricing for managerial/component inputs;
- resource imbalances – resulting in a failure by one party to dedicate managerial time or finance to the activity;
- exchange rate fluctuations – resulting in lowering of expected returns for one party;
- conflicting strategic objectives and hidden agendas – all too often firms enter into joint ventures for reasons which they do not publicise to their partner and this inevitably results in a lack of trust and in failure of the venture;
- the relative strategic importance of the venture – leading to conflict over control of the operation.

It is clear, then, that failure to embrace the challenges posed by cooperation will ultimately result in the demise of the venture. Indeed, some industry observers now suggest that project-based alliances are preferable to the pursuit of long-term business alliances, which tend to be fraught with problems, not least because flexibility can be hard to achieve since it means constantly re-evaluating expectations and outcomes:

'Purely contractual agreements offer little flexibility, unless they are constantly renegotiated, a cumbersome and often irritating process. Contracts, though, by limiting the partners' commitment, can be terminated at a relatively low cost. Flexibility may thus be achieved through belonging to a network of companies, engaging in flexible short-term contracts, provided these companies know each other well enough to limit transaction costs.'   (Doz *et al.*, 1990)

The trend in business seems to be so much in this direction that Handy (1994) has concluded:

'When intelligence is the primary asset, the organisation becomes more like a collection of project groups, some fairly permanent, some temporary, some in alliance with other parties.'

BEST PRACTICE MANAGEMENT

Boyacigiller and Adler (1995) point to an interesting limitation in the understanding of multinational management – management, as an academic subject, is biased towards the cultural understanding of the American way of doing things. In the English-speaking world a strong focus on the largest English-speaking community is unsurprising, and likewise the ignorance of all that is not translated into English. The economic power of the USA through the 1950s and 1960s led to the development of models and theories that can be considered peculiarly American in nature. As international activity spread to the multinational enterprises of Europe and Japan, new and equally culturally bound and self-referring theories of business developed.

It is only in the last decade or so that theorists and businesses alike have begun to learn and make the effort to learn from their international neighbours that there are many ways of doing business and the key is not to try to persuade the world that a particular way is best, but rather that an amalgam of different elements, together delivering 'best practice', may, or even must, be the ultimate goal.

In the West in the early 1980s interest in Japanese management practices grew rapidly, the key question asked being: What makes the Japanese so successful? This led to an exploration of the various facets of Japanese management and questions regarding the transferability of these facets to non-Japanese business. In many ways this hunger for knowledge was unremarkable. In 1987 Japan produced over 10 per cent of world GDP, compared with a figure of only 2 per cent 20 years earlier. Japan's share of world exports rose from 7 per cent in 1962 to 16 per cent in 1990, and in 1989 the outflow of Japanese foreign direct investment totalled US$67.5 billion (up from an average of US$3.6 billion throughout the 1970s). The question for Western firms was to what extent could this formula be copied or, indeed, should it be copied as a means of attaining global success? Now that the Japanese bubble has burst and America has shown that in technology, particularly in services that for decades have been more important than manufacturing from the perspective of the early twenty-first century, this attention to Japan seems misplaced, but it is only with the benefit of hindsight that this is obvious. Academics and managers alike failed to see that the Japanese excelled only in manufacturing and only in specific sectors, but they provided important lessons even so.

Japanese management practices

> 'We are going to win and the industrial West is going to lose out: there's nothing much you can do about it, because the reasons for failure are within yourself ... for you, the essence of management is getting the ideas out of the heads of the bosses into the hands of labour ... for us, the core of management is precisely the act of mobilising and pulling together the intellectual resources of all employees ... only by drawing the combined brainpower of all employees can a firm face up to the turbulence and constraints of today's environment.'
>
> (Konosuke Matsushita, *The Economist*, 6 March 1993)

This quotation from a top Japanese executive demonstrates that Japan's success in the 1980s may partly have been attributable to a totally different managerial ethos, an integral part of the local business culture. This immediately cast doubt over the ability of Western firms simply to replicate Japanese working practices in Western organisations. Nevertheless, it was possible to distinguish between the 'hard' production techniques that could be copied relatively easily and the 'soft', more intangible cultural framework in which the Japanese economy operated.

Production techniques utilised so successfully in Japan are ironically not unique. Many of them were introduced into Japan with US aid packages and technology transfer deals after the Second World War, particularly the quality control philosophy and associated business methodologies. They were implemented enthusiastically by Japanese managers after being adapted to suit the Japanese cultural preference for group and teamworking – the concept of *wa* which is about belonging, cooperation, harmony and achievement.

Oliver and Wilkinson (1992) identify four groups of factors characteristic of Japanese industry:

- **Manufacturing methods** – including total quality control, quality circles, in-process controls such as statistical process control, just-in-time delivery and management systems and continuous improvement – *kaizen*.

- **Organisational structures and systems** – including management accounting, which does not simply inform but forces improvements, research and development, led by powerful *susha* (project leaders). In addition organisational structures are flatter.

- **Personnel practices** – including lifetime employment, longer working hours and commitment to consultation and improvement.

- **Wider social, political and economic conditions** – incorporating enterprise unions, buyer–seller relationships, government support and economic structures, including an integral banking system.

Manufacturing methods

The first of these areas constitutes the most tangible elements of the Japanese business system. The practices focus on quality and efficiency and, as such, have the potential to enhance competitiveness. It is these, more than the other factors highlighted, which have been transferred to the West. Table 19.2 outlines the nature and scope of the most commonly utilised business practices.

Organisation structures and systems

The main distinguishing feature of Japanese organisations is their flat structure, which promotes a 'hands-on' management ethos and management by consensus. This 'bottom-up' approach to management reflects the belief that workers have the potential to improve the quality of their work. This consensus mentality and team approach to business is reflected in narrow salary differentials between the top and bottom of the organisation.

Nevertheless, while teams are used to solve problems and aid company efficiency this is not at the expense of personal leadership and individual champions of industry. Many leading Japanese companies have attained their position in world markets as a result of strong leadership.

Management accounting procedures also differ radically from those typically found in Western organisations. They are extremely product-focused and involve activity-based costing programmes rather than the 'cost plus' variant. This gives organisations greater flexibility to adapt to changes in the business environment and reflects a market-driven rather than profit-driven view of organisational development. This approach is part of the reason why Japanese firms have tended to have a longer-term view of business development, planning being based on the development of market share rather than on quick returns on capital, which can often preclude new investment and development.

However, tendencies to overemphasise the long termism of the Japanese economy were soon realised:

> *'A far-sighted Japan and a myopic America make a tidy contrast, but one with little basis in fact. By and large, Japanese managers are at least as much obsessed with short-term results as their American counterparts ... They have arrived where they are today not by rigidly adhering to predetermined long-range strategies, but by paying*

scrupulous attention to performance on a monthly or even weekly basis – performance measured not against a three- or five-year plan, but against budget, against return on sales, against competitor performance.'　　　　　　　　　　　　　　(Ohmae, 1982)

It is therefore the difference in approach to measuring profits rather than profit concerns themselves which distinguish between Japanese and Western firms. Whereas Western firms tend to concentrate on return on investment (ROI), Japanese organisations concentrate on return on sales (ROS).

A final area of interest is the links developed between manufacturing companies and their suppliers. As outlined earlier in the chapter, cooperation, either formal (through joint development agreements) or informal (through shared communica-

Table 19.2 Japanese manufacturing techniques

MANUFACTURING TECHNIQUE	OVERVIEW
Total quality control	The despecialising of the business function. Responsibility for quality remains in its 'natural' place, namely where production is performed. It incorporates all business functions with the aim being customer satisfaction, both internal to the organisation (downstream business units) and external to the company (intermediaries and final customers).
Quality circles	These are small groups, usually between five and ten people, who meet voluntarily to try to find ways to improve quality and productivity. Members are trained in statistical analysis and problem-solving techniques.
Statistical process control (SPC)	This system is used to assist in the control of production processes in order to achieve less variation in output and to ensure quality. SPC involves operators periodically sampling their own production, not with a view to accepting or rejecting it but in order to produce a chart of how the process itself is behaving. In addition to reducing scrap and reworking costs, minimising variation in components can improve product performance significantly.
Just-in-time (JIT) production	'The JIT idea is simple: produce and deliver finished goods in time to be sold, subassemblies just in time to be assembled into finished goods, fabricated parts just in time to go into the subassemblies and purchase materials just in time to be transformed into fabricated parts' (Schonberger, 1982). The system requires predictable and planned demand, or production flexibility, to cater for changes in demand.
***Kanban* production system**	This system involves containers for holding stock and cards for initiating production. This means that the amount of stock in the system can be varied by altering the number of cards in the system. In this way materials are pulled through the production process according to the demand for final assembly rather than pushed through by an inflexible production plan.
Flexible working	In Japanese firms this includes teamworking (or cellular manufacturing). This is facilitated by multiskilled workers who can be rotated between jobs. The system simplifies workflow allowing workers to be moved to alleviate bottlenecks and ensure a continuous flow of production.

tion and assistance), can be regarded as quasi-internalisation of up-stream business functions. The Japanese have developed very sophisticated mechanisms for cooperating with contractors and suppliers to the extent that they have even supported foreign direct investment programmes for their 'partner' organisations to service their business needs in overseas markets.

In the last few years, and particularly since the onset of the Asian financial crisis as Japan has increasingly stagnated, America's telecommunications and technology revolution attention has reverted to American management practices. In particular, the USA is now seen as the leading provider of services, the sector that long ago eclipsed manufacturing and contributes almost three-quarters of GNP in all developed economies. Moreover, a growing proportion of all trade is now in services, ironically particularly in those very financial services of banking and insurance so troublesome for the Japanese.

Personnel practices

Japanese personnel practices are very suited to manufacturing organisation. They rely on cooperation, not mere compliance. The concept of 'collectivism' starts in the family and extends to the business organisation, where mutual dependence and loyalty are central features. Within such groups there is a strict hierarchy, based on seniority, where those lower down the organisation (or family) have a duty to their elders which must be repaid through diligence and loyalty. Seniority is also the basis for promotion.

Loyalty gives rise to a sense of belonging and concern over the future welfare of the group, which results in a committed and motivated workforce working for the good of the company (group) rather than the individual. Loyalty also leads to lifetime employment as workers and managers feel tied to common goals rather than individual development and career progression.

The best Japanese companies are highly dependent on the contribution of their skilled, flexible workforce. Core workers are protected and nurtured because they are viewed as a critical resource. They face tough selection and induction procedures and ongoing training but in return they enjoy secure contracts and attractive remuneration packages. Nevertheless, profit-linked bonus schemes can result in broad differentials in pay between boom and slump periods.

The question arises as to how far such practices are helpful in developing services, in focusing on the individual consumer and in tailoring business to the uniqueness of services, when services lack the homogeneity of products and where production and consumption are seen to be simultaneous.

Wider social, political and economic considerations

The term '**Japan Inc**' was coined in response to the coherence and interrelatedness of Japan's economic effort. Western organisations, which for many years believed that Japan was closed to Western business, have used this term to describe the highly protectionist nature of the Japanese economy, wherein the Ministry of Trade and Industry has carved out comfortable cartel-like markets devoid of the threat of Western competition. The reality, however, is far more complex.

First, it is important to allay the myth that the Japanese market is devoid of competition. Domestic competition among Japanese firms is highly aggressive and, while many industries are characteristically oligopolistic in nature (tending to lead to oligopolistic-style strategies), this has more to do with the **keiretsu groups**, which are broad-based conglomerates stemming from the activities of large and wealthy industrial families. Companies within these groups are highly interrelated through a complex array of cross-shareholdings and directorships. Each *keiretsu* involves a number of disparate industries including manufacturing organisations, banking institutions, trading companies and service firms. There is, therefore, great potential for synergy within *keiretsu* groups as skills and resources can be drawn from a wide pool of industrial and commercial activity. The 22 existing groups account for a substantial proportion of the economy, are extremely influential and constitute the international face of Japan.

However, this is not the full picture. Outside the *keiretsu* groups the economy boasts a very high proportion of small firms and family firms that make up half of the employment in Japan. They enjoy long-term relationships with the *keiretsu* groups, although, significantly, they are vulnerable and tend to suffer in periods of economic downturn. As these firms are subcontractors and suppliers to the major economic groups they are a significant feature of the total Japanese business system. For example, in the late 1980s Toyota manufactured approximately 4.5 million cars and employed 65,000 workers. General Motors, on the other hand, needed 750,000 employees to produce 8 million cars. The difference may be explained by the value of the car produced by the suppliers – one-quarter for General Motors but one-half for Toyota.

A key feature of the *keiretsu* group is the integral nature of the banking sector. With banks being part of the conglomerate they are tied into the success and the failure of the group. So Japanese firms tend to enjoy more favourable banking rates than their economic counterparts overseas though this has tied them in with the fortune of the banks. In addition, the *keiretsu* groups have strong links with powerful state bureaucracies which involve joint decision making and consultation. This gives the main economic groups a leading voice in industrial policy and development, which ensures that political policy takes into account the needs of industry and commerce but also any reluctance to tackle unpalatable problems like those of massive unperforming loans.

Western business practices

Table 19.3 provides a summary of key Japanese principles and a comparison with Western business practices. For the sake of convenience this comparison treats 'Western business practice' as a single common entity. It has already been suggested in this chapter, however, that there are distinct differences in culture between the developed markets of the West. How, then, can such an agglomerative analysis provide a useful foundation for understanding business practices? The answer to this lies in the focus of analysis. What is being discussed here is corporate culture and business practice, which shows a higher degree of commonality between Western nations than social and economic culture. Nevertheless, differences between nations do exist and where these are deemed important they are given due regard.

Individualism

The benefits of individualism have been well proven in Western organisations. The notion of entrepreneurial spirit is not only welcomed, it is actively encouraged because as the tendency for individuals to compete against each other frequently

Table 19.3 Japanese-style versus Western-style management

JAPANESE STYLE	WESTERN STYLE
Organisational principles	
1. The firm viewed as a collective body; total devotion of the individual to the firm, i.e. joining the firm, not hiring by contract.	1. Functionalist organisation of individuals as specialists.
2. Human-centred, not functionalist-centred organisation.	2. Cooperative work system based on division of labour; subdivision and standardisation of jobs.
3. Stress on cooperative teamwork.	3. Pyramid-shaped bureaucracy.
4. Indeterminate job description and job standing (authority and responsibility); generalist-oriented.	4. Clearly defined job description and job standing (authority and responsibility).
5. Japanese-style adaptation of modern bureaucracy.	5. Employment of contract ('give and take' commercial exchange).
Decision making and communication	
1. Collective decision making (bottom-up consensus-type decision making as seen in the *ringi* system).	1. Top-down decision making and one-way orders (no consideration given to opinions at the lower echelons).
2. Verbal and non-verbal communication (*nemawashi* or behind-the-scenes manoeuvres; information transmitted by implicit understanding, gut decision).	2. Autocratic authority at the top; expanded power of the bureaucracy.
3. Collective work performance system (common-room system; total membership participation and planning).	3. Individual responsibility and competition (fair-play principles).
4. Exemption from responsibility (seat of authority obscure; no one takes responsibility).	4. Strong owner consciousness (the company's president is also a hired hand).
5. Separation of ownership and management (no real power in officers' meetings and general stockholders' meetings).	5. Local armament by lawyers (legal specialists).
6. 'Japan Inc' (collusive relationships of government, business and labour).	
Personnel system/labour management	
1. Life-long employment (no layoffs but there is flexibility by means of part-time and temporary employees).	1. Employment of people only at times when needed; layoffs in bad times.
2. Seniority-based promotion system (evaluations for promotions are quite comprehensive; they stress not just work results but incentive and effort, as well as reflecting capability).	2. Wages and job compensation according to competency (efficiency system) with no relationship to age and seniority.
3. Seniority wage system (stress is placed not just on compensation for labour but on overall exhibition of ability); stress on fringe and welfare benefits.	3. Seniority system at times of promotion and layoffs.

▶

4. Extensive employee training and education.	4. Labour unions are functionally organised by craft and job type; unions safeguard the individual's life and rights.
5. Enterprise labour unions; cooperation between labour and management.	5. Much tension in labour–management relations.

Human relations and values

1. Groupism (the group comes first; value placed on the group; the individual is devoted heart and soul to the group) and mutual dependence.	1. Individualism (ultimate value placed on the individual; devotion and loyalty to the group are weak).
2. Concurrence of the firm's goal and the individual's life goal (devotion to the group; prestige, sense of security; morale pursuant to participation; co-prosperity idea; love of company spirit).	2. To the individual the firm is nothing more than a means to obtain wages and to the firm the individual is like a piece of machinery, a tool.
3. Stress on harmony in human relations (emphasis on feelings and motives, warm human relations, mutual consent of all members and linking of hearts).	3. Human relations in the workplace are simply artificial relations for work purposes; relations cease outside of the company.
4. Egalitarianism in substance (little chance for class discrimination; small earning differentials).	4. Egalitarian in form (strong class consciousness, competition for equal opportunity).
5. Strong desire for the elevation of quality and efficiency.	5. Purpose of life resides in the family and leisure; strong community consciousness.

Source: Based on H Mirza (1984) 'Can – should – Japanese management practices be exported overseas?', *The Business Graduate*, January.

gives rise to the development of new ideas. In the commercial organisation this means new products and technologies. This supports the notion that individualism promotes benefits for society.

Nevertheless, individualism has its drawbacks. First, it tends to promote mobility between organisations as employees attempt to build impressive work records and move up the management ladder at a faster rate than their peers. This produces managers with broad general management experience but limited knowledge and understanding of the workings of an individual company. Nevertheless, mobility can mean that Western managers are exposed to a wide array of differing business practices as they move between organisations. This mirrors the situation in Japan, to some extent, although here mobility tends to be controlled within organisations by senior managers rather than at the personal level.

Second, it dilutes continuity in management with new personnel frequently replacing old and constantly moving business departments in a different direction. This can be unsettling to the workforce and overall morale, with concomitant adverse effects on productivity.

Finally, individualism may make it difficult to build cooperation, both within and outside the company. With cooperation between business departments and between organisations becoming an increasingly important feature of global business activity there is a case for concern regarding Western managers' ability to adapt from a competitive to a cooperative mentality.

Given the above it is not difficult to see why there has been a renewed interest in the development of teamworking. Management education increasingly stresses the importance of the ability of managers to work closely together and to recognise that bringing to bear multiple perspectives on issues at hand is a powerful tool. In an international context where cultural differences need to be recognised and accounted for, bringing together parties from different cultures is even more important, but easier in societies where heterogeneity rather than homogeneity is the tradition.

Communication and employee involvement

Traditionally employee involvement in Western business management has been somewhat limited, with organisations demonstrating classic hierarchical structures, decisions being made at a senior level and executed by the workforce. Interestingly the Social Chapter of the single European market initiative attempts to redress this balance and create a more harmonious relationship between managers and workers. The UK has been vehement in its criticism of this proposal, partly because it is seen as rejuvenation of union activity through the 'back door'. The Conservative government of the 1980s worked hard to dilute the power of UK trade unions in an effort to eradicate union interference in working practices, which frequently led to industrial action and lost output. Their criticisms, however, appear to have missed the point. Employee involvement is not so much about empowering the workforce to take action against management as to providing an environment in which employees are encouraged to take a greater interest in the long-term success of the organisation.

Germany provides a direct corollary to the UK case. It has broadly adopted the concept of 'co-determination' where, in companies of more than 2000 employees, the law dictates that 50 per cent of representation on supervisory boards must come from employees other than management. In the early stages of introduction there was a great deal of management scepticism, not least because worker representatives have to be given access to full company information, including objectives and strategic direction. An indirect benefit of worker participation is its ability to protect firms from hostile takeovers.

In the USA, slow take-up of employee involvement programmes is partly due to union resistance. Rather than favour teamwork programmes, certain unions have seen them as a covert means of 'union-busting' by changing the nature of employee interaction. Interestingly, the programmes of employee involvement being implemented in the USA are beginning to diverge from those in Japan:

> *'In American-style teamwork, for example, workers not only gain a more direct voice in shop floor operations – as in Japan. They also take over managerial duties, such as work and vacation scheduling, ordering materials, and hiring new members.'*
>
> (*Business Week*, 10 July 1989)

In essence, American systems are building on Japanese principles in such a way that they fit with local cultural conditions. By empowering employees in this way, companies are combining the benefits of cooperation and teamwork with individualism and entrepreneurship.

Training and development

As the demands on firms are changing and increasingly requiring more flexible manufacturing and work practices, teamwork, as already noted, and multiskilling are essential if firms are to remain competitive. This means training the workforce in a variety of skills so that it can react quickly to changes in models and production runs as in service requirements. Harnessing the knowledge and expertise of in-house managers can reduce the cost of such training considerably. SP Tyres in Birmingham, a company which has introduced teamwork and flexible manufacturing, has an extensive and very cost-effective training programme:

'This is because most of it is done relatively inexpensively in-house by multidisciplinary teams, led by senior managers. These teams take responsibility for training other members of staff, often in areas outside their occupational expertise.'

(*Financial Times*, 3 January 1990)

Wider education and training issues are also of relevance. Japan's managerial educational system stresses life-long learning programmes which provide for ongoing training once, and usually only once, individuals have left the formal education system. In the West it is the German education system which is held up as an example of good practice. A key feature of the system is the close relationship between business organisations and educational institutions, and the high propensity of organisations to make in-house provision for training their employees. This runs the gamut from the extensive apprenticeship system to management training programmes, supported by university and polytechnic staff but conducted in the workplace. The main benefit of such industry–education cooperation is that it allows individuals to be trained in the necessary skills for their career/job role as well as meeting the skills training needs of the organisation, while also creating company loyalty. Moves in other countries to encourage greater cooperation between industry and education are testament to the benefits that can be derived. Failure of managers to consider the educational needs of their workforce is likely to result in long-term problems for the organisation as the skills required of workers are continually changing in response to developments in technology and global economic conditions.

Western short-termism

In the late 1980s and early 1990s, before the USA managerially eclipsed Japan, Western short-termism, though sometimes denied, had often been accused of being the root cause of failings in Western relative competitiveness. A study on the competitiveness of British industry (Buckley *et al.*, 1992) concluded that the short-term mentality of many British businesses restricted investment and development in such a way that full exploitation of advantages was not possible. The UK stock market was frequently cited as a major contributory factor in this short-term mentality, with companies being constantly judged on their share performance rather than on their long-term potential. The other major contributory factor is obviously Western business culture which, as outlined above, tends to measure company performance in terms of ROI rather than on more market and growth-led dimensions, but, while there is some truth in these allegations (which continue, despite the revival in Western competitiveness), aspiration to be long-termist may, in an increasingly unpredictable world, be equally unwise.

In many ways the plethora of articles on 'Japanese success' have been misleading. Many implicitly assumed that everything about Japanese management was better than anything the West could offer. This belied the fact that America continued to boast a larger number of multinational companies and that the UK remained the second-largest foreign direct investor in the world economy.

Nevertheless, it is said that the Japanese have never been too proud to learn from their Western counterparts (and this needs to continue to be true if Japan is to return to growth) and this is perhaps the key lesson, not the idea that Japanese management practices are inherently 'better'. Japanese management has been a continually developing phenomenon which has often drawn on Western input. Peters and Waterman's *In Search of Excellence* (1982) described the practices employed by the most successful US corporations and sold 50,000 copies within two days of the Japanese translation being published, and Ohmae (1982) reported Japanese managers remarking on similarities between their companies and the 'excellent' ones in the USA.

The message for firms, therefore, is to pursue good business practice regardless of its source. The Japanese never did have and do not now have a monopoly over 'best practice' and, while they have developed successful mechanisms for manufacturing management, each firm has to adopt policies which fit with all of its national, industry and corporate culture.

It should be stressed that no country's business system can be replicated in another country. Subtle ambiguities of culture and different ways of thinking (which mean many things cannot be precisely defined) and acceptance of constant dynamism, as distinct from seeking an end to a process, underpin the concept of constant improvement (Fry, 1991). Rather, any country's success should act as a catalyst to other nations to pursue the development of 'lean organisations' with the capability for global competitiveness.

Perhaps all firms should take a lead from companies such as IBM which, for many years, pursued strategies sometimes labelled 'Japanese'. The 'IBM way' was described by Bassett (1986) as 'exactly the opposite of the Japanese method' because the company culture was based on individualism rather than collectivism. Nevertheless, efficiency and quality are key elements of company strategy and there are perhaps grounds to suggest:

> *'Japanese and American management is 95 per cent the same and differs in all-important respects.'* (Takeo Fujisawa, co-founder of the Honda Motor Company)

Differences lie in approach rather than practice.

That said, responsiveness to changes in the environment remain key. International operators seem no less immune to bubbles, financial crises and busts than their domestic counterparts. Developed-country authorities cannot always be expected to ignore the hollowing out of their manufacturing any more than can their developing country equivalents accept the obstacles their own businesses face in penetrating developed markets. Indeed, none can ignore major developments such as EU enlargement and the rise and rise of countries such as India and China.

SUMMARY

This chapter has outlined many of the complexities of multinational management, which essentially centre on managing organisations in a diverse and dynamic global environment.

■ Readers should now understand something of the importance of managing in an ever-changing global environment, be aware of the decision-making challenges facing managers with regard to developing strategies which cater both for environmental change and cultural diversity and have some knowledge of varying business practices employed by firms around the globe – practices which are now converging and merging to make international firms more efficient and effective in their global operations.

■ It should be apparent that management of multinational and international firms requires continual change and adaptation. The economic world is not static and thus, in order to remain competitive, managers must constantly look for new strategies and business practices that allow such changes to be turned into opportunities rather than threats. Resting on the laurels of past business success or simply attempting to capitalise on monopolistic technologies is not sufficient to carry firms into the future.

■ Innovating organisational structures and strategies are just as important as developing new products and technologies, such that the 'winners' in the new global order will be those firms adept at managing change rather than those intent on managing fixed resources.

Review and discussion questions

1 *With environmental change serving as a key exogenous factor in organisational decision making, how can managers develop business systems which allow them to prepare for, and adapt to, such change?*

2 *How may managers ensure that they do not lose their competitive advantage by deciding to 'externalise' key parts of the value chain?*

4 *The literature on international business is awash with examples of failed joint ventures between firms. How, then, can the increased trend towards joint venture activity be justified?*

5 *Why are firms beginning to reject hierarchical organisational structures in favour of flatter, functional-centred business systems?*

6 *To what extent can any country's management practices be transferred to multinational firms?*

7 *Are management practices employed in particular parts of the world intrinsically 'superior' or 'inferior' to those employed elsewhere?*

CASE STUDY

On the globalisation of business

It is widely recognised that over the last quarter of the twentieth century some major changes have occurred in the character of contemporary capitalism, as the political-economic order established in the wake of World War Two came under increasing pressure, leading in turn to questions about the viability and morality of the post-Enlightenment project of modernity. This was registered in phrases such as 'the crisis of Fordism' and 'the crisis of the welfare state'. The references to crisis raised disturbing questions as to the sustainability of existing arrangements (even more so as recognition of the ecological limits to mass production and consumption lifestyles began to emerge) and about what might replace them, ushering in an era of 'post-isms' (post-Fordism, post-colonialism, post-modernism, for example). Furthermore, they also raised questions as to the adequacy of existing forms of knowledge and ways of understanding political, economic and social life, generating further 'post-isms' (post-positivism, post-structuralism and so on).

Over the same 25 years, and linked to the explosion of post-isms, there was a growing recognition within the social sciences of the importance of spatiality to cultural, economic, political and social life. The difference that place and space make became of central concern across much of the social sciences. This reflected a growing assertion that the spatial was too important to be left to geography, the 'traditional' disciplinary locus of concerns with questions to do with the production and meanings of space and territory. The net result was a remarkably vibrant and productive cross-disciplinary debate on the centrality of the spatiality of social life, especially within Europe. There had previously been recognition that spatial variation was important (at scales ranging from the micro to macro), but there had also been a strong tendency to conceptualise space as a pre-formed container into which these various processes were then poured and sedimented. Now, however, there was an increasing recognition of the importance of the social production of place and space and of varied spatial scales as integral to the constitution of economies and societies, drawing on long-established work, primarily in human geography. As part of this, there were growing claims as to the significance of both supra-national and sub-national spatial scales and interest in the complex ways in which the sub-national and supra-national became combined with the national in complex multiscalar architectures of economies and societies and systems of governance and regulation.

A strong strand running through all this is a debate that revolved around concepts such as 'globalisation', 'Europeanisation' (especially as this relates to the formation, widening and deepening of the European Union) and 'transnationalisation'. Such concepts are intended to register recognition that a formerly international political economy, constructed around the building blocks of national economies, polities and societies, and multinational forms of corporate organisation, is being transformed to create new, qualitatively different forms of supra-national organisation. Of these new concepts, however, it is fair to say that 'globalisation' has generated the most heat, if not always corresponding light, as it has become a site of fierce theoretical and political disagreement and debate. 'Globalisation' is a strongly contested concept, with no consensus as to its meaning and significance (or even as to its spelling), not least because analytical and theoretical concerns are often elided (deliberately or inadvertently) with political and normative claims.

Proponents of 'globalisation' often disagree amongst themselves as to its meaning and most significant aspects, while others simply challenge the validity and utility of the concept. Few would now subscribe to the simplistic view that 'globalisation' implied global homogenisation (of cultures, markets, production structures, fashions and tastes) as an almost automatic consequence of the annihilation of space by time due to technological innovations in transport and ICT. Recognition of this, however, simply raises a more difficult question: how best to conceptualise and comprehend the more complex and multiscalar geographies of a globalising world? While 'the national' is no longer unquestioningly prioritised, and almost automatically accorded methodological and onto logical pre-eminence, there are various responses to this. Some argue, for example, that 'the national' remains the critical spatial scale in understanding contemporary political-economies, albeit in transformed relations with social actors constituted at other spatial scales. Others emphasise the centrality of sub-national spatial scales, such as the urban and regional, as the central nodes within an emergent global economy. Indeed, the most sophisticated theorisations are those that focus upon the multi-scalar organisation of contemporary political economies, and seek to establish empirically which scales and processes are dominant in a given conjuncture via careful, theoretically informed empirical analysis rather than seeking theoretically and/or politically to pre-empt the answer to this question.

Source: Extract from R Hudson (2002) 'On the Globalization of Business', *British Journal of Management*, December, 13 (4), pp. 362–6.

FURTHER READING

Emmott, B, Crook, C and Michelthwait, J (2002) *Globalisation: Making Sense of an Integrating World: Reasons Effects and Challenges*, **Economist Books.**
A detailed study of globalisation and its effects.

Hutton, W and Giddens, A (2000) *On the Edge*, **London: Jonathan Cape.**
A collection of essays about what globalisation means.

Kynge, J (2007) *China Shakes the World: The Rise of a Hungry Nation*, **Phoenix.**
The development and growth of the Chinese economy.

Legrain, P (2003) *The Open World: The Truth About Globalisation*, **Abacus.**
A point of view on globalisation.

Luce, E (2006) *In Spite of the Gods: The Strange Rise of Modern India*, **Little Brown.**
The development of India in the global economy.

WEBSITES

http://internationalecon.com/
Straightforward explanations of international trade.

http://www.ilo.org/
The website of the International Labour Organisation which provides comprehensive information on international business.

http://www.odci.gov/cia/publications/factbook/
The World Factbook provides information about countries.

http://libweb.uncc.edu/ref-bus/vibehome.htm
Virtual international business and economic sources with links to internet sources on international business.

http://www.internationalist.com/business/
The Center for International Business provides information about international business.

CHAPTER 20

Managing in the twenty-first century

Outcomes

Having read this chapter, you will be able to:

- discuss the universality of the role of managers;
- summarise the skills required in management;
- analyse the development of careers in management;
- understand the importance of management theories;
- explain the results of flatter management structures as organisations face the challenges of their business environment;
- discuss management ideas in the context of the need for managers to take advantage of changing circumstances.

THE ROLE OF A MANAGER

The management role is as old as history, although it only became the subject of serious study in the late nineteenth century. The organisation of the building of the pyramids in the years before 2000 BC, the exploits of generals such as Alexander the Great around 300 BC and the development of great civilisations and empires all over the world through history required management at all levels. The extent to which management is universal and involves generic skills is a point of argument and discussion. Is managing a commercial organisation all that different from managing one in the public sector? Is managing a football team very different from managing a hospital or university? There is no doubting the views of Socrates who suggested by his usual method of asking questions that successful businesspeople and generals perform much the same functions (Exhibit 20.1).

Socrates went further to argue that

> *'the management of private concerns differs only in point of number from that of public affairs. In other respects they are much alike, and particularly in this, that neither can be carried on without men, and the men employed in private and public transactions are the same.'*   (Adair, 1989)

The management role has always involved decision making, choice, supervision and control and has always been much more than a purely operational function. In the future, as in the past, it will include the need to forecast and plan, to organise, to command and coordinate. The role does not mean following instructions without question or carrying out routine tasks as is the case in an operational job – it does mean making decisions between different courses of action. A manager has been described as a person who decides what needs to be done and who arranges for someone to do it – and clearly a managerial job offers opportunities for making choices in what is done, how it is done and when it is done. All of this is within the context of an organisation, its corporate and ethical structure and its external environment.

It is possible to 'measure' a management job by the length of time the manager is left to work alone before the work is checked for quality. This 'time–space discretion' may be a few hours for a supervisor or foreman, a few days for junior and middle managers, up to weeks or months for senior managers. Generally speaking the more choices a manager has then the further up the management hierarchy he or she has climbed. A junior manager has a limited area of choice and limited means to manoeuvre, but the management function can be said to have clearly entered a job at the moment when a significant amount of decision making and choice enters the role.

Promotion in an organisation normally means an increase in the management function, so that decision making and choice become an increasing part of the job. The move from 'player' to 'manager' requires a considerable adjustment, one which many people find difficult to make. The brilliant salesperson, for example, may not be a good sales manager: his or her expertise is in the process of selling and making decisions within that framework not in the organising, controlling and decision making required to be a manager. At the next stage, top managers are concerned much more with planning and organising and will spend relatively little time supervising, while middle managers may spend fairly even amounts of time on planning, organising, directing and controlling. Again, the change in role will involve an adjustment which may be hard to make.

Exhibit 20.1 Socrates

NICOMACHIDES: Isn't it like the Athenians? They have not chosen me after all the hard work I have done since I was called up, in the command of company or regiment, though I have been so often wounded in action. They have chosen Antisthenes, who has never served in a marching regiment nor distinguished himself in the cavalry and understands nothing but money making.

SOCRATES: Isn't that a recommendation? Suppose he proves capable of supplying the men's needs?

NICOMACHIDES: Why, merchants also are capable of making money, but that doesn't make them fit to command any army.

SOCRATES: But Antisthenes also is eager for victory, and that is a good point in a general. Whenever he has been a choir-master, you know, his choir has always won.

NICOMACHIDES: No doubt, but there is no analogy between the handling of a choir and of an army.

SOCRATES: But you see, though Antisthenes knows nothing about music or choir training, he showed himself capable of finding the best experts in those activities. And therefore if he finds out and prefers the best men in warfare as in choir training, it is likely he will be victorious in that too; and probably he will be more ready to spend money on winning a battle with the whole state than on winning a choral competition with his tribe.

NICOMACHIDES: Do you mean, Socrates, that the man who succeeds with a chorus will also succeed with an army?

SOCRATES: I mean that, whatever a man controls, if he knows what he wants and can get it he will be a good controller, whether he controls a chorus, an estate, a city or an army.

NICOMACHIDES: I would never have thought to hear you say that a good business man would make a good general.

SOCRATES: For the good business man, through his knowledge that nothing profits or pays like a victory in the field, and nothing is so utterly unprofitable and entails such heavy loss as a defeat, will be eager to seek and avoid what leads to defeat, prompt to engage the enemy if he sees he is strong enough to win; and above all, will avoid an engagement when he is not ready.

Source: Adapted from J Adair (1989) *Leaders*, Guildford: Talbot Adair Press.

The so-called 'Peter principle' can come into play as people are promoted. This suggests that people tend to be promoted to their level of incompetence – that is, just above the point at which they can cope, a point where they can no longer cope. Luckily this is not always the case but it is essential for managers to discover the level at which they are confident in their ability and can be a success. This is not an easy process because ambition and higher salaries will encourage managers to seek promotion perhaps to a point where they are no longer successful. At the same time, senior managers may promote more junior managers because of their performance at that level.

Organisations have introduced training and development programmes to prepare managers for more senior levels and to attempt to assess their suitability for promotion. The armed services have had this procedure in place for many years in order to decide who should become an officer and then be promoted at every level. This type of process establishes a structured management career, which is reflected in some large companies but is becoming rarer as managers take more responsibility for their own development. John Kotter (2001) has described most US corporations at the present time as 'over-managed and underled', so that managers need to develop their capacity to exercise leadership. Kotter argues that successful corporations do not wait for leaders to emerge, they actively seek out people with leadership potential and expose them to career experiences designed to develop that potential. However, strong leadership with weak management can be worse, or no better, than strong management with weak leadership. An organisation needs both strong management and strong leadership, there needs to be an understanding of the differences between the two so that people can be developed appropriately.

Management is about coping with complexity, while leadership is about coping with change. The two overlap so that strategic management, for example, is about developing strategies that create a fit between an organisation and its environment, and ideally both leadership and management are required for this to be successful (see Zaleznik, 2004). However, while management can provide the organisation and control once a strategy has been developed, it requires leadership to decide on new strategies when the environment alters. As a result of the spread of globalisation, the development of new technology and increasing levels of competition, the organisational environment has become more volatile and major changes have become more and more necessary. This requires more leadership. A clear illustration of this difference between management and leadership is that while in peacetime an army can survive on good administration and management, in wartime an army needs leadership at all levels.

MANAGEMENT SKILLS

Managers need a diversity of skills because of the complexity of the job, including conceptual skills which involve planning and thinking, and the ability to see the organisation as a whole and the relationship of its various parts. They need to understand how their particular role fits into the total organisation. As managers are promoted, the ability to think strategically becomes more important, so that even if they find it difficult to provide leadership they can understand the leader's role. The software company Microsoft has been said to reflect, and is perhaps dependent on, the strategic decisions of Bill Gates, founder and chairman. With modern technology he is able to spread his ideas throughout the whole giant organisation via e-mail, for example the decision to move into the superhighway of communication and information technology. The senior vice-president for US sales and marketing has been quoted as saying

> *'each part of the company has a life of its own, but Bill is the glue that holds it all together.'*
> (Schlewder, 1990)

As managers are promoted into more senior positions they must develop conceptual and strategic skills or their performance will be poor and they will effectively have reached their level of incompetence, and they will not be able to become leaders. This is the problem of promoting a highly competent and successful deputy into the top position, whether this is as the CEO of a company, the head coach of a sports team or the headteacher of a school. The deputy may remain a good 'manager' but may prove to be a hopeless 'leader'. Managers have to organise, control and problem solve, while leaders have to motivate and inspire and provide direction.

In organising and controlling people, the ability to work with people is an essential skill. People management skills are demonstrated by the way a manager is able to motivate, coordinate and communicate with other people. This not only involves distributing work and resolving conflicts but also coaching and encouraging people. Managers have to relate to a wide range of people, employers, colleagues, more senior managers, customers, suppliers and members of the community – they need what has, in the last decade, been called 'emotional intelligence'. They need to have social skills to enable them to be comfortable in a range of situations, to represent the organisation confidently, to focus people's efforts on the objectives of the organisation and to encourage teamwork and a high level of motivation in order to provide for the needs of customers.

> *'Every businessperson knows a story about a highly intelligent, highly skilled executive who was promoted into a leadership position only to fail at the job.'* (Goleman, 1998)

And they may also know about someone with fewer obvious intellectual abilities and technical skills who, when promoted, has succeeded. Goleman's view is that the majority of effective leaders had one thing in common – 'emotional intelligence'. He has identified five components of this emotional intelligence and these are summarised in Exhibit 20.2.

Technical skill is the understanding of proficiency in the performance of specific tasks, whether they are concerned with product engineering, marketing or finance. These skills include specialised knowledge, analytic ability and competence in processes and procedures applied to solving problems. Such skills are more important for junior and middle managers than for senior management where human and conceptual skills are more important. However, most managers have to prove themselves in a technical area before they are given the opportunity to exhibit their conceptual and human skills. Goleman (1998) argues that IQ and technical skills are 'threshhold capabilities' in the sense that they are the entry-level requirements for executive positions. A manager can have the best training, an incisive and analytical mind and smart ideas but still not make a successful leader. A leader must have self-management skills (self-regulation and motivation) and be able to manage relationships with other people (empathy and social skills). These skills can be developed as a result of correctly focused training programmes which concentrate on changing behavioural habits and developing skills such as 'listening' and 'motivating'.

Exhibit 20.2 The components of emotional intelligence

Component	Definition	Characteristics
Self-awareness	an understanding of your own moods and their effect on others	self-confidence, realistic self-assessment
Self-regulation	the ability to control impulses and to think before acting	integrity, open to change
Motivation	a propensity to pursue goals with energy and persistence	strong drive to succeed, optimism and commitment
Empathy	the ability to understand people	expertise in retaining talent, service to customers, cross-cultural sensivity
Social skills	proficiency in managing relationships and in negotiating common ground	effectiveness in leading change and team building

Source: Based on D Goleman (1998) 'What makes a leader?', *Harvard Business Review*, November/December.

MANAGEMENT CAREERS

Management careers tend to evolve through a series of stages. These can either be seen as a fairly straightforward move from exploration through establishment and maintenance to decline; or as a more complex process of transition which occurs every five or seven years. Individual careers do not, of course, necessarily follow either of these patterns exactly, but these patterns do help in understanding where managers are in their careers and what shape the future may be.

The first stage is one of **exploration**, which occurs at the beginning of a career and is characterised by self-analysis and the exploration of the different types of available jobs. This is a stage which most people experience in their late teens and into their twenties. They may hold part-time jobs while at school or college which help them to understand about work and the type of job they may want or want to avoid if possible. The first full-time job is often not the one that people settle into these days (in contrast to the pre-1940s) and there may be some experimentation with various jobs before a career begins to be established.

A career can be seen as a sequence of work experiences which accumulate over a person's working life more or less successfully. The second stage is when the career path is **established**. This is typically when people are aged between the middle twenties and middle thirties. Jobs may now establish a pattern where the experiences of the exploration stage are put into practice and each job is sought as a progression on the previous one. Promotion is sought in the same company or in different companies and a career pattern begins to develop.

The third stage in career evolution is the **maintenance** stage where the established career pattern is maintained and nurtured. The manager's career may stabilise at this stage, grow or even stagnate. It is at this point that careers may reach a plateau where there is little further development. The last stage is the **decline** stage which usually occurs near retirement when people may not be able to maintain prior performance levels because of a loss of interest or difficulty in keeping their job skills up to date. The maintenance stage may occur at any age from the mid-thirties or forties onwards, while decline may set in during the forties, fifties or not until the sixties.

The career plateau occurs when a person becomes stuck in a particular job where the likelihood of promotion or major development is very low. In unskilled and semi-skilled work, the career plateau can start in the twenties when physical energy and motivation are at their greatest and can last until a person's forties or fifties when these factors are decreasing and the period of decline begins. In these types of work, typically seen in areas such as building and construction, earning levels may be highest in a person's twenties and thirties with a levelling off or decline thereafter. Managers hope to continue to increase their real earnings well into their fifties, but their career plateau may arrive sooner than this because of a level of ability or bad luck or poor assessment by superiors. Most people will experience it in one way or another because there is a tendency for there to be more candidates for higher-level positions than there are positions available, so that as managers rise up the hierarchical pyramid even highly successful ones eventually reach a career plateau. This is the case in terms of promotion and with flatter organisations the number of promotional steps has declined in most organisations. However, companies can no longer afford to keep large numbers of 'plateaued' managers with the consequence that redundancy and early retirement become a feature of management careers (see Figure 20.1).

Figure 20.1 Career stages

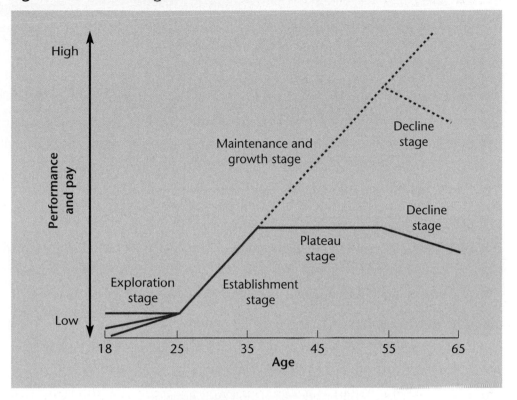

In practice, managers may reach their career plateau at any time because any promotion may prove to be the last at junior, middle or senior management level. Pay levels may reflect this situation as well so that real pay reaches a maximum as the plateau is reached. It is important for managers to recognise that they have reached this stage and to make the most of it. The plateau can be made much more interesting if sideways moves and changes in job roles are possible, or fresh opportunities open up by changing jobs or taking on new developments.

The Levinson model of career evolution (Levinson *et al.*, 1978) suggests that adult life involves a series of transitions in a fairly predictable sequence every five to seven years (see Exhibit 20.3).

The plateau in their career which managers may reach in their forties or fifties can lead to the mid-life crisis or the 'age 50 transition', and perhaps a relatively early decline. Some managers move from one job to another in an attempt to find an area of growth, while others attempt to maintain their interest in a role in which they have become expert. They have to accept that younger managers may overtake them and that they are not going to reach the top of their career path. Levinson's model may act as a guide to pitfalls and opportunities ahead, and to some extent these stages are 'proved' by the exceptional cases which are highlighted in pop music and film careers. A pop group may compress all these stages into a few short years so that they reach the top of the charts and their highest pay levels in their twenties. They then reach a brief plateau and a quick decline from which they may never recover. The more talented groups 're-create' themselves for new audiences every few years, while others move into different areas of the entertainment industry.

Exhibit 20.3 Levinson model of career evolution

- **Age 17–22 Early adult transition** – assertion of independence, breaking away from family ties. Those who prolong parental ties may underperform in their careers

- **Age 22–28 Entering the adult world** – a preoccupation with entering the adult world, education completed and career selection begins

- **Age 28–33 Age 30 transition** – review of career and life progress and feeling of last chance to change career

- **Age 33–40 Settling down** – job and career advancement takes precedence

- **Age 40–45 Mid-life transition** – another period of review, possible mid-life crisis

- **Age 45–50 Entering middle adulthood** – consolidation of period of review, with a possible sense of fulfilment

- **Age 50–55 Age 50 transition** – possible crisis or review of previous periods of transition

- **Age 55–60 Combination of middle adulthood** – relatively stable, with preparation for retirement

- **Age 60–65 Late adult transition** – retirement with review and reflection on career

- **Age 65+ Late adulthood** – evaluation and summing up

Source: D J Levinson, C N Darrow, E B Klein, M H Levinson and B McKee (1978) *The Seasons of a Man's Life*, New York: Knopf. Reprinted by permission of Sterling Lord Literistic Inc. Copyright © by Daniel Levinson.

It is obviously necessary for all managers to analyse their career aims and objectives, to be clear about their own abilities and shortcomings, to be realistic about the opportunities that are available and accept the fact that no one can be as interested in an individual's career as that particular person is. For an ambitious manager a career needs to be planned so that the correct steps can be taken at the right moments, but these plans are unlikely to succeed without a realistic analysis of what opportunities exist and what talents are on offer. In their study of management careers Cappelli and Hamori (2005) confirm that there have been major changes since William H Whyte wrote his 1956 classic book *The Organisation Man*, with hints of change in the 1970s clearly emerging in the 1980s and 1990s. Top executives in the top companies are now generally younger than their predecessors in the 1980s, more of them are female and they have reached the top faster increasingly moving from one company to another as their careers develop. Fewer managers are 'organisation men' employed and developed by one large corporation throughout their adult lives.

The advanced economies have changed dramatically in the last 50 years from an industrial base to a service base and towards the so-called 'knowledge economy' where companies need to be at the forefront of technology, information, knowledge sharing and learning. The typical top executives in the news today are leading companies mainly in such areas as retailing, airlines and computer software. Capelli and Hamori note that certain types of companies in general offer better chances for promotion than others. Growing companies offer the best prospects for promotion, along with young companies – and while marketing was seen as an advantageous route to the top in the 1970s, finance has been the best route since then. Companies such as

> *'General Electric, Procter & Gamble and the like provide extensive training and development opportunities. They also offer relatively long promotion ladders – hence the common notion that these "academic companies" are great to have been from.'*
> (Capelli and Homari, 2005)

The right time to move from a company is obviously a difficult and individual decision, but as the average age of executives falls then delays in promotion become more damaging. Other factors which can be taken into account in making decisions are such matters as the future of the company and its stage in its life cycle, along with consideration of the length of time already spent in the company:

> *'Research suggests that the odds of advancement fall as a person's tenure in a job grows. Individuals who advance to the top tend to be amongst the youngest in their cohorts – possibly because talent and ability get spotted early, possibly because of "halo" or reputation effects.'*
> (Capelli and Hamori, 2005)

While it may seem at first glance that the 'delayering' of company structure would provide greater opportunities for internal promotion, there may be a view that the gap between moving from one layer to another is too great in terms of experience and competencies, so that the company recruits from outside. An account manager may find that the way to the role of sales manager or sales director is blocked because there are no meaningful intermediary jobs in the company where the ability to manage people and to take responsibility for profit and loss can be proved. Small companies may provide more opportunities than large companies for proving ability in these areas.

MANAGEMENT DEVELOPMENT

In 1987 the Institute of Management (renamed the Chartered Management Institute since it received a Royal Charter in 2002) reported on the importance of managers to the economy of a country:

> *'One of the most important resources possessed by a nation is its managerial skills. Ideas can be turned into wealth when combined with effective management. The ability to create more wealth is vital if the growing expectations of society are to be met. Those services which spend the wealth must also be well managed to ensure the maximum benefit from the resources available.'*   (Constable and McCormick, 1987)

This report found that over 10 per cent of the working population were in managerial roles in Great Britain. Since then this proportion has continued to grow as more people are required to manage other people, physical resources, financial resources and information, ideas and knowledge. The report highlighted the lack of systems for management development in the UK compared to other industrial countries, a situation that has not changed dramatically in the last two decades in spite of a variety of initiatives.

In the last 20 years there have been a number of initiatives to promote management development, but the world of work has become more competitive as well as more flexible and volatile and hours of work have increased for many managers rather than fallen. An article in *Guardian Weekend* (12 June 2004) based on her book *Willing Slaves: How The Overwork Culture is Ruling Our Lives* (Bunting, 2004) asked the question 'why haven't wealth and technological development brought us leisure?' The argument is that from John Maynard Keynes to Alvin Toffler, thinkers predicted that the twenty-first century would be an 'age of leisure' and that with the expansion of automation and the rapid developments in computer technology there were concerns about how people would usefully fill their time. In fact in the last decade or so hours at work have increased rather than fallen:

> *'The office is now where the heart is, not the home, as the complexities of the workplace demand an ever larger share of our emotional resources.'*   (Bunting, 2004)

The demands of a job have been measured in terms of time and effort, to which now has to be added its emotional demands. This has partly been due to the growth of the service economy plus the emphasis on a customer focus, and partly as a result of the shake-up of the structure of enterprises and their physical organisation. An open-plan office alters the relationship between the boss and the team, while 'flatter' organisations require the individual to have qualities of empathy, persuasion and communication skills. At the same time areas of work such as call centres, with a demand for consistent politeness and friendly helpfulness, have been one of the fastest growing sources of employment. Increasing demands on people's time at work have been seen as an obstacle to initiatives in management and staff development such as Investors in People and the 'learning organisation':

> *'Often managers and employees were faced with many competing demands on their time and energy, which they had simultaneously to negotiate. These pressures can lead to role strain, or what we have described as "initiative overload."'*   (Bell et al., 2002)

Initiatives in the development of managers have included those developed as a result of *The Making of British Managers* (Constable and McCormick, 1987) and *The Making of Managers* (Handy, 1987) which led to the formation of the National Forum for Management and in 1988 its executive arm, the Management Charter Initiative (MCI). Also during this period Investors in People, a state-sponsored workplace training initiative, encouraged managers to achieve a base level of good practice in the development of employees, while the 'National Targets for Education and Training' were published as a result of the Confederation of British Industry (1989) report *Towards a Skills Revolution* with the objective of making 'lifetime learning a reality throughout the workforce'. At the same time there was an increase in the number of MBAs on offer, although a report by the Chartered Management Institute (Mann, 2006) found that the boom time for MBA salaries had waned from increases of 39 per cent in 2002 to 18 per cent in 2004. This had been partly because employers who paid for their employees' MBA studies, which usually involved a contractual obligation, did not need to offer a large reward on graduation. At the same time the increase in the number of people holding MBAs may have dampened salary increases. The average age for those taking the MBA in Europe was found to be 26 to 27. A *Times* newspaper sponsored survey was reported by the CMI to have found that 'base salaries increase sharply between three and five years after graduation' and that 'average salaries three to five years after graduation were 53 per cent higher than graduates' pre-MBA salaries' (Mann, 2006).

However in spite of these and subsequent initiatives, a CMI report published in 2005 found that only 20 per cent of UK managers had a management-related qualification (Kennett, 2006). Other results showed that experience at work was more valuable for managers than natural ability, and that business performance was improved when management development was linked to business strategy. At the same time organisations such as Investors in People, the British Quality Foundation and the Learning and Skills Council supported the link between investment in management development and improved business performance.

The largest companies, such as Shell and ICI, have recognised the need for management development for a long time but there remains a difference between the demand for management development by employers and the demand by individuals. From the employers' point of view, their interest is in managers obtaining skills rather than qualifications. Some employers have been found to be opposed to qualifications because they made managers potentially more mobile. Individuals, on the other hand, want to obtain qualifications as well as skills in order to build up their curriculum vitae and to increase their opportunities in the job market. Employers have tended to emphasise job experience and innate ability as the most important factors contributing to creating an effective manager, although training would help. Education and management training has also been recognised to play an important part in broadening a manager's perspective, especially in a situation in which many managers obtain much of their experience within a single function. They may be experts in managing areas of production, or sales or finance, but may have very little knowledge across these functional borders. This not only limits the number of potential senior managers with a width of experience but can also encourage a blinkered perspective amongst managers, so that, for example, they know about production but little about the finances that provide investment and facilities.

The idea that management might become a 'profession' similar to medicine or the law has been floated at times without much support from major companies. The possibility that their managers could accumulate qualifications which might not be closely related to their actual work has sometimes been felt to be a distraction from their main occupation, so that while MBAs and other management qualifications have expanded in availability and in the number of managers obtaining them, they are often studied as a result of individual initiative rather than organisational support. In support of the Charter Group Initiative in the 1980s and 1990s, the president of the Board of Trade threw out a challenge to companies to develop the talents of their managers as an essential part of their business strategy. In practice, a survey of 258 chief executives, carried out for the *Sunday Times* (Smith, 1997), found that British managers did not have the skills to obtain the full potential from their businesses. This survey suggested that they lacked the vision and were too concerned with cost-cutting to build their businesses. The majority of the chief executives thought that the business, social and economic environment in Great Britain had created a culture in which cost-cutting was the driving force for managers instead of the development of the skills to manage growth and innovation. They believed that leadership and a strategic vision were by far the most important skills while, in practice, managers were better versed in technical and financial skills.

As managers have had to take more responsibility for and control over their careers, they have had to chart their own path through management development, balancing qualifications and courses with work experience to build up a curriculum vitae which will propel them into the first interview for a job. After this the result of subsequent interviews will depend on a manager's communication and presentational skills, the quality of the other candidates for a job and whether or not a person's 'face fits', that is whether or not the people already in a company feel that they can work with a particular candidate. A *Management Today* survey (Kennett, 2006) found that nearly half the 1000 managers surveyed from a mixture of private and public sector organisations were very ambitious and another quarter were moderately ambitious. However, over half were not actively seeking promotion and nearly 70 per cent did not want their boss's job. In five years' time, 27.1 per cent thought they would be in the same organisation in a more senior role, 19.1 per cent thought they would be running their own business, 17.4 per cent thought they would be in the same job or a similar job in another organisation and 7.7 per cent thought they would have retired. The Loyalty and Alliances Manager of BP, who had survived a radical restructuring in the company, was quoted in the survey as saying:

> *'change has become a way of life. It never stops – we have to continually reinvent ourselves. Just like Tesco. Or Madonna.'*　　　　　　　　　　　　　　(Kennett, 2006)

So just as an organisation has to restructure to keep up with the competition, so ambitious managers have to make sure that their development retains their competitiveness in the job market.

MANAGEMENT THEORIES

Why should managers be interested in management theories?

→ Chs 1 & 7　Management theories were discussed briefly in Chapters 1 and 7 where it was noted that they have been particularly important since the Industrial Revolution. The need for a systematic approach to management arose as a result of the development of new machinery and the concentration of great quantities of raw materials and large numbers of workers in one place. Workshops, and then factories, produced goods in large quantities which had to be distributed widely, while the move from a self-sufficient economy to one based on the division of labour created a need for organisation and control. The development of economic theories based on the factors of production developed by Adam Smith in *The Wealth of Nations* (1776) emphasised the relationship between the separate elements in the production of goods and services.

However, although the Industrial Revolution emphasised the need for a systematic approach to management, in fact through history every action that managers have taken and every plan they have developed has been based on some theory either in the back of their minds or in the forefront of their thinking, so that they anticipate that the actions they are planning will lead to the results they expect. In practice, managers will often deny this by claiming that they are pragmatic problem-solvers working 'in the real world' and not theorising academics (!). This denial arises out of the view that 'theoretical' is more or less the same as 'impractical' – while, in fact, a 'theory' is a proposition waiting to be 'proved' it is a speculation on what will happen as a result of certain actions (Christensen and Raynor, 2003).

A theory is a statement, arising out of research into past actions and ideas, predicting which actions will lead to what results and why. A military general plans a campaign and orders an attack on the enemy on the basis of a theory or a prediction of what will happen. If the general has different ideas in his mind then he will organise his campaign differently and use a different approach in his assault on the enemy.

At the beginning of the Second World War, the French military command still had ideas and military theories based on First World War campaigns where there had been a relatively static form of warfare, whereas the German military command had new ideas based on mobility. The French thought they were impregnable behind fixed fortifications, which the German army simply drove around. A study of any military campaign shows that the most successful generals are those who, in modern jargon, 'think outside the box' and to do this they need to understand what is in the 'box' in the first place. This is why history, or 'knowing what has happened before' and what 'actions have led to what results', is important. For example, in developing a competitive advantage an organisation may consider that instead of competing in existing, highly competitive, markets where it has struggled to survive, they might be better off creating an uncontested market space and creating new demand

Good theories are valuable because they help in the making of predictions. Gravity is a theory, or a statement of cause and effect, which makes it possible to predict that if a person steps off a cliff they will fall, without the need to try it to see what happens. Theories also help in the understanding of the present in order to interpret what is happening and why it is happening. Theories are based on research into a subject or a problem that needs to be understood, attempting to identify a cause and effect relationship and trying to predict one from the other. Bad theories are underresearched and poorly understood and the foundation for asserting cause and effect is weak, while good theories are well researched with cause and effect proved effectively so that the theory can be used as the basis for action. For example, it is useful to know about the theory of gravity in order to avoid walking near the edge of a cliff! Good management theories are useful in order to understand why people make particular decisions and as a guide to action. Concepts can guide practice.

Management as a science

The science of management is today based on the view that 'what can't be measured isn't worth doing'. This is a view supported by Professor Sir Roland Smith, but even this apparently 'up-to-date' theory has been described by John Harvey-Jones as being out of date (see Chapter 1). This is partly because of the echoes thrown forward from the 1960s when there was a management view that everything could be measured and that success would follow improvements in systems of measurement, particularly accountancy. The modern version of this theory has been greatly encouraged by developments in information technology which has vastly increased the potential for measurement. Although all managers have to accept the need for business accounts and the application of statistics in making decisions, at the same time they must consider the derivation and accuracy of the numbers presented to them. At times it may be sensible to override all the facts and figures that are available. For example, Sony produced the Walkman against the evidence of market research which suggested that the product would not be successful. This example does not invalidate market research but puts it in its place as one of a number of factors in the management decision-making process.

→ Ch. 1

Managers have to operate in the situation in which they find themselves:

> *'The difficulty is that there can never be any single correct solution to any management problem, or any all-embracing system which will carry one through a particular situation or period of time.'*
>
> (Harvey-Jones, 1993)

The fact is that over the years management styles and fashions change and business environments alter. As a subject of study and analysis, management can be seen as a mongrel form of social science, borrowing as necessary from other social sciences, and because it is concerned with people and their behaviour there is an element of unpredictability about the whole process.

Scientific management developed at the end of the nineteenth century when skilled workers were in short supply in the USA and, in order to meet demand, productivity needed to be expanded by increasing the efficiency of the workers who were available. In order to do this, Frederick W Taylor (1856–1915) developed a body of principles which came to be known as '**Taylorism**'. He based his managerial system on production-line time studies. He analysed each job by breaking it down into its component parts and then designed the quickest and best methods of operation for each part. By doing this he was able to establish how much workers should be able to do with the equipment and materials available, and how far pay could be related to levels of productivity.

This process developed into a 'differential rate system' based on greater pay for greater productivity which in turn, it was argued, would lead to greater profits. The higher payments would continue, Taylor thought, because they were 'scientifically correct' rates set at a level that was best for the company and the worker. Increased profits would encourage companies to expand and ensure continued employment for those workers able to meet the required productivity standards. Those who did not meet these standards would easily find work, in his opinion, because of the shortage of skilled workers. This process is what might be referred to now as a form of performance-related pay – it is interesting to note that Taylor decided to put his ideas into effect as a private consultant as early as 1893.

One well-documented example of his work as a consultant management engineer was with the Simonds Rolling Machine Company. In one operation, 120 women inspected bicycle ball-bearings. Taylor's approach was to study and time the movements of the best workers; he then trained the rest of the workers in the methods of their more effective colleagues and transferred or laid off the poorest performers. He introduced rest periods during the working day and a differential pay rate system. The results were increases in productivity, quality, earnings and morale and a fall in costs (see Exhibit 20.4).

The problem with Taylor's approach was that it did lead to lay-offs, and there was the fear that increased productivity would mean that the available work would be completed even sooner causing more lay-offs. By 1912 opposition to Taylorism led to strikes and to hostile members of the US Congress asking for explanations of his ideas and methods. Taylor stated that his philosophy rested on a few basic principles.

- **The development of a true science of management, so that the best method for performing each task could be determined.**
- **The scientific selection of workers so that each worker would be given responsibility for the task for which he or she was best suited.**
- **The scientific education and development of the worker.**
- **Intimate, friendly cooperation between management and labourer.**

Taylor's views are summarised in his book *Scientific Management* (1947). He believed that for these principles to succeed there needed to be a change in working attitudes and practices, 'a complete mental revolution' on the part of management and employees. He felt that the concentration of effort should not be on profit but that both management and labour should concentrate on increased production,

Exhibit 20.4 The Taylor

- Monitor, study, tim

- Train the other wo

- Introduce changes   ase
  productivity

which he believed would mean that profits would rise to an extent where management and labour would no longer have to compete for them.

This need for change was at the heart of the problem with the Taylor approach, because changing attitudes is notoriously harder than changing practices. Although the new technology was adopted by management, Taylor's philosophy was not. Increases in productivity in fact often led to lay-offs or changes in pay rates that left workers producing more output for the same income. The proponents of scientific management did not take into account the actual needs of people at work sufficiently. They assumed that the prime motivation for work was pay and that provided there was an increase in their pay then workers would be happy. In fact modern views suggest that workers wanted then, as they do now, to have satisfaction in their work, to have good working conditions and to feel they have a say in matters which directly affect them. Modern management practices are based on consulting people and giving them responsibility for their work, while scientific management was based on telling people how to increase their earnings, training them and then expecting them to go ahead and do it (see Table 20.1).

Contributors to scientific management extended Taylor's work. For example, Henry Gantt (1861–1919) reconsidered and developed his incentive system and produced the Gantt chart to record a worker's progress. Frank Gilbreth (1868–1925) extended Taylor's research on time and motion problems, and his wife Lillian (1878–1972) focused on the scientific selection, training and placing of employees to provide the precursor to present-day human resources management. Lillian Gilbreth, in particular, developed as well as extended scientific management. However, the basic theory remained the concept of the division of labour and the belief that, by specialising in certain tasks, a team of people can outproduce the same number of people each performing all the tasks. The highly productive

Table 20.1 'Taylorism'

ARGUMENTS FOR:	PROBLEMS WITH:
Use of technology	Attitudes
Productivity increases	Lay-offs
Motivation: pay	Motivation: satisfaction, working conditions, control
Telling employees	Consulting employees
Long-term benefits	Focus on work design, training

modern assembly line is a direct descendant of these ideas. The ideas of efficiency propounded by scientific management, such as time and motion studies, promoted awareness of the equipment and physical movement involved in a task, while the emphasis on the training of workers recognised the importance of ability and its development in increasing productivity. The focus on work design has encouraged managers to have a fresh look at the way a job is done and has pointed the way towards the idea of the professional manager.

Administrative management

Of course, Frederick Taylor was concerned largely with the detail of organisational functions and how they could be managed to provide benefits for the whole company. Other contemporary ideas were based on the whole organisation and the influence of the management of this on company functions and effectiveness.

In classical organisation theory it was believed that managerial practice fell into certain patterns that could be identified and analysed. Henri Fayol (1841–1925), for example, was a contemporary of Taylor but was interested in the management of large groups of people rather than organisational functions. Fayol believed that 'with scientific forecasting and proper methods of management, satisfactory results were inevitable'. He insisted that management was a skill like any other, so that managers were not born but made. Once the underlying principles were understood and a general theory of management formulated then management could be taught. This was a major change in views of leadership as well as management and forms the basis of many modern attitudes.

Fayol divided business operations into units which he described as technical, commercial, financial, security, accounting and managerial, all of which were closely dependent on one another. His primary focus was on the management of the operational areas which he defined in terms of five functions:

- **planning** – a course of action for the organisation to meet its goals;
- **organising** – to ensure the availability and coordination of the material and human resources of the organisation to put the plans into effect;
- **commanding** – to provide direction to employees;
- **coordinating** – to ensure that the resources and activities of the organisation work together to achieve the desired goals;
- **controlling** – to monitor the plans and ensure they are being achieved.

Compared with Taylor, Fayol had a comprehensive view of management very similar to modern ideas. This comprehensive view was being developed at much the same time by Max Weber (1864–1920) in Germany. His ideas were based on the structure of the organisation, or the 'bureaucracy', which was characterised by:

- **a clear definition of authority and responsibility**
- **a chain of command**
- **selection based on qualifications, training and examination**
- **appointed officials working for fixed salaries**
- **strict rules, disciplines and controls.**

Weber wanted to depersonalise management in order to promote a uniformity which would provide for the fair and equal treatment of all workers. His 'bureaucracy' was designed to provide stability and certainty in an organisation and his model of management has contributed to organisational thinking over the last 100 years, particularly in large national and multinational companies.

The Hawthorne effect

In the late 1920s and early 1930s, American researchers such as Elton Mayo (1880–1949) emphasised the concept of 'social man' to complement the classical concept of 'rational man'. Although it was recognised that personal economic needs remained an important source of motivation, it was emphasised that social needs, such as job satisfaction and work group pressures, were also very important. These social factors placed a heavy emphasis on management style – on how managers operated as well as what they did. Elton Mayo was involved in the famous 'Hawthorne experiments' which were an important study in human behaviour at work and are still influential today. This was a series of experiments carried out mainly at Weston Electric's Hawthorne plant near Chicago. The early studies were carried out by company engineers in collaboration with the National Academy of Sciences, with problems posed by this initial research then investigated by a team of researchers led by Elton Mayo, F J Roethlisberger and W J Dickson of Harvard in the period between 1927 and 1932.

The research was to examine the effects of changes in lighting on the productivity of workers. These were divided into two groups so that the control group could be exposed to a consistently well-lit workplace, while the experimental group worked under varied lighting conditions. The results of the experiment were ambiguous because although the productivity improved when the test group's lighting conditions were improved, the increases were erratic. There was also a tendency for productivity to continue to increase when lighting conditions were made worse. To add to the confusion, the control group's productivity also rose as the test group's lighting conditions were changed even though there was no change in their lighting. Similar results were achieved in a new set of experiments which varied wages, rest periods and the length of working days and weeks for the test group. Mayo and his associates decided that financial and other incentives and changes were not causing productivity improvements. They believed that a complex chain of attitudes was involved in the productivity increases, with the main factor arising from the situation that the groups had been singled out for special attention, so that a group pride developed which motivated them to better performance (see also Chapter 12).

→ Ch. 12

The phenomenon, known as the '**Hawthorne effect**', suggests that employees work harder when they believe that management is concerned about their welfare and when managers pay special attention to them. It was also concluded that the social environment of workers and their informal work groups had a positive influence on productivity. Many employees found their work dull and meaningless but their social links with co-workers imparted some meaning to their working lives. This reinforced Mayo's concept of the 'social man' motivated by social needs and responding more to work group pressures than to management control. The Hawthorne experiments have exerted a profound influence on the way managers approach their jobs in that they have focused attention on the development of people-management skills. In terms of motivation, follow-up experiments only served to illustrate the complexity of the issue. Attention is now given to working conditions and to motivation, and while the experiments did not solve any problems they did highlight relatively neglected areas where management could have an important influence.

Behavioural theory: the organisation of people

Some of the classical theories of management appear inappropriate for considera-tion today, but they developed when organisations were relatively stable and existed in relatively predictable environments. As working situations have changed and become more unsettled, classical theories have become less relevant but have still left their mark on management thinking. The administrative approach shifted the emphasis of management thinking towards considering the organisation as a whole. This was followed by more people-oriented ideas and a human relations approach which is more in tune with present-day ideas on styles of management.

Early contributors to this included Mary Parker Follett (1868–1933) who asserted that the hierarchical distinction between managers and subordinates was artificial and obscured a natural partnership between labour and management. In her view they shared a common purpose as members of the same organisation, and she stressed the interdependence among their activities and functions. She considered that leadership should not be based on authority but on the superior knowledge and ability of the manager.

Other managers, such as Chester I Barnard (1886–1961), carried these ideas fur-ther. He became president of New Jersey Bell in 1927 and through his experience as a manager and his reading he developed the view that an organisation could operate efficiently only when its goals *and* the aims of the individuals working for it were kept in balance. He put an emphasis on both the individual worker as the strategic factor in organisations and the importance of individuals working in groups. This was a clear statement of the behavioural view that 'the organisation is people'.

While management theories and styles have altered over the years, the basic management problems have remained the same. One of these is to increase produc-tivity in order to increase output and to compete successfully. The scientific management approach was to consider this mainly as an engineering problem, while the behavioural management approach considered it to be concerned more with people. The latter rediscovered the views of Robert Owen who, in the early 1800s, managed several cotton mills in New Lanark in Scotland. In the new facto-ries that had developed as a result of the Industrial Revolution, working conditions for employees were very poor and Owen saw the manager's role as one of reform. He built better housing for his workers, opened schools for their children and reduced the number of hours in the standard working day. He believed that by improving conditions there would be increased productivity and profits, so that while other managers concentrated on technical improvements he stressed that the manager's best investment was in the workers. In fact his methods did work in that his factories were profitable, but it took a long time for people to apply these ideas more generally.

Responsive management

In order to create more responsive organisations, many companies have shed man-agement layers and have created a 'flat' or 'flatter' organisation. The objective has been to create a leaner, more flexible organisation which could cope with the chal-lenges of change and increased competition. These changes have brought new problems with companies feeling that they face a range of increasing challenges:

- the rate of change is speeding up
- customers are becoming more demanding
- more markets are becoming global
- environmental and social pressures are increasing.

Many companies have been turning to the flat organisation as an alternative to the conventional hierarchical structure in an attempt to maximise the use of staff. The philosophy of the flat organisation is based on breaking down the tiers of the hierarchy and ensuring that more staff have a broader base of skills, eliminating the need for many specialisms. Rewards are based on outcomes and value added rather than work.

The Chartered Management Institute reports have revealed a gap between the perceptions which senior managers had of how their staff coped with the changes and the reality of those trying to implement them. Middle and junior managers felt that they were receiving conflicting signals, for example by being under pressure both to improve customer satisfaction and to achieve staff reductions and cost savings. In a survey carried out by *Management Today* (Kennett, 2006) it was found that most 'middle managers' (that is, managers between senior managers and junior managers – which means most managers!) were happy in their work in spite of concerns about the pressure they were under and their feeling that their bosses had entrenched views. 'Even though it is very hard work, it is also very satisfying' was a typical response. The rationale for being a manager was having the ability to make a positive difference to colleagues and the company's performance. One response was: 'I enjoy the power, the decision making, and having the influence – and the challenge.' Another response: 'It gives me the power to change things. I spent years moaning about managers. Now I realise how important good management is to the success of any service.' This survey confirmed that for middle managers, as for senior managers, having autonomy was a major source of job satisfaction. They liked to be given responsibility, to be allowed to do what they thought was best. At the same time the most respected bosses were those who gave their managers space to work in their own way, while those who micromanaged were the most disliked.

At the same time, managers were being asked to do more with less. When a layer of management is taken out then previous workloads and responsibilities are often simply passed on to those who remain without a systematic reassessment of priorities and resources. It was found that extra training was seldom provided so that managers were expected to work harder without being equipped to work smarter. The *Management Today* survey (Kennett, 2006) found that half the managers identified their biggest challenge as working with too few resources. One response, from a manager in a design company, was: 'in a service company, you tend to be slaves to your clients'. The survey also found that managers said that initiatives were imposed from above with little understanding of the repercussions further down the organisation.

At the same time, many organisations were found to be clinging to traditional boundaries and practices, despite the awareness of the need to change. For example, an earlier survey showed that 90 per cent of managers agreed that issues and problems no longer corresponded with traditional functional boundaries, while 73 per cent thought that functional specialists and departments must be maintained. There was a wide recognition that managers required new skills, although little help was provided for them to acquire these. In fact 95 per cent of respondents agreed that 'managers need to be equipped with new skills', and 97 per cent 'that management development will become increasingly important'. Figure 20.2 shows the changes that managers thought were important to enable their organisations to respond better to challenges in the business environment.

In most areas managers believed that their organisations ought to have been doing more than they were in terms of teamwork, networking, flexibility and ensuring the interdependence of both functions and organisations. Only in creating slimmer and flatter organisations was there a view that the organisation might do a little less. At the same time, the qualities that managers were felt to need supported to these views. It was considered that future managers should possess:

- a broad perspective on the organisation's goals
- flexibility
- adaptability
- the ability to communicate
- an understanding of the business environment
- a balanced perspective.

Figure 20.2 Changes that enable organisations to respond better to challenges in the business environment

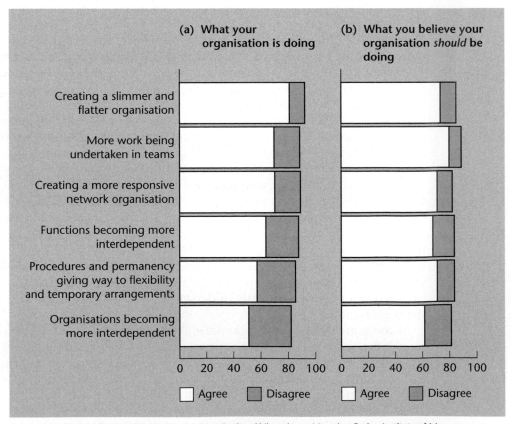

Source: C Coulson and T Coe (1991) *The Flat Organisation: Philosophy and Practice*, Corby: Institute of Management. Reproduced with permission of the Chartered Management Institute (formerly the Institute of Management).

Nine out of ten of the respondents believed that managers would need to be:

- **able to assume greater responsibility**
- **able to contribute to teams**
- **aware of ethics and values**
- **able to handle uncertainty and surprise.**

As Figure 20.3 shows, there was strong agreement about the importance of qualities such as good communications skills, flexibility and adaptability, whereas tolerance of ambiguity and specialist expertise were felt to be less important.

The survey exposed contradictions in the views of respondents about flatter and leaner organisations. While most respondents thought that they should be moving to a flexible network organisation with a breaking down of functional barriers, only 10 per cent thought that the multiskilling implied by this process was very important. While two-thirds of respondents felt that developing human potential was very important to managing change, only one-quarter were committed to ongoing learning as a very important management quality. In fact, it can be argued that what is required to promote success is a highly skilled and adaptable workforce, whose skills are continually updated in order to respond to the even faster pace of change.

Figure 20.3 Importance of particular management qualities

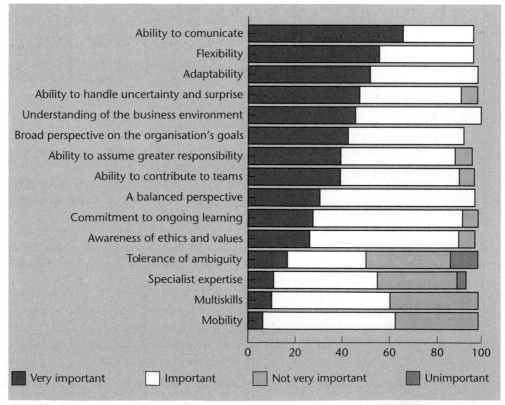

Source: C Coulson and T Coe (1991) *The Flat Organisation: Philosophy and Practice*, Corby: Institute of Management. Reproduced with permission of the Chartered Management Institute (formerly the Institute of Management).

Similar problems were exposed in terms of teamworking skills and the importance of vision and mission to an organisation. More work was seen to be in teams, but the ability to work in teams was seen as very important by only 36 per cent of respondents. More training and support were needed in this area, as they were in terms of vision and mission, where to be effective the mission had to be compelling, shared and realistic. As organisations flatten their hierarchical pyramids, the report identified that managers were not necessarily being equipped with the skills to work in the new managerial environment.

MANAGEMENT IDEAS

Management ideas and techniques come in and out of fashion and writers such as Pascale (1991) have agreed that management ideas have acquired the 'velocity of fads' in the post-1945 period. This has been attributed to the rise of so-called professional management based on the premise that a set of generic concepts underpinned management everywhere. At the same time there was the view that there were instant solutions to management problems and these have been packaged in the form of conferences and workshops, books and software offering a mass market of managerial techniques. In these there is the suggestion that a day spent on 'time management' will completely alter the ability of a manager to organise working time and improve productivity; the attendance at a conference on 'selling techniques' with 2000 other potential super salespeople will enable managers to sell 'ice-cream to Eskimos'; listening to cassette tapes and following the instructions of computer discs will increase 'brain power' sufficiently to enable managers greatly to increase their potential advancement.

> *'Today the bewildering array of fads pose more serious diversions and distractions from the complex task of running a company. Too many modern managers are like compulsive dieters, trying the latest craze for a few days, then moving relentlessly on.'*
> (Byrne, 1986)

The search for panaceas to management problems may arise from increasing competition or from individual needs. Competition may encourage the adoption of new ideas before they are well tested. Organisations may be forced by a fear of competition to experiment with a variety of solutions in order to obtain a competitive advantage. This is obviously likely to be particularly the case in periods of recession but may occur at any time in a particular sector. The 'solutions' may be imitated quite widely and even institutionalised through government support. Support for quality management, for example, has moved through quality circles, team building, the Management Charter, Investors in People, benchmarking and so on.

Alex Ferguson, the manager of Manchester United, has been quoted as saying: 'management is all about control. Success gives you control and control gives you longevity as a manager' (Gwyther and Saunders, 2005). Also involved in this success has been control over his players on and off the football pitch. At the same time, Pina e Cunha *et al.* (2006) have suggested that 'surprise' is an underestimated element in organisations. They define 'surprise' in terms of

> *'being taken unawares without preparation, with no anticipation beforehand.'*

Whereas the usual approach to management problems is to anticipate and predict, plan and control, the problem is that an organisation faced with a 'surprise' may be confused and hesitant and therefore at a disadvantage. Managers should on the one hand be 'prepared' for surprises as these are defined, and on the other the organisation should not be fearful of surprises but welcome the opportunities they may represent as well as the dangers. Although by definition a surprise is an event for which a manager is not prepared, if the manager and the organisation are encouraged to be sufficiently flexible and alert they should be able to deal with it.

Management programmes to do with people whether customers or employees – 'putting people first', 'participatory management', 'customer service through staff development' – have been constantly replenished and refurbished; 'new ideas' are needed. Individuals may view a new idea as a method of enhancing their careers. A new idea needs a 'champion' who promotes its adoption within a company and this enables an individual to be a star. For a time the champion becomes an expert to whom other managers have to turn for understanding of the new technique or system. The introduction of a new technique can provide a defence against the accusation that management is not up to date and trying every available method of meeting competition. Also, new ideas may be seen as offering relatively quick solutions to different problems. As managers are promoted from their specialist function, they may look for 'quick-fix' ideas and techniques as a way of exerting an immediate influence.

The whole process can be seen as a superficial approach to deep-seated problems. While it may be sensible to look for up-to-date ideas as hooks on which to hang long-term solutions, it may not be sensible to believe that most problems can be easily solved. A study of the management of change shows that while people's behaviour may be altered fairly quickly, for a time at least, changing their attitudes will take much longer. For example, a customer-care programme can encourage employees to smile and to answer consumer questions promptly and positively, but if attitudes have not changed this may be a thin veneer which disappears once things begin to go wrong. This does not mean that the programme should not be introduced, but it does mean that it needs to be considered as a long-term programme.

'A review of the more popular "new" management ideas of the 1980s shows that many of them represent new wine in old bottles. The total number of bottles remain the same, but each is refilled with new contents.'   (Huczynski, 1993)

This has not changed in the twenty-first century with the emphasis on such ideas as performance measurement, target setting and a focus on the customer. Huczynski argues that a management idea which addresses an individual's own needs is likely to have the greatest impact. This suggests that management ideas should be packaged on this basis. For example, quality management was popular in the 1980s, packaged in terms of the idea of quality circles because it integrated elements of group leadership, teamworking, problem solving, delegating and so on (see Table 20.2).

A further perspective on management ideas can be obtained by comparing short courses, such as those on time management, against MBA-type programmes. The former type of course may be perceived as too relevant, while the latter may be perceived as threatening because MBA-type programmes are based on research and the objective assessment of management performance. This could expose managerial weaknesses and undermine a manager's positive image. In practice, organisations which provide short courses often focus on individual managers and emphasise success in order to promote a feeling of well-being. The development of this positive feeling may be more important than the actual content of the course.

Table 20.2 Management ideas classified by personal impact

INNER SELF	OUTER SELF	INTERPERSON	GROUP	ORGANISATION
Self-confidence	Rapid reading	Delegating Communicating		
Stress management	Writing skills	Appraising	Group leadership	Quality management
Learning styles	Assertiveness Problem solving Decision making Goal setting	Motivating Interpersonal skills Negotiating	Running meetings Team working	Searching for excellence Customer care Managing change

Most impact ⟵————————————————————⟶ *Least impact*

Source: Based on A Huczynski (1993) *Management Gurus*, London and New York: Routledge. Reprinted with permission.

It can be argued that the whole search for management principles is not designed to maximise profit but to legitimise the manager's role. Mant (1979) argues that managerial literature went beyond the description and categorisation of management tasks and engaged in manufacturing:

> '*A mythology about executive work, sedulously nourished by the management consultants, business school professors and so on. Executives like the myth and are prepared to pay good money to have it reinforced.*'

The myth concerned rational, scientific decision making and relied on creating a theory of management which underpinned the practice of management. In fact, of course, there are a number of theories of management, some of which contradict each other. These can be summarised in a slightly different form which suggests that there are four main views of management (based on Watson, 1986).

- **Management as science** – successful managers are those who have learned the appropriate body of knowledge and have developed an ability to apply acquired skills and techniques. This view has been supported by scientific management and classical administrative theory.

- **Management as art** – successful managers are those born with appropriate intuition, intelligence and personality which they develop through the practice of leadership. Leadership skills can be developed although not taught.

- **Management as politics** – successful managers are those who can work out the unwritten laws of life in the organisational jungle and are able to play the game so that they win. Managers are involved in power struggles and in competition for scarce resources with fellow managers.

- **Management as magic** – successful managers are those who recognise that nobody really knows what is going on and who persuade others of their own powers by calling up the appropriate gods and by engaging in the expected rituals. Charismatic leadership can be seen in this context.

Experienced managers know that successfully playing the role may involve all four of these approaches. Intuition will play a part, as will information, persuasion, charisma and personality. Intelligence is important along with communication as well as an understanding of other people, the games they play and their attitudes and prejudices. It helps to acquire skills in running meetings, in negotiating, in finance and personnel policies and it is important to be aware of techniques of selling and marketing for creating popular products and services. Successful managers learn from successes and failures and never stop learning, and see themselves as serving others, supporting them as well as leading them in order to achieve certain objectives.

In an article in 1994 Sir Geoffrey Chandler argued that:

> *'Drivers have licences, doctors seven years' training and the Hippocratic Oath, businessmen the seat of their pants. And pants can be very successful. The history of business and industry is starred with self-made figures whose lack of formal education, abundant determination and acute intuition are part of the folklore.'*

The article continues by pointing out that driving and medicine are, of course, dangerous to others, while business too can make or break the lives of individuals and communities. Yet the UK tends to allow the management of business to be amateur without universal standards of competence and training. In France, Germany and Japan, on the other hand, there are much higher levels of qualification and training of both management and workforce. In the USA the belief in self-development has gone hand in hand with a belief in education as a route to success. The Wharton School of Business was founded in 1881, Harvard in 1908, while the London Business School was not opened until in 1965.

> *'Just as a driving licence doesn't make a good driver, so an MBA doesn't make a good manager.'*
> (Chandler, 1994)

In response to industrial and commercial globalisation, and competition from other countries, the 'lifelong learning' initiative was introduced in the UK in 1998 in another attempt to improve education and training. The objectives included the expansion of further and higher education numbers by half a million by the year 2002, the launch of a University of Industry (UFI) by 1999 and the establishment of Individual Learning Accounts. ILAs had the aim of widening participation in education and training, while the UFI was designed as an open-all-hours one-stop shop for training based on a freephone service giving information and advice on a range of lifelong learning courses at convenient places near where people live. The UFI has been described as the first college to be built in cyberspace!

Analysis needs to be balanced by intuition and by an understanding of people. A manager does not need to have heard of Theory X and Theory Y to know that people respond better to persuasion and encouragement than coercion, but if a manager does not have this intuitive understanding then training in the theories of management and in the practical experiences of managers can lead to a rational understanding of the most successful methods.

With organisational restructuring, the career expectations of managers have changed dramatically. The connection between how well a manager performs and job security has been shaken. There has been a shift from managers being secure in their jobs if they did not make mistakes to job security based on performance measurement, to losing a job irrespective of performance because of organisational requirements. In the past, middle managers in particular were reasonably paid, had job security and could expect a slow but steady rise in pay even if they had reached their career plateau. This is no longer the case. Faith in the orderly, single-company career path has been lost.

Managers have now to take control of their own careers to an extent unknown in the past. They have to become entrepreneurial about their own careers, and entrepreneurial managers have to create a product or service of value. Instead of seeing career development as moving up a hierarchy, entrepreneurial managers now see progress in their careers as the territory grows below them, as the demand for their services grows, as their pay increases. These managers may become traditional entrepreneurs in developing their own business, or modern entrepreneurs developing their own 'consultancy' based on their skills and ideas but they all have to make sure that they obtain the training and experiences they need in order to remain 'employable' and 'in demand':

> *'Hereafter, the employee will assume full responsibility for his own career – for keeping his qualifications up-to-date, for getting himself moved to the next position at the right time, for putting away funds for retirement, and, most daunting of all, for achieving job satisfaction. The company, while making no promises, will endeavour to provide a conducive environment, economic exigencies permitting.'*   (Kiechael, 1987)

In many cases managers have been able to move out of companies and then be re-employed by them as independent advisers or consultants. These developments are threatening for many people but hold out considerable benefits for those managers able to take advantage of the situation as the economic environment, international competition and the global environment change. The major challenge from a management perspective is to create a situation where managers welcome change and are in a position to take advantage of it.

MANAGEMENT CONCEPTS AND PRACTICES

In facing the challenges to management, **leadership** plays an essential part because it is through this quality that the strands of an organisation can be drawn together for a productive outcome. Leadership creates the climate of an organisation and affects its culture and it has been suggested that this is a result of 'emotional intelligence' – that is the ability of leaders to manage themselves and their relationships with others efficiently. This is as a result of self-awareness, self-management, social awareness and social skill. Good leadership and good management are essential in the success of any organisation, big or small, public or private, social, charitable or profit-making.

Self-awareness is felt to include emotional awareness, which is the ability of leaders to understand their emotions and to recognise their impact in work situations. It also includes a realistic self-evaluation of strengths and weaknesses and self-confidence. Self-management includes such matters as self-control, a consistent display of honesty and integrity, facing up to responsibilities, skill at adjusting to changing situations and overcoming obstacles, and a drive to meet internal standards of excellence and to seize opportunities. Social awareness includes empathy with other people and their feelings, taking an active interest in their concerns while navigating the politics of working life and recognising the needs of customers. Social skills involve taking charge of situations, inspiring and persuading people, helping to develop others, listening and communicating, helping to resolve conflicts and competence at promoting cooperation and building teams.

Managers with a strong 'emotional intelligence' are able to provide leadership and meet the challenges presented by changing circumstances. It is often, in practice, difficult and unnecessary to separate the role of manager from that of leader.

> *'Just as management without leadership encourages an uninspired style, which deadens activities, leadership without management encourages a disconnected style, which promotes hubris.'*   (Gosling and Mintzberg, 2003)

Research into the appointment of company chief executives (Bennis and O'Toole, 2000) argues that many are appointed on the basis of their past record rather than on their leadership qualities. They may have had financial successes or have been excellent deputies but if they are to lead an organisation they require other qualities. They need to inspire confidence, to be able to delegate, to develop leadership qualities in others, to energise others and to communicate well. Social awareness in a manager helps in the focus on customers and the understanding required in order to provide consumer benefits. Managers can help their organisations to recognise and seize opportunities by inspiring and supporting innovation.

There is a view (for example Hayward, 2004) that the future of management may be dominated by short-term considerations. It can be argued that in many cases organisations follow their cynical self-interest and this approach embraces both managers and customers.

> *'In an environment where marketing directors are said to enjoy an average tenure of only eighteen months, and the average employee in the UK has been in eight different jobs by the age of 32, who cares about the long term?.'*   (Hayward, 2004)

Consumer loyalty and respect for many organisations is fragile as a result of the strong feeling that many companies have not responded to signals that consumers have been sending out about both their behaviour and their products. Customers learn to be short term and expedient in the companies they choose: 'The next generation is being brought up to switch brands and suppliers at the drop of a hat, and this will alter the dynamics of all businesses' (Hayward, 2004).

> *'Marks and Spencer may have thought the good times were bound to last as they passed the £1 billion profit mark for the first time in 1997. But the seeds of future disappointment were already being sown. A TV documentary at that time, showing chairman Sir Richard Greenbury testing prototype puddings and inspecting lingerie, suggested a complacent culture where too much power lay in the hands of one person. M&S lacked the agility and responsiveness to satisfy changing customer demand in a rapidly changing market.'*   (Stern, 2005)

The problems of stores such as M&S have been reflected by the rapid expansion of the 'value' sector, retailers such as TK Maxx ('labels for less'), Primark ('look good, pay less') and Matalan ('high street quality at half the price') as well as Asda and Tesco. 'Our customers have voted with their wallets' (Asda executive quoted in Walsh, 2005). These companies concentrate on cheap supplies, reducing overheads, large quantities, cheap prices and ruthlessly following the customer lead. 'managers don't change business – customers do, customers are in the driving seat' (Stern, 2005).

Management is complicated and confusing:

> *'be global, managers are told, and be local. Collaborate, and compete. Change perpetually, and maintain order. Make the numbers while nurturing your people.'*
>   (Gosling and Mintzberg, 2003)

The present era is one of continuous innovation where knowledge is the key asset whose exploitation can determine success for many companies (Miles *et al.*, 2000). In order to be effective, managers need to face up to these juxtapositions and challenges to arrive at an integration of these seemingly contradictory concerns and it can be argued that to do this they have to focus on concept as well as practice. Strategic thinking and implementation promotes a sustainable competitive advantage by providing a structure which develops people and helps to produce a climate in the organisation which encourages quality and achievement. Gosling and Mintzberg (2003) argue that managers need what they refer to as 'mind-sets', which are conceptual frameworks from which action can be applied. These include a 'reflective mind-set' which means that they need to stop and think before acting, and an 'analytical mind-set' which considers all the relevant factors before putting an idea into practice. They also need a 'worldly mind-set' which is less general than the idea of globalisation and which makes allowance for the fact that there are many ways of seeing and doing things. Managers also need to be collaborative and to be action-oriented in terms of a sensitive awareness of the organisation and its context so they can harness the abilities of the people they manage and set and maintain a direction.

> *'Managers are important to the extent they help other people do the important work of developing products and service'*   (Gosling and Mintzberg, 2003)

and they can bring out the abilities of people and their enthusiasm. Lesley-Ann Thompson, the Marketing and Events Manager of Ely Cathedral, has been quoted (in Kennett, 2006) as saying:

> *'my role is largely about bringing out people's potential. I look after about eighty cathedral guides – volunteers who come here from different backgrounds and for different reasons. I work out why they are interested in the cathedral and press the right buttons.'*

Her own background was managing European communications for MCI, the telecoms company, organising a team of staff across ten countries:

> *'coming to the cathedral from that high-level capitalist company was a jolt back to earth – and a great learning experience for me.'*

King (2007) has argued that managers should not allow the danger of making a mistake to inhibit an initiative – it is healthier to expect to make mistakes from time to time. Ideas about what to do in any situation have to arise from somewhere and it is assumed that effective management is based on good ideas, while ineffective management is based on poor ideas. Vandenbosch *et al.* (2006) have suggested that managers fall into archetypes according to their ideas and they way they think. These include the 'incrementalists' who place a great deal of importance on what they already know, they are experience-based decision makers. 'Consensus builders' are managers concerned with gaining agreement – they look for harmony and unity. 'Searchers' are concerned with objectivity – they look for ideas and attempt to resolve conflicting views rather than win people over. 'Debaters' believe that good decision arises from discussion and experiment, while 'assessors' do not take anything for granted, everything is open to question.

These different management types or 'mind-sets' can be seen as ways of looking at the roles of a manager. Incrementalists may generate low-risk workable solutions to problems, while consensus builders may be good at implementing solutions once they have been agreed. Debaters can be successful in generating ideas as well as foreseeing problems, while searchers may move too much between ideas to ensure a successful innovation, and assessors may be too critical for many of their ideas to survive. These types may overlap and merge into one another. Managers need a battery of qualities in order to be successful:

> *'These include intelligence, energy, confidence and responsibility' and 'a willingness to suffer the painful consequences of unpopular decisions.'* (Pearce, 2001)

Management is not an exact science, but nor is it a complete mystery and managers can develop and be developed so that they lead effectively. The goal is to create managers who can transform bold strategic, financial and organisational objectives into reality.

SUMMARY

- This chapter places management and careers in management in context. It summarises the links and differences between management and leadership. It discusses how far it is possible to see management as a transferable skill which can be applied with success to a variety of circumstances so that a manager has the ability to manage any type of organisation.

- The career paths of managers can be viewed in different ways. It is useful for individual managers to understand the opportunities and obstacles that they face.

- In many countries the role of the manager and career paths have, to a greater or lesser extent, been affected by company re-engineering and the move to 'flatter organisations'.

- It is important for managers to understand the role of management theories, while management ideas can be considered in terms of organisational as well as personal needs and the management role can be seen as constantly evolving in response to change.

Review and discussion questions

1 *Is it possible for a manager to manage any type of organisation successfully, or is it necessary to have knowledge and experience of the area to be managed?*

2 *What are the most important skills a manager requires?*

3 *Do management careers follow a pattern because of organisational, individual or other factors?*

4 *What qualities are required for managers to cope with the development of flatter organisations?*

5 *Are past theories of management of any assistance to managers in the twenty-first century?*

6 *Of what use are management ideas and concepts in the practice of management?*

CASE STUDY

Loss of faith in managers

When we asked 140 MBA students at the London Business School to describe their career ambitions, only six aspired to management positions in established corporations. Most hoped to derive professional satisfaction by constantly broadening and deepening their personal portfolio of skills, and by contributing to society in meaningful ways. As managers in established companies, they felt, they could neither develop personally nor contribute to social and economic progress.

It is easy for corporate executives to write these students off as arrogant or naïve. Easy but dangerous. Managers must confront the reality that the best and the brightest from other professional schools, universities and technical programmes are not joining established companies. This inability to attract and retain talented young people is only one symptom of a more profound challenge to managers of large corporations – society has lost faith in them.

The evidence of lost faith is overwhelming. Corporate executives fare poorly in polls of public trust. We admire football players for their multimillion pound contracts, but vilify managers who prosper from performance-based incentives. The best selling Dilbert series argues that management positions exist as places where the least competent employees can do the least harm.

This crisis of faith in management has serious implications, not only for business, but for society as a whole. Unless the tide is turned, firms will not replenish their management ranks with talented young people; executives will find themselves increasingly hemmed in by regulations designed to limit their influence; and managers will lose faith in themselves. These trends could hobble the large businesses that now represent society's main engine of economic progress.

From its beginnings in the nineteenth century, management has stood out as the ungainly stepchild among the professions. The goal of law is justice, the goal of medicine health. Management, in contrast, lacks a clear idea. Professionals in other fields may fall short of their lofty goals, but at least they have ideals to fall short of. Some argue that managers create wealth for society, but this goal too easily blurs into personal greed, so losing social legitimacy and inspirational power. Moreover, few managers of large companies are seen to be gener-

ating new economic value. In contrast to entrepreneurs who are lionised for creating wealth and institutions *de novo*, managers of ongoing concerns are viewed as mere rentiers, living off their companies' past legacy like dissolute heirs squandering the family fortune.

Bill Gates becomes a cult hero by creating Microsoft, while Michael Eisner wins at best grudging recognition for transforming Disney from a tired theme park in the US to a global creative powerhouse. The spate of recent restructuring, layoffs and divestment has further eroded confidence in managers. Through repeated bouts of restructuring many managers have elevated efficiency to the corporation's highest goal. While they are a necessary means, operational efficiencies rarely succeed as a goal to attract, impassion and retain motivated employees.

Moreover, employees in contracting companies see few attractive opportunities for professional development. Nor, in an age of layoffs and downsizing, do employees trust companies to manage their careers for them.

The first step in reversing this growing crisis of faith is to recognise that corporations and their managers act as the primary engine of social and economic progress. Progress requires innovative combinations of resources, technologies and knowledge to create new products and services. Innovation requires human will and creativity to impose change on the world. While individual entrepreneurs often provide the initial creative spark, large organisations are generally necessary to stoke the flame. Apple computers started in a garage, but the Macintosh was produced by an established company, as were the Walkman, synthetic fabrics and AZT. Placing societal progress at the heart of the company's vision and purpose is not a public relations gimmick. Rather the ideal of progress underpins the success of the companies we most admire. The precise vision of progress varies across companies, with different companies aspiring to change the world through technological innovation (Honda, Merck, Sony, 3M), social activism (The Body Shop, Ben & Jerry's) and empowering the underdog (Mary Kay Cosmetics, Ikea, Wal-Mart). These visions of progress infuse organisations with a sense of purpose that allows them to attract, motivate and retain committed employees.

Inertia is the enemy of progress. Past insights ossify into clichés, processes lapse into routines and commitments become ties that bind companies to the same course of action. Perhaps the most vital and fulfilling element of a manager's job is to prevent inertia. To seize the promise of the future, managers must constantly overcome the burdens of the past.

A manager's role, therefore, is not to toil long and hard to make the inevitable happen. His or her job is to make happen what otherwise would not happen.

Source: Financial Times, 6 June 1997, © Donald Sull and Sumantra Ghoshal. Reprinted with permission.

FURTHER READING

Cappelli, P and Hamori, M (2005) 'The new road to the top', Harvard Business Review, January.
A discussion of research into management promotion.

Christensen, C M and Raynor, M E (2003) 'Why hard-nosed executives should care about management theory', Harvard Business Review, September.
A discussion of the importance of management theory for managers to operate successfully.

Drucker, P (1998) Managing in Time of Great Change, New York: Plume.
The challenge facing managers by a 'classic' author.

Gosling, J and Mintzberg, H (2003) 'The five minds of a manager', Harvard Business Review, November.
Making sense of the complicated world of the manager.

Kennet, M (2006) 'View from the middle', Management Today, March.
A report on a survey into the opinions of managers on their work.

WEBSITES

http://www.inst-mgt.org.uk
The website of the Institute of Management providing information about its services and publications.

http://www.ifslearning.com
Information about the Financial World publication.

APPENDIX: HOW TO PASS MANAGEMENT EXAMS

WHAT IS AN EXAMINATION?

Examinations involve answering questions over a few hours on what has been learnt over a much longer period of time. They are tests of the ability to extract the main points from this learning and put the relevant material into a coherent argument that answers the questions set. The examiners are attempting to discover whether or not the person taking an examination (the examinee) has remembered and understood the subject which has been studied. In doing this they set questions which cover the arguments and facts included in the subject syllabus.

An examination is a method of assessment. Other methods include assignments, essays, projects, a presentation, a thesis, an adjudicated discussion or case study.

OBTAIN THE SYLLABUS

It is essential to obtain the syllabus for the subject being studied because it will list what has to be studied and what will be examined. It is also important to know the form and structure of the examination.

- How will questions be asked?
- Will there be a choice?
- How many questions have to be answered?
- Will there be multiple-choice questions?
- Will there be essay questions?
- Will the examination cover the whole syllabus? If not, which parts will it cover?
- Will the examination be open-book or not?
- How long is the examination?
- Are there compulsory questions?
- Are there more marks for some questions than others?
- Will there be short-answer questions?
- Will there be calculations? If there are (in statistics and accountancy for example) what aids can be taken into the examination (calculators or laptops for example)

TYPES OF QUESTIONS

There is a growing tendency for examiners to ask a variety of types of questions, but most management examinations are of the essay or report type – that is they ask for a number of questions to be answered in a continuous piece of writing or a report.

It is important to know the exact form of essay which is favoured – whether it should be continuous or more of a report style. A report style can include headings and subheadings, summaries and notes. If multiple-choice questions are asked it is worth answering every question even if the answer is not known – with this type of question there is always a chance of guessing the correct answer! Marks are awarded for correct answers and it is unusual for marks to be deducted for wrong ones.

OPEN-BOOK EXAMINATIONS

Many management examinations are of the open-book type because examiners in management subjects believe that understanding the concepts of a subject is more important than memorising facts or arguments. These examinations have their own difficulties. The fact that books and notes can be used may make it appear easier but in fact all that happens is that the expectations of the examiner change. It is assumed that facts will be correct and that arguments and discussion points will be well covered because they do not depend on memory. The test will be in terms of marshalling the arguments and facts.

The main problem in these examinations involves time and selection. If an examinee has prepared well by deciding which books to take into the exam and by marking the relevant pages and making relevant notes, then there will be no problems involving a lack of material or information. This means that the important strategy is to organise the time available wisely and select the information and arguments to include in the answer.

EXAMINATION STRATEGY

Before the examination it is important to:

■ leave plenty of time to revise;
■ consider what questions are likely to be asked;
■ if possible obtain a previous examination paper;
■ consider the form of the questions.

During the examination it is essential to:

■ answer the question that is asked and not the question you hoped would be asked;
■ read the instructions carefully to be sure how many questions have to be answered and which (if any) are compulsory;
■ answer all the required questions and try to spend the same time on each of them if they are allocated the same mark;
■ make a plan of an answer so that it has a beginning, a middle and a conclusion;
■ decide exactly what the examiner wants in answer to a question – it helps to look for key words such as describe, analyse, calculate and so on;
■ keep calm!

GLOSSARY

Accounting standards A set of accounting rules.

Accruals Amounts which are owing at the year (period) end – e.g. vehicle repairs, light and heating not yet paid for.

Activity-based costing Overheads are shared out according to cost drivers, a cost driver being the activity that causes a cost to be incurred.

Ansoff matrix An analysis to provide managers with an indication of the type of policy they should follow for new or existing products or services, with respect to market penetration, product development, market extension and diversification.

Appropriations (profit and loss account) Sharing out the net profit before tax between the stakeholders – taxation, dividends paid and proposed, transfers to reserves, and retained earnings.

Artificial intelligence Any form of information technology which attempts to emulate human behaviour, such as reasoning, communication or sensory perception.

Attitude survey A survey, usually conducted by questionnaire, to elicit employees' opinions about issues to do with their work and the organisation.

Audit The prevention and detection of errors and fraud by using the verification of assets and liabilities, checking on the delegated authority, obtaining explanations, checking documents and systems of internal control and reporting – e.g. the statutory Auditors' Report of a company.

Authorised share capital *See* Share capital.

Authoritarian management A management style which is task oriented and stresses the quality of the decision over the wishes of subordinates.

Balance sheet A statement of assets and liabilities extracted from an organisation's accounting records as at a particular moment in time.

Balanced scorecard A **management system** that enables companies to develop a strategy and translate it into action based on the internal business processes and external outcomes in order to improve strategic performance and results continuously.

Bandwidth The measure of how much information a communications channel can carry in a given time.

Batch A group of products with similar characteristics.

Behavioural aspects of budgeting The way in which budgets affect people – e.g. in terms of motivation, the achievement of targets, participation, etc.

Benchmarking An objective measure of performance – a measure which can be used for comparability purposes.

Boston matrix A classification of products or services into categories – stars, problem children, cash cows, dogs – to indicate performance and prospects with respect to market share and market growth rate. It can also be amended to illustrate the financial life cycle of a company.

Breakeven model The breakeven point is the point where total revenue equals total cost (TR = TC). A breakeven model expresses TC and TR mathematically allowing the decision maker to calculate the breakeven point.

Budget A plan expressed in money showing expected future income, expenditure and the capital to be employed.

Budgetary control The establishment of budgets, and the frequent and continuous comparison of actual results with budget targets.

Business ethics A set of moral principles or values in business activity and business organisations, which interact with society and vary from organisation to organisation, country to country, over time, etc.

Business process re-engineering (BPR) An improvement philosophy that recommends the redesign of processes to meet customer needs.

Capacity The maximum level of value-adding activity that an operation is capable of over a period of time.

Capital budgets Budgets for the finance required for projects, expansion etc.

Capital expenditure The amount spent on fixed assets – e.g. buildings and equipment.

Capital investment appraisal A review of capital projects using one or a number of methods – e.g. the payback method and the net present value method – but also taking into account other information.

Capital reserve *See* Reserves.

Capital structure The mix of financing which is used by companies and which has an impact on gearing.

Cash budget Also known as a cash flow forecast, it attempts to predict what the cash and bank balances will be for a specific period, usually for between 3 and 12 months.

Cash cow A company's product or service that has a high market share and low market growth in a reasonably stable market (*see* Boston matrix).

Cash flow statement The historic statement showing where the cash has come from and gone to over the financial period – not to be confused with the cash budget/cash flow forecast.

Cause–effect diagram *See* Ishikawa diagram.

Cell layout Locating transforming resources with a common purpose together in close proximity.

Chaos theory A situation in which broad patterns are predictable but detailed features within these broad patterns are completely unknown.

Charismatic leadership The style of leadership which relies on personal vision and energy to inspire followers.

Coercive power The power that results from the ability to punish people who don't behave as required.

Communications (in organisations) The provision and passing of information and instructions which enable an organisation to function efficiently and employees to be properly informed about developments. It covers information of all kinds, the channels along which it passes and the means of passing it. It also takes into account formal and informal mechanisms and processes that operate between employers, managers and employees.

Communication (physical) The transmission of information from a sender to a receiver in such a way that both can share and have a common understanding of the information. For this to occur both sender and receiver have to share a common symbol set so that the information has the same meaning to both.

Companies Act A legislation and a component of the rules governing companies in England and Wales which sets out the responsibilities of the companies and their directors.

Company politics The game-playing, sabotaging, negative, blaming, non-cooperative behaviour that goes on in hundreds of interactions in organisations.

Competitive advantage The significant advantages that an organisation possesses over its competitors which allow an organisation to add more value than its rivals in the same market.

Competitive forces strategy A strategy of competitive advantage through differentiation, cost leadership or a combined strategy concentrated on a narrow target market. It was developed in the 1980s by Michael Porter and is based on the idea of five competitive forces in an organisation's environment – threats from new market entrants and substitute products, bargaining power of buyers and suppliers, and rivalry among competitors.

Connection power The power that results from personal and professional access to key people.

Continuous improvement An approach to operations improvement that builds on small incremental steps.

Control chart A statistical technique intended to monitor and assess the variation in a given process so that the decision maker can make a judgement as to when the process requires action or intervention. The chart uses recalculated limits to define the expected variation around some average level of process performance.

Control system An organised set of components, both human and technological, that work together to achieve the desired goals.

Core competencies The distinctive group of skills and technologies that enables an organisation to provide particular benefits to customers and deliver competitive advantage.

Corporate social responsibility (CSR) Concerned with business ethics, organisational values, corporate equity and equality.

Cost control systems Systems such as budgeting and standard costing which involve setting targets, comparing them with the actual performance and reporting the variances to management.

Cost and management accounting The costing of products and services, and the provision of information for planning, control and decision-making purposes.

Cost of capital Made up of all the costs of the permanent and long-term capital – e.g. ordinary shares, retained earnings, debentures. There are various ways of calculating this.

Cost of sales Sales revenue less the direct cost of the product or service. There are a number of possible combinations.

Country club management A management style based on a belief that the most important leadership activity is to secure the voluntary cooperation of group members in order to obtain high levels of productivity.

Creative accounting Using accounting concepts, policies, etc. to paint a picture of the financial situation which is different from that which really exists. Also called 'window dressing'.

Culture *See* Organisational culture.

Current assets Stocks of raw materials, debtors, prepayments, short-term investments, cash and bank balances shown in the balance sheet.

Current liabilities Debts due to be paid within the next 12 months – e.g. creditors, accruals, proposed dividends, taxation owing.

Current ratio The ratio of current assets to current liabilities.

Customer benefits Customers are not so much looking for particular products and services, they are looking for the benefits that these may be able to provide.

Customer profitability analysis A technique which assesses the profit yield from customers primarily to provide management with information about distribution of revenues, costs and profits among customers.

Customer pyramid An inverted pyramid hierarchy in which customers are at the top and management is at the base, management's role being to devolve power and decision making to self-managed teams at the point of production or customer service with the aim of providing the best quality or service and gaining competitive advantage.

Customers Whoever receives benefits from an organisation's products and services.

Data Logically defined, abstract symbols whose meaning is clarified by their context.

Decision tree A decision support tool that shows decisions and their possible consequences and likelihoods.

Delayering The removal of layers of management and administration in an organisation's structure.

Delegation The act by which a person or group of persons possessing authority transfers part of that authority to a subordinate person or group.

Delphi technique A qualitative forecasting technique where panels of experts are asked their opinions of a new product/service, and then the average of these groups of opinions is used as a base for arriving at a judgement of the future of the product/service.

Departmentalisation The grouping of jobs, tasks, processes and resources into logical units for performance of an operation.

Depreciation Spreading the cost of a fixed asset – such as machinery, fixtures and fittings – over its useful life.

Directors' remuneration All the salaries, fees, bonuses, etc. due or paid to a company's directors for the period in question.

Directors' report Their report to shareholders in their company's annual published report and accounts.

Discounts receivable Discounts received from suppliers for prompt payment of their account.

Dividend A reward for shareholders for investing/risking their money in a company.

Division of work The breaking down of tasks into component parts so that individuals are responsible for an activity or limited set of activities instead of the whole task.

Downsizing Reducing the size of the workforce of an organisation without necessarily reducing the output.

Efficiency ratios Indicate the way in which the assets are being managed including working capital management.

Emergent strategy A strategy in which the financial objective is unclear and its elements develop as the strategy proceeds.

Emotional intelligence The ability of leaders to manage themselves and their relationships with others efficiently. The quality which includes self-awareness, self regulation, motivation, empathy and social skills.

Employee engagement The extent to which an individual identifies with, and feels a part of, the organisation.

Empowerment The devolution of power and decision making to those lower down in the organisation.

Encoding The process of turning information into a form that can be communicated to another.

Environment That which is not part of a system and cannot be controlled by the system but which can have a significant effect on the system.

Environmental audit A check on the environmental performance of an organisation and on the performance of the management system.

Equal opportunities Everybody should be treated equally in employment situations, whether they are men, women, married or single, of different ethnic or religious backgrounds, or different sexual orientations.

Expectancy model theory Motivation is a function of the expectancy of reaching a certain outcome multiplied by the value of the outcome for that person.

Expected value The weighted average payoff from a number of alternative outcomes where the weight is the probability of each outcome.

Expert power The power that comes from the superior expertise that a leader has or is believed to have.

Expert systems An attempt to apply computer systems to support what people do in arriving at a solution to a problem.

Federal organisation A variety of individual organisations or groups of organisations allied together by a common approach and mutual interest, which can provide a way for relatively small organisations based on core workers to obtain the advantages of large companies.

Feedback Information about the outputs from a process which is used to determine how the workings of the process should be modified to ensure that it achieves its goals.

Financial analysis Tends to use ratio analysis to compare financial performance internally and externally.

Financial management Looks in particular at financing decisions and investing decisions, and covers working capital management, the valuation of companies, dividend policy and take-overs and mergers etc.

Fishbone diagram *See* Ishikawa diagram.

Fixed assets Assets purchased to be used in the business and which are not intended for resale – e.g. freehold land and buildings, plant, machinery, equipment, fixtures and fittings, motor vehicles.

Fixed position layout Moving transforming resources to the position of the product or service.

Flatter management Aims to reduce the layers of control and of approval and veto over decision making, to speed up decision making and push the point of decision nearer to the point of action.

Forcefield analysis A technique used to highlight forces that are either driving movement toward a goal (driving forces) or blocking movement toward a goal (hindering forces).

Forcefield theory In any organisation there are forces for change and forces resisting change.

Four Cs model The effectiveness of outcomes to human resource management can be evaluated under four headings – commitment, competence, congruence and cost-effectiveness.

Four Ps *See* 'P'.

Fuzzy logic A branch of decision theory that deals with situations where boundaries cannot be clearly defined.

Gatekeeper A person who is responsible for an important information junction – e.g. controlling the flow of information which reaches top management.

Gearing The proportion of debt (i.e. long-term liabilities and preference shares) to debt plus equity (equity being ordinary share capital plus reserves).

General reserve *See* Reserves.

Globalisation The process whereby an organisation's operations span the world and the strategic position of competitors in national markets is influenced by their overall global positions.

Goal Something that is desired and which we act to achieve.

Goal-setting theory A theory of motivation that predicts the intensity and direction of effort on task performance. The theory argues that specific, difficult goals are better than vague or 'do your best' goals. Important moderating factors are feedback about progress towards goal achievement and a person's commitment to achieving a goal.

Goods Tangible entities that are the output from the transformation process.

Gross profit This is the difference between the sales figure and the cost price of the sales – sometimes referred to as the 'mark-up' when expressed as a percentage of sales or cost.

Halo effect An assumption that because a candidate has a desirable characteristic (e.g. smart appearance) then he or she must be equally good in all other areas.

Hawthorne effect Employees work harder when they believe management is concerned about their welfare and when managers pay special attention to them.

Headhunting Contacting and actively recruiting personnel from another organisation.

Hierarchy How components are connected together and ordered at increasing levels of accumulation in a system.

Hierarchy of relative prepotency The classification of human needs by motivating factors, as proposed in 1942 by Abraham Maslow, an American organisational psychologist.

Hierarchical pyramid The hierarchical pyramid places the most numerous and, in management terms, the most junior people at the bottom of the pyramid and the least numerous, and most senior, people at the top.

Horizontal integration When an organisation acquires its competitors or forms a close association with another organisation at the same stage of production or in the same competitive area.

Human resources management Concerns the human side of enterprises and the factors that determine workers' relationships with their employing organisations.

Impoverished management This does not provide leadership in a positive sense but believes in a laissez-faire approach, relying on previous practice to keep the organisation going.

Individualism index A culture index by Geert Hofstede defined as the relationship between the individual and the group to which he or she belongs, or the preference for living and working in collectivist or individual ways.

Induction The process of introducing recruits to an organisation and explaining their role within it.

Information Data components brought together in a particular structural relationship that gives an overall meaning not contained in its individual components.

Information power The power that results from personal and professional access to key information.

Inspirational leadership Exercised by people who stimulate those around them to purposeful action without recourse to a power or authority base, and who change the way people understand the world around them and relate to each other.

Intelligent systems *See* Artificial intelligence.

Intended strategy A strategy consisting of a set of actions planned to achieve well-defined organisational goals.

Interest payments Payments to the providers of loans, debentures and overdrafts.

Internal rate of return The rate which gives a net present value equal to the initial investment – i.e. a net present value of nil.

International Accounting Standards A set of accounting rules that meets the needs of the international financial and business communities and are particularly acute to the needs of international corporations that are obliged to satisfy many different requirement simultaneously in each country in which they operate.

Internet An international network of computer services providing a range of communication (such as e-mail) and information (such as the World Wide Web) systems.

Interviewing A conversation with a purpose.

Intranet An internal organisational version of the Internet protected by passwords and restricted to employees and customers. Parts of it may be limited to one group or another. It usually contains various communications to employees, such as the company strategy, vision and values as well as bulletins and other useful information. It can also contain interactive packages, training programmes, employee selection programmes and an internal e-mail facility. It is increasingly being used by organisations as a virtual meeting medium, replacing teleconferencing.

Investments Money lent by individuals or organisations to a company, usually as quoted or unquoted shares or loans.

Ishikawa diagram Named after Kaoru Ishikawa, it shows the causes of a certain event. Such diagrams are used to identify improvements in a process or situation. Also called a fishbone diagram or a cause–effect diagram.

Issued ordinary share capital *See* Share capital.

Japan Inc A term coined in response to the coherence and interrelatedness of Japan's economic effort.

Jobbing Processes that deal with high variety and low volumes of products or services.

Job satisfaction A psychological label that refers to a job holder's perceptions about, and satisfaction with, job-related characteristics such as pay and reward policies, promotion prospects, management styles, leadership behaviours, resource allocation, etc.

Joint consultative committee (JCC) A body made up of employee representatives and management which meets regularly to discuss issues of common interest.

Just-in-time production A technique concerned with improving production efficiency and reducing waste by minimising storage through careful planning and purchasing to meet the exact requirements of the customer, internal or external.

Just-in-time systems Systems which ensure that stock is delivered from suppliers only when it is required so that stock is not stored and held in reserve.

Kaizen The process of continuous improvement in production.

Kanban **production system** A system of production where containers hold stock for initiating production so that the amount of stock in the system can be varied by altering the number of cards in the system. Thus materials are pulled through the production process according to the demand for final assembly, rather than pushed through by an inflexible production plan. From the Japanese *kanban* meaning 'card'.

Keiretsu **groups** Broad-based Japanese conglomerates stemming from the activities of large and wealthy industrial families having a high degree of synergy as skills and resources are drawn from a wide pool of industrial and commercial activity.

Key success factors Those resources, skills and competencies of an organisation in an industry that are essential to deliver success in the market.

Knowledge management The retention, exploitation and sharing of knowledge in an organisation that will deliver sustainable advantage.

Leadership The process of motivating other people to act in particular ways in order to achieve specific goals.

Learning organisations Organisations skilled in continually seeking knowledge deficiencies, acquiring knowledge and modifying their behaviour to reflect this new knowledge.

Legitimate power The power that comes from the socially accepted duty for people to obey the leader.

Leverage The term used in the USA for 'gearing'.

Leveraging The exploitation by an organisation of its existing resources to their fullest extent.

Life cycle analysis Products and services, after they are introduced, tend to pass through periods of growth, relative stability and then decline.

Liquidity ratio Indicates an organisation's ability to pay its debts as the debts become due.

Long-term debt Long-term loans and debentures – debentures are a special type of long-term loan, the holders being protected by a Deed of Trust.

Make-to-order organisation Produces goods based on customer demand.

Make-to-stock organisation Produces goods and stores them as inventory.

Management The process of planning, organising, leading and controlling people so that there is a productive outcome to work.

Management accounting The more modern predetermined cost and management accounting systems such as budgeting and standard costing.

Management by objectives (MBO) Describes a set of procedures that begins with objective setting and continues through performance review.

Management by walking about (MBWA) Management by observation.

Management information system (MIS) An information system which deals with the control of so-called 'routine', 'structured' or 'day-to-day' operations.

Marginal costing A system which separates fixed and variable costs. Only the variable costs – those that vary directly with the production of the product – are included in the product costs.

Market The group of actual or potential customers who are ready, willing and able to purchase a commodity or service.

Market extension Occurs when an offer is introduced into a market segment other than the one in which it is currently positioned.

Market penetration Involves either increasing sales to existing users or finding new customers in the same market.

Market positioning Often seen in terms of market share as a precursor to profits (*see* Positioning).

Market research The planned systematic collection, collation and analysis of data designed to help the management of an organisation to reach decisions about its operation and to monitor the results of these decisions.

Market segmentation The identification of specific parts of a market and the development of different market offerings that will be attractive to these segments.

Marketing The management process responsible for identifying, anticipating and satisfying customer requirements profitably.

Marketing audit A formal review of everything that has affected or may affect the organisation's marketing environment, internal marketing system and specific marketing activities.

Marketing mix The appropriate combination, in particular circumstances, of product, price, place and promotion (and people, process and physical evidence).

Marketing orientation In which the marketing function is at the centre of the structures of an organisation integrating the work of all the other functions.

Masculinity index A culture index by Geert Hofstede defined as pertaining to societies in which social gender roles are clearly distinct – men are supposed to be assertive, tough and focused on material success. *Femininity* pertains to societies in which women are supposed to be more modest, tender and concerned with the quality of life.

Maslow's hierarchy *See* Hierarchy of relative prepotency.

Mass Processes that provide a high volume of goods or services with low variety.

Materiality Whether or not an amount of income or expenditure is of a significant value – e.g. in making the decision to treat an item as revenue or capital expenditure in the accounts.

Maximax criterion A method used in decision analysis for maximising the largest payoff from some decision situation.

Maximin criterion A method used in decision analysis for maximising the minimum payoff from some decision situation.

Metastrategy The underlying orientation of the organisation towards its environment.

Middle-of-the-road management A style of management which believes in compromise so that decisions are taken only if endorsed by subordinates.

Minimax regret criterion A method used in decision analysis for minimising the maximum regret from some decision situation.

Mission statement A single short statement by an organisation giving the purpose of its activity.

Model A simplified representation of reality created for the purpose of explanation.

Net present value The present value of the cash flows less the initial cost of the investment/project being evaluated.

Net profit before tax Gross profit, plus other income, less all expenses, including any adjustment to the provision for bad and doubtful debts, depreciation, interest payable (other than dividends) and directors' remuneration.

Network Two or more ICT devices connected by wire, optical cable or radio so that they can intercommunicate.

Networking Interacting for mutual benefit, usually on an informal basis, with individuals and groups internal and external to the organisation.

Neural networks Computer or software designs that mimic the working of the human brain.

Noise A range of factors that can lead to a message being distorted or difficult to understand.

'O' (six) of markets Occupants, objects, occasions, organisations, objectives, operations.

Open and closed systems These reflect the extent to which an organisation interacts with its environment.

Operation A process, method or series of acts, especially of a practical nature.

Operations management The activities, decisions and responsibilities of managing the production and delivery of products or services.

Operations managers Those responsible for producing the supply of goods or services in the organisation. They make decisions regarding the operations function and the transformation processes used.

Ordinary shares *See* Share capital, Ordinary shares.

Organisational behaviour modification Used to improve work-related performance such as productivity quality and absenteeism.

Organisational culture The generally accepted beliefs and assumptions that have evolved over time and which represent the organisation's collective experience – also influenced by the wider cultural, political, economic and environmental context in which the organisation operates.

Organisational development A management-supported, long-term effort to improve an organisation.

Organisational politics Deliberate efforts made by individuals and groups to use power in pursuit of their own interests.

Outsourcing The decision by an organisation to buy in products or services from outside, rather than supply them from within the organisation. The practice of handing over the management and operation of certain functions to a third party.

'P' (four or seven) in the marketing mix Product, price, place, promotion; and people, process and physical evidence.

Participatory theory of leadership The involvement of employees in solving organisational problems.

Particularism A cultural dimension which prevails in a culture where unique circumstances and relationships are more important considerations in determining what is right and good than abstract rules – it is the opposite cultural dimension to universalism (*see* Universalism).

Path–goal theory of leadership Attempts to predict how different types of rewards and leadership styles affect the performance of subordinates.

Payback The time taken for an investment/project to repay its original cost.

Payoff table A table showing the payoffs for all combinations of a decision problem.

Peer group appraisal Work performance assessment by a colleague of equal occupational status to the employee being assessed.

Performance appraisal Establishes objectives for an individual or a group and judges performance on how well they have been achieved.

Performance management Systems designed to establish individual objectives which assist the achievement of corporate objectives and monitor progress on accomplishing them.

PERT (program evaluation review technique) Helps managers to schedule large-scale projects.

PESTLE factors The political, economic, social and technological aspects of an organisation's environment.

Place Where the final exchange takes place between the seller and the purchaser.

Politics See Company politics

Positioning (organisational) Where the organisation sees itself and its products and services in the market.

Power distance index (PDI) A culture index by Geert Hofstede defined as the extent to which the less powerful members of institutions and organisations within a country expect and accept that power is distributed unequally.

Privateness The degree to which an organisation depends on direct charges to consumers and direct market dealing rather than taxed funds.

Process The activities required to manufacture or deliver a product or service.

Process layout Locating similar transforming resources together to meet the processing needs of different products or services.

Product layout Locating transforming resources in a sequence as defined by the processing activities of the product or service – also known as 'line'.

Productivity The most common measure of operations management performance, defined as the ratio of output to input – output means results achieved; input means resources consumed.

Products Tangible objects whose sale involves a change of ownership.

Product/service portfolio The products and services that an organisation decides to offer to customers.

Professional service Provide bespoke knowledge-based services involving high customer contact.

Profit and loss account The account in which the profit or loss for the period is computed and shared out between the various stakeholders.

Profitability index The present value of the cash flows divided by the cost of the original investment.

Profitability ratios These indicate the return on capital employed and the productivity of the capital employed.

Project Using clear start and end points to reach a defined goal by using predefined activities and resources.

Provision for bad and doubtful debts An amount which is charged in the profit and loss account and then deducted from debtors in the balance sheet to give debts recoverable a more realistic value.

Publicness How far an organisation is in the public sector – reflected by the degree to which it depends on taxed funds.

Quality An attribute of a product or service which ensures that it is attractive in the eyes of the customer.

Quality circle A group of people that meets regularly to identify and solve its own work-related problems and implement its own solutions with management approval.

QUEST analysis (quality in every single task) Everybody in an organisation is a 'customer' and 'supplier' and receives products and services from colleagues within the organisation.

Ratio analysis Used to assess and compare financial performance by companies (*see* Profitability ratios, Liquidity ratios, Efficiency ratios and Capital structure).

Re-engineering Instead of trying to improve coordination between departments organised into vertical functions, the organisation is structured into a collection of horizontal processes each of which takes orders and delivers a product or a service.

Referent power The power that comes to someone who is a role model for others.

Regression analysis Designed to estimate one variable on the basis of one or more other variables.

Regret The loss due to not making the best decision.

Reserves Ploughed back profits which have been retained and reinvested in the business.
    Capital reserve Not available for distribution as dividend – e.g. share premium, revaluation reserve.
    General reserve Available for distribution as dividend.

Retained earnings The amount ploughed back into the business after the deduction of all other appropriations – e.g. taxation, dividends, transfers to general reserve.

Reward power The power that results from the ability to reward required behaviour.

Risk analysis The analysis of a situation where there are several possible outcomes and the probability of their occurrence is unknown – the uncertainty that arises when a particular action may lead to one of several outcomes.

Sampling A sample is anything less than a full survey of a 'population'.

Sampling variation Relates to the difference in results that might be expected by taking different samples of whatever is being measured.

SARAH The change process in terms of shock, anger, rejection, acceptance and help.

Scientific management An analytic approach to problems of organisation emphasising the codification of routine tasks – based on the work of Frederick Winslow Taylor (*see* Taylorism). He believed that managers must accept full responsibility for planning, organising and supervising work, based on the reduction of people's tasks into rules, laws and formulae.

Self-disclosure Sharing information about yourself with others to improve trust and communication.

Self-fulfilling prophecy A prophecy where people believe that something will happen – they act on this view and their actions mean that it does happen.

Services Intangible processes that do not result in a change of ownership – intangible entities that are the output from the transformation process.

Service shops Medium variety, medium volume service processes.

Seven Ps *See* 'P'.

Shamrock organisation A form of organisation composed of three interlocking leaves in the sense of three distinct groups of workers.

Share capital Consists of ordinary shares and preference shares:
    Authorised share capital The maximum number of shares that a company can issue.
    Issued share capital The number of shares which have been issued by a company.
    Ordinary shares The owners of these shares have voting rights and receive dividends.
    Preference shares Usually fixed interest and no voting rights.

Share premium account When shares become fully paid, this account represents the difference between the total amount received for the shares and the face (or par) value of those shares.

Six Os *See* 'O'.

SMART objectives Those which are specific about what is to be accomplished, measurable differences, attainable target, results oriented and time limits established.

SOHO 'Small office, home office' market.

Span of management The number of people or units for whom a manager is responsible.

SPECTACLES Social, political, economic, cultural, technological, aesthetic, customers, legal, environmental and sectoral factors in an organisation's environment.

Stakeholders People or groups who have an interest in an organisation – e.g. in the private sector the shareholders, the tax authorities, the directors, the employers, the providers of finance, the creditors etc.; and in the public sector, the government, taxpayers, the 'public', employees and employers, etc.

Standard costing A predetermined system which uses standard quantities of labour, materials, etc. at standard rates/prices and compares these at regular intervals with actual performance.

States of nature Uncontrollable future events that determine the outcome of a decision.

Statistical process control (SPC) A technique for the statistical monitoring of a process.

STEP factors Social, technological, economic and political factors in an organisation's environment (*see* Spectacles).

Strategic analysis The complexity arising out of ambiguous and non-routine situations with organisation-wide rather than operationally specific implications.

Strategic business plan This outlines the process of allocating resources in an organisation in order to achieve its strategic objectives.

Strategic change The implementation of new strategies that involve substantive changes beyond the normal routines of the organisation.

Strategic decisions These decisions are concerned with achieving an advantage for an organisation in the long term.

Strategic drift When the actual strategy of an organisation drifts further and further away from the strategy needed for success.

Strategic fit The matching of the activities and resources of an organisation to the environment in which it operates.

Strategic leadership Motivating people to move in a particular direction in order to achieve particular objectives.

Strategic management The decisions and actions used to formulate and implement strategies that will provide a competitively superior fit between the organisation and its environment to enable it to achieve organisational objectives.

Strategic marketing This involves moving the organisation from its present position to a more competitive one where it has a competitive advantage.

Strategic plan Provides an idea of an organisation's overall direction, the way it is planning to develop if it is able to control matters, its overall purpose and objectives.

Strategic planning A formal planning system for the development and implementation of the strategies related to the mission and objectives of the organisation.

Strategy A sense of purpose, looking ahead, planning, positioning, fit, leverage and stretching.

Stretch When resources are used in challenging ways to build up a number of core competencies.

STRETCH target An impossibly difficult goal that requires people to adopt a completely new approach to achieve it.

Suggestion scheme Schemes whereby employees are encouraged to make suggestions or put forward ideas to improve workplace efficiency and organisational effectiveness – many organisations that operate such schemes give rewards for the best suggestions.

Supply chain management The interrelationship between suppliers and customers.

Sustainable competitive advantage An advantage over competitors that cannot be easily eliminated.

SWOT analysis Highlights the internal strengths and weaknesses of an organisation from the customers' point of view as they relate to external opportunities and threats.

Synergy One plus one = three – e.g. joining two companies together could bring about greater efficiency.

System A way of viewing a complex accumulation of components that brings structure and understanding to the whole.

Systems approach Managers focus on the role that each part of an organisation plays in the whole organisation rather than dealing separately with each part.

Tacit knowledge Knowledge held by individuals but which has not been shared with others in the organisation.

Taguchi method Helps to quantify the loss due to lack of quality of a performance characteristic, with the objective of identifying the real cause of the problem.

Taylorism The division of work into measurable parts so that standards of work performance can be defined (named after F W Taylor).

Team A group of two or more people who interact with each other for a particular purpose.

Team briefing Regular meeting of groups of between four and 15 people based round a common production or service area. Meetings are usually led by a manager or supervisor and last for no more than 30 minutes, during which information is imparted, often with time left for questions from employees. A method used within organisations to cascade information to all employees quickly.

Team management A style where there is a belief that tasks need to be carefully explained and decisions agreed with subordinates to achieve a high level of commitment.

Teleconferencing A system whereby meetings, lectures, presentations and similar events are performed between individuals and groups in different geographical locations via television satellite links. Because of expense many organisations are turning to intranets for similar functions.

Theory X Managers who tend to believe that people have an inherent dislike of work, regarding it as necessary for survival and avoiding it whenever possible.

Theory Y Managers who believe that people see work as a natural phenomenon, that they accept responsibility and, in fact, seek it.

Three other Ps *See* 'P'.

Total absorption costing A costing system which charges all of the production overheads, and possibly other overheads, to the cost of the product/service.

Total quality management An intensive, long-term effort to transform all parts of the organisation in order to produce the best product and service possible to meet customer needs.

Tough-guy culture An organisation made up of individuals (entrepreneurs) who are prepared to take high risks and quick feedback.

Trait theories Based on the personal characteristics of leaders.

Transactional leadership The leader determines what subordinates need to do in order to achieve their own and organisational objectives and then classifies these requirements and helps subordinates to become confident of reaching their objectives.

Transformation process The activity that changes inputs into outputs – this is the most commonly used theoretical model of operations management.

Transformational leadership The leader, using his/her personal vision and energy, inspires people to do better than they would have expected by raising motivation and the importance of the value of people's tasks within the organisation.

Transformed resources Resources that are converted in a process – usually materials, information and customers.

Transforming resources The resources that act on the transformed resources to carry out the transformation process – normally classified into facilities and staff.

Treasury function The function responsible for investing surplus cash short term – e.g. for 24 hours or one week or one month.

Triple I organisation Based on intelligence, information and ideas which form the intellectual capital represented by the core workers.

Uncertainty avoidance index (UAI) A culture index by Geert Hofstede defined as involving the creation of rules and structures to eliminate ambiguity in organisations, and support beliefs promising certainty and protecting conformity. This means that human beings try in various ways to avoid uncertainty in their lives by controlling their environment through rules and regulations.

Undistributed profits Those profits which have been ploughed back and reinvested in the business.

Universalism A cultural dimension whereby people believe that what is true and good can be discovered, defined and applied everywhere. It is the opposite cultural dimension to particularism (*see* Particularism).

Valence In expectancy theory of motivation, the perceived attractiveness or the value a person places on the rewards on offer for pursuing a particular course of action.

Variance analysis The frequent comparison of budgets and/or standards with actual performance and the reporting of the variances to management.

Variety The range of different products or services that a process produces.

Vertical integration The acquisition by an organisation of another that is further back in the stages of production or further forward – such as an organisation acquiring its raw material suppliers or its distributors.

Vision statement *See* Mission statement.

Volume The level of output from a process.

Window dressing *See* Creative accounting.

Working capital Current assets less current liabilities.

Works councils Committees made up either solely of workers or of joint representatives of workers, management and shareholders which meet, usually at company level, to discuss a variety of issues relating to workforce matters and sometimes general, wider-ranging organisational issues. They are usually supported by legislation which compels organisations to set them up.

X theory *See* Theory X.

Y theory *See* Theory Y.

Zero-based budgeting A system where managers are forced to justify and prioritise their requirements.

Zero defects An error-free approach to quality control – 'doing it right first time'.

REFERENCES AND USEFUL READING

CHAPTER 1

Argyris, C (2000) *Flawed Advice and the Management Trap*, Oxford: Oxford University Press.

Barnard, C I (1938) *The Functions of the Executive*, Cambridge, MA: Harvard University Press.

Beer, M and Nohria, N (2000) 'Cracking the code of change', *Harvard Businesss Review*, May/June.

Betts, P W (1999) *Supervisory Management*, Prentice Hall.

Binney, G, Wilke, G and Williams, C (2005) *Living Leadership*, Prentice Hall.

Christensen, C M and Overdorf, M (2000) 'Meeting the challenge of disruptive change', *Harvard Business Review*, March/April.

Drucker, P F (1988) 'The coming of the new organization', *Harvard Business Review*, January/February.

Drucker, P F (1998) *Managing in a Time of Great Change*, New York: Plume.

Dunkerley, D (1975) *The Foreman: Aspects of Task and Structure*, London: Routledge and Kegan Paul.

Fayol, H (1930) *Industrial and General Administration*, Geneva: International Management Institute.

French, W L and Ball, C H (1984) *Organization Development: Behavioral Science Interventions for Organization Improvement*, Englewood Cliffs, NJ: Prentice Hall.

Gilbreth, L M (1914) *The Psychology of Management*, New York: Stangus & Walter.

Hales, C (1999) 'Why do managers do what they do? Reconciling evidence and theory in accounts of managerial work', *British Journal of Management*, December, 10 (4).

Hales, C (2000) *Managing Through Organisations*, Thompson Learning.

Hamel, G and Prahalad, C K (1994) *Competing for the Future*, Boston, MA: Harvard Business School Press.

Hannagan, T J (2006) 'Leadership and environmental assessment in further education', *Journal of Further and Higher Education*, 10 (4).

Harvey-Jones, J (1993) *Managing to Survive*, London: Heinemann.

Kerr, S, Hill, K D and Broedling, L (1986) 'The first-line supervisor: phasing out or here to stay?' *Academy of Management Review*, 11 (1).

Kotter, J P (2007) 'Leading change: why transformation efforts fail', *Harvard Business Review*, January.

Lewin, K (1951) *Field Theory in Social Science*, New York: Harper & Brothers.

Lowe, J (1992) 'Locating the line: the front-line supervisor and human resource management' in Blyton, P and Turnbull, P (eds) *Reassessing Human Resource Management*, London: Sage.

Mayo, E, Roethlisberger, F J and Dickson, W J (1939) *Management and the Worker*, Cambridge, MA: Harvard University Press.

Mescon, M H, Albert, M and Khedouri, F (1985) *Management: Individual and Organizational Effectiveness*, New York: Harper & Row.

Michailova, S and Hutchings, K (2006) 'National cultural influences on knowledge sharing: a comparison of China and Russia', *Journal of Management Studies*, 43 (3), May.

Ouchi, W (1981) *Theory Z: How American Business Can Meet the Japanese Challenge*, Reading, MA: Addison-Wesley.

Owen, B (2001) 'The first-line manager – redefining the role', Proceedings of the NEBS Conference *Growing Organisations: Managing the Challenges*, Nottingham, March: NEBS Management.

Parker Follett, M (1941) *Collected Works*, New York: Harper & Brothers.

Pearce, J A and Robinson, R B Jr (1989) *Management*, New York: McGraw-Hill.

Peters, T (1987) *Thriving on Chaos*, London: Macmillan.

Peters, T and Waterman, R (1982) *In Search of Excellence*, New York: Harper & Row.

Pettigrew, A M (1988) *The Management of Strategic Change*, Oxford: Blackwell.

Pettigrew, A M, Ferlie, E and McKee, L (1992) *Shaping Strategic Change*, London: Sage.

Smith, R (1993) 'Windsor Business Forum', *Cable Telecom*.

Stern, S (2005) 'Let's reclaim the "M" word', *Management Today*, April.

Weber, M (1947) *The Theory of Social and Economic Organizations*, New York: Free Press.

Zaleznik, A (2004) 'Managers and leaders: are they different?', *Harvard Business Review*, January.

CHAPTER 2

Adair, J (1989) *Great Leaders*, Guildford: Talbot Adair Press.

Allen-Mills, T (2005) 'Neutron Jack (and his wife) tell it like it is, *Sunday Times*, 3 April.

Bass, B M (1985) 'Leadership: good, better, best', *Organizational Dynamics*, 3.

Bass, B M and Avolio, B (1994) *Improving Organisational Effectiveness Through Transformational Leadership*, Sage.

Bass, B M and Avolio, B (1997) 'Shatter the glass ceiling: women may make better managers' in Grint, K (Ed) *Leadership: Classical, Contemporary and Critical Approaches*, Oxford University Press.

Bennis, W G (2004) 'The seven ages of the leader', *Harvard Business Review*, January.

Bennis, W G and Nanus, B (1986) *Leaders*, New York: Harper & Row.

Bennis, W and O'Toole, J (2000) 'Don't hire the wrong CEO', *Harvard Business Review*, May/June.

Bennis, W G and Thomas, R J (2002) 'Crucibles of leadership', *Harvard Business Review*, September.

Binney, G, Wilke, G and Williams, C (2004) *Living Leadership: A Practical Guide for Ordinary Heroes*, Financial Times Prentice Hall.

Blackhurst, C (2005) 'Allan Leighton', *Management Today*, September.

Blackhurst, C (2005a) 'Philip Green', *Management Today*, October.

Blake, R R and Mouton, J S (1985) *New Management Grid III: The Key to Leadership Excellence*, Houston, TX: Gulf Publishing.

Bolchover, D (2005) 'Woodward's winning ways in the management game', *Sunday Times*, 19 June.

Boyd, R (1987) 'Corporate leadership skills: a new synthesis', *Organizational Dynamics*, 1.

Burgoyne, J and James, K T (2006) 'Towards best or better practice in corporate leadership development: operational issues' in 'Mode 2 and design science research', *British Journal of Management*, 17 (4).

Council for Excellence in Management and Leadership (2002) 'Managers and leaders: raising the game', available at http://www.managementand leadershipcouncil.org/press/release2.htm.

Deal, T and Kennedy, A D (1982) *Corporate Cultures: The Rites and Rituals of Corporate Life*, Reading, MA: Addison-Wesley.

Donnell, S and Hall, J (1980) 'Men and women as managers: a significant case of no significant difference', *Organizational Dynamics*, Spring.

Drucker, P F (1992) *Managing for the Future*, Oxford: Butterworth-Heinemann.

Fiedler, F (1968) 'The leader's psychological distance and group effectiveness' in Cartwright, D and Zander A (eds), *Group Dynamics*, New York: Harper & Row.

Fiedler, F (1971) 'A theory of leadership effectiveness', *Administrative Science Quarterly*, September.

Fiedler, F and Chemers, M M (1974) *Leadership and Effective Management*, Upper Saddle River, NJ: Pearson Education.

Fleishman, E A (1953) 'Leadership climate, human relations training behaviour', *Personnel Psychology*, 2.

Ghiselli, E (1971) *Explorations in Managerial Talents*, Santa Monica, CA: Goodyear.

Goleman, D (2000) 'Leadership that gets results', *Harvard Business Review*, March/April.

Hamm, J (2006) 'The five messages leaders must manage', *Harvard Business Review*, May.

Handy, C (1991) *The Age of Unreason*, London: Century.

Handy, C (1993) *Understanding Organisations* (4th edition), London: Penguin Books.

Hannagan, T J (2006) 'Leadership and environmental assessment in further education', *Journal of Further and Higher Education*, 30 (4), November.

Heifetz, R and Linsky, M (2002) 'A survival guide for leaders', *Harvard Business Review*, June.

Hersey, P (1998) *The Situational Leader*, Escondido, CA: Center for Leadership Studies.

Hersey, P, Blanchard, K and Johnson, D (2001) *Management of Organizational Behavior: Leading Human Resources,* 8th edition, Upper Saddle River, NJ: Prentice Hall.

House, R (1971) 'A path–goal theory of leadership effectiveness', *Administrative Science Quarterly*, September.

House, R and Mitchell, T (1974) 'Path–goal theory of leadership', *Journal of Contemporary Business*, Autumn.

Kelly, S, White, M, Martin, D and Rouncefield, M (2006) *Leadership Refrains: Patterns of Leadership*, Sage Publications.

Kim, W Chan and Mauborgne, R (2003) 'Tipping point leadership', *Harvard Business Review*, April.

Kotter, J P (2001) 'What leaders really do', *Harvard Business Review*, December.

McGregor, D, (1960) *The Human Side of Enterprise*, New York: McGraw-Hill.

Management Today (1993) 'Present bearers of the leadership mantle', November.

Manz, C (1986) 'Self-leadership: towards an expanded theory of self-influence processes in organizations', *Academy of Management Review*, 2 (3).

Manz, C and Sims, H (1987) 'Leading workers to lead themselves: the external leadership of self-managing work teams', *Administrative Science Quarterly*, 32.

Massie, J L and Douglas, J (1977) *Managing: A Contemporary Introduction*, Englewood Cliffs, NJ: Prentice Hall.

Moore, J F (1997) *The Death of Competition: Leadership and Strategy in the Age of Business Ecosystems*, New York: Harper Business.

Nanus, B (1995) *Visionary Leadership*, San Francisco, CA: Jossey-Bass.

Nicholls, J (1993) 'The paradox of leadership', *Journal of General Management*, 18 (4), Summer.

Pearce, J and Robinson, R (1987) 'A measure of CEO social power in strategic decision making', *Strategic Management Journal*, May/June.

Peters, T (1987) *Thriving on Chaos*, London: Macmillan.

Peters, T and Waterman, R (1982) *In Search of Excellence*, New York: Harper & Row.

Pfeffer, J (1977) 'The ambiguity of leadership', *Academy of Management Review*, 2 (1).

Porter, M E, Lorsch, J W and Nohria, N (2004) 'Seven surprises for new CEOs', *Harvard Business Review*, October.

Ricie, R, Instone, D, and Adams, J (1984) 'Leader sex, leader success and leadership process: two field studies', *Journal of Applied Psychology*, February.

Rooke, D and Torbert, W R (2005) 'Seven transformations of leadership', *Harvard Business Review*, April.

Schein, E H (1985) *Organisational Culture and Leadership*, Jossey-Bass.

Scholz, C (1987) 'Corporate culture and strategy – the problem of strategic fit', *Long Range Planning*, 20 (4).

Smircich, L and Morgan, G (1982) 'Leadership: the management of meaning', *Journal of Applied Behavioural Science*, 18 (2).

Stogdill, R and Coons, A (1957) *Leader Behavior: Its Description and Measurement*, Columbus, OH: Ohio State University, Bureau of Business Research.

Tannenbaum, R and Schmidt, W (1973) 'How to choose a leadership pattern', *Harvard Business Review*, May/June.

Vroom, V H and Jago, A G (1988) *The New Leadership: Managing Participation in Organizations*, Englewood Cliffs, NJ: Prentice Hall.

Vroom, V H and Yetton, P W (1973) *Leadership and Decision Making*, Pittsburgh, PA: University of Pittsburgh Press.

Waldman D A, Siegal, D S and Javidan, M (2006) 'Components of CEO transformational leadership and corporate social responsibility', *Journal of Management Studies*, 43 (8), December

Weber, M (1947) *The Theory of Social and Economic Organizations*, New York: Free Press.

Welch, J and Welch, S (2006) *Winning*, Harper Collins.

Wood, M (2005) 'The fallacy of misplaced leadership', *Journal of Management Studies*, 42 (6).

Yukl, G (1999) 'An evaluation of conceptual weaknesses in transformational and charismatic leadership theories', *Leadership Quarterly*, 10 (2)

Zaleznik, A (2004) 'Managers and leaders: are they different?', *Harvard Business Review*, January.

CHAPTER 3

Bennis, W (1966) 'The coming death of bureaucracy', *Think*, November/December.

Bergman, B and Klefsjo, B (1994) *Quality: From Customer Needs to Customer Satisfaction*, Maidenhead: McGraw-Hill.

Bhote, K R (1997) 'What do customers want anyway?', *American Management Association*, March.

Clarke, K (1993) 'Survival skills for a new breed', *Management Today*, December.

Davey, J (2006) 'Leahy's global shopping spree', *Sunday Times*, 17 December.

Davidson, A (2006) 'The down and out tycoon', *Sunday Times*, 10 December.

Egar, G (1994) 'Hard times contracts', *Management Today*, January.

Farjoun, M (1998) 'The independent and joint effects of the skill and physical bases of relatedness in diversification', *Strategic Management Journal*, 19.

Faulkner, D and Johnson, G (1992) *The Challenge of Strategic Management*, London: Kogan Page.

Gulati, R and Oldroyd, J B (2005) *Harvard Business Review*, April.

Hammer, M and Champy, J (1993) *Re-engineering the Corporate: A Manifesto for Business Revolution*, London: Nicholas Brealey.

Handy, C (1989) *The Age of Unreason*, London: Pan Books.

Heller, R (1994a) 'Customer focus means commitment to constant change', *Management Today*, January.

Heller, R (1994b) 'The manager's dilemma', *Management Today*, January.

Heskett, J L, Sasser, W E and Schlesinger, L A (1997) *The Service Profit Chain: How Leading Companies Link Profit and Growth to Loyalty, Satisfaction and Value*, New York: Free Press.

Kanter, R M (1989) *When Giants learn to Dance: Mastering the Challenges of Strategy, Management and Careers in the 1990s*, Unwin.

Kay, J (1997) 'Produced to price', *Financial Times*, 13 June.

Kilburn, D (1994) 'Japanese management', *Management Today*, January.

Lee, H L (2004) 'The triple-A supply chain', *Harvard Business Review*, October.

Lucas, E (2007) 'Listen to customers and act on what you hear', *Professional Manager*, Chartered Management Institute, 16 (2).

McGregor, D (1960) *The Human Side of Enterprise*, New York: McGraw-Hill.

Miles, R F, Snow, C C, Miles, G (2000) 'The future organisation', *Long Range Planning*, 33.

Peppers, D and Rogers, M (1997) *The One to One Future: Building Relationships One Customer at a Time*, New York: Doubleday.

Peters, T and Waterman, R (1982) *In Search of Excellence*, New York: Harper & Row.

Porras, J I and Collins, J C (1996) 'Building your company's vision', *Harvard Business Review*, September/October.

Prahalad, C T and Ramaswamy, V (2000) 'Co-opting customer competence', *Harvard Business Review*, January/February.

Prem, R L and Butler, J E (2001) 'Is the resource-based "view" a useful perspective for strategic management research?', *Academy of Management Review*, 26.

Pugh, D S and Hickson, D J (1976) *Organisational Structure in its Context: The Aston Programme 1*, Farnborough: Saxon House.

Raynor, M A (1998) 'That vision thing: do we need it?', *Long Range Planning*, June.

Reichleld, F F (1996) *The Loyalty Effect: The Hidden Force Behind Growth, Profits and Lasting Value*, Boston, MA: Harvard Business School Press.

Salz-Trautman, P (1994) 'The manager's dilemma: Germany', *Management Today*, January.

Scott, W R (1987) *Organizations: Rational, National and Open Systems*, Englewood Cliffs, NJ: Prentice Hall.

St John, C H and Harrison, J S (1999) 'Manufactuirng-based relatedness, synergy and coordination', *Strategic Management Journal*, 18.

Stimpert, J L and Duhaime, L M (1997) 'In the eyes of the beholder: conceptualization of relatedness held by the managers of large diversified firms', *Strategic Management Review*, 18.

Tempest, S, Barnatt, C and Coupland, C (2002) 'Grey advantage: new strategies for the old', *Long Range Planning*, 35.

Thackray, J (1994) 'Strategic concepts', *Management Today*, January.

Toffler, A (1970) *Future Shock*, New York: Random House.

Welch, J and Welch, S (2006) *Winning*, Harper Collins.

Young, R (1993) 'Jobs for life', *Professional Manager*, Institute of Management, November.

Zander, I and Zander, U (2005) The inside track: on the important (but neglected) role of customers in the resource-based view of strategy and firm growth', *Journal of Management Studies*, 42 (8).

CHAPTER 4

Adair, J (1989) *Great Leaders*, Guildford: Talbot Adair Press.

Ansoff, I (1969) *Corporate Strategy*, Penguin.

Bichard, M (2000) 'Creativity, leadership and change', *Public Money and Management*, April/June.

Boyne, G A (2004) 'A 3Rs strategy for public sector turnaround: retrenchment, repositioning and reorganisation', *Public Money and Management*, April.

Boyne, G A, Farrell, C, Law, J, Powell, M and Walker, B (2003) *Evaluating Public Sector Management Reforms: Principles and Practices*, Buckingham: Open University Press.

Bryson, J M (1995) *Strategic Planning for Public and Non-profit Organisations*, Jossey-Bass.

Carvel, J (2003) *The Guardian*, 3 March.

Chambers (1992) *Maxi Dictionary*, Chambers.

Cook, S (2004) 'Public attraction', *Management Today*, January.

Davidson, A (2005) 'Simon Thurley', *Management Today*, November.

Deal, T and Kennedy, A D (1982) *Corporate Cultures: The Rites and Rituals of Corporate Life*, Reading, MA: Addison-Wesley.

Dopson, S and Stewart, R (1990) 'Public and private sector management: the case for a wider debate', *Public Money and Management*, Spring.

Doyle, M, Claydon, T and Buchanan, D (2000) 'Mixed results, lousy process: the management experience of organisational change', *British Journal of Management*, 11, September.

Dunleavy P and Hood C (1994) 'From old public administration to new public management', *Public Money and Management*, Summer.

Foster, W and Bradach, J (2005) 'Should non-profits seek profits?', *Harvard Business Review*, February.

Hannagan, T J (2003) 'Strategic change in further education', *Doctoral Thesis*, Milton Keynes: Open University.

Hannagan, T J (2006) 'Leadership and environmental assessment in further education', *Journal of Further and Higher Education*, 30 (4), November.

Heymann, P B (1987) *The Politics of Public Management*, New Haven, CT and London: Yale University Press.

Laing, A and Hogg, G (2002) 'Political exhortation, patient expectation and professional execution: perspectives on the consumerisation of health care', *British Journal of Management*, 13 (2).

McNulty, T and Whittington, R (1992) *Managing Strategic Change in Public and Private Sectors*, Coventry: Local Government Centre, University of Warwick.

Meek, V L (1988) 'Organisational culture: origins and weaknesses', *Organisation Studies*, 9 (4).

Moore, M H (1995) *Creating Public Value: Strategic Management in Government*, Cambridge, MA and London: Harvard University Press.

Newman, J (1994) 'Beyond the vision: cultural change in the public sector', *Public Money and Management*, April/June.

Nowak, S (2006) 'A leader has to make the direction clear', *Professional Manager*, May.

Peters, T J and Waterman, R H (1982) *In Search of Excellence*, New York: Harper & Row.

Pettigrew, A M (1990) 'Is corporate culture manageable?' in Wilson, D and Rosenfeld, R (eds) *Managing Organisations: Text, Readings and Cases*, London: McGraw-Hill.

Pollitt, C and Bouckaert, G (2000) *Public Management Reform*, Oxford: Oxford University Press.

Reeves, F (1997) *Further Education as Economic Regeneration*, Wolverhampton, Bilston College Publications in association with Education Now Publishing Cooperative.

Porter, M E (1996) 'What is strategy?', *Harvard Business Review*, November/December.

Saint-Martin, D (2000) *Building the New Managerialist State*, Oxford: Oxford University Press.

Saunders, A (2006) 'Fixing the tube', *Management Today*, October.

Schein, E H (1992) *Organisational Culture and Leadership*, San Francisco, CA: Jossey-Bass.

Stacey, R D (1999) *Strategic Management and Organisational Dynamics* (3rd edition), London: Pitman.

CHAPTER 5

Argyris, C (2000) *Flawed Advice and the Management Trap*, Oxford: Oxford University Press.

Beer, M, Voelpel, S C, Leibold, M and Tekie, E B (2005) 'Strategic management as organisational learning: developing fit and alignment through a disciplined process', *Long Range Planning*, 38.

Blackhurst, C (2006) 'Charles Allen', *Management Today*, March.

Campbell, A, Devine, M and Young, D (1990) *A Sense of Mission*, London: Hutchinson.

Cyert, R M and March J G (1963) *A Behavioral Theory of the Firm*, Prentice Hall.

Daft, R L (1994) *Management* (3rd edition), Orlando, FL: Dryden Press.

Drucker, P F (1961) *The Practice of Management*, London: Mercury Books.

Evans, P and Wursten, T S (1997) 'Strategy and the new economics of information', *Harvard Business Review*, September/October.

Foster, T R (1993) *101 Great Mission Statements*, London: Kogan Page.

Goold, M, Campbell, A and Alexander, M (1994) *Corporate-Level Strategy: Creating Value in the Multibusiness Company*, New York: John Wiley.

Gupta, A K and Govidarajan, V (1984) 'Business unit strategy, management characteristics and business unit effectiveness at strategy implementation', *Academy of Management Journal*, 27.

Hamel, G (1996) 'Strategy as revolution', *Harvard Business Review*, July/August.

Hamel, G (1997) 'Killer strategies that make shareholders rich', *Fortune*, June 23.

Hamel, G and Prahalad, C K (1989) 'Do you really have a global strategy?', *Harvard Business Review*, July/August.

Hamel, G and Prahalad, C K (1993) 'Strategy as stretch and leverage', *Harvard Business Review*, March/April.

Hannagan, T J (2001) *Mastering Strategic Management*, Palgrave.

Harris, I C and Ruefli, T (2000) 'The strategy/structure debate: an examination of the performance implications', *Journal of Management Studies*, June.

Herrmann, P (2005) 'Evolution of strategic management: the need for new dominant designs', *International Journal of Management Reviews*, 7 (2), June.

Joyce, P (1999) *Strategic Management for the Public Services*, Buckingham: Open University Press.

Joyce, P (2000) *Strategy in the Public Sector*, New York: John Wiley.

Kald, M, Nilsson, F and Rapp, B (2000) 'On strategy and management control: the importance of classifying the strategy of the business', *British Journal of Management*, 11 (3), September.

Kelly, J (2000) 'Every little helps', *Long Range Planning*, 33.

Miles, R E and Snow, C C (1978) *Organisational Strategy, Strategy and Process*, McGraw-Hill.

Mintzberg, H (1973) 'Patterns in strategy formulation', *Management Science*, 24.

Mintzberg, H (1987) 'The strategy concept I: five Ps for strategy', *California Management Review*, 30.

Mintzberg, H (2000) *The Rise and Fall of Strategic Planning*, Harlow: FT Prentice Hall.

Mintzberg, H and Waters, J H (1985) 'Of strategies deliberate and emergent', *Strategic Management Journal*, 6.

Ohmae, K (1996) *The Mind of the Strategist: The Art of Japanese Business*, New York: McGraw-Hill.

Orit, G and Gilbert, J L (1998) 'Profit pools: a fresh look at strategy', *Harvard Business Review*, May/June.

Pascale, R T and Sternin, J (2005) 'Your company's secret change agents', *Harvard Business Review*, May.

Pearce, J A and Robinson, R B Jr (1989) *Management*, New York: McGraw-Hill.

Peterof M A (1993) 'The cornerstone of competitive advantage: a resource-based view', *Strategic Management Journal*, 14.

Peters, Tom (1992) *Liberation Management*, Basingstoke: Macmillan.

Peters, T and Waterman, R (1982) *In Search of Excellence*, New York: Harper & Row.

Porter, M E (1980) *Competitive Strategy: Techniques for Analyzing Industries and Competitors*, New York: Free Press.

Porter, M E (1985) *Competitive Strategy*, New York: Free Press.

Porter, M E (1990) *The Competitive Advantage of Nations*, New York: Free Press.

Porter, M E (1996) 'What is strategy?', *Harvard Business Review*, November/December.

Porter, M E (1998) *Competitive Advantage: Creating and Sustaining Superior Performance*, New York: Free Press.

Prahalad, C K and Hamel, G (1990) 'The core competence of the corporation', *Harvard Business Review*, May/June.

Rappaport, A (1997) *Creating Shareholder Value: A Guide for Managers and Investors*, New York: Free Press.

Ringland, G (1998) *Scenario Planning: Managing for the Future*, New York: John Wiley.

Schwartz, P (1996) *The Art of Long View: Planning for the Future in an Uncertain World*, New York: Doubleday.

Segal-Hom, S (1998) *The Strategy Reader*, Buckingham: The Open University/Blackwell.

Simons, R (1990) 'The role of management control systems in creating competitive advantage new perspectives', *Accounting, Organisations and Society*, 15 (1).

Stacey, R D (1999) *Strategic Management and Organisational Dynamics* (3rd edition), Harlow: FT Prentice Hall.

Stalk, G and Lachenauer, R (2004) 'Five killer strategies for trouncing the competition', *Harvard Business Review*, April.

Zimmerman, J with Tregee, B (1997) *The Culture of Success: Building a Sustained Competitive Advantage by Living Your Corporate Beliefs*, Maidenhead: McGraw-Hill.

CHAPTER 6

Anthony, S D, Eyring, M and Gibson, L (2006) 'Mapping your innovation strategy', *Harvard Business Review*, May.

Beer, M, Voelpel, S C, Leibold, M and Tekie, E R (2005) 'Strategic management as organisational learning: developing fit and alignment through a disciplined process', *Long Range Planning*, 38.

Bessant, J (2005) 'Enabling continuous and discontinuous innovation: learning from the private sector', *Public Money and Management*, January.

Buchanan, D, Fitzgerald, L, Ketley, D, Gollop, R, Jones, J L, Lamont, S S, Neath, A and Whitby, E (2005) 'No going back: a review of the literature on sustaining organizational change', *International Journal of Management Reviews*, 7 (3), September.

Butcher, D and Clarke, M (2001) *Smart Management: Using Politics in Organisations*, Basingstoke: Palgrave.

Chartered Institute of Public Finance and Accountancy (1992) *Business Plans: A Move in the Right Direction*, London: CIPFA.

Doyle, M, Claydon, T and Buchanan, D (2000) 'Mixed results, lousy process: the management experience of organisational change', *British Academy of Management*, 11, September.

Drucker, P F (1955) *The Practice of Management*, London: Heinemann.

Drucker, P F (1988) 'The coming of the new organization', *Harvard Business Review*, January/February.

Drucker, P F (1998) 'The discipline of innovation', *Harvard Business Review*, November/December.

Elbanna, S (2006) 'Strategic decisions-making: process perspectives', *International Journal of Management Reviews*, 8 (1).

Evans, P and Wurster, T S (1997) 'Strategy and the new economics of information', *Harvard Business Review*, September/October.

Faulkner, D and Johnson, G (1992) *The Challenge of Strategic Management*, London: Kogan Page.

Fayol, H (1949) *General and Industrial Management*, London: Pitman Publishing.

Finlay, P (2000) *Strategic Management*, Harlow: FT Prentice Hall.

George, C (1972) *The History of Management Thought*, London: Prentice Hall.

Goold, M, Campbell, A and Alexander, M (1994) *Corporate-Level Strategy: Creating Value in the Multibusiness Company*, New York: John Wiley.

Greiner, L E (1972) 'Evolution and devolution as organizations grow', *Harvard Business Review*, July/August.

Grundy, T (1992) *Corporate Strategy and Financial Decisions*, London: Kogan Page.

Grundy, T (1993) *Implementing Strategic Change*, London: Kogan Page.

Hamel, G (1996) 'Strategy as revolution', *Harvard Business Review*, June/August.

Hamel, G and Prahalad, C K (1994) *Competing for the Future*, Boston, MA: Harvard Business School Press.

Hannagan, T J (2001) *Mastering Strategic Management*, Basingstoke: Palgrave/Macmillan.

Harris, I C and Ruefli, T W (2000) 'The strategy/structure debate: an examination of performance implications', *Journal of Management Studies*, June.

Jacobs, R L (2002) 'Institutionalising organisational change through cascade training', *Journal of European Industrial Training*, 26.

Jelinek, M (1979) *Institutional Innovation*, New York: Praeger.

Kaplan, R S and Norton, D P (1996) *The Balanced Scorecard: Translating Strategy into Action*, Boston, MA: Harvard Business Press.

Kay, J (1997) 'Know your place', *Financial Times*, 27 June.

Kotler, J P (1995) 'Leading change: why transformation efforts fail', *Harvard Business Review*, 73.

Lahteenmaki, S, Toivonen, J and Merja, M (2001) 'Critical aspects of organisational learning research and proposals for its measurement', *British Journal of Management*, 12 (2), June.

McDonald, M (1992) *Strategic Marketing Planning*, London: Kogan Page.

Marquanett, I A (1990) 'Corporate planning challenges', *Journal of Business Strategy*, June.

Mintzberg, H (1973) *The Nature of Managerial Work*, New York: Harper & Row.

Mintzberg, H (2000) *The Rise and Fall of Strategic Planning*, FT Prentice Hall.

NHS Modernisation Agency (2002) *Improvement Leaders' Guide to Sustainability and Spread*, Ancient House Printing Group.

Moore, M H (2006) 'Breakthrough innovations and continuous improvement: two different models of innovative processes in the public sector', *Public Money and Management*, January.

Nutt, P C (2000) 'Decision-making in public, private and third sector organisations: finding sector dependent best practice', *Journal of Management Studies*, January.

Ohmae, K (1996) *The Mind of the Strategist: The Art of Japanese Business*, London: McGraw-Hill.

Pettigrew, A M (ed) (1988) *The Management of Strategic Change*, Oxford: Basil Blackwell.

Pettigrew, A M, Ferlie, E and McKee, L (1992) *Shaping Strategic Change: Making Change in Large Organisations – The Case of the National Health Service*, London: Sage.

Porter, M E (1996) 'What is strategy?', *Harvard Business Review*, November/December.

Porter, M E (1998) *Competitive Advantage: Creating and Sustaining Superior Performance*, Free Press.

Professional Manager (2007) 'We need to see innovation as a broadly spread capacity across the economy', *Chartered Management Institute*, 16 (1).

Stacey, R D (1999) *Strategic Management and Organisational Dynamics* (3rd edition), Harlow: FT Prentice Hall.

Stone, B (1997) *Confronting Company Politics*, Basingstoke: Palgrave.

CHAPTER 7

Atkinson, P E (1990) *Creating Culture Change: The Key to Successful Total Quality Management*, London: FS Publications.

Beer, M, Voelpel, S C, Leilbold M and Tekie, E B (2005) 'Strategic management as organisational learning', *Long Range Planning*, 28.

Belbin, R M (1981) *Management Teams – Why They Succeed or Fail*, London: Heinemann.

Belbin, R M (1993) *Team Roles at Work*, London: Butterworth Heinemann.

Bergman, B and Klefsjo, B (1994) *Quality from Customer Needs to Customer Satisfaction*, Maidenhead: McGraw-Hill.

Buchanan, D, Fitzgerald, L, Ketley, D, Gollop, R, Jones, J L, Lamont, S S, Neath, A and Whitby, E (2005) 'No going back: a review of the literature on sustaining organizational change', *International Journal of Management Reviews*, 7 (3), September.

Camison, C (1998) 'Total quality management and cultural change: a model of organisational development', *International Journal of Technology Management*, 16 (4).

Cartwright, R (2002) *Mastering Team Leadership*, Basingstoke: Palgrave.

Collard, R (1989) *Total Quality Success Through People*, London: IPM.

Collier, P M (2006) 'In search of purpose and priorities: police performance indicators in England and Wales', *Public Money and Management*, June.

Confederation of British Industry (1980) *The Will to Win*, CBI.

Confederation of British Industry (1990a) *Investors in People*, London: CBI.

Confederation of British Industry (1990b) *Working for Customers*, London:CBI.

Crosby, P B (1978) *Quality is Free*, Maidenhead: McGraw-Hill.

Crosby, P B (1997) 'Quality management' in Kimbler, J, Grenier, R W and Heldt, J J (eds) *Quality Management Handbook*, New York: Marcel Dekker.

Deming, W E (1982) *Quality, Productivity and Competitive Position*, Cambridge, MA: MIT Press.

Deming, W E (1986) *Out of the Crisis*, Cambridge, MA: MIT Press.

Department of Employment (1988) *Employment for the 1990s*, Cm 540, London: HMSO.

Department of Employment (1990a) *Managing Quality*, London: DoE.

Department of Employment (1990b) *Investors in People: The Context*, November, London: DoE.

Department of Employment (1990c) *Investors in People Briefing Document 1*, November, London: DoE.

Drucker, P F (1968) *The Practice of Management*, London: Pan.

Galgano, A (1994) *Companywide Quality Management*, Portland OR: Productivity Press.

Harrington, H J (1996) *The Complete Benchmarking Implementation Guide: Total Benchmarking Management*, Maidenhead: McGraw-Hill.

Harris, I C and Ruefli, T W (2000) 'The strategy/structure debate: an examination of performance implications', *Journal of Management Studies*, June.

Heikman, R G and Creighton-Zoller, A (1998) 'Diverse self-directed work teams: developing strategic initiatives for 21st century organisations', *Public Personnel Management*, Summer.

HMSO (1999) *Learning to Succeed: A New Framework for Post-16 Learning*, Cm 4392, June, London: HMSO.

Hoerschemeyer, D (1989) 'The four cornerstones of excellence', *Quality Progress*, 22 (8).

Hume, C and Wright, C (2006) 'You don't make a pig fatter by weighing it – performance management: the experience of the youth justice board', *Public Money and Management*, June.

Imai, M (1997) *Gemba Kaizen: A Common Sense, Low-Cost Approach to Management*, Maidenhead: McGraw-Hill.

Ishikawa, K (1984) *What is Total Quality Control the Japanese Way?*, Englewood Cliffs, NJ: Prentice Hall.

ITT (1981) *Circle News*, March.

Juran, J M (1970) *Quality Planning and Analysis*, Maidenhead: McGraw-Hill.

Juran, J M (1992) *Juran on Quality by Design: The Next Steps for Planning Quality into Goods and Services*, New York: Free Press.

Juran J M (ed) (1995) *A History of Managing for Quality: the Evolution, Trends and Future Directions of Managing for Quality*, Milwaukee: ASQC Press.

Juran, J M and Gryna, F M (1993) *Quality Planning and Analysis*, New York: McGraw-Hill.

Katzenbach, J R and Smith, D K (1993) *The Wisdom of Teams*, Boston: Harvard Business School Press.

Martiboye, R J (1989) *Leadership and Quality Management: A Guide for Chief Executives*, London: Department of Trade and Industry.

Mohamed, Z (1998) *Benchmarking for Best Practice: Continuous Learning through Sustainable Innovation*, Oxford: Butterworth-Heinemann.

Morland, J (1981) *Quality Circles*, London: The Industrial Society.

Oakland, J S (1986) *Total Quality Management*, London: Heinemann.

Peters, T J (1987) *Thriving on Chaos*, Basingstoke: Macmillan.

Peters, T J and Waterman, R H (1982) *In Search of Excellence*, New York: Harper & Row.

Schneier, C E, Beatty, R W and Baird, L S (1987) *The Performance Management Sourcebook*, New York: Human Resource Development Press.

Stoner, J A and Freeman, R E (1989) *Management*, Englewood Cliffs, NJ: Prentice Hall.

Taguchi, G (1986) *Introduction to Quality Engineering*, OECD, Paris: Asian Productivity Organisation.

Tuckman, B W and Jensen, M A C (1977) 'Stages of small group development revisited', *Group and Organisational Studies*, 2.

Waterman, R H (1988) *The Renewal Factor*, New York: Barton.

Webb, I (1991) *Quest for Quality*, London: The Industrial Society.

CHAPTER 8

Ansoff, I (1989) *Corporate Strategy*, Harmondsworth: Penguin.

Ash, K (2007) 'Show and tell', *Daily Telegraph*, 20 January (M10).

Bremner, R (2004) 'Fiat and BMW: a tale of two dynasties', *Management Today*, January.

Creech, P B (1995) *The Five Pillars of TQM: How to Make TQM Work for You*, New York: Plume.

Crosby, P B (1996) *Quality is Still Free*, New York: McGraw-Hill.

Drucker, P F (1993) *Managing for the Future*, Oxford: Butterworth-Heinemann.

Grant, A W and Schlesinger, L A (1995) 'Realise your customers' full profit potential', *Harvard Business Review*, September/October.

Foster, D and Davis, J (1994) *Mastering Marketing*, Basingstoke: Macmillan.

Giroux, H (2006) 'It was such a handy term': management fashions and pragmatic ambiguity', *Journal of Management Studies*, 43 (6), September.

Hamel, G and Prahalad, CK (1994) *Competing for the Future*, Boston, MA: Harvard Business School Press.

Hannagan, T J (1992) *Marketing for the Non-Profit Sector*, London: Macmillan.

Hannagan, T J (1999) *The Effective Use of Statistics: A Practical Guide for Managers*, London: Kogan Page.

Heller, R (1994) *The Fate of IBM*, New York: Little, Brown.

Henley Centre and Chartered Institute of Marketing (1993) *Customer Loyalty*.

Hume, C and Wright, C (2006) 'You don't make a pig fatter by weighing it – performance management: the experience of the youth justice board', *Public Money and Management*, June.

Kay, J (1995) *Why Firms Succeed: Choosing Markets and Challenging Competitors to Add Value*, Oxford: Oxford University Press.

Kotler, P (1986) *Principles of Marketing* (3rd edition), Englewood Cliffs, NJ: Prentice Hall.

Kotler, P (2001) *Kotler on Marketing*, New York: Free Press.

Kotler, P (2005) *Marketing Management: Analysis, Planning, Implementation and Control* (12th edition), Englewood Cliffs, NJ: Prentice Hall.

Kotler, P and Armstrong, G (2006) *Marketing: An Introduction* (8th edition), Englewood Cliffs, NJ: Prentice Hall.

Kotler, P, Rackham, N and Krishnaswamy, S (2006) 'Ending the war between sales and marketing', *Harvard Business Review*, July/August.

Lancaster, G and Massingham, L (1988) *The Marketing Primer*, Oxford: Heinemann.

McDonald, M (1992) *Strategic Marketing Planning*, London: Kogan Page.

Myers, J H (1996) *Segmentation and Positioning for Strategic Marketing Decisions*, New York: American Marketing Association.

Nunes, P F and Cespedes, F V (2003) 'The customer has escaped', *Harvard Business Review*, November.

Oliver, G (1980) *Marketing Today*, London: Prentice Hall.

Peters, T and Waterman, R (1982) *In Search of Excellence*, New York: Harper & Row.

Porras, J I and Collins, J C (1996) *Building Your Company's Vision*, Boston, MA: Harvard Business School, September/October.

Pullig, C, Simmons, C J and Netemeyer, R G (2006) 'Brand dilution: when do new brands hurt existing brands?', *Journal of Marketing*, 70, American Marketing Association.

Raynor, M A (1998) 'That vision thing: do we need it?', *Long Range Planning*, June.

Thomas, M J and Whaite, N E (eds) (1989) *The Marketing Digest*, Oxford: Heinemann.

Rein, I, Kotler, P, Stoller, M and Hamlin, M (2006) *High Visibility: Improving Your Personal and Professional Bid*, McGraw-Hill

Slywotzky, A J (1996) *Value Migration: How to Think Several Moves Ahead of the Competition*, Boston, MA: Harvard Business School.

Smith, A (1776) *An Inquiry into the Nature and Causes of the Wealth of Nations*, London: Strahn and Caddell.

Volkner, F and Sattler, H (2006) 'Drivers of brand extension success', *Journal of Marketing*, American Marketing Association, 70, April.

Wilmshurst, J (1984) *The Fundamentals and Practice of Marketing*, Oxford: Heinemann.

Zimmerman, J with Tregee, B (1997) *The Culture of Success: Building a Sustained Competitive Advantage by Living Your Corporate Beliefs*, New York: McGraw-Hill.

CHAPTER 9

Barnard, C (1938) *The Functions of the Executive*, Cambridge, MA: Harvard University Press.

Belbin, R M (1996) *The Coming Shape of Organisation*, London: Butterworth-Heinemann.

Belbin, R M (2003) *Team Roles at Work*, London: Butterworth-Heinemann.

Butcher, D and Clarke, M (2001) *Using Politics in Organisations*, Basingstoke: Palgrave.

Chinges, P T (1997) *Paying for Performance: A Guide to Compensation Management*, New York: John Wiley.

Collier, P M (2006) 'In search of purpose and priorities: police performance indicators in England and Wales', *Public Money and Management*, June.

Daft, R (2007) *Understanding the Theory and Design of Organisations*, Mason, OH and London: Thomson South Western.

Davidow, W H and Malone, M S (1992) *The Virtual Corporations: Structuring and Revitalizing the Corporation for the 21st Century*, New York: Harper Business.

Drucker, P F (1955) *The Practice of Management*, London: Heinemann.

Edwards, M R (2005) 'Organisational identification: a conceptual and operational review', *International Journal of Management Reviews*, 7 (4), December.

Fayol, H (1949) *General and Industrial Administration*, London: Pitman Publishing.

Grisham, J (1992) *The Firm*, London: Random House, Arrow Books.

Ghoshal, S (1997) 'Strategic learning with scenarios', *European Management Journal*, 15 (6), December.

Harris, I C and Ruefli, T W (2000) 'The strategy/structure debate: an examination of the performance implications', *Journal of Management Studies*, June.

Harvey-Jones, J (1993) *Managing to Survive*, London: Heinemann.

Hume, C and Wright, C (2006) 'You don't make a pig fatter by weighing it – performance management: the experience of the youth justice board', *Public Money and Management*, June.

Jones, R A, Jimmieson, N L and Griffiths, A (2005) 'The impact of organisational culture and reshaping capabilities on change implementation success: the mediating role of the readiness to change', *Journal of Management Studies*, 42 (2).

Joyce, W F (1999) *Mega Change: How Today's Leading Companies Have Transformed Their Workforces*, New York: Free Press.

Kafka, F (1994) *The Trial* (new edition), Harmondsworth: Penguin.

Kaplan, R S and Norton, D P (1996) *The Balanced Scorecard: Translating Strategy into Action*, Boston, MA: Harvard Business School Press.

Kerr, S (1997) *Ultimate Rewards: What Really Motivates People to Achieve*, Boston, MA: Harvard Business School Press.

Lipnock, J and Stamps, J (1997) *Virtual Teams: Reaching Across Space, Time and Organizations in the Technology*, New York: John Wiley.

Miles, R E, Snow, C C and Miles, G (2000) 'The future organisation', *Long Range Planning*, 33.

Mullin, R (1996) 'Knowledge management: a cultural revolution', *Journal of Business Strategy*, September/October.

Nonaka, I and Takeuchi, H (1995) *The Knowledge-creating Company: How Japanese Companies Create the Dynamics of Innovation*, Oxford: Oxford University Press.

Parker Follett, M (1941), *Collected Works*, New York: Harper and Brothers.

Smith, A (1776) *An Inquiry into the Nature and Causes of the Wealth of Nations*, London: Strahn and Caddell.

Stone, B (1997) *Confronting Company Politics*, Basingstoke: Palgrave.

Studeman, F (1997) 'In search of a modern structure', *Financial Times*, June 27.

Thompson, P and Wallace, T (1996) 'Redesigning production through team working', *International Journal of Operations and Production Management*, 16 (2), February.

Tuckman, R W (1965) 'Developmental sequence in small groups', *Psychological Bulletin*, 58 (6).

Wenger, E C and Snyder, W M (2000) 'Communities of practice: the organizational frontier', *Harvard Business Review*, January/February.

CHAPTER 10

Addison, J T and Belfield, C R (2002) 'What do we know about the new European Works Councils? Some preliminary evidence from Britain', *Scottish Journal of Political Economy*, 49 (4): 418–44.

Ainley, J (1992) 'Asking staff to survey management style', *Involvement and Participation*, 612: 10–11 and 19.

Alston, J P (1985) *The American Samurai: Blending American and Japanese Management Practice*, Berlin: Walter de Gruyter.

Anderson, P A (1999) *Non-Verbal Communication: Forms and Functioning*, Mountain View: Mayfield.

Argyle, M (1990) *Bodily Communication* (2nd edition), London: International Universities Press Inc.

Barnum, C and Wolniansky, N (1989) 'Taking cues from body language', *Management Review*, 78 (6) pp. 59–61.

Bicknell, D (2000) 'What should companies do about staff internet abuse?', *Computer Weekly*, November: 16.

Burgoon, J K (1991) 'Relational message interpretations of touch, conversational distance and posture', *Journal of Non-Verbal Behaviour*, 15: 233–59.

Chen, C Y and Lindsay, G (2000) 'Viruses, attacks, and sabotage: it's a computer crime wave', *Fortune*, 141 (10): 484–6.

Child, J (2005) *Organisation: Contemporary Principles and Practice*, Oxford: Blackwell Publishing.

Clampitt, P G (2005) *Communicating for Managerial Effectiveness*, Newbury Park, CA: Sage Publications Inc.

Crichton, M (1993) *Rising Sun*, London: Arrow.

Czerny, A (2004) 'Woolworths aims to involve staff', *People Management*, 13, June 30.

Dawson, S (1996) *Analysing Organisations* (3rd edition), Basingstoke: Macmillan Press Limited.

DeVito, J A (1989) *The Interpersonal Communication Handbook*, New York: Harper & Row.

Ekman, P and Friesen, W V (1975) *Unmasking the Face: A Guide to Recognising Emotions from Facial Clues*, New Jersey: Prentice Hall Inc.

Emmott, M (2006) *Engaging Personalities* available at: http:\\www.cipd.co.uk/cande/annual/conference/_daily_wed_005.htm

Francesco, A M and Gold, B A (1998) *International Organisational Behaviour: Texts, Readings, Cases and Skills*, New Jersey: Prentice Hall Inc.

Gilbert, G N (1980) 'Being interviewed: a role analysis', *Social Science Information*, 19: 227–36.

Goffman, E (1990) *The Presentation of Self in Everyday Life*, London: Penguin Books Ltd.

Graves, L (1993) 'Sources of individual differences in interviewer effectiveness: a model and implications for future research', *Journal of Organisational Behaviour*, 14: 349–70.

Greenberg, J and Baron, R A (2000) *Behaviour in Organisations. Understanding and Managing the Human Side of Work* (7th edition), London: Prentice Hall International.

Gross, R D (2005) *Psychology: The Science of Mind and Behaviour* (5th edition), London: Hodder & Stoughton Educational.

Gudykunst, W B and Ting-Toomey, S (1988) *Culture and Interpersonal Communication*, Newbury Park, CA: Sage Publications Inc.

Guirdham, M (1990) *Interpersonal Skills at Work*, Hertfordshire: Prentice Hall International (UK) Ltd.

Guirdham, M (2002) *Interactive Behaviour at Work*, Harlow: Pearson Education Limited.

Gunter, B G and van der Hoeven, R (2004) 'The social dimension of globalisation: a review of the literature', *International Labour Review*, 143 (1/2): 7–42.

Hall, E T (1966) *The Hidden Dimension*, New York: Doubleday & Company.

Hargie, O and Dickson, D (2004) *Skilled Interpersonal Communication: Research, Theory and Practice*, Hove: Routledge.

Hargie, O, Saunders, C and Dickson, D (1994) *Social Skills in Interpersonal Communication*, London: Croom Helm.

Harris, T E (2002) *Applied Organisational Communication: Principles and Pragmatics for Future Practice* (2nd edition), New Jersey: Lawrence Erlbaum & Associates Inc.

Harris, P R and Moran, R T (2000) *Managing Cultural Differences* (5th edition), Houston: Gulf Publishing.

Hartley, P (1999) *Interpersonal Communication* (2nd edition), London: Routledge.

Heslin, R and Alper, T (1983) 'Touch: a bonding gesture' in Wiemann, J and Harrison, R (eds) *Non-Verbal Interaction*, London: Sage Publications Ltd.

Hill, C and O'Brien, K (1999) *Helping Skills: Facilitating Exploration, Insight and Actions*, Washington DC: American Psychological Association.

Hill, S (1991) 'Why quality circles failed but total quality management might succeed', *British Journal of Industrial Relations*, 29 (4): 541–68.

Hinton, P R (1993) *The Psychology of Interpersonal Perception*, London: Routledge.

Hyman, J and Mason, B (1995) *Managing Employee Involvement and Participation*, London: Sage Publications Ltd.

Kim, D and Kim, H (2004) 'A comparison of the effectiveness of unions and non-union works councils in Korea: can non-union employee representation substitute for trade unionism?', *International Journal of Human Resource Management*, 15 (6). 1069–93.

Kimble, C E and Seidel, S D (1991) 'Vocal signs of confidence', *Journal of Non-Verbal Behaviour*, 15: 99–105.

Kirkman, B L, Rosen, B, Gibson, C B, Tesluk, P E and McPherson, S O (2002) 'Five challenges to virtual team success: lessons from Sabre Inc.', *Academy of Management Executive*, 16 (3): 67–79.

Klotz, V (1988) 'Staff suggestion schemes', *International Labour Review*, 127 (3): 335–53.

Kreitner, R, Kinicki, A and Buelens, M (2002) *Organisational Behaviour* (2nd European edition), Maidenhead: McGraw-Hill Education.

Lengel, R and Daft, R (1988) 'The selection of communication media as an executive skill', *Academy of Management Executive*, August: 225–32.

Luft, J (1970) *Group Processes: An Introduction to Group Dynamics*, Palo Alto: National Press Books.

Marsh, R M (1996) *Reading the Japanese Mind*, Tokyo: Kodansha International.

Marsh, A A, Elfenbein, H A and Ambady, N (2003) 'Non-verbal "accents": cultural differences in facial expressions of emotion', *Psychological Science*, 14 (4): 373–6.

McCormick, J (1987) 'Decisions', *Newsweek*, 17 August: 62.

McShane, S L and Von Glinow, M (2003) *Organisational Behaviour: Emerging Realities for the Workplace Revolution*, New York: McGraw-Hill.

Melamed, J and Bozionelos, N (1992) 'Managerial promotion and height', *Psychological Reports*, 71: 587–93.

O'Conaill, B, Whittaker, S and Wilbur, S (1993) 'Conversations over video conferences: an evaluation of the spoken aspects of video-mediated communication', *Human Computer Interaction*, 8: 386–428.

Orr, J E (1990) 'Sharing knowledge, celebrating identity: community memory in a service culture' in Middleton, P *et al.* (eds) *Collective Remembering: Memory in Society*, London: Sage Publications Ltd.

Palmer, M T and Simmons, K B (1995) 'Communicating intentions through non-verbal behaviours ', *Human Communication Research*, 22: 128–60.

Pearlson, K E and Sounders, C S (2001) 'There's no place like home: managing Tele-Commuting paradoxes', *The Academy of Management Executive*, 15 (2): 117–28.

Robbins, S P and Hunsaker, P L (2003) *Training in Interpersonal Skills: Tips for Managing People at Work* (3rd edition), New Jersey: Prentice Hall Inc.

Seiter, J S (1999) 'Does communicating non-verbal disagreement during an opponent's speech affect the credibility of the debater in the background?, *Psychological Reports*, 84: 855–61.

Seiter, J S (2001) 'Silent derogation and perceptions of deceptiveness: does communicating non-verbal disbelief during an opponent's speech affect perceptions of debaters' veracity?', *Communication Research Reports*, 7 (2): 203–9.

Swartz, N (2006) 'E-mail hampers productivity', *Information Management Journal*, 40 (2): 22.

Thomas, A (2005) 'Henkel's innovative team briefing programme', *HR Review*, 5 (1): 10–11.

Thomas, A and Bull, P (1981) 'The role of pre-speech posture change in dyadic interaction', *British Journal of Social Psychology*, 20: 105–11.

Van Maanen, J (1991) 'The smile factory: work at Disneyland' in Frost, P J, Moore, L F, Louis, M R, Lundberg, C C and Martin, J (eds) *Reframing Organisational Culture*, Newbury Park, CA: Sage Publications Inc.

Watson, K W and Barker, L L (1984) 'Listening behaviour: definition and measurement' in Bostrom, R N (Ed) *Communication Yearbook*, Newbury Park, CA: Sage Publications Inc.

Yamada, H (1997) *Different Games, Different Rules*, New York: Oxford University Press.

CHAPTER 11

Age Partnership Group (2006) *Be Ready Personnel Organiser*, Department for Work and Pensions.

Atkinson, J (1984) 'Manpower strategies for flexible organisations', *Personnel Management*, 16 (8), 28 (24).

Becker, B E, Huselid, M A, Ulrich, D (2001) *The HR Scorecard: Linking People, Strategy, and Performance*, Boston MA: Harvard Business School Press.

Beer, M, Spector, B A, Lawrence, P R and Walton, R E (1985) *Human Resource Management*, New York: Free Press.

Bernardin, H J and Russell, J (1993) *Human Resource Management: An Experimental Approach*, Maidenhead: McGraw-Hill.

Boerlijst, G and Meijboom, G (1989) 'Matching the individual and the organisation' in Herriot, P (ed), *Assessment and Selection in Organisations: Methods and Practice for Recruitment and Appraisal*, Chichester: Wiley.

Boxall, P and Purcell, J (2003) *Strategy and Human Resource Management*, Basingstoke: Palgrave Macmillan.

Brandon, P and Leonard, S (2007) '100 best companies to work for', *The Sunday Times*, 11 March.

Burn, D (1996) *Benchmarking the Human Resources Function*, Hutchin Technical Communication.

Cherrington, D J (1995) *The Management of Human Resources* (4th edition), Hemel Hempstead: Prentice Hall International.

CIPD (2007) *Employee Engagement: A Facts Sheet*, London: Chartered Institute of Personnel and Development.

Coussey, M (2000) *Getting the Right Work–Life Balance: Implementing Family Friendly Practices*, London: Chartered Institute of Personnel and Development.

Cressey, P (1998) 'European Works Councils in practice', *Human Resource Management Journal*, 8 (1).

Denison, D R (1996) 'What is the difference between organizational culture and organizational climate? A native's point of view on a decade of paradigm wars', *Academy of Management Review*, 21.

Duddington, J (2003) *Employment Law*, Harlow: Pearson Education.

European Commission (1991) *Protection of the Dignity of Women and Men at Work*, Commission Recommendation 92/131/EEC of 27 November, Official Journal 49 of 24/02/1992.

Ferris, G R and Buckley, R M (1996) *Human Resources Management: Context, Functions and Outcomes*, Hemel Hempstead: Prentice Hall.

Fletcher, C and Williams, R (1992) 'The route to performance management', *Personnel Review*, 24 (10).

Flynn, M and McNair, S (2007) *Managing Age a Guide to Good Employment Practice*, London: TUC/CIPD.

Fraser, J M (1954) *A Handbook of Employment Interviewing*, London: Macdonald & Evans.

Gennard, J and Judge, G (2005) *Employee Relations* (4th edition), London: CIPD.

Graham, H T and Bennett, R (1998) *Human Resources Management* (9th edition), London: FT Pitman Publishing.

Greenberg, J and Baron, R A (1997) *Behaviour in Organisations: Understanding and Managing the Human Side of Work*, Hemel Hempstead: Prentice Hall.

Guest, D (1987) 'Human resource management and industrial relations', *Journal of Management Studies*, 24 (5).

Harrison, R (2002) *Learning and Development* (3rd edition), London: Chartered Institute of Personnel and Development.

Johnson, R W and Neumark, D (1997) 'Age discrimination, job separations, and employment status of older workers', *Journal of Human Resources*, 32 (4).

Kinnie, N and Lowe, D (1990) 'Performance related pay on the shop floor', *Personnel Management*, 21 (11).

Legge, K (1989) 'Human resource management: a critical analysis' in Storey, J (ed), *New Perspectives on Human Resource Management*, London: Routledge.

Leopold, J (2002) *Human Resources in Organisations*, Harlow: FT Prentice Hall.

Machin, S (2000) 'Union decline in Britain', *British Journal of Industrial Relations*, 38 (4).

McGregor, D (1957) 'An uneasy look at performance appraisal', *Harvard Business Review*, 35 (3).

Patterson, M G, West, M A, Lawthorn, R and Nickell, S (1997) *Impact of People Management Practices on Business Performance*, London: Chartered Institute of Personnel and Development.

Pecci, R, Bewley, H, Gospel, H and Willman, P, (2005) 'Is it good to talk? Information disclosure and organisation performance in the UK', *British Journal of Industrial Relations*, 43 (1).

Pedler, M, Burgoyne, J and Boydell, T (1991) *The Learning Company: A Strategy for Sustainable Development*, New York: McGraw-Hill.

Pettigrew, A and Whipp, R (1991) *Managing Change for Competitive Success*, Oxford: Blackwell.

Philpott, L and Sheppard, L (1992) 'Managing for improved performance' in Armstrong, M (ed), *Strategies for Human Resource Management*, London: Kogan Page.

Pilbeam, S and Corbridge, M (2002) *People Resourcing: HRM in Practice* (2nd edition), Harlow: FT Prentice Hall.

Plender, J (1997) 'Bullies in the boardroom', *Financial Times*, 15 July.

Reid, M A and Barrington, H (1999) *Training Interventions: Promoting Learning Opportunities* (6th edition), London: Chartered Institute of Personnel and Development.

Robinson, D, Perryman, S and Hayday, S (2004) *The Drivers of Employee Engagement*, Brighton: Institute for Employment Studies.

Rodger, A (1952) *The Seven Point Plan*, London: National Institute of Industrial Psychology.

Schein, E (1985) *Organization Culture and Leadership*, San Francisco, CA: Jossey-Bass.

Schneier, C E, Shaw, D G and Beatty, R W (1991) 'Performance measurement and management: a tool for strategy execution', *Human Resource Management*, 30 (4).

Schuler, R S (1992) 'Linking people with the strategic needs of business', *Organisational Dynamics*, Summer.

Schuler, R S and Walker, J W (1990) 'Human resources strategy: focusing on issues and actions', *Organisational Dynamics*, Summer.

Senge, P M (1990) *The Fifth Discipline: The Art and Practice of The Learning Organization*, New York: Doubleday.

Stroh, C K and Caliguiri, P M (1998) 'Strategic human resources: a new source of competitive advantage in the global arena', *International Journal of Human Resource Management*, 9 (1).

Truss, C, Soane, E and Edwards, C (2006) *Working Life: Employee Attitudes and Engagement*, Research report, London: Chartered Institute of Personnel and Development.

van Ham, J, Paauwe, J and Williams, R (1986) 'Personnel management in a changed environment', *Personnel Review*, 15 (3).

Walton, J (1999) *Strategic Human Resource Development*, Harlow: FT Prentice Hall.

Willey, B (2003) *Employment Law in Context: An Introduction for HR Professionals* (2nd edition), Harlow: FT Prentice Hall.

CHAPTER 12

Adams, J S (1965) 'Inequity in social exchange' in Berkowitz, L (ed), *Advances in Experimental Social Psychology*, 2, New York: Academic Press.

Alderfer, C P (1969) 'An empirical test of a new theory of human needs', *Organisational Behaviour and Human Performance*, 4.

Andrasik, F, Heimberg, J S and McNamara, J R (1981) *Behavior Modification of Work and Work-Related Problems*, New York: Academic Press.

Arnolds, C A and Boshoff, C (2002) 'Compensation, esteem valence and job performance: an empirical assessment of Alderfer's ERG theory', *International Journal of Human Resource Management*, 13 (4).

Arvey, R D, Bouchard, T J, Segal, N L and Abraham, L N (1989) 'Job satisfaction: environmental and genetic components', *Journal of Applied Psychology*, 74.

Balcazar, F, Hopkins, B L and Suarez, Y (1986) 'A critical objective review of performance feedback', *Journal of Organisational Behaviour Management*, 7.

Balliod, J and Semner, N (1994) 'Turnover and patterns of job change among computer specialists', *Zeitschrift für Arbeits und Organisations Psychologie*, 38 (in German).

Bandura, A (1977) *Social Learning Theory*, Englewood Cliffs, NJ: Prentice Hall.

Bandura, A (1982) 'Self-efficacy mechanism in human agency', *American Psychologist*, 37.

Bandura, A (1986) *Social Foundations of Thought and Action: A Social-Cognitive Theory*, Englewood Cliffs, NJ: Prentice Hall.

Blau, G (1993) 'Operationalizing direction and level of effort, and testing their relationships to individual job performance', *Organizational Behaviour and Human Decision Processes*, 55.

Boonzaier, B, Ficker, B and Rust, B (2001) 'A review of research on the job characteristics model and the attendant job diagnostic survey', *South African Journal of Business Management*, 32 (1).

Boswell, R B, Roehling, M V, Lepine, M A and Moynihan, L M (2003) 'Individual job-choice decisions and the impact of job attributes and recruitment practices: a longitudinal field study', *Human Resource Management*, 42.

Boudreau, J W, Boswell, W R, Judge, T A and Bretz Jr, R D (2001) 'Personality and cognitive ability as predictors of job search among employed managers', *Personnel Psychology*, 54.

BrKich, M, Jeffs, D and Carless, S A (2002) 'A global self-report measure of person–job fit', *European Journal of Psychological Assessment*, 18.

Caldwell, D F and O'Reilly, C A (1990) 'Measuring person–job fit with a profile-comparison process', *Journal of Applied Psychology*, 75.

Campion, M A and McClelland, C L (1993) 'Follow-up and extension of the interdisciplinary costs and benefits of enlarged jobs', *Journal of Applied Psychology*, 78 (3).

Carr, S C, McLoughlin, D, Hodgson, M and MacLachlan, M (1996) 'Effects of unreasonable pay discrepancies for under and overpayment on double demotivation', *Genetic, Social and General Psychology Monographs*, 122 (4).

Clegg, C W and Wall, T D (1990) 'The relationship between simplified jobs and mental health: a replication study', *Journal of Occupational Psychology*, 63.

Clements, C, Wagner, R J and Roland, C C (1995) 'The ins and outs of experiential learning', *Training & Development*, 49.

Cooper, A C, Gimeno-Gascon, F J and Woo, C Y (1994) 'Initial human and financial capital as predictors of new venture performance', *Journal of Business Venturing*, 9.

Cooper, M D (1992) 'An examination of assigned and participative goal-setting in relation to the improvement of safety in the construction industry', *Unpublished PhD Thesis*, School of Management, UMIST.

Cooper, M D (1998) *Improving Safety Culture: A Practical Guide*, Chichester: Wiley

Cooper, M D (2006) 'Exploratory analyses of the effects of managerial support and feedback consequences on behavioural safety maintenance', *Journal of Organizational Behaviour Management*, 26 (3).

Cooper, M D, Robertson, I T, Duff, A R and Phillips, R A (1992) 'Assigned or participative goals: do they make a difference?', *British Psychological Society*, Annual Occupational Psychology Conference, Liverpool, 3–5 January.

Cooper, M D, Phillips, R A, Sutherland, V J and Makin, P J (1994) 'Reducing accidents using goal-setting and feedback: a field study', *Journal of Occupational and Organisational Psychology*, 67.

Cooper, M D, Robertson, I T and Tinline, G (2003) 'Recruitment and selection: a framework for action' in Fletcher, C (ed) *The Essential Business Psychology Series*, London: Thompson Learning.

Cooper, M D, Farmery, K, Johnson, M, Harper, C, Clarke, F L, Holton, P, Wilson, S, Rayson, P and Bence, H (2005) 'Changing personnel behaviour to improve quality care practices in an intensive care unit', *Therapeutics and Clinical Risk Management*, 1 (4).

Deming, W E (1986) *Out of the Crisis*, Cambridge, MA: MIT Press.

Dive, B (2002) *The Healthy Organization: A Revolutionary Approach to People and Management*, London: Kogan Page.

Duff, A R, Robertson, I T, Cooper, M D and Phillips, R A (1993) *Improving Safety on Construction Sites by Changing Personnel Behaviour*, HMSO Report Series CRR51/93, London: HMSO.

Erez, A and Judge, T A (2001) 'Relationship of core self-evaluations to goal-setting, motivation and performance', *Journal of Applied Psychology*, 86.

Erez, M and Zidon, I (1984) 'Effect of goal-acceptance on the relationship of goal-difficulty to performance', *Journal of Applied Psychology*, 69.

Hackman, J R and Oldham, G R (1975) 'Development of the job diagnostic survey', *Journal of Applied Psychology*, 60.

Hackman, J R and Oldham, G R (1976) 'Motivation through the design of work: test of a theory', *Organisational Behaviour and Human Performance*, 16.

Hackman, J R and Oldham, G R (1980) *Work Redesign*, New York: Addison-Wesley.

Hamel, G and Prahalad, C K (1993) 'Strategy as stretch and leverage', *Harvard Business Review*, March/April.

Harder, J W (1992) 'Play for pay: effects of inequity in a pay for performance context', *Administrative Science Quarterly*, 37.

Hauenstein, N M and Lord, R G (1989) 'The effects of final offer arbitration on the performance of major league baseball players: a test of equity theory', *Human Performance*, 2.

Hayes, N (2001) *Managing Teams: A Strategy for Success*, London: Thompson Learning.

Heckhausen, H, Schmalt, H D and Schneider, K (1985) *Achievement Motivation in Perspective*, New York: Academic Press.

Herzberg, F, Mausner, B and Syndorman, B B (1959) *The Motivation to Work*, New York: Wiley.

Hinds, J-M (1995) *Hinds Model of Company Success: How to Overcome Boredom Through Instant Teams and Transform Your Workplace*, London: Millennium Books.

Holstein, B B (1997) *The Enchanted Self*, Amsterdam: Harwood.

Jenkins, J M (1993) 'Self-monitoring and turnover: the impact of personality on intent to leave', *Journal of Organizational Behaviour*, 14.

Jessup, P A and Stahelski, A J (1999) 'The effects of a combined goal setting, feedback and incentive intervention on job performance in a manufacturing environment', *Journal of Organisational Behaviour Management*, 19 (3).

Joinson, C (2001) 'Making sure employees measure up', *HR Magazine*, 46 (3).

Judge, T A and Bono, J E (2001) 'Relationship of core self-evaluation traits – self-esteem, generalized self-efficacy, locus of control, and emotional stability – with job satisfaction and job performance: a meta-analysis', *Journal of Applied Psychology*, 86.

Judge, T A and Illies, R (2002) 'Relationship of personality to performance motivation: a meta-analytic review', *Journal of Applied Psychology*, 87.

Kemp, N J, Wall, T D, Clegg, C W and Cordery, J L (1983) 'Autonomous work groups in a greenfield site: a comparative study', *Journal of Occupational Psychology*, 56.

Kini, R B and Hobson, C J (2002) 'Motivational theories and successful total quality initiatives', *International Journal of Management*, 19 (4).

Kinnie, N, Hutchinson, S and Purcell, J (2000) 'Fun and surveillance: the paradox of high commitment management in call centres', *International Journal of Human Resource Management*, 11 (5).

Klawsky, J D (1990) 'The effects of sub goals on commitment and task performance', *Proceedings of the 11th Annual Graduate Conference in Industrial/Organizational Psychology and Organizational Behavior*.

Klein, H J, Wesson, M J, Hollenbeck, J R and Alge, B J (1999) 'Goal-commitment and the goal-setting process: conceptual clarification and empirical synthesis', *Journal of Applied Psychology*, 84 (6).

Kohn, M L and Schooler, C (1982) 'Job conditions and personality: a longitudinal assessment of their reciprocal effects', *American Journal of Sociology*, 87.

Korman, A K (1970) 'Towards a hypothesis of work behavior', *Journal of Applied Psychology*, 54.

Korman, A K (1976) 'Hypothesis of work behavior revisited and an extension', *Academy of Management Review*, 1.

Ladd, D, Jagacinski, C and Stolzenberg, K (1997) 'Differences in goal-level set for optimists and defensive pessimists under conditions of encouragement', *Proceedings of the 18th Annual Graduate Conference in Industrial/Organizational Behavior*, 18.

Leach, D J, Wall, T D and Jackson, P R (2003) 'The effect of empowerment on job knowledge: an empirical test involving operators of complex technology', *Journal of Occupational and Organisational Psychology*, 76.

Levin, I and Stokes, J P (1989) 'Dispositional approach to job satisfaction: role of negative affectivity', *Journal of Applied Psychology*, 74.

Locke, E A and Latham, G P (1990) *A Theory of Goal-Setting and Task Performance*, Englewood Cliffs, NJ: Prentice Hall.

Locke, E A and Latham, G P (2002) 'Building a practically useful theory of goal-setting and task motivation', *American Psychologist*, 57 (9).

Locke, E A, Latham, G P, and Erez, M (1988) 'The determinants of goal commitment', *Academy of Management Review*, 13.

Locke, E A, Frederick, E, Buckner, E and Bobko, P (1984) 'Effect of self-efficacy, goals, and task strategies on task performance', *Journal of Applied Psychology*, 69.

Locke, E A, Shaw, K M, Saari, L M and Latham, G P (1981) 'Goal-setting and task performance: 1969–1980', *Psychological Bulletin*, 90.

Luthans, F and Kreitner, R (1975) *Organizational Behavior Modification*, Glenview, IL: Scott, Foresman.

Luthans, F and Martinko, M (1987) 'Behavioural approaches to organisations' in Cooper, C L and Robertson, I T (eds), *International Review of Industrial and Organisational Psychology*, (Vol 2), Chichester: Wiley.

Maloney, W F and McFillan, J M (1995) 'Job characteristics: union–non-union differences', *Journal of Construction Engineering and Management*, 121.

Maslow, A H (1942) 'A theory of human motivation', *Psychological Review*, 50.

Matsui, T, Okada, A and Kakuyama, T (1982) 'Influence of achievement need on goal-setting, performance and feedback effectiveness', *Journal of Applied Psychology*, 67.

McClelland, D C (1961) *The Achieving Society*, Princeton, NJ: Van Nostrand.

Medcof, J W and Hausdorf, P A (1995) 'Instruments to measure opportunities to satisfy needs, and degree of satisfaction of needs, in the workplace', *Journal of Occupational and Organisational Psychology*, 68.

Mendelson, J L, Barnes, A K and Horn, G (1989) 'The guiding light to corporate culture', *Personnel Administrator*, 34 (7).

Mount, K M, Barrick, M R and Stewart, G L (1998) 'Five-factor model of personality and performance in jobs involving interpersonal interactions', *Human Performance*, 11.

Nadler, D A and Lawler, E E (1979) 'Motivation: a diagnostic approach' in Steers, R M and Porter, L W (eds) *Motivation and Work Behavior* (2nd edition), New York: McGraw-Hill.

Nicholson, N, Fenton-O'Creavy, M, Soane, E and Willman, P (2000) 'Risk and performance among city traders', *ESRC Risk and Human Behaviour Newsletter*, 7.

O'Brien, R M, Dickson, A M and Rosow, M P (eds) (1982) *Industrial Behavior Modification: A Learning-based Approach to Industrial Organizational Problems*, Boston, MA: Allyn and Bacon.

Orpen, C (1994) 'Interactive effects of work motivation and personal control on employee job performance and satisfaction', *Journal of Social Psychology*, 134 (6).

Orpen, C (1997) 'Interactive effects of communication, quality and job involvement on managerial job satisfaction and work motivation', *Journal of Psychology*, 131 (5).

Parker, S K and Wall, T D (1998) *Job and Work Design: Organizing Work to Promote Well-being and Effectiveness*, London: Sage.

Pinder, C C (1984) *Work Motivation*, Glenview, IL: Scott, Foresman.

Pritchard, R D, Jones, S D, Roth, P L, Stuebing, K K and Ekeberg, S E (1988) 'Effects of group feedback, goal-setting, and incentives on organisational productivity', *Journal of Applied Psychology*, 73.

Ragins, B R and Cotton, J L (1999) 'Mentor functions and outcomes: a comparison of men and women in formal and informal mentoring relationships', *Journal of Applied Psychology*, 84.

Rakestraw, T L and Weiss, H M (1981) 'The interaction of social influences and task experience on goals, performance, and performance satisfaction', *Organisational Behaviour and Human Performance*, 27.

Ray, P S, Bishop, P A and Wang, M Q (1997) 'Efficacy of the components of a behavioral safety program', *International Journal of Industrial Ergonomics*, 19.

Reid, D H and Parsons, M B (1996) 'A comparison of staff acceptability of immediate versus delayed verbal feedback in staff training', *Journal of Organisational Behaviour Management*, 16 (2).

Renn, R W and Fedor, D B (2001) 'Development and field test of a feedback seeking, self-efficacy, and goal-setting model of work performance', *Journal of Management*, 27.

Rentsch, J R and Steel, R P (1998) 'Testing the durability of job characteristics as predictors of absenteeism over a six-year period', *Personnel Psychology*, 51.

Robertson, I T and Sadri, G (1993) 'Managerial self-efficacy and managerial performance', *British Journal of Management*, 4.

Robertson, I T, Smith, J M and Cooper, M D (1992) *Motivation: Strategies, Theory and Practice*, London: Institute of Personnel Management.

Roe, R A, Zinovieva, I L, Dienes, E and Ten Horn, L A (2000) 'A comparison of work motivation in Bulgaria, Hungary, and The Netherlands: test of a model', *Applied Psychology: An International Review*, 49.

Roethlisberger, F J and Dickson, W J (1939) *Management and the Worker*, Cambridge, MA: Harvard University Press.

Rosenthal, R (2002) 'Covert communications in classrooms, clinics, courtrooms and cubicles', *American Psychologist*, 57.

Sadri, G and Robertson, I T (1993) 'Self-Efficacy and work-related behaviour: a review and meta-analyses', *Applied Psychology: An International Review*, 42.

Smither, R and Lindgren, H C (1978) 'Salary, age, sex, and need for achievement in bank employees', *Psychological Reports*, 42.

Stadler, R (1994) 'Berufliche Veranderungen bei Computerfachleuten' (Job changes among computer specialists), *Unpublished Master's Thesis*, University of Bern, Department of Psychology.

Stahl, M J (1983) 'Achievement, power and managerial motivation: selecting managerial talent with the job choice exercise', *Personnel Psychology*, 36.

Stajkovic, A D and Luthans, F (1997) 'A meta-analysis of the effects of organizational behavior modification of task performance', *Academy of Management Journal*, 40.

Stajkovic, A D and Luthans, F (2003) 'Behavioral management and task performance in organizations: conceptual background, meta-analysis, and test of alternative models', *Personnel Psychology*, 56.

Thomas, Ken (2003) *Intrinsic Motivation at Work: Building Energy and Commitment*, New York: Berrett-Koehler Publishers Inc.

Thompson, K R, Hochwarter, W A and Mathys, N J (1997) 'Stretch targets: what makes them effective?', *The Academy of Management Executive*, 11 (3).

Townsend, A (2001) 'Get out of the office', *Management OHS&E*, 5 (4).

Vroom, V H (1964) *Work and Motivation*, New York: Wiley.

Wall, T D and Martin, R (1987) 'Job and work design' in Cooper, C L and Robertson, I T (eds), *International Review of Industrial and Organisational Psychology* (2), Chichester: Wiley.

Wall, T D, Kemp, N J, Jackson, P R and Clegg, C W (1986) 'An outcome evaluation of autonomous working groups: a long-term field experiment', *Academy of Management Journal*, 29.

Warr, P (1996) 'Employee well-being' in Warr, P (ed), *Psychology at Work* (4th edition), London: Penguin.

Weldon, E and Yun, S (2000) 'The effects of proximal and distal goals on goal level, strategy development', *Journal of Applied Behavioral Science*, 36 (3).

Wood, R E, Mento, A J and Locke, E A (1987) 'Task complexity as a moderator of goal-effects: a meta-analysis', *Journal of Applied Psychology*, 72.

Wright, S M and Carrese, J A (2002) 'Excellence in role modelling: insight and perspectives from the pros', *Canadian Medical Association Journal*, 167 (6).

Zhou, J (1998) 'Feedback valence, feedback style, task autonomy, and achievement orientation: interactive effects on creative performance', *Journal of Applied Psychology*, 83.

CHAPTER 13

Ambrosini, V (1998) *Exploring Techniques of Analysis and Evaluation in Strategic Management*, Hemel Hempstead: Prentice Hall.

Clemen, R T and Kwit, R C, (2001) 'The value of decision analysis at Eastman Kodak Company, 1990–1999', *Interfaces*, September/October.

Coles, S and Rowley, J (1995) 'Revisiting decision trees', *Management Decisions*, 33 (8).

Dickson, T (ed) (1999) *Mastering Global Business*, London: FT Management.

Drucker, P F (1992) *Management*, Oxford: Butterworth-Heinemann.

Johnson, G and Scholes, K (2002) *Exploring Corporate Strategy* (6th edition), Harlow: FT Prentice Hall.

Mintzberg, H and Quinn, J B (1996) *The Strategy Process: Concepts, Contexts and Cases*, Hemel Hempstead: Prentice Hall.

Pidd, M (2001) *Tools for Thinking*, Chichester: John Wiley & Sons.

Richardson, C (1991) 'Staffing the front office', *Operational Research Insight*, 4 (2).

Stonebraker, J S (2002) 'How Bayer makes decisions to develop new drugs', *Interfaces*, November/ December.

CHAPTER 14

Babbage, C (1832) *On the Economy of Machinery and Manufacturers*, London: Charles Knight.

Charnes, A, Cooper, W W and Rhodes, E (1978) 'Measuring the efficiency of decision making units', *European Journal of Operational Research*, 2.

Christopher, M (1998) *Logistics and Supply Chain Management*, London: FT Prentice Hall.

Cousins, P, Lamming, R, Lawson, B and Squire, B (2007) *Strategic Supply Management: Theories, Concepts and Practice*, Harlow: Pearson.

Denzler, D (2000) 'Shell One: operations management circa 2000', http://www.clubpom.com, accessed 20 October 2000.

Evans, J R (1997) *Production/Operations Management: Quality, Performance and Value*, St Paul, MN: West Publishing Company.

Fogarty, D W, Hoffmann, T R and Stonebraker, P W (1989) *Production and Operations Management*, Cincinnati, OH: South-Western Publishing.

George, C S Jr (1968) *The History of Management Thought*, Englewood Cliffs, NJ: Prentice Hall.

Gilgeous, V (1997) *Operations and the Management of Change*, Harlow: FT Prentice Hall.

Greasley, A (2006) *Operations Management*, Chichester: John Wiley and Sons Ltd.

Hackman, J R, Oldham G, Janson, R and Purdy, K (1975) 'A new strategy for job enrichment', *California Management Review*, 17 (4), Summer.

Hammer, M and Champy, J (1993) *Re-engineering the Corporation*, New York: Nicholas Brealey Publishing.

Harrington, H J (1991) *Business Process Improvement*, New York: McGraw-Hill.

Harris, N D (1989) *Service Operations Management*, London: Cassell.

Hill, T J (1991) *Production/Operations Management* (2nd edition), London: Prentice Hall.

Hill, T J (1993) *Manufacturing Strategy* (2nd edition), Basingstoke: Macmillan.

Ishikawa, K (1985) *What is Total Quality Control? The Japanese Way*, translated by D J Lu, Englewood Cliffs, NJ: Prentice Hall.

Johnston, R and Clark, G (2005) *Service Operations Management* (2nd edition), Harlow: FT Prentice Hall.

Kaplan R and Norton D (1996) *The Balanced Scorecard*, Boston, MA: Harvard Business School Press.

Lamming, R C (1996) *Beyond Partnership – Strategies for Innovation and Lean Supply*, London: Prentice Hall

Lockyer, K, Oakland, J and Muhlemann, A, (1992) *Production and Operations Management* (6th edition), London: Pitman Publishing.

Murdick, R G, Rendern, B and Russell, R S (1990) *Service Operations Management*, Needham Heights, MA: Allyn & Bacon.

Moriarty, P and Kennedy, D (2002) 'Performance measurement in public sector services: problems and potential', *Performance Management Association Conference*, Boston, MA: Centre of Business Performance.

Poister, T H (2003) *Measuring Performance in Public and Non-profit Organisations*, John Wiley and Sons.

Porter, M E (1985) *Competitive Advantage: Creating and Sustaining Superior Performance*, New York: Free Press.

Schmenner, R W (1986) 'How can service businesses survive and prosper?', *Sloan Management Review*, Spring.

Schonberger, R (1996) *World Class Manufacturing: The Next Decade*, New York: Simon & Schuster.

Schonberger, R J and Knod, E M (1994) *Operations Management: Continuous Improvement* (5th edition), Burr Ridge, IL: Richard D Irwin.

Schroeder, R G (1993) *Operations Management* (4th edition), New York: McGraw-Hill.

Schroeder, R G (1999) *Operations Management: Contemporary Concepts and Cases*, London: McGraw-Hill.

Scott Myers, M (1991) *Every Employee a Manager* (3rd edition), San Diego, CA: University Associates.

Shostack, G L (1977) 'Breaking free from product marketing', *Journal of Marketing*, April.

Skinner, W (1969) 'Manufacturing – the missing link in corporate strategy', *Havard Business Review*, May/June.

Slack, N (1983) 'Operations management and curriculum design', *Management Education and Development*, 14 (1).

Slack, N (1989) 'Focus on flexibility' in Wild, R (ed) *International Handbook of Production/Operations Management*, London: Cassell.

Slack, N (1991) *The Manufacturing Advantage*, London: Mercury Books.

Slack, N and Lewis, M (2002) *Operations Strategy*, Harlow: FT Prentice Hall.

Slack, N, Chambers, S, Harland, C, Harrison, A and Johnston, R (2001) *Operations Management* (3rd edition), London: FT Prentice Hall.

Slack, N, Chambers, S and Johnston, R (2004) *Operations Management* (4th edition), Harlow: FT Prentice Hall.

Slack, N, Chambers, S, Johnston, R and Betts, A (2006) *Operations and Process Management*, Harlow: FT Prentice Hall

Smith, A (1776) *An Inquiry into the Nature and Causes of the Wealth of Nations*, London: Strahn and Caddell.

Taylor, F W (1911) *The Principles of Scientific Management*, New York: Harper.

Underwood, L (1994) *Intelligent Manufacturing*, Wokingham: Addison-Wesley with the Economist Intelligence Unit.

Waters, D (1996) *Operations Management*, Reading, MA: Addison-Wesley Longman.

Wheelwright, S C and Hayes, R H (1985) 'Competing through manufacturing', *Harvard Business Review*, January/February.

Wild, R (1989) *Production and Operations Management* (4th edition), London: Cassell.

Wren, D A (1972) *The Evolution of Management Thought*, New York: Ronald Press.

CHAPTER 15

Forsyth, R (ed) (1989) *Expert Systems* (2nd edition), London: Chapman Hall.

Harry, M J (1990) *Information and Management Systems*, London: Pitman Publishing.

Harry, M J S (2001) *Business Information: A Systems Approach*, Harlow: FT Prentice Hall.

Olle, T W, Hagelstein, J, MacDonald, I G, Colette, R, Sol, H G, VanAssche, F J and Verrijn-Stuart, A A (1988) *Information Systems Methodologies*, Wokingham: Addison-Wesley.

Levinson, P (1997) *The Soft Edge: A Natural History and Future of the Information Revolution*, Routledge.

Postman, N (1993) *Technopoly: the Surrender of Culture to Technology*, New York: Vintage Books.

Turban, E, Leidner, D, McLean, E and Wetherbe, J (2006) *Information Technology for Management: Transforming Organizations in the Digital Economy* (5th edition), Wiley Higher Education.

Verard, R (1984) *Pragmatic Data Analysis*, Oxford: Blackwell Scientific.

Winston, H W (1984) *Artificial Intelligence*, Reading, MA: Addison-Wesley.

Zadeh, L (1965) 'Fuzzy sets', *Information and Control*, 8.

CHAPTER 16

Atkinson, A, Kaplan, R, Matsumura, E and Young, S (2007) *Management Accounting*, Harlow: FT Prentice Hall.

Britton, A and Proctor, R (2006) *Financial Accounting with Managerial Accounting for Business Decisions*, Harlow: FT Prentice Hall.

Chadwick, L (2001) *Essential Financial Accounting for Managers*, Harlow: Pearson Education Limited.

Drury, C (1998) *Management Accounting for Business Decisions*, London: Thomson Learning.

Elliott, B and Elliott, J (2006) *Financial Accounting, Reporting and Analysis* (2nd edition), Harlow: FT Prentice Hall.

Elliott, B and Elliott, J (2007) *Financial Accounting and Reporting* (11th edition), Harlow: FT Prentice Hall.

Hussey, J and Hussey, R (1998) *Business Accounting*, Basingstoke: Macmillan Business.

Horne, J van and Wachowicz, J (2005) *Fundamentals of Financial Management*, Harlow: FT Prentice Hall.

Nobes, C and Parker, R (2006) *Comparative International Accounting* (9th edition), Harlow: FT Prentice Hall.

Weetman, P (2006) *Management Accounting*, Harlow: FT Prentice Hall.

Zahirul Hoque, Z (2006) *Strategic Management Accounting* (2nd edition), Harlow: FT Prentice Hall.

CHAPTER 17

Allen, P (2007) *Your Ethical Business: How to Plan, Start and Succeed in a Company with a Conscience*, NGO Media.

Anthony, P D (1998) 'Management education: ethics versus morality' in Parker, M (ed) *Ethics and Organisations*, London: Sage.

Argyris, C (1964) *Integrating the Individual and the Organization*, New York: John Wiley.

Armour, J and McCahery, J A (2006) *After Enron: Improving Corporate Law and Modernising Securities Regulation in Europe and the US*, Hart Publishing.

Bennis, W (1972) 'A funny thing happened on the way to the future' in Thomas, J and Bennis, W (eds) *The Management of Change and Conflict*, Harmondsworth: Penguin Books.

Bloom, H, Calori, R and de Woot, P (1994) *Euromanagement: A New Style for the Global Market*, London: Kogan Page.

Burke, T, Maddock, S and Rose, A (1993) 'How ethical is British business?', *Research Working Paper*, 2 (1), University of Westminster.

Burns, T and Stalker, G (1963) *The Management of Innovation*, London: Tavistock Press.

Chryssides, G D and Kaler, J H (1993) *An Introduction to Business Ethics*, London: Chapman & Hall.

Department of Trade and Industry (DTI) (2002) *Business and Society: Corporate Social Responsibility Report*, London: DTI.

DiMaggio, P J and Powell, W (1983) 'The iron cage revisited: institutional isomorphism and collective rationality in organisational fields', *American Sociological Review*, 48.

Donaldson, J (1989) *Key Issues in Business Ethics*, San Diego, CA: Academic Press.

Donaldson, J and Waller, M (1980) 'Ethics and organisation', *Journal of Management Studies*, 17 (1).

Eichenwald, K (2005) *Conspiracy of Fools: A True Story*, Broadway Books (Bantam Doubleday).

ENDS (1993) 'Jury still out on responsible care', *Industry Report*, ENDS 222, July.

Friedman, M (1963) *Capitalism and Freedom*, Chicago, IL: Phoenix Books, University of Chicago Press.

Fox, L (2004) *Enron: The Rise and Fall*, New York: John Wiley and Sons.

Guardian (2007) 'Principles and profit are given the green light' and 'The new M&S Ethical Fund', *Money Guardian*, 24 February.

Hartley, R F (1993) *Business Ethics: Violations of the Public Trust*, New York: John Wiley.

Holloway, R J and Hancock, R S (1968) *Marketing in a Changing Environment*, New York: John Wiley.

Hopkins, M (2003) *The Planetary Bargain: Corporate Social Responsibility Matters*, London: Earthscan.

Husted, B W and Salazar, J de J (2006) 'Taking Friedman seriously: maximising profits and social performance', *Journal of Management Studies*, 43 (1), January.

Kroeber, L and Kluckhohn, L (1952) *Culture*, New York: Vintage Books.

Kynaston, D (1999) *City of London: Illusions of Gold 1914–1945 London*, Chatto and Windus.

Lawton, A (1998) *Ethical Management for the Public Services*, Buckingham: The Open University Press.

Lawton, A (2006) 'Ethics and public management – 25 years on', *Public Money and Management*, January.

Luthans, F (1985) *Organizational Behaviour* (4th edition), New York: McGraw-Hill.

Markham, J W (2006) *A Financial History of Modern US Corporate Scandals: Enron to Reform*, M E Sharpe.

Martinson, J (2007) 'Penny Newman: The ethical coffee chief turning a fair profit', *Guardian*, 9 March.

McLean, B and Elkind, P (2004) *The Smartest Guys in the Room: The Amazing Rise and Scandalous Fall of Enron*, Harmondsworth: Penguin Books.

Michie, R (1999) *The London Stock Exchange: A History*, Oxford: Oxford University Press.

Mintzberg, H (1979) *The Structuring of Organizations*, New York: Prentice Hall.

Mole, J (1990) *Mind Your Manners: Culture Clash in the Single European Market*, London: The Industrial Society.

Nolan Committee (1995) *Standards in Public Life, 1*, First report of the Committee on Standards in Public Life, London: HMSO.

Phelps-Brown, H (1990) 'The counter revolution of our time', *Industrial Relations*, 29 (1).

Porter, M E and Kramer, M R (2006) 'Strategy and society', *Harvard Business Review*, December.

Raw, C (1977) *Slater Walker: An Investigation of a Financial Phenomenon*, New York: Harper & Row.

Raw, C, Hodgson, G and Page, B (1971) *Do You Sincerely Want to be Rich? The Full Story of Bernard Corbfield and IOS*, Random House.

Reeves, R (2005) 'Just a shot of ethicality', *Management Today*, December.

Sampson, A (1977) *The Arms Bazaar*, London: Coronet Books.

Sampson, A (1982) *The Money Lenders: Bankers in a Dangerous World*, London: Coronet Books.

Smith, A (1776) *An Inquiry into the Nature and Causes of the Wealth of Nations*, London: Strahn and Caddell.

Smith, C (2003) 'Corporate social responsibility: whether or how?', *California Management Review*, 45 (4).

Sorell, T (1998) 'Armchair applied philosophy and business ethics' in Cowton, C and Crisp, R (eds), *Business Ethics: Perspectives on the Practice of Theory*, Oxford: Oxford University Press.

Stark, A (1993) 'What's the matter with business ethics?', *Harvard Business Review*, May/June.

Tweedale, P (2000) *Magic Mineral to Killer Dust: Turner and Newall and the Asbestos Hazard*, Oxford: Oxford University Press.

Warren, R and Tweedale, G (2002) 'Business ethics and business history: neglected dimensions in management education', *British Journal of Management*, 13 (3), December.

Welford, R J (1989) 'Growth and the performance participation nexus: the case of UK producer cooperatives', *Economic Analysis and Workers' Management*, 23.

Welford, R J (1992) 'Linking quality and the environment: a strategy for the implementation of environmental management systems', *Business Strategy and the Environment*, 1 (1).

Welford, R J (1994) 'Barriers to the improvement of environmental performance' in Welford, R J, *Cases in Environmental Management and Business Strategy*, London: Pitman Publishing.

Welford, R J, Prescott, K and Mercado, S (2001) *European Business: An Issue-based Approach*, Harlow: FT Prentice Hall.

Westing, J H (1968) 'Some thoughts on the nature of ethics in marketing' in Mayer, R (ed), *Marketing Systems*, 1967 Winter Conference Proceedings, Chicago, IL: Marketing Association.

Windsor, D (2006) 'Corporate social responses: three key approaches', *Journal of Management Studies*, 43 (1), January.

Zadek, S (2001) *The Civil Corporation: The New Economy of Corporate Citizenship*, London: Earthscan and the New Economics Foundation.

CHAPTER 18

Boiral, Oliver (2006) 'Global warming: should companies adopt a proactive strategy?' *Long Range Planning*, 39.

BSI British Standards (1996) *Environmental Management Systems Handbook: A Guide to the BS EN ISO 14000 series*, London: BSI.

European Commission (2001) *Environment 2010: Our Future, Our Choice*, communication from the Commission to the Council, the European Parliament, the Economic and Social Committee and the Committee of the Regions, On the Sixth Environment Action Programme of the European Community, Proposal for a Decision of the European Parliament and of the Council Laying down the Community Environment Action Programme 2001–2010, Brussels, 24 1 2001 COM (2001) 31 Final, Brussels: European Commission.

European Commission (2002) *Choices for a Greener Future: The European Union and the Environment*, Brussels: European Commission Directorate-General for Press and Communications.

Hoffman, A J (2002) 'Examining the rhetoric: the strategic implications of climate change policy', *Corporate Environmental Strategy*, 9 (4).

Hoffman, A J (2005) 'Climate change strategy: the business logic behind voluntary greenhouse gas reductions', *California Management Journal*, 23 (3).

Hopkins, M (2003) *The Planetary Bargain: Corporate Social Responsibility Matters*, London: Earthscan.

Jordan, A, Wurzel, R K and Zito, A R (2003) 'New instruments of environmental governance? National experiences and prospects', *Environmental Politics*, 12 (1), Spring.

Luo, X and Bhattacharya, C B (2006) 'Corporate social responsibility, customer satisfaction, and market value', *Journal of Marketing*, 70, October.

Moxen, J and Strachan, P A (1998) *Managing Green Teams: Environmental Change in Organisations and Networks*, Sheffield: Greenleaf Publishing.

The New Economics Foundation (2004) *Climate Change: A Corporate Impact Survey*, London: New Economics Foundation.

Roddick, A (1991) 'In search of the sustainable business', *Ecodecision*, 7.

Strachan, P A, Haque, M, McCulloch, A and Moxen, J (1997) 'The eco-management and audit scheme: recent experiences of UK participating organisations', *European Environment*, 7 (25).

Strachan, P A, Sinclair, I and Lal, D (2003) 'Managing ISO 14001 implementation in the United Kingdom continental shelf (UKCS)', *Corporate Social Responsibility and Environmental Management*, 10.

Welford, R J (1992) 'A guide to environmental auditing', *Supplement to European Environment*, 8 (4).

Welford, R J (1993) 'Breaking the link between quality and the environment', *Business Strategy and the Environment*, 2 (4).

Welford, R J (1998) *Corporate Environmental Management 1: Systems and Strategies*, London: Earthscan.

Welford, R J, Prescott, K and Mercado, S (2001) *European Business*, Harlow: FT Prentice Hall.

Wheeler, D (1992) 'Environmental management as an opportunity for sustainability in business – economic forces as a constraint', *Business Strategy and the Environment*, 1 (4).

Williams, J O and Goliike, U (1982) *From Ideas to Action, Business and Sustainable Development*, ICC Report on the Greening of Enterprise, London: International Chamber of Commerce.

World Commission on Environment and Development (1987) *The Brundtland Report*, or *Our Common Future*, Oxford: Oxford University Press.

CHAPTER 19

Bartlett, C A and Ghoshal, S (1990) 'Managing innovation in the transnational corporation' in Bartlett, C A, Doz, Y and Hedlund, G (eds), *Managing the Global Firm*, London: Routledge.

Bartlett, C A, Doz, Y and Hedlund, G (1990) *Managing the Global Firm*, London: Routledge.

Bassett, P (1986) *Strike Free: New Industrial Relations in Britain*, Basingstoke: Macmillan.

Beamish, P W, Killing, P, Lecraw, D J and Crookell, H (1991) *International Management: Text and Cases*, Homewood, IL: Irwin.

Bloom, H, Calori, R and de Woot, P (1994) *Euromanagement: A New Style for the Global Market*, London: Kogan Page.

Boyacigiller, N A and Adler, N J (1995) 'The parochial dinosaur: organisational science in a global context' in Jackson, T (ed), *Cross Cultural Management*, Oxford: Butterworth-Heinemann.

Buckley, P J, Pass, C and Prescott, K (1992) *Servicing International Markets: Competitive Strategies of Firms*, Oxford: Blackwell.

Calori, R, Atamer, T and Numes, P (2000) *The Dynamics of International Competition – From Practice to Theory*, London: Sage.

Davis, S M (1992) 'Managing and organising multinational corporations, 1979' reprinted in Bartlett, C A and Ghoshal, S (eds), *Transnational Management*, Homewood, IL: Irwin.

Dicken, P (1992) *Global Shift. The Internationalisation of Economic Activity* (2nd edition), London: Paul Chapman.

Doz, Y, Prahalad, C K and Hamel, G (1990) 'Control, change and flexibility: the dilemma of international collaboration' in Bartlett, C A, Doz, Y and Hedlund, G (eds), *Managing the Global Firm*, London: Routledge.

Dunning, J H (1988) *Explaining International Production*, London: George Allen & Unwin.

The Economist (1993) 'The Japanese economy – from miracle to mid-life crisis', *The Economist*, March 6.

Edelshain, D J (1995) 'British corporate currency exposure and foreign exchange risk management', *Unpublished PhD Thesis*, London Business School.

Freeman, C and Hagedoorn, J (1992) *Globalization of technology*: working paper, Maastricht Research Institute on Innovation and Technology.

Fry, E (1991) 'Subtlety and the art of Japanese management', *Business Credit*, October.

Graham, J (1988) 'Japanisation as mythology', *Industrial Relations Journal*, 19 (1).

Grant, R M (2002) *Contemporary Strategy Analysis* (4th edition), Oxford: Blackwell.

Halliburton, C and Hünerberg, R (1987) 'The globalisation dispute in marketing', *European Journal of Marketing*, 5 (4).

Handy, C (1994) *The Empty Raincoat: Making Sense of the Future*, London: Arrow.

Hedlund, G (1986) 'The hypermodern MNC – a heterarchy?', *Human Resource Management*, 25 (1), Spring.

Hedlund, G and Rolander, D (1990) 'Action in heterarchies: new approaches to managing the MNC' in Bartlett, C A, Doz, Y and Hedlund, G (eds), *Managing the Global Firm*, London: Routledge.

Hill, C W L (1997) *International Business: Competing in the Global Marketplace*, Homewood, IL: Irwin.

Hofstede, G (1983) 'The cultural relativity of organisational practices and theories', *Journal of International Business Studies*, Autumn.

Hudson, R (2002) 'On the globalisation of business', *British Journal of Management*, 13 (4), December.

Hymer, S (1960) 'The international operations of national firms: a study of direct investment', *Doctoral Dissertation*, Boston: Massachusetts Institute of Technology.

Johanson, J and Vahine, J (1977) 'International processes of the firm: a model of knowledge development and increasing foreign market commitment', *Journal of International Business Studies*, 8.

Levitt, T (1983) 'The globalisation of markets', *Harvard Business Review*, May/June.

Mirza, H (1984) 'Can – should – Japanese management practices be exported overseas?', *The Business Graduate*, January.

Ohmae, K (1982) *The Mind of the Strategist: Art of Japanese Business*, Harmondsworth: Penguin.

Oliver, A and Wilkinson, S (1992) *The Japanisation of British Industry: New Developments in the 1990s* (2nd edition), Oxford: Blackwell.

Perlmutter, H V (1969) 'The tortuous evolution of the multinational corporation', *Columbia Journal of World Business*, 29 (1).

Peters, T and Waterman, R (1982) *In Search of Excellence*, New York: Harper & Row.

Porter, M E (1990) *Competitive Advantage of Nations*, London: Macmillan.

Porter, M E (1991) 'Towards a dynamic theory of strategy', *Strategic Management Journal*, 12 (2).

Porter, M E, Takeuchi, H and Sakakibara, M (2000) *Can Japan Compete?*, Basingstoke: Macmillan.

Ricks, D A and Mahajan, A (1984) 'Blunders in international marketing', *Long Range Planning*, February.

Schonberger, R (1982) *Japanese Manufacturing Techniques*, New York: Free Press.

Trompenaars, F (1993) *Riding the Waves of Culture: Understanding Cultural Diversity in Business*, London: Nicholas Brealey Publishing.

Valla, J P (1986) 'Industrial firms in European markets: the French approach to Europe' in Turnbull, P W and Valla, J P (eds), *Strategies for International Industrial Marketing*, New York: Croom Helm.

Vandermerwe, S (1993) 'A framework for constructing Euro-networks', *European Management Journal*, 11 (1), March.

Vernon, R and Wells, L T Jr (1991) *The Manager in the International Economy* (6th edition), Upper Saddle River, NJ: Prentice Hall.

Welford, R and Prescott, K (1996) *European Business: An Issue-based Approach*, London: Pitman Publishing.

Young, S, Hamill, J, Wheeler, C and Davies, R (1989) *International Market Entry and Development: Strategies and Management*, Hemel Hempstead: Harvester.

CHAPTER 20

Adair, J (1989) *Leaders*, Guildford: Talbot Adair Press.

Barnard, C (1938) *The Functions of the Executive*, Cambridge, MA: Harvard University Press.

Bartlett, C A and Ghoshal, S (2000) 'Going global, lessons from late movers', *Harvard Business Review*, March/April.

Bell, E, Taylor, S and Thorpe R (2002) 'A step in the right direction? Investors in People and the learning organisation', *British Journal of Management*, 13 (2).

Bennis, W and O'Toole, J (2000) 'Don't hire the wrong CEO', *Harvard Business Review*, May/June.

Bunting, M (2004) *Willing Slaves: How the Overwork Culture is Ruling Our Lives*, London: HarperCollins.

Byrne, J A (1986) 'Business fads: what's in and what's out', *Business Week*, January 20.

Cappelli, P and Hamori, M (2005) 'The new road to the top', *Harvard Business Review*, January.

Chandler, Sir G (1994) 'The business of book-learning', *Management Today*, November.

Christensen, C M and Raynor, M E (2003) 'Why hard-nosed executives should care about management theory', *Harvard Business Review*, September.

Confederation of British Industry (1989) *Towards a Skill Revolution*, London: CBI.

Confederation of British Industry (1992) *World Class Targets*, London: CBI.

Constable, J and McCormick, R (1987) *The Making of British Managers*, London: British Institute of Management and Confederation of British Industry.

Coulson, C and Coe, T (1991) *The Flat Organisation: Philosophy and Practice*, Corby: Institute of Management (now Chartered Management Institute).

Fahey, L and Randall, R M (1998) *Learning from the Future: Competitive Foresight Scenarios*, New York: John Wiley.

Further Education Unit (1994) *Tackling Targets*, London: FEU.

Garvin, D A (1993) 'Building a learning organization', *Harvard Business Review*, July/August.

Ghoshal, S and Sull, D (1997) 'Loss of faith in managers?', *Financial Times*, 6 June.

Goleman, D (1998) 'What makes a leader?', *Harvard Business Review*, November/December.

Gosling, J and Mintzberg, H (2003) 'The five minds of a manager', *Harvard Business Review*, November.

Gwyther, M and Saunders, A (2005) 'United they stand?', *Management Today*, April.

Hamel, G and Prahalad C K (1994) *Competing for the Future*, Boston, MA: Harvard Business School Press.

Handy, C (1987) *The Making of Managers*, London: Manpower Services Commission, National Economic Development Council, British Institute of Management.

Harvey-Jones, J (1993) *Managing to Survive*, London: Heinemann.

Hayward, M (2004) 'I showed them the future and they ignored it', *Management Today*, September.

Hesselbein, F, Goldsmith, M and Beckhard, R F (2000) *The Organization of the Future*, San Francisco, CA: Jossey-Bass.

Huczynski, A A (1993) *Management Gurus*, London and New York: Routledge.

Imai, M (1997) *Kaizen: The Key to Japan's Competitive Success*, Maidenhead: McGraw-Hill.

Kennet, M (2006) 'View from the middle', *Management Today*, March.

Kiechael III, W (1987) 'Your new employment contract', *Fortune*, 6 July.

King, W J (revised by Shakoon, J G) (2007) *The Unwritten Laws of Business*, Profile Books.

Kotter, J P (2001) 'What Leaders Really Do', *Harvard Business Review*, December.

Levinson, D J, Darrow, C N, Klein, E B, Levinson, M H and McKee, B (1978) *The Seasons of a Man's Life*, New York: Knopf.

Lucas, E (2006) 'Good managers born or made?', *Professional Manager*, 15 (4), Chartered Institute of Management.

Mann, S (2006) 'Doing your MBA sums', *Professional Manager*, 15 (1), Chartered Institute of Management.

Mant, A (1979) *The Rise and Fall of the British Manager*, London: Pan.

Mayo, E (1953) *The Human Problems of an Industrial Civilization*, New York: Macmillan.

Miles R E, Snow, Charles C and Miles, G (2000) 'The future organisation', *Long Range Planning*, 33.

Mullin, R (1996) 'Knowledge management: a cultural revolution', *Journal of Business Strategy*, September/October.

Nicholson, N (2000) *Managing the Human Animal*, London: Texere.

Nonaka, I and Takeuchi, H (1995) *The Knowledge-Creating Company*, Oxford: Oxford University Press.

O'Dell, C and Grayson, C J (1998) *If Only We Knew What We Know: The Transfer of Internal Knowledge and Best Practice*, New York: Free Press.

Parker Follett, M (1941) *Collected Works*, New York: Harper and Brothers.

Pascale, R T (1991) *Managing on the Edge*, Harmondsworth: Penguin.

Pearce, W H (2001) 'The hard work of being a soft manager', *Harvard Business Review*, December.

Peters, T and Waterman, R (1982) *In Search of Excellence*, New York: Harper & Row.

Pina e Cunha, M, Clegg, S R and Kamoche, K (2006) 'Surprises in management and organisation; concepts, sources and a typology', *British Journal of Management*, 17 (4).

Pirie, M (1994) *20–20 Vision: Targets for Britain's Future*, London: Adam Smith Institute.

Prahalad, C K and Hamel, G (1990) 'The core competence of the corporation', *Harvard Business Review*, May/June.

Ringland, G (1998) *Scenario Planning: Managing for the Future*, New York: John Wiley.

Schlewder, B (1990) 'How Bill Gates keeps the magic going', *Fortune*, June 18.

Schwartz, P (1996) *The Art of the Long View: Planning for the Future in an Uncertain World*, New York: Doubleday.

Senge, P M (1994) *The Fifth Discipline: The Art and Practice of the Learning Organization*, New York: Doubleday.

Smith, A (1776) *An Inquiry into the Nature and Causes of the Wealth of Nations*, London: Strahn and Caddell.

Smith, D (1997) 'Managers lack proper skills', *Sunday Times*, 14 September.

Stern, S (2005) 'Forever changing', *Management Today*, February.

Taylor, F W (1947) *Scientific Management*, New York: Harper & Brothers.

Vandenbosch, B, Saatcioglu, A and Fay, S (2006) 'Idea management: a systematic view', *Journal of Management Studies*, 43 (2), March.

Walsh, F (2005) 'The low-cost revolution', *Management Today*, March.

Watson, T J (1986) *Management Organisation and Employment*, London: Routledge.

Whyte, W H (1956) *The Organization Man*, New York: Doubleday.

Zaleznik, A (2004) 'Managers and leaders, are they different?', *Harvard Business Review*, January.

INDEX